Art in Renaissance Italy

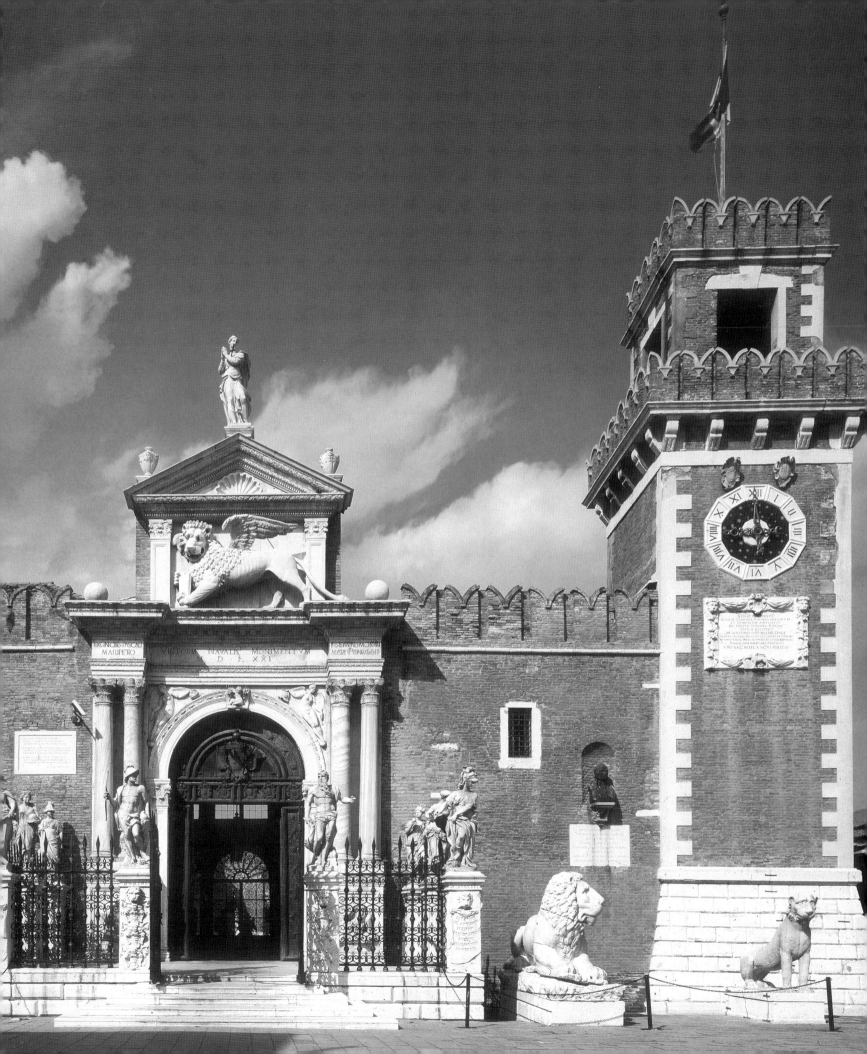

Art in Renaissance Italy

Second Edition

JOHN T. PAOLETTI & GARY M. RADKE

HARRY N. ABRAMS, INC., PUBLISHERS

For Rebecca and Sarah and Lydia

Library of Congress Cataloging-in-Publication Data
Paoletti, John T.
    Art in Renaissance Italy / John T. Paoletti, Gary M. Radke—2nd ed.
        p. cm.
    Includes bibliographical references and index.
    ISBN 0-8109-1390-9
    1. Art, Italian. 2. Art, Renaissance—Italy. 3. Italy—Civilization—1268–1559. I. Radke,
Gary M. II. Title.

N6915 .P26 2001
709'.45'09024—dc21   2001022405

 This book was designed and produced by
Calmann & King Ltd, London
www.calmann-king.com

Senior managing editor: Richard Mason
Designer: Ian Hunt
Jacket designer: Pentagram
Picture researcher: Sue Bolsom
Typesetter: Fakenham Phototypesetting, Norfolk, UK

Frontispiece: Arsenal Gateway (detail), 1457/58–1460, Venice.
Marble and Istrian stone. © Cameraphoto Arte, Venice.

Printed and bound in China

10   9   8   7   6   5   4   3   2   1

 Harry N. Abrams, Inc.
100 Fifth Avenue
New York, N.Y. 10011
www.abramsbooks.com

Contents

3

Art and Society:
The Later Fourteenth Century   129

4

Fashioning Images of Rulership
and Authority:
The Early Fifteenth Century   173

5

Elaborating Local and
Classical Traditions:
The Mid-Fifteenth Century   229

6

Splendor and Magnificence:
The Later Fifteenth Century   279

7

Rivaling Ancient Rome:
The Early Sixteenth Century   347

8
Renewing the City:
The Mid-Sixteenth Century   409

9
Innovation and Reform:
The Later Sixteenth Century   451

Preface

For four centuries the history of art produced in Renaissance Italy has been presented as a series of biographies of individual artists. Formulations such as *"Michelangelo's* David," *"Leonardo's* Last Supper," *"Palladio's* Villa La Rotonda" ring true to modern ears, because they celebrate the creative individuality of these masters and their works. But in structuring histories of Renaissance art around artists, rather than according to the places in which they worked, the persons and institutions whom they served, and the societal expectations they met—the point of view taken in this text—historians have often failed to indicate that the critical interrelations of these social forces with the arts gave them a compelling visual life over time. Italian Renaissance artists were no more solitary geniuses than are most architects and commercial artists today. They understood that they might gain personal recognition and fame from their creations. They also knew that their patrons—civic leaders in the case of the *David*, the Duke of Milan with the *Last Supper*, and a wealthy churchman for the Villa La Rotonda—expected even greater renown for their patronage and their astute exploitation of the visual arts.

Our point of view—that art must be seen in terms of its patronage and the specific times and circumstances in which it was created—is hardly new to art history. Many specialized studies and a number of more geographically and chronologically limited books have used such an approach. This volume, however, provides a comprehensive, fully illustrated, pan-Italian consideration of art from the thirteenth through the sixteenth century. We have broadened our consideration of the diverse traditions of cities throughout Italy, rather than focusing primarily on Florence (which has too often been used to make other centers, even well-recognized ones such as Venice and Rome, seem like cultural and artistic satellites of the Tuscan capital). Expanded geographic and stylistic parameters provide a richer picture of art produced in Renaissance Italy, including works of Florentine art that have previously been accorded marginal or problematic status. We have also rejected rigid separation of the arts by media, preferring to discuss painting, sculpture, and architecture as complementary arts, recognizing that most artists worked in a variety of forms and that they and their patrons regularly thought in terms of ensembles, not isolated masterpieces.

To set our selected works of art more firmly into their original historical fabric, we have added several special features to this book. Wherever possible, captions indicate the patron as well as the artist who created the work. "Contemporary Scene" boxes give a glimpse of daily life during the Renaissance, suggesting some of the sociological "givens" that affected people's view of the world: their religious practices, how they entertained themselves, the foods they ate, and more. "Contemporary Voice" boxes provide actual period texts, drawn not just from literary figures and the theorists and historians who wrote about art but also from authors who wrote for more mundane purposes, tempering the elite bias that a focus on patronage—or, in previous texts, on artistic genius—can sometimes bring to art-historical discussions.

In this book we hope to make the familiar seem more intriguing and the unfamiliar more comprehensible. The picture we present necessarily includes a recognition of the ambiguities and paradoxes inherent in reconstructing past events. Chronological boundaries for each chapter are somewhat arbitrary, like all such divisions, but in general they reflect sociopolitical shifts caused by changes of governmental structures or rulers in the various cities covered. Thus the dates in the chapter titles are approximate and have to be adjusted for each of the city-states discussed.

Some readers may find that works of art they consider important—even crucial—to an understanding of the history of Renaissance art are not discussed in our text. Such "omissions," in tandem with the addition of unusual works of art, are inevitable in a book that attempts to change the very mode of presentation of the material by expanding its scope. We hope that readers will see in our selections a manifestation of the truly challenging intellectual and artistic richness of the Renaissance. The intention of this book is to provoke questions about approach and stylistic development, not to provide a new canon. We are living in a particularly vital time in historical thinking, when old prescriptive boundaries have been breached. It is critically important to participate in the adventure of these changes.

As is the case with most books of this nature, we have not footnoted the text. However, we have included a bibliography at the end, thereby recording the main source materials we have used and our profound debt to earlier scholars. This bibliography could well be treated as a guide to further reading and understanding of the art and ideas presented in the book. We have also provided a glossary of technical terms which are highlighted in the text in boldface type.

The problem of translating Italian terms into English is always an issue in books on the Renaissance. By and large we have favored English terms and English forms of names according to common usage. In the rare instances of technical terms that do not have an exact equivalent we have provided an approximate translation in the text the first time the word appears, but we then continue to use the Italian term because of its specificity. Nomenclature changed during the period under discussion, but by and large family surnames were not used. Thus artists are referred to in the text either by first name (Michelangelo and not Buonarroti), or by nickname where it was or has become the accepted form (Veronese and not Paolo Cagliari), or by surname (Vasari) if that has become customary usage. There are confusing instances in which an artist's patronymic has become transformed in modern usage to a surname: thus Simone di Martino now commonly appears as Simone Martini. In these very few cases usage in the text varies, but the bibliographical references clarify how one can search for more information on the artist.

From the outset of this project Rosemary Bradley, formerly of Calmann & King, was a quietly encouraging first editor. We owe her an enormous debt of gratitude. Melanie White took over editorial responsibilities for the book after it was in process and provided firm and helpful direction at critical moments when a gargantuan project threatened to overwhelm us all. We have also been privileged to work with Lesley Ripley Greenfield, our ever-attentive editor at Calmann & King, and with the ever-supportive Julia Moore at Abrams; we are grateful for their assistance and kind encouragement in realizing this project. Most particularly we wish to thank Ursula Payne who with kindly persistence, an impeccable eye for accuracy, and good humor guided us through the endless details of editing the first edition; the text is the better because of her perceptive work. For the second edition Richard Mason has guided the editorial process with a sure hand, assisted by Michael Bird and Ian Hunt, the designer. We are grateful for their help. Susan Bolsom has been the photo editor for both editions and we are deeply appreciative of her indefatigable efforts and keen eye.

Special thanks go to students at Wesleyan University and Syracuse University who read the text of the first edition critically and perceptively: Adam Borden, Jennie Diamond, Rachel Posner, Melea Press, and Lisa Rubino at Wesleyan and Sharon Brind, Alexis Drosu, Holly Hurlburt, Jennifer Mosher, and Nathan Peek at Syracuse. The following seminar students at Syracuse also helped in the revisions for the second edition of the text and deserve our gratitude: Ilya-Karina Bonet, Elizabeth Butler, Rahel Elmer Reger, Julia Gardner, Caroline Hillard, Alexandra Korey, Laura Macaluso, Lia Markey, Melissa Moreton, Lisa Neal, Soonie Olson, Jenny Patten, Kimberly Santoro, Melanie Taylor, Anne Weatherly, and Julie Zappia. Monica Hahn-Koenig, Holly Hurlburt, Tricia Shapiro, and Sheena Simpson helped as researchers and their work is particularly appreciated. We also warmly acknowledge secretarial assistance from Marilyn Bergett, Linda Straub, Brenda Keating, Carol Kearney, and Tricia Irvine, who kept the project humming.

Many of our colleagues have read and commented on various aspects of this text. We are immensely grateful for their generous offers of assistance and for their criticism. Listing them by name hardly seems appropriate gratitude, but we hope that their students will see their names and realize the dedication of their teachers to their teaching and to their discipline. In particular we would like to note Steven Bule, Jill Carrington, Anthony Colantuono, Roger Crum, Anne Derbes, Phillip Earenfight, Patricia Emison, Adrian Hoch, Ellen Longsworth, Sarah McHam, Susan McKillop, Anita Moskowitz, Gabriele Neher, Jonathan Nelson, Joy Pepe, James Saslow, Richard Turner, Mary Vaccaro, and Shelley Zuraw. David Gillerman also read portions of the text at various stages of its evolution and consistently offered trenchant, critical, and creative suggestions.

We would like to thank Caroline Bruzelius, the former director of the American Academy in Rome, and the entire staff of the Academy for their hospitality and assistance at a critical moment in the generation of this book, and Suzanne Boorsch of the Metropolitan Museum of Art for sharing her knowledge of printed images of Rome and for supplying urgently needed illustrative material. We are also appreciative of the assistance of Denise Allen and Peggy Fogelman in obtaining the images of the lost-wax process that appear in the Introduction (Fig. 27), and to Francesca Bewer for the diagram and succinct text of that process.

The staffs of numerous libraries have also been of enormous assistance in helping us to find the extraordinary range of research materials necessary for the writing of a book such as this one. Among the most supportive were Kathleen Stefanowicz and the late Steven Lebergott of the interlibrary loan office of the Olin Library of Wesleyan University, Susanne Javorski, the art reference librarian at Wesleyan, and Randy Bond at the Fine Arts Library of Syracuse University.

Of course our greatest gratitude goes to our wives, Nancy Romig Radke and Leslie Hiles Paoletti, who watched this book grow from the outset, heard more about the difficulties of putting nearly four centuries of Italian art between two covers than they ever needed to know, and still managed to encourage us in our work. While this book is dedicated to our children, it also belongs to them.

John Paoletti, Gary Radke, February 2001

Introduction:
Art in Context

Art mattered in the Renaissance. Viewers expected works of art to be meaningful, purposeful, and functional, not just beautiful. Visual imagery was so important—and the physical manufacture of work's of art so complicated—that artists very rarely worked alone. They collaborated with one another and with a wide range of patrons, responding sensitively to the differing civic, social, political, and historical contexts in which they worked. Art mattered because it was the product of an entire society. It both forged and reflected societal values.

The governing point of view in this text—that works of art were made to serve the particular purposes of those who commissioned them—makes the form as well as the content of the art directly dependent on its use. Formal properties such as composition or figural form that we might now view merely as aesthetically pleasing were often intended as part of the moral or political content of the work. That is not to say that aesthetic pleasure had no role to play in people's perceptions of works of art. Texts of the period suggest just the opposite. At the end of the fifteenth century Matteo Colaccio, a Sicilian, visited Padua and wrote of his pleasure at seeing the wood **intarsia** choir stalls in the church of Sant'Antonio (the Santo):

> [I] am almost struck dumb with admiration. Everything seems real to me, I cannot believe it is feigned. I come closer, and run my hands over them all . . . near the angel Gabriel and Mary, you admire branches with such leaves and fruit that nature does not produce truer . . . Who could be sated of admiring that silk veil stretched over a chalice, both for the color and for the fineness of the weave, all in folds of purple, and for those sinuous folds produced by the inequality of the falling ends?

Aesthetics, however, were not the driving force behind the commission and creation of works of art. Quite mundane or awkward images of a Madonna and Child may have been just as efficacious as devotional objects as those generally admired images that have come to define the Renaissance artistic canon. Copies after works by acknowledged masters (see Fig. 2) provide a welcome antidote to the elitist bias that a focus on wealthy patrons imposes on artistic production in the Renaissance.

They also document the diffusion of art throughout Renaissance society and highlight the innovations and exceptional quality of those works that have dominated historical discussion since the sixteenth century.

Attempts to imagine how objects and monuments of the past were seen in their own day are important, even

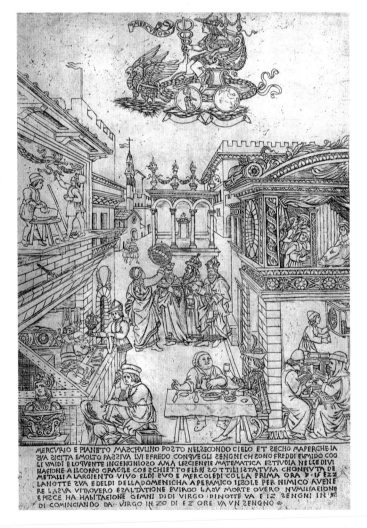

1 *Mercury*, c. 1460, attributed to BACCIO BALDINI. Engraving, 12¾ × 8½" (32.4 × 22 cm) (© British Museum, London)

The artist has placed this imaginary scene before the actual main civil piazza of Florence. In the background on the left is the crenellated façade of the Palazzo della Signoria and the now destroyed church of San Piero Scheraggio, and in the center background is the Loggia della Signoria.

though it is impossible to reconstruct precisely the original visual impact of these works, especially if they have been removed from their original location. Any commission for a work of art during the Renaissance manifested not only the wishes of the purchasers but also the history of the site into which it was to be placed. Where the site was a public place its history might stretch as far back as the mythic beginnings of the city where it was located. Where the site combined private and corporate activity—for example, a private chapel in a monastic church—the collective histories and wishes of both patron and host religious order influenced the final form of the work produced. Most art of the period reflects this rich historical, familial, communal, and social fabric.

Renaissance art obviously spoke more immediately to its contemporaries than it does to a modern viewer. The images and attributes of saints, classical heroes, or local rulers, along with their symbolic meanings, were part of an individual's intellectual equipment in the culture of the time. For example, St. John the Baptist could be identified by his gaunt features, short hair shirt, and thin reed staff; St. Catherine of Alexandria by the spiked wheel on which her prosecutors attempted to torture her. Such images of saints not only made them recognizable, but also recalled the popular stories connected with their lives, thus speaking directly to story-telling traditions and to the imagination of the viewer.

Works of art existed over time, since worshipers stood before devotional images repeatedly and citizens daily passed public statues of their rulers. The messages of these works must have been thoroughly assimilated, if only unconsciously, by every observer. Insofar as images tended to be repeated in similar form over long periods of time, even personifications of abstract concepts such as Justice (holding a sword or scales, or both) became clearly recognizable to a wide population.

It is worth noting that only a very small percentage of works of art from the Renaissance survives. Perhaps the highest losses occur among mass-produced objects, often by students within a master's shop, and, in the case of sculpture, made of inexpensive materials such as stucco or plaster (Fig. 2), that replicated or imitated already accepted models. Thus repetitive images were far more pervasive than surviving evidence suggests. It is also important to note that many Renaissance paintings and sculptures carried labels, sometimes simple captions identifying the figures represented and at other times long and discursive inscriptions not only identifying the event depicted but interpreting it as well. Mutually reinforcing exchanges between word and image (see Figs. 1.36 and 2.14) were common and open important avenues for understanding. People at all levels of society, whether literate or not, simply could not fail to assimilate the tenets of religious and civic belief that had governed their society for generations.

Much of the surviving art of the Renaissance is fragmentary, requiring an active effort on the part of the viewer to reconstruct not only the original object but also the context in which it existed. Altarpieces have been broken apart for multiple sales; public sculpture has been defaced as the political figures represented fell out of favor (as recently occurred in the separating states of the former Soviet Union); and buildings have been renovated and rebuilt to accommodate new owners or needs. A large category of visual history has simply disappeared. Figurated banners, large-scale plaster sculpture, temporary parade architecture, and floats built for special occasions rarely outlived the events for which they were produced. It is also true that in Italy nineteenth-century restorers often excessively stripped sculpture of pigmentation and buildings of decorations, while at the same time they misleadingly repainted damaged paintings in order to make them appear whole (a practice still current).

Efforts of reconstruction must work two ways: they need to address how public spaces accumulate meaning over time as events occurring in them become part of their history, and they must strip away later additions to works of art despite what such additions tell us of the history of their own time. Any reconstruction must also consider the possibility that time has added a distancing quality of venerability to works of art. When excessively devout viewers scratched out the faces of Judas, or the "bad" thief crucified with Christ, or an accompanying devil in paintings of his Passion, that act of disfigurement illustrated the effectiveness of the image in conveying the message of the narrative. In some cases, a work of art also had, in its original context, a practical dimension often lost through its history. For example, mules were allowed to cross through the Cathedral of Florence, through the side doors and across the nave, so as to avoid the longer exterior route around the building. People might be in awe of religious images and sacred sites, but they also had very emotional and pragmatic reactions to them.

Contrary to the implications of museum displays, works of art were not always stationary. Many were portable. Small painted devotional images, such as **diptychs** or **triptychs**, could be carried from a city palace to a country villa and could be opened or closed as required. Wooden figures of the crucified Christ could be taken down from the support of the cross and treated as if they were real bodies in liturgical dramas on Good Friday. Works of art were functional in this culture and could, therefore, be renewed or even discarded according to need. Thus miracle-working images were simply replaced as they became damaged over time in order to maintain devotional practice.

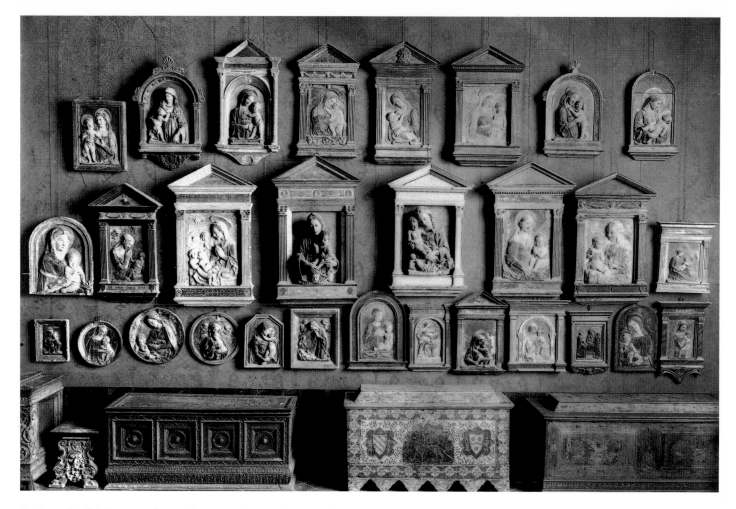

2 Museo Bardini, Florence, nineteenth-century photographic view of the interior showing plaster and stucco casts of Virgin and Child reliefs

These repeated images document the mass-production market for such popular objects during the fifteenth century (as well as their replication—and forgery—during the late nineteenth and twentieth centuries).

Consideration of the function of works of art has important implications for a discussion of style. Once a compositional form became associated with an image or iconography—such as the seated elect on either side of the frontal Divinity in Last Judgment scenes—it was extremely difficult to dislodge, whatever stylistic developments may have occurred elsewhere. Moreover, different social groups within a culture used style as a form of identification, as they still do. Thus multiple functions and contexts led to multiple styles, rather than to a single unified period style.

Patronage

The functional nature of art within any society underlines a particular aspect of its creation. In virtually all cases a work of art was commissioned, rather than produced by the artist on his own initiative. By and large art was not made to be art but because someone had a particular need for it. Thus this book treats patronage as a critical definer of context. "Patronage" is a complicated term and does not articulate as clearly as it might the complex set of social exchanges that it encompasses for the period under consideration. The Italian language uses two terms to make the concept clear. The first, *clientelismo*, is construed in the political sense to mean a series of exchanges, or favors granted, which bind the participating bodies—patron and client—together. Intricate and carefully observed social, political, economic, and even religious conventions of the Renaissance demanded such exchanges, not only within particular social groups, but up and down the social scale. The social cohesion that they provided was an antidote to the frequent violent factionalism that permeated Renaissance cities. A second term, *mecenatismo*, refers exclusively to the purchase of works of art and the support of artistic projects. The word derives from the name of Gaius Cilnius Maecenas (c. 70–8 B.C.E.), renowned for his enormous wealth and luxurious living. It was this sense of patronage that the fifteenth-century sculptor and architect Filarete (Antonio Averlino) referred to when in a provocatively gendered simile he referred to the patron as the father and the artist as the mother of the work of art. In a hierarchically structured and patriarchal society such as that of Renaissance Italy it was clearly the patron, not the artist, who was perceived, until late in the period, as the dominating figure in artistic creation.

It is in the overlap of these two concepts of *clientelismo* and *mecenatismo* that patronage of the arts during the Renaissance functioned. Commissioned works of art, whether generated by the state, the Church, monastic communities, civic and corporate groups such as guilds, or private individuals, were conceived with specific goals in mind and were meant to convey publicly specific messages often more complex than their subjects would indicate. Private patrons could present works of art to the Church with the expectation that God and the saints would reward their gifts with salvation. New research indicates that, despite the dominant role of the male in Renaissance society, women, following the examples of earlier female patrons—notably in the Early Christian and late medieval periods—did commission works of art, including extensive and costly architectural projects and altarpieces and frescoes where they appear in significant numbers as donors. Rulers could beautify their cities as manifestations of their legitimacy, power, and generosity with the expectation that their subjects would support their continued supremacy. And religious orders, particularly new ones anxious to demonstrate their presence within the culture and the sanctity of their founders (and thus their own legitimacy), were also important patrons within the urban culture of the period, providing expansive church interiors where their stories could be told and where the laity could, through impressive donations, assert their own positions within the cultic life of the city. Each commission set up particular interrelationships and exchanges, sometimes primarily between patron and artist—as, for instance, in the commission of a private portrait; sometimes between patron, monastic community, and artists—as in a fresco cycle for a private chapel in a monastic church. Art was an integral part of the functioning social and political fabric. It provided visual structures for the patterns that governed not only earthly life, but life in the hereafter as well.

Viewers' reactions might be determined by their understanding of the patron's generosity, wealth, or power; the efficacy of the monastic order or guild in ensuring social stability; the artist's degree of skill or genius; or the depicted saint's perceived ability to intercede with God. At the center of this network of social relationships stood the work of art. To it the human participants brought, consciously or unconsciously, a complex set of historically accepted conventions of representation which were circumscribed by tradition and by pre-existing models. History—of the patron, of the site, of the typology to which the image belonged—is an unseen but critical factor in the creation of works of art in the Renaissance (and in fact for all pre-modern periods).

Artists' Workshops

An anonymous print of the late fifteenth century (Fig. 1) depicts the arts in a time of active production and prosperity under the guidance of their patron, the god Mercury, whose chariot floats in the sky and whose earthly spokesman, Hermes Trismegistus, is represented in discussion below. In the upper floor of the building at the right an organist energetically plays away, assisted by a young man working the bellows. Below them a book dealer shows his wares to a customer; one assumes that the scribes in his employ are hidden deeper in the building, busily copying manuscripts. On the building opposite a painter decorates the façade with a garland and ribbon pattern, part of inscribed and pigmented pattern work known as **sgraffito**, while an assistant prepares pigments for him. Below them is a sculptor's studio with a somewhat tattered young master kneeling in front, carving a marble bust of a woman. Inside the sculptor's shop young pupils, called *garzoni*, staff the sales counter where wares, including the bust of a man (most likely made of painted wood or terracotta) and more practical ewers and salvers, are being sold to maintain a steady income for the shop. One young *garzone* is practicing his drawing skills. In a somewhat schematic manner this print shows that the arts—broadly interpreted to include all objects of visual or material culture—were part of an economic as well as a cultural exchange during this period. Their production was structured within traditional workshops headed by a master craftsman and staffed by a team of artisans at various stages in their training. The image of the solitary artist-genius, popularized in the nineteenth century, has little place in Renaissance Europe.

The Image of the Artist   Although the image of the artist represented in the print of the workshops is essentially true, it is one that underwent significant change during the fifteenth and sixteenth centuries. Comparison between a relief showing a traditional sculptor's workshop by Nanni di Banco (Fig. 3) and the *Self-Portrait* of the sculptor Baccio Bandinelli (Fig. 5) suggests both the evolving role of artists within their own society and their own perception of that role. Although artists had long held positions of civic responsibility within their city-states, Nanni's relief concentrates on the craft aspect of the sculptor's studio, with each worker assigned specific tasks to ensure an efficiently operating shop. The craftsmen are all dressed in working clothes and attend to their duties with true single-mindedness. A little more than a century later, Bandinelli's self-portrait shows the artist seated in an impressive classical architectural setting pointing to a drawing of two male nudes, perhaps representing Hercules and Cacus, the subject of one of

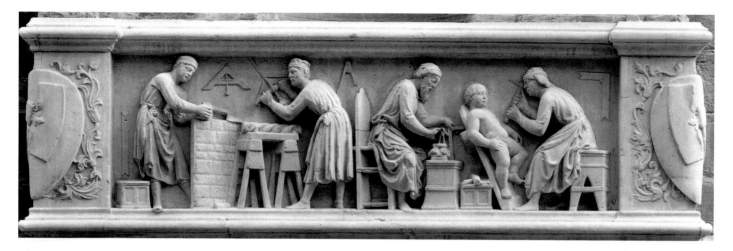

3 *Sculptor's Workshop*, c. 1416, commissioned by the Arte dei Maestri di Pietra e Legname from NANNI DI BANCO for the base of the guild niche at Or San Michele, Florence. Marble

Bandinelli's most famous sculptures (see Fig. 7.49). The well-dressed artist, seated in a classicizing architectural setting, seems to be giving a lecture about the drawing, or perhaps about *disegno*, the art of drawing, more as an academician or philosopher than as a craftsman. In fact nowhere in the painting is there any indication of the tools of his trade, although Bandinelli has self-consciously demonstrated his technical virtuosity in the complicated pose of his own body, in the wrinkles along the edges of the drawing, and in his ability to depict a drawing (a medium in which he was particularly well known) in oil paint. Bandinelli presents himself as a gentleman wearing the gold chain and shell pendant of the chivalric Order of St. James. Clearly in the interval between the relief by Nanni di Banco showing craftsmen struggling with their stone and the painting by Bandinelli showing the artist as a socially prominent commentator on the arts, the artist's perception of his role within society had changed.

Not only did the role of the artist within the culture change during the Renaissance, but the very notion of who could operate within this craft tradition changed as well; the word "artist" as we use it did not exist during this period, but referred instead to grammarians. Women, traditionally excluded because of their sex, became increasingly visible and critically accepted as major contributors to an evolving profession, even though depictions *of* actual women remained remarkably bound by long-standing traditions of decorum within a patriarchic culture. Sofonisba Anguissola's painting of her teacher, Bernardino Campi, painting her portrait (Fig. 6) is a wry commentary on the very structures of artistic production, a story within a story, so to speak, that points to male construction of female form. Anguissola's gaze rivets the viewer of the painting, forcing consideration of what

appears to be the inscribing of male authority on the body of the female. Campi's gaze complicates matters, however, since as he paints he looks out of the painting towards what the picture indicates must be his subject, Anguissola. In the finished painting, however, Anguissola also looks directly at the viewer. Thus the viewer in front of the painting plays a double role: that of the subject of the painting within the painting, namely Anguissola herself, and of an engaged viewer—watched by both Campi and Anguissola—made complicit in Anguissola's destabilizing of contemporary social norms.

For, as the actual painter of the canvas, Anguissola placed her head higher than Campi's. Thus, according to the social rules of the period concerning position, she was conferring on herself a status greater than her teacher's—both in terms of social position and in terms of artistic accomplishment. Anguissola's assertion of superiority is ironically underscored by the aligned placement of the two visible hands in the painting: Campi's identifies him as someone who works with his hands for a living, whereas Anguissola's—holding a pair of gloves—indicates her nobility (her father was a member of the minor nobility of Cremona and she herself was soon to be an attendant of the Infanta Isabella of Spain and a lady-in-waiting to Elizabeth of Valois, the wife of Philip II, in whose court she lived from 1559 to 1580).

Anguissola herself was the real painter of the canvas, yet she has hidden her active right hand in the painting and made her head, the seat of the intellect, slightly larger than Campi's. Thus, Anguissola's construction in the painting of her own artistic and social status as a woman is paired with her presentation of the changing role of the artist from manual labourer to conceptual creator, an inversion of the patriarchal norms voiced by Filarete a century earlier: as presumed patron of the painting

Art and Offerings

People in the Renaissance expected to leave something of themselves in their churches: not just prayers and offerings but physical mementos and records of direct engagement with the power of God and the saints. As is evident in Carpaccio's painting *The Vision of Prior Ottobon in Sant'Antonio di Castello* (Fig. 4), churches contained a wide variety of objects and furnishings, most of them donated by the pious laity. Since rights to altars were sold to the wealthy in perpetuity, new and old donations intermingled, often resulting in a mixture of styles on a single wall. In Carpaccio's painting, different-sized Gothic polyptychs occupy the first two bays at the right. A much taller and classically framed altarpiece from later in the period dominates the third bay. Its position, closest to the choir screen—and therefore to the high altar—confirms the impression that this was the costliest altar of the three, certainly more prestigious than the modest altar in the corner next to the entrance wall. Families who could not afford their own altar might have sufficient funds to hang a painting on one of the columns of the nave arcade, in the manner of the framed plaque (in this case perhaps an official Church notice or decree) located on the column at the center of the painting, much like those in Florence Cathedral (see Fig. 2.16).

Many worshipers also felt impelled to leave *ex votos* (symbolic thank offerings) in their churches. Candles, flags, banners, medals, miniature representations of body parts, and scale models of ships fill the upper reaches of the first two bays of Carpaccio's church, while others hang across the choir screen. Objects were strewn over and around images, testifying to "graces received": healings, miraculous interventions, protection from danger, and successful births. At certain very powerful shrines—for example, the altar of the Madonna in the Church of the Annunziata in Florence—worshipers left sculpted and painted portraits of themselves so that they could be perpetually present in the church. An industry of mannequin makers, working faces and hands in wax, provided full-scale, clothed representations of illustrious devotees, including Lorenzo de' Medici who commissioned figures of himself for the convent church of the Chiarito, dressed in the actual bloodstained clothes he had worn during the unsuccessful attempt on his life in the Pazzi Conspiracy of 1478. Like most people of his time, Lorenzo believed in publicly displaying his gratitude for divine intervention and protection.

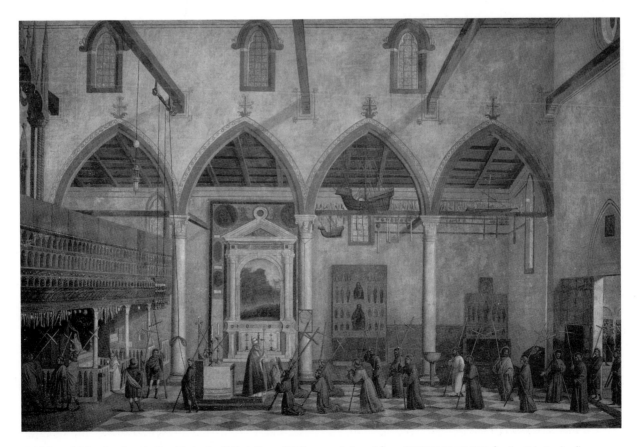

4 *Vision of Prior Ottobon in Sant'Antonio di Castello*, c. 1515, commissioned from VITTORE CARPACCIO for Sant'Antonio di Castello, Venice. Oil on canvas, 47½ × 68½" (121 × 174 cm) (Accademia, Venice)

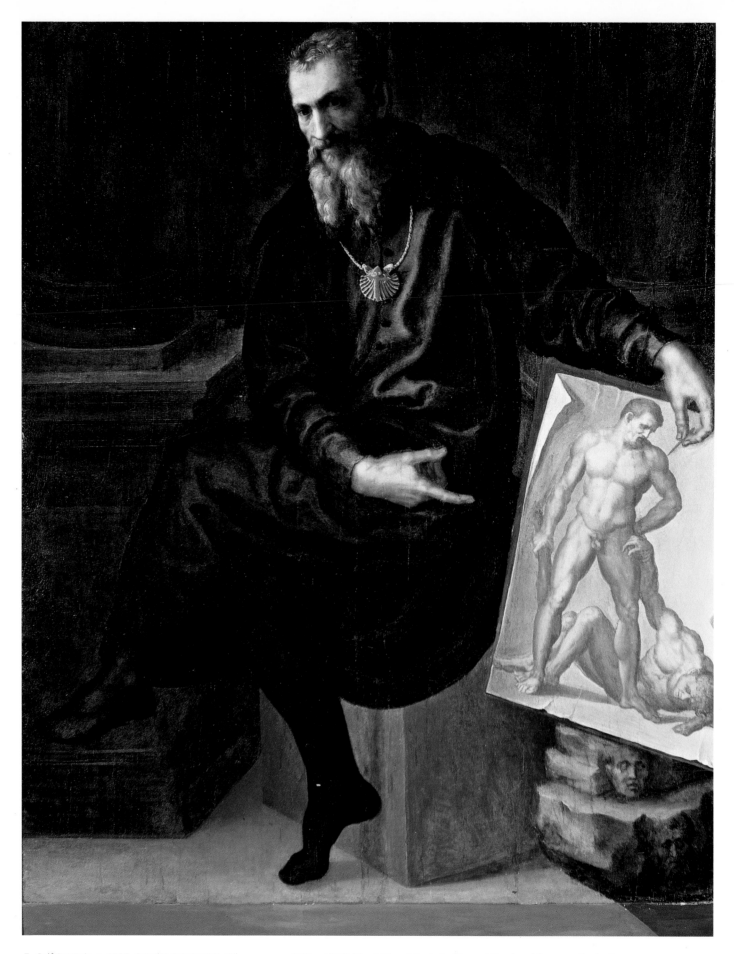

5 *Self-Portrait*, c. 1530, BACCIO BANDINELLI. Oil on canvas, 57⅞ × 44" (147 × 112 cm) (Isabella Stewart Gardner Museum, Boston)

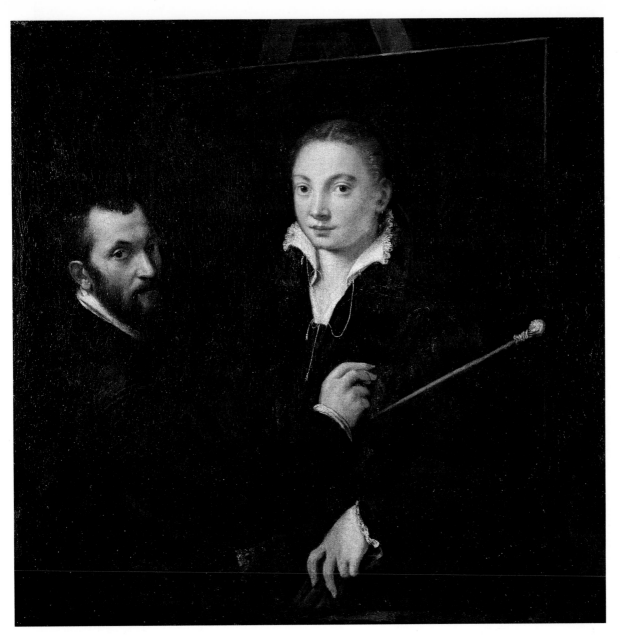

6 *Bernardino Campi Painting Sofonisba Anguissola*, late 1550s, SOFONISBA ANGUISSOLA. Oil on canvas, 42½ × 43" (108 × 109 cm) (Pinacoteca Nazionale, Siena)

within the painting she is the "father" of the image, and as the actual artist she is also the "mother."

Workshop Training Despite changes in the social position of the artist and in the ways that artists thought about their work, the actual production of art remained remarkably unchanged during the Renaissance. In many instances workshops passed from father to son or uncle to nephew, from generation to generation. A group portrait by Bernardino Licinio (Fig. 7) shows the artist with his nephews, whom he is trying to teach. The boy on the left holds a drawing done from the model of a classical sculpture held by Licinio, while the older boy with the worried look at the right tries to complete a similar drawing. On the drawing of the younger boy are the words "Oh, look how good this drawing is" while that of the older boy bears an inscription stating how difficult drawing is.

The strength of the workshop system for preserving what was valued as artistic expression from generation to

generation was clearly articulated by Cennino Cennini around 1410 in the preface to a painting manual that he wrote called *Il Libro dell'arte* (*The Craftsman's Handbook*). There Cennino says that he "was trained in this profession for twelve years by my master, Agnolo di Taddeo (Gaddi; 1333–96) of Florence; he learned this profession from Taddeo (Gaddi; active 1332–63), his father; and his father was christened under Giotto and was his follower for four-and-twenty years . . ." Families of artists, such as the Licinio and the Gaddi, and interlocking family workshops were not unusual for the period. Such structures made for remarkable continuity over time and assured a coherent style in large projects like the sculptural and painted decoration of large churches, where many artists had to work together. Whether in the sixteenth century or the fourteenth, in workshops such as these imitation was valued rather than deprecated.

Master painters and sculptors normally accepted apprentices in their early teens. In exchange for their

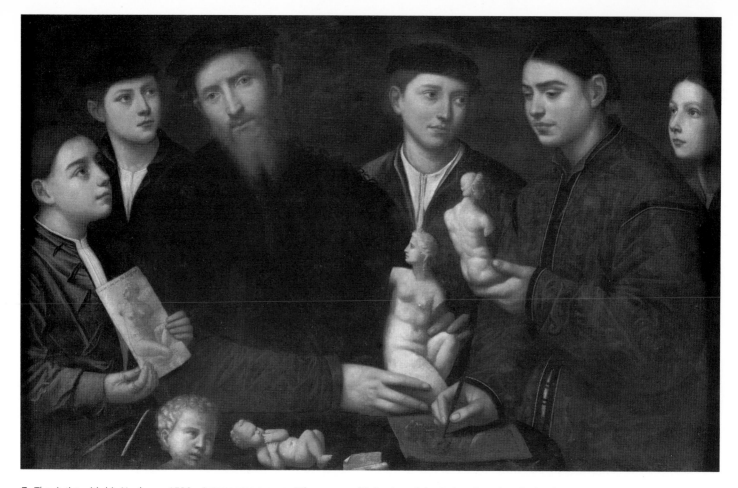

7 *The Artist with his Nephews*, 1530s, BERNARDINO LICINIO. Oil on canvas (Collection of the Duke of Northumberland, England)

assistance in the shop, the master gave his pupils training in his particular craft, room and board, and occasionally a modest salary. A contract of 1467 between the father of an apprentice named Francesco and the painter Francesco Squarcione outlines the expectations placed on both teacher and student. Squarcione agreed:

> . . . to teach . . . Francesco . . . the principle of a plane with lines drawn according to my method, and to put figures on the said plane, one here and one there, in various places on the said plane, and place objects, namely a chair, bench or house, and get him to understand these things, and teach him to understand a man's head in foreshortening by isometric rendering, . . . and teach him the system of a naked body, measured in front and behind, and to put eyes, nose, mouth and ears in a man's head at the right measured places, and teach him all these things item by item as far as I am able and as far as the said Francesco will be able to learn . . . and always keep him with paper in his hand to provide him with a model, one after another, with various figures in lead white, and correct these models for him, and correct his mistakes.

Training progressed from quite menial tasks to learning drafting and modeling skills, how to prepare materials and how to use necessary tools. If the pupils learned quickly and well, the master assigned them specific tasks in the major commissions on which he was working, eventually allowing them full collaborative status. In some instances work coming from a large studio was totally the product of student assistants; the master's signature on such works usually indicated only that he had provided an initial design and perhaps some guidance along the way. Students could also produce copies of their master's works to sell over the counter (see Fig. 1). The seemingly endless number of Madonna and Child images in both painting and sculpture (see Fig. 2) give ample testimony of this practice, which both allowed the students to test their craft and propagated the fame of the master. The few extant artists' account books of the period attest to the careful records kept by masters of their assistants' work. As assistants grew older they hired themselves out at day wages; some, like Taddeo Gaddi or Leonardo da Vinci, functioned as virtually independent artists while remaining affiliated with their teacher's shop.

Contracts The master of a workshop not only had to teach and manage students, but also had to oversee a wide range of subcontracting operations. Sculptors and architects had to arrange for the quarrying and delivery of stone, which could involve large numbers of day laborers.

An Artist's Life

In *The Craftsman's Handbook* (c. 1410), Cennino Cennini not only instructs painters in the techniques of their calling but also advises them on the proper attitude to their work and a way of life conducive to success in it.

CHAPTER II

It is not without the impulse of a lofty spirit that some are moved to enter this profession, attractive to them through natural enthusiasm. Their intellect will take delight in drawing, provided their nature attracts them to it of themselves, without any master's guidance, out of loftiness of spirit. And then, through this delight, they come to want to find a master; and they bind themselves to him with respect for authority, undergoing an apprenticeship in order to achieve perfection in all this. There are those who pursue it, because of poverty and domestic need, for profit and enthusiasm for the profession too; but above all these are to be extolled the ones who enter the profession through a sense of enthusiasm and exaltation.

CHAPTER III

You, therefore, who with lofty spirit are fired with this ambition, and are about to enter the profession, begin by decking yourselves with this attire: Enthusiasm, Reverence, Obedience, and Constancy. And begin to submit yourself to the direction of a master for instruction as early as you can; and do not leave the master until you have to.

CHAPTER XXIX

Your life should always be arranged just as if you were studying theology, or philosophy, or other theories, that is to say, eating and drinking moderately, at least twice a day, electing digestible and wholesome dishes, and light wines; saving and sparing your hand, preserving it from such strains as heaving stones . . . . There is another cause which, if you indulge it, can make your hand so unsteady that it will waver more, and flutter far more, than leaves do in the wind, and this is indulging too much in the company of woman. Let us get back to our subject. Have a sort of pouch made of pasteboard, or just thin wood, made large enough in every dimension for you to put in a royal folio, that is, a half; and this is good for you to keep your drawings in, and likewise to hold the paper on for drawing. Then always go out alone, or in such company as will be inclined to do as you do, and not apt to disturb you. And the more understanding this company displays, the better it is for you. When you are in churches or chapels, and beginning to draw, consider, in the first place, from what section you think you wish to copy a scene or figure; and notice where its darks and half tones and high lights come; and this means that you have to apply your shadow with washes of ink; to leave the natural ground in the half tones; and to apply the high lights with white lead.

(from Cennino Cennini. *The Craftsman's Handbook* [*Il Libro dell'arte*]. Trans. Daniel V. Thompson, Jr. New York: Dover Publications, 1960, pp. 2, 3, 16)

On occasion sculptors also subcontracted the painting of objects carved by themselves to specialists in this kind of work. Painters had to work with carpenters to procure frames and panels. At each step of the way the master craftsman was responsible for the economics of the transaction and had to be able to figure such costs into the final price of his work.

Contractual arrangements often required the artist to submit a drawing (in the case of painting and sculpture) or a model (in the case of sculpture and architecture) to give the patron a clear idea of what he or she could expect for the finished product. Presentation drawings, as they are called, are significantly different from the sketches that an artist might make preliminary to a finished compositional scheme. They had the weight of a legal document, as did models. Sculptural and architectural models were often subcontracted to a professional craftsman, so that their detailing would be accurate. Comparison of presentation drawings to finished products, as in Taddeo Gaddi's *Presentation of the Virgin in the Temple* (Figs. 8 and 9) and Lorenzo Vecchietta's full-scale drawing for the building committee of the Ospedale della Scala in Siena of the bronze tabernacle which he proposed to make for the altar of the hospital chapel (Figs. 10 and 11), show that the designs of presentation drawings were expected to be adhered to rather closely.

Surviving contracts describe virtually nothing of the complicated exchanges that must have occurred in a highly stratified society between patron and artist in establishing the content and meaning of the work of art. They are for the most part bare-bones business contracts, meant to have legal weight should either artist or patron default. The terms frequently mention that the work is to be done by the artist's own hand, a recognition of the workshop practices of the period, and they stipulate the quality of the pigments and how much gold or lapis lazuli should be used. Contracts sometimes specify the subject of the commission (although in most cases that is assumed, given prior discussion) and also give a final date for completion of the work, along with terms of payment and indication of penalties for failure to meet the terms of the contract. The production of art was to a great extent an economic transaction. Whether fulfilling a public or private commission, the artist had to be ever vigilant in ensuring his just compensation. Litigation was not unusual in Renaissance shops; artists frequently brought in outside specialists to adjudicate a just price for their work because of a complaining patron, and patrons brought suit because an artist failed to meet the stipulated deadline for the delivery of the work.

Despite the tightly structured and remarkably tenacious workshop system, some individual artists did achieve reputations of international stature. Giotto not only painted in his native Florence but was called to Padua, Milan, and Naples as well. Gentile da Fabriano traveled to Venice and to Florence and was finally called to the papal court in Rome. Antonello da Messina worked in Naples and Venice as well as his native Sicily. And Michelangelo had invitations from both the French king and the Turkish sultan in Constantinople (modern Istanbul) for his services. Thus, while some shops were of remarkable longevity, others were put together quickly to meet the needs of a particular commission overseen by a visiting artist. The peripatetic careers of such artists were in part responsible for transplanting personal styles to new locations, for the artists trained local craftsmen as

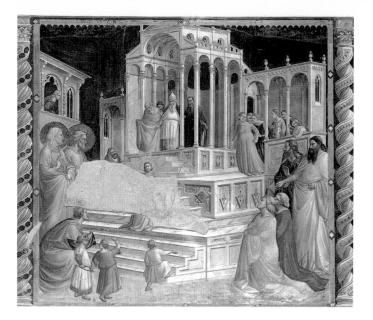

9 *Presentation of the Virgin in the Temple*, c. 1332, commissioned by the Baroncelli family from TADDEO GADDI for the Baroncelli Chapel, Santa Croce, Florence. Fresco

they moved from city to city. Conversely artists could absorb new stylistic ideas from the places to which they traveled, thus enriching both their own work and ultimately the artistic language of their home city.

Historiography and Methodology

The dissemination of artistic ideas was supported by the ever-increasing production of artistic treatises, especially after the introduction of the printing press in Italy in the later fifteenth century, and by the establishment in the mid-sixteenth century of artistic academies where theory could be proposed and debated by both artists and intellectuals interested in the arts. These two forces—the treatise and the academy—helped to transform the perception of the arts from a craft-based to an intellectual activity.

First among the Renaissance treatises was Leon Battista Alberti's *De Pictura*, written in Latin in 1435 and translated into Italian in 1436 as *Della Pittura*. The Latin text—dedicated to Gianfrancesco Gonzaga of Mantua—indicates that Alberti first thought of the educated patron as his audience (Filarete's "father"). The Italian translation dedicated to the artists from whom Alberti had learned his practical information (see page 206) retained the classical references which lard the original Latin text and initiated the formal transformation of the arts from manual skills to intellectual endeavor.

With the proliferation of treatises (especially on architecture for which the Roman architect, Vitruvius, provided a well-known model then existing in multiple manuscript copies), writers moved increasingly toward theoretical issues and then to recording the recent history of the

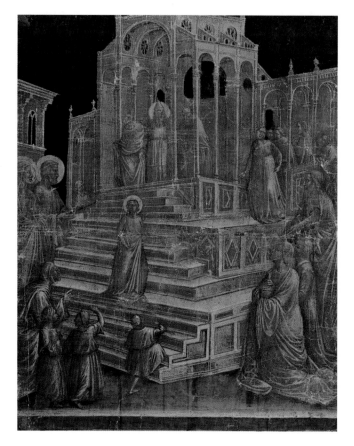

8 *Presentation of the Virgin in the Temple*, c. 1332, TADDEO GADDI. Presentation drawing for the fresco in the Baroncelli Chapel, Santa Croce, Florence; silverpoint with white highlighting, green and blue pigments on green prepared paper, 14¼ × 11½" (36.4 × 28.3 cm) (Musée du Louvre, Cabinet des Dessins, Paris)

10 (left) *Eucharistic Tabernacle* for the altar of the Chapel of the Ospedale della Scala, Siena, 1467, LORENZO VECCHIETTA. Presentation drawing; tempera and oil on cloth, 138 × 35" (352 × 89 cm) (Pinacoteca Nazionale, Siena)

11 (right) *Eucharistic Tabernacle*, 1467–72, commissioned under the rector Niccolò Ricoveri from LORENZO VECCHIETTA for the altar of the Chapel of the Ospedale della Scala, Siena. Bronze (Siena Cathedral)

Although originally on the altar of the hospital chapel, the tabernacle was moved in 1506 to the high altar of Siena Cathedral, where it replaced Duccio's *Maestà* (see Fig. 2.19).

arts that flourished so spectacularly during this period. The sculptor Lorenzo Ghiberti seems to have been the first to have attempted such a. history in his autobiography, left unfinished at his death in 1455. In his short manuscript he essentially lists artists whose accomplishments he believed had been markers in the development of the arts, much as Cennini listed his own personal artistic lineage going back to Giotto. This "great man" approach to history was developed into a full-scale biographical model one hundred years later by Giorgio Vasari in his *Lives of the Artists*, first published in 1550 and then revised and greatly expanded for a second edition of 1568. The *Lives* has provided a dominating critical and historical framework for understanding Italian art. Despite a challenging array of new theoretical approaches to this art—and to the entire field of art history—Vasari's narrative has been remarkably tenacious within the critical literature and therefore deserves some attention.

Vasari's Three Ages

Vasari ordered the history of Renaissance art into three distinct—and progressive—periods or "ages" as he called them, which essentially divide history by century from the fourteenth into the sixteenth century. For Vasari the arts of antiquity provided a model of excellence which had been debased by what he referred to as the "barbarian" style of the Middle Ages. Their revival began with Giotto in the fourteenth century, matured in the work of artists such as Masaccio and Donatello in the fifteenth century, and culminated in the work of Michelangelo in the

C O N T E M P O R A R Y   V O I C E

Terms of Employment

Although contracts between patrons and artists varied considerably, even within the same town, the following contract, between the Prior of the Ospedale degli Innocenti in Florence and the painter Domenico Ghirlandaio, is fairly typical. This was for a painting of the *Adoration of the Magi* (which may still be seen at the Ospedale today).

Be it known and manifest to whoever sees or reads this document that, at the request of the reverend Messer Francesco di Giovanni Tesori, presently Prior of the Spedale degli Innocenti at Florence, and of Domenico di Tomaso di Curado [Ghirlandaio], painter, I, Fra Bernardo di Francesco of Florence, Jesuate Brother, have drawn up this document with my own hand as agreement contract and commission for an altar panel to go in the church of the abovesaid Spedale degli Innocenti with the agreements and stipulations stated below, namely:

That this day 23 October 1485 the said Francesco commits and entrusts to the said Domenico the painting of a panel which the said Francesco has had made and has provided; the which panel the said Domenico is to make good, that is, pay for; and he is to colour and paint the said panel all with his own hand in the manner shown in a drawing on paper with those figures and in that manner shown in it, in every particular according to what I, Fra Bernardo, think best; not departing from the manner and composition of the said drawing; and he must colour the panel at his own expense with good colours and with powdered gold on such ornaments as demand it, with any other expense incurred on the same panel, and the blue must be ultramarine of the value about four florins the ounce; and he must have made and delivered complete the said panel within thirty months from today; and he must receive as the price of the panel as here described (made at his, that is, the said Domenico's expense throughout) 115 large florins if it seems to me, the abovesaid Fra Bernardo, that it is worth it; and I can go to whoever I think best for an opinion on its value or workmanship, and if it does not seem to me worth the stated price, he shall receive as much less as I, Fra Bernardo, think right; and he must within the terms of the agreement paint the predella of the said panel as I, Fra Bernardo, think good; and he shall receive payment as follows—the said Messer Francesco must give the abovesaid Domenico three large florins every month, starting from 1 November 1485 and continuing after as is stated, every month three large florins . . . .

And if Domenico has not delivered the panel within the abovesaid period of time, he will be liable to a penalty of fifteen large florins; and correspondingly if Messer Francesco does not keep to the abovesaid monthly payments he will be liable to a penalty of the whole amount, that is, once the panel is finished he will have to pay complete and in full the balance of the sum due.

(from Michael Baxandall. *Painting and Experience in Fifteenth-Century Italy*. Oxford: Oxford University Press, 2nd ed., 1988, p. 6)

---

sixteenth century. For Vasari perfection in the arts consisted of the ability to reproduce forms in a naturalistic manner while adding an ineluctable aspect of grace to figural movement and to emulate, if not surpass, the artistic accomplishments of ancient Greece and Rome.

Given the biographical format of Vasari's *Lives*—and perhaps also the fact that he was himself a painter and architect—it is not surprising that individual creative genius governs his presentation. Vasari chose each artist either because he provided new forms for the arts, or because he carried a new idea into a more complete phase of development, or because he produced important new milestones along a continually developing path for the arts. There is but one woman, Properzia de' Rossi (1490 Bologna–c. 1530 Bologna) to whom Vasari gives a "life"—albeit a brief one (see Contemporary Voice, p. 26)—in the 1550 edition, with only passing reference to a few other female artists added to this account in the second edition. By using biography as a structure for his history Vasari borrowed a narrative literary form that had its own history and traditions, including the freedom to invent stories when the facts of the subject's life were not available. The lives of the saints were other conventional models for Vasari's biographies, so artists often appear as *exempla*, moral and otherwise, of artistic behavior, individual genius, and—importantly for Vasari—elevated status. By Vasari's time an artist like Michelangelo was referred to as "divine," his genius as an artistic creator metaphorically compared with the power of the original Creator.

In recent historiography Vasari's three "ages" have been supplanted by such unhelpful terms as "proto-Renaissance," "early Renaissance," and "High Renaissance." By implying a linear conception of history, loosely related to a biological model of birth and maturity, terms such as these are misleading. To define any work of art as "proto" or even "early," for example, is to define it by its relationship to something else, not by its own inherent qualities. Similarly, to describe a work of art as "high" is to suggest that it is qualitatively better than anything previous, once again diminishing the effective power of earlier works.

Despite Vasari's occasional forays outside Tuscany, the *Lives* is essentially about Florentine and other Tuscan artists, perhaps not surprising since Vasari dedicated the book to Cosimo I de' Medici, the ruler of Tuscany and his patron. It is easy to come away from a reading of the *Lives* believing that the Renaissance was essentially a Florentine phenomenon which did not spread to other areas of Italy and Europe until late in the fifteenth and on into the sixteenth century. Artistic developments and works of extraordinary power in major cities such as Milan or Naples which are integral to an understanding of the artistic history of the period seem to have no place in Vasari's scheme of history, a bias which this book seeks, at least in part, to redress. His Tuscan bias may have its uses in defining certain stylistic innovations, but it plays havoc with the wealth of differing artistic styles in the peninsula, where individual cities functioned as separate states, each with its own traditions, forms of government, and history of artistic patronage. Given the different artistic styles of the various Italian city-states any simple definition of the Renaissance becomes problematic at best.

Vasari's biases are evident in his biography of Properzia de' Rossi. His narration of this extraordinary woman's life and works is relatively short, partly because she was a woman, but also because she did not work in Florence or Rome. In his biography, Vasari initially idealizes Properzia's character and education. He paints a perfect picture of a perfect Renaissance woman: delicate, musically talented, and "excellent not only in household matters . . . but also in sciences without number." At the same time, Vasari's Properzia is subjected to the narratives of her own art, in this case her relief of *Joseph and Potiphar's Wife* for San Petronio, Bologna (Fig. 12). Like the biblical character, Properzia was supposedly spurned by "a handsome young man, who seemed to care but little for her," and the relief "was a great satisfaction to herself, thinking that with this illustration from the Old Testament she had partly quenched the raging fire of her own passion." It was difficult for most men, not just Vasari, to believe that women could be both creative and virtuous.

Documents confirm that Properzia did indeed have a fiery, even unconventional spirit. In 1520 she and her lover (the documents call her his "concubine") were charged with entering and destroying the garden of her neighbor. In 1525 she and a male painter friend were arrested for having trespassed on the property of another painter, where she threw paint in his face and scratched his eyes. She spent her last years penniless in Bologna's Ospedale di San Giobbe.

But does this information actually provide an adequate insight into the meaning of the relief? While Properzia may indeed have exploited her own experience to carve a powerful, determined Potiphar's wife, payments indicate that some of her compositions were carved from models provided by other artists. She is unlikely to have chosen the subject herself. It is more likely that it was assigned to her by men on the building committee of San Petronio. And to many viewers who were unaware of the political machinations within the workshops of the Fabbrica, it was merely a story among many from the Old Testament extolling male virtue. Looking at a work of art in a broader context than Vasari did, not just as a reflection of the maker's biography, is more likely to reveal its fuller significance.

Terminology

A critical issue in the study of Italian art of the fourteenth through the sixteenth century centers around the word "Renaissance," a term that immediately generates controversy and that has produced some of the most acrimonious historical debate of the last fifty years. Meaning "rebirth," the word "Renaissance" first appeared in a historical context in 1855, in the seventh volume of Jules Michelet's *Histoire de France*, which he titled *La Renaissance*. Michelet's Renaissance, however, dealt with the emerging French nation of the sixteenth century, not the politically fragmented Italy of the fourteenth and fifteenth centuries. In 1860 Jacob Burckhardt used Michelet's terminology in his *Kultur der Renaissance in Italien* ("The Civilization of the Renaissance in Italy"), still a foundation text for the period. Burckhardt's exclusive focus on Italy from the fourteenth to the sixteenth century provided both the time frame and the location that have determined virtually all modern discussions both of the term and of the phenomena of the Renaissance. The title of the book, moreover, conflates in one word, "civilization," the art and the politics of the period as visualizations of the modern state. It is the expansion of this Burckhardtian approach, with a more inclusive interpretation of the meaning of culture, that governs more modern approaches to the period.

Since "Renaissance" remains in current usage it is useful to try to unpack some of its meaning. It is a curious term for a historian to use for it implies a definitive rupture in the historical flow. Such a conception of history has its roots in fourteenth-century Italy, where it was used to serve very specific purposes. In 1336, in a poem called "Africa," Petrarch wrote that the grandsons of his contemporaries would be able to walk out of "this slumber of forgetfulness into the pure radiance of the past." Such an assertion suggests three things: the beginning of a new age in history, the existence of the Dark Ages (another historical term essentially empty of meaning), and a time frame of three generations (Vasari's three "ages") for the revival of the arts and learning of classical antiquity. Together these concepts came to define the Renaissance. In their roles as collectors and editors of antique texts, as well as writers, Petrarch and his successors laid the foundations for the *studia humanitatis*, known by the technical term "humanism." From its origins in the fourteenth century, humanism flourished for the next two hundred years. It was fundamentally the study of the literary style,

moral content, and political theory of classical antiquity, although the texts of the Church Fathers were also carefully and critically studied. Writers from Petrarch to Vasari reclaimed the antique as an ideal of form and urged its revival in art and letters. Vasari even used the Italian word for rebirth (*rinascita*) in the *Lives*. There he claimed, however, not just the perfection of antique forms, but their closer temporal relation to the moment of Creation itself.

C O N T E M P O R A R Y   V O I C E

Fashioning the Female Artist

This account of the life of a female artist is fraught with contradictions. Somewhat ludicrously, Vasari asserts that Properzia de' Rossi carved peach pits because she possessed a formidable intellect, neglecting to note that as a woman she had extremely limited access to the usual sculptor's materials and training. Two examples of her pit carving survive: one a cherry pit with dozens of small bearded faces carved on it (Museo degli Argenti, Pitti Palace, Florence), the other a jeweled escutcheon of the Grassi family set with peach pits (Museo Civico Medievale, Bologna).

Nor have they [women] been too proud to set themselves with their little hands, so tender and so white, as if to wrest from us the palm of supremacy, to manual labours, braving the roughness of marble and the unkindly chisels, in order to attain to their desire and thereby win fame; as did, in our own day, Properzia de' Rossi of Bologna, a young woman excellent not only in household matters, like the rest of them, but also in sciences without number, so that all the men, to say nothing of the women, were envious of her.

This Properzia was very beautiful in person, and played and sang in her day better than any other woman of her city. And because she had an intellect both capricious and very ready, she set herself to carve peachstones, which she executed so well and with such patience, that they were singular and marvellous to behold, not only for the subtle-

ty of the work, but also for the grace of the little figures that she made in them and the delicacy with which they were distributed. And it was certainly a miracle to see on so small a thing as a peach-stone the whole Passion of Christ, wrought in most beautiful carving, with a vast number of figures in addition to the apostles and the ministers of the Crucifixion. This encouraged her, since there

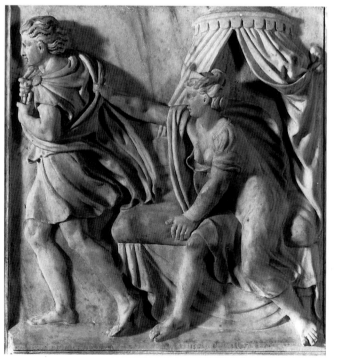

12 *Joseph and Potiphar's Wife*, c. 1525–26, commissioned by the Fabbrica of San Petronio, Bologna, from PROPERZIA DE' ROSSI for the façade of San Petronio. Marble, 1'9" × 1'11" (0.54 × 0.58 m) (Museo di San Petronio, Bologna)

Properzia was paid for two sibyls, two angels, and one relief on August 4, 1526.

were decorations to be made for the three doors of the first façade of S. Petronio, all in figures of marble, to ask the Wardens of Works, by means of her husband, for a part of that work; at which they were quite content, on the condition that she should let them see some work in marble executed by her own hand. . . . In this, to the vast delight of all Bologna, she made an exquisite scene, wherein—because at that time the poor woman was madly enamoured of a handsome young man, who seemed to care but little for her—she represented the wife of Pharaoh's Chamberlain, who, burning with love for Joseph, and almost in despair after so much persuasion, finally strips his garments from him with a womanly grace that defies description. This work was esteemed by all to be most beautiful, and it was a great satisfaction to herself, thinking that with this illustration from the Old Testament she had partly quenched the raging fire of her own passion. . . She also made two angels in very strong relief and beautiful proportions, which may now be seen, although against her wish, in the same building. In the end she devoted herself to copper-plate engraving, which she did without reproach, gaining the highest praise. And so the poor love-stricken young woman came to succeed most perfectly in everything, save in her unhappy passion.

(from Giorgio Vasari. *Lives of the Most Eminent Painters, Sculptors, and Architects*. Trans. Gaston de Vere, ed. Kenneth Clark. New York: Harry N. Abrams, 1974, vol. II, pp. 1044–48)

When Vasari called up the antique as a source of perfection it was not simply because of its formal properties, but because it reflected the divine more clearly than any later art could.

Yet modern historians have quite rightly begun to stress the continuities between historical periods rather than the disjunctions noted by writers like Petrarch and Vasari. Established iconographical types, such as the Last Judgment, for example, show few signs of change in compositional pattern from their initial formulation to their disappearance, even if figural style differs over time. Scholars, lawyers, and doctors used textual sources from both antiquity and the Middle Ages as foundations for their own thinking and writing, tying them to the past even as they attempted to interpret and expand upon these earlier ideas. History was deeply felt as an influential force for cultural and social definition. Petrarch's extreme formulation is but one manifestation that earlier ideas were so pervasive in the culture that the writer felt a need to distance himself in a stark manner from their influence by relegating them to some imagined dark age. More recently historians have supplanted the term "Renaissance" with "early modern," which may raise as many problems as it solves, but which has the benefit of changing the terms of discourse from rebirth or revival to continuity with the present (although the use of "early" does raise the specter of a simple evolutionary model for history).

The term "Renaissance" will be used in this book as a convenient designation of a chronological period, not as a description of style. Social, political, religious, and psychological self-perceptions were vastly different from one city-state to another and from the beginning of the fourteenth to the end of the sixteenth century. Elsewhere in Europe, new nation states were forming, making the Italian pattern of independent city-states anachronistic by 1600. The once monolithic Christian community splintered into several independent churches. An economic system focused on the Mediterranean since antiquity collapsed with the gradual enlargement of the Islamic Ottoman Empire, with explorations around the coast of Africa, and with the European "discovery" of the Americas. And the tenaciously held notion of a geocentric universe eventually gave way to new scientific investigations that revealed the earth as merely a satellite of the sun. In a world where such fundamental challenges to people's self-perceptions were occurring, to define the Renaissance in the arts as a phenomenon based on naturalistic representation, reverence for classical antiquity, and Vasari's notion of perfection is myopic. The history of the period is enormously exciting, but its events, its artistic creations, and its lessons are even more compelling if they are seen in a context that includes multicultural variables from city to city.

It is important to underscore here that the art of the Renaissance, like that of other historical periods, represents a marriage of intellect and craft. Artistic forms do not flow automatically from the hand of the artist but are carefully structured by an incisive, critical, and open intellect. Michelangelo emphasized the importance of the artist's intellectual genius when, in 1546, he wrote complaining of the pressures being placed on him to finish his sculpture for the tomb of Julius II: ". . . a man paints with his brains and not with his hands, and if he cannot have his brains clear he will come to grief."

Following Vasari's approach, art historians have concentrated on those artists who either departed from the stylistic conventions in which they were trained or invented new ways of representing their subjects or combined accepted modes of representation in new and powerfully effective ways. Such innovations were, however, part of a complicated pattern of response to the demands of the patrons and the commissions. In a situation in which an artist's ability to pursue his career was dependent upon the receipt of commissions, any novel form of representation needed to find a positive and knowledgeable response from the patron. Stylistic and iconographical innovations remain intriguing because of their sheer imaginative and aesthetic power and because that power was joined to a web of social, religious, and political events. It is the typical, however, rather than the exceptional, that in many ways governs our lives. Examining the exceptional work of art in the context of the typical enhances the meaning of each.

When Vasari wrote his *Lives* he essentially foreclosed discussion of the Renaissance by declaring his own era—Michelangelo's era—an age of artistic perfection. Today, renewed study of Italian Renaissance art calls for continued re-evaluation not only of the arts themselves, but also of past histories and of the many new critical methodologies for interpreting them. Since this art raises fundamental issues about perception and self-promotion (whether of the individual or the state), the interpenetration of the spiritual and the physical worlds, and the models appropriate for carrying a given meaning, the ability to understand these arts provides a window into understanding our own world as well as that of Renaissance Italy.

Materials and Methods

Although individual workshops for painting, sculpture, and architecture had some procedures and structures in common, they all required considerable skill in organizing specialized group activity. Artists were sometimes productive in more than one medium, but each art had its own set of problems to solve and each its own types of materials. Moreover, virtually all artistic workshops undertook a variety of jobs in order to ensure their commercial viability. Painting shops are a case in point. In addition to large-scale fresco cycles or free-standing paintings, the Renaissance painter could be engaged in painting works of sculpture, preparing presentation drawings for sculptors and architects, producing small devotional images or large-scale cloth banners (see Fig. 5.46), decorating household furniture (Fig. 13), and devising and producing festival decorations.

The Painting Studio

Wall Painting Among the most complex projects undertaken during the Renaissance was the painting of **fresco**. Fresco (literally "fresh") is simply painting on wet plaster. This medium was used to decorate large wall areas of both public and private buildings. The wall, usually of rough stone and cement, was first prepared by the application of a layer of rough plaster, called the *arriccio*. Then a finer layer of wet plaster, called *intonaco*, was laid on the *arriccio* in sections; each section was painted, using pigments mixed with water, and allowed to dry before a new

section was begun. Painters worked from the top down to avoid dripping on an already finished surface. Ensuring that pigment was always laid on a plaster of equal wetness was important for guaranteeing that the colors would dry evenly to the same tone over the entire fresco. This process meant that each patch of wet plaster (called a *giornata*, or "day's work"—though in many cases more than one was completed in a day) slightly overlapped the edge of the adjacent patch. Areas of complicated painting, such as faces, are relatively small, whereas simple expanses of sky or landscape are quite large. These overlaps allow modern restorers to trace the progress of the painting from beginning to end by plotting the sequence of the overlaps. Sometimes frescoes were painted on plaster surfaces that were already dry. Called *fresco secco* (dry fresco) to distinguish it from *buon fresco* (good, or true, fresco), this technique was used most often for corrections and for fine details, on costume, for example. It was much less durable than *buon fresco*.

Such sizable paintings, in which timing was of critical importance, took careful planning and involved a number of assistants. A precise plan in the form of a drawing, or of many drawings, was required so that the composition would fit exactly on the designated wall. Painting at

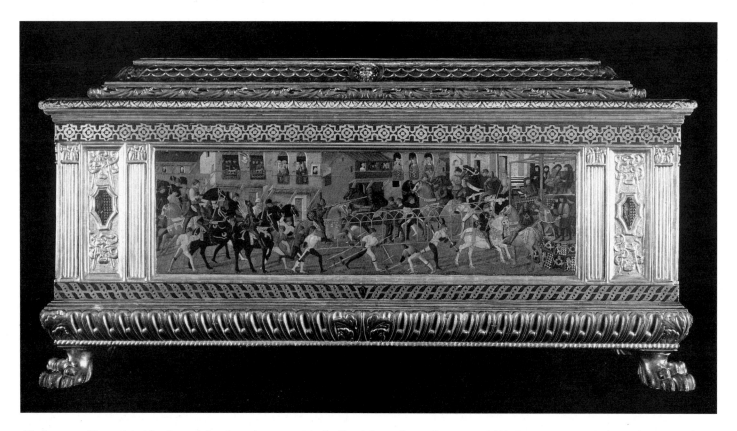

13 *Cassone* with a painted front panel showing a tournament in the Piazza Santa Croce, Florence, c. 1460. Tempera on panel, chest 40 × 80 × 14" (103 × 203 × 66 cm), panel 15 × 51" (38 × 130 cm) (National Gallery, London)

The gold has been renewed on the chest. Originally, the armor of the knights participating in the tournament was silver.

wall size involved a problem comparable to that of carving a large-scale sculpture from a small model: how to transfer the figures in a small drawing to a large wall. One way of doing this was simply to place a grid of squares over the drawing, like the one Uccello used for his monumental commemorative fresco of Sir John Hawkwood (Fig. 14). With the help of an enlarged grid, containing

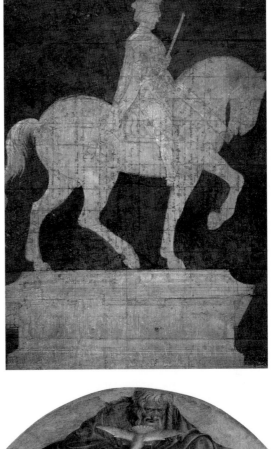

14 *Sir John Hawkwood*, c. 1436, commissioned by the Signoria of Florence from PAOLO UCCELLO for Florence Cathedral. Preparatory drawing, squared with a stylus, for the fresco; silverpoint heightened with white on a light green, prepared ground, 18 × 13″ (46 × 33 cm) (Gabinetto dei Disegni, Galleria degli Uffizi, Florence)

15 *St. Jerome and the Trinity*, 1455, commissioned by Girolamo Corboli from ANDREA DEL CASTAGNO. Preparatory *sinopia* drawing (now detached from wall) for fresco, 9′ 9″ × 6′ 7″ (2.97 × 1.78 m) (Cenacolo di Sant' Apollonia, Florence)

16 *St. Jerome and the Trinity*, 1455, commissioned by Girolamo Corboli from ANDREA DEL CASTAGNO for the Corboli Chapel, Santissima Annunziata, Florence. Fresco (now detached from wall), 10′ 10″ × 6′ 10½″ (3 × 1.79 m)

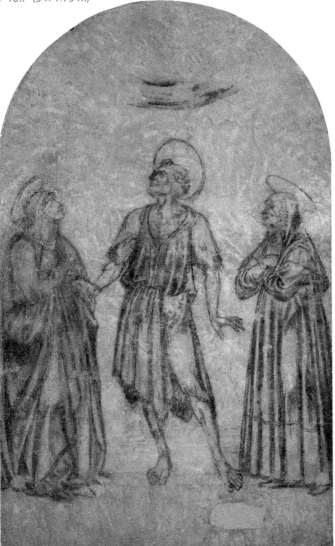

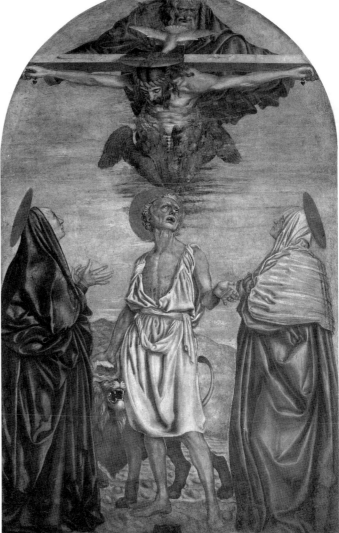

the same number of squares as the drawing and applied to the wall, the painter could then transfer each square of the drawing onto the wall. Another method was to draw directly onto the *arriccio* with a burnt-orange pigment called *sinopia* ("cinnobar"), most likely referring to a pre-existing drawing of the whole composition. The painter could then cover the *arriccio* with sequential patches of painting, remembering the outlines of the covered part of the *sinopia* and joining the new painting to adjacent areas of *sinopia*. Recent restoration techniques allowing the upper layer of a fresco to be detached from the *arriccio* have revealed a wealth of *sinopia* drawings from the fourteenth century, when this technique seems to have been most often employed. The use of the *sinopia* drawing as a preparation for the final fresco allowed the artist some freedom to alter his composition as he went along, as Castagno's frescoes for Santissima Annunziata demonstrate (Figs. 15 and 16).

In the fifteenth and sixteenth centuries the **cartoon** (from an Italian word *cartone* indicating heavy paper)

seems to have replaced the *sinopia* underdrawing as a way of transferring the artist's conception to the wall. Cartoons were full-scale simplified drawings of sections of the final fresco. The image could be transferred to the wall in one of two ways. The artist could place an individual cartoon against the wet plaster and draw with a stylus over the lines, thus leaving an incision in the plaster; once painted over, the marks of the stylus are hardly noticeable except in sharp raking light (Fig. 17). Alternatively, the artist could prick holes in the lines of his drawing, then place the drawing against the wet plaster and pound a small bag made from very fine cloth and filled with charcoal dust against the drawing; in this technique, called pouncing, the dust penetrated the pricked holes, leaving a small dotted outline of the composition on the wet plaster. These charcoal dots could then be painted over; close, detailed inspection of the finished frescoes often reveals these charcoal dots beneath the finished surface (Fig. 18), but, even more than the marks of the stylus, they are difficult to read at a distance.

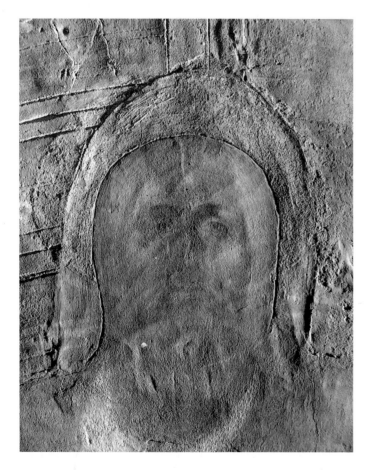

17 *Trinity*, c. 1425, commissioned by a member of the Lenzi family from MASACCIO for Santa Maria Novella, Florence. See also Fig. 4.60

This detail of the head of God in a raking light shows the stylus marks on the wet plaster, outlining the head and marking the vaulting system.

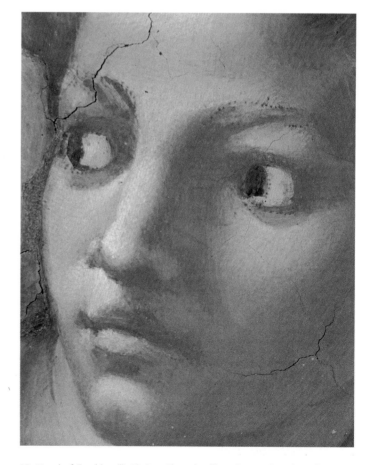

18 *Head of Eve* (detail), Sistine Chapel ceiling, Rome, Creation of Adam, 1508–12, commissioned by Julius II from MICHELANGELO. Fresco

The charcoal dots from the pricked cartoon are evident in the eyebrows.

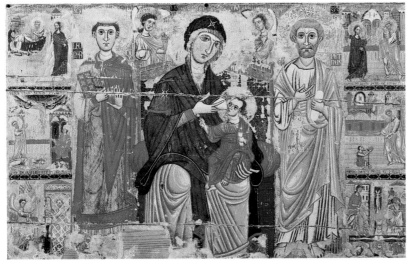

19 *Magdalene Altarpiece*, second half of thirteenth century, MAGDALENE MASTER. Tempera on panel, 41¼ × 63″ (104.9 × 160 cm) (University Purchase from James Jackson Jarves, Yale University Art Gallery, New Haven)

The presence of the youthful St. Leonard at the Virgin's right side suggests that the painting was made for the high altar of San Leonardo, Arcetri, just outside Florence. The Magdalene Master is a generic term for a style rather than a reference to a single artist.

Panel Painting   Panel painting, although a very different medium from wall painting, and serving very different functions, also required careful stages of preparation before paint could be applied to the surface. The wooden support for the painting and the frame that was attached to it were either ordered from a woodworker to the specification of the painter or provided by the patron who had procured it from a woodworker. The selection of the wood—usually poplar—and its curing were important aspects of the work; improperly aged panels could warp and crack, causing damage to the painted surface. When the painter received the raw wood panel, often with its framing and decorative elements already in place, he and the members of his shop had to prepare it for painting. They covered the surface with fine linen onto which they brushed a coarse layer of **gesso** (*gesso grosso*) made from ground plaster and glue. This layer acted as a base for the application by brush of several layers of very fine gesso (*gesso sottile*), continuously applied to the surface before any one layer dried completely. When the gesso surface had hardened it was scraped and polished to give it a very smooth finish. The various layers of this built-up surface can be seen in a much-damaged altarpiece of Mary Magdalene (Fig. 19) where raw panel, linen, and gesso surface all show through the abraded surface and where even the burn mark of a candle gives some hint of the damages to which such paintings were prone. Decorative details such as haloes or borders of costumes or even inscriptions could be built up on this surface with plaster

(*pastiglia*) so that they became a low relief on the panel. This technique was used in fresco as well.

It was customary to make a drawing of the planned painting with fine charcoal on the gesso surface. This could be erased and altered as required. Once the painter was satisfied with the drawing, it could be reinforced and clarified with ink. No unfinished panels bearing such drawings have survived, but X-rays of existing paintings often reveal traces of drawings beneath the surface.

Large areas of gilding were applied before the painting began (see Fig. 2.1). Areas to be gilded were painted with red **bole**, which was suspended in a liquid medium of **glair**, or size. The bole gave added luster to the thin foil of gold leaf which merely had to be pressed onto its wet surface in order to adhere. A preparatory layer of green pigment was laid down on areas that were to represent flesh, so that when the pink flesh tones were painted over it the interaction of the color opposites gave vitality to the skin. In paintings where the layers of skin tone have now worn away the green under-modeling lies exposed in a manner never intended by the artist. The medium used for panel painting was **tempera**, in which the pigments were suspended in a medium of egg yolk. Tempera was a slow, painstaking process, as the short, repeated strokes that make up any surface of one of these panels attests.

Once the painting was finished, metal punches could be used to add decorative borders around the individual panels, to the haloes, or to the clothing of the figures. This decorative surface, like the raised plaster areas of the panel, caught and reflected the light from candles and oil lamps in a shimmering manner intended to intensify the otherworldly quality of the images and, more practically, to make them legible in the darker areas of churches.

Oil Painting   By the mid-fifteenth century Italian artists in Naples, Venice, and Florence began to incorporate the technique of oil painting into their repertoire. Although at first used on panel, oil painting was later more often employed with a cloth support such as linen. In this technique pigments are suspended in an oil medium, often linseed oil, giving an easy fluidity of application and allowing corrections and adjustments as the painting progresses. Using oils, a painter could apply successive layers of paint to the surface. This not only made it easy to change the composition of the picture but also allowed greater richness of color, as the overlapping tones interacted with one another. The effect of light penetrating the various layers of paint or playing over the glazes that the painter also applied to the surface achieves a luminous brilliance that would have been appreciated by artists seeking an evermore naturalistic effect.

Mosaic and Stained Glass No material was more reflective and resplendent than mosaic (see Fig. 1.1). In this medium, as in the production of stained-glass windows (both much more common in Italy than is usually supposed), a master painter provided a full-scale cartoon for a glass specialist to translate into his medium. In order to piece together the image, the mosaicist employed tiny squares of colored glass called tesserae, some of them with gold or silver leaf sandwiched between sheets of glass. These tesserae were set in a plaster ground, their individual surfaces deliberately set at irregular angles the better to catch and reflect in a shimmering manner the irregular light of candles and oil lamps. A master window glazer cut larger pieces of blown glass into irregular pieces and joined them together with canes of lead. Either he or, occasionally, the painter who had provided the cartoon would add the lines and shadows of the figures to be depicted in **grisaille**, a dark pigment that was fused at high heat onto the glass itself. Thus, although individual panes of colored glass might give local color to individual features of the narrative, the details were presented in monochrome. For a culture in which light carried implications of the divine, reflective mosaic and glass were highly effective media for carrying sacred narratives.

The Sculpture Workshop

Sculpture workshops were arguably the most complex and diverse of the Renaissance. A sculptor might choose to work in stone, wood, terracotta, stucco, plaster of Paris, papier-mâché, wax, bronze, gold, or silver (see Fig. 3.1), although most limited themselves to one or two of these media. Moreover, the work could be figural or purely decorative, free-standing or relief, a colossal exterior statue or a very small medal. The artist could be paid a specified amount of money for a figural work or a price per given unit of measurement if he were providing decorative sculpture such as moldings. Some sculptors cast bronze within the shop, others subcontracted out the casting once a finished model was ready. The shop could be a private one, owned by an independent master, or it could be one established under the auspices of a building committee for a large building in need of decoration, such as a cathedral. In the former case the artist could control and govern who worked in the shop, bringing in new talent as the need demanded and letting others go when there was no work. As with painting workshops, the result of this system of training under a master was designed to produce a uniform shop style, in which everything produced had the look of the master.

In a large, corporate shop, artists of different training, style, and even national background were often hired to work side by side in an effort to complete large decorative programs as quickly as possible. Although a certain amount of consistency would be lent to such programs by the initial selection of the artists and by the supervision of the *capomaestro*, or head of the shop, it was more important to get the work done than to have complete uniformity of style, as Alfonso I's triumphal arch in Naples (see Fig. 6.5) demonstrates. Nanni di Banco's relief for the Arte dei Maestri di Pietra e Legname (Stone and Wood Workers' Guild) in Florence (see Fig. 3) shows that there was also division of labor within the shop, with some artists adept at architectural detailing such as twisted columns, others being entrusted with the leafy details of capitals, and still others with figures.

Stone sculpture required the sculptor either to travel to the quarry himself or to send a trustworthy assistant in order to find a block of stone not only the right size and shape but also without imperfection such as veins of minerals which would jeopardize the structural integrity of the work once it was complete. The stone had to be quarried and shipped, often over large distances, requiring travel both by boat and by oxcart (Fig. 20). With tolls based on weight or size having to be paid along the way, it was important that the sculptor not order more than was necessary for the commission. Once the rough stone arrived at the shop, assistants could begin to block out the figure, using a model in wax or terracotta provided by the master or a rough drawing on the block itself. For figural sculpture, points were marked on the model, usually at the knees, the buttocks, and the shoulders. These points were then transferred and enlarged to the scale of the large block by mechanical and mathematical devices (Fig. 21). Similar techniques could also be used to replicate ancient sculpture.

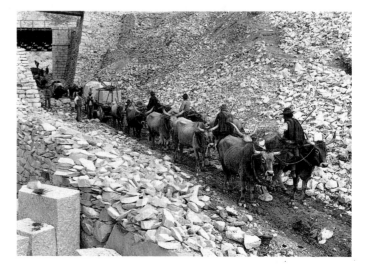

20 Transportation of Carrara marble by ox-cart, shown in a nineteenth-century photograph

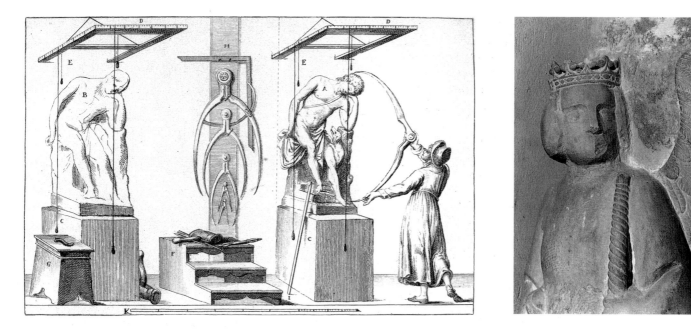

21 Transferring from a model to a block of stone, from FRANCESCO CARRADORI, *Istruzione elementare per gli studiosi della scultura*, Florence, 1802

22 Tomb monument of Carlo of Calabria, detail showing the unfinished head of Charity, 1332–33, commissioned by the House of Anjou from TINO DA CAMAINO. Marble (Santa Chiara, Naples)

The sculptor worked in from the block of the stone, constantly refining the form, first working with drills and pointed chisels and then progressing to chisels with finer and finer claws (cutting edges) as the carving became more delicate. Stone rough from the chisel had to be smoothed, using files and abrasives such as pumice. Finally, polishing with straw and cloth gave the surface its smooth character which over time took on a luster. In some rare instances unfinished sculpture was actually installed (Fig. 22), giving the modern historian some idea of how the carvers went about shaping the figure from the large block and carving the stone. In most cases sculptors painted their completed marbles, either to clarify the separation of figures from background, in the case of relief sculpture, or to add naturalistic details of color to the white marble of figural sculpture (Fig. 23). Often this amounted simply to gold detailing of architecture, of drapery borders, and of haloes. Most of this **polychromy** has subsequently worn away or been effaced in later "cleaning" projects, leaving a quite misleading notion of how Renaissance sculpture originally looked.

Sculptors also worked in wood, a medium that has only recently received serious scholarly attention. Most wooden figures, carved from sections of the trunks of trees, were virtually life-sized. In order to prevent major cracks in the figures as the wood aged and slowly dried, the tree trunk was often hollowed out from the back, allowing the figure to be more pliable in responding to changes in temperature and humidity. Wooden sculpture

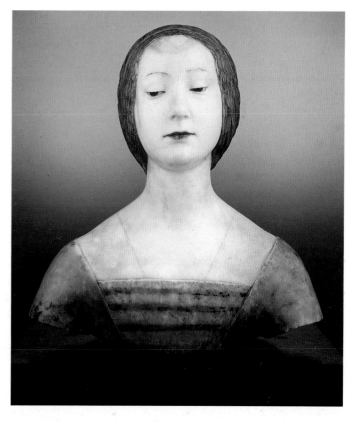

23 *Isabella of Aragon* (?), c. 1490, FRANCESCO LAURANA. Marble, height 17¼" (44 cm) (Kunsthistorisches Museum, Vienna)

could be pieced together from several logs, especially for crucifixes, in which the arms of the figure extended out from the main core of the body and thus needed to be carved from separate pieces of wood. In all cases wood sculpture was completely painted, so that the figure imitated as accurately as possible the human form it represented. This required that the wood surface be covered with gesso or with a fine linen fabric which itself was then covered with gesso; that plaster surface could then be colored much the same as a panel painting. It was not unusual for a sculptor to subcontract out the painting of wooden sculpture to workshops that specialized in such tasks as part of the mass production of devotional objects and painted furniture. Wooden statues were often completed by the addition of metal attributes (St. Peter's keys, for example) or by clothing, heightening the sense that the naturalistically painted figure was a human presence. Not surprisingly, given the fragile, flammable nature of wood and of fabric, most of these wooden figures have been lost.

What remains, however, opens rich reconsideration of how this sculpture functioned as part of religious rituals such as processions and liturgical drama. Many figures were clothed in special costumes for festival days, blurring the boundary between the real and the represented. Some wooden crucifixes were carved with arms attached on pins, so that the body could be removed from the cross, the arms folded down, and the Christ "buried" as part of the liturgy for Good Friday (Fig. 24). Some of these

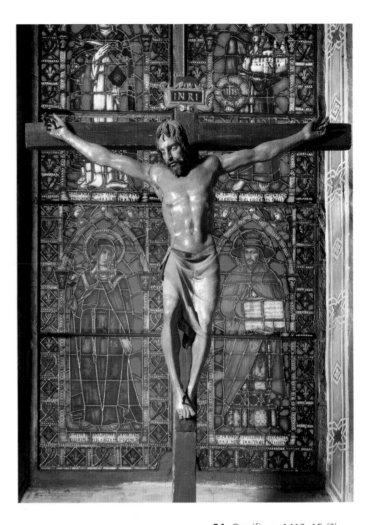

24 *Crucifix*, c. 1412–15 (?), DONATELLO. Painted wood, height 6' 6" (1.68 m) (Santa Croce, Florence)

Like many other statues carved in wood, this sculpture was overpainted with a brown pigment to simulate bronze by a later generation attempting to confer value on the work and to transform its realistic rendering of the human body into a classical one.

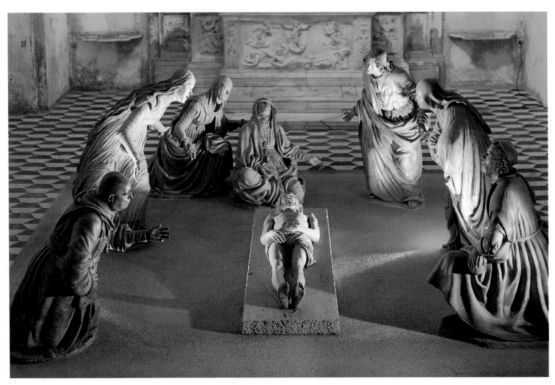

25 *Lamentation*, 1492–94, commissioned by Alfonso II of Naples from GUIDO MAZZONI for the Chapel of Alfonso II and Gurello Orelia (now Chapel of the Sepulchre), Church of Monteoliveto, Naples. Terracotta

The life-size kneeling figure on the left is a portrait of the patron, Alfonso II, in the role of Joseph of Arimathea.

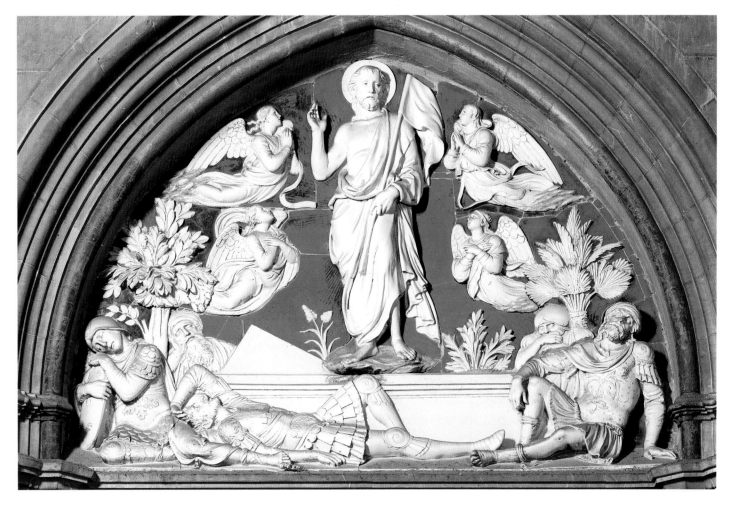

26 *Resurrection*, 1442–45, commissioned by a building committee of the cathedral (Opera del Duomo) from LUCA DELLA ROBBIA for a lunette over the door to the north sacristy, Florence Cathedral. Glazed and polychromed terracotta, 6′ 7″ × 8′ 8¼″ (2 × 2.65 m)

crucified Christ figures were even carved with a smooth scalp so that wigs of real human hair could be added, just as loincloths of real material were sometimes used.

Terracotta sculpture, like wood sculpture, was also brightly painted. The earliest extant examples of such sculpture come from the second half of the fifteenth century. Because of the fragile nature of terracotta very little remains of what must have been a sizable production in this medium. Generally independent figural sculpture in terracotta is life-sized (Fig. 25). During the fifteenth century the shop of Luca della Robbia developed a way of glazing terracotta sculpture so that it became quite durable and could be used for both exterior and interior spaces. Although the colors of the glazes were limited, they added brilliant polychromatic possibilities to this humble medium, and increasingly large-scale work in terracotta remained popular well into the sixteenth century —not only figures and reliefs (Fig. 26) but whole altarpieces as well.

Bronze Sculpture   Bronze sculpture of the Renaissance varies in size from small medals which can be held in the palm of the hand to large free-standing public sculpture. Most bronze statues are hollow shells of metal; smaller ones may be cast solid. Benvenuto Cellini's *Autobiography and Treatises* and Vannoccio Biringuccio's *De la pirotechnia* (1540) described how to make them, and technical examination of Renaissance bronze sculptures has confirmed them to be lost-wax casts (Fig. 27). The lost-wax process (from French *cire-perdue*) can be divided into "direct" and "indirect" casting, although written evidence and technical studies indicate that variations were used. The "direct" method is a straight translation of an original and unique wax model into a unique metal cast. In the "indirect" method, the wax model used for casting is made by taking an intermediary, reusable mold from the original model, which introduces another procedural step. This method permits the production of multiple casts and preservation of the original model.

The Renaissance sculptor (or workshop) produced a hollow wax model (A) either by hand or with a reusable mold. The wax model was rigged with a network of wax rods, or "sprues" (B). These create the passageways through which the wax, metal, and air circulate in the fire-resistant mold placed around the model. If the figure was hollow, metal core pins were inserted through the wax into the internal mold or "core" made of fire-resistant, or "refractory," material such as sandy clay (B); pins project on the inside and outside of the wax shell and hold the core in place. The sprued wax was embedded in refractory mold material (C). The mold was heated (D) to dry it thoroughly and melt out the wax. Meanwhile, the founder liquefied the alloy of copper and tin (often zinc and lead as well) in a crucible, or furnace. He poured molten bronze through the funnel created by the casting cup until it filled the cavity created in the mold by the wax (E). Once the metal solidified, the newly cast figure was broken out of the mold (F) and freed of its oxidized metal, network of sprues, and other imperfections (G). It was repaired, cleaned up, and any separately cast parts joined.

When the cooled bronze was freed from the mold the air tubes, now filled with solid bronze, had to be cut away and the entire rough surface of the bronze (Fig. 28) filed,

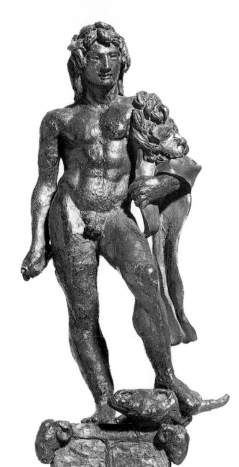

28 *Hercules*, 1470s, ANTONIO DEL POLLAIUOLO. Bronze, height of figure 11¾" (30 cm); height of figure and base 17¼" (44.1 cm) (© Frick Collection, New York)

The surface of the bronze is unfinished. Small, precious table bronzes such as this were regarded as collectors' items from the last decades of the fifteenth century, as a representation of the owner's fascination with, and knowledge of, antiquity.

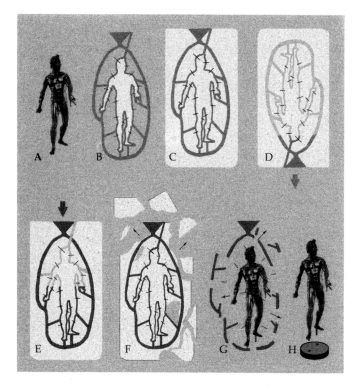

27 The lost-wax casting process

The lost-wax process allowed the sculptor to replicate a wax model in the permanent—and very expensive— material of bronze, but with a hollow core that saved on both material and also weight, important for transport costs (see Contemporary Voice box, p. 433).

chased, polished, and given a patina (sometimes varnish, sometimes colored oil) to enhance the luminous surface of the material. Before patinating, fine details of costume or of facial features could be incised into the bronze sculpture and gilding, if required, could be added (see Fig. 5.5). Given the technical complications of bronze casting, professional casters (sometimes bell-makers and at other times artillery specialists) were often given the job of turning the sculptor's models into their final form—yet another example of the collaborative nature of artistic production in this period.

Drawings

Drawings served important functions in painting and sculpture workshops. They could be used to train the *garzoni* to draw the figure (see Fig. 30)—as Squarcione's contract with his pupil Francesco indicates (see page 20)—or they could be records of motifs for use by both the master and his students (Fig. 29) or for manufacture in other shops. These drawings were kept in notebooks, functioning essentially as model books which could be lent, facilitating the transfer of ideas and motifs from one artistic studio to another or even from one city to another. Drawings, some at full scale, were often employed by architects and sculptors as models for the assistants in the shop to use in completing large projects. Documents indicate that Jacopo della Quercia had full-scale drawings of his intentions for the *Fonte Gaia* (see Fig. 4.66) placed on an interior wall of the town hall in Siena, both so that his patrons would know what to expect of the finished fountain and so that his assistants would know what to carve during the master's absences from the city. For obvious reasons no traces of such drawings remain: they were utilitarian steps in a process which, when complete, made them obsolete.

The history of drawings during this period suggests that they served an exclusively functional role until the beginning of the sixteenth century, when patrons, bent on forming a collection of work by artists of major importance, seemed satisfied, if not completely happy, to have a drawing by a chosen artist if they could not persuade him to deliver a painting. Thus Isabella d'Este pestered Leonardo da Vinci for a painted portrait, but received, ultimately, only a drawing. Vasari seems to have been the first person actively to collect drawings, which he pasted down in notebooks, then framed and even embellished with ink drawing of his own, as part of his

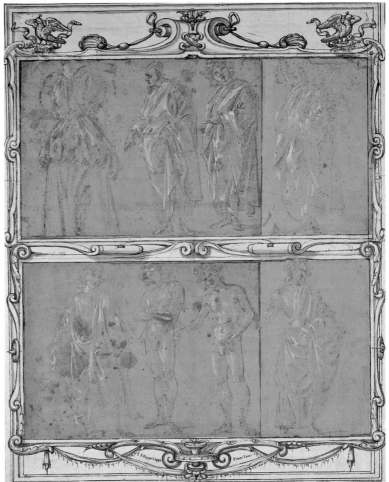

30 A page from GIORGIO VASARI'S drawing book in which he pasted drawings from his collection and added frames to structure a composition on the page (Christ Church, no. 1338, fol. 240r, Oxford)

The drawings are in silverpoint on prepared paper by Filippino Lippi, c. 1475.

record of the genius of the artists about whom he wrote (Fig. 30).

Even before Vasari began collecting, however, there were clearly some drawings that were meant to be appreciated not just for their technical competence and their contractual value, but for their beauty as well. Different from sinopia drawings, which were painted over in large fresco cycles (see Figs. 15 and 16), and different from model book drawings (see Fig. 29), some presentation drawings are so stunning in their use of prepared colored paper and coloristic highlights (see Fig. 8) that one must assume that they were meant to convince the patron of the artist's abilities as much by their sheer aesthetic splendor as by their promise of a finished product that would suit the patron's needs. Some workshop drawings of the later fifteenth century (see Fig. 30) are drawn on richly colored paper in silverpoint, a very fine wire of silver used like lead that oxidizes to leave a refined and elegant line on the paper; the richness of the medium with its white wash highlighting gives drawings such as these a shimmering quality of changing light that belies their mundane subjects of studio models.

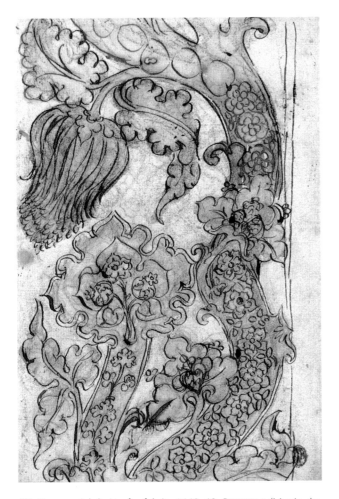

29 Ornamental design for fabric, 1448–49, PISANELLO (Musée du Louvre, Cabinet des Estampes, Paris)

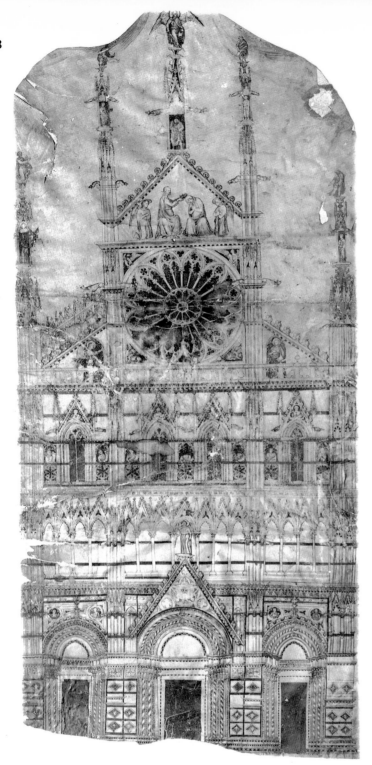

31 Façade of the Baptistry of Siena, c. 1316–17. Presentation drawing; ink on parchment (Museo dell'Opera del Duomo, Siena)

Architecture

Although the term "architect" does appear in some formal documents of this period, there seems not to have been a prescribed course of training for this position. Many architects began their careers as sculptors (Lorenzo Maitani, Filippo Brunelleschi, Bernardo Rossellino, Michelangelo, Jacopo Sansovino) or as painters (Giotto, Bramante, Raphael). Some, such as Brunelleschi or

Leonardo, seem to have had a thorough grasp of engineering; others most likely used master builders, whose practical expertise guided a building's progress.

Constructing a building during the Renaissance was a collaborative process, as it is today, which involved many teams of people directed by an architect or master builder and—in the case of a public building—by the commissioning officials. The initial conception for a new building could be visualized for a patron or a building committee in two ways. An architect might provide a presentation drawing (perhaps one drafted by someone else under his direction, comparable to practice today) which gave precise indications of his design; a drawing on parchment for the façade of the Sienese Baptistry (Fig. 31) is one of the few remaining examples of such drawings. Another practice was to provide a model of the planned building, which would give the patron a sense of the three-dimensional substance and detail of the planned structure. Wooden models such as that for Brunelleschi's dome of the cathedral of Florence (Fig. 32) were made by professional woodworkers from the designs of the architect. Stucco or clay models could be made within the shop of the architect. Before finished drawings or models were presented to the patron, however, there were undoubtedly numerous sketches and preliminary plans

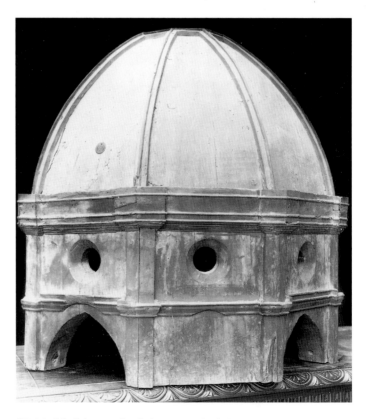

32 Model of the cupola of Florence Cathedral, c. 1420, commissioned by the Opera del Duomo from BRUNELLESCHI. Wood (Museo dell'Opera del Duomo, Florence) (see Fig. 4.46)

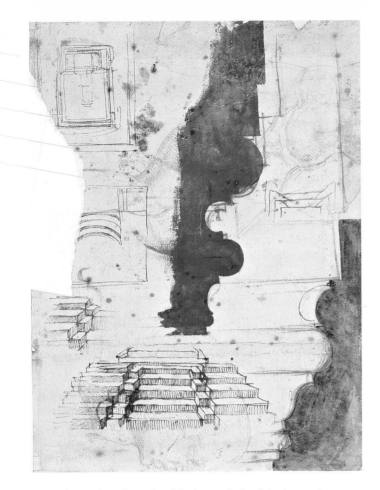

33 Design projects for stairwell in the vestibule of the Laurentian Library, Florence (see Fig. 7.49), c. 1523, commissioned by Pope Clement VII from MICHELANGELO. Black ink, red pastel, and watercolor, 12' 7" × 9' 2" (3.9 × 2.8 m) (Casa Buonarotti, Florence)

The drawings show early phases in the development of Michelangelo's thinking about the design possibilities for the stairwell. The watercolor drawings are templates for column bases that would have been replicated (sometimes on metal), cut out in profile, and used by stone carvers as directions for their work.

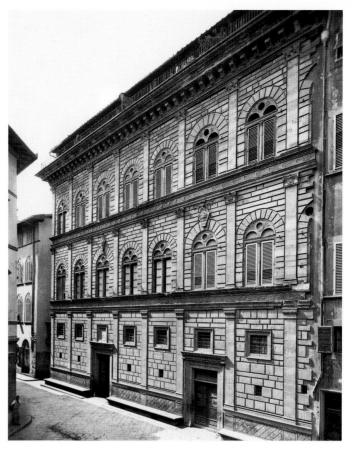

34 Palazzo Rucellai, Florence, c. 1450, commissioned by Giovanni Rucellai from LEON BATTISTA ALBERTI

made by the architect for the project. Regardless of the numbers of drawings that may have existed, including detailed solutions of specific aspects of the building used by artisans on the site (Fig. 33), there must have been a certain amount of on-the-spot problem solving by the master builder and the craftsmen.

Since there was little open space within the walls of Italian cities, builders had to accommodate their new structures to already existing buildings on the site. Sometimes this amounted only to wrapping a skin of stone or stucco around one or more pre-existing structures and re-ordering the new façade on the street—as in the façade of the Palazzo Rucellai in Florence (Fig. 34) by Leon Battista Alberti. One can still see the ragged right edge of the building where construction was halted—ostensibly because the Rucellai had failed to acquire the adjacent building in order to complete it. Interior remodeling would also be required in order to accommodate the new spacing of windows and doors on the street or to transform a row of houses belonging to more than one

owner into a building for a single extended family. Even new churches were built on the foundations of earlier ones which they replaced, sometimes extending the earlier structure considerably in proportions, retaining the earlier measurements and thus adding a formal constraint to the architect's imaginative freedom. The economics of building, then as now, often dictated such continued reuse, as did the fact that complete destruction of pre-existing structures would have been too time consuming.

Like Roman architecture, Italian architecture of the late Middle Ages and the Renaissance does not necessarily reveal its true structural system, which often lies hidden beneath a decorative veneer. Even when the heavy wood beams that supported the floor or ceiling above, or the wooden trusses that supported the gabled roofs of churches, were revealed, they were normally painted and sometimes carved or even covered with a decorative plaster overlay (see Fig. 1.21) that took attention away from their supporting function. The façade (literally "facing") of a church generally demonstrates a primary characteristic of Renaissance architecture, namely that it was to have a public and distinctive character within the urban landscape and that that character need not be congruent with what lay behind. Thus a church façade could, for example, extend far above the rest of the building (see Fig. 1.16) in order to give it increased prominence within the city.

An architectural project required large teams of crafts-men, laboring over long periods of time. Since major buildings took decades to complete, they were often the product of several different architects. Even if a single architect saw a project through from beginning to completion, he was, himself, responsible for overseeing a constantly changing body of workmen including quarriers, carriers, masons, stonecarvers, and provisioners (Fig. 35). In the case of public buildings all of this work, including its financing, was overseen by a specially elected committee called the **Opera**. Often the head of that body, the *operaio*, was elected for life. The membership of the Opera changed frequently, thus guaranteeing a range of expertise for any major building project.

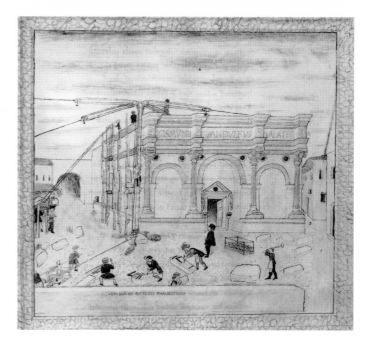

35 Drawing of the reconstruction of San Francesco, Rimini (see Fig. 6.7), c. 1455, GIOVANNI BETTINI (Bibliothèque de l'Arsenale, Paris)

Other Workshops

Although painting, sculpture, and architecture dominate histories of art, to some degree because of early histories like Vasari's *Lives*, it is important to remember that the visual culture of the Renaissance was enriched by a range of other arts as well. Such objects as banners and armor for frequent processions or tournaments; temporary stage sets and other constructions in wood and plaster of Paris for civic ritual; tapestries to cover large walls and shut out the cold; carved and painted furniture; jeweled reliquaries manufactured by goldsmiths for liturgical use (and often later destroyed for their precious materials); liturgical vessels and vestments; manuscript illumination; even pilgrims' amulets and souvenirs were all part of the lived experience of the people of this period and must also be considered integral to their visual language.

Perhaps the most significant technical artistic innovation during this time was the print. Coincident with the invention of printing, this medium allowed a rapid dissemination of images over a geographically wide area and, it might be argued, an increasing internationalism of artistic language.

During the Renaissance the most widely used print media were the woodcut and the engraving, both of which came to prominence in Italy in the 1470s. In the former, the desired image was drawn on a smooth piece of wood. The artist would then carve away part of the wood, leaving only the drawn lines standing in relief. These raised areas of the block were inked and the block printed, giving a reverse of the block's image on the paper.

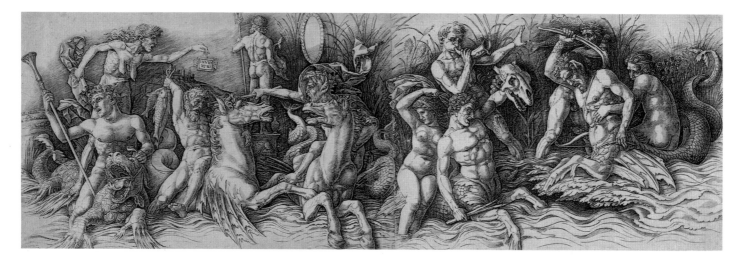

36 *Battle of the Sea Gods*, 1470s, ANDREA MANTEGNA. Engraving and drypoint, 11⅛ × 32⅜" (28.3 × 82.6 cm) (Duke of Devonshire Collection, England)

The print is made from two plates, printed on separate sheets of paper and joined at the center. The raging female figure of Envy (upper left) has led to the suggestion that the print represents a competition between rival engravers. Whatever Mantegna intended as content for the print, it is clear that it is an exercise in wit, for the powerful, classical sea gods do battle with bones and knots of fish, hardly capable of defending them, while a standing statue of Neptune, the god of the sea, turns his back on the whole scene.

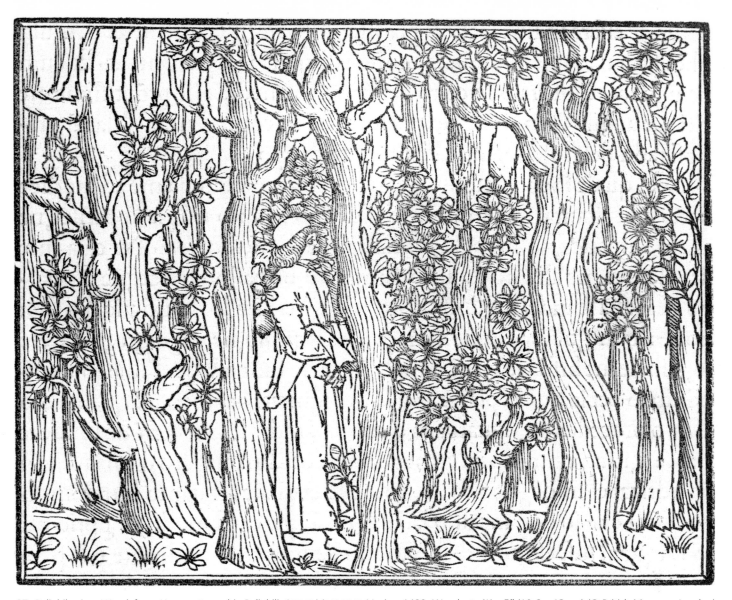

37 *Poliphilus in a Wood*, from *Hypnerotomachia Poliphili*, ALDUS MANUTIUS, Venice, 1499. Woodcut, 4¼ × 5" (10.6 × 13 cm) (© British Museum, London)

The Aldine Press was one of the foremost European printing houses at the end of the fifteenth century and throughout the sixteenth century. It was a center of classical scholarship; among the visitors to the Press was Erasmus of Rotterdam, who carefully edited texts published there.

Normally the result produced an unmodulated line of dense black ink on the surface of the paper (Fig. 37).

Engraving, a technique related to the decorative work of the goldsmith, reverses the principle of the woodcut. On a metal plate—most often copper—the artist first drew the design, then engraved the lines with a **burin**, a triangular-shaped instrument like an awl. A viscous ink was then pushed into the incised grooves and the surface of the plate wiped clean. Pressure in the printing press forced the paper slightly into these grooves, where it picked up the ink, again producing a reverse image (Fig. 36). In both woodcut and engraving the plates could be used repeatedly until the intense pressure of the printing press caused them to distress and crack. Like the prints themselves, the plates could also travel from place to place. And in a number of instances images were pirated as they entered the mass market, so that it is not unusual to see plates from one book appearing in another with minimal changes. Ultimately the print allowed artists to reach a much larger audience than they did with their private commissions. The printing process also had the effect of enhancing the status of artists since they often delegated to craftsmen the job of producing prints from their drawings, thus helping to forge the distinction between the "pure" artist, who conceives and creates an image, and the artisan who gives it final form.

Changing social, political, and economic forces caused shifts in artistic production which, from the thirteenth to the sixteenth century, gave artists an increasingly prominent social role. While endowing artists with almost heroic stature, these changes also marginalized their position in the culture by distancing them from the job of creating objects that played important roles in the culture. This dichotomy, a product of the Renaissance, has come to dominate our attitude toward the artist's role and makes reconstruction of the social exchanges implicit in works of Renaissance art an important part of this understanding.

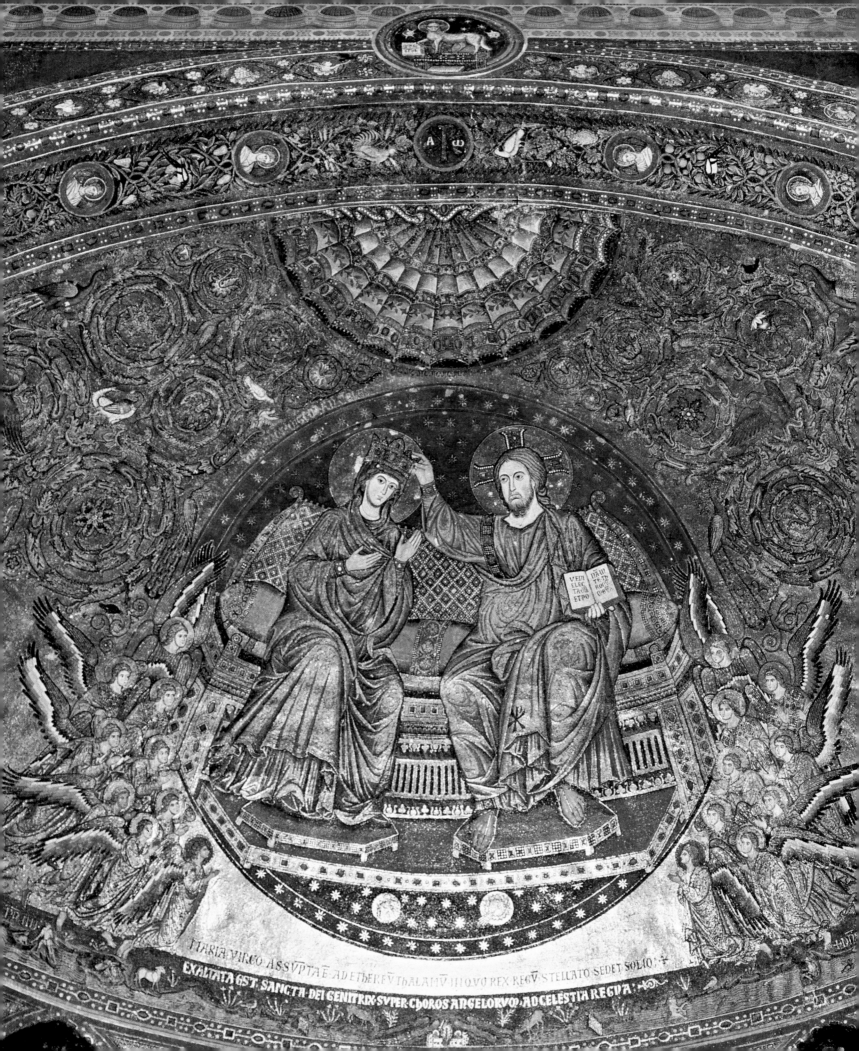

1
Traditions and Innovations: The Thirteenth Century

Italy as we know it did not exist in the Renaissance. There were no "Italians" in the modern sense—only Venetians, Milanese, Florentines, Sienese, Romans, Neapolitans, and other groups whose identities were defined by the city-state or territory in which they lived. City-states dominated the peninsula, each possessing and cherishing a distinct history, dialect, set of popular traditions, social and governmental structures, economy, and artistic and cultural expectations.

Geography and history conspired to keep city-states apart. Although nothing but the broad Lombard and Paduan plains separate Venice and Milan, the two cities effectively occupied two different worlds. Venetians took advantage of their site on the Adriatic Sea to tie the city's economic and cultural life to the eastern Mediterranean, especially Constantinople and Crete, whereas Milan looked the other way, standing as it did just south of a pass in the Alps on one of the major routes through Burgundy to Paris. The Appenine Mountains, running down the central spine of the peninsula, split east from west, while hilltops, affording natural protection from invaders, were crowned with many insular towns. The jagged coastline played its own part in isolating one maritime Italian state from another. Little wonder that the political unity of Italy in ancient Roman times was only vaguely remembered throughout the Renaissance and that the modern nation of Italy (unified as late as 1870) has had to work so hard to hold itself together.

At the same time, Italy's geography and history also distinguished it from the rest of Europe. The Italian peninsula is a distinct geographical feature, jutting freely into the Mediterranean Sea. At its north the Alps establish a formidable barrier, protecting Italy from the colder climate of northern Europe and from easy military invasion.

The history of this land stretched back over two thousand years; and the fact that its people had been united in ancient Roman times meant that they were conscious of sharing a common cultural heritage. In 1347 Cola di Rienzi (1313–54), the fiery Roman civic leader and advocate of reviving a "sacred Italy," invited representatives from all the major cities of the peninsula to meet in Rome to confirm their common Roman citizenship; twenty-five accepted. The cities saw each other as rival siblings rather than separate nations.

By the thirteenth century every city on the peninsula had already created and accumulated centuries of artistic and cultural traditions that gave each a distinctive personality in the eyes of contemporaries. This process of self-definition continued unabated through the Renaissance, constantly refreshed by active commercial and diplomatic exchange between cities and with states far beyond the peninsula. Concurrently, a measure of unity was imposed by newly founded religious orders, whose monastic communities spread throughout the length of the peninsula. In all of this the arts served as the primary means for cities, corporate bodies, religious orders, and individuals to convey ideas about themselves and their place in the world (and throughout the Christian world and its colonies). A recognisable visual language provided a way of expressing governing structures in a competitive urban environment.

Types of Cities

The Italian city-states fall into three broad political categories: 1) republics, such as Venice, Florence, and Siena; 2) states ruled by a sovereign, such as Naples, Milan, and many small principalities of northern Italy; and 3) the

1.1 *Coronation of the Virgin* (detail), c. 1294, commissioned by Nicholas IV from JACOPO TORRITI for the apse of Santa Maria Maggiore, Rome. Mosaic. See also Fig 1.35.

Papal States, including Rome, under the temporal authority of the pope. This categorization offers a useful way of thinking about Italian cities which indicates their similarities as well as differences. While Naples and Milan, for example, are farther from one another than any other two cities discussed in this book, their ruling families inter-married, and artistic activity at both courts centered around exalting the ruler and his dynasty. These two cities, as we shall see in Chapter 2, offer ample opportunities for comparing and contrasting the distinctive ways artists and patrons maneuvered within comparable social and political structures. A similar situation applies in the republics. Venice, Florence, and Siena often emphasized differences in their topography, local history, legends, and artistic traditions, yet all three cities were concerned with promoting a communal ideal, linking Church and state, and generally giving citizens a stake in their city's fashioning and embellishment. Papal Rome was different again, the city's thousands of years of history and unique position as the capital of western Christendom deeply conditioning the character of art that was produced there.

Venice, Florence, and Siena: Communal Myths and Institutions

In the thirteenth and fourteenth centuries increasing urbanization prompted Venice, Florence, and Siena to expand their boundaries and to create new streets, public spaces, churches, and government buildings, essentially transforming the cities into the urban spaces we now know. The major physical features of these cities suggest the general texture of urban environments throughout Italy at the time. Even more important, changes in Venice, Florence, and Siena show how citizens gave splendid and monumental expression to their city's most deeply treasured foundation myths, saintly protectors, and corporate values, thereby promoting their respective communal ideals to insure civic unity.

Three early views of Venice, Florence, and Siena (Figs. 1.2–1.5) show each city as a discrete entity. Venice is bounded by the waters of its lagoon, naturally defended by its site on islands off the Adriatic coast. Founded on inhospitable alluvial soil during the invasions of Italy in the fifth century, the city grew through massive land reclamation efforts organized by its government. Considerable civic resources were also committed to constructing and maintaining an impressive commercial and military fleet.

Florence, being located in a valley, on the river Arno, required more in the way of man-made defenses. Its leaders girdled their city with walls fortified with towers. The fortifications visible in Fig. 1.4 were built in the late thir-

teenth century to replace a twelfth-century ring of fortifications that itself had replaced the outgrown limits of the city's cramped ancient Roman core (see page 490). Great gates with double and triple sets of iron-studded wooden doors and imposing metal grates opened at daybreak to admit travelers and farmers from the countryside. The city shut tight again at dusk.

Siena also depended upon walls to define its limits, but its hilltop site provided additional natural fortification. Long curving streets follow the contours of the three main hills upon which the city is built. The city's primary religious building, the Cathedral, stands out on the horizon, dominating the oldest area of settlement, which was first occupied by the ancient Etruscans. Newer neighborhoods grew out like fingers on the other hills, progressively linked together by substantial brick walls which came to encircle the entire area.

All cities depended upon surrounding farmland for basic provisions. Siena, for example, sits in the midst of an agricultural district long known for its production of high-quality wine and olive oil. Even in Venice there were large garden plots, assuring some self-sufficiency, especially during the frequent wars that disturbed commerce.

Ready access to water was essential, too. The Arno River provided Florence with drinking water and fish, as well as a means of washing and dyeing raw materials in the production of woolen goods, which dominated the Florentine economy. Although not completely navigable, the Arno also facilitated transporting products to and from the Tyrrhenian Sea, approximately 50 miles (80 kilometers) to the west. In Venice the waters of the lagoon served as the breeding ground for fish, mollusks, and waterfowl. An S-shaped channel, the Grand Canal, provided essential access from the city's large harbor into the well-protected commercial center of the city at the Rialto (literally "high bank") Bridge. Drinking water was drawn from wells and cisterns as it was in riverless cities like Siena (which also built aqueducts to feed public fountains).

Buildings most closely associated with the communal government stood out on the horizon, regularly taller and more massive than any other structures in town. In the prints of Florence and Venice, a tall *campanile*, or bell tower, in front of the major church marks the religious heart of the city. For symbolic and practical reasons, government headquarters were located nearby. Church and state functioned together, citizen committees overseeing the construction and embellishment of the city's main churches as well as the more obviously governmental structures.

Early views of Italian cities indicate that they were densely populated, buildings being "packed in, not scattered but continuous, stately and adorned in a stately

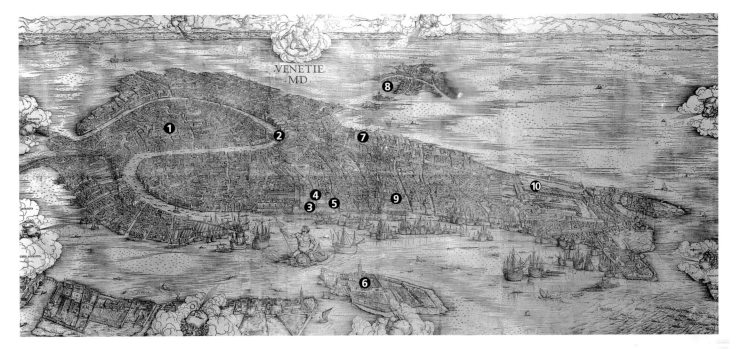

1.2 and **1.3** *Map of Venice*, 1500, JACOPO DE' BARBARI, published by the Nuremberg merchant Anton Kolb. Woodcut, 53 × 111" (134.5 × 281.8 cm) (Museo Correr, Venice)

1 Santa Maria Gloriosa dei Frari (Franciscan) and Scuola Grande di San Rocco; **2** Rialto Bridge; **3** Piazzetta San Marco; **4** Piazza San Marco; **5** Ducal Palace; **6** San Giorgio Maggiore; **7** Santi Giovanni e Paolo (Dominican) and the Scuola Grande di San Marco; **8** San Michele in Isola; **9** San Zaccaria; **10** Arsenal

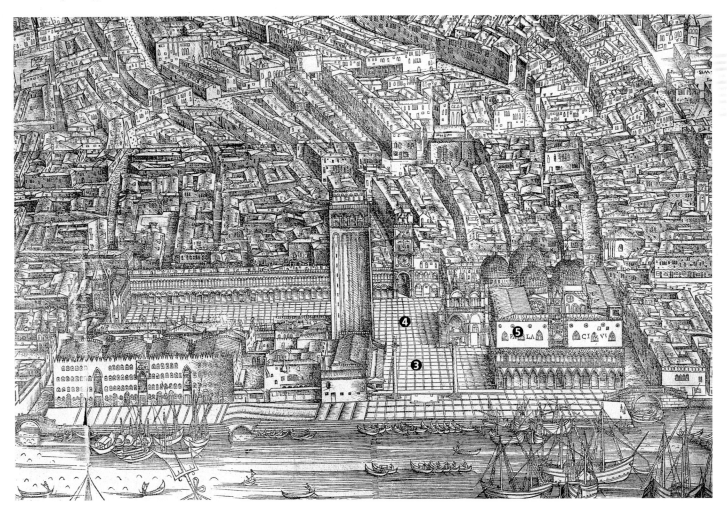

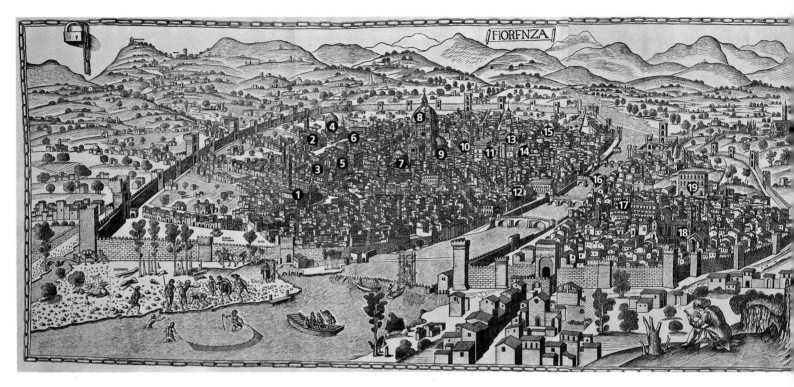

1.4 *Chain Map of Florence*, detail, 1480, anonymous. Woodcut (Galleria degli Uffizi, Florence)

1 Santa Maria Novella (Dominican); **2** San Marco (Dominican); **3** San Lorenzo; **4** Santissima Annunziata (Servite); **5** Medici Palace; **6** Innocents' Hospital; **7** Baptistry; **8** Cathedral; **9** Campanile; **10** Or San Michele; **11** Marzocco; **12** Santa Trinità; **13** Palazzo della Signoria; **14** Loggia della Signoria; **15** Santa Croce (Franciscan); **16** Ponte Vecchio; **17** Santo Spirito; **18** Church of the Carmine; **19** Pitti Palace; **20** San Miniato

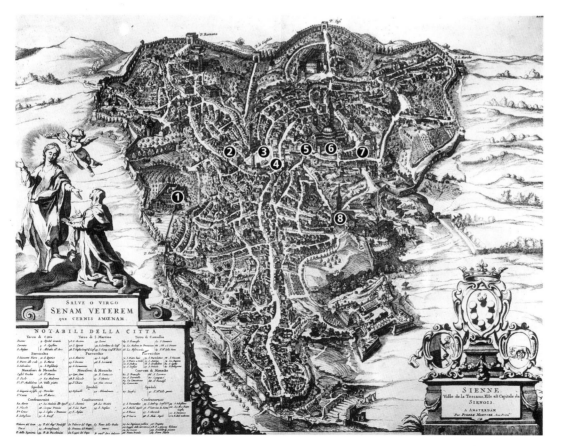

1.5 *View of Siena*, eighteenth century, produced by PIERRE MORTIER. Engraving (Museo Civico, Siena)

The Medici coat of arms at the bottom right was imposed on Siena by the Florentine dukes in the mid-sixteenth century.
1 San Francesco (Franciscan); **2** Palazzo Pubblico; **3** Campo; **4** Fonte Gaia; **5** Baptistry; **6** Cathedral; **7** Ospedale della Scala; **8** San Domenico (Dominican)

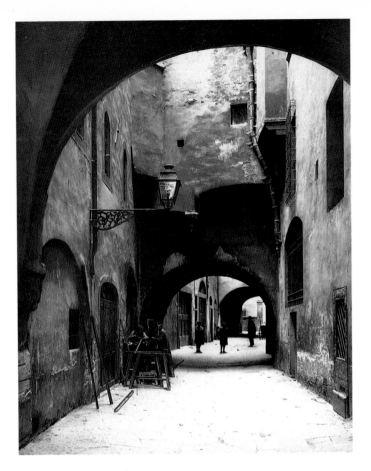

1.6 Via dei Girolami, Florence

Space was at such a premium in parts of Florence that the inhabitants of some neighborhoods built enclosed bridges and balconies—known as *sporti* (seen in the photograph)—out over public streets. City officials attempted to discourage such practices by imposing fines, but many people chose to pay the fines rather than lose precious living space. Workshops on ground level spilled out into the street.

manner," as the schoolmaster Bonvicino da Riva put it in a laudatory description of Milan. A view of the Via dei Girolami in Florence (Fig. 1.6) shows the narrow, wayward character of most streets. Shops opened directly onto the street, allowing merchants to display their wares on counters which could be shuttered tightly at night. Living quarters were located above or adjacent to most people's places of employment, assuring a heterogeneous population throughout the city. Even so, each neighborhood was dominated by a few wealthy families. Their private towers, which served as status symbols and as fortified perches in the frequent battles among competing clans, soared above the streets. In Venice, which was remarkably successful in promoting civic harmony and where shifting alluvial soil made their construction a daunting challenge, people had no reason to erect such structures.

Physical order in all cities was controlled by ordinances that imposed height restrictions on buildings and fined citizens for structures that hung out over the streets or obstructed public thoroughfares. Sometimes statutes even dictated window types and other common features

in important sites such as public squares. In 1266 the Venetians paved over pre-existing canals to form an enormous piazza in front of St. Mark's Basilica, and three years later they restored the palace of the procurators (high-ranking citizens charged with the embellishment and maintenance of St. Mark's and its surrounding public buildings and squares) to give a unified façade on the north side of the piazza, both important physical manifestations of governmental authority. Whatever the legislation, it had essentially two purposes: to bring safety and well-being to the population and to present the city as a whole as an ordered and successful polity enhancing its reputation to the world at large.

Shaping and embellishing public squares was an important manifestation of governmental authority. The Venetians began the process in the 1160s and 1170s, well in advance of similar projects in most other Italian cities. Piazzas were also essential sites for public processions (Fig. 1.7). Through these recurring events citizen groups affirmed their solidarity with the city as a whole. Conversely, the city's enemies, such as criminals and traitors, were often executed in public squares, demonstrating governmental authority over life and death.

Civic Myths and Patron Saints

Numerous factors other than the practical governed the forms of urban development during this period. Chief among them were the myths—particularly myths of foundation—which individual cities developed to narrate their past history. Cities also chose different Christian saints as their protectors and as guarantors of well-being into the future.

Every city had its patron saint, with an important church devoted to his or her cult. Saints were believed to provide divine protection and assistance to cities and their citizens, warding off pestilence, protecting food supplies, ensuring military victories, and generally supporting civic as well as personal needs.

Venice: St. Mark and His Basilica

The standard depiction of Venice (see Figs. 1.2, 1.3) shows the city with its formal point of entrance from the sea. A visitor coming from the sea would have been greeted by the façade of the Doge's Palace (labeled on the bird's-eye view as Pala[zzo] Civi[co], "civic palace") with its ceremonial and honorific loggia for the doge at the center of its upper level. Immediately to the left are two columns, topped by statues of St. Theodore (actually a fragment of a Roman cuirass figure with later additions to

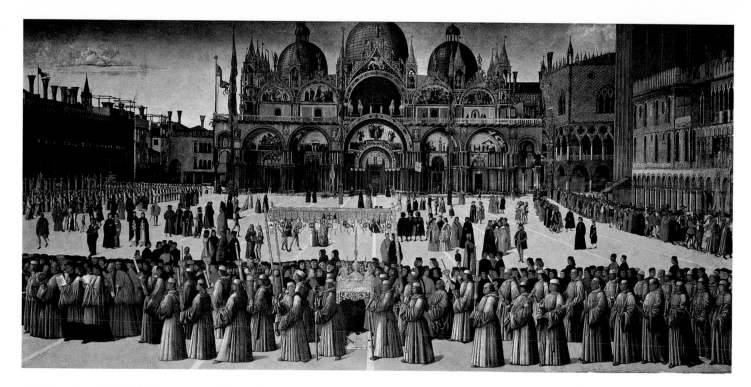

1.7 *Procession in St. Mark's Square*, part of the cycle *Miracoli della Croce*, 1496, commissioned by the Scuola di San Giovanni Evangelista, Venice, from GENTILE BELLINI. Oil on canvas, 10' 7" × 14' (3.67 × 7.45 m) (Galleria dell'Accademia, Venice)

San Marco is the church structure in the background; the palace of the Procurators is on the left.

transform it into one of Venice's oldest patron saints) and the Venetian lion of St. Mark (actually a Persian chimera, a spoil of war, also with later reworkings). The columns form a processional gateway into the city, but the statues look toward the city, not toward the sea. They simultaneously direct movement into the Piazzetta San Marco, which moves along the flank of the Ducal Palace to St. Mark's, and confer the city's protection on people leaving the city. Moreover, they were clearly visible to legislators inside the Doge's Palace; an early account indicates that when they saw the lion of St. Mark struck by lightning during one of their sessions, they took it as a very bad omen indeed.

A female personification of Justice carved in a roundel at the center of the flank of the Doge's Palace along the Piazzetta announced to any visitor that the city was ordered on firm principles of government. These principles are underscored by a statue of St. Michael the Archangel at the corner of the Doge's Palace closest to the column statues and by carved figures of the Judgment of Solomon at the far corner of the palace. There the Piazzetta meets the large central space of the city in front of St. Mark's basilica, dedicated to the city's major patron saint.

St Mark's (see Fig. 1.7) was officially the chapel of the doge, the head of the Venetian government, whose palace

---

The Image as Document

In the prologue to the second part of *Les Estoirs de Venise*, a history of the Venetian Republic written between 1267 and 1275, the chronicler Martin da Canal argues for the importance of painted as well as written accounts of events.

I will tell you the deeds and battles that the Venetians carried out in those days [of Doge Ranieri Zeno, r. 1253–68] just as I have recounted the deeds and undertakings of their ancestors because there are many people in the world who would like to know of these things, and this is not possible—for one man has died, a second is dying and a third is being born, and thus one cannot recount to everyone what has happened in those times—unless it is made known to them by means of writing or painting. We see writings and paintings with our eyes, so that when one sees a story painted or hears a naval or land battle recounted or reads about the deeds of his ancestors in a book, he seems to be present at the scene of battle. And since events live, thanks to paintings and oral accounts and writing, I have undertaken to occupy myself with the deeds that the Venetians have accomplished in the service of the Holy Church and in honor of their noble city.

(from Patricia Fortini Brown. "Painting and History in Renaissance Venice." *Art History*, 7 [1984]: pp. 263–94 [extract p. 265])

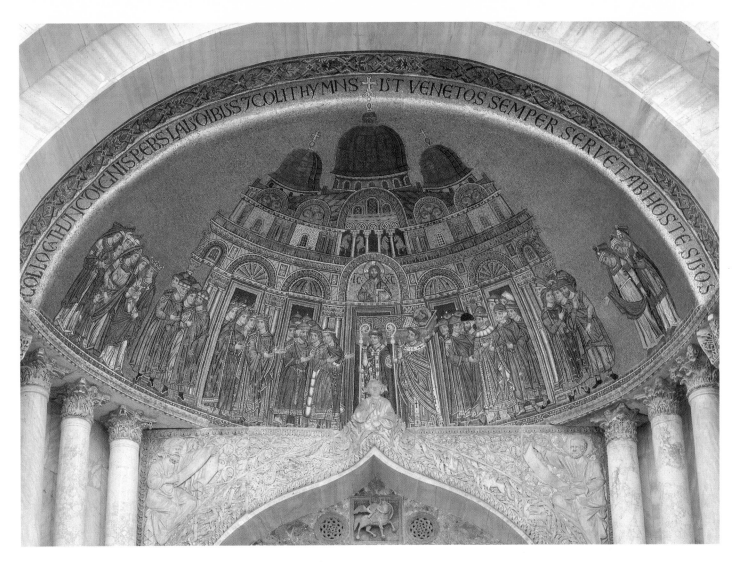

1.8 *Translation of the Relics of St. Mark*, c. 1270, commissioned by the Procurators of St. Mark's for the left portal of St. Mark's, Venice. Mosaic

it adjoined. According to legend, two merchants, called Buono of Malamocco and Rustico of Torcello (names obviously fabricated—the "Good Man" and the "Rustic," from islands in the archipelago owing allegiance to Venice) stole the body of St. Mark from Alexandria in Egypt and carried it back to Venice. In 828/29 they presented their saintly relic not to the patriarch (head of the Venetian Church) but to the doge, thus linking St. Mark inextricably to the state. It was the doge who ordered the construction of the basilica to house the saint's remains.

The transferal of St. Mark's relics into the church is represented in a mosaic over the far left portal of the basilica (Fig. 1.8). One of the most accurate architectural representations of the thirteenth century, the mosaic shows the church before it received the elaborate white cresting and **tabernacles** that have crowned the façade since the fifteenth century. Nevertheless the late eleventh-century church is clearly identifiable. Its central and subsidiary domes link it to the well-known form of earlier Byzantine churches deriving from Constantine's Church of the Apostles in Constantinople, an appropriate model for a church dedicated to St. Mark who was himself an apostle.

While the patriarch guides the body of St. Mark into the basilica, the doge, recognizable in his domed red hat and splendid red and gold vestments to the right of center, joins throngs of Venetian leaders who participate in the miraculous event.

Some time between 1267 and 1275 a Venetian chronicler, Martin da Canal, cited the mosaic to establish the validity of the basilica's foundation myth: "And if some of you wish to verify that those things happened just as I told you, come to see the beautiful church of St. Mark's in Venice, and look at it in front, because this story is written there just as I have told it to you." Art rivaled the written word as a record of civic traditions.

Local myth and legend also surrounded four ancient life-sized gilt bronze horses, represented clearly over St. Mark's central entrance in the mosaic and in Bellini's painting of the Piazza San Marco (see Fig. 1.7). Plundered from the Hippodrome in Constantinople in 1204 during the Fourth Crusade, the horses held pride of place on a platform from which the doge made public pronouncements. Because the animals were bridleless and thus triumphantly free, Venetians saw them as consummate emblems of Venetian independence and liberty. As military loot they also testified to the success with which Venice defended and extended its power.

What is clear from this civic imagery is that Venice looked to Constantinople and the Byzantine east for many of its models. Alone among Italian city states in seeming not to have an actual Roman history, the Venetians formulated myths as fantastical and charming as the city itself. New archaeological excavations ten feet below the ground line of the modern city, however, have revealed Roman streets and traces of other habitation dating to c. 200, sites that were buried as inhabitants of the city continuously built up the islands to escape the encroaching sea. As the old remains of the city disappeared the Venetians replaced the actual and most likely dimly remembered real Roman history of the city with a new mythology of place, claiming another "Rome"—that founded by Constantine in the east—as a model. This model, far more impressive than the modest remains of Roman Venice suggest, simultaneously asserted an ancient history and yet distinguished Venice from other city states in Italy as unique in its classical heritage.

Florence: St. John the Baptist and the Baptistry

Florence did have a Roman history, one which is physically manifest in the grid plan of its central core, that of the Roman military *castrum* or camp. Florentines literally walked on Roman streets. Founded by Roman soldiers during the Roman republic of the first century B.C.E. and named Florentia (*Fiorenza*, with its double meaning of "flower" suggesting beauty and "flowering" suggesting fertile development), the city claimed a continuous existence back into Roman antiquity. This history, and especially its republican origins, became a constant reference in political discourse and subsequently in the visual arts. Antique stylistic and iconographical quotations in Florence, far from being simply literary or aesthetic, were tied to a history constructed as politics. As early as the twelfth century Hercules with his club appeared on the Florentine state seal with the inscription *Herculea Clava Domat Florencia Prava* ("Hercules' club subdues Florence's wickedness"), a clear statement of the difficulties of controlling unruly and factional urban populations during the late Middle Ages.

Like Venice, Florence's urban plan embodied critical social messages. Cathedral and town hall are at opposite ends of the main east–west street of the Roman grid with the guild oratory of Or San Michele situated on the same axis (see map, page 490). Church, state, and corporate economy, the structuring elements of this body politic, therefore control the urban spine from which all other

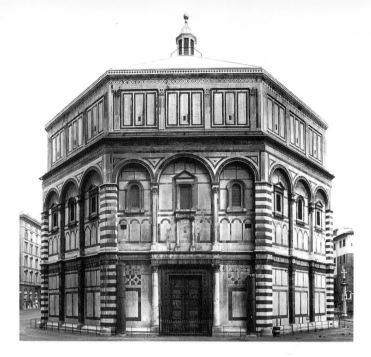

1.9 Baptistry, Florence, c. 1059–1150

features extend. Urbanistically they are united, just as they were in terms of their operations, with members of the leading families of Florence acting as governors of their guilds, elected officials in the town hall, and members of the building committees of the cathedral. Despite their individual spaces within the urban fabric, boundaries between Church and state were clearly permeable. The same seamless interaction that characterized relations within the state can be seen in the overlapping of antique past and Christian present.

Florence's patron was St. John the Baptist. The city's Baptistry of San Giovanni dedicated to him served as a primary site of civic and religious self-identification (Fig. 1.9), overshadowing the city's cathedral, which was a relatively modest structure until its rebuilding in the fourteenth and fifteenth centuries. At San Giovanni one became a Christian and a Florentine at the same time, the Baptistry serving as the single place of baptism for the entire city. Although completed in its present form in the late eleventh and twelfth centuries, the building's foundations date back to the fifth century. Florentines believed that the building had served originally as a temple dedicated to Mars—a belief that reflects Florentine pride in their Roman past as well as their belief that the city would be victorious in its military endeavors, guided as it was by the god of war. The Baptistry's marble cladding, its use of classically detailed pilasters, friezes, and tabernacles, along with the reuse of actual Roman columns in its interior and flanking its entrances, served to reinforce the impression of great antiquity.

The maintenance and embellishment of the Baptistry was entrusted to the wealthy Arte del Calimala (Wool Merchants' Guild), which oversaw the Opera di San Giovanni (the building works of the Baptistry). This initiated a pattern that was to see the guilds assume responsibility for a number of major ecclesiastical buildings in the city. Guilds not only monitored and regulated commerce but also dominated the city government. In this manner, mercantile values came to dominate the city.

Throughout the thirteenth and early fourteenth centuries guild officials endowed the vaulted surfaces and balustrades of the Baptistry's interior with glittering mosaics (Fig. 1.10). The mosaics may have been designed by a Florentine artist steeped in the Byzantine tradition (Coppo di Marcovaldo [active 1260–76 Siena, San Gimignano, and Orvieto] is frequently suggested), but artists trained in Venice who possessed special expertise in this medium are likely to have executed them. An official act of 1301 commissioned a certain Constantinus and his son to work on the Florentine mosaics and to invite other artists from Venice to join them. Civic loyalty did not impede artists from working in rival towns; then, as now, they went where there was work. Patrons may actually have sought out foreign artists in a spirit of competitiveness.

The mosaics, covering the whole area of the octagonal dome in concentric bands, depict significant moments in Christian history from the Creation to the Last Judgment. Directly above the opening into the apse and the altar

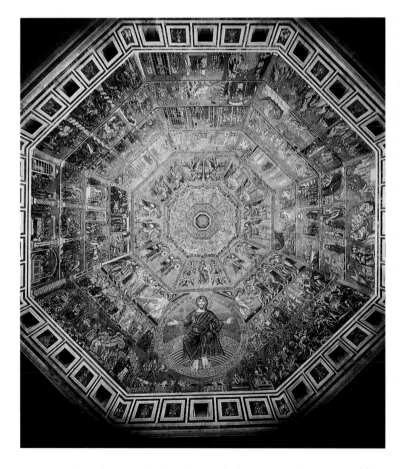

1.10 Baptistry, Florence, showing the mosaics by Coppo di Marcovaldo (?) in the vaults, late thirteenth to early fourteenth centuries

looms a colossal figure of Christ in Judgment, his divinity marked by the crackling light shining from the gold striations of his stylized robes. At his feet naturalistic figures of the dead rise from their tombs on the last day. Christ's awesomely contorted hands and feet extend toward the gold and patterned circular band as if he majestically encompassed the boundaries of the universe. He welcomes with outstretched palm the elect in the vault segment to his right and condemns the damned in the vault segment to his left with the back of his hand. The five vault segments that complete the dome contain bands of narratives depicting the Creation and Old Testament narratives through the story of Joseph, the life of John the Baptist, and the life of Christ. Although there are naturalistic touches in the narrative depictions, the imposing iconic figure of Christ dominates the dome and offered Florentines a glimpse of the grandeur of God's universe and a sense of their place in it.

Siena: The Virgin Mary and the Cathedral

Siena's foundation myth, like Florence's, traces its history back to antiquity. But unlike Florence's historical basis for a constructed history, Siena's is mythological, claiming that the city had been founded by Senius and Aschius, the sons of Remus, one of the twin founders of Rome. Thus Siena claims a history virtually as old as Rome's. Fleeing their uncle, Romulus, after having stolen the shrine of the She-wolf in Rome, Senius (from whom the city took its name) and Aschius were protected on their journey northwards by a white cloud during the day and a black cloud at night, a part of the myth recalled by Siena's heraldic crest, the *balzana*, divided horizontally with a white field above and a black one below. The brothers brought the She-wolf to Siena, where they provided an appropriate temple to house it. The myth is recalled repeatedly on the façade of Siena's town hall with sculpted images of Romulus and Remus being suckled by the She-wolf and with the *balzana* appearing under each arch (see Fig. 4.68).

In 1260, just before a decisive victory over their archrivals, the Florentines, at Montaperti, the Sienese dedicated their city to the Virgin Mary. Thereafter the citizens saw the Virgin as their protectress, dedicating their cathedral (Figs. 1.11 and 1.12) to her Assumption into heaven. As in Venice and Florence, where citizen groups had taken responsibility for religious buildings dedicated to their patron saints, in Siena the *operai* (building supervisors) were mostly laymen chosen by the city government. They kept accounts and supervised work. Citizens were also expected to contribute time and money to the cathedral's construction, including a twice-yearly commitment to

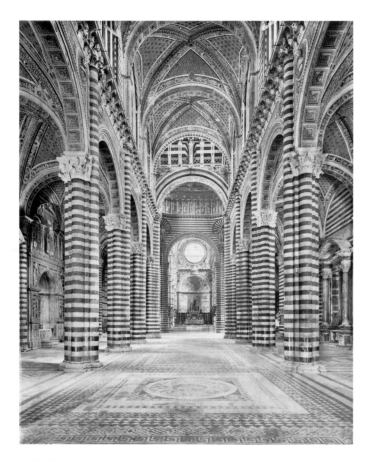

1.11 Siena Cathedral, complete by the 1260s, vaults raised and apse expanded c. 1355–86, commissioned by the Operai of Siena Cathedral

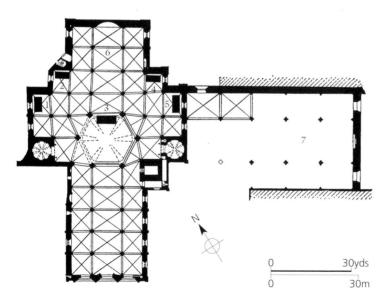

1.12 Siena Cathedral, plan. **1** Chapel of San Savino, Pietro Lorenzetti, *Birth of the Virgin*; **2** Chapel of Sant'Ansano, Simone Martini, *Annunciation*; **3** Main altar, Duccio, *Maestà*; **4** Chapel of San Vittorio, Bartolomeo Bulgarini, *Nativity*; **5** Chapel of San Crescenzio, Ambrogio Lorenzetti, *Purification of the Virgin*; **6** Baptistry on level below; **7** Projected nave of enlarged church, planned 1321–22, foundation laid 1339, work halted 1348

provide carts and beasts of burden for transporting building materials to the site.

Siena Cathedral was structurally complete by the 1260s, giving the city a decisive edge over Florence where the new cathedral was not even begun until 1296. Unlike most cathedrals previously built in central Italy, which generally had plain columnar supports and a wooden truss support for the roof, Siena's Duomo (as an Italian cathedral is often called) boasts **compound piers** supporting round **diaphragm arches** and a vaulted ceiling. These elements may reflect the example of a number of monastic complexes built by northern European monks around Siena or perhaps sources as far away as Germany or southwest France, where similar construction was popular. Siena's traders and bankers conducted business across Europe, and the cathedral suggests their awareness of contemporary architectural developments in France and Germany. On the other hand, the alternation of black and white marble stripes on the piers and walls (interior and exterior) is characteristically Italian, having been used in Pisa and Orvieto cathedrals, for example. It may also intentionally echo the *balzana*.

The Pulpit   In 1265 the Sienese hired Nicola Pisano (c. 1220–1284) to design and carve a new marble pulpit for their cathedral (Fig. 1.13). Nicola seems to have begun his career in the southern Italian workshops established by the Holy Roman Emperor Frederick II (1194–1250). The classically oriented ideals Nicola learned in the imperial court there served him well in his first documented commission, a marble pulpit completed and signed in 1259/60 for the Pisa Baptistry (Fig. 1.14). Pisano's reputation as a highly talented sculptor and head of an efficient workshop must have brought him to the attention of the Sienese Opera.

Both pulpits consist of a polygonal platform raised on columns and faced with marble reliefs depicting key moments in the life of Christ, culminating in scenes of the Crucifixion and the Last Judgment beneath the lectern. In Siena, however, Nicola substantially elaborated the original scheme. The Siena pulpit is octagonal, whereas Pisa's is hexagonal, with a corresponding increase in the number of reliefs from five to seven; each panel includes more figures and episodes, and the figures are freed more completely from their stony matrix. In both pulpits he demonstrated a knowledge of Gothic architectural forms such as the **trilobed cusping** on the arches under the relief panels and in the attached triple columns placed between each relief at Pisa, but the Siena pulpit is more thoroughly Gothic in details. Unlike the Pisa pulpit, with its rigid separation of relief panels and columnar frames (not unlike the architectural separation of narrative reliefs on Roman triumphal arches), the Siena

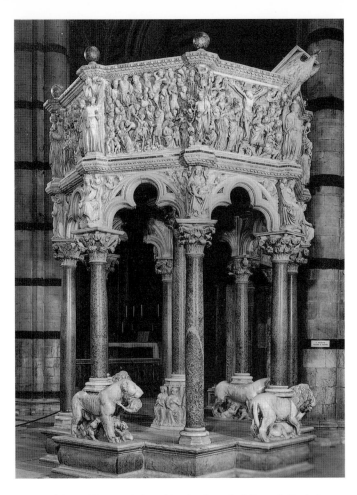

1.13 Pulpit, 1265, commissioned by the Operai of Siena Cathedral from NICOLA PISANO for Siena Cathedral. Marble

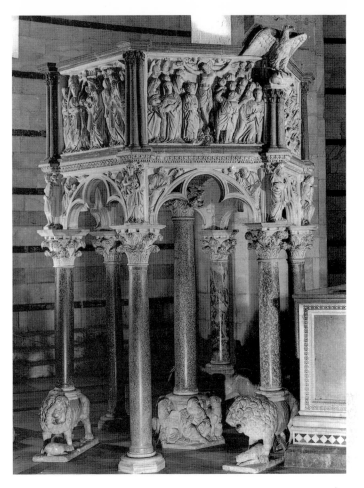

1.14 Pulpit, 1259/60, commissioned by Bishop Federico Visconti from NICOLA PISANO for the Baptistry, Pisa. Marble, height c. 15′ (4.6 m)

pulpit follows the example of Gothic church portals, transforming the columnar divisions into human figures and unifying the entire surface of the pulpit. Nicola may well have made a trip to northern France, as his son Giovanni is later thought to have done, for images such as the writhing crucified Christ can be traced to earlier examples of this type in the Île de France.

Nicola's Sienese patrons may have demanded that their pulpit be more internationally attuned than had the Pisans, who were much more tied to their classical artistic traditions. In Pisa the cathedral exemplifies the Tuscan **Romanesque** style, its façade covered with rows of small marble columns. Ancient sarcophagi filled the civic cemetery next to the Baptistry (see Figs. 3.14 and 3.15). Siena's relationship with the ancient world was more ambivalent. In the early fourteenth century the Sienese set a newly discovered statue of Venus on public display, but when the city began to suffer ill-fortune the populace attributed the turn of events to the statue. It was taken from the column, smashed, and buried in Florentine territory by night, so that its powerful magic could work against Siena's traditional enemy.

The pulpits of Pisa and Siena also differ from one another in the emotional tenor of their figures. The Pisa reliefs are restrained, the figures set largely parallel to the picture plane. Their neatly creased, classicizing drapery

and broad, idealized facial features contribute to a sense of calm order. In Siena, by contrast, Nicola explored a greater range of emotion. In the Crucifixion relief Christ hangs heavily from the cross, which emphasizes his suffering, rather than appearing as he did in Pisa with his arms and hands outstretched as if in triumph. In *The Massacre of the Innocents* (Fig. 1.15), a violent story which

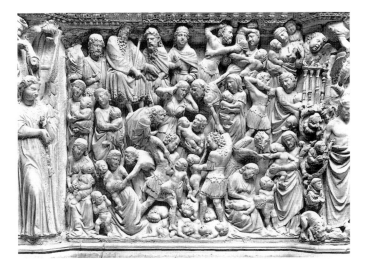

1.15 *Massacre of the Innocents*, detail from the pulpit, 1265, commissioned by the Operai of Siena Cathedral from NICOLA PISANO for Siena Cathedral. Marble, 33½ × 38¼″ (85 × 97 cm)

appears on the Siena pulpit but not at Pisa, soldiers thrust daggers into writhing babies. Mothers tear their hair in grief. Space flows around all the figures, who seem capable of more independent movement than appears possible for the weighty figures of the Pisa relief. This relief, in its vertical piling up of figures, suggests that Nicola had looked carefully at late Roman battle sarcophagi on which figures are similarly disposed.

Since Vasari, historians of the Renaissance have tended to respond more positively to the Roman classicizing style of Nicola's Pisa pulpit than to his work in Siena, because the Renaissance was construed as a revival of the early Roman antique. However, the classical traditions embodied in the Pisa reliefs constituted but one strand to which Renaissance artists and patrons turned for inspiration. The Gothic naturalism, movement, and expressivity of the Siena reliefs document other possibilities.

The Cathedral Façade   Around 1284 Sienese officials placed Nicola's son, Giovanni (1245/50 Pisa–1319 Siena), who had collaborated with his father on carving in Siena and played an active role in other major commissions in

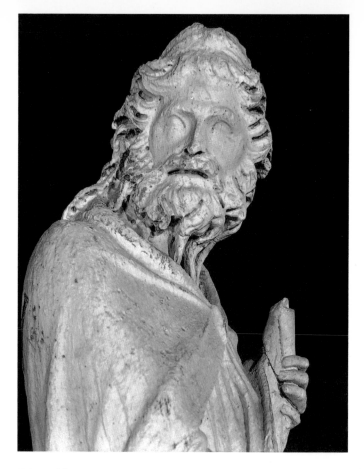

1.17 Isaiah, c. 1284, commissioned by the Operai of Siena Cathedral from GIOVANNI PISANO for the façade of Siena Cathedral. Marble, height of entire figure 6′ 2⅜″ (1.89 m) (Museo dell'Opera del Duomo, Siena)

Bologna, Perugia, and Pisa, in charge of providing a façade for Siena Cathedral (Fig. 1.16). With its triple portals and dramatically rising gables Giovanni's façade demonstrates a familiarity with northern Gothic models. But the relatively modest width of the cathedral's nave and aisles left little room for sculptural decoration around the portals, in the Gothic tradition. Instead Giovanni conceived an ensemble of figures on narrow platforms just above the portals and extending around the turreted sides of the façade. Many of Giovanni's sibyls, prophets, and other Old Testament figures seem to be engaged in conversation with one another and with the world below. Giovanni knew that the figures would be seen from a good distance below, so he dramatically exaggerated their poses and carving and positioned them to lean forward into space. In the figure of Isaiah, for example (Fig. 1.17), Giovanni peppered the prophet's beard with numerous drill holes which enhance the dramatic play of light and shadow across and around the face. In spite of the statue's weathered surface, its expressive facial features still evoke a prophet's impassioned exhortations.

The City Hall

Throughout much of their early history the communal governments of Florence and Siena met in churches,

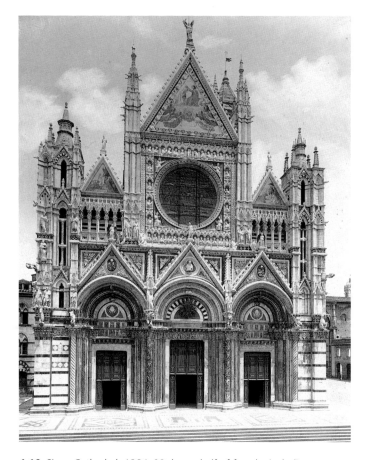

1.16 Siena Cathedral, 1284–99, lower half of façade, including statues, commissioned by the Operai of Siena Cathedral from GIOVANNI PISANO (originals now in Museo dell'Opera del Duomo, Siena)

another indication of the close links between Church and state. By the end of the thirteenth century such improvised arrangements no longer sufficed, and in the following century local governments constructed city halls for their own use (Figs. 1.18–1.20). These buildings have many features in common, being more or less rectangular in plan and somewhat blocky in form. All had courtyards on their ground floors and an impressive hall for meetings of citizens' councils on the upper floor. They also included one or more chapels, meeting space for smaller administrative groups, government offices, and residential quarters for government leaders.

At the same time, each city hall offered a distinctive image for its civic government. In Florence the resolute masonry walls and exaggerated battlements of the Palazzo della Signoria (begun in 1296) powerfully express the need to uphold and defend civic liberty from any and all assailants. Even though Arnolfo da Cambio (c. 1245 Colle di Val d'Elsa–1302? Florence), the architect for the Palazzo della Signoria, had studied with Nicola Pisano and was recently back from Rome where he had worked for the pope (see Fig. 1.40) and high-ranking cardinals (see Fig. 1.38), there is no hint of classical form in the building. It remains resolutely traditional using indigenous castle

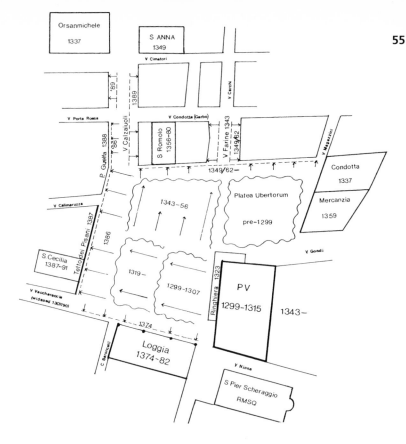

1.19 Piazza della Signoria, Florence, and the area surrounding the Palazzo della Signoria. Plan of spatial expansion during the fourteenth century (from Marvin Trachtenberg, *Dominion of the Eye: Urbanism, Art, and Power in Early Modern Florence*)

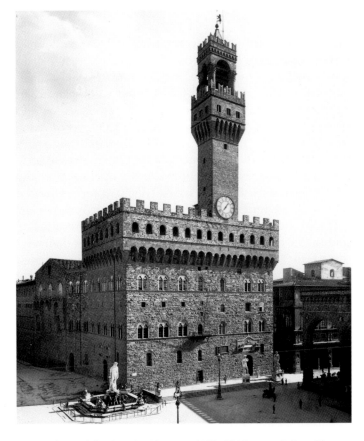

1.18 Palazzo della Signoria, Florence, 1299–1310, commissioned by the Florentine government from ARNOLFO DI CAMBIO

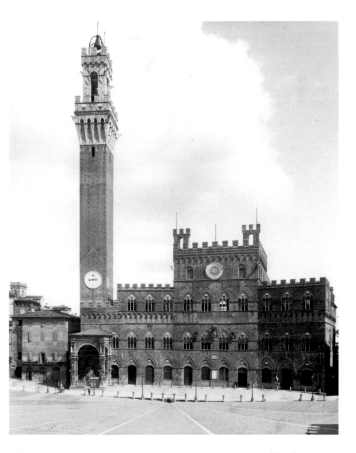

1.20 Palazzo Pubblico, Siena, begun 1298, commissioned by the Sienese government

architecture as its vocabulary, not unlike its predecessor building, the Palazzo del Podestà, known today as the Bargello. When the Palazzo della Signoria was built the city was deeply factionalized between Guelf and Ghibelline parties. The first nominally supported the popes and the latter were generally loyal to the medieval German emperors but both fought battles over local issues. The merchant class, wresting power from the predominately aristocratic Ghibellines in the late thirteenth century, erected the tower of the Palazzo della Signoria off-center on the stump of a pre-existing Ghibelline tower, symbolically triumphing over the rival faction.

The Signoria not only demolished the palace structures of the Ghibelline Uberti family at the site, but over a period of years continued to acquire property around the site of the new Palazzo della Signoria (see Fig. 1.19). This spatial extension into the fabric of the city accomplished a number of things: it essentially erased the existence of the Uberti from the center of the city; it added a grandeur to the building by isolating it from any nearby structures, both giving it a visual prominence in the city and making it safer; it provided a public space for the citizenry to gather in front of the town hall to hear the decisions of their governors; it brought the building—through its piazza—to the edge of the major north–south axis of the city, thus linking it with the cathedral; it allowed the long west façade of the building to become the new entrance façade of the building rather than the shorter northern side; and it allowed multiple points of view of the building as it was approached by different routes through the city, most notably coming from the cathedral and from the Ponte Vecchio and the other side of the Arno.

This concern for marking the building on the wider urban landscape is evident in the tower of the Palazzo della Signoria, taller than any other tower in the city (see Fig. 1.18); its height is actually measurable on the ground since it determined the distance from the corner of the building to the street entering the piazza from the cathedral and Or San Michele. Its position off the center axis of the west side of the building also meant that it was framed by another street entering the piazza from the thoroughfare that connected the Ponte Vecchio to the Old Market of the city. Carefully calculated vistas sharpened awareness of the superiority of this tower and of the power of the factions that had ordered its construction.

For its city hall, Siena chose visual seduction over the brute strength of Florence's civic fortress. Brick walls gently bend to embrace the amphitheater-shaped Piazza del Campo which it faces. Thin marble columns supporting Gothic arches decorate the windows. As in Florence, crenellations declare that this is a place of security and safety—as indeed it needed to be since the priors actually lived in the building and were subject on occasion to physical attack from the population. An astonishingly tall bell tower—clearly surpassing the height of the civic tower of their rival city Florence—extends from the left wing of the building, dominating other such structures which spiked the urban landscape. A later chapel beneath the tower extends out into the public square and indicates the fusion of Church and state in this city dedicated to the Virgin. In a city tightly packed within its medieval walls, the expansion of the Campo in front of the Palazzo gives a measure of the importance of rule extending out from the building to the population congregating before it. At the same time, this extraordinary sloping shell-like space—a natural concavity at the meeting of Siena's three hills—suggests the power that reciprocally flowed from the citizenry to their representative government. The Campo hosted not only meetings of the body politic but also public religious and sporting events. Public sermons (see Fig. 4.68) supported by the state again manifested the connections between religion and politics, calling divine favor upon the entire urban community. Events such as the wild bare-backed horse race around the Campo were a way both to entertain the population and to channel aggressions in a crowded and populous space.

Mendicant Orders

At the same time that communal governments were investing heavily in churches dedicated to their patron saints and constructing massive city halls, they also played instrumental roles in building projects for new urban religious orders, most notably the Franciscans and Dominicans. Named for their founders, Francis of Assisi (c. 1181–1226) and Dominic de Guzman from Spain (c. 1170–1221), these orders dedicated themselves to public charity and teaching. Both the Franciscans and the Dominicans were reformers, who sought to correct the isolation of much of medieval monasticism—which retreated from the world in closed communities—by espousing radical poverty and working within cities. Rather than relying on income from investments in land and businesses, as many orders did, the Franciscans and Dominicans were mendicants (persons who beg for alms). All their worldly goods were held in trust by the papacy, so that even when they began to receive major bequests from rich citizens they were technically able to remain distant from the corrupting influence of money. The mendicants' obvious piety, simplicity, and concern for the common folk of the towns earned them broad popularity. They served as powerful ambassadors to the laity, preaching a compassionate theology which reinforced orthodoxy and loyalty to the Church. While their churches grew to monumental proportions to accommodate the huge following that these

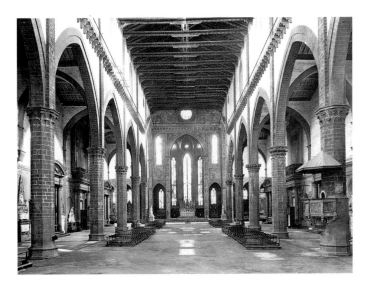

1.21 Santa Croce, Florence, begun 1294, commissioned by the Franciscans with the support of the Florentine government and private citizens, probably from Arnolfo di Cambio

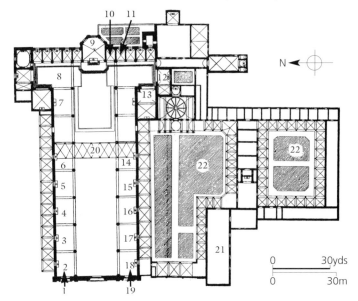

1.22 Santa Croce, Florence, plan of church and convent showing fourteenth-century chapel dedications and sixteenth-century nave chapel renewals

1 Zanchini Chapel, Bronzino, *Christ in Limbo*; **2** da Verrazzano Chapel, Naldini, *Entombment*; **3** Medici Chapel, Santi di Tito, *Resurrection*; **4** Berti Chapel, Santi di Tito, *Supper at Emmaus*; **5** Guidacci Chapel, Vasari, *Incredulity*; **6** Asini Chapel, Stradano, *Ascension*; **7** Biffoli Chapel, Vasari, *Pentecost*; **8** Risaliti Chapel, Macchietti, *Trinity*; **9** Alberti Chapel, Agnolo Gaddi, *Legends of the True Cross*; **10** Bardi Chapel, Giotto, *Life of St. Francis*; **11** Peruzzi Chapel, Giotto, *Lives of St. John the Evangelist and St. John the Baptist*; **12** Baroncelli Chapel, Taddeo Gaddi (and Giotto), *Life of the Virgin*; **13** Castellani Chapel, Various artists, *Lives of the Saints*; **14** Pazzi Chapel, Minga, *Agony*; **15** Corsi Chapel, Barbiere, *Flagellation*; **16** Zati Chapel, Coppi, *Ecce Homo*; **17** Buonarroti Chapel, Vasari, *Way to Calvary*; **18** Alamanneschi Chapel, Santi di Tito, *Crucifixion*; **19** Dini Chapel, Salviati, *Deposition*; **20** Choir screen (destroyed 1565); **21** Refectory, Taddeo Gaddi, *Last Supper and Tree of Life*; **22** Cloisters

two new religious orders enjoyed, they were sited away from cathedral and town hall, as if to give them independence from local civic pressure, and often at opposite ends of the walled city, as if to give the new mendicant messages the widest reach within the urban fabric.

Santa Croce and Santa Maria Novella in Florence The Dominicans and Franciscans became major rivals, however: the Franciscans emphasized a mystical, personal faith while the Dominicans articulated Christian theology in more rational, philosophical terms, their opposing sites in the city further emphasizing their rivalry. In Florence the Franciscan church of Santa Croce (Figs. 1.21 and 1.22) was begun on the eastern side of the city in 1294; the Dominicans built their church of Santa Maria Novella in the western part (Figs. 1.23 and 1.24). Both churches are cavernous enlargements of earlier monastic structures on their sites, attesting to the growth of both city and monastic orders. The Florentine government allotted substantial subsidies to the construction of both these buildings, so they must be read as civic monuments as well as monastic churches, indications of the city's beneficial cultic life. In fact, when Santa Croce was still unfinished in the 1430s, city officials lamented how poorly its delay reflected on the city as a whole.

Both churches are extraordinarily large, reflecting the size of the congregations who came to hear the preaching for which both orders were renowned, but they are also relatively restrained in their decoration, compared to the rich marble striping of Siena Cathedral or the marble- and mosaic-encrusted surfaces of the Florentine Baptistry. Both churches are laid out in modified **cruciform** plan, with a shallow apse, whose simple rectangular forms appropriately recall the geometric severity of churches built for the Cistercians, an older religious order that had

also promoted ecclesiastical reform. At Santa Maria Novella the nave wall is pierced only by simple oculi, and hardly a molding protrudes from its flat surface. Similarly at Santa Croce the open wooden truss roof and unelaborated lancet windows project an image of relative austerity, albeit on a monumental scale. Recalling the great Early Christian basilicas of Rome in their large size, these mendicant order churches testify to a desire to animate the institutional Church with the values of an earlier era.

Defining St. Francis The Franciscans worked diligently to develop a compelling image of their charismatic founder, St. Francis. Francis was renowned for dramatic gestures. When he decided to dedicate himself to a religious life he stripped himself naked in a public square and returned his clothes to his father. Following traditional Christian teaching, Francis believed that he could come closer to God by rejecting worldly goods and committing himself to a severe regimen of prayer, meditation, fasting, and mortification of the flesh. In 1224, just two years before his death, he manifested marks on his hands, feet, and side corresponding to the wounds of Christ. The stigmata, as these wounds are called, marked Francis

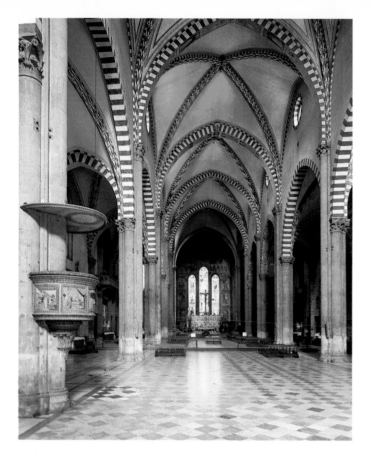

1.23 Santa Maria Novella, Florence, founded before 1246, nave begun after 1279, commissioned by the Dominicans with the support of the Florentine government and private citizens

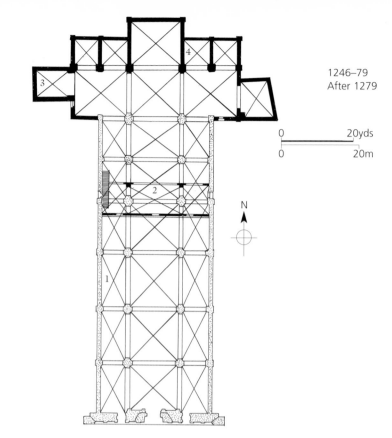

1246–79
After 1279

0   20yds
0   20m

N

1.24 Santa Maria Novella, Florence, plan

1 Lenzi Chapel, Masaccio, *Trinity*; **2** Choir screen (destroyed 1565); **3** Strozzi Chapel, Andrea and Nardo di Cione, *Last Judgment*, *Paradise*, and *Hell*; **4** Strozzi Chapel, Filippino Lippi, *Scenes from the Life of St. Philip and St. John*, Benedetto da Maiano, Tomb of Filippo Strozzi

in the eyes of some of his followers as a second Christ (*alter Christus*). At the same time Francis showed genuine compassion for individuals who were not as disciplined as he, celebrating the positive aspects of earthly life. He expressed an especially profound love of natural beauty. The words of Francis's *Canticle of the Sun*, a mystical poem in which he addresses "brother sun and sister moon," suggest the immediacy with which he embraced the natural universe.

For the Church, promoting the cult of St. Francis meant controlling and enhancing his image. In 1228 Pope Gregory IX (1227–41) commissioned a biography of the saint from Thomas of Celano. Official biographies, commissioned by the papacy at the time of canonization and read on a saint's feast day, were primary vehicles for allowing the Church to ensure that the proper lessons were drawn from a saint's life. Celano's work gave a gritty portrait of a man with foibles and weaknesses who was also a formidable miracle worker. Sixteen years later Celano began extensive revisions of the life, softening his emphasis on Francis's asceticism and dispensing with any posthumous miracles so as to focus on Francis's saintly acts during his lifetime.

Francis's official image was finally codified in 1260 with the commissioning of a third and canonical—that is, final and definitive—biography from Bonaventure of Bagnoreggio, a young Franciscan and future Minister General of the Order. Taking familiar stories from

Francis's life but framing them metaphorically, Bonaventure composed a mystical portrait of the saint as a modern Elijah, Moses, John the Baptist, angel of the Apocalypse, and faithful imitator of Christ. He admitted Francis's radical commitment to poverty and simplicity but emphasized how Francis had worked within the institutional Church to effect his reforms. In Bonaventure's work, known as the *Legenda Maior*, Francis's radical life was tamed and fitted for use by the official Church.

The First Franciscan Art   Art produced for Franciscans and their supporters also underwent notable changes as artists and patrons attempted to find the most effective ways to communicate visually who Francis was and what he stood for. The earliest signed and dated representation of St. Francis is an altarpiece produced in 1235 by Bonaventura Berlinghieri (active 1228–74), an artist from Lucca noted for his highly stylized, icon-like representations (Fig. 1.25). Although the work was created only nine years after Francis's death, the central standing image of Francis shows nothing of the saint's renowned good humor and accessibility. Instead, Francis appears highly formal, even forbidding, in a rigid frontal pose emphasizing his asceticism—a style considered suitable for an altarpiece, an image for contemplation and worship.

The figure conforms to the traditions of Byzantine art, reflecting the popularity of types that were invented and popularized in the Eastern Byzantine Empire following the collapse of the Western Roman Empire in the fifth century. These types were disseminated by Byzantine settlements in Italy and reinforced by renewed contacts between East and West during the Crusades.

Byzantine religious art is noted for the aura of sanctity and mystery with which saints are portrayed, consciously attempting to recall and repeat their features so as to retain the essence of their original prototype: presumed portraits of the actual saints painted in ancient times.

The iconic aspects of Byzantine art were well suited to emphasizing the spiritual aspects of Francis. The identification of Francis is achieved through the knotted cord of his brown habit, his tonsure and beard, and the stigmata on his hands and feet. The sternness of the saint's looming figure is mitigated by the three small scenes to either side of it. These more lively images were meant to be read as stories, providing insight into Francis's popular deeds and miracles and the reasons he was to be revered. For example, Francis is shown receiving the stigmata from a seraph. The positioning of this event at the upper left (that is, to the saint's right) suggests that it was the most important in Francis's life. Other scenes depict the saint preaching to birds and making various miraculous cures—a blending of the official and the popular, but all

within a narrative context meant to convey the historical facts of miraculous events, thus demanding a more animated and naturalistic style than did the central iconic figure of Francis.

The same general compositional scheme of the altarpiece was used for many other depictions of saints in this period, including St. Clare (c. 1194–1253), the founder of the second (or female) order of Franciscans known as the Poor Clares (Fig. 1.26). Clare was a noblewoman of Assisi. When she became a follower of St. Francis in 1212 and began her religious order, she apparently intended to create a female community comparable to the original Franciscans. Francis insisted, however, that the Poor Clares live in strict *clausura*, cloistered away from the world. Clare's community, too, grew to a sizable one, and she was known as a miracle worker. When she was canonized in 1255, just two years after her death, Pope Alexander IV (1254–61) commissioned Thomas of Celano to write her official biography. Figure 1.26, dated to the 1280s, represents St. Clare in much the same manner as Berlinghieri's painting of St. Francis. A central iconic image of the saint on a gold ground is flanked by eight scenes from her life taken from Celano's biography. Her history throughout the narrative panels—the first to represent a contemporary female saint—is tied to St. Francis.

CONTEMPORARY VOICE

Francis as Another Christ

In this typical passage from his life of St. Francis (known as the *Legenda Maior* because it superseded all other lives of the saint), St. Bonaventure engages the reader with rich anecdotal detail, at the same time making clear the symbolic and religious implications of all he reports.

On the feast of the Exaltation of the Holy Cross, while he was praying on the mountainside, Francis saw a Seraph with six fiery wings coming down from the highest point in the heavens. The vision descended swiftly and came to rest in the air near him. Then he saw the image of a Man crucified in the midst of the wings, with his hands and feet stretched out and nailed to a cross. Two of the wings were raised above his head and two were stretched out in flight, while the remaining two shielded his body. Francis was dumbfounded at the sight and his heart was

flooded with a mixture of joy and sorrow. He was overjoyed at the way Christ regarded him so graciously under the appearance of a Seraph, but the fact that he was nailed to a cross pierced his soul with a sword of compassionate sorrow. . . .

Eventually he realized by divine inspiration that God had shown him this vision in his providence, in order to let him see that, as Christ's lover, he would resemble Christ crucified perfectly not by physical martyrdom, but by the fervor of his spirit. As the vision disappeared, it left his heart ablaze with eagerness and impressed upon his body a miraculous likeness. There and then the marks of nails began to appear in his hands and feet, just as he had seen them in his vision of the Man nailed to the Cross. His hands and feet appeared pierced through the center with nails, the heads of which were in the palms of his hands and on the instep of each foot, while the points stuck out on the opposite side. The heads were black and round, but

the points were long and bent back, as if they had been struck with a hammer; they rose above the surrounding flesh and stood out from it. His right side seemed as if it had been pierced with a lance and was marked with a livid scar which often bled, so that his habit and trousers were stained. . . .

True love of Christ had now transformed his lover into his image, and when the forty days which he had intended spending in solitude were over and the feast of St. Michael had come, St. Francis came down from the mountain. With him he bore a representation of Christ crucified which was not the work of an artist in wood or stone, but had been reproduced in the members of his body by the hand of the living God.

(from Marion A. Habig. *St. Francis of Assisi: Writings and Early Biographies*. Chicago: Franciscan Herald Press, 1973, pp. 730–2)

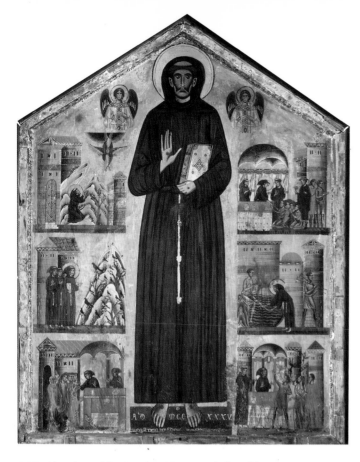

1.25 *Altarpiece of St. Francis*, 1235, commissioned from BONAVENTURA BERLINGHIERI for San Francesco, Pescia. Tempera on panel, 60 × 45¾″ (1.52 × 1.16 m)

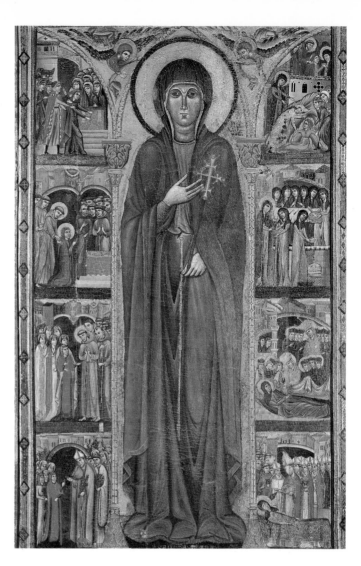

1.26 *Altarpiece of St. Clare*, 1280s, probably commissioned by the Clarissan sisters of the monastery of Santa Chiara, Assisi. Tempera on panel, 9 × 5½′ (2.73 × 1.65 m)

Her parents' disapproval of her wish to follow Francis, depicted at the upper left, mirrors his confrontation with his father, for example, and her death and funeral rites on the two panels to the lower right are depicted in a way comparable to those of Francis. Yet the middle two narrative panels on the right, depicting Clare's miraculous feeding of her religious sisters and her death, place her solely in the company of women. She is presented as a model of chastity, as well as obedience, having accepted Francis's demands that her order be cloistered.

Still, the unknown painter commissioned by the Poor Clares to depict their founder gave her a livelier and more approachable presence than we find in any early image of Francis. St. Clare is depicted within an architectural niche, almost as if she were modeled in space, much like painted wooden figures sometimes used as the centers for elaborate multi-paneled altarpieces. The top side panels are arched, creating the illusion that the sides are wings that could be folded in to match the arch behind Clare's head. The painting thus has the characteristics of small, private, portable devotional images, appropriate for the cloistered nuns, and at the same time the scale of a major pilgrimage object honoring an important saint. Clearly the tensions between the intercessory power of this woman and the traditional submissive role assigned to women in the society (and underscored again and again in Celano's biography) underlie this image of St. Clare.

Crucifixes

The Dominicans did not develop a personal cult around their founder and thus commissioned relatively few images of St. Dominic. They joined the Franciscans, however, in encouraging the production of large, painted crucifixes to be hung above the high altar or placed atop the monumental rood screens that divided the apse and their choir stalls from the nave (later removed from most churches following liturgical reforms in the sixteenth century). As the essential image of Christ's sacrifice, crucifixes were common features in all medieval churches. The mendicants built upon this tradition, while propagating a newly compassionate representation of Christ's suffering and death. One of the most poignant of these was painted by the Florentine artist Cimabue (Cenni de Pepi; active 1260s–1302 Florence, Arezzo, Assisi, Pisa, and Rome) for the church of San Domenico in Arezzo (Fig. 1.27). Very little is known about Cimabue's life, but his works indicate that he and his patrons were deeply impressed by Byzantine art. The type of suffering Christ (*Christus*

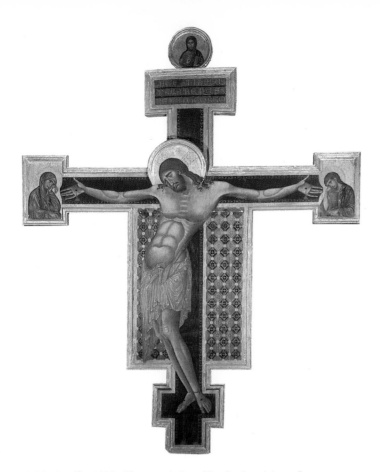

1.27 *Crucifix*, 1270s (?), commissioned by the Dominicans from CIMABUE for San Domenico, Arezzo. 11′ × 8′ 9″ (3.36 × 2.67 m)

patiens) he created for Arezzo had already appeared in Byzantine art in the eleventh century. It gained popularity in Italy only in the early thirteenth century, when the emotional and immediate spirituality of reformers like saints Dominic and Francis encouraged worshipers to identify with Christ more closely. Previously crucifixes had presented a regal, live Christ triumphant on the cross (hence the term *Christus triumphans* for this type of crucifix). Cimabue's image speaks in quieter, more human terms. Christ's head slumps forward in death, his long hair piling in tight curls on his broad shoulders. Strong lines indicate the muscles in his arms, chest, and abdomen. His body is weighty, sagging far to the left of the cross's central axis. The image communicates sadness, not eternal power, and compels individual identification with Christ's sufferings—behavior exemplified by the grieving half figures of the Virgin Mary and St. John in rectangular panels at the ends of the arms of the cross.

Altarpieces Dedicated to the Virgin

Images of the enthroned Madonna and Child reflect the intense popularity of the Virgin and her cult in this period. Like crucifixes, altarpieces of the Madonna and Child document a growing interest in imagining religious images in more human terms. They were also increasingly large, in accordance with the increasing spaciousness of mendicant

churches and the need for devotional objects to be clearly visible to all. While early altarpieces like those dedicated to Francis and Clare were relatively modest in scale, eight- and ten-foot (two-and-a-half to three-meter) high altarpieces of the Virgin became common in the second half of the thirteenth century. One of these, commissioned from the Sienese artist Guido da Siena (active 1262/67– 1280s Siena), stood on the high altar of San Domenico in Siena (Fig. 1.28). As the chief devotional image within the church the image is suitably iconic. The Virgin's narrow facial features and the tight net of gold fishbone patterns that originally embellished her garments reflect traditional Byzantine types (see Fig. 19), as does the bust of Christ flanked by angels in the gable of the altarpiece. More recent Byzantine innovations in depicting space may have inspired Guido to show the splayed side of the Virgin's throne. Overall, however, Guido's style was much more insistently linear than any contemporary Byzantine models. Certain of the tighter elements of the altarpiece may have been consciously—or at least appropriately—chosen to make the work look older and therefore more venerable and potentially more efficacious than it otherwise might have been. The panel carries the date 1221, which does not refer to the date of its creation but rather to the death of St. Dominic, the founder of the order that commissioned the work. The power of new, more naturalistic models is evident, however, insofar as the faces of this Madonna and Child were repainted in the early fourteenth century to correspond to the softer naturalism that the next generation of Sienese artists found in a closer study of Byzantine and Gothic models. Greater lifelikeness eventually gained the upper hand.

Cimabue's Altarpiece for Santa Trinità   By the 1280s the new scale of altarpieces popularized in mendicant churches had been adopted for those in other churches as well. The visual impact and devotional effectiveness of these large images clearly recommended them to religious leaders. For the Vallombrosan church of Santa Trinità in Florence, Cimabue created a twelve-foot (three-and-a-half-meter) high image of the *Enthroned Madonna and Child* (Fig. 1.29). His Florentine altarpiece employs Byzantine types, but is distinctive, however, insofar as it depicts a deeper and more complex space around the figures. Cimabue also rediscovered the original purpose of gold highlights and linear embellishments in much of Byzantine painting. Rather than using the typical fishbone striations merely as abstract patterns on the surface of the painting, Cimabue understood that gold highlights referred directly to actual folds and creases in drapery. Equally important is his use of crisp lines to construct space around and in front of the Madonna. The platforms under her feet and the oblique angles created by the arms

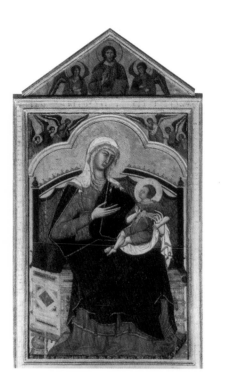

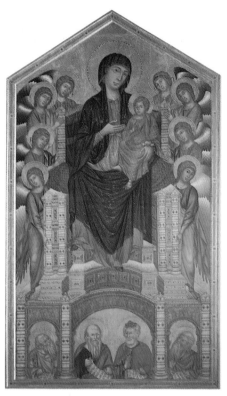

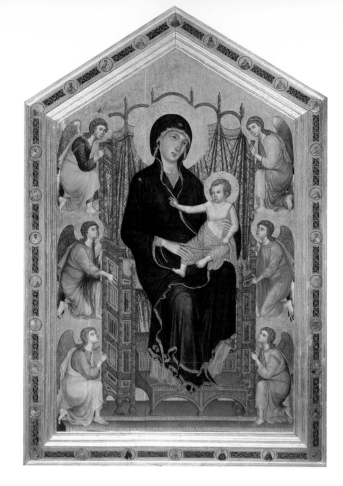

of her **architectonic** throne suggest a degree of perspective, although some spatial ambiguities result: in what plane, for example, are the Old Testament prophets below the throne? Cimabue's altarpiece, with its shimmering gold throne flanked by the muted violet and pastel robes of the angels, retains the ability of Byzantine art to evoke the transcendent nature of the divine. At the same time, it makes the incarnation of God in Christ through Mary more believable through a new emphasis on humanly observable phenomena.

Duccio's Altarpiece for the Confraternity of the Laudesi

On April 15, 1285 the Confraternity of the Laudesi, a lay group associated with the Dominicans in Florence and dedicated to charitable work and praise of the Virgin, commissioned a huge altarpiece for their chapel in the right transept of Santa Maria Novella. They called upon a young Sienese artist, Duccio di Buoninsegna (active c. 1278–1318 Siena), to provide a suitable image (Fig. 1.30). Duccio may have trained with either Cimabue or Guido da Siena, but his work breaks notably with that of his predecessors. His new, more naturalistic style—particularly in the rendering of facial features—was to dominate Sienese painting for much of the early fourteenth century.

Duccio's enthroned Madonna and Child—now familiarly known as the *Rucellai Madonna* because of its subsequent placement in a chapel belonging to the Rucellai family—reveals in its frame the special concerns of the Laudesi. It displays thirty small roundels depicting

1.28 (left) *Enthroned Madonna and Child*, c. 1260, commissioned by the Dominicans from GUIDO DA SIENA for the high altar of San Domenico, Siena. Main panel, 9′ 4½″ × 6′ 4″ (2.86 × 1.93 m) (Chapel of St. Bernard, San Domenico, Siena)

In many cases, the faces of figures in such devotional paintings were so heavily abraded by repeated cleaning that the green underpaint was revealed. In this case the heads of the Madonna and Child were actually repainted at a slightly later date to make them conform to the style of Duccio.

1.29 (middle) *Enthroned Madonna and Child (Maestà)*, 1280s, commissioned from CIMABUE for Santa Trinità, Florence. Tempera on panel, 11′ 7″ × 7′ 4″ (3.53 × 2.24 m) (Galleria degli Uffizi, Florence)

1.30 (right) *Enthroned Madonna and Child (Maestà)*, 1285, commissioned by the Confraternity of the Laudesi from DUCCIO for their chapel in Santa Maria Novella, Florence. Tempera on panel, 14′ 9⅛″ × 9′ 6⅛″ (4.5 × 2.9 m) (Galleria degli Uffizi, Florence)

saints who include St. Catherine of Alexandria (a favorite saint in Dominican contexts), St. Dominic (the founder of the Dominican order), St. Zenobius (a patron saint of Florence), and St. Peter Martyr (founder of the confraternity).

Comparison of Duccio's altarpiece with Cimabue's large panel for Santa Trinità reveals some of the shifts taking place in Italian painting at the end of the thirteenth century. Whereas Cimabue tied his figures to a Byzantine model, with smooth ovoid shapes defining the structure of the faces and with crisp, angular gold striations used to model drapery, Duccio seems to have looked to French models as well. Although the facial features of his figures betray sources similar to Cimabue's in their abstracted shapes, the drapery of the figures adheres much more closely to the physical forms beneath. The border of the Virgin's robe, carefully tooled in gold, ripples in a sinuous pattern which seems to delight in graceful curvilinear movement for its own sake; while suggesting the folds of the fabric it also "works" as an elegant surface pattern. Even the soft shift of the axes of the Virgin's body (compare Cimabue's Madonna, who is aligned on a single axis, apart from her right leg) suggests new concern for activating the figure. Duccio enhances the incipient concern for shading and modeling seen in the work of his Sienese predecessor Guido da Siena to create a volumetric, though simplified, treatment of the human form.

That said, it is probably just as important to recall how similar such devotional images were, rather than to emphasize their differences. Duccio's and Cimabue's altarpieces purposefully presented similar subject matter in similar ways in order to allow worshipers to forge a coherent image of the divine. The power of these altarpieces derived in no small part from the collective image they left on the minds of the faithful. Looming out of the semidarkness of countless churches, the Madonna and Child became familiar, accessible, and omnipresent, a highly effective means of approaching God.

Rome: Artists, Popes, and Cardinals Renewing the Church, 1277–c.1310

No city in Italy could boast as rich and complex a history as Rome. A fifteenth-century woodcut emphasizes its papal and imperial monuments (Fig. 1.31). The palace of the popes (clearly labeled *palatium pape*) stands on the horizon immediately to the right of Old St. Peter's Basilica, burial site of the Apostle who was the first pope. The prominent position of these structures on the Vatican hill reflects the city's domination by the papacy. Major monuments of Roman antiquity stretch across the foreground of the print, documenting the city's former grandeur. Many of these had acquired or been given Christian significance. At the far left appears a corner of the Colosseum (sacred site of Christian martyrdom), followed by the dome and portico of the Pantheon (rededicated as a church to the Virgin Mary) and the column of Trajan (an ancient monument to one of the Roman emperors whom Christians recognized as "good"). At the far right stands the huge drum-shaped Castel Sant'Angelo, originally the mausoleum of the Emperor Hadrian but later endowed with fortifications by several popes. Hefty ancient walls continued to define the city's limits.

Even so, Rome was but a shell of its former self. Whereas other cities repeatedly outgrew and expanded

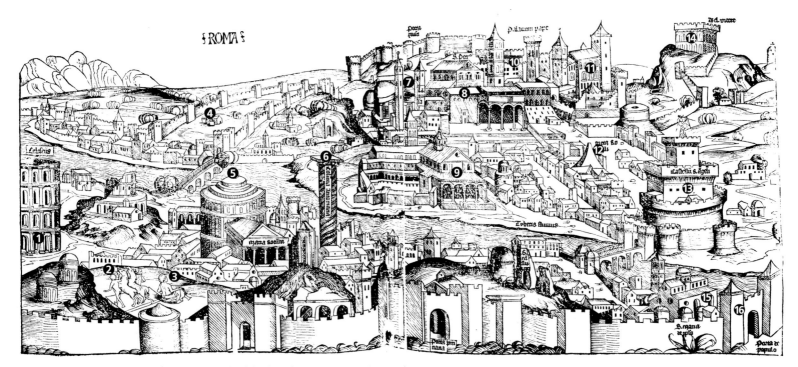

1.31 *View of Rome*, from Hartmann Schedel, *Liber chronicarum*, 1493. Woodcut

1 Colosseum; **2** Quirinal Hill (and *Horse Tamers*); **3** *Nile River God* (now on Capitoline Hill); **4** Trastevere; **5** Pantheon; **6** Column of Marcus Aurelius; **7** Obelisk of Augustus; **8** Old St. Peter's; **9** Hospital of Santo Spirito; **10** Sistine Chapel; **11** Papal Palace; **12** Tomb of Romulus (destroyed 1496); **13** Castel Sant' Angelo; **14** Belvedere of Innocent VIII; **15** Santa Maria del Popolo; **16** Porta del Popolo

their ancient and medieval walls, Rome rattled around inside them. Huge fields of ruins stood starkly in what once had been densely populated neighborhoods; sheep and cows grazed in the remains of the imperial fora. Most of the population clustered together in the neighborhood at the bend on the Tiber River where the Vatican met the old imperial city.

The woodcut shows a good number of houses in front of the Vatican, along with a porticoed church-like building and enormous courtyard that made up the papal hospital of Santo Spirito, an institution committed to public charity. As effective rulers of Rome, the popes, who claimed that their temporal rulership of the state had been conferred on them by Constantine before he moved the capital of the Empire to Constantinople in the fourth century, were responsible for all aspects of life in the city. Although the Roman Senate continued to exist as the official civic government, real control over the city was exercised by the pope and a few very strong factionalized feudal families such as the Colonna and the Orsini.

Artistic patronage in Rome was determined by the peculiar nature of papal authority, which was both religious and secular, local and international, and by the papacy's need to respond to the political demands of the Senate and the leading families. The lineage of the papacy, although continuous and unbroken since Peter, the first pope, was non-dynastic, a pope being elected for life by the cardinals, his major subordinates within the hierarchically organized institution of the Church. Presumably as a celibate, a pope had no heirs to whom the office could descend. The cardinals and the popes were not always Roman or even Italian, a situation that led inevitably to power struggles between the popes and local families who sought favorable treatment from the papacy. Thus the popes had to construct a lineage, associating themselves with the histories and deeds (including artistic commissions) of their predecessors, so as to underscore the continuity of the office and their unbroken connections with its previous holders. Given these concerns and the imposing, ubiquitous reminders of past glory, it is not surprising that art and culture in Rome were often highly traditionalist.

The Revival of Rome under Nicholas III

In 1277 Cardinal Giangaetano Orsini, a member of one of Rome's most powerful families, ascended the papal throne as Nicholas III—an event that was to stimulate a revival of Rome. His immediate predecessors had been mainly Frenchmen, who were unwelcome in Rome. In the three years of his papacy Nicholas initiated a major expansion to the popes' palace at the Vatican as well as

the restoration of Early Christian frescoes at the papal basilicas of St. Paul's Outside the Walls and St. Peter's. Construction at or near St. Peter's served both personal and papal needs. By concentrating his efforts at the Vatican, rather than at St. John Lateran, the official cathedral of Rome, Nicholas underscored the papacy's descent from St. Peter, whose cult centered around the Vatican's own basilica. At a practical level Nicholas's work in the Vatican also benefited from the fact that the Orsini, his family, controlled a district of the city directly across the Tiber, thus giving him a strong power base in the city. Nicholas himself had served as an archpriest at St. Peter's, and numbers of his relatives had been buried there.

Nicholas's additions to the papal palace in the Vatican were substantial. Archaeologists have determined that much of the basic structure of the palace was determined by him, although it was significantly altered over succeeding centuries. Nicholas's palace included a large chapel, audience hall, and state chambers, surrounded by a great park. Some of the decorations of Nicholas's chambers survive above later dropped ceilings (Fig. 1.32). In one of the frescoes lively birds play amid leafy garlands; in another, a corbeled arcade runs along the top of the wall. These motifs appear again and again in Roman medieval art. But unlike their immediate predecessors, which had become increasingly linear and schematized from repeated copying and imitation, these motifs are

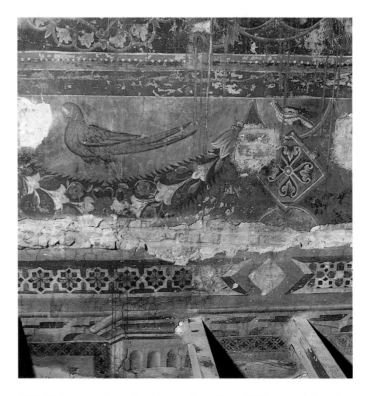

1.32 Birds, garlands, and architectural motifs, c. 1277, commissioned by Nicholas III for the Vatican Palace, Rome. Fresco

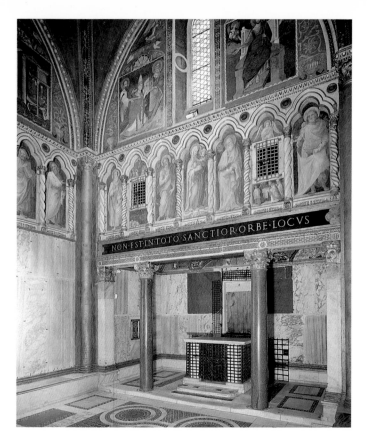

1.33 Sancta Sanctorum, 1278, commissioned by Nicholas III from MASTER COSMATUS for the Lateran Palace, Rome (Scala Santa)

The stairs leading up to this chapel originally served as the entrance to the medieval Lateran Palace. Legend said that they had come from Pilate's house in Jerusalem, where Christ was said to have walked on them. Out of respect, pilgrims climb the steps on their knees.

vigorous and animated. Some, especially the birds, seem almost to be drawn from life. The leafy garlands, on the other hand, derive from a renewed acquaintance with antique frescoes that Nicholas's artists were restoring next door in St. Peter's. What appeared new was actually very old. This conscious revival of a late antique style gave formal unity to the decorative program at the Vatican and, more importantly, recalled the early days of the Church in Rome—an association with positive meaning for Nicholas as he sought to reestablish the papacy in Rome.

The Sancta Sanctorum A major earthquake in 1278 offered Nicholas III the opportunity to rebuild the Sancta Sanctorum, the popes' private chapel at the Lateran Palace (Fig. 1.33). Nicholas graciously conceded recognition to his builder, Cosmatus, in a marble plaque on the side wall. The architect provided the pope a compact cubical space where decorations again link Nicholas to his predecessors by carefully blending old and new. The chapel is covered with "modern" cross-ribbed vaulting, but the vaults themselves spring from reused Roman columns in the corners of the basically square space. The rectangular apse is marked by a marble entablature supported on reused porphyry columns, an Egyptian stone so expensive and highly prized that in ancient times its quarrying and

use were under the direct control of the emperors. Nicholas had the words "NON EST IN TOTO SANCTIOR ORBE LOCUS" ("There is not a holier place in the entire world") inscribed on the architrave, referring to the fact that here the popes housed one of Christianity's most sacred relics, the Acheropita, a presumed true portrait of Christ. Two of Nicholas's most powerful thirteenth-century predecessors, Innocent III (r. 1198–1216) and his successor Honorius III (r. 1216–27), had enshrined the image in gold, silver, and bronze. Now Nicholas rebuilt the chapel for its adoration, both linking himself to his predecessors and graphically proclaiming his contact with Christ, his ultimate source of authority.

Frescoes recounting stories of saints whose relics were kept in the Sancta Sanctorum cover the side walls of the chapel. Gold mosaics add luster to the vaults over the altar. A fresco portrait of Nicholas kneeling with Saints Peter and Paul at his sides admits the pope to the perpetual company of the Savior and the saints (Fig. 1.34). He presents a model of his chapel to Christ who sits

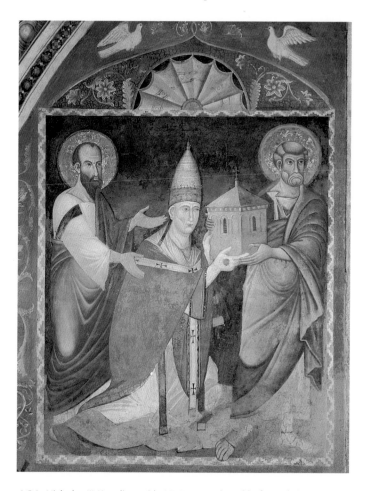

1.34 *Nicholas III Kneeling with SS. Peter and Paul before Christ,* 1277–80, commissioned by Nicholas III for the Sancta Sanctorum, Lateran Palace, Rome. Fresco (Scala Santa)

Nicholas is accompanied by the papal patrons, St. Peter and St. Paul.

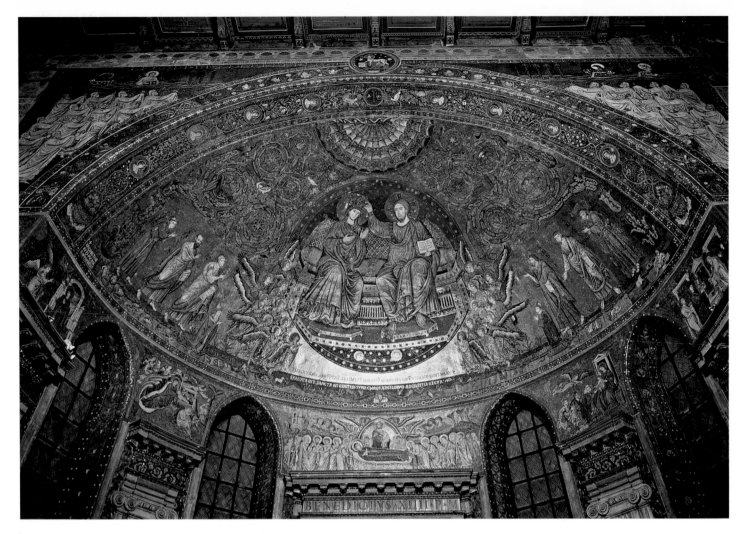

1.35 *Coronation of the Virgin*, c. 1294, commissioned by Nicholas IV from JACOPO TORRITI for the apse of Santa Maria Maggiore, Rome. Mosaic. See also Fig. 1.1

enthroned in a paired fresco on this same wall (see Fig. 1.33). Nicholas's portrait is a highly personable image, confident and relaxed in a manner that none of the scores of earlier representations of popes as donors had been.

Nicholas IV at Santa Maria Maggiore

Pope Nicholas IV (r. 1288–92), a Franciscan monk from Ascoli, continued the cultural policies of Nicholas III. His major focus was Santa Maria Maggiore, the papal basilica in the neighborhood controlled by the Colonna family, who effectively adopted this non-Roman pope, a redressing of urban power after the earlier Orsini pope. Nicholas replaced the old apse at Santa Maria Maggiore with a larger, more impressive structure that included a transept, enhancing its similarities to Old St. Peter's. He lined the apse with marbles and mosaics by the Roman painter and mosaicist Jacopo Torriti (active 1270–1300 Rome) depicting the *Coronation of the Virgin* in a star-studded blue orb (Fig. 1.35; see also Fig. 1.1). Imperially clad figures of the Virgin and Christ sit upon a golden throne softened with scarlet and blue cushions. Raising his right hand to

the Virgin's head, Christ completes the coronation of his Queen of Heaven while angels steady the celestial sphere. The Latin inscription below it comes from the liturgy for the August 15 feast of the Assumption of the Virgin, the anniversary of the traditional founding of the basilica. It calls explicit attention to key elements in the representation: the Virgin's assumption to the heavenly throne, the starry realm of Christ the King, the chorus of angels, and the Virgin's royal status. This depiction of the Virgin as the Queen of Heaven can also be seen as a reference to Mary as Ecclesia, or the Church, the bride of Christ, a metaphor based on the Old Testament *Song of Songs*. In this role Mary/Ecclesia appears as co-ruler with God, like him capable of granting salvation. It is a powerful image of the Church controlling Christian destiny and, by extension, of the popes who were its head.

To the left of the central image a small figure of Nicholas in a scarlet coat and papal tiara appears in the kneeling pose of the patron before the standing figures of saints Peter and Paul, who appear to be presenting the pope to the celestial court. To the left of these saints Torriti represents the plainly clad and tonsured figure of St. Francis, an appropriate inclusion for a patron who had begun his ecclesiastical career as a Franciscan. At the right a miniaturized Cardinal Jacopo Colonna kneels before another pair of saints, John the Baptist and John the Evangelist; at the far right St. Anthony of Padua, another Franciscan, completes the Franciscan "bracketing" of the scene.

Torriti's full, soft forms and the poses of his figures recall the Byzantine imperial style of the mid-1260s that had abandoned the characteristally insistent linear patterns of Byzantine art. The mosaic's lush green **rinceaux** (stylized, scrolling vine patterns) sprout red flowers and give roost to splendid paradisiacal birds—peacocks, cranes, and partridges. These motifs and the water flowing from river gods along the base of the mosaic suggest that late classical models also formed part of the mosaicists' repertoire. Here, in fact, the artists may have been replicating or even reusing elements from the original fifth-century apse. Obviously, neither Byzantine nor late antique models had outlived their usefulness, primarily because both were still vibrant, living traditions.

Patrons from the Papal Curia

Commissions by two cardinals at their titular churches in Rome document the competitive spirit that prevailed among patrons at the papal court. Toward the end of the thirteenth century, at Santa Maria in Trastevere, Cardinal Bertoldo Stefaneschi commissioned the Roman painter Pietro Cavallini (Pietro dei Cerroni; c. 1240/50–1330s) to renovate the church's mid-twelfth-century apse mosaic with a band of scenes from the life of the Virgin below it. Cavallini was an artist of considerable genius, who has been under-appreciated by many art historians—partly, no doubt, because he was largely unknown by Vasari, who credited many of Cavallini's innovations to the Florentine artist Giotto. Cavallini made his reputation working for Pope Nicholas III, restoring Early Christian frescoes in the papal basilica of St. Paul's Outside the Walls, works that disappeared when that church burned in 1823. There Cavallini's task seems to have been to replicate badly deteriorating Early Christian images, thus training himself to be able to produce that stylistic vocabulary—essentially a late Roman one—at will. That experience allowed him to give Byzantine prototypes new vitality and a greater sense of movement, enhancing their three-dimensionality and heightening the human interaction among them.

In one of the scenes at Santa Maria in Trastevere, the *Birth of the Virgin* (Fig. 1.36), Cavallini placed St. Anne (the mother of Mary), her attendants, and the infant Virgin in three tightly connected planes parallel to the picture surface: the maids preparing the child's bath far

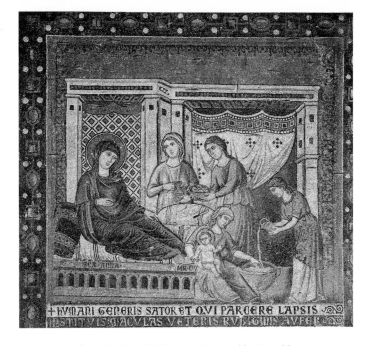

1.36 *Birth of the Virgin*, c. 1290, commissioned by Bertoldo Stefaneschi from PIETRO CAVALLINI for the transept wall of Santa Maria in Trastevere, Rome. Mosaic

forward, the large reclining figure of St. Anne in the middle, and two more servants behind the bed. The parted curtain at the far right implies further space beyond this densely clustered composition, as does the space around the stage-like architecture and its receding diagonals. The effect is both noble and domestic. Intimate in its scale, the scene communicates dignity and solemnity through the strong vertical and horizontal lines of its architectural setting.

Around the same time that Cavallini was working on these mosaics, the French cardinal Jean Cholet engaged him to create a larger and more extensive cycle of frescoes for his titular church of Santa Cecilia, also in Trastevere. Frescoes were cheaper than mosaic, but the scope of this project was larger. For the nave walls of Santa Cecilia, Cholet commissioned a now-ruined cycle of Old and New Testament scenes, directly imitative of established models that Cavallini knew intimately from the papal basilicas. The entire back wall of the church was reserved for a *Last Judgment* (Fig. 1.37), a subject traditionally placed in that location to complete the cycle of Christian history begun in the biblical scenes on the side walls.

Enough of the *Last Judgment* survives to give a solid understanding of this mature phase of Cavallini's art. Christ sits at the center of the composition, flanked to left and right by enthroned apostles. Beneath them, in areas now obscured, angels attend to persons who are about to be saved on Christ's right (the viewer's left), while on the other side devils take possession of the bodies of the damned. Cavallini's debt to the increasing naturalism of northern Gothic art of the period is evident throughout these frescoes, especially in some of the drapery folds. However, neither Gothic sources nor the Byzantine

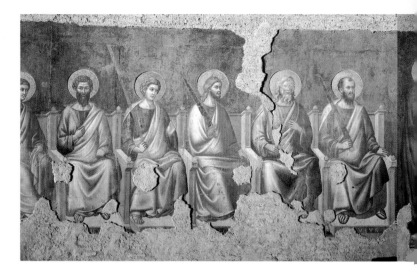

1.37 (right) *Last Judgment*, c. 1290, commissioned by Jean Cholet from Pietro Cavallini for Santa Cecilia in Trastevere, Rome. Fresco

prototypes that clearly inspired the iconography of his frescoes (see, for example, the similar subject in the Florentine Baptistry; Fig. 1.10) fully explain the warmly modeled reality of his figures, the way drapery actually seems to flow volumetrically around them, the deep thrones in which each of the figures sits, the effective way that bright light from either side of the composition throws them into relief, and the remarkable coherence of his overall composition. These we must credit to Cavallini's own genius. Rather than merely mimicking what he found in artistic models around him, he was synthesizing them, learning their lessons, and applying them in novel ways to his own work.

Cardinal Cholet also hired the Florentine sculptor/ architect Arnolfo di Cambio (c. 1245– 1302?) to create a new *baldacchino* (baldachin), or altar canopy, for his church (Fig. 1.38). Arnolfo was well qualified for the job, having worked as an assistant in the workshop of Nicola Pisano before creating an impressive *baldacchino* for the papal basilica of St. Paul's Outside the Walls in 1285. The

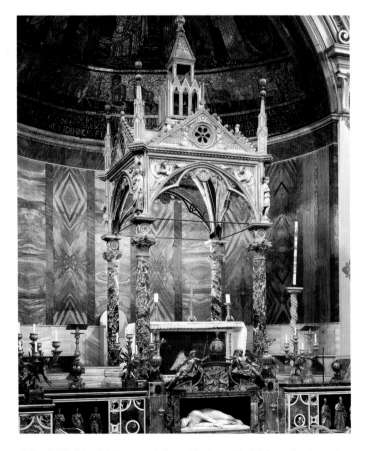

1.38 Baldachin, 1293, commissioned by Jean Cholet from Arnolfo di Cambio for Santa Cecilia in Trastevere, Rome. Marble

canopy at Santa Cecilia (1293) deftly combines classical Roman and French Gothic elements. Like earlier such canopies, the structure is supported on four ancient Roman columns. Arnolfo inserted delicate bar tracery under the tentatively pointed main arches, transformed the corners of the canopy into pinnacles, and edged the gables with sprouting Gothic **crockets** (stylized leaves). Traditional Roman elements are also used to decorative effect. Beribboned laurel wreaths hover at the apex of each arch, and **impost blocks** over the capitals raise the canopy's height, lessening the apparent weight of the structure upon the richly mottled columns. This is another work of brilliant synthesis, well suited both to its Roman setting and to a non-Roman patron at the international papal court.

Pope Boniface VIII and an Imperial Language of Power

Pope Boniface VIII (1294–1303), himself an active patron of the arts while still a cardinal, set a new standard for unabashed pomp and visual splendor. It is probably just a quirk of history that Boniface is the first pope whose luxurious possessions—including pheasant-plumed fans; goblets encrusted with garnets, enamels, and sapphires; knives with handles of ivory, coral, sandalwood, jasper, and lapis lazuli—are documented. Much of this he must have inherited from his predecessors. But there was something imperial about the material display of his papacy, as well as his own demeanor and brash confidence in the unassailability of the papacy. He would have been as comfortable on the ancient Palatine Hill among the emperors as he was at the Lateran and Vatican palaces. The apocryphal report that he once announced "I am the emperor" does not stray far from his actual estimation of himself and the papacy.

Like his predecessors, Boniface spent money on building repairs and renovations, the most famous of which

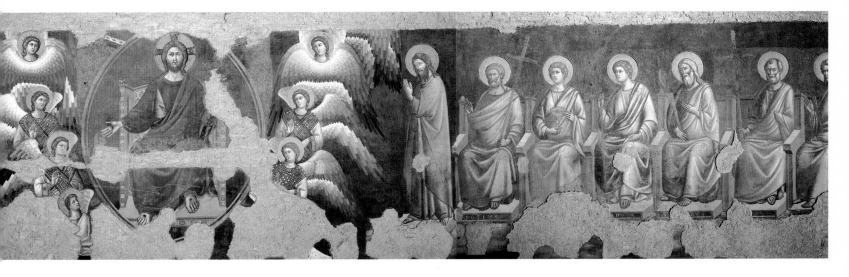

was the construction of a new Benediction **loggia** at the Lateran Palace (Fig. 1.39). Boniface emblazoned the loggia (used by the pope to bless the faithful) with imperial parasols and the coat of arms of his family, the Caetani, and supported it both physically and symbolically with reused ancient columns. Sculptural figures of saints Peter and Paul flanking the loggia's gable emphasized the pope's rightful succession to apostolic power.

A portrait bust from Boniface's tomb, which he commissioned before his death, tells us yet more about papal ambitions in this period (Fig. 1.40). Boniface's tomb monument in the chapel of St. Boniface in Old St. Peter's included this vivid image of benediction along with a recumbent effigy of the pope and a mosaic in which saints Peter and Paul recommended him to the Virgin and Child. The message of these three images is clear: the

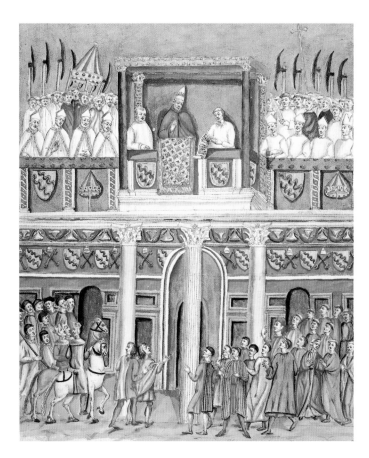

1.39 *Pope Boniface VIII Imparting a Blessing from the Benediction Loggia at the Lateran*, seventeenth-century miniature recording the composition of a fresco, c. 1300, inside the Benediction Loggia at the Lateran Palace, Rome (Biblioteca Ambrosiana, ms. F. inf. 227, 8v, Milan)

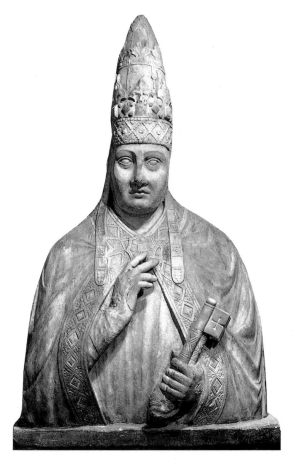

1.40 *Portrait Bust of Pope Boniface VIII*, c. 1300, commissioned by Boniface VIII from ARNOLFO DI CAMBIO for his tomb monument at the altar of St. Boniface in Old St. Peter's, Rome. Marble (Vatican Grotto)

Art and Miracles

During the Renaissance, as in other periods, art was on occasion vested with supernatural powers. A carved wood image of the *Christ Child* (Fig. 1.41) preserved at the Franciscan church of the Aracoeli in Rome, was rushed to the bedside of mortally ill children and credited with numerous miraculous recoveries. Reliquaries (see Fig. 2.41) were carried through the streets to stave off plague and military threats. The *Madonna of Impruneta* in the countryside outside Florence was regularly brought into the city to control the weather, and the *Madonna and Child* at Or San Michele in Florence (see Fig. 3.25) intervened when nature got fully out of control, saving devotees from drowning in the city's frequent floods.

The figures of miracle-working images exhibited great sympathy for their human devotees and themselves manifested very human characteristics: they could be saddened and weep; they could close their eyes when offended; they bled; they could be jealous and moody, refusing their normal thaumaturgical activities if not accorded appropriate respect. Above all, they were fiercely loyal, protecting cities, communities, and individuals from natural and human disasters.

Ironically the works credited with effecting miraculous cures, assisting in the accomplishment of difficult or perilous tasks, or protecting devotees from harm or misfortune were most often works with little or no aesthetic pretension. The very power of the miracle existed in some large measure in surprise. Just as miracles could not be planned, miracle-working images could not be manufactured. They had their greatness thrust upon them. And their very ordinary quality, embedded in the life of the community, helped to lend them power and veracity. Although an artist might sometimes be called upon to update or

enhance a miracle-working image, as was the case with Bernardo Daddi's *Madonna and Child* for Or San Michele,

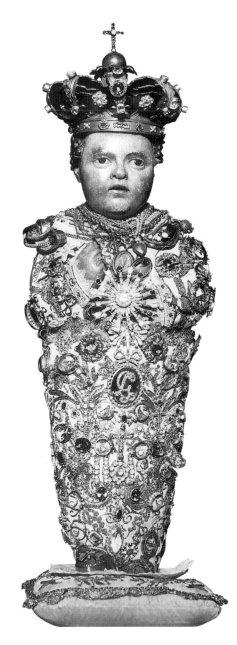

1.41 *The Bambino of Aracoeli*, second half of the fifteenth century, commissioned by the Franciscans of Santa Maria d'Aracoeli, Rome. Polychromed wood

Legend has it that the sculpture was carved from wood from the Mount of Olives in Jerusalem.

the "creation" of miraculous images was largely a popular phenomenon.

The divine chose to dwell in images serendipitously, but once an image began working miracles, it could be kept efficacious through devout reverence. Figures like the *Christ Child* in Rome were dressed in elegant outfits and fitted with crowns. Statues of the Madonna were adorned with necklaces and earrings. Often the object was enhanced architecturally. Santa Maria dei Miracoli in Venice (see Fig. 6.39) was built to house what had been a simple devotional image on a street corner. At Santa Maria delle Carceri in Prato the original wall upon which the Madonna had been painted was deemed so sacred that it was incorporated physically into the structure of the fifteenth-century church, even though the curve of the original apse did not correspond to the geometry of the new structure.

How did the Church tolerate what seems to most modern viewers extraordinarily pagan and idolatrous behavior? Christians believed that God had taken on human form in their savior Christ, and that God continued to act directly and sometimes dramatically in the lives of believers. Church authorities maintained, in spite of what much of the general public might have believed, that the images themselves did *not* perform miracles. Instead, God and his saints worked *through* images. Theologians distinguished between reverence and worship, only the latter being due to God. In countering charges of paganism at the end of the sixth century, Gregory the Great had insisted that physical representations of the deity were merely aids to contemplation of the divine, not direct manifestations of divinity itself. Statues and paintings were allowed, even encouraged, because they invited reverence and served didactic purposes, especially for the illiterate.

individual pope may die but the dignity of his office, manifest in the bust by the papal tiara and keys, lives on. While the mosaic speaks of Boniface's personal admission to salvation, his bust implies the eternal efficacy of his benediction for others. His mortal body was placed in its tomb, but the papacy which he had embodied was to live forever. The conceit of Boniface VIII's tomb was sophisticated, stopping just short of self-exaltation. Little wonder his enemies charged him with idolatry. A less than sympathetic eye would see only Boniface, not the papacy, represented in the bust.

These confident images belie Boniface's stormy relations with the Roman aristocracy, especially the Colonna, whose stronghold at nearby Palestrina he leveled and began to replace with a new papal estate. The Colonna's French allies then actually attacked the pope in his own palace in Anagni. Only his valiant defiance saved the day. Awaiting his would-be captors in full papal regalia and thus projecting the image of authority which appeared in his tomb monument, Boniface forced his attackers to humiliate the papacy as well as himself. Learning of this affront, the local townspeople, who held little affection for Boniface the man, rose up to defend the office he represented. Still, neither Boniface nor the papacy emerged unscathed. He died soon thereafter, a broken and bitter man. Broken, too, was the confidence of the papacy in its ability to manage its affairs in Rome. Subsequent popes–especially those who did not come from Roman families–found it impossible to control the Eternal City and its often hostile, competing clans.

Images for the Church during an Absent Papacy

Offered a safe haven at Avignon in 1306, Pope Clement V moved the institutional offices of the papacy to that small French town, beginning what was to be more than a century of exile. Without the patronage of popes and cardinals, major construction and artistic production in Rome could be sustained only with great difficulty. As it became increasingly evident that the papal court was well established in Avignon, new artistic enterprises in Rome slowed to a trickle.

Nevertheless popes and cardinals engaged in various attempts throughout the fourteenth century to reclaim and renovate their traditional seat of authority. Cardinal Jacopo Stefaneschi—brother of Bertoldo, who had enhanced Santa Maria in Trastevere—commissioned a large mosaic for the atrium of Old St. Peter's (Fig. 1.42), along with a double-sided altarpiece (Fig. 1.43) probably intended for the canons' choir in the nave of the building at the boundary of the transept. Both works included a kneeling portrait of the cardinal and should be seen as attempts by Stefaneschi to reassert the rightful place of the papacy in Rome while commemorating himself as he approached death.

Stefaneschi turned to the shop of the Florentine artist Giotto di Bondone (c. 1267/75 Vespignano–1337 Florence) for each of these commissions, perhaps because artists like Torriti and Rustici, already with established records of success in mosaic, had died or because Cavallini had already moved to Naples, where he was in the employ of the Angevin court by 1308. The literary tradition recounted by Dante and Vasari that Giotto had been a student of Cimabue needs to be supplemented by the fact that Cimabue was recorded in Rome in 1272 and that the older artist was technically working for the papacy in the late 1270s when he was painting in Assisi. Giotto may well have visited Rome before the Jubilee Year of 1300, at the height of Cavallini's new stylistic experiments at Santa Cecilia in Trastevere. Thus it is not surprising

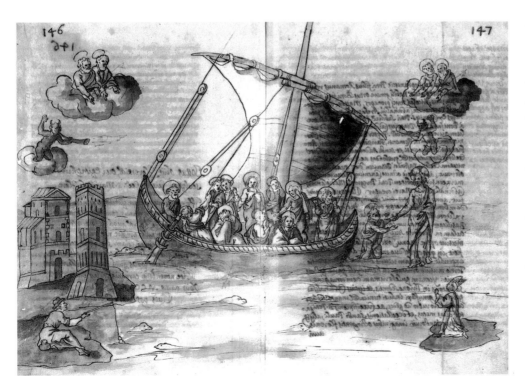

1.42 *Navicella*, commissioned by Jacopo Stefaneschi from GIOTTO, drawing after the lost original mosaic for the atrium of Old St. Peter's, Rome (Vatican Library, Vat. Barb. Lat. 2733, fols. 146v/147r, Rome)

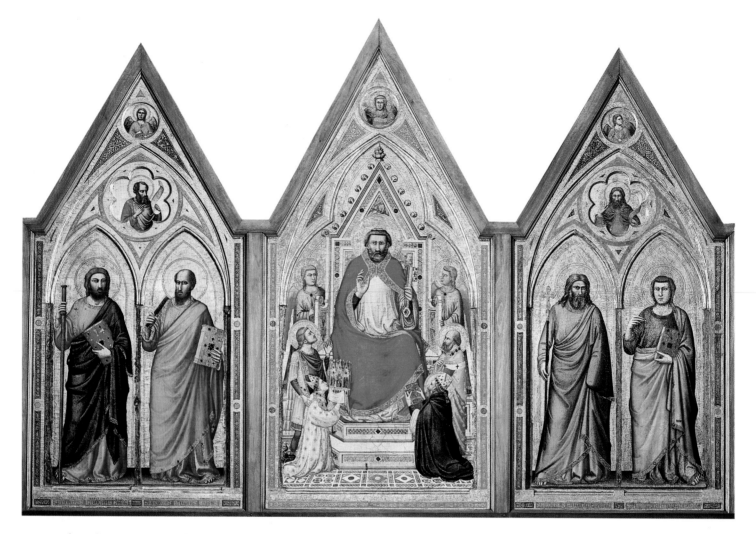

1.43 *Stefaneschi Altarpiece*, early fourteenth century, commissioned by Jacopo Stefaneschi from GIOTTO, probably for the canon's choir of Old St. Peter's, Rome. Tempera on panel, 7′ 2½″ × 8′ ½″ (2.2 × 2.45 m) (Pinacoteca, Vatican)

This two-sided altarpiece was intended for viewing from both within the canon's choir and from the transept, which it adjoined. The panels were originally set in much more elaborate frames.

that Giotto's style seems to owe so little to extant work in Florence of the this period, but a great deal to the innovations of Roman style under Cavallini and perhaps also Rustici. Both Giotto and Cavallini were obviously inspired by classical art, using light boldly to create increasingly massive and three-dimensional figures. By the time of Stefaneschi's commissions Giotto had achieved an international reputation.

Giotto's mosaic, now lost, originally decorated the inner, gateway façade of the courtyard in front of St. Peter's (see Fig. 9.28, far right). It represented the Navicella ("little ship"), an image of the Church in perilous times supported by the command of Christ. Just as Peter did not drown in the turbulent waters around the fishing boat when he went forward to greet Christ, who had been miraculously walking on the water, so the Roman Church expected the papacy to survive all challenges. Although based on a pre-existing work, the theme had a special poignancy at this time, which was known as

the Babylonian Captivity of the papacy. The scope and scale of the work were overwhelming, occasioning awed commentary well into the sixteenth century. Surviving fragments suggest that subtle colors and impressionistic devices heightened the mosaic's dramatic effects.

Stefaneschi's altarpiece, signed by Giotto but attributed to his workshop, paired two images of papal authority: an enthroned Christ flanked by scenes of the martyrdoms of St. Peter and St. Paul on one side and an enthroned St. Peter and flanking saints on the other, echoing one another to make clear the identification between Christ and his papal successors. Illusionistic space in the altarpiece was kept to a minimum; St. Peter raises his right hand in benediction, while in the left he holds the oversized keys that symbolized his and the papacy's authority (see Fig. 1.40). Peter's staring visage and rigid, frontal placement against an imposing marble throne further emphasize his supremacy, as does his enlarged size, relative to the donor portrait of Cardinal Stefaneschi on

Peter's right, who reverently presents a miniaturized version of the altarpiece. On St. Peter's left St. Peter Morone submits a deluxe manuscript which may represent Stefaneschi's biography of this papal saint.

Although the popes were not to return permanently to Rome for over a century, imagery like this continued to mark the city as the rightful capital of Western Christendom. Rome's relics, ancient monuments, papal basilicas, and works of art spoke powerfully throughout the papal absence.

Assisi: Papal Influence outside Rome

The Church of San Francesco

St. Francis's canonization in 1228 virtually demanded that a church in his honor—as a focus for devotion to the most popular of Italian saints—be built in his home town of Assisi. The issue of ownership of property such

as churches and convents had already divided the Franciscans within Francis's own lifetime. On the one side were the Spiritualists, who wished to maintain the vow of absolute (or apostolic) poverty upon which Francis had founded his order. On the other side were the Conventualists, for whom the success of the order in terms of its numerous communities throughout the Christian world indicated the need for permanent established churches and convents. In order to satisfy Francis's vow of poverty and yet meet the need for a cult church for Francis's relics and a home church for the Franciscan order, the papacy became the nominal patron and "owner" of the Basilica of San Francesco; the church was by deed a papal basilica, not a Franciscan church. The close relationship between the Franciscans and the papal hierarchy ensured that the church containing the mortal remains of the poor man of Assisi was one of the most lavishly conceived structures of its time, although St. Francis's tomb, unlike the tomb of any other monastic founder during this period (see Fig. 2.60), was hidden from view in the crypt of the building. Poverty and

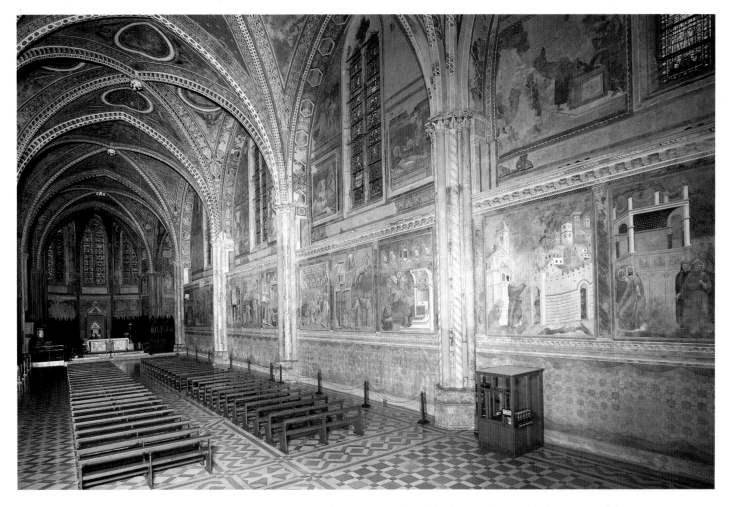

1.44 Upper Church, San Francesco, Assisi, begun 1228, consecrated 1253, commissioned by the Franciscans with the support of the papacy

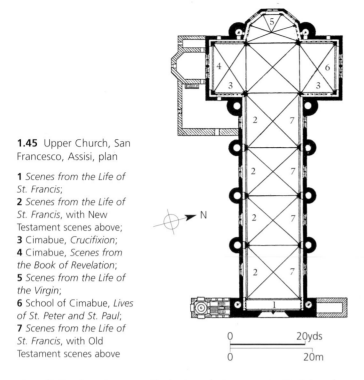

1.45 Upper Church, San Francesco, Assisi, plan

1 *Scenes from the Life of St. Francis*;
2 *Scenes from the Life of St. Francis*, with New Testament scenes above;
3 Cimabue, *Crucifixion*;
4 Cimabue, *Scenes from the Book of Revelation*;
5 *Scenes from the Life of the Virgin*;
6 School of Cimabue, *Lives of St. Peter and St. Paul*;
7 *Scenes from the Life of St. Francis*, with Old Testament scenes above

chapel, an architectural form given one of its best-known expressions at about the same time in Paris in Louis IX's splendid Sainte Chapelle (1240s). Thus although San Francesco is ostensibly a Franciscan site—the home church of the order—it must also be seen as a princely papal site, with all that this implies for its decoration.

The architecture itself is rather simple, with large expanses of wall providing large surface areas suitable for elaborate fresco cycles (see Fig. 1.44). The present proliferation of chapels in the lower church was added over time. Both the lower and upper churches were laid out basically in the form of a tau (see Fig 1.45), the T-shaped cross which had inspired Francis's own design of his friars' habits. The broad, low bays of the nave and the stubby transepts culminate in a shallow five-sided apse, whose number recalls the five wounds of the crucified Christ and by extension Francis's own stigmata.

simplicity barely prevailed at a shrine controlled by the papacy.

Preparations for the construction of the Basilica of San Francesco (Fig. 1.44) began even before Francis's canonization in 1228. Pope Gregory IX is recorded as having built a papal residence within the adjoining monastic complex, and a papal throne sits within the church's apse. The aisleless, double-storied structure of the church (Fig. 1.45) was immediately recognizable as a palatine

Apse and Transept Frescoes   Many of the artists responsible for the early decoration of the Basilica of San Francesco in Assisi had connections with papal Rome, either as natives of the city or as artists who had worked there. The most important of these was the Florentine Cimabue, who was in Rome by 1272. Assisted by his workshop, he was largely responsible for the apse and transept decoration of the upper church. Befitting Francis's special devotion to the Virgin, the apse presents apocryphal stories of her death and afterlife flanking the centrally placed papal throne. One of these, the *Coronation of the Virgin*, repeats the imagery seen in Roman basilicas (see Fig. 1.35) and may also indicate the papal presence in this building. Five scenes from the lives of saints Peter and Paul in the south transept, now largely ruinous, also underscored the Franciscans' Roman and papal associations by reproducing the same subjects and virtually the same compositions as the papal frescoes in the courtyard of Old St. Peter's.

Representations of the Crucifixion appear in both transepts, underlining Francis's identification with Christ and his sacrifice. Cimabue's work is still compelling (Fig. 1.46), in spite of the fact that the lead white

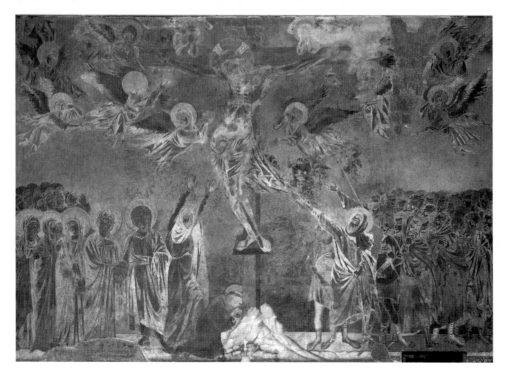

1.46 *Crucifixion*, after 1279, commissioned by the Franciscans from CIMABUE for the transept of the Upper Church, San Francesco, Assisi. Fresco, 17 × 24′ (5.18 × 7.32 m)

St. Francis and the Christ Child

In this passage from Bonaventure's *Legenda Maior*, St. Francis is credited with having created the first Nativity scene, or crèche, in the little village of Greccio, halfway between Rome and Assisi, in 1223. The presence of real animals in the scene and the devotional atmosphere led the worshipers to believe that the Christ Child himself lay in the crib.

Three years before he died St. Francis decided to celebrate the memory of the birth of the Child Jesus at Greccio, with the greatest possible solemnity. He asked and obtained the permission of the pope for the ceremony, so that he could not be accused of being an innovator, and then he had a crib prepared, with hay and an ox and an ass. The friars were all invited and the people came in crowds. The forest re-echoed with their voices and the night was lit up with a multitude of bright lights, while the beautiful music of God's praises added to the solemnity. The saint stood before the crib and his heart overflowed with tender compassion; he was bathed in tears but overcome with joy. The Mass was sung there and Francis, who was a deacon, sang the Gospel. Then he preached to the people about the birth of the poor King, whom he called the Babe of Bethlehem in his tender love.

A knight called John from Greccio, a pious and truthful man who had abandoned his profession in the world for love of Christ and was a great friend of St. Francis, claimed that he saw a beautiful child asleep in the crib, and that St. Francis took it in his arms and seemed to wake it up.

The integrity of this witness and the miracles which afterwards took place, as well as the truth indicated by the vision itself, all go to prove its reality. The example which Francis put before the world was calculated to rouse the hearts of those who are weak in the faith, and the hay from the crib, which was kept by the people, afterwards cured sick animals and drove off various pestilences. Thus God wished to give glory to his servant Francis and prove the efficacy of his prayer by clear signs.

(from Marion A. Habig. *St. Francis of Assisi: Writings and Early Biographies*. Chicago: Franciscan Herald Press, 1972, pp. 710–11)

---

pigments have oxidized, reversing the original relationships of light and dark. Everything is windblown and charged with dramatic intensity. At the very center the painter chillingly contrasts the deathly, sinuous slump of Christ's body with a loincloth that flaps freely in the howling wind. Mary Magdalene to the left and the Roman centurion, Longinus, who recognized Christ's divinity from the tumultuous circumstances of his death, thrust their arms desperately toward Christ. Angels bring the moment to its final fevered pitch, fretting, twisting, and crying in response to this universal tragedy. Only Francis, kneeling at the foot of the cross, finds solace in the moment of horror. Crowds press in from either side, but Francis, miraculously transported in time to the moment of the Crucifixion, clings to the foot of the cross, as if the intensity of his devotion had collapsed time, allowing him to participate fully in this crucial event in Christian history, just as he participated in Christ's passion by carrying the stigmata on his own body.

Nave Frescoes   From a functional point of view the nave of the upper church at Assisi was separate from the apse and transepts. As in most medieval churches, a large screen, now removed, created a barrier at the end of the nave beyond which most laypeople were not allowed to pass. The areas beyond this—the choir stalls and apse with the high altar—were for the exclusive use of the friars.

The subject matter of the frescoes painted on the nave walls in the upper church pairs Old Testament stories on the right side with the life of Christ on the left, repeating the subject and compositional order of narratives of the major Early Christian basilicas in Rome and expanding upon subject matter also treated in stained glass windows in the apse and transepts. The nave scene of *Esau Being Cheated of His Birthright* (Fig. 1.47), like Cavallini's work in Rome at this same time, structures the narrative in successive stages of receding architectural volumes. Neat crisp folds wrap around the reclining figure of Isaac, evoking the images of majestic classical prototypes. The tremulous and hesitant gesture of the blind and blankly staring Isaac as he gradually realizes that he has been duped into giving the birthright to Jacob rather than to his first-born, Esau, marks an important moment in the depiction of psychological awareness and emotional intensity, a naturalistic development very different from the frescoes of the transept and apse of the building.

Below the Old and New Testament scenes are other stories obviously directed toward the ever-growing crowd of pilgrims visiting San Francesco: an extensive cycle of the life of St. Francis stretching around the entire lower part of the nave and entrance walls. Although it is not clear by whom and when they were painted—suggested dates range from the 1290s well into the fourteenth century—the twenty-eight scenes present the story of the saint in a

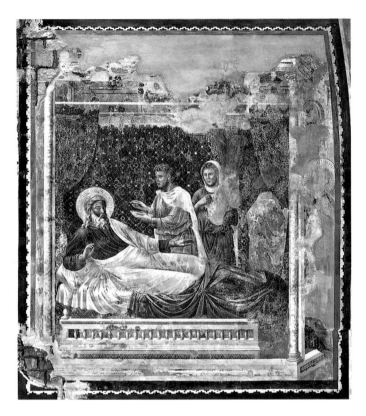

1.47 *Esau Being Cheated of His Birthright*, 1290s (?), commissioned by the Franciscans from the so-called ISAAC MASTER for the upper right wall of the nave of the Upper Church, San Francesco, Assisi. Fresco

straightforward and highly accessible manner. Each scene is accompanied by an inscription beneath its painted molding from Bonaventure's official biography of Francis, the *Legenda Maior*. The frescoes have a noticeably institutional emphasis, repeatedly illustrating St. Francis's respect for Church authority by presenting the episodes of his life before popes and cardinals. Francis's sanctity is recognized through an extended depiction of his death, funeral rites, and canonization. Avoiding poetic and mystical images, these frescoes are overtly didactic, intended to tell an officially sanctioned version of the saint's life.

The style of the frescoes is particularly well suited to their task. Impressively naturalistic and illusionistic, they communicate with unprecedented eloquence. Francis himself had urged his followers to imagine their religious experience in visual, tangible terms. In the scene of the *Crib at Greccio* (Fig. 1.48) we see Francis constructing the first Nativity scene before the altar of the little church at Greccio for a Christmas Eve mass in 1223 (see p. 75). In this painting the friars in the rear of the choir enclosure open their mouths wide as if singing the Christmas liturgy; the clergy and a townsman near the altar canopy bend to get a closer look; town leaders bear witness by their sober presence; and a group of women, normally not given entrance to this sacred part of the church, crowd

forward through a central doorway. The broad solidity of their bodies seems to occupy actual space—an impression greatly enhanced by rear views of a pulpit and crucifix that lean out into the nave. Candles, festoons, and other small details of clothing and architecture help to make the scene visually compelling.

The time and degree of collaboration required to produce a decorative program as complex as that of the church of San Francesco make it difficult to specify who may have been responsible for any particular section. In many ways that is as it should be. Artists at Assisi were not asked to produce highly individual or idiosyncratic works; rather, they were working together with their Franciscan and papal patrons to create a broad, visual biography for Francis of Assisi. Whereas previous generations of worshipers had focused much of their devotion on local Early Christian martyrs, the thirteenth century turned for inspiration to Francis and other contemporary preaching saints, such as the Spaniard St. Dominic. Both Francis and Dominic inspired enthusiasm for a renewed,

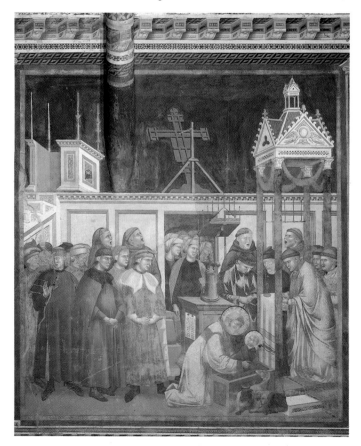

1.48 *Crib at Greccio*, late thirteenth to early fourteenth century, commissioned by the Franciscans from the so-called ASSISI MASTER for San Francesco, Assisi. Fresco

Conspicuously absent in this cycle of St. Francis's life are the many stories that Bonaventure tells about St. Francis's extreme asceticism and self-mortification. Instead, the frescoes emphasize Francis's compassionate nature and his support of the institutional Church.

more accessible religious experience. The search for means to express these new and vivid ideas, though linked to the great traditions of the Church, proved extremely fertile ground for artistic experimentation.

Synopsis

Italy in the thirteenth century was already highly urbanized, its citizens the beneficiaries and exploiters of thousands of years of recorded and mythologized history. Every city had an ancient past which was both remembered and re-invented to suit the purposes of its ruling classes, providing a structure in which citizens found a sense of their identity. Writers such as Martin da Canal in Venice make it clear that citizens were extraordinarily proud of their cities, attentive to how streets, buildings, and their decoration, along with commercial activity, contributed to a city's glory. Art and architecture manifested each city's values, its aspirations, and its pretensions.

Artists in these historically rich centers were just as likely to renovate, enhance, restore, enlarge, and reclaim pre-existing works as they were to create completely new ones. Thus the Venetians continued to commission mosaics for the already splendid Basilica of St. Mark, just as the Florentines commissioned new ones for their venerable Baptistry. The popes rebuilt, restructured, and redecorated their nearly thousand-year-old basilicas. When new projects were begun—Siena Cathedral and San Francesco in Assisi, for example—there was an expectation that these too would consume the energy of several generations, that they were built both for present needs and for the future.

The scale of art and architectural commissions changed dramatically over the course of the thirteenth century as cities increased in population and the economics of existence moved from the country to the city. As Venice continued to reclaim land around its islands and to carve an enormous piazza out of the urban fabric in front of St. Mark's, Florence built new walls. In Rome Nicholas III enlarged the palace at the Vatican, determining the size and scale of papal residences there for the next three centuries. Larger churches and palaces demanded larger altarpieces, more extensive fresco cycles, and grander ensembles of sculpture. The sheer numbers of persons engaged in the building trades and in the figural arts must have increased dramatically.

Artists and patrons drew on a vast range of models for their inspiration. These included works from antiquity, ranging from imperial classicism to late Roman figural and compositional types; Byzantine models, with their iconic power of pose, increasingly softened by volumetric modeling, and reinterpreted in altarpieces and crucifixes especially; Gothic art and architecture, which inspired the naturalism and emotionalism of Nicola Pisano and his son Giovanni.

Throughout the thirteenth century artistic styles varied widely depending upon particular circumstances. The function of a work greatly affected how, when, and where stylistic possibilities might be explored. Thus narrative subjects were regularly livelier than devotional images created in the same region or even by the same artist. The differences among Cimabue's emotionally restrained crucifix for San Domenico, Arezzo, his tormented fresco of the *Crucifixion* for the Upper Church in Assisi, and his majestic, but essentially immutable, *Enthroned Madonna and Child* for Santa Trinita depend directly on subject, type, and function. Similar distinctions applied in architecture, where the simple preaching halls of the mendicant friars were deliberately less elaborately structured and richly ornamented than the city's cathedral.

In the end, art and architecture did not take and could not have taken a predictable, let alone a single, path of development. Within each city different commissions demanded different skills and creative approaches, sometimes traditionalist, at other times more openly innovative; sometimes extremely parochial, at other times distinctly cosmopolitan. In each city locally available materials—glass and imported stone in Venice, Carrara marble and local sand-colored limestone in Florence, soft red brick in Siena, fragments of ancient buildings in Rome—had a major effect on the look and feel of the city. The lagoon of Venice, the river valley of Florence, the carefully tended countryside surrounding Siena, and the hills of Rome also helped to give each place its distinctive character. While artists could and did work in more than one locale, they necessarily responded to such changing environments. Even when we know about an artist's previous work and have a firm grasp of a city's traditions and visual character, the real excitement in understanding the artistic history of this period comes in seeing how artists responded to the demands of a particular commission.

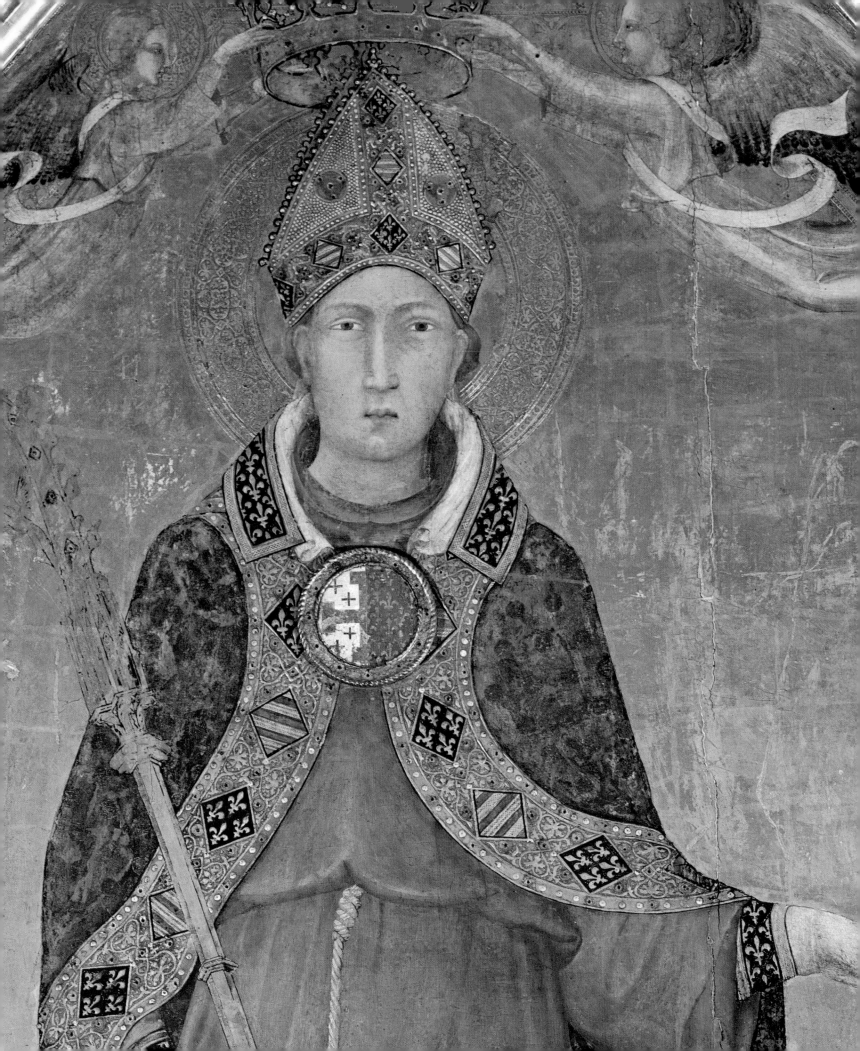

2

Varieties of Style and Patronage: The Early Fourteenth Century

The first half of the fourteenth century presents a complex picture of several different artistic styles coexisting, intermingling, and occasionally competing, within a complex pattern of patronage. Responding to the demands of differing commissions and to the traditions of style and iconographic patterns which lay behind them, artists continued to produce works of art that could be progressive or sensibly traditional, cosmopolitan or closely tied to local expectations.

The formal innovations of space and mass evident in painting in Rome and Assisi in the thirteenth century were developed in Padua, Florence, Naples, and Milan by Giotto and his followers. In Siena, at the same time, Duccio di Buoninsegna invented a competing style which blended Byzantine prototypes with elements of the graceful Gothic style then flourishing in France. His pupil Simone Martini expanded this elegant style, gaining reknown for Sienese art at the Angevin court in Naples and at the papal court of Avignon, where he determined the course of painting for much of the next century. Interchange with northern European centers also informed Italian architecture, although the sunny Italian climate and a long tradition of fresco painting continued to favor buildings that were more massive and mural than their northern counterparts.

While the Church continued to play a crucial role in commissioning works of religious art, it was increasingly obliged to consider and adapt to the wishes of a powerful mercantile middle class, who provided the funds for new commissions within monastic and ecclesiastical centers. Rich individual patrons enhanced their status while glorifying God; powerful city-states identified themselves visually with the saints, invoking their protection; governments underscored their legitimacy with memorable images in which divine and civic virtues were combined.

Princes and magistrates, too, engaged in visual propaganda, using display and artistic virtuosity to reflect glory upon themselves, their families, and the cities they ruled.

Padua and Florence: Private Patronage

One of the earliest documented assimilations of the newly naturalistic style of painting first seen in Rome and Assisi occurred in the small university city of Padua, west of Venice. The city traced its history back to the mythic figure of Antenor, a Trojan soldier who, according to Virgil, sailed westward after the Trojan War, ultimately to found Padua. A massive medieval sarcophagus honoring Antenor still stands in the city. Thus Padua's constructed history is one that consciously imitates the myth of Rome's founding by the Trojan prince Aeneas, although the Roman historian Livy, himself born in Padua, claimed that the city had been founded only in 302 B.C.E., successfully resisting a Spartan attack the following year. Padua flourished during the Republic and the Empire. It became a commune in the eleventh century and retained that status until the Carrara family took control of the city in 1318. Padua's university was founded in 1222, which makes it the second oldest in Italy after Bologna (1119). Its faculties of law, medicine, physical science (especially optics), and classics made it one of the most important intellectual centers in Italy; Galileo was but one of its more notable teachers. St. Anthony, the most popular Franciscan saint besides St. Francis himself, died in Padua in 1231; a basilica in his honor, now known as the Santo, was begun in 1232 and soon became one of the most frequented pilgrimage sites in Europe.

2.1 *Altarpiece of St. Louis of Toulouse* (detail), c. 1319, commissioned by Robert of Anjou from SIMONE MARTINI. Tempera on panel, with a gilt-glass morse and now-lost paste pearls and gems on the cope; main panel 78¾ × 54¼" (200 × 138 cm), predella 22 × 54" (56 × 138 cm) (Gallerie Nazionali di Capodimonte, Naples). See also Fig. 2.50.

The Scrovegni (Arena) Chapel

One of the city's leading banking families was the Scrovegni. Their head in the late thirteenth century was Reginaldo Scrovegni, whose flagrant usury earned him a place in Dante's *Inferno* (Canto XVII, 43–78) as the most notorious practitioner of this sin. Reginaldo's son Enrico continued initially in his father's footsteps, but later became troubled by the possible consequences of his actions. In 1302, by way of expiation for his ill-gotten gains, he began to erect a family chapel dedicated to the Virgin of Charity (Santa Maria della Carità). Because the Scrovegni Chapel, like the adjacent (later demolished) Scrovegni Palace, was erected on the site of the old Roman arena, it has come to be known also as the Arena Chapel.

Work on the chapel apparently proceeded quickly, since there is a document recording the dedication of the site in 1303 and a record of March 1304 of indulgences granted by Pope Innocent XI to visitors to the chapel. The chapel was formally dedicated on March 25, 1305, the feast of the Annunciation. For the dedication of the Scrovegni Chapel the High Council of Venice, Padua's neighbor to the east, agreed to lend tapestries to enhance the festivities for the occasion. This support from the Venetian state and from the pope in the building project indicates the extraordinary social and financial power of the Scrovegni family.

To decorate the interior of his chapel (Fig. 2.2), Scrovegni hired Giotto di Bondone of Florence who may also have been the architect for the chapel since it is little more than a simple barrel-vaulted box designed to accommodate an extensive fresco cycle. Giotto's commission was to paint scenes of the redemption of humanity, beginning with the annunciation to the Virgin in the arch wall at the front of the chapel, continuing with the Life of the Virgin and the Life of Christ on the side walls, and ending with a Last Judgment filling the entire entrance wall of the chapel. This fresco cycle is the earliest work universally accepted as being by the hand of Giotto.

The cycle begins on the arched wall framing the altar. God the Father (painted on a wooden panel now thought to date from much later in the century, perhaps replacing an original glass window) sits enthroned at the apex of the arch, about to begin the work of human redemption. On the left side of the arch His messenger, the Angel Gabriel, announces the impending birth of Christ to Mary, who appears to the right of the arch. These figures, in their illusionistic projecting stage-like architectural boxes, exchange greeting and response, setting up a dramatic interplay across the chapel. The two narrative cycles of the Life of the Virgin and the Life of Christ start on the wall to the right of the altar and continue in a clockwise

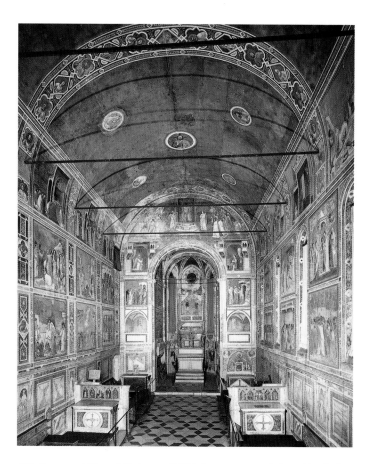

2.2 *Scrovegni Chapel*, Padua, c. 1305, frescoes commissioned by Enrico Scrovegni from GIOTTO

direction on the left. The Life of the Virgin occupies the top row and that of Christ the next two. On the lowest part of the walls are fictive marble panels, framing monochrome paintings of the virtues on the south side of the building (the right side looking toward the altar), and their corresponding vices, on the north wall—rendered so as to resemble relief carving.

In constructing his narratives, Giotto gave them an extraordinary sense of unity through a careful use of perspective. A diagram of the altar wall (Fig. 2.3) shows that each scene is organized according to a unified **two-point perspective** scheme which orders the architecture of all levels of the wall and also unites both sides of the building in a single co-ordinated scheme of diagonal lines. The same is true for the side walls where, for example, the architecture depicted in all the frescoes is conceived as if it were to be viewed from the center of the chapel. Thus the perspective is slightly distorted in the outer two scenes of the south wall to compensate for the viewer's angle of vision. In each frame, however, the architecture extends equally deeply into space, so that there is a consistency to the depth of the illusionistic field from one scene to another. The same is true of landscape, where it appears.

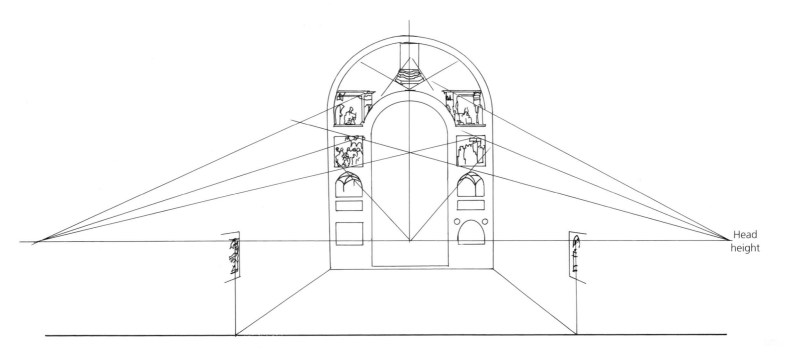

2.3 *Scrovegni Chapel*, Padua, perspective scheme of the front wall (after Adriano Prandi)

Head
height

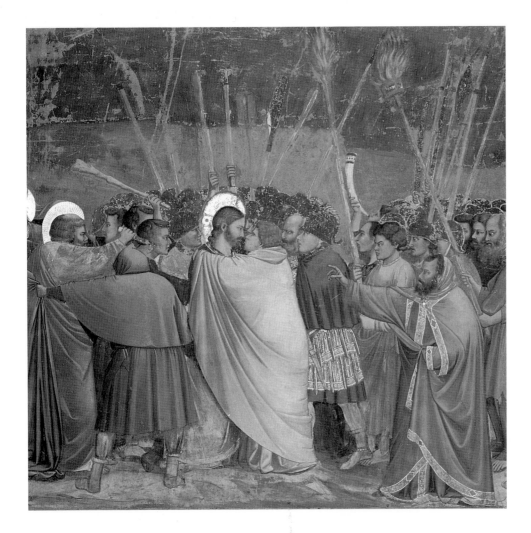

2.4 *The Kiss of Judas*, c. 1305,
commissioned by Enrico Scrovegni from
GIOTTO for the Scrovegni Chapel, Padua.
Fresco, 6' 6¾" × 6' ¾" (2 × 1.85 m)

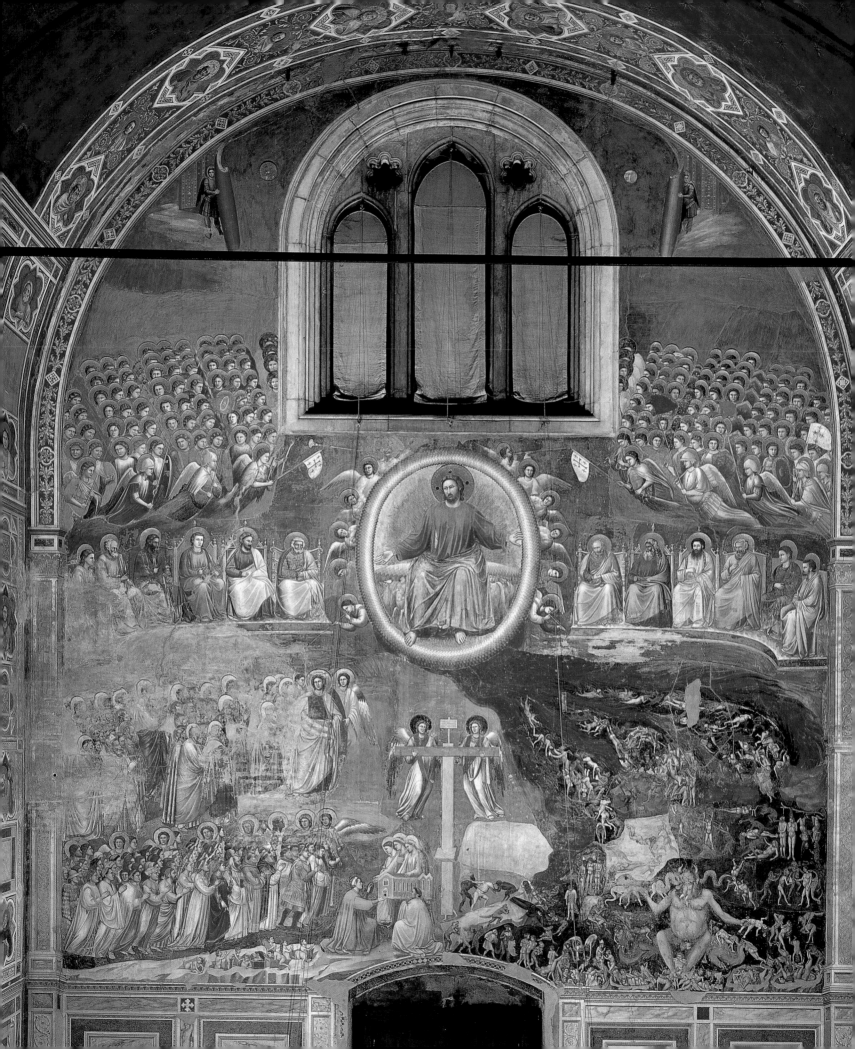

In the adjacent panels of the *Lamentation* and the *Noli Me Tangere* the landscape also seems to continue behind the painted architectural frames and to drive the narrative forward from one panel to the next.

Giotto has also found powerful ways to focus on the human drama that unfolds, scene by scene, through the chapel. In the *Kiss of Judas* (Fig. 2.4), for example, the narrative is the only scene at the third level that takes place in a landscape, and it is positioned at the center of the wall, directly in front of the viewer whose position in the chapel is determined by the perspective organization of the entire wall. Not only has Giotto located the beginning of the Passion in a critical position on the wall—ironically above the figure of Justice in the bottom row—but he has also dramatized the event by such means as the brilliant yellow cloak of Judas, which virtually obliterates the figure of Christ, and the stereotypical characterizations of good and evil presented by the handsome features of Christ and the brutish face of Judas. The psychological intensity of the event is heightened, at the left of the scene, by Peter's act of violence: cutting off the ear of the high priest's servant.

The *Last Judgment*, which occupies the entire entrance wall (Fig. 2.5), presents the culmination of the process of redemption begun on the altar wall of the chapel. Christ sits in majesty in the center, flanked to his left and right by choirs of angels and seated Apostles. Below him and to his right are the elect, to whom he gestures. In the lower right quadrant of the wall is a vision of hell with a large personification of evil devouring the damned. Just over the door of the chapel at the bottom center of the fresco Giotto has depicted Enrico Scrovegni in the kneeling pose of a donor, presenting his chapel in the metaphorical form of a model to three haloed figures: Gabriel, the Virgin of Charity, and the Virgin Annunciate, the latter two embodying the double dedication of the chapel. The two figures of the Virgin are crowned, as is the allegorical figure of Charity on the lower south wall of the Chapel. The Virgin of Charity wears a dalmatic, the liturgical robe of the deacon, who in the early Church was responsible for dispensing alms (or charity); the Virgin also wears that costume in the Annunciation on the altar wall and in the Visitation fresco just beneath it, as if the very act of redemption initiated at the moment of the Annunciation was an act of charity. Although there is some dispute about the identification of these three figures, there can be no doubt about the importance of the Virgin Annunciate for this chapel and for Scrovegni's intentions.

The eccentric placement of Scrovegni, the heavenly figures, and his model seems to be explained by the fact that on March 25, the feast of the Annunciation, a beam of light enters the building from the south window nearest the entrance wall and falls on the *Last Judgment* in the area between the donor and the model, a sign of divine approval for the gift that Scrovegni is making.

Scrovegni's repentance is conveyed not only by the image of himself as donor but also by two representations of Judas which point up the dangers of ill-gotten gains. In the depiction of hell and its denizens, he is shown hanging from a tree, and he appears again on the altar wall opposite, receiving the thirty pieces of silver for betraying Christ—a panel that is out of sequence in the narrative. By placing these two images of Judas to either side of the imagined viewer, Giotto underscored the moral message of the chapel.

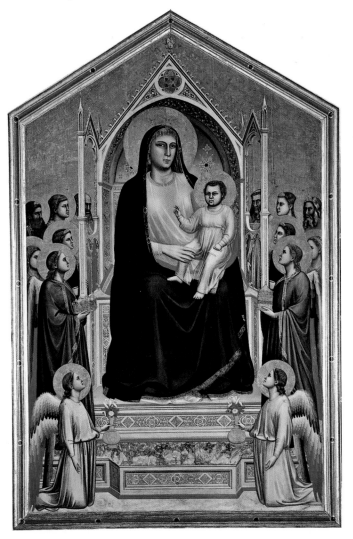

2.5 (opposite) *Last Judgment*, c. 1305, commissioned by Enrico Scrovegni from GIOTTO for the Scrovegni Chapel, Padua. Fresco, 32′ 9¾″ × 27′ 6¾″ (10 × 8.4 m)

2.6 *Ognissanti Madonna and Child* (*Maestà*), c. 1310–15, painted by GIOTTO for the high altar of the Ognissanti Church in Florence. Tempera on panel, 10′ 8″ × 6′ 8¼″ (3.2 × 2 m) (Galleria degli Uffizi, Florence)

The power of the Scrovegni chapel frescoes lies partly in the all-enveloping nature of the work. It also derives from the psychological intensity of the individual scenes. Like the painter of the Isaac stories in Assisi (see Fig. 1.47), Giotto has infused the familiar biblical stories with a human poignancy which helps to transform these stories of remote history into comprehensible and moving events.

In this respect Giotto provided a drama comparable to the *tableaux vivants* and stylized performances which had taken place in front of the former chapel on the site and which most likely continued within the Scrovegni chapel once it was completed: the panel of God the Father, high on the altar wall, is actually a wooden door from which an actor representing an angel would appear. From this level he could be lowered by ropes threaded through holes in the ceiling immediately in front of the door to the floor below. The ephemeral action of such liturgical dramas found permanent form in Giotto's frescoes.

The Ognissanti *Madonna and Child*

Giotto translated the monumental style of the Scrovegni frescoes to the altarpiece in his large *Madonna and Child* for the Church of the Ognissanti in Florence (Fig. 2.6). Although the specific patron is unknown, the church was the headquarters of the Umiliati, a mendicant order that was renowned for its wool production as well as its acts of charity. The painting is normally dated to c. 1310 on the basis of style. The stolid Virgin, her robes draping heavily over her limbs to reveal the masses of the body beneath, is formally very much like the Christ figure in the *Last Judgment* of the Arena Chapel. Although Giotto used the conventional gold background seen in previous Maestà images, he eliminated the decorative patterns of light in Guido da Siena's and Cimabue's versions of this same subject (see Figs. 1.28 and 1.29) and the decorative border arabesques seen in Duccio's *Maestà* (see Fig. 1.30). Moreover, he conceived space in a completely volumetric manner, so that the Gothic throne in which the Virgin and Child sit enframes the figures, providing a believable volume for their bodies. Rather than the vertical columns of angels in the earlier paintings, Giotto has placed the angels around the throne, their spatial depth indicated in part by the fact that the foreground angels partially obscure those behind them and in part by the volumes of their individual forms. Giotto's radical transformation of the style of the devotional image so evident in the Ognissanti *Madonna and Child* (and perhaps in other paintings now lost) marks an important moment in the acceptance of his new style in Tuscan panel painting at the beginning of the fourteenth century.

The Santa Croce Frescoes and Altarpiece

Like Enrico Scrovegni, wealthy Florentines also commissioned major fresco cycles as manifestations of their hopes for salvation—and of their social position. The strongest and wealthiest citizens of Florence had very early allied themselves with the Franciscan and Dominican orders through family members who had become friars; these prominent families established their presence within urban monastic churches such as Santa Croce (see Fig. 1.21) and Santa Maria Novella (see Fig. 1.23) by endowing them with chapels. Although these chapels were built with funds from the Commune and with pious donations for the general construction of the church, the religious orders ultimately sold them to private families who could be relied on to decorate them in a way that would bring honor to the church and to the monastic community resident there. Such chapels were held as family property by the heirs of the founders until they were sold or the family died out. The size of such a chapel and its proximity to the high altar indicated the prominence of the family who owned it and established in a clearly propagandistic manner its position of honor within the religious, social, and economic fabric of the city.

The programs for the frescoes decorating these chapels were subject to the approval of the order that maintained the church. Both private patron and monastic community had audiences to address. An artist had to be aware of the interlocking network of patron, religious order, audience, and site; and he himself added yet another level of complexity as his own vision gave form to these relationships.

The Bardi Chapel   The first chapel to the right of the choir of Santa Croce (begun 1294; Fig. 2.7) belonged to the Bardi family, who controlled one of the most famous banking houses in Europe until its collapse in 1346, caused in part by the failure of the English king to repay his extensive outstanding loans. They commissioned Giotto to decorate its walls with scenes from the life of St. Francis. Later other members of the family were to contribute another chapel to the left of the high altar and a third quite large chapel at the end of the left transept. Clearly the various branches of the family were determined to declare their prominence in their quarter of the city by the magnitude of their patronage. The fresco cycle depicting events in the life of St. Francis, the patron saint of the order that oversaw the church, indicates, however, that the Franciscans were able to dictate the subject matter for the painted decorations of their building regardless of how important the individual families were who owned the chapels, just as they did for the chancel (the story of the True Cross) and the chapel to its left (the stories from the Life of the Virgin) both of which depict subjects central to Franciscan spirituality.

The date of the Bardi Chapel frescoes is uncertain. Giotto apparently joined the Florentine guild of the *Medici e Speziali* (the Pharmacists and the Spice-sellers, where painters purchased their pigments), in 1327; however, the frescoes may have been begun as early as 1320. The frescoes cannot be dated on the basis of stylistic comparison with other Giotto works since the only earlier extant frescoes securely attributed to him are those in the Arena Chapel in Padua of around 1305, leaving too great a gap in time between their proposed dates for meaningful comparison.

Giotto divided the side walls of the Bardi Chapel into three levels. The episodes from the life of St. Francis move from top to bottom and from left to right, beginning with Francis's renunciation of his earthly goods and ending with his posthumous appearances. Giotto treated the width of the wall as a single expanse for the presentation of one narrative episode, rather than dividing the surface into separate framed narrative panels as he had done in Padua. In all of the scenes Giotto used architecture to strengthen the narrative, much as did the painters of the nave frescoes in the upper church in Assisi (see Figs. 1.47, 1.48). In the lower scenes in the Bardi Chapel such as the *Trial by Fire* (Fig. 2.8) Giotto extended the architecture to the very borders of the pictorial space, using it not only to provide a unified and symmetrical framework for the narrative, but also to highlight or focus on dominant figures in the stories and to create a consistent spatial depth from one tier of the chapel to the next. Giotto also increased the scale of the architecture in relation to the figures, so that the figures take up only about half of the height of each scene. These compositional devices give the narrative a monumental scale. The figures themselves are fully modeled, with drapery falling in sensuous, heavy folds over their bodies. Although Giotto tends to place his figures in a shallow band of space within the architectural frame, their gestures, as well as their positions and grouping, create a sense of volume, particularly in relation to the blank surfaces of the architecture, which run parallel to the picture surface. This relief-like device is one that Giotto, like contemporary sculptors, must have learned from looking at ancient Roman sculpture.

Giotto also shows himself to be a masterful story teller and student of human psychology. Anger, sorrow, confusion, amazement, and even boredom are among the many emotions and reactions he registers in the body language and faces of his figures. In the *Trial by Fire*, which tells the story of Francis's challenge to the Islamic priests of the Egyptian Sultan to prove their faith by walking through fire, Francis, at the far right, is the embodiment of stalwart devotion to his beliefs. He shields his eyes from the heat of the fire blazing in front of him and lifts his gown, ready to step into the flame. His companion, hands clenched within his habit and head tilted to the side, seems both to implore the saint to refrain from such a rash act and pray for God's protection should he go through with it. Giotto shows the Sultan at the center of the composition to be in conflict by having him point across his body to Francis and look askance in the opposite direction at his own priests as they skulk out of the scene at the left. A turbaned servant reinforces the Sultan's challenge with his hand, too, pointing back towards Francis, while the priest next to him holds his cloak up high as if to protect himself from such a dangerous test. His companion to the left puts one hand to his ear, unwilling even to hear the challenge. Packed into a very few figures, then, is a psychologically rich narrative, both compelling and believable because of the humanity of its protagonists.

The Peruzzi Chapel Not to be outdone by the Bardi, Donato di Arnoldo Peruzzi, a leader of another Florentine banking family, left funds in his will for the construction of a chapel immediately to the right of the Bardi Chapel. For this, his grandnephew, Giovanni di Rinieri Peruzzi, commissioned Giotto to paint scenes from the lives of John the Baptist (on the left wall) and John the Evangelist (on the right wall), one of whom was presumably his patron saint. The frescoes probably date from the early 1320s; the left wall may have been painted considerably before the right one. These frescoes were painted *a secco* and much of the surface has flaked away, precluding any detailed stylistic analysis. They reveal a compositional order significantly different from that which Giotto had used in the Bardi Chapel. The *Ascension of St. John the Evangelist* (Fig. 2.9) illustrates a popular story claiming that the Evangelist rose live into heaven, cheating death, the only Apostle to have escaped martyrdom. Rather than stretch the architectural framework of the composition skin-like over the wall surface, as he had done in the Bardi Chapel, Giotto gave the architecture in the Peruzzi frescoes a three-dimensional mass, constructing it along diagonal axes which continually thrust into the pictorial space. The true purpose of this device can be understood only if the chapel and its paintings are seen as a whole, as they would be when viewed outside the chapel from the transept of the building (see Fig. 2.7). Then one can see that the diagonal axes of the painted architecture move from the entrance wall to the rear wall of the chapel providing a convincing illusion of space, rather than the puzzling and awkward zigzags of architectural forms dominating photographs taken of the frescoes

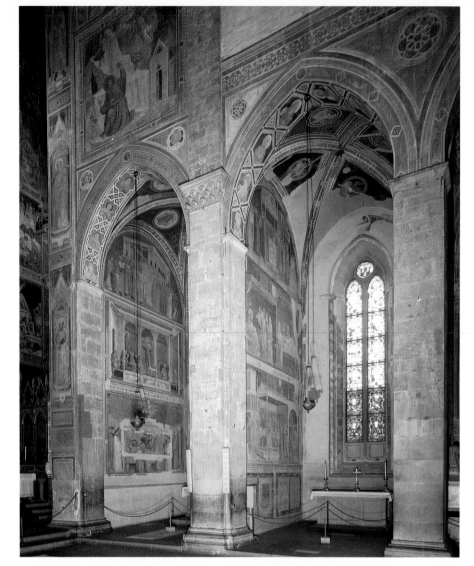

2.7 Bardi (left) and Peruzzi (right) chapels, Santa Croce, Florence, seen from the transept, showing GIOTTO'S fresco cycles.

Giotto painted a fresco of the *Stigmatization of St. Francis* on the outside wall of the chapel over the arch, which identifies the dedication of the chapel from a distance and at the same time provides the Franciscans with a large-scale image within the church itself of a defining moment in the life of their patron and founder.

2.8 *Trial by Fire*, c. 1320, commissioned presumably by Ridolfo di Bartolo de' Bardi from GIOTTO for the Bardi Chapel, Santa Croce, Florence. Fresco, 9' 2" × 14' 9" (2.8 × 4.5 m)

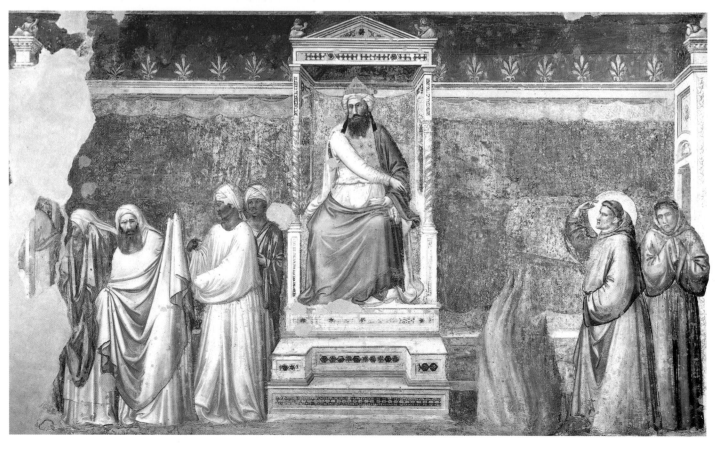

straight-on. The activation of the architectural frame creates spaces through which individual figures and groups of figures can move, adding greater realism to the narrative.

In the *Feast of Herod* (Fig. 2.10) these devices give Giotto space to portray the tower in which John the Baptist is imprisoned on the far left, the banquet hall in the center where Salome danced so alluringly that Herod

offered her anything she might desire (it turned out to be the head of the Baptist), and, on the right, an anteroom where Salome kneels and presents the head to her mother, who had suggested the request because of her anger over the Baptist's criticism of her illicit relationship with Herod. To ensure that the three episodes are joined together in a single narrative, rather than read as unrelated events, Giotto positions figures at the two junctures

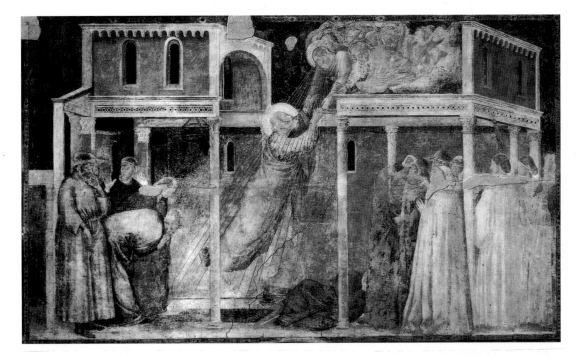

2.9 *Ascension of St. John the Evangelist*, 1320s, commissioned by Giovanni di Rinieri Peruzzi from GIOTTO for the Peruzzi Chapel, Santa Croce, Florence. Fresco, 9′ 2¼″ × 14′ 9⅛″ (2.8 × 4.5 m)

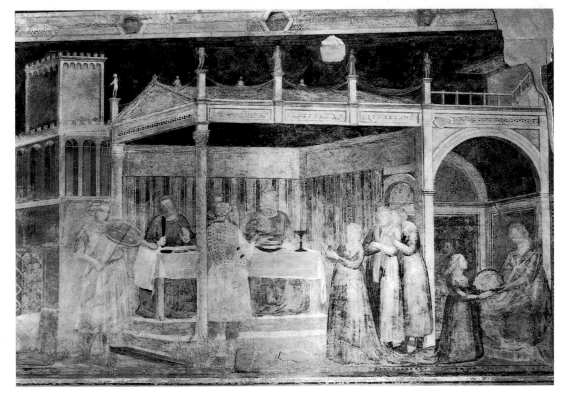

2.10 *Feast of Herod*, 1320s, commissioned by Giovanni di Rinieri Peruzzi from GIOTTO for the Peruzzi Chapel, Santa Croce, Florence. Fresco, 9′ 2¼″ × 14′ 9⅛″ (2.8 × 4.5 m)

between the three spaces: a viol-playing musician at the left and onlookers at the right, underscored by the trains of Salome's skirts, which seem to join as she is first seen standing at the left and then kneeling on the right.

The Baroncelli Chapel Giotto's work had an important influence on the frescoes for the chapel of yet another of Florence's leading banking families, the Baroncelli.

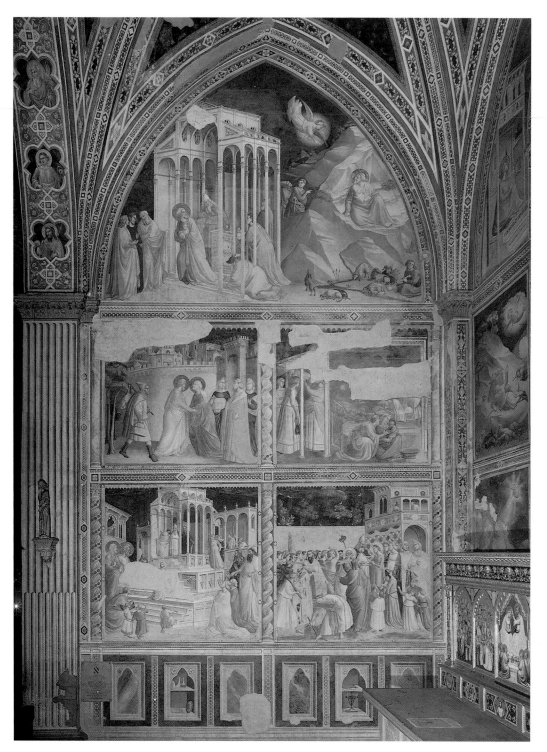

Their chapel, at the end of the right transept, is decorated with scenes from the life of the Virgin, painted by Giotto's leading pupil, Taddeo Gaddi (active *c.* 1328–66), from 1332 to 1338 (Fig. 2.11). Taddeo most likely took charge of Giotto's Florentine workshop when Giotto went to Naples in 1328. The Baroncelli frescoes provide yet more evidence that the style of Giotto and his pupils had found favor with the Franciscans and with their eminent patrons. While depicting the lives of saints in a suitably reverent manner, the new style managed also to give them a naturalistic, human quality.

The scenes depicted on the wall of the Baroncelli Chapel narrate highly involved legends about the Virgin's early life. At the upper left her father, Joachim, is driven from the Temple in Jerusalem, clutching a sacrificial lamb which has been rejected by a scowling priest. Joachim and his wife Anna were childless and therefore presumably cursed by God. At the right, Joachim has gone into exile in the barren countryside where an angel appears in the sky announcing that his aged wife will bear a child after all, a scene obviously invented to correspond to the later annunciation of Christ's conception to Mary herself and the announcement of Christ's birth to the shepherds. The story continues in the second tier, where the couple grasp one another's arms as they stride toward an eager reunion outside the walls of

2.11 *Scenes from the Life of the Virgin*, 1332–38, commissioned by the Baroncelli family from TADDEO GADDI for the Baroncelli Chapel, Santa Croce, Florence, detail of left wall. Fresco. See also Figs. 8 and 9.

Jerusalem. To the right, Anna has given birth, and nurse-maids admire the baby Mary in front of her mother's bed. Mary is soon a little girl and reappears in the lower tier (see also Figs. 8 and 9), mounting the huge steps of the temple, where legend had it that she was cared for and educated by nuns. Her youth and childhood conclude in marriage to Joseph at the bottom right. The story continues on the right (actually the back window) wall of the chapel with the *Annunciation* at the top and the announcement of Christ's birth to the shepherds below, as well as other episodes from Christ's youth.

The Baroncelli Chapel frescoes, like the earlier Peruzzi cycle, were conceived to be seen from the transept, as the architecture in the top and bottom tiers indicates. Because the Baroncelli Chapel is deeper than the chapels that extend along the length of the transept, Taddeo was constrained to divide the wall surface into separately framed scenes in the conventional manner rather than extending individual narratives the entire width of the wall. He chose to do so with a series of twisted columns, whose witty *trompe-l'oeil* effect demonstrate the painter's consciousness of his ability to transform a flat surface into architectural volume and spatial depth. Taddeo's architecture is more thinly membered and much more vertical than the massive forms that characterize Giotto's frescoes in Santa Croce.

Taddeo Gaddi seems to delight in unusual effects, such as the luminaristic effects of the *Annunciation to Joachim* and of the night scene of the shepherds. Perhaps the most interesting scene is that of the *Marriage of the Virgin* at the lower right of the composition on the chapel's left wall. Here the decorum of earlier painted narratives in Santa Croce has been abandoned in favor of a more contemporary interpretation. The noisy crowd and the mocking *charivari* ritual of raucous music-making accompanying the bridal couple—with ribald suggestions of the pair's sexual union—suggest not a biblical event but, rather, Italian wedding celebrations of the time. Joseph, the old bridegroom, is being publicly ridiculed for foolishly marrying a pregnant woman—an element of sharp Florentine humor that must have amused the viewers.

The impression created by the transept chapel decorations in Santa Croce seen as a whole is that of a fairly consistent stylistic development over the course of some twenty years. Since most of the chapels were painted by Giotto and his students, it is apparent that the church's clergy and lay patrons appreciated the attention to narrative detail and increasingly naturalistic presentation of the new style.

The Santa Croce Altarpiece   This impression is tempered by the fact that the original altarpiece for the main altar of the church, a depiction of the Virgin and Child flanked by saints, was painted not by Giotto or a member of his studio, but by a Sienese painter, Ugolino di Nerio (active 1317–27; d. 1339?), who had trained in Duccio's workshop. This training is perhaps most clearly evident in the predella panels which virtually replicate similar images from Duccio's *Maestà* for the main altar of the cathedral of Siena (see Fig. 2.19). Although Ugolino's altarpiece is now completely dismembered, its original form is known from an eighteenth-century drawing (Fig. 2.12). Why, given the adventurous cycles of frescoes in the family chapels to the left and right of the main altar, did the Franciscans and the donor family (most likely the Alberti, another very powerful Florentine banking family) retain Ugolino? Significantly, Ugolino also provided the altarpiece for the high altar of Santa Maria Novella, so the Dominicans, as well as the Franciscans, must have had a reason for what would appear to be a very conservative choice of painter, especially when placed in the context of other paintings in the transept chapels. It seems likely that while the friars were quite glad to have narrative scenes rendered in a naturalistic manner, they felt that an image intended to be the object of devotion should retain the iconic, hieratic quality that had served this purpose so well in the past. Different needs occasioned different styles, each designed to elicit different reactions. Their

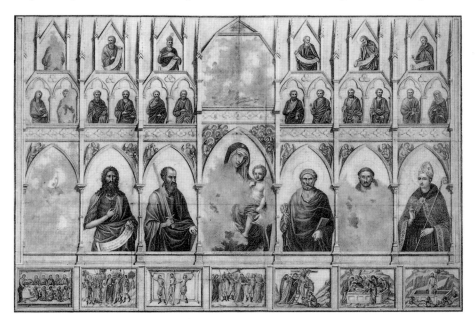

2.12 *Santa Croce Altarpiece*, c. 1324–25, eighteenth-century drawing of the lost painting by UGOLINO DI NERIO (Biblioteca Apostolica Vaticana, Rome, Vat. Lat., 9847, fol. 92r)

coexistence as part of a complete decorative program suggests an assumption on the part of ecclesiastical patrons that worshippers could read different visual languages concurrently and use them as different, but equally valid, routes to spiritual truths.

The Ugolino altarpiece makes the altarpiece of *The Coronation of the Virgin* (Fig. 2.13) for the Baroncelli Chapel only a decade or so later seem almost revolutionary. Below the central panel of the *Coronation* is an inscription reading: "Op[us] Magistri Iocti d[e] Flor[enti]a" ("This is the work of Master Giotto of Florence"). Although stylistic and technical weaknesses suggest that Giotto did not actually paint this altarpiece, the inscription does indicate the active involvement of his workshop. He may have provided the design for the panel, if not for the whole chapel. Unlike Ugolino's painting of the iconic Virgin and Child flanked by isolated individual saints, the Baroncelli altarpiece presents a completely unified field across its five panels, more akin to the *Maestà* paintings of Duccio and Simone Martini (see Figs. 2.19 and 2.23). More importantly the Baroncelli altarpiece depicts an event involving the Virgin—her Coronation—rather than simply presenting her as an object of adoration, as in the iconic figures of Ugolino's altarpiece and of virtually every other extant altarpiece of the time. This may explain why the two central protagonists are treated in a full and volumetric manner, with drapery hanging heavily from their limbs and falling in deep folds, while the numerous figures in the side panels are layered in a flattened space which precludes imagining fully dimensional bodies beneath their heads. This stylistic throwback to an earlier period is not entirely explained by the painting's attribution to Giotto's workshop, rather than to the master himself. Its use of

traditional formulas for the depiction of the figures in the side panels seems, rather, a deliberate attempt to emphasize the miraculous aspects of the event depicted and the devotional purpose of the altarpiece, in contrast to the narrative naturalism of the central figures or of the frescoes on the walls of the chapel. Here, as in Fig. 2.12, the style responds to the function of the painting rather than following an unbroken development toward naturalism.

The contrasts in the styles of the Ugolino and the Baroncelli altarpieces illustrate the distinguishing characteristics of Sienese and Florentine painting and the differing but compatible styles in Tuscan painting in the 1320s and 1330s. They also reflect the different intentions of the patrons—in the one case the Franciscan order, clinging to traditional religious images as a solemn backdrop for the celebration of the mass at the high altar, in the other wealthy, private donors celebrating the lives of Christ, the Virgin, and patron saints, keen to be in the vanguard of artistic developments. In the family chapels of Santa Croce, the dominance of the new style points to its eventual triumph.

The Refectory Frescoes Two other frescoes in the monastery of Santa Croce underscore the range of styles available to Florentine artists and patrons. For the end wall of their refectory the Franciscans commissioned Taddeo Gaddi probably in the 1330s to paint a *Last Supper*, an appropriate subject for the friars' dining hall. Above the *Last Supper* Gaddi painted a *Tree of Life* (the *Lignum vitae*; Fig. 2.14), a devotional subject derived from the writings of the Franciscan St. Bonaventure. To reinforce both its Franciscan and refectory context, the mystical tree is surrounded by a depiction of St. Francis's

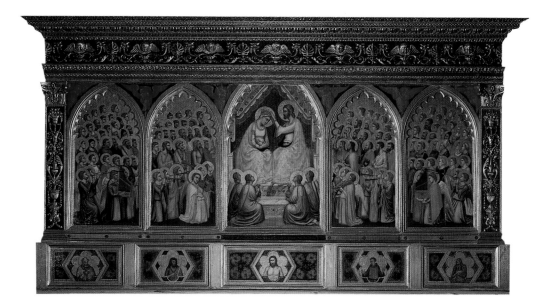

2.13 *Coronation of the Virgin*, c. 1332–38, commissioned by the Baroncelli family from the workshop of GIOTTO as the altarpiece for the Baroncelli Chapel, Santa Croce, Florence. Tempera on panel, 6' ¾" × 10' 7⅞" (1.85 × 3.23 m)

The frame of the painting was substantially altered in the fifteenth century when its original elaborate Gothic framework was transformed into a classicizing rectangular format that was more suited to the tastes of that time. The figures of angels in the spaces between the arched panels that had once been covered by the Gothic frame were added at that time.

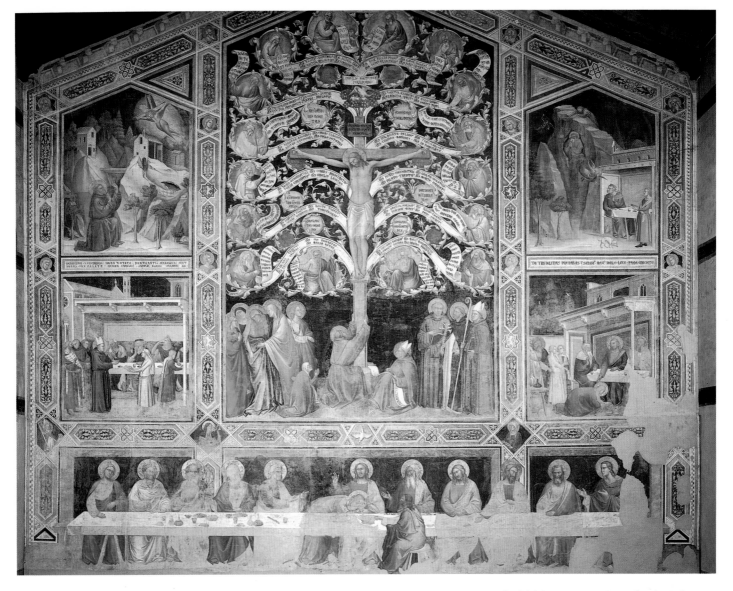

2.14 *Last Supper, Tree of Life*, and *Four Miracle Scenes*, c. 1330–40, commissioned by Mona Vaggia Manfredi (?) from TADDEO GADDI for the Refectory, Santa Croce, Florence. Fresco, 36′ 9″ × 38′ 3″ (11.2 × 11.7 m) (Museo dell'Opera di Santa Croce, Florence)

stigmatization at the upper left and three holy events that take place at meals, including the penitential image of Mary Magdalene washing the feet of Christ with her tears at the lower right.

The *Last Supper* below is remarkable for its startling illusion of high relief. The painter has thrust the figures into space in front of the wall, rather than creating a spatial platform or cavity behind it, in the usual way. Thus the figures, larger than any others on the wall above them, project into the space of the friars who would have been taking their meals in this room, bridging the gap between image and reality.

Immediately above, the *Tree of Life* includes at its lower level volumetric groups of figures creating both actual and contemplated reactions to the event of the Crucifixion being depicted. Conspicuous among them is a kneeling female donor, dressed in the robes of a Franciscan tertiary

(the lay order of Franciscans); she is slightly smaller in scale than the saintly, haloed figures at the foot of the cross. Given the presence of Manfredi coats of arms on the fresco, this woman has been identified as Mona Vaggia Manfredi, who died in 1345 and was buried in Santa Croce. Her presence in this important fresco exemplifies the critical role women played throughout this period as donors, either in their own right as secular patrons or nuns, or as executors for their husbands' estates. Despite contemporary Florentine regulations stipulating that women could act in financial matters only through an appointed male agent, many cases of women commissioning large-scale works of art have recently come to light.

Surrounding the crucifix in the *Tree of Life* are banderoles (unfurled scrolls) and stylized branches that carry texts and weave around medallions bearing images of prophets and yet further inscriptions calling on the viewer to contemplate the mystery of Christ's sacrifice. Any illusion of space is counteracted by the repetitive curves of the branches, which create a flat surface against the wall itself, almost as if the wall had become a flat page of text only incidentally illuminated by the portraits in the medallions. These figures have something of the stylized anonymity of those in Ugolino's altarpiece, despite their more naturalistic three-quarter poses. The painting is didactic and non-narrative in its straightforward presentation of Bonaventure's text and relies as much on word as on image to convey its message. Taken together, the *Last Supper* and the *Tree of Life* present a virtual compendium of the pictorial possibilities available to painters in the first half of the fourteenth century. They also caution against seeing an unbroken development toward a naturalistic style either within the Giotto workshop or in the world of ecclesiastical patronage. Whatever stylistic predilections painters might have had they had to respond to the conventions of the subject matter and the religious purpose in order to insure that their paintings would be legible to a visually literate community.

Florence and Siena: Promoting Church and State

Florence: The Duomo

The cathedral of Florence (Figs. 2.15 and 2.16), called the Duomo (from Latin *domus*, "house," and implying both the house of God and the residency of the local bishop), was conceived as a civic monument as well as a religious one, being built and financed by the Florentine Republic and the Woolworkers' Guild (the *Arte della Lana*). Although plans to build a new cathedral were discussed as early as 1285 and the building committee (Opera del Duomo) was operating by 1294, the construction of the building did not begin until 1296. The new building was to surround and replace the small medieval church of Santa Reparata, which itself had supplanted an early Christian structure built next to the walls of the ancient Roman city. City officials planned the new building to be large enough to hold the entire Florentine population, which in the early 1300s may have numbered as many as 90,000. Funds were raised through the imposition of a special tax on all personal property. In the project's early years, the twelve major guilds exerted managerial control over it, but in 1331 the Woolworkers' Guild was given charge of the building; from that time forward this guild had responsibility for building, decorating, and main-

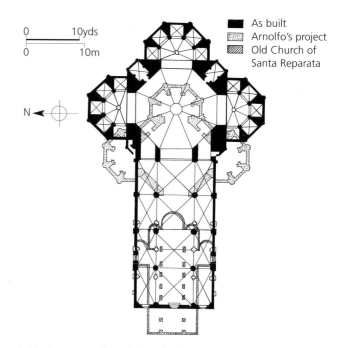

2.15 *Florence Cathedral*, plan showing stages in the construction

1 Chapel of St. Zenobius; **2** Chapel of the Arte della Lana, dedicated to St. Stephen; **3** Chapel of the Parte Guelfa; **4** and **5** North and South Sacristies; **6** Current position of John Hawkwood Monument

taining the structure, an arrangement that guaranteed lay control over it. The archbishop of Florence officiated at services in the Duomo, but he had little control over much of its form.

The building history of the Duomo is complicated and controversial. Arnolfo di Cambio (c. 1245 Colle di Val d'Elsa–1302? Florence?), a Tuscan sculptor and a student of Nicola Pisano who had been active in Rome at the end of the thirteenth century, was apparently the original architect of the new building, since he appears as *capomaestro* (chief master of the shop) of the project in a document of 1300. The first plan of the Duomo, as it can be reconstructed from the first two bays of the existing building, apparently called for a wooden **truss** roof structure comparable to that used in the Florentine church of Santa Croce (see Fig. 1.21) and in the Early Christian basilicas of Rome where Arnolfo had previously worked. Arnolfo's project was most likely continued after his death under the jurisdiction of a committee drawn from the twelve guilds.

In 1334 the Arte della Lana appointed Giotto *capomaestro* of the structure. The document of appointment also names Giotto as architect for the city walls, for fortifications, and for whatever other civic structures might be ordered by the governors of Florence, indicating the general esteem in which Giotto was held since he had no (known) experience as an architect. Giotto initiated work on the Duomo's free-standing bell tower, the Campanile. This enlargement of the original project suggests compe-

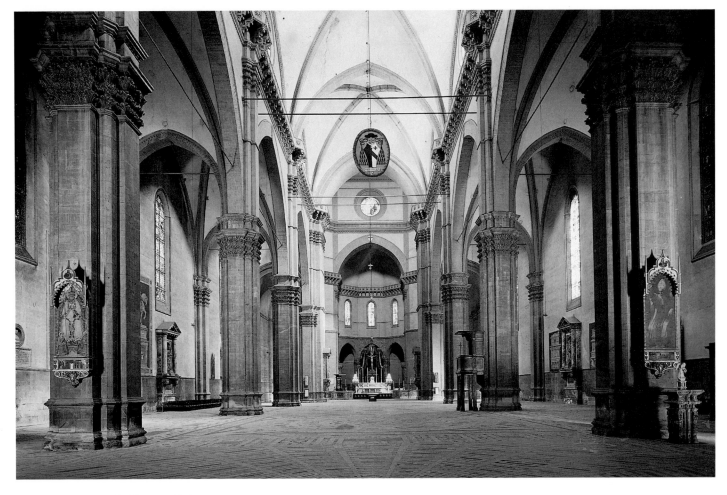

2.16 *Florence Cathedral*, begun 1296.

The first architect was Arnolfo da Cambio; a revised plan of 1357 was built under Francesco Talenti.

tition with neighboring Pisa whose campanile—now familiarly known as the Leaning Tower of Pisa—was begun in 1173. Work was suspended on the Pisa tower when its sandy subsoil caused it to begin tilting and was not resumed until 1275. The completion of both towers at roughly the same time, in the 1350s, further suggests an element of civic rivalry.

Unfortunately we cannot define precisely what Giotto and his successor, Andrea Pisano, may have planned for the cathedral building itself, since the present building follows plans of 1357 and 1365, drawn up after their involvement in the project. It is unlikely that by mid-century much more than the first two bays of the building had been completed. The change at that time from a traditional Tuscan timber beamed roof to the existing Gothic stone vaults suggests a new internationalism on the part of patron and guild. The size and scale of the building and its projected dome would have given the Duomo a prominence equal to or surpassing all but St. Mark's in Venice and Old St. Peter's in Rome. At the same time the polygonal **tribunes** that radiate from the central

area of the building beneath the dome are unmistakable references to the neighboring octagonal Baptistry (see Fig. 1.9), echoing the Roman references of the earlier building and placing the Duomo firmly within Florence's architectural traditions.

Andrea Pisano's Baptistry Doors The Arte del Calimala (Wool Merchants' Guild) was responsible for maintaining and decorating the Baptistry. Dating possibly from the sixth century, the Baptistry had been given its green and white marble cladding in the eleventh and twelfth centuries, and now the Calimala embarked on another project for its embellishment: a magnificent bronze door for the south entrance to the building. The commission for this door was given to Andrea di Ugolino da Pontedera, known as Andrea Pisano (c.1295 Pontedera–1348 Orvieto?; Fig. 2.17). The date of 1330 inscribed on the doors records the date of the commission; the work for this enormous project actually continued until 1336 when the doors were finally put in place. The magnitude of this project was clearly meant to assert

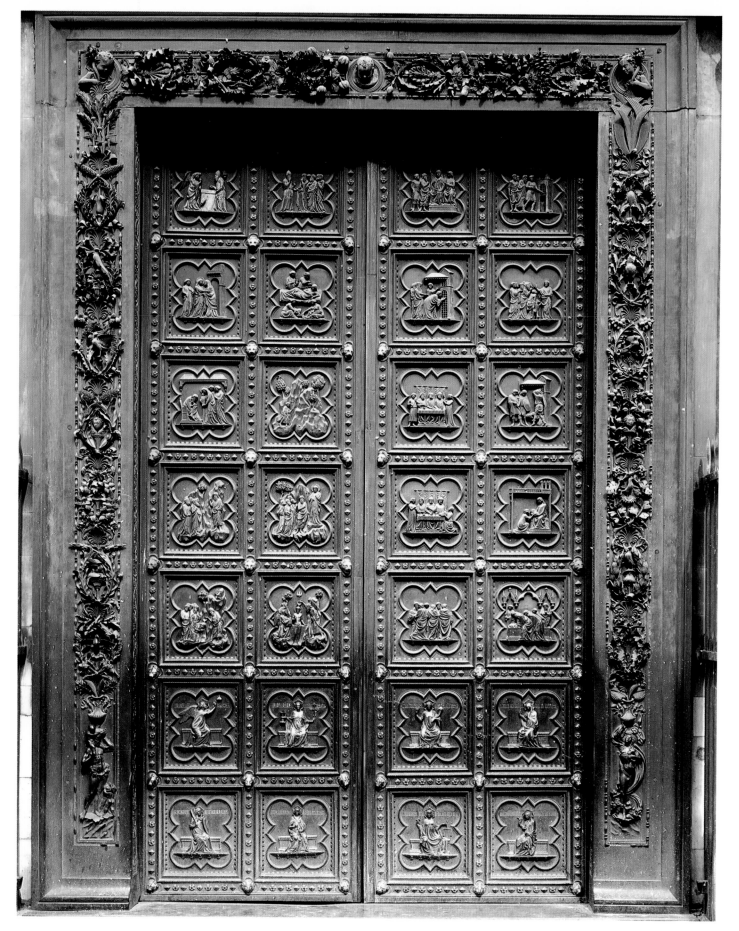

2.17 *South doors*, 1330–36, commissioned by the Arte del Calimala from ANDREA PISANO for the Baptistry, Florence. Gilt bronze

the power of the Calimala in the Duomo precincts, just at the time when the guild had lost control of the cathedral itself to the Arte della Lana.

Andrea's doors contain twenty-eight quatrefoil panels, twenty of which narrate the life of St. John the Baptist, the patron saint of the building and also of the city of Florence. The bottom eight panels depict seated personifications of virtues. At the interstices of the panels are decorative lions' heads, recalling the *marzocco*, or shield-bearing lion, which was one of the emblems of the city. Within each of the quatrefoils Andrea created a carefully structured composition of nearly free-standing figures moving across a narrow platform, like a stage. Each relief is enhanced by gilding, which is applied not only to the figures but also to the architecture and landscape features to distinguish them from the bronze background. The figures are indebted to Giotto's treatment of form in the determined articulation of their bodies beneath the drapery and in the psychological intensity of their participation in the event depicted.

Andrea was also clearly influenced by Gothic art from north of the Alps. The quatrefoil shape of the panels is itself reminiscent of reliefs on cathedral façades such as those of Amiens, Rouen, and Auxerre. The decorative border patterns of the drapery in Andrea's panels are also similar to northern Gothic forms, as is the lyrical simplicity of the figures. Like many other artists, Andrea may have traveled to France or Germany, where he could have seen this sculpture for himself. He could also have had access to a northern style through imported portable objects such as reliquaries; having trained as a goldsmith (he is called *orefice* in the documents), Andrea would have looked at such work very carefully. Or he might have assimilated such stylistic elements from contemporary Italian artists—including Giotto—who had already made them integral to their own work. By the time Andrea acted as an independent sculptor at the South Doors, he was clearly a mature artist who had completely integrated both classical and contemporary elements into his personal style. He was thus able to provide the Calimala with a sculptural work not only of amazing technical virtuosity but of great artistic sophistication, rivaling medieval examples such as the bronze doors for the cathedral of Pisa.

For the Campanile, designed by Giotto and still under construction, Andrea provided a series of reliefs to decorate its exterior at approximately the time he succeeded Giotto as the director of the architectural project. The program was encyclopedic, including the seven Sacraments, seven virtues, seven planets, seven Liberal Arts, and seven Mechanical Arts. Andrea included the art of weaving (Fig. 2.18) in the Mechanical Arts, a clear reference to the guild responsible for working with the Opera del Duomo on

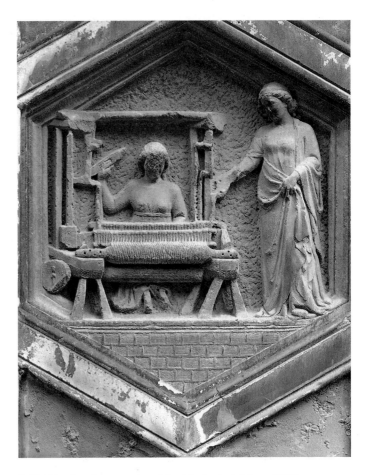

2.18 *Weaving*, from a series of the Mechanical Arts, c. 1337, commissioned by the Opera del Duomo from ANDREA PISANO for the exterior of the Campanile, Florence. Marble, 33 × 27" (83 × 69 cm) (Museo del Opera del Duomo, Florence)

the decorative project and to a craft that had contributed so much to Florence's prominence. The loom and the figures are arranged to maintain the plane of the relief, giving the scene an austere directness. The drapery of the standing figure falls in simple folds reminiscent of drapery in classical sculpture, while the elegant curves of its borders evoke the formal elements of the Gothic style.

Siena: Duccio's *Maestà*

While the Florentines were just beginning work on the Duomo, the Sienese were launching extensive decorative programs for both their cathedral (structurally largely complete by the mid-1200s) and their new town hall which were to establish a style for the city quite distinct from that of Florence.

On October 9, 1308, the head of the cathedral workshop signed a contract with Duccio for a large altarpiece for the cathedral's main altar, then under the dome. The main panel of the altarpiece which depicts the Virgin in Majesty, is now known simply as the *Maestà* (Fig. 2.19). It expresses visually the dedication of the city to the Virgin

The Procession of the *Maestà*

The completion of Duccio's *Maestà* in 1311 and its installation in the Duomo occasioned a city-wide celebration. The panel was removed from Duccio's workshop on the outskirts of the city and carried in procession to its designated position above the cathedral's high altar. This contemporary account reflects not only the splendor of the occasion but also the inseparable connections between civic and religious life in European cities during the Middle Ages and Renaissance.

At this time the altarpiece for the high altar was finished, and the picture which was called the "Madonna with the large eyes," or Our Lady of Grace, that now hangs over the altar of St. Boniface, was taken down.

Now this Our Lady was she who had hearkened to the people of Siena when the Florentines were routed at Monte Aperto [the battle of Montaperti, 1260], and her place was changed because the new one was made, which is far more beautiful and devout and larger, and is painted on the back with the stories of the Old and New Testaments. And on the day that it was carried to the Duomo the shops were shut, and the bishop conducted a great and devout company of priests and friars in solemn procession, accompanied by the nine *signori*, and all the officers of the commune, and all the people, and one after another the worthiest with lighted candles in their hands took places near the picture, and behind came the women and children with great devotion. And they accompanied the said picture up to the Duomo, making the procession around the Campo, as is the custom, all the bells ringing joyously, out of reverence for so noble a picture as is this. And this picture Duccio di Niccolò the painter made and it was made in the house of the Muciatti outside the [city] gate . . . . And all that day they stood in prayer with great almsgiving for poor persons, praying God and His Mother, who is our advocate, to defend us by their infinite mercy from every adversity and all evil, and keep us from the hands of traitors and of the enemies of Siena.

(from Charles Eliot Norton. *Historical Studies of Church-Building in the Middle Ages.* New York: Harper & Brothers, 1880, pp. 144–5)

made formal at the time of the Battle of Montaperti against the Florentines in 1260. Duccio's altarpiece followed six years after his commission for another altarpiece of the same subject for the chapel of the ruling council of Siena (the *Nove* or Nine) in the Palazzo Pubblico (town hall). Thus both cathedral and town hall repeat the same imagery, attesting to the continuous interpenetration of sacred and secular art in Italian city states of this time.

Because the *Maestà* occupied a free-standing position under the dome, it was painted on both sides. Its bright colors, set against luminous gold backgrounds in the iconic tradition, and its original elaborate gilded frame with finials punctuating the space between the uppermost panels must have shone brilliantly against the somber black and white marble interior of the cathedral, bathed in the light streaming down from the windows of the dome (later, sadly, filled in). Additional, colored light from the huge round stained glass window depicting the *Death, Assumption, and Coronation of the Virgin*, also by Duccio, in the east wall of the building, would have given it an almost magical radiance. Thus painting and window functioned together to glorify Siena's patron, the Queen of Heaven.

The front of the *Maestà* shows the enthroned Virgin and Child, flanked by saints and angels. The main panel is surmounted by truncated figures of Apostles and, at the next level up, by separate panels showing scenes from the life of the Virgin. Small panels depicting angels may originally have crowned each of these scenes. Among the figures flanking the Virgin in the main panel are other saints: Ansanus, Savinus, Crescentius, and Victor who kneel in the front row. Though relatively obscure members of the saintly hierarchy, these are patron saints of Siena, and their prominence indicates that this was as much a civic as an ecclesiastical commission. This fact is spelled out in the inscription on the Virgin's footstool: "Holy Mother of God, be the cause of peace to Siena, [and] of life to Duccio because he has painted thee thus."

The prominence of Duccio's name on the face of the altarpiece is a measure of his status as one of Siena's most renowned citizens and serves as a reminder that artists, particularly in Siena but throughout Italy as well, had long marked both their pride in their work and their piety by placing their names in conspicuous positions on their work. The prominence of famous artists within the civic life of the period is borne out by documents recording high fees for the leading artists and even by indications that some on occasion served as political emissaries for their city-states. With the *Maestà* Siena at last had a work by Duccio that could compare with the *Rucellai Madonna* (see Fig. 1.30), which he had made for the Compagnia dei Laudesi in Florence more than twenty years earlier.

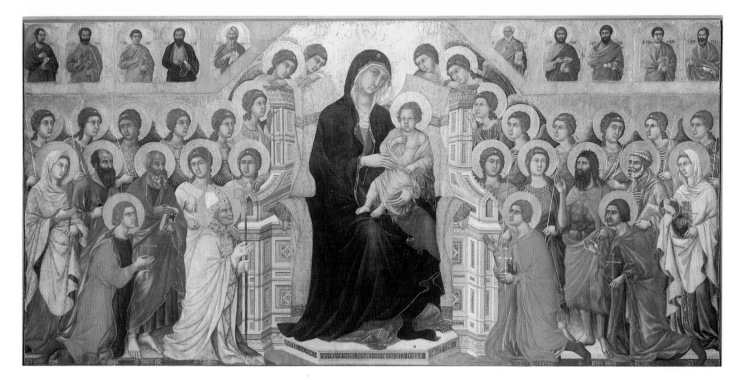

2.19 *Maestà* (front side), 1308–11, commissioned by the Opera del Duomo from DUCCIO for the high altar of Siena Cathedral. Tempera and gold leaf on panel, 7 × 13' (2.13 × 3.96 m) (Museo dell'Opera del Duomo, Siena)

The *Maestà* shows some traces of the style of the earlier painting in the folds of the veil around the Virgin's face, in the tendril-like gold border of the cloak, in the gold striations of the Virgin's gown (just visible under her robe), and in the luxuriousness of the materials used. In the *Maestà*, however, the faces are both fuller and softer,

and the throne is more satisfyingly three-dimensional. There is also a conscientious effort to suggest the rounded volumes of the figures and their spatial relationships through their overlapping forms.

The development of Duccio's style seen by comparing the *Ruccellai Madonna* and the *Maestà* may owe something

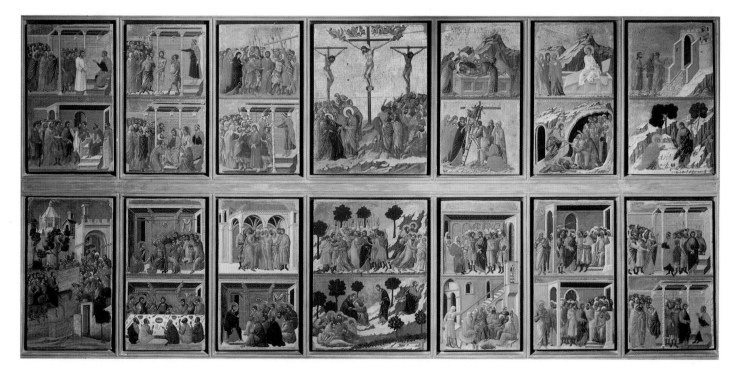

2.20 *Maestà* (reverse side)

The altarpiece was removed from the cathedral in 1771, when it was sawn into several smaller pieces. The heraldic crest of the Opera of the cathedral probably appeared on the original frame.

to a trip to Paris he may have made in the intervening years. There are documentary references to a "Duch de Siene" (Duccio of Siena) in Paris in 1297 which coincide with his absence from any documentary reference in Siena between 1295 and 1302. Thus it appears that Duccio traveled north to see for himself the fully developed Gothic style of the French court.

The reverse side of the *Maestà* (Fig. 2.20) is composed of separate panels depicting events in the life of Christ. Various students assisted Duccio on these panels (as well as on those for the front of the altarpiece) in a collaboration that helped to perpetuate the distinctive Sienese school of painting into the next generation. However, it must have been Duccio himself who devised the compositional scheme, ensured consistency in the

individual panels, and gave a clear visual form to the stories depicted.

A comparison of Duccio's work on the *Maestà* with the work of other artists reveals some interesting similarities. On the reverse of the *Maestà*, the central icon of Christianity, the *Crucifixion*, is placed on the central axis and is given twice the space of the other panels, as it was in the fresco cycle in Old St. Peter's in Rome. Although schematized, the architecture of the individual panels provides a uniform geometrical frame and spatial envelope for the actions depicted and is consistent with the most current developments of depictions of space. Even the space that Duccio leaves at the top of panels such as the *Last Supper* (Fig. 2.21) compares with similar treatment in the Isaac panels in Assisi (see Fig. 1.47) or

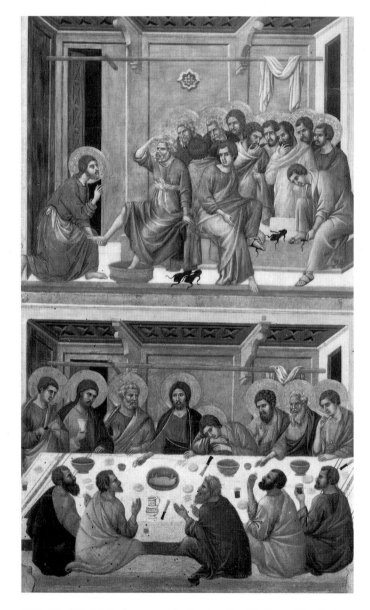

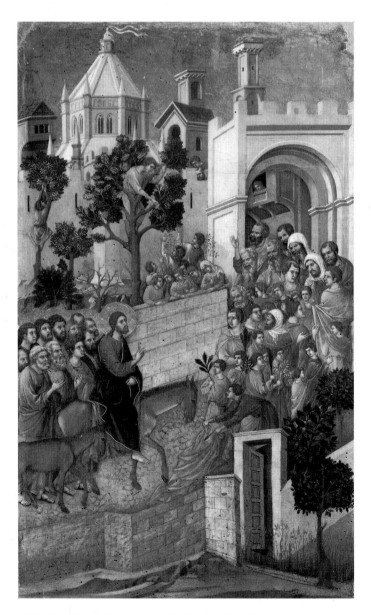

2.21 *Maestà*, detail of reverse side showing the *Washing of the Feet* and *Last Supper*, 1308–11, 40 × 21" (102 × 53 cm)

2.22 *Maestà*, detail of reverse side showing the *Entry into Jerusalem*, 1308–11, 40 × 22" (102 × 56 cm)

Giotto's painted architecture in the Scrovegni Chapel. Although landscape features tend to be simple schematic rock forms, they give a consistent sense of spatial depth from panel to panel, bringing additional unity to the various events of the narrative. Most compelling, of course, is the dramatic response to events with which Duccio invests the scenes. In the *Entry into Jerusalem* (Fig. 2.22), for example, each of the participants is intensely focused on his response to the event. There is a clear axis of movement from left to right and a naturalistic, even anecdotal, rendering of the figures and their activities. The figures of the two young men in the trees suggest either that Duccio knew Giotto's rendering of this same subject in Padua or that both artists used a similar model.

Simone Martini's *Maestà* for the Palazzo Pubblico The power of Duccio's *Maestà* and its symbolic value for the

city is clearly evident in the fact that soon after it was finished the governing body of the Nine commissioned Simone Martini (c. 1284 Siena–1344 Avignon) to paint a fresco of the same subject (Fig. 2.23) for the main meeting room of their newly completed town hall (see Fig. 1.20). Simone had trained in Duccio's workshop and had assisted in the painting of the *Maestà* for the cathedral. The historical conditions for his own *Maestà* clearly mandated that he imitate Duccio's previous depiction of this subject and perhaps also the earlier *Maestà* by Duccio (1302) in the chapel of the Nine. Simone included exactly the same saints who appear in Duccio's great *Maestà* and arranged them in much the same order. The imitative nature of Simone's work was determined by the needs of the program, which undoubtedly called for consistency in the depiction of the city's protectress. Here in the town hall, as in the cathedral, the image served a propagandis-

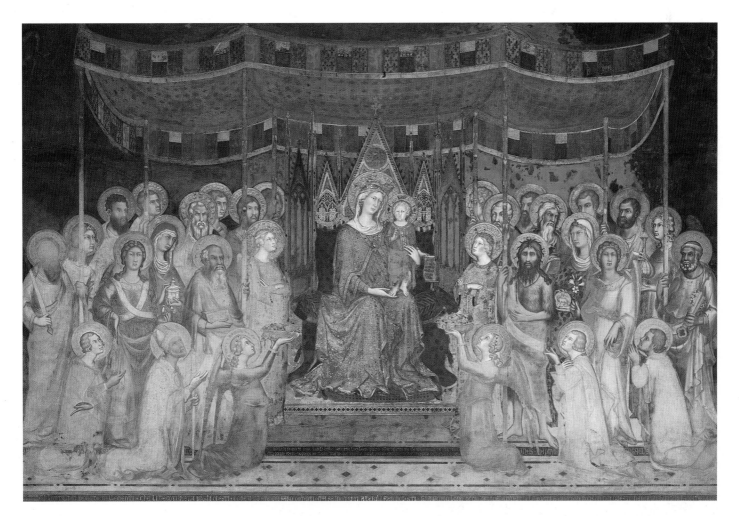

2.23 *Maestà*, c. 1315, repaired and repainted in 1321, commissioned presumably by the governing body of the Nine from SIMONE MARTINI for the Sala del Consiglio (Room of the Council), Palazzo Pubblico, Siena. Fresco, 25' × 31' 9" (7.62 × 9.68 m)

Damage to the fresco over time was caused by the storage of salt in basement rooms of the Palazzo Pubblico beneath the fresco. Moisture carried the salt up through the inner walls of the building and caused crystals to form beneath the surface of the paint. These pushed the pigment forward and damaged the structural integrity of the plaster. The Christ Child holds an actual parchment scroll that has been adhered to the surface of the fresco: it reads: "Love Justice you who judge the earth."

tic purpose. The inscription at the base of the throne of the Virgin in Simone's *Maestà*, "The angelic little flowers, the roses and the lilies which adorn the heavenly fields do not delight me more than righteous council," is an exhortation to the rulers of the city who met in this room to carry out their responsibilities in a just and equitable manner.

Two rondels painted in the center of the dado of the wall beneath the border, although badly damaged and repainted, carry a message presumably painted by Simone or one of his assistants. They contain images of the seal of the Captain of the People, a rampant lion, and of the Communal Seal of the city of Siena with the Virgin and Child flanked by candle-bearing angels surrounded by a Latin inscription which reads: "The Virgin protects Siena which she has long marked for favor." Unlike the Virgin in Duccio's *Maestà*, Simone's Virgin wears a crown, her queenly status appropriate in a room dedicated to the business of government.

In his *Maestà* Simone integrated some of the spatial realism and corporeality of earlier painting in Florence, Rome, and Naples into the Sienese style, although there is no evidence that he had yet visited these cities. In contrast to the compressed and stacked quality of Duccio's figures, all of whom line up in even rows, Simone's angels and saints have more space between one another and are organized so that they create diagonal rows from front to back of the composition, thus emphasizing the deep stage-like space formally constructed by the *baldacchino* which covers the entire group. Simone also structured the folds of the material clothing his figures to make them appear fuller and more weighty than Duccio's sinuous, decorative draperies although he follows Duccio in including complicated folds and pooling of fabric at the base of his figures.

The elaborate Gothic throne in which the Virgin and the Christ Child are placed also differs from Duccio's heavy marble throne, which recalls indigenous Tuscan architecture. The thin window-like arches of Simone's throne suggest the elaborate frames of contemporary altarpieces and the Gothic architecture of Naples, then under the control of the Angevin dynasty, with which Siena had long-standing political alliances. Simone, in fact, moved to Naples shortly after completing this fresco.

The Palazzo Pubblico in San Gimignano   The success of Simone's *Maestà* is suggested by its repetition in the Palazzo Pubblico of San Gimignano, a small hill town then a dependency of Siena. In 1317–18 Simone's some-

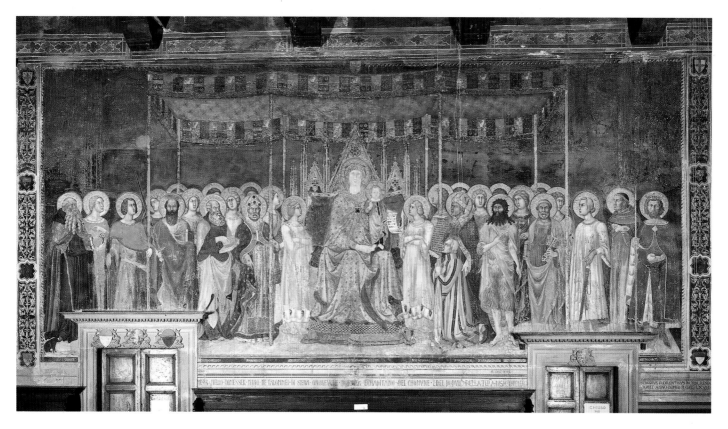

2.24 *Maestà*, 1317–18, commissioned by Nello di Mino Tolomei from LIPPO MEMMI for the Palazzo Pubblico, San Gimignano. Fresco

The paired figures to the left and the right were added by Bartolo di Fredi when the fresco was enlarged in 1367. The fresco was repaired along the lower edge in the 1460s by Benozzo Gozzoli, who may have repainted the heads of the two figures to the far right.

time collaborator and later his brother-in-law, Lippo Memmi (active 1317–c. 1350 Siena), was commissioned by Nello di Mino Tolomei, then *podestà* (chief magistrate) and Captain of the People in San Gimignano, to paint a *Maestà* in the town hall there (Fig. 2.24). Lippo adjusted the composition of Simone's fresco to accommodate the different commission. He replaced the Sienese patron saints in the front row with Nello, kneeling in a donor pose, and with St. Nicholas (Nello's patron saint) standing behind him. St. Gimignano, the patron saint of the city, stands at the left of the Virgin, and the coat of arms of the Tolomei family appears in the *baldacchino* above. If nothing else this rather pedestrian painting indicates how powerful the language of civic imagery was. By placing the copy of Simone's *Maestà* in the town hall of San Gimignano, Nello made very clear Siena's political control over the small town and his power as legate in enforcing that control.

The Sala della Pace: "Good Government" One of the most elaborate decorative programs for the Palazzo Pubblico of Siena was painted by Ambrogio Lorenzetti

(active 1317–48 Siena), who was Sienese by birth, but who had worked in Florence where he enrolled in the painters' guild in the 1330s. In 1338 the Nine commissioned Lorenzetti to fresco their own meeting room (the Sala dei Nove, or the Sala della Pace [Room of Peace]), which adjoins the room in which Simone had painted his *Maestà*. The Nine, who led the Sienese government from 1287 to 1355 and whose membership changed every two months, were drawn from the Sienese aristocracy, despite repeated attempts to widen the sources of representation. Legislation of 1318 made them responsible for "the ordering and reformation of the whole city and *contado* ('countryside') of Siena." For the Sala dei Nove Lorenzetti designed an allegorical fresco cycle underscoring the benefits of good government and the dangers of bad government.

The cycle consists of three frescoes: the *Allegory of Good Government*, the *Effects of Good Government in the City and in the Country*, and *Bad Government and the Effects of Bad Government in the City*. The *Allegory of Good Government* (Fig. 2.25) occupies one short wall of the room and is the central image in it. A complicated and fragmented work,

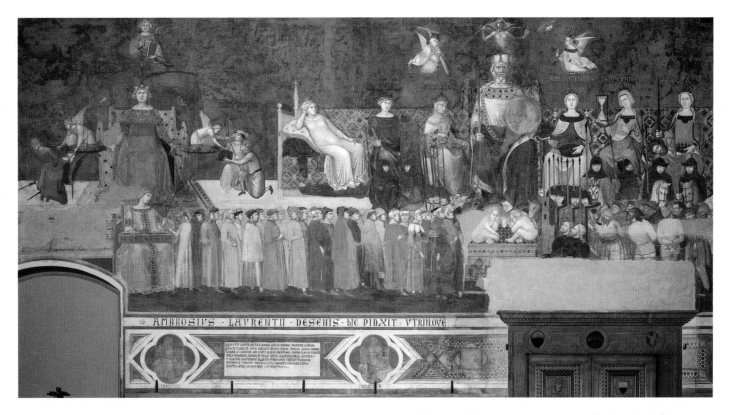

2.25 *Allegory of Good Government*, 1338–40, commissioned by the governing body of the Nine from AMBROGIO LORENZETTI for the Sala della Pace (also known as the Room of the Nine), Palazzo Pubblico, Siena. Fresco, length c. 25′ 3″ (7.7 m)

The text in the lower border of the fresco reads: "This holy virtue [of Justice] where she rules, induces to unity the many souls [of the citizens], and they, gathered together for such a purpose, make the Common Good their Lord; and he, in order to govern his state, chooses never to turn his eyes from the resplendent faces of the Virtues who sit around him. Therefore to him in triumph are offered taxes, tributes and lordship of towns; therefore, without war, every civic result duly follows—useful, necessary, and pleasurable." (Trans. Diana Norman)

Art and Violence

Contrary to what appears in idealized cityscapes, such as Ambrogio Lorenzetti's *Effects of Good Government* (see Fig. 2.27), Renaissance cities were rife with raucous behavior and sometimes violence. Rivalries with competing city-states and intense local political factionalism often led to armed conflict within the city itself as well as on the battlefield. It was not always clear who posed a greater danger: the soldiers of an opposing city-state or one's neighbors.

In an attempt to control violence within their jurisdictions, city governments passed laws limiting the carrying and use of arms. To enable people to let off steam, they also provided officially sanctioned opportunities for engaging in violent and often dangerous behavior. Rules were relaxed especially during Carnival, a festival in late winter just before the start of the penitential season of Lent. During Carnival men were allowed to dress as women, slaves as masters, laity as clergy.

As seen in Figure 2.26, a late sixteenth-century Venetian print, neighborhood groups and city officials also organized thrilling—and cruel—spectator sports. In the right foreground young men run up a bridge and leap to grasp a tethered goose by its neck; both successful and unsuccessful participants landed unceremoniously in the canal below. At the left, two masochistic figures on a platform submit themselves to clawing by a cat strapped to a board. Just behind them dogs bait a bear. In the background spectators run from an enraged bull. In the center square, citizens enjoy a gentler pastime, a hip-rocking dance.

Although coarse and often inhumane, these events appealed to a wide audience, including the noblewomen shown here perched in windows and balconies overlooking the scene. City officials were proud of such events. For example, when King Henry III of France visited Venice in 1574 he was treated to a stick fight. Representatives from the two major factions in the city—one claiming to have their origins on the mainland, the other from the islands in the lagoon—donned rough iron helmets and chain mail before fighting for control of the top of the Carmini Bridge. The king called off the event after three hours, saying that it was less violent than an actual battle but more dangerous than a game really should be.

In Rome visitors and citizens enjoyed the vicarious terror of watching wild horses run down the Via del Corso (Street of the Race) to the base of the Capitoline Hill. Siena was—and still is—famous for men on horseback careening around the Piazza del Campo to claim the city's *palio* (ceremonial banner). In Florence tournaments held in the large squares in front of the mendicant churches of Santa Croce and Santa Maria Novella were a bit more ritualized in their violence, though the public could indulge its taste for blood and physical contact by cheering on their neighborhood players in the annual rugby-like soccer matches staged in the city's piazzas. Sometimes these events got out of hand, occasionally leading to riots—as hotly contested games may do even today—but for the most part they reinforced civic and group solidarity, domesticating and limiting civic violence.

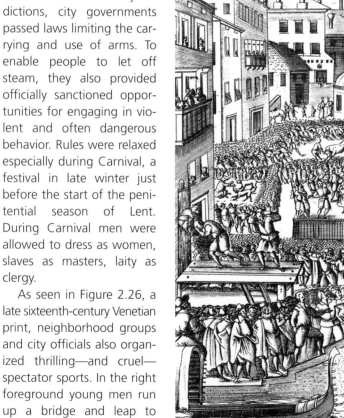

2.26 *From* GIACOMO FRANCO, *Habiti d'huomeni et donne venetiane con la processione della serenissima signoria et altri particolari cioe trionfi feste ceremonie publiche della nobilissima città di Venetia*, Venice, 1600s, reprint 1878. Engraving

it lacks a single compositional focus and thus must be read episodically. The largest image on the wall, and therefore, according to the hierarchies of the period, the most important, is the seated male figure on the right, who is clothed in the heraldic black and white colors of Siena and identified with gold lettering, halo-like around his head, as CSCV, or *Comune Senarum Civitas Virginis* ("The Sienese Commune, the City of the Virgin"). The Commune, or in this case the *Buon Comune* or Good Government, is flanked left and right by six female personifications of virtues, each clearly labeled above her head. Above the head of the *Buon Comune* float three much smaller winged figures identified as the three cardinal virtues: Faith, Charity, and Hope. Thus the state manifests an ideal of Christian virtue.

In depicting the *Buon Comune* flanked by virtues, Lorenzetti adopted a configuration typically used for the Last Judgment. Thus anyone reading his image would see the *Buon Comune* as omnipotent, like the central figure of God in the Last Judgment (see Fig. 2.5), and would also read the Commune as judge. To underscore this reading Lorenzetti included bound criminals at the lower right of the composition (to the *Buon Comune's* left side) and the upright citizens, or—to use Last Judgment iconography—the elect, at the *Buon Comune's* right side. Moreover, the inscription over the heads of the criminals repeats that of the communal seal depicted in the border of Simone's *Maestà* in the next room and underscores verbally the protection of the Virgin and of the Commune that represents her. Civil and moral law come together in this image. The imagery provides a complex diagrammatic representation of the late-medieval commune, based on the reality of its citizen members, a divinely sanctioned order, and an abstract conception of the State. The responsibility of the Nine was to make this order manifest in Siena.

At the left side of the fresco a female figure of Justice sits in much the same pose as the *Buon Comune*. An admonitory inscription taken from the opening of the Book of Wisdom, "Choose Justice, you who judge the land," arches over the figure. Justice looks up at the winged figure of Wisdom above her head, who holds scales labeled as distributive and commutative justice. A female figure of Concord sits at her feet. Across the bottom of the fresco, from Concord to the right edge, Sienese citizens move two by two in a peaceable procession, concord being the natural result of the governance whose structure is visualized metaphorically above their heads.

Lorenzetti's style demonstrates how well he had managed to integrate some of the stylistic principles of Giotto into his own work—not surprisingly, as he had worked in Florence from 1321 to 1327 and again from 1332 to 1334. Figures are naturalistically rendered (especially the citizens and soldiers) and fully modeled, their volumetric

solidity enhanced by the depth of the benches on which they sit or by their three-quarter poses. Yet this fresco also contains non-naturalistic elements, such as the use of changing scale to suggest the relative importance of different people. Lorenzetti's use of perspective is tentative: figures move sequentially across the fresco surface on a narrow platform with no delineation of background at all, although they themselves are treated volumetrically; thus they are placed in an environment completely at odds with their own figural style. In fact the fresco as a whole is non-narrative and the individual allegorical figures are conventional, just as allegory is an artificial, conventional, and formal literary device. It is only in the lowest tier of the fresco where the quasi-historical figures of the citizens of Siena appear, that the fresco utilizes completely naturalistic stylistic conventions.

To provide visible proof of the efficacy of the abstract concepts of the *Buon Comune* fresco, Ambrogio painted a long two-part fresco of the *Effects of Good Government in the City and in the Country* on the adjacent long wall to the right (Fig. 2.27). This is a busy scene of everyday urban and rural life, crammed with an extraordinary richness of detail: with masons and carpenters constructing buildings, cobblers making shoes, a teacher instructing his class, visitors to the city strolling through it, while outside the walls peasants tend the crops and wealthy citizens ride through the countryside. It is a fascinating panorama of the late-medieval city-state at work, a purely secular painting, with no indication of the religious rituals that punctuated the citizens' lives. As historical narrative, it represents civic life and noteworthy events on which the city could reflect with pride and a strong sense of its identity.

On the wall opposite the *Effects of Good Government* and to the left of the *Buon Comune* Ambrogio painted another fresco called *Bad Government and the Effects of Bad Government in the City* (Fig. 2.28), which uses the same forms and compositional devices as the other frescoes in the room, but inverts them. The malevolent-looking figure representing Bad Government, pointedly labeled as Tyranny (a noun gendered as feminine in Italian) is enthroned like the *Buon Comune* and stares hieratically out at the observer. Neither male nor female, it is fanged, cross-eyed, and porcine, clearly bloated with corruption. In place of the cardinal virtues, personifications of Avarice, Pride, and Vainglory fly over its head. Tyranny is flanked by clearly labeled seated figures representing Cruelty, Treason, and Fraud at the left and Frenzy, Divisiveness, and War at the right. A bound figure representing Justice lies at its feet. The city to its left is falling into ruin, robbers roam the streets, and, in the foreground, a group of ruffians drags a woman by her hair. Even in its now ruinous condition the image conveys a dire warning.

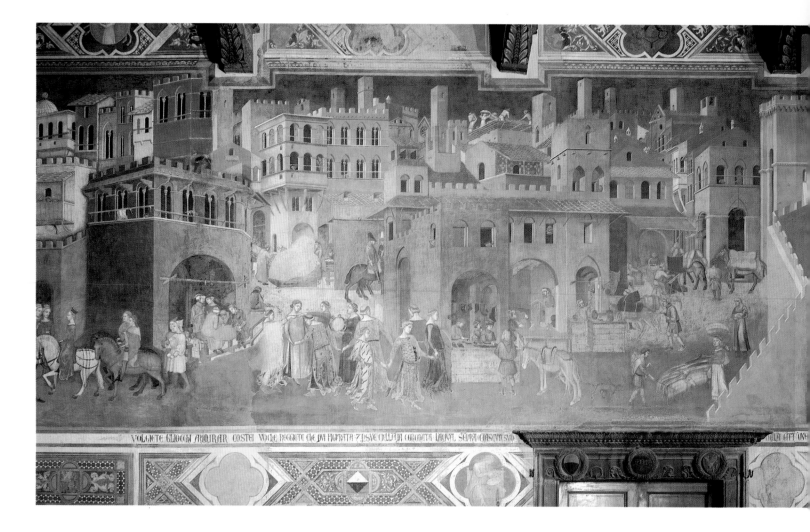

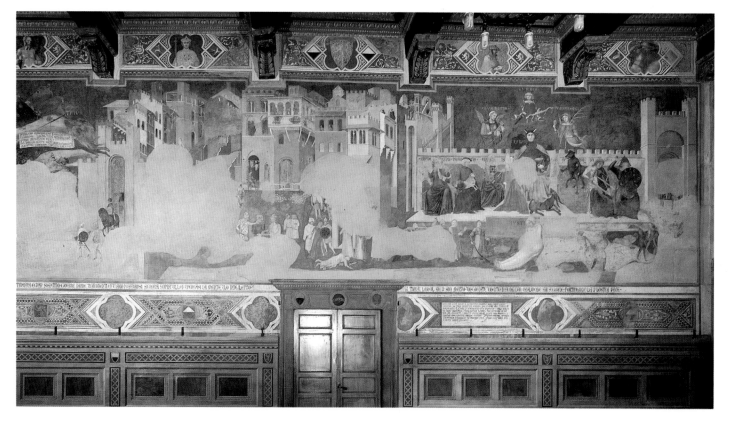

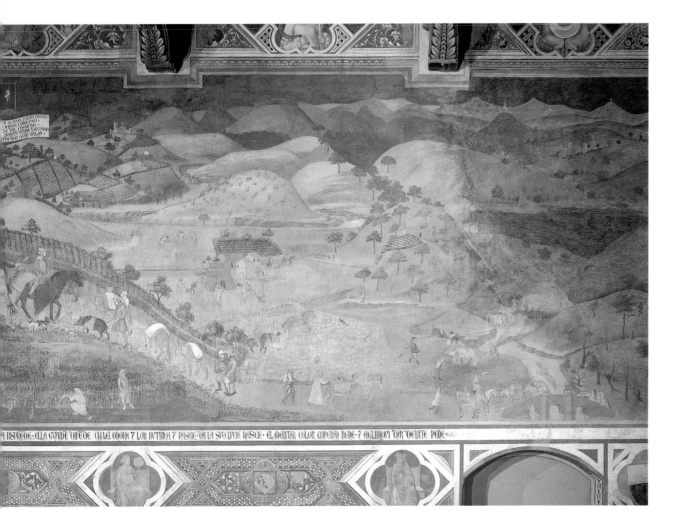

2.27 *Effects of Good Government in the City and in the Country*, wall to the right of the *Allegory of Good Government*, Sala della Pace (Room of the Nine), Palazzo Pubblico, Siena, detail. Fresco, length c. 46′ (14 m)

Securitas (Security), flying in the air at the city gate holding a gibbet with a man hanging from it, also holds a scroll that reads: "Without fear every man may travel freely and each may till and sow, so long as this commune shall maintain this lady [Justice] sovereign, for she has stripped the wicked of all power." (Trans. Diana Norman)

2.28 (left) *Bad Government and the Effects of Bad Government in the City*, wall to the left of the *Allegory of Good Government*, Sala della Pace (Room of the Nine), Palazzo Pubblico, Siena, detail. Fresco

There is reason to believe that the inscriptions along the bottom border of each fresco are modern restorations, although they may reproduce original texts. Timor (Fear) in the upper left corner, facing Security across the room, holds a scroll that reads: "Because each seeks only his own good, in this city Justice is subjected to Tyranny; wherefore, along this road nobody passes without fearing for his life, since there are robberies outside and inside the city gates." In the border a text reads: "There, where Justice is bound, no one is ever in accord with the Common Good, nor pulls the cord straight; therefore it is fitting that Tyranny prevails. She, in order to carry out her iniquity, neither wills nor acts in disaccord [sic] with the filthy nature of the Vices, who are shown here conjoined with her. She banishes those who are ready to do good and calls around herself every evil schemer. She always protects the assailant, the robber, and those who hate peace, so that her every land lies wasted." (Trans. Diana Norman)

Altarpieces: Conventions and Contexts   Other works by Simone Martini and Ambrogio Lorenzetti further illustrate the point that different iconographical conventions and contexts govern artistic style in the fourteenth century. In the late 1320s the officials of the Siena cathedral workshop devised a plan to complete the central space of the cathedral, furnishing it with more altars and altarpieces. Four altars, situated symmetrically in the transept and flanking the main altar under the dome, were to be dedicated to the four patron saints of Siena (see Fig. 1.12) depicted in the foreground of Duccio's *Maestà*. The altarpieces for the four altars were to depict important events in the life of the Virgin, whose image as eternal heavenly queen graced the main altar. These are the first altarpieces of this period to utilize such a narrative structure rather than a standard icon such as a Virgin and Child or a standing saint. The program for the four altars repeats the iconography of a now lost series of frescoes once on the exterior wall of the main hospital in Siena, the Ospedale della Scala, facing the façade of the cathedral. This repetition, like the *Maestà* paintings for the cathedral and town hall, continually reasserted the city's dedication to the Virgin and ensured its protection.

In 1333, after having traveled to Naples where he worked for the Angevin king, and to Assisi where he painted in the church of San Francesco, Simone completed an altarpiece depicting the *Annunciation* (Fig. 2.29) for one of the cathedral altars, that of St. Ansanus. Despite its abraded surface, the painting is still astonishing for its opulence. The gold of the haloes is richly tooled, so that light refracts from the **punch work** and seems literally to radiate. Gabriel's robe is intricately worked with gold, and his flowing cloak is richly patterned in plaid.

The *Annunciation* shows an initially puzzling retreat from the naturalism of the *Maestà* Simone had painted for the Palazzo Pubblico some eighteen years earlier. The weighty quality of both figures and drapery in that fresco contrasts sharply with the nervous and febrile linear qualities of the figures in the *Annunciation*, particularly the near-impossible twisting of the body of the Virgin herself, although the faces in both the fresco and the panel painting share the same hard, ovoid structure.

The explanation for this apparent stylistic shift may lie in the purpose that the altarpiece served. Because the *Annunciation* was intended to function as a narrative extension to Duccio's *Maestà* on the high altar, Simone echoed the style of the earlier painting in order to provide a unified decorative program for the cathedral. It must have been easy for Simone, who had been trained in Duccio's shop and who had, himself, painted parts of the *Maestà*, to adopt the visual language of that painting which so dominated the interior of the cathedral. Thus, like Duccio's *Maestà*, Simone's *Annunciation* uses a gold background and elongated figures, the edges of whose drapery create a sinuous surface pattern quite independent of the bodies beneath.

The mutability of style during this period can be seen again in Simone's frescoes for the Montefiore Chapel in the lower church at Assisi (Fig. 2.30), painted for the Franciscan cardinal Gentile Partino da Montefiore (d. 1312) and variously dated from 1312 to c. 1330. The cycle depicts events in the life of St. Martin of Tours. When compared to both earlier and later work by Simone these frescoes demonstrate clearly that he had access to a variety of stylistic possibilities and used them as they were appropriate to the subject matter of his painting. For this narrative sequence he employed a naturalism reminiscent of the work of Giotto. Although the musicians standing at the right of *The Investiture of St. Martin* are dressed in rich

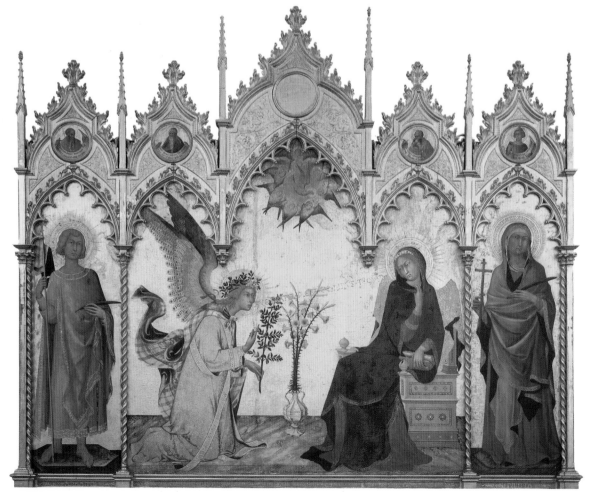

2.29 *Annunciation*, c. 1329/31–33, commissioned, presumably by the Opera del Duomo, from SIMONE MARTINI for the altar of St. Ansanus, Siena Cathedral. Tempera and gold leaf on panel, 10′ × 8′ 9″ (3 × 2.67 m) (Galleria degli Uffizi, Florence)

The flanking figures of St. Ansanus and St. Margaret (?) may have been painted by Lippo Memmi, Simone's brother-in-law and assistant. They were already cut from the central panel by the eighteenth century. The present frame is modern.

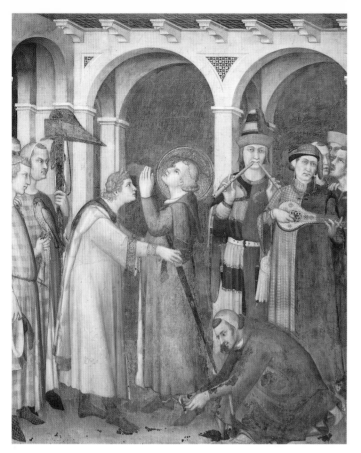

2.30 *The Investiture of St. Martin*, c. 1320–30, commissioned by Gentile Partino da Montefiore from SIMONE MARTINI for the Lower Church, San Francesco, Assisi. Fresco, width c. 9′ 2¼″ (2.8 m)

decorative robes befitting princely retainers (St. Martin here being made a knight), they betray their concern for singing the notes correctly by their worried facial expressions and the difficulty of blowing through the pipes by bulbous cheeks. The volumetric density of the figures and the carefully structured architectural frames were most likely painted in the years between the Gothic elegance of Simone's *Maestà* and his *Annunciation*, thus precluding any simple description of his style as moving in a linear fashion toward naturalism.

By 1342, when Pietro Lorenzetti (active 1306–48 Siena), the brother of Ambrogio, completed his *Birth of the Virgin* (Fig. 2.31) for the altar of St. Savinus (see Fig. 1.12) in Siena's cathedral, the stylistic unity for the overall program for the cathedral altars had been breached. Pietro's Florentine training dominates this painting and suggests that the new naturalistic style was beginning to win favor even in Siena. Like Simone's *Annunciation*, Pietro's *Birth of the Virgin* is divided into three panels; but unlike Simone, whose three panels are each self-contained, Pietro has created a unified illusionistic space

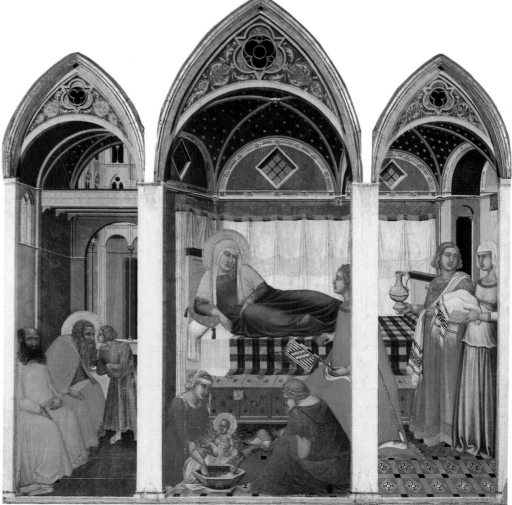

2.31 *Birth of the Virgin*, c. 1335–42, commissioned by the Opera del Duomo from PIETRO LORENZETTI for the altar of St. Savinus, Siena Cathedral. Tempera on panel, 6′1½″ × 5′ 11½″ (1.87 × 1.82 m) (Museo dell'Opera del Duomo, Siena)

across the three panels and treated his subject with all the anecdotal detail familiar in Florentine painting of this time. His only apparent debt to local Sienese traditions is his use of richly decorative details such as those of the floor tiling and the bedclothes. The stylistic differences between Simone's and Pietro's altarpieces can be explained in several ways: differences of artistic training and personal style; the artists' willingness or unwillingness to transform their individual styles to conform to that of an existing image at the site; and, politically, from the wishes of the Nine to suggest close relations with their erstwhile rival Florence, to which they were allied as members of the Tuscan League by the time Pietro received his commission. In any event, the altarpieces around Duccio's *Maestà*, which also include a *Purification of the Virgin* (1342) by Ambrogio Lorenzetti and a later *Nativity* (c. 1361) by Pietro's student Bartolomeo Bulgarini (active 1337–78 Siena), provided the Sienese with a telling display of the richly varied work of their greatest painters and of the greatness of their own city.

Sculpture

Tino di Camaino (c. 1280 Siena–1337 Naples), a leading early fourteenth-century Sienese sculptor trained in the workshop of Giovanni Pisano, was *capomaestro* of the cathedral workshop of Siena in 1319–20. His only authenticated work in that city is the marble tomb of Cardinal Riccardo Petroni (d. 1314), begun around 1318. The Petroni Tomb (Fig. 2.32) would originally have been partly painted, and areas such as the decorative borders of the cardinal's chasuble would have been filled with colored glass paste, giving the monument greater impact within the cathedral's somber black and white interior than it now has. The front face of the Petroni Tomb carries three reliefs of biblical narrative, whose subject matter—the *Noli Me Tangere*, the *Resurrection*, and the *Incredulity of St. Thomas*—all relate to the Resurrection and are thus appropriate for a funerary monument. In their massive and blocky forms the figures of the Petroni Tomb seem more like those of the marble pulpit of the cathedral carved by Nicola and Giovanni Pisano, Arnolfo di Cambio, and Lapo (see Fig. 1.13) than the elongated and restless figures by Giovanni Pisano and his workshop decorating the cathedral's façade. The images on the tomb and their arrangement derive in part from papal and curial tombs, particularly in details such as the angels holding apart the curtains that surround the figure of the dead cardinal. Using a tomb type imitating Roman sources and most often seen in the papal city, the Petroni Tomb suggests the international language of the Church, while its style refers to an earlier decorative program in the cathedral.

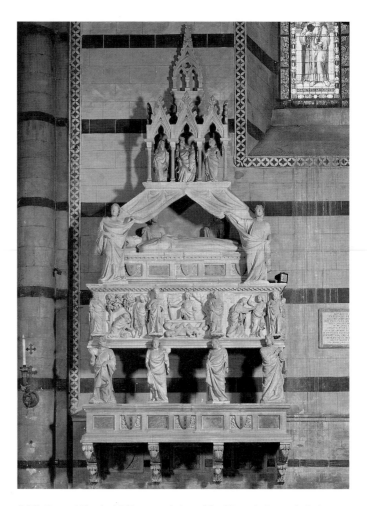

2.32 *Petroni Tomb*, 1318, commissioned by Riccardo Petroni's heirs from TINO DA CAMAINO for Siena Cathedral. Marble, height 51⅛" (130 cm)

Arezzo: The Tarlati Tomb   In contrast to the Petroni monument, no devout imagery adorns the Tarlati Tomb (c. 1329–32; Fig. 2.33) by three Sienese sculptors, Agostino di Giovanni (active 1310–c. 1347), Agnolo di Ventura (active 1312–49), and Agostino's son, Giovanni d'Agostino (c. 1311–c.1347), in the Duomo of Arezzo. A grandiose monument glorifying the reign of the Tarlati family in Arezzo and in particular Bishop Guido Tarlati who is buried in it, the tomb strains the boundaries of propriety for personal commemoration. For one thing, it is enormous, filling one entire bay wall of the cathedral. The monument bears sixteen narrative reliefs representing important events in the history of the Tarlati family and of Arezzo under Guido Tarlati's tenure as bishop. The effect is strongly reminiscent of the imperial reliefs on Roman triumphal arches, although here rather flatly carved. In some of the panels, such as the *Comune in Signoria* (Fig. 2.34) where a prisoner at the right is about to be beheaded while another, kneeling, pleads his case before the seated judge, the sculptors used compositional

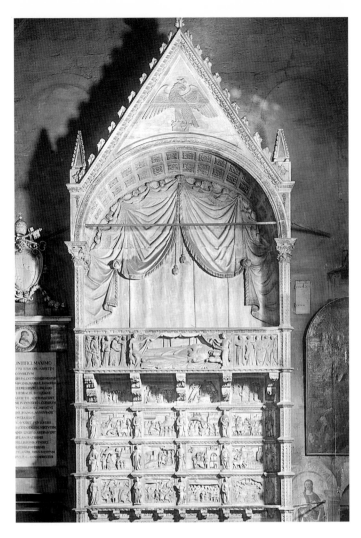

2.33 *Tarlati Tomb*, c. 1329–32, commissioned by Guido Tarlati's brother, Pietro Saccone, from AGOSTINO DI GIOVANNI, AGNOLO DI VENTURA, and GIOVANNI D'AGOSTINO for Arezzo Cathedral. Marble

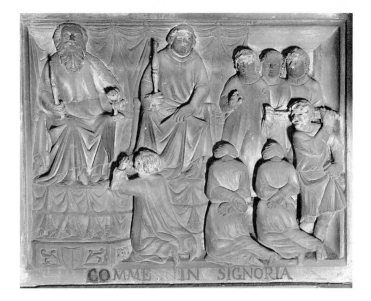

2.34 *Tarlati Tomb*, detail showing the *Comune in Signoria*. Marble relief

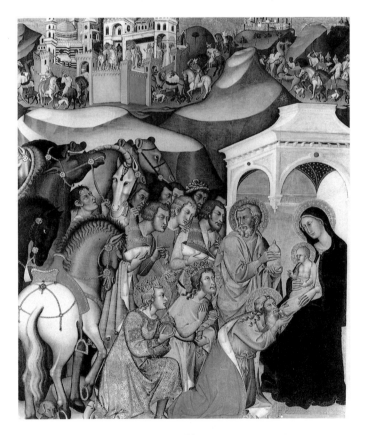

2.35 *Adoration of the Magi*, 1390s (?), BARTOLO DI FREDI. Tempera on panel (Pinacoteca Nazionale, Siena)

devices comparable to those in Lorenzetti's *Allegory of Good Government* to indicate the stability of Arezzo's government under the Tarlati. The only other contemporary instance of non-biblical narrative reliefs on tombs are found on those of major saints, where events from the saint's life are depicted. Guido Tarlati's tomb was unique in the unabashedly secular character of its decoration. Significantly, it was not imitated.

The Tarlati Tomb marks an early appropriation by an individual (the commissioner, Pier Saccone, the bishop's brother and executor) of civic imagery for use as propaganda for one family. The political intent of the tomb and its reliefs was not lost on the citizens of Arezzo, who defaced the monument when the Tarlati were finally expelled in 1341.

Later Sienese Painting

Sienese painting in the second half of the fourteenth century perpetuates the figural styles established earlier in the century by Duccio and Simone Martini despite the work of the Lorenzetti brothers, as if the efficacy of the images depended upon recognizable models. This conservatism may have been a reaction to the political uncertainty that prevailed after the expulsion of the Nine in 1355. For example, the *Adoration of the Magi* (1390s?; Fig. 2.35) by Bartolo di Fredi (active 1353–97 Siena) employs the same curiously stylized rock-like structures for mountains, compressed space, arabesque curves of drapery, and

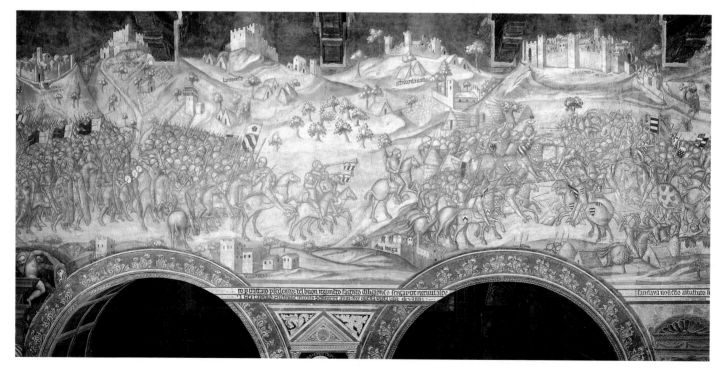

2.36 *Madonna and Child*, 1362, NICCOLÒ DI SER SOZZO and LUCA DI TOMMÉ. Tempera and gold leaf on panel (Pinacotecca Nazionale, Siena)

elongated figures previously encountered in Duccio's *Maestà* (see Fig. 2.19). Almost as if in conscious opposition to Florentine style, painters such as Niccolò di ser Sozzo (active 1334–63 Siena) and his sometime collaborator Luca di Tommé (active 1356–89 Siena) created altarpieces (Fig. 2.36) that to all intents and purposes are indistinguishable from those of the earlier part of the century. They are a measure of the wealth of the city and its patrons, who were able to afford the lavish use of gold in these paintings. They may also reflect an attitude on the part of the Sienese that their distinctive style of painting was a civic treasure to be cherished and maintained as a political act of self-definition distinguishing Siena, through its art, from its neighboring—and rival—city-states.

Ever aware of their history, the government of Siena commissioned the painter and miniaturist Lippo Vanni (active 1341–75 Siena) to record their victory in the Val di Chiana over English mercenaries in 1363 (Fig. 2.37). His monochromatic fresco, like many such civic images painted exclusively in central Italian town halls, records the progress of the battle and the disposition of the troops episodically across the wall; it is a graphic chronicle of the event rather than a naturalistic reconstruction, with cities carefully labeled and the armies identified by the heraldic flags of their leaders. Here, then, we have yet another approach to painting—it, too, like iconic objects of devotion, religious narrative, and political allegory—determined by the function it was intended to serve.

2.37 *Victory of the Sienese Troops at the Val di Chiana in 1363*, c. 1364 (?), LIPPO VANNI, Sala del Mappamondo, Palazzo Pubblico, Siena. Fresco

Naples and Milan: Images of Dynasty, Power, and Magnificence

Republics like Florence and Siena were hardly alone in exploiting the arts to express civic values. In autocratically controlled city-states like Naples and Milan, art and architecture were calculated to promote the centralized power and authority of a single ruler. His will, not the collective decisions of leading citizens, determined the city-state's policies and actions. The ruler was advised by aristocrats and highly educated bureaucrats who constituted his court, but he determined its character, having final say on every governmental decision, from new trade agreements to the design of the court livery worn by those who served him.

Courts were very agreeable places of employment for artists. Recent scholarship suggests that appreciation for individual artistic genius had its origin in aristocratic and royal courts, where distinctive accomplishment was extravagantly rewarded, rather than in the more consensual, relatively egalitarian world of the Italian republics. Unlike republics, where artists were viewed mainly as craftsmen and had to seek individual commissions on an entrepreneurial basis, courts usually guaranteed artists' salaries, food, and lodging and provided enhanced social status by association with the ruler. To be sure, court artists often had to create works on short notice and needed to please their employer, but so did their counterparts working in the mercantile republics. Artists sensitively gauged the needs of their patrons.

Taken together, artistic commissions in Naples and Milan demonstrate a wide range of strategies for securing and extending political power over a sometimes recalcitrant citizenry. By importing artists from northern Europe and luring the best artists from other Italian centers—Cavallini, Giotto, and Simone Martini, for example—patrons in Naples and Milan enriched their cities and broadened the range of artistic styles available across the Italian peninsula.

Naples: The Court and the Importation of Artists

The best early view of Naples, the so-called *Tavola Strozzi* of 1464 (Fig. 2.38), shows a city that shares numerous similarities with the cities we have already examined. A dense urban fabric, partially dating from its ancient Greek past, accommodates many churches, including several major mendicant complexes crowning the city's skyline. Walls and a fortified harbor provide impressive defense. The single most prominent building, however, is not the city's cathedral, which housed the miracle-working remains of its patron saint, Gennaro, but the seaside fortress, the Castel Nuovo (completed in 1284), which served as the residence of the kings of Naples. Situated apart and aloof from the rest of the city, this structure embodied both the power and the wariness of an autocratic ruler. Even the most fortified of the republics' city halls, the Palazzo della Signoria in Florence (see Fig. 1.18), stood accessible and vulnerable on a major civic

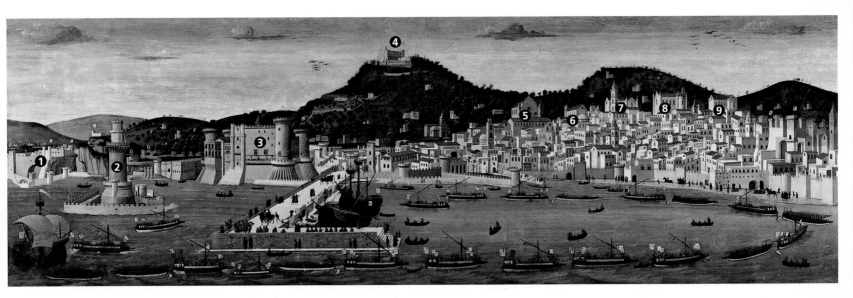

2.38 *Panorama of Naples (Tavola Strozzi)*, 1464. Tempera on panel (Gallerie Nazionali di Capodimonte, Naples)

1 Castel dell'Ovo; **2** Molo di San Vincenzo; **3** Castello Aragonese (Castel Nuovo); **4** Certosa di San Martino; **5** Santa Chiara; **6** San Domenico Maggiore; **7** San Lorenzo Maggiore; **8** Duomo; **9** San Giovanni a Carbonara

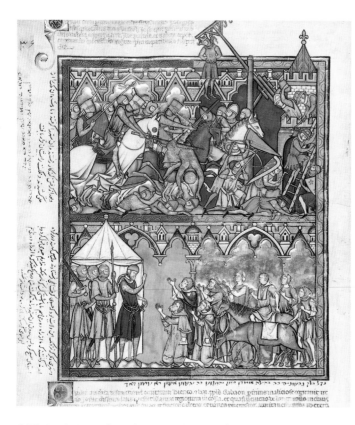

2.39 *Battle Scene from the Book of Joshua*, from an *Old Testament Picture Book*, c. 1250, commissioned by a royal patron in Paris. Vellum, 15⅜ × 11¾" (39 × 30 cm) (Pierpont Morgan Library, ms. 638, fol. 10V, New York)

Parisian artists were major exporters of portable works of art, including manuscripts and small devotional panels in ivory.

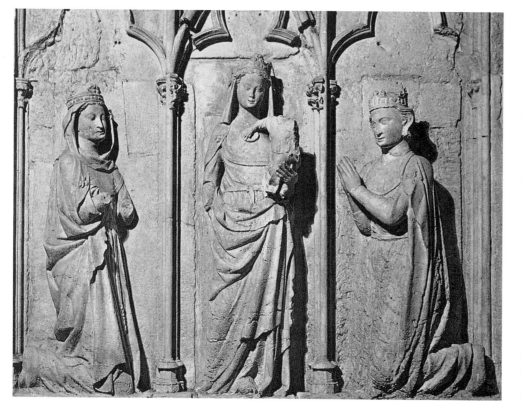

square. Here, by contrast, several lines of defense surrounded the imposing castle of the king of Naples in order to isolate and protect him from his subjects.

The Neapolitan court in the late thirteenth century was dominated by foreigners. In 1264 Pope Clement IV (r. 1264–68) granted Charles of Anjou, brother of King Louis IX of France and the first of the Angevin kings of Naples, sovereignty over all of southern Italy (the so-called Kingdom of the Two Sicilies). King Charles hired artists to help him validate his new dynasty, sustaining his rule not only with military subsidies from the papacy but by a policy of political and cultural imperialism. Charles placed Frenchmen in charge of all his government agencies, and he also imported French masters and craftsmen to undertake his artistic projects. (When he founded several new monasteries he even insisted that the monks come from France.) Local artists were allowed only menial tasks; the literal importation of Gothic forms which Charles required demanded workers from abroad.

Some works of art were imported from France—among them some illuminated manuscripts displaying the confident and festive forms characteristic of Parisian art. An Old Testament picture book produced in Paris around 1250 probably made its way to Naples by the late thirteenth century (Fig. 2.39). The miniatures in this manuscript are extremely large, leaving barely enough room for an Italian scribe to add a few lines of text identifying each scene. The detail shown, of a battle, captures the dynamic energy of the conflict. Clear and brilliant color, complex poses, and entangled figures command attention in a manner that may recall destroyed wall paintings and other large-scale compositions from mid-thirteenth century Paris.

Fragments of a royal tomb for the French queen Isabella of Aragon suggest the sophistication of sculpture in southern Italy during Charles's reign (Fig. 2.40). A royal stonecarver was probably dispatched to Cosenza soon after January 28, 1271, when Isabella died there. Her husband, Philip III (nephew of Charles of Anjou; r. 1270–85), took her bones back with him to the royal burial

2.40 *Philip the Bold and Isabella of Aragon Kneeling before the Virgin*, 1271–76, commissioned by Philip III from a Parisian sculptor for Cosenza Cathedral

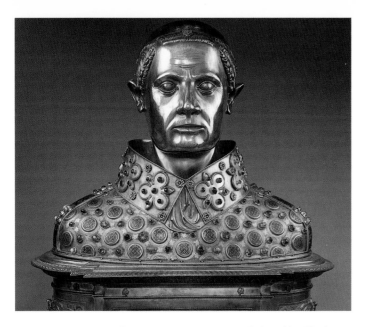

2.41 *Reliquary Bust of San Gennaro*, 1304, commissioned by Charles II of Anjou from ETIENNE GODEFROYD, GUILLAUME DE VERDELAY, and MILET D'AUXERRE. Gold and silver with inlaid enamel and multicolored jewels (Cathedral Treasury, Naples)

Relics were carried through city streets on festival days and in times of peril.

church of St. Denis, outside Paris, but he left her entrails in Cosenza, following the common French practice of dispersing royal bodies for entombment and hence commemoration and recognition in several locations.

Life-sized portraits of the French king and queen kneel before an under-life-sized Virgin and Child. The heads of the royal couple are placed deferentially lower than Mary, the Queen of Heaven, but the larger size of the king and queen accentuates their royal status. The figures' alert demeanor and the soft but precise folds of their garments invite comparison with such famous works of the 1260s as the regal *Vierge Dorée* of Amiens Cathedral or the life-sized prophets that stand gracefully before the piers inside Louis IX's Sainte Chapelle in Paris. Like them, the Cosenza figures were surely intended to be painted in the bold, rich colors and patterns seen in the *Old Testament Picture Book* (see Fig. 2.39).

Charles and members of his court were active as patrons of luxury arts. Continuing this practice, in 1304, Charles's son and successor, Charles II (1254–1309), commissioned three Provençal goldsmiths, Etienne Godefroyd, Guillaume de Verdelay, and Milet d'Auxerre, to produce a reliquary bust of the patron saint of Naples, San Gennaro (Fig. 2.41). Probably intended to mark the one-thousandth anniversary of the saint's martyrdom and thus to link the Angevin dynasty directly to Naples' most ancient and sacred Christian history, the figure consists of a head even more lifelike than the representation of Philip the Bold at Cosenza. Because the reliquary was intended to hold the surviving bones of the saint's cranium—its head is hinged just between its tonsure (ritualistically shaved head) and tight wavy hair—it has good reason to suggest as much as possible the actual features

of the saint. Slight bags under the eyes and lines to their sides, along with somewhat sagging cheeks, offset the otherwise traditional conventions of saintly passivity and immobility. What might be read as merely bejeweled splendor is in fact a cunning use of color and rich materials to associate the saint and the Angevin dynasty. The head emerges from a broad collar enlivened with blue and red gems (the Angevin heraldic colors) set on multi-lobed decorations that recall the royal fleur-de-lys, a motif that recurs across the saint's chest and shoulders in red and blue inlaid enamels alternating with different-colored gems. As the faithful offered their prayers to this image of their city's patron, they also saw emblems of their kings—rulers who exploited the divine to reinforce their reign.

Architectural Commissions in Naples

The Angevin kings expected members of their court to sponsor works in the French style. In 1270 three of Charles I's courtiers, Jean d'Autun, Jean de Lyon, and Guy

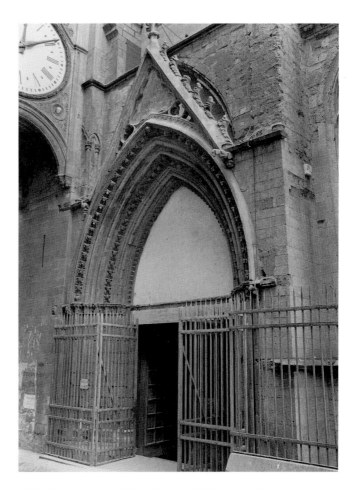

2.42 Side portal, Sant'Eligio, Naples, 1270, commissioned by Jean d'Autun, Jean de Lyon, and Guy de Bourguignon

de Bourguignon, hired French master masons to supervise the erection of a church and hospital for war veterans near King Charles's new public markets—that is, in the southeastern corner of the city relatively near the harbor. Dedicated to three of royal France's most revered saints, Eloi (or Eligio, the name by which it is now known), Denis, and Martin of Tours, it exemplifies the elegance of Gothic architecture. The interior boasts finely detailed, extremely graceful cross-ribbed vaults supported by stylishly narrow and highly pointed arches. On the exterior, a side portal (Fig. 2.42) features multiple arches crowned by a steep gable as well as ornamentation based on designs of the 1260s used on the north transept of Notre Dame in Paris.

For San Lorenzo Maggiore, Naples's largest Franciscan church, Charles I's architects began the work in the king's preferred northern mode, exploiting the sophisticated technology of flying buttresses to support a complex sys-

tem of vaults over a soaring choir (Figs. 2.43 and 2.44). But so much effort must have gone into trying to make the buttresses from the weak local tufa (volcanic stone) that French masons did not attempt as many fine details as at Sant'Eligio. Thus already by the early 1280s Charles's attempts to impose French style were being compromised by local exigencies. Tracery designs at San Lorenzo Maggiore show the direct influence of St. Denis in Paris, but the execution of the leafwork and capitals was increasingly standardized and repetitive rather than newly invented. The cavernous nave and its unarticulated walls bring to mind Franciscan churches throughout Italy (Santa Croce in Florence, for example; see Fig. 1.21).

As construction proceeded into the fourteenth century at San Lorenzo Maggiore and at other churches in Naples, Charles I's strategy of artistic imperialism gave way to more expedient practices of accommodation and coexistence. French Gothic forms continued to fill win-

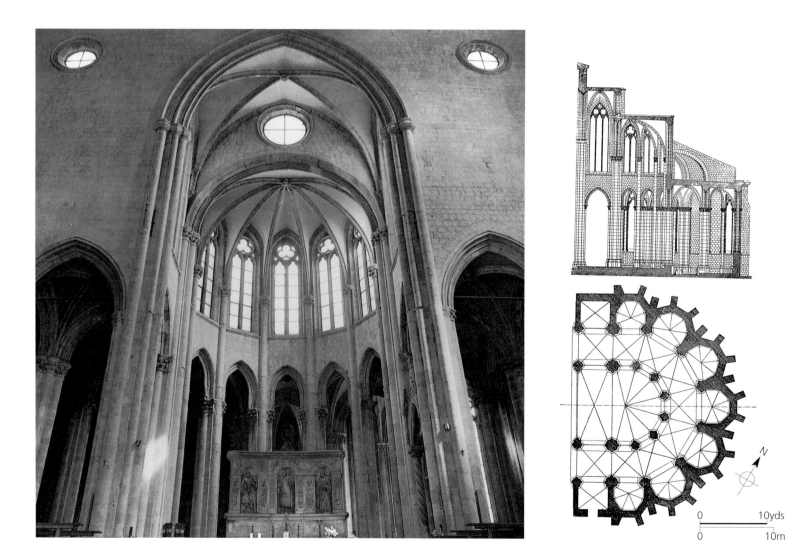

2.43 San Lorenzo Maggiore, Naples, begun early 1280s, commissioned by the Franciscans with support from Charles I and Charles II of Anjou and their court

2.44 San Lorenzo Maggiore, Naples, elevation and plan

dows and serve as decorative details, but only the elegant and refined spirit, not the structure, of earlier Gothic buildings prevailed. Charles's children and grandchildren continued to admire aspects of French culture, but as the Angevins found themselves comfortably ensconced in Naples, it made sense for them to take greater interest in artistic developments in Italy than those in France. The period of outright importation of French styles and workmen, then, was relatively short-lived, but it added significant new forms to the visual repertoire available to Neapolitan artists and patrons.

Consolidating Angevin Rule: A Queen's Commissions

Charles of Anjou's son, Charles II, oversaw the completion of many of his father's building projects, while his wife, Queen Mary of Hungary (d. 1323), initiated an active tradition of royal female patronage in Naples. Founding the convent of Santa Maria Donnaregina in 1307, she provided a propitious site for her own retirement and eventual burial close by the city's cathedral (Figs. 2.45 and 2.46). As at San Lorenzo, the apse of Mary's church was conceived as a luminous cage for stained glass, its brightness made especially compelling by the lower, dark nave that precedes it. Above the nave, and necessitating the construction of piers and vaults that darken it, is a substantial nuns' choir. While lay worshippers entered the church and spent much of the mass in semi-darkness, Mary and her fellow nuns found them-

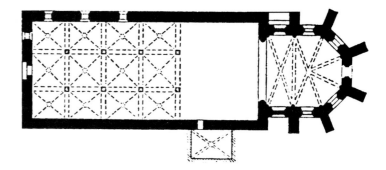

2.46 Santa Maria Donnaregina, Naples, plan

selves surrounded by the glowing stained glass windows and an extensive but poorly preserved fresco cycle. Adapting the general scheme of Cavallini's frescoes at Santa Cecilia in Rome (see Fig. 1.37), the program includes a *Last Judgment* on the back wall, Old and New Testament scenes in three tiers on the side walls, saints' lives beyond them, and a celestial vision above the apse. The nuns' view of the apse and saints was partially obscured by a screen at the end of their choir, but the rest of the imagery was constantly visible. Deriving from the grand schemes of papal Rome, and therefore full of historical resonance, the frescoes provided these religious women with a rich compendium of subjects for contemplation and meditation.

Cavallini and Giotto in Naples The frescoes at Santa Maria Donnaregina document the impact of Pietro Cavallini's arrival in Naples in 1308, the narrative scenes having been painted by a large coterie of his followers and artists from other centers. A series of prophets that includes King David (Fig. 2.47) may come directly from Cavallini's hand. Like the faces of the apostles in the *Last Judgment* at Santa Cecilia in Rome (see Fig. 1.37), David's visage is evocatively rendered. Soft shadows, delicate highlights, rounded volume, and the shift of the figure's eyes make for a compelling, even riveting portrayal.

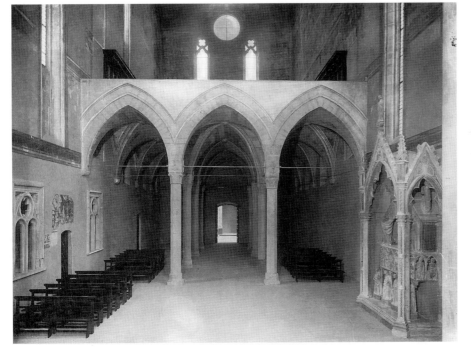

2.45 Santa Maria Donnaregina, Naples, founded 1307, commissioned by Queen Mary of Hungary

The queen's coats of arms appear in the keystones of the vaults. She is buried in a handsome tomb within the church (see Fig. 2.54).

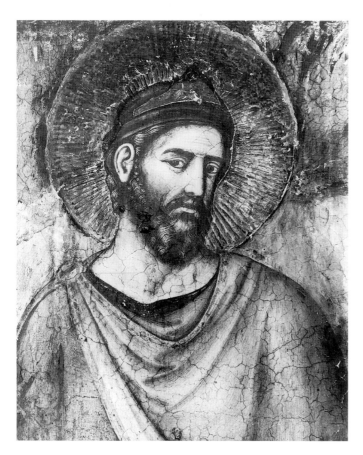

2.47 *David*, detail of the head, after 1308, commissioned by Queen Mary of Hungary from Pietro Cavallini for Santa Maria Donnaregina, Naples. Fresco

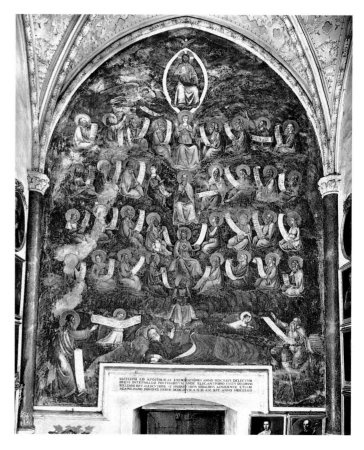

2.49 *Tree of Jesse*, c. 1320, commissioned by Uberto d'Ormont from Lello da Orvieto for Naples Cathedral. Fresco

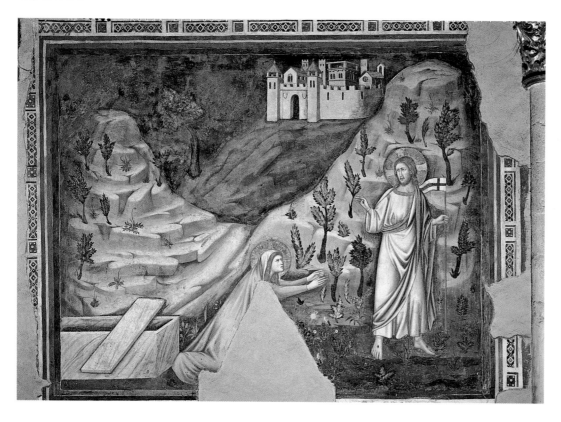

2.48 *Noli Me Tangere*, c. 1310, probably commissioned by Cardinal Landolfo Brancaccio from a Follower of Giotto for his family chapel in San Domenico Maggiore, Naples. Fresco

Other scenes in the chapel depict events in the lives of the apostles Andrew and Peter.

Unfortunately, only a small portion survives of the painting produced in early fourteenth-century Naples that decorated the many new buildings erected by the Angevins. Judging from this remnant our loss of the others is an artistic disaster. The fragmentary, undocumented, and contested works that remain indicate that Angevin rulers and other Neapolitan patrons commissioned works that were second to none in Italy, both in their quantity and quality. Giotto, for example, was a member of the royal household from December 1328

until 1332, actively producing frescoes and panel paintings, now lost. His imprint, though not his hand, is clearly visible in frescoes produced by one of his followers in the Brancaccio Chapel in San Domenico Maggiore, a royal foundation of 1283 (Fig. 2.48). In the *Noli Me Tangere* (literally, "do not touch me," Christ's command to Mary Magdalene when she encountered him newly resurrected) the artist exploits landscape as a foil for human interaction much as Giotto had done at the Scrovegni Chapel in Padua (see Fig. 2.2). The composition is anchored around the imploring figure of the Magdalene, her triangular form repeated in the hill on which she kneels before Christ. The lid of Christ's tomb, set in the lower left of the panel, propels the action up the hill from left to right. In the background a substantial walled city, presumably Jerusalem, glimmers in contrast to the darker hill on which it is set. While the vegetation remains highly schematic, the drapery of the figures is convincingly modeled in light and shade as it falls softly around their bodies. The intensity of the gazes exchanged by the holy figures also compares with the increasing attention to psychological awareness seen first in the frescoes at Assisi (see Figs. 1.47 and 1.48) and later in Giotto's works (see Fig. 2.4).

The enduring impact of both Cavallini's and Giotto's innovations can be seen in the work of Lello da Orvieto, who, like so many artists, was called to Naples from central Italy. Around 1320 Lello painted his impressive *Tree of Jesse* (Fig. 2.49) on the side wall of the Chapel of St. Paul in Naples Cathedral for Archbishop Uberto d'Ormont. The subject would not initially appear to lend itself very well to naturalistic depiction; it is a genealogical table of Christ's ancestors, reaching back to the Old Testament patriarch Jesse, from whom the tree issues. Christ's ancestors are placed, as always, up the central trunk of the tree; prophets, sages, and

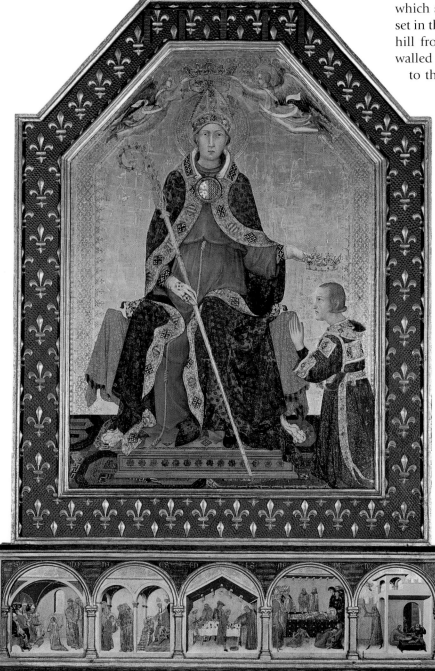

2.50 *Altarpiece of St. Louis of Toulouse*, c. 1319, commissioned by Robert of Anjou from SIMONE MARTINI. Tempera on panel, with a gilt-glass morse and now-lost paste pearls and gems on the cope; main panel 78¾ × 54¼" (200 × 138 cm), predella 22 × 54" (56 × 138 cm) (Gallerie Nazionali di Capodimonte, Naples). See also Fig. 2.1.

The patterns inscribed in the gold surface around the perimeter of the main panel, on the saint's halo, his mitre, and the crown he holds over the head of King Robert were produced with dies that were repeatedly punched into the surface. Punch marks often differ from one artist's studio to another.

saints fill its branches. Unlike most earlier representations of this subject, however, Lello's tree has real life and substance. The figures actually seem to sit or recline upon the soft, cushion-like foliage, and they turn to one another and gesticulate, showing off their scrolls or pointing to the figure of Christ at the very top of the composition. At the bottom left of the wall we see a figure from the back striding into the scene, inviting the viewer to imagine him- or herself doing the same. The figure of Jesse (now greatly damaged) reclines in the middle. To the right a man on horseback also raises his hand and draws us into this very palpable vision. Similar in composition to Taddeo Gaddi's *Tree of Life* in the refectory of Santa Croce in Florence (see Fig. 2.14), Lello's work is also didactic but more approachable and visually alluring, bearing witness to the warm humanity of Cavallini and Giotto's schools in Naples.

Robert of Anjou

When Robert of Anjou succeeded to the throne of Naples in 1309 he continued the lavish patronage of his parents and completed the transformation of the city into one of the most impressive in Europe. Known as Robert the Wise, King Robert was a highly learned ruler, a characteristic recorded by both Dante and Petrarch. Robert's assumption of power in southern Italy, although planned by his father, Charles II, was not completely uncontested. He was, in fact, the third son; his oldest brother, Charles Martel (named after the illustrious Frankish ruler), had died in 1295, leaving a young son, (see p. 482) Carobert (Carlo Roberto) to succeed him as heir to the thrones of both Hungary and Naples. Charles II, however, refused to accept his grandson as his successor. Charles II's second son, Louis, was especially devoted to the Franciscan order and renounced his claim to the throne of Naples in the summer of 1296 in order to join the Franciscans. A few months later, Pope Boniface VIII made a reluctant Louis bishop of Toulouse. Scarcely had Louis arrived in his diocese when, on August 19, 1297, he died. This left Robert the designated heir to Charles II.

The Altarpiece of St. Louis   Soon after Louis's death, his father launched a campaign to have him canonized, a project pursued with equal vigor by his brother Robert after Charles II's own death. Louis was finally proclaimed a saint in April 1317 by John XXII in Avignon; he thus joined with other canonized members of his family, including Louis IX of France (his grandfather's brother) and Queen Elizabeth of Hungary (the great-aunt of Sancia of Majorca, Robert's wife), to form a heavenly pantheon of support for the Angevin household. To exploit

the saintly connection and so enhance his family's legitimacy, Robert commissioned a huge altarpiece depicting his older brother placing the crown on his head. Given Robert's close political ties to Siena, it is not surprising that he called Simone Martini, Siena's leading painter, to Naples to paint this monumentally scaled panel.

In Simone's *Altarpiece of St. Louis of Toulouse* (Fig. 2.50; see also Fig. 2.1), the saint is seated in a rigid frontal pose. His staring immobility recalls earlier saints' altarpieces (see Figs. 1.25 and 1.26) and implicitly declares his status as an intercessor with God. Despite placing diagonals on the floor to create perspective and treating his head, hands, and abdomen volumetrically, Simone makes it clear that St. Louis belongs to a realm outside normal time and space. Louis's left hand and the royal crown it touches hover against the elaborately tooled gold ground. This is obviously celestial space, as indicated by the angels at the top of the altarpiece, who award an even more precious heavenly diadem to Louis. The coronation of the king thus parallels the crowning of God's saint, lending divine sanction and protection to Robert's rule.

The extraordinary luxury of the painting—especially in the richly embroidered and gold-tooled cloak which Louis wears over the drab brown tunic of a mendicant Franciscan—conveys clearly that this is a royal image. Angevin territorial claims also figure prominently in it. The frame of the painting (original) surrounds the two brothers with the Angevin crest of the gold fleur-de-lys on a blue ground. The red and yellow heraldic colors of Provence, of which Louis was count, and the crest of the city of Jerusalem, to which the Angevins laid claim, also appear on the clasp of Louis's cloak, indicating the breadth of Robert's realm.

The Development of a Local School of Painting

It was not until the next generation of painters in Naples that the city could claim one of its own as a major contributor to the arts. The life of Roberto d'Oderisio (active c. 1330–1382 Naples) is not well documented, but he seems to have worked primarily during the third quarter of the fourteenth century. He is perhaps most famous for his expressionistic devotional paintings and for the frescoes attributed to him in the Church of the Incoronata (Fig. 2.51). There the principles of space, volume, and narrative focus advanced by Giotto and his followers in the first half of the century, along with the elegance of Simone Martini, have been completely integrated into the work of a southern Italian painter. At the center of the awkwardly shaped spandrel of the ceiling vaults Roberto shows a knight taking the hand of his bride in matrimony. (Unfortunately, her torso and

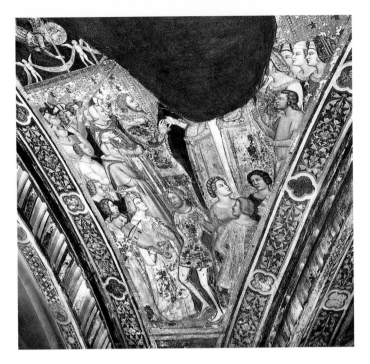

2.51 *The Sacrament of Marriage*, c. 1350–75, probably commissioned by a royal patron from ROBERTO D'ODERISIO for the Church of Santa Maria dell'Incoronata, Naples. Fresco

face, as well as that of the officiating priest, have been destroyed.) Crowding around them—men behind the groom, women behind the bride—are witnesses, many convincing enough to be portraits. Trumpeters, flag bearers, musicians, and dancers enliven the scene and document the lavishness of the Angevin court.

Monastic Sites of Royal Patronage

As part of their duties as divinely ordained rulers of Naples, Robert and his wife, Sancia of Majorca (1286–1345), built impressive monastic churches within the city. Queen Sancia was particularly instrumental in promoting the Franciscan order. Her commissions constitute an important chapter in the history of artistic patronage by women, begun by her mother-in-law Queen Mary of Hungary. Sancia apparently used her own inheritance as well as her dowry money to underwrite building costs, virtually independent of male control. The best-known of

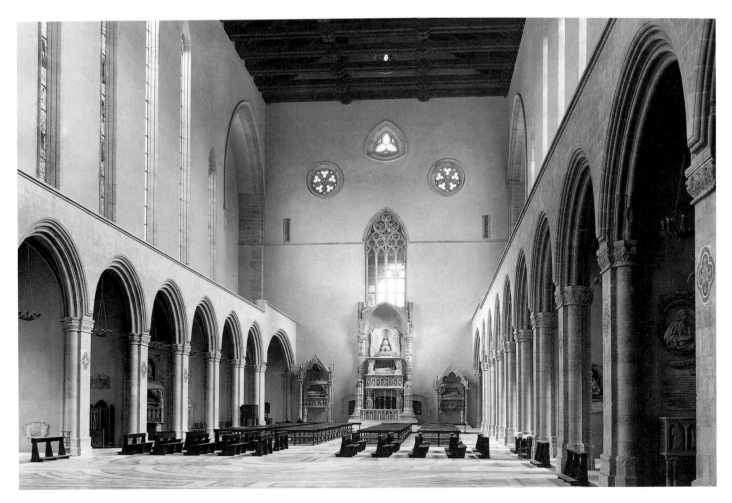

2.52 Santa Chiara, Naples, 1310, commissioned on behalf of the Franciscans by Sancia of Majorca probably from GAGLIARDO PRIMARIO

The church was severely damaged by bombs in World War II. Although its structure has been faithfully reconstructed, most of the church's extensive painted and sculptural decoration was destroyed.

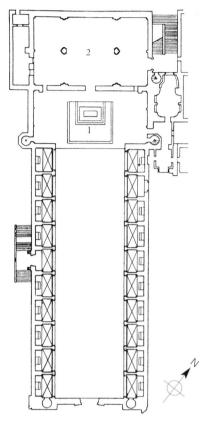

2.53 Santa Chiara, Naples, plan

1 High altar and Tomb of King Robert of Anjou of Naples; **2** Nuns' choir

Sancia's churches is that of Santa Chiara (Figs. 2.52 and 2.53), one of four convents she patronized in Naples. Although founded in 1310 for the Poor Clares, the female Franciscans, it ultimately expanded to a double convent, housing both men and women, and became a safe haven for the renegade Spiritual Franciscans, who espoused extreme poverty. Sancia herself had been a Clarissan novice before her marriage to Robert of Anjou in 1309, which explains her passionate support of the order through her artistic patronage of a church dedicated to the order's founder, St. Clare.

The architect of the church was most likely the Neapolitan, Gagliardo Primario (active 1306/7–48), an artist whose name appears in court documents but about whom little is known. Because the interior of the building was almost totally transformed during the baroque period and the structure itself bombed during World War II, the present church must be examined with care. Nonetheless, the reconstructed interior is one of the purest manifestations of the Italian Gothic style. The long, single-aisled nave is covered with a truss roof, as are the interiors of many other Franciscan Italian churches, such as Santa Croce in Florence (see Fig. 1.21). The walls, although massive in the typical Italian style, are pierced with tall lancet windows. The apse end of the building is

flat, and the windows in the center wall rise high to accommodate the multi-storied tomb of Robert of Anjou. From the sequestered choir behind, the nuns could view the elevation of the Host during Mass in the church. Sancia was particularly devoted to the Eucharist, and had originally wished to dedicate the church to Corpus Christi (the Body of Christ). It may have been the Queen's intervention that gave the nuns at Santa Chiara an unprecedented direct view of the high altar, allowing them to see as well as to hear mass.

Angevin Tombs

Probably as a result of the challenge to Robert's claims to the throne of Naples by his nephew, Carobert, the king continued to bolster his dynastic status with imposing works of art. As part of this strategy, he transformed the

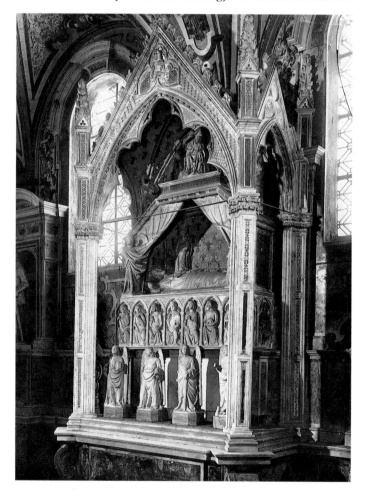

2.54 Tomb of Mary of Hungary, 1325, commissioned by Robert of Anjou from GAGLIARDO PRIMARIO and TINO DA CAMAINO for Santa Maria Donnaregina, Naples. Marble

The church in which this tomb is located was founded by the queen. A monumental balcony across the back of the church allowed resident nuns to worship unseen and undisturbed by the laity.

interior of Santa Chiara into a burial church for his branch of the house of Anjou. In fact, he seems to have intended to fill all of Naples with images of his family, which had ruled the city for a mere three generations. The campaign of sculpture was impressive, especially given the short period of its execution during Robert's reign. No fewer than ten members of the royal family had tomb monuments constructed in various Neapolitan churches during the twenty-year span between 1325 and 1345.

The Tomb of Mary of Hungary The first of the royal Angevin tombs in Naples was erected for Robert's mother, Mary of Hungary (Fig. 2.54). Because his grandfather, Charles of Anjou, had established a local school of builders, there was a competent architect on hand, Gagliardo Primario, to design the tomb's structure; but the king was obliged to go outside Naples to obtain the services of Tino da Camaino for the sculpture. Tino moved to Naples from Siena in 1323 and spent the remaining fourteen years of his life in Angevin employ. The tomb of Mary of Hungary was placed in Santa Maria Donnaregina, the church that Mary herself had built and into whose monastic community she retired after her husband's death in 1309 (see Fig. 2.45).

The sculpture on Mary's tomb emphasizes her success at providing male heirs: rulers not only for all of southern Italy but for Hungary as well—not to mention a saint. The sarcophagus is decorated with niches holding seated figures of her seven sons (tellingly her five daughters are not represented). As one might expect, St. Louis of Toulouse, her second son, occupies the central position of honor. To Louis's right—a position, then as now, connoting honor and privilege—sits a crowned Robert of Anjou holding symbols of royal power. To Louis's left sits Charles Martel, king of Hungary at his death in 1295. To the left of Robert of Anjou are Philip of Taranto and Pietro Tempesta, and to the right of Charles Martel are Giovanni di Durazzo and Raimondo Berengario. The side panels of the tomb show relief figures of court counselors, suggesting the queen's active involvement in affairs of state. The tomb chest itself is supported by figures of four virtues, standard funerary iconography of the time. Mary's own effigy has the long, curving lines of late Gothic forms. Her face is a crisply modeled ovoid reminiscent of the work of Simone Martini. The figures of the sons, however, derive from standard seated ruler iconography; they are repetitive and severe in their frontality, with heavily massed draperies, characteristic of Angevin monuments of this period.

The Tomb of Robert of Anjou The construction of Robert's own tomb in Santa Chiara (Fig. 2.55), undoubtedly planned, in intention if not in fact, before his death

in 1343, was formally overseen by his granddaughter and successor, Giovanna I. The sculptors Pacio and Giovanni Bertini (documented 1343–45), like Tino, with whom they probably trained, and most of the other artists in Robert's employ, came from outside the region of Naples, in their case from Florence. The tomb is impressive not only because of its size but also because it looms over the main altar in front of the nuns' choir at the east end of the church. It thus is the focal point for a visitor entering the building, occupying a site normally reserved for the church's patron saint. The tomb now bears three carved images of Robert: a relief of the seated king at the center of the sarcophagus (obscured in Fig. 2.55), a

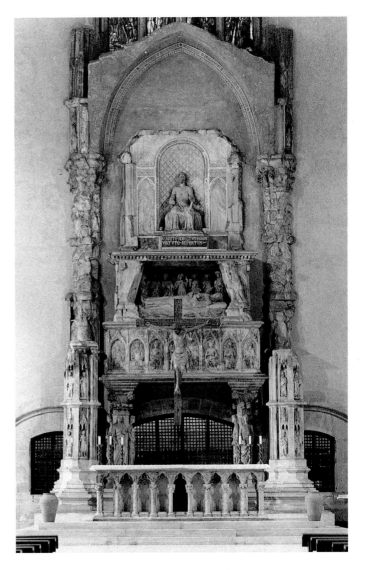

2.55 Tomb of King Robert of Anjou of Naples, planned c. 1343 (damaged in August 1943), commissioned by Giovanna I at the behest of Robert of Anjou from PACIO and GIOVANNI BERTINI of Florence for Santa Chiara, Naples

The grate in the wall behind the tomb allowed the cloistered nuns in the choir beyond to see the high altar during the celebration of the mass.

recumbent effigy on the sarcophagus itself and, above this, a free-standing seated (live) ruler under a canopy. Originally a fourth figure of the king, kneeling in a donor pose to the right of a Madonna and Child, appeared at the summit of the monument.

Like Simone's altarpiece depicting St. Louis of Toulouse, Robert's tomb indicates that he and his artists were intensely conscious of the power of traditional imagery to carry meaning. In the upper, seated figure of the king, Robert assumes a rigid pose derived from Roman antiquity and reserved for rulers. The Latin inscription at his feet translates, "Behold King Robert, recognized by his virtue." The use of the Latin term *virtus* is appropriate for a Christian tomb, with its hope for the afterlife, but may also refer to the original Roman meaning of the word, manliness, and its traditional connotations of strength and valor, concepts appropriate for a king.

The effigy of the dead king shows him crowned but also barefoot and in the tunic of a Franciscan friar, the clothes he had chosen for his burial. Whereas the crown symbolizes his secular power, the friar's tunic marks his devotion to the Franciscan order. Robert is depicted on the burial chest for yet a third time in relief in the center niche. He is flanked on the right by his first wife and his son and daughter-in-law. To the left of Robert, at his more prestigious right side, are the two main patrons of his tomb and this church: Sancia of Majorca, his second wife, who survived him by two years, and his successor and granddaughter Queen Giovanna I, as well as an unidentified male figure. At the sides of the chest are figures of two infants. Since Robert had the tombs of his son and daughter-in-law constructed in Santa Chiara, he was visually and actually surrounded by his family.

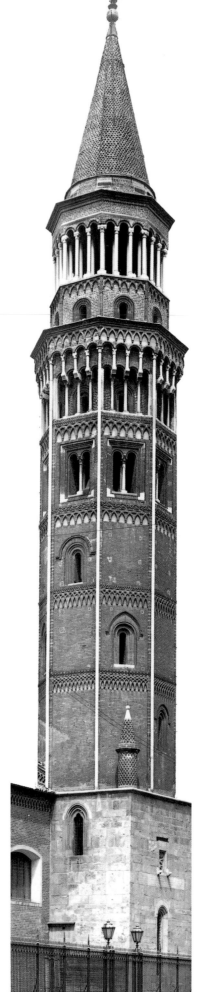

2.56 Tower, after 1330, commissioned by Azzone Visconti for San Gottardo, Milan

Milan: The Visconti

Milan, Italy's other dominant center of autocratic rule in the Renaissance, has always been open to innovation and a center of international exchange. Because the city has been rebuilt and reinvigorated so frequently, very few of its medieval and Renaissance neighborhoods survive. Still, Milan played a key cultural, economic, and political role in the Renaissance as a major commercial and industrial center. Especially renowned for the production of high-quality armor and armaments, the city also imported and developed rice and silk production from Asia.

As elsewhere in Italy, Milan's key civic monuments—the cathedral and ducal castle—date from the fourteenth and fifteenth centuries. Their grand scale owes much to Milan's proud Roman and medieval past. In the fourth century the Roman emperor Constantine chose Milan, over Rome, as his capital in the West. Strategically well placed in relation to northern Europe but protected to the north by the Alps, and with a population of nearly 100,000, Milan justly assumed the title of a new Rome. Conquered by the itinerant Lombards, it survived as an important civic center, eventually becoming a republic that led a federation of northern Italian city states, the so-called Lombard League. Eleventh-century Milan saw the design and construction of some of the very first rib vaults in Europe at the basilica of Sant'Ambrogio, dedicated to the city's first bishop and patron saint, Ambrose.

In the late thirteenth century, Milanese politics became increasingly dominated by struggles between two rival aristocratic clans: the Della Torre and the Visconti. In 1277 the Visconti, who were to rule Milan until the mid-fifteenth century, seized power, finally defeating their foes in 1294. The Visconti were of ancient Milanese stock, many of their number having served as archbishops of the city, giving the family a power within the city that it ultimately transformed into political rulership. Unlike the Angevins, who represented a foreign presence in Naples, they identified themselves with local traditions and were especially attentive to the city's imperial legacy and the reputation of her local saints. Splendor and magnificence were two hallmarks of their patronage.

Azzone Visconti and the Idea of Magnificence The first surviving, large-scale works of Visconti patronage date from the rule of Azzone Visconti (d. 1339), who revived the idea of a Lombard League with Milan as its capital. Seeking to forge a collective identity for the Milanese state, he embarked on a program of constructing churches, towers, and other public buildings, paving streets, and opening squares. The centerpiece of his building program was a palace complex close to Milan's cathedral. An extraordinarily detailed and vivid description of the palace by Azzone's court advisor, the Dominican friar Galvano Fiamma, admits us to the Milanese court. Fiamma both describes Azzone's palace and justifies its grandeur. Adopting Aristotle's notion of magnificence, Fiamma says that private expenditure by the prince is intended to create a kind of public magnificence that serves the common good. Investment in a palace with ample accommodation for court officials and offices impresses the public and keeps them from wishing to attack the ruler. Devoting funds to churches, which in Azzone's case included the reconstruction of Milan cathedral's bell tower, which had lain in ruins for several generations, confirmed his status as a pious, Christian prince.

Only the tower of San Gottardo (Fig. 2.56) survives from Azzone's palace complex, but, with its traditional Lombard crown of marble columns and an angel holding a banner with the Visconti coat of arms (which Fiamma says originally crowned it), it exemplifies Azzone's magnificence. The top of the tower included a clock with bells that rang out at every hour, defining time for the entire community. The chapel's interior was especially lavish: a choir with ivory paving and pulpits, stained glass windows, gold and silver reliquaries, and liturgical vessels encrusted with pearls, all now destroyed.

The adjoining Visconti palace was equally impressive. Fiamma describes in detail the exotic birds and animals that Azzone kept in cages in the palace, the lush gardens and numerous fountains, and all the other features intended to arouse wonder and awe in the beholder. When he boasts that blacksmiths, scribes, sculptors, glaziers, carpenters, and various other craftsmen all actually lived in the complex, the extent of Azzone's dedication to magnificent display becomes clear. Workers needed to be close at hand not only to decorate the palace but to provide the trappings for processions and ceremonies that took place regularly throughout the city, extending Azzone's splendid image wherever he went.

CONTEMPORARY VOICE

In Praise of Magnificence

The lavish expenditure of Azzone Visconti was not—according to his supporter Galvano Fiamma—inspired merely by a desire for self-glorification. A very respectable justification for such display could be found in the writings of the revered Greek philosopher Aristotle (384–322 B.C.). In the fourth book of Aristotle's *Nicomachean Ethics*, the philosopher praises lavish expenditure by those possessed of great wealth, provided its object is worthy: "The magnificent man is an artist in expenditure . . . he will think how he can carry out his project most nobly and splendidly, rather than how much it will cost and how it can be done most cheaply."

Fiamma demonstrates how his employer has applied Aristotle's precepts to his own residence:

Azzo Visconti, considering himself to have made peace with the Church and to be freed from all his enemies, resolved in his heart to make his house glorious, for the Philosopher says in the fourth book of the *Ethics* that it is a work of magnificence to construct a dignified house, since the people seeing marvellous buildings stand thunderstruck in fervent admiration, as is stated in the sixth book of the *Politics*. And from this they judge a Prince to be of such power that it is impossible to attack him. A magnificent habitation is also an appropriate place of residence for a multitude of officials. In addition, it is required of a magnificent prince that he build magnificent,

honourable churches, for which reason the Philosopher says in the fourth book of the *Ethics* that the honourable expenses which a magnificent prince should defray pertain to God. For this reason Azzo Visconti began work on two magnificent structures, the first for the purpose of divine worship, that is a marvellous chapel in honour of the Blessed Virgin, and a magnificent palace, fitting to be his dwelling.

(from Galvano Fiamma. "On the Magnificence of Buildings." Chapter 15 of *Opusculum de rebus gestis ab Azone, Euchino et Johanne Vicecomitibus*. Louis Green. "Galvano Fiamma, Azzone Visconti, and the Revival of the Classical Theory of Magnificence." *Journal of the Warburg and Courtauld Institutes*, 53 [1990]: p. 101)

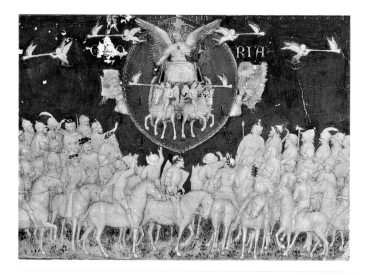

2.57 *Vainglory*, from Francesco Petrarch, *De Viris Illustribus*, after 1336, manuscript recording composition of frescoes in the palace of Azzone Visconti, Milan, originals probably by GIOTTO (Bibliothèque Nationale, ms. Lat. 6069, Paris, presentation copy, 1379, frontispiece "A")

Fiamma describes the multi-storied palace in meticulous detail, even including the washrooms. Its gardens included a courtyard ringed with paintings of the Punic wars. Another fresco of Vainglory celebrated the fame of Azzone in the company of Charlemagne and the leading founders of ancient cities. An idea of what part of this painting may have looked like can be gained from an illustration of Vainglory in a central chariot surrounded by an entourage of excited horsemen which is preserved in a later presentation copy of Petrarch's *Trionfi* (Fig. 2.57). There is good reason to think that the original may have been by Giotto, who was sent to Milan by the Signoria of Florence in 1335, having earlier decorated parts of the interior of the Angevin kings' castle in Naples. Seen variously from the back, side, and head on, the horsemen turn to one another and gesticulate in highly convincing ways.

Giotto's legacy also is clearly evident in a page illustrating the *Death of Jacob and Joseph* from the *Liber Pantheon of Goffredo da Viterbo*, an encyclopedic text copied in Milan in 1331, and dedicated by its scribe to Azzone (Fig. 2.58). The illustration displays an extraordinary range of human emotions and comportment. At the top and bottom left, female mourners throw themselves in expressive abandon on the corpses of Jacob and Joseph. At the bottom, men wait on a bench outside the death chamber, not yet aware of what has occurred, even though a man carrying a wood and rope bier on his back is already making his way up the rocky path. Among the seated men a figure stands as if to share the news, while another, who is presented almost entirely from the back, cranes to hear the message. The wait has been too long

for another, however, who slumps over in bored dejection, providing a dramatic foil to the concern on the face of his companion to the right and the outright anguish communicated by the upraised hands and tilted head of the next.

Azzone Visconti's Tomb   Azzone's image of princely magnificance continued in death. His tomb (Fig. 2.59) was placed in the palace chapel of San Gottardo, which he had so lavishly embellished. Attended by angels, his effigy rests on the cover of the sarcophagus, which is further decorated with relief sculpture commemorating his reign. At the center is Milan's patron, St. Ambrose (340–97), sheltering two seated figures, possibly Azzone's successor Lucchino Visconti (1292–1349) and the Holy Roman Emperor Ludwig of Bavaria (r.1314–46), from whom he had received the prestigious title of imperial vicar, or deputy. To his right and left kneel personifications of the cities that owed him allegiance, including Como, Brescia, and Monza, presented by their patron

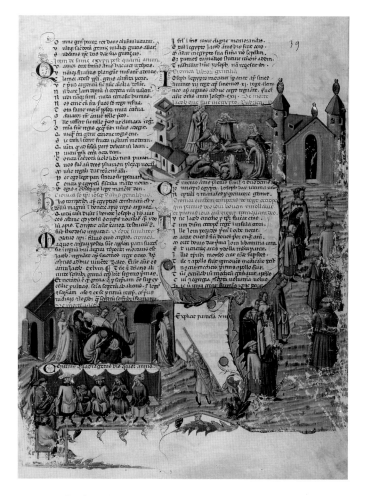

2.58 *Death of Jacob and Joseph* from the *Liber Pantheon of Goffredo da Viterbo*, 1331, commissioned by Azzone Visconti. Vellum (Bibliothèque Nationale, ms. Lat. 4895M, fol. 39, Paris)

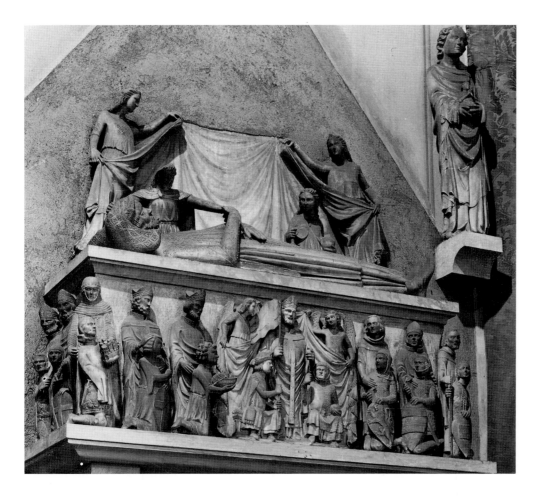

2.59 Tomb of Azzone Visconti, c. 1342–44, commissioned by Azzone's brother, Archbishop Giovanni Visconti, for San Gottardo, Milan

The tomb was originally brightly painted and crowned by a baldachin. It carried the inscription: "In this tomb is buried the nobleman Azzo Anguiger, a man mild in his rule, sometimes gentle, sometimes cruel: he girded the city with walls, and accepted kingly power: he punished crimes and built fortresses: he deserves a long life, if it were in the fates that virtue could endure for many years." (trans. Ellen Longsworth)

saints. Although Visconti rule was not as neatly hereditary as in royal states—Azzone's realm was divided at his death among competing cousins—the tomb conveys the implied hope that his legacy would endure.

Embellishment of the City　Azzone's example encouraged other prominent Milanese to contribute to the artistic embellishment of the city. An outstanding example of this was a new freestanding tomb that Dominicans commissioned to honor St. Peter Martyr (Fig. 2.60) at Galvano Fiamma's Dominican convent of Sant'Eustorgio. Peter Martyr was a famous inquisitor who was murdered in 1252. In 1253 a modest tomb for his miracle-working body had been set up in the left aisle of Sant'Eustorgio, where it attracted great crowds of pilgrims. In the climate of artistic magnificence established by Azzone and promoted by Fiamma in the mid-1330s, the tomb must have seemed inadequate for the second most important saint of the order after St. Dominic himself. The friars wished to emulate the Bolognese tomb of their founder, and to this end they secured the services of a Tuscan artist, Giovanni di Balduccio (active 1317–49), who, as a collaborator of Giovanni Pisano in Pisa, had a reputation as a designer of impressive tomb monuments.

The king and queen of Cyprus, Azzone Visconti, and his uncle Archbishop Giovanni Visconti all made major contributions toward the project for St. Peter Martyr's tomb and are represented on the lid of the sarcophagus kneeling alongside paired saints. Their figures, however, are barely noticeable in the context of this spectacular composition, which bears the stamp of the Dominicans' wish to promote the cult of their saint. The sarcophagus containing the body of the saint is raised above the ground so that it would be visible even when thronged by crowds seeking to touch it. It is supported by eight caryatids representing the virtues, each elegantly posed and turned toward the center of the monument. Doctors of the Church, saints, and angels appear as statuettes around the monument, which is crowned by a tabernacle holding a seated Madonna and Child flanked by saints Dominic and Peter Martyr.

Reliefs on the front of the sarcophagus depict the saint's funeral, his canonization, and his miraculous intervention in a storm at sea. They make it clear that the saint's remains are both highly efficacious and sanctioned by Church authority. In the funeral scene, supplicants with bent hands holding crutches and seated on wooden walkers seek to be healed through sheer proximity to the

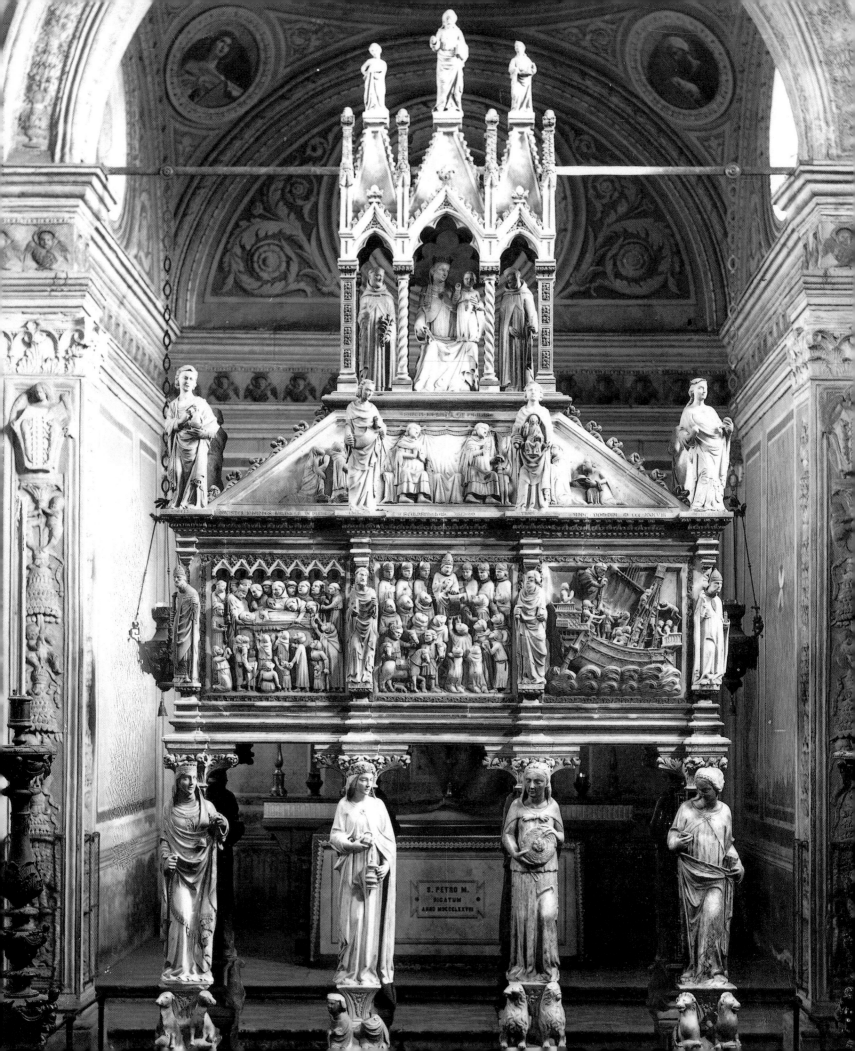

saint's body. The canonization scene places central attention on the pope and on a banderole representing the papal bull admitting Peter Martyr to the ranks of sainthood. As the papacy's strong right arm in supporting orthodoxy, the Dominicans naturally tended to underscore their direct ties to the institutional Church. The maritime miracle at the right may even be a reference to the Navicella (see Fig. 1.42), with the sea calmed not by Christ but by the order's own saint. It is certainly an odd subject for a landlocked city like Milan, but most appropriate for the Dominicans, who used such imagery in other important commissions such as the Chapter House of their monastery in Florence (see Fig. 3.23).

In its splendor, the tomb of St. Peter Martyr epitomises the taste for grandeur and display that the Visconti and their supporters brought to the city-state of Milan in the fourteenth century. Like their Angevin counterparts, they relied heavily on painters and sculptors from central Italy, but the Visconti also employed large numbers of local builders and craftsmen. Unfortunately, most of their work has been lost. Still, descriptions by writers like Fiamma make it clear that the Visconti court spent lavishly on the arts, enhancing Milan's already considerable reputation for imperial pomp and grandeur.

Synopsis

The first forty years of the fourteenth century saw intense artistic activity in all of Italy's major cities, save Rome, which had lost its major source of patronage when the papacy moved to Avignon in 1308. Venice might appear to be another notable exception, because of the relative paucity of Venetian works surviving from this period. Yet Venetians reclaimed land for new neighborhoods, expanded civic shipbuilding facilities, and supported the new mendicant orders as they gained popularity among the general populace. Piazza San Marco remained the single most impressive public space in Italy despite the urbanistic schemes of Siena's Piazza del Campo and the still small but successively enlarged Piazza della Signoria in Florence.

Civic officials and Church authorities across Italy were obviously sensitive to and aware of one another's accomplishments. Giotto's documented activity in Padua, Milan, Assisi, Rome, and Naples, as well as his native Florence, is another indication of the interconnectedness of cultural and political life in this period. Simone Martini's international reputation, earned by accomplishments in Siena, Naples, and Avignon, was promoted at the papal court by his friend, the literary scholar and student of the classics, Francesco Petrarca (known in English as Petrarch). Dante's banishment from Florence to Ravenna in this period for political reasons led to his writing the greater part of his *Divine Comedy* in exile, furthering the development of a pan-regional Italian language.

Sophisticated awareness of a wide variety of artistic styles and modes of presentation afforded patrons rich expressive possibilities. A single church like the Franciscan basilica of Santa Croce in Florence included a main altarpiece by a Sienese follower of Duccio as well as frescoes by Giotto and his school; the building itself evoked the forms of Rome's Early Christian basilicas and Gothic decorative details imported from France. In turn, Florentine and Sienese sculptors carved impressive tombs in Naples and Milan, encouraged by explicit appeals—the first since antiquity—to classical concepts of magnificence and display. Artists enlivened many works with increasingly naturalistic figures and settings of the sorts first explored in Rome in the late thirteenth century, adapting and adjusting them to the conventions of allegory and devotional imagery as well as to narratives, each achieving slightly different but no less successful results. Artists remained conscious of the way traditional imagery could convey important messages in a powerfully convincing manner; they did not jettison the old for the new. Thus Ambrogio Lorenzetti presented civic values in Siena's town hall both in a highly structured allegory and in a freer narrative explication of familiar daily life. By the mid-fourteenth century, then, artists and their patrons had greatly expanded the options available for powerful and effective visual communication, so much so that their successors would spend much of the rest of the fourteenth and early fifteenth centuries refining and exploiting them.

2.60 (opposite) Tomb of St. Peter Martyr, 1330s, commissioned by the Dominicans of Sant'Eustorgio with the support of noble patrons from GIOVANNI DI BALDUCCIO for Sant'Eustorgio, Milan. Marble.

The tomb was originally located in its own chapel along the left aisle of the church.

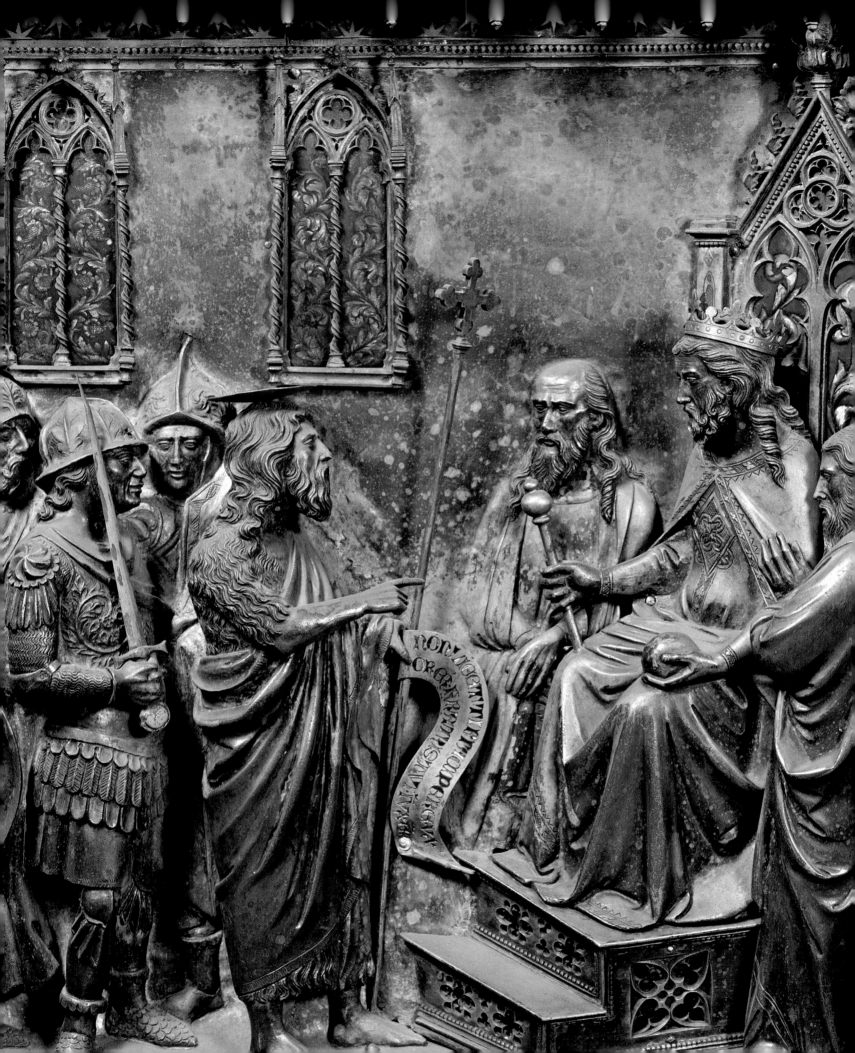

3
Art and Society:
The Later Fourteenth Century

Artists and patrons in the later decades of the fourteenth century devoted themselves with unprecedented vigor and tenacity to the production of complex works of art. In the face of a much less expansive economy and numerous natural disasters—including floods, famine, and the outbreak of the bubonic plague in 1348—artists and patrons remained committed to a large-scale artistic production. Since significant population loss placed increased wealth in the hands of survivors, governmental officials and individual patrons were able to invest heavily in elaborate works of art, whether at miracle-working shrines like Or San Michele in Florence or in secular commissions there like the huge new Loggia della Signoria. In Venice the major seaward wing of the Doge's Palace was rebuilt in the open and confident forms it still displays today. The city government called on sculptors from Lombardy who were providing north Italian despots with life-sized portraiture on heroically scaled tombs to enhance the Doge's Palace with some of the most lifelike sculpture of the age. Narrative fresco cycles continued to grow in vivacity and naturalism as well, especially at the pilgrimage center of the Santo in Padua, where Altichiero produced some of the most stunning portrait likenesses of the Renaissance.

Allegorical representations gained widespread popularity in central Italy, dwarfing earlier, discreet schemes in both size and complexity. Gothic decorative vocabulary grew ever more complex, adding colorful and intricate patterning to nearly every commission—including projects as diverse as the reinstallation of Byzantine enamels on the high altar of St. Mark's in Venice and the completion of the campanile of Florence Cathedral. It was an era that spent extravagantly on the arts, often to confirm existing hierarchies and traditional values. In unsettled times the visual arts provided effective vehicles for giving order to an increasingly complicated world.

Venice: Images of the State and the Individual

Throughout the fourteenth and well into the fifteenth century, Venetian artists amplified themes and images that underscored the republic's commitments to its own traditions of consensus and oligarchy. Threatened by earthquakes, flood, famine, and plague, as well as by wars with Crete and Genoa, the Venetian state continued to promote and maintain political and social stability: not without reason did Venetians dub their city "La Serenissima"—the "most serene" republic.

At the same time, expanding definitions of the office of doge gave the head of the Venetian state an increasingly powerful and visible role in the city. A key player in this development was Andrea Dandolo (doge 1343–54). A literary scholar (he was a friend of Petrarch's), Dandolo articulated the ideal of the doge as the personification of the Venetian state. In his *Chronica extensa*, a major history of the republic, Dandolo emphasized how individual doges gave glory to Venice. In their accomplishments, the abstract ideal of the ducal office took on concrete, particularized form, newly celebrated by Dandolo.

The *Pala d'Oro*

Andrea Dandolo made his concept of the ducal office evident in a major artistic project that built upon the work of several of his predecessors. This was the embellishment of the *Pala d'Oro*, the great golden altarpiece above the high altar of the doges' own chapel, St. Mark's Basilica (Fig. 3.2). The original altarpiece, consisting of a number of enameled gold panels depicting saints, had been

3.1 Silver altar (detail), 1366–77, commissioned by the Arte del Calimala from LEONARDO DI SER GIOVANNI, BETTO DI GERI, and others for the Baptistry, Florence. Silver on a wooden base, front face 3′ 9¼″ × 8′ 7″ (1.15 × 2.62 m). (Museo dell'Opera del Duomo, Florence.) See also Fig. 3.24.

commissioned in 976 in Constantinople by Doge Pietro Orseolo I. A later doge, Ordelafo Falier, enlarged the altarpiece in 1105, and yet more panels—including some looted from Constantinople after the Venetians' conquest of that city—were added in 1209. In its present dazzling form, however, the *Pala d'Oro* dates from 1345, when Andrea Dandolo added a sumptuous Gothic-style gold frame, some new enamels, and an enormous number of pearls and precious stones, including rubies, sapphires, and emeralds. He also added two inscription blocks, commemorating his own contribution and those of his predecessors.

The central figure of the altarpiece, an enthroned Christ, pays homage to the past through its iconic Byzantine pose, but Dandolo's goldsmith, working in the *cloisonné* enamel technique established in the earlier panels, enhanced the figure with crisply pleated drapery, carefully placed feet, and three-dimensional cast fingers and hands, making the entire figure distinctly more lifelike than the similarly positioned Christ in the earlier mosaics of the Florence Baptistry, for example (see Fig. 1.10). On the *Pala d'Oro* gems and pearls adorn Christ's halo, his

throne, and the open book on his lap. Meticulously cast golden leaves and a filigree border in the lozenge around Christ wed flowing Gothic curves to Byzantine splendor.

Dandolo called on Paolo Veneziano (active 1333–58 Venice) and his workshop to provide painted wooden panels to cover the enamels on non-feast days. Paolo came from a family of painters; he is among the first to be documented as an official civic artist. Particularly striking is the panel depicting the rediscovery of St. Mark's relics within the basilica (Fig. 3.3). At the center the doge and the Venetian patriarch kneel before an altar on which stands a small golden **polyptych**. St. Mark's head and hand emerge from a niche in one of the marble and porphyry piers behind it. Pious crowds of prelates, city officials, and citizens look on, one on the far left leading the gaze of his compatriots with an outstretched arm and hand pointing toward the saint. The precise rendering of the basilica's marble screens, balconies, and apse, its window of leaded glass roundels, and its standing saint in a glowing gold niche suggests that the work served partly as documentation, anchoring the event depicted in a setting immediately recognizable to Venetians.

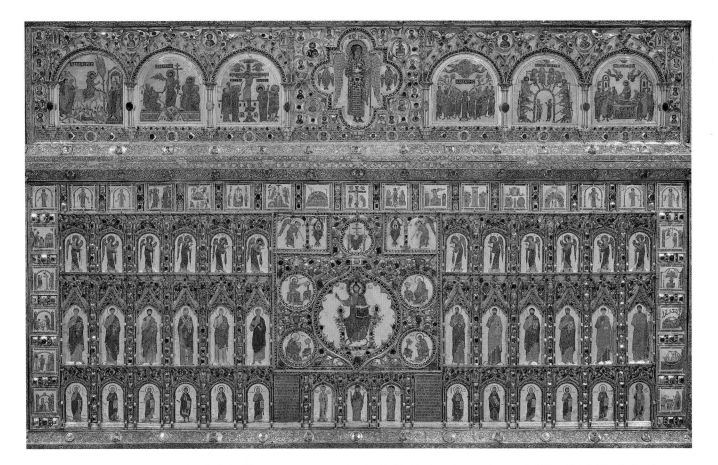

3.2 *Pala d'Oro*, 1345, restored and embellished by ANDREA DANDOLO for St. Mark's, Venice. Gold and enamel, 137 × 55" (348 × 140 cm)

The Venetians were the first to set objects like these on top of altars instead of attached to the front of the altar table.

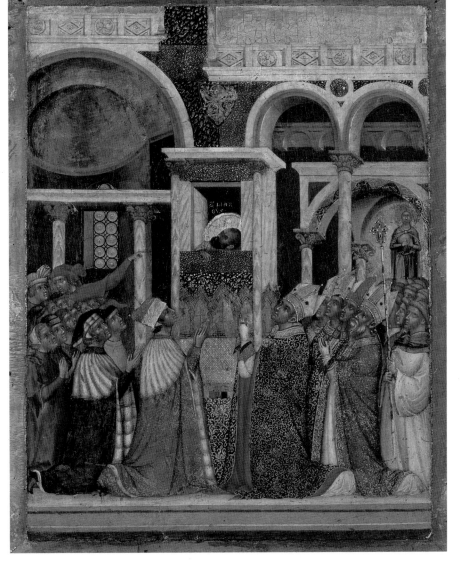

3.3 *Rediscovery of the Relics of St. Mark,* signed and dated April 22, 1345, commissioned by Doge Andrea Dandolo from PAOLO VENEZIANO and his sons LUCA and GIOVANNI for part of the cover of the *Pala d'Oro,* St. Mark's, Venice. Tempera on panel

Altarpieces were regularly covered during parts of the year, especially during penitential seasons, although most much more simply than this example.

models for storytelling, relaxing some of the figures in a manner reminiscent of northern Gothic art.

Dandolo's contributions to the Baptistry were completed by his funerary monument (Fig. 3.5 and on the right side wall in Fig. 3.4), which he was planning shortly before he died. Unlike the tomb monuments of all his predecessors, Dandolo's tomb celebrates the individual holding the ducal office. It is the first to provide an effigy of the deceased doge and to incorporate other features long seen on important tombs elsewhere in Italy: angels parting a cloth of honor, niches, and narrative reliefs. A lengthy inscription below the tomb is one of the earliest to laud the specific achievements of a doge. The elected nature of the ducal office in republican Venice discouraged any representation of the doge as a living figure comparable to those of absolutist rulers (see Fig. 2.55). Yet Andrea Dandolo's monument marks a bold step in that direction. At the center of the sarcophagus sits an enthroned Madonna and Child, a gentle but persuasive image of authority. The city's traditional founding date of March 25, the feast of the Annunciation, is represented by a statuette of the Angel Gabriel on the right-hand corner of the sarcophagus and one of the Virgin on the left. The effigy of Dandolo, the statuettes, and narratives of the martyrdom of Andrea's patron saints, John the Evangelist and Andrew, are fluidly carved and convincingly three-dimensional; originally their forms and the lush leafwork surrounding them were made even more vivid by polychrome decoration.

St. Mark's Baptistry

In St. Mark's Baptistry, which Dandolo selected as his burial site, he replaced earlier fresco decorations with mosaics (Fig. 3.4) inspired by Byzantine models. Seated evangelists occupy the entrance arch, while the central cupola bears an image of Christ in Glory surrounded by a ring of standing Apostles depicting the *Mission of the Apostles.* Smaller figures next to each Apostle, one submerged to his chest in a baptismal font and the other standing before a miniaturized building, graphically illustrate Christ's command to the Apostles that they preach and baptize. The international theme would have resonated with the Venetians, whose commercial activities and political ambitions extended across the Mediterranean. Scenes narrating episodes from the life of St. John the Baptist on the side walls share the same gold backgrounds and miniaturized settings as the cupola mosaics and the Crucifixion on the end wall, ensuring decorative unity, but the mosaicists turned to more recent

The Church of Santi Giovanni e Paolo

Andrea Dandolo was the last doge to be buried in St. Mark's. Many of his successors (twenty-five of them) chose instead the church of Santi Giovanni e Paolo (Fig. 3.6), making this Dominican church (whose name is commonly shortened to San Zanipolo in the Venetian

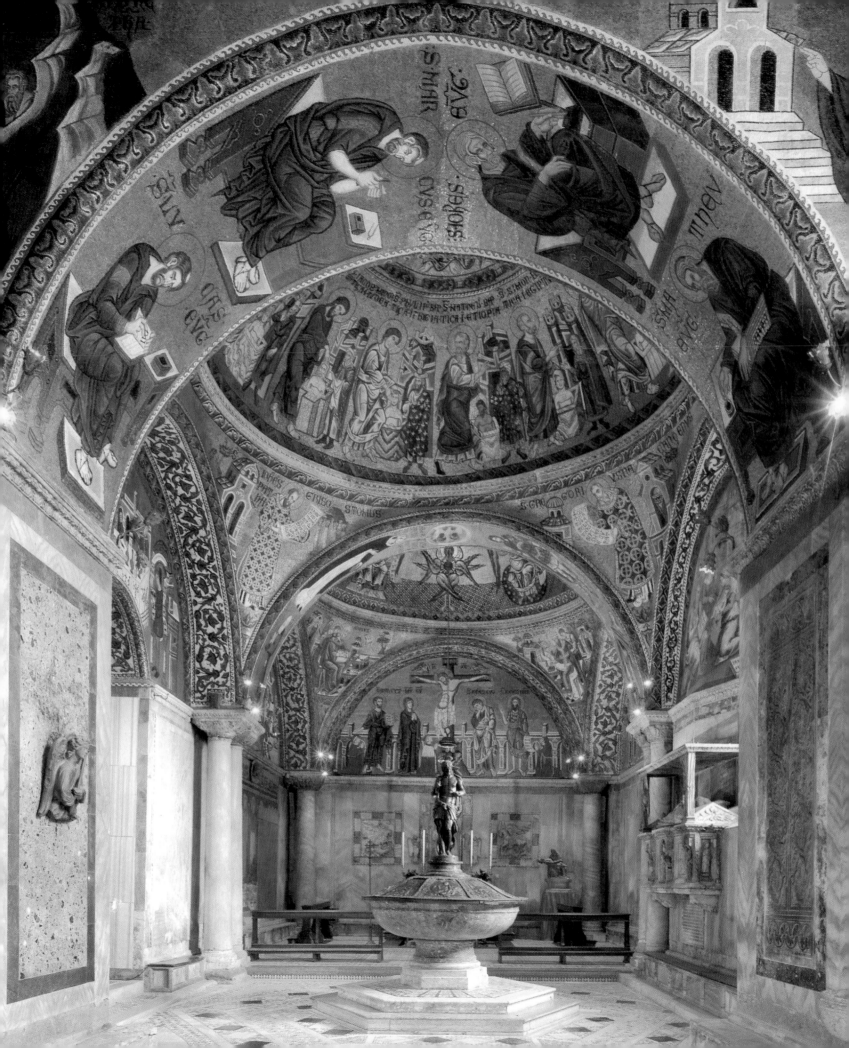

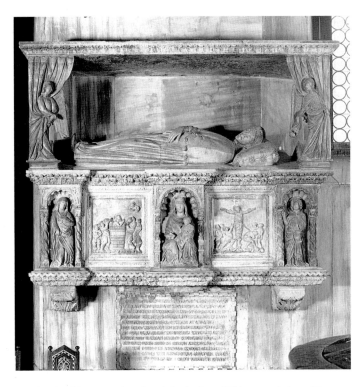

3.5 Tomb of Doge Andrea Dandolo, before 1354, commissioned by Andrea Dandolo for the Baptistry, St. Mark's, Venice. Marble

The inscription beneath the tomb reads: "This small space of a cold tomb contains the limbs of the valorous one whom the venerable army of virtues never deserted. Tenets for him were probity, judgment, penetrating intelligence, moderation, and deeds of nobility of high renown, and noble work. He secured for the country long-lasting honor for which he is worthy of memory. And because his shining deeds resound to the nations throughout the world, the pen allows the recording of many meritorious things worthy of recounting. Andrea, to whom the noble house of Dandolo gave birth, worthy in every respect of the Venetian state, when the seventh day of September, in 1354, he died." (Trans. Debra Picus)

dialect) the third major focus of civic ritual after St. Mark's and the Doge's Palace. The church was begun around 1333, and the crossing and apse must have been complete by the early 1360s, when Giovanni Dolfin (doge 1356–61) was buried in a tomb on one of the side walls of the choir. In its spaciousness and lofty vaulting, the church resembles others built by and for the Dominicans, such as Santa Maria Novella in Florence (see Fig. 1.23). In Venice, however, the vast open space is especially remarkable given the wet, sandy subsoil on which it had to be built. Although mainland models inspired the soaring nave arcade, cross vaults, polygonal apse (with complex window tracery), and transept chapels, local structural compromises included building both the piers and the outer walls of relatively lightweight brick, rather than stone, and the vaults of wood, and tying the entire structure together with an insistent grid of wooden

3.4 (opposite) Baptistry, St. Mark's, Venice, 1342–54, mosaics and tomb commissioned by Andrea Dandolo

The bronze baptismal font is a later addition, commissioned from Jacopo Sansovino c. 1545, but produced by his workshop.

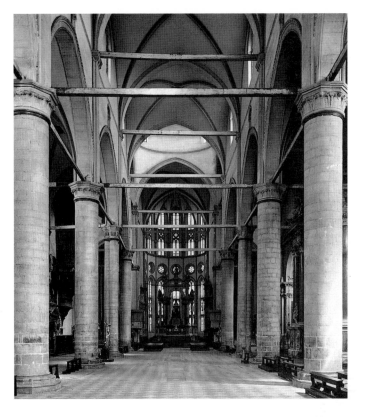

3.6 Santi Giovanni e Paolo, Venice, begun c. 1333, commissioned by the Dominicans

beams at both the height of the capitals and the springing of the vaults. A Byzantine-style dome was later added over the crossing to stress Venetian traditions, but the overall impression is Gothic spatial expanse, a testament to the strong influence of northern artistic models and international expectations that mendicant churches would be suitably large to accommodate their increased following.

The Doge's Palace

In 1340 the Venetian Senate decided to rebuild a large portion of the Doge's Palace (Fig. 3.7) so as to provide more ample space for gatherings of the Great Council. Like the church of San Zanipolo and the *Pala d'Oro*, the palace displays many Gothic features—in this case notably the rich arcading on the first two storeys. Above, a taut skin of interlocking, diamond-patterned pink and white stone further softens any appearance of weight and mass. At the roof line, the usual severe crenellations are replaced by fanciful flames of white stone. The effect is exotic and may owe some of its flavor to Islamic precedents, of which the seafaring Venetians would have been well aware. Venetian Gothic is well-laced with Eastern luxury. Reversing normal expectations of a heavy ground story to support less weighty areas above, the open arcades suggest a levitated structure in which light and air

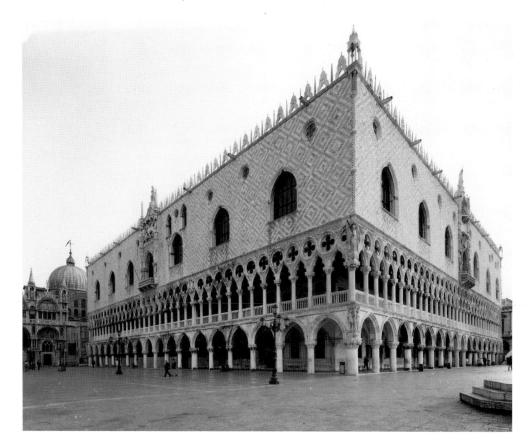

3.7 Doge's Palace, Venice, 1340–1438 (extension toward St. Mark's begun 1424), commissioned by the Venetian government

move around freely even at the corners, where a slightly enlarged pier deftly provides the necessary feeling of stability. The building is a visual tour de force, celebrating the confident Venetian state and the security of its maritime site. The date of 1344 inscribed on one of the ground floor capitals indicates that work moved ahead under Doge Andrea Dandolo. Just what the building looked like by the time he died, however, is highly debatable. The structure was still unroofed in July 1348 when the Senate ordered the building to be covered and debris to be hauled away. Five days later, the project was cut short by the onset of plague. Work resumed in February 1350 and must have been completed by 1365 when the Paduan artist Guariento di Arpo (active 1338–68/70 Padua) was commissioned to fresco the interior walls.

As if to anchor the palace—and certainly to take advantage of its exposed outer corners—the builders incorporated sculptural groups into either end of the arcade facing the lagoon. Both commemorate human weakness and frailty, the rationale for the establishment and rule of government. At one end stand Adam and Eve with the Archangel Michael. At the other appears the *Drunkenness of Noah* (Fig. 3.8). The three-quarter relief is divided into two planes by a sturdy grapevine which undulates back and forth, playing along the limits of the virtual corner of the building. At the left is the drunken figure of a slightly under-life-sized Noah, whose limp right hand spills the wine that has inebriated him. To the right, one son covers

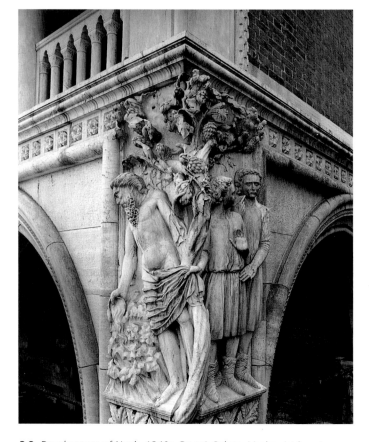

3.8 *Drunkenness of Noah*, 1340s, Doge's Palace, Venice. Istrian stone

Noah's third son is depicted on another relief across the arch to the right (not visible in this illustration).

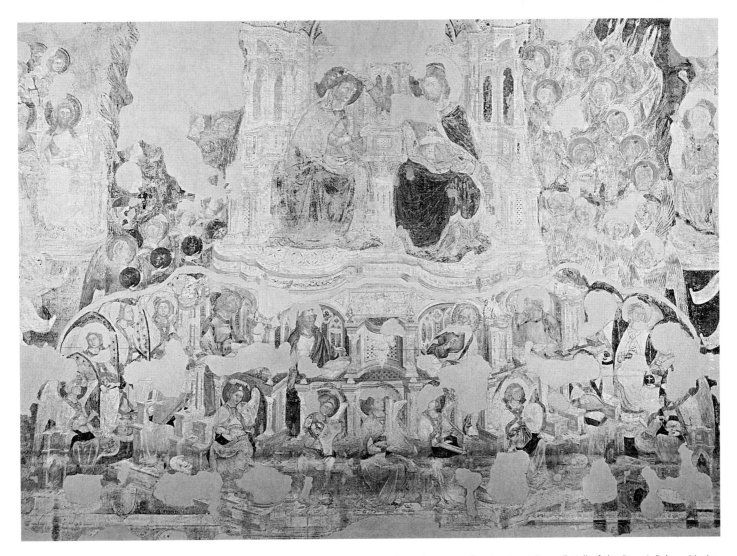

3.9 *Coronation of the Virgin*, 1365, commissioned by the Venetian government from GUARIENTO for the Great Council Hall of the Doge's Palace, Venice. Fresco (anteroom to the Great Council Hall)

his naked father and begs indulgence for him, while the other shows himself to be a disapproving moralist. The soft, fleshy body of Noah, the intricate carving of the vine, and the sturdy portrait-like presence of Noah's sons are so compelling that the relief has sometimes been given a much later date, well into the early fifteenth century. Recent studies, however, have noted convincing similarities between this group and smaller figures on the capitals of the building's lower arcade dating from the 1340s. Also at this time, Lombard sculptors in Verona were creating highly complex sculptural groups (see Fig. 3.36). Venice and some of its north Italian neighbors stood in the vanguard of sculptural production.

Painting in the Doge's Palace

To decorate the interior of the palace's Great Council Chamber, the Venetian Senate turned in 1365 to Guariento di Arpo, an expert in fresco who had worked for the Carrara family in Padua and at the Church of the Eremitani there. Guariento's imposing *Coronation of the*

Virgin (Fig. 3.9) was irreparably damaged by fire in 1577, but the general composition can still be made out in fragments that were found behind Tintoretto's huge replacement painting of *Paradise* (see Fig. 8.30) and that were then removed to another room, where they can now be seen. Still impressive in its size (over 70 by 20 feet [21.3 by 6 meters]) the fresco must have had a tremendous impact in its pristine state and its dominant position on the end wall of the Great Council Hall. It is a multi-tiered extravaganza, spreading out from an elaborate double Gothic throne containing the figures of Christ and the Virgin, an image of authority with clear roots in papal Rome. Dozens of music-making angels occupied small traceried niches in the flaring substructure of the throne. Painted Gothic arches resting on the actual corbels contained the upper limits of rank upon rank of fiery-winged angels and saints. The subject is the same as Jacopo Torriti's thirteenth-century composition at Santa Maria Maggiore in Rome (see Fig. 1.35) and reminiscent of Nardo di Cione's *Paradise* in the Strozzi Chapel in Florence (see Fig. 3.17). But Guariento has enlivened the scene with Christ reaching across the niche to crown the

Virgin and by the spectacularly undulating forms of the architectural elements. Heaven is alive with energetic forms. In functional context Guariento's fresco is more like Simone Martini's *Maestà* in the Palazzo Pubblico in Siena (see Fig. 2.23), celebrating the state and its emblem, the Virgin. In Venice, however, the image carried particular force because the Virgin was understood not only as a protectress of the state but as its very embodiment. Her purity was seen as analogous to Venice's unblemished history of independence, and the authority given to the Queen of Heaven was understood as a representation of divine favor and authority awarded to Venice itself. A typically Venetian Annunciation bracketed Guariento's composition and bust-length portraits of the doges around the Council Chamber complemented the main work.

Accompanying Guariento's *Coronation* on the side walls of the Great Council Hall were twenty-eight frescoes recounting the stories of battles between Pope Alexander III and the Emperor Frederick Barbarossa, who were reconciled by Doge Sebastiano Ziani in 1177—all destroyed by fire in 1577. The documentary record regarding the slowly executed project is quite slim, and only drawings and sketches suggest the details of some of its compositions. Still, the project is worth examining, for it offers important insights into Venetian ways of thinking about narrative art in this governmental setting.

A drawing (Fig. 3.10) has been convincingly linked with scenes commissioned between 1409 and 1415 from the young painter Pisanello (Antonio Pisano; c. 1395 Pisa or Verona–1455 Rome?), who had received his training in Verona. As Guariento had done in his *Coronation*, Pisanello gave the event depicted—Emperor Frederick Barbarossa being implored by his son for peace—an elaborate setting. The complicated set of arches and balconies recalls the tradition of architectural rendering in late fourteenth-century Paduan paintings by another Veronese-trained artist, Altichiero da Zevio (active 1369–84; see Fig. 3.48). The main action and naturalistic placement of the figures also conforms to relatively recent Paduan precedents, but in essence the scene corresponds person by person to what can be reconstructed of the same scene in an earlier cycle in a chapel in the palace. The action in each painting centered around the seated emperor stretching out his arm to the left in response to his son's entreaties for peace. Two secular figures and one in monastic dress accompanied them in both cycles. The consistency from one image to the other emphasized the historical accuracy of the representation and made the subject recognizable—much as artists portraying the Nativity or other well-known biblical subjects usually arranged their figures in set, familiar patterns.

As an official state painter, Jacobello del Fiore (active 1400–39 Venice), a follower of Guariento in the

International Gothic style, received the respectable salary of 100 ducats a year from the Venetian government. In 1421 he painted an *Enthroned Justice Flanked by St. Michael the Archangel and the Angel Gabriel* (Fig. 3.11) for the offices of the Magistrato del Proprio, the civil and criminal court in the Doge's Palace, where it hung above the judges' benches, confirming and enhancing their juridical authority. The panel is extraordinarily lavish, a painted counterpart to the recently completed sculptural extravaganza above the façades of St. Mark's (see Fig. 1.7). Jacobello turns and twists drapery and banderoles even more voluptuously than on the façades. He also employs richly worked gilt **pastiglia** (raised plaster detailing) on the armor and breastplates of all three figures, making them stand out from the surface in glittering relief.

Jacobello's painting, repeating the imagery of a marble relief tondo on the exterior of the Ducal Palace, conveys a

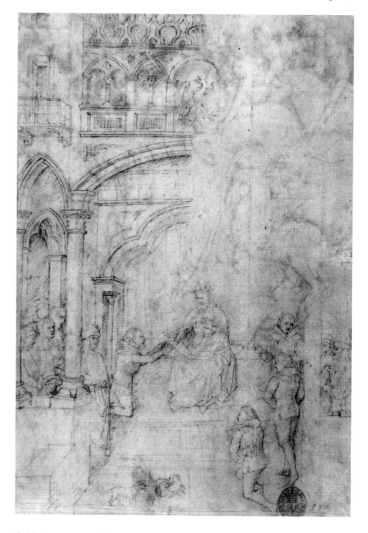

3.10 *Emperor Frederick Barbarossa Receiving the Entreaties of His Son for Peace*, c. 1409–15, drawing reflecting composition of commission by the Council of Ten to PISANELLO for the Great Council Hall, Doge's Palace, Venice. 10¾ × 7¼″ (27.5 × 18.4 cm) (Sloane Collection, © British Museum, drawing number 5226–57v, London)

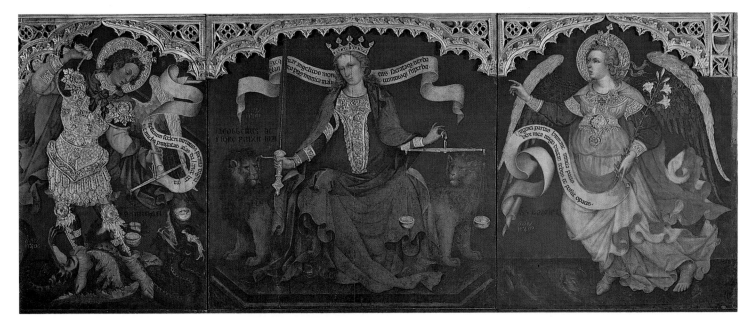

3.11 *Enthroned Justice Flanked by St. Michael the Archangel and the Angel Gabriel*, 1421, commissioned by the Magistrato del Proprio from JACOBELLO DEL FIORE for their offices in the Doge's Palace, Venice. Panels with gold work; Justice 6′ 9¾″ × 6′ 4¼″ (2.08 × 1.94 m), Gabriel 6′ 9¾″ × 5′ 4″ (2.08 × 1.63 m), Michael 81¾ × 52¼″ (208 × 133 cm) (Galleria dell'Accademia, Venice)

Government offices regularly contained paintings the subject matter of which encouraged officials to act wisely and diligently. The crowned Justice says: "I shall obey the admonitions of the angels and the words of Holy Writ, dealing gently with the devout, angrily with the wicked, and proudly with the vainglorious". Gabriel's scroll at the right carries the following message: "My voice [brought] the message of peace to the Virgin's birth; she entreats you as a leader in troubled matters." Michael the Archangel's scroll at the left reads: "Punishment to crime, worthy rewards to virtues, and he gives to me purged souls with kindly lance."

clear message equating Venice with Justice, a point made explicit by three long inscriptions accompanying each of the figures. Justice is seated in a rigid iconic pose familiar from images of law and power (see Fig. 2.25) and flanked by the lions of St. Mark/Venice, here further referenced to the throne of Solomon which was supported by lions. The Angel Gabriel, on the right, holding a lily, turns and gestures toward the figure of Justice, who in Venetian eyes was identified with the Virgin Mary and with Venice itself; thus the angel's gesture is a reminder of Venice's legendary founding on the Feast of the Annunciation. His banderole terms the Virgin birth as "a message of peace" and implores her for guidance in difficult situations. St. Michael, like the central figure, holds a set of scales and asks Justice/Venice/the Virgin to award damages or inflict penalties according to the merits of each case, recommending purified souls to her benevolence and balanced decision.

Enhancements to St. Mark's

St. Mark's Basilica continued to attract lavish civic expenditure and elaboration. Although the church had been structurally complete at the end of the thirteenth century, generation after generation worked a proliferation of decorative and narrative detail into its fabric. Unlike Florence and Milan, whose unfinished cathedrals still stood gapingly open to the sky, St. Mark's had long been structurally complete.

In 1394 the brothers Pierpaolo (active 1383–1403 Mantua, Bologna, and Venice) and Jacobello dalle Masegne (active 1383–c. 1409 Mantua, Bologna, and Venice) finished a new choir screen for the basilica (Fig. 3.12). Sons of a Venetian stonemason, they seem to have been aware of contemporary developments in Tuscan sculpture as well as local traditions in Venice. An inscription indicates that the doge and two of the officers responsible for oversight of the building chose the brothers and were the sponsors of the project.

The general arrangement of the choir screen, with its paneled balustrade, columnar supports, and surmounting figures of Apostles, conforms to local traditions. The creative challenge for the Dalle Masegne was to enhance the traditional composition in such a way that the new screen was both more splendid than its predecessor and still harmonious with the rest of the basilica. Thus the screen echoes the basilica's marble-faced walls, geometric inlays, attached columns (in the lowest level), and broad horizontal bands of decoration. The spiritual intensity of the much earlier standing Apostles in the mosaics above animates the statues on the top of the screen. Their taut, thin form, and almost metallically bright, crisp finish also evoke the previous metalwork of liturgical vessels, reli-

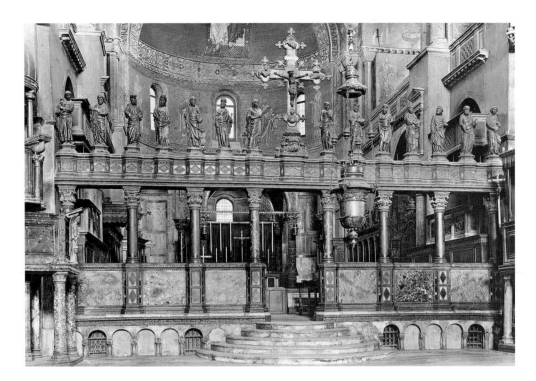

3.12 Choir screen, 1394, commissioned by Antonio Venier with Pietro Cornaro and Michele Steno, Procurators of St. Mark's, from PIERPAOLO AND JACOBELLO DALLE MASEGNE for St. Mark's, Venice

The crucifix over the center of the screen is a work in silver; the flanking statues are carved from marble. An inscription states that the work was made "in the time of the excellent lord Antonio Venier, by the grace of God, Doge of Venice, and of the noblemen the lords Pietro Cornaro and Michele Steno, honorable procurators of the blessed and most holy church of the Evangelist St. Mark."

quaries, and the famous *Pala d'Oro* (see Fig. 3.2) glimmering behind them. At the same time, the statues are more lifelike in pose and demeanor than earlier works, encouraging emotional and psychological engagement with the crucified Christ and the mourning Virgin at the center.

On the exterior of the church the Venetians began gothicizing the structure, in 1384, by adding spiky columnar tabernacles to the upper edges of the north (left) façade, continuing these around all three of the exposed façades (compare Figs. 1.7 and 1.8). Sculptural embellishment of this area continued into the 1420s. Local Venetian carvers were joined by sculptors from Tuscany and Lombardy, all of whom submerged much of their individuality for the benefit of the overall scheme. The addition of these tabernacles may have been suggested by the fact that the corners of St. Mark's were already marked by open two-story porches with attached columns on the lower level and by similar smaller structures at its upper corners. Economically building on pre-existing forms, the Venetians thus validated tradition even as they embraced innovation. The tabernacles epitomize Venetian Gothic exuberance, with their gracefully poised, cone-shaped roofs, each encircled with a corona of decorative, flame-shaped crenellations. Similar canopied tabernacles were inserted into the depressions between each arch of the façades. As was the custom on church façades throughout Europe, and also on many royal and noble tombs, figural sculpture occupied these airy perches. The Venetians also added Gothic peaks of billowing marble fronds over the rounded crowns of the brick walls. Bust-length prophets, many holding elaborately twisted and flapping ban-

deroles, rise from every other crest. The Venetians showed themselves adept in employing fashionable Gothic forms without, however, having to sacrifice any of the pre-existing structure or accumulated decoration. Even the coverings over the domes, rebuilt after a fire in 1419, retained their unmistakably Veneto-Byzantine character when they were raised to a greater, more stylish height and capped with fanciful little cupolas resembling inflated parachutes. Paradoxically, this building, with its idiosyncratic mixture of Byzantine and Venetian Gothic styles, achieves a sense of imminent levitation that many a purely Gothic church, despite flying buttresses and soaring vaults, fails to equal.

Santo Stefano

The attractiveness of St. Mark's frothy stonework to Venetian patrons is evidenced by its imitation—in both stone and paint—in other buildings. An example of simulated stonework can be found in the Augustinian church of Santo Stefano (Fig. 3.13). Exact dating of the structure of the church is uncertain, though it was evidently restored and expanded in the early fifteenth century. Bands of florid leaf work, painted in *grisaille* (grey and white) to resemble unpainted stonework, follow the arcading of the nave. Above each cusp rides a bust-length figure of a saint and fluttering banderoles mimicking the St. Mark's façade but reduced in number and limited to exemplary Augustinians. Painted **diaper** patterns of repeated geometrical units on the upper walls evoke the

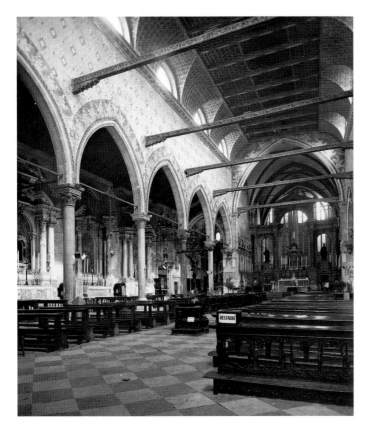

3.13 Santo Stefano, Venice, c. 1407, commissioned by the resident Augustinian friars

Most of the architectural decoration of this interior is painted, not carved.

real stone patterns on the Palazzo Ducale. Thus the decoration, in its economy, suggests monastic poverty while still underlining ties to the Venetian state.

The church's wooden ceiling is also characteristically Venetian, though few other examples have survived centuries of fires and renovation. Resembling the inverted keel of a large boat, it reflects local expertise in ship building and provides an elaborately profiled but relatively lightweight covering which respects the structural difficulties of building in this island city. Its apparent **coffering** (that is, its division into small square panels) is also carried out in paint rather than three-dimensionally, an excellent example of how patrons without a great deal of money could create effects emulating the city's more expensive and prestigious monuments. In spite of troubled times, the late fourteenth and early fifteenth centuries were obviously a period of great creativity in Venice.

Pisa and Florence: Morality, Judgment, and Crisis

The second half of the fourteenth century in Tuscany did not see the formidable stylistic innovations that characterize the art of the early years of the century. The reasons for this apparent leveling off of artistic energy are embed-ded in the social fabric of the culture and the needs of patrons. Bankruptcies in two leading Florentine banking houses, drought and famine in the middle years of the 1340s throughout Tuscany, the onset of the Black Death in 1348 and its repeated recurrence, a papal interdict against Florence, and the revolt of that city's wool workers in 1378 all delivered shocks to the social order. Nonetheless the actual structures of the Tuscan political order remained remarkably resistant to change through the fourteenth century. The colossal unfinished building projects like the cathedral and the church of Santa Croce in Florence initiated at the end of the thirteenth century still dominated the city and challenged the patronage of city leaders. The buildings required sculptural and painted decoration to give precision to their meanings and form to the myths that lent individual city-states their distinctive character.

The Camposanto Frescoes in Pisa

Extensive decorative programs begun in Pisa in the 1330s were made possible by Pisa's wealth as a major shipping power. Foremost among them were the frescoes of the Camposanto ("holy field"), the enclosed burial ground adjacent to the cathedral, which tradition claims contains earth brought from the Holy Land, thus making it literally a holy field. Strong Dominican influence over the University of Pisa determined the theological content of the Camposanto frescoes since the Dominicans apparently assisted in devising their program. Although the site was heavily damaged during the bombings of World War II, enough remains of the frescoes on the walls of the portico which surrounds the interior courtyard of the Camposanto—much like a cloister—to assess their importance. The earliest of them depict the story of the Passion of Christ, the *Triumph of Death* (Fig. 3.14), and the *Last Judgment* (Fig. 3.15)—fitting themes for a burial ground. Although these frescoes have been attributed to Francesco Traini (active 1300s Pisa), a local painter trained in Sienese workshops, and to Buffalmacco (active 1315–36 Pisa), a painter known more through literary texts than through any documented work, there is little secure evidence to support these claims.

The *Triumph of Death* is painted on a wall facing a short axis of the loggia. Since it is the same width as the loggia, the fresco is a framed focal point of attention as one moves through the space; it must have been considered an important image within the overall program. To the left of the *Triumph of Death* is a Crucifixion, a juxtaposition indicating that the frescoes in this corner of the Camposanto form a narrative of salvation. The *Triumph of Death* is an extraordinary mixture of disparate scenes, few of them ostensibly about death. A riding party of noble men and women occupy the left front plane; since they face left they are oblivious of the maimed peasants at the lower center of the fresco. Elsewhere in the picture hermit monks, a group of courtiers and musicians, and flying angels and demons seem unaware of each other. There is little or no attempt at either compositional or narrative unity. Yet the individual scenes and characters are powerful, the work of an artist with both vision and skill.

Close reading of the fresco indicates a wealth of meanings and metaphors. The courtly group of men and women on horseback in the left foreground of the painting have encountered three dead bodies lying in coffins. The artist's concern for naturalistic detail is typified by the male rider who holds his nose because of the offensive odor of the corpses, each in a different state of decompo-

sition. These figures represent an old visual and literary tradition in which the living are forced to confront their own mortality by an encounter with death. This theme is made didactically clear by the appearance of the hermit saint Macarius, at the very left of the composition; he holds out a scroll with an inscription that translates: "If your mind will be well aware, keeping here your view attentive, your vainglory will be vanquished and you will see pride eliminated. And, again, you will realize this if you observe the law which is written."

The juxtaposition of St. Macarius and the hunting party indicates that despite the naturalism and descriptive coloring of the figures, a moral allegory—not a simple narrative—is being presented here. Behind and above the band of aristocrats a group of hermits—praying, meditating, and milking a doe—occupy a peaceful hillside retreat, where even the falcon and the rabbit seem to

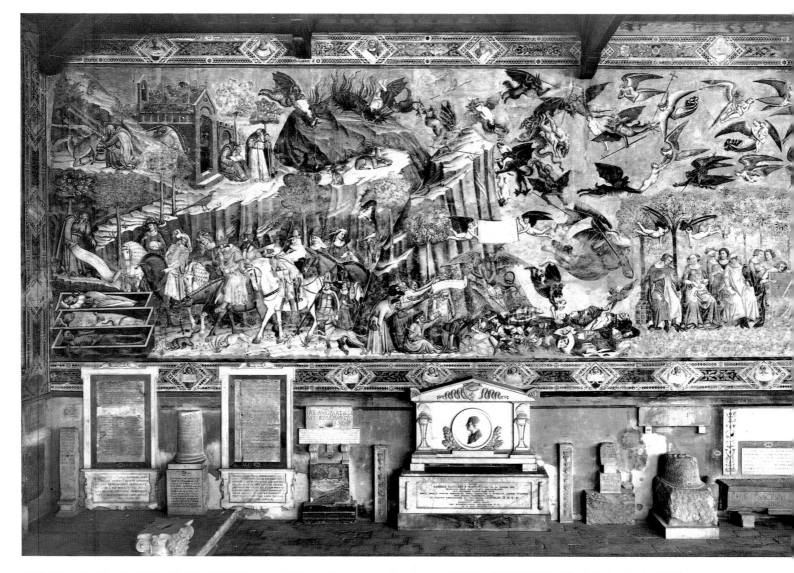

3.14 *Triumph of Death*, 1330s, MASTER OF THE TRIUMPH OF DEATH, Camposanto, Pisa. Fresco, 18' 6" × 49' 2" (5.64 × 15 m) (state prior to 1944)

coexist in harmony. The tranquil hermits, who spend their lives preparing for salvation, are clearly meant to be read in contrast to the surprised nobles who evidently —given their startled reactions to the corpses before them—have given little thought to death and the afterlife.

Just to the right of the maimed peasants at the center of the painting lies a heap of dead bodies, whose ascending souls are being fought for by hosts of flying demons and angels. A female figure of Death carrying a scythe lunges vengefully toward a serene party of courtly figures seated in an orange grove, listening to a musician playing a psaltery. While Death prepares to destroy their insouciance, the crippled peasants at the center beg to be freed from their earthly miseries. Their words appear on banderoles that they hold: "Since prosperity has completely deserted us, O Death, you who are the medicine for all

pain, come to give us our last supper!" Death, then, is seen as merciful as well as vengeful.

Landscape plays an important metaphorical role in the fresco, one aspect representing virtue, the other vice. The hermits' landscape is severe and rocky, one of retreat and asceticism. By contrast, the courtiers' landscape, at the right, is luxuriant, with its carpet-laid ground and fruit-bearing trees. One is a landscape of prayer, the other a landscape of pleasure. Moreover the courtiers— arranged flatly over the surface in a row different from the narrative at the left of the fresco—are given attributes that allow us to read them as a collective symbol of the sin of "luxury," or lust. The central woman, dressed in a pink gown, holds a lap dog, a slang reference, linguistically, to female genitalia, while the men hold hunting birds, a well-known and popular phallic reference since the term for bird was used colloquially to refer to the phallus in

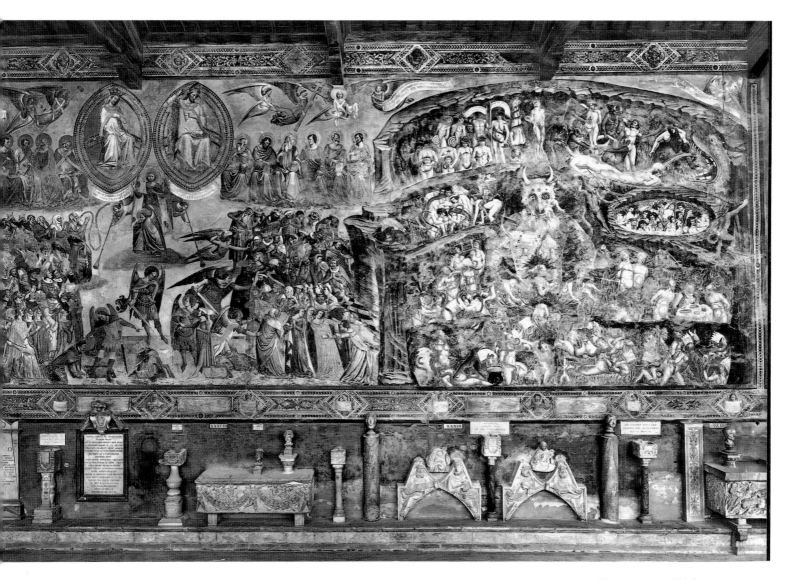

3.15 *Last Judgment*, 1330s, Master of the Triumph of Death, Camposanto, Pisa. Fresco, 19′ 8″ × c. 50′ (6 × c. 15 m) (state prior to 1944)

medieval Italian (and other European languages), as it is now. Comparable scenes of lovers are often depicted on contemporary luxury objects such as ivory combs and cosmetic boxes, attesting to the familiarity of such iconography at this time. The complex warnings against luxury and lust as impediments to salvation in this fresco seem aimed at the wealthy Tuscan banking and mercantile class. At this same time the new mendicant orders, the Franciscans and Dominicans, were focusing attention on holy voluntary poverty, recalling the asceticism of the early Church Fathers.

The fresco immediately to the right of the *Triumph of Death* is an extraordinary *Last Judgment* (see Fig. 3.15) in which the entire right half of the painting is given over to a representation of hell. Christ, in contrast to his frontal pose usual in depictions of the Last Judgment, is here shown turning toward the damned. His left hand points to the wound in his side, a gesture recalling Thomas's placing of his hand in the wound as a proof of Christ's resurrection and thus of the possibility of salvation for all humans. Christ is accompanied in a paired mandorla by a figure of the crowned Virgin, who represents Ecclesia, the institutional Church, just as she does in Torriti's mosaic in Santa Maria Maggiore in Rome (see Fig. 1.35). Here, too, the crowned Virgin/Ecclesia appears as co-regent with Christ. This powerful image conforms to the teaching that the papacy was the absolute power within the institutional Church—a tenet vigorously supported by the Dominicans—and suggests Dominican influence in this series of frescoes.

The part of the fresco representing hell has areas that also suggest Dominican intervention in support of orthodoxy and of the power of a united Church. Although most of the inscriptions that originally identified the figural groups in hell have worn away, two at the top left of the image read "Antichrist" and "Niccolo"; the figure identified as Niccolo is being hacked to pieces by demons and is further described by an inscription indicating that he loves Muhammad. These two figures have been identified as Muhammad and the **antipope**, Nicholas V, who had been in Pisa in 1328. The Pisans supported the Avignon papacy and therefore regarded the Rome-based rival claimants as schismatic. Nicholas's debased presence in this fresco is a further sign of orthodoxy. The catalogue of sins represented by horrifically tortured figures cascading over the wall, each punishment duly identified with an inscription, has the same scholastic completeness to it as Dante's narration of the fate of the damned in the *Inferno*. This detailed and didactic representation of hell may indicate an academic religious figure (possibly the Dominican monk and poet Fra Domenico Cavalca, of the convent of Santa Caterina in Pisa) as an advisor for the painting.

Santa Maria Novella in Florence

Just as the Dominicans had influenced the development of the arts in Pisa, so also did they provide an environment for some of Florence's most extensive projects of the late 1300s. The transept and surrounding altars of their church of Santa Maria Novella, although begun at the same time as the Franciscans' Santa Croce, apparently took longer to complete. It was only in the mid-fourteenth century that the sanctuary and the chapel at the north end of the transept were complete and ready to receive their decoration (see Fig. 1.24), long after Giotto and Taddeo Gaddi had completed their major fresco cycles at Santa Croce.

The Strozzi Chapel and the Black Death   At the north end of the transept Andrea di Cione, known as Orcagna (active 1343/44–68 Florence), and his brother, Nardo di Cione (active 1343–66 Florence), heads of a very large and active workshop, provided the altarpiece and frescoes for the Strozzi Chapel, one of the most important decorative programs of its time. The Strozzi Chapel (Fig. 3.16) looks today much as it did when it was completed in 1357. It is raised over what had originally been the communal burial ground for the Dominican friars affiliated with Santa Maria Novella and it is dedicated to St. Thomas Aquinas, arguably the most important Dominican saint after Dominic himself and St. Peter Martyr. The codifier of Church theology and a leading figure in the philosophy of scholasticism, Thomas had been canonized in 1323. This chapel provided an important opportunity for an exposition of Dominican thought.

The wall facing the entrance to the chapel is divided vertically by a large central lancet window whose stained glass shows a standing Virgin and Child, the primary devotional image of the Dominicans, and, below them, a standing figure of St. Thomas Aquinas. The frescoes on this wall depict the *Last Judgment*, with Christ appearing at the apex of the window arch. Below him are the Virgin and St. John the Baptist with the Apostles, whose preaching and proselytization the Dominicans, also known as the Order of Preachers, emulated. To the left of the window on the lowest tier of the fresco are the haloed elect and on the right the tormented figures of the damned.

Dominican commitment to orthodoxy, order, and the institutional Church is evident on the left wall of the chapel. There a *Paradise* (Fig. 3.17) shows the elect arranged row upon row, around and beneath the figures of the enthroned Divinity and the Virgin. Both figures are crowned; the figure of God even holds a scepter. In this configuration the Virgin—or metaphorically, Maria Ecclesia (the Church)—shares unmistakably the power of the Godhead on the model familiar from Roman thirteenth-century mosaics (see Fig. 1.35). Tellingly, at the bottom right of the fresco an angel leads a female donor figure into the ranks of the elect in Paradise, not unlike Mona Vaggia Manfredi in Taddeo Gaddi's refectory fresco in Santa Croce (see Fig. 2.14) and Fina Buzzacarini in the Paduan Baptistry. Although there is no clear documentary evidence of a patron for the Strozzi Chapel and its decoration, this donor figure strongly suggests the involvement of a female member of the family in the

commission. On the right wall of the chapel, opposite the *Paradise*, is a depiction of hell. Like the *Last Judgment* fresco in the Camposanto in Pisa, Nardo di Cione's vision of hell places each of the major sins in a separate ledge-like compositional frame which creates its own illusion of depth. A torment fitting the nature of the sin racks the body of each figure. Nardo also carefully labeled each of the sins so that there would be no doubt about what was being represented, again repeating the scholastic catalogue seen at Pisa and the enumeration of punishments of Dante's *Inferno*.

Orcagna's *Strozzi Altarpiece* (Fig. 3.18), which still stands on the chapel's altar, also incorporates iconography relating to both the Dominican order and the Last Judgment. It is a richly decorative painting, with tooled gold background, gold punchwork imitating embroidered fabric, and large areas of expensive lapis lazuli blue. The sheer opulence of the painting indicates its importance. At the center of the altarpiece is a figure of God, seated rigidly and frontally in a radiant mandorla of cherubim, suspended in a light-filled heaven which defies specific spatial description. On his right he is flanked by a crowned Virgin (the dedicatee of the church) in a Dominican habit who presents her protégé St. Thomas Aquinas, to him. St. Thomas (who should perhaps be understood as representing the Dominican order as a whole) kneels before God in a typical donor pose. To God's left St. Peter kneels to receive the keys that symbolize his office—and his power—as pope. Behind Peter is St. John the Baptist, the two forming a group that balances that of the Virgin and St. Thomas. The saints in the outermost compartments of the altarpiece include St. Michael the Archangel, a figure weighing the relative merits of the elect and the damned in Last Judgment iconography; St. Catherine of Alexandria, a saint especially dear to the Dominicans; St. Lawrence, whose hagiography includes the curious tale that on each Friday he descends from heaven to purgatory to release one soul from torment; and St. Paul, who, when paired with Peter, often personifies the papacy. Thus the saints at the outer edges of the painting are, like St. Thomas and St. Peter, references to the Dominicans and their support of the papacy as well as to death and the Last Judgment.

The blank, staring aspect of the central figure of the painting and its placement in an undefined space has suggested quite reasonably to some scholars a throwback to thirteenth-century saints' altarpieces (see Fig. 19). When such interpretations of this iconic representation are coupled with the notion that style developed progressively along the naturalistic lines evident in the paintings of Cavallini and Giotto, however, they lead to a misleading hypothesis that the *Strozzi Altarpiece* represents a radical shift in style away from the innovations of these

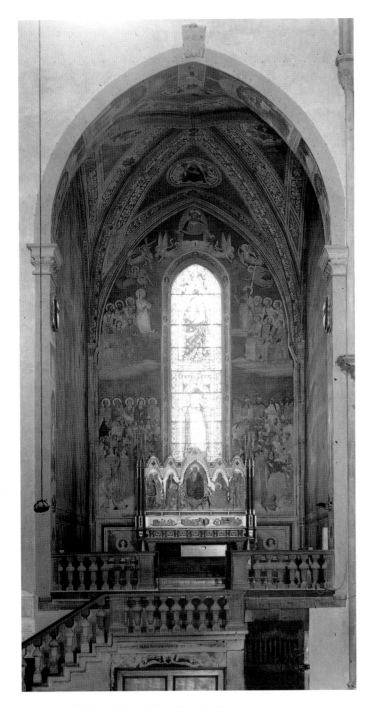

3.16 Strozzi Chapel, Santa Maria Novella, Florence

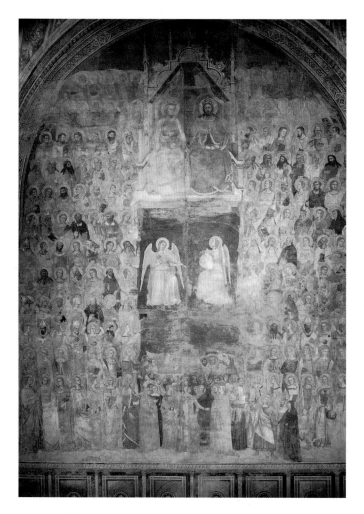

3.17 *Paradise*, c. 1355, NARDO DI CIONE, Strozzi Chapel, Santa Maria Novella, Florence. Fresco

artists. A common explanation for this presumed retrograde style places its cause in the psychological devastation brought about by the catastrophic mortality rates of the bubonic plague. The Black Death—so called because of the color of the lesions that it caused on the bodies of the plague victims—struck central Italy in 1348, following upon years of bad crops and famine. It had begun in central Asia and had been carried to Europe by Italian trading ships traveling from the Crimea to the Italian peninsula. In the virulent form that the plague took during the summer months of 1348, infected persons, bitten by engorged fleas carried by brown rats, usually developed red-ringed black buboes or lesions in the groin or the armpits and died within a matter of days, leaving no time for either spiritual or material preparation.

Boccaccio (1313–75), perhaps the most gifted writer in central Italy in the mid-fourteenth century, described the ravages of the plague in the first book of the *Decameron*. He indicated not only the rapacity of the disease itself but also the social breakdown that accompanied it:

. . . people behaved as though their days were numbered, and treated their belongings and their own persons with equal abandon. Hence most houses had become common property, and any passing stranger could make himself at home as naturally as though he were the rightful owner. But for all their riotous manner of living, these people always took good care to avoid any contact with the sick. All respect for the laws of God and man had virtually broken down and been extinguished in our city. For like everybody else, those ministers and executors of the laws who were not either dead or ill were left with so few subordinates that they were unable to discharge any of their duties.

The sick and the dying were left untended out of fear; normal rituals of prayer and penance surrounding death which acted as a transition to the afterlife were largely suspended; and the very continuity of the family and community seemed threatened by the irrational violence of the disease. One contemporary explanation for the plague, as Boccaccio noted, was that it was a "punishment signifying God's righteous anger at our iniquitous way of life."

The plague was particularly virulent during the summer months of 1348, then abated during the colder winter season. Carried to other parts of Europe through trade, the plague reached England and Scandinavia in the early 1350s and appeared as far east as Poland at about the same time. Although it then appeared to have run its course, the plague had not died out. Especially destructive epidemics were recorded in Italy in 1363 and 1400, and minor outbreaks occurred throughout this period and well into the sixteenth century.

Historians have tended to concentrate on the 1348 occurrence of the Black Death because it is the first example of plague in the modern period; because literary accounts of it, such as Boccaccio's *Decameron*, are so vivid; because death was both inevitable and quick once the disease was contracted; and because the mortality rate in that year was so high. In Tuscany, for example, a conservative estimate places the death rate in the cities (always greater than in the country) at 60 percent of the population. A contemporary observer wrote of 1,800 people dying in Florence on the feast of St. John the Baptist (June 24), the patron saint of the city, and another 1,800 the following day. Even allowing for exaggeration, in a city of fewer than 100,000 people those numbers are startling, especially given the duration of the plague through the summer months.

Advocates of the long-accepted theory that the plague had a major impact on the style and iconography of the visual arts have often used the iconic and flattened forms of the central figures of the *Strozzi Altarpiece* and the

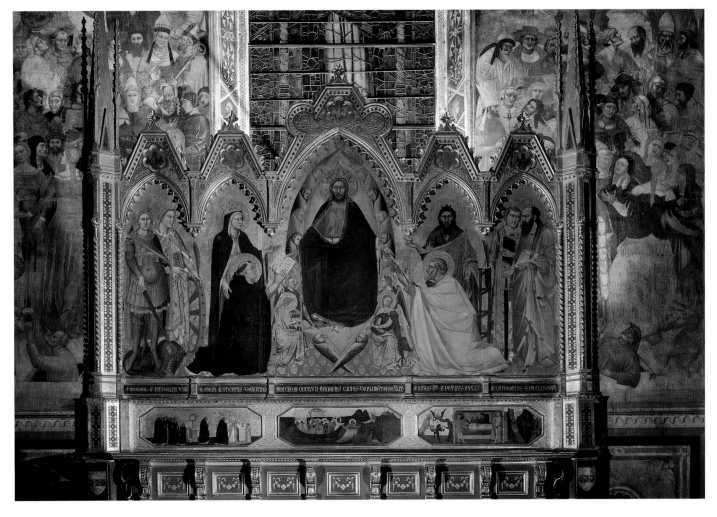

3.18 *Strozzi Altarpiece*, 1354–57, ANDREA DI CIONE (called ORCAGNA), Strozzi Chapel, Santa Maria Novella, Florence. Tempera on panel, 9' × 9' 8"
(2.74 × 2.95 m)

horrific presentation of hell in the Pisa *Last Judgment* (see Fig. 3.15; now dated *prior* to the plague) as evidence to support the theory. But if the 1348 plague had truly been as influential in the arts as some critics have suggested, stylistic and iconographic references similar to those of these two paintings should also occur in works of art from other parts of Italy, where the plague had mortality rates nearly as high as those in Tuscany. Since this seems not to have been the case, it seems unlikely that the style used for the figure of Christ in the *Strozzi Altarpiece* was primarily a response to the plague.

From the transept of the church the *Strozzi Altarpiece* is seen together with the *Last Judgment* wall (see Fig. 3.16). The figure of God in the altarpiece can be seen as the seated Judge which the lancet window precluded in the fresco of the *Last Judgment* on the wall behind. Read this way, the stylistic particulars of the figure stand well within the conventions of this subject matter. Paintings such as Simone Martini's *St. Louis of Toulouse Altarpiece* (see Fig. 2.50) or Ambrogio Lorenzetti's *Allegory of Good*

Government (see Fig. 2.25) also depict images of rulership and judgment in a conventional hieratic form. In fact the Dominicans employed a similar type of figure for the first major altarpiece dedicated to St. Thomas for their church in Pisa. In this painting, once attributed to Francesco Traini but now to Lippo Memmi (Fig. 3.19), St. Thomas is also seated in a spatially ambiguous mandorla, and his flattened pose is decidedly different from virtually all of the other figures in the painting. This convention of the seated, hieratic figure was repeatedly used in illustrations in legal treatises during this period. There the figure of God as the fountainhead and provider of civil and canon law is seated with a king at his left and a pope at his right in the same flattened compositional arrangement as the central three figures of the *Strozzi Altarpiece*. Thus Orcagna and his Dominican patrons apparently wished to use this visual convention of authority to convey the orthodoxy of the order's teaching through the writings of St. Thomas and to suggest the special relationship between the order and the papacy. It is telling in

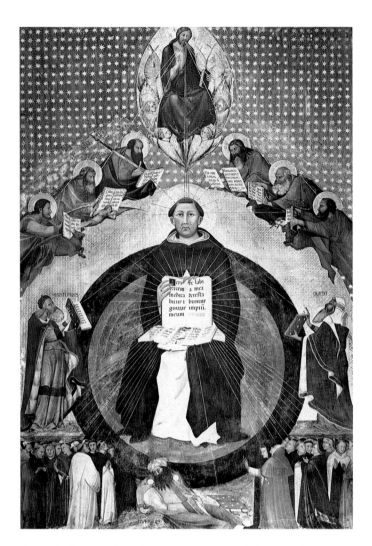

3.19 *Glorification of St. Thomas*, c. 1355, commissioned by the Dominicans from LIPPO MEMMI, formerly attributed to Francesco Traini, for Santa Caterina, Pisa. Tempera on panel

To Thomas's right, in the conventional position of honor, is Aristotle. Plato is to Thomas's left while Averroes is at his feet

Memmi's depiction that Averroes, an Arab philosopher used to represent heresy, is humiliated (literally 'on the ground') beneath the feet of Thomas, who holds his own writings in his lap.

A close reading of the *Strozzi Altarpiece* reveals that the figures, other than those framed by the central three arches, are not flat, nor are they situated in a spaceless environment. On the outer edges St. Michael the Archangel and St. Catherine, in particular, are fully volumetric and naturally posed, typical of current developments in the depiction of human figures. Orcagna's use of both naturalistic and iconic styles in his altarpiece is governed by the function each figure performs within the work. Given the multiple messages that the altarpiece conveys—including the devotional needs of the Strozzi family who endowed the chapel, the establishment of the Dominican St. Thomas

Aquinas as an important saint within the Christian hierarchy, the Dominicans' alliance with the papacy, and their support of orthodoxy—it is not surprising that the painting conflates several conventions of style and iconography.

The Guidalotti Chapel Also within the precincts of Santa Maria Novella is another major fresco cycle from the middle years of the fourteenth century. In 1365–67 Andrea Bonaiuti (Andrea da Firenze; active 1346 Florence–after 1379 Florence) painted the walls of the Guidalotti Chapel (Fig. 3.23) in the church's cloister. Andrea was an esteemed member of his profession, serving on an advisory panel of painters to Florence Cathedral and as a consul of his guild. Here he was called on to decorate a space that was used as a burial chapel for the Guidalotti family and also as a chapter house for the resident Dominican community. Mico [Buonamico] Guidalotti's tomb slab still remains on the floor before the altar; the inscription filling its border indicates that he was a merchant who had the chapel built and painted. It adds, tellingly, that he was buried in a Dominican habit, a privilege allowed him as much for his generosity, one assumes, as for his goodness. Andrea's impressive and remarkably well-preserved frescoes provide a compendium of the stylistic possibilities in painting in this period.

A *Crucifixion* narrative (Fig. 3.22) decorates the altar wall of the chapel. Opposite it, on the entrance wall, is a cycle narrating the life of St. Peter Martyr (c. 1205–52; Fig. 3.20), a Dominican saint particularly venerated in Florence, where he had been perhaps the most popular preacher of his day. In the *Way of the Cross* and the *Harrowing of Hell*, which occupy the lower part of the *Crucifixion*, architecture and landscape create a convincing illusion of depth behind the figures. In the Crucifixion scene itself the crosses of the two thieves create recessional axes into space, although the actual space depicted is relatively shallow. The thieves twist convulsively on their crosses while a group of figures runs from an attacking soldier at the right. The *Preaching of St. Peter Martyr* depicts an event that occurred in the piazza outside Santa Maria Novella. The saint stands in a pulpit (rendered with careful attention to perspective) while the listening figures, crowded into the space around him, twist and turn, actively gesturing in response to his sermon. Figures in both the Crucifixion and Peter Martyr frescoes respond in ways that enhance the emotional aspects of these events. They have all of the naturalism and dramatic intensity that characterize figures in the most advanced painting of the century.

Completely different compositional structures appear in the frescoes on the side walls of the chapel. In the *Apotheosis of St. Thomas* (Fig. 3.21) on the left wall of the chapel, St. Thomas sits enthroned in a Gothic aedicule

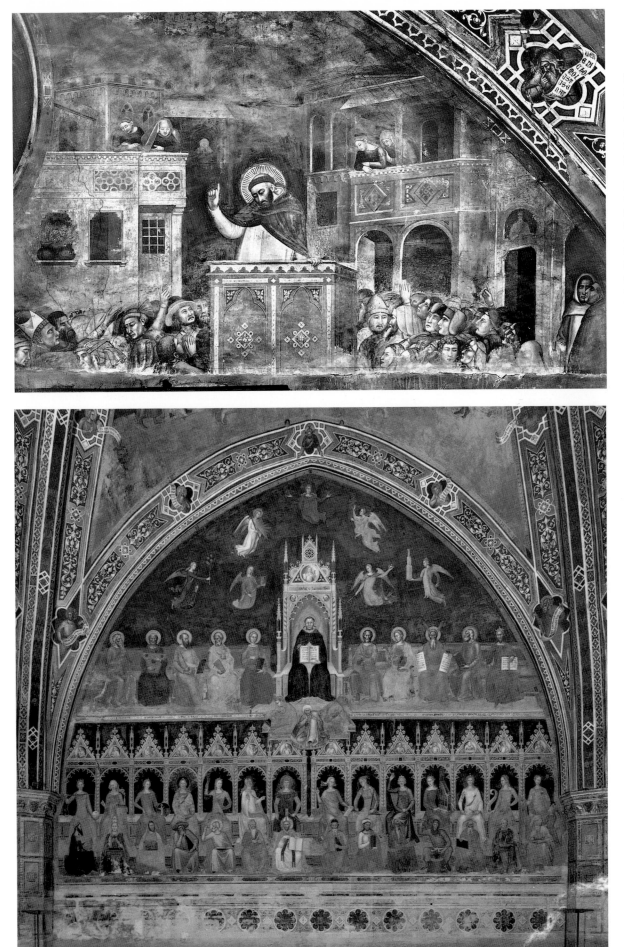

3.20 *Scenes from the Life of St. Peter Martyr*, detail, c. 1365–67, chapel construction and fresco decoration provided for in the 1355 will of Buonamico (Mico) Guidalotti; frescoes subsequently commissioned from ANDREA BONAIUTI (called ANDREA DA FIRENZE), for the entrance wall of the Guidalotti Chapel, Santa Maria Novella, Florence. Fresco, width 38′ (11.6 m)

3.21 *Apotheosis of St. Thomas*, c. 1365–67, chapel construction and fresco decoration provided for in the 1355 will of Buonamico (Mico) Guidalotti; frescoes subsequently commissioned from ANDREA BONAIUTI (called ANDREA DA FIRENZE), for the left wall of the Guidalotti Chapel, Santa Maria Novella, Florence. Fresco. width 38′ (11.6 m) flanked by figures of Apostles and prophets. Comparison of this fresco with the *Glorification of St. Thomas* (see Fig. 3.19) suggests that Thomas's flattened frontal pose was canonic and that his word is law, the definer of orthodoxy for the Church. The configuration of a centrally placed figure flanked by smaller figures spread out in a row is familiar from Last Judgment imagery and from works such as Lorenzetti's *Buon Comune* (see Fig. 2.25). In the *Apotheosis* St. Thomas is also accompanied by personifications of virtues, who float in the sky overhead. At his feet there are representations of Sabellius, Averroes, and Arius, leaders of well-known religious groups considered by the papacy—and thus by the Dominicans—as heretical. Below St. Thomas are seated figures, seven representing the divisions of theology and seven of the liberal arts; below each is seated the historical personage who best

represents the theological or scholarly concept. Thus the emperor Justinian is seated before the figure of Civil Law, St. Augustine before Theology, Pythagoras before Arithmetic, Euclid before Geometry, and Cicero before Rhetoric. Given the prominent role that the Dominican order played in education during this period, it is no surprise to see knowledge personified and codified in this

3.23 (opposite) *Way of Salvation*, c. 1365–67, chapel construction and fresco decoration provided for in the 1355 will of Buonamico (Mico) Guidalotti; frescoes subsequently commissioned from ANDREA BONAIUTI (called ANDREA DA FIRENZE), for the right wall of the Guidalotti Chapel, Santa Maria Novella, Florence. Fresco, width 38' (11.6 m)

This chapel, built as a chapterhouse for the monastery as well as a funerary chapel, is now commonly called the Spanish Chapel because in the sixteenth century it was a place of worship for the Spanish colony in Florence.

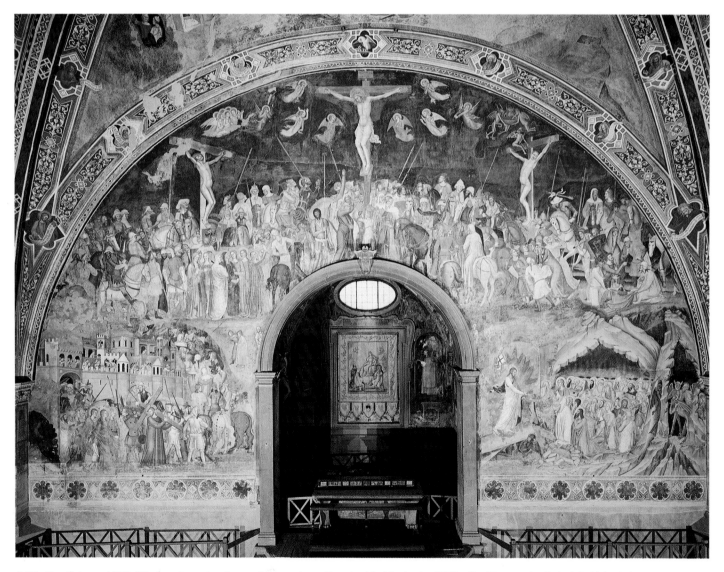

3.22 *Crucifixion* c. 1365–67, chapel construction and fresco decoration provided for in the 1355 will of Buonamico (Mico) Guidalotti; frescoes subsequently commissioned from ANDREA BONAIUTI (called ANDREA DA FIRENZE), for the altar wall of the Guidalotti Chapel, Santa Maria Novella, Florence. Fresco, width 38' (11.6 m)

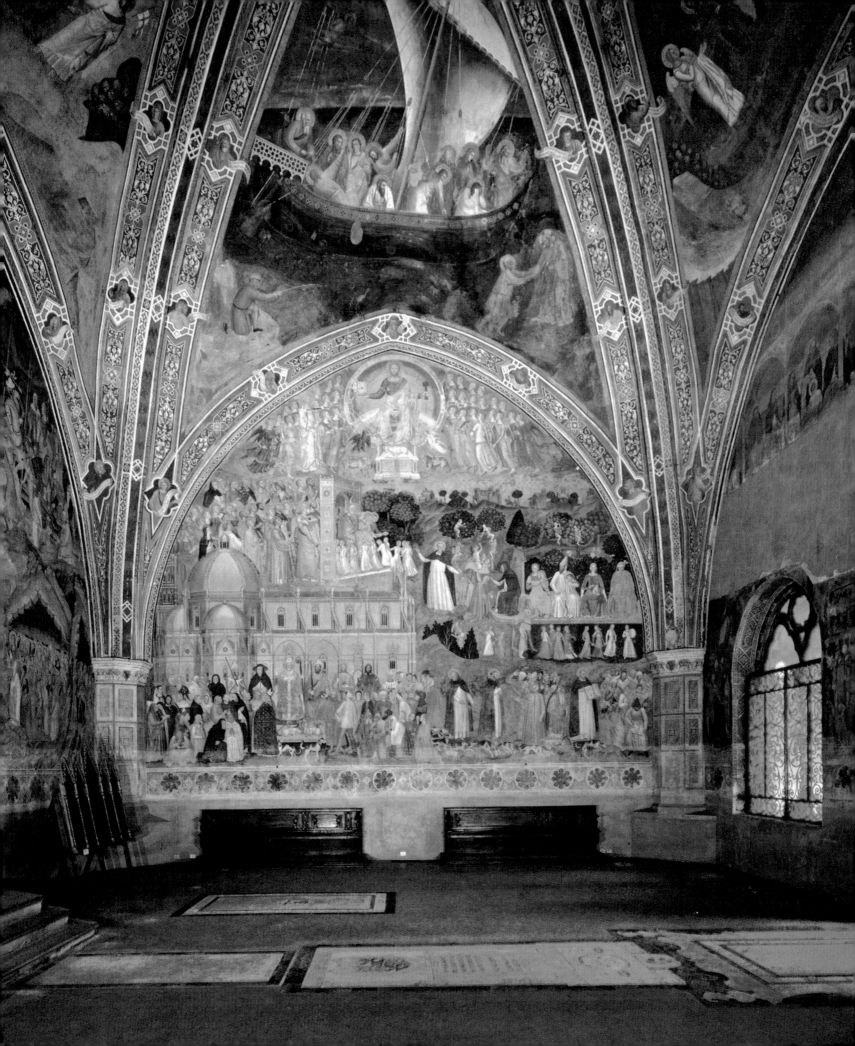

way with St. Thomas. Yet despite the orthodox, didactic content of this fresco Andrea allowed himself some artistic experimentation, overlapping the painted architectural frame of the fresco with fictive thrones as if to suggest that they actually extend out from the wall, thus pushing figures illusionistically into the space of the room.

The fresco on the wall opposite the *Apotheosis* represents the *Way of Salvation* (see Fig. 3.23). It is unlike any of the other three walls of the room in the way that it is divided compositionally into several different areas. Figures change scale radically from one group to the next and include both hieratic and natural types. In some areas space is compressed parallel to the picture plane, as in the foreground; in others it is three-dimensional, as in the treatment of the landscape at the upper right. Each section of the fresco seems to illustrate some different aspect of Dominican activity and belief, strung along in no immediately apparent order, but often brought into focus by the familiar white and black robes of the Dominican monks, whose punning black and white dogs, the *Domini canes* ("Dogs of God"), rush about at their feet at the bottom of the composition chasing the wolves of heresy.

In the lower left quadrant of the wall a representation of the Florence Duomo, unfinished at this time, symbolizes the universal Church. The Duomo provides a backdrop for a group of seated figures whose relative status is conventionally indicated by size. In the center of this group are the pope (probably Innocent VI; r. 1352–62) and the emperor, Charles IV. The pope sits slightly higher than the emperor, a clear indication of the Dominican belief in the supremacy of the spiritual ruler over the temporal one. Cardinal Giles Albornoz, the most important papal diplomat in Italy during this period, is seated in a position of honor immediately to the pope's right. Other religious and temporal leaders flank this central group and provide another unmistakable image of authority within the chapter house, comparable to the *Apotheosis of St. Thomas* on the opposite wall. Above the Duomo the elect are welcomed into heaven by St. Peter, a juxtaposition making clear the Church's authority in providing salvation. The Dominicans figure prominently as the lay person's guide on this journey. In the lower right corner of the fresco Dominicans are preaching and converting heretics. Above them, another Dominican points to

CONTEMPORARY VOICE

The Bridge of Salvation

In this passage from *The Dialogue*, by St. Catherine of Siena, the metaphor of a stepped bridge represents Christ the Redeemer. St. Catherine (1347–80) was a Dominican nun and the author of several devotional works and poems. It was largely through her influence that Pope Gregory XI was persuaded to return to Rome from Avignon. She was interrogated about her sometimes unorthodox beliefs by Dominican inquisitors in the Chapterhouse at Santa Maria Novella.

Then God eternal, to stir up even more that soul's love for the salvation of souls, responded to her:

Before I show you what I want to show you, and what you asked to see, I want to describe the bridge for you. I have told you that it stretches from heaven to earth by reason of my having joined myself with your humanity, which I formed from the earth's clay.

This bridge, my only-begotten Son, has three stairs. Two of them he built on the wood of the most holy cross, and the third even as he tasted the great bitterness of the gall and vinegar they gave him to drink. You will recognize in these three stairs three spiritual stages.

The first stair is the feet, which symbolize the affections. For just as the feet carry the body, the affections carry the soul. My Son's nailed feet are a stair by which you can climb to his side, where you will see revealed his inmost heart. For when the soul has climbed up on the feet of affection and looked with her mind's eye into my Son's opened heart, she begins to feel the love of her own heart in his consummate and unspeakable love . . . . Then the soul, seeing how tremendously she is loved, is herself filled to overflowing with love. So, having climbed the second stair, she reaches the third. This is his mouth, where she finds peace from the terrible war she has had to wage because of her sins.

At the first stair, lifting the feet of her affections from the earth, she stripped herself of sin. At the second she dressed herself in love for virtue. And at the third she tasted peace.

So the bridge has three stairs, and you can reach the last by climbing the first two. The last stair is so high that the flooding waters cannot strike it—for the venom of sin never touched my Son . . . .

When my goodness saw that you could be drawn in no other way, I sent him to be lifted onto the wood of the cross. I made of that cross an anvil where this child of humankind could be hammered into an instrument to release humankind from death and restore it to the life of grace. In this way he drew everything to himself: for he proved his unspeakable love, and the human heart is always drawn by love.

(from Susan Noffke. Trans. *Catherine of Siena: The Dialogue*. New York: Paulist Press, 1980, pp. 64–5)

the heavenly reward awaiting confessed and absolved Christians. Four courtly figures seated in a bower mid-right are reminiscent of the elegantly dressed nobles listening to music in the Camposanto frescoes in Pisa (see Fig. 3.14), and may represent the worldly life before conversion. They provide the antithesis to the good work of the Dominicans.

The seated figure of the judging Christ in the apex of the fresco conspicuously displays the keys of papal power. In the vault above him is a depiction of the *Navicella*. This image of the Church as the ship of state or the vessel of salvation is the same subject depicted by Giotto in Old St. Peter's at the beginning of the century (see Fig. 1.42). The compositional linkage of the *Navicella*, the judging Christ, and the relative positions of the two frescoes may be a metaphor for the support given to the Church by the Dominicans.

In this room, where the Florentine Dominican community met regularly, where novices were received into the order, where each friar confessed his sins to the prior and to the community, these frescoes provided a constant message of indoctrination for the monastic community. They provided a model for preaching in the person of St. Peter Martyr, a model for learning in the figure of St. Thomas, and incentives to obedience to the institutional Church. Whereas the Crucifixion fresco contains imagery fitting for Mico Guidalotti's funerary chapel, the *Way of Salvation* and the other frescoes emphatically assert the Dominicans' control of this important space. Each of the subjects given to Andrea da Firenze presented him with different narrative and allegorical demands. It is not surprising that he responded with such variations of style from one wall to another.

Social Upheaval and Civic Works in Florence

Florentine history for the later decades of the fourteenth century is punctuated with moments of social upheaval. In 1363 the plague struck again with particular severity. In the next decade the Florentines opposed the papacy over control of land, leading to a papal interdict on the city from 1376 to 1378. This meant that normal liturgical functions were suspended; among other prohibitions, the dying could not be confessed and the Eucharist could not be exposed, thus effectively closing the routes of salvation for the populace. Even the bells of the churches were silenced, which in a late-medieval city not only eliminated the one sound that could communicate over a large area, but effectively limited the ability of people to measure their days. (The two years of the interdict are known as the War of the Eight Saints to honor the eight governors of the city, who staunchly maintained what

they perceived to be Florentine independence from an encroaching neighboring power, namely the papacy.)

Then in 1378 the wool workers (*ciompi*) revolted against the guild (the Arte della Lana) that controlled their livelihoods and against the owners of their shops, causing a political eruption known as the Ciompi Revolution, which essentially toppled the upper classes from political power. When, in 1381, the wealthy classes regained control of the government they punished the workers with particular ruthlessness.

In this environment, the city's major building projects were subject to delays. Work at the Duomo seems to have progressed in fits and starts during the fourteenth century, with repeated changes in plans and challenges to the already established program. In mid-1355 a committee of twelve laymen and artists was appointed to judge the feasibility of a model for the choir end of the building that had been submitted earlier that year by Francesco Talenti (active 1300s). In 1357 a new plan with three bays in the nave had been approved, and by this time the octagonal crossing and the surrounding spaces had already been assigned. In 1366 three concurrent commissions were charged with developing a new plan, which apparently was agreed upon in 1368 when competing designs were ordered to be destroyed. At various times plebiscites were held to choose the best of competing models—an indication of civic investment in the planning of the Duomo. The model of 1368 gave the Duomo its present form of a four-bayed nave (see Fig. 2.16). Its three equal-sized tribunes, the cluster of polygonal shapes that make up the eastern end of the Duomo, echo the shape of the Baptistry and suggest a deliberate intention to create a harmonious group of forms in the heart of the city.

In 1366, the same year that the commission initiated the last plan for the Duomo, the Arte del Calimala commissioned the goldsmiths Leonardo di ser Giovanni (active 1358–71 Florence), Betto di Geri (active 1366–1402 Florence), and others to make a large silver-covered altar (Fig. 3.24; see also Fig. 3.1) for the Baptistry. Conceived on a lavish scale meant to demonstrate the guild's economic power in the city, the altar was not finished until the sixteenth century. Rectangular reliefs depicting scenes from the life of St. John the Baptist, to whom the building is dedicated, were set into the front and sides of the altar; the architectural frame is composed of numerous Gothic niches, each containing a small statuette. The reliefs differ significantly from those on the same subject created by Andrea Pisano for the south doors of the Baptistry (see Fig. 2.17); their architectural backgrounds offer more illusionistic spaces for the action, all of which appears to take place behind the plane of the relief rather than in front. Clearly these sculptors must have closely studied contemporary narrative painting.

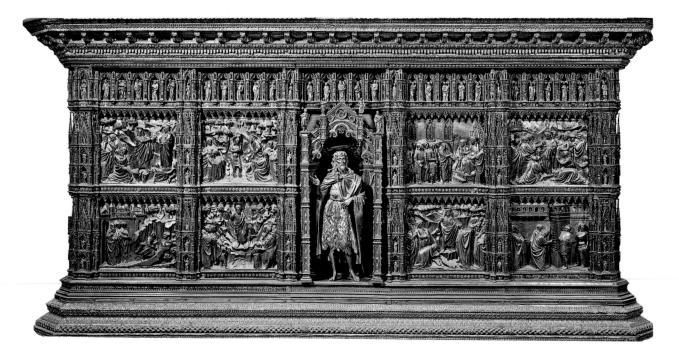

3.24 Silver altar, 1366–77, commissioned by the Arte del Calimala from LEONARDO DI SER GIOVANNI, BETTO DI GERI, and others for the Baptistry, Florence. Silver on a wooden base, front face 3' 9¼" × 8' 7" (1.15 × 2.62 m) (Museo dell'Opera del Duomo, Florence). See also Fig. 3.1.

The central niche figure of St. John the Baptist was added to the altar in 1452; the sculptor is Michelozzo di Bartolomeo.

A comparison with the *Pala d'Oro* in Venice (see Fig. 3.2) indicates that, while the Silver Altar is not as lavish in its coloration or in the variety of its component parts, it does share a repetition of form, and an insistent multiplicity of similar units, as if sheer opulence was itself the *raison-d'être* of the commission. On the other hand, the restrained geometry of the Silver Altar subordinates the myriad Gothic niches containing tiny statuettes to an overall structural order. This allows the narrative reliefs of the life of the patron saint of the church and of the city to read through the richness of the decoration, appropriate for the altar of a building that is itself inscribed with a severe if bold geometrical design (see Fig. 1.9). Six of the eight panels on the front of the Altar show a figure dominating the narrative from the center of the panel. The central niche with the statuette of St. John the Baptist is framed with scenes from his life, recalling early saints' altarpieces (see Figs. 1.25 and 1.26), as if the reuse of an earlier compositional format—and perhaps even the squat figural types seen in the reliefs—were appropriate for the decoration of this Romanesque building.

Or San Michele

Or San Michele was originally simply an open loggia built in 1337 around a modest architectural tabernacle protecting a miracle-working image of the Madonna and Child, then in the grain market of the city. The upper stories of the building were added after the plague of 1348 as a granary to protect against famine. Located in the heart of the city on an axis extending from the cathedral to the town hall, Or San Michele functioned as a guild church to which each of the guilds contributed an image of its patron saint to mark its participation at the site. The most important single addition to Or San Michele at this time was an architecturally scaled marble tabernacle (Fig. 3.25), to house a painting already at the site by one of the most successful students to come from Giotto's workshop, Bernardo Daddi (active c. 1320–48 Florence). Daddi's painting had replaced an earlier miracle-working image of the Virgin and Child around 1346. The tabernacle, built with donations made after the plague of 1348, has an inscription on its back under a large relief of the *Burial and Assumption of the Virgin* (Fig. 3.26) dating it to 1359 and bearing the name of Orcagna. A railing was added to the tabernacle in 1366, protecting it from the milling crowds that often filled the building's ground floor—at that time not yet completely walled in. The dome that crowns the tabernacle may echo a proposed design for the dome of the unfinished cathedral—much like the dome in Andrea da Firenze's fresco of the *Way of Salvation*, completed at about the same time (see Fig.

3.25 (right) Tabernacle, c. 1355–59, ANDREA DI CIONE (called ORCAGNA), Or San Michele, Florence. Marble, inlaid stone, and glass

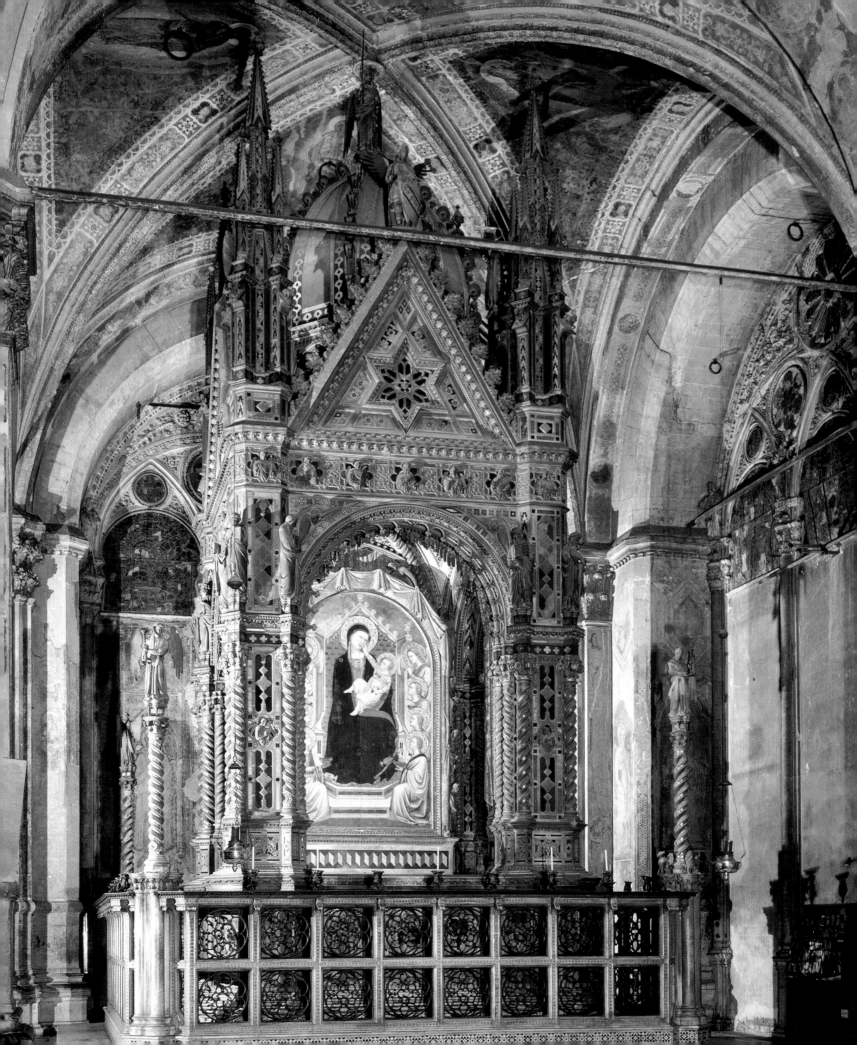

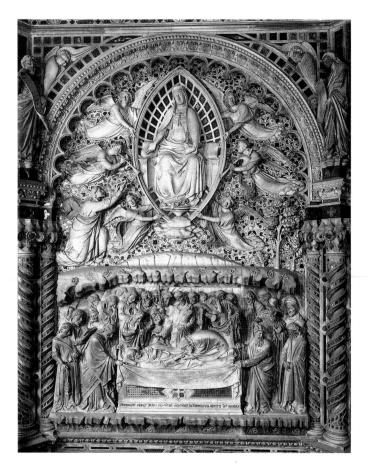

3.26 Tabernacle, c. 1355–59, detail of back wall showing the *Burial and Assumption of the Virgin*, ANDREA DI CIONE (called ORCAGNA), Or San Michele, Florence. Marble, inlaid stone, and glass

3.23). The form of Orcagna's tabernacle underscores the importance of the Duomo's construction in the artistic life of the city.

Despite awkward passages which betray the contributions of several members of Orcagna's workshop, the sculpture on the tabernacle is notable for its naturalism. Even where conventional patterns of composition dictate form and where abstract patterns of mosaic make up the background, as in the *Assumption of the Virgin*, the figures have a sense of volumetric fullness that places them in the tradition of painting established by Giotto and also exemplified by Orcagna's own painting style. The Virgin, for example, the masses of her limbs clearly evident beneath the drapery, extends her hand toward the kneeling St. Thomas as she prepares to hand him her belt, proof that it is really she who is being lifted into heaven. Even given his flattened profile pose, the volumes of Thomas's body betray the urgency of his action.

By contrast, the paintings in Or San Michele, which were designed to cover virtually every surface of the interior, including its piers, show what appear to be deliberate inclusions of an iconic or non-naturalistic style.

A typical example is *St. John the Evangelist* (Fig. 3.27), painted by Nardo di Cione's student Giovanni del Biondo (c. 1333/35 Florence–1399 Florence) for the Arte della Seta (the Silk Manufacturers' and Goldsmiths' Guild), which was attached to a pier immediately facing the tabernacle. St. John is seated frontally against a gold ground, in a familiar pose and style for the period. Although the painting is somewhat awkward in its handling of form, it is clear that Giovanni was attempting to create an intense, emblematic image of the patron saint for Or San Michele, appropriate for a building conceived as an expression of the power of the guilds in Florence.

Unlike other images of St. John, Giovanni's painting includes figures of Pride, Avarice, and Vainglory trampled under the feet of the seated saint. These vices are the same ones that appear flying over the head of tyranny in the Lorenzetti fresco of *Bad Government* in Siena (see Fig. 2.28). Thus it appears likely that the powerful Arte della Seta—far from commissioning a simple devotional image—deliberately used iconography related to civic order. The dating of the altarpiece is problematic, although current opinion places it, on the basis of style and the history of Or San Michele, to the years around 1381, shortly after the Ciompi Revolution and the papal interdict. The Arte della Seta, governed by the same social class that had been threatened by the *ciompi*, here seems to equate its own image with political and social stability. If, indeed, that was the intended message, it would explain the frontal pose of the saint. A political message has supplanted the religious one normally conveyed by this pose. The painting is thus a reminder of the inextricable connections between the civil, corporate, and religious spheres of the Italian communes of this time. Here in Or San Michele, one of the major centers of corporate and religious activity in Florence, the guilds clearly articulated their central, powerful role in the city's life. If there is a conservative reaction in the painting styles of the fourteenth century in Florence, this is it, and it is tied to issues of power and hierarchy similar to those explored by the Dominicans in Santa Maria Novella.

Family Commissions

After the Ciompi Revolt of 1378, the disruptions caused by the papal interdict in 1376–8, and the restitution of the oligarchy in 1381, a family's public presence was a matter of some consequence. Thus it is not surprising that during the last two decades of the fourteenth century prominent families continued to commission large fresco cycles for their chapels. The style used for these cycles established a pattern for fresco painting in Florence that was to last well into the fifteenth century.

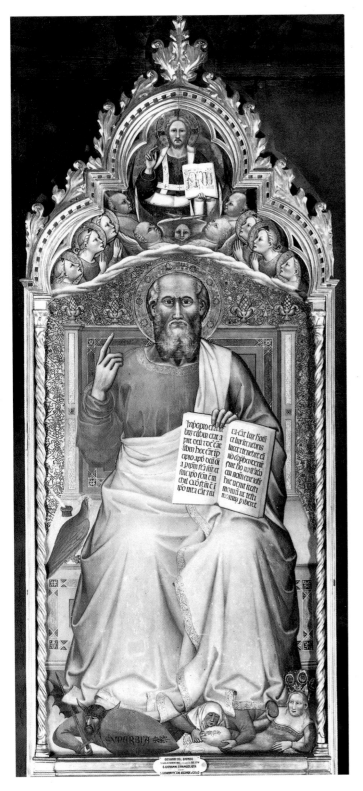

3.27 *St. John the Evangelist*, c. 1381, commissioned by the Arte della Seta from GIOVANNI DEL BIONDO for Or San Michele, Florence. Tempera on panel, 92 × 41" (234 × 104 cm) (Galleria dell'Accademia, Florence)

The Castellani Chapel When Michele di Vanni Castellani wrote his will in 1383 he stipulated that his heirs build and decorate a new chapel at Santa Croce to honor him and their family. As many as four painters, including Agnolo Gaddi, Taddeo Gaddi's son, may have worked on the chapel, an indication that there was some pressure to have the project completed quickly. Each bay of the side walls of the chapel has a narrative program of a different saint especially revered by the Castellani family (John the Baptist, Nicholas, Anthony Abbot, and John the Evangelist). Figures and spatial environments throughout the chapel recall the Giottesque tradition— not surprising given the fact that Gaddi's father had been trained by Giotto.

Immediately to the left of the entrance to the chapel is an image of *St. John on Patmos* (Fig. 3.28) which presents a virtual quotation from Giotto's Peruzzi Chapel frescoes, just across the transept (see Fig. 2.7). Rather than merely slavishly copying a venerated painting tradition, however, the Castellani's artists may have been seeking to link their patrons to earlier oligarchic Florentine families, represented by the Peruzzi. The stylistic similarities between the frescoes might suggest an equal status of the patrons but, more importantly, an unbroken leadership of oligarchic families, despite the Ciompi Revolt (during which the Castellani Palace had been burned). The inclusion in the Castellani frescoes of St. Louis of Toulouse, the patron saint of the oligarchic Guelf Party, and of St. Anthony Abbot, whose feast day marks the day of the return of the oligarchy to power after the Ciompi Revolt, supports an interpretation of this decorative program tied to the political fortunes of the family. The Castellani had managed to retain their mercantile and economic power and would have had every reason to see itself in the tradition of the powerful banking families from the beginning of the century.

The *Legend of the True Cross* The sanctuary of Santa Croce (just visible at the left of Fig 2.7) is decorated with a huge fresco cycle depicting the *Legend of the True Cross*, by Agnolo Gaddi (active 1369–96 Florence). Lack of documentary evidence precludes precise dating of the cycle; however, the Alberti family is mentioned in early records pertaining to the chapel, and their crest is carved on its piers, so it is more than likely that they, in conjunction with the Franciscans, were the patron family of this cycle, which illustrates the dedication of the church to the Holy Cross (Fig. 3.29). Since members of the Alberti family were exiled by the oligarchy in 1387 for their liberal political views and since there seems to be no break in the pictorial unity of the frescoes themselves, they were probably either completed before 1387 or not begun until members of the family returned to the city and felt the

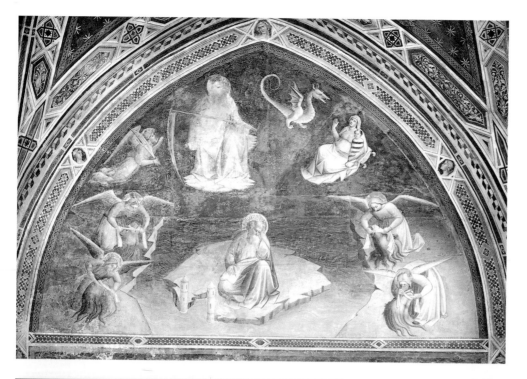

3.28 *St. John on Patmos*, c. 1385–90, commissioned by the Castellani family for the Castellani Chapel, Santa Croce, Florence. Fresco

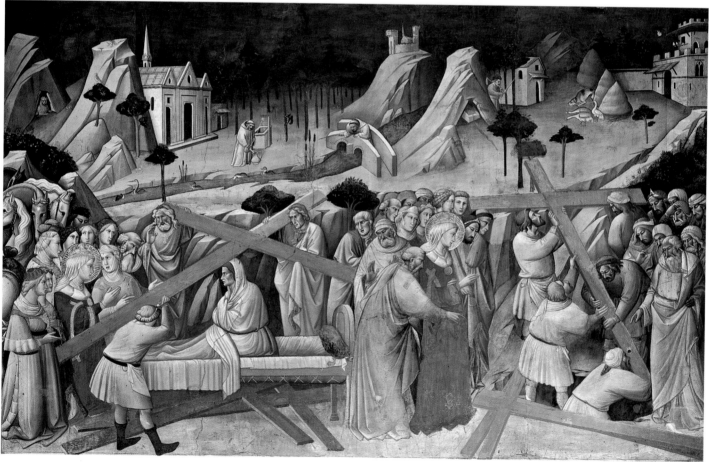

3.29 *Discovery of the True Cross*, before 1387, Agnolo Gaddi, choir, Santa Croce, Florence. Fresco

St. Helena, the Emperor Constantine's mother, discovers the True Cross and the two crosses of the thieves crucified with Christ at the right of the fresco. At the left, she identifies which of the three crosses is the True Cross as it miraculously brings a dead man back to life.

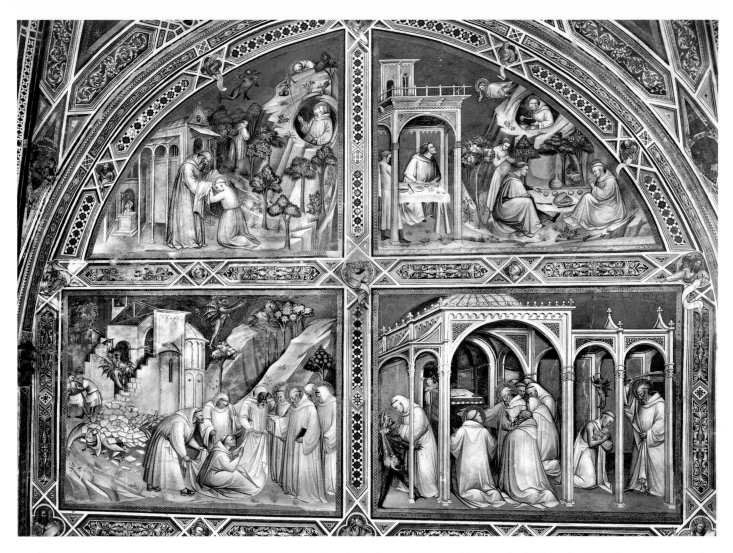

3.30 *Scenes from the Life of St. Benedict,* 1386–88, showing *St. Benedict Retires to Subiaco and is Given the Habit by the Monk Romano; St. Benedict Visited by a Monk Sent by God on Easter Day; St. Benedict Founds Monte Cassino and Resurrects a Monk Crushed by a Falling Wall;* and *St. Benedict Exorcises a Possessed Monk,* commissioned by Benedetto degli Alberti from SPINELLO ARETINO for the sacristy of San Miniato al Monte, Florence. Fresco

moment opportune to reassert their presence with this high-profile act of patronage.

Agnolo Gaddi's portrayal of the *Legend of the True Cross* was derived from a collection of the thirteenth-century religious writings by Jacopo da Voragine known as the *Golden Legend.* The frescoes provided the pictorial model which the Franciscans followed for the next century. The narrative tells the story of Christ's cross which, according to tradition, was made from a tree planted over Adam's grave by his son Seth. Although Solomon had intended to use this tree in his temple, it was made into a bridge instead. When the Queen of Sheba crossed the bridge she had a vision that the Savior would be crucified on its wood and that the kingdom of the Jews would then cease to exist—a prediction that led Solomon to have the wood buried. It was recovered, however, and fashioned into Christ's cross, which was ultimately stolen by the Persian king Chosroes. Chosroes was subsequently defeated by Heraclius, who returned the cross to Jerusalem. In order to depict the complexities of this tale Agnolo spread the

narrative across the entire width of the wall, with groups of figures moving from left to right depicting different episodes, but with the background landscape and architecture providing a single unifying frame for the painting.

Agnolo's figures derive their essentially static style from his father's frescoes in the Baroncelli Chapel (see Fig. 2.11), although his own hand is evident in their elongated, elegant poses, their grouping to suggest volumes in the landscape, and their placement in full, open spaces. Throughout the frescoes there are examples of compellingly individualized facial features which suggest that they were drawn from life. The individual scenes are suffused with light which enhances the solidity of buildings and landscape features against the dark background. The colors of the costumes are lighter than in earlier frescoes, lending the entire cycle a vivacity commensurate with the animation of its figures. These frescoes mark the end of a long development of fourteenth-century painting in Santa Croce which, beginning with Giotto's frescoes for the Bardi Chapel (see Fig. 2.8), established new ways of realizing narrative. By transforming that tradition they provided a model for the generation of painters working into the first two decades of the fifteenth century.

Frescoes at San Miniato   The influence of Agnolo's refined and elegant style is evident in a fresco cycle of the life of St. Benedict in the sacristy of the church of San Miniato al Monte (Fig. 3.30). Painted by Spinello Aretino (Spinello di Luca Spinelli; 1350/52 Arezzo–1410 Florence), the cycle was commissioned by Benedetto degli Alberti before he and other male members of his family were exiled in 1387. St Benedict was the patron saint of both Benedetto and of the Olivetan Benedictines who, along with the Arte del Calimala, had charge of the church. The scenes concentrate on miracles associated with St. Benedict, including his resurrection of a monk killed by a falling wall and his exorcism of a monk possessed by a devil. In each case evil is represented by a winged fiend that Benedict has managed to expel through his own holiness. The same thinly membered, detailed, and miniaturized architecture that characterizes Agnolo Gaddi's work serves as a frame for the episodes in Spinello's cycle. The buildings, like the figural groupings, usually have one face parallel to the picture surface, their adjacent sides, on a diagonal, leading the eye deeper into space. The figures, like those in Agnolo's *True Cross* cycle but unlike Agnolo's elongated and softly swaying figures, are grouped episodically across the painting and call to mind the slow, heavy movement and weighty massing typical of Giotto and his followers.

Although the Castellani and the Alberti were political opponents—the former allied to the faction that exiled the latter—the commissions of the two families are remarkably similar, suggesting that social position rather than political persuasion was a determinant of style. Of course the choice of Agnolo Gaddi for the Santa Croce frescoes may have been determined by the resident Franciscans, just as the prior of the Olivetans at San Miniato seems to have been responsible for selecting Spinello, who had already worked for the Olivetans in Arezzo. The commissioning of major public fresco cycles was rarely a simple matter between a single patron and an artist.

Other Civic Imagery

Even secular painting had different audiences. There was a large category of painting intended to record specific historical events that took place at or near the sites they decorated within the city. Most of these are now lost, but the few that do survive suggest that their painters were aware of the special demands that the genre made on style. One of these, the *Orphans Assigned to their New Parents* (Fig. 3.31) was painted in 1386 by Niccolò di Pietro Gerini (active 1366–1415 Florence) and Ambrogio di Baldese (1352–1429 Florence) for the charitable Confraternity of the Misericordia. The fresco originally decorated the exterior of the confraternity building (which itself appears in the painting) immediately across the street from the Baptistry. Gerini, whose artistic roots lay in the art of both Andrea Orcagna and Taddeo Gaddi, clearly made an effort at naturalism, despite the rather stolid figures. Gerini's children react in differing animated ways to their new mothers, while the adults act in a decorous manner, presumably befitting their new roles as parents. Of course, given what we know of the often horrendous conditions for lower-class children and orphans during this period, this image is most likely more a wished-for model than a representation of fact.

Gerini ordered the figures into different groups, depending on their activity, blocking them within the lines of the background architectural units, in order to structure the reading of the narrative. At the same time, he crowded the figures at the foreground of the composition, framed the confraternity members in the arches of the honorific loggia of their building to indicate their status, depicted the building itself rather schematically (although leaving no doubt about its identity), and included at the far left a tower-like structure decorated with figures representing Adam and Eve perhaps as symbolic models for the new parents depicted in the fresco. The cramped space is unlike other Florentine narrative painting of the time and suggests a forced and somewhat stylized visual concentration on the act of charity taking place. Thus, as conventional as Gerini's style in this fresco may now appear, he was responding to the needs of a public painting of an historical event. His understanding of convention made him one of the most sought-after painters of his time, working for the major guilds as well as for monastic communities.

Another important project of this period was a now-lost fresco cycle of twenty-two *Uomini Famosi* ("famous men"), commissioned in about 1385 for the Audience Chamber of the Signoria in the Palazzo della Signoria. It was to be paralleled by an unexecuted series of sculpted monuments to famous Florentines in the Duomo. Coluccio Salutati, the chancellor (official secretary) of the city of Florence and a pupil of Boccaccio, most likely helped to plan the cycle, and he provided a series of epigrams to accompany each figure. Based on Petrarch's *De viris illustribus* ("On Illustrious Men"), Salutati's choice of figures included Alexander the Great, Augustus, Brutus, Cicero, Constantine, and Charlemagne. There are echoes of Florentine history in the choices of the figures, since the city's foundation myths included stories of its having been settled both at the time of Caesar and at the time of Charlemagne. Salutati also included Dante, Petrarch, and Boccaccio, native sons, among the *Uomini Famosi* as examples of Florence's greatness. His rehabilitation of these figures by placing them in a Florentine pantheon ignores some of the more controversial aspects of their careers for the republic (Dante, for example, having died in exile) in his desire to claim the major figures of fourteenth-century humanism and letters for Florence.

Outside the Palazzo della Signoria, civic imagery took a somewhat more traditional turn in the sculptural decoration for the newly completed Loggia della Signoria (see Fig. 1.4 and at the far right of 1.18). The Loggia was begun in 1373/74 and is remarkable for its time in its monumental scale, recalling not only Roman triumphal arches but the remains of ancient ruins such as the Basilica of Constantine. Standing at a right angle to the Palazzo Vecchio, it served not only to frame important public civic events but to define one side of a heroically scaled piazza then still being carved out of the heart of the city (see Fig. 1.19). Seven seated figures of virtues in star-studded hexafoils decorate the **spandrels** between the arches. Originally painted and set on a colored ground, these reliefs were designed by Agnolo Gaddi and were carved in 1386–7 by Giovanni d'Ambrogio (active 1382–1418 Florence) and Jacopo di Piero Guidi (active 1376–1412 Florence), each of whom later became a *capomaestro* of the cathedral workshops. Giovanni's *Prudence* (Fig. 3.32) sits in a three-quarter pose, giving

her heightened three-dimensionality against the flat patterned surface and within the niche's complex triangular lobed frame. Andrea Pisano's Virtues for the south door of the Baptistry (see Fig. 2.17) found their successors in these figures for the Loggia della Signoria. The ease in their presentation is a clear sign that the principles of form introduced nearly a century earlier by artists working in Rome, Padua, and Florence had now been fully assimilated.

Secular Painting

In frescoes commissioned for private houses, different stylistic tendencies could and did exist. A more artificial style was often favored in these works. A case in point is the *Story of the Chastelaine de Vergi* (Fig. 3.33); painted high on the walls around a room in the Palazzo Davanzati, it illustrates a thirteenth-century French chivalric romance—subject matter diffused throughout Italy (see Fig. 3.39). Based loosely on the story of Pyramus and Thisbe, two ill-fated lovers in Ovid's *Metamorphoses*, the tragic tale tells of a secret love between the Chastelaine and a young knight. When the knight refuses the advances of the Duchess of Burgundy, the wife of his liege lord, and tells the duke both of the duchess's infidelity and of his own secret love, the duchess drives the Chastelaine to her death. The grief-stricken knight commits suicide. The duke, convinced of his wife's guilt, kills her; he then joins the Knights Templars. The figures in the

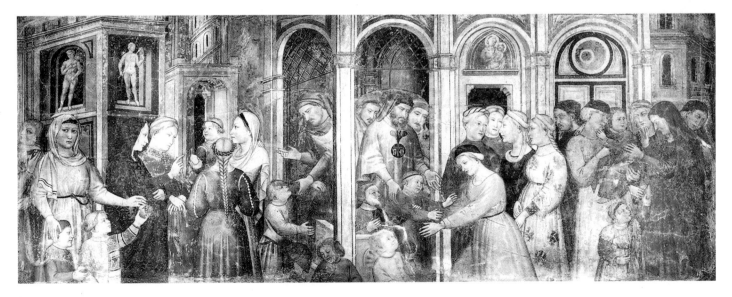

3.31 *Orphans Assigned to their New Parents*, 1386, commissioned by the Confraternity of the Misericordia from NICCOLÒ DI PIETRO GERINI and AMBROGIO DI BALDESE for the façade of their headquarters. Fresco (Museo del Bigallo, Florence)

The fresco was removed from the exterior of the building in 1777 and partially destroyed at that time. The male figure in the center arch wears the insignia of the Misericordia. The Confraternity of the Misericordia merged with the Orfanotrofio del Bigallo in 1425, but subsequently re-emerged as a separate entity in 1527, building new confraternal structures and leaving its original building to the Bigallo, by which name it is now known.

fresco are depicted in a very narrow space under a fictive loggia. Stylized trees are centered within each arch and fan out to conceal any possible background space. A bed and chessboard are tipped up in defiance of the spatial system created by the loggia. This medieval romance and its depiction within a private home clearly demanded a style different from civic and biblical narratives. Both styles—the naturalistic and the artificial—existed concurrently, both were commissioned by the ruling class, and both respond to the particular subjects they treat and the functions they were meant to serve.

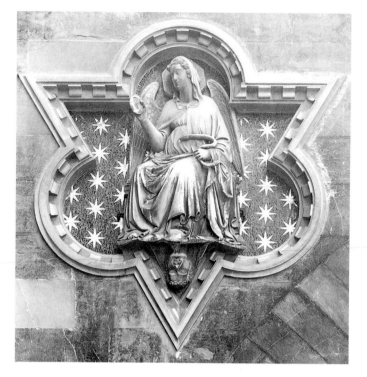

3.32 *Prudence*, 1386, GIOVANNI D'AMBROGIO (after a design by AGNOLO GADDI), Loggia della Signoria (now also called the Loggia dei Lanzi), Florence. Marble

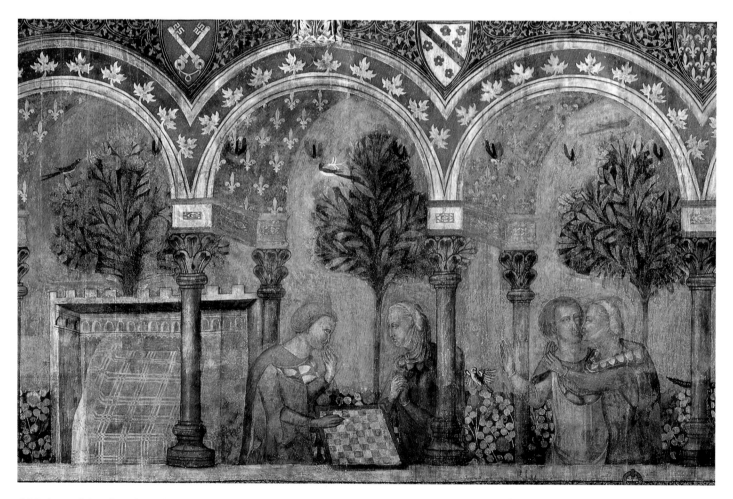

3.33 *Story of the Chastelaine de Vergi*, c. 1395, Palazzo Davanzati, Florence. Fresco

Milan and Pavia: The Visconti

The Milanese court grew especially grand. The city's Visconti lords exploited the rich agricultural resources of the north Italian plains and demanded monetary tribute from subject towns and cities in order to aggrandize their position among the European aristocracy. Although many at the courts of England and France viewed the Visconti as opportunistic upstarts, there was no denying their wealth. Royal coffers in those two countries were being bled by the Hundred Years' War (begun in 1337); so when the Visconti provided handsome dowries to accompany the marriage of both their male and female children, the offers were rarely refused. The Visconti soon boasted familial ties to many of the great houses of Europe. Acting the part of princes, they spent lavishly on courtly display and art and architecture, as well as on maintaining frighteningly efficient military forces and effective regional government.

The Altarpiece of the Magi The Visconti enhanced their exalted status through art and pageantry. They showed special interest in the cult of the Three Magi (wise men) or Three Kings, who had brought gifts to the infant Jesus. Every year on the feast of the Epiphany (January 6) they sponsored a procession of three "kings" across the city to a representation of Herod's palace constructed among the ancient Roman columns in front of the Early Christian church of San Lorenzo; from there the procession moved down the street and out the city gate to Sant'Eustorgio, where the kings adored a figure of the Christ Child in a crib at the high altar. Accompanied by large crowds and exotic beasts, including monkeys and baboons borrowed from the Visconti menagerie, the parade then swung around the city and reentered through the Porta Romana.

In 1347 the Scuola dei Magi, a prestigious lay group dedicated to the Three Kings, commissioned a marble altarpiece for their chapel in the church of Sant'Eustorgio (Fig. 3.34) which had once held the supposed relics of the Magi themselves in a huge stone sarcophagus. The altarpiece suggests the popular character of the Magi's cult in Milan. Carved in a direct, even slightly naive manner (note, for example, the rather stumpy figures and the crowded composition on the left), the narrative begins in the right panel with the Magi making their way through densely carved hills in the background to an

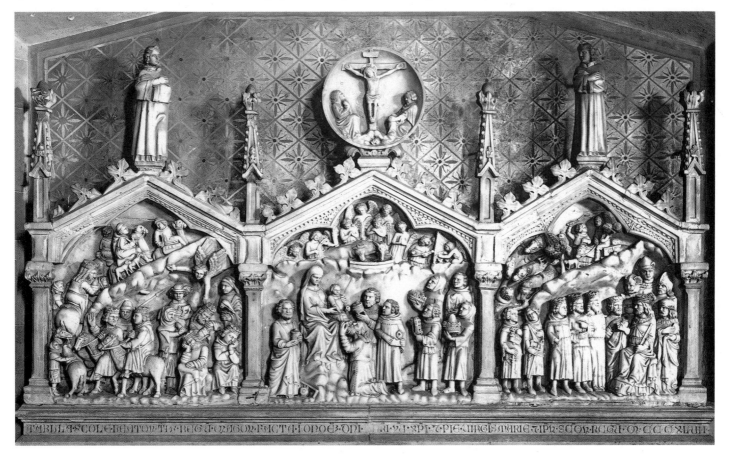

3.34 *Altarpiece of the Magi*, 1347, commissioned by the Scuola dei Magi for Sant'Eustorgio, Milan. Marble, 2' 3½" × 7' 2½" (70 × 220 cm)

Even though the church's relics of the Three Kings had been stolen several centuries earlier by Germans, who then built an elaborate shrine for them in Cologne, the Milanese continued to pay homage to the Magi.

audience before King Herod. The central relief shows the Magi fervently adoring the Christ Child and presenting their gifts. At the left an angel commands the sleeping kings not to return to Herod but to seek another way home, again back into the compacted hillside at the upper left of the relief.

The Equestrian Monument of Bernabò Visconti
Sometime before 1363 Bonino da Campione (active after 1357, d. after 1397), a Lombard sculptor who had worked in the shops of Milan Cathedral, produced a life-sized equestrian statue of Bernabò Visconti as part of the Milanese ruler's funerary monument (Fig. 3.35). As Lord of Milan, Bernabò was a fierce and domineering ruler, intimidating his subjects with attack dogs and boasting of the fact that he had sired more than thirty illegitimate children. He had no trouble dominating his much more reticent cousin Galeazzo Visconti, with whom he shared rulership in Milan and its territories. Galeazzo wisely set up primary residence at Pavia, a safe distance of 22 miles (35 kilometers) from Bernabò in Milan.

It was a common north Italian custom to celebrate local leaders with individualized equestrian images. These were usually placed over doorways and on top of tomb monuments outside churches (Fig. 3.36), but Bonino's statue of Bernabò was designed to stand above the high altar of the Milanese church of San Giovanni in Conca. In claiming such an exalted site, normally reserved for royalty (see Fig. 2.55), Bernabò displayed a remarkable arrogance.

The horse and rider, carved from a single block of stone, rise above a sarcophagus whose main face shows Bernabò being presented by St. George, his patron saint, to the crucified Christ. The relief on the back depicts a subject equally suited to the sacrificial connotations of an altar and the funereal connotation of the monument itself: Christ as the Man of Sorrows (a bust-length figure of Christ displaying the wounds of the Crucifixion), flanked by saints. Stylistically, the stark and immovable horse and rider differ remarkably from the more naturalistically carved reliefs, where the figures stand in front of their frames and give some illusion of distance through their diminishing size. Once again, a more iconic mode was adopted for the image of authority, a more relaxed mode for narrative and devotion.

Part of the statue's magisterial authority also derives from the equestrian type itself, which since ancient Roman times had been associated with imperial power. An example of this genre, well known to the Visconti, was the equestrian statue of Emperor Septimius Severus (146–211), popularly known as the Regisole ("sun king"), which stood in Pavia until it was destroyed in 1796. Bonino exploited and even transcended the conventions

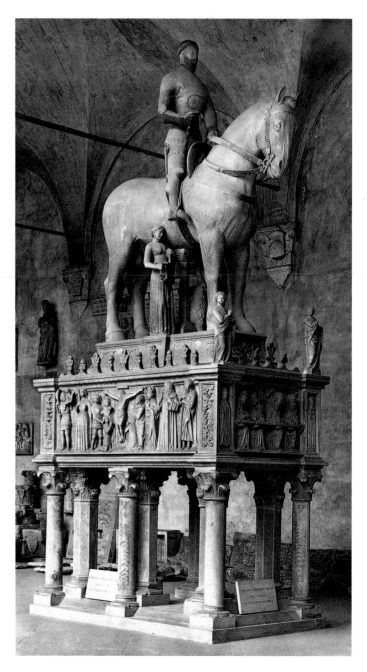

3.35 *Equestrian Monument of Bernabò Visconti*, before 1363, commissioned by Bernabò from BONINO DA CAMPIONE for the high altar of San Giovanni in Conca, Milan. Marble, height (including sarcophagus and columnar supports) 19′ 8″ (6 m) (Castello Sforzesco, Milan)

of this form; he shows Bernabò not merely seated astride the horse but standing erect in the stirrups—a force to be reckoned with. From the nave of the church, Bernabò would have been seen in profile, the standard view on coins and medals, and another, more subtle reminder of his authority. Gold and silver patterns on the horse, rider, sarcophagus, and supporting columns suggested costly metal. At the same time, Bonino disarmed the viewer with numerous realistic details, such as the horse's parade drapery bunching on its barrel chest, the delicately incised hairs of its mane, and minute attention to Bernabò's armor—all serving to vivify this imposing icon of power.

The Cansignorio della Scala Monument in Verona
Both Bonino and Bernabò may have been inspired in this commission by the impressive series of equestrian-topped tomb monuments that the lords of Verona, the della Scala, had begun erecting to themselves in the 1320s, next to the church of Santa Maria Antica. Indeed Bonino's success in Milan seems to have brought him to the attention of Cansignorio della Scala, who commissioned him, sometime before 1375, to produce the most splendid of the series (Fig. 3.36). An outsized tabernacle surrounds Cansignorio's sarcophagus and effigy, his worldly remains guarded by figures of warrior saints in tabernacles. On one end of the sarcophagus, just beneath the head of his effigy, a relief shows the popular knightly saint George (who had also been shown recommending Bernabò Visconti to Christ) assuring Cansignorio's entrance into heaven by presenting him to the Virgin. A Coronation of the Virgin provides an aptly regal image on the other end, while the road to salvation is represented by scenes from the life of Christ on the sides. Virtues and angels holding della Scala coats of arms fill the upper niches, rising to the base of Cansignorio's equestrian portrait, a triumphant image for the della Scala dynasty. The entire monument is thoroughly Gothic. Bonino rejected the square plan and relatively restrained decoration of earlier canopied monuments in favor of a complex polygonal plan, open tabernacles, tall spires, and steeply pointed gables to house his graceful figures, clad in soft and swaying drapery.

The Castello Visconteo   Not to be outdone by either his cousin Bernabò Visconti or the lords of Verona, Galeazzo II Visconti of Milan erected an imposing new residence in Pavia in the 1360s (Fig. 3.37). Pavia provided Galeazzo with a seat of power independent of his overbearing cousin and with an enhanced aura of legitimacy, since the city was the traditional capital of the Lombard kings, who ruled this region from the sixth to the eleventh century.

Galeazzo's new residence, the Castello Visconteo, was erected on the edge of town next to the city wall. It measured a formidable 465 feet (142 meters) across and was nearly as deep; its four corners (of which only two remain) were buttressed by square towers (Fig. 3.38). For its time it is an extraordinarily regular structure, both in plan and elevation. Despite these and other fortifications, including a moat, drawbridge, and **crenellations**, the structure had more the air of a palace than a castle: its long, two-storied façade, pierced with large Gothic-style

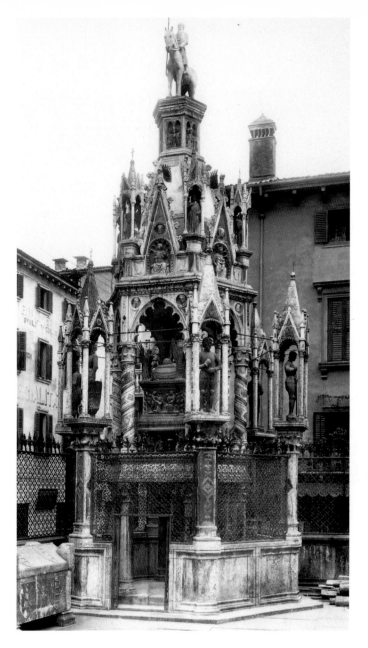

3.36 *Funerary Monument of Cansignorio della Scala*, before 1375, commissioned probably by Cansignorio from BONINO DA CAMPIONE, outside Santa Maria Antica, Verona

This monument stands amidst a large number of others in a cemetery adjacent to the entrance of the church.

windows, would have offered scant protection against attackers. While borrowing Gothic forms from northern Europe, the builders of the Castello Visconteo drew also on conservative Lombard precedents, barely pointing the arches of the courtyard's lower arcade and inserting traditional plate tracery into the rounded arches of the upper story. These round motifs recall late thirteenth-century civic buildings.

In general, secular architecture of the late fourteenth century is neither as structurally nor as stylistically progressive as church architecture, with its intricate and florid tracery; and the design of Galeazzo's palace/castle, like that of most secular buildings, emphasized functionality over beauty. The ground and subterranean areas served as

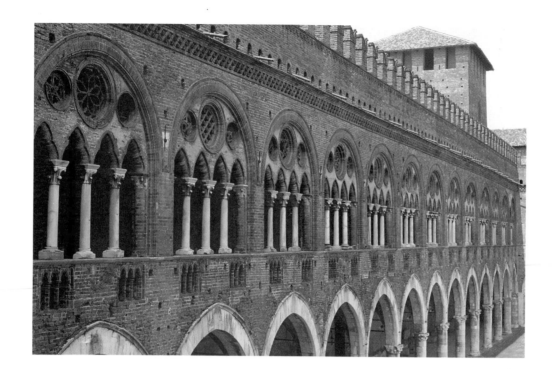

3.37 Castello Visconteo, Pavia, courtyard, 1360, commissioned by Galeazzo II Visconti

cellars, stables, storerooms, and prison. The courtyard was large enough to serve as an arena for jousts, tournaments, and grand banquets of over a dozen courses, served in great splendor. The upper story consisted of a single row of rooms, which provided audience and administrative space as well as apartments for Galeazzo and his extended family. Only fragments of the original sumptuous deco-

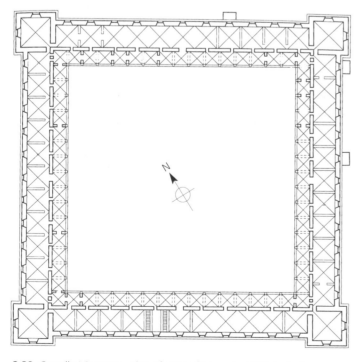

3.38 Castello Visconteo, plan of upper floor as in 1469, including reconstruction of destroyed wing

ration survive, but it included mounted knights, geometric designs, heraldic devices, a panoramic view of the city of Pavia, and numerous portraits of Galeazzo. This profusion of images must have made the simple structure appear more splendid and various than it actually was. The entire complex impressed Petrarch, one of Galeazzo's many illustrious guests, as "the most noble production of modern art." This opinion probably referred both to the building itself and to its contents, including a renowned manuscript library which was among the very largest in Europe. An inventory taken in 1426 listed 988 manuscripts, 371 of which still survive.

Manuscript Illumination Galeazzo, Bernabò, their wives, and other Visconti family members were notable patrons of manuscript illumination. When Bernabò married his daughter, Valentina, to Louis of Touraine in 1389, her luxurious trousseau included manuscripts as well as the usual jewels and embroidered robes. Among the most splendid of the manuscripts commissioned by the Visconti court in Milan is an illustrated copy of the knightly romance, the *Legend of Guiron le Courtois* (Fig. 3.39). Bernabò's monogram, which appears on his tomb and on coins minted during his reign, has recently been noticed within the manuscript, revealing a gentler side of Bernabò's otherwise daunting personality. In this work we again encounter the image of the soldier on horseback, but instead of conveying intimidation and power, the image is used to illustrate a fable about the mysterious helmeted knight known as Fieramonte at the court of Artù.

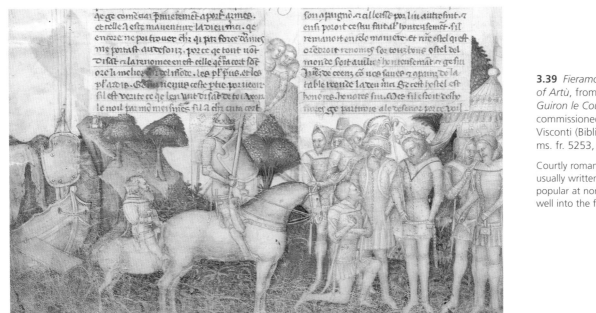

3.39 *Fieramonte at the Court of Artù*, from the *Legend of Guiron le Courtois*, 1389, commissioned by Bernabò Visconti (Bibliothèque Nationale, ms. fr. 5253, fol. 2V, Paris)

Courtly romances, which were usually written in French, were popular at north Italian courts well into the fifteenth century.

The illumination shown, rendered with light strokes and colored with pastel delicacy, packs a great deal of narrative information into a relatively constricted space. Fore-, middle- and background merge compactly behind the words of the text, itself arranged in two columns which seem to lie directly on the picture plane. Beneath the right column Blioberis kneels before the king to ask permission to challenge the mysterious horseman, who in courtly fashion is accompanied by a dwarf riding on his own miniature steed. Behind them and to the left rests the ship that has brought them across the sea to this encounter. Between the two columns of text, ladies of the court stand in a wooden enclosure awaiting the tournament that will soon follow, while at the far right the king's retainers exchange knowing and worldly glances. The high etiquette, stylized costume, and conventionalized behavior of life at court emerge clearly from this illumination.

In a slightly more popular vein but still informed by the same precious and courtly sensibilities as the Guiron manuscript is an illustration of *Spring* (Fig. 3.40) from a *Tacuinum Sanitatis*, an illustrated health handbook owned by Verde Visconti, Bernabò's daughter and the wife of Leopold of Austria. Perhaps dating to the 1380s, Verde's copy of this popular manual—one of the first mass-produced texts after the invention of printing in the fifteenth century—uses naturalistic shorthand to provide instructions on medical self-help. Following the conventions of this sort of manuscript, which limit space and extraneous detail in order to focus on one subject, the picture depth is shallow and the background is left blank. A young woman with long blond hair casually tied in the back smells a flower while her male companion, stylishly clad in long pointed shoes and a scallop-edged cloak, holds a hunting bird and points to a spring landscape beyond a wattled fence. The illumination and accompanying text are succinct and direct, the greenery swept across the page

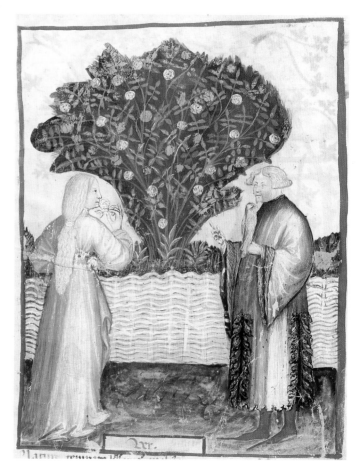

3.40 *Spring*, from a *Tacuinum Sanitatis* (illustrated health handbook), 1380s (?), commissioned probably by Verde Visconti (Bibliothèque Nationale, ms. lat. 6977A, fol. 103, Paris)

in broad outlines, the meandering branches sketched casually on the darker ground. On other pages little traceried and paneled buildings provide just enough context to highlight the ingredient or element being described, selectively emphasizing features or characteristics important to the reader.

Art and Gastronomy

A Renaissance Italian would hardly recognize modern Italian food. Tomatoes, potatoes, corn, green and red peppers, certain kinds of white beans, chocolate, and coffee—all native to the Americas—were unknown in Europe until the sixteenth century. The diets of rich and poor alike centered around meat and fish, which were usually dried and salted—the most efficient means of preserving foods before modern refrigeration. Heavy doses of spices, rose water, and flower petals helped to disguise off-flavors. Soups, stews, and porridges were the mainstays of most people's diets; a spit-roast capon was enough of a luxury that Sienese officials chose it, along with fresh peas, to impress Lorenzo Ghiberti when they were courting him for work in their Baptistry in 1417.

No part of an animal was left unutilized. In Figure 3.41, two women in long aprons prepare tripe—the one on the left scraping the cow's stomach, while another on the right boils it in a large cauldron. Their product is deposited in rectangular and round bowls made of wood or ceramic, though the plate being presented at the table in the background may just as likely be a trencher made of stale bread. Broth or juices softened the bread and made it edible. Small rolls—any leftovers of which would be ground into crumbs for thickening dishes—accompanied meals, along with plenty of wine.

As now, medical professionals offered advice about diet. Each food was associated with a particular "humor" or physical and psychological tendency related to one of the four essential elements: earth, fire, air, or water. For example, the hardworking businessman Francesco Datini of Prato was counseled by his physician to avoid fruit of all sorts because its "cold and wet" properties would lead to lethargy and putrification of the blood. Melon, berries, cherries, figs, almonds, honey, wine, and mint were allowed in small quantities because they were somewhat "warmer." Bacelli beans (which Datini

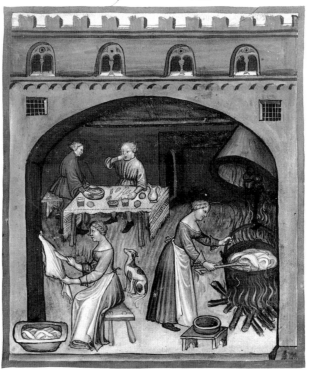

adored), apples, chestnuts, and pears were completely off-limits.

Table manners were informal: many dishes were eaten communally and with the fingers, as seen in the picture. In 1290 Fra Bonvicino da Riva wrote an admonition that was often repeated well into the sixteenth century: "Thou must not put either thy fingers into thine ears, or thy hands to thy head. The man who is eating must not be scraping with his fingers at any foul part." Although every table was set with at least one large knife—also visible in the illustration—forks were relatively rare. Imported from the Byzantine East by a princess named Theodora, who married Doge Domenico Selvo (1071–84), they were two-pronged and gold, and initially struck Venetians as superfluous. However, forks became fashionable in Italy in the fifteenth century when the ecumenical councils of the 1430s and the fall of Constantinople in 1453 brought many Greek Byzantines to Italy. The fork did not gain wide acceptance in the rest of Europe until the eighteenth century, which earned Italians the reputation of being particularly elegant eaters.

3.41 *Preparing Tripe*, from a *Tacuinum Sanitatis* (illustrated health handbook), late fourteenth century, Lombardy (Österreichisches Nationalbibliothek, ms. ser. nov. 2. 644, fol. 81, Vienna)

Padua: The Carrara Court

Francesco da Carrara, lord of Padua from 1350 to 1388, also encouraged the arts and learning in his city, becoming a close friend and avid correspondent of the internationally renowned poet and scholar Petrarch, who lived in and around Padua from 1370 until his death in 1374. Conversations and correspondence with Petrarch probably encouraged Francesco to join other north Italian rulers in exploiting aspects of Roman art and history to support his regime. When Francesco's son recaptured Padua in 1390 after a two-year break in the Carrara family's rule, he commissioned the coining of small medals (Fig. 3.42), the first of their kind of the Renaissance, portraying himself in the guise of a Roman emperor. Earlier Francesco had used Petrarch's collection of biographies of famous Romans (*De viris illustribus*) as the basis for a series of frescoes in the Carrara palace. The narrative scenes seem to have followed chivalric types such as appear in the Milanese Guiron manuscript (see Fig. 3.39), depicting Roman history in contemporary rather than

antique dress. Classical content did not require classical form. Each famous Roman was accorded an individual portrait; and the cycle included one of Petrarch as well. The original fresco survives in highly damaged and altered form. It is better known through a precise manuscript illumination (Fig. 3.43). Here Petrarch occupies a highly coherent and illusionistic space which recalls types first created by Giotto at the Scrovegni Chapel (see Fig. 2.2). The scholar sits before a desk on which he turns the pages of a manuscript, other volumes ready at hand on a circular stand to his left. His pet dog curls up comfortably in front of a storage chest. Diagonally placed ceiling beams lead the eye back to a closet whose open doors reveal other volumes. The open panel of a window with precisely rendered leaded glass roundels admits light and air into the homey interior. All these details lend a remarkable anecdotal realism to the image, unusual for painting of this time.

The Padua Baptistry   Padua's ruler did not neglect his city's religious buildings. For the decoration of the Padua Baptistry (Figs. 3.44 and 3.45), which he and his wife chose as their burial place, Francesco da Carrara turned to the Florentine painter and late follower of Giotto, Giusto de' Menabuoi (active 1349–90 Padua). By 1370 Giusto was at work in the church of the Eremitani in Padua, where he may have come to Francesco's attention. The commission for the Baptistry frescoes was instigated around 1378 by Francesco's wife, Fina Buzzacarini. She appears in one of the frescoes kneeling before the Madonna as the putative patron, while her last will and testament indicate that she left all decisions about the decoration and its execution to her husband. Her presence in the birth scene from the Life of St. John the Baptist and the unusually large number of women

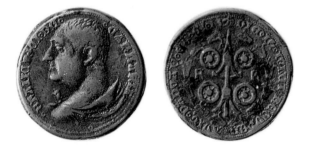

3.42 Medal of Francesco da Carrara, Lord of Padua, c. 1390. Silvered bronze, 1¼" (33 mm) (© British Museum, London)

The emblem on the reverse is a highly stylized representation of a four-wheeled cart, or *carro*, a reference to the Carrara family.

Illustrious Men

In 1379, five years after the death of Petrarch, his good friend and literary executor, Lombardo della Seta (d. 1390), produced the first manuscript version of the poet's unfinished *Uomini Illustri* ("Illustrious Men"). The preface that Lombardo provided for the work dedicated it to the lord of Padua, Francesco il Vecchio Carrara, and paid graceful tribute to the frescoes that Francesco

had commissioned as a visual complement to these biographies.

As an ardent lover of the virtues, you have extended hospitality to these *viri illustres*, not only in your heart and mind, but also very magnificently in the most beautiful part of your palace. According to the custom of the ancients you have honored them with gold and purple, and with images and inscriptions you have set them up for admiration . . . .

To the inward conception of your keen mind you have given outward expression in the form of most excellent pictures, so that you may always keep in sight these men whom you are eager to love because of the greatness of their deeds.

(from Theodor E. Mommsen. "Petrarch and the Decoration of the Sala Virorum Illustrium in Padua." *Art Bulletin*, 34 [1952]: pp. 95–116 [extract p. 96])

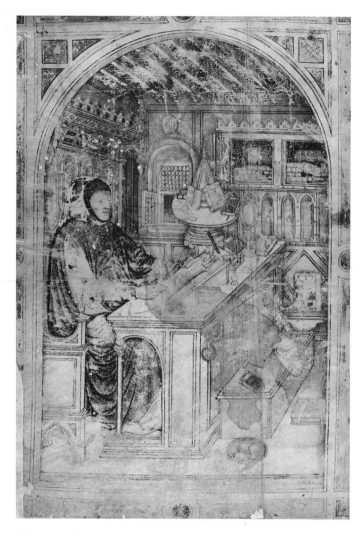

3.43 *Petrarch in His Study*, manuscript illumination recording the composition of frescoes commissioned by Francesco da Carrara for the Sala Virorum Illustrium, Carrara Palace, Padua (Hessische Landes- und Hochschul-Bibliothek, Handschriftenabteilung Codex 101, fol. 1v, Darmstadt, Germany)

Although Florence claimed Petrarch as one of the city's most famous sons, he spent most of his life at the papal court in Avignon, France, and in northern Italy.

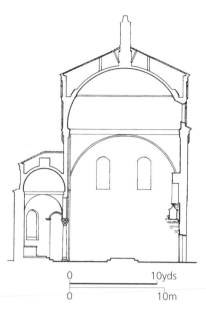

3.44 Bapistry, Padua, east-west section (after Giotto)

3.45 (below) *Dome of Heaven*, 1370s, commissioned by Francesco da Carrara at the behest of his wife, Fina Buzzacarini, from GIUSTO DE' MENABUOI for the Baptistry, Padua. Fresco

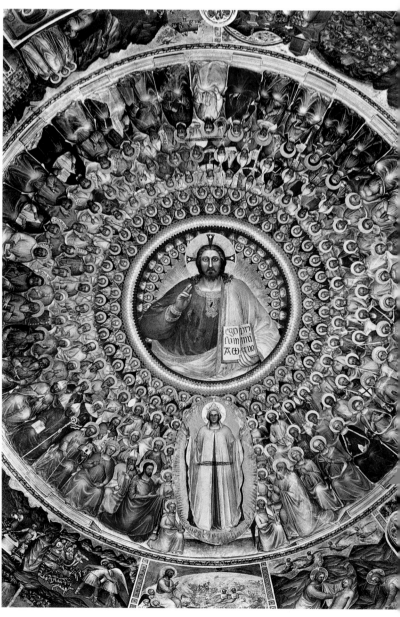

in other scenes suggest that her husband was honoring her wishes.

The Padua Baptistry is a centrally planned structure with a domical vault supported on **pendentives**. Giusto and his assistants covered every wall surface of the Baptistry with frescoes. They were also commissioned to paint the altarpiece for the small adjoining sanctuary—itself centrally planned in imitation of the main structure. One of the primary themes of the program is the end of time, the Day of Judgment, when the elect will join Christ in his kingdom. Concentric tiers of saints and angels ring the center of the dome, whose height is enhanced by the progressive diminution of the figures' sizes toward the central, looming figure of the blessing Christ. Directly beneath him and on axis with the Baptistry's entry door and Fina's tomb (subsequently destroyed and replaced by an inscription) hovers the Virgin in a glowing gold mandorla. In the sanctuary the theme is made explicit with illustrations of the Apocalypse, including the dead being called from their graves and schematic representations of the frightening beasts that loom so large in the biblical account of the end of the world.

Patronage at the Santo: The St. James (San Felice) Chapel The Lupi clan, who served the Carrara as *condottieri* (mercenary soldiers), claimed prize patronage sites at the Basilica of Sant'Antonio—the Santo—Padua's famed pilgrimage church, and its adjacent cemetery. For the decoration of their burial chapels, the Lupi chose a more innovative style than was used so successfully in the solemn space of the Baptistry, hiring the adventurous Altichiero da Zevio (active 1369–93 Verona and Padua).

Some of Altichiero's most impressive works line the walls of the chapel that Bonifazio Lupi commissioned from the sculptor and builder Andriolo de' Santis (active 1342–75; Fig. 3.46). Located in the right transept of the Santo, directly opposite the miracle-working tomb of St.

Anthony in the left transept, the chapel was dedicated to Bonifazio's patron saint, St. James. Scenes from James's life occupy the side walls, while the altar wall is dominated by an enormous Crucifixion. Appropriately for the chapel's function as a burial place, a small fresco of the dead Christ being lowered into his tomb occupies the wall over the tomb of Bonifazio's predecessors to the left, while a Resurrection provides a more hopeful image for the patron's own tomb to the right, completing the frescoed Passion cycle for the chapel.

The *Crucifixion* extends across three of the five bays above the altar, functioning as an enormous altarpiece. Though rich in anecdotal detail and portrait-like renderings, the fresco does not include the crosses of the two thieves who were crucified with Christ, concentrating instead on the central sacrifice. The cross is set in the foreground of a broadly coherent space which extends in greater and greater depth as it moves to either side, culminating in a hilltop castle on the far right and a firmly rendered and believably scaled pedestrian bridge, city gate, walls, and towers on the far left.

Throughout the frescoes Altichiero captures and communicates a depth of emotional intensity that is

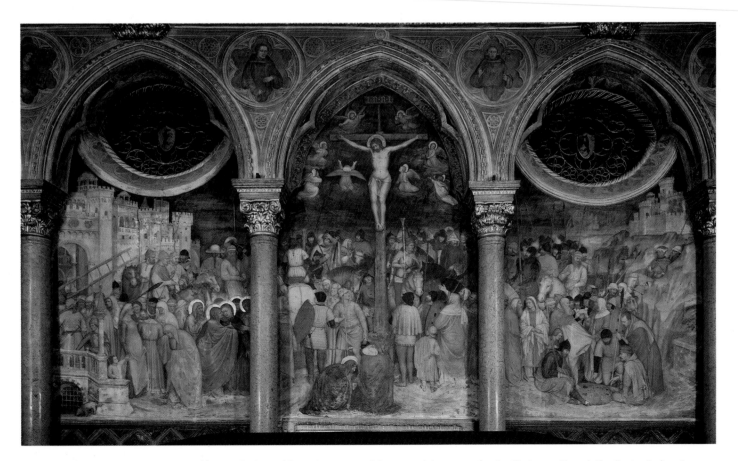

3.46 *Crucifixion*, 1370s, commissioned by Bonifazio Lupi from Andriolo de' Santis and Altichiero for the St. James Chapel, the Santo, Padua. Fresco
The current dedication to San Felice dates from the early sixteenth century.

unmatched throughout most of the Renaissance. At the foot of the cross and directly at eye level, Mary Magdalene arches her red-cloaked back in horror mixed with adoration. Her companion in blue slumps in despair, experiencing Christ's sacrifice in her own way. Other figures stand and gawk, kept in line by efficient guards and soldiers on horseback behind the cross. Soldiers at the right lean over their dice, intent on winning the prize of Christ's seamless white garment, which is being stretched and tested by custodian priests behind them. A cowled figure holding a lance bends over them—almost certainly a portrait, as is the equally individualized guard crouched in front of him. Shot colors on the clothing of many of the figures—yellow highlights on pink, blue on green, for example—intensify the compelling realism of the scene. The Crucifixion becomes horrifyingly real, a visual parallel to the fiery sermons and intense devotional practices of the Franciscans and their exemplary saint, Anthony of Padua, to whom the basilica is dedicated.

St. Anthony of Padua   Anthony's ability to stir the emotions of worshipers through realistic, down-to-earth imagery was legendary. After his death, in 1231, his jaw and tongue were preserved and then later encased in transparent reliquaries, so that they would be visible to the faithful (Fig. 3.47). They were believed to have been miraculously spared from decomposing—visible signs of the saint's close and special relationship to God. By approaching the relics and either contemplating or touching them, a devotee hoped to gain access to the sanctity associated with them. The reliquary made in 1349 to contain Anthony's jaw features a crystal globe in which one can see the jaw, contained in a golden enameled and bejeweled bust. The rest of his body was buried in a stone sarcophagus which the faithful were encouraged to touch. Throngs of pilgrims still flock to the Santo because of their belief in St. Anthony's ability to intervene in everyday events, dispelling imminent danger and healing illness. As at virtually all major pilgrimage sites, they have always left behind gifts and tokens of his interventions (small paintings, miniaturized versions of healed limbs and body parts, abandoned crutches, and even richly jeweled necklaces and diadems like those on the jaw reliquary), adding their own visual contributions to the ensemble created by artists and patrons.

Thus the ultra-realism of Altichiero's frescoes played into expectations that the divine could be experienced in the here and now. Although the actual workings of God remained mysterious even in miracle-working shrines like the basilica of the Santo, God's volitional intervention on the part of humankind allowed and even encouraged naturalistic depiction and illusionism.

The Oratory of St. George   Altichiero's success in the frescoes for St. James's Chapel led to his receiving a subsequent commission in 1377 for a mortuary chapel, next door to the Santo, from another member of the Lupi clan, Raimondino. These frescoes, too, impress with their convincing depiction of complex architectural spaces, the variety of demeanor shown by the figures, and the individuality of their characterization. In the scene of *St. George Baptizing King Servius* (Fig. 3.48) the saint is dressed as a contemporary knight. He stands before a precisely detailed Gothic church whose arches and vaults are picked out in alternating red and white. The realism was enhanced by silver gilt, now darkened, on the footed basin before which the king kneels. Members of his family and the court look on—each evidently a portrait likeness, each responding intently and individually to the event. To the far right and left, other onlookers, also responding appropriately according to their age, rank, and proximity to the action, stand in and around a handsomely delineated courtyard. The scene is full, but not overcrowded, the space coherently structured with remarkable assurance, and the figures rendered with particular integrity—all in all a major narrative achievement.

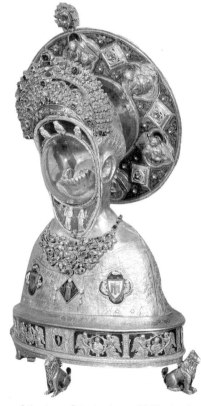

3.47 Reliquary of the jaw of St. Anthony, 1349, the Santo, Padua. Gold, enamel, jewels, and crystal

A companion reliquary displayed the saint's tongue. Both reliquaries honored St. Anthony's legendary preaching skills.

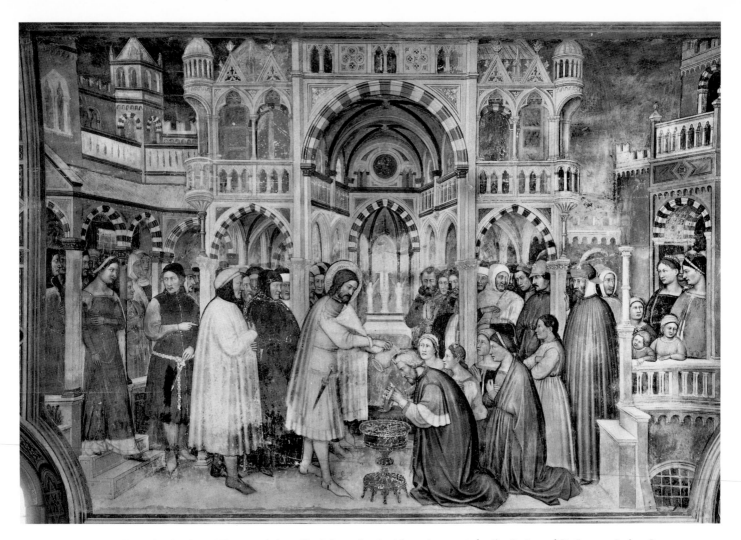

3.48 *St. George Baptizing King Servius*, 1377, commissioned by Raimondino Lupi from ALTICHIERO for the Oratory of St. George, Padua. Fresco

A multi-tiered marble tomb with statues of members of the Lupi family once stood in the center of the oratory. It was so ornate that later pilgrims confused it with a saint's shrine.

Synopsis

Too often the second half of the fourteenth century has been viewed as a period of little significance for the development of Renaissance art. Neglecting the impressive tombs of north Italian despots, the compellingly naturalistic fresco cycles in Padua, and the celebratory imagery of the Venetian state, art historians have taken a myopic view of art production in this period, in large part because of what they misperceived as conservative and reactionary elements in Florentine and Sienese painting.

In the face of unsettled political, social, and economic conditions, patrons continued to invest heavily in art. Building projects were only temporarily suspended during periods of plague and political turmoil: the Florentines expanded their Duomo project after mid-century, for example, and the Venetians resumed construction and decoration of the Doge's Palace after outbreaks of plague. Vast bequests enriched miracle-working shrines at Or San Michele in Florence and at the Basilica of St. Anthony in Padua. The sheer dimensions of wall surfaces covered by fresco increased dramatically, from Guariento's enormous *Coronation of the Virgin* in the Great Council Hall of Venice to the Dominican allegories in the Guidalotti Chapel at Santa Maria Novella in Florence.

Local leaders spent extravagantly on the arts for purposes of self-promotion in such projects as the huge Loggia della Signoria in Florence and the palace of Galeazzo Visconti in Pavia. Roman ideas of grandeur, first promoted by scholars including Petrarch, manifested themselves in the immense scale of such structures and in the cycles of famous heroes, equestrian images, and coins that appeared in many cities. Throughout the Italian peninsula there was a new emphasis on commemorating individuals, whether in the aborted cycle of monuments to famous local sons in the Florentine cathedral, the tomb of Doge Andrea Dandolo in Venice, or the exuberant monuments of the lords of Milan and Verona. Far from marking a hiatus between the generation of Giotto and the early fifteenth century, the second half of the fourteenth century was an era of intense creative activity.

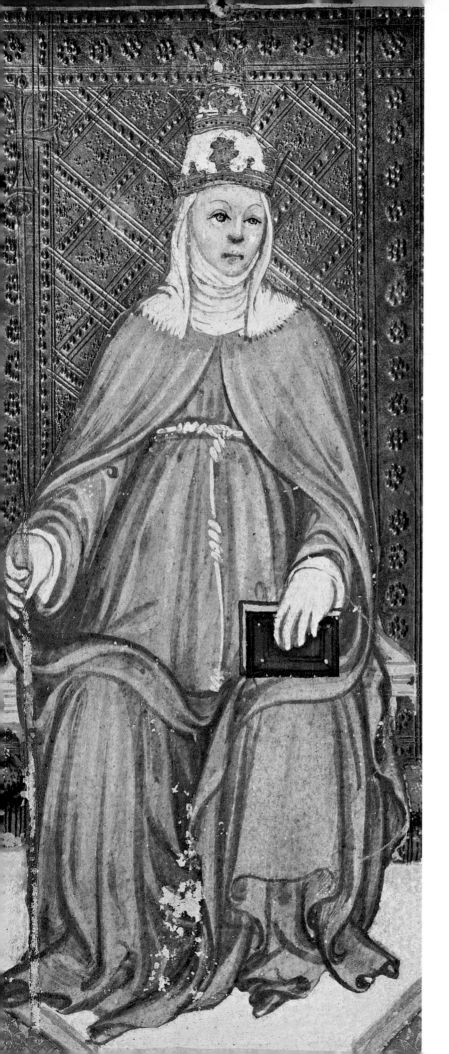
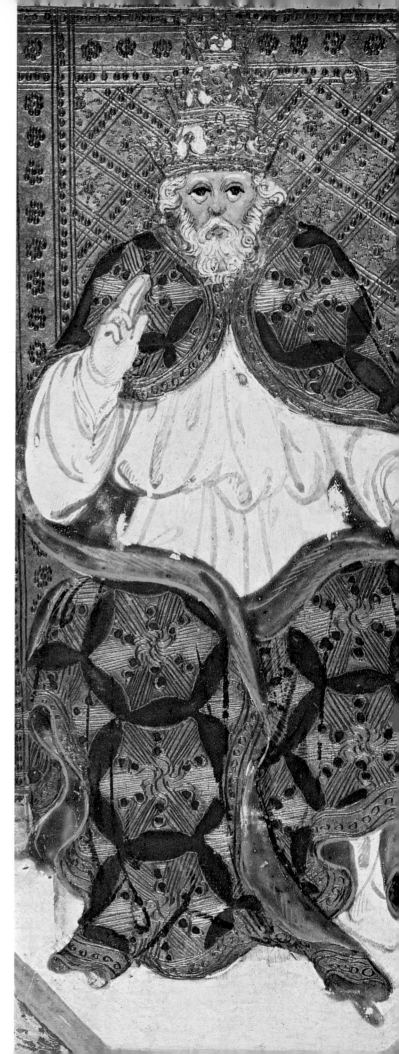

4
Fashioning Images of Rulership and Authority: The Early Fifteenth Century

At the end of the fourteenth and beginning of the fifteenth century, civic energies were directed toward completing and decorating the large-scale public buildings—city halls, cathedrals, and mendicant basilicas—begun during earlier periods of rapid urban growth. Milan was somewhat unusual insofar as its newly proclaimed duke, Giangaleazzo Visconti, initiated the construction of a new cathedral at this time, but his actions should be understood at least in part as an attempt to keep Milan apace of earlier projects in other cities.

Wealthy families and lay groups played significant and expanding roles in enhancing the appearance of cities throughout the peninsula, in private chapels and family residences as well as in designated portions of public projects. The vast majority of private patrons expected painting and sculpture to conform to the aesthetic of the elegant International Style, with its carefully balanced compositions, naturalistic detail, and artifice. Renowned practitioners found work across Italy: Michelino da Besozzo in Milan and Venice, his son in Naples; Gentile da Fabriano in Venice, Florence, and Rome.

These years also saw artists and patrons fascinated with eclectic combinations of styles and motifs, studying ancient Roman models, for example, but usually presenting them in chivalric garb. In Florence, sculpture made between 1410 and 1430 for the guild oratory of Or San Michele suggests that the International Gothic style implied social status not only for individual but for corporate patrons as well. The Florentine architect Brunelleschi was a stylistic maverick in applying a classical vocabulary to his buildings, but in his most stunning architectural achievement—the dome of Florence Cathedral, designed for the Arte della Lana—he used pointed Gothic arches and a drum decorated with a marble veneer much like the rest of the pre-existing building.

Coexistence of competing styles well into the fifteenth century is attested by the work of the great psychological and visual realist Masaccio, who shared his important commissions with Masolino, an exponent of the more elegant International Style.

The Courts: Gothic and Classical Inspirations

One of the most striking aspects of art at the courts in the early fifteenth century was the extraordinary adaptability of the International Gothic style. Developed in northern Europe and given its most prestigious form at the highly cultured court of the dukes of Burgundy, this style combined sumptuous patterns and materials with linear artifice and a close study of nature. All across Europe, from Paris, Burgundy, Germany, and Hungary to southern Italy, artists embedded detailed studies of flora and fauna within disembodied extravaganzas of color and pattern. Refined, complex forms were as at home in architecture (notably window tracery), sculpture, and wall painting as they were in the luxury art of manuscript illumination. Much of this was a logical outgrowth of dual Gothic tendencies towards naturalism and stylization, but sophisticated patrons now looked at these works in new ways. Both north and south of the Alps scholars were moving ahead with Petrarch's project to recover the ancient past. Reading classical authors, they were struck by Greek and Roman descriptions of art and nature that seemed to confirm their own predilections for the extravagant and gorgeous. They also learned of the significance of artistic types, such as the portrait medal, which had fallen into disuse with the passing of the ancient world. For the

4.1 (opposite) *Papessa and Pope* (tarot cards), 1441–47, commissioned by Bianca Visconti and Francesco Sforza. Gold leaf and paint on parchment pasted to papier-mâché board, each 6½ × 2¾″ (17 × 7 cm) (Pierpont Morgan Library, New York)

most part uninterested in serious archaeology, artists, architects, and patrons cared little about the visual discrepancies we now recognize between the art of their own day and that of the ancient past. Instead, their new learning allowed them to appreciate works of art in the International Gothic style with heightened sensitivity and delight.

Milan: Giangaleazzo Visconti

Milan set the pace and tone for much courtly art in early fifteenth-century Italy. The political situation in the city favored commitments to both the monumental and decorative arts. In 1385 Giangaleazzo Visconti, son of Galeazzo Visconti who had earlier ruled Pavia, united the rule of Milan and Pavia. Ten years later the Hapsburg emperor, Wenceslas, proclaimed Milan a duchy, the only one of its time in Italy. Giangaleazzo earned his title of Duke through military acumen, diplomatic treachery, and a substantial contribution to the imperial treasury, giving him greater autonomy than other Italian princes. Already master of most of Italy north of the Apennines save Venice when he accepted the ducal crown, Giangaleazzo soon extended his dominion well into central Italy, securing Pisa and Siena and laying siege to Florence. By 1402 he was poised to unify northern and central Italy under a single ruler, and he might have done so had he not died suddenly in the summer of that year.

Giangaleazzo seemed an unlikely person to achieve such international prominence. He cut a very poor public figure. Retiring and secretive, more a thinker than a soldier, he was, however, a supreme strategist, entering into alliances both to subdue rivals and to learn the vulnerabilities of his allies, themselves often his next targets. Giangaleazzo even feigned a religious conversion in order to overthrow his fearsome uncle, Bernabò (see Fig. 3.35), ambushing him during a faked religious procession around Milan.

As a patron of the arts Giangaleazzo followed and expanded upon the precedent set by his father, Galeazzo, adding to the decoration of the family residence in Pavia (see Fig. 3.37), commissioning

some new impressive buildings of his own, and supporting the luxury arts of manuscript illumination, ivory carving, and goldsmithery. Giangaleazzo also emulated the cultural sophistication of Burgundy and the Île-de-France. Married at a young age to Isabelle, daughter of King John II of France (r. 1350–64), through whom he assumed the title of Comte de Vertus in Champagne, he further tied the Visconti to the French crown through the marriages of his niece and his daughter to French royalty. Not surprisingly, he gauged Milanese accomplishments by international standards.

The Certosa of Pavia Soon after assuming the title of Duke of Milan, Giangaleazzo launched plans for the grandest of his commissions, the Certosa of Pavia (begun 1396). He intended this huge Carthusian monastery—which was not completed until well into the fifteenth century (Fig. 4.2)—to serve as his dynasty's mausoleum, emulating Jean de Berry, Duke of Burgundy, who had, in 1383, founded another Carthusian monastery, the Chartreuse de Champmol, for the same purpose. Giangaleazzo chose a site on the edge of ducal hunting grounds outside the city of Pavia, confirming his family's associations with the town while at the same time ensuring exclusive control over the monastery. The first order of business was to erect quarters for the monks, who

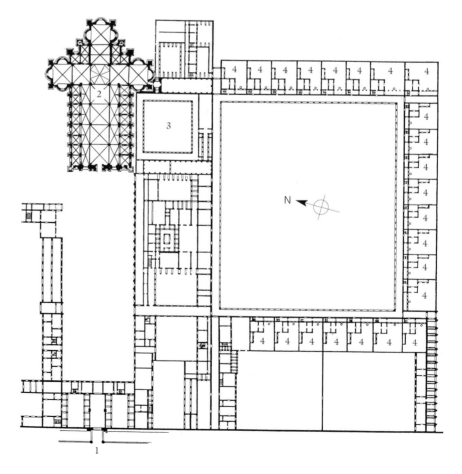

4.2 Certosa, Pavia, plan, begun 1396, commissioned by Giangaleazzo Visconti

1 Main entrance; **2** Church of Santa Maria; **3** Small cloister; **4** Monks' cells

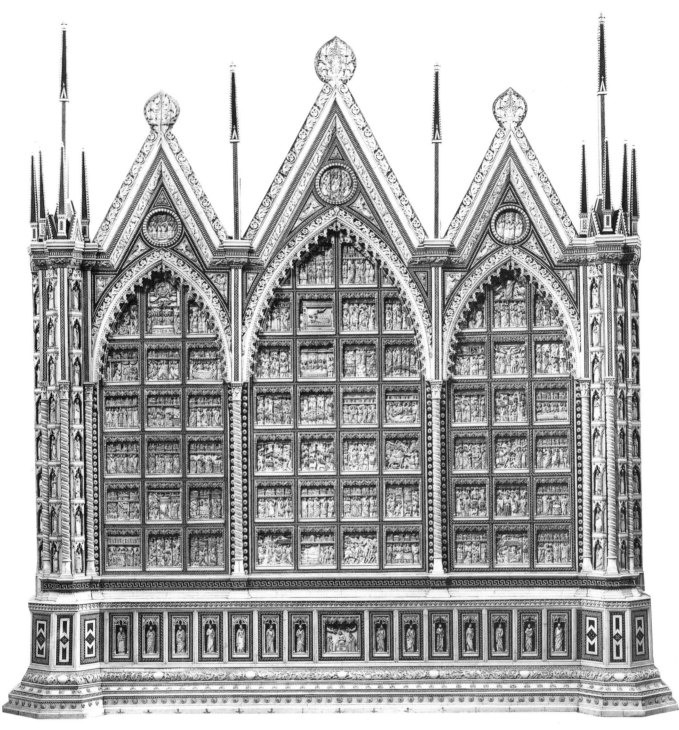

4.3 Ivory altarpiece, 1390s, commissioned by Giangaleazzo Visconti from BALDASSARE DEGLI EMBRIACHI for the Certosa, Pavia. Elephant ivory and ebony

were committed to a solitary life of prayer and meditation. Each individual was given a small three-room dwelling, complete with individual garden—generous accommodation by monastic standards, which must have enhanced the sincerity with which the monks prayed for the souls of deceased Visconti. Construction then began on the church. Although the present building is largely a product of much later intervention by other Milanese dukes, Giangaleazzo's ivory altarpiece (Fig. 4.3), which was to stand on the high altar in close proximity to his

tomb, survives in nearly pristine form. It, too, follows a Burgundian precedent, Jean de Berry having ordered similar triptychs from the same artist, Baldassare degli Embriachi (active 1390–1409 Florence and Venice), for Champmol and Poissy in 1393. Ivory was a favorite medium among noble patrons, who appreciated its expense and luxury, while the Carthusian monks would have approved the purity of its color, embellished only with gold and some ebony inlay, which conformed to their tendency to avoid worldly color and pattern.

The Pavia triptych is extraordinarily large for a work in ivory, constructed of thousands of pieces of carved elephant tusk. The architectural frame, reminiscent of Giotto's design for the Florence Campanile and reflecting Baldassare's training in Florence before he set up his own workshop in Venice, contains fifty-four niches for saints. The panel at the left contains eighteen reliefs depicting stories from the life of the Virgin; the one on the right, an equal number from the life of Christ. In the large central panel appear scenes from the lives and legends of the Three Kings, a subject chosen by Giangaleazzo to recall the Milanese cult of the Magi and, by association, to emphasize his own princely patronage. Most of the incidents in his altarpiece are carved from several narrow pieces of ivory. The Magi narrative was so important, however, that Baldassare and his workshop carved several of its reliefs from much larger pieces of ivory, joined with great ingenuity, which facilitated the inclusion of larger elements and more expressive interchange among the figures. In the scene of *The Magi Being Greeted on their Return Home* (Fig. 4.4) the eldest Magus leans well forward to extend his hands across the juncture of two broad pieces of ivory, grasping the outstretched arms of a younger man who has come out to meet him. They exchange joyful greetings, their emotion echoed by a child with upraised arms and a loyal dog who turns a perky head up toward his master. Another hound runs beneath the Magus's gold-caparisoned steed, a familiar image in courtly art. In spite of the precious medium and miniature scale, the relief's illusionistic space is deep and complex. In the background a deer appears in a cleft of one of the

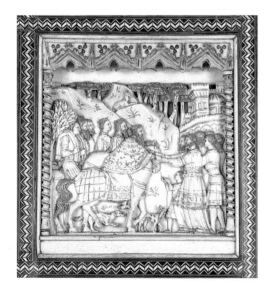

4.4 *The Magi Being Greeted on their Return Home*, detail of the ivory altarpiece, 1390s, commissioned by Giangaleazzo Visconti from BALDASSARE DEGLI EMBRIACHI for the Certosa, Pavia. Elephant ivory and ebony

mountains, and trees give way to rooftops and towers as the procession nears the city.

Milan Cathedral Architecture   Giangaleazzo Visconti would have liked to have left the impression that everything splendid in Milan and its domains was a result of his leadership, but there were other noteworthy patrons of Milanese art and architecture. Foremost was the Fabbrica or building committee of Milan's cathedral. Led by the archbishop and supervised by a semi-autonomous citizens' council, which by 1395 numbered 300 members, the Fabbrica allowed a certain amount of artistic self-determination in this otherwise autocratically controlled city, encouraging the entire population to identify with a single project that exalted the city. Surviving account books record donations ranging from large sums given by aristocrats down to a few coins contributed by a prostitute. Because a splendid cathedral could be of propagandistic value to the duke, he, too, was happy to facilitate its construction. He provided subsidies and exclusive access to important quarries. In acknowledgement of his contributions, the Visconti emblem of a radiating sun appears in the center of the lancet window behind the cathedral's high altar (Fig. 4.5). Otherwise the cathedral, like others throughout Europe, is a civic monument.

The archbishop and leading citizens of Milan had been laying plans for a new cathedral for several decades before work began on it in 1386, but Giangaleazzo's predecessor, Bernabò, had declined to support the project. Giangaleazzo was of another opinion. Soon after seizing power from Bernabò in 1385 he instituted several measures that endeared him to the citizenry, including lowering taxes and reforming the city's law code, as well as agreeing to the construction of a new cathedral. In September of the next year the foundations were being dug, led by Simone da Orsenigo (active 1380s–90s) and advised by Bonino da Campione and other local artisans. Day laborers were assisted by alternating troops of volunteer workers drawn from the city's guilds and parishes.

The building is both profoundly Lombard and distinctly international, grounded in Roman and Romanesque architectural ideas but executed with northern Gothic detail. The double-aisled nave and ambulatory follow the precedent of the large Romanesque cathedrals at the Lombard cities of Piacenza and Cremona (Fig. 4.6). Vast space spreads into the double side aisles. The structure appears solid and massive, northern Gothic verticality and insubstantiality countered and balanced by huge capitals that crown the piers with statues set within Gothic niches. Small broad clerestory windows assure that the upper reaches of the vaults remain in mysterious shadow, just as they had in such Romanesque churches as Milan's own Sant'Ambrogio.

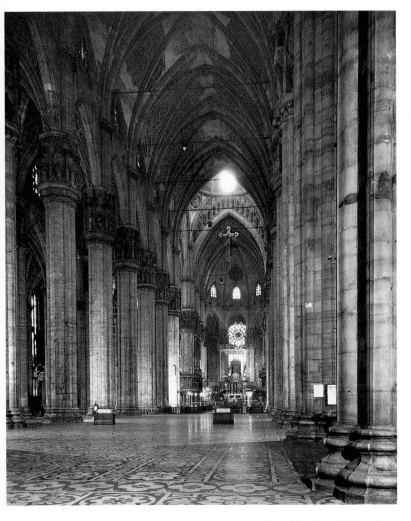

4.5 Milan Cathedral, begun 1386, commissioned by the Fabbrica of Milan Cathedral with the support of Giangaleazzo Visconti from SIMONE DA ORSENIGO and BONINO DA CAMPIONE

The interior is extremely dark for a Gothic church because the builders refused to use flying buttresses which they found ugly.

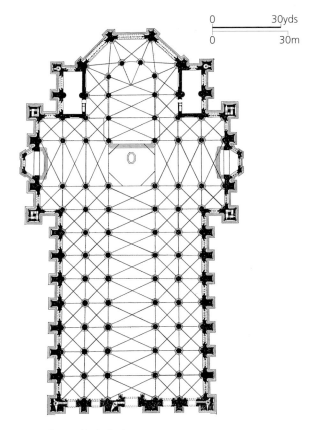

4.6 Milan Cathedral, plan

The complex piers of bundled colonettes, the highly pointed arches above them, and the thin, flamelike tracery patterns in the apse windows, however, were clearly inspired by transalpine models. Just as Giangaleazzo emulated the French aristocracy, the Fabbrica called upon architects from across northern Europe to advise on the construction of their cathedral. In 1389 they first turned to Paris, engaging Nicholas de Bonaventure; the next year they called upon a Master Johann from the German city of Freiburg; in 1391 and 1392 candidates were sought from Cologne and Ulm, finally resulting in the hiring of Heinrich Parler of Schwäbisch-Gmünd, who was working in Prague. He was succeeded by Jean Mignot of Paris, who was unusual in lasting several years on the job.

The design and construction process was filled with acrimony, vividly documented in the minutes of meetings held in 1392, 1400, and 1401. The Fabbrica had very clear ideas about the kind of building it wanted, and so did the northern European architects. Both sides based their recommendations regarding the shape of the building on ideal geometric schemes of squares and triangles, but neither had the ability to calculate accurately the actual forces at work within the building. Typical of Italian cathedrals in this period, the plan had been established, foundations laid, and piers built before final decisions were made about the size and shape of the vaulting or the kind of buttressing that would be required to sustain it. In 1392 Heinrich Parler declared that the piers were not sufficiently strong to support the desired superstructure, which he, like Nicholas de Bonaventure of Paris before him, imagined to consist of a high nave and low side aisles steadied in typically northern fashion by flying buttresses. But local opposition to flying buttresses is documented in 1400, when the Fabbrica criticized the exterior of Notre Dame in Paris. The Milanese preferred a lower and broader church with higher side aisles which would make the structure essentially self-supporting. They also defended the unusual proportions of the nave piers and capitals in anthropomorphic terms, insisting that the capital (or head) be several times larger than the base (or foot). Thus, the weightiness of the present building and the unusual form of its piers are direct expressions of clearly expressed local aesthetic preference.

Milan Cathedral Sculpture   From the start the cathedral project entailed an ambitious sculptural program. Masters were enlisted both locally and from abroad to carve figures for pinnacles and for reliefs between the traceried windows. Interior walls and the tabernacled capitals of the nave piers were likewise embellished with sculpture. Much of this sculpture has a linear quality—the result of the method used in commissioning it. The Fabbrica first engaged painters and manuscript illuminators to produce drawings for sculptural decoration; these were then auctioned to sculptors who offered the best price for what was expected to be competent but not necessarily innovative work. When the sculpture was complete it was presented to the Fabbrica for comparison with the initial drawing.

For sculpture intended to occupy a prominent position, the Fabbrica was more selective. In 1419 they gave the very experienced master carver Jacopino da Tradate (active 1401–40 Milan and Mantua) a commission to produce a nearly twice-life-sized high relief carving of Pope Martin V for the interior of the cathedral (Fig. 4.7). Martin had dedicated the high altar in October 1418, an event that the duke and all of Milan had obvious reason to commemorate. While adhering to the convention of a frontal and enthroned pose for the pope, Jacopino enlivened the image with cascades of drapery on the back and sides of the throne and over the majestic figure of the pontiff. Apart from the purposefully rigid pose and fixed gaze of the pope, every element has been carefully observed from nature and rendered with the utmost fidelity. Martin's legs and his raised right arm and hand, offering his blessing in perpetuity, extend realistically into space; his torso has weight and presence. A rectangular frame and a two-tiered corbel display lushly undercut foliage.

Manuscript Illumination   Manuscript illuminators led the way in promoting and popularizing the conventions of the International Style that Jacopino exploited in his sculpture. One of its earliest exponents in Lombardy was Giovannino dei Grassi (active 1380s–1398 Milan), a multi-talented illuminator and painter who provided designs for Milan Cathedral. Around 1395 Giovannino produced a prayer book for Giangaleazzo Visconti, whose portrait, surrounded by the blazing device of the Visconti family, appears with a text from Psalm 118 (Fig. 4.8). Typical of the International Style and of manuscript illumination in this period, the page includes a variety of artistic modes: some highly conventionalized, others strikingly naturalistic. Giangaleazzo's portrait, for example, is precisely rendered in profile. Derived from the tradition of Roman coins and medals, this formal pose allowed the ruler's distinctive features to be easily recognized by his subjects (see Fig. 3.42).

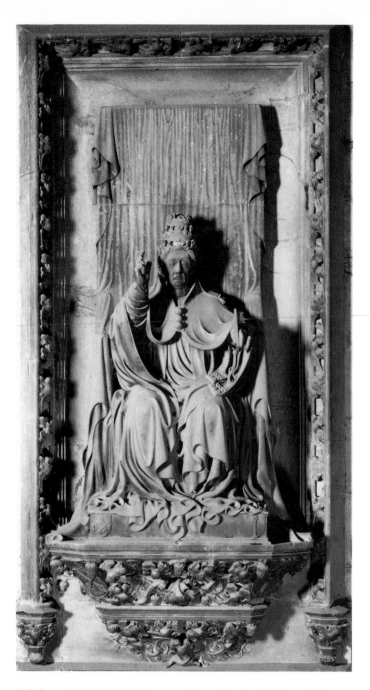

4.7 *Pope Martin V*, 1419–21, commissioned by the Fabbrica of Milan Cathedral with the encouragement of Filippo Maria Visconti from JACOPINO DA TRADATE for Milan Cathedral. Marble, twice lifesize

A much more fanciful and delicate decorative mode informs the illumination at the center of the text. Anchored at its four corners by the Visconti coat of arms, the basically square field supports a spiraling ribbon carrying the French fleur-de-lys and framing King David, traditionally regarded as the author of the psalms. The setting is illusionistic enough to suggest a shallow cavity of space within the initial, but linear and decorative enough to respect the graphic demands of the letter it is enhancing. The *bas de page*, or lowest range of the manuscript, is most detailed and realistic. This was considered a less important area of a manuscript since it did not include written text. Three of Giangaleazzo's hunting

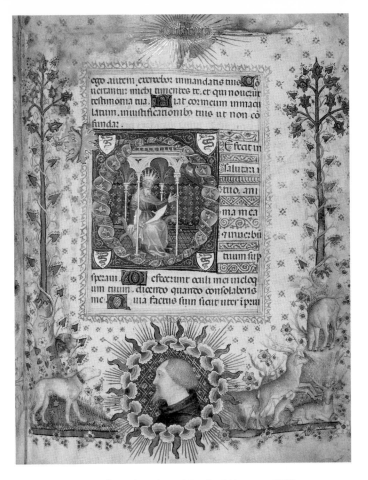

4.8 Psalm 118:81, from the *Visconti Book of Hours*, c. 1395, commissioned by Giangaleazzo Visconti from GIOVANNINO DEI GRASSI. Tempera and gold on parchment, 9¾ × 6⅞" (24.7 × 17.5 cm) (Banco Rari, Biblioteca Nazionale, 397, fol. 115, Florence)

This small book fits easily in one's hands. It was used for personal devotions on a regular schedule throughout the day.

dogs on the left raise their muzzles in anticipation of pursuing the deer on the right. One of their quarry leaps across the rocky setting, while another, radically foreshortened in the background, grazes contentedly; yet another two sit in the foreground. The differing modes of depiction on a single page are obviously conscious choices, as is confirmed by a page of animal studies from Giovannino's own sketchbook (Fig. 4.9). At the top, a pack of hunting dogs viciously attacks a wild boar which itself seems to have mortally wounded a hound whose muzzle is thrown back in agony at the top of the group. On the lower half of the page, in contrast, a leopard set in a garden and chained to a radiant circle is a heraldic design and therefore much calmer and more stylized. Giovannino and his Lombard contemporaries were so renowned for their meticulous renditions of animals from life that this kind of work came to be known throughout Europe by the French term *ouvraige de Lombardie* ("Lombard work"), a noteworthy achievement in this otherwise French-dominated art.

The most widely known Lombard illuminator of the early fifteenth century was Michelino da Besozzo (Michelino Molinari; active 1388–1445 Milan). Time has not been kind to Michelino's reputation. Much of his work has been destroyed, and the surviving examples are of a fragile preciosity that runs counter to the classicizing trend traditionally accepted as typical of Renaissance art. But the early humanist Umberto Decembrio singled out Michelino's art as superior to all others, and the Duke of Berry even sent his agent to interview Michelino; the agent returned with the report that Michelino was "the most excellent painter among all the painters in the world." Such hyperbole cannot be taken completely on face value, but there is no denying that European connoisseurs were dazzled by Michelino's artistry. He began his career in Pavia, went to Venice where he was in contact with Gentile da Fabriano, and then received major commissions in Milan. After the death of Giangaleazzo and during the troubled reign of Giovanni Maria Visconti (r. 1401–12), Michelino took his practice to Vicenza and Venice, an area highly receptive to his refined, delicate style. He returned to Milan in 1418, where he worked until his death at mid-century.

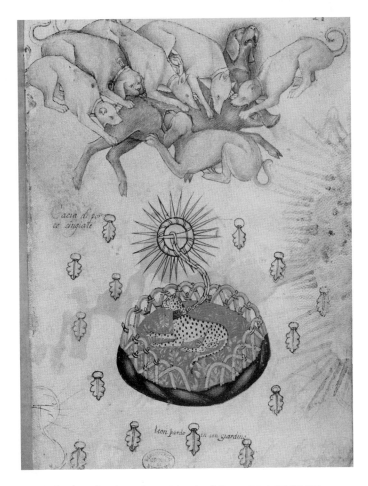

4.9 Animal studies, from the notebook of GIOVANNINO DEI GRASSI, 1390s. 10¼ × 6¾" (26 × 17.5 cm) (Biblioteca Civica, ms.Δ, VII, 14 = Φ 9–6, Bergamo)

A page from the *Eulogy for Giangaleazzo Visconti* (Fig. 4.10; see also Fig. 4.1), written by an Augustinian monk, Pietro da Castelletto, and illuminated by Michelino, exemplifies the refined sensibilities that appealed to aristocratic patrons. Framing the text is a garland of flowers with fragile leaves and threadlike tendrils. In the upper rectangular field a cloth of honor overlaid with the imperial and Visconti coats of arms forms the delicate backdrop for the culminating event of Pietro's eulogy, Giangaleazzo's heavenly coronation by the Christ Child. The Christ Child is the most robust of all the figures, everyone else having been reduced—apart from their firm hands and heads—to wraith-like forms, perhaps to convey the ethereal nature of heavenly existence. In the decorated initial below, a more substantial and clearly earthbound Pietro da Castelletto addresses his fellow Augustinians, his hands firmly grasping a pen and the pulpit from which he speaks. Clearly, Michelino had a

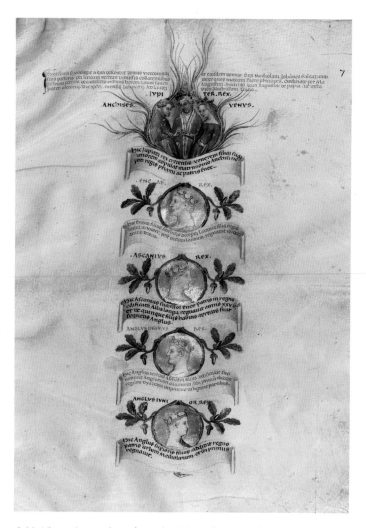

4.11 Visconti genealogy, from the *Eulogy for Giangaleazzo Visconti*, 1402/03, commissioned by the Visconti court from MICHELINO DA BESOZZO. 14¾ × 9½" (37.5 × 24 cm) (Bibliothèque Nationale, ms. lat. 5888, fol. 7, Paris)

repertoire of styles, employed as appropriate for different subjects.

Michelino's work, closely related to similar art at the Valois courts in France, had obvious appeal for patrons like the Visconti, with their dynastic ambitions and royal marriage alliances. The opening page of the Visconti genealogy from the *Eulogy* (Fig. 4.11) lines up profile images inspired by Greco-Roman coins and medals to trace the Visconti lineage from its legendary origins in the marriage of the Trojan prince Anchises and the goddess Venus, performed by Jupiter. The mythic couple and Jupiter appear at the top of the manuscript, depicted, in Michelino's refined manner, as contemporary aristocrats; the same delicacy informs the Roman profiles of the Visconti. These antique references—evidence of humanist activity at the Visconti court—are deftly integrated, through Michelino's deceptively casual manner, into a medieval legend.

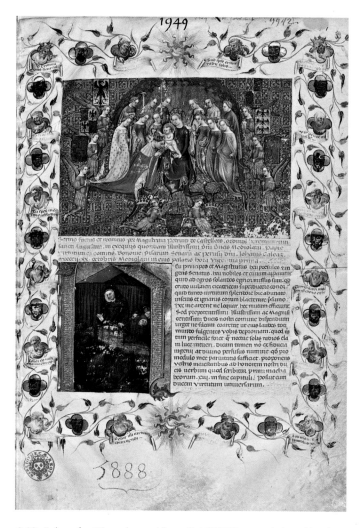

4.10 *Eulogy for Giangaleazzo Visconti*, 1402/03, commissioned by the Visconti court from MICHELINO DA BESOZZO. 14¾ × 9½" (37.5 × 24 cm) (Bibliothèque Nationale, ms. lat. 5888, fol. 1, Paris).

Secular Frescoes The extent to which the International Style left an imprint on northern Italy can be appreciated by examining a fresco cycle by an unknown painter in the city of Trent in the foothills of the Alps, north of Verona. Commissioned sometime between 1391 and 1407 by the city's prince-bishop, George of Lichtenstein, the frescoes cover the walls of one of the large towers in his residence, the Castello del Buonconsiglio. They represent the twelve months of the year (Fig. 4.12). The paintings, sensitively restored in 1534, provide a rare opportunity to experience vicariously the life and artistic sensibilities of early fifteenth-century courtiers.

The wooden beams, intervening ceiling panels, walls, and window surrounds all pulsate with decoration. Tall, thin, twisted colonettes divide one month's representation from another, set above a fictive dado that seems to be hung with brightly colored, brocade fabric. Once again, we encounter a natural world constructed with careful artifice, reminiscent of earlier illustrations of the *Tacuinum Sanitatis* type (see Fig. 3.40), a famous copy of which was owned by Prince-Bishop George. The scenes shown here represent, from left to right, the months of April, May, June, and July. In the April landscape amorous noble couples cavort on a floral field. Behind them rises a fortress, perhaps representing one of Prince-Bishop George's dependencies. Similar representations appear in luxurious Burgundian manuscripts of this time, such as the Limbourg Brothers' *Très Riches Heures* for the Duke of Berry. In the scenes of June and July, however, hardly an aristocrat is present, for work under the scorching summer sun was delegated largely to peasants. The carefree amusements of the aristocrats contrast tellingly with the vigorous labor of the peasants, who often appear smaller than the aristocrats—not only because the artist wished to suggest some depth in the scenes but also because of the peasants' lower social status.

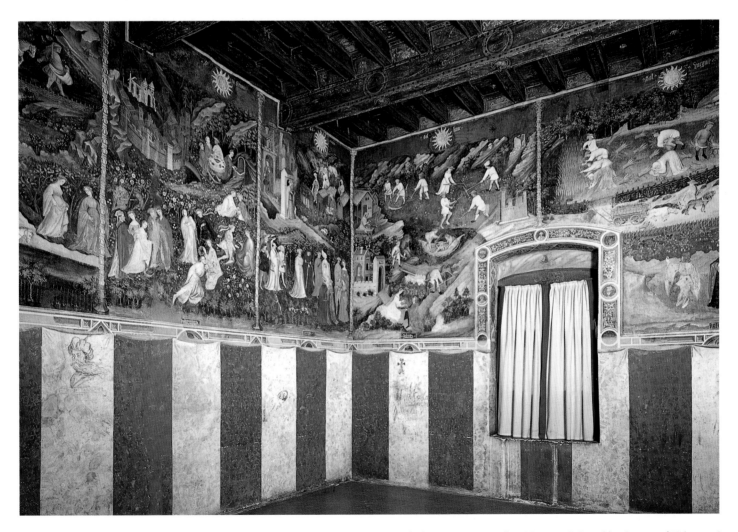

4.12 *Representations of the Twelve Months*, detail showing April, May, June, and July, between 1391 and 1407, commissioned by George of Lichtenstein for the Castello del Buonconsiglio, Trent. Fresco

A snowball fight in the January scene (not shown here) is one of the earliest surviving representations of a snow scene in western European art.

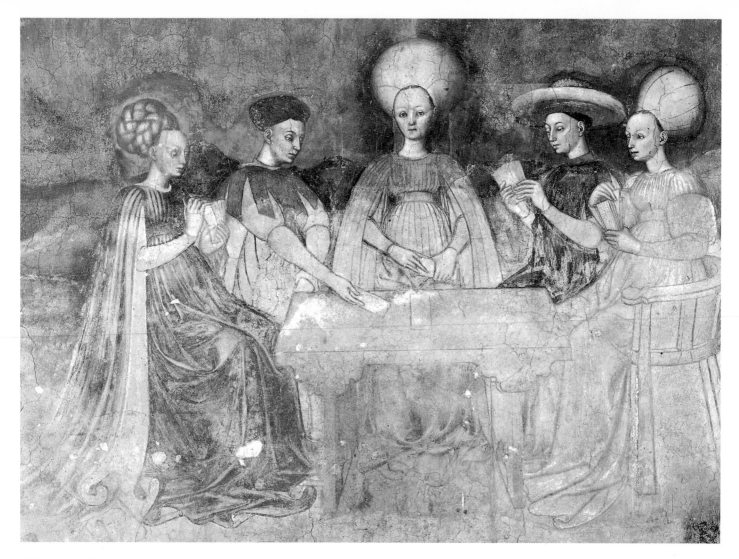

4.13 *Men and Women Playing Cards*, 1430s (?), commissioned by the Borromeo family for the Casa Borromeo, Milan. Fresco

Literary sources describing the decorations of other palaces in this period suggest that these figures may represent members of the Borromeo family.

Aristocratic pastimes included playing party games that required both skill and sometimes cunning deceit. Elegant depictions of some of these entertainments appear inside the Casa Borromeo in Milan (Fig. 4.13). The Borromeo family were wealthy merchants who had been ennobled at the beginning of the fifteenth century. The frescoes, located in one of the living halls probably destined for use by female members of the family, depict women and men amusing themselves by batting balls, chasing one another in a game of tag, and, in this illustration, playing cards. The figures, remote and emotionless in their fashionable clothing and headdresses, sit in a vast landscape whose vegetation is limited to three perfect trees on each wall. Since women in this period were expected to be modest and demure, their activities are performed in a highly ritualized manner, graceful and balletic even in the more energetic scenes. The frescoes both mirrored contemporary behavior and, no doubt, encouraged similar comportment from the room's occupants.

The figures in the Casa Borromeo frescoes are playing with tarot cards painted on stiff paper showing different figures and symbols (swords, goblets, coins, and batons) carrying specific numeric values. Widely diffused in the fifteenth century, they were used for games of skill and chance, each pictorial card representing a vice, virtue, force of nature, or mythical character. Most were produced as block prints, but for aristocratic clients like the Borromeo, illuminators provided hand-painted and gilded versions. A splendid set, still almost intact, was created by an unidentified artist between 1441 and 1447 for Bianca Visconti, daughter of Duke Galeazzo Maria Visconti, and her husband, Francesco Sforza (Fig. 4.14). The pair shown represents an enthroned female figure known as the Papessa or female pope, identifiable by her papal tiara and brown mendicant robes. Medieval legend claims that a woman had once been elected pope by disguising her gender. Here she plays the female counterpart to the pope, much as the Virgin Mary complemented Christ. Associated with the moon, the Papessa represented

Commissions of King Ladislas   Little art survives from the late fourteenth century in Naples, a mark of the continuing struggles that accompanied the shift in leadership within the kingdom. By the early fifteenth century, however, the Durazzesco King Ladislas (r. 1399– 1414) had brought relative peace to southern Italy, a situation conducive to a major increase in artistic activity. In Naples he chose to underline his family's dual Hungarian and Angevin lineage in a series of frescoes (by a now-unknown artist) depicting the life of his patron saint and first king of the Hungarians, St. Ladislas (Fig. 4.15). Ladislas's decision to patronize a chapel at the Angevin royal site of Santa Maria dell'Incoronata and to decorate it with scenes from the life of a Hungarian saint should be seen as an attempt both to co-opt the Angevin lineage and to assert his Durazzesco heritage.

One section of the fresco cycle, *St. Ladislas I of Hungary Declared King by the Will of the Entire Magyar People in 1077*, suggests the enthusiasm and unanimity with which Ladislas of Naples hoped his subjects would greet him. At the center his namesake, St. Ladislas, strides briskly through the crowds, his bearing designed to communicate saintly modesty at all this public adulation. In the tradition of the major narrative cycles of the Paduan school of the 1380s, large crowds of highly individualized persons bracket the composition and lead the eye into deep space by their smaller scale. The painted architecture situates the exuberant scene, anchoring it in the left and right foreground with waist-high platforms and in the rear with soaring Gothic windows and flying buttresses. The tall, attenuated forms of many of the onlookers attest to the popularity of International Gothic models in Naples.

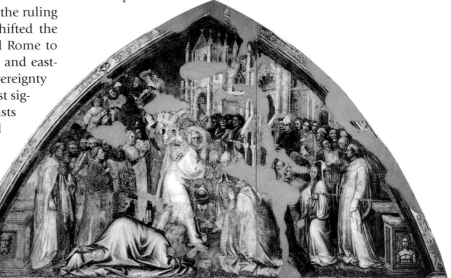

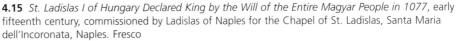
4.15 *St. Ladislas I of Hungary Declared King by the Will of the Entire Magyar People in 1077*, early fifteenth century, commissioned by Ladislas of Naples for the Chapel of St. Ladislas, Santa Maria dell'Incoronata, Naples. Fresco

4.14 *Papessa and Pope* (tarot cards), 1441–47, commissioned by Bianca Visconti and Francesco Sforza. Gold leaf and paint on parchment pasted to papier-mâché board, each 6½ × 2¾" (17 × 7 cm) (Pierpont Morgan Library, New York)

knowledge, intuition, divinatory power, penetration of mysteries, recognition, secret knowledge, wisdom, and common sense. Given the patriarchal bias of medieval and Renaissance society, she was, nevertheless, one of the lowest-valued figural cards, only the King of Carnival and the Fool ranking lower.

Naples: King Ladislas, Queen Giovanna

In the late fourteenth century, a new branch of the ruling Angevin family in Naples, the Durazzeschi, shifted the artistic orientation of the city from France and Rome to northeastern Italy, the Visconti court in Milan, and eastern Europe, where the Neapolitans claimed sovereignty over Hungary. Artistically, Milan proved the most significant of these foci, since a number of artists who had trained in the Lombard capital received major commissions at the Neapolitan court. Serving the needs of the royal court and its emulators among the nobility and clergy, artists were encouraged to study earlier works and at times even to reuse them. This eclectic approach produced art and architecture that pulsated with vitality, often producing theatrical, scenographic effects, especially when painting and sculpture were combined in lavish ensembles.

Aristocratic Patronage Courtiers and clergy contributed significantly to the embellishment of Naples under King Ladislas. The foremost patron after the royal family was Cardinal Enrico Minutolo, who as archbishop of Naples sponsored the carving of elaborate new portals for the façade of Naples Cathedral. The main portal (Fig. 4.16), dating from 1407, is a spectacular, composite affair designed by Antonio Baboccio (c. 1351 Piperno–1435), a native of Piperno, south of Rome, who had probably worked previously in Milan. The program focuses upon two images of the regal Virgin, an enthroned Madonna and Child in the **tympanum** and a representation of her coronation in the **oculus** above. Although the choice of subject may seem surprising in a cathedral dedicated to the Neapolitan bishop-saint Gennaro, it is consistent with the flourishing cult of the Virgin in Europe generally and may reflect Minutolo's own previous position as cardinal archpriest of Santa Maria Maggiore in Rome. Smaller statues of saints in tabernacles to the sides of the doorway represent several of the city's other protectors, though a number owe their inclusion personally to Cardinal Minutolo—which suggests that the archbishop of Naples had more direct control over the decoration of his cathedral than did prelates in Siena and Florence, who deferred to civic authorities. Minutolo himself kneels in the tympanum before the Virgin and Child. Just below, his coat of arms shares a place of honor with busts of the four Evangelists, along with the seal of the cathedral and the coat of arms of King Ladislas, a schematic representation of social negotiation in this city.

Baboccio's overall design resembles the exuberant work of Milanese carvers, especially in the gable, where music-making angels carved in high relief surround the oculus containing the Coronation of the Virgin. Fleshy leaves sprout along the edges of the gable; crimped ribbons of stylized cloud gather into frothy bouquets in the spandrels.

In addition to these Milanese elements, the portal incorporates reused antique porphyry columns, two crouching lions probably appropriated from the dismantled tomb of Charles Martel by the school of Nicola Pisano and a Madonna and Child by the Sienese sculptor Tino da Camaino (c. 1285–1338). All of these elements attest to the eclecticism of Neapolitan art in the early 1400s, and to its desire to link the present to the past.

Similar eclecticism, as well as exuberance, characterizes the Palazzo Penna, erected in 1406 by Antonio Penna, the king's secretary (Fig. 4.17). Its entire lower story is faced with smooth **rustication**, the upper blocks of which carry incised decoration. Three rows at the height of the doorway bear a feather pen (a literal rendition of his family name—Penna—and an apt emblem for the king's secre-

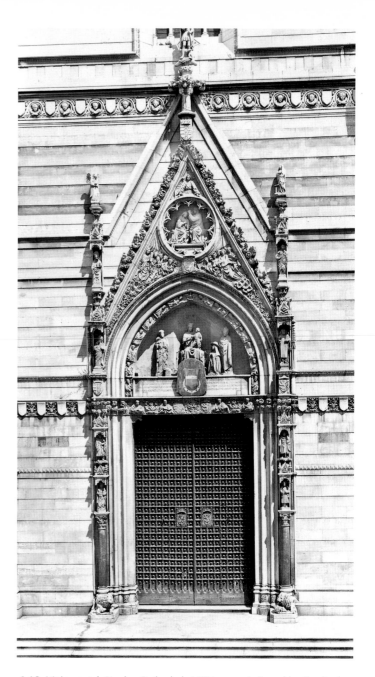

4.16 Main portal, Naples Cathedral, 1407, commissioned by Cardinal Enrico Minutolo from ANTONIO BABOCCIO. Marble

Baboccio reused some small figures from an earlier monument to supplement his own carvings.

tary). The vast majority carry the fleur-de-lys of the Angevin/Durazzesco dynasty. The rustication is surmounted by an arched corbel frieze which displays the devices of Penna's employer, King Ladislas—a rare privilege in the highly stratified courtly society of Naples. Within its simple rectangular frame the stilted arched doorway (characteristic of Durazzesco building) is carved from white marble. It carries a fluttering ribbon on which Penna flaunts his literary knowledge and anticipates criticism with an epigram by the classical author Martial: "You who pull faces and find it disagreeable to read such words, may you envy everyone else, jealous man, and may no one envy you."

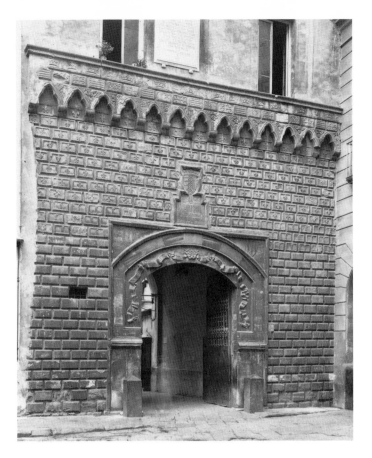

4.17 Palazzo Penna, Naples, 1406, commissioned by the royal secretary Antonio Penna

The facade was originally lavishly painted and gilded.

Queen Giovanna II and the Monument to King Ladislas

The standard for such display was set by the royal court, which since at least the time of Robert the Wise had been noted for its exploitation of visual splendor. King Ladislas's sister and successor, Queen Giovanna II (r. 1414–35) saw to it that Ladislas's tomb monument, begun in 1414 and completed in 1428, would set new standards for royal grandeur (Fig. 4.18). Her sculptors—among them the stone carvers Andrea (Andrea da Firenze; 1388–c. 1455 Florence) and Matteo Nofri from Florence—followed a plan probably laid out by a Neapolitan. Occupying virtually the entire height and breadth of the chancel of the church of San Giovanni a Carbonara, the monument competes locally with its Neapolitan predecessors and internationally with the multi-storied tombs of the della Scala in Verona (see Fig. 3.36), the equestrian monuments of the Visconti in Milan (see Fig. 3.35), and the canopied extravaganzas of the dukes of Burgundy in Dijon. The tomb represents an amplification of the tomb of Robert the Wise (see Fig. 2.55), with a life-sized statue of the queen sitting next to her brother in the second level, whereas Robert's earlier tomb had shown the king alone. Giovanna's portrait, like Robert's enthroned effigy, is blocky and severe, an unassailable image of regality, her individuality repressed to express the dignity of her office and lineage.

The monument culminated dramatically in the triumphant equestrian image of King Ladislas himself at its apex. As in Michelino da Besozzo's genealogy for the Visconti (see Fig. 4.11) and the inscription on the Palazzo Penna, ancient Roman ideas are presented in chivalric garb. Following Roman imperial custom, the words "Divus Ladislus" appear on the tomb. Thus Giovanna claims universal rank for her brother—shocking arrogance for the tomb of a Christian ruler. He raises his sword in victory as his heavily caparisoned horse

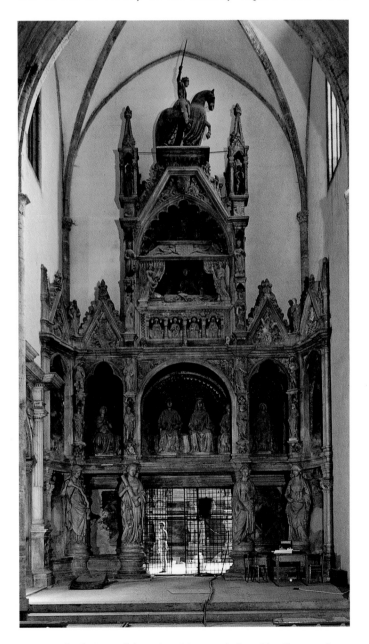

4.18 Tomb of King Ladislas, 1414–28, commissioned by Giovanna II from ANDREA AND MATTEO NOFRI and others for the chancel of San Giovanni a Carbonara, Naples. Marble

The Caracciolo Chapel is located behind the tomb wall, through the iron grate. The high altar originally stood in front of the tomb.

(originally polychromed) leads him forward to victory. The heroic and classical/pagan themes are encapsulated in the concluding line of his epitaph: "his soul, single and free, sought starry Olympus."

One would never sense from this splendid assertion of power that Giovanna's reign was particularly difficult, challenged throughout by her barons and then by a competitor of her own making, Alfonso of Aragon, whom she adopted as her successor. Alfonso ousted her from the throne after a long struggle and thus established a new, Aragonese, dynasty in Naples.

The Caracciolo Chapel   Queen Giovanna's transformation of the chancel of San Giovanni a Carbonara encouraged high court officials to erect their own tombs in the same church. One of them, the queen's lover and chief advisor, and the court's grand seneschal, Sergianni Caracciolo, built his family's burial chapel directly behind the high altar and Ladislas's tomb. It was a piece

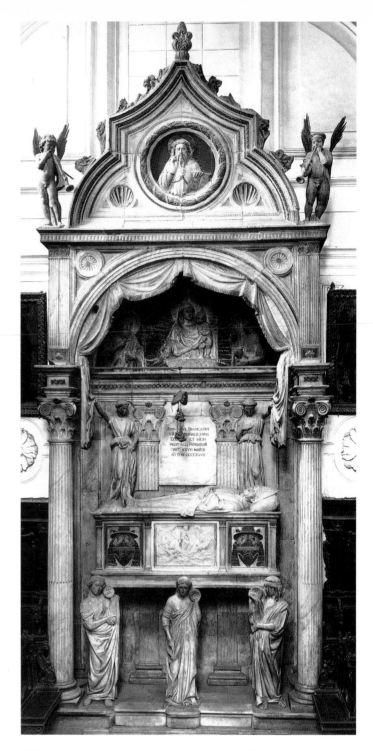

4.20 Tomb of Cardinal Rainaldo Brancacci, c. 1425, commissioned by Rainaldo Brancacci from LEONARDO DONATELLO and MICHELOZZO for Sant'Angelo a Nilo, Naples. Marble, height of each caryatid c. 5' 5" (1.65 m)

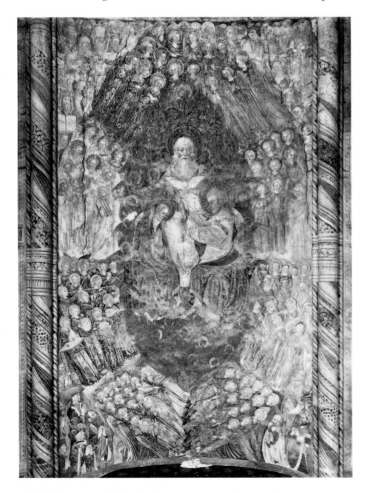

4.19 *Coronation of the Virgin*, c. 1428, commissioned by Sergianni Caracciolo from LEONARDO DA BESOZZO for the Caracciolo Chapel, San Giovanni a Carbonara, Naples. Fresco

Besides appearing in the fresco, Sergianni is represented nearly life-size in a statue standing atop his tomb in the chapel.

of exquisite courtly ambiguity, at once modest, since the chapel is almost invisible from the nave, and yet shrewdly opportunistic in its effective conversion of Ladislas's monument into an enormous triumphal frontispiece for his own chapel. The polygonal plan of Caracciolo's chapel may deliberately recall the form of ancient Roman imperial mausolea, giving the structure another level of exalted status.

Inside the Caracciolo Chapel every surface is covered with pattern and color. Three rows of frescoes adorn the walls. The top two include scenes from the life of the Virgin by Leonardo da Besozzo (active 1421–88 Milan and Naples), son of Michelino, the renowned Milanese painter, miniaturist, and building master (see Figs. 4.10 and 4.11). His presence in Naples in 1428 demonstrates the artistic connections between the two courts. In the *Coronation of the Virgin* (Fig. 4.19) Leonardo employed interlocking and curving patterns similar to those that Baboccio had used in his music-making angels on the Naples Cathedral portal (see Fig. 4.16), though softened with his own version of the delicate features and finely spun detail for which his father was famous. Sergianni appears several times in the frescoes as patron and witness to the sacred events. In the *Coronation* he kneels in his best damasks and furs at the bottom left of the angelic aureole, accompanied by portraits of other courtiers and the sensitive, searching features of adoring saints.

The Brancacci Tomb   It was for this same courtly clientele that the Florentine sculptural team of Donatello (Donato di Niccolò di Betto Bardi; 1386? Florence–1466 Florence) and Michelozzo (Michelozzo di Bartolommeo; 1396 Florence–1472 Florence) began, around 1425, to design a tomb monument for Cardinal Rainaldo Brancacci (Fig. 4.20). The cardinal selected burial in a frescoed chapel, Sant'Angelo a Nilo, at his newly endowed hospital near the Brancacci family home in the center of Naples. Donatello had been working for some time in a rigorously classicizing and naturalistic manner, very different from the works of artists such as Baboccio, Leonardo da Besozzo, and most of their contemporaries

in Florence. The Brancacci tomb shows this influence in the classical, fluted columns and paired **pilasters** which the sculptors integrated into the otherwise typically Neapolitan tomb. At the same time, the juxtaposition of convex and concave lines in the pediment creates a stylish late Gothic effect. The tomb's principal decorative element, a blessing Christ in glory in a round frame, finds a direct parallel in Baboccio's portal for the cathedral (see Fig. 4.16). Although the poses of the winged putti blowing trumpets at its sides may be classically inspired, they serve the same kind of decorative function as the pinnacle figures on the Ladislas tomb and the cathedral portal. This is definitely not a work intended for the sculptors' native Florence, where surviving tombs are not usually supported by caryatids nor crowned by such an elaborate canopy. The tomb's type corresponds to other important tombs in Naples and Rome. Its eclectic fusion of classical and Gothic elements perfectly suited the sophisticated Neapolitan court.

Verona

Verona, ancient stronghold of the della Scala family—or Scaligeri, as they are known (see Fig. 3.36)—fell in the late fourteenth century to the expansionist campaigns of Milan's lord Giangaleazzo Visconti, only to become one of Venice's mainland possessions in 1405. Artistically, however, the city remained in the orbit of the courts, due in no small part to the artistic leadership of Vittore Pisano, called Pisanello (c. 1395 probably Pisa–1455

Praise for Pisanello

Pisanello's work received an enthusiastic reception among north Italian humanists, many of whom were heavily influenced by the Greek scholar Manuel Chrysoloras (c. 1355–1415). Chrysoloras popularized the Greek tradition of *ekphrasis*, or extended, descriptive praise. Because of the compatibility between Pisanello's work and humanist rhetoric, it was he—not the classicizing Donatello, Brunelleschi, or their compatriot Masaccio—who received most praise from early Italian humanists, even out of Verona.

A good example of *ekphrasis* survives in a description of Pisanello's work by Guarino da Verona (1370–1460), Chrysoloras's most famous pupil.

. . . you equal Nature's works, whether you are depicting birds or beasts, perilous straits and calm seas; we would swear we saw the spray gleaming and heard the breakers roar. I put out a hand to wipe the sweat from the brow of the labouring peasant; we seem to hear the whinny of a war horse and tremble at the blare of trumpets. When you paint a nocturnal scene you make the night-birds flit about and not one of the birds of the day is

to be seen; you pick out the stars, the moon's sphere, the sunless darkness. If you paint a winter scene everything bristles with frost and the leafless trees grate in the wind. If you set the action in spring, varied flowers smile in the green meadows, the old brilliance returns to the trees, and the hills bloom; here the air quivers with the songs of birds.

(from Michael Baxandall. *Giotto and the Orators.* Oxford: Clarendon Press, 1971, pp. 92–3. Trans. from *Epistolario di Guarino Veronese.* Ed. R. Sabbadini. Venice, 1915, pp. 554–7)

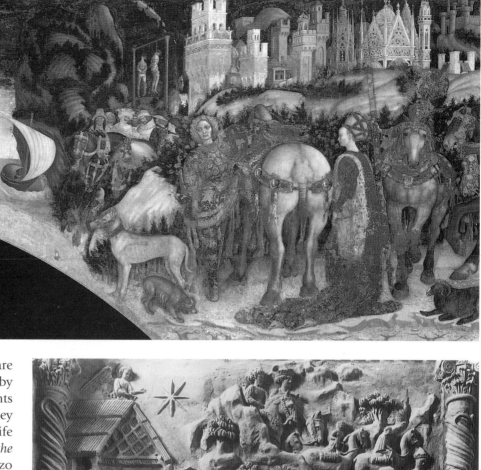

4.21 *St. George and the Princess*, 1430s, commissioned by the Pellegrini family from PISANELLO for the exterior of the entry arch into the Pellegrini Chapel, Sant'Anastasia, Verona. Fresco (now in sacristy)

probably Rome). An artistic virtuoso, Pisanello worked across the breadth of Italy, from Milan to Verona, Mantua, Ferrara, and even the republic of Venice, as well as Rome and Naples. In the 1430s Pisanello collaborated with a Florentine sculptor, Michele da Firenze (master of the Pellegrini Chapel; active 1404– 1443), on the decoration of the Pellegrini Chapel in the church of Sant'Anastasia in Verona. Over the entrance arch of the chapel, Pisanello painted a fresco of *St. George and the Princess* (Fig. 4.21), now removed to the church's sacristy. The walls of the chapel are lined with twenty-four terracotta reliefs by Michele. The reliefs narrate mainly events from the Passion and Resurrection. They also include a few scenes from the early life of Christ (Fig. 4.22). In the *Adoration of the Magi* Michele reverses his master Lorenzo Ghiberti's portrayal of the same subject from the second set of bronze doors for the Baptistry in Florence (see Fig. 4.31, third scene on the third row from the bottom). He also adds charming, almost naïve detail quickly modeled in the terracotta: a parade of the Magi and their entourage among the hills at the upper right; lilies, ferns, and flowers growing as large and larger than the trees; and an angel and eight-pointed star above a thatched shed sheltering the obligatory ox and ass. Amidst the panels, originally brightly painted, appear standing saints and a large kneeling portrait of the patron. Both Pisanello and Michele fill their spaces to overflowing, celebrating their inventive and depictive powers and apparently striving for what we would now say verges on sensory overload. Diversity and complexity have here taken precedence over dramatic unity and coherence.

Michele's terracotta scenes, recalling the early manner of Lorenzo Ghiberti, are modeled in very high relief. Many anecdotal details, originally brightly painted, seem to leap out at the viewer. Similarly, although Pisanello's fresco centers on the figure of St. George and the elegantly garbed princess to the right of his horse, there is much to distract the eye: a body of water at the far left and a

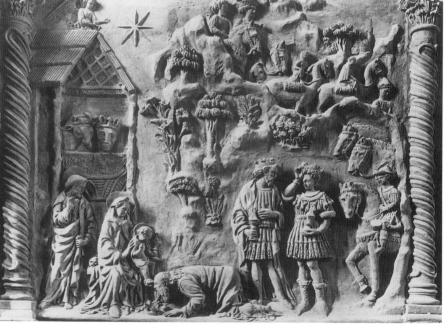

4.22 *Scenes from the Life of Christ*, detail of the *Adoration of the Magi*, 1430s, commissioned by the Pellegrini family from MICHELE DA FIRENZE for the Pellegrini Chapel, Sant'Anastasia, Verona. Terracotta

Pisanello and Michele probably collaborated on this project, which is typical of multi-media decorative complexes in this period. Besides providing a fresco for the entrance to the chapel, the painter may have participated in polychroming the relief sculpture.

boat sailing toward shore; horsemen whose physiognomy suggests they may come from eastern Europe or Asia; two hanged men on gallows; a shining, magical city of Gothic towers and delicate tracery in the background; and hunting dogs rendered with loving accuracy.

Art and Punishment

Pisanello drew these figures of hanged men (Fig. 4.23) as preparatory studies for his fresco of St. George in Verona (see Fig. 4.21). Carefully observed and detailed, they depict one of the grimmer aspects of life in medieval and Renaissance Europe, where the executions of criminals were public events and where bodies or parts of bodies were left on view in the landscape or in designated parts of the city as warnings to the population at large against breaking the law. London Bridge, for example, often carried decapitated heads exposed on spikes. And at the Senator's Palace of the Capitoline Hill in Rome men were tortured by having their hands tied behind their backs with a rope, by which they were then hoisted into the air and then repeatedly dropped a certain distance. This punishment, called *strappato*, tore the muscles of their arms, yet the men were left hanging from the façade of the building between applications of the torture. Bodies placed on wheels, with their limbs brutally broken over the rim, the bones piercing the skin, were erected on tall poles on open fields where they attracted carrion-eating birds.

Pisanello's fresco shows the gallows placed outside the city wall, as was the usual custom, in order that the criminal dead should not defile the city itself. Thus punishment put the tres-passer literally outside the bounds of the society. Moreover, it denied to the criminal the normal transitional rites of Christian burial which were meant to usher the soul into the afterlife. Even though confraternities assumed the duty of praying with and for the condemned prisoner, and even accompanied him up the ladder to the gibbet with exhortations to repentance, the final act of execution left the criminal alone and unattended, spatially and spiritually separated from the community (see Fig. 5.33). Pisanello's drawing also graphically suggests the degradation of the con-demned men, as some of their garments fall away, revealing their nakedness. Prostitutes were often punished by being stripped to the waist and paraded through the streets as a form of public humiliation. In times of insurrection people were sometimes hanged from windows of the town halls where they had moments earlier been sentenced to death—swift justice in a period of inflamed passions. In Florence paintings of hanged criminals were painted on the façades of the Palazzo del Podestà (the governor's palace, now known as the Bargello) and the Palazzo della Signoria.

Both Castagno and Botticelli are known to have painted such images; Castagno was even known as Andrea of the Hanged Men, supposedly for the number, if not the fame, of his works in this genre. Accompanying inscriptions identified the criminals, and the images remained as a long-term reminder, not only of the individuals but of the shame that they had brought to their families. These portraits of infamous men, as they were known, served as a vivid counterpart to the portraits of virtuous citizens that decorated the walls of family chapels and the façades of confraternities and churches (see Figs. 3.31 and 4.51). In their own way they are a measure of the power of the visual image to convey messages about civil order.

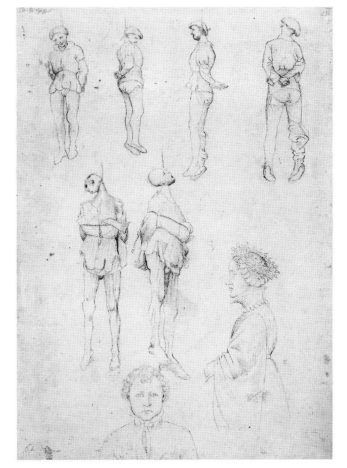

4.23 *Hanged Men and Two Portraits*, 1430s, PISANELLO. Metalpoint and pen on paper, 11¼ × 7¾" (26.6 × 19.7 cm) (© British Museum, no. 1895.9.15.441, London)

Ferrara

During the 1430s and 1440s Pisanello also came into close contact with humanist scholars at the court of Leonello d'Este (1404–50) in Ferrara. Tutored from childhood by Guarino of Verona, Leonello possessed a sharp mind and an intense love for the classical past. He collected antique coins and jewels and constructed a special study in which to examine and enjoy them. Leonello also turned learning and cultural achievements to political ends. His first major artistic enterprise upon assuming the title of marquis of Ferrara and Modena in 1441 was to commission from two Florentine sculptors, Antonio di Cristoforo and Niccolò Baroncelli (both active in the 1440s and 1450s), a now destroyed bronze equestrian sculpture, the first since antiquity, in honor of his father, Niccolò d'Este. An inscription lauded Niccolò d'Este as "three times creator of peace" and gave credit to the civic authorities who financed the project, testifying to the Este family's successful efforts in cultivating a reputation as amicable rulers both at home and abroad.

Medals for Leonello d'Este   In Ferrara Pisanello produced portraits and helped to revive the ancient art of the medal. Pisanello was inspired both by humanist studies and contemporary pageantry, specifically the visit of the Byzantine Emperor John VIII Paleologus to Ferrara during the great ecumenical council begun there in 1438. Dedicated to reuniting the Orthodox and Western branches of Christendom, and thus lending support to the Byzantine rulers as their empire was crumbling, the conference brought great numbers of Eastern officials to Ferrara. Pisanello made sketches of many of them, and thus was able to give the image of the Byzantine emperor which appeared on one of his medals (Fig. 4.24) a striking air of authenticity.

Humanists may have suggested the medallic form to Pisanello and Leonello, understanding that the genre had been favored by the ancient Roman emperors. They also would have known of large gold medallions commemorating the emperors Heraclius and Constantine which the Parisian goldsmith Michelet Saulmon (active 1375–1416) had created for the duke of Burgundy at the beginning of the century. Following both ancient and medieval examples, then, Pisanello placed John Paleologus in profile on the obverse (front), surrounded by an identifying inscription (in Greek). On the reverse (back) Paleologus again appears in profile, on his horse, stopping to pray at a roadside cross. He is also shown departing across the rock-strewn landscape at the left. Inscriptions in both Latin and Greek name Pisanello as the medal's creator.

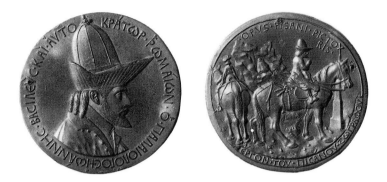

4.24 Medal of Emperor John VIII Paleologus, obverse and reverse, c. 1438, perhaps commissioned by Leonello d'Este from PISANELLO. Bronze, diameter 4" (1.03 cm) (Museo Nazionale del Bargello, Florence)

Medals were produced in a variety of media, ranging from relatively inexpensive, soft metals, like lead, to precious silver and gold.

The custom of issuing commemorative medals was now becoming re-established—as we have seen, for example, in the small classicizing medals of Francesco da Carrara in Padua (see Fig. 3.42). But whereas the rulers of Padua appeared in Roman guise, Pisanello chose to commemorate a living individual in contemporary garb. Pisanello's "revival" of the ancient Roman medal consisted of taking a form that the Paduan and Burgundian courts had already salvaged from antiquity and giving it a contemporary aspect. Stylistically, Pisanello's medals were not Roman at all—an incongruity of little concern to a courtly patron who doubtless saw himself as a fancier, not a slavish imitator, of antiquity.

Leonello d'Este popularized Pisanello's medals, using them as diplomatic gifts to cement relationships with dignitaries throughout Europe. In one example, announcing Leonello's marriage to Mary of Aragon, natural daughter of King Alfonso of Naples (Fig. 4.25), Pisanello anchors his patron's bust in the Latin words "Leonello d'Este Marquis" across his shoulders. The qualifying descriptor "of Ferrara and Modena" appears in the curve beneath.

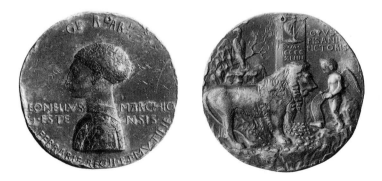

4.25 Medal of Leonello d'Este, obverse and reverse, 1444, commissioned by Leonello d'Este from PISANELLO. Bronze, 4" (1.03 cm) (Museo Nazionale del Bargello, Florence)

The abbreviation GE R AR hovers like a coronet above his head, a clever rendition of the Latin words for "Son-in-law of the King of Aragon." The obverse provides, as do many of Pisanello's medals, a charming commentary on the event. At the right Cupid patiently points out musical notes on a scroll to a very meek lion, tail between his legs, who is learning to sing—an ingratiatingly modest image of the awkward but diligent bridegroom Leonello ("little lion"). In the background an eagle (one of the devices of his father-in-law) keeps watch, while the king of the beasts learns his new role. Dated 1444 and carrying Leonello's personal emblem of the column and sail on a **stele**, the work is inscribed with Pisanello's name above Cupid's head.

Mantua

Another important center of artistic activity was the court of Mantua, situated on the edge of three marshy lakes in the midst of the plain between Milan and Venice. Well connected to other cities on the Paduan plain by waterways, it was a popular pilgrimage site, for the Mantuans claimed to own a relic of the Precious Blood of Christ, supposedly brought to the city by Longinus, the soldier who had pierced Christ's side. But Mantua's low-lying topography was susceptible to floods, plagues, and threats from outside powers, so its rulers, the Gonzaga family, hired themselves out as *condottieri* first to one competing city-state and then to another, juggling alliances and securing enormous fees in the bargain. At the same time, the Gonzaga encouraged literary studies, softening their reputation as mercenaries by trading on the history of the city as the birthplace of the Roman poet Virgil. As elsewhere, chivalric and humanist values co-inhabited the same court.

Frescoes in the Sala Pisanello Around 1447–48 Ludovico Gonzaga, who had become marquis of Mantua in 1444, commissioned Pisanello to paint a series of frescoes for the main reception hall of the Palazzo Ducale (Fig. 4.26). The Lancelot Cycle frescoes tell the story of Bohort, cousin of the legendary Lancelot.

The paintings depict a tournament in which Bohort defeats sixty opponents in order to acquire the right to marry a princess. Admiring ladies stand in viewing boxes on the left wall, where knights, all carefully labeled in French, have assembled from great distances to take part in the contest. Above each wall appears a frieze of heraldic devices, dominated by Ludovico's personal emblem of the flower and heraldic collar of the German imperial Order of the Swan, of which he and his wife, Princess Barbara of Brandenburg, were the only Italian members. The focus on a brave, noble, and successful knight can be seen as a graceful compliment to Ludovico's activities as a *condottiere*. The Arthurian legends were also popular in Mantua because the knights' search for the Holy Grail was linked in the

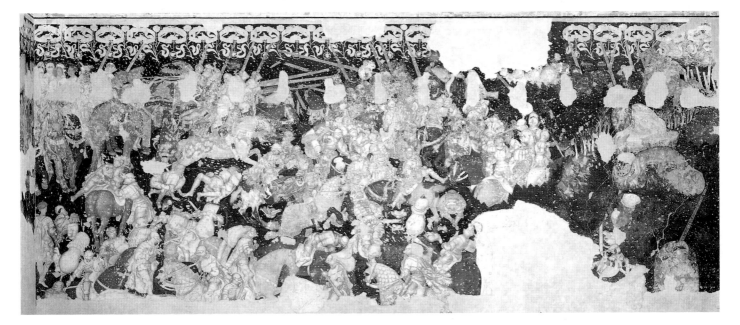

4.26 *Legend of Lancelot*, c. 1447–48, commissioned by Ludovico Gonzaga from PISANELLO for the Palazzo Ducale, Mantua. Fresco

The surviving figures are missing a good deal of final detail that would have been added *a secco*. They are also in a somewhat damaged state, having been plastered over following the collapse of a ceiling in 1480; they were rediscovered only in the 1960s.

popular imagination to the relic of the Blood of Christ which the city protected.

Violent but bloodless, the Lancelot Cycle would have provided the Gonzaga family with both a chivalric model and a lavish backdrop for courtly events. Pisanello imagined the tournament as a great mêlée of knights and other people, capturing the spirit of the written texts and their rich detail. Figures—seen from above, below, behind, and to the side—charge, lurch, turn, and fall. They are evenly disposed, tapestry-like, over the wall. Almost all semblance of depth is foregone in favor of a two-dimensional surface, although buildings are placed on a diagonal to emphasize their volume, and individual figures are carefully modeled. Fragments of faces peer out from helmets that would once have been bright with silver foil. Foreshortening dramatizes the fate of those knights who have fallen to the ground. Pisanello never completed the frescoes because he was called to work in the royal court of Naples. Nonetheless, these works reveal the richness of his imagination and suggest the appeal of his art throughout Italy.

Florence: Expressions of the Restored Republic

By the end of the fourteenth century such major building projects as the Cathedral, Or San Michele, and the Palazzo della Signoria had radically changed the urban fabric of Florence. Eager to bring these buildings to completion, the Florentines embarked on commissions of public sculpture through the 1430s which were to be among the most ambitious in its history.

The republican form of government which had been challenged by the Ciompi Revolt of 1378 had been restored by the early 1380s, returning a wealthy oligarchy to power within the bureaucratic structures of the city. Although Giangaleazzo Visconti of Milan threatened Florentine territories during the mid-1390s, the last two decades of the century were marked by economic prosperity and relative peace. It was not until 1402 that Visconti's troops moved into Florentine territory, having already taken control of major cities like Bologna to the north and Siena to the south in a drive to place the entire northern half of the Italian peninsula under Visconti domination.

The Florentine republic responded to the Visconti attack by closing its gates and refusing to capitulate as neighboring cities, fearful of sack by Visconti's formidable army, had done. For a mercantile city dependent on the importation of raw materials and the export of finished products of silk and wool for its economic livelihood, this closure represented an extraordinary commitment to the concept of a republican form of government as opposed to a princely (and military) dictatorship by an occupying foreign power. The humanist chancellor of the republic, Coluccio Salutati, whose responsibilities included the public articulation of government policy, couched the decisions of the government in terms of the city's Roman history. As heirs to the ancient Roman republic, Florence having been founded by republican troops fleeing an imperial take-over of Rome during the first century B.C.E., the Florentines were destined to repeat their history by resisting Visconti. This appeal to history and to the ideal of a republic demanded that the Florentines wall themselves in during the summer with dwindling food supplies and scarce water. These sacrifices were apparently divinely vindicated when Visconti died quite suddenly in September 1402, lifting Florence from its Milanese siege and giving new power to the idea of the republic as Florence's form of government, in fact, its very self-definition.

The threat of control by a foreign power repeated itself later in the decade, this time from King Ladislas of Naples who by 1409 had taken control of Rome and of the papal states in Umbria just to the south of Tuscany. Worries about his designs for a unified Italy under his control governed Florentine foreign policy until King Ladislaw's death in 1414. By 1420 Filippo Maria Visconti had renewed the Milanese plans for territorial expansion initiated by his father. He was successful in surrounding the Florentine state to the north and the east, ultimately defeating the Florentine troops in 1424. Only the alliance of Venice with Florence in 1425 stemmed the Milanese advances. In the face of continued threats to their independent existence through the first quarter of the century it is not surprising that Florentine artists and patrons sought a new visual language to convey their hard-won republican ideals in the most important civic sites of the city.

Decoration for the Cathedral

The first site to bear this new language was the Porta della Mandorla, an entrance abutting the tribune on the north side of Florence Cathedral (Fig. 4.27). The sculpture decorating this portal is unmistakably classical, the outer jambs being covered with a foliate pattern framing figures depicting the heroic labors of Hercules. Hercules had first appeared representing the Florentine state in the twelfth century, when a standing nude figure of the god began to appear on the city's official seal. A series of classicizing figures decorates the inner reveals of the door, the most notable of which is a small nude Hercules with the

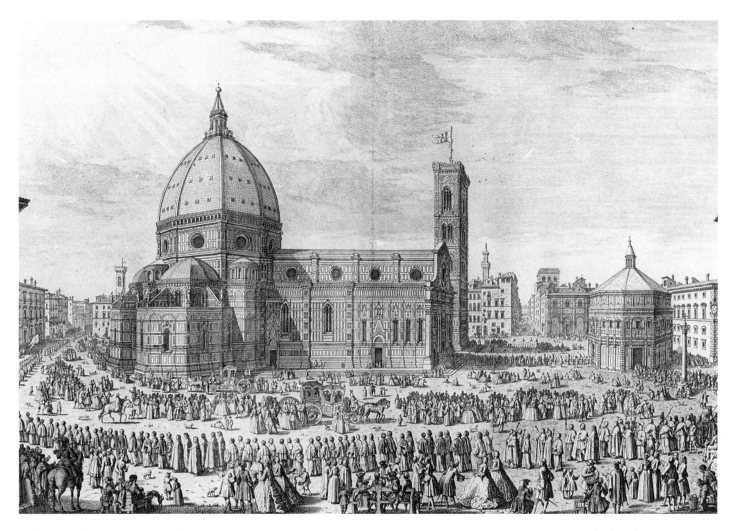

4.27 (above) Florence Cathedral, 1754, GIUSEPPE ZOCCHI. Etching

This view shows the north flank of the cathedral and the north tribune with a reconstruction of the program of buttress statues. The Baptistry is to the right. The axial street extending into the distance from the piazza between the cathedral and the Baptistry moves past Or San Michele, whose rectangular mass rises midway at the right. The street ends at the piazza of the Palazzo della Signoria, whose tower is just visible in the far distance.

4.28 (right) *Hercules*, detail of the Porta della Mandorla, 1391–97, commissioned by the Opera del Duomo, sometimes attributed to NICCOLÒ LAMBERTI, for the north flank of Florence Cathedral. Marble

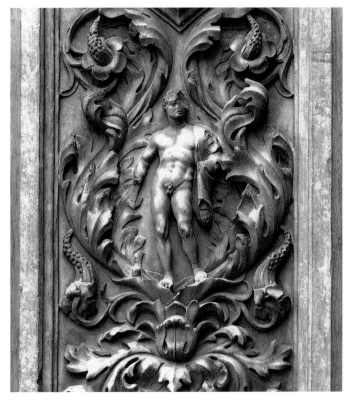

skin of a lion he had slain draped over his shoulder (Fig. 4.28), very similar to his image on the Florentine seal. The antique figural style of the Hercules, with its *contrapposto* pose and naturalistically modeled musculature, contrasts with the overall decorative program of the Porta della Mandorla, which includes simplified Gothic angel head reliefs and curling banderoles. Different stylistic forms coexist in the sculptural decoration of the door, as they would continue to do in Florentine art throughout the fifteenth century.

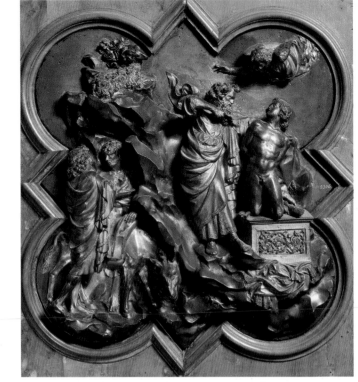

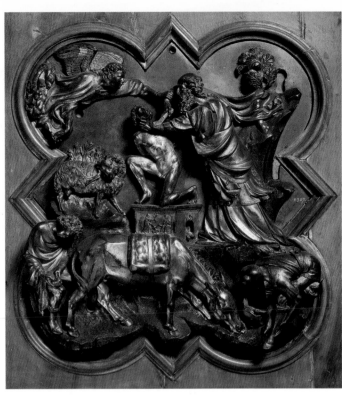

4.29 *Sacrifice of Isaac*, 1401–3, competition panel, commissioned by the Arte del Calimala from LORENZO GHIBERTI for the doors of the Baptistry, Florence. Parcel-gilt bronze, 17¾ × 15″ (45 × 38 cm) (Museo Nazionale del Bargello, Florence)

4.30 *Sacrifice of Isaac*, 1401–3, competition panel, commissioned by the Arte del Calimala from FILIPPO BRUNELLESCHI for the doors of the Baptistry, Florence. Parcel-gilt bronze, 17¾ × 15″ (45 × 38 cm) (Museo Nazionale del Bargello, Florence)

The Competition for the Second Baptistry Doors

In 1401 the Arte del Calimala initiated a competition for a second set of bronze doors for the Baptistry. Significantly, the competition for this enormously expensive undertaking was opened just at the time that Milanese troops were advancing on the city. Thus the competition may have been a way for the Arte del Calimala to vie for prestige with the Arte della Lana, which was in charge of the Duomo, or a way to manifest civic solidarity in enhancing the beauty of the city at the time of threat, or both. The Arte del Calimala stipulated that each contestant was to submit a relief showing the sacrifice of Isaac. The subject depicts the moment when Abraham, ordered by God to sacrifice his son, is about to plunge the knife into Isaac's neck, but is stopped by the miraculous intervention of an angel. The reliefs were to employ the quatrefoil format used by Andrea Pisano in his first set of doors from sixty-five years earlier (see Fig. 2.17), an attempt to make a coherent decorative program for the exterior of the Baptistry.

The two extant competition reliefs were both submitted by young artists trained as goldsmiths: Lorenzo Ghiberti (Lorenzo di Cione di ser Buonaccorso; 1378 Florence–1455 Florence) and Filippo Brunelleschi (1377 Florence–1446 Florence). Each was destined to make a major impact on the art of Florence, Ghiberti as a sculptor in bronze and Brunelleschi as an architect and inventor of scientific perspective. Their two reliefs encapsulate alternative possibilities of style in early fifteenth-century Florence (Figs. 4.29 and 4.30). Both artists portray the subject on a flat background similar to Andrea Pisano's treatment of figures and ground. Both seem fascinated with repeated curves of drapery, which are independent of the body beneath; the edges of drapery in Brunelleschi's relief flutter in the wind to heighten the drama of the event. But there are also differences. Ghiberti's Isaac, like the Porta della Mandorla Hercules, is a model of classical form, his sleek torso turning slowly on its axis to face Abraham. Brunelleschi's figures, however, are positioned—even twisted—to reinforce the surface of the plane. Their exaggeration gives an appropriately nervous feeling to the relief, especially at the point where the angel grasps Abraham's wrist—locked in place on the central axis—just as he is about to plunge the dagger into his son's throat. The servant in the lower left of Brunelleschi's relief, a direct quotation from an ancient Roman bronze, the *Thorn Puller*, disguises its origins with elaborate drapery folds, suggesting the complexity of classical allusions during this period.

In the end Ghiberti gained the commission for the doors, maintaining that he had won the competition outright; Brunelleschi's biographer, Antonio Manetti, claimed that the Arte del Calimala had called the competition a tie. Whatever the facts, the lyrical quality of Ghiberti's figures, his decorative treatment of form,

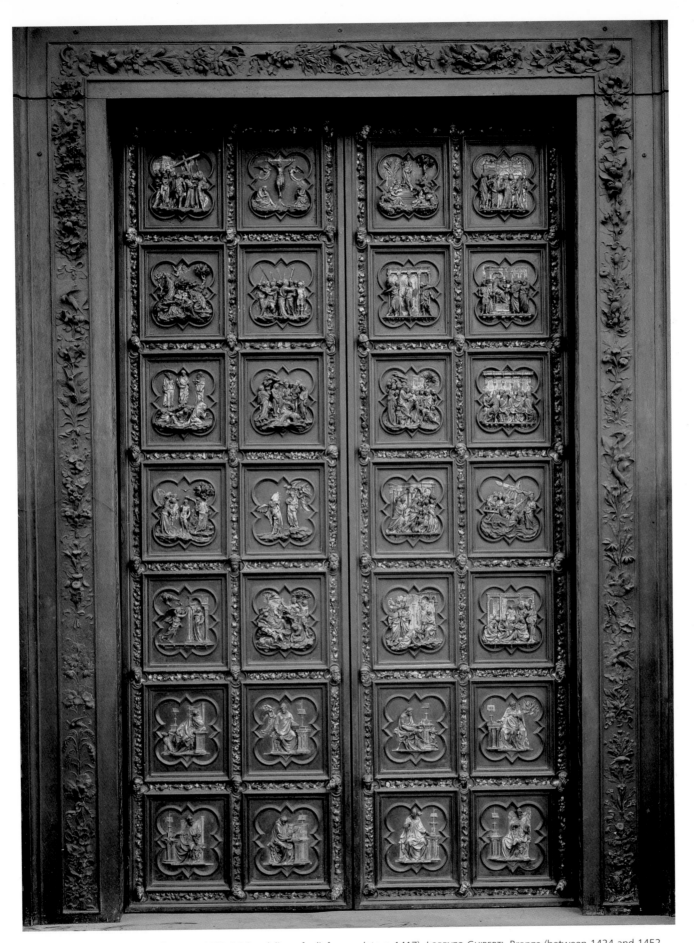

4.31 North doors, Baptistry, Florence, 1403–24 (modeling of reliefs complete c. 1417), LORENZO GHIBERTI. Bronze (between 1424 and 1452 set into the east face of the Baptistry)

Ghiberti versus Brunelleschi

In these two accounts of the competition for the second set of doors for the Florence Baptistry—one by Ghiberti (written c. 1450) and the other by Brunelleschi's biographer, Antonio Manetti (written c. 1480)—we get a flavor of the intense rivalry that this contest engendered between these two great artists.

First, Ghiberti's version:

In my youth in the year of Christ 1400, because of the corrupt air in Florence [plague] and the bad state of the country, I left that city with an excellent painter whom Signor Malatesta of Pesaro had summoned. He had had a room made which was painted by us with great care. . . . However, at this time my friends wrote me that the governors of the church of S. Giovanni Battista [the Baptistry] were sending for skilled masters whom they wished to see compete. From all countries of Italy a great many skilled masters came in order to take part in this trial and contest. I asked permission of the prince and my companion to leave. The prince, hearing the reason, immediately gave me permission [to go]. Together with the other sculptors I appeared before the Operai of [the Baptistry]. To each was given four tables of bronze. As the trial piece the Operai and the governors of the church wanted each [artist] to make one scene for the door. The story they chose was the Sacrifice of Isaac. . . . To me was conceded the palm of the victory by all the experts and by all those who had competed with me. To me the honor was conceded universally and with no exception. To all it seemed that I had at that time surpassed the others without exception, as was recognized by a great council and an investigation of learned men. . . . It was granted to me and determined that I should make the bronze door for this church.

This I executed with great care. This is my first work: the door with the frame around it cost about twenty-two thousand florins. Also in the door are twenty-eight compartments; in twenty are stories from the New Testament, and at the bottom are the four Evangelists and the four [church] Doctors, and around the work are a great number of human heads. With great love the door was diligently made, together with frames of ivy leaves, and the door jambs with a very magnificent frame of many kinds of leaves. The work weighed thirty-four thousand pounds. It was executed with the greatest skill and care.

And from Brunelleschi's point of view:

Filippo sculpted his scene in the way that still may be seen today. He made it quickly, as he had a powerful command of the art. Having cast, cleaned, and polished it completely he was not eager to talk about it with anyone. . . . It was said that Lorenzo was rather apprehensive about Filippo's merit as [the latter] was very apparent. Since it did not seem to him that he possessed such mastery of the art, he worked slowly. Having been told something of the beauty of Filippo's work he had the idea, as he was a shrewd person, of proceeding by means of hard work and by humbling himself through seeking the counsel . . . of all the people he esteemed who, being goldsmiths, painters, sculptors, etc. and knowledgeable men, had to do the judging. While making [his scene] in wax he conferred and . . . tried to find out how Filippo's work was coming along. He unmade and remade the whole and sections of it without sparing effort. . . .

Since none of [the judges] had seen Filippo's model they all believed that Polycleitus—not to mention Filippo—could not have done better [than Lorenzo]. . . . However, when they saw [Filippo's] work they were all astonished and marveled at the problems that he had set himself: the attitude, the position of the finger under the chin, and the energy of Abraham; the clothing, bearing, and delicacy of the son's entire figure; the angel's robes, bearing, and gestures and the manner in which he grasps the hand; the attitude, bearing, and delicacy of the figure removing a thorn from his foot and the figure bending over to drink—how complex these figures are and how well they fulfill their functions (there is not a limb that is not alive). . . .

Those deputized to do the judging changed their opinion when they saw it. However, it seemed unfeasible to recant what they had said so persistently [i.e. that Lorenzo's would surely win]. . . . Gathering together again they came to a decision and made the following report to the Operai: both models were very beautiful and for their part, taking everything into consideration, they were unable to put one ahead of the other, and since it was a big undertaking requiring much time and expense they should commission it to both equally and they should be partners. When Filippo and Lorenzo were summoned and informed of the decision Lorenzo remained silent while Filippo was unwilling to consent unless he was given entire charge of the work. On that point he was unyielding. . . . The officials threatened to assign it to Lorenzo if he did not change his mind: he answered that he wanted no part of it if he did not have complete control, and if they were unwilling to grant it they could give it to Lorenzo as far as he was concerned. With that they made their decision. Public opinion in the city was completely divided as a result.

(from Ghiberti. *Commentaries.* In Elizabeth G. Holt. *A Documentary History of Art.* New York: Doubleday, 1957, pp. 156–8; and from Antonio Manetti. *The Life of Brunelleschi.* Ed. Howard Saalman. University Park: Pennsylvania State University Press, 1970, pp. 46, 48, 50)

and his superbly detailed workmanship (his relief was cast as a single piece, Brunelleschi's was composed of separately cast elements) embodied the most advanced visual language in Europe at the time. These factors must have suggested to the Arte del Calimala that he was ideal for the job. By the time Ghiberti signed his contract for the doors, at the end of 1403, the Calimala had changed the subject matter from an Old Testament to a New Testament narrative, the life of Christ, to complement Andrea Pisano's life of John the Baptist on the

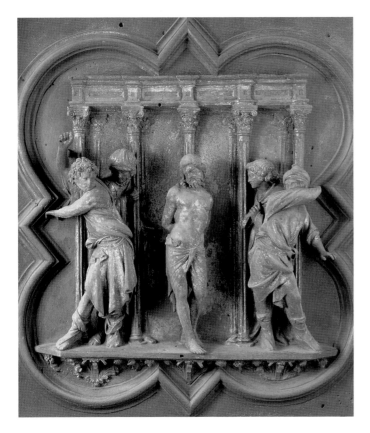

4.32 *The Flagellation of Christ*, detail from the north doors of the Baptistry, Florence. Bronze, 20½ × 17¾" (52 × 45 cm)

south doors. Modeling, casting, gilding, and finishing of the doors lasted until 1424, when they were finally installed on the east face of the Baptistry facing the cathedral (Fig. 4.31).

Over the twenty-one years Ghiberti spent creating the reliefs, his ideas for them evolved. In *The Flagellation of Christ* (Fig. 4.32), one of the last reliefs to be designed, he placed the figures against an architecture of Corinthian columns, thus establishing a simple and regular internal order within the outer quatrefoil frame and allowing a more focused view of the subject—quite different from the *Sacrifice of Isaac*, in which the servants, the angel, and Abraham and Isaac occupy separate areas. Throughout the doors, however, Ghiberti continued to reveal his fascination with decorative details, swirls of drapery, craggy landscapes, and thickly foliated trees.

Cathedral Sculpture

The pursuit of new projects at the Duomo brought two young sculptors to prominence: Nanni di Banco (c. 1374/80–85 Florence–1421 Florence) and Donatello. Nanni learned his trade in the cathedral workshops assisting his father who was also a sculptor. Donatello's origins

are more obscure, although he is first documented in Pistoia in 1401, where he was arrested for hitting another man over the head with a club. He subsequently worked in Ghiberti's workshop on the Baptistry doors. On January 24, 1408, the Opera del Duomo commissioned Nanni (along with his father) to carve a figure of Isaiah to be placed high on the outside of the cathedral, on one of the buttresses of the north tribune (see Fig. 4.27) as one of a program of twelve Old Testament figures. A month later Donatello received a commission for a David for the same location. Nanni's unusually youthful *Isaiah* (Fig. 4.33) was finished by the end of the year, Donatello's *David* (Fig. 4.34) by June 1409, beginning a decade of apparently close collaboration between the two sculptors which led to a new style for free-standing figural sculpture. The swaying figures of *Isaiah* and *David* are distinctly Gothic in their stances. One essentially mirrors the other,

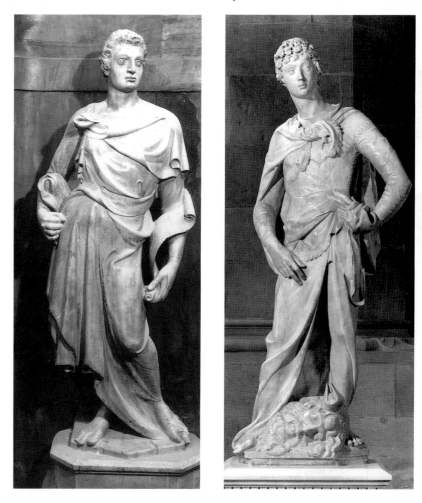

4.33 (left) *Isaiah*, 1408, commissioned by the Opera del Duomo from NANNI DI BANCO for the north buttress of Florence Cathedral. Marble, height 6' 4" (1.93 m) (Florence Cathedral)

4.34 (right) *David*, 1408–9, commissioned by the Opera del Duomo from DONATELLO for the north buttress of Florence Cathedral. Marble, height 6' 3" (1.91 m) (Museo Nazionale del Bargello, Florence)

4.35 *St. Luke*, 1408–15, commissioned by the Opera del Duomo from NANNI DI BANCO for the façade of Florence Cathedral (seen straight on). Marble, height 6' 9½" (2.07 m) (Museo dell'Opera del Duomo, Florence)

4.37 *St. Mark*, 1408–15, commissioned by the Opera del Duomo from NICCOLÒ LAMBERTI for the façade of Florence Cathedral (seen straight on). Marble, height 8' 1½" (2.17 m) (Museo dell'Opera del Duomo, Florence)

although Nanni used strong swags of drapery whereas Donatello only partially covered the figure with drapery, pressing it close to the torso and leg in order to reveal the physical form of the youthful warrior. The Opera found neither of these two statues acceptable, ostensibly because they were too small to be seen from the street below, despite their life-sized scale. Legibility was important.

To test empirically the appropriate size for the buttress statues the Opera commissioned Donatello to make a larger statue of Joshua. Made of terracotta, which was both inexpensive and quick to model, then whitened with gesso and paint to make it look like marble, the *Joshua* was in place on the north tribune by 1410, where it remained until it disintegrated, most likely in the eighteenth century. Nearly 18 feet (5.5 meters) tall, this colossal figure was clearly intended to capture the viewer's attention from the street below. It must also have been a matter of civic pride to the Florentines to have in their city a statue rivaling the heroic-sized sculptures of antiquity.

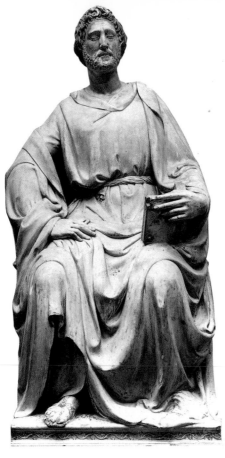

4.36 *St. John*, 1408–15, commissioned by the Opera del Duomo from DONATELLO for the façade of Florence Cathedral (seen from below). Marble, height 6' 10½" (2.1 m), width at base 34½" (88 cm) (Museo dell'Opera del Duomo, Florence)

Also at the end of 1408 the Arte della Lana began commissioning sculpture for the unfinished façade of the Cathedral, engaging Nanni di Banco, Donatello, and Niccolò Lamberti (c. 1370 Florence–1451 Florence) each to make a seated Evangelist for the niches on either side of the main door (Figs. 4.35–4.37). Once again Donatello and Nanni made figures similar to one another, although in a style significantly changed from their earlier work. Notable in both Donatello's *St. John* and Nanni's *St. Luke* is the awareness that the figure would be seen from below and thus require adjustments in form—or optical corrections—to accommodate the viewer's angle of vision (as seen in Fig. 4.36). Thus when seen straight on, the torso of the *St. John* is too long, the drapery rather ponderous, and the hands limp (as seen in Figs. 4.35 and 4.37). When seen from below, however, St. John's outward glance seems to respond to a vision, his torso nests back into the lower sections of the figure, and the curving drapery between the legs not only opens up the mass of the stone but connects with the arms to lock the figure together in an oval frame which also drives attention to the saint's head. In both figures the drapery creates pockets of real space and hangs heavily over the armature of the body, endowing the physical form beneath it with a sense of power. The heads of the figures are also strikingly bold, inspired by ancient portrait types that the two sculptors were beginning to explore.

Of these three sculptors, Lamberti had worked longest in the Duomo workshops. His response to what he must have perceived as competition from younger artists was to produce a *St. Mark* that is a technical tour de force and a mark of his knowledge of the International Style. Extravagantly decorative curves and folds of drapery cascade over the figure and even spill over the base. Straps hang off the Gospel, and the saint's right hand extends freely in space. For all its technical brilliance, however, the *St. Mark* is a curiously static figure. By 1416 Lamberti had moved to Venice, where the decorative properties characteristic of this work well suited the elaborate program for the façade of St. Mark's (see Fig. 1.7). He ceded his position in the Florentine Cathedral shops to a new group of sculptors, whose more classical style was commensurate with the political rhetoric of the state.

Or San Michele

In 1406 the Signoria (governors) of Florence, impatient to bring the decorative program of the guild church of Or San Michele to completion, declared that those guilds owning rights to niches on the exterior of the building

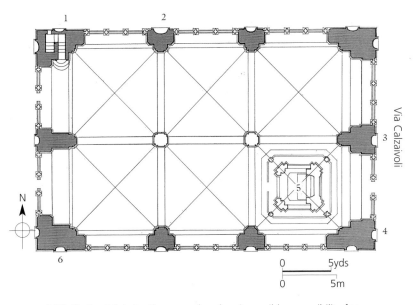

4.38 Or San Michele, Florence, plan showing guild responsibility for exterior niches

1 Arte dei Corazzai, Donatello, *St. George*; **2** Arte dei Maestri di Pietra e Legname, Nanni di Banco, *Four Crowned Saints*; **3** To 1459, Guelf Party, Donatello, *St. Louis of Toulouse*. After 1459, Mercanzia (Merchants' Court), Verrocchio, *Christ and St. Thomas*; **4** Arte del Calimala, Ghiberti, *St. John the Baptist*; **5** Tabernacle, c. 1355–59, Andrea di Cione, called Orcagna (see Fig. 3.25); **6** Arte dei Linaiuoli, Donatello, *St Mark*

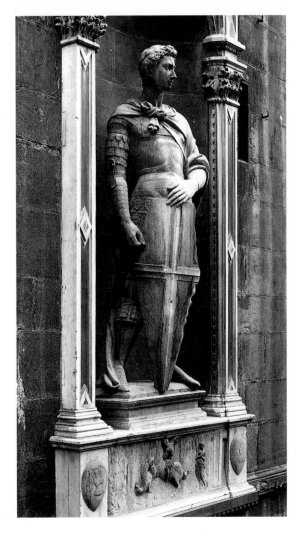

4.39 Niche of the Arte dei Corazzai with *St. George*, c. 1410–15 (?), and relief of *St. George Slaying the Dragon*, c. 1417, commissioned by the Arte dei Corazzai from DONATELLO for the north side of Or San Michele, Florence. Marble, statue height 6' 10¼" (2.09 m), relief 15¼ × 47¼" (39 × 120 cm) (the statue is now in the Museo Nazionale del Bargello, Florence; the relief is still in situ)

should fill them with statues of their patron saints within ten years. Only five of the fourteen niches had been completed by 1406, even though they had been assigned to the individual guilds as early as 1339. Over the next two decades Ghiberti, Donatello, and Nanni each contributed three statues to this program (Fig. 4.38), giving the guilds an important presence on the city's major thoroughfare.

Donatello's *St. George* for the Arte dei Corazzai (Armorers' Guild) (Fig. 4.39), perhaps begun shortly after 1410, originally carried a real sword and wore a real protective helmet—both produced by the guild. Although it has become a commonplace to discuss this figure as a manifestation of the new civic humanism in Florence responding to the military threats of Giangaleazzo Visconti and King Ladislas, it seems more reasonable to place this statue within the chivalric traditions of late Gothic realism, exemplified by the warrior knights placed on the tomb of Cansignorio della Scala in Verona (see Fig. 3.36) or depicted in the frescoes of Altichiero in

Padua (see Fig. 3.48). The chivalric treatment of the legend of St. George is also evident in Donatello's relief beneath the statue's niche, which depicts the saint slaying the dragon that had been menacing the elegantly posed princess at the right of the relief. Employing a *schiacciato* ("squashed") relief for the first time in his career, Donatello created with barely incised lines a sense of atmospheric space receding into the far distance, a transfer of painterly conventions to low sculptural relief which was to have lasting impact.

The contrast with Nanni's relief under the adjacent niche for the Stone and Woodcarvers' Guild (see Fig. 3) is remarkable. Whereas Nanni, Ghiberti, and Brunelleschi conceived of relief as a series of figurines set against a background, Donatello treats the marble as though it were malleable wax or clay (materials he would have worked with in Ghiberti's casting shop). The soft flow of forms on the surface suggests rather than defines space, veiling both his figures and their setting with atmospheric effects—even before such devices were used in painting.

Donatello's *St. Mark* of c. 1411–13 for the Arte dei Linaiuoli (Linen Weavers' Guild) (Fig. 4.40) shows a thorough integration of classicizing principles in the sculptor's work. The classical *contrapposto* pose, with the weight resting on one foot, and the turn of the figure suggest that the saint is about to move out of the niche. At the same time Donatello anchored his figure with strong verticals in the columnar folds of material covering the saint's right leg. The drapery adheres closely to the chest and arms, revealing the contours of the body despite the heavy folds and crimped border. The intensity of the saint's expression and the realistic modeling of his hands, with their veins pulsing just beneath the skin, re-create the human form in a highly naturalistic manner.

More than a century later the novelty of the *St. Mark* was still notable to Vasari, who invented a story that Donatello's patrons were displeased with the sculpture, presumably because they did not find it finished enough, craft here being the motivation behind the criticism. According to Vasari, they asked him to recarve the face. In the story Donatello placed a screen before the sculpture already in place in its niche and, hidden from view, pretended to recarve the face. When he revealed the statue in its niche, guild officials were most pleased with the effect—even though Donatello had only made chiseling noises and thrown a handful of marble dust down from the scaffold. Vasari's tale of artistic genius unappreciated by unknowledgeable patrons is most likely a literary fiction, but it does point to the revolutionary nature of Donatello's vivid naturalism, noted by another writer contemporary to Vasari, who claimed that Donatello himself was so impressed with one of his statues for the Campanile, the so-called *Zuccone*, that he exclaimed, "Speak, damn you, speak!"

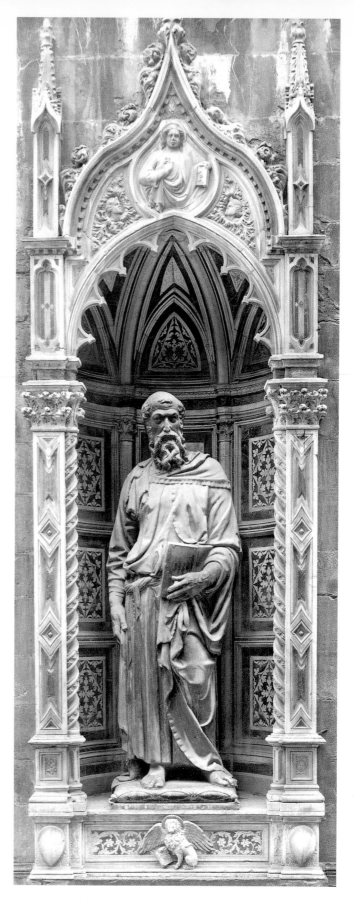

4.40 Niche of the Arte dei Linaiuoli with *St. Mark*, 1411–13, commissioned by the Arte dei Linaiuoli from DONATELLO for the south side of Or San Michele, Florence. Marble, figure height 7′ 8¾″ (2.36 m) (original now in Museo di Or San Michele, Florence; copy in the niche)

The niche was commissioned from the stonecarvers Perfetto di Giovanni and Albizzo di Pietro in 1411. They received 200 florins for the work; Donatello received 100 florins for his statue of David (see Fig. 4.34).

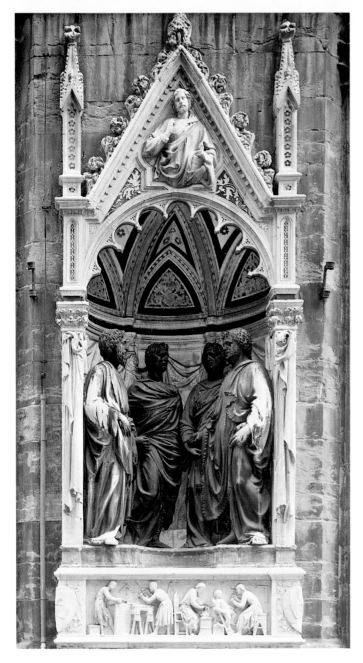

4.41 Niche of the Arte dei Maestri di Pietra e Legname with *Four Crowned Saints*, c. 1414–16, commissioned by the Arte dei Maestri di Pietra e Legname from NANNI DI BANCO for the north side of Or San Michele, Florence. Marble, figure height 6' (1.83 m) (original group now in the Museo di Or San Michele, Florence; niche now empty)

Nanni's *Four Crowned Saints* (Fig. 4.41), for the niche of the Arte dei Maestri di Pietra e Legname at Or San Michele, represents four Christian artists of the third century who were asked by the emperor Diocletian to produce a pagan image. Refusing to do so, they were condemned to be beheaded. Nanni chose the moment of the men's dawning awareness of their fate. The Roman gravity in the three older men is played against the more active pose of the youngest figure—calm resignation paired with defiance. Each figure presents the viewer with a different possible response to adversity, but as a group they suggest duty accepted and discharged; the Christian tale becomes a metaphor for responsible citizenship. Stylistically, the classicizing manner in which the *Four Crowned Saints* are depicted is appropriate for figures who lived in antiquity.

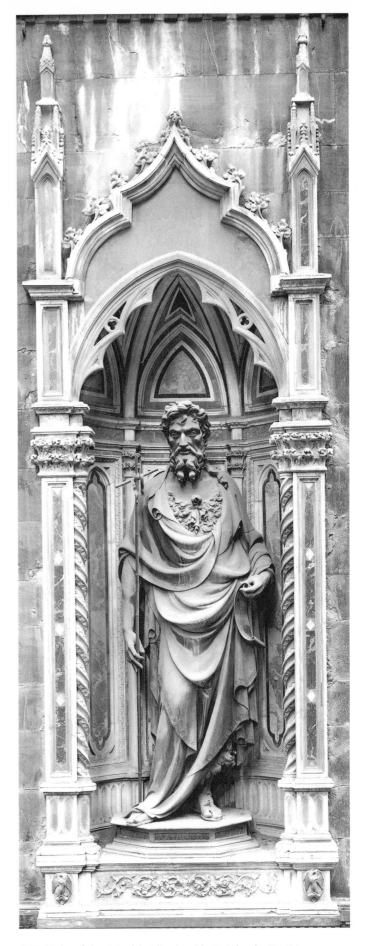

4.42 Niche of the Arte del Calimala with *St. John the Baptist*, c. 1412/13–17, commissioned by Arte del Calimala from GHIBERTI for the east side of Or San Michele, Florence. Bronze, height 8' 4¼" (2.55 m) (original Museo di Or San Michele, Florence; niche now empty)

The Arte del Calimala chose Ghiberti in 1412 to make their statue of *St. John the Baptist* (Fig. 4.42) for Or San Michele—a natural choice since he was then already in their employ for the bronze doors for the Baptistry. They thus chose a sculptor whose fluid, elegant style contrasted with the more severe classicism of the other artists at work on sculpture for the building. The repeated elongated curves of the Baptist's drapery (on the border of which Ghiberti inscribed his name) and the carefully arranged S-curves of his hair and of his hair-shirt focus attention on graceful patterns, a reflection of the International Gothic style, perhaps appropriate for a guild whose governors were among the wealthiest citizens of the city.

Ghiberti's continuation of a late Gothic drapery style into the late 1420s, despite the successes of the classicizing forms of Donatello and Nanni di Banco, is normally treated as a manifestation of his personal stylistic predilections. However Ghiberti's commissions at Or San Michele were from the major and most powerful guilds of the city (he produced another bronze statue, of St. Matthew, for the Arte del Cambio [Bankers' Guild]), whereas Donatello's and Nanni's were from minor guilds, a distinction in status clearly suggested by the costly medium of bronze used by Ghiberti. The social hierarchy of the guilds, therefore, may also have acted as a determinant of style for the Or San Michele niche statues.

Donatello's *St. Louis of Toulouse* (Fig. 4.43) was commissioned in the early 1420s by the Guelf Party, a political union with a long and illustrious history in the city. The *St. Louis* was the only statue on Or San Michele not made for a guild. Completely gilded, it outstripped the other niche figures in its visual impact. For the statue Donatello and his partner, Michelozzo (1396 Florence–1472 Florence), designed an unremittingly classicizing niche with Corinthian pilasters, decorative swags, and flying **putti**. The statue, cast in several pieces, is unlike any other at Or San Michele. Donatello's use of bronze for this statue placed him in direct competition with Ghiberti, then the acknowledged master of this medium in Florence; his overworked volumetric folds provide a clear alternative to Ghiberti's treatment of fabric. Unlike the ascetic *St. Louis of Toulouse* known to history (see Fig. 2.50), Donatello's figure is completely enveloped in elaborate vestments, almost as if the saint's reluctant acceptance of the office of bishop, here represented by his regalia, has overwhelmed his personal dedication to Franciscan poverty. The sculptor's emphasis on the power of St. Louis's office provided a visual analogue to the power of the Guelf Party in Florence during the early part of the century.

The Foundling Hospital

The extensive sculptural programs for the Duomo, the Baptistry, and Or San Michele were matched by new building projects which were to change the fabric of the city of Florence as much as the building of the cathedral and the Palazzo della Signoria and the transformation of Or San Michele had done in the fourteenth century. The leading architect for this transformation was Filippo Brunelleschi. By 1419 he was at work for the Arte della Seta (Silk Manufacturers' and Goldsmiths' Guild) for their special benefice in the city, the Foundling Hospital (Ospedale degli Innocenti; Fig. 4.44), an orphanage where unwanted children could be left anonymously to be cared for by guild charity. The history of such charitable institutions goes back to the thirteenth century, when cities were forced to provide shelter and care for an increasing population of poor and unwanted (see Fig. 3.31). Located in what was then a relatively underdeveloped part of Florence, the Foundling Hospital stands at a

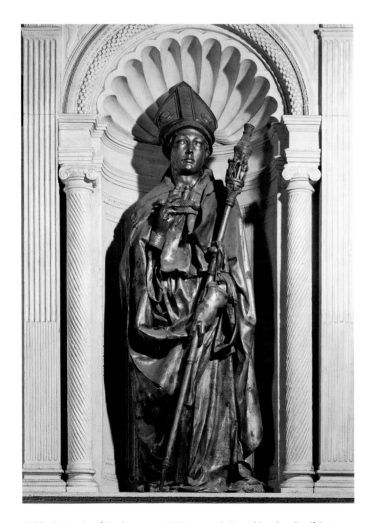

4.43 *St. Louis of Toulouse*, c. 1423, commissioned by the Guelf Party from DONATELLO for the east side of Or San Michele, Florence. Fire-gilt bronze, height 8′ 8¾″ (2.66 m) (Museo di Santa Croce, Florence)

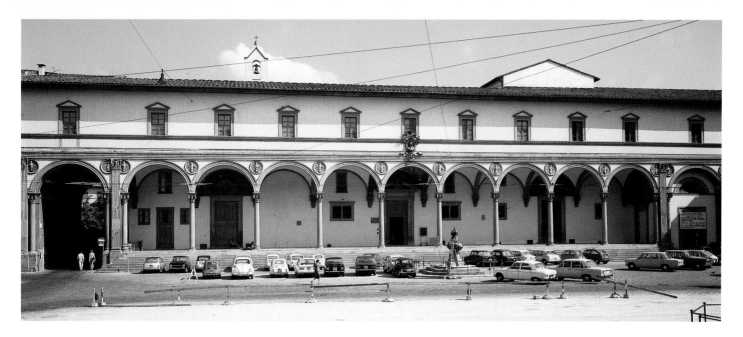

4.44 Foundling Hospital, Florence, begun 1421, commissioned by the Arte della Seta from FILIPPO BRUNELLESCHI

right angle to the church of the Santissima Annunziata, which housed a miracle-working image of the Annunciation and which was one of the main pilgrimage sites in the city. At this site Church and corporate foundation work hand in hand to define the character of the city as divinely favored and civically responsible, demonstrating the reciprocal relations between God and citizen in architectural terms.

The loggia that Brunelleschi designed for the hospital is not, in its basic form, unusual. This type of structure seems to have been used consistently in late medieval hospitals. Street loggias providing shelter for pedestrians were common in other Italian cities, particularly Bologna, Padua, and Venice. The question of the sources that may have inspired the graceful rhythms of Brunelleschi's Foundling Hospital loggia has been much debated. Art historians have traditionally searched for ancient Roman precedents for specific characteristics of Brunelleschi's architecture to support the idea that the Renaissance was essentially a revival of antiquity. Yet there is little in the massing of Brunelleschi's architecture that can easily be associated with Roman forms, despite details of column capitals and mouldings that imitate Roman ornament. Evidence suggests that he was not only familiar with Byzantine architecture, especially as manifested in Venice, but perhaps also in Constantinople itself, and that he knew building techniques practiced by the Persians. The row of domed vaults in the porch of the Foundling Hospital, for example, can be compared with a similar arrangement in the **narthex** of St. Mark's in Venice, where slightly pointed arches support six small domes. Since Brunelleschi cannot be traced either in documentation or in works of art between 1404 and 1415, he may well have traveled far more widely than Rome, where he is traditionally thought to have lived during this time. At home he was certainly impressed by the abstract classicism of

the revetment on Florence's Baptistry (see Fig. 1.9) that, in the sharp alternation of light and dark geometric forms, he imitates in the architectural membering of the Hospital.

The building itself is a remarkably light one, given the stone and masonry architecture of the city. Each of the members—columns, arches, window enframements—is thin, a fact of the plans alluded to in the documents, which specifically provide for iron tension rods to brace the arches of the portico. The sole exceptions to this thin membering are the heavy cornice above the arches and the strong Corinthian pilasters that gird the structure at the left and right. The cornice runs the entire length of the building and ties the façade structure together compositionally as well as giving a defining frame for the piazza on which the building stands. The cornice, unusually, in fact turns 90 degrees at the edges of the building, forming an actual bordering frame for the property. Glazed terracotta roundels from the della Robbia workshop of babies in swaddling clothes (*innocenti*) fill the spandrels between the arches and identify the purpose of the building.

Brunelleschi presumably envisioned a rectangular piazza in front of the Foundling Hospital and Santissima Annunziata—one that was not built until the sixteenth century. In the 1420s such a piazza would have been unusual as an unencumbered space in the city, although significantly the Loggia della Signoria (see Fig. 1.18) and the Palazzo della Signoria defined the governmental piazza in much the same way. A more likely precedent for Brunelleschi's plan is the Piazza San Marco in Venice (see Fig. 1.7), which was also flanked by loggias, with the Basilica forming the boundary of one short side of the square, just as the Annunziata did in Florence. Rectangular piazzas flanked by arcades also formed part of ancient Roman fora and were used frequently thereafter in Christian sites such as the atrium in front of Old

Art and Childbirth

Having children was a much less private concern in the Renaissance than it is today. Since infant mortality was high (like mortality as a whole, due to disease and war), both Church and state encouraged parents to have large families. Childlessness was interpreted as a mark of disfavor with God; moreover, it weakened the community's chances for survival and advancement. City governments in both Florence and Venice, for example, established brothels on the principle that lusty young men not yet in a financial position to marry (which they normally did in their thirties) could reinforce their heterosexuality and eventually become fathers. Civic foundling hospitals cared for abandoned and orphaned children, training them for basic trades essential to the city's economic well-being.

Not surprisingly, the birth of a new child was marked by ceremony and celebration, the mother often receiving gifts from visitors (see the figures behind the bed in Cavallini's *Birth of the Virgin*, Fig. 1.36)—who might include city officials as well as friends and relatives. The most common gifts for a new mother were sweets and fruits presented on a keepsake *desco da parto* (birth dish) made of wood or ceramic. Sometimes guests offered beverages from a matching flask or pitcher. Often painted on both

front and back, the dishes showed scenes of the mother presenting the new child to guests and/or allegorical and literary themes extolling love and virtue. The parents' coats of arms often appear as well, tying the individual birth to its familial context. In Florence, all sorts of items designed specially for infants and young mothers were available, from practical items such as wooden bowls to embroidered linens to charms and amulets for a successful birth.

4.45 *The Birth of Hercules, surrounded by Fortune and Seven Planetary Gods, with Virtues Below*, c. 1555, central Italian. Earthenware (Victoria and Albert Museum, London, Salting Bequest, cat. no. 1006 C. 2223–1910)

The sixteenth-century ceramic plate in Figure 4.45 is rare in showing at its center the actual birthing process, rather than the more usual post-partem washing of the child which appears in works such as Pietro Lorenzetti's *Birth of the Virgin* (see Fig. 2.31). Childbirth was women's business. Midwives, not doctors, attended to mothers, the midwife sitting on a small stool in front of the mother, who herself was comforted and encouraged by other women. Until the early sixteenth century, women often sat on one another's laps to give birth. With increasing awareness of ancient practices, they adopted birthing chairs, set in front of the elaborately draped matrimonial bed.

In this example, birthing takes on cosmic significance. Roman planetary gods occupy ovals around the inner rim—for example, Jupiter at the top, Mars at the left, and Venus at the right. On the outer edge, inscriptions in Italian praise virtue, personified by reclining figures on the bottom half of the rim. ("Without virtue, illustrious valor, and art the seed of Minerva and Mars is not born; he whom plainly you see here is born of you to be the flower of the age.") Exuberant putti on the upper half effectively suggest the joys of a world filled with numerous healthy children.

St. Peter's. It is perhaps not accidental that the church of the Annunziata was one of the major pilgrimage churches of Florence, just as St. Peter's was in Rome, and thus needed occasionally to accommodate large numbers of visitors in its precincts. The Arte della Seta was therefore provided with an especially grand space which proclaimed its charity and wealth not only to the city but to foreign pilgrims as well.

Brunelleschi's Dome

While working on the Foundling Hospital, Brunelleschi also supervised the work for which he was—and is—most famous, the dome, or **cupola**, of Florence's Cathedral (Fig. 4.46). Although a large dome had been planned for the cathedral at least from the mid-fourteenth century, no architect had apparently solved the problem of

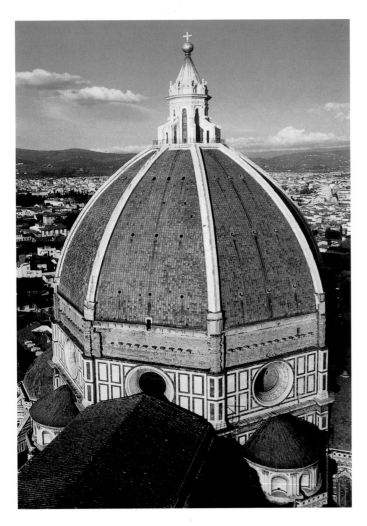

4.46 Dome of the Cathedral, Florence, 1418–36, commissioned by the Opera of the Cathedral and the Arte della Lana from FILIPPO BRUNELLESCHI, 100' high (30.5 m), 459' diameter (140 m)

The dome was closed at the oculus in 1436. The Opera accepted Brunelleschi's new model for the lantern of the dome in that year, but the lantern is largely the work of Michelozzo di Bartolomeo, who took over the project at Brunelleschi's death in 1446. Work on the lantern continued through the 1450s. The gilt bronze ball surmounting the lantern was designed and fabricated by Andrea del Verrocchio between 1468 and 1471.

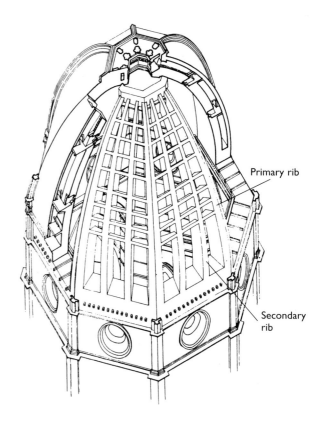

4.47 Dome of the Cathedral, Florence, isometric view, after PIERO SANPAOLESI

how to vault such a large space; the diameter of the octagonal crossing measures nearly 140 feet (43 meters), almost as great as the Pantheon in Rome.

Having worked on plans for this project from 1417, Brunelleschi submitted in 1418 a model that did not require the usual temporary wooden scaffolding or **centering** (see Fig. 32). Brunelleschi's scaffolds cantilevered from the base of the drum and were moved upward as the dome progressed in a series of horizontal courses. This audacious plan ultimately won him the commission, but, as had been the case with the early history of the cathedral itself, progress was not smooth at the outset. A change in the overseeing committee in 1419 occasioned an open competition for the project in which Donatello and Nanni di Banco participated. Brunelleschi's model for this competition was topped with a gilt banner bearing the Florentine lily, an indication of the civic component of the commission. A

decision by the building committee in 1420 gave responsibility for the project jointly to Brunelleschi, Ghiberti, and a master mason, Battista d'Antonio, the last an assertion of practical know-how as a guard against Brunelleschi's theory and Ghiberti's minimal experience in architecture. What the committee intended as fruitful collaboration ended in tense and frayed relations between Brunelleschi and Ghiberti until, according to Brunelleschi's biographer, he used a clever ruse to demonstrate Ghiberti's architectural incompetence, thus finally taking charge of the building of the dome.

Construction began in 1420 and continued until August 1436, when the dome was closed at the level of the lantern. At that time the city ordered trumpeters and pipers to play for a great feast for the workmen, the building committee, and the priests of the cathedral. This ceremony was the last in a series that had begun when Pope Martin V had sent the cathedral a branch of miniature roses fashioned of gold (now in the Cathedral Museum) to mark the extraordinary efforts of the city to complete the dome. With the imminent completion of the dome, Pope Eugenius IV, then resident in the city, rededicated the cathedral to Santa Maria del Fiore (St. Mary of the Flower) on March 25, 1436 (the feast of the Annunciation). The name derives from the name of the city, Firenze or then Fiorenza, meaning flowering. For this

In Praise of Artists

Alberti wrote his text first in Latin in 1435 and then translated it into Italian in 1436 so that his artist friends could read it. The prologue to the *Della Pittura (On Painting)* is both a recognition of the genius of a new generation of Florentine artists and a paragone or competitive comparison between the present and the antique past.

I used to marvel and at the same time to grieve that so many excellent and superior arts and sciences from our most vigorous antique past could now seem lacking and almost wholly lost. We know from [remaining] works and through references to them that they were once widespread. Painters, sculptors, architects, musicians, geometricians, rhetoricians, seers and similar noble and amazing intellects are very rarely found today and there are few to praise them. Thus

I believed, as many said, that Nature, the mistress of things, had grown old and tired. She no longer produced either geniuses or giants which in her more youthful and more glorious days she had produced so marvellously and abundantly.

Since then, I have been brought back here [to Florence]—from the long exile in which we Alberti have grown old—into this our city, adorned above all others. I have come to understand that in many men, but especially in you, Filippo [Brunelleschi], and in our close friend Donato the sculptor [Donatello] and in others like Nencio [Ghiberti], Luca [della Robbia] and Masaccio, there is a genius for [accomplishing] every praiseworthy thing. For this they should not be slighted in favour of anyone famous or of long-standing in these arts. Therefore, I believe the power of acquiring wide fame in any art or science lies in our industry and diligence more than in the times or in the gifts of nature. It must be admitted

that it was less difficult for the Ancients—because they had models to imitate and from which they could learn—to come to a knowledge of those supreme arts which today are most difficult for us. Our fame ought to be much greater, then, if we discover unheard-of and never-before-seen arts and sciences without teachers or without any model whatsoever. Who could ever be hard or envious enough to fail to praise Pippo the architect on seeing here such a large structure, rising above the skies, ample to cover with its shadow all the Tuscan people, and constructed without the aid of centering or great quantity of wood? Since this work seems impossible of execution in our time, if I judge rightly, it was probably unknown and unthought of among the Ancients.

(from Leon Battista Alberti. *On Painting*. Trans. and ed. John Spencer. New Haven: Yale University Press, 1956, pp. 39–40)

dedication the Flemish composer Guillaume Dufay wrote a motet that referred both to Martin's gift and to the presence of Eugenius who "with his own hands . . . dedicate[d] this immense temple." Thus the grandeur of this building project was honored by none other than the popes, granting renown to the building within the Christian community and adding to the magnificence and reputation of the city of Florence.

Although Brunelleschi's dome is considered one of the masterpieces of Renaissance architecture, it deviates from classical precedents. It is pointed, rather than hemispherical, and employs ribs—eight visible and sixteen concealed (Figs. 4.46 and 4.47)—in a manner similar to the construction of Gothic vaults. Other construction features include the use of stone and chain girdles at several levels to counteract the lateral thrust of the dome's weight, a complex herringbone pattern of brickwork (known only in Persian architecture at this time) to reduce cracks due to settling, and double shell construction (also used in Persian architecture) to minimize weight and simultaneously to provide access for maintenance.

All of these details were laid out in two long legal memoranda in 1420 to ensure that the work on this novel project would be carried out in exacting detail.

Specifications about thickness of walls, curvature of the dome, width of space between the double shell (ceiling/roof) construction, the type of stone used for reinforcement, the placement of the chain girders, the type of brickwork and the weight of each brick, and details of water drainage are all noted, as is the intention voiced at the very outset that the dome be "magnificent and swelling," a result of the extra height given to the exterior shell by its raised curve. There is even a note that the ceiling was to be built to accommodate mosaics, indicating that at least some envisioned the interior of the dome matching the dome of the Baptistry (see Fig. 1.10), just as the floor plan of the cathedral imitated the earlier structure. The technology of the dome, more than its stylistic properties, however, won Florence enormous prestige and gave it an architectural wonder comparable, if not surpassing, its Tuscan neighbors and rivals, Siena and Pisa. When Leon Battista Alberti wrote metaphorically in his *Della Pittura* of 1436, the year of the closing of the oculus, that the dome "covered the entire Tuscan people with its shadow," he referred not just to the size of the structure, which stands over the skyline of the city and can be seen from a great distance, but also to the cultural, economic, and technological hegemony of Florence over the entire region. More than the glory of God was at stake in Brunelleschi's project for the dome of the cathedral.

The Cathedral Interior

Military expenditures in Florence's efforts to stave off the threatening advances of Filippo Maria Visconti after 1420 eventually led to a shortage of funds for large public projects and, in 1427, to a moratorium on new sculptural programs for the Duomo. However, the prospect of completing the building's dome and the end of a protracted war with the neighboring state of Lucca, which lasted

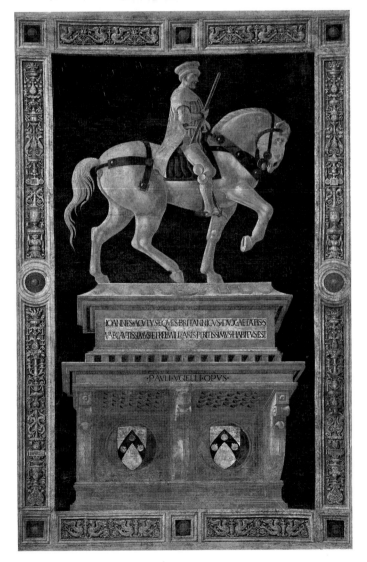

4.48 *Sir John Hawkwood*, 1436, commissioned by the Opera del Duomo from PAOLO UCCELLO for Florence Cathedral. Fresco, without frame 24' × 13' 3" (7.32 × 4.04 m)

The frame was added in the sixteenth century, most likely in 1524 by Lorenzo di Credi; the fresco was detached from the wall in 1842 and transferred to canvas. See Figs. 2.15 and 2.16 for location in the Duomo—originally slightly higher than the current placement.

from 1429 to 1433, encouraged the Opera to initiate new decorative projects for its interior in the 1430s.

Sir John Hawkwood (Fig. 4.48), a huge fresco on the left wall of the cathedral, was one of these projects. It was commissioned from Paolo Uccello (Paolo di Dono; 1387 Florence–1475 Florence), yet another artist to have emerged from Ghiberti's workshop. He was a master of painting and mosaic, and was renowned for his obsessive study of perspective. His fresco commemorates an event relating to the security of the state. John Hawkwood (known in Italian as Giovanni Acuto, d. 1394) was an English mercenary soldier (*condottiere*) employed by Florence, and responsible for staving off early threats to Florentine independence by Giangaleazzo Visconti. In gratitude, the Opera del Duomo agreed in 1393 to construct a marble tomb for Hawkwood after his death—one of a series of eight monuments of famous men projected for the cathedral. This plan was simplified in 1395 when the Opera instead commissioned Agnolo Gaddi and Giuliano d'Arrigo (Pesello; 1367–1446) to paint a fresco depicting Hawkwood on horseback, a commission that mirrors a painted series of *uomini famosi* ("famous men") in the Palazzo della Signoria.

In March 1433, as the dome of the cathedral was nearing completion, the Opera announced a competition to replace the existing Hawkwood fresco, and in May 1436 Uccello was told to begin work on the project. A drawing squared for transfer (see Fig. 14) that Uccello prepared for the fresco suggests that he had learned this technique from Brunelleschi, whose biographer notes the architect's use of squared paper to record ancient Roman buildings. This is the earliest extant squared drawing, although Masaccio must also have used the technique since there are remains of incised grid lines on the *Trinity* fresco (see Fig. 4.60), just as there are on the Hawkwood monument. Uccello's fresco was complete in 1436, at the time of the cathedral's consecration. Like Masaccio's *trompe l'oeil* chapel of the *Trinity*, Uccello's fresco of Hawkwood, although painted in monochrome, is a convincing replication of three-dimensional shapes—in this case a bronze equestrian monument. Although Uccello depicted the base of the illusionistic monument from below, he portrayed the horse and rider in profile, adding an iconic power to the figure. As part of a tradition of equestrian portraits of *condottieri* and despotic rulers (see Fig. 3.35), the fresco flirted with a type of image that could easily have been misinterpreted in the republic, with its distrust of tyrants; thus the Opera stipulated that the inscription state that Hawkwood was English, and thus that he was a hireling, rather than someone who had risen to power from within the state. The inscription uses words from Plutarch which describe the Roman Republican hero of the Second Punic War, Fabius Maximus Cunctator, who

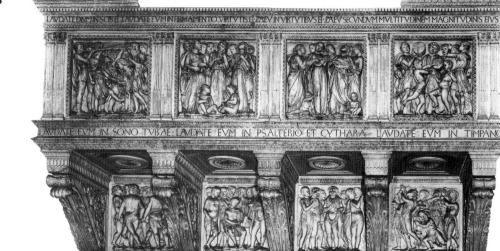

4.49 *Cantoria*, 1430–38, commissioned by the Opera del Duomo from LUCA DELLA ROBBIA to go above the south sacristy door of Florence Cathedral. Marble, overall 10′ 9″ × 18′ 4″ (3.28 × 5.6 m), upper reliefs 44½ × 36¾″ (103 × 93.5 cm), lower reliefs 38¾ × 37″ (98.5 × 94 cm) (Museo dell'Opera del Duomo, Florence)

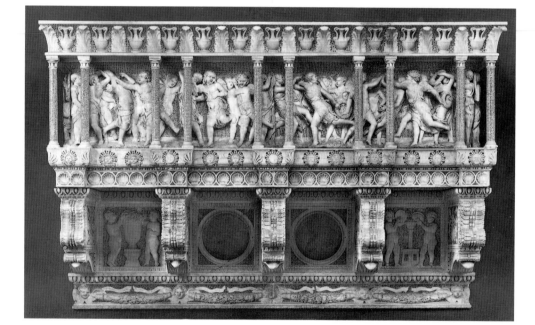

4.50 *Cantoria*, 1433–c. 1440, commissioned by the Opera del Duomo from DONATELLO to go above the north sacristy door of Florence Cathedral. Marble and mosaic with bronze heads, overall 11′ 5″ × 18′ 8½″ (3.48 × 5.70 m); frieze of putti, front 38½ × 205½″ (98 × 522 cm), sides 38½ × 52″ (98 × 132 cm) (Museo dell'Opera del Duomo, Florence)

The two *cantorie* were removed from the cathedral in 1688 on the occasion of the wedding of Ferdinando de' Medici with Violante Beatrice of Bavaria. Parts of the marble architectural framing of Luca's pulpit were used for repair work at the cathedral; one piece was found in the lantern of the Baptistry. The upper cornice of the *cantoria* is modern, and diverges from Donatello's original design, which consisted of repeated paired dolphins and a stylized leaf pattern.

had had a bronze statue raised in his honor in Rome by the state and thus implicitly identifies Florence as a new Rome, as well as honoring Hawkwood. The Opera ensured that the successes of the state would form part of the decoration of the new cathedral and that the ecclesiastical space would also be perceived as a civic space controlled by the state, in this case through the Arte della Lana.

The Opera also ordered two shallow marble *cantorie*, or singing galleries, by Luca della Robbia (Luca di Simone di Marco; 1399/1400 Florence–1482 Florence) and Donatello (Figs. 4.49 and 4.50) to be placed over the north and south sacristry doors. Both *cantorie* are richly carved with relief sculpture, but they are strikingly different in style. Luca received the contract for his *cantoria* in 1430. Although Luca's career before the commission for the *cantoria* is unknown, he may have trained in the cathedral workshops under Nanni di Banco. His invention of

polychromed glazed terracotta as a medium for sculpture was certainly indebted to Donatello's experimental *Joshua* for the north tribune of the cathedral (see p. 198). His *cantoria* illustrates Psalm 150, "Praise ye the Lord," each figured panel depicting one verse of the psalm. The formal classicism of the architecture framing the panels, the Roman lettering of the inscriptions, and the toga-like clothing of the musicians counter the lively anecdotalism of some of the panels. In one, adolescent boys cluster around a single hymn book—a reminder that a confraternity of young boys associated with the Duomo had responsibility for singing the canonical hours there.

Donatello was not awarded the commission for his *cantoria* until July 1433, partly because he had been in Rome for over a year. His contract stipulated that his *cantoria* should follow Luca's in its design of multiple panels. But by 1435 Donatello seems to have decided to substitute a continuous relief of dancing putti (actually

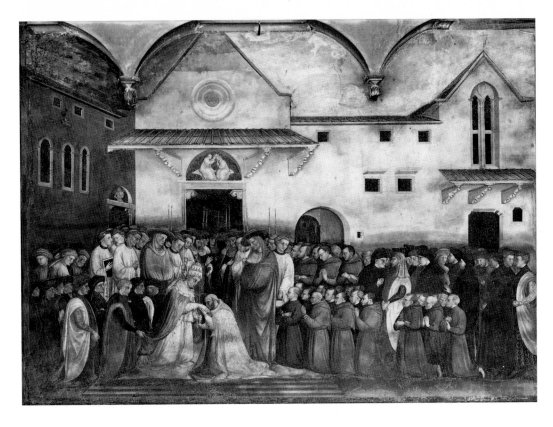

4.51 *Consecration of St. Egidio*, 1430s, BICCI DI LORENZO, Ospedale di Santa Maria Nuova, Florence. Fresco

The small shed-like roof extending out from the façade of the church behind the pope may have been intended to protect the terracotta tympanum figures of the *Coronation of the Virgin* sometimes attributed to Dello Delli.

then in the cloister of that church. From written accounts and drawings it appears that Masaccio, like Bicci, painted ranks of prominent citizens participating in what was both a religious and a civic event, where ritual demonstrated both the Florentines' religious devotion and their communal solidarity. The *Consecration* is in the same class of painting as Gerini's fresco for the Confraternity of the Misericordia (see Fig. 3.31), a straightforward history painting, as opposed to a moral and civil allegory such as Lorenzetti's *Buon Comune* (see Fig. 2.25), in which citizens also appear. The particularized facial features and row-like organization of the figures indicate that Bicci and his patrons intended to present a formal record of the participants as an *exemplum* of the harmony among different groups within the state. It thus served a purpose similar to Lorenzetti's allegory, but makes its point in the context of a specific time and place. It also indicates that the event and its patrons were important enough to warrant Martin V's participation in the consecration.

carved from two stones) screened by paired columns. Although the figures evoke Roman antiquity, the architectural frame contrasts strikingly with the classicizing pilasters of Luca's *cantoria*. Stylized and compressed leaf patterns, repetitive and flattened decorative motifs, and a surface covered with colored mosaic suggest, rather, Early Christian and medieval art. Fresh from his experiences in Rome, Donatello may have used the context of his *cantoria* to re-create some of the forms and images he had seen there, especially in the cloisters of the papal basilicas of St. John Lateran and St. Paul's Outside the Walls. It is a measure of Donatello's reputation that he was able to diverge from his contractual arrangements with the Opera and so provide such an anomalous work of sculpture for the Duomo. His *cantoria* was the last of the major sculptural projects for the cathedral begun during the high point of the republic in the early fifteenth century.

Other Civic Imagery

Communal pride, so evident in the cathedral and its extensive decorative programs, was not always so grandly displayed. A series of frescoes containing clearly recognizable portraits of prominent citizens, the first extant example of which is the *Consecration of St. Egidio* (Fig. 4.51) by Bicci di Lorenzo (c. 1373 Florence–1452 Florence) provided another means for Florentine citizens to mark important events in their city and to fashion a visual record of civic leadership. The fresco derives from Masaccio's lost monochrome (*terra verde*) fresco of the Consecration of Santa Maria del Carmine (c. 1424–27),

Family Commissions

In the preface to his manual on painting, written at the turn of the fifteenth century, Cennino Cennini expressed pride in the long tradition to which he belonged:

> I was trained in this profession for twelve years by my master, Agnolo di Taddeo [Gaddi] of Florence; he learned this profession from Taddeo, his father; and his father was christened under Giotto, and was his follower for four-and-twenty years; and that Giotto changed the profession of painting from Greek [Byzantine] back into Latin, and brought it up to date; and he had more finished craftsmanship than anyone has had since.

Tenaciously held traditions such as Cennino's shaped subsequent thinking about artistic development during the fifteenth century and have obscured consideration of clearly developed alternatives to the Giottesque tradition outlined in so linear a manner by Cennino.

As the Florentine oligarchy became stronger after crushing the Ciompi Revolution and successfully thwarting the Milanese threats to the city's liberty, noticeable stylistic changes occurred in Florentine painting, as frescoes for the Bartolini-Salimbeni Chapel in Santa Trinità (Fig. 4.52) make clear. These frescoes were painted by Lorenzo Monaco (Lorenzo the monk, born Piero di Giovanni; c. 1370 Siena?–1425/30 Florence), who may have been trained by Agnolo Gaddi or as an illuminator in the scriptorium of Santa Maria degli Angeli, where he was a monk. Completed between 1420 and 1424, Lorenzo's paintings of events from the Life of the Virgin cover an earlier fresco cycle by Spinello Aretino believed to have been commissioned by Bartolomeo Salimbeni in 1390—almost as if the family were seeking to assert its status by assimilating a new style associated with the

courts in the north. The painted architecture of the Bartolini-Salimbeni frescoes extends over the entire narrative, stepping back along sharp diagonals, while the row of figures moves in a gradual diagonal back into space, a composition that suggests Lorenzo's close study of Agnolo Gaddi's frescoes at Santa Croce (see Fig. 3.29). Lorenzo's debt to earlier sources is also evident in the figure of St. Joseph, whose gathered yellow cloak falls in two large curves and then loops along the ground. The altarpiece for this chapel (Fig. 4.53) recalls the miracle-working image at Santissima Annunziata in Florence, recast in the earlier Sienese Gothic forms of Simone Martini's *Annunciation* (see Fig. 2.29) in its decorative details and elongated figures, with their long S-curves and arabesque drapery edges. Apart from the fact that Lorenzo came from Siena, the reason for the references to Simone's altarpiece, then still in Siena's cathedral, is not clear. In painting as in sculpture, however, the juxtaposition of recent Florentine and older Sienese references in one chapel suggests how thoroughly painters in Florence had assimilated the International Gothic style imported from

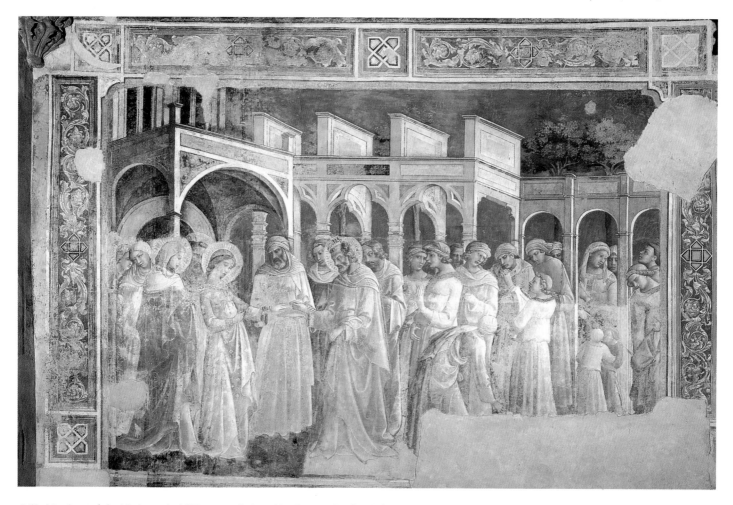

4.52 *Marriage of the Virgin*, early 1420s, commissioned by the Bartolini family from Lorenzo Monaco for the Bartolini Chapel, Santa Trinità, Florence. Fresco, 6' 10½" × 7' 6½" (2.1 × 2.3 m)

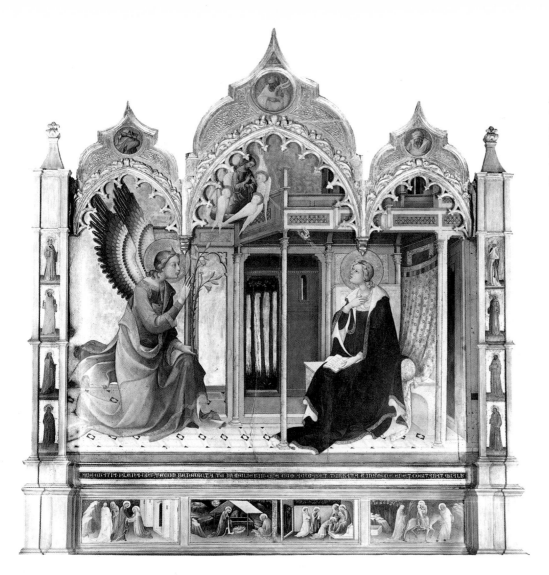

4.53 *Annunciation*, early 1420s, commissioned by the Bartolini family from LORENZO MONACO for the Bartolini Chapel, Santa Trinità, Florence. Tempera on panel, 9′ 10″ × 8′ 11¾″ (3 × 2.74 m)

France, and how such a style might distinguish a new group of patrons from others of their contemporaries.

Lorenzo's elegant style reached maturity in his very large altarpiece of the *Coronation of the Virgin* (Fig. 4.54) for the high altar of his conventual church of Santa Maria degli Angeli in Florence. In both the Santa Maria degli Angeli altarpiece and the Bartolini Chapel frescoes, the patrons apparently regarded Lorenzo's style as the most novel in Florentine painting of their time. The church of Santa Maria degli Angeli is itself referred to in the altarpiece both by the many angels who accompany the saints and by the white robes of the Virgin, which evoke the white monastic robes of the Camaldolite order, whose church it was. In Lorenzo's *Coronation* the edges of the figures' garments have an animation quite independent of the actual movement of the figures. Although the composition of the painting is quite conventional, the figures display a new fluidity in their poses and in the movements of their drapery which is suggestive of the International Style then being employed in sculpture by Ghiberti and Niccolò Lamberti (see Figs. 4.42 and 4.37). Surface patterns vie for attention with the volumes of the figures; even the superimposition of figures tends to read as pattern. Brilliant, light-toned color and the lavish use

of gold and expensive ultramarine blue pigment would have made the painting a strong focal point in the church and would also have testified to its importance and to the donor's extraordinary generosity.

The Strozzi Chapel At the beginning of the fifteenth century Onofrio Strozzi was head of the wealthiest family in Florence. When he died in 1418 he had already initiated work on his family burial chapel at Santa Trinità—which was also to serve as the church's sacristy. The chapel and much of its decoration were commissioned by Onofrio's son, Palla Strozzi. Documentary evidence indicates that Ghiberti was the architect—a choice that may reflect the fact that Palla Strozzi served as a member of the committee that ordered Ghiberti's north doors for the Baptistry (see Fig. 4.31).

The centerpiece of the chapel was the *Adoration of the Magi* (Fig. 4.55) by one of Italy's leading proponents of the International Gothic style, Gentile da Fabriano (Gentile di Niccolò di Massio; c. 1385 Fabriano–1427 Rome). Befitting the work of an artist who had enjoyed great success in Venice (where he painted narratives in the Great Council Hall) and the court of Pandolfo Malatesta in Brescia, it is one of the most lavish paintings made in

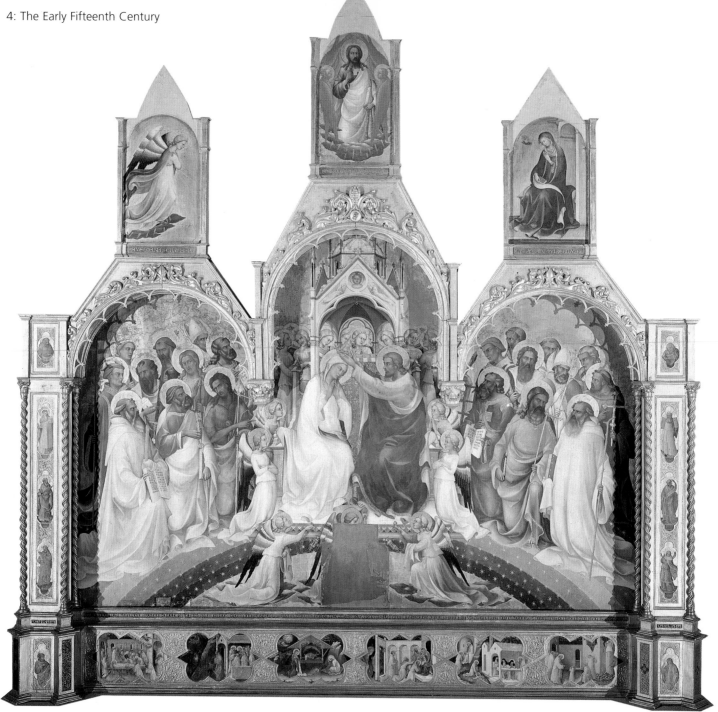

4.54 *Coronation of the Virgin*, 1414, commissioned by a member of the Della Frasca family (perhaps Domenico di Zanobi) to honor Zanobi di Ceccho della Frasca and other members of the family from LORENZO MONACO for the main altar of Santa Maria degli Angeli, Florence. Tempera on panel, 16' 9½" × 14' 9" (5.12 × 4.5 m) (Galleria degli Uffizi, Florence)

The inscription that runs along the base of the painting reads: "This picture was made for the soul of Zanobi di Ceccho della Frasca and his family in compensation for another altarpiece that was placed in this church for him. The work is by Lorenzo di Giovanni, a monk of this order, and his [shop]. He painted it in the year of our Lord 1413, in the month of February, during the time of Matthew's priorate of this monastery."

fifteenth-century Florence, a manifestation of the Strozzi's enormous wealth. The altarpiece luxuriates in gold, elaborate tooling, patterned costumes, and decorative details, which even adorn its frame. The opulence of Gentile's *Adoration* should not, however, obscure two other critical aspects of the painting, typical of the work he produced during his Florentine years: the suffusion of light throughout the composition and the beautifully modeled figures whose features are subtly put in relief by the play of light upon them, effects already evident in Gentile's earlier works. These effects and the softness of colors in the *Adoration* differ from Lorenzo Monaco's sharper tonalities, setting Gentile's painting apart from the leading painter in Florence at the time. Another noteworthy

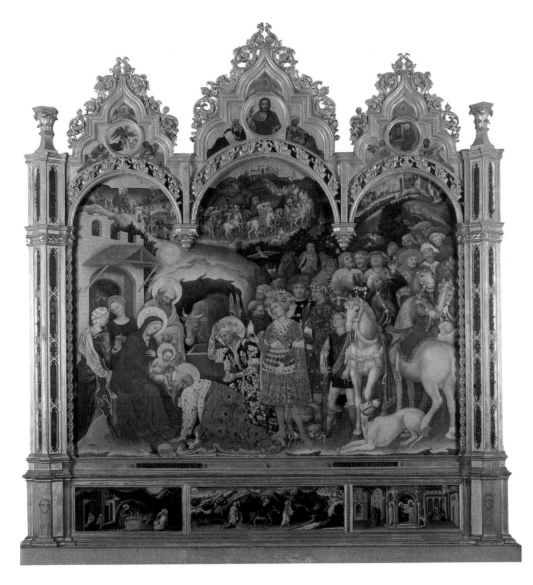

4.55 *Adoration of the Magi*, 1423, commissioned by Palla Strozzi from GENTILE DA FABRIANO for the Strozzi Chapel, Santa Trinità, Florence. Tempera on panel, 9' 10" × 9' 3" (3 × 2.82 m) (Galleria degli Uffizi, Florence)

feature is the aristocratic quality of both subject and treatment. Not only does it have a regal cast of characters in the Three Kings, but it portrays the event with the full panoply of princely life, including hunting dogs, pet monkeys, and falcons, although the Strozzi were bankers.

The impact of this painting was enhanced by its position inside a chapel whose exterior decorative details mark an early and tentative exploration of a classical vocabulary. Thus the "public face" of the chapel presents a gravity appropriate for a civic leader, while the splendor of the altarpiece inside expresses more freely the private aspirations of the family.

Soon after completing the *Adoration of the Magi*, Gentile painted an altarpiece, now dismantled, for the main altar of San Niccolò sopr'Arno, over which Bernardo di Castello Quaratesi had property rights. The *Quaratesi Altarpiece* (Fig. 4.56) is signed and dated to 1425 on the center panel and may have been commissioned by one of Bernardo's heirs after his death in 1423. It is much more conventional in its composition than the Strozzi *Adoration*, with the Madonna and Child enthroned between the patron saints of the family and the church.

Despite the traditional gold ground behind the saints and the schematic pattern of the floor on which they stand, their volumetric treatment in space (which originally would have been even greater with wooden colonnettes between the panels creating an arcaded loggia) gives them a presence unlike those of previous altarpiece figures. Although St. Nicholas (second from the left, and in the place of honor to the Virgin's right) appears in an iconic frontal pose as the patron saint of the church, the other figures turn and gesture in a manner more naturalistic even than Ghiberti's *St. John the Baptist* (see Fig. 4.42), which they resemble in certain details of drapery. The same natural quality can be seen in the Virgin and Child, who, although seated on a throne covered with four different patterns which tend to flatten space, are fully modeled and spatially convincing. The projecting knees of the Virgin catch the light from the left, the drapery hanging heavily between them, and the smooth faces are delicately modeled with red highlights on the cheeks blurring into a soft pink. The gray shadows on the figures' left darken imperceptibly as they help to structure contour.

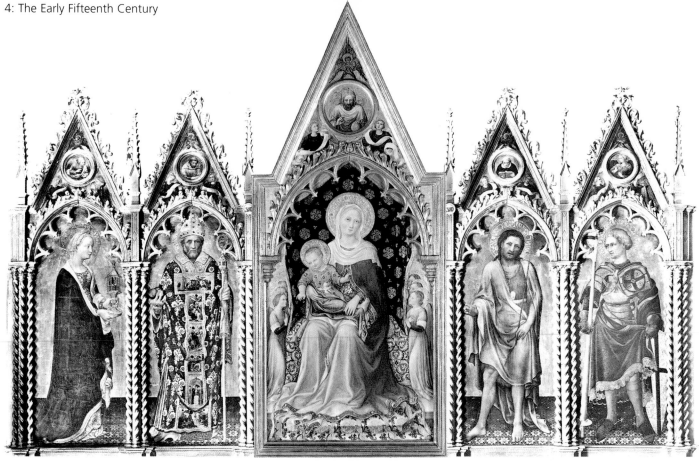

4.56 *Quaratesi Altarpiece* (reconstruction), 1425, commissioned by a member of the Quaratesi family from GENTILE DA FABRIANO for the high altar of San Niccolò sopr'Arno, Florence. Tempera on panel, center panel, including frame, 87½ × 32½" (222.7 × 83 cm)

The Virgin and Child is in the National Gallery, London (on loan from Her Majesty the Queen); Mary Magdalene, St. Nicholas, St. John the Baptist, and St. George are in the Galleria degli Uffizi, Florence.

Masaccio and the Brancacci Chapel   At about the time that Gentile painted the *Quaratesi Altarpiece*, a young revolutionary Florentine painter now known as Masaccio (Tommaso di ser Giovanni di Simone Guidi; 1401 San Giovanni Val d'Arno–1428 Rome) began to explore new ways of representing the real world on a two-dimensional surface. His career was very short, although he is known to have been painting by the age of sixteen. His first extant major commission was for a large multi-paneled altarpiece completed in 1426 for the choir screen of a chapel in the Carmelite church of Santa Maria del Carmine in Pisa that belonged to a notary of that city.

Like Gentile, Masaccio was obliged to use a gold background—still considered necessary for the iconic figures of an altarpiece. He placed his Madonna and Child (Fig. 4.57) in an architectural throne whose ornaments of Corinthian capitals and rosettes and strygyl base distinguish it from those in earlier Florentine paintings of the enthroned Virgin (see Fig. 2.6). Her arms create an oval, opening a volume into which the child fits. The full volumes and heavy massing of the drapery over her clearly defined body show that Masaccio had looked carefully at the sculpture of his friend Donatello (see Fig. 4.36). The play of light over facial features is indebted to

Gentile, although Masaccio heightened the effect of light with the strong shadows created by the left side of the throne and by the figures themselves. This meticulous treatment of light and shadow attests to Masaccio's concern for naturalism, seen also in the amusing gesture of the Christ Child stuffing grapes (a Eucharistic symbol) into his mouth, much as any child would do.

Masaccio's frescoes for the Brancacci Chapel in Santa Maria del Carmine, Florence, another Carmelite church (Fig. 4.58), mark a milestone in the history of wall painting. They enhance Giottesque traditions of naturalism with new vitality, not merely in their formal properties of space and volume, but also in the psychological intensity that permeates the narrative. The frescoes were assigned to Masaccio, and to a slightly older Florentine painter now known as Masolino (Tommaso di Cristofano di Fino; 1383 Panicale di Val d'Arno–c. 1440 Castiglione Olona) who may have received early training in the workshop of Agnolo Gaddi and who was employed in Ghiberti's workshop between 1407 and 1415. The nicknames given the two painters—Masaccio being a derogative form of Maso perhaps connoting slovenliness or brutishness, Masolino being another diminutive of Maso contrarily implying gentleness—are responses to their

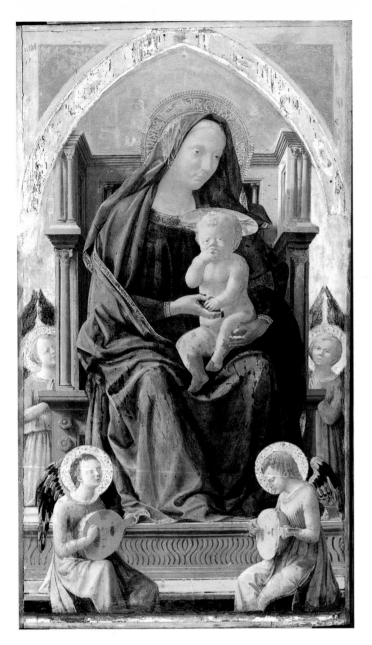

4.57 *Pisa Altarpiece*, center panel, 1426, commissioned by ser Giuliano di Colino degli Scarsi da San Giusto from MASACCIO for a chapel in Santa Maria del Carmine, Pisa. Tempera on panel, center panel 53 × 28¾" (135 × 73 cm)

The center panel of the Madonna and Child is now in the National Gallery, London; the predella panels and the saints from the frame supports are in the Staatliche Museen, Berlin; the Crucifixion is in the Gallerie Nazionali di Capodimonte, Naples; and the figure of St. Andrew from the second story of the polyptych is in the J. Paul Getty Museum, Malibu; only the figure of St. Paul remains in Pisa, at the Museo Nazionale.

distinctive painting styles and have colored understanding of their work since the sixteenth century. The simplified opposition that the nicknames establish takes little account of the fact that the artists worked together on more than one occasion and thus that their patrons would have assumed that their collaboration would produce a harmonious work.

The Brancacci Chapel was created through a bequest of Pietro Brancacci, who died in 1367. Because of the deaths of Pietro's sons and his brothers by the mid-1390s,

ownership of the chapel eventually passed to his nephew, Felice Brancacci, and it is generally believed that he was the patron who commissioned the frescoes from Masolino and Masaccio. Until his second marriage to Lena di Palla Strozzi (the daughter of Gentile's patron for the *Adoration of the Magi*) Felice was closely allied to Cosimo de' Medici. He also had strong connections to the papal court, in part through two members of his family who were cardinals and also through another relative who was the head of the Dominican order in Florence. When Palla Strozzi was exiled from Florence in 1434, Felice was charged with political intrigue against the new Medici regime, ostensibly because of his Strozzi marriage alliance. He was himself exiled from the city in 1435, when the frescoes were still unfinished, and his goods were confiscated by the state, precluding any further work on the decoration of the chapel.

Most of the frescoes of the Brancacci Chapel depict scenes from the life of St. Peter, the patron saint of the original donor, Pietro Brancacci. Masolino seems to have been the first of the two artists to be commissioned. He painted the vaults and the lunettes of the chapel, all of which were destroyed in a fire of 1748. Of the extant frescoes Masaccio was responsible for the left wall, Masolino for the right wall; it appears both painters worked on the altar wall. Although Masolino was already working on the frescoes by 1425, he had left for Hungary by September of that year, perhaps never to return to them; Masaccio went to Rome in 1427, leaving his part of the commission also unfinished.

Old Testament subjects of the Temptation of Adam and Eve by Masolino and the Expulsion from Paradise by Masaccio are depicted on the entrance arch to the chapel—a reminder of the Original Sin. Standard comparisons between the two frescoes (Fig. 4.58, top left and right; Fig. 4.59 left) propose that Masolino represented the end of the Gothic tradition and Masaccio the beginnings of a new and more powerful tradition of figural representation in Florence. Although there may be some truth to this characterization, it is clear from other family chapels and from the ongoing careers of painters such as Lorenzo Monaco and Gentile da Fabriano that an elegant style was still in great demand in Florence and that Masolino was responding to this stylistic disposition as he assimilated the gently modeled forms and coloration of Gentile's work into his own painting. Masaccio's figures seem to have no precedent in contemporary painting; again, as in the *Pisa Altarpiece*, his naturalistic human forms show, rather, the influence of Donatello. The muscular Adam in the *Expulsion* bends and turns at the same time, racked with shame and fear; he creates a core of space with his body that is directed to the right even though his right leg drags behind his body, as if

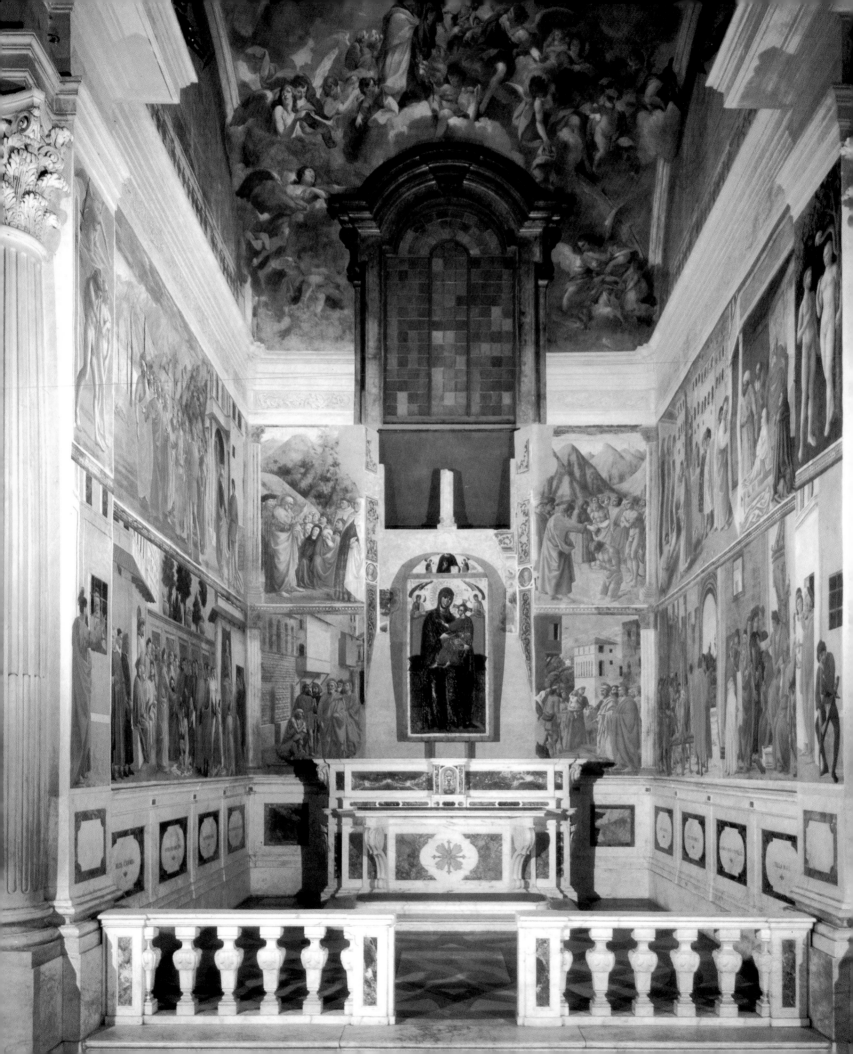

4.58 (opposite) Brancacci Chapel, plan originated by Pietro Brancacci, partially painted c. 1424–27 by MASOLINO and MASACCIO (FILIPPINO LIPPI painted the lower right wall and the unfinished part of the lower left wall in the mid-1480s), Santa Maria del Carmine, Florence. Fresco

Recent cleaning of the chapel was begun in 1984 and completed in 1990.

attempting to slow the inevitable expulsion. Eve attempts to hide her nakedness while her face is contorted in a paroxysm of grief. Modeled on a classical *Venus pudica* type, she is schematic as a physiological representation, but compelling as an expressive psychological depiction.

In *The Tribute Money* (see Fig. 4.59; taken from Matthew 17:24–27), Masaccio depicts Christ's commands to Peter as events already realized. In the center the messenger from the Temple asks Christ for the yearly tax for maintaining the Temple in Jerusalem. Christ, claiming to be free from the tax, nonetheless orders Peter to catch a fish, shown in the middle distance on the left where Peter opens the mouth of the fish to find the coin of tribute. On the right Peter pays the tax collector the coin, actually worth twice the required tax.

Masaccio's landscape is missing the leaves that were originally painted *a secco* on the trees, but the overall effect remains remarkable for its realism. Colors fade into a hazy monochromatic distance where hills meet sky, creating an atmospheric perspective analogous to that attempted in stone by Donatello in his St. George relief (see Fig. 4.39). The crisply delineated architecture on the right serves to frame Peter and the tax collector.

In the central group of figures Christ anchors the composition, being the focal point of the narrative, as he directs an unwilling Peter to pay the Temple messenger. Peter's pose echoes that of Christ, the gesture of their right arms directing attention to the next scene in the narrative.

The paired gestures imply an equation between Christ's authority and Peter's, an assertion of the legitimacy of papal power. Furthermore, in both instances where Peter confronts the temple tax collector, their two bodies are mirror images of one another. This opposition strengthens the narrative by locking the two protagonists of the story into a single compositional unit. The figural opposition also serves to enhance the three-dimensional quality of the image by providing enough information for the viewer to construct mentally a fully rounded pair of figures—front and back in one case, right and left sides in the other. Masaccio modeled his forms' surfaces so that light plays smoothly over them, leaving dark pockets of shadow in the drapery and soft convexities of flesh in the figures, thus adding to the dramatic impact of the story.

There have been attempts to see in *The Tribute Money* references to the institution of a state tax based on a declaration of income and assets (the *catasto*) first taken in 1427. However, these are unconvincing for the simple reason that the Brancacci would have been allied to the faction opposing the tax. A more likely interpretation connects this particular scene with Pope Martin V's 1423 agreement that the Florentine Church be subject to state tax. The cycle as a whole may refer simply to the original donor of the chapel, Pietro Brancacci, or it may reflect Felice Brancacci's close connections to the papacy, here represented by St. Peter. The presence of Carmelite monks in some of the frescoes is a clear reference to the order that had charge of the church, suggesting that they too had a role to play in their creation. In these powerful images Masaccio transformed the traditions of monumental narrative painting, opening up alternatives to the style exemplified by the Bartolini-Salimbeni frescoes (see Fig. 4.52), painted at about the same time.

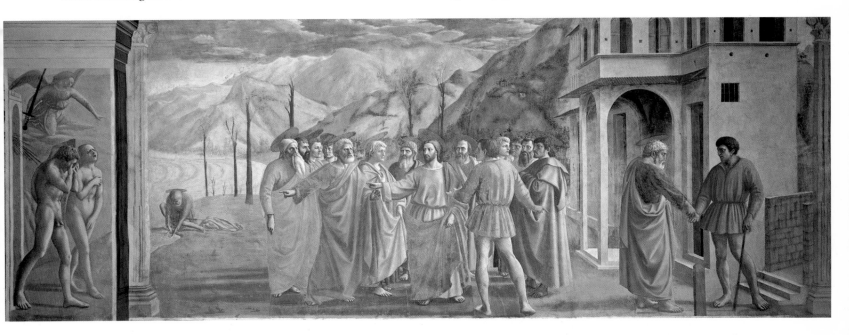

4.59 *Expulsion* and *The Tribute Money*, MASACCIO, Brancacci Chapel, Santa Maria del Carmine, Florence. Fresco, 8' 4⅜" × 19' 7⅜" (2.54 × 5.97 m)

The *Trinity* and Single-Point Perspective

Perhaps Masaccio's best-known painting is the one for which there is the least concrete information. The *Trinity* (Fig. 4.60) was painted on the left wall of the church of Santa Maria Novella. During Vasari's remodeling of the church in the 1560s Masaccio's fresco was covered by a stone tabernacle and a painting, which were not removed until 1860–61. At that time the *Trinity* was detached from the wall, suffering severe damage in the process. Because there is an early record of a tomb slab for Domenico Lenzi and his family placed in the pavement in front of the fresco's original position in 1426, the kneeling donor figure on the left side of the *Trinity* is generally assumed to be Lenzi, and the figure at right his wife.

The *Trinity* depicts a small chapel containing the Three Persons of the Trinity, with God the Father standing above and behind the Son on the Cross, as if presenting him to the worshiper, and the dove of the Holy Spirit hovering above Christ's head. The painted chapel provided the patron and his wife with a substitute for a real one, which either they could not afford to build or—because the wall on which it is painted is contiguous with the cloister—was architecturally unfeasible. However, from Santa Maria Novella's side door, directly opposite the fresco, then used as a major entrance to the building, the fictive chapel of the *Trinity* would have resembled a real space.

At the foot of the cross stand Mary and John the Evangelist, as they do in more literally rendered Crucifixion scenes. Here separated from that narrative context they appear to be contemplating a religious icon, with Mary looking out toward the viewer and gesturing toward the crucified Christ. All of the sacred figures exist behind the architectural frame, separated in their own space, while the donor and his wife kneel on a ledge in front of it, thereby illusionistically sharing the viewer's space. At the base of the painting is a fictive altar supported by four thin columns; beneath it is an open sarcophagus supporting a skeleton whose inscription warns, "What you are now I once was, what I am now you will be." Thus tomb, donors, and devotional image are spatially sequenced to take the viewer into the sacred space of the Trinity.

The means of achieving this fusion of real and depicted space lie in part in Masaccio's ability to render his figures as if they are three-dimensional as he did in *The Tribute Money*. Equally important is his use, for the first time in the history of painting, of a fully developed single-point perspective system. The development of this linear system for the representation of space occurred when the increased realism of the figures demanded a commensurate realization of their surroundings. Single-point perspective, despite its importance, must be seen as part of a

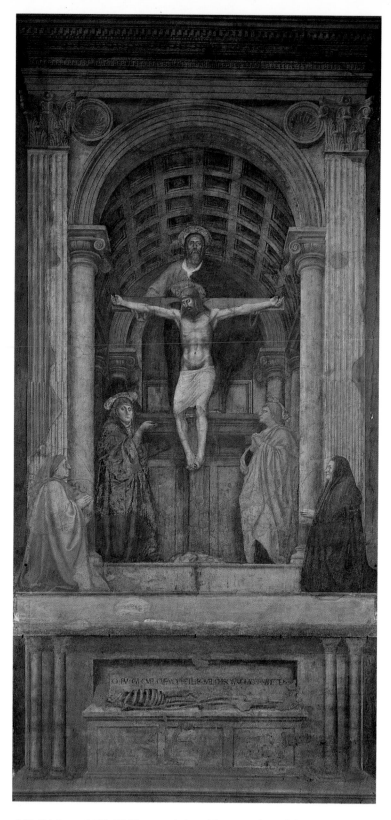

4.60 *Trinity*, c. 1426–27 (?), commissioned by a member of the Lenzi family from MASACCIO for Santa Maria Novella, Florence. Fresco detached from the wall, 21' 10⅝" × 10' 4¾" (6.67 × 3.17 m)

whole development and as one of a number of pictorial devices that artists might use—or not use—in depicting their subjects.

The single-point perspective system was invented by the architect Filippo Brunelleschi. Since a fully developed, rationalized space does not appear in painting until the *Trinity*, Brunelleschi's invention should perhaps be dated to around 1424–25; the actual development of single-point perspective must have taken place over some time.

Reconstruction of the history of this pictorial invention stems from Antonio Manetti's life of Brunelleschi, written in the 1480s, in which the author describes two small panels painted by Brunelleschi: one of the Palazzo della Signoria, the other of the Baptistry. In each, the building was set within its surrounding urban context. According to Manetti, Brunelleschi painted the panel of the Baptistry by standing some 6 feet (2 meters) inside the main doors of the cathedral. He either looked directly across the small piazza that separates the two buildings or into a mirror with his back to the Baptistry so that what he painted was a replica of the mirrored image. From this vantage point Brunelleschi saw not only the east face of the Baptistry (where Ghiberti's first bronze doors were placed in 1424; see Fig. 1.9) but also the streets and markets to the left and right. The geometrical regularity and precision of the decorative elements of the Baptistry would certainly have aided the construction of the demonstration panel. Manetti describes the panel as half a *braccia* (literally "arm," a Florentine unit of measure) or approximately a foot (30 centimeters) square, painted with a miniaturist's care, with the sky made of reflective burnished silver so that "the [mirrored] clouds seen in the silver are carried along by the wind as it blows." It appears that Brunelleschi's concern was to re-create an illusionistic reality (on a small scale) as closely as possible.

Manetti also says that the panel was intended to be viewed from the back, by looking through a hole drilled at the central vanishing point at a mirror held up in front of it (Fig. 4.61). This would have achieved three goals. First, it closed the viewer's vision to the panel itself, excluding any surrounding and competing "reality." It also required the viewer to use only one eye, thus making the illusion of space in the panel more vivid. And, as Manetti points out, the distance between panel and mirror was to be approximately one *braccia*. Since the actual distance between the Baptistry and the spot where Brunelleschi painted the image was 60 *braccia* and the image represented an actual width of 30 *braccia*, the relationship of distance between the panel and the viewer's eye and the width of the panel was 2:1 just as the represented distance was 2:1, thus again helping to replicate the vision of reality. The concept of the vanishing point—the point in the distance, appearing at eye level, where lines in the field of vision appear to converge—is implied in this construction. Behind the construction of the perspective panel lie Brunelleschi's careful measurements which ensured that actual spatial relationships were translated to their proportional equivalents as the panel

was seen in the mirror. Clearly this is not a system that translates easily to ordinary painting.

In Masaccio's *Trinity* the problems of applying Brunelleschi's system, based on real buildings, to an imaginary space, in which figures play a major part, remain partially unresolved. It is difficult to imagine where God the Father is standing or how his position in space relates to Christ's. The **orthogonal** lines (diagonal lines moving to the centric point) of the vaulting system, however, all meet at a point somewhat below the base of the cross—roughly at the eye level of the viewer. The perspective system not only creates a space inside the picture, but positions the viewer in the space before the painting as well, dictating a position out from the painting on a center line toward which the Virgin gazes. Despite the unresolved aspects of perspective in this painting, Masaccio—perhaps with the assistance of Brunelleschi, who was a friend—had established a mode of pictorial representation in the *Trinity* that was to dominate European visual language until the nineteenth century.

Masaccio's accomplishments were bought with a price. His down-to-earth vision probably struck many contemporaries as startlingly forthright and certainly underdecorated. Lacking the allure and graceful artifice evident in works of Lorenzo Monaco and Gentile da Fabriano, Masaccio's paintings would have taken some getting used to, just as had the sober beauty of a Madonna by Giotto which Petrarch earlier claimed could only be appreciated by sophisticated viewers. Predictably, Masaccio's new style did not fully displace the International Gothic style until several decades later, when artists found ways to make the new manner as visually rich and opulent as the work of Masaccio's competitors.

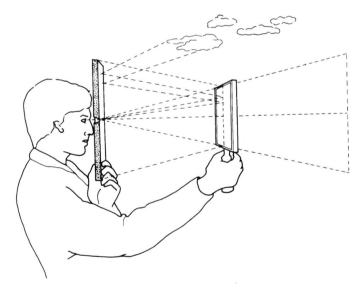

4.61 Drawing showing FILIPPO BRUNELLESCHI's perspective panel of the Baptistry held before a mirror and viewed from behind through a peep-hole (after Alessandro Parronchi)

Siena: Renewing the Image of the Commune

It is a standard and understandable tradition to compare Siena to Florence in the fifteenth century and to emphasize the remarkable conservatism of Sienese art at this time. That the Sienese themselves were conscious of Florentine innovations in the arts is testified to by their several attempts to bring Florentine artists to Siena to work on major commissions. As in other city-states, however, the conditions for making art in Siena and the messages it was intended to convey differed considerably from those in Florence, and they explain why Sienese art of the fifteenth century focused so strongly on the traditions and accomplishments of the previous century.

Siena's Political System and the Palazzo Pubblico

The system of government in Siena changed significantly and repeatedly during the last half of the fourteenth century. The Nine were driven from power in 1355 to be followed by a troubled period of coalition under the Dodici (the "Twelve"), merchants who were assisted in their roles as governors by twelve nobles. The reform

government led by the *popolo minuto*, or "little people," which took over in 1368, itself fell from power in 1386, leading to a period of instability that made it easy for Giangaleazzo Visconti of Milan to take control of the city in 1399. The Sienese regained control of their city only in 1404 with a coalition republican government led by ten Priors, which brought some order to political life in the city for the remainder of the century.

Siena's economy did not have an international base in the fifteenth century, but was focused on local trade and banking. Although risks were low, so were growth prospects. As the second most populous city in Tuscany after Florence, with a population of about 13,000 within its walls, Siena benefited from a relatively narrow discrepancy between rich and poor, which gave it an appearance of civic harmony and prosperity throughout the century.

Restoration of the republic after 1404 enabled the Priors to turn toward an extensive embellishment of the Palazzo Pubblico. This work amounted to a reaffirmation of civic ideals, drawing on earlier traditions depicted within the Palazzo Pubblico and at the same time adding new humanist overtones to the Sienese stylistic repertoire. Among the first of the commissions for the building was that contracted in 1406 for the redecoration of the chapel located next to the room in which Simone Martini's *Maestà* (see Fig. 2.23) was painted. In 1302 this chapel had been provided with an altarpiece also of a *Maestà* by Duccio. In 1406–07 Taddeo di Bartolo (1362/63 Siena–1422 Siena), perhaps a student of Bartolo di Fredi (see Fig. 2.35), decorated its walls with frescoes of scenes from the life of the Virgin, the city's patron saint (Fig. 4.62). These employ fourteenth-century conventions of spatial organization and figural composition, although the drapery style suggests the weight and mass of material in a way similar to that which Giovanni d'Ambrogio was already using in his sculpture in Florence (see Fig. 3.32). The wiry outline of the figures and their sharp, angular

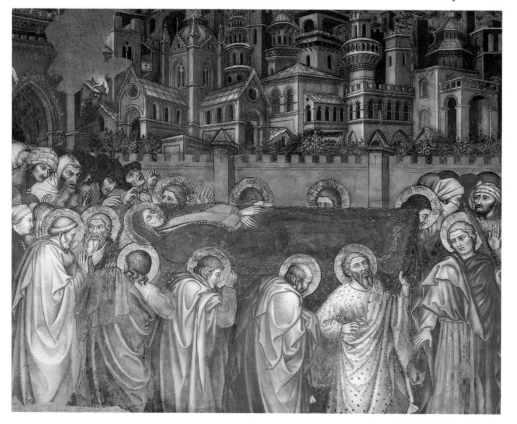

4.62 *The Funeral of the Virgin*, 1406–7, commissioned by the Priors from TADDEO DI BARTOLO for their chapel, Palazzo Pubblico, Siena. Fresco, 10' 6" × 11' 4" (3.2 × 3.45 m)

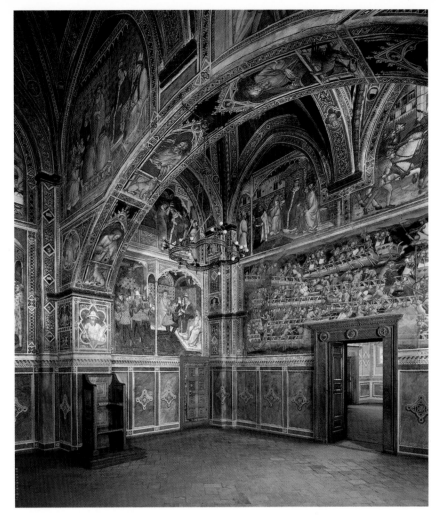

4.63 *Scenes from the Life of Alexander III*, 1407, commissioned by the Priors from SPINELLO ARETINO for the Sala dei Priori, Palazzo Pubblico, Siena. Fresco

poses appear consistently in Taddeo's work. Along with the stylized or blank backgrounds in the frescoes these features would have given the decorative program of the town hall a stylistic consistency spanning over a century.

In 1407 the Priors commissioned Spinello Aretino (assisted perhaps by his son, Parri Spinelli, 1387 Arezzo–1453 Arezzo) to paint the walls of their meeting room, the Sala dei Priori (Fig. 4.63). Spinello had previously worked in Florence (see Fig. 3.30) and was the first non-Sienese artist to be employed on major commissions in Siena during the fifteenth century. The subject matter of the two-tiered frescoes, which cover all four walls of the room, concerns the Sienese pope Alexander III Bandinelli (r. 1159–81); this is the same pope who appears in several Venetian fresco cycles, for it was Doge Ziani who had reconciled Alexander with the Holy Roman Emperor Frederick Barbarossa (r. 1152–90). Supposedly this subject was chosen as the result of a visit of Pope Gregory XII to Siena, the frescoes being intended to remind the current incumbent of a Sienese citizen who had been pope and who had even brought the fearsome Barbarossa to his knees. They fit the needs of a civic site by honoring one of its famous citizens, and they may also serve contemporary history by suggesting a comparison between Alexander's alliance with the Lombards and the Priors' Milanese alliance with the Visconti. The frescoes' Florentine sense of spaciousness, their massive, solid figures, and naturalistic details indicate that historical narrative demanded a dramatic and naturalistic style.

In 1413–14 the Priors again turned to Taddeo di Bartolo to paint a cycle of paintings for the antechapel of the Palazzo Pubblico, a space that functioned as an important passage between other rooms of the palace. The Priors thought this space important enough to assign Pietro de' Pecci, a lawyer and teacher in Siena, and Cristoforo di Andrea, the city's chancellor, as advisors to Taddeo in determining the fresco program. On one wall Taddeo painted allegories of Justice and Magnanimity under the two arches; beneath each he placed a figure from Roman history exemplifying the concept (Fig. 4.64). Each group of Roman heroes is labeled with an inscription in Latin, and each figure bears a further Latin inscription below his feet. The inscriptions between M. Curius Dentatus and F. Furius Camillus claim them as founders of Siena, while others under Cicero and Cato speak of their fight for liberty, and justice. Despite the elaborate humanist program, with its complex Latin messages, the figures belong to the medieval tradition of the *uomini famosi*. The soldiers' elaborate costumes follow chivalric painterly traditions rather than historical accuracy. The one inscription in Italian in this room which might have been readable by Siena's counselors is placed between the two groups of heroes and urges them to look to the example of Rome, to seek for the common good and to emulate the examples of just counsel. Given Siena's recent history, it is significant that the central message of the inscription is a plea for unity. It is also significant that the Priors commissioned a Sienese artist whose style places the imagery well within traditional formal conventions of Sienese painting.

The *Fonte Gaia*

Civic commissions in Siena were not limited to the Palazzo Pubblico. In December 1408 the Sienese sculptor Jacopo della Quercia (1371/75? Siena–1438 Siena), according to Ghiberti one of the competitors for the

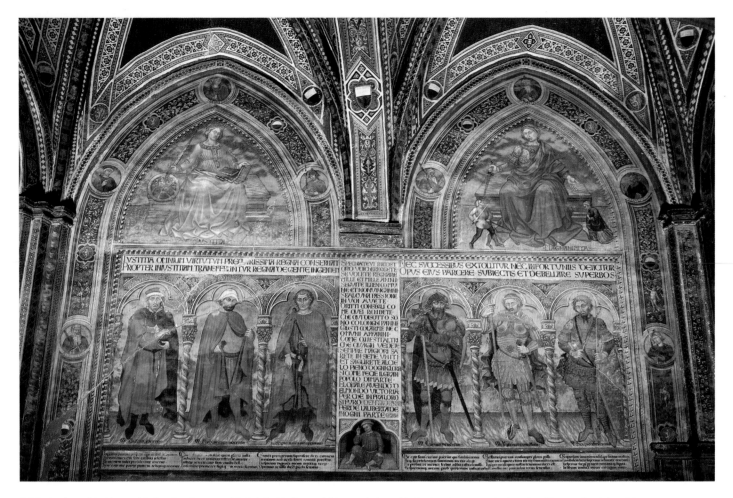

4.64 *Justice with Cicero, M. Porcius Cato, and P. Scipio Nasica* and *Magnanimity with Curius Dentatus, Furius Camillus, and Scipio Africanus*, 1413–14, commissioned by the Priors from TADDEO DI BARTOLO for the antechapel, Palazzo Pubblico, Siena. Fresco, each lunette 8' 10¼" × 10' 6" (2.7 × 3.2 m)

doors of the Florentine Baptistry in 1401, was commissioned to design and carve the reliefs for a large public fountain, now known as the *Fonte Gaia* ("Happy Fountain"), to be situated on the Piazza del Campo opposite the town hall (Fig. 4.66). The design for the fountain was set at the time of the contract, and a full-scale drawing for it was made on an interior wall of the Palazzo Pubblico. Modifications and changes in the contract occurred in 1409, but Quercia seems not to have begun actual work on the project until 1414, shortly after he had to leave a project in Lucca because of accusations against him and his assistant, Giovanni da Imola, of theft, adultery, and sodomy. The project dragged on until 1419, to the exasperation of the commissioners.

Even in its now-ruined state the *Fonte Gaia* conveys some of the splendor which it originally added to the center of Siena and underscores the civic imagery important for such a site. A central relief of the Virgin and Child recalls the city's dedication to Mary and the imagery of most of its civic commissions. She is flanked to the left and right by niches containing figures of virtues, much as

Lorenzetti's *Buon Comune* (see Fig. 2.25) is flanked by allegorical personifications. Although the original plan called for figures of Gabriel and the Virgin Annunciate facing one another at the ends of the wings, a revision ordered in 1415 substituted reliefs of the *Creation of Adam*, and the *Expulsion from Paradise* (Fig. 4.65). The *Expulsion* adds an important focus on Justice to the fountain, again echoing the theme of the *Good Government* fresco in the Palazzo Pubblico. Quercia had most likely looked carefully at the work of Donatello and Nanni di Banco in Florence and incorporated the new style of active, weighty, and expressively modeled form that appeared in their figures for the façade of the Florence Duomo (see Figs. 4.36 and 4.35) and at Or San Michele (see Figs. 4.40 and 4.41). Local references are equally important, however. The rounded, soft forms of Quercia's bodies refer to Etruscan terracotta sculpture most likely already available to Quercia from looted local tomb sites. The heavy, decorative drapery of the Virtues echoes the reliefs of the Liberal Arts formerly decorating the base of the Cappella di Piazza immediately across the

Campo from the *Fonte Gaia*. For a civic commission such references to indigenous history would naturally have been appropriate. Partly because of Quercia's ability to assimilate such divergent stylistic components into his work, his position in the history of art has been somewhat marginalized, despite the power of his sculpture and the obviously high reputation that he enjoyed in his own time.

The Baptismal Font

A decision by the Opera del Duomo in 1414 to construct a new baptismal font (Fig. 4.67) for Siena's Baptistry was not implemented until 1416, when the Sienese invited Lorenzo Ghiberti to visit the city as an advisor to the project and ultimately as its designer. Early in 1417 Ghiberti sent a trial relief to Siena, indicating that a full-scale sculptural model of the font already existed. The Opera had clearly been impressed with Ghiberti's project for the doors of the Florentine Baptistry, and, not to be outdone by Florence, they hired the same sculptor to decorate their own baptistry. The commission is a measure of the competition between the two cities, here being played out in artistic terms with art functioning as politics. In 1417—as if to maintain their pride in local artists—the Opera commissioned four bronze reliefs for the hexagonal font: two from Quercia and two from the workshop of a local

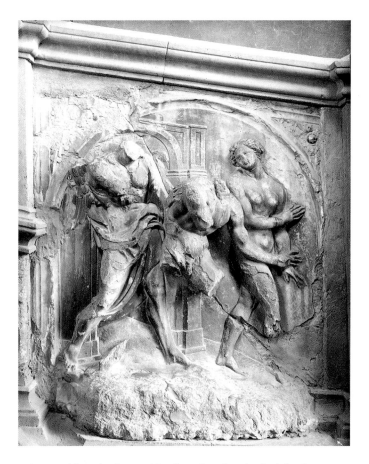

4.65 *Expulsion of Adam and Eve from Paradise*, detail of the *Fonte Gaia*, Ospedale della Scala, Siena

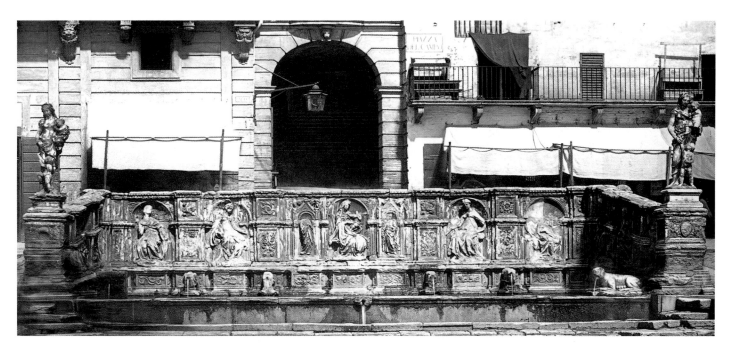

4.66 *Fonte Gaia*, 1408–19, commissioned by the Priors from JACOPO DELLA QUERCIA for the Piazza del Campo, Siena. Marble, center span 33′ 4″ wide (10.15 × 5.55m) (Ospedale della Scala, Siena)

The fountain was removed in 1858 and replaced by a modified replica made between 1858 and 1868 by Tito Sarocchi.

Sienese goldsmith, Giovanni di Turino (1384 Siena–c. 1455 Siena). Only then did they award Ghiberti his commission for the last two reliefs of the font. The Opera's motive, like that of the Florentine Opera in the commissions for the Evangelists for the façade of the Duomo (see pages 198–199), was to add a competitive charge between artists in the hope that the work would be completed promptly. Donatello entered the project in 1423, when he was awarded a commission for a relief assigned to Quercia. His presence in the project must have been intended as a provocation to Ghiberti who, like Quercia, had done virtually nothing on his reliefs for the font. By 1427 all six reliefs were in place, thanks to pressure and threats from the Opera and legal proceedings against Quercia for violating the terms of his contract, which had stipulated delivery of his reliefs within two years.

Ghiberti's *Baptism of Christ* (Fig. 4.69) for the font was the pivotal work between his quatrefoil reliefs for the Florence Baptistry's north doors (see Fig. 4.31) and his later square reliefs for its east doors, the *Gates of Paradise* (see Figs. 5.2–5.5). By the time that he had been awarded the commission for the second pair of doors, his reliefs for the Siena font had already provided him with a new compositional format for his pictorial relief sculpture. Ghiberti completely gilded his Siena reliefs, as he was later to do with those for the *Gates of Paradise*. But his *Baptism of Christ* suggests that Ghiberti had also looked carefully at the relief sculpture of Donatello, particularly the *schiacciato* carving exemplified by the latter's St. George relief at Or San Michele. Although Ghiberti's Christ figure is in high relief, the angels floating above his head disappear into the background as if into space.

Donatello's *Head of the Baptist Brought Before Herod* (Fig. 4.70) for the Siena font was one of his first bronze sculptures (roughly contemporaneous with his *St. Louis of Toulouse*; see Fig. 4.43). His relief is an investigation of the single-point perspective system recently invented by his friend Brunelleschi although the orthogonals cluster toward the empty center of the relief rather than meeting at a single focal point, as if to split the composition apart, leaving Herod and the severed head of the Baptist at the left and Salome at the right. In fact the man at the right with his hand on his hip illustrates the system of perspective that Alberti was to write about in his *Della Pittura* of 1435, one that, because of its simplicity, supplanted the empirical mathematical system of Brunelleschi. According to Alberti, an artist should use a figure standing on the ground line of the composition as the numerical module for the composition by dividing it into six units, each measuring a head in length. This measure derives from submitting observed human proportions to

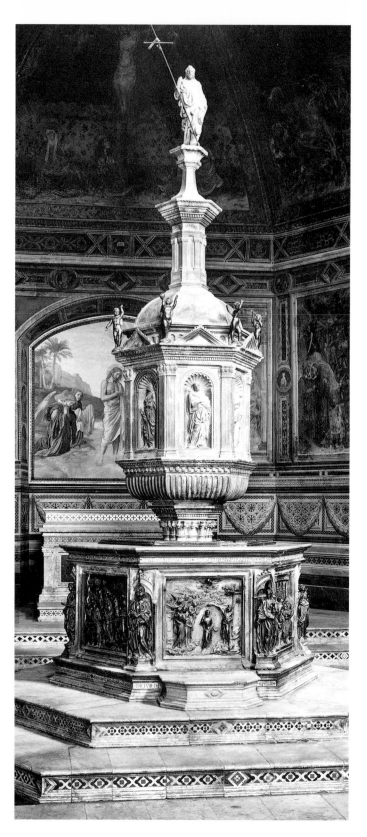

4.67 Baptismal font, basin 1416–27, commissioned by the Opera del Duomo and designed by LORENZO GHIBERTI, with reliefs by GHIBERTI, JACOPO DELLA QUERCIA, DONATELLO, and GIOVANNI DI TURINO, for the Baptistry, San Giovanni, Siena. Gilt bronze reliefs in a marble frame

The tabernacle, added to the font, was designed by Quercia and begun in 1427; work was complete by 1434. Donatello was also responsible for two of the Virtues at the corners of the font and for three of the musical angels at the cornice of the tabernacle.

Art and Popular Piety

Throughout the history of organized religion, preachers of extraordinary skill and charisma have from time to time emerged to capture the imagination and fervor of large audiences. The Franciscan friar San Bernardino of Siena (1380–1444), like St. Francis and St. Peter Martyr before him (see Fig. 3.20), drew large crowds who were captivated by his passionate calls for repentance. In many instances civic authorities or clergy would hire such preachers to deliver sequences of sermons during special liturgical seasons such as Lent. Thus townspeople had the opportunity to hear ideas recapitulated and developed over several days. Scribes often transcribed the sermons as they were delivered, giving modern historians texts that must closely approximate the sentiments and energies of the speaker, if not all of his actual words.

In Siena in 1427, Bernardino gave a number of sermons standing in a temporary pulpit which had been erected in front of the Palazzo Pubblico. In these sermons he preached not only moral reform but also civic peace. Sano di Pietro's small painting of one of these occasions (Fig. 4.68) shows a rich curtain draped across much of the lower façade of the town hall, before which are seated the priors of the city. Men and women kneel in devoted attention to Bernardino's words—and were chastised by the preacher when they failed to pay attention. The sexes are separated by a barrier

which extends from Bernardino's pulpit across the piazza (here called the Campo, or field) which forms the very heart of the city. The stone surfaces of the buildings must have carried the sound of Bernardino's voice to distant

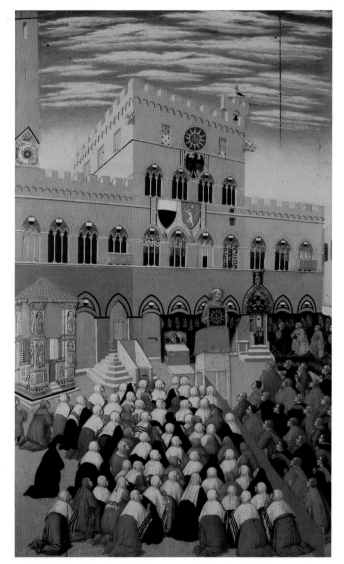

4.68 *St. Bernardino Preaching in the Campo*, 1445–47, probably commissioned by the Confraternity of the Virgin from SANO DI PIETRO. Tempera on panel, 63¾ × 40" (162 × 101.5 cm) (Chapterhouse, Siena Cathedral)

This may have been a side panel to a large triptych for the confraternity's assembly rooms located beneath the hospital of Santa Maria della Scala, opposite the cathedral.

members of his audience, just as they amplify sound today. Bernardino holds an emblem of a radiant sun surrounding the initials IHS, signifying Christ—one that he consistently used in his preaching, and which was copied in reduced amulet form for his devotees to carry away as a reminder of his exhortations to repentance. So persuasive were Bernardino's arguments in support of civic obedience that the grateful governors of the city agreed to place his symbol high on the façade of the Palazzo Pubblico, where it still remains. Despite Bernardino's popularity, however, street gangs—called Noise and Scratch—continued to exist in Siena and to threaten the civic concord which Ambrogio Lorenzetti had depicted in the Room of the Nine (see Fig. 2.25) in the town hall.

Bernardino's impact on popular piety in Siena was so great that he was canonized in 1450 by Pius II, another Sienese citizen. At the festivities honoring the event, numerous paintings of the saint were commissioned, and a lifesized figure of Bernardino accompanied by music-making angels was hoisted along the wall of the Palazzo Pubblico, from the ground to a representation of Paradise at the top of the building, as if Bernardino were floating into Heaven where God the Father waited to receive him. This tableau vivant was so successful that it was repeated with the image of St. Catherine when she was canonized in 1461.

an average and thus creating an ideal form. Two of these head units—a third the height of the body—then provide the measure of the divisions of the ground line of the composition (marked on Fig. 4.70) from which the artist can then extend orthogonals to a central vanishing point. Thus it appears that Alberti's treatise, written nearly a decade after Donatello designed his Siena relief, recorded well established studio practice.

In the highly emotional scene in which a severed head is brought on a platter to the birthday feast of Herod where food is shown on plates flanked by knives, each figure in the foreground reacts intensely to the horrific sight. Contrary to the focus that single-point perspective normally brings to a composition, Donatello has used it here to create a wedge separating the two figural groups in the foreground—the dance at the right and the result at the left—and to direct the viewer to a second perspective grid formed by the two left arches that frame in flashback fashion earlier moments of the narrative with the musician of the dance in the mid-ground and the head of the Baptist being carried to the feast in the background. Donatello both knew the conventional rules of the newly formulated single-point perspective and manipulated and inverted them to enhance the expressionistic aspects of the story. Critical here is that artificial perspective was controlled by human measure and that the figure in Donatello's work provided the measuring basis for con-

struction of illusionistic architecture framing the narrative. The Sienese Opera clearly benefited from the competition on the font reliefs, having provoked each of the artists into new investigations of style which were to influence their later careers.

In 1425, before Quercia had even finished the model for his relief for the font, he accepted a commission for a colossal project of decorating the main door of the church of San Petronio in Bologna (Fig. 4.71), a project that continued well into the sixteenth century (see also Fig. 12). The *Expulsion* (Fig. 4.72) derives from Quercia's own relief on the *Fonte Gaia* (see Fig. 4.65), but the figures have become more muscular and tense, as if to compensate for the greater distance between this work and a hypothetical viewer looking at the whole door. Here, as in other reliefs for the portal, the lingering lyricism of the Sienese style is transformed by the expressive animation and the heroically proportioned bodies of the figures. Quercia had breathed new life into the Sienese style, but he had done so outside the city of Siena. In his native city, instead, patrons continued to favor works that reminded them of the city's golden age, now nearly a century past. Proud of their local traditions and thus feeling no compulsion to replace the major monuments of earlier generations, the Sienese tied their independence to their own distinctive artistic language, leading to a remarkably static visual style during the course of the century.

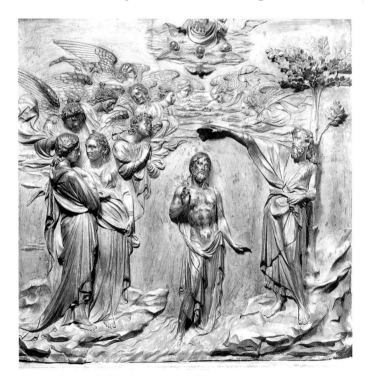

4.69 *Baptism of Christ*, detail of the baptismal font, c. 1423–27, LORENZO GHIBERTI, San Giovanni, Siena. Gilt bronze, 31 × 31" (79 × 79 cm)

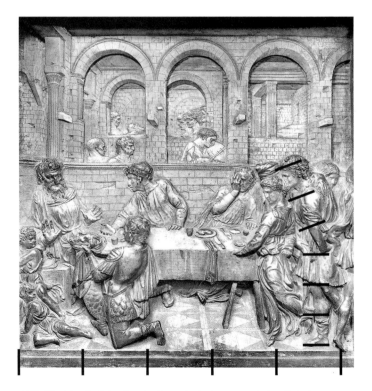

4.70 *The Head of the Baptist Brought Before Herod*, detail of the baptismal font, with perspective measures superimposed, 1423–27, DONATELLO, San Giovanni, Siena. Gilt bronze, 23½ × 23½" (60 × 60 cm)

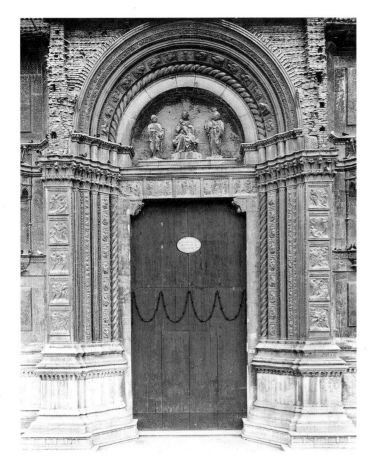

4.71 Main portal, 1425–39, commissioned by Louis Aleman, papal legate in Bologna and archbishop of Arles, from JACOPO DELLA QUERCIA for San Petronio, Bologna. Marble

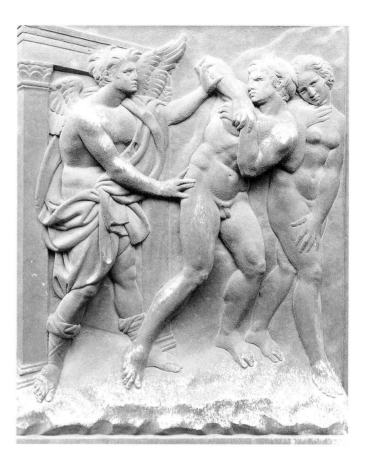

4.72 *Expulsion of Adam and Eve from Paradise*, detail of the main portal, mid-1430s, JACOPO DELLA QUERCIA, San Petronio, Bologna. Marble, height 39 × 36½" (99 × 92 cm)

Synopsis

Often the early fifteenth century is hailed as a moment of historic redefinition for the history of art. It is, but in a very different way than is usually suggested. Rather than marking the demise of the Gothic, neatly supplanted by the more "modern" mode of classical revival pioneered in Florence, the era was dominated by the International Gothic style. Embraced across the entire Italian peninsula, it was the first fully pan-Italian aesthetic since antiquity. True to its name, the International Style found proponents and enthusiasts from Milan and Venice in the north through Florence and Siena south to Naples, and linked all these centers to the visual culture of one another and the northern European courts. Whether adding Gothic crests and peaks to the façade of St. Mark's in Venice, enlivening Pope Martin V's imposing sculptural portrait in Milan Cathedral with billowing arabesques of drapery, providing lavish altarpieces and chapels for the wealthy Strozzi and Salimbeni families in Florence, or honoring King Ladislas in Naples with a sumptuous tomb, artists joined Gothic decorative forms to exquisite naturalism. As before, they adjusted their works to fit local traditions and specific typological and functional expectations, but these tasks were made easier by newly converging stylistic expectations. Florentine sculptors like Niccolò di Piero Lamberti and Andrea and Matteo Nofri found ready audiences for Florentine Gothic forms in Venice and Naples respectively; Michelino da Besozzo, from Milan, Pisanello, from Verona, and Gentile da Fabriano, from the Marches on Italy's east coast, were renowned throughout Italy.

Classical forms promoted in Florence at this time did set the course for the development of a subsequent, pan-Italian revival of antique classical style, only fully achieved a century later. However, in a peninsula of self-aware and individualistic city-states, Florentine exponents of classicism were more probably seeking to define their city as distinct from other cities rather than offering a visual language to join them together. Assimilation and adaptation of the possibilities of this new classical language took much of the rest of the century.

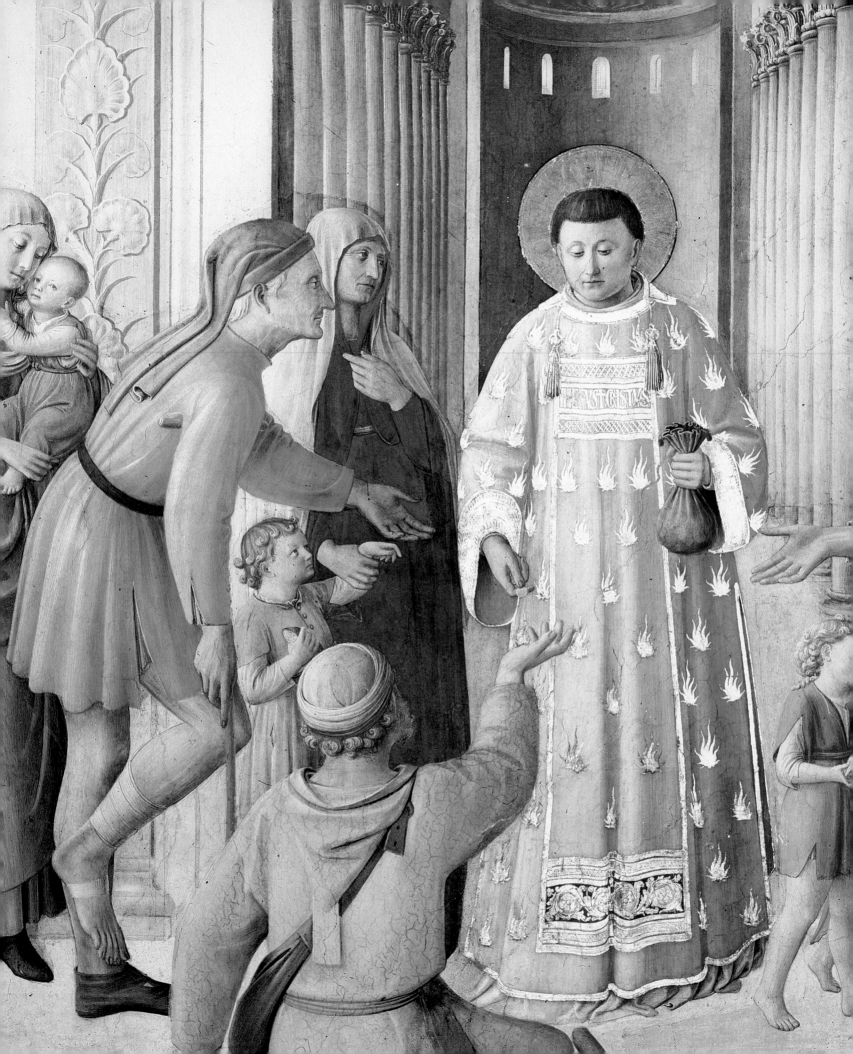

5
Elaborating Local and Classical Traditions: The Mid-Fifteenth Century

In the mid-fifteenth century there was a growing interest in antique artistic sources and the meanings of social and cultural predominance which many of them implied. Donatello created the first bronze nude since antiquity in Florence, and portrait sculpture in both Venice and Florence adopted the verism of Roman republican prototypes. Commissions for bronze equestrian monuments in Ferrara and Padua also reflected patrons' desires to emulate ancient prototypes, though the hero on horseback was already well known in contemporary rather than ancient garb from numerous fourteenth-century tomb monuments. This Roman world was vividly and vigorously resurrected in frescoes in Padua by the young Andrea Mantegna, perhaps the most single-minded exponent of a classical vocabulary in Italy during this time. In newly revived papal Rome, artists, conscious of the special history of the city, made reference to Early Christian models as well as ancient Roman ones.

The persistence of Gothic traditions is, however, equally evident in the popularity of chivalric themes throughout this period of revival and experimentation. In Florence Benozzo Gozzoli portrayed the Medici as part of the courtly train of the Three Magi. In Pienza Pope Pius II modeled the interior of his new cathedral on the Gothic hall churches he had seen in Austria. Doge Francesco Foscari's grand residence in Venice emulated the Doge's Palace, attesting to patrons' recognition of these Gothic buildings as key emblems of civic identity. This was not an era of stylistic purity but one of lively pluralism that showed respect for both the recent and the distant past.

Florence: Civic and Personal Commissions under the Medici

The Florentine republic and its civic and guild structures had initiated an extraordinary series of commissions during the early years of the fifteenth century, culminating in the completion of the dome of the cathedral in 1436. Factionalism, exacerbated by the dispute over the institution of the *catasto* in 1427, eventually erupted in 1433 and changed the structures of power within the city in ways that were to affect its remaining history. In that year the leaders of the oligarchy managed to win enough power in the government to exile the leading male members of the Medici family who were the apparent leaders of the *popolano* ("populist") faction. The acknowledged head of the Medici, Cosimo di Giovanni (see genealogical chart, p. 486) left Florence for Venice in October. The Medici were strong enough politically, however, to reverse the tables despite their absence from the city. In 1434 Cosimo returned triumphantly to Florence only to exile his opponents in turn as a first step to his eventual control of the political life of his city, control which was passed on to his son Piero and grandson Lorenzo. Among those banished from Florence were Palla Strozzi and Felice Brancacci, who had been the patrons of some of the more audacious artistic projects in the city just a few years before their exile (see Figs. 4.55 and 4.58). The decades after 1434 were a critical period in the history of Florentine art which helped to establish imagery—and new styles—for the changing power structures in the city, simultaneously maintaining traditional images of church and state to suggest continuity and stability, as if the republic had remained unchanged over time.

5.1 *St. Lawrence Receiving the Treasures of the Church* and *St. Lawrence Distributing Alms* (detail), 1448–c. 1455, commissioned by Nicholas V from FRA ANGELICO for the Chapel of St. Lawrence (now known as the Chapel of Nicholas V), Vatican Palace, Rome. Fresco. See also Fig. 5.36

The *Gates of Paradise*

In 1425, shortly after completing the second set of bronze doors for the Baptistry (see Fig. 4.31), Ghiberti received a commission from the Arte del Calimala for the third and final set (Fig. 5.5). At the time of the commission, Leonardo Bruni, the chancellor of the city of Florence (see Fig. 5.6), wrote to the Board of the Calimala: "It is my opinion that the twenty stories of the new doors . . . should mainly have two qualities: one, that they should show splendor, the other that they should have significance. By splendor I mean that they offer a feast to the eye through variety of design: significant I call those which are sufficiently important to be worthy of memory." Ghiberti certainly satisfied Bruni's demands.

Originally, these doors, like the two earlier sets, were intended to include twenty-eight panels; however, in the early stages of the commission the number was reduced to ten. They depict Old Testament stories, with statuettes of individual prophets and sibyls placed in the frames of each door. Instead of the quatrefoil frames used for his first doors, Ghiberti used a new square format for these reliefs, based on the ones he was then producing for the baptismal font in Siena (see Fig. 4.69). Ghiberti's second set of doors was completely gilded—like the Siena reliefs, but unlike the reliefs for his first doors in which only the raised surfaces were gilded.

It took Ghiberti twenty-seven years (1425–1452) to complete these doors. When they were finished, their extraordinary splendor won them pride of place on the east side of the Baptistry, facing the cathedral (see Fig. 1.9; his original doors for that site were moved to the north side). The space between the Florentine Baptistry and the cathedral was known in Italian as the *paradiso* because of its use as a cemetery during the late Middle Ages, giving Ghiberti's doors the name by which they are usually known, the *Gates of Paradise*.

Each panel of the *Gates of Paradise* depicts several episodes of a Biblical narrative (Fig. 5.2). In the panel depicting the story of the rival brothers Jacob and Esau, the latter's loss of his birthright through the deceit of Rebecca and Jacob is placed in the foreground, with Isaac's blessing of Jacob being positioned at the right of the composition. Esau appears both in the near foreground and in the far background, at right, as he goes off to hunt game for his father. The *schiacciato* relief deriving from Donatello's sculpture and the single-point perspective system allow the space to recede illusionistically, the figures becoming flatter as well as smaller as they move into the distance. The grouping of figures also helps to create a sense of space as the four women at the left pose dance-like in a circle and as Esau moves diagonally toward his father and into the space of the relief at the

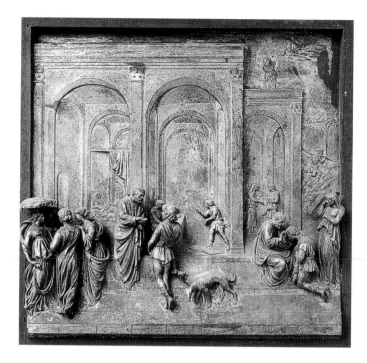

5.2 East doors, detail of *Isaac* panel. 31¼ × 31¼" (79 × 79 cm)

center. At the same time the figures of the woman at the left and of Rebecca at the right spill out over the frame, suggesting continuity between the space outside the frame and the space inside it.

In both the *Jacob and Esau* and the *Joseph* panels, located at the mid-point of the doors, the architecture is structured on a single-point perspective scheme. The perspectival plans of the two panels work together (Fig. 5.3) to unite both valves of the doors. Such a scheme places the viewer at a particular position in space toward which the faces of Ghiberti and his son, Vittorio, gaze from small roundels in the frame of the door between the two narrative panels. Thus Ghiberti structured the perspective system so that the viewer focuses both on the narrative and on its creator (whose name is also incised under the relief).

The subject matter of the *Meeting of Solomon and Sheba* at the bottom right of the doors (Fig. 5.4) is rarely depicted in this period, leading to speculation that it was included deliberately to represent the union of the Eastern and Western churches, which was announced on the steps of the Florence Duomo on July 9, 1439, as the fruition of a Church council which had met there. Virtually the entire Byzantine court, including the Emperor of Byzantium, John VIII Paleologus (see Fig. 4.24), had traveled from Constantinople to participate in this council. The Eastern Church is metaphorically represented by Sheba, the queen who came to Solomon "from the East," while the Western Church is represented by Solomon. The figures in the mid-ground, separated by parapets, align in formal, diagonal rows at either side of Solomon and Sheba, enhancing the sense of spatial recession. The figures in the foreground—perhaps representing those come to hear the reading of the decree of union—jostle for glimpses of the meeting. The doors ultimately were placed to face the steps of the Duomo where the decree of union had been read.

Although there are certain classicizing stylistic details evident in the east doors—some of the heads in the roundels of the frame, the nude figure of Samson in the niche in the right frame, the architecture in the central two panels—they are overshadowed by Ghiberti's continued fascination with elegant sweeps of drapery, repeating cascades of decorative folds, and gently swaying figures that stem from the late International Gothic style in which he had been trained. Thus the immediate favorable response to the doors when they were installed in 1452 suggests the continued viability of the late Gothic style over time. More than simply providing a stylistic cohesion with the two other doors of the Baptistry, their craftsmanship spoke of accomplishments approaching Brunelleschi's technical feats for the dome of the cathedral. Moreover, the brilliance of gold over virtually the entire surface of the doors was both a fitting introduction to the gilt dome of the interior of the Baptistry (see Fig. 1.10) and a public statement of the wealth and power of the Merchants' Guild that had commissioned them.

The Tomb of Leonardo Bruni

The new classicizing style was more wholeheartedly embraced in the Tomb of Leonardo Bruni (Fig. 5.6). Unlike earlier monuments to civic figures intended for or built in the Duomo, this tomb was placed in Santa Croce. This humanist scholar (1370–1444) had been chancellor of Florence from 1427 until his death. His tomb was presumably commissioned by the Signoria and is traditionally ascribed to Bernardo Rossellino (1407/10 Settignano–1464 Florence), the head of a family of stone carvers from one of the quarry towns in the hills outside Florence. The figure of the dead Bruni appears on his funerary bier, clutching to his chest his history of Florence, written as part of his duties as chancellor. He is crowned with a laurel wreath, a symbol of undying fame because the laurel leaf was reputed never to wither. During Bruni's funeral, in imitation of ancient Roman ceremonies, Gianozzo Manetti (1396–1459), one of Florence's leading humanists and political figures, had actually closed his oration by placing a crown of laurel on the head of the dead Bruni.

The carved effigy is a remarkable work of portraiture. Bruni's face, turned to catch the light coming from the

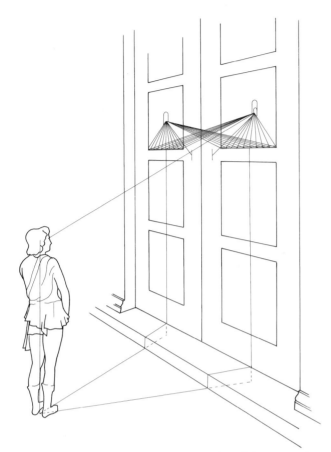

5.3 East doors, Baptistry, Florence, reconstruction of the perspective system, with a figure standing before them (after ALESSANDRO PARRONCHI)

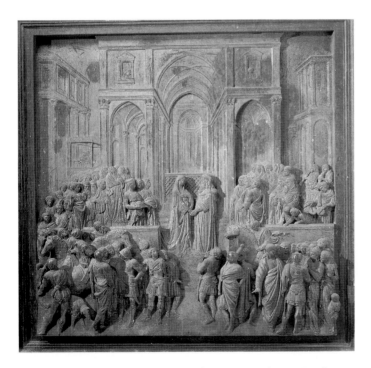

5.4 East doors, detail of *Solomon* panel. 31¼ × 31¼" (79 × 79 cm)

232

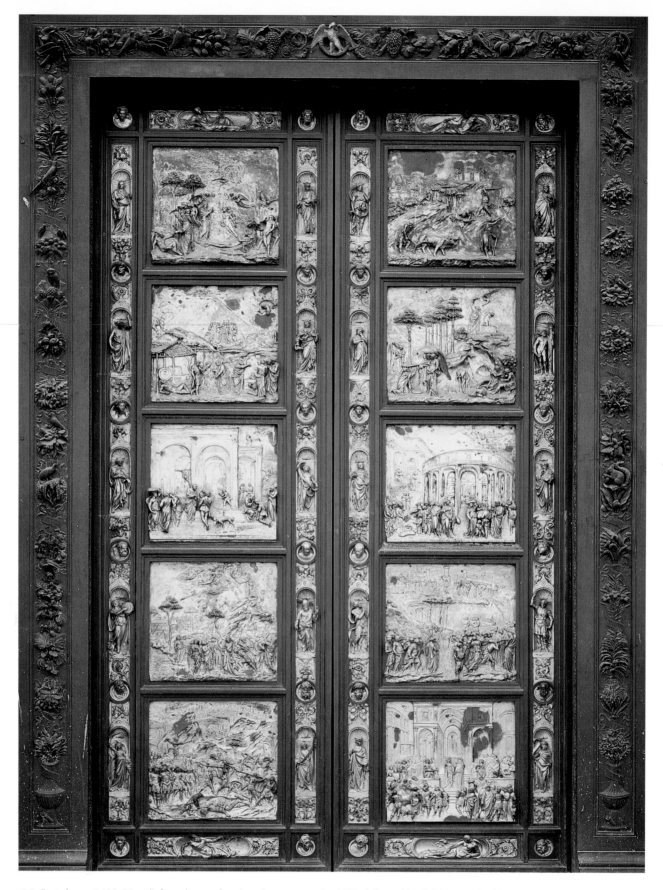

5.5 East doors, 1425–52, reliefs and some framing elements cast by 1436, followed by finishing and gilding, commissioned by the Arte del Calimala from LORENZO GHIBERTI for the Baptistry, Florence. Gilt bronze (Soprintendenza and Museo dell'Opera del Duomo, Florence)

A replica has now replaced the original doors on the Baptistry. This photograph was taken before the originals were removed for restoration. It is still unclear whether the doors will be completely reassembled after all of the panels have been cleaned or whether the component parts will be exhibited separately.

nave of the church, is uncannily lifelike, with its bulbous nose and slightly crooked mouth. The decorative elements of the tomb, however, are carefully chosen to eulogize Bruni, and by extension the state. The arch that frames the tomb evolves, in its profusion of rich classicizing detail, the splendor of ancient Rome. Two robust putti support a wreath enclosing a lion, the Florentine civic symbol of the *marzocco* (a heraldic lion whose name is believed to be a corruption of *Martocus*, "little Mars"—the Roman god of war). Other lions appear in the roundel below the sarcophagus and in its supports. The eagles supporting the bier recall the Roman symbol of a soul carried to the afterlife by an eagle. The only specifically Christian reference in the decorative program for the tomb is the roundel of the Virgin and Child under the arch. Nowhere on the tomb is Bruni's family name given; he is simply "Leonardus," deracinated as a symbol for the state whose history he holds in his hands.

In this case the overt classicism of the iconography and of the decorative forms must have been considered appropriate for the classical scholar and for the chancellor of a republic whose history extended back to ancient republican Rome. Like Uccello's *Hawkwood Monument* (see Fig. 4.48) of the previous decade, the classical vocabulary of Bruni's tomb called up important myths of the state.

The Medici

The rise to power of the Medici in Florence began in 1418 when Giovanni di Bicci de' Medici (c. 1360–1429) became the banker to the papacy and established the wealth of the family on a sure footing. Giovanni's son, Cosimo (1389–1464), steadily increased the control of his family over the political fortunes of Florence after his return from exile in 1434, leading eventually to their *de facto* rulership of the city until they were ousted in a revolt in 1494.

Cosimo and his heirs worked carefully to maintain control of the government through an elaborate political network supported by their wealth. They also sought to dismantle or dominate power bases in the city that were threats to their control. Ultimately the Medici brought the city under their influence, without, however, disturbing the appearances of the formal structures of government which had been in place for two centuries. In name Florence remained a republic, while in practice the Medici functioned rather like princes in their rule over it. The Medici surrounded themselves with visual images denoting rulership, although they steadfastly maintained that they were ordinary citizens within the republic. The differences between appearance and reality could not help but affect the art produced within the city.

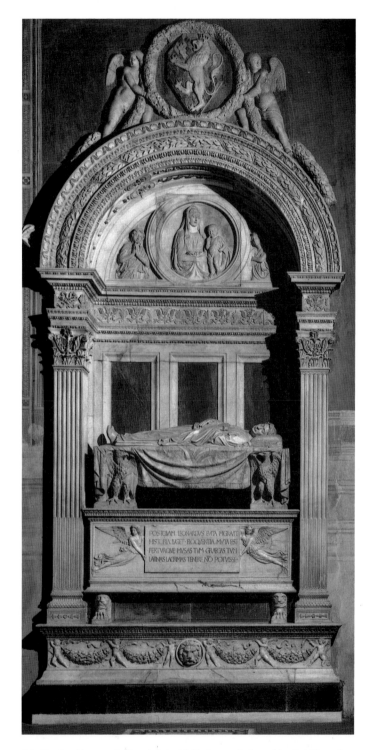

5.6 Tomb of Leonardo Bruni, late 1440s, commissioned by the Signoria (?), most likely with the assistance of Bruni's native city, Arezzo, and his family, from BERNARDO ROSSELLINO for Santa Croce, Florence. Marble, height 23′ 3½″ (7.15 m)

Bruni's epitaph, inscribed on the sarcophagus, reads: "After Leonardo departed from life, history is in mourning and eloquence is dumb, and it is said that the Muses, Greek and Latin alike, cannot restrain their tears."

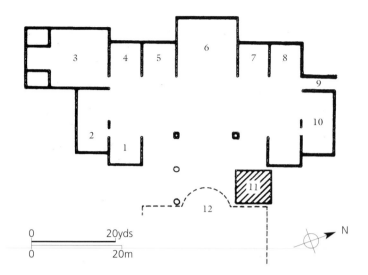

5.7 San Lorenzo, Florence, first plan of transept area (1418) showing chapel ownership and pre-existing Romanesque church

1 Martelli; **2** Medici; **3** Medici (Sacristy): **4** Neroni; **5** Rondinelli; **6** Medici after 1442 (Canons' choir); **7** della Stufa; **8** Ciai; **9** Ginori corridor; **10** Ginori; **11** Belltower;   **12** Romanesque church of San Lorenzo

San Lorenzo The beginnings of extensive Medici patronage of the arts are associated with Giovanni di Bicci de' Medici. Sometime around 1418 a group of citizens living in the neighborhood of the church of San Lorenzo decided to act together to rebuild their parish church. Led by Giovanni, each member of the group agreed to contribute funds for the construction of his family's chapel around the transept of the proposed new structure. Giovanni agreed to build the **sacristy** of the new building as a family burial site and also to build an adjacent double chapel at the end of the transept (Fig. 5.7). This gave the Medici patronage rights over a traditionally important part of the building—the sacristy—and also over much more space than any other family participating in the project.

The building already at the site was an eleventh-century Romanesque church, itself a replacement for an Early Christian basilica dedicated in 393 by no less a person than St. Ambrose, who had also consecrated Florence's first bishop. San Lorenzo, then, represented the entire Christian history of Florence—more so, even, than the Duomo, which had a later foundation. Awareness of that history is critical for any understanding of the evolution of San Lorenzo as a site of patronage throughout the Renaissance.

Brunelleschi's plans for San Lorenzo are somewhat unclear, since he died before the nave of the building was begun. But the transept, the chapels around the transept, and sacristy are his and are instructive for what they tell of the layers of meaning embedded in Renaissance architecture. For example, the rectangular chapels and main altar area extending from the transept derive from the plans of mendicant churches in Florence and elsewhere (see Fig. 1.24). The essentially basilical plan of the building is certainly not unusual, but the arrangement of arches springing continuously along the nave from one column capital to the next (Fig. 5.8) and the uninterrupted wall

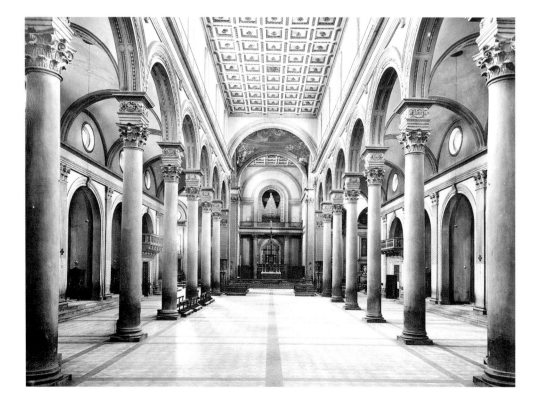

5.8 San Lorenzo, Florence, 1418–c. 1466, original project commissioned by Giovanni di Bicci de' Medici and others from FILIPPO BRUNELLESCHI; nave built by Cosimo de' Medici after 1442, modifying original plan

between the arches and the row of clerestory windows recall major Early Christian buildings in Rome such as St. Paul's Outside the Walls. Brunelleschi's original plan for the building apparently called for side walls unbroken by chapel spaces, another feature that would have made the plan similar to Early Christian basilicas. The juxtaposition of cool white stucco in the spandrels and other flat surfaces with the warm slate coloring of the *pietra serena* arches and pilasters may derive from the black and white exterior decoration of Romanesque architecture in Florence, such as the Baptistry, which was later used for the Duomo as well (see Fig. 1.9).

The two-color scheme also helps to clarify the building's modular structure. Among the structural elements moving the viewer through the space is a narrow **cornice** projecting from the wall above the nave arcade, which moves unbroken from the entrance wall of the building to the transept, giving a strong longitudinal pull while at the same time unifying the space of the nave. A band of white stucco separates the cornice from a thin **string-course** that lies over the arches. These horizontal elements separate the clerestory from the arcade and lift the weight of the clerestory visually from the lower part of the building, giving it a lightness and buoyancy augmented by the light flooding in through the clerestory windows. The arches of the nave arcade spring from impost blocks, which creates the impression that they are floating above the columns that actually support them, and thus have a longitudinal momentum of their own. Brunelleschi's decorative forms—capitals, mouldings—are pure classical revivals; like the Early Christian references, they may reflect the time he spent in Rome after 1404 measuring and drawing ancient buildings. Rather than being mere architectural quotation, however, these references tie San Lorenzo stylistically to its earliest history.

Work that had begun so earnestly on the transept of San Lorenzo in 1418 had all but ceased by the time of Giovanni di Bicci's death in 1429. In 1442 Cosimo declared that he would himself pay for the construction of the new building. In doing so he assumed property rights over the main altar area and he stipulated that no family crest other than that of the Medici appear in the church. Cosimo's assumption of the building costs effectively transformed San Lorenzo into a Medici structure, despite the presence of families who maintained control of the chapels along the transept. Insofar as the building marks the site of the first Christian church in Florence, dedicated in 393, Cosimo also symbolically appropriated the entire religious history of the city for his family; the princely overtones of this act recall royal foundations such as St. Denis, outside Paris, or the Visconti patronage of the Certosa of Pavia. In a city that called itself a republic, this form of patronage must have seemed extraordinary.

The Old Sacristy The sacristy of San Lorenzo built for Giovanni de' Medici (now called the Old Sacristy; Fig. 5.9) was designed as a family mausoleum as well as a sacristy. It contains the tombs of Giovanni and his wife, Piccarda de' Bueri, who are buried beneath the dome. The centralized plan of the Old Sacristy relates it to the Baptistry in Padua (see Fig. 3.44), where its patrons, Francesco I da Carrara and Fina Buzzacarini, were buried. The exterior of the lantern of the Old Sacristy has a curious spiraling decoration which refers to the structure built over the tomb of Christ in Jerusalem; thus it provides a symbol of resurrection and suggests the hopes of the Medici for their afterlife.

Even the architectural details of the sacristy contribute to the theme of resurrection. The architectural **membering** in the chapel (non-load-bearing since it is applied to a stone rubble construction) suggests structure, but at each place where weight and gravity might be evident Brunelleschi manipulated the forms to create lightness and a vertical drive. The *pietra serena* ring from which the dome springs does not touch the main arches of the room, a thin margin of white stucco allowing it to float free. The bases of these arches are separated from the pilasters in the corners of the room—theoretically their supports—by a protuding heavy cornice. The cornice is itself split by a series of roundels with painted stucco reliefs of cherubim, again alleviating mass and lifting the upper part of the room from the lower. The effect throughout the room is one of light and lightness.

Although the Old Sacristy was substantially complete at the time of Giovanni di Bicci's death in 1429, it owes most of its subsequent decoration to his sons Cosimo and Lorenzo (not to be confused with Lorenzo the Magnificent, Cosimo's grandson). The activity of the two brothers in the Old Sacristy reveals important new patterns of patronage. Donatello's roundel depicting the *Apotheosis of St. John* (Fig. 5.10), one of four placed in the pendentives of the Sacristy, shows how crucial the function and shape of a space is to the form of a design placed within it. The complex perspective system seems a deliberate confusion of Brunelleschi's single-point perspective system since there is more than one vanishing point suggested by the receding background orthogonals. However, since the relief is placed on a surface curving over the head of the viewer, the orthogonals of the foremost building point to the roundels of the Evangelists on the adjacent walls. The vertical edges of the buildings in the *Apotheosis* are not quite plumb, but angle slightly toward a center line which, when projected from the curving pendentive into space, directs attention to the lantern, whose resurrection symbolism Brunelleschi had made explicit by its curious spiraling shape. The classically inspired sarcophagus of Giovanni de' Medici and his wife, Piccarda,

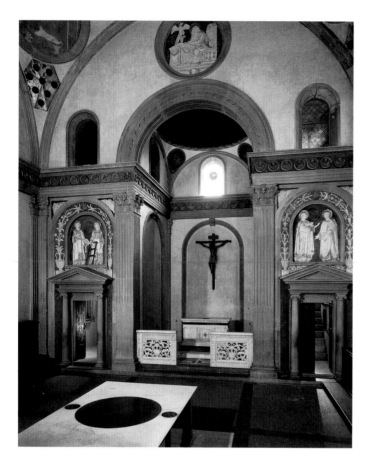

5.9 Old Sacristy, San Lorenzo, Florence (after restoration), c. 1418–28, commissioned by Giovanni di Bicci de' Medici from FILIPPO BRUNELLESCHI. Central square room c. 37' 9" × 37' 9" (11.5 × 11.5 m)

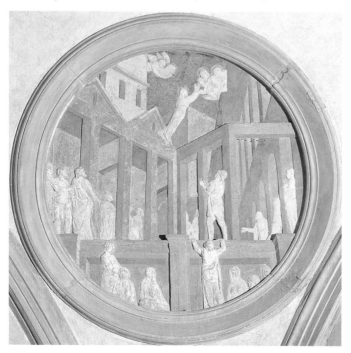

5.10 *Apotheosis of St. John* (after restoration), before 1433, probably commissioned by Cosimo and Lorenzo de' Medici from DONATELLO for the Old Sacristy, San Lorenzo, Florence. Painted stucco, diameter 7' 6" (2.15 m)

lies directly below the lantern, emphasizing the patrons' hopes for eternal life. The inscription on it names both Cosimo and his brother Lorenzo as its commissioners (see genealogical chart, page 486), jointly discharging their filial responsibilities. In a social system in which the oldest son became the head of the family upon the death of the father, this manifestation of equality speaks quietly but eloquently about the unity of the Medici family and deflects attention from Cosimo's leadership role just at the time when he was also beginning his consolidation of political power in the city.

The brothers' presence in the sacristy is also marked by other visual signs. Large stucco reliefs over small doors on either side of the altar wall present dramatically posed standing figures of saints Lawrence and Stephen on the left (Fig. 5.11) and saints Cosmas and Damian on the right. These figures could simply be titular saints—Lawrence (Lorenzo), for the church in which they appear and Cosmas and Damian, the doctors (*medici*), for the family that had built the Old Sacristy. These saints, however, are also the patron saints of Lorenzo and Cosimo, who probably commissioned these reliefs after their father's death, the sons appearing in the guise of their

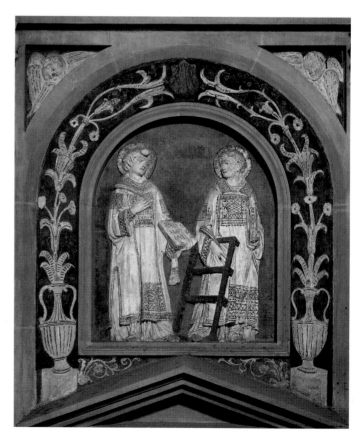

5.11 *St. Lawrence and St. Stephen* (after restoration), between 1434 and 1443 (?), commissioned by Cosimo and Lorenzo de' Medici from DONATELLO for the Old Sacristy, San Lorenzo, Florence. Painted stucco, 7' 6" × 5' 11" (2.15 × 1.8 m)

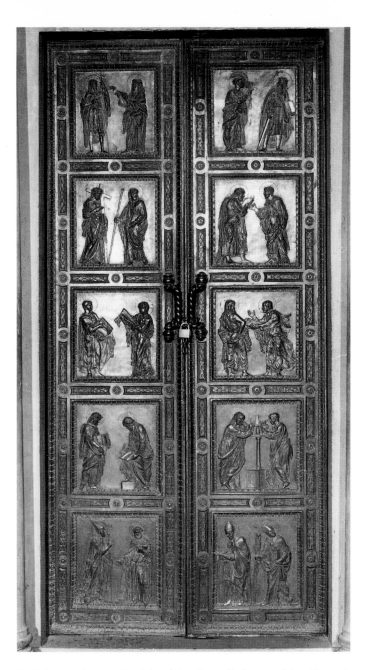

5.12 Bronze doors to the right of the altar with figures of Apostles and the Doctors of the Church, between 1434 and 1443, commissioned by Cosimo and Lorenzo de' Medici from DONATELLO for the Old Sacristy, San Lorenzo, Florence. Bronze, 92½ × 43" (235 × 109 cm)

patron saints just as Giovanni does in the roundel of St. John the Evangelist above the altar arch.

Beneath each of these reliefs is a set of bronze doors, each containing ten panels with paired standing and gesticulating figures. The one on the right (Fig. 5.12) under Cosmas and Damian has figures of Saints John the Baptist and John the Evangelist at the top left and Saints Peter and Paul at the top right. St. John the Evangelist could refer to Giovanni di Bicci and the chapel's dedication or to Cosimo's son, also named Giovanni. John the Baptist unmistakably alludes to the patron saint of Florence and marks the first time that the Medici had joined their own iconography with that of the city. St. Peter refers to Cosimo's other son, Piero, and the paired

Peter and Paul to the papacy, an appropriate reference for the papacy's bankers and for a family that had been a strong supporter of Pope Eugenius IV, then resident in Florence. But what ultimately appears is a dynastic line from Giovanni, high in the altar arch, to Cosimo on the stucco relief, to Piero and Giovanni on the bronze doors (see Fig. 5.9). Nowhere in previous Florentine art are dynastic lines so graphically articulated.

The choice of bronze for the two doors was itself a daring gesture. Bronze had previously been reserved for important civic commissions, notably the Baptistry doors. The Medici thus appropriated a medium that, in itself, gives this space a civic resonance. Although all of these references appear in a sacristy, a site traditionally used to enhance a powerful family's status and mark their devotion and hopes for the afterlife, the Medici subtly seem to have invested their sacristy with extra dimensions of civic and dynastic power.

But the initial plans for San Lorenzo and the sacristy should be seen as something more than a neighborhood and family project. It was just at the time that Giovanni di Bicci had agreed to build the sacristy with Brunelleschi as his architect that Onofrio Strozzi (died 1418) and his son Palla were engaged in building the sacristy at SS. Trinità with Ghiberti as his architect. Familial and political rivalries were joined with artistic rivalries. The Medici and the Strozzi were members of opposing political factions in the city. Although in 1418 the Strozzi were considerably wealthier than the Medici, the Old Sacristy was considerably larger and more insistently classicizing than the Strozzi commission. The sheer scale of the Medici architectural project at San Lorenzo gave the family an architectural prominence in the city far surpassing the Strozzi. This insistence on public generosity was part of the strategy of Giovanni de' Medici's son Cosimo at this same time. Cosimo acted as one of four operai for the commission of Ghiberti's *St. Matthew* for the Bankers' Guild at Or San Michele; a forced assessment of guild members in 1420 indicates that Medici contributions were significantly more generous than those of the Strozzi. Even in a commission contracted by a guild, family and personal rivalries played important roles. The different styles used by the two families for their commissions thus underscore the use of style as a signal of different factions in the social order.

San Marco   Cosimo's activities at San Lorenzo were not his only endeavors at church-building. When the Dominican Order took charge of the dilapidated monastery of San Marco in 1436, Cosimo hired Michelozzo di Bartolommeo (1396 Florence–1472 Florence) to rebuild it. Cosimo also added a library (which he then helped to fill with books), a cloister, a

C O N T E M P O R A R Y   V O I C E

A Job Application

This letter from the painter Domenico Veneziano to Piero di Cosimo de' Medici illustrates the groveling expected of artists (until quite recent times) when addressing important patrons. Amid all the flattery, however, the writer tries earnestly to convey his superiority to other candidates—or at least their unsuitability because of existing commitments. However, Domenico's plea went unheeded: the commission for the *San Marco Altarpiece* (see Fig. 5.13) went to Fra Angelico.

To the honorable and generous man Piero di Cosimo de' Medici of Florence, . . . in Ferrara.

Honorable and generous Sir. After the due salutations. I inform you that by God's grace I am well, and I wish to see you well and happy. Many many times I have asked about you, . . . and having first learned where you were, I would have written you for my comfort and duty. Considering that my low condition does not deserve to write to your nobility, only the perfect and good love I have for you and all your people gives me the daring to write, considering how duty-bound I am to do so.

Just now I have heard that Cosimo [de' Medici, Piero's father] has decided to have an altarpiece made, in other words painted, and wants a magnificent work, which pleases me very much. And it would please me more if through your generosity I could paint it. And if that happens, I am in hopes with God's help to do marvelous things, although there are good masters like Fra Filippo [Lippi] and Fra Giovanni [Angelico] who have much work to do. Fra Filippo in particular has a panel going to Santo Spirito which he won't finish in five years working day and night, it's so big. But however that may be, my great good will to serve you makes me presume to offer myself. And in case I should do less well than anyone at all, I wish to be obligated to any merited punishment, and to provide any test sample needed, doing honor to everyone. And if the work were so large that Cosimo decided to give it to several masters, or else more to one than to another, I beg you as far as a servant may beg a master that you may be pleased to enlist your strength favorably and helpfully to me in arranging that I have some little part of it . . . and I promise you my work will bring you honor. . . .

By your most faithful servant Domenico da Venezia painter, commending himself to you, in Perugia, 1438, first of April.

(from Creighton E. Gilbert. *Italian Art 1400–1500*. New York: Prentice-Hall, 1980, p. 5)

chapter room, a bell tower, a bronze bell, and church furnishings, including an imposing altarpiece by Fra Angelico (Guido di Piero; c. 1395 Vicchio–1455 Rome) for the main altar.

The *San Marco Altarpiece* (Fig. 5.13) was badly abraded through faulty restoration in the nineteenth century, yet it is still remarkable for what it says of Fra Angelico's work and of his patron's wishes. In some sense the image is profoundly traditional, with a centrally placed group of the Virgin and Child flanked by angels and saints. This may befit the work of a painter who was a Dominican monk living at San Marco, where he also painted devotional images in the cells of the cloister in which the monks lived. Yet the setting of the *San Marco Altarpiece* has an arrestingly open, spacious quality. The architectural throne, with its shell niche framing the Virgin and Child, is large and decorated with classical garlands and Corinthian pilasters. Space expands not only into the distance, but also behind and around the figures. A single-point perspective defined by the lines in the carpet both establishes a deep spatial stage for the figures and focuses on the hand of the Virgin, tellingly placed in front of her womb, as if to emphasize the Incarnation of Christ and her maternity, a central concern in Dominican theology. The inscription from the Dominican Little Office on the hem of the Virgin's garment emphasizes this tenet: ". . . like a vine I caused loveliness to bud, and my blossoms became glorious and abundant fruit." The background landscape, framed by patterned draperies, is remarkably naturalistic in its depiction of trees, of the sea meeting the land, and of the sunlit sky. It too relates to a holy text; in the Old Testament book of Ecclesiasticus, Wisdom says, "I have grown tall as a cedar on Lebanon, as a cypress on Mount Hermon; I have grown tall as a palm in Engedi, as the rose bushes of Jericho; as a fine olive in the plain, as a plane tree I have grown tall" (24:13–15). The illusionistic draperies, tied to the frame at the upper left and right, refer to contemporary altarpieces, which were actually covered by cloth, drawn open only on festival days. Here, by contrast, the mood would always be jubilant, a stage set for the adoration of the Child whose redemption of the world is symbolized by the crucifix on the small tabernacle door that interrupts the composition at the bottom.

The draperies of the kneeling figures, with their thick folds and weightiness, suggest that Fra Angelico, for all the tranquility of his images, had looked carefully at the more dramatic painting of Masaccio. Such features as the hanging cloth behind the figures and the expressive modeling of the faces also suggest that he had studied the work of Gentile da Fabriano. His simplified oval faces also indicate that he was familiar with Sienese painting—especially with the work of Sassetta (1392 Cortona–1450 Siena), with whom he had shared a commission at the Dominican monastery in Cortona in 1438.

Although there are obvious differences in spatial organization and figural structure between Fra Angelico's *San Marco Altarpiece* and Gentile's *Adoration of the Magi* (see Fig. 4.55) painted for Palla Strozzi, the Medici altarpiece has a sense of opulence no less finely calibrated than the Strozzi. Rich gold-embellished draperies hang not only at the left and right of the composition but behind the Virgin and Child as well. Gold is used generously in the haloes of the figures, as it was originally in the borders and surfaces of many of the robes worn by them. The luxuriousness of the arboreal landscape is matched by the richness of the patterning on the cloth separating it from the figures and of that on the carpet.

It is worth noting, however, that instead of choosing the courtly subject matter of the Magi, Cosimo ordered a traditional *sacra conversazione* for his altarpiece. The sobriety of the figures is appropriate for their Dominican location, yet their poses give them the gravity of Roman statesmen, unlike the lively, elegant figures in the *Strozzi Altarpiece*. Cosimo and Fra Angelico seem deliberately to have employed a visual language that could be seen as an alternative to that used by the leading member of the oligarchy—and yet at the same time to have incorporated some of the signs of wealth and social prestige that characterize the Strozzi commission.

As in the decoration for the Old Sacristy (see Figs. 5.10, 5.11, and 5.12) there is a dynastic "subtext" in the imagery in the *San Marco Altarpiece*. Its patron, Cosimo de' Medici, appears in the guise of St. Cosmas kneeling in the traditional position of the donor in the left foreground of the painting. John the Evangelist, standing second from the left, probably represents Giovanni di Bicci, Cosimo's father; and St. Lawrence, at the far left with his grill leaning against his right leg, Cosimo's brother, Lorenzo, who died in 1440, shortly before the painting was completed. The red balls on a gold ground of the Medici family crest appear along the border of the rug at the bottom of the altarpiece. The red and white floral garlands hanging at the top of the painting, although most likely referring to Ecclesiasticus, also represent the heraldic colors of the city of Florence, uniting Medici and civic imagery once again.

Thus, just before taking control of the main altar of San Lorenzo in 1442, Cosimo also visually appropriated the high altar of San Marco, just a short distance away from his home, further enhancing his presence in the city. Medici patronage, also marked by the appearance of their crest on the exterior of the monastic buildings attached to this church, served as a public reminder of the family's power as well as their generosity.

The Medici Palace When, about 1445, Cosimo de' Medici began to build his palace (Figs. 5.14 and 5.15) on the Via Larga (now the Via Cavour), he had apparently already hired and dismissed Brunelleschi as its architect, supposedly because Brunelleschi had provided a model for too grand a structure. Yet the palace that Cosimo built was more splendid than any in the city, leading to recent speculation that Brunelleschi's project placed the palace opposite the church of San Lorenzo rather than on its current site. Such a configuration of church and palace, given Cosimo's take-over of San Lorenzo, would have referenced to a well-known architectural iconography of authority most typically seen in juxtapositions of bishops' palaces and cathedrals, a message that would have been too blatant for Cosimo, who maintained that he was merely an ordinary citizen of the republic, despite his *de facto* control over the state.

Cosimo replaced Brunelleschi with Michelozzo, who had begun his career as a founder in the Florentine mint before becoming one of Ghiberti's many assistants and, in 1423, a partner in Donatello's workshop. He may have appealed to Cosimo because he could work in Brunelleschi's manner, but was more malleable than the senior architect. The palace he designed for Cosimo is striking in its use of extremely heavy rusticated masonry on the ground story, which gives the building a fortress-like aspect—softened in the increasingly refined treatment of surface on the stories above. The rustication of the lower story is typical of Florentine palazzi of the fourteenth and early fifteenth centuries, a conservative element suggesting Cosimo's adherence to tradition and his equality with other citizens who had built similar, if smaller, palaces. Yet the extreme heaviness of the rustication and the double lancet windows of the upper stories can be found only at the Palazzo della Signoria (see Fig. 1.18), thus linking the Medici architecturally with the city's main site of sovereignty. None of this vocabulary is classical in form, although some have seen the unrelieved rustication as an echo of the massive wall around the back of the Forum of Augustus in Rome, thus lending further suggestions of rulership to the Medici inhabitants.

Deviating from normal building practice in Florence, Cosimo built his palace from the foundations up, having destroyed whatever pre-existing structures were on the site. A more common practice was for owners to acquire adjacent properties, which they then enveloped with a thin facing of stone; this presented a unified façade to the street while the interior spaces maintained some of the haphazard arrangements of the original buildings. A renovation and restructuring of family properties begun by

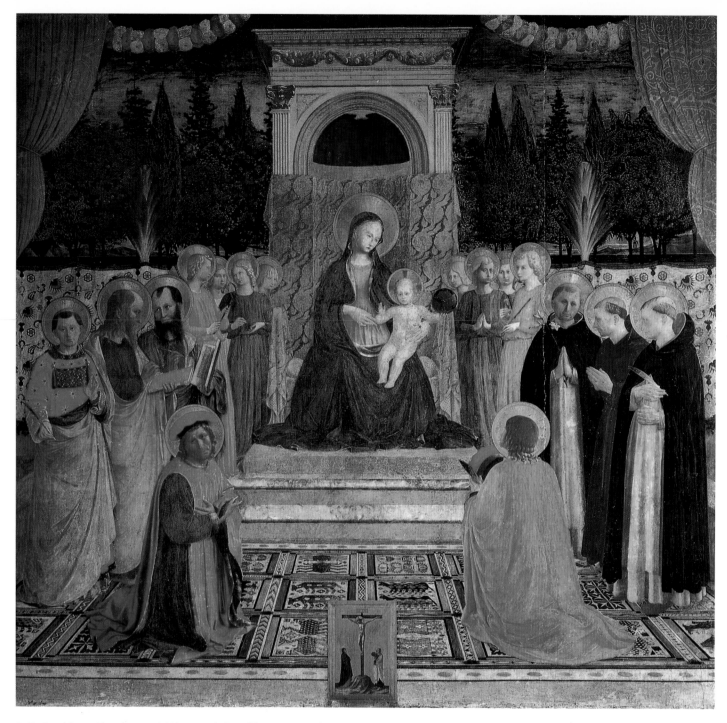

5.13 *San Marco Altarpiece*, c. 1440, commissioned by Cosimo and Lorenzo de' Medici from FRA ANGELICO for the high altar of San Marco, Florence. Tempera on panel, 7' 2⅜" × 7' 5⅜" (2.2 × 2.27 m) (Museo San Marco, Florence)

The painting was badly damaged in an early restoration, leaving its surface stripped.

Giovanni Rucellai (see Fig. 34) just shortly after work began on the Medici Palace demonstrates both the innovative and the traditional aspects of the latter. The masonry blocks of the Palazzo Rucellai form a veneer over the surfaces of a row of buildings; this façade ends raggedly at the right in anticipation of the purchase of another property. Each story is separated into bays by pilasters, with a different order of capital used at each level—a hierarchy also used on the Colosseum in Rome. Thick cornices decorated with classicizing ornament divide the stories. The uniformity of the Rucellai façade also disguises the commercial function of the ground floor implied by rustication by removing the differentiation of surface treatment between the stories so carefully maintained in the Medici Palace. Both palazzi, however, like their predecessors in Florence, present a block-like solidity on the street that suggests the unity of the family living behind the façade and declares their presence in the city. Such families, of course, normally included at least two generations of males, with their wives, children, and servants.

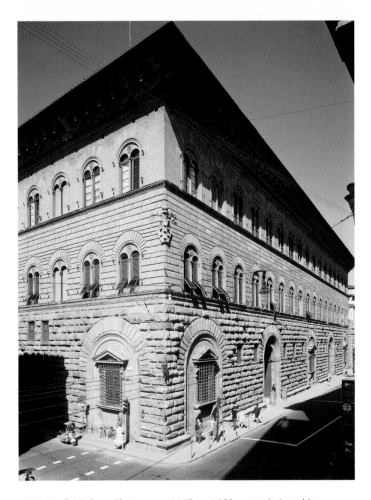

5.14 Medici Palace, Florence, c. 1445–c. 1460, commissioned by Cosimo de' Medici from MICHELOZZO

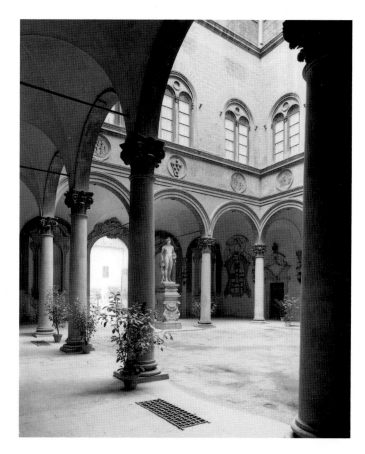

5.15 Medici Palace, Florence, courtyard

The central courtyard of the Medici Palace (see Fig. 5.15) is strikingly different from the exterior of the building. Here the novelty of the building becomes obvious in the refined classical detailing of the arcade which completely surrounds the courtyard, and in the sculpted roundels suggesting ancient Roman gems that decorate the frieze above the arcade. Whether Cosimo and Michelozzo drew on local sources for this courtyard or on courtyards that they would have seen in northern Italy during Cosimo's exile in 1433–34, the size, the uniform order, and the allusions to classical forms were new to Florentine architecture.

Portrait Busts   Cosimo was the patron for the architecture of the Medici Palace, but his son Piero apparently took responsibility for the lavish decoration of its rooms. One of Piero's earliest commissions marks his inventiveness. He employed Mino da Fiesole (1429 Papiano–1484 Florence), who may have trained under Michelozzo and thus within the influence of Donatello, to carve marble portrait busts of himself (Fig. 5.16) and his brother Giovanni. Piero's portrait is a vivid portrayal of the actual features of the man combined with a stoic vitality in his firmly set features and turning head. It was fairly common practice at this time to make life masks or death

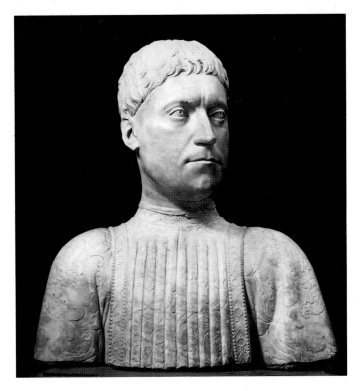

5.16 *Piero de' Medici*, 1453, commissioned by Piero de' Medici from MINO DA FIESOLE. Marble, height 21½" (55 cm) (Museo Nazionale del Bargello, Florence)

masks of important people from wax or plaster of Paris; but Piero's bust, finished in 1453, marks the first example in marble to recall antique Roman portraits, a model appropriate for a citizen of a republic. Somewhat earlier medals of rulers (see Fig. 4.25), also modeled on Roman sources, may also have influenced Piero's commission. The vertical borders of his clothing are carved with Piero's personal crest of a diamond ring with a ribbon woven through it bearing the word SEMPER (Latin for "always"). The message of Medici permanence rings loud and clear to anyone who might have thought that Medici power in republican Florence was a passing aberration.

Donatello's Bronze *David* and *Judith and Holofernes*
Donatello's bronze *David* (Fig. 5.17) is one of the best-known of the Medici commissions and yet one of the most perplexing. It is first recorded in 1469 in a description of the wedding festivities of Piero's son, Lorenzo, and Clarice Orsini. The slightly smaller than life-sized statue then stood on a column in the courtyard of the Medici Palace, although the figure may well have been made for another site. The sleekly sensual depiction of the adolescent David, who stands in a languid pose, his left foot carelessly resting on Goliath's severed head, is remarkable for its naturalism. Donatello departed from tradition by presenting David nude, in the manner of a classical hero. Yet despite references to antique column statues and to the antique gems carved on Goliath's helmet, the treatment of the body does not recall the idealized male nudes of antiquity. This is a slim, pre-pubescent boy, not a powerful man. The unusual representation of the *David* suggests it conveyed more than the usual meanings attached to this subject.

Piero and Donatello were, of course, aware that Donatello's earlier marble statue of David (see Fig. 4.34) stood in the Palazzo della Signoria, placed in front of a wall which was painted blue and decorated with gold fleurs-de-lys, one of the symbols of Florence. David had become a metaphor for the city, strong in protecting its freedoms from external threat. Piero's placement of the *David* in the private context of the palace thus appropriated civic imagery for the Medici. Contemporary awareness of this strategy of appropriation can be found in two later events. In 1476 Lorenzo and Giuliano de' Medici sold to the Signoria a traditionally clothed bronze David by Andrea del Verrocchio (1435 Florence–1488 Venice), also in the Medici collections, for placement in the Palazzo della Signoria, thus parting with the less problematic of their two Davids. In 1495, after the expulsion of the Medici from the city, the Signoria transported Donatello's *David* to the courtyard of the Palazzo della Signoria, a new inscription making explicit recognition of the state iconography carried by the statue.

Some modern historians have challenged the identity of the figure as David, proposing Mercury instead. Depictions of Mercury from the fifteenth century show the god with a particular hat called a petasus, similar to that worn by the *David*. A viewer's position beneath the statue would have made the decapitated head barely visible and its identity as Goliath or Argo hard to ascertain.

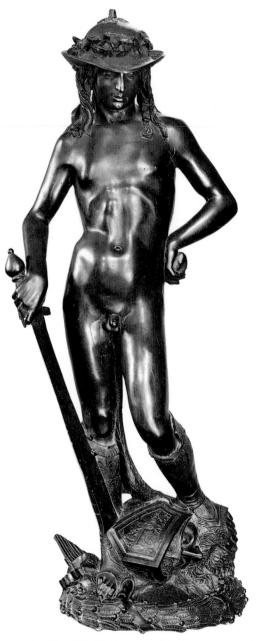

5.17 *David*, 1460s (?) (dates from the late 1420s to the early 1460s have been proposed for the figure), commissioned most likely by Piero de' Medici from DONATELLO. Bronze, height 5' 2¼" (1.58 m) (Museo Nazionale del Bargello, Florence)

Recent discussion of the statue suggests that the head of Goliath is a self-portrait of the artist. An inscription, now known from manuscript sources, was in the fifteenth century on the base of the *David*: "The victor is whoever defends the fatherland. God crushes the wrath of an enormous foe. Behold! A boy overcame a great tyrant. Conquer, o citizens!"

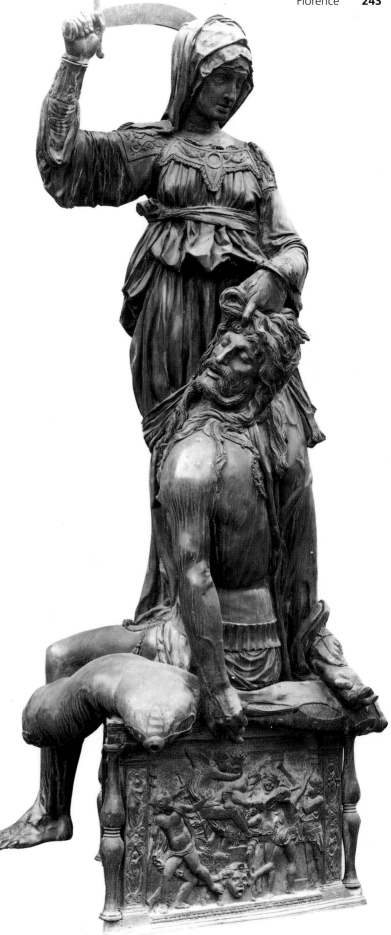

5.18 *Judith and Holofernes*, late 1450s (?), commissioned most likely by Piero de' Medici from DONATELLO for the garden of the Medici Palace. Bronze with traces of gilding, figure group height 7' 9" (2.36 m) (Palazzo della Signoria, Florence)

A second inscription on the original column supporting the sculpture read: "Kingdoms fall through luxury, cities rise through virtues; behold the neck of pride severed by the hand of humility." When the statue was moved to the Palazzo della Signoria in December 1495 a new inscription was placed at the top of its new base: "The citizens placed this example of public health [here in] 1495."

Interpretation of the statue as a Mercury would allow the Medici to avoid the charge of appropriation of public imagery for private use, Mercury being the patron god of merchants as well as of the arts (see Fig. 1), and thus an appropriate symbol for the family. In fact, the statue did not have to read *either* as David *or* as Mercury, but could have been read as *both*.

The placement of the *David* in the Medici Palace court-yard resonates with the marriage festivities of 1469. For the wedding feast the women were seated in the second floor of the palace, looking down into the courtyard—just as Michal, David's wife, looked from her balcony at her husband. This then would have transformed the *David* into Lorenzo, a youthful hero growing into a wise ruler, just as the young king in the palace chapel frescoes evokes Lorenzo's role as courtier in the 1459 civic procession honoring the Pope and Galeazzo Sforza. The multiple meanings evoked by the *David* typify the complex interweaving of personal and public imagery in Medici commissions.

Paired with the *David* in Medici imagery was Donatello's bronze statue of *Judith and Holofernes* (Fig. 5.18). As a woman who saved the Jewish nation from foreign domination by slaying the Assyrian general Holofernes, Judith is obviously a counterpart of David. In that respect she is also a civic icon. Intended as a fountain sculpture in a small garden within the palace complex, the statue is an early example of sculpture meant to be seen in the round, with no single viewpoint fixed for the observer. Judith's heavy garments contrast with the near nakedness and overtly sensual fleshiness of Holofernes. Judith's foot is placed squarely on Holofernes's groin as her hand rises for the second time to strike at his already partially severed head. As part of a fountain, the statue would have had water trickling from spouts in the faces of the triangular base on which the figures are placed—a startling addition of a gurgling sound to the already grisly scene. The sculpture could be interpreted simply as virtue overcoming vice; however, a political meaning is clearly implied by the inscription that Piero originally placed on the group: "Piero, son of Cosimo, has dedicated the statue of this woman to that liberty and fortitude bestowed on the republic by the invincible and constant spirit of the citizens."

244

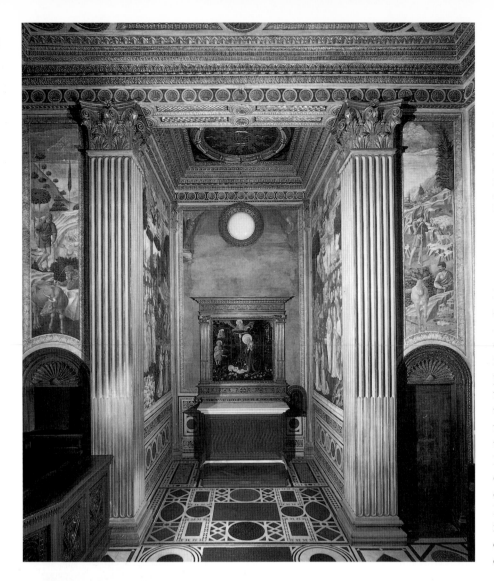

5.19 Medici Chapel, Medici Palace, Florence, c. 1459, frescoes commissioned by Piero de' Medici from BENOZZO GOZZOLI

The original altarpiece for the chapel was an *Adoration of the Christ Child* by Filippo Lippi (now at the Staatliche Museen Preussischer Kulturbesitz, Berlin); a copy by the Pseudo Pier Francesco Fiorentino replaces the original.

Decoration of the Medici Palace The small chapel of the Medici Palace (Fig. 5.19) is strikingly ornate. The elaborately coffered and gilded ceiling and the richly inlaid marble floor centered around a porphyry disk form a suitably grand setting for the spectacular frescoes on the walls. Beginning on the right wall of the chapel and moving clockwise around the room are frescoes by a pupil of Fra Angelico, Benozzo Gozzoli (Benozzo di Lese; c. 1420 Florence–1497 Pistoia) depicting the procession of the Magi to Bethlehem. With one king and his retinue occupying each wall, the procession directs the viewer to the altarpiece, which depicts the Adoration of the Christ Child.

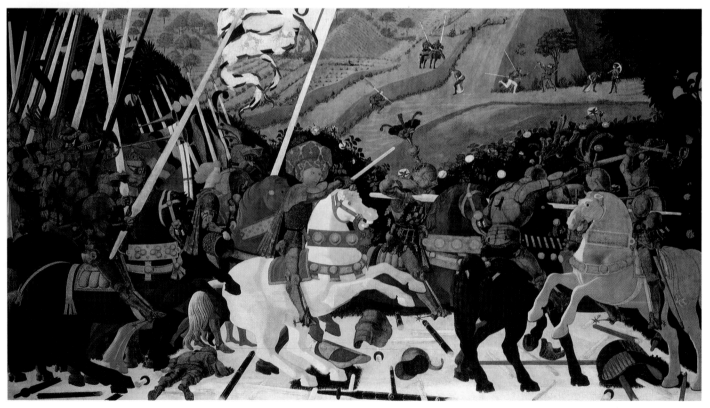

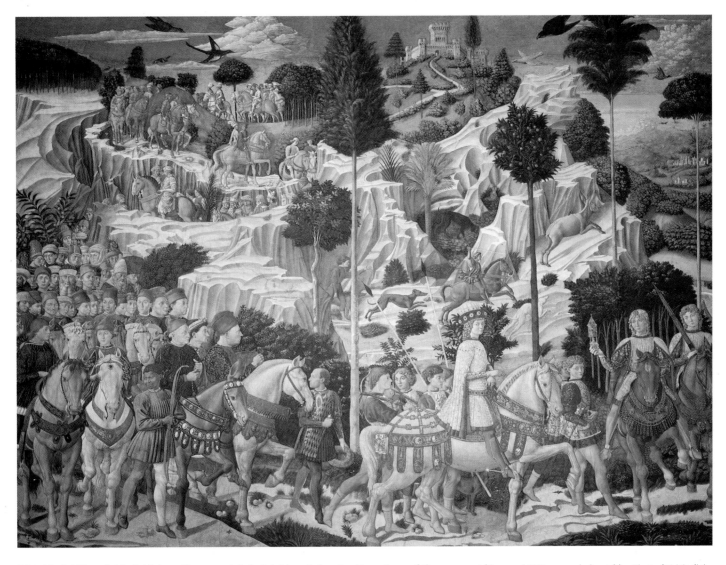

5.21 Medici Chapel, Medici Palace, Florence, detail of right wall showing the retinue of the youngest king, c. 1459, commissioned by Piero de' Medici from BENOZZO GOZZOLI. Fresco

The artist appears in the third row at the left in a red hat looking directly out toward the viewer.

The wall with the youngest king (Fig. 5.21) is particularly lavish in its treatment of costume, recalling the treatment of the same subject (see Fig. 4.55) commissioned by Palla Strozzi. Piero seems to have appropriated both the subject matter and the style of the earlier painting, as if to supplant the exiled Palla Strozzi by assuming the very pictorial vocabulary that had characterized his commission.

5.20 (opposite) *The Battle of San Romano*, 1430s (?), by PAOLO UCCELLO. Oil on panel, 6' × 10' 7" (1.83 × 3.23 m) (National Gallery, London)

New archival discoveries indicate that Lorenzo purchased the Uccello paintings from another owner. Whatever the meanings of the paintings may have been for the previous owner, it is nevertheless clear that they were intended as part of an overall decorative ensemble in Lorenzo's living quarters.

The two mounted figures behind the young king are Piero de' Medici, on the white horse, and Piero's father, Cosimo, on the donkey. Piero's son, Lorenzo, appears in the second row at the left in three-quarter view, wearing a red hat, his ski-jump nose a clear mark of his identity. Although there is considerable dispute over the identity of the young king, he probably represents a second idealized ten-year-old Lorenzo (1449–92), Piero's first son, who, in luxurious costume, had ridden the lead horse during an elaborate public ceremony staged by Piero in 1459 to honor Pope Pius II and Galeazzo Maria Sforza of Milan, both then visiting Florence. This role as one of the Magi would have been appropriate for Lorenzo, since he had been baptized on January 6, 1449, the feast of the Magi. Moreover the men of the Medici family belonged to the Company of the Magi, a confraternity that processed through the city each year on that feast day, from the monastery church of San Marco, where relics of the Magi were kept, past the Medici Palace, to the Baptistry. Thus this fresco in the private chapel of the Medici, where Cosimo sometimes greeted visiting dignitaries, gave a noticeably royal cast to the family while at the same time celebrating their civic generosity and religious devotion.

Other rooms in the palace conveyed equally complex messages. Inventories of the period indicate that a room marked as Lorenzo's was decorated with three large paintings by Paolo Uccello showing the battle of San Romano (1432). The victorious general, Niccolò da Tolentino, appears in one of them (Fig. 5.20) with a banner carrying his device of a knot floating above his head. Uccello's paintings of this battle have a curiously frozen, doll-like quality. The geometrically simplified humans and animals and the carefully arranged angles of the fallen lances indicate the painter's reputed obsessive interest in the new science of perspective. Behind the figures at the left of the panel shown are trees bearing bright oranges, a fruit known during this time as *mala medica*, or "medicinal apple." Since the Medici name means "doctors," it was natural for them to choose this fruit as their symbol.

In addition to their charm these battle scenes are important because such subject matter was at that time depicted in the palaces of princes (see Fig. 4.26) and on the walls of town halls (see Fig. 2.37) to commemorate state military victories. Thus Lorenzo's room seems to have conflated not only citizen and prince but also private room and public council chamber, giving the family a visual language of rule.

An even more obvious appropriation of civic imagery can be seen in a small table bronze of *Hercules and Anteus* (Fig. 5.22) made for the Medici by Antonio del Pollaiuolo (Antonio di Jacopo Benci; c. 1432 Florence–1498 Rome), who produced paintings, metalwork, embroidery designs, and engravings. Hercules had been represented on the state seal of Florence since the end of the thirteenth century. Pollaiuolo's sculpture depicts the defeat of Anteus, achieved by lifting him off the ground, since Anteus derived his strength from his mother, Earth (Ge). Every muscle in the contorted bodies of the men is tense, emphasizing the ferocity of their struggle although not indicating that Pollaiuolo had actually made anatomical studies, as some have claimed. The detailed modeling of the bronze, polished to a high luster, fragments reflected light in a manner that further heightens the tension. The statuette is a technical tour de force. The centrifugal motion of Anteus's legs and both antagonists' arched backs enlivens the space around the figures. In medium as well as subject matter, such bronze statuettes, imitative of antique examples, mark an innovation in Florentine

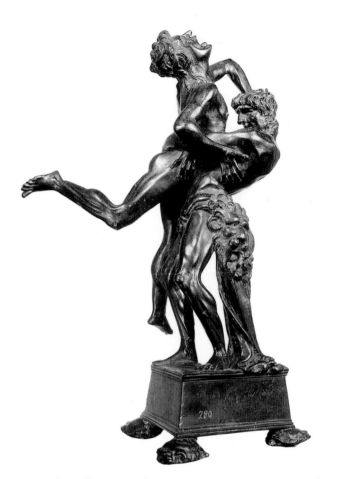

5.22 *Hercules and Anteus*, early 1470s (?), commissioned by the Medici from ANTONIO DEL POLLAIUOLO. Bronze, height 17¾" (45 cm) (Museo Nazionale del Bargello, Florence)

sculpture and the extension of a classical vocabulary into the domestic interior.

Cosimo and Donatello's Late Work Although Piero had taken charge of most Medici painting and sculpture commissions by the mid-century, his father, Cosimo, was, according to Vasari, responsible for one last, critically important commission, that for the reliefs now on two bronze pulpits in San Lorenzo (Figs. 5.23 and 5.24). The original commission for the reliefs modeled and cast by Donatello and his assistants is still unclear, since they were not completed at the time of Donatello's death in 1466 and were not incorporated into pulpits until 1515. Suggestions that they were begun as reliefs for a tomb for Cosimo, which would have been placed in the choir of San Lorenzo, or for the high altar are compelling, but as yet unsubstantiated. Their delayed placement in the church resulted in their having minimal impact on near-contemporary sculpture.

The reliefs on the south pulpit (Fig. 5.23) narrate the Passion and Crucifixion of Christ, while those on the north pulpit (Fig. 5.24) contain scenes of the

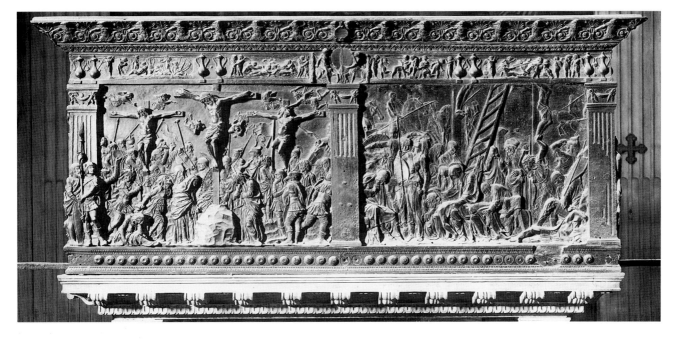

5.23 South pulpit, c. 1460–66 (placed on present column supports between 1558 and 1564; completed with reliefs by later sculptors), commissioned by Cosimo de' Medici from DONATELLO for San Lorenzo, Florence. Bronze, 48 × 145″ (123 × 292 cm)

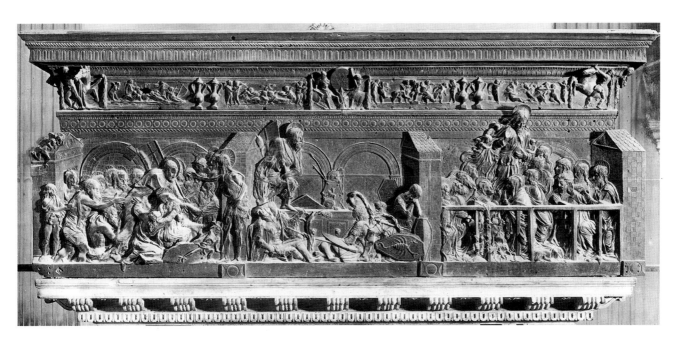

5.24 North pulpit, c. 1460–66 (placed on present column supports between 1558 and 1564; completed with reliefs by later sculptors), commissioned by Cosimo de' Medici from DONATELLO for San Lorenzo, Florence. Bronze, 54 × 110½″ (137 × 280 cm)

Harrowing of Hell, the Resurrection, the Ascension, and the Martyrdom of St. Lawrence. The reliefs for both pulpits are extraordinary in their expressionistic, occasionally violent, portrayal of these events. The action is compressed into a compacted space; the figures writhe and lunge. Drapery details and physical features seem gouged into the bronze, as if Donatello were deliberately rejecting the heavy volumes characteristic of his early work. The compositions of some reliefs are abruptly cut at the edges, leaving figures sliced in half, as if the image continued beyond the frame. Donatello also placed figures in front of the pilasters separating the reliefs of the south pulpit so that they blur the boundaries between what is outside and what is inside the frame. In these reliefs Donatello has taken the expressionistic aspects of his earlier reliefs for the baptismal font in Siena (see Fig. 4.70) and for the high altar of the Santo in Padua (see Fig. 5.58) to increased intensity. These convulsive images provided a startling contrast to the detached calmness of contemporary altarpieces and fresco cycles.

Painting at Mid-Century

Given the enormous wealth of the Medici and the Strozzi, their patronage was inevitably on a grander scale than that of other prominent Florentine families. The work of Filippo Lippi (c. 1406 Florence–1469 Spoleto), whose workshop was one of the most active and notable ones in Florence during these years, does, however, suggest the character of work commissioned by these other families.

Filippo's earliest dated work is known as the *Tarquinia Madonna* (Fig. 5.25) because of its location in the town of that name. Presumably painted as a private devotional image for the Florentine archbishop Giovanni Vitelleschi, who was born in the town, the painting demonstrates the range of stylistic possibilities available to an artist working in the 1430s in central Italy. Filippo's early training may have occurred in the workshops of the church of Santa Maria del Carmine in Florence, since he had joined the Carmelite order in 1421, shortly before Masaccio and Masolino painted the Brancacci Chapel (see Fig. 4.58). A payment in 1434 for an unspecified painting produced during a stay in Padua, where he apparently was acquainted with the local painter Squarcione, indicates that he was already an established painter by that time. The Virgin of the *Tarquinia Madonna* demonstrates Filippo's assimilation of the massive sculptural forms of Masaccio's painting; the realistically lively Christ Child shows the influence of Donatello's sculpture, especially his *cantoria* (see Fig. 4.50) for the Duomo, then being carved. The smoothly ovoid shape of the Virgin's head suggests that Filippo had also looked carefully at contemporary Sienese painting by artists such as Sassetta during his stay in that city as sub-prior of the Carmelite order there in 1428–29. The steeply tipped perspective of the framing architecture and the meticulous details of jewelry and embroidery, with their glistening spots of reflected light, implies that he also had models of Flemish painting in mind—not surprising, given the vigor of Florentine commerce with Flanders.

Filippo's larger-scale work shows the same fusion of solid figures with refined elegance. The *Coronation of the Virgin* (Fig. 5.26), commissioned for the high altar of Sant'Ambrogio in Florence by Francesco Maringhi, the prior of the church, shows a celestial coronation with a group of saints in the frontal plane of the composition

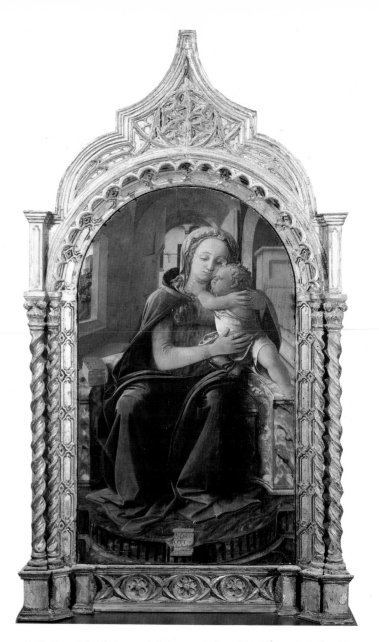

5.25 *Tarquinia Madonna*, 1437, commissioned by Giovanni Vitelleschi from FILIPPO LIPPI. Tempera on panel, 45 × 25½" (114 × 65 cm) (Palazzo Barberini, Galleria Nazionale, Rome)

and the patron kneeling in reverence at the lower right. St. Ambrose, the patron saint of the church, is standing at the left; St. John the Baptist, the patron saint of Florence, is standing in front of Maringhi in the right foreground. Rather than employing the squared frame used by Fra Angelico for the *San Marco Altarpiece* (see Fig. 5.13), Filippo ordered his composition in a traditional manner, with arches separating the coronation itself from the accompanying angels and saints. Even the figural grouping of the angels is conventional, as they line up row upon row in a manner not far removed from Simone Martini's *Maestà* (see Fig. 2.23), painted a century earlier or Lorenzo Monaco's *Coronation of the Virgin* (see Fig. 4.54). Every surface in the painting, whether architectural or figural, is manipulated for decorative purposes. Elaborate costumes, intricate folds of material, and animated poses make this one of the most extraordinary

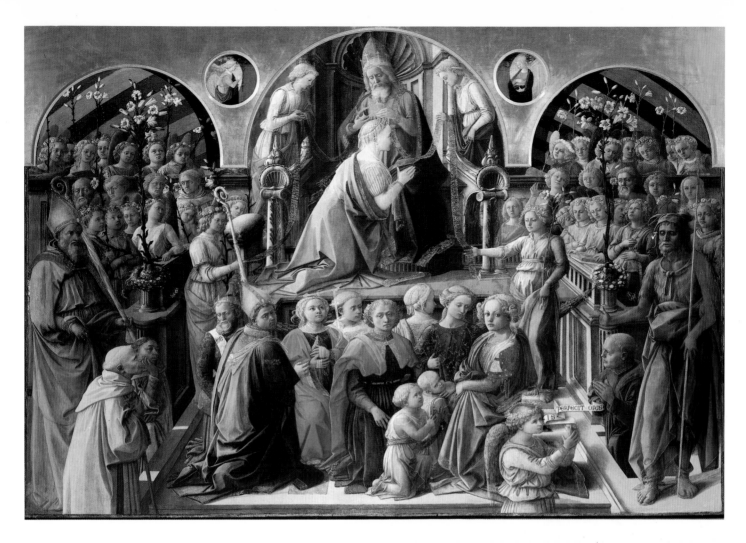

5.26 *Coronation of the Virgin*, 1447, commissioned by Francesco Maringhi from FILIPPO LIPPI for the main altar of Sant'Ambrogio, Florence. Tempera on panel, 6′ 7″ × 9′ 5″ (2 × 2.87 m) (Galleria degli Uffizi, Florence)

Florentine altarpieces of the mid-century. Most notable, perhaps, is the profusion of gold over the surface (much of which has since disappeared). Thick gold buttons, gold threaded through fabric, and gold stippling and gold dust in the haloes and the surfaces of the costumes give the painting an opulence comparable to that of the Strozzi *Adoration of the Magi* (see Fig. 4.55), but with a textured quality not achievable with gold leaf.

A contemporary of Filippo Lippi's whose work also appealed to Florentine patrons was Domenico Veneziano (c. 1405 Venice?–1461 Florence). He was apparently born in or near Venice, as his nickname indicates, but received his training in Rome and Florence. His *St. Lucy Altarpiece* (Fig. 5.27) was painted for the high altar of the small church of Santa Lucia dei Magnoli to replace a painting of 1332 by Pietro Lorenzetti. The presence of Florence's two patron saints, John the Baptist and Zenobius, suggests that the patron of the altarpiece wished to be seen as a supporter of the city's traditions.

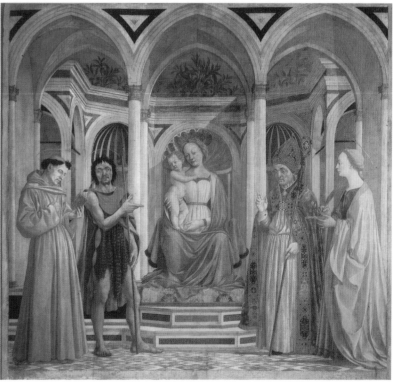

5.27 *St. Lucy Altarpiece*, c. 1445–47, DOMENICO VENEZIANO, originally on the main altar of Santa Lucia dei Magnoli, Florence. Tempera on panel, 6′ 6″ × 6′ 9½″ (1.98 × 2.07 m) (Galleria degli Uffizi, Florence)

The *St. Lucy Altarpiece* bears some similarities to the work of Filippo Lippi in the simplification of the physical features of the women, in the fascination with jeweled and embroidered detail in the cope and miter of St. Zenobius at the right, and in the general volumetric massing of drapery forms. Yet the whole mathematically controlled environment of this picture seems suffused with a white light quite different from Filippo's darker interiors. Art historians have tended to see Domenico's coloration as a reflection of his Venetian background, yet there is little in Venice to which it can be compared. A far more likely source is the painting of Fra Angelico, then arguably the leading painter in Florence.

Narrative Frescoes   The conservative nature of narrative frescoes in mid-fifteenth-century Florence is exemplified by a cycle painted by Andrea del Castagno (c. 1419 Castagno–1457 Florence) for the cloistered Benedictine nuns of Sant'Apollonia (Fig. 5.28). Despite the idiosyncratic expressions and gestures of the individual figures—Castagno first won attention for his evidently compelling portrayals of hanged men painted on the exterior walls of

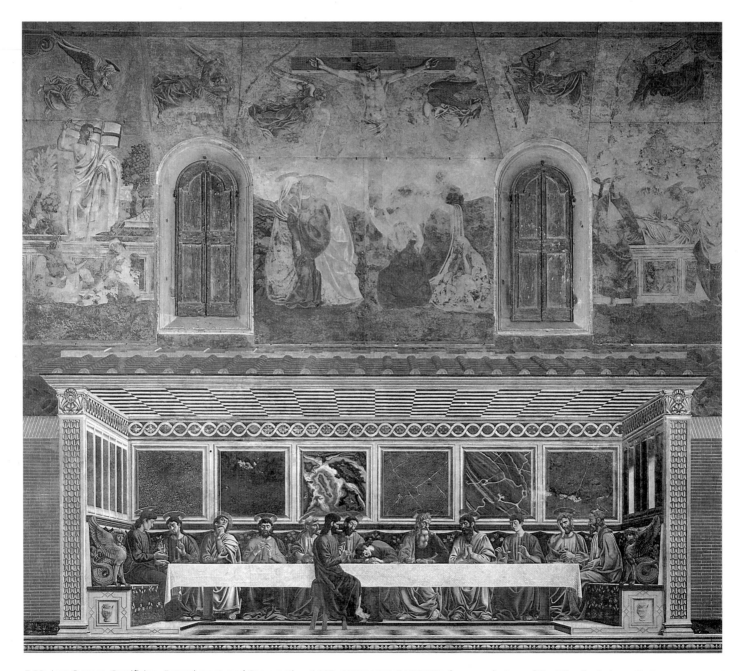

5.28 *Last Supper, Crucifixion, Entombment*, and *Resurrection*, 1447, ANDREA DEL CASTAGNO, former refectory of Sant'Apollonia (now Castagno Museum, Florence). Fresco, 30' 2¼" × 31' 6" (9.2 × 9.6 m)

the Bargello which provoked his nickname, Little Andrea of the Hanged Men—the *Last Supper* has a static quality reminiscent of the fresco of the same subject by Taddeo Gaddi (see Fig. 2.14) in the refectory of Santa Croce from a century earlier. The space is more deeply rendered and more insistent in its perspective organization, but the scene, like Gaddi's, comes forward illusionistically from the wall, as if on a constructed stage. The frescoes of the *Crucifixion* above are somewhat more dramatic in the agitated movements of the figures, the naturalism of the nude crucified Christ, and the sharp contrasts of light and shadow. Here too, however, the figures are pushed forward to the front of the composition, with the distant landscape either hidden by the figures or schematically rendered in order to concentrate the viewer's attention on the event. Although the nuns of this community came from some of the city's most prominent families and could thus commission (either themselves or through the generosity of their families) one of Florence's best-known painters, the commission is one that reinforces established traditions, the better to inspire piety and devotion.

Given the radical changes in Florentine political structures beginning with Cosimo de' Medici's return from exile in 1434, it is hardly surprising that Florentine art of the 1430s and 1440s is so varied in its forms. It is not only that artists such as Domenico Veneziano came to Florence from other cities or that Florentine artists spent time abroad (Ghiberti in Venice, 1425, Uccello in Venice, 1425–c. 1430, Filippo Lippi in Padua, 1434, Castagno in Venice, 1442–43, Donatello in Rome, 1432–33, and in Padua, 1443–53), or that patrons commissioned and collected paintings from the new generation of Flemish artists such as Jan van Eyck (c. 1389–1441) and Rogier van der Weyden (1400–64) which influenced the remarkably fluid styles of mid-fifteenth-century Florentine painting. New alignments within the political fabric of the city during these years demanded new visual expressions for families seeking to find their place within the changing social structures of Medicean Florence. An extended period of peace and increased wealth gave patrons new opportunities for embellishing their environments and for fashioning a social aristocracy in imitation of the example set by the Medici. It is no accident that while the artistic projects of the first part of the century included many corporate and civic commissions, those of the middle years of the century were predominantly private.

Santa Maria Novella Façade

Despite the dominating presence of the Medici family in Florentine architectural projects during the early and middle years of the century, other families also initiated important building programs. Members of the Pazzi family built the chapter house for the monks at Santa Croce (known as the Pazzi Chapel and left unfinished after the downfall of the family in 1478; now no longer thought to be by Brunelleschi); Folco Portinari built the hospital of Santa Maria Nuova (see Fig. 4.51); the Pazzi and the Spinelli built large and important palaces. But perhaps the most notable of the patrons was Giovanni Rucellai, known best for four impressive architectural projects: the façade of his palace (see Fig. 34) which, despite its incomplete surface, began a radically new ordering of the traditional Florentine palace with antique cornices and a rising complexity of capitals from the ground story to the roof line—like its repeated arches reminiscent of the Colosseum in Rome; the triple arched loggia modeled on the Loggia della Signoria built across from the palace as a frame for important public family events; the façade of Santa Maria Novella (Fig. 5.29); and his tomb chapel in the church of San Pancrazio, a miniature version of the Tomb of the Holy Sepulchre in Jerusalem.

The façade of Santa Maria Novella—the only completed church façade in fifteenth-century Florence—was designed by Leon Battista Alberti, who was apparently the house architect for Giovanni Rucellai since he was responsible for all four of the projects (with the possible intervention

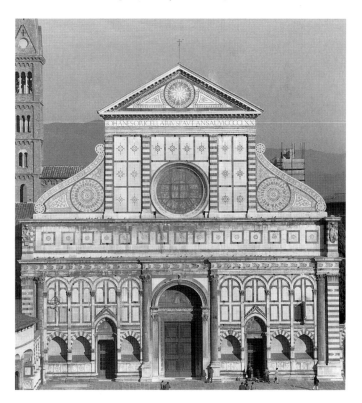

5.29 Santa Maria Novella, façade, 1458–70, commissioned by Giovanni di Paolo Rucellai from LEON BATTISTA ALBERTI

The inscription across the façade of the building reads: "Giovanni Rucellai, son of Paolo, [made this] in the year of Salvation 1470."

of Bernardo Rossellino in the execution of the palace façade). A number of problems faced Alberti in designing this façade. Chief among them was the desire to unify the low side aisles of the building with the high Gothic nave of the church in a coherent compositional structure, here done in part with the architectural scrolls that curve from high in the upper structure to the exterior edge of the lower story. The busyness of the decoration disguises the fact that Alberti designed a modular façade whose main unit—the second story temple form—is a perfect square with the width equal to the height from the top of the pediment to the cornice that forms its base. This module and measures derived from it are repeated a number of times in the units for the decorative elements of the façade, further unifying the overall composition.

Alberti also clearly struggled to provide a modern—that is classicizing—façade for the Gothic church of Santa Maria Novella. The pedimented structure rising into the upper story of the façade imitates Roman classical temple forms, despite the rose window of the old building that

interrupts the classical order. Alberti used a Roman religious building type as the model for his modern religious building, giving some sense of a decorum in architectural imitation. The black marble columns that extend the height of the first story at the left and right ends of the façade and flanking the main portal are also classical insofar as they are capped with Corinthian capitals. On the other hand, Alberti was constrained to retain the medieval *avelli* or tombs running the length of the façade because the patron family of the two side doors, the Baldesi, thought that their commission granted them rights to the entire façade. The law suit that the Baldesi brought against Giovanni Rucellai was solved in part because Alberti found a way to incorporate their earlier decoration into his new design. Alberti and Giovanni Rucellai also chose to refer to the indigenous Florentine Romanesque exterior design of geometrical units of white and black marble, like the Baptistry and cathedral and, in this case, like San Miniato al Monte, all revered structures in the city. Even the Corinthian columns can be seen as part of the decorative ensemble of the Baptistry, an instance of the difficulty of sepa-

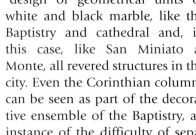
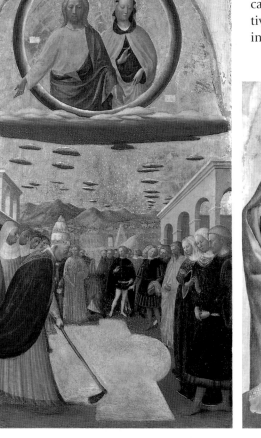
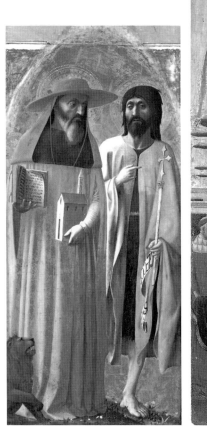
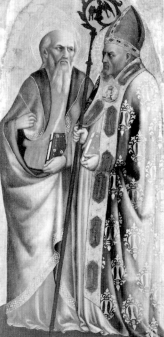

5.30 *Santa Maria Maggiore Altarpiece*, commissioned by Martin V (?) from MASOLINO (with collaboration by MASACCIO) for the high altar (?) of Santa Maria Maggiore, Rome, c. 1423–27. Shown in the illustration is the *Founding of Santa Maria Maggiore*, tempera on panel, 56¾ × 30" (144 × 76 cm) (Gallerie Nazionali di Capodimonte, Naples), flanked by side panels representing *St. Jerome and St. John the Baptist* (attributed to MASACCIO) (left) and *St. John the Evangelist and St. Martin of Tours* (right). Tempera, oil, and tooled gold on panel, 45¼ × 21" (155 × 55 cm) and 39⅜ × 32½" (100 × 52 cm) (National Gallery, London, and John G. Johnson Collection, Philadelphia Museum of Art)

rating out Tuscan Romanesque from classical Roman and a warning about reading classicizing forms in Florence exclusively as antique, even when the architect is a humanist scholar trained in antique forms and texts. Thus the façade of Santa Maria Novella—like Cosimo's palace, but unlike the Palazzo Rucellai—was in large measure conservative, designed to place the building solidly within the established history of the city and its unique history of ecclesiastical building decoration.

Rome: Re-establishing Papal Power

The election to the papacy of Martin V (Oddo Colonna; see Fig. 4.7) at the Council of Constance in 1417 ended more than 100 years of disruption within the Church, which had begun in 1308 with the removal of the papal court to Avignon, and was followed in 1378 by the Great Schism. Martin was a member of one of Rome's oldest and most powerful families, the Colonna, which gave him a local power base. When he finally entered Rome in September 1420, he found a city that was essentially an urban backwater, having suffered a century of neglect by the papal court, which had been its chief source of artistic patronage.

Following patterns well established for his office, Martin (r. 1417–31) selected traditional sites of papal patronage—a tacit recognition that although the papacy was essentially an absolute monarchy it was an elected, not a dynastic one, and that his legitimacy thus depended upon establishing a strong link with his predecessors. In 1427 Martin issued a bull ordering building and restoration at the Lateran Palace, St. John Lateran, St. Paul's Outside the Walls, and the portico of Old St. Peter's. In choosing these major sites of earlier papal patronage, with the continuity that this implied, Martin attempted to draw a veil over the papacy's absence from Rome during the previous century.

Martin V's Santa Maria Maggiore Altarpiece

At the basilica of Santa Maria Maggiore, located in the traditional Colonna enclave in the city and previously the recipient of Colonna patronage under Nicholas IV (see Fig. 1.35), Martin (or another member of his family) commissioned a large double-sided altarpiece (Fig. 5.30) from the Florentine painters Masolino and Masaccio (there being no local school of artists because of the papacy's century-long absence from the city). Presumably intended for the main altar, the *Santa Maria Maggiore*

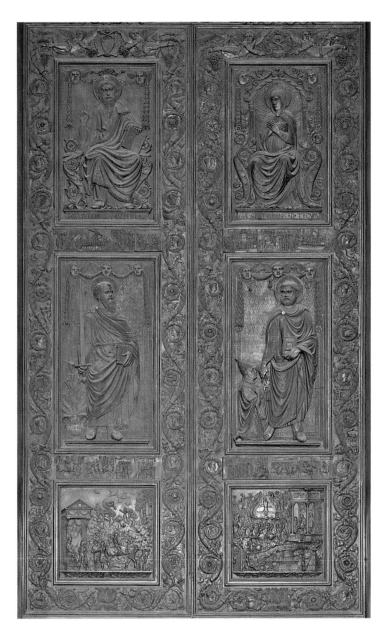

5.31 Doors of Old St. Peter's, 1445, commissioned by Eugenius IV from FILARETE (ANTONIO AVERLINO) for the main entrance of Old St. Peter's, Rome. Silver-gilt bronze, 20′ 8″ × 11′ 9″ (6.3 × 3.58 m) overall (St. Peter's, Rome)

Altarpiece was the first such painting to be commissioned in Rome since the *Stefaneschi Altarpiece* for the canons' chapel of Old St. Peter's over a century earlier (see Fig. 1.43). Masolino was chiefly responsible for this now-dismembered triptych, although Masaccio contributed figures for at least one of the side panels. The central panel of the altarpiece facing the congregation depicted the Assumption of the Virgin, an appropriate subject for a Marian basilica. From the nave of the building this subject would have aligned with the mosaic of the Coronation of the Virgin in the apse (see Fig. 1.35). On the central panel of the side of the altarpiece facing the apse is a depiction of the foundation of the church by Pope Liberius, with the Virgin and Christ looking down from a celestial roundel. This event took place, according to legend, in August 352, when a miraculous fall of snow formed the plan of the building on the ground. The same subject is depicted in the mosaics on the façade of the basilica; the altarpiece thus emphasizes the continuous history of the church from its Early Christian foundation.

In the panel to the right of the *Foundation* is a figure of St. Martin of Tours, dressed in his bishop's regalia. His cope is embroidered with heraldic Colonna columns (the meaning of the family name), which—along with his strongly characterized features—suggests that this figure may also be a portrait of Martin. All the figures share the intense expressions and weighty presence of those in the Brancacci Chapel frescoes (see Fig. 4.58), despite being placed on a gold ground in an iconic, rather than a narrative, context.

Eugenius IV (r. 1431–47)

Martin's successor, Eugenius IV, was a Venetian by birth and was not accepted by the Roman population at his election in 1431. By 1434 his popularity had reached such a low ebb that in June of that year he fled the city, disguised as a monk, sailing down the Tiber in a little boat. He was received by the city of Florence, where he lived until his success in uniting the Eastern and Western Churches at the Council of Ferrara-Florence in July 1439 (see page 230) gave him enough support to consider returning to Rome, which he finally did in 1443.

Eugenius's major artistic commission was for a set of silver-gilt bronze doors for the main entrance to Old St. Peter's (Fig. 5.31). Although presumably commissioned from Filarete (Antonio Averlino, c. 1400 Florence–1469 Rome?) before Eugenius fled Rome in 1434, the doors were not completed and installed until 1445.

The upper two panels represent enthroned figures of God and the Virgin. Here the Virgin is again a metaphor for the Church, as in late medieval Roman apse mosaics (see Fig. 1.35). The papal saints, Peter and Paul, are the subjects of the central panels. Eugenius IV, his name clearly inscribed, kneels as a donor before St. Peter, his predecessor and the saint to whom the church is dedicated. Below each of the saints is a narrative relief depicting the scene of his martyrdom, echoing similar painted images in the then extant atrium of Old St. Peter's. Silvering and inlaid colored glass originally brightened the major reliefs of the door.

Filarete's doors for St. Peter's could not be more different from Ghiberti's breathtakingly naturalistic doors for the Florentine Baptistry (see Figs. 4.31 and 5.5), which he must have known. The four isolated single figures in the upper four panels are flattened against an essentially blank background and are posed in a stiff, iconic manner, deliberately alluding to an Early Christian style, appropriate for this building, built in the mid-fourth century. The two large narrative reliefs of martyrdom have the slightly disjointed quality of Roman relief friezes from Trajan's Column. It is clear that Filarete wished to convey a sense of distance and spatial recession, despite the vertical perspective he employs. In the narrow horizontal strips between the panels, Filarete inserted diminutive narrative scenes of the Holy Roman Emperor Sigismund in Rome in 1433 for his coronation in St. Peter's (Fig. 5.32) and of the arrival of the Byzantine court in Italy for the meeting of the Council of Ferrara-Florence. Eugenius's concern to have these important successes of his reign accurately and fully recorded is evident in the careful labeling of people and places in the reliefs and in the portraits they contain. The curving foliate pattern filling the outside frames of the doors is related to stylized imperial Roman examples, although the figurative and animal forms that enliven it are naturalistically rendered. Within the circular curves of the vegetation, Filarete included roundels of male and

5.32 Doors of Old St. Peter's, detail of left valve under St. Paul showing *Emperor Sigismund Returning to the Castel Sant'Angelo*, with Antonio de Riddo, the castellan, at the left, and the emperor and the pope approaching him on horseback

Eugenius's coats-of-arms are shown on the right shield hanging from the portal of the castle. The inscription above the relief refers to the union of the Greek, Armenian, and Ethiopian churches with Rome as a result of the Council of Ferrara-Florence.

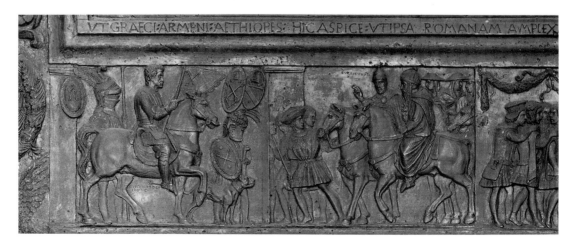

female heads, some of which derive from ancient Roman coins, extending the interest in medallic art that had already appeared in northern Italy in the late fourteenth century (see Fig. 3.42) and which was being promoted in Filarete's lifetime by Pisanello (see Figs. 4.24 and 4.25). Contemporary and biblical history, then, rely on models that support the claims of the papacy to rulership by making Roman imperial forms an official papal language.

A Cautionary Fresco

Sixteenth-century drawings of now-lost frescoes from the left transept of St. John Lateran give some sense of the use of pictorial imagery to record contemporary events in fifteenth-century Rome. The frescoes represented the arrest and execution, in 1438, of two men who had stolen precious gems from the reliquary busts of saints Peter and Paul kept in the tabernacle over the main altar of the basilica. The criminals were taken to the church of Santa Maria in Aracoeli on the Capitoline Hill, stripped of their clothing before the high altar, placed in a wooden cage (Fig. 5.33), and taken to the Campo dei Fiori, one of Rome's oldest and most popular open markets. There, after having had their right hands cut off, they were burned at the stake while an accomplice was hanged from a tree.

The original frescoes thus commemorated a theft that had occurred in the very place in which they were painted and indicate that contemporary secular events could form part of the decorative program within a church. This narrative is portrayed in a straightforward, didactic, and hard-hitting manner—although its warning of the punishments awaiting those who stole Church property was not always heeded: Filarete himself was charged with stealing the reliquary head of St. John from the Lateran in 1447 and had to flee Rome. Pope Eugenius's coat-of-arms, prominently displayed in the fresco, also suggests a warning to anyone who would dare to attack the papacy, whose church this was, an offence tantamount to the gross sacrilege of defiling relics.

Nicholas V (r. 1447–55)

One of Nicholas V's first actions upon his election to the papacy in 1447 was to declare that the year 1450 would be a Jubilee Year—an event designed to focus attention on the strength of the Church and on Rome, much as the first Jubilee of 1300 had done. The Jubilee also necessitated the renovation of the city in order to accommodate the thousands of pilgrims that were expected (and that did arrive). Nicholas's vision of the city as a metaphor for

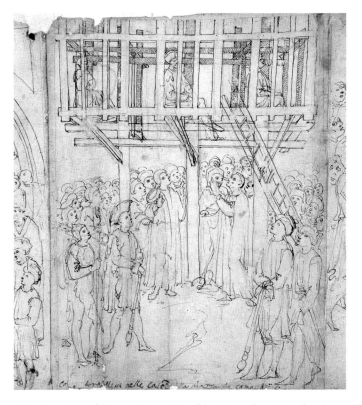

5.33 *Execution of Capocciola and Garofalo*, sixteenth-century drawing after a fresco commissioned by Angelotto da Foschi in 1438–40 for St. John Lateran, Rome. Ink on paper glued to cardboard (Archivio Capitolare Lateranense, Rome)

The drawn record of these destroyed frescoes suggests the existence of other contemporary secular history painting almost all of which is now lost.

papal power concentrated on both the civic and the religious centers of Rome, symbolizing the dual nature of the office of the papacy as both civil and ecclesiastical.

As early as 1447 Nicholas had launched several building projects on the Capitoline Hill, stamping his presence on the site of the civic government of Rome. He restored the Senators' Palace and built and planned new towers for its corners, and he built a new palace fronted by a portico for the conservators (civic magistrates) of the city (Fig. 5.34). Nicholas lost no time in placing his personal heraldic crest on the face of the Senators' Palace, making clear his wish to control the civil as well as the ecclesiastical bureaucracies in Rome.

Simultaneously Nicholas initiated major architectural projects at the Vatican. These consisted of new fortifications for the Vatican to protect it from outside attack and from internal Roman factionalism (Fig. 5.35), a renewal of the area from Old St. Peter's to the Tiber, designed to house the Curia (the administrative offices of the Church), a new wing and decorations for the Vatican Palace, substantial enlargements and repairs for Old St. Peter's, and a large new piazza in front of St. Peter's to accommodate pilgrims and to provide a suitably grand

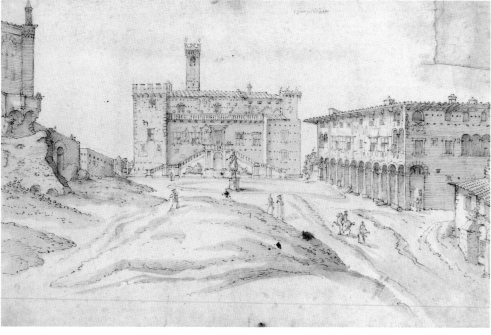

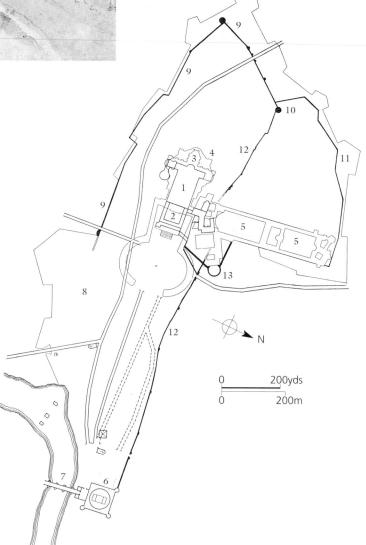

5.34 The Capitoline Hill, Rome, as it appeared c. 1554–60, showing the Senator's Palace with left corner tower and bell tower built by NICHOLAS and the Conservators' Palace (Musée du Louvre, Cabinet des Dessins, Paris)

space for papal appearances. In these plans Nicholas may have been helped by Alberti, then a member of the Curia and an acquaintance of the pope's from their days together in the humanist circles of Florence.

Nicholas's plans for the enlargement of Old St. Peter's show the grandeur of his vision. His new choir increased the length of the nave of the basilica by a third; new transepts would have provided substantial additional space around the main altar marking the burial site of St. Peter in the crypt below. Like his predecessor Nicholas III (r. 1277–80), Nicholas V intended to enhance the burial site of Peter, thus emphasizing his lineage from the first pope and underscoring the continuous spiritual power of the papacy. To this end, he had four large columns taken from the Pantheon to St. Peter's, an acquisition asserting equality between Nicholas and the emperor Hadrian, builder of the Pantheon—one that would have been an important opening salvo in the transformation of the Vatican into a new imperial city. Nicholas also planned to move the ancient obelisk erected by the emperor Augustus, then at the side of Old St. Peter's, to the piazza in front of the basilica. With these Roman remains Nicholas asserted claims to the temporal power of the Roman emperors just as he claimed the spiritual power of Peter.

Fra Angelico in Rome

On the upper floor of his addition to the Vatican Palace Nicholas commissioned Fra Angelico to paint a fresco cycle of the lives of saints Lawrence and Stephen in his small private chapel (Fig. 5.36; see also Fig 5.1). The choice of these saints ties Nicholas V's chapel to Nicholas III's Sancta Sanctorum (see Figs. 1.33 and 1.34), which also contains frescoes of these two early Christian deacon-saints. Fra Angelico's frescoes contain images of

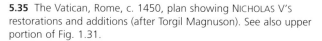

5.35 The Vatican, Rome, c. 1450, plan showing NICHOLAS V'S restorations and additions (after Torgil Magnuson). See also upper portion of Fig. 1.31.

1 Old St. Peter's; **2** Atrium of Old St. Peter's; **3** Nicholas V's plan for enlarging apse and transept areas of Old St. Peter's; **4** New St. Peter's; **5** Belvedere Courtyard; **6** Castel Sant'Angelo; **7** River Tiber; **8** Janiculum Hill; **9** Leonine Wall rebuilt by Nicholas V; **10** Vatican Hill; **11** Wall of Nicholas III around the Pomerium; **12** Leonine Wall; **13** Great Tower of Nicholas V

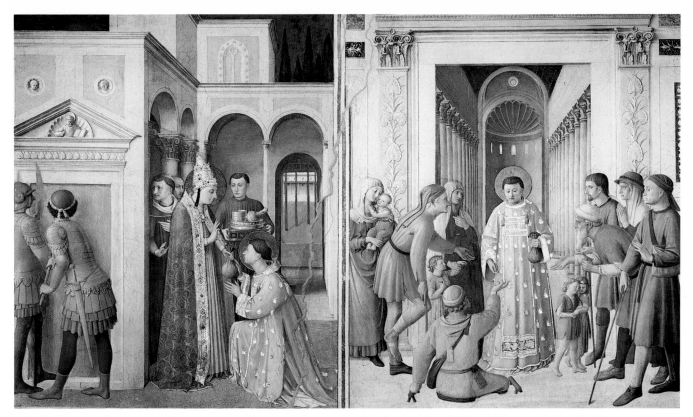

5.36 *St. Lawrence Receiving the Treasures of the Church* and *St. Lawrence Distributing Alms*, 1448–c. 1455, commissioned by Nicholas V from FRA ANGELICO for the Chapel of St. Lawrence (now known as the Chapel of Nicholas V), Vatican Palace, Rome. Fresco. See also Fig. 5.1.

the ordination of each saint and the distribution of alms by them, emphasizing the power of the pope to confer office, as well as the charity offered by the Church.

The gold details of St. Lawrence's dalmatic (the costume of a deacon) and the cope worn by Sixtus II give some indication of the original luxury of this chapel. Fra Angelico's figures stand in a narrow apron space close to the picture plane, their grouping and solid forms, rather than the schematic architecture, giving the scenes their spaciousness. Behind St. Lawrence, Fra Angelico included a simplified image of the nave of St. Peter's and Nicholas's project for the choir. The classicizing details of the painted architecture, like Nicholas's choice of Alberti as his architect, suggest that while Nicholas sanctioned the destruction of ancient Roman monuments in order to provide building materials for new structures, he also saw the potential for borrowing antique stylistic references to represent a new state controlled by a strong ruler.

Pius II (r. 1458–64)

St. Peter's continued to be a focus of papal commissions by Nicholas V's successors. After the mid-fifteenth century, two popes, Pius II and Paul II, began new decorative programs both outside and in the building, which increased the number of sites for pilgrims' devotion and which further emphasized the concept of papal rulership.

Pius II (Aeneas Sylvius Piccolomini) was away from Rome for eighteen months shortly after his election,

attending the Congress of Mantua, where he attempted—unsuccessfully—to interest European leaders in a crusade. On his return to Rome in 1460 he immediately began major building and decorative programs at St. Peter's, which were to go on for the remainder of the century. The real incentive for his work in the basilica seems to have been his knowledge that in May of that year, when the Turks invaded the Peloponnesus, Thomas Paleologus, a member of the imperial family of Constantinople, had rescued the relic of the head of St. Andrew, St. Peter's brother, from its burial place in Patras, in Greece. Pius had immediately sought to have the head brought to Rome. To reunite it with relics of the heads of saints Peter and Paul, then in the Lateran, would represent a union of Eastern and Western churches against the Turks and would have supported Pius's ardent wishes for a crusade to reclaim the Holy Lands for Christianity. Pius received the relic in a carefully staged series of public processions during Easter week of 1462. By then St. Peter's already bore the stamp of his patronage.

Pius had begun his work at St. Peter's by transforming the area before the atrium of the old basilica into a magnificent piazza. He also planned a benediction loggia, which was to extend across the entire façade of the atrium (see Fig. 1.31), and a grand staircase leading to it. This project realized the grand scheme of Nicholas V for the enhancement of the site, although the stairs, built with marble quarried from the Colosseum, were not of the imperial porphyry and green marble specified for Nicholas's plan.

Ruins and Dreams

Ancient Rome had always held power over the imaginations of pilgrims to the city and of the humanist scholars who studied its history. Poggio Bracciolini (1380–1459) wrote this lament on the fickleness of fortune in 1430, just as the papacy was beginning to re-establish itself in the city and to restore some of its most venerated structures. Poggio's Rome, however, was not the Rome of the popes but the Rome of the emperors, sadly all but disappeared by the time of his writing. At the heart of Poggio's text is an implied claim that contemporary civilization was a quiet echo of what it had been during antiquity. He also insinuates that a reconstruction of ancient Rome, known to him more through ancient texts than through actual monuments, was to be gained through precise scholarship and the collecting and accurate reading of inscriptions—an area in which he criticizes no less a humanist than Petrarch.

Not long ago, after Pope Martin left Rome shortly before his death for a farewell visit to the Tuscan countryside, and when Antonio Lusco, a very distinguished man, and I were free of business and public duties, we used to contemplate the desert places of the city with wonder in our hearts as we reflected on the former greatness of the broken buildings and the vast ruins of the ancient city, and again on the truly prodigious and astounding fall of its great empire and the deplorable inconstancy of fortune. And once when we had climbed the Capitoline hill, and Antonio, who was a little weary from riding, wanted to rest, we dismounted from our horses and sat down together within the very enclosures of the Tarpeian ruins, behind the great marble threshold of its very doors, as I believe, and the numerous broken columns lying here and there, whence a view of a large part of the city opens out. . . .

"You may turn all the pages of history, you may read all the long-drawn-out records of the authors, you may examine all the historical annals, but you will find that fortune offers no more striking example of her own mutability than the city of Rome, the most beautiful and magnificent of all those that either have been or shall be, the city which was described by Lucian, the learned Greek author, when he was writing to a friend of his who wanted to see Rome, as not so much a city as a bit of Paradise. How much the more marvellous to relate and bitter to behold, how the cruelty of fortune has so transformed its appearance and shape, that, stripped of all beauty, it now lies prostrate like a giant corpse, decayed and everywhere eaten away.

"Surely this city is to be mourned over which once produced so many illustrious men and emperors, so many leaders in war, which was the nurse of so many excellent rulers, the parent of so many and such great virtues, the mother of so many good arts, the city from which flowed military discipline, purity of morals and life, the decrees of the law, the models of all the virtues, and the knowledge of right living. She who was once mistress of the world is now, by the injustice of fortune, which overturns all things, not only despoiled of her empire and her majesty, but delivered over to the basest servitude, misshapen and degraded, her ruins alone showing forth her former dignity and greatness. . . .

Yet truly these buildings of the city, both public and private, which it seemed would vie with immortality itself, now in part destroyed entirely, in part broken and overturned, since very few are left which preserve their original greatness—these buildings were believed to lie beyond the reach of fortune. . . .

Then I answered, "You may well wonder, Antonio, at the injury wrought by fortune on this mother of cities, now so cruelly damaged that, as I wander through it today, surveying it, I am compelled not only to marvel but to lament that almost nothing survives intact, that there are so few remains of the ancient city, and those half-consumed and lying in ruins. For of all the public and private buildings of this once free city, only some few broken remnants are seen. . . .

The pyramid set in the walls of the city near the Porta Ostia [is one]; this is the noble tomb of C. Cestius, a member of the college of priests, and the letters inscribed on it refer to it as a work completed in one hundred and thirty days, from the will of Ponthus Clamela.

I am the more amazed, since this inscription still survives entire, that the most learned Francesco Petrarca wrote in one of his letters that this is the tomb of Remus. . . .

"This will perhaps seem trivial, but it moves me greatly, that to these monuments I may add—of the once almost innumerable colossi and statues, of both marble and bronze (for it is less surprising that silver and gold statues were melted down), which were erected in honour of illustrious men because of their greatness of character, not to mention the various figures set up by the state for the sake of art and public enjoyment—only these five marble statues, four in the baths of Constantine, two standing beside horses—the work of Phidias and Praxiteles [the Horse Tamers]—two reclining [the Nile and the Tigris River Gods] and the fifth in the forum of Mars, a statue which today bears the name of this forum. And there is only one gilded bronze equestrian statue, which was presented to the Lateran basilica by Septimius Severus. [Equestrian statue of Marcus Aurelius now on the Capitoline.]

"It is indeed most grievous and scarcely to be related without great amazement that this Capitoline hill, once the head and center of the Roman Empire and the citadel of the whole world, before which every king and prince trembled, the hill ascended in triumph by so many emperors and once adorned with the gifts and spoils of so many and such great peoples, now lies so desolated and ruined, and so changed from its earlier condition, that vines have replaced the benches of the senators, and the Capitol has become a receptacle of dung and filth. . . .

The forum, which, properly speaking, was the most famous place in the city, after the laws had been passed which called the people together and created the magistracy and the distinguished assembly, has become, by the malignity of fortune, a neglected desert, here the home of pigs and wild deer, and there a vegetable garden."

(from "The Inconstancy of Fortune", in Latin Writings of the Italian Humanists. Ed. F. A. Gragg. New York: Charles Scribner's Sons, 1927)

To bracket each end of the stairs, Pius commissioned Paolo Romano (Paolo di Mariano di Tuccio Taccone, active c. 1445–70) to carve colossal statues of Peter and Paul. Although little is known of Paolo Romano he was responsible, along with collaborators such as Mino da Fiesole and Isaia da Pisa (active 1447–64 Rome), who migrated to Rome from other cities at this time, for a number of important sculptural commissions in the Rome of Pius II. These works—mainly tomb monuments and altars for reliquaries—were to serve as propaganda transforming Roman church interiors into a visual history of its powerful elites.

Paolo's statue of St. Paul was carved between 1461 and 1462 for the right side of the stair base (Fig. 5.37). The rhetorical bombast of its aggressive pose would have projected over the immense space of the piazza. Its rigid drapery folds bear the same relationship to Early Christian sculptural style as do Filarete's main doors of St. Peter's (see Fig. 5.31), suggesting a consistent referencing over time to the fourth-century origins of the basilica.

To prepare for the placement of St. Andrew's head inside St. Peter's, Pius cleared the interior of the building of hundreds of years of accreted decoration, had its more important monuments moved to the side walls, and commissioned Paolo Romano and Isaia da Pisa to make a tabernacle and altar for the relic (Fig. 5.38). The *Reliquary Tabernacle of the Head of St. Andrew* was destroyed when the new St. Peter's was built, leaving only remnants of its original sculpture. The iconic appearance of this sculpture again recalls the favored Early Christian

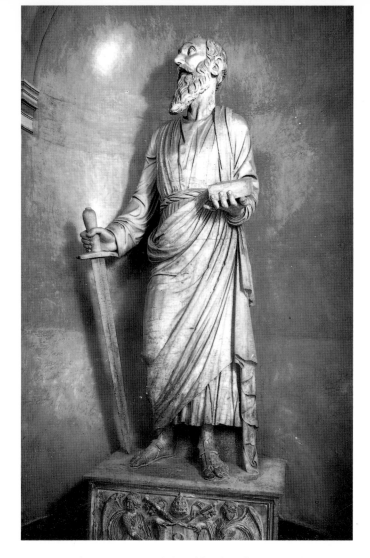

5.37 *St, Paul*, 1461–62, commissioned by Pius II from PAOLO ROMANO for the right side of the stairs of Old St. Peter's, Rome. Marble (Vatican Apartments, Rome)

The statue originally carried gilt attributes; the right arm carrying the sword was raised.

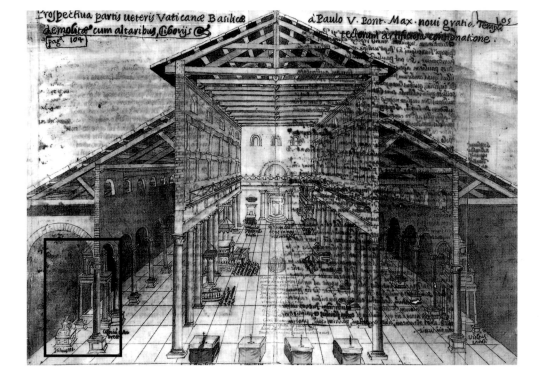

5.38 *Reliquary Tabernacle of the Head of St. Andrew*, c. 1463, commissioned by Pius II from PAOLO ROMANO and ISAIA DA PISA (with GIOVANNI DALMATA) from GIACOMO GRIMALDI, *Descrizione della Basilica Antica di S. Pietro in Vaticano*, 1619 (Vatican Library, Vat.Barb.Lat.2733, fols. 104v/105r, Rome)

The tabernacle is visible in this drawing of 1619 in the left aisle of Old St. Peter's (indicated by the superimposed black box) before the destruction of this remaining part of the early Christian building to make way for Carlo Maderno's nave. The door at the end of the nave connected Old St. Peter's with the new building begun in 1506.

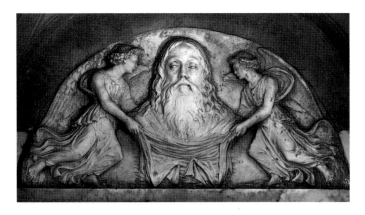

5.39 *Reliquary Tabernacle of the Head of St. Andrew*, relief, c. 1463, Isaia da Pisa, one of three by different artists that originally formed the upper faces of the tabernacle. Marble (Grotte Vaticane, Rome)

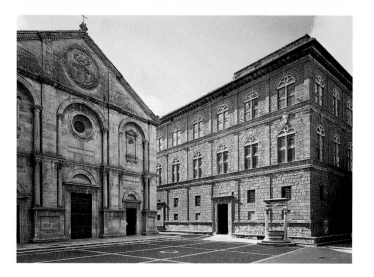

5.40 Main square, Pienza, c. 1462, commissioned by Pius II from Bernardo Rossellino

style (Fig. 5.39). In form, the monument copied earlier reliquary tabernacles, such as the one over the main altar of St. John Lateran housing relics of the heads of saints Peter and Paul. This form raised the relic high in the church, so that crowds of people could see it, and also provided security for the precious reliquary which contained it.

Pienza Although Sienese, Pius had actually been born in a small hill town south of Siena called Corsignano. Beginning in 1459, he attempted to establish this town as a papal seat. In 1462 he rechristened it Pienza in honor of himself, raised it to a bishopric, and hired Bernardo Rossellino, who had previously worked in an elaborated classicizing style in Florence (see Fig. 5.6), to transform its center into a suitably coherent setting for the town's new status. Rossellino's plan was determined in part by pre-existing streets, by the medieval town hall at the site, and by the precipitous drop of the hill where Pius planned a new cathedral. To either side of the cathedral Rossellino placed the bishop's palace and Pius's own palace, forming a trapezoidal piazza (Fig. 5.40), flanked by images of civil and ecclesiastical power. Pius's own coat-of-arms is prominently placed in the gable of the cathedral, whose triple-arched façade recalls ancient Roman triumphal arches. Each structure of this program refers to well-established building types: like the humanist rhetoric in which Pius had been trained, clarity of meaning is enlivened by variety of form. The interior of the papal palace, intended as a pleasant country retreat, renounces the formality of the public square, being built around a courtyard whose south side opens onto a garden and a view of Monte Amiata in the distance. Although the cathedral has a classical appearance, its plan derives from German Gothic hall churches that Pius had admired during his travels for the papal Curia in Austria. In his *Commentaries* Pius describes the church

and its decorations fully, providing virtually the only description by a Renaissance patron of his or her architectural accomplishments.

On the church's interior, whitewashed to give it a sense of light, Pius commissioned five altarpieces by painters he referred to as "illustrious Sienese artists." The *Assumption of the Virgin* (Fig. 5.41) is by Vecchietta (Lorenzo di Pietro;

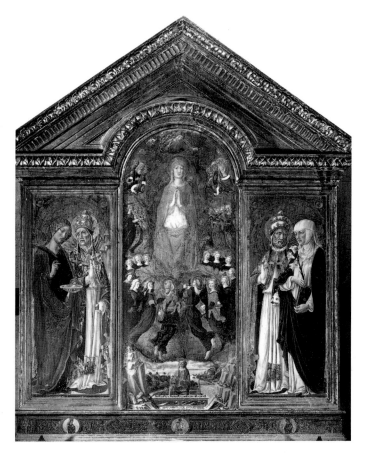

5.41 *Assumption of the Virgin*, 1463, commissioned by Pius II from Vecchietta for the second chapel on the left of the nave of Pienza Cathedral. Tempera on panel, 9' 2¼" × 7' 4½" (2.8 × 2.5 m)

1410 Siena–1480 Siena), a painter, sculptor, and architect who later produced the extraordinary bronze tabernacle for the Ospedale della Scala in Siena (see Fig. 11) that was to mark one of the first substantive explorations for this new piece of ecclesiastical furnishing. Like Masolino's *Santa Maria Maggiore Altarpiece* (see Fig. 5.30), Vecchietta's painting depicts the Assumption in the center panel, flanking it with side panels of standing saints, thus connecting this church to one of the major papal basilicas in Rome. The appearance of St. Catherine of Siena (c. 1347–80) at the right of the altarpiece refers to Pius II, who canonized her in 1461, as does, nominally, the figure of Pius I next to her, leaving little doubt about the painting's patron.

Despite the fact that the Pienza altarpieces were completed in 1463, their style recalls that of the great Sienese artists of the beginning of the previous century—not surprising since Pius clearly had in mind a contemporary reprise of the program of altarpieces around the main altar of Siena's Duomo (see Fig. 1.12). The lyrical poses of Vecchietta's figures, the simple ovoid shapes of their heads, the arabesques of drapery, and the gilded background of the panels stamp a Sienese presence in Pienza as clearly as does Pius's heraldic device on the façade of the cathedral. However, Vecchietta's stately lateral saints indicate his exposure to Florentine painting of mid-century, as does the deeply receding landscape at the base of the central panel.

Cardinals' Commissions

Cardinals in the papal court were also expected to enhance the beauty of Rome by commissioning new buildings and new painting and sculpture for existing structures. Perhaps the most powerful cardinal in Rome during the mid-fifteenth century was the Frenchman Guillaume d'Estouteville. For the basilica of Santa Maria Maggiore, d'Estouteville commissioned a marble baldachin from the Florentine sculptor Mino da Fiesole to cover the main altar (Figs. 5.42 and 5.43), similar to the one by Arnolfo di Cambio in Santa Cecilia in Trastevere (see Fig. 1.38). Now dismembered, the tabernacle had marble reliefs on each of its upper faces depicting events related to the basilica, like earlier tabernacles in St. Peter's and St. John Lateran.

Duplicating the imagery of Masolino's and Masaccio's *Santa Maria Maggiore Altarpiece* (see Fig. 5.30) and the mosaic on the façade of the basilica, Mino carved a relief for the ciborium to face the nave depicting the miraculous August snow that yielded the plan of the basilica. Behind two groups of figures the architecture creates a deep perspective, leaving the center of the composition open for the fall of snow, with God and the Virgin initiating the miracle from above. D'Estouteville, archpriest of Santa Maria Maggiore, looks out of the relief immediately to the right of the pope, here a portrait not of Liberius but of Pius II. The lateral arrangement of the figures, their

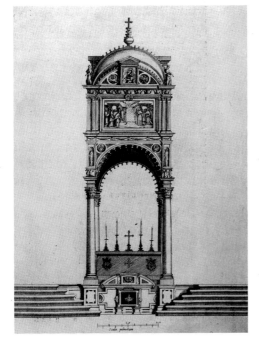

5.42 Tabernacle for Santa Maria Maggiore, c. 1461–63, reconstruction by Paolo de Angelis, *Basilicae S. Mariae Maioris . . . descriptio et delineatio, auctore Paulo de Angelis*, Rome, 1621, 93

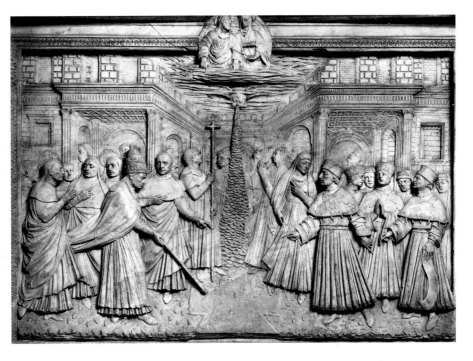

5.43 Tabernacle for Santa Maria Maggiore, detail showing the *Miraculous Fall of Snow*, c. 1461–63, commissioned by Guillaume d'Estouteville from Mino da Fiesole for Santa Maria Maggiore, Rome (now immured in the wall of the apse of the basilica)

placement in front of an architectural backdrop, and the alignment of their heads all evoke classical Roman relief style and testify to a renewed and energetic investigation of the antique in the court of Pius II.

The French cardinal, who had hoped to be elected pope in the conclave of 1458 which elected Pius II and who retained that hope throughout his lifetime, claimed the focal point of one of the major pilgrimage sites of the city, declaring his wealth and his power—as well as his generosity—on no uncertain terms. Although there could only be one leader of the church, there were many aspirants for the throne of St. Peter, and their worthiness could be proclaimed at least in part through their artistic patronage.

Paul II (r. 1464–71)

Pius died in Ancona in August 1464, while preparing to embark on a crusade to return the Holy Land to the Christians. His successor, the Venetian Pietro Barbo, who took the name Paul II, had been made cardinal by his uncle, Eugenius IV, and was thus the first of the Renaissance popes whose road to office was clearly paved by the widespread—and accepted—practice of nepotism.

Paul II's activity as a patron of the arts had begun during his years as a cardinal in Rome. His keenness for the art, archaeology, and coins of ancient Rome led him to collect antique gems and coins; by the time of his death he had amassed the foremost collection of this kind in Italy. During his papacy he paid for major restorations of the Pantheon, repairs to the gilt bronze equestrian statue of Marcus Aurelius (in 1466–68), and a restoration of the Arch of Titus (in 1466). He also enacted civic statutes aimed at the protection of Roman antiquities—until then simply used as quarries for new building projects.

In 1455, before his election to the papacy, Paul had begun building his cardinal's palace in Rome, next to his titular church of San Marco. The palace, possibly designed by the poorly documented Jacopo da Pietrasanta or Francesco del Borgo, was never completed, despite Paul's expanded plans for it after he became pope in 1464 (Fig. 5.44). The courtyard of the Palazzo Venezia (as it is known because of Paul's Venetian origins), with its super-imposed arcades and applied half columns, is reminiscent of the Colosseum. Ample open arches would have provided a grand interior courtyard to the palace, every detail of which imitated ancient Roman architectural forms. In 1467 Paul arranged for the red porphyry sarcophagus of Santa Costanza (now in the Vatican Museums) to be moved to the piazza in front of San Marco. Paul's appropriation of this Roman imperial tomb, traditionally thought to be that of Constantine's

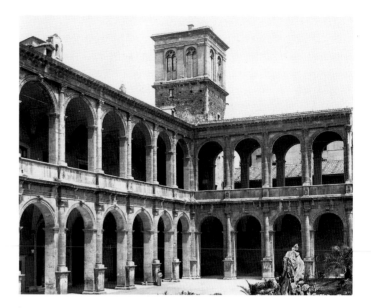

5.44 Palazzo Venezia, Rome, begun 1455, commissioned by Pietro Barbo (later Paul II) from JACOPO DA PIETRASANTA or, more probably, FRANCESCO DEL BORGO

own daughter, suggests that he intended his own palace, in the heart of Rome, to carry imperial connotations of rulership and power.

A Roman School of Painting

During the papacy of Paul II the beginnings of a flourishing Roman school of painting were firmly established. The leaders in this development were Antoniazzo Romano (Antonio Aquili, active c. 1452–1512) and Melozzo da Forlì (Melozzo degli Ambrosi; 1438 Forlì–1498 Forlì). Both painters spent part of their early careers painting copies of Madonna and Child paintings piously thought to have been painted by St. Luke himself—the sort of mass-market painting that one might expect in Europe's leading pilgrimage city. At the same time, each sought to assimilate the innovations of style brought to Rome by painters visiting the papal court.

Antoniazzo's fresco cycle of the life of St. Francesca Romana (1384–1440) was painted in 1468 for a group of lay women founded by Francesca Romana who lived together and dedicated themselves to acts of charity around the city. It tells the story of a Roman matron who had lived the life of a nun after her husband's death. In the *Communion of St. Francesca Romana* (Fig. 5.45) it is easy to see why these frescoes, with their simplified architecture and gentle, rather doll-like figures, were long confused with the work of Benozzo Gozzoli, one of Fra Angelico's assistants at the Vatican Palace. A didactic label in late Gothic lettering explicates the events por-

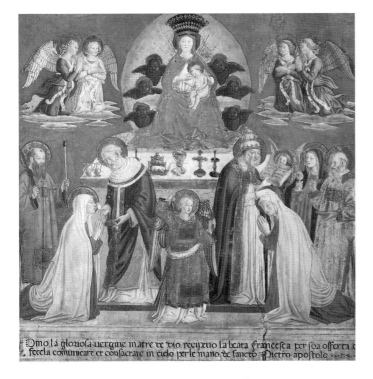

5.45 *Communion of St. Francesca Romana*, 1468, ANTONIAZZO ROMANO, Oratory of the Oblates of San Francesca in the Tor de'Specchi, Rome. Fresco

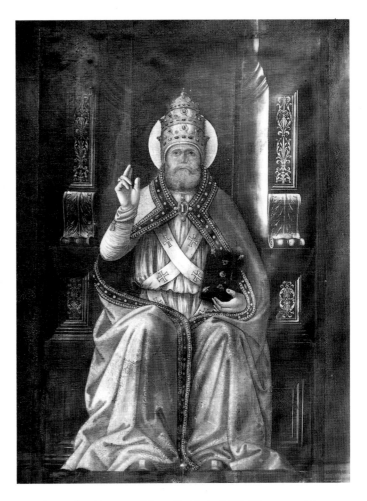

5.46 Processional banner of Pope St. Mark, 1469–70, presumably commissioned by Paul II from MELOZZO DA FORLÌ for San Marco, Rome. Tempera on red silk

trayed in Italian rather than Latin, indicating that it was addressed to the female residents of the house. As the first depictions of a saint whose cult had been authorized only in 1460 (she was not canonized until 1608) these frescoes clearly suggest the patrons' wish to establish a canonical history of her life and miracles as a support to the canonization process. The *Communion* depicts two of these miracles. At the left, as a response to St. Francesca's devotion, the Virgin, seated in glory at the apex of the triangular composition, sends St. Peter to give the saint Communion; St. Paul, dressed as a deacon, but holding his identifying sword, looks on. At the right St. Peter, dressed in full papal regalia, has arrived to consecrate St. Francesca in her religious life. The fresco cycle is a somewhat naive and straightforward rendition of the saint's life, bearing little resemblance to the classicism practiced in architecture and sculpture at this time, but appropriate for its didactic purpose.

A processional banner depicting the Roman Pope St. Mark (r. 336; Fig. 5.46), painted at about the same time as the St. Francesca cycle by Melozzo for Paul II's titular church of San Marco, and probably at his command, suggests the possibilities for including classical forms in traditional contexts. The banner shows the patron saint of the church in a hieratic frontal pose, seated in full regalia on a classicizing throne. The rigid pose—reminiscent of late Roman imperial portraits—does not, however, detract

from the full-blown naturalism of the figure, with its deep folds of drapery and fleshy, craggy face. The classical decoration that covers every surface of the throne probably derives more from the early work of Mantegna (see Fig. 6.22) than it does from any painting that Melozzo might have seen in Rome. In the spring of 1459 Piero della Francesca was in Rome, painting in one of the rooms recently constructed by Nicholas V and perhaps also in Santa Maria Maggiore; his frescoes in the Vatican palace may have provided a model for the monumentally scaled figures that appear in the *Pope St. Mark* banner and that would develop fully in Melozzo's work of the 1470s.

Beginning with Nicholas V the popes and the cardinals embarked on a series of monumental architectural and sculptural projects in an effort to restore the papacy to a world-wide power while still tied to traditional devotional and spiritual practices. Melozzo's processional banner shows the beginnings of convergence of these different concerns and the possibilities for a new style in painting as well.

Venice and the Veneto: Affirmations of Past and Present

In the mid-fifteenth century artists once again mined Venice's rich past to uncover new possibilities for enhancing and reinforcing its traditions. In this endeavor, the Venetians—newly allied militarily with Florence and Siena against Visconti Milan—cautiously experimented with central Italian artistic models. Those models that had no immediate applicability were either rejected or ignored. At the same time, the presence in Padua of the Florentine master Donatello and the emerging enthusiasm for classical antiquity began to have an impact. Once domesticated in the Veneto, *all'antica* works were in a position to transform the art of Venice as well.

The Doge's Palace

Only a year after taking office in 1423, Doge Francesco Foscari (r. 1423–57) demolished the entire twelfth-century wing of the Doge's Palace between St. Mark's Basilica and the fourteenth-century wing facing the lagoon. Although the Senate had committed itself to this action before Foscari took office, it was a bold and daring act in tradition-conscious Venice. To compensate for this rip in Venice's otherwise continuous historical fabric and to ensure visual unity, the new wing faithfully repeated the distinctive design of the fourteenth-century palace, with its graceful Gothic loggia and pink and white stone diaper patterns (see Fig. 3.7). The seam between the two structures is nearly invisible; a sculptural roundel depicting *Venice Enthroned as Justice*, above one of the columns on the side facing the Piazzetta, marks the spot. The column capitals, which echo or repeat the subjects of the lagoon façade, celebrate the richness and variety of life lived in a good and just society. Besides emphasizing consistency and stability, this continuation of the fourteenth-century wing on the Piazzetta side greatly enhanced the presence of the palace (the largest civic palace in Italy), giving it a majestic air, rivaling the enormous scale of the palaces of Venice's chief rival, Milan (see Fig. 3.37).

Sculpture on the Palace   Doge Foscari's extension of the Doge's Palace required the collaboration of several workshops to carve great numbers of capitals and vast expanses of tracery. By the mid-1430s work must have been sufficiently advanced to award two special commissions, one for a near life-sized sculpture of the *Judgment of Solomon* (Fig. 5.47) at the corner of the building nearest St. Mark's and another virtually adjacent to it for a new monumental portal, now known as the Porta della Carta

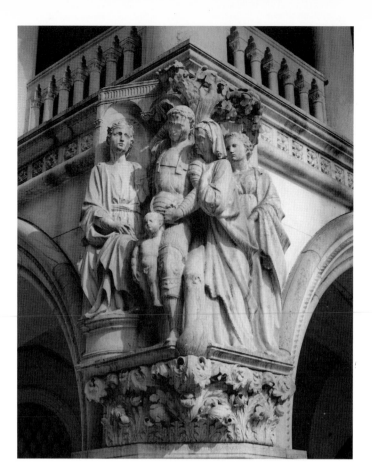

5.47 *Judgment of Solomon*, 1430s, commissioned under Francesco Foscari, possibly from BARTOLOMEO BON THE ELDER, for the Doge's Palace, Venice. Istrian stone

(Fig. 5.48), which opens into the palace's courtyard. There is general agreement that the *Judgment of Solomon* was carved first, but there is little agreement about the identity of the sculptor, who may have been a Florentine, a Lombard, or the Venetian sculptor Bartolomeo Bon the elder (c. 1400/10 Venice–1464/65 Venice), creator of the portal and a member of an important family of stonemasons. The melding of these regional traditions in a single unified composition suggests a situation of artistic collaboration and exchange as vital as had existed in Assisi and Rome at the end of the thirteenth century.

The *Judgment of Solomon* is set at an angle around the corner of the palace so as to be fully visible to anyone approaching the entrance from St. Mark's. It depicts the story in which two women appeal to Solomon, each claiming to be the mother of a child. The king blandly orders a soldier to cut the baby in half and give one half to each woman, whereupon the true mother, aghast, relinquishes her claim to save the child's life. The drama is eloquently conveyed by the facial expressions of the main participants: Solomon appears impassive, befitting impartial justice; the true mother, horrified, as she leans forward to prevent the soldier from obeying the order; the imposter at the far right, dispassionate.

The biblical/historical portrayal of the virtues of the Venetian state seen in the *Judgment of Solomon* is

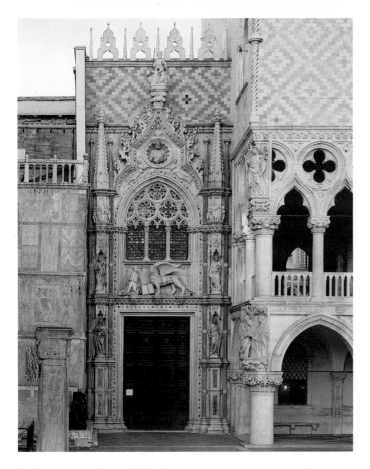

5.48 Porta della Carta, 1438–42, commissioned by Francesco Foscari from BARTOLOMEO BON the elder, for the Doge's Palace, Venice. Red and white marble and Istrian stone

The head of the doge and the winged lion were knocked down by Napoleonic troops; the present forms are modern replacements.

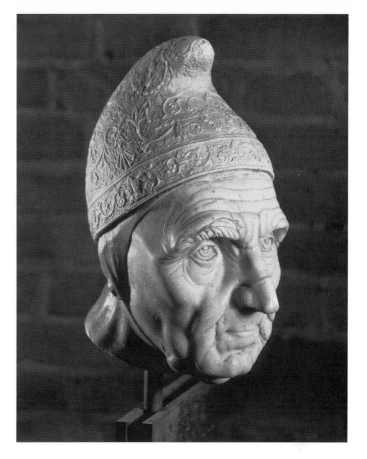

5.49 Head of Francesco Foscari, 1438–42, commissioned by Francesco Foscari from BARTOLOMEO BON the elder, for the Porta della Carta, Doge's Palace, Venice. Marble, 1' 2" high (0.36 m) (Museum of the Doge's Palace)

The end of the doge's nose and much of his left eyebrow are modern replacements.

complemented in more contemporary form on the Porta della Carta (see Fig. 5.48). This magnificent doorway, the new formal entranceway into the Doge's Palace, celebrates Venetian ideals with characteristic panache. Tall Gothic niches along the side borders hold female personifications of the virtues of Temperance, Charity, Fortitude, and Prudence. Over the entrance the larger than lifesized figure of Doge Foscari kneels before the Lion of St. Mark, clearly conceived as the servant of the state. Above them, the crisp tracery of the tripartite window, with its quatrefoil roundels, recalls that on the palace's loggia. A segmented Gothic pediment above it frames three angelic figures displaying a bust of St. Mark. Putti cavort up the portal's final ascent to the seated figure of Justice, who originally rose free against the sky as did the finials of the flanking turrets.

The creator of this splendid composition, Bartolomeo Bon the elder, proudly carved his name on the doorway's architrave. He received the contract along with his father and teacher, Giovanni, on November 10, 1438; the work was complete in 1442. Bartolomeo came from a family of stoneworkers, his earliest surviving work being a wellhead for the Ca' d'Oro, which shows an appreciation of the work of Lorenzo Ghiberti. Bon became Venice's leading

local sculptor and architect, capable of working in a wide variety of modes. His vigorous portrait of Foscari on the Porta della Carta captures every well-earned wrinkle of this indomitable doge (Fig. 5.49). Lips and mouth firmly set, the veins on his temples pulsing with life, Foscari's eyes are intent on the Lion of St. Mark. We are clearly in the presence of a living individual, the proud and determined leader of the Venetian state. At the same time that Pisanello was immortalizing the features of north Italian princes on bronze medals (see Fig. 4.25) Bon offered his own essay in portraiture. Foscari's features are recorded with documentary accuracy—not to celebrate him as an individual, for such self-aggrandizement by the doge was officially proscribed by the state, but as the chief representative of the republic.

Palazzo Foscari

Like most political leaders, however, Francesco Foscari was neither modest nor self-effacing. The palace he built for himself and his family, starting in 1450 (Fig. 5.50), openly imitates the Doge's Palace, both in tracery on its façade and the placement of its main reception halls

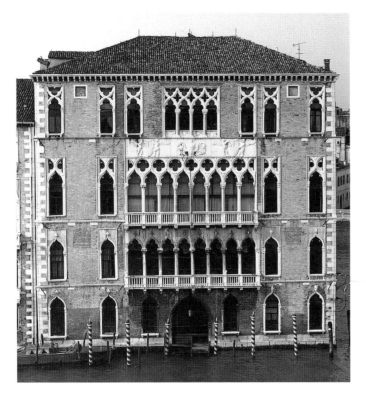

5.50 Palazzo Foscari, Venice, begun 1450, commissioned by Francesco Foscari

5.51 (opposite) Ca' d'Oro (Palazzo Contarini), Venice, 1421–37, commissioned by Marino Contarini from GIOVANNI AND BARTOLOMEO BON, MATTEO RAVERTI, and others

The façades of this and other Venetian noble palaces were regularly enhanced with gold leaf, bright colors, and varnish.

The Ca' d'Oro

Foscari's penchant for splendor had a long tradition in Venice. The Palazzo Contarini is known as the Ca' d'Oro ("house of gold"; Fig. 5.51) because of the gold leaf that originally embellished the intricate carving on its façade. Even without the gold, its luxurious tracery and inlaid marbles give the Ca' d'Oro a blithe extravagance. This was the home of Marino Contarini, scion of one of Venice's most venerable noble families, who took personal responsibility for overseeing the entire project. It was a confident and aggressive assertion of his family's wealth and social prestige, built on the Grand Canal, the city's most important thoroughfare.

The basic organization of the palace follows a well-established type (Fig. 5.52). As with many small and moderate-sized Venetian Gothic palazzi, the façade is asymmetrical. The main entrance, on the ground floor, is sheltered by the simplest of the three loggias. Behind it is the *androne*, a great open hall, which served the practical purpose of receiving and dispensing shipments of goods; alongside were assorted storerooms. (Many Venetian nobility owed their fortunes to trade, unlike their counterparts elsewhere in Europe.) Farther back is a courtyard and garden. Above the *androne*, fronted by another loggia—the most elaborate of the three, with its quatrefoil tracery—is the *gran salone*, the main reception hall, flanked by smaller reception rooms; this floor is known as the *piano nobile* in Italian. The upper floors contain more private rooms. Providing adequate light for all these rooms was problematical, given the scarcity of land and the narrowness of flanking canals, which meant that palaces stood close together. For this reason the façades were designed with large windows.

As was common practice in Venice, Contarini issued contracts to builders, sculptors, and painters. He entrusted the tracery of the main loggia to Matteo Raverti (active 1389–1434), one of the chief sculptors at Milan Cathedral and perhaps a contributor to the sculptural program of the Doge's Palace. To simulate the sheen of marble, painters applied white lead and oil to the Istrian stone. Red Verona marble details were oiled to bring out their richest tonalities, and the balls on the façade's parapet, along with the window finials, capitals, and architectural moldings were all gilded. Though more extravagant than most private residences in Venice, it epitomizes the luxuriant tenor of much Venetian art.

at the top of the double-tiered loggia. The geometric orderliness of the façade, balancing symmetrically arranged windows on either side of the central loggias, was typical of larger Venetian palaces. Classicizing putti display the Foscari coat of arms on a large relief which runs across the façade, echoing Florentine forms. Like their smaller counterparts on the Porta della Carta, they document a taste for the antique that was just beginning to be felt in Venice at this time, although still mainly restricted to decorative elements.

The form and extraordinarily large size of the palace permanently associated Foscari and his family with the office of doge. Cosimo de' Medici was making similar claims for his family in Florence, where the Medici Palace (see Fig. 5.14) clearly evoked associations with the Palazzo della Signoria. Foscari may have felt free to stretch the limits of typical Venetian luxury, since he held the ducal office longer than any of his predecessors. He was also enamored of pomp and display. Foscari's reception in 1438 for the Byzantine Emperor John VIII Paleologus stupefied even the Venetians, who were accustomed to lavish pageantry: twelve floating theaters accompanied the doge's *Bucintoro* ("barge") in welcoming the imperial visitor.

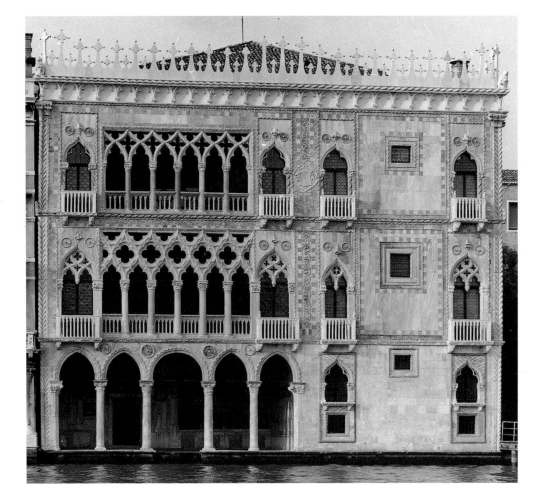

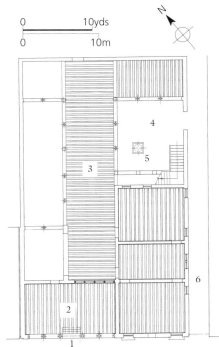

5.52 Ca' d'Oro, Venice, plan of lower floor

1 Grand Canal; **2** Entrance portico (*riva*); **3** Central hall (*androne*); **4** Courtyard; **5** Well-head; **6** Alleyway (Calle di Cà Giustinian)

C O N T E M P O R A R Y   V O I C E

Finishing Touches

Today the Ca' d'Oro remains one of the most beautiful of Venetian *palazzi*, with its exquisite white marble tracery. One can scarcely imagine how spectacular it must have appeared when completed—lavishly painted and gilded according to the specifications laid down by its owner, Marino Contarini.

This is the work which . . . Marin Contarini . . . wishes to be done in the painting of the façade of his house at Santa Sofia on the Grand Canal.

And firstly to gild all of the little balls that are on top of the crenellation, and to gild all of the discs of the crenellations that are below the flowers.

And to gild the rosettes which are at the bottom of the little arches.

And to gild all of the leaves of the two large capitals at the corners, which have the lions on the top.

And to fill in the background of the said capitals with fine ultramarine blue.

And in the same way to gild the two lions which are above the said capitals, with the [Contarini] arms that they hold in their paws, the which arms I wish to be finished with ultramarine blue.

And the plinths where the said lions are positioned I wish to be gilded at the front.

And below, I wish it to be fine ultramarine blue with small gold stars. . . .

And next I wish to be gilded the rope mouldings on the twenty roundels, and the balls, and also twelve flowers, all gilded.

And next I wish to be gilded the large coat of arms, that is, the shield with the dentils and foliage, and I wish the stripes to be of ultramarine blue applied in two coats so that it will appear excellent; and this is all the work that I wish to be gilded on the said façade.

And next I wish that all of the crowning cornice . . . to be finished with white oil paint,

and that all of the crenellations are to be darkened in the manner of marble. . . .

And then I wish that all of the red stonework that is in the said façade and all of the red dentil [courses] are to be finished with oil and varnish so that they appear red.

And then I wish that all of the roses and vines that are on the said façade are to be finished with white oil paint, and to paint the fields with black oil paint so that it appears well. . . .

All of which work is to be done by *maestro* Zuan da Franza, painter, of Sant'Aponal, all at his own expense, and I intend that the said *maestro* is to use ultramarine blue at a cost of XVIII ducats per pound, and he is to receive for his work as described 60 gold ducats.

(from Richard J. Goy. *The House of Gold: Building a Palace in Medieval Venice.* Cambridge: Cambridge University Press, 1992, pp 287–8)

The Cappella Nova

In 1430 Doge Foscari enlisted the assistance of two noble allies and procurators of St. Mark's to create a new chapel in the left transept (Fig. 5.53), probably as an *ex voto* to the Virgin after a failed assassination attempt on March 11, 1431 (1430 Venetian style since the new year did not begin until March 25). Known as the Cappella Nova, or "New Chapel," until the seventeenth century, when it was taken over by the Confraternity of the Mascoli whose name it now bears, the barrel-vaulted chapel contains a suave marble altarpiece showing the Madonna and Child flanked by two saints, perhaps Evangelists. An inscription above them records the names of the chapel's founders and the foundation date. Mosaics surrounding an oculus in the lunette and on the barrel vault depict scenes from the life of the Virgin. Variegated marble covers the lower walls; the original traceried balustrade still survives at the chapel's entrance.

The chapel's decoration demonstrates the power of Venice's Byzantine past, which continued to furnish models for figures and compositions while also providing a matrix in which to incorporate new forms imported from outside the republic. In charge of the mosaic decorations was the Venetian painter and mosaicist Michele Giambono (Michele di Taddeo or Michele di Giovanni Bono; 1400 Venice–c. 1462 Venice). In the *Annunciation*, depicted in the lunette, Giambono sets Gabriel and Mary on a bare stage against a gold ground, overlooked by God the Father and the descending dove of the Holy Spirit, reminiscent of the hauntingly powerful, isolated Byzantine-style figures who hover in the mosaics elsewhere in the east end of the church. Giambono's quietly introverted figures also display a melancholy air characteristic of Venetian-Byzantine figural art.

We know nothing about Giambono's training, but by the time he was working on the mosaics in Foscari's Cappella Nova he had developed a unique personal style which blends Byzantine traditions with the art of Jacobello del Fiore and Gentile da Fabriano, who had worked in Venice before moving on to Florence and Rome. Eschewing the more elaborate and contrived aspects of the work of his predecessors—their artificially fluttering hems and complicated silhouettes—Giambono invented equally precious but more languid figures whose drapery clings to their bodies and moves in response to their actions.

In the scenes of the *Birth of the Virgin* and her *Presentation in the Temple* on the left side of the barrel vault, Giambono faced the challenge of depicting a continuous narrative. These stories had been very rarely represented in Venetian art up until this time. For inspiration, Giambono thus turned to the most extensive and best-known Virgin cycle in Venetian territory, Giotto's frescoes in the Scrovegni Chapel in Padua (see Fig. 2.2). In the background and to the left of the *Birth of the Virgin*, the same patient servant waits outside the birthing chamber, which has been modernized with balconies, porches, and Gothic tracery that relate both to contemporary architecture and to the complex architecture of late-fourteenth-century Paduan frescoes (see Fig. 3.48). More important, he took into consideration the fact that the chapel's location in the corner of the basilica's left transept and the marble barrier in front of it forced most viewers to look at the composition from outside the chapel and to the right. Thus he set his action and the Virgin's birthplace obliquely across the field of vision, encouraging onlookers to move into the action as it evolves continuously from left to right. The clear colors of the figures' garments stand out against the grey and white buildings, making the composition easy to read in spite of its complex settings. The continuous gold background unites the scenes as well, joining them in a long rectangular field which conforms to the format of the other narratives in the church.

The Scuola della Carità

The most prolific painters of mid-fifteenth century Venice were Antonio Vivarini (c. 1418 Murano–1476/84 Venice) and his brother-in-law Giovanni d'Alemagna (d. 1450 Padua). They ran an extremely well organized shop that specialized in multi-tiered, multi-paneled altarpieces and fanciful Gothic frames, which they subcontracted to various woodworkers. In 1446 they signed and dated a large panel painting of the *Madonna and Child with Saints* for the wall behind the officers' bench of the recently expanded *albergo* (officers' meeting room) of the Scuola della Carità (now part of the Accademia painting gallery; Fig. 5.54). Resembling an altarpiece—which it is not—but functioning like Simone Martini's *Maestà* in the Palazzo Pubblico in Siena (see Fig. 2.23) as an inducement to good decision-making, this monumental painting shows the four doctors of the Church (saints Gregory and Jerome at the left, Ambrose and Augustine at the right) in a courtyard around a massive Madonna and Child.

While the unified space in the Scuola della Carità painting may have been inspired by a now dismembered altarpiece that the Florentine artist Filippo Lippi had created for a church in Padua in the 1430s, the two Venetian artists put their model to a different use as emblem of the Scuola. The Virgin's celestial court is vividly rendered with marbled pink and grey architecture, rich deep colors, costly robes, gilt *pastiglia*, and lovingly observed plant life. Unlike Venetian altarpieces of this and earlier periods, the

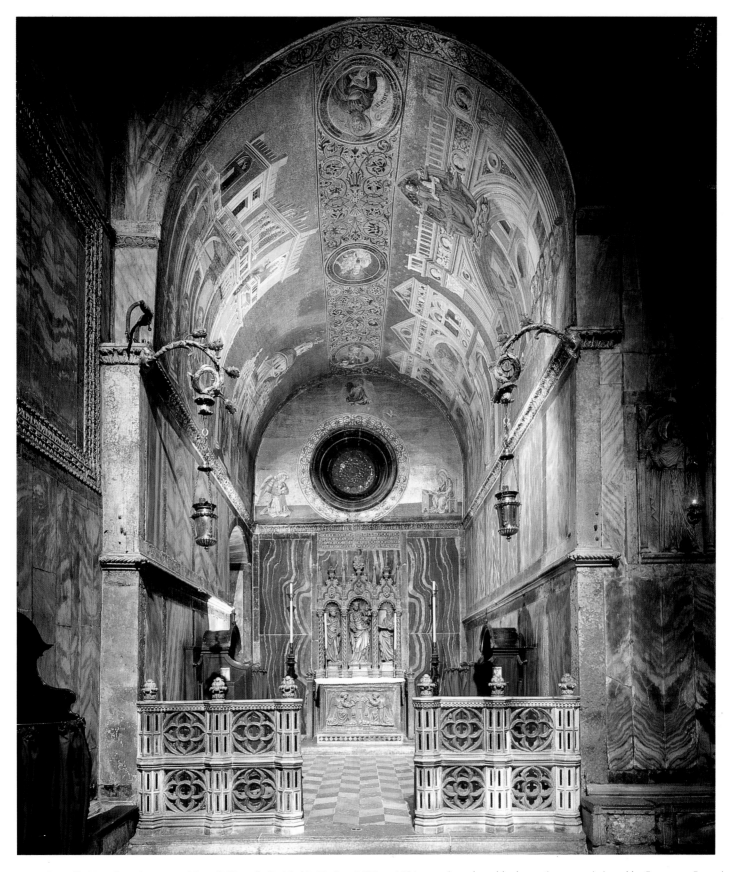

5.53 Cappella Nova (now known as Mascoli Chapel), St. Mark's, Venice, 1431–c. 1451, mosaic and marble decoration commissioned by Francesco Foscari from MICHELE GIAMBONO and others

This multi-media complex of colored marbles and mosaics survives almost completely intact.

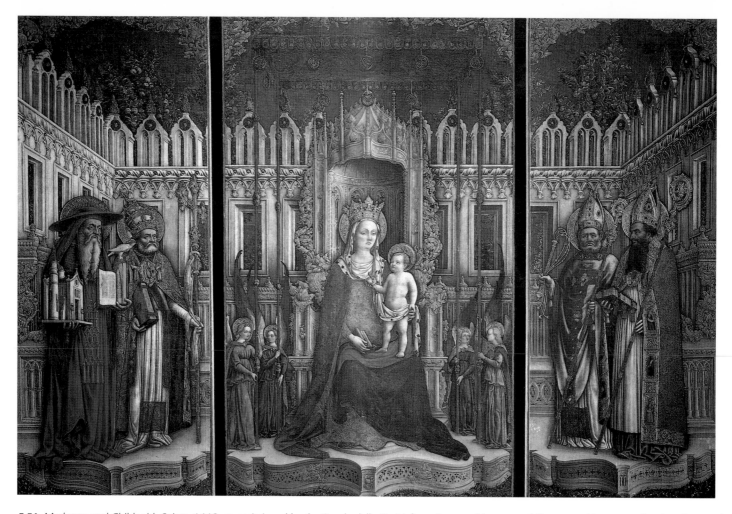

5.54 *Madonna and Child with Saints*, 1446, commissioned by the Scuola della Carità from Antonio Vivarini and Giovanni d'Alemagna for the *albergo* of the Scuola della Carità, Venice. Oil on panel, 11' 3½" × 15' 7¾" (3.44 × 4.77 m) (Galleria dell'Accademia, Venice)

work represents the supernatural in a physically specific world. Whatever naturalness the space conveys is countered, however, by the elaborately curved platform on which the figures stand. Theater and display here play an important role, much as the corporate rituals and charitable activities of the Scuola manifested religious fervor in the physical reality of the city.

Jacopo Bellini

Jacopo Bellini (c. 1400 Venice–1470/71 Venice) was an even greater synthesizer than Vivarini and Giovanni d'Alemagna, equally at home with Byzantine, Gothic, northern European, and central Italian types and modes. He was the foremost student of Gentile da Fabriano and the founder of an artistic dynasty, being the father of both Gentile and Giovanni Bellini and father-in-law of Andrea Mantegna. Jacopo's *Madonna and Child Surrounded by an Aureole of Angels* (Fig. 5.55), probably created as a private devotional object, reveals several aspects of his artistic personality. Still in its original frame, the image expresses a sadness typical of Veneto-Byzantine Madonnas. A shower of gold dots flickers across the Virgin's robe, evoking the

glimmer of Venetian mosaics. The painting also betrays Jacopo's study of northern European paintings. As in certain works by Jan van Eyck and his school, the figures are set behind a parapet which sharply defines the pictorial space. The Child's pleasant, open demeanor and soft, golden curls captivate and charm, even as the Virgin keeps him in the realm of the holy by holding her hand in front of and across his little body.

Jacopo was also a prolific draftsman. A series of 220 drawings by him has been preserved in two volumes, one set on parchment, the other on white paper. They seem to have been created for his own study, not preparatory to any specific commissions, nor necessarily for the instruction of students in his studio. Jacopo purchased the paper unbound but in quires (sets of twenty-four or twenty-five sheets), working on the drawings over several decades. His widow called these works "drawn paintings," an apt characterization of their status as works of art in their own right. They are the first works of their kind.

One of the principal artistic challenges that Jacopo addressed in his drawings was how to adapt scientific perspective to Venetian and Paduan preferences for imagining narrative in highly complex environments (see Fig. 3.48), a tradition that grew out of a belief in the

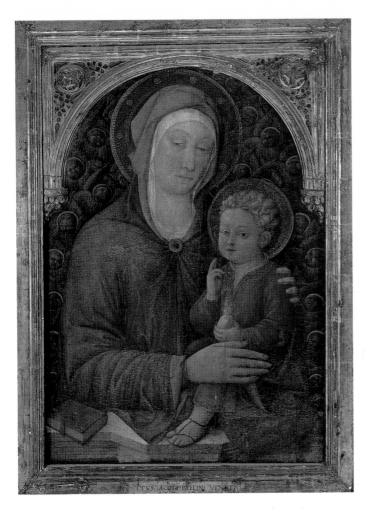

5.55 *Madonna and Child Surrounded by an Aureole of Angels (Madonna of the Cherubim)*, 1450s, JACOPO BELLINI. Tempera on panel, 37 × 26" (94 × 66 cm) (Galleria dell'Accademia, Venice)

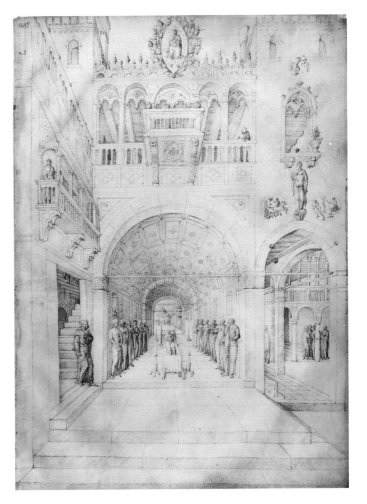

5.56 *Dormition of the Virgin*, c. 1450, page from the notebooks of JACOPO BELLINI. Leadpoint on parchment with later pen retouchings, 16¾ × 11¼" (42.5 × 28.5 cm) (Musée du Louvre, Paris)

documentary value of art. To be true to life, narratives in the Venetian tradition needed to be complicated and filled with anecdotal detail. In a drawing of the *Dormition of the Virgin* (Fig. 5.56) representing the display of the Virgin Mary's corpse, Bellini constructs an expansive urban space in which all diagonal lines merge toward a single vanishing point at the eye level of the figures within the drawing, just as prescribed by Alberti in his *Della Pittura*. But Bellini was not content to create the spare and highly focused compositions preferred by Tuscan artists. He shows, instead, a typically Venetian delight in complex architecture. These buildings appear irregular, spontaneous: they are filled with figures going about their business—one on a balcony, another coming down the stairs, another group gathered far to the right background around the column of an arcade.

In the midst of this rich world Bellini placed the apostles mourning over the body of the deceased Virgin Mary, whose soul in the form of a miniaturized body is received by Christ in the small aureole of angels at the very top of the drawing. Just below it rises a radically foreshortened balcony seen from below. This introduces a new dimension. Paradoxically, what had seemed natural and true-to-life suddenly becomes contrived and disturbing, much as

the fallen soldiers and regularly arranged lances on the ground in Paolo Uccello's panel paintings (see Fig. 5.20) appear artificial. It is all too clear that scientific perspective is also *artificial* perspective, closely approximating human sight but neither replicating it nor accounting for its tendency to "correct" what people see in terms of their prior knowledge of it. Jacopo began to domesticate scientific perspective in such compositions but still left room for experimentation.

The Cappella Nova in the late 1440s

Jacopo's spatial experiments account for the mosaics added to the right side of the barrel vault in the Cappella Nova in St. Mark's (Fig. 5.57), probably between 1448 and 1451. As in Giambono's compositions in the chapel of the early 1430s (see Fig. 5.53), the field contains two major scenes, the *Visitation* at left and the *Dormition* at right. The two scenes are conceived separately, however, each placed before its own illusionistic architectural backdrop.

The distinctive manners of the Florentine painter Andrea del Castagno (see Fig. 5.28), of Michele Giambono

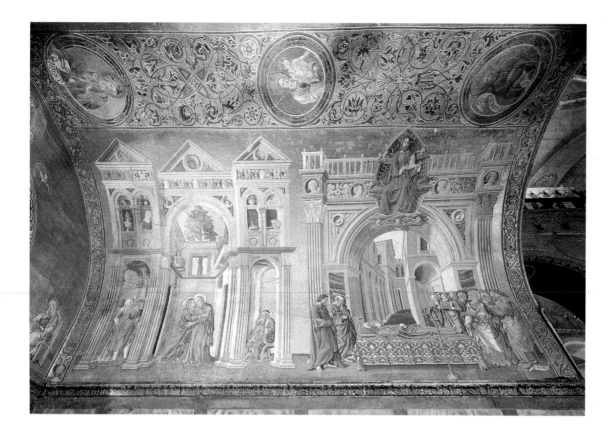

5.57 *Visitation* and *Dormition of the Virgin*, 1448–51, commissioned from JACOPO BELLINI, ANDREA DEL CASTAGNO, and MICHELE GIAMBONO for the right half of the barrel vault of the Cappella Nova (Mascoli Chapel), St. Mark's, Venice. Mosaic

(see Fig. 5.53), and of Jacopo Bellini, all three of whom worked on the full-scale preparatory cartoons for the mosaics, are visible in the *Dormition*. Although depicting the same subject as Bellini's drawing, the composition for the Cappella Nova mosaic is evidently not by him but by Castagno. Florentine in conception, it gives prominence to the main actors. Castagno's composition is decidedly more dramatic and legible than Bellini's, but it sacrifices faithful rendition of visual experience and spatial expansiveness for visual clarity. Castagno places only two Apostles to the left of his powerfully large figure of the deceased Virgin—the huddled groups at right bear the imprint of Giambono's and Bellini's intervention. The seated figure, God the Father, who in Bellini's drawing had appeared as a small figure hovering at a believably great height above the buildings, now comes close to the viewer, as do the Apostles and the Virgin's bier.

The most convincing current theory to account for the presence of this radically foreign artistic conception in St. Mark's suggests that Castagno received the commission from Francesco Foscari when he was working for Elena Foscari, the sister of the Doge, at the nunnery of San Zaccaria in Venice between 1440 and 1442. Castagno probably produced the cartoon for the Cappella Nova mosaics before leaving Venice in 1442, though the project was left to languish until the late 1440s, when Venice was more receptive to Florentine style. Then Bellini and Giambono added their own figures to the right side, sug-

gesting either that Castagno left the work unfinished or that it was damaged in the intervening years and that the Venetians preferred seeing figures subordinate to their setting, as in Jacopo's drawings, rather than dominating it. They also added a little balustrade atop the triumphal arch to soften its Tuscan severity.

Jacopo Bellini seems to have been assigned the task of designing the *Visitation* mosaic to accompany Castagno's composition. The work tells us much about the Venetian response to Castagno's example. Except for the classicizing language of its architectural elements and the large scale of its figures, the entire scene reads as a rather severe critique of Castagno's work. Mary and Elizabeth encounter one another *in* the space under the central arch, not in front of it, the area behind them enlivened with a variety of doors, windows, a balcony, a flowering window box, and a framed view of a tall tree, rather than Castagno's plain and deserted street façades. Bellini also included chambers at the left and right for witnesses to the sacred encounter, so important to Venetian documentary expectations. In the upper story a young woman looks on from a window filled with objects, more of which appear, along with a monkey, on the right. The composition is as legible as Castagno's but even more delightful and intriguing to explore.

At mid-century Venetian artists were increasingly cognizant of and ready to experiment with scientific perspective and classical vocabulary. Not only Jacopo Bellini but also the builders of the Palazzo Foscari and the carvers of the Porta della Carta showed interest in incorporating new elements into their works. At the same time, traditional commitments to visual richness and elaboration, as well as an ongoing tendency toward synthesis, meant that new elements were not merely adopted but fused with older ones. Eclectic combinations of style and motifs were never richer nor more varied.

Donatello in Padua

The influence of artistic developments in Padua may have caused Jacopo Bellini and his Venetian contemporaries to begin exploring ways to use scientific perspective and classicizing elements in their compositions. Since 1444 the Florentine sculptor Donatello had been working in that city, where he was to remain for a decade. Padua was not only a dependency of Venice (since 1403) but also the site of a renowned university, at which Venetian scholars earned their degrees.

The city was a major center of humanist studies. Petrarch had spent his last years in Venice and Padua and was commemorated in a remarkably detailed and spatially convincing painting in the Carrara palace (see Fig. 3.43). The Paduans' active promotion of the cult of St. Anthony had also encouraged the exploitation of very realistic modes of presentation, Altichiero's late fourteenth-century frescoes in the Santo being among the most illusionistic and lifelike of their day (see Fig. 3.46). Donatello's own active, passionate interest in antiquity, human psychology, and the convincing representation of reality made him an ideal candidate to undertake work in Padua. However, it was probably his technical expertise, specifically in bronze casting, which first brought Donatello to the attention of local authorities, who commissioned from him a bronze equestrian statue and works for the high altar of the Santo. His affinity with local traditions and his genius for expanding upon them ensured that his works were more than mere technical achievements.

The Santo Altarpiece   The entire ensemble for the high altar of the Santo (Fig. 5.59) was modeled and cast in less than two years, temporarily assembled for the saint's feast day on June 13, 1448, but still not completely chased and polished when Donatello left Padua in 1454. Intended to give glory to the city's beloved, miracle-working saint, the altar included four large reliefs of St. Anthony's miracles, six lifesized statues (three Franciscans, including Anthony, and three other local saints), a limestone relief of the Lamentation at the tomb, and bronze reliefs of the symbols of the Evangelists and of music-making angels. It was a sculptor's tour de force of free-standing and relief sculpture, all set within an elaborate architectural framework as if the figures existed on a liturgical stage.

Donatello's relief of *The Ass of Rimini* (Fig. 5.58) for the altar tells the story of a man who doubted the Church's doctrine of Transubstantiation, that is, the miraculous but actual, physical presence of Christ in the sacrifice of the Mass. When St. Anthony displayed a consecrated Host to the man's donkey, as he is shown doing in the center of

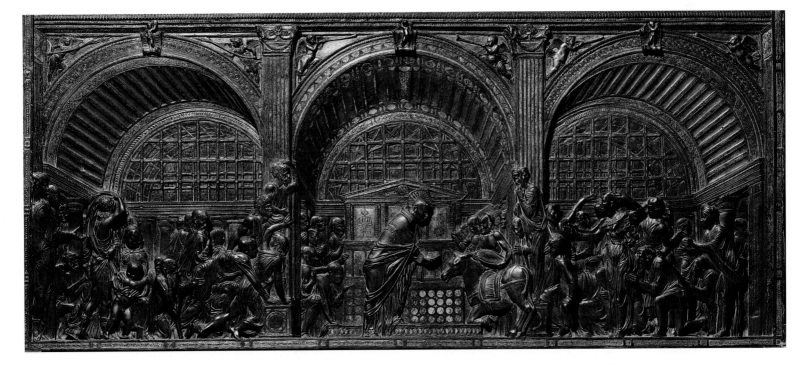

5.58 *The Ass of Rimini*, 1446–53, detail of the high altar, the Santo, Padua, commissioned by the governors of the Santo from DONATELLO. Bronze, partially gilt, 22½ × 48½" (57 × 123 cm)

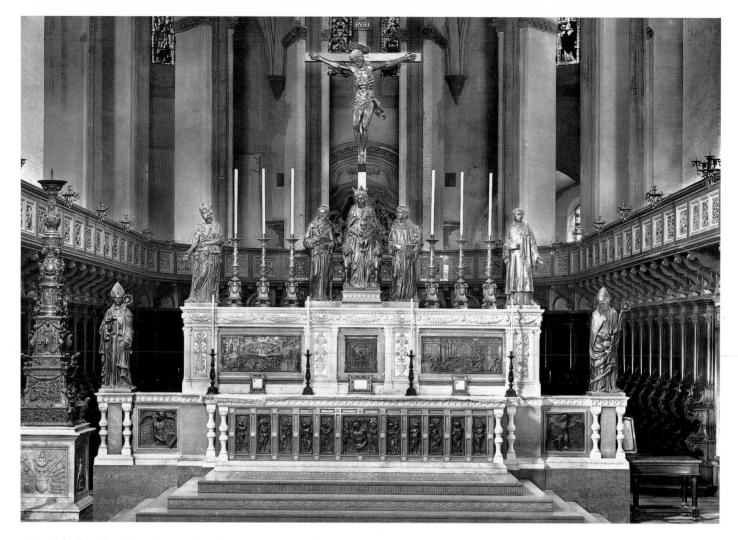

5.59 High Altar, the Santo, Padua, 1446–53, commissioned by the governors of the Santo from DONATELLO. Bronze, partially gilt

The arrangement of the statues does not correspond to their original disposition, which included an architectural canopy for most or all of the figures, perhaps roughly comparable to the architectural structuring of Mantegna's *San Zeno Altarpiece* (Fig. 5.62). Donatello's bronze crucifix was not part of the altar program.

the relief, the beast recognized the divine presence and fell to its knees. Church doctrine was confirmed and heresy refuted by a beast of burden—a reminder of St. Francis's own use of animals in his preaching and miracles and a confirmation of Anthony's effectiveness as a defender of orthodoxy.

Donatello imagined the event as both momentous—and therefore worthy of a grand setting—and emotionally and spiritually transforming, as suggested by the intense, personal reactions of the attending figures. The action takes place before three huge barrel vaults, whose monumentality suggests those of the Basilica of Maxentius in the Roman Forum. Donatello enlivened the cavernous space with classical pilasters, putti in the arches' spandrels, and rectangular coffering which leads the eye back to iron grates through which yet deeper spaces can be seen. The strategic application of gilding keeps the complex architecture legible.

Jacopo Bellini would probably have been impressed by Donatello's architectural setting—its masterly perspective and deep spatial recession—but he would surely have noted that Donatello only partially integrates his figures into the space, most of them seeming to stand right on the front edge of the picture plane. What is more, the relief's emotionalism might have seemed indecorous to Venetians, no matter how effective and appropriate it was to its location in a major site of pilgrimage and miracles.

On the other hand, Donatello's *Madonna and Child*, around which his other figures on the altar are grouped, is traditionally iconic in its composition, representing in its strict frontality the allegory of Mary as the Throne of Wisdom as she supports an equally severely frontal Christ Child. The Madonna is both formidable and approachable. As regal as a Byzantine empress in her headdress of winged cherubs, she presents the worshiper with the true and palpable body of Christ, a literal counterpart to the presentation of the Host in the relief discussed above. As the worshiper approaches the altar, the Madonna rises from her throne, her right leg slightly bent behind her, so that we can see the baby Jesus in all his humanity. Surrounded by the parting drapery of her gown, the Christ Child seems born before our very eyes.

The Gattamelata Monument   While Donatello and his large workshop were producing the altar for the Santo, they were also engaged in creating an over-life-sized bronze equestrian statue of the Paduan-born leader of the Venetian army, Erasmo da Narni, known to history by his nickname Gattamelata ("honeyed cat"; Fig. 5.60). The earliest recorded payments for this work date from 1447; in 1453 the work was appraised and in place. It was financed by the late general's wife and son but made possible only by authorization of the Venetian government. The epitaph composed by the humanist Giantonio Porcello de' Pandoni for Gattamelata's tomb inside the Santo phrased it succinctly: "The Senate and my pure faithfulness rewarded me with worthy gifts and an equestrian statue."

Occupying a prominent position in the piazza in front of the Santo, the monument to Gattamelata is extraordinary in many ways. Not only is it a major technical and artistic achievement—the first surviving monumental bronze equestrian statue since antiquity—but it confers the Roman imperial dignity of this form to a person of less than sovereign status, the Venetian republic's hired military leader. Previous Venetian *condottieri* had been portrayed in contemporary guise, in much more humble materials, and inside churches; exterior equestrians throughout northern Italy had been reserved for rulers such as the Scaligers (see Fig. 3.36) or Niccolò III d'Este, whose bronze monument in Ferrara (now destroyed) was commissioned by Leonello d'Este shortly before Donatello began work in Padua. Donatello not only added some Roman features to Gattamelata's armor, he also created an idealized portrait of a Roman hero, much more restrained in its commitment to realism than Bartolomeo Bon's equally powerful but graphically candid head of the man Gattamelata served, Doge Foscari (see Fig. 5.49). He sits astride a massive horse, whose pose and features suggest a crossbreed of the horses on the façade of St. Mark's and the heftier animal ridden by Marcus Aurelius in the Piazza del Campidoglio in Rome. In this formidable image the state and the individual are inextricably fused.

It is, however, a curious monument for a man who more than once fled from the enemy and who was far from Venice's greatest military hero (not to mention one who bore a nickname so suggestive of slyness). It has been suggested that Donatello made more of the commission than he should have, that it became a pretext for his own evocation of the grandeur of antiquity, which in some ways it is. But placed at the entrance to the Santo, Padua's most cherished shrine, Donatello's re-imagined Gattamelata offers an image that could please Paduan and Venetian alike. By removing Gattamelata from the present and recasting him as an ancient hero, Donatello avoided calling attention to the facts—discomforting to

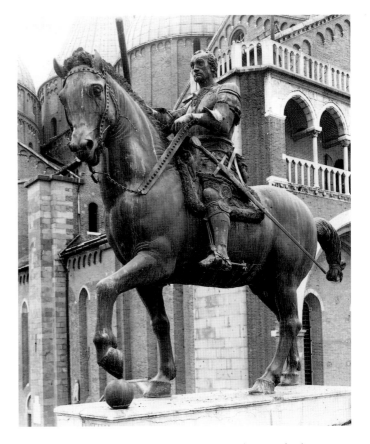

5.60 *Equestrian Monument to Erasmo da Narni* (Gattamelata), 1447–53, commissioned by his wife and son from DONATELLO to be placed outside the Santo, Padua. Bronze, height 12′ 2″ (3.7 m)

This is a cenotaph monument. Gattamelata's actual tomb monument and burial site are located inside the Santo.

both parties—that Gattamelata represented the military force of Venice, which had conquered Padua, and that he was actually less successful as a soldier than the Venetians hoped he might be. Significantly, the monument never received an inscription, which would have tied it to a specific time and place. Instead, Gattamelata is every hero, an embodiment of virtue, the noble Roman who exhibits self-control, dignity, and pride in everything he does, a model for all viewers whatever their political or ideological allegiance. The pious pilgrim might even have imagined him as the Christian emperor Constantine, whose identity had long been confused in Rome with the equestrian statue of Marcus Aurelius.

Mantegna in Padua

Ancient Roman sculpture also inspired a young Paduan, Andrea Mantegna (1430/31 Isola di Cartura, Padua–1506 Mantua), who created paintings of unprecedented archaeological accuracy, learning from the example of Donatello, of his father-in-law, Jacopo Bellini, and of

Francesco Squarcione, an artist entrepreneur who was his teacher and adoptive father. Mantegna's first major fresco cycle, scenes from the lives of saints James and Christopher for the mortuary chapel of Antonio di Biagio degli Ovetari in the church of the Eremitani, Padua, was almost completely destroyed in World War II. Pre-war photographic documentation and surviving fragments in the chapel, however, indicate that all the scenes took place in distinctly classical settings.

The patron of the chapel, Ovetari's widow, Imperatrice, reacted strongly to Mantegna's work. She raised a lawsuit against Mantegna when the artist failed to show all twelve Apostles in a scene of the Assumption of the Virgin on the apse wall. From the start she allotted half of the frescoes to the well-established Venetian team of Antonio Vivarini and Giovanni d'Alemagna, who had provided the impressive polyptych for the Scuola della Carità in Venice (see Fig. 5.54). Their richly decorative manner dominated the vault. Probably so as to expedite the work, Mantegna and a young Paduan artist, Niccolò Pizzolo (1421–53), were assigned the other half of the chapel. But when Giovanni d'Alemagna died in 1450, Vivarini decided to abandon the project, leaving the creations of the younger artists to dominate the chapel.

Taking into account an actual viewing position slightly above eye level, Mantegna imagined the scene of *St. James Being Led to His Execution* from a worm's eye view (Fig. 5.61), that is, from beneath the figures' feet, who seem to loom above us. The effect is dramatic and unsettling. The coffered barrel vault of a triumphal arch at the left and the cornice of a large house at the right sweep in bold angles down and into the picture space. A Roman soldier at the far right belligerently moves the crowd out of the way, while another, in front of the saint, raises his hands amazed at the miraculous conversion and healing of the man kneeling at the saint's feet. The events seem to take place at only an arm's reach from the picture plane, a distance Mantegna nearly eliminated in the adjacent scene of the saint's execution, where he placed the martyr's head in the extreme foreground, just before it was to be severed. High drama, a recurrent theme in Paduan narrative fresco painting, had found a powerful new exponent.

Predictably, Mantegna's accomplishments—especially his mastery of perspective—brought him wide attention and praise. Writers such as Alberti and the Paduan Michele Savonarola (not the famous religious reformer with the same surname) used perspective, with its foundation in mathematics, theory, and philosophy, as one of their primary bases for claiming that painting was a liberal (i.e. intellectual) art rather than a mechanical one (i.e. a craft). Such a distinction must have mattered a great deal in a university town like Padua, as did Mantegna's studious evocation of ancient Roman models. Paduan

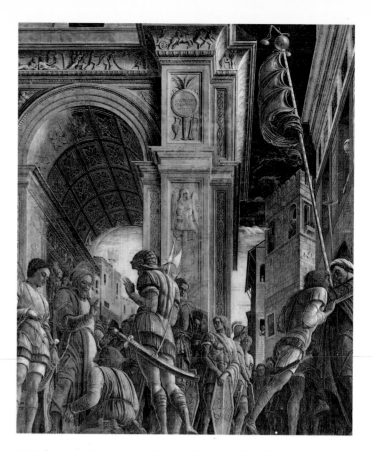

5.61 *St. James Being Led to His Execution*, c. 1455–56, commissioned by Imperatrice Ovetari from ANDREA MANTEGNA for her husband Antonio's burial chapel in the Church of the Eremitani, Padua. Fresco

Only shattered fragments of the original fresco cycle still survive, carefully reassembled after extensive bomb damage during World War II.

scholars had been active in antiquarian studies for well over a century, having in 1315 revived the ancient practice of crowning a poet laureate and long having celebrated famous citizens like the historian Livy (59 B.C.E.–C.E.17) whose supposed bones were discovered in a local monastery in 1413. The itinerant scholar Cyriac of Ancona, who had traveled around the Mediterranean collecting inscriptions and making drawings of Roman ruins, affirmed local interest in elegant Roman epigraphy. Paduan scholars delighted in these acts of learning and revival. On one occasion Mantegna and some friends dressed up and imagined themselves as Romans while they spent a carefree day boating on Lake Garda.

Mantegna in Verona

Soon after completing the frescoes in the Ovetari Chapel, Mantegna was given an opportunity to work with the Venetian nobleman Gregorio Correr, who was abbot of the monastery of San Zeno in Verona. Correr was a serious humanist scholar and man of advanced tastes. For him, Mantegna imagined a fully classicizing, spatially unified altarpiece (Fig. 5.62), perhaps comparable in its disposition of figures to the original structuring of Donatello's altar of the Santo in Padua (see Fig. 5.59) and

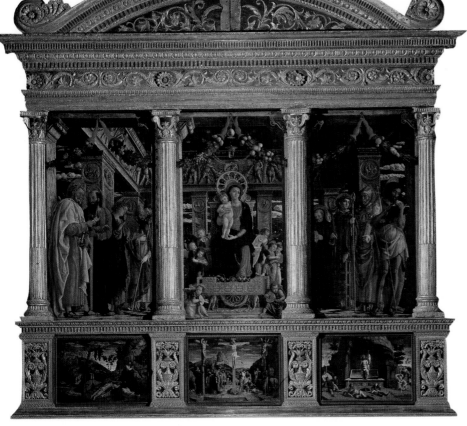

5.62 *San Zeno Altarpiece*, 1456–59, commissioned by Gregorio Correr from ANDREA MANTEGNA for the high altar of San Zeno, Verona. Tempera on panel, height 7' 2½" (2.2 m)

The predella panels are copies of the originals, which are now in France.

poses he positions the throne of the Madonna and Child well forward in the central panel, giving Mary and Christ a prominence that serves traditional religious expectations in new, more illusionistically convincing ways. The altarpiece also sings with bright color—reds, yellows, and greens—probably both in response to local critics who had complained that the Eremitani frescoes looked like tinted statues and owing to the fact that panel painting allowed Mantegna to produce richer, brighter tones than were possible in fresco.

Synopsis

differing from the compartmentalized type that the artist had provided for a more traditionalist patron in Padua just a year or two earlier. The work consists of a Madonna and Child enthroned in the midst of a courtyard and surrounded by standing saints. The wooden frame is sumptuously gilded, as was the regular practice for altarpieces; but instead of using the still-popular pinnacles and elaborately cusped, pointed arches that continued to surround most north Italian altarpieces well into the 1470s, Mantegna followed Donatello's lead and framed his subjects with classically detailed pedestals, fluted columns, a rich architrave, and a curved pediment terminating in graceful volutes. The unusually large fields of the rectangular predella panels clearly evoke the scale of Donatello's narrative reliefs on the Santo altar (see Fig. 5.58).

The frame of the *San Zeno Altarpiece* serves as a portico to a marble courtyard that embraces the entire pictorial field of the altarpiece, the frame and the courtyard just barely separated from one another by swags of fruit and vegetables. In the main panel of the triptych, Mantegna once more simulates Roman architecture and sculpture, both for the throne of the Madonna and Child, flanked by Donatellesque angel musicians, and for the carved roundels and putto frieze which appear on and above, respectively, the sturdy rectilinear piers. His command of perspective allows him to lay out the inlaid marble floor with masterly foreshortening and to place the saints in the two flanking panels back along the sides of the portico and well into the space. For devotional and hieratic pur-

In the mid-fifteenth century patrons in Italy increasingly cultivated a taste for ancient Roman subject matter and style, enriching and enlarging rather than limiting or narrowing their stylistic options. Most artists freely blended new subjects and decorative motifs with old, Mantegna's rigorous visual archaeology being the exception that proves the rule. While the figures in Ghiberti's panels for the *Gates of Paradise*, for example, inhabit a world ordered according to classical principles of design, they retain the elegance of the International Gothic style. Many works make no reference to classical antiquity: the battle scenes painted by Paolo Uccello and the unpretentious narratives of Antoniazzo in Rome, for example. In Mantegna's own Padua and even more so in nearby Venice, Byzantine models continued to inspire works of deep contemplative value.

Understanding of this period, then, is enhanced by discarding the familiar model of antique revival as the definer of advanced style. Nor should Florentine artistic developments be used as a standard against which to measure the art of other city-states. While the work of Florentines was widely admired and studied in this period—thanks both to the dissemination of works and to travel by artists to and from Florence—these works were freely adapted to their local environment. Jacopo Bellini's visual "critique" of Castagno's work in Venice's Cappella Nova cautions against using any single standard to evaluate Renaissance art, underscoring the critical thought and deliberation about artistic production in this period.

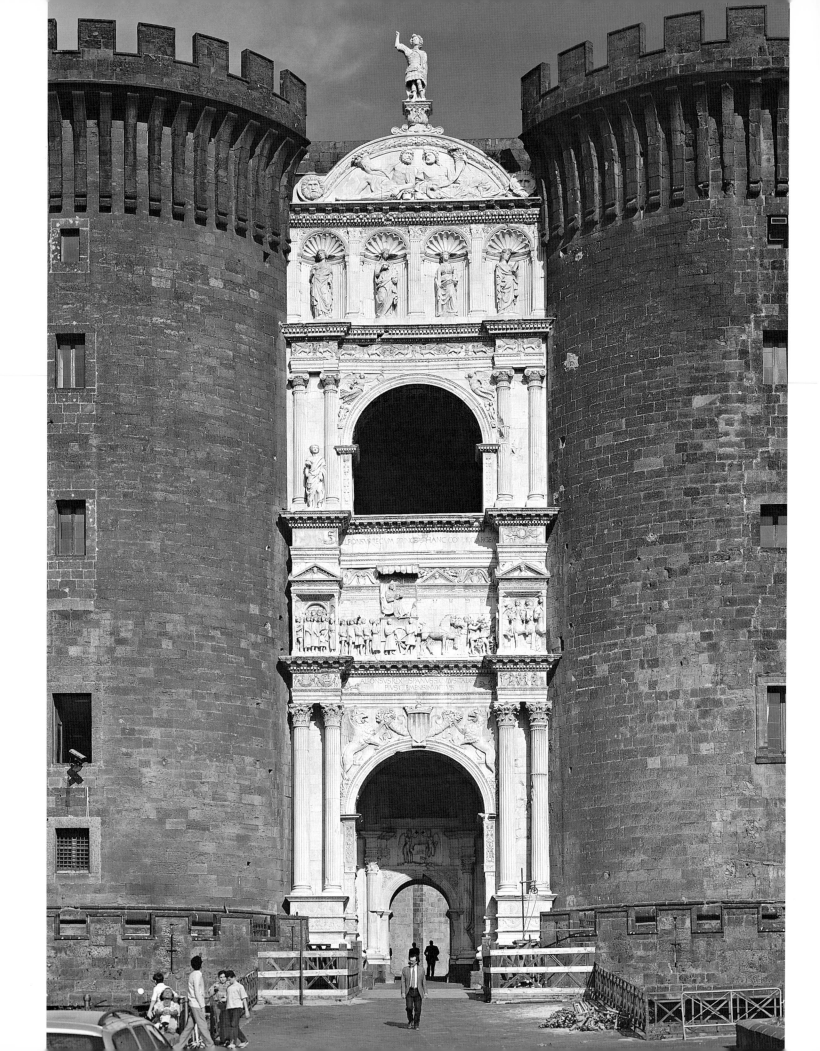

6
Splendor and Magnificence: The Later Fifteenth Century

The character of artistic production in the later fifteenth century testifies to the unprecedented tranquility of the political scene, at least by Italian standards. Though powerful individuals led the governments of each city and occasionally sought to gain an upper hand over one another—Pope Sixtus IV, for example, acted as a silent partner in an unsuccessful coup against the Medici—their power was for the most part well balanced and manifested itself in confident and celebratory works. Patrons often indulged a growing passion for antiquity, which included a marked increase in collecting ancient objects. They also took advantage of artists' uncanny skill at feigning natural appearances in their art. Building on the visual achievements of Flemish artists, Italians such as Antonello da Messina and Giovanni Bellini mastered the relatively new technique of oil painting. Jacopo Bellini and Vittore Carpaccio in Venice offered eyewitness accounts of life in their cities, flattering patrons with impeccably lifelike renditions of the world in which they worked and worshiped. Domenico Ghirlandaio in Florence and Melozzo da Forlì in Rome offered similar essays of clear-headed realism, given a classicizing gloss by Mantegna in Mantua.

In the courtly environment surrounding Lorenzo de' Medici, the effective though unofficial head of the Florentine government, no less than in the actual courts of northern and southern Italy and at the papal Curia, artists often shaped reality even more poetically. Sandro Botticelli and Pinturicchio composed fetchingly beautiful and appropriately unnatural allegories and extensively elaborated history paintings. In Naples and Rimini architects faced Gothic structures with faithful renditions of Roman triumphal arches. In Milan, Leonardo da Vinci and Bramante took courtly grandeur to new heights for Ludovico Sforza, creating monumental works that gave substance to the otherwise shaky underpinnings of his rule. The awe-inspiring barrel-vaulted nave of Sant'Andrea in Mantua, the lavish interior courtyard of the Doge's Palace in Venice, and the enormous scale of the Cancelleria Palace in Rome openly imitated the splendor of the rulers of Roman antiquity, setting new standards for competitive display.

The Courts: Art Reflecting the Ruler

Every Renaissance court reflected and embodied the values of its prince. Physical structures, decorations, court ceremony, and festivities all worked together to enhance a prince's reputation as well as give pleasure. Every aspect of a ruler's activities and his surroundings were shaped to be manifestations of the prince himself.

In the second half of the fifteenth century, Alfonso of Aragon (the new king of Naples), Sigismondo Malatesta of Rimini, Borso d'Este of Ferrara, Federico da Montefeltro of Urbino, and the Gonzagas of Mantua brought this ideal of the perfect identity between a prince and his court to even clearer and more felicitous expression, favoring artists who exploited naturalism and classical references to create works of art that characterized their rule. At the same time, courtly mores placed restrictions on images of consorts, including such extraordinary individuals as Battista Sforza in Montefeltro Urbino and Isabella d'Este in Gonzaga Mantua. Examining works that reflect both male and female perspectives, then, affords broader insights into the role that patronage and social expectations played in the production of works of art.

6.1 (*opposite*) Castello Aragonese (Castel Nuovo), Triumphal Arch of King Alfonso of Aragon, Naples, 1453–58 and 1465–71. See also Fig. 6.5.

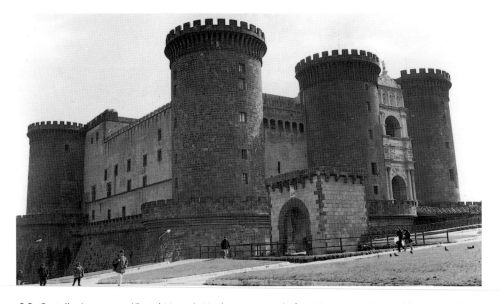

6.2 Castello Aragonese (Castel Nuovo), Naples, renovated after 1443, commissioned by King Alfonso I

Alfonso's Triumphal Arch extends between the two towers at the far right. A great fortified forecourt once stood in front of the castle.

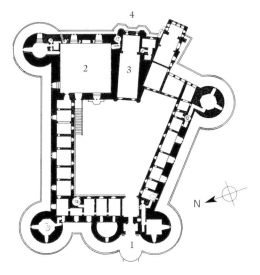

6.3 Castello Aragonese (Castel Nuovo), Naples, plan of upper floor

1 Triumphal arch; **2** Sala dei Baroni; **3** Chapel; **4** Harbor

Naples and the Court of Alfonso the Magnanimous

On July 5, 1421, the childless Queen Giovanna II of Naples adopted Alfonso of Aragon (c. 1396–1458) as her heir, giving him claim to a kingdom that stretched across the Mediterranean, from Spain to Italy. Two years later Giovanna had second thoughts about empowering the already formidable Aragonese king, preferring instead to recognize the claims of her Angevin cousins. It took twenty years of fierce fighting before Alfonso was able to ride in triumph through his new capital city in 1443, and he was determined that his artistic projects would both proclaim and ensure his sovereignty.

Alfonso repeated the early Angevin strategy of importation and imposition. He allotted the construction of the castle's greatly enlarged moats and new, defended forecourt, the so-called Citadella, to Italians, but followed the examples of fortifications in Spain and southern France in the renovations of the castle (Figs. 6.2 and 6.3). Renamed the "Castello Aragonese" for its new owner, the building was at once fortress and palace, the congenial home to studies of ancient philosophy, literature, and rhetoric, as well as the site of cold-blooded scheming and battle plans. It presents a resolutely military aspect, providing lofty interior spaces and efficient defense against newly powerful cannons. By contrast, its entryway suggests an ancient triumphal arch, celebrating Alfonso's conquest of the city (Fig. 6.1). The five enormous towers at its corners rise from splayed bases which functioned as defense against heavy artillery.

The castle's most important ceremonial space, the Sala dei Baroni (Fig. 6.4), occupies one corner of the building, which faces an ample interior courtyard. Its stunning star vault is the work of the Catalan architect Guillermo Sagrera (active 1397 Felanity, Mallorca–1454 Naples). He began the work in 1452; it was fully complete by April 15, 1457, when Alfonso inaugurated the space with a banquet in honor of his nephew. Sagrera's experience as architect of the cathedral of Palma in Mallorca and his designs for the thin, spiraling piers of that city's Lonja del Mar served him well as he undertook the task of vaulting the 85-foot (26-meter)-square space to a height of nearly 92 feet (28 meters). Sagrera transformed the square space into an octagon by constructing **squinches** in its corners. He then sent eight main ribs springing directly out of the wall, creating an impression of organic spontaneity. The vaults are subdivided into smaller units, all the ribs converging toward a central oculus. Carved bosses bear the devices of King Alfonso and punctuate the inner points of the star. No wonder Pope Pius II exclaimed that even the palace of Darius, ancient King of Persia, could not have been grander. Although the room's structure was clearly Gothic, its scale and daring structure rivaled the most celebrated accomplishments of antiquity.

An Arch for a Humanist Ruler   Within his formidable and splendid castle Alfonso gathered some of the fifteenth century's most renowned humanist scholars. Intensely interested in the study of Greek and Latin literature, Alfonso had Caesar's *Commentaries* read to him on the battlefield and even claimed, somewhat

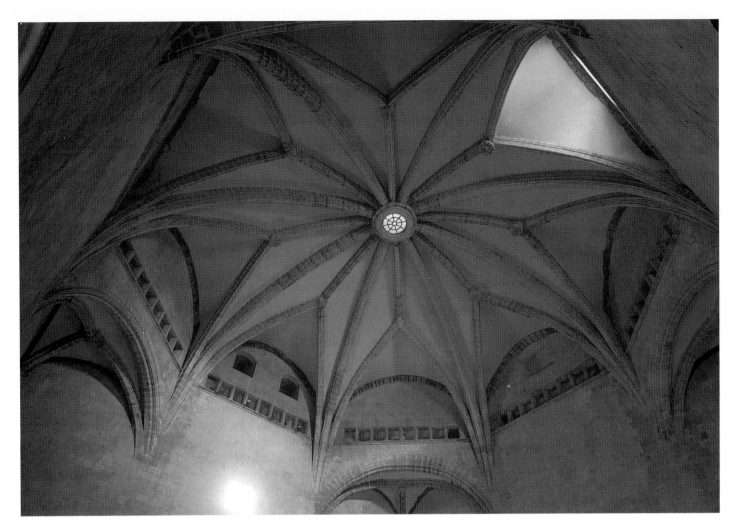

6.4 Sala dei Baroni, Castello Aragonese (Castel Nuovo), Naples, begun 1452, commissioned by Alfonso I from GUILLERMO SAGRERA

An intense fire in 1909 destroyed many of the more subtle architectural details, which included intricate keystones and balustrades filled with complicated tracery.

disingenuously, to have learned more about war from the ancient authors than he had from practical experience. Every day after dinner, he and his coterie of scholars retired to his library to engage in spirited, often heated, exchange.

In 1453 Alfonso's interests in ancient civilization began to take on substantive form in a triumphal arch built as the entrance to his castle (see Fig. 6.1). This was intended to commemorate the temporary arch that had been erected in front of the cathedral when he entered the city in triumph in 1443. Typifying Alfonso's dependence on Spanish staff, the Catalan master Pere Joan (active 1400–58) oversaw the project. Under his direction Pietro da Milano (c. 1410 Milan–c. 1473 Naples), a Lombard sculptor who had spent his early years working in Ragusa in Dalmatia, organized and supervised the work of at least five master sculptors and no less than thirty-three assistants. Sculptural work was allocated block by block to different workers, ensuring the speedy completion of the project.

The multiple-storied arch, made of white marble, fills the opening between two of the main towers of the castle. The lower section accurately imitates an actual Roman monument, the Augustan Arch of the Sergii at Pula, in modern Croatia, which Pietro may have seen while working in Dalmatia, before going to Naples. Paired fluted Corinthian columns stand on pedestals to either side of the **barrel-vaulted** entrance, itself enhanced with classical coffers, while a relief of *The Triumphal Entry of Alfonso into Naples* (Fig. 6.5) decorates the **attic story** of this arch. Allegorical statues were to fill the niches above the upper arch. In this relief, groups of figures, all carefully coordinated in size and scale, even though carved by different hands, enact an idealized and simplified version of Alfonso's triumphal entry into Naples a decade earlier. The sculptors evoke the character and decorum of early Roman imperial reliefs in the proud, calm bearing of nobles who process behind Alfonso, enthroned and elevated on a canopied processional cart, and in the more active figures of the musicians and horsemen who lead the way. The fire at Alfonso's feet, however, comes from Arthurian legends popular at all the Italian courts and represents the Siege Perilous ("dangerous seat") which could be occupied safely only by Sir Galahad, the knight destined to find the Holy Grail. Since Alfonso now occupied that seat symbolically, he was to be seen as

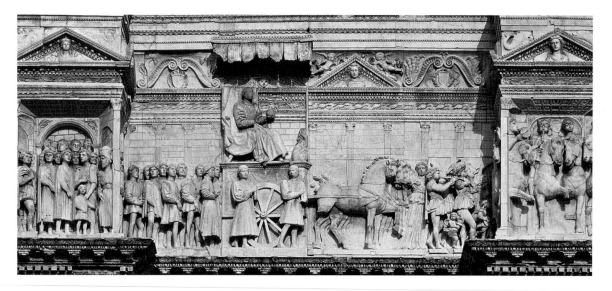

6.5 *Triumphal Entry of Alfonso of Aragon into Naples*, 1453–58, upper story sculpture 1465–66, commissioned by Alfonso I from PERE JOAN, PIETRO DA MILANO, and others for the Triumphal Arch, Castello Aragonese (Castel Nuovo), Naples. Marble

a chivalric hero as well as a Roman victor. Thus antique and medieval traditions merged to create a powerful image of kingly rule. It is not surprising that Alfonso's medals carried an inscription labeling him the "godly" (*divus*) Alfonso.

Rimini

In Rimini, a small papal vassalage on the Adriatic coast, antiquity and chivalry also proved effective tools of propaganda for Sigismondo Pandolfo Malatesta (1417–68), one of the most notorious despots of the Renaissance. Sigismondo (whose surname means "bad head") was flagrantly disloyal to those who engaged his services as a *condottiere* and inflicted appalling cruelties on his enemies. His use of art, literature, and classical learning for unrepentent self-promotion was one of his more endearing qualities. He so outraged Pius II that the pope publicly condemned him to hell during his lifetime. Still, papal vilification of Sigismondo cannot be taken at face value, especially since he maintained good relations with other popes and rulers. He even appears in Gozzoli's frescoes for the Medici family chapel in Florence (see Fig. 5.21, where he is the horseman at the far left). Sigismondo seems to have been well liked by the citizens of Rimini, who reveled in the way their leader claimed equal footing with the great powers of the Italian peninsula.

Recently scholars have been able to separate Sigismondo's artistic activities from his character in order to appreciate them on their own terms. The key to understanding Sigismondo lies in his renovation of the church of San Francesco in Rimini, the traditional burial place of the Malatesta lords (Figs. 6.6 and 6.7). Usually called by the inappropriate term Tempio Malatestiano

("Malatesta Temple"), a term invented in the nineteenth century to characterize the building as a paganizing monument to Sigismondo Malatesta himself, the church should preferably be known as the Rimini Temple, the title that appears on medals cast to commemorate its foundation and in dedicatory inscriptions on the sides of the church which report that Sigismondo "erected at his magnanimous expense this temple to the Immortal God and to the City, and left a memorial worthy of fame and full of piety." Sigismondo was fulfilling a vow he had made during wars between Florence, Venice, and the Sforza contingent of Milan on one hand and Naples, the Pope, and the Visconti of Milan on the other. He emerged as the decisive player, switching sides in 1447 to fight for the eventual victors, the Florentines, which may explain why both the architecture and its sculptural decoration were commissioned from Florentine artists, and why he appears in the Medici Chapel fresco.

At first Sigismondo seems to have intended only to erect a chapel to his name saint, Sigismund, but by 1450 he had committed himself to a grander project: renovating the old church of San Francesco with classical elements. He contracted the humanist architect Leon Battista Alberti (1404–72) for the design, but entrusted the supervision of the construction (see Fig. 35) to the builder and artist Matteo de' Pasti (active 1441–64). Alberti's solution was to wrap the entire existing Gothic church in a marble classical skin, articulated with arches. Alberti also intended to erect a massive hemispherical dome modeled on the Pantheon over a new choir, although that part of the project was never accomplished. The façade evokes the forms of an actual Roman Augustan gate in Rimini—an indication of Sigismondo's rulership intentions. On the church, fluted attached columns divide the lower part of the façade into three arched bays. The spandrels above the arches are decorated with roundels, while

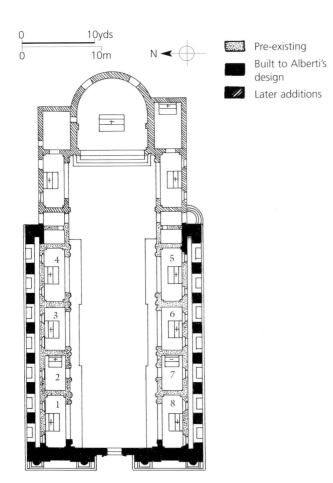

6.6 San Francesco (the Rimini Temple), Rimini, plan

1 Chapel of the Ancestors; **2** Chapel of the Virgin; **3** Chapel of the Playing Children; **4** Chapel of the Arts and Sciences; **5** Chapel of the Planets; **6** Chapel of San Michele; **7** Cella of the Relics; **8** Chapel of San Sigismondo

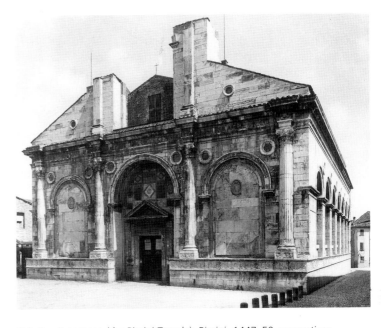

6.7 San Francesco (the Rimini Temple), Rimini, 1447–50, renovations commissioned by Sigismondo Pandolfo Malatesta from LEON BATTISTA ALBERTI and MATTEO DE' PASTI

a triangular pediment marks the door. Alberti enhanced this imperial imagery with geometric inlays of serpentine and porphyry, again recalling Roman precedents in their design and material. For the upper part of the façade Alberti planned a broad pediment with an arch at the center (not completed), flanked by fluted pilasters. The central arch may have been intended to frame the tomb of Sigismondo's saintly brother, Galeotto Roberto, whose miracle-working tomb then stood in front of the original church. The triumphant imagery, suggesting victory over death, thus would have combined Christian and familial themes, much as Robert of Anjou had done in the previous century in Naples (see Fig. 2.50).

The rebuilt church was to include the tombs of Sigismondo, his mistress and, later, wife Isotta degli Atti, and other members of the family. On the outside, arches along the side of the church, which allowed light to enter the

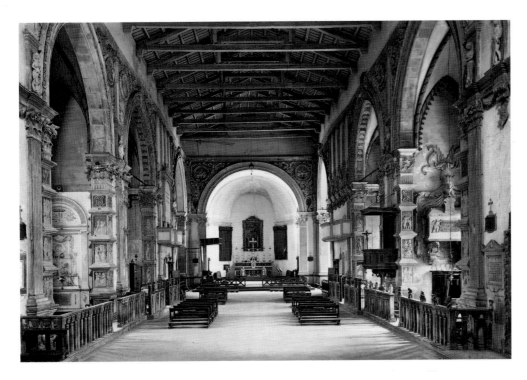

6.8 San Francesco (the Rimini Temple), Rimini, 1450s–60s, renovations commissioned by Sigismondo Pandolfo Malatesta from AGOSTINO DI DUCCIO. Marble

The exposed wooden trusses in the ceiling and the rib vaults partially visible in the side chapels all pre-date Malatesta's renovations, having been part of an existing Franciscan church on the site.

interior, each framed a sarcophagus recalling in their shape ancient types visible in nearby Ravenna, once capital of the Western Roman Empire. The sarcophagi were reserved for illustrious humanist scholars and members of the court, including Basinius of Parma, author of the epic *Hesperis* about Sigismondo's exploits as a *condottiere*, and the military writer Roberto Valturio, who catalogued much of Sigismondo's war machinery. Another tomb contained the supposed remains of the contemporary Greek philosopher Gemisthus Plethon.

A more ornate, chivalric character prevails in the interior of the church (Fig. 6.8), designed by Agostino di Duccio (1418 Florence–after 1481 Perugia), a student of Donatello's who had earlier worked in Modena. Whereas Alberti had concealed the Gothic elements of the pre-existing church with a classical skin, Agostino, like most of his contemporaries, preferred to apply classical vocabulary over and around Gothic structure, retaining pointed arches and framing double tiers of Gothic window tracery with classical rinceaux. Agostino's manner is lavish, enhanced by polychromy and the recurrent appearance of coats of arms, chivalric helmets, and such exotic motifs as elephants, the Malatesta family emblem.

Ferrara

Few Renaissance princes were as enamoured of courtly display as Borso d'Este (1413–71). Renowned for his broad smile and splendid attire, Borso moved freely among his subjects in full court dress, winning loyalty and admiration through a conscious display of the princely virtues of magnificence and jocundity. Succeeding his equally image-conscious but more restrained and scholarly half-brother Leonello (see Fig. 4.25 and genealogical chart, page 485) as Marquis of Ferrara in 1450, Borso acted the part of a great prince. He was totally convinced of the innate nobility of Ferrara and its Este family rulers, deploying his charm and vast wealth to earn the title of Duke of Modena and Reggio (1451) and recognition as the first Duke of Ferrara (1471).

Ferrarese art under Borso was frankly extravagant and flamboyant, high-pitched, coloristic, and full of decorative verve. While some observers found Borso's penchant for luxury a bit overwhelming—Pope Pius II snidely remarked that Borso wished merely to appear rather than to be grandiose and generous—there was no denying the opulence of the Ferrarese court.

Borso's Bible   Borso committed himself and his artists to upholding and enhancing the accomplishments of his predecessors, a strategy for maintaining dynastic power that is made explicit in his commission for the dec-

oration of a deluxe illuminated Bible (Fig. 6.9). Borso's ducal chamberlain made a contract with Taddeo Crivelli (active 1451–died before 1479 Bologna) and his assistant, Franco de' Russi (active c. 1453–82), illuminators who had earlier worked for the Malatesta family on the Adriatic coast. The contract stipulated not only the usual matters of format, price, and completion date of the work, but also instructed the artists to emulate a deluxe French Bible that scholars have identified as a work illuminated by Belbello da Pavia for Borso's father Niccolò III. Since the two Bibles are quite different in the arrangement of their pages, spatial conceptions, and specific style, the artists must have been asked not to copy the earlier work but to use it as a standard of excellence to equal or exceed. Borso's splendor was to be measured in terms of the most elaborate work previously produced at the Este court.

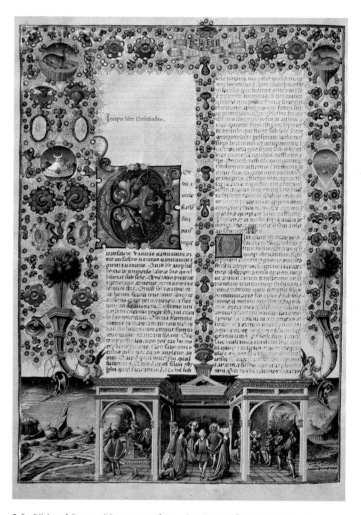

6.9 *Bible of Borso d'Este*, page from the *Song of Songs*, 1455–61, commissioned by Borso d'Este from TADDEO CRIVELLI and FRANCO DE' RUSSI (Biblioteca Estense, Ms. V.G. 12 = Lat. 422, I, fol. 284r, Modena)

The Bible was produced in two large volumes at two different rates of remuneration, the higher one reserved for the opening pages of each book of the Bible.

The opening page of the Old Testament book of *Ecclesiastes* is clearly marked on a fluttering orange ribbon in the center of the upper border and in red lettering in the left column. An enormous floriated initial begins the text itself, surrounded in the border by equally brilliant, nearly enameled flowers laid on a ground of fine gold filigree. Teardrop-shaped openings reveal heraldic imagery: a deer and leopard in the upper corners reclining on woven baskets of green grass recall much prior courtly imagery (see Fig 4.9). Lavender cornucopiae and a golden vase improbably but splendidly tie the border to an equally fantastic but more illusionistic landscape and pavilion below.

Inside the pavilion courtiers and their ladies perform a circle dance accompanied by trumpeters at the right. At the left, however, the king for whom they perform looks away, contemplating the golden glow of the sky. He is the wise ruler of the text of *Ecclesiastes*, who heeds the writer's condemnation of all wordly accomplishment and pleasure as "vanity of vanities". How ironic and yet telling for a patron so enamored of display as Borso. No matter how gorgeous his world, God's realm is more wondrous yet.

Borso's extravagant Bible with its more than 1000 illuminations served as a splendid personal devotional object. The Bible also contributed handsomely to Borso's public reputation for great works, what contemporaries called his magnificence. It was shown to ambassadors and carried by Borso when he went to Rome at the end of his life to be invested as Duke of Ferrara. Since Borso spent most of his reign working to make Ferrara a duchy, he had to look, act, and spend like a duke, being especially conscious of the example of the dukes of Milan and Burgundy, who were also lavish patrons of manuscript illumination (see Fig. 4.8). The Bible's great expense, some 5000 ducats or fully one hundred times the average yearly rent for an entire house in Ferrara, placed him firmly in their league.

Palazzo Schifanoia   Around 1465 Borso began renovating a late-fourteenth-century pleasure palace in the southeast corner of Ferrara. Known as the Palazzo Schifanoia (literally "away with boredom" but implying casting one's cares to the wind), the palace had traditionally been used as a guest house and site for court entertainments. Substantial remains of its decorative program can still be admired in the main reception hall, the so-called Hall of the Months (Figs. 6.10, 6.11), and the smaller audience hall and antechamber to Borso's private apartment, the Hall of the Stuccoes (Figs. 6.11, 6.12). As its name

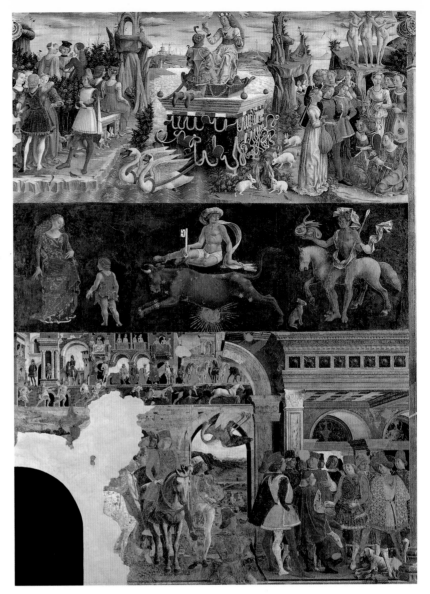

6.10 Hall of the Months, detail of April and May, 1469–70, commissioned by Borso d'Este from FRANCESCO DEL COSSA, ERCOLE DE' ROBERTI, and others according to designs probably provided by COSMÈ TURA for the Palazzo Schifanoia, Ferrara. Fresco, width of each 13' 2" (4 m)

The figures in the dark middle band represent phases of the astrological calendar ruled by Taurus, the Bull.

implies, the Hall of the Stuccoes is renowned for a wide band of stucco (plaster) decoration that wraps around the room just below an intricately carved, polychromed, and gilded coffered ceiling bearing shields with Borso's personal emblems. The stuccoes are rare survivors of a type of decoration that was quite popular in Renaissance palaces, because it could achieve the bold sculptural effects of carved wood without the expense. Here, putti stand amid cornucopias and thick garlands which serve as a kind of celestial court of honor for female personifications of virtues enthroned in shell-topped niches: Charity, Faith, and Hope on the wall contiguous with the duke's chambers and Fortitude, Prudence, and Temperance on the wall adjoining the reception hall.

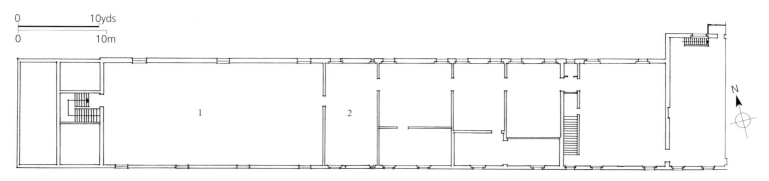

6.11 Palazzo Schifanoia, Ferrara, plan of upper floor

1 Hall of the Months; **2** Hall of the Stuccoes

In a sense, the decorative program of the palace was not complete unless Borso himself was present. Borso saw himself as the embodiment of Justice, the only virtue absent from the iconographic program of the Hall of Stuccoes. Dressed lavishly, in keeping with the splendor of his surroundings, he would have greeted his most important guests in this room and then have had the pleasure of leading them back into the larger main reception room, where the fresco cycle began with a portrayal of the duke and his courtiers under a portal clearly labeled "Justice." Art and court life were perfect mirrors of one another.

The principal subject of the Hall of the Months (see Fig. 6.10), was an astrological and calendrical cycle resembling schemes such as those at Trent in the early fifteenth century (see Fig. 4.12). The cycle runs counterclockwise around the room, beginning with March, the first month of the year in most Renaissance calendars. It and the adjacent scene of April are the best preserved paintings, hav-ing been executed largely in *buon fresco* by an enterprising local artist, Francesco del Cossa (c. 1435 Ferrara–1476/77 Bologna). The lower band of the central bay representing April is dominated at the right by a classically detailed white, green, and pink pavilion, suggesting the Este's armorial colors of red and green. In its center foreground stands the rotund, smiling Borso and a group of courtiers; his coat and those of two of the more splendid youths are embellished with real gold. A doorway cut into the wall at the left truncates a balancing composition of Borso engaged in the hunt, both a literal depiction of an aristocratic activity and a metaphorical allusion to Borso's maintenance of peace in the countryside as well as in the city. The two scenes pivot around the ruins of a classical arch, behind which stretches a vast landscape and in front of which sits the charming figure of a courtier, his crossed legs seeming to extend out into the viewer's space. Above the hunting scene Cossa has squeezed in a representation of the Palio di San Giorgio, an annual race among the city's neighborhoods. Roman ruins at the left blend with a medieval tower and crenel-lated wall, suggesting, along with the Roman arch at the center of the full panel, that Ferrara is heir to ancient glories now revivified under the virtuous Borso d'Este.

All these mundane activities are given a celestial gloss in the upper zone of the wall by a representation of the Triumph of Venus, her float drawn into safe harbor by a

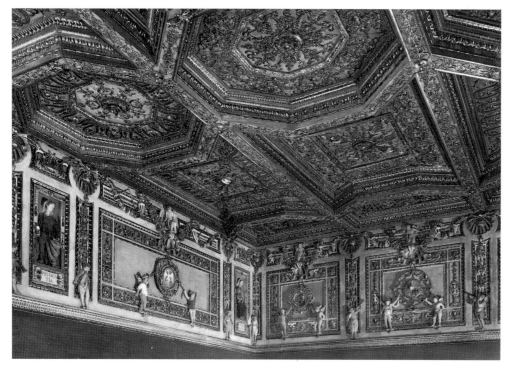

6.12 Hall of the Stuccoes, 1467, commissioned by Borso d'Este from DOMENICO DI PARIS and BUONGIOVANNI DA GEMINIANO for the Palazzo Schifanoia, Ferrara. Stucco with polychromy and gilding

pair of swans. A knight in golden armor kneels before her, chained as her prisoner. He is probably to be understood as Mars, the god of war, who according to Tito Vespasiano Strozzi's *Borsiade* (a classicizing biography of Borso) objected to Jupiter's pronouncement that Borso would usher in a reign of peace. Venus, goddess of love, persuaded Mars to change his mind. Amorous young couples confirm that Venus and Borso have triumphed. Numerous pairs of rabbits, renowned for their fecundity, graze across the lavender and green landscape.

Borso had very good reason to be pleased with Cossa's work. It was visually alluring, learned, witty, and filled with intriguing detail. It may come as a surprise to learn, then, that Cossa complained about being paid by the square foot for his efforts, rather than by time or by figure, and that his requests for additional compensation fell on deaf ears. A persuasive theory suggests that Cossa was paid on this basis because the duke's salaried court artist, the slightly older Cosmè Tura (c. 1430 Ferrara–1495 Ferrara), provided detailed drawings for each of the compositions. Cossa was expected to execute them diligently, not necessarily inventively. Modern critics appreciate the superior workmanship of Cossa's frescoes—they are largely done in *buon fresco* instead of the less demanding *al secco* technique used by the other artists active in the room—but unfortunately for Cossa the supply of competent painters in Ferrara far exceeded demand. Borso may well have appreciated Cossa's stunning illusionistic effects but it was not in his economic self-interest to pay for more than had been requested.

Urbino

The relative isolation of Urbino, a small hill town 48 miles (77 kilometers) inland from the central Adriatic coast, required that its lord, Federico da Montefeltro (1422–82), cast a wide net for artistic talent. Fortunately, Federico had numerous contacts. His success as a military captain and diplomat was matched by a reputation for being especially humane and learned. He employed artists and architects from many Italian states, as well as northern Europe, and created a great library at Urbino, purchasing many of his deluxe editions from the humanist bookseller Vespasiano da Bisticci in Florence.

A double portrait by the highly intellectual provincial genius Piero della Francesca (c. 1415 Sansepolcro–1492 Sansepolcro), a native of Borgo San Sepolcro in the Papal States, west of Urbino, presents both Federico da Montefeltro and his recently deceased wife Battista Sforza (Fig. 6.13). Piero adopted the traditional convention of profile representation appropriate to the couple's high status, giving dignity to Federico's less than handsome features.

(Not only did Federico suffer from a skin disease, but he had lost his right eye and part of the bridge of his nose in a tournament in 1450.) The couple also benefit from the cool light and geometrical clarity that Piero learned during his student days in Florence working in the shop of Domenico Veneziano (see Fig. 5.27).

Piero pairs the couple heraldically. In each case their collars are aligned with the horizon, linking them subtly but firmly to continuous but distinct physical worlds. Federico appears before a glowing world of lakes, rivers, and boats which would allow him to venture far beyond the hills of Urbino. Battista, who had been his most trusted confidant and had attended to affairs in Urbino during his frequent absences, is shown in front of an enclosed and fortified landscape denoting traditionally proscribed limits of female activity. The heavy shadows may allude to her recent death. Both landscapes recall elements in popular portraits by Hans Memling of Bruges (c. 1440–94), an indication of Piero's acquaintance with northern European painting and of its high prestige at Federico's court.

On the reverse of the diptych Federico and Battista appear in two sober triumphs (Fig. 6.14). This type of image was popularized by Petrarch's poems on the Triumphs of Love, Chastity, Death, Fame, Time, and Divinity. It appears frequently in small-scale works such as manuscripts and the panels decorating *cassoni*, recalling grand public festivals. Latin inscriptions in fine Roman capital letters indicate Federico's high respect for the written word. His triumph celebrates active, masculine rulership, personified by the four women sitting on his chariot: the cardinal virtues Justice, Prudence, and Strength facing out and forward; Temperance seen from the back facing into a landscape similar to the one shown in Federico's portrait on the other side of the panel. Battista, too, rides in front of a landscape that is a continuation of that shown in Federico's triumph but, once again, dominated by earth rather than water. She is deeply engaged in reading what is probably a prayerbook. Her inscription, written in the past tense—in contrast to Federico's living present—extols her modesty and her role as the famous man's spouse. The source of her fame is the traditional feminine virtue of Chastity, underscored by the unicorns drawing her cart. Facing outward at the front of the chariot and emphasizing her piety is Faith. Pride of place, however, is given to an unusual depiction of Charity, a woman clad in a dark dress and holding a pelican, a bird which, according to legend, picks its breast until it bleeds so as to give sustenance to its young—an apt image for a woman whose numerous pregnancies may, according to later writers, have caused her death at the age of twenty-six. Although not securely identified, the two women standing behind the figure of Battista

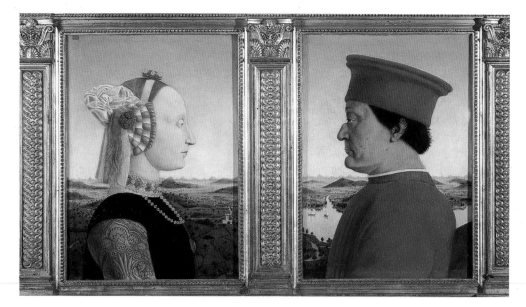

6.13 *Battista Sforza and Federico da Montefeltro*, c. 1472, commissioned by Federico da Montefeltro from PIERO DELLA FRANCESCA. Oil and tempera on panel, each 18½ × 13" (47 × 33 cm) (Galleria degli Uffizi, Florence)

The paintings are not in their original frames, which may have been hinged like a book.

ment. Two jutting cornices, one in shadow at the upper left of the painting and the other in light on the right, suggest that Federico may instead be kneeling in the nave just in front of them all, distinguishing his human status from that of the holy figures and angels.

The impressive ostrich egg hanging from the shell-topped apse can be understood as an image of birth and resurrection, the emergence of a baby bird from an egg symbolizing both Christ's miraculous Virgin Birth and his dramatic release from the tomb. Ostrich eggs were, in fact, often hung in many chapels dedicated to the Virgin during the Middle Ages and Renaissance (see Fig. 4). The egg in this painting may have also served as a veiled heraldic device, for one of Federico's personal emblems was the ostrich itself.

The altarpiece has been trimmed slightly at the sides and by fully one-ninth of its height (an entire plank of wood) at the bottom. Even so it impresses with its remarkably large, ample space. In only one case did Piero alter normal proportions, enlarging the figure of the Madonna so that she is larger than life-size. Identified closely with the building in which she sits, she should be understood as an embodiment of both this building and

may be intended to personify her much-lauded modesty and piety.

Also dating from the period soon after Battista's death, when Federico may have been contemplating his own mortality, is an altarpiece by Piero della Francesca (Fig. 6.15). Mesmerizing in its stillness, the altarpiece shows Federico kneeling in glinting armor before the enthroned Madonna and Child, in the company of mainly mendicant and penitential saints (John the Baptist, Bernardino, and Jerome on the left; Francis, Peter Martyr, and John the Evangelist on the right). Piero constructs his imaginary space with great precision. The saints and Madonna and Child sit and stand in the crossing of a meticulously detailed church reveted with marble panels, fluted pilasters, and classical moldings. Coffered barrel vaults cover the transept arms and chancel behind them, where accompanying angels stand on more darkly colored pave-

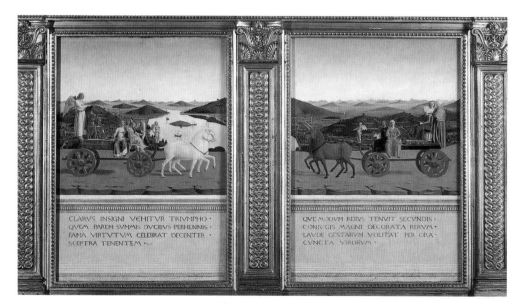

6.14 *Triumphs of Federico da Montefeltro and Battista Sforza* (reverses of Fig. 6.13), c. 1472, commissioned by Federico da Montefeltro from PIERO DELLA FRANCESCA. Oil and tempera on panel, each 18½ × 13" (47 × 33 cm) (Galleria degli Uffizi, Florence)

Beneath each of the triumphal carts, inscriptions in Latin appearing to be carved in Roman capitals extol the gendered virtues of Federico da Montefeltro and Battista Sforza. Federico's reads: "He that the perennial fame of virtues rightly celebrates holding the scepter, equal to the highest dukes, the illustrious, is borne in outstanding triumph." Battista's reads: "She that kept her modesty in favorable circumstances, flies on the mouths of all men, adorned with the praise of the acts of her great husband."

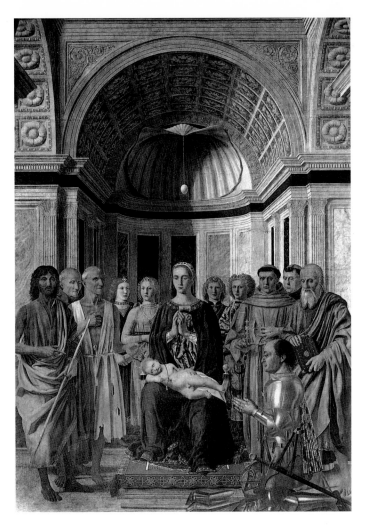

6.15 *Enthroned Madonna and Saints Adored by Federico da Montefeltro*, c. 1472–74, commissioned by Federico da Montefeltro from PIERO DELLA FRANCESCA, perhaps for Federico's burial chapel. Oil on panel, 8′ 2″ × 5′ 7″ (2.51 × 1.72 m) (Pinacoteca di Brera, Milan)

Federico was buried in the church of San Bernardino, which he founded outside the walls of Urbino.

The Palazzo Ducale The restrained elegance and balanced order of Piero's imagined architecture mirrored actual forms in Federico's palace in Urbino, which dominates the city both physically and symbolically (Figs. 6.16 and 6.17). Federico built the palace in several stages. Much of the work in the western part of the complex, designed as early as 1465 by the Dalmatian architect Luciano Laurana (c. 1420/25 Vrana, Dalmatia–1479 Pesaro), required substantial engineering since it follows the edge of a steep valley that separates the earlier part of

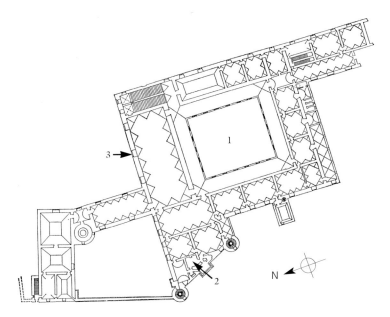

6.16 Palazzo Ducale, Urbino, plan of upper floor

1 Courtyard; **2** *Studiolo*; **3** Entrance on lower floor; **4** Hanging garden

the universal Church for which it stands. In kneeling here in front of the Virgin, Federico is clearly pledging his devotion not just to the Madonna but to the institutional Church—a wise move indeed, as he sought in these very years to dispel suspicions of disloyalty that had fallen upon him because of his service against the papacy in the battle of Rimini in 1469. As the loyal son of the Church, he offers his gleaming armor and pious soul to the Madonna representing the Church. Federico's offering was both accepted and rewarded when in 1474, at the time of the completion of the painting, Pope Sixtus IV named him **Gonfaloniere** of the Holy Roman Church.

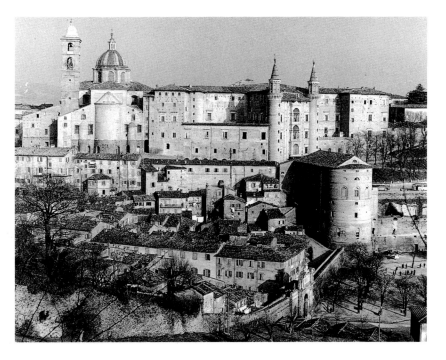

6.17 Palazzo Ducale, Urbino, western façade, mid-1450s–80s, commissioned by Federico da Montefeltro from LUCIANO LAURANA, FRANCESCO DI GIORGIO, and others

the palace, begun in 1447, from a fortification to the north. On the west side, facing the main road that circled around the city from the coast, Laurana erected a ceremonial façade for the palace, both proudly militaristic in its twin multi-storied, round towers and frankly celebratory and classicizing in the four superimposed arches at the center. Perhaps inspired to take advantage of the hillside site by Pius II's works at Pienza and certainly wishing overtly to recall the comparable imagery of King Alfonso's arch in Naples (see Fig. 6.1), Laurana's design allows ample space between the individual elements and opens the arches to serve as loggias, both for enjoying a splendid sunset and for giving Federico platforms on which he could appear high above guests approaching and entering the city.

Laurana's design for the palace's central courtyard is justly famous for its lucidity and understated elegance, again in keeping with Federico's own character (Fig. 6.18). Five bays wide and six bays deep, it offers the appearance from one of the shorter sides of being a perfectly balanced square, thanks to the effects of perspective foreshortening. Originally this part of the palace was only two stories tall; even with the additional two stories, the space is much lighter and more open than any of its Central Italian counterparts—a perfected distillation of elements from new Tuscan trends (the graceful arcade, whose proportions recall those in Brunelleschi's Foundling Hospital, see Fig. 4.44, and the courtyard of the Palazzo Medici, see Fig. 5.15) and from Rome (for example, the rectangular window frames, broad pilasters, and handsome brickwork of the Cancelleria courtyard). Laurana gave the corners of the arcade an increased sense of stability with L-shaped piers, faced with pilasters.

The handsome inscription running around both frieze levels of the courtyard was not added until after 1474, when Federico was formally named Duke of Urbino, but in many ways it sums up the intentions of Federico and his architect. It gives his titles as Duke of Urbino and Gonfaloniere of the Holy Roman Church and says that hav-

ing won all his battles, assisted by the virtues of Justice, Clemency, Liberality, and Religion, Federico "built this house to his glory and that of his successors." This was not so much a boast as a matter of fact, bolstered by a wish to impart something enduring to posterity. The remarkable harmony between Federico's wishes and Laurana's talents produced architecture that has impressed generations of visitors as a metaphor for humanity and intelligence.

Inside the palace Federico and his guests enjoyed several handsome suites of rooms. On the lower level were a small series of ancient-style baths, heated by an underground furnace, so that he could follow the approved Roman sequence of hot, warm, and cold water. On the middle level are two tiny rooms, one called the Chapel of Pardon and the other dedicated to the classical Muses. Federico found nothing incompatible about his Christian and Roman-inspired beliefs, preferring a syncretist view which found value in a wide range of thought and revelation.

The crowning glory of Federico's private suite was his *studiolo* ("small study"; Fig. 6.19). The densely carved, gilded, and coffered ceiling carries Federico's personal emblems and an inscription giving his noble titles and the date 1476, the decoration being part of extensive renovations and enhancements begun in 1474. As was the case in Leonello d'Este's much earlier, but now destroyed, *studiolo*, the lower walls are lined in *trompe l'oeil*

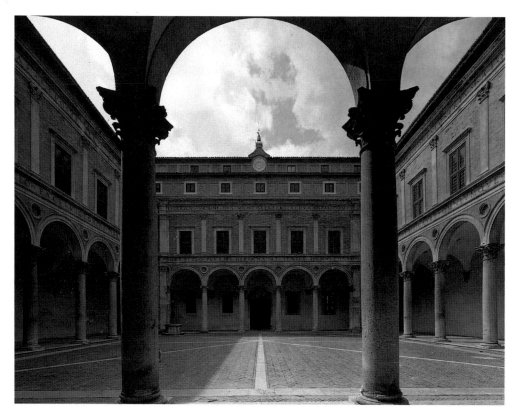

6.18 Palazzo Ducale, Urbino, courtyard, mid-1460s, commissioned by Federico da Montefeltro from LUCIANO LAURANA

The clock and small square windows of the top story are not original.

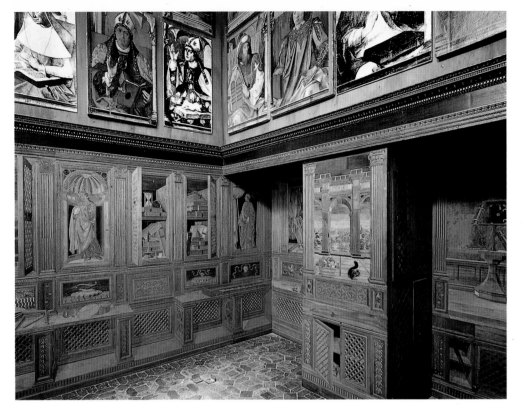

6.19 *Studiolo*, 1476, commissioned by Federico da Montefeltro probably from the workshop of GIULIANO DA MAIANO (inlaid woodwork) and from JUSTUS OF GHENT (panel paintings) for his private quarters in the Palazzo Ducale, Urbino. Intarsia, height 7' 3" (2.21 m)

Most of the original paintings are represented by large photographs, the originals having been removed to museums throughout Europe. Federico himself appears in the intarsia panel set in the left niche of the room.

wood intarsia. Books, scholarly equipment, musical instruments, and even Federico's armor are all convincingly rendered, mimicking the actual objects kept behind the cupboard doors and even the small work table that folded down in the right niche. It is a breathtaking essay in perspective, composition, and craftsmanship, probably executed by Florentine craftsmen in the workshop of the architect and woodworker Giuliano da Maiano (1432 Maiano–1490 Naples), following designs by several artists, including Botticelli. Tellingly, a book stand is portrayed over Federico's desk, an appropriate contemplative image contrasting with emblems of the active life, Federico's armor, momentarily consigned to a closet but partially falling on the counter in the left niche.

To modern eyes the intarsia shown at center right may look like merely an elaborate still life of a basket of fruit and a squirrel set on the edge of a carefully constructed piazza and monumental classical arcade, but the unusual presence under the scene of a panel of interlocking Gothic fretwork—by 1476 associated primarily with religious architecture and choir stalls—suggests that this composition should be read allegorically, along with the images of the active and contemplative life to either side of it. The squirrel's habits of industriousness and saving for the future (in this case represented by the full basket of fruit) made the animal a recognized image of the prudent ruler. The state for which he provides is founded in religion, alluded to by the Gothic fretwork, and embodied in the idealized city square and also in the view of the luminous landscape and city in the background. Because of Federico's pious thought and prudent actions his realm will flourish.

Above these allegories two rows of paintings depict paired exemplars of the major fields of scholarly learning from antiquity through Federico's own time, arranged much as the books were arranged in his own library. Typically, classical and Christian authorities were juxtaposed. Since the scheme consists of portraits, for which northern European artists were particularly renowned, Federico commissioned most of the paintings from a Flemish artist, Justus of Ghent (Joos van Wassenhove; active 1460–80), who came to work at Federico's court. In the *studiolo*, then, Federico brought together a wide range of learning, both ancient and modern, Christian and pre-Christian, and also several contemporary artistic styles. To Federico our categorically opposed labels of "ancient" and "modern," "Italian" and "Flemish," "Gothic" and "Renaissance" would have seemed strangely and unnecessarily exclusive. Neither he nor the artists who worked for him were disturbed by the variety within his decorative scheme. If anything, rich diversity gave the scheme much of its particular power.

Mantua

The Gonzaga family, who ruled Mantua, were equally supportive of stylistic and cultural variety, having long nourished and exploited chivalric themes and Gothic forms (see Fig. 4.26). From the mid-1460s, however, classical forms began to predominate, promoted by Leon Battista Alberti and Andrea Mantegna. Thoroughly committed to classical ideals, these artists offered Ludovico Gonzaga a unique opportunity to reshape visual imagery in the city.

Sant'Andrea   In 1470 Alberti produced designs for the basilica of Sant'Andrea (Figs. 6.20 and 6.21) in the center of Mantua. The site was particularly important to

Ludovico Gonzaga because it stood close by the Gonzaga palace and contained a relic, the supposed Blood of Christ, that had been recognized as genuine by a papal council that met in Mantua in 1459. Alberti accurately understood Ludovico's criteria and addressed the main practical considerations in a letter of October 1470:

> I understood in these days that your Highness and these your citizens were thinking of building here at Sant'Andrea. And that your principal intention was to have a great space where many people would be able to see the Blood of Christ. I saw that *modello* of Manetti's. I liked it. But to me it does not seem suited to your intentions. Ponder and imagine this which I send you. This will be more capacious, more lasting, more worthy and more felicitious. It will cost much less. This type of temple was known among the ancients as the Etruscan. Should you like it, I shall see to drawing it up in proportion.
>
> (Translated in Eugene Johnson, *Sant'Andrea in Mantua*, p. 8)

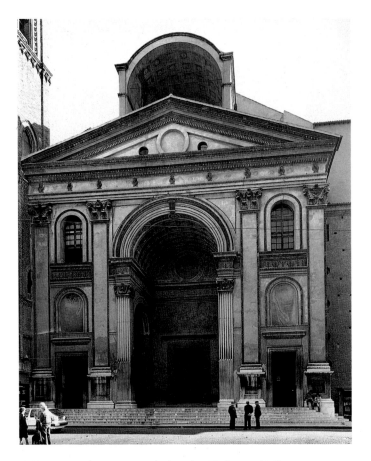

6.20 Sant'Andrea, Mantua, designed 1470, begun 1472, commissioned by Ludovico Gonzaga from LEON BATTISTA ALBERTI, construction overseen by LUCA FANCELLI

The peculiar arch rising above the pediment imitates the barrel vault of the nave of the building.

What patron could resist so solicitous and level-headed a proposal—for a building that would be both grander and less expensive than originally projected!

Alberti's design for the façade of Sant'Andrea, like that of his Rimini Temple for Sigismondo Malatesta (see Fig. 6.7), draws its inspiration from Roman triumphal arches, but the Mantuan church takes the idea much further, its design at once more monumental and more complex, adapting a classical form rather than seeking to replicate it. The huge central arch of the exterior portico, with its coffered barrel vault, prefigures the height and vault of the nave. It is flanked by proportionately smaller openings, which also correspond to the church's internal structure, and by a **giant order** of paired Corinthian pilasters. Their smooth surface complements the richly coffered surfaces of the arch, while their height helps to unify the different levels of the composition. A boldly framed triangular pediment crowns the façade.

Inside the church Alberti honored his promise to provide excellent visibility of the high altar and its sacred relic, creating a broad, single-aisled space covered with a 60-foot (18.3-meter) wide coffered barrel vault, notably the largest since classical times. To support it, he followed Roman precedent, using not columns but huge piers,

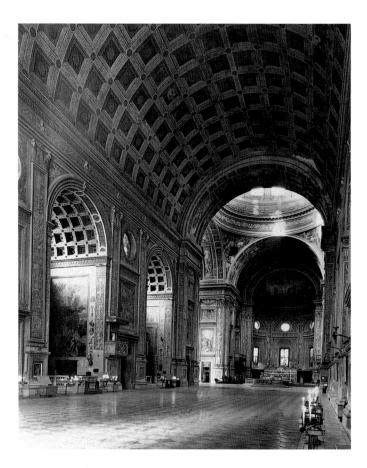

6.21 Sant'Andrea, Mantua

between which he placed side chapels. Alberti's careful coordination of elements throughout the entire structure, interior and exterior alike, as well as his use of large, bold forms, gave Ludovico Gonzaga the distinction of being patron of the first truly monumental, classicizing structure of the fifteenth century.

Mantegna Ludovico Gonzaga's taste for classical antiquity had been stimulated by his resident court artist, Andrea Mantegna. Hired in 1457 to replace Pisanello, who had left for Naples nearly a decade earlier, Mantegna finally entered Ludovico's service in 1460. Ludovico's humanist education prepared him to appreciate Mantegna's classicism; however, in the late 1450s Mantegna's paintings were novel, their sculptural toughness quite different from the dreamy idealism of much court painting (see Fig. 6.10). At this time the duchess of Milan was sending her court painter Zanetto Bugatto (active 1450s–1476) to Bruges to study with Rogier van der Weyden, not Rome to study ancient sculpture. In hiring Mantegna, then, Ludovico Gonzaga was taking something of a risk, especially for the head of a small court that had heretofore followed, rather than led, artistic fashion. The gamble worked: Mantegna gave exemplary service to

the Gonzaga court for forty-six years. For it, he produced some of his most celebrated works.

In 1465 Mantegna began to paint the walls of Ludovico's newly renovated bedroom and audience chamber—what contemporaries called the Camera Picta ("painted chamber"; Fig. 6.22) in the Castello di San Giorgio. Mantegna worked on the frescoes for almost nine years, a singularly long time for the sort of commission that was usually carried out in a matter of months as a prince prepared for a wedding or state visit. The main intent of the frescoes must have been to glorify the Gonzaga family. Mantegna makes this clear in the inscription which he depicted as carved Roman letters on a gold plaque over the entrance to the room:

> For the illustrious Ludovico, second Marchese of Mantua, best of princes and most unvanquished in faith, and for his illustrious wife Barbara, incomparable glory of womanhood, his Andrea Mantegna of Padua completed this slight work in the year 1474.

This "slight" work (in the obsequious language required of artists until modern times) was, in fact, a grand paean both to Mantegna's employer and to his own talents as

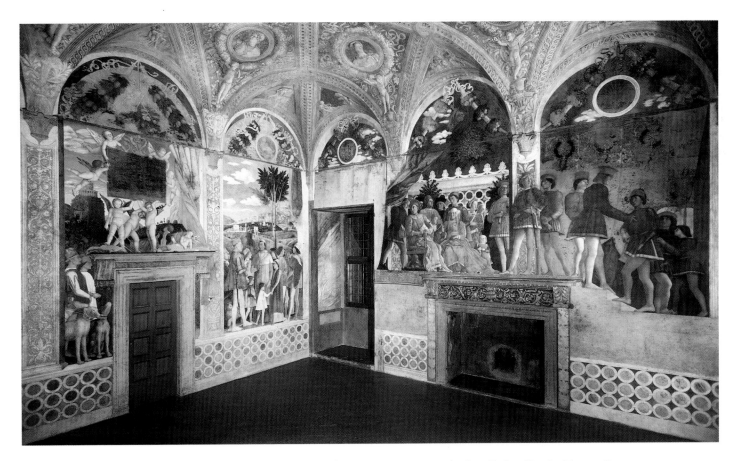

6.22 Camera Picta, 1465–74, commissioned by Ludovico Gonzaga from ANDREA MANTEGNA for Castello San Giorgio, Mantua. Fresco

illusionist, portraitist, and consummate court artist. The frescoes in the Camera Picta became instantly famous, attracting just the sort of positive attention to Mantua that Ludovico had been cultivating since early in his reign.

The room is a masterpiece of *trompe l'oeil*. On two adjacent walls, which served as background for Ludovico's bed, Mantegna painted splendid gold brocade curtains, a visual link with the actual bed hangings. From his bed, Ludovico could gaze at the panorama depicted on the other two walls, in which he, his wife, their children, courtiers and attendants appear engaged in various activities. The exact subject of these court scenes remains in dispute; they may relate to events surrounding the raising of Ludovico's son Francesco to the cardinalate (he is shown in the scene to the right of the door) but do not seem to portray any one event as it actually happened. The effect is rather like a publicity film of life at the Gonzaga court, with its members going about their "normal" business and leisure pursuits. Mantegna has used the mantel over the fireplace as the support for a dais, on which Ludovico himself sits with his wife, Barbara of Brandenburg, surrounded by their children, court advisers, and even a female dwarf. In contrast to his elegantly dressed wife and courtiers, Ludovico wears a simple dressing gown and slippers—perhaps an allusion to the room itself, as his semi-private domain; he holds a letter possibly bearing the news of his son's appointment or perhaps news of the sudden illness of his employer, Francesco Sforza of Milan. He turns his head to hear what an attendant or messenger is saying. At the right of the scene, courtiers control the approach to Ludovico from steps that descend from the dais.

Above these images of courtly life, Mantegna transformed the simply vaulted ceiling into a brilliant display of faux stucco work (Fig. 6.23). A network of "ribs," apparently embossed with scrollwork, divides the ceiling into segments which are filled with a profusion of ornament. The eight main fields each carry a bust of one of the first eight Roman emperors, surrounded by a laurel wreath carried on the back of a winged putto. All of these elements are painted in *grisaille* against gold backgrounds and modeled as though lit from below so as to simulate relief sculpture. The spandrels between the vaults bear more fictive reliefs showing the deeds of the classical heroes Arion, Orpheus, and Hercules. Clearly Mantegna and Ludovico wished to associate the Gonzaga reign with the grandeur of Roman antiquity, but it must have been a rather tenuous connection, for Roman literary sources make it clear that the character and deeds of some of these emperors made them somewhat dubious models for an enlightened Christian ruler. Nevertheless, the grandeur and the classical image must have been effective.

The *gravitas* is delightfully shattered by the oculus at the center of the ceiling—a spectacular example of aerial perspective. Here Mantegna imagines a view into a blue sky through an elaborate balustrade, alive with cavorting putti. Their foreshortened bodies illustrate most strikingly Mantegna's mastery of *di sotto in su* construction (depiction of objects as though seen from far below). Mantegna draws us further into his make-believe world with the playful putti sticking their heads through openings of the balustrade and with the smiling faces of three servants and a plant-filled washtub balancing perilously on a pole, on the other side of which a court lady seems to be whispering to a visitor or court retainer from Eastern lands. Is the curiosity of the viewer below about to be punished with a shower of greenery—or, worse yet, by a crashing fall of the washtub itself? Mantegna's visual joke suggests that looking is a potentially dangerous exercise—while at the same time he rewards it with all the artistry at his command.

After Ludovico's death in 1478, Mantegna continued to work for his successors, fueling their growing passion for antiquity. Court humanists instilled a fervent love of ancient art and literature in both their male and female students, many of whom became discerning collectors and connoisseurs of antique gems, cameos, and sculpture, as well as medals and paintings of ancient subjects. Chief among them was the young marchesa of Mantua, Isabella d'Este (1474–1539), who had been reared at the court of Ferrara. Her husband, Francesco Gonzaga, grandson of Ludovico, was a military man who had few scholarly interests of his own, but even he encouraged the production of revivalist works, though they were tellingly different from those commissioned by Isabella.

As we saw in Piero's double portrait of Federico da Montefeltro and Battista Sforza (see Figs. 6.13 and 6.14), the virtues, deportment, and activities associated with a ruler and those associated with his consort were quite distinct. Although both men and women collected small-scale works of art, men were largely responsible for erecting buildings and attending to public self-promotion; women more usually commissioned devotional works and organized court entertainments and musical events. These distinctions are evident in two works created by Andrea Mantegna: a series of nine large paintings entitled the *Triumphs of Caesar*, for Francesco Gonzaga (Fig. 6.24), and *Pallas Expelling the Vices from the Garden of Virtue*,

6.23 (right) Camera Picta, ceiling, 1465–74, commissioned by Ludovico Gonzaga from ANDREA MANTEGNA for Castello San Giorgio, Mantua. Fresco

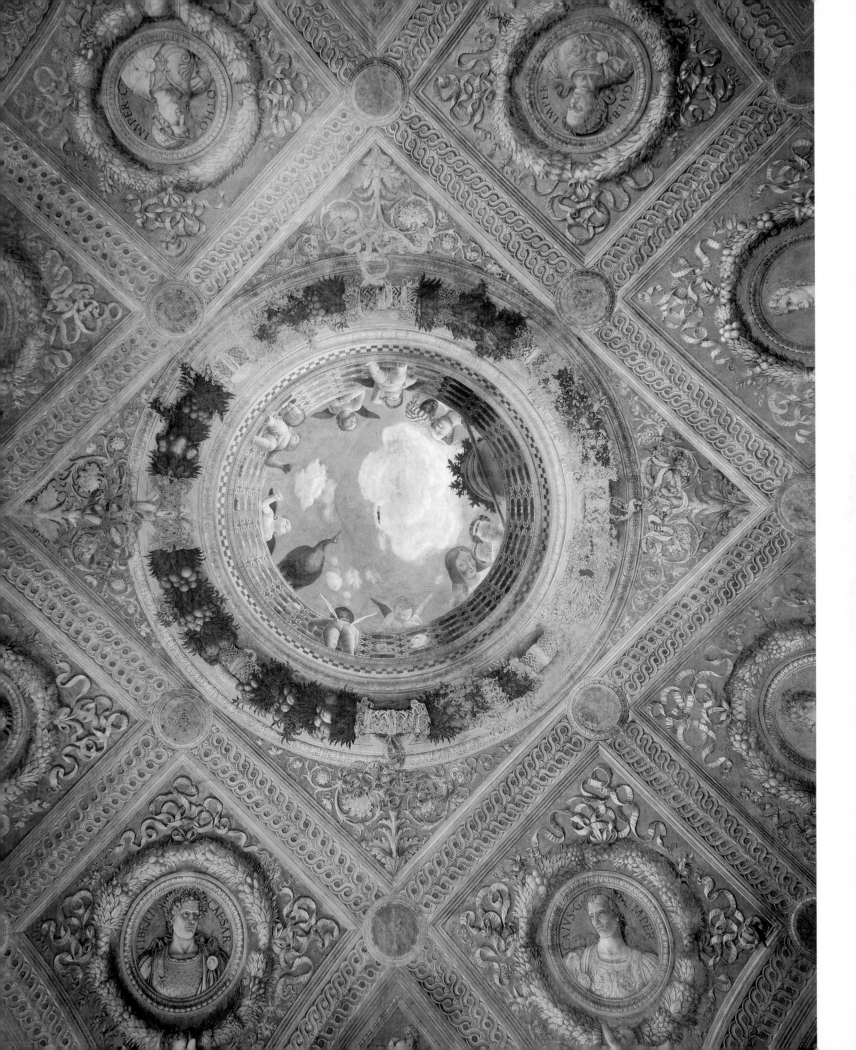

commissioned by Isabella d'Este (Fig. 6.25). The *Triumphs* paintings have been badly damaged over the centuries, partly through clumsy restoration, but in their present condition they still eloquently convey Mantegna's goal: to present Caesar's triumphal return from the Gallic Wars with the utmost authenticity. His close study of ancient sculptural reliefs can be seen in the accurate Roman togas and armor worn by the participants in the first painting, *The Picture Bearers*. Acquaintance with Flavio Biondo's scholarly research on ancient Rome informed his long, straight trumpets, the standards topped with bronze statuettes, and banners carrying images of captured cities. All of the paintings are extremely bold and lifelike, intended for public display.

Mantegna's painting for Isabella, by contrast, was conceived and executed in more precious and delicate terms, destined for the restricted realm of the *studiolo* where she kept her collection of small luxury objects. Isabella's

court advisor, the poet Paride da Ceresara, devised a program of classical allegories for the room, one of which was awarded to Mantegna. The painting is crammed with anecdotal detail and communicates allegorically, rather than in the historic mode of the *Triumphs*. It illustrates dramatically the traditional assumption that the leader's consort was responsible for upholding moral values in the court, while giving this idea a new twist. Popular wisdom held that education was incompatible with female virtue; but here, in a painting intended for the first known *studiolo* created for a woman, Pallas Athene, goddess of wisdom and war, strides forward to banish the vices from her realm. Her handmaids lunge toward Lust, represented by the languorous, nearly nude female standing on the back of a centaur. As befits the room of a lady, the vices are depicted with a nice balance of repulsiveness and good taste; their genitals are discreetly hidden or miniaturized, as in the case of the typically lascivious satyr

Fighting for Chastity

When Isabella d'Este commissioned Perugino to paint the conflict between Love and Chastity for her *studiolo* in Mantua, she clearly had in mind a definitive treatment of the subject. Her letter to Perugino is exhaustive in its specifications, although she does leave a few minor details to his own judgment and acknowledges that he might find it difficult to accommodate all the figures. Perugino dutifully followed Isabella's instructions, documenting a patron's power to define artistic activity.

Our poetic invention, which we greatly want to see painted by you, is a battle of Chastity against Lasciviousness, that is to say, Pallas and Diana fighting vigorously against Venus and Cupid. And Pallas should seem almost to have vanquished Cupid, having broken his golden arrow and cast his silver bow underfoot; with one hand she is holding him by the bandage which the blind boy has before his eyes, and with the other she is lifting her lance and about to kill him. By comparison Diana must seem to be having a closer fight with Venus for victory. Venus has been struck by Diana's arrow only on the surface of the body, on her crown and garland, or on a veil she may have around

her; and part of Diana's raiment will have been singed by the torch of Venus, but nowhere else will either of them have been wounded. Beyond these four deities, the most chaste nymphs in the trains of Pallas and Diana, in whatever attitudes and ways you please, have to fight fiercely with a lascivious crowd of fauns, satyrs and several thousand cupids; and these cupids must be smaller than the first, and not bearing gold bows and silver arrows, but bows and arrows of some baser material such as wood or iron or what you please. And to give more expression and decoration to the picture, beside Pallas I want to have the olive tree sacred to her, with a shield leaning against it bearing the head of Medusa, and with the owl, the bird peculiar to Pallas, perched among the branches. And beside Venus I want her favourite tree, the myrtle, to be placed. But to enhance the beauty a fount of water must be included, such as a river or the sea, where fauns, satyrs and more cupids will be seen, hastening to the help of Cupid, some swimming through the river, some flying, and some riding upon white swans, coming to join such an amorous battle. On the bank of the said river or sea stands Jupiter with other gods, as the enemy of Chastity, changed into the bull which

carried off the fair Europa; and Mercury as an eagle circling above its prey, flies around one of Pallas's nymphs, called Glaucera, who carries a casket engraved with the sacred emblems of the goddess. Polyphemus, the one-eyed Cyclops, chases Galatea, and Phoebus chases Daphne, who has already turned into a laurel tree; Pluto, having seized Proserpina, is bearing her off to his kingdom of darkness, and Neptune has seized a nymph who has been turned almost entirely into a raven.

I am sending you all these details in a small drawing, so that with both the written description and the drawing you will be able to consider my wishes in this matter. But if you think that perhaps there are too many figures in this for one picture, it is left to you to reduce them as you please, provided that you do not remove the principal basis, which consists of the four figures of Pallas, Diana, Venus and Cupid. If no inconvenience occurs I shall consider myself well satisfied; you are free to reduce them, but not to add anything else. Please be content with this arrangement.

(from D.S. Chambers. *Patrons and Artists in the Italian Renaissance*. London: Macmillan, 1970, pp. 136ff.)

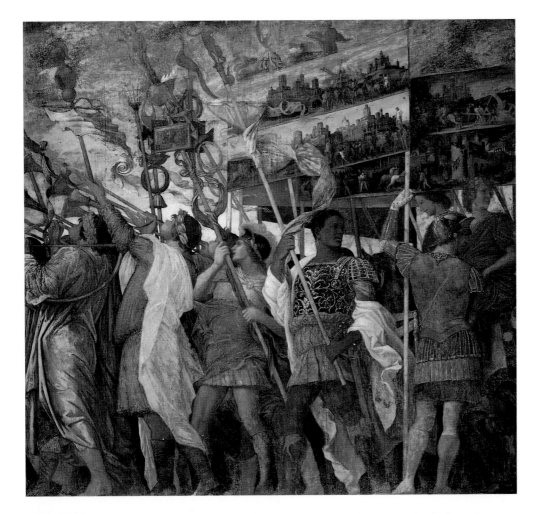

6.24 *The Picture Bearers*, canvas 1 of the *Triumphs of Caesar*, 1490s, commissioned by Francesco Gonzaga, perhaps following the lead of his grandfather, Ludovico, from ANDREA MANTEGNA for the Corte Vecchia of the Palazzo Ducale, Mantua. Distemper on canvas, 8′ 8¾″ × 9′ 1½″ (2.66 × 2.78 m) (The Royal Collection, London, © Her Majesty Queen Elizabeth II)

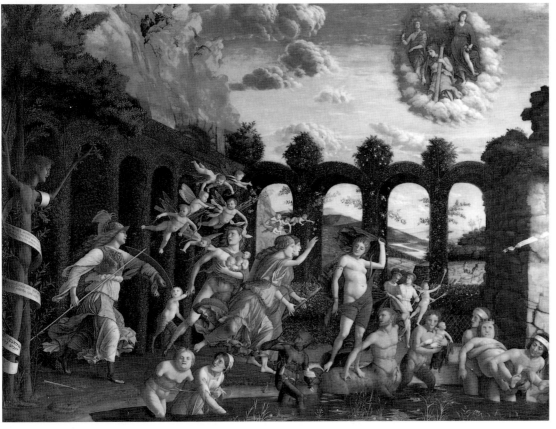

6.25 *Pallas Expelling the Vices from the Garden of Virtue*, c. 1499–1502, commissioned by Isabella d'Este from ANDREA MANTEGNA for her *studiolo* in the Palazzo Ducale, Mantua. Tempera on canvas, 5′ 3″ × 6′ 3½″ (1.6 × 1.92 m) (Musée du Louvre, Paris)

The theological virtues (Faith, Hope and Charity) appear in the cloud in the upper right corner of the painting.

carrying a baby at the right of the painting. Some of them are identified pictorially—for example, the armless Sloth being dragged by a servant—while others are identified with labels.

Given the relatively modest funds at her disposal, Isabella relied on letter-writing campaigns to secure many of the works for her collections, snatching what she could from artists' estate sales and hounding other artists for whatever they might release to her. Her patronage was thus less systematic than that of some of her male counterparts, but was ironically prophetic of a subtle shift beginning to take place in the relationship between patron and artist—artists becoming gradually more independent and, as we shall see in later chapters, occasionally willful.

Venice:
Heir of East and West

In 1457 the extraordinarily long dogeship of Francesco Foscari came to an abrupt and ignominious end as the old man was forced from office following several scandals and the execution of his son for treason. Always a controversial figure, especially in his commitment to creating a mainland empire for Venice, Foscari was vindicated in the next decade as Venice's holdings on the Italian mainland began to turn a profit. Friuli, Treviso, Padua, Vicenza, Verona, Brescia, Bergamo, Crema, and Ravenna all now contributed to Venice's ability to support the costs of continuing battles with the Ottoman Turks, who by 1477 were on the verge of attacking the city. Astute military action and calculated negotiations led to a peace treaty in 1479, reinvigorating Venetian trade and ensuring investments in the arts.

At the same time, Venetian artists and patrons undertook a major new synthesis of their traditional stylistic preferences. The fall of Constantinople to the Ottoman Empire in 1453 had brought large numbers of Eastern scholars and immigrants to the city, encouraging the city to fashion itself as the rightful successor to the glory of the fallen Byzantine Empire. In the 1460s and 1470s

this vision began to be expressed in works that exploited ancient Roman architectural and decorative vocabulary while also making repeated reference to the city's own past. Gothic forms diminished in frequency, but when they were used it was with a reverent appreciation for their associative meanings. The same was true for Byzantine models and motifs, which were exploited, in painting as well as architecture, for their capacity to communicate both religious and civic values.

The Arsenal

The first structure built in Venice that consciously adopted ancient and Byzantine models was a new entrance to the Arsenal (Fig. 6.26), the massive civic shipyards. Signaling a distinct stylistic break with the Gothic extravagance of Francesco Foscari (see Figs. 5.48 and 5.50), the new gateway announced Venice's claims to imperial dominion. Doge Pasquale Malipiero (r.1457–62), whose name appears proudly in the dedicatory inscription to either side of the portal, surely recognized the triumphal significance of its form, as did other Italian rulers who also built structures inspired by ancient Roman arches in these decades (see Figs. 6.1, 6.5, 6.7, and 6.17). Indeed, the Venetians later celebrated their leading role in the Battle of Lepanto, where they finally crushed Islamic forces threatening to control the entire Mediterranean, by adding another inscription above the doorway in 1571. As heirs to the Byzantine Empire, the Venetians flanked their gateway with columns crowned by Byzantine-inspired **basket capitals**, not classical ones. Venetians were as much heirs of the East as the West.

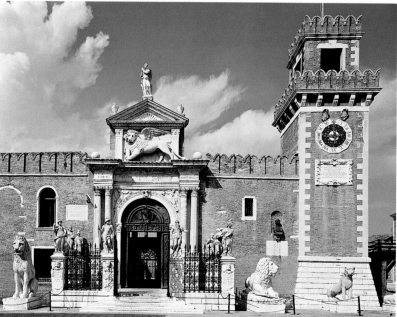

6.26 Arsenal Gateway, 1457/58–1460, commissioned by Doge Pasquale Malipiero and the Avogadori di Comun (Leone Molin, Albano Capello, and Marc'Antonio Contarini) for the entrance to the Arsenal, Venice. Marble and Istrian stone.

Later additions include the sixteenth-century statue of Santa Giustina above the pediment, the terrace with Mars and Neptune added in 1682, bronze doors commemorating the Venetian reconquest of the Morea in the 1690s, and lions brought to Venice from Athens.

Religious Architecture

Patrons seized upon Early Christian as well as Byzantine models for much religious architecture in this period, as is evident at the monastery church of San Michele in Isola (Figs. 6.27 and 6.28). It was rebuilt beginning in 1469 by Mauro Codussi (c. 1440 Lenna–1504 Venice), who came to Venice from the subject city of Bergamo and became an outstanding proponent of a new classical style. The façade's classically inspired pilasters and arched upper story, masking the side aisles and top of the nave, suggest Codussi's acquaintance with Leon Battista Alberti's designs for the Rimini Temple (see Fig. 6.7), but the general scheme may just as credibly derive from the traditional shape of Venetian parish church façades, many of which culminated in arches over the nave and side aisles. More original is Codussi's sure handling of rustication even of the pilasters, which gives the façade's lower story a weight and monumentality reminiscent of some palace façades (see Fig. 34). The upper story is ingeniously modeled: the pilasters that frame the central portion of the façade wrap around the corners to suggest piers,

seemingly grasped by the moldings of the flanking arches; the arches themselves are embellished with fluting.

The simple columnar supports and ample nave arcade of the interior (Fig. 6.29) recall other Venetian churches (see Fig. 3.13), now classicized with a flat ceiling and round arches. The patron, Abbot Pietro Donà, spent extensive time in Ravenna reforming the abbey of Sant'Apollinare in Classe. The Early Christian and Byzantine basilicas of that city provided stylistic means for this monastic reformer to link his home abbey with the early, presumably purer, days of Christianity. The resulting space resembles Brunelleschi's Santo Spirito and San Lorenzo in Florence (see Fig. 5.8), but Codussi's space feels different because he seems to have thought of the church interior as a unified spatial volume rather than as an interplay of carefully articulated and positioned walls and arcades. Exploiting the soft white color of Istrian stone, Codussi's supports blend with, rather than stand out from, the gently illuminated space.

In 1483, five years after completing his work at San Michele, Codussi was given responsibility for the even more prestigious project of completing the new church of the Benedictine convent of San Zaccaria, begun in 1458 by the Venetian builder Antonio di Marco Gambello (active 1458–81 Venice) but stalled for decades. The abbess, Lucia Donà, was a relative of the abbot of San Michele in Isola and like most of the nuns came from a prominent Venetian family. The unusually complex form

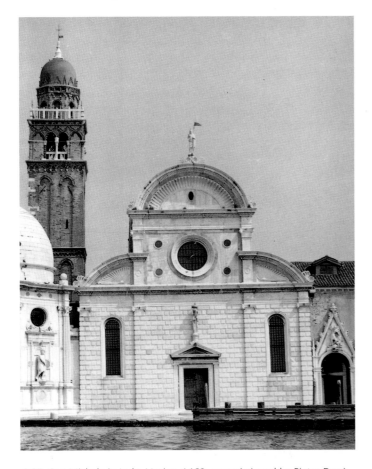

6.27 San Michele in Isola, Venice, 1469, commissioned by Pietro Donà from MAURO CODUSSI

The church now serves as the mortuary chapel for Venice's island cemetery.

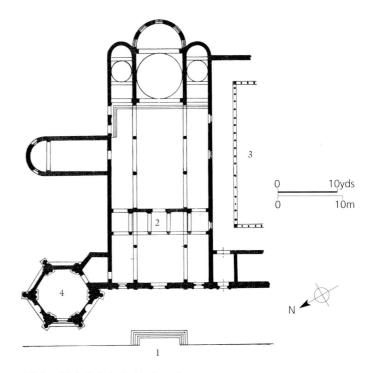

6.28 San Michele in Isola, Venice, plan

1 Lagoon; **2** Choir screen; **3** Cloister; **4** Emiliani Chapel (later addition)

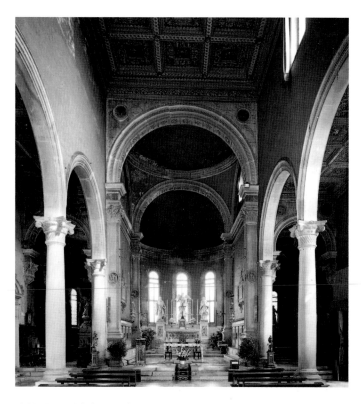

6.29 San Michele in Isola, Venice.

This photograph was taken from just inside the *barco* (choir screen) that still divides the entrance end of the church from the rest of the nave.

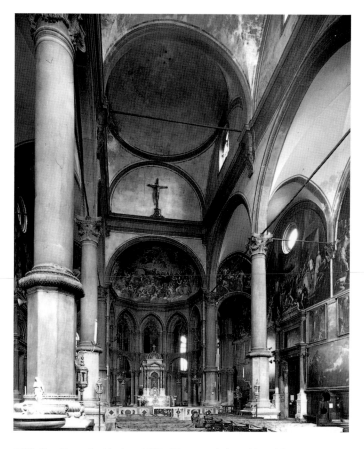

6.30 San Zaccaria, Venice, 1458–89, commissioned by Abbess Lucia Donà and the resident Benedictine nuns from ANTONIO DI MARCO GAMBELLO, succeeded by MAURO CODUSSI

Dark paintings along the nave walls were added in later centuries. Candle smoke has also distorted the brightness of the space, darkening the columns and arches, which are made of light-colored Istrian stone, not the gray stone commonly used in central Italy.

of the church's apse and choir (Fig. 6.30) can be explained by San Zaccaria's special place in Venetian history and ceremony. Not only were a number of Venice's earliest doges buried there, but the Benedictine nuns had ingratiated themselves with the Venetian state by donating part of their gardens as the site for St. Mark's Basilica. In recognition of the nuns' generosity, which also included the creation and donation of the first ducal *corno* ("ceremonial hat"), the doge and the city's senators made an annual procession to the church on Easter afternoon. There they paid homage to a symbolic replica of Christ's sepulchre located over the high altar (today marked by a sixteenth-century domed *tempietto*). To accommodate this crowd, Gambello had designed the apse with an **ambulatory** and radiating chapels, a feature of pilgrimage churches such as the Santo in Padua. Codussi's hand is evident around the ambulatory in the clusters of antique marble columns which carry basket capitals recalling those at San Michele. Above them rise polygonal piers and a pointed arched arcade containing Gothic tracery, consciously archaic elements meant to associate the new choir with the past. Above, Codussi turned to even more ancient, Byzantine, models, crowning the apse with a semi-dome and squeezing ovoid hemispheres into the bays of the ambulatory, evidence of a Byzantine revival that pervaded much Venetian church architecture well

into the early sixteenth century. In the three-aisled nave, which may have been laid out by Gambello before Codussi took over, the columnar supports stand on high pedestals, like the commemorative columns in the ancient fora of Rome and Constantinople. Their imperial associations are made explicit by eagles carved on the capitals, repeating forms that appeared in the earlier, twelfth-century church and were said to have been granted to the nuns by the Byzantine emperors.

Painting

In a society as conscious of tradition as Venice, the success of new works depended on their ability to evoke and blend with the past. So as Codussi was meeting his patrons' desires to incorporate Early Christian, Byzantine, and Gothic elements into classically informed buildings, painters, too, were creating works that effectively married classical and non-classical forms.

One alternative, promoted by Antonio Vivarini's younger brother Bartolomeo Vivarini (active 1440–1501 Venice) and embraced by his primarily aristocratic patrons, was to accentuate classicizing forms with lush decoration and highly pitched color, making them visually compatible with the dynamic, swirling forms of gilt, Gothic frames that had long been popular in his family's workshop. The figures in the *St. Mark Altarpiece* (Fig. 6.31), which Bartolomeo Vivarini produced for the Corner family's chapel at the Franciscan church of Santa Maria Gloriosa dei Frari, explicitly recall the work of Andrea Mantegna (see Fig. 5.62) in their demeanor, poses, and clinging drapery, but all their garments are on fire with color. The sky behind the figures glints like gold, shifting dramatically from nearly white on the horizon to midnight blue at top. The carving on St. Mark's marble throne, though inspired by classical models, is as dense and tightly wound as the tracery on the altar's frame. The altarpiece "works" visually because Vivarini thought of his panels and their frame as an integral, decorative whole. In a sense, then, his altarpiece is more like Mantegna's *San Zeno Altarpiece* than might first appear: the panels in each would be incomplete without their frames.

The same is true of a series of altarpieces produced in the 1470s by one of Venice's most talented and adaptable painters, Giovanni Bellini (1429/30 Venice?–1507 Venice), Jacopo's son and Mantegna's brother-in-law. Giovanni continued to pay homage to Venetian traditions even as he transformed the relationship between painting and frame. In the *San Giobbe Altarpiece* (Fig. 6.32), commissioned by the Confraternity of St. Job, Giovanni set his figures before a glimmering, mosaic- and marble-encrusted apse which evokes the same traditions as the domes and columns at San Zaccaria, underlining the continuity of Venetian and Byzantine history. At the same time, Bellini ruptures the traditional Venetian conception of an altarpiece as a collection of distinct panels, a tradition with venerable Byzantine roots in the famous *Pala d'Oro* on the high altar of St. Mark's (see Fig. 3.2). Imagining a unified space which had previously appeared rarely in works such as Vivarini's *Enthroned Madonna, Child and Saints* at the Scuola della Carità (see Fig. 5.54), Bellini now systematically coordinated his illusionistic architecture with an actual stone frame—also probably designed by him. The sense of reality is heightened by the light entering the painting from the right, as though from the actual windows in the church. St. Francis, at the left, reveals the stigmata on his hand and seems to invite the worshiper to draw nearer, further bridging the gap between reality and painting.

Giovanni's approach in creating this altarpiece may have been influenced by several factors. Foremost among these must have been circumstances at San Giobbe itself, which was rebuilt for the reforming Observant branch of the Franciscan order beginning in the mid-fifteenth century. Giovanni's painted architecture reflects the simple, classicizing forms of the church's domed **chancel**, burial place of Doge Cristoforo Moro (r. 1462–71), but he enriches the basic vocabulary with a coffered barrel-vault, marble panels, and mosaics. Perhaps Bellini's patrons asked him to create an altarpiece that would compete openly with the chancel, since Doge Moro had dislodged the altar of St. Job from the apse.

Bellini's innovative solution was favored by the altarpiece being commissioned from a confraternity rather than an aristocratic patron. As was the case earlier in the century for the niche sculptures at Or San Michele in Florence (see Figs. 4.39–4.43), where the lesser guilds commissioned works from the stylistic mavericks Donatello and Nanni di Banco while the major guilds appreciated the more ornate manner of Ghiberti, so in Venice aristocratic

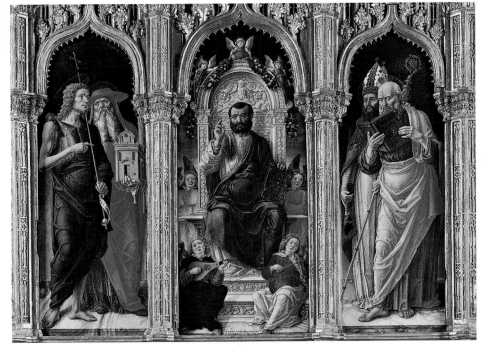

6.31 *St. Mark Altarpiece* (detail), 1474, commissioned by the Corner family from BARTOLOMEO VIVARINI for the Corner Chapel, Santa Maria Gloriosa dei Frari, Venice. Tempera on panel, central panel 65 × 26¾" (165 × 68 cm), side panels 65 × 22½" (165 × 57 cm)

6.32 *San Giobbe Altarpiece*, before 1478, commissioned by the Confraternity of St. Job from GIOVANNI BELLINI for San Giobbe, Venice. Oil on panel, 15′ 4″ × 8′ 4″ (4.71 × 2.58 m) (Galleria dell'Accademia, Venice)

The original stone frame for this altarpiece remains *in situ*—but empty—in the church of San Giobbe.

families like the Corner at the Frari imposed their taste for the Gothic while Bellini worked with more experimental models and forms for less formidable patrons.

Undoubtedly, formal, artistic considerations also influenced the *San Giobbe Altarpiece*. Bellini was the son of an artist who had undertaken many experiments with scientific perspective (see Fig. 5.56). In addition, around 1475 he encountered the work of Antonello da Messina (c. 1430 Messina–1479 Messina), a Sicilian probably trained in the Flemish manner in Naples, who may have been invited to Venice by Pietro Bon, a galley owner and Venetian consul in Tunis. Bon commissioned Antonello

to produce an altarpiece for San Cassiano (Fig. 6.33), which originally contained eight standing saints and an enthroned Madonna and Child. Because the altarpiece has been cut down and dismembered, it is impossible to reconstruct Antonello's spatial setting, but the remaining figures share much in common with Bellini's. At the left a bishop saint, like St. Francis in the *San Giobbe Altarpiece*, looks out at the worshiper, and Antonello's Madonna and Child both raise their hands, beckoning the viewer to approach and receive their blessing. Antonello, like Bellini, composes with light, describing full forms, free of the linear quality characteristic of earlier painting. Exploiting the technique of painting with oils, which he probably learned in Naples and which he promoted in Venice (though it had already been introduced there), Antonello made his paintings glow with luminous detail, even catching reflections and refractions on transparent objects such as crystal and glass.

Scanty documentation does not permit an exact reconstruction of the events that led to the similarities between Antonello's and Giovanni Bellini's work. Both artists seem to have learned from one another and to have shared common artistic goals. Bellini, for one, may have been aware of contemporaneous Central Italian paintings such as Piero della Francesca's altarpiece for Federico da Montefeltro (see Fig. 6.15), but rather than placing his figures in front of the apse, as Piero did, he, like Antonello, placed his figures within it in his father's typical Venetian manner (see Fig. 5.56). The resonant color and occasional impressionistic effects, such as the daubs of paint which Bellini uses to suggest the sheen of mosaic tesserae, diverge significantly from Piero's cool colors and characteristically precise, Tuscan delineation.

Antonello's mastery of the oil medium and its suitability for describing objects both precisely and softly is most evident in his best-preserved work, a small panel showing St. Jerome in his study (Fig. 6.34). Although the work is documented in a Venetian collection in 1529, Antonello may have brought it with him from southern Italy as a demonstration piece. The architectural setting recalls Neapolitan models, as does the framing arch, which resembles the popular depressed form seen around the entrance to the Palazzo Penna in Naples (see Fig. 4.17). He counterfeits the natural flaws and joining of their stone material both with paint and with tiny gashes and incisions in the panel's surface. The still, contemplative mood seems almost sacral, reinforced by the fact that Jerome has removed his shoes and left them at the base of the stairs. Warm, glowing light picks out his books, the containers, and the edges of the vaults. Strikingly similar to work by van Eyck and Memling (to whom sixteenth century sources say it was sometimes attributed), the painting reveals its Italian origin in Antonello's

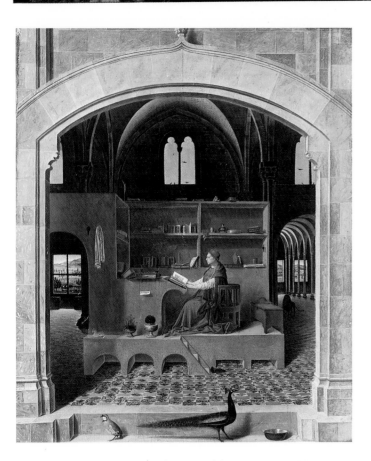

6.33 *Enthroned Madonna and Child with Saints*, 1475–76, commissioned by Pietro Bon from ANTONELLO DA MESSINA for San Cassiano, Venice. Oil on panel, three fragments; center Madonna 45¼ × 25″ (115 × 63 cm), left 21¾ × 13¾″ (55.5 × 35 cm), right 22¼ × 14¼″ (56.8 × 35.6 cm) (Kunsthistorisches Museum, Vienna)

6.34 *St. Jerome in his Study*, before 1475 (?), ANTONELLO DA MESSINA. Oil on lime, 18 × 14⅛″ (46 × 36 cm) (first documented in a Venetian collection in 1529, now National Gallery, London)

expert use of scientific perspective. Laying out a grid of tiles that leads to open windows and views of idyllic landscapes and birds gliding against clear blue skies, Antonello fully tames the problems of spatial description, just as he domesticates Jerome's lion, strolling in the shadows at the right.

Giovanni Bellini and his patrons, too, responded positively to Flemish realism and the new luminous capacities of the oil medium. In one of his panels, commissioned for a patron who must have had a profound appreciation of Franciscan symbolism (Fig. 6.35), St. Francis stands in the midst of a landscape which is replete with the complex symbolic allusions of Flemish art—plants, animals, and household objects alluding to Franciscan ideals of poverty and humility. Resembling a stigmatization (a depiction of St Francis receiving the wounds of Christ), this scene may be, rather, a meditation on Francis's identification with creation. It is dawn, the rocks a cool gray-green, except where the first rays of the sun begin to warm the earth. Francis stretches out his arms and looks skyward, where, in traditional Franciscan stigmatizations, one would expect to find a seraph (see Fig. 1.25), perhaps eliminated when the panel was cut down on top or just as likely absent from the original scheme. There are none of the traditional lines linking the saint's wounds to Christ's; neither does the saint's head carry a halo. Natural beauty and light are sufficient, here, to describe the divine, which Francis himself had done in his *Canticle of the Sun*.

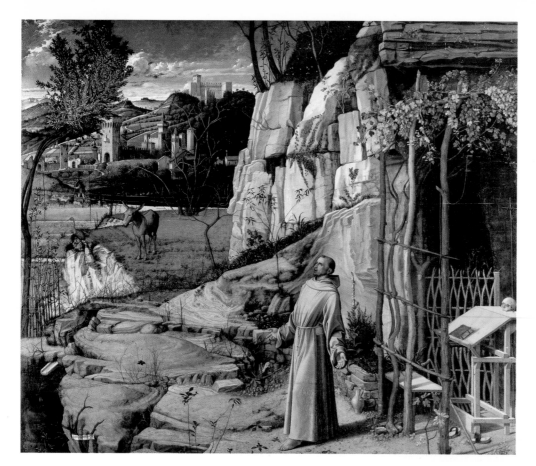

This was but one of many modes in which Bellini conceived his religious paintings. The artist's prolific output of devotional paintings dedicated to the Madonna and Child ranged from highly naturalistic to iconic images. His *Madonna Lochis* (Fig. 6.36) negotiates several modes, blending the melancholy of a transcendent, shimmering Byzantine Madonna with the energy of a wriggling Christ Child, evocative of Hellenistic sculpture. As in an earlier painting by his father (see Fig. 5.55), the Madonna is seen at half length, as in Byzantine icons, but the traditional immobility of such figures is ruptured by the lively Christ Child who seems to be crawling away from her. Placing her right hand under Christ's slightly exposed genitals, the Madonna calls the viewer's attention to his indisputably human as well as divine nature. Warm light resolves the inherent tension in the subject and unifies its iconic and narrative modes.

The *Scuole* and Lay Commissions

Purely narrative painting in late fifteenth-century Venice is best studied today in works produced for the **scuole**, charitable lay organizations which were dominated by the citizen class (nobles being explicitly prohibited from holding office in the *scuole*). It should be kept in mind, however, that these paintings may appear to modern historians to have been more prominent within their own culture than they actually were, because other

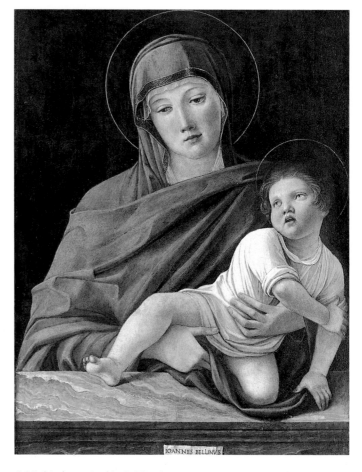

6.36 *Madonna Lochis*, 1470s, GIOVANNI BELLINI. Tempera on panel, 18½ × 13¼" (47 × 34 cm) (Accademia Carrarra, Bergamo)

contemporary large narrative works in the Doge's Palace were destroyed in a fire of 1577. There was a great deal of civic-minded competition among the *scuole* in this period, each seeking to enhance its own position within the city as well as contribute to the city's overall fame. Giovanni Bellini and his older brother Gentile (c. 1429/30–1507) were members of the Scuola Grande di San Giovanni Evangelista, for whose officers' meeting room Gentile produced the *Procession in St. Mark's Square* (see Fig. 1.7). Gentile is less renowned than Giovanni as an artistic innovator, but because of his seniority in the family he preceded Giovanni in receiving governmental honors, including the opportunity in 1479 to sign the long-sought peace treaty that ended the Turkish wars with Sultan Muhammad II, whose portrait Gentile painted.

Gentile Bellini was a superb draftsman who fed a voracious Venetian appetite for documentary works of art. In his panel for San Giovanni Evangelista, Gentile commemorates the annual procession of all the *scuole* and leading citizens marking the feast of Corpus Christi. Members carry the Scuola's cherished relic of the True Cross, protected by a red canopy, across the Piazza San Marco. White robes declare their group identity, while portrait likenesses distinguish each individual—a long-standing tradition in group portraits of *scuole* members. In fact, the painting depicts a specific historical event: a miracle that occurred in 1444, when a terminally ill child was cured when his father—shown in red to the right of the canopy—dropped to his knees to adore the relic. In Florentine art (see Fig. 6.49) the miracle would have been set front and center, the occurrence rearranged for narrative emphasis. Here, instead, Gentile sets the event in real time and space, the surrounding crowds and minute description of the buildings on the piazza testifying to the truth of the miracle. Just as Venetian historians in this period preferred to intersperse family matters with public events, recording history in chronicles as it occurred rather than separating public from private and organizing their writings by grand schemes, so Gentile, like his brother Giovanni (see Fig. 6.35), portrays the divine intervening naturally in the world around him.

The bustle of urban life dominates the paintings for the Scuola Grande di San Giovanni Evangelista. In the *Miracle at Rialto* (Fig. 6.37) Vittore Carpaccio (c. 1460/66 Venice?–1525/6 Venice) records every plank of the city's principal wooden drawbridge (replaced by the present bridge in 1588–92) and catalogues numerous variations on Venetian chimney pots. Carpaccio's precise training is not known, but he was clearly influenced by the work of both Giovanni and Gentile Bellini. As in Ambrogio Lorenzetti's earlier allegories in Siena (see Fig. 2.27), Carpaccio celebrates the living city, catching figures on rooftops as well as in gondolas and on the streets. Almost incidentally the relic of the Holy Cross performs another miracle, this time on a balcony at the left. Other surviving paintings by Carpaccio for smaller *scuole*, in this same anecdotally rich manner, suggest that

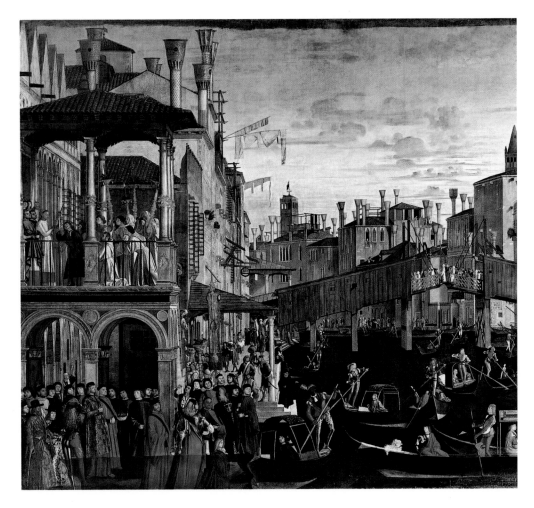

6.37 *Miracle at Rialto*, c. 1494, commissioned by the Scuola Grande di San Giovanni Evangelista from VITTORE CARPACCIO for the *albergo* of their Scuola, Venice. Oil on canvas, 11' 11¾" × 12' 9¼" (3.65 × 3.89 m) (Galleria dell'Accademia, Venice)

Carpaccio seems to have taken great delight in depicting the decoratively designed chimney tops that vented Venetian fireplaces.

the Venetian public as a whole enjoyed imagining sacred events in familiar settings.

During the late fifteenth and early sixteenth centuries, costs for building and enlarging the *scuole* which contained these paintings grew so high that the government allowed the major *scuole* to increase their income by enlarging their membership and by classifying their building projects as "charitable works." This freed them from some of their prescribed spending on the poor and destitute. The standard for elaboration was established by the Scuola Grande di San Marco in construction projects to replace buildings destroyed by fire on the night of March 31, 1485. The new façade (Fig. 6.38) is composed in two distinct but related units, reflecting the larger structure of the main meeting hall (*sala del capitolo*) on the left and the smaller rooms used by the officers (*sala dell'albergo*) on the right. The project was assigned to the workshop of Pietro Lombardo (Pietro Solari; c. 1435 Carona–1515 Venice). As his name suggests, Pietro hailed from Lombardy, as did most of the stoneworkers in Venice, who were attracted by guild laws enacted in the 1460s prohibiting the importation of work from outside the lagoon but encouraging outsiders to move to Venice. Pietro, who did much to popularize classical architectural forms, was a sculptor as well as an architect, enriching his compositions with delicate carvings. On the façade of the Scuola Grande di San Marco his son Tullio (c. 1455 Venice–1532 Venice) revived the ancient custom of *trompe*

l'oeil relief sculpture, uniting the outer panels of each section of the façade in perspective compositions focusing on their respective doorways. True to the Scuola's dedication, lions (symbol of St. Mark) emerge from fictive barrel vaults at the sides of the main entrance. St. Mark himself baptizes and cures the sick in illusionistic porticoes on the right, a subject chosen to emphasize the charitable activities of the Scuola. As in Giovanni Bellini's *San Giobbe Altarpiece* (see Fig. 6.32) Tullio's illusionism is one with its framing, blurring distinctions between real architecture and its representation.

The Lombardi were well known to the citizen leaders of the Scuola Grande di San Marco because of their previous work in the same neighborhood on the votive church of Santa Maria dei Miracoli (Fig. 6.39). A precious jewel box of a building, the structure was erected by local citizens to house a miracle-working image of a Madonna. Originally located at the corner of a local shop, the image proved so prodigiously beneficent—believers were rescued from sure death and evil deeds were short-circuited by her miraculous intervention—that neighbors decided to erect a church and convent to protect and honor the Madonna's image. Lay worshipers occupied the lower zone of the rectangular nave; the resident Clarissan nuns worshipped from an enclosed balcony at the back of the nave opposite the unusually high, raised presbytery. Like the earlier Clarissans at Santa Maria Donnaregina in Naples (see Figs. 2.45, 2.46), they enjoyed a privileged

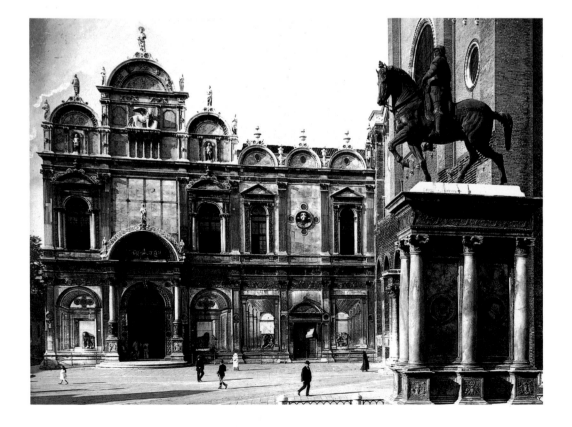

6.38 Scuola Grande di San Marco, Venice, 1485–90s, commissioned by the Scuola Grande di San Marco from PIETRO AND TULLIO LOMBARDO, succeeded by MAURO CODUSSI in 1490

On the right can be seen the Monument to Bartolomeo Colleoni, 1479–96, commissioned by the Venetian Senate from Andrea del Verrocchio. The casting and base were completed by Alessandro Leopardi, for the Piazza SS. Giovanni e Paolo, Venice. Bronze and marble.

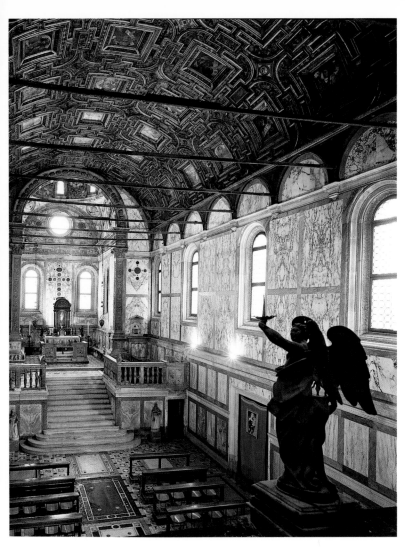

6.39 Santa Maria dei Miracoli, Venice, 1481–5, commissioned by members of the local neighborhood from PIETRO LOMBARDO and his sons for their own devotions and those of resident Clarissan nuns

position from which to pray for the souls of fellow citizens. Inspired by the Florentine example of Brunelleschi's Old Sacristy (see Fig. 5.9), the chancel is crowned by a centralized dome on pendentives. It is enriched with delicate reliefs and decorations, and marble revetments that recall the interior of St. Mark's.

Ducal and State Commissions

Whereas earlier generations had hesitated to provide even an effigy of the leader of the republic, wealthy Venetian families now emulated aristocrats at the Italian courts by commissioning multi-level monuments for their illustrious relatives. In 1476 Filippo Tron, son of Doge Niccolò Tron (r. 1471–73) commissioned a tomb (Fig. 6.40) from Antonio Rizzo (before 1440 Verona–1499 Foligno?), who had begun his career in Verona working for Gregorio Correr, the humanist patron of Mantegna's *San Zeno Altarpiece* (see Fig. 5.62), and who subsequently designed a number of other tombs for prestigious Venetian nobles.

Located on the left wall of the Frari's chancel, the Tron tomb consists of five tiers of sculpture, arranged in a classically restrained but imposing 49-foot (15-meter) high composition. The sculpture includes representations of the Annunciation (a traditional allusion to the founding of Venice), the Resurrection, virtues, and warriors. The doge is represented both by a recumbent effigy, and by a life-sized standing portrait—the latter previously reserved in Venice for military heroes. A highly legible, laudatory inscription set above the statue and below the doge's sarcophagus justifies this manner of portraying him, emphasizing Tron's acquisition of Cyprus and active participation in the war against the Turks. The inscription also commemorates his controversial reform of Venetian

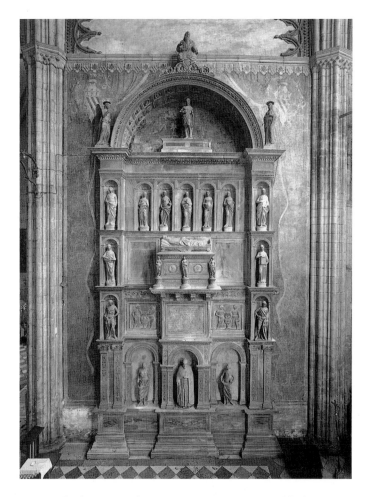

6.40 Tomb of Doge Niccolò Tron, 1476–80, commissioned by his son Filippo Tron from ANTONIO RIZZO for the chancel of Santa Maria Gloriosa dei Frari, Venice. Marble

The inscription beneath the sarcophagus reads: "Nicolò Tron was an unexcelled citizen, an unexcelled senator, an unexcelled prince of the aristocracy. Under his most blessed leadership, the most flourishing state of the Venetians received Cyprus into its empire. With the king of the Parthians, he joined arms against the Turks. He restored the value of money with his living image. His son Filippo has erected this well-earned monument to his most innocent shades for divine aid in everlasting perpetuity." (Trans. Debra Pincus)

coinage, on which he placed his own portrait—common in autocratic states (see Fig. 3.42) and visually sanctioned by roundels of Roman rulers on Tron's sarcophagus but so contrary to traditional Venetian values that the practice was outlawed for his successors. Doges were expected to serve and promote the state and their office, not themselves or their family.

Although the Venetian government continued throughout this period to limit the doge's actual power, he was presented to outsiders as the prestigious head of state. In 1485 the Senate decreed that the forthcoming coronation of Doge Marco Barbarigo (r.1485–6) and the reception of ambassadors and visiting dignitaries would take place on a new staircase in the courtyard of the Doge's Palace which was on an axis with the Campanile of St. Mark's and the Porta della Carta (see Fig. 5.48). The design of this staircase (Fig. 6.41) was assigned to Rizzo, who made the authority of the doge and the government implicit by locating a prison cell under its landing, putting eight personifications of Victories in relief on the projecting ends, and covering the sides with colored marbles and dense, classicizing ornament featuring marine and military motifs that allude to Venetian control of both land and sea. The huge statues of Neptune and Mars, produced by teams of sculptors working under Jacopo Sansovino and placed there in 1576, emphasized this theme and gave the stairway its name, the Scala dei Giganti. The arms of the Barbarigo family are also greatly in evidence, Agostino Barbarigo (r.1486–1501) having succeeded his brother Marco as doge in 1486 in an unprecedented and potentially worrisome election for a state that viewed ruling dynasties with abhorrence. The Barbarigo brothers' penchant for grandeur did little to assuage such fears.

The challenge of providing a suitably princely dwelling for the doge also affected the style of Mauro Codussi, who is now believed to have designed the wing of the palace to which the staircase rises. Site supervision was entrusted to Rizzo. This wing, containing the doge's living quarters, had burned down in 1483. The basic organization of the façade derives from the opposite, Gothic wing of the palace, to which Codussi paid homage by placing a pointed arcade on the *piano nobile*, above one with round arches, as he had done in the apse of San Zaccaria (see Fig. 6.30). The decoration of the façade is unusually sumptuous, extolling the doge and the Venetian state while serving to distract the eye from the uneven window sequences, determined by the existing interior organization of the palace.

Venetians always remained wary of individual commemoration. When Bartolomeo Colleoni, their famed military captain and successor to Erasmo da Narni ("Gattamelata"; see Fig. 5.60), left a substantial bequest

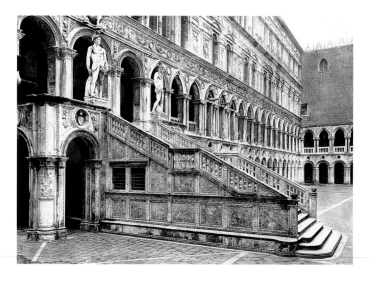

6.41 Scala dei Giganti, 1485, commissioned by the Venetian government from ANTONIO RIZZO for the courtyard of the Doge's Palace, Venice

to the city on the condition that he be honored with an equestrian monument in Piazza San Marco, city fathers demurred. They saved face, however, by authorizing its erection in the square in front of the Scuola Grande di San Marco, not in front of the basilica (see Fig. 6.38). This was an extremely honorable site insofar as it paralleled the position of the Gattamelata monument in front of the Santo in Padua. What is more, the site was in Venice itself, the *scuola* was newly rebuilt, and the adjacent church of SS. Giovanni e Paolo (see Fig. 3.6) was a major ducal burial site.

Verrocchio, who had replaced Donatello's *St. Louis of Toulouse* with his *Incredulity of St. Thomas* group at Or San Michele in Florence (see Fig. 6.43), totally rethought the older master's staid and noble Gattamelata monument, creating a dynamic work that seems about to charge off its pedestal. Emulating the energy and lithe musculature of the late antique bronze horses that stood on the façade of St. Mark's, Verrocchio lifted his horse's left leg and hoof high off the ground. The considerable technical feat of casting the work was realized by the local Venetian bronze founder Alessandro Leopardi, who also supervised the erection of the handsome, columniated marble pedestal on which the work stands. Standing high in his stirrups, Colleoni glares imperiously at potential foes. The exaggerated folds and intense eyes of his jowly face recall another specifically Venetian precedent: the hyperrealistic portrait of Doge Francesco Foscari on the Porta della Carta (see Fig. 5.49). Verrocchio establishes new ground, however, in effectively suggesting the inner workings of Colleoni's mind and spirit. Numerous commentators have credited the young Leonardo da Vinci, who worked in Verrocchio's shop, for this innovation.

Florence: The Golden Age under Lorenzo the Magnificent

When Lorenzo de' Medici took charge of his family, on the death of his father Piero in 1469, he was just twenty years old. Although a masterful political tactician, Lorenzo did suffer one serious threat to his power in the city. On Easter Sunday of 1478, members of the Pazzi family and their cohorts, having been encouraged by Pope Sixtus IV, attacked Lorenzo and his younger brother Giuliano during mass in the cathedral. Giuliano was murdered, suffering twenty-seven knife wounds, but Lorenzo, though wounded, managed to escape. The Pazzi Conspiracy, as the attack is known, was brutally put down, with Medici supporters rallying in the streets of the city. The men responsible for the attack were either murdered or sent into exile. One insurrectionist even fled as far as Constantinople, only to be extradited to Florence by the sultan as a favor to Lorenzo; he was hanged from a window of the Palazzo della Signoria as a warning to any others who might challenge Medici hegemony. Lorenzo's power clearly extended far beyond the walls of the city and remained unchallenged after the Pazzi Conspiracy until his death in 1492.

Known as Lorenzo "the Magnificent" in his own lifetime because of the extensiveness of his patronage and his position within the social structures of Florence, Lorenzo was a friend of famous writers, notably the Platonist Marsilio Ficino (1433–99); Lorenzo himself wrote poetry, based on classical and traditional Tuscan models. Although he commissioned relatively few paintings and sculptures, Lorenzo used his family's resources to fund new architectural projects and to amass a collection of antique carved gems and goblets made from semiprecious stones which was one of the most remarkable of its time. He also advised a number of other families in their commissions, encouraging the arts even when works were to enhance the prestige of others—and establishing himself as the arbiter of taste within the city.

The Tomb of Piero and Giovanni de' Medici

Lorenzo's first major commission, the tomb of his father and his uncle (Fig. 6.42), was one he undertook with his brother Giuliano about 1470. The sculptor for the project was Andrea del Verrocchio (1435–88), who was to remain active in Medici commissions. The tomb was placed in an open arch in the wall between the Old Sacristy of the church of San Lorenzo and the double chapel owned by the Medici in the adjacent transept (see Fig. 5.7, nos. 3 and 2). The red porphyry sarcophagus

is decorated by lush bronze acanthus leaves and circular green marble inserts. It is supported by lion feet, and the platform on which it rests is itself supported by four bronze tortoises. Piero's heraldic diamond ring modeled

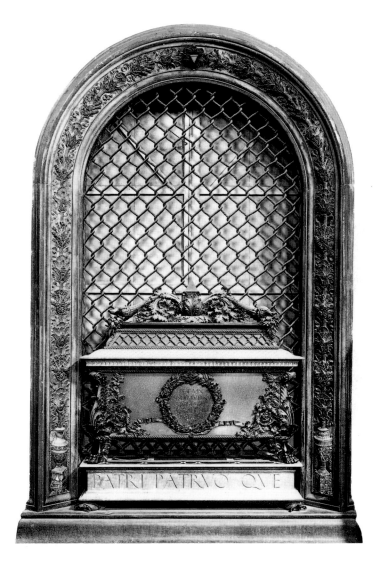

6.42 Tomb of Piero and Giovanni de' Medici, c. 1470–72, commissioned by Lorenzo and Giuliano de' Medici from ANDREA DEL VERROCCHIO for San Lorenzo, Florence. Marble, red porphyry, green serpentine, bronze, and pietra serena; height of arch 14' 9¼" (4.5 m), width of plinth 7' 10¾" (2.41 m), depth of plinth 42½" (108 cm)

The inscription running around the marble base reads: "Lorenzo and Giuliano, sons of Piero, placed [this tomb here] for their father and their uncle MCCCCLXXII [1472]." The inscription on the green serpentine tondo facing the sacristy (as in the illustration) reads: "Piero lived 53 years, 5 months, and 10 days; Giovanni lived 42 years, 4 months, and 28 days." The inscription on the similar tondo on the other side of the tomb reads: "To Piero and Giovanni de' Medici, sons of Cosimo Pater Patriae H[oc] M[onumentum] H[eredem] N[on] S[equatur]." This last formula, like all the Latin on the tomb, is pure classical Latin, indicating a refined and erudite classicist as the author. As a legal formula it indicates that the property is inviolable and cannot pass to its neighbors. It is thus a learned humanist translation of Piero's motto "Semper" ("always") into an appropriate antique indication of permanence built on legal right.

in bronze tops the sarcophagus. Every detail of the monument bespeaks imperial power. Red porphyry is a material that was reserved in antiquity for the sarcophagi of emperors and their families. Pope Paul II had already recognized this significance in Rome (see page 262). The lion is a traditional symbol of sovereignty and had been used as a Florentine state symbol for at least two centuries. Even the tortoises, attached to the motto *Festina lente* ("Hurry slowly"), refer to Augustus and Constantine, from whom Piero had adopted the motto. In commissioning this tomb monument, Lorenzo and Giuliano proved that they had learned their lessons well, for the tombs of both their grandfather and their great-grandfather (see Fig. 5.9) had employed red porphyry, albeit in a more indirect manner. The security of Lorenzo's position allowed him to be more flagrant in his use of the material than his more cautious predecessors had been. The opulent, elegant style characteristic of this tomb was to develop in the following years into a symbol of a golden age under Lorenzo; however, at the beginning of his career a number of styles existed concurrently in Florence, each of which offered possibilities for future development.

The Mercanzia Niche at Or San Michele

In 1463 the guilds' juridical tribunal, known as the Mercanzia, bought the niche belonging to the Guelf Party at Or San Michele and commissioned Verrocchio to replace Donatello's *St. Louis of Toulouse* (see Fig. 4.43) with a new bronze group, the *Incredulity of St. Thomas* (Fig. 6.43). Piero de' Medici had been involved in this project from its outset, and before his death his place on the building committee was taken by his son Lorenzo, so it is not surprising that the *St. Louis*, the most important public symbol of the Guelf Party, a competing political entity, was removed. Placed on the façade of Santa Croce, a center of Guelf activity, the image of the Franciscan St. Louis could be assimilated into the Order's iconography and thus be drained of its political potency.

Verrocchio's Christ and St. Thomas have a monumentality commensurate with Donatello's splendidly classical niche in which they stand, projecting outward from its confines. Thomas's gently curving position, as he moves to place his finger in the wound in Christ's side, has some of the same lyricism as figures painted by Filippo Lippi in his later career. This subject frequently appeared in Tuscan town halls as a symbol of justice, and was thus appropriate for the Mercanzia. Yet the complicated folds of material, the flowing curls of the men's hair, and the extraordinarily realistic and sensual details of the men's bodies suggest a courtly language far removed from the

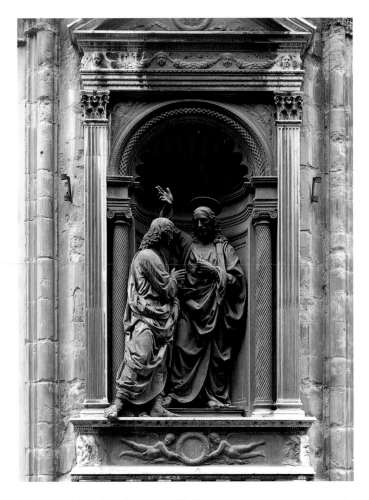

6.43 *Incredulity of St. Thomas*, 1465–83, commissioned by the tribunal of the Mercanzia from ANDREA DEL VERROCCHIO for their niche at Or San Michele, Florence, bought from the Guelf Party. Bronze, height (Christ) 7' 6½" (2.3 m), (Thomas) 6' 6¾" (2 m) (Museo di Or San Michele; copy now in niche)

severities of the law as if style were separating the idea of justice from its earlier civic context.

The Devotional Image

Beginning in the early 1470s, Verrocchio's pupil Leonardo da Vinci (1452 Vinci–1519 Amboise) began to make his presence felt in his teacher's workshop. His first major commission, an *Adoration of the Magi* (begun 1481; Fig. 6.44) for the Augustinian canons of the convent of San Donato at Scopeto, just outside Florence, marks a significant moment of innovation in the tradition of the altarpiece. Although Leonardo left the work unfinished with just the underdrawing and initial ground painted in, it reveals his mastery of composition and form. The painting shows the Virgin and Child seated, surrounded by the retinue of the Magi, who kneel to present their gifts.

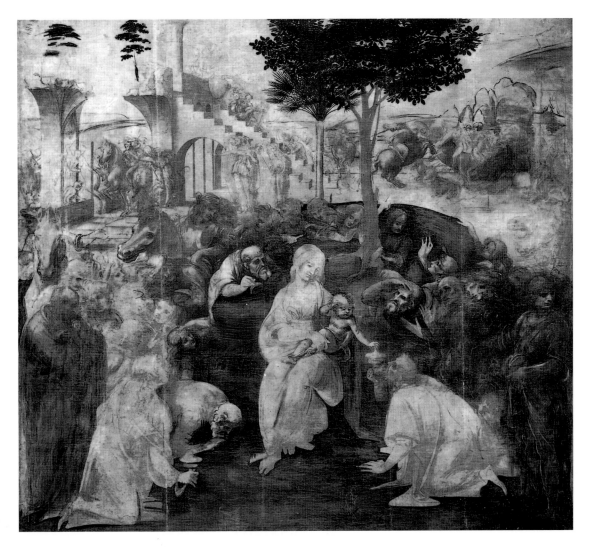

6.44 *Adoration of the Magi*, begun 1481, left unfinished in 1482, commissioned by the Augustinian monks of San Donato a Scopeto from LEONARDO DA VINCI. Panel, 8' × 8' 1" (2.44 × 2.46 m) (Galleria degli Uffizi, Florence)

The head of the Virgin is at the center of the composition, and her body marks the apex of a triangle created by the kneeling figures. Despite the active, gesturing poses of the other figures and the subordinate scenes in the distance, the main protagonists are locked into a stable compositional order which focuses the viewer's attention on them. In addition to the diagonal movement into the composition, the figures themselves contribute, through their poses, to the illusion of space. The Virgin's head and body are composed of a series of oval shapes, nesting one inside another—head inside upper torso inside the curve of the arms. Each of these shapes turns in opposing, tilting directions, creating not only a convincingly rounded figure, but also a sense of energy in the surrounding space.

Leonardo's concern for unifying his composition extended to the extensive use of the painterly device of *sfumato* ("smokiness") where washes of pigment create shadows so dense that they blur the borders between one form and another, fusing them as if their physical forms were as continuous as the space created by the residual

perspective scheme in the upper left. Although *sfumato* is technically a finishing operation, the underdrawing of the *Adoration* indicates that even at the early stages of the painting Leonardo was preparing to use this revolutionary technique.

By 1482 Leonardo had left Florence for Milan, however, and his painterly innovations were not assimilated into the studio traditions of the city until he returned nearly twenty years later. The *Adoration*, for all of its excitement, was an event without an immediate sequel.

A contemporary painting of the same subject by Sandro Botticelli (Alessandro di Mariano Filipepi; 1445 Florence–1510 Florence; Fig. 6.45), a pupil of Filippo Lippo, is much more typical of its time, although its relatively small devotional size may have something to do with its style. Botticelli—also a student of Verrocchio—ordered his composition, too, along a carefully plotted triangle, in this case reinforced by the beams of the decaying classical architecture of the stable, a reference to the passing of the Old Law into the New with the birth of Christ. Each of the figures, however, is linearly separated

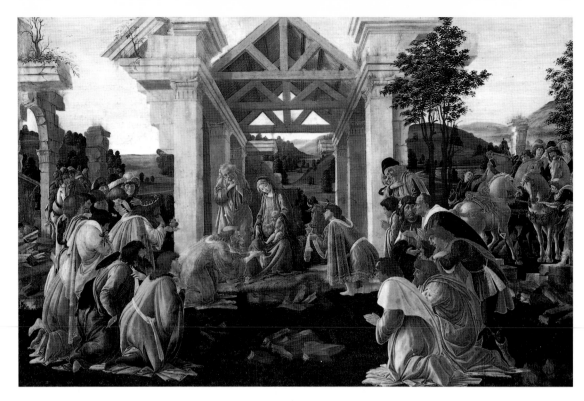

6.45 *Adoration of the Magi*, early 1480s, SANDRO BOTTICELLI. Tempera and oil on panel, 27⅝ × 41" (70 × 104 cm) (Andrew W. Mellon Collection, © 1996 Board of Trustees, National Gallery of Art, Washington, D.C.)

from its adjacent form, the traditional Florentine sense of *disegno* (in this case "drawing with line" to define a sculptural volume) isolating rather than uniting solid forms. Clarity of color and a landscape that looks like a stage backdrop, rather than a continuous extension into space, are other traditional aspects of this work. Along with the artificiality of the background, the Virgin has an unnaturally elongated torso, which gives her a courtly elegance somewhat at odds with the biblical stable, but echoed in the elaborated drapery folds of the surrounding figures. This somewhat chilly artificiality with a motion seemingly stilled in space is typical of Botticelli's work through his career.

The potentialities for this elegant and somewhat airless depiction of narrative can be seen in the work of Filippino Lippi (1457/58 Prato–1504 Florence), the son of Fra Filippo Lippi and the nun Lucrezia Buti, who was to become one of the most sought after painters of Central Italy. His *Vision of St. Bernard* (Fig. 6.46) was commissioned by Piero del Pugliese, who appears at the lower right of the composition in the conventional—albeit remarkably naturalistic—profile pose of the donor. Bernard is seated in an ascetic stony landscape. His library shelves are outcroppings of rock which also conceal grotesque demons (at right). Their evil work is foiled by the miraculous aid that the Virgin gives to the tired St. Bernard. Lippi used cool earth colors for most of the painting, except for the donor, whose red cowl calls attention to him despite his humbled position in the abyss implied at the lower edge of the painting, and for the Virgin and angels, whose brilliant primary-colored red, yellow, and blue clothing, decorated with gold, makes them the focus of the viewer's attention as well as of St.

Bernard's. The elongated figure of the Virgin, her elegant gestures and smooth ovoid face, and the lyrical movement of the angels create an atmosphere of aristocratic refinement—comparable to Botticelli's *Adoration*—which was to characterize Florentine altarpieces for the remainder of the century.

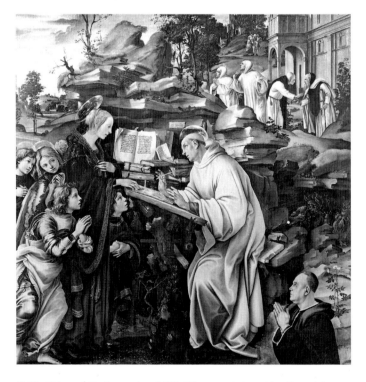

6.46 *Vision of St. Bernard*, c. 1485–90, commissioned by Piero del Pugliese from FILIPPINO LIPPI for a chapel in the Church of Le Campora, Marignole (outside the Porta Romana, Florence, and belonging to the Badia Fiorentina), owned by Piero del Pugliese from 1479. Panel, 6' 10" × 6' 5" (2.08 × 1.96 m) (Badia Fiorentina, Florence)

Portraiture

The stylistic differences evident in devotional paintings by Leonardo and Botticelli also appear in portraiture. Leonardo's *Ginevra de' Benci* and Ghirlandaio's *Giovanna dei Tornabuoni* (Figs. 6.47 and 6.48) illustrate the different possibilities for portraiture during this time. Leonardo painted a perfected and perhaps idealized representation of the physical appearance of Ginevra, whose alabastrine and simplified ovoid head is haloed with a bush of juniper (the homophonic *ginepro* in Italian), thus clearly identifying her. A sickly woman, Ginevra faces the viewer with a calm, if not chilly, expression, the triangular shape of her carefully posed body enhancing the air of stillness generated by her fixed gaze. A sun-filled landscape, reminiscent of Flemish painting of the time, provides a spacious and scintillating backdrop to the portrait as Ginevra is placed on a very slight diagonal responding both to the space and to the possibility for movement suggested by the glints of light shimmering through her hair. Giovanna, on the other hand, sits in stiff profile within a confining architectural (domestic) setting. Although each detail of figure and costume is meticulously presented, the bright overall light and the ram-rod pose give the figure an unnatural formal quality. Giovanna is dressed formally in an extraordinarily luxurious costume, her hair arranged both artfully and meticulously, and she wears a

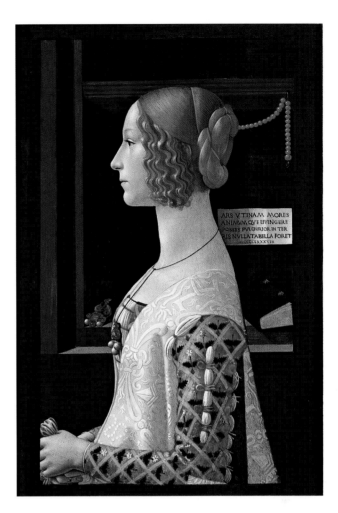

6.48 *Giovanna de' Tornabuoni*, 1488, commissioned from DOMENICO GHIRLANDAIO. Tempera on panel, 76 × 50 cm (Museo Thyssen-Bornemisza, Madrid)

large jewel around her neck with another in the cupboard behind. Both dress and jewels function as symbols of her husband's wealth, telling details in that the painting is a posthumous portrait. She is both subject of the portrait and object of social status within the wealthy mercantile and banking culture of Florence. Her very body is encased by metaphors of male success. The inscription from Martial on the small paper behind Giovanna reinforces the idea of her role. It reads: "O art, if you were able to depict the conduct and the soul, no lovelier painting would exist on earth." Thus Giovanna's conduct and the pureness of her soul—glossed by the presence of the book of hours in the cupboard behind her (and paired with the jewel to suggest both propriety and beauty)—surpass the powers of art to depict. Clearly implied, however, is the notion that art has succeeded in depicting everything else of importance.

Ginevra, on the other hand, is rather more simply attired, with little conspicuous evidence of the wealth of her family on her body, suggesting that the painting lies

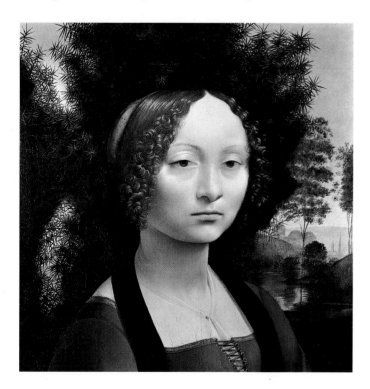

6.47 *Ginevra de' Benci*, c. 1474? and 1478/80, commissioned from LEONARDO DA VINCI. Oil and tempera on panel, 15′ ⅛″ × 14′ ½″ (3.82 × 3.67 m) (National Gallery of Art, Washington)

outside the bounds of formal portraiture commissioned to mark significant events in the sitter's life. An inscription on the reverse of the painting reads "Beauty Adorns Virtue" and describes a timeless state of being for the sitter, not unlike that implied for Giovanna. The motto is carried on a scrolling ribbon that twines around a small juniper branch and extends left and right to a circlet made of a stem of laurel and palm frond. This emblem, it turns out, is also personal to Pietro Bembo, the Venetian ambassador to Florence on two separate occasions (1475–6, 1478–80). Bembo's own motto, similar to Ginevra's, was "Virtus et Honor" ("Virtue and Honor") and was originally the decoration on the reverse of the portrait before Ginevra's device was painted over it, suggesting an exchange of the painting between them. Whatever the platonic relationship shared by Bembo and Ginevra (both were married), the painting functioned as a special mark of the friendship between the two— Ginevra, like Bembo, was apparently a poet—and thus exists outside the conventions so carefully adhered to by Ghirlandaio for domestic or marriage portraits.

Fresco Cycles

Two styles predominate in the large fresco cycles painted for family chapels during this period, although in each there is an overwhelming sense of the wealth and social status of the patron. Francesco Sassetti was the general manager of the Medici bank. His burial chapel, in the church of Santa Trinità, painted by Domenico del Ghirlandaio (Domenico Bigordi, 1449 Florence–1494 Florence) is composed of scenes from the life of St. Francis, Francesco's patron saint (Fig. 6.49). It is one of the most elaborate fresco cycles of the period. Sassetti and his wife, Nera Corsi, are buried in **all'antica** black marble sarcophagi embedded in the left and right walls of the chapel; their portraits as kneeling donors are painted on either side of the altarpiece much as Masaccio had earlier portrayed the Lenzis in his *Trinity* painting (see Fig. 4.60). The altarpiece itself, representing the *Adoration of the Shepherds*, also includes a number of classical references, attesting to Sassetti's reputation as a patron of classical scholarship.

The fresco on the altar wall just under the vault depicts the confirmation of the Franciscan Rule, while the one immediately below it shows Francis's miraculous resuscitation of a boy of the Spini family (a hagiographic invention). In each case the scene is depicted in a Florentine location; the confirmation shows the Piazza della Signoria in the background (although the event took place in Rome), and the supposed miracle in the Piazza Santa Trinità shows the church to the right and the

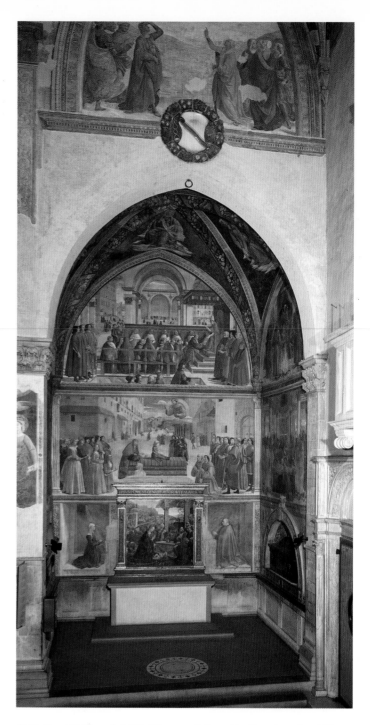

6.49 Sassetti Chapel, 1483–86, commissioned by Francesco Sassetti, with frescoes by DOMENICO DEL GHIRLANDAIO and black marble tombs attributed to GIULIANO DA SANGALLO, for Santa Trinità, Florence

Palazzo Spini (with the child falling from a window) in the left background. Ghirlandaio treated these scenes as historical narratives, placing contemporary Florentines in rows at the left and right as witnesses to the scenes. The clarity and didacticism of their portrayal are reminiscent of historical frescoes such as the *Consecration of Sant'Egidio* (see Fig. 4.51). Sassetti appears at the right of the confirmation with his young son. Immediately to his right stands Lorenzo the Magnificent, and entering the space from a sunken stairway are Lorenzo's three children in the company of their tutors, led by Poliziano. This

prominence in the city, Filippo embarked on a number of artistic projects, his funerary chapel being among the most lavish. The chapel's frescoes, best seen from a distance, were painted by Filippino Lippi between 1487 and 1502. Their elaborate classicizing illusionistic architecture and fictive sculptural reliefs frame a stained glass window showing large figures of the dedicatory saints, John and Philip (Filippo), also designed by Lippi. Beneath the window and behind the altar, Benedetto da Maiano provided a marble tomb whose simplicity of form belies its costly materials and ambiguous position. From outside the chapel the black marble sarcophagus appears to lie beneath the altar table, rather than behind it; this position is normally reserved for specially venerated persons such as saints. The arch containing a white marble **tondo** of a Virgin and Child flanked by flying angels is the same width as the altar and thus "reads" as a carved rather than painted altarpiece for the chapel.

On the left wall of the chapel the *Raising of Drusiana* (Fig. 6.51, a subject which also appears in one of Donatello's tondi for the Old Sacristy) tells of St. John's miraculous revival of a dead woman—appropriate for a funerary chapel, but also metaphorically referenced to the Strozzi's return to Florence after over thirty years of exile. All the figures are in animated poses, their costumes elaborate confections adding both energy and elegance to the scenes. The imagined Roman architecture is also intricately detailed, an echo of Filippino's experiences in

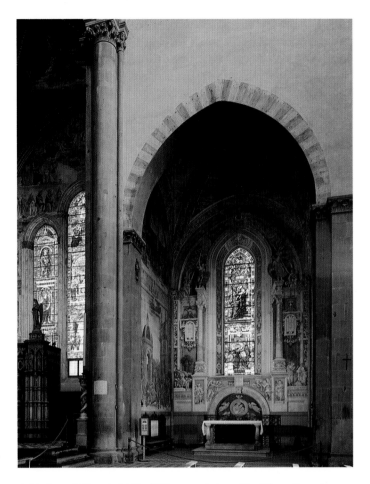

6.50 Strozzi Chapel, 1487–1502, commissioned by Filippo Strozzi, with frescoes of the lives of St. Philip (right) and St. John (left) by FILIPPINO LIPPI and tomb and relief tondo of the Madonna and Child by BENEDETTO DA MAIANO, for Santa Maria Novella, Florence

fresco provides unquestionable evidence of Sassetti's status as a close associate of the city's *de facto* ruler, Lorenzo's position alluded to in a fresco high on the transept of the youthful, victorious David standing on a pedestal with an inscription dedicating it "to the safety of the fatherland and to Christian glory." It also gave Lorenzo a visible presence in the city (and outside his own neighborhood) without the possibility of a charge that he was asserting himself in ways inappropriate for a private citizen. The stately propriety of the narratives is enhanced by the richness of the clothing worn by the young Florentine women in the *Miracle* scene and by the opulence of the overall program with its gold highlights and marble sculpture.

The Strozzi Chapel in Santa Maria Novella (Fig. 6.50 and see Fig. 1.24 no. 4) illustrates an alternative style in frescoes for family chapels. Filippo Strozzi, its patron, returned to Florence in 1466 from the exile that had been imposed on the Strozzi by the Medici, first in 1434, then renewed in 1458. In order to re-establish his family's

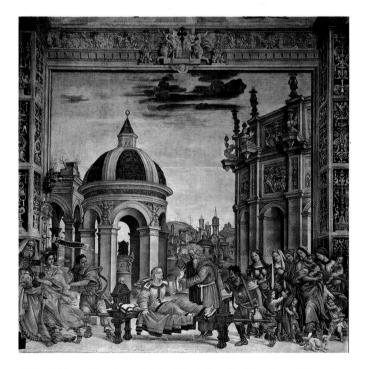

6.51 *Raising of Drusiana*, detail of the left wall of the Strozzi Chapel, commissioned by Filippo Strozzi from FILIPPINO LIPPI for Santa Maria Novella, Florence. Fresco

Rome during the time these frescoes were painted. The fabulous settings for the narratives and allegories lend a sense of elegance and richness to the Strozzi Chapel which makes the Sassetti Chapel appear staid and decorous by comparison—a manifestation of civic virtue as opposed to the courtly splendor that characterized Strozzi Florentine commissions. The two fresco cycles provide a stylistic measure of traditional values from a family that had been central to the Medicean power structure (the Sassetti), as opposed to pictorial novelty from a patron whose family (the Strozzi) had recently returned from a prolonged exile decreed by the Medici. Filippo Strozzi asserted a fantastical all'antica style which definitively set him apart from Medicean public painting in the city while at the same time recalling the opulence of earlier Strozzi commissions such as Gentile da Fabriano's *Adoration of the Magi* (see Fig. 4.55).

The Strozzi Palace

Filippo Strozzi's other great commission was the building of a family palace in the heart of Florence (Fig. 6.52). The building was most likely designed by Giuliano da Sangallo (c. 1445 Florence–1516 Florence) who, with his brother Antonio, provided a wooden model for the build-

ing in 1489. By the time of this commission, Sangallo had already built a number of other palaces in the city, including that of the Florentine Chancellor, Bartolomeo Scala, and he had worked on a number of architectural projects for Lorenzo the Magnificent. Sangallo's training had been as a woodcarver, but by 1465 he had traveled to Rome to study classical antiquity, his extensive notebooks now being one of the most important sources available to document the appearance of these monuments in the fifteenth century. Sangallo was assisted on the Strozzi Palace by Cronaca (Simone Pollaiuolo; 1457 Florence–1508 Florence), who had also spent an extended period of time (c. 1475–85) in Rome studying ancient monuments.

The exterior cornice of the building provided by Cronaca derives from the Forum of Nerva, a classical cap for a building that otherwise retains a conventional Florentine severity of masonry structure on the exterior, most notable in the smaller Medici Palace (see Fig. 5.14). Here the rustication is carried up through all three stories, the last use of an entirely rusticated façade in Florence. The plan (Fig. 6.53) shows that the building is symmetrical along its short central axis, each half designed for one of Filippo's two sons—a bold statement of dynastic continuity in the city after the family's long exile. Filippo Strozzi supposedly asked Lorenzo de' Medici's advice on the building of his palace and was encouraged by him to pursue the project. Thus Filippo believed that he had avoided possible reprisals from the Medici for an architectural project which overshadowed the Medici Palace in size, and Lorenzo gained the reputation of artistic arbiter.

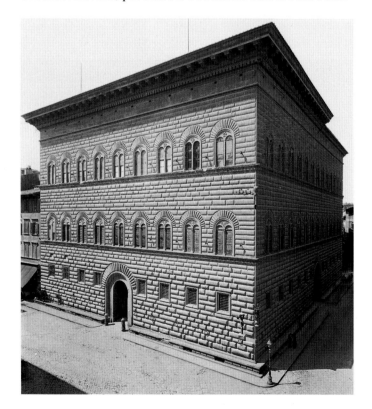

6.52 Palazzo Strozzi, Florence 1489–1507, commissioned by Filippo Strozzi from GIULIANO DA SANGALLO with contributions from CRONACA (SIMONE DEL POLLAIUOLO)

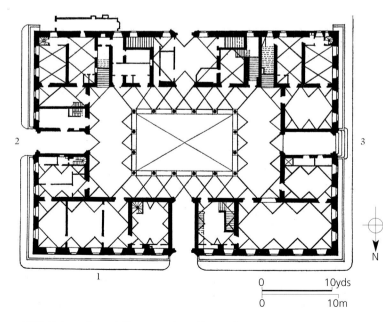

6.53 Palazzo Strozzi, Florence, plan of lower floor

1 Via Strozzi; **2** Piazza Strozzi; **3** Via Tornabuoni

Classical Antiquity as a Topos for the Golden Age

One of the critical innovations of the late fifteenth century was the transformation of mythology into large-scale imagery. Despite considerable scholarly attention, the meaning of many of these mythological paintings remains elusive. *Primavera* (Fig. 6.54) by Sandro Botticelli is a case in point. The painting (whose title means "Spring") seems to have belonged to Lorenzo di Pierfrancesco de' Medici, a cousin of Lorenzo the Magnificent. It presents a tapestry-like frieze of figures on a flowered ground. Space is pushed to the frontal plane by the grove of orange trees (the *mala medica*) behind the figures. Venus, the goddess of love, stands slightly to the right of center, with Cupid aiming his arrow over her head. She is haloed by a laurel bush, a homophonic reference (*lauro* in Italian) to Lorenzo. At the far right, an icy blue Zephyrus, the wind god, begins his embrace of Chloris, the spring nymph. A leafy vine extending from her mouth mingles with the blooms on Flora's dress, beside her, suggesting that the two women are two manifestations of the single concept of fertility. The Three Graces, to the left, are the counterpart of Flora and Chloris on the right side of the painting. Mercury completes the composition at the far left, perhaps part of the same extended family iconography as Donatello's David–Mercury in the Medici Palace (see Fig. 5.17). There is little interaction between the figures, and Mercury, the Graces, Venus, and the group at the right remain isolated from adjacent figures. The elongated proportions of the figures, their attenuated limbs, and the sensuousness of costume and landscape make this painting one of the most self-consciously artificial images of the century. The reading of the painting is episodic, moving from one figure to another. Connections are rarely made, leaving the viewer to pair figures and embroider the narrative freely, while necessarily displaying his or her classical learning.

The overt, albeit cool, eroticism of the female figures, whose diaphanous drapery does more to reveal than to conceal their bodies; the rape of Chloris at the right (and her subsequent marriage to Zephyrus); the entwined fingers of the Graces, and the location in the Garden of Venus suggest to some historians that the painting might

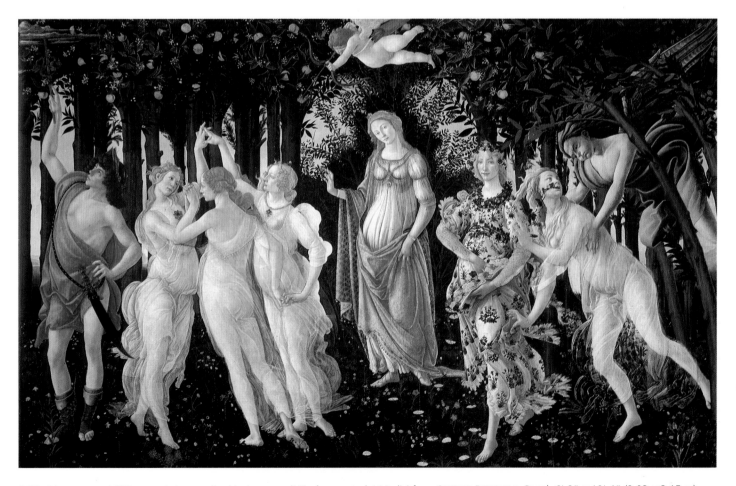

6.54 *Primavera*, c. 1482, commission ascribed to Lorenzo di Pierfrancesco de' Medici from SANDRO BOTTICELLI. Panel, 6' 8" × 10' 4" (2.03 × 3.15 m) (Galleria degli Uffizi, Florence)

Art and the Collector

Since a reverence for classical antiquity was a natural outgrowth of humanist scholarship and education during the Renaissance, it is not surprising that collectors began to assemble objects such as ancient Greek and Roman sculpture, gems, and coins, both for study and as signs of their learning and culture. Already in the early fourteenth century Oliviero Forzetta (1300–72), a merchant from Treviso, was seeking such objects from dealers in Venice. In the mid-fifteenth century, the sculptor Lorenzo Ghiberti claimed in his *Commentaries* to have a small collection of ancient sculpture, and Donatello was sometimes called upon to appraise the authenticity and value of newly discovered works. Artists became important players in the burgeoning market for objects of ancient art. Since large-scale free-standing ancient sculpture was still extremely rare in the early fifteenth century, collections tended to be of smaller objects such as gems and coins, as well as reliefs and fragments. Thus the precious appearances of the collections echoed those amassed in the previous century by the French royal house and the dukes of Berry. Because of their rarity, such objects were greatly

prized and aroused a competitive spirit among individual collectors. Piero de' Medici's illegitimate brother, Carlo, complained that he had been forced to relinquish a collection of important Roman coins because Pope Paul II wanted them for himself. Lorenzo the Magnificent subsequently triumphed in this collectors' contest when he bought virtually all of Paul's collection from his successor, Sixtus IV.

Agents were active for private collectors, seeking to provide their employers with the best examples of classical sculpture and often resorting to overstatements of value and to outright stealing to achieve their goals. Although small objects such as coins were kept in private studies, marbles were placed in the gardens of private palaces, often in a random manner. When the *Laocoön* was discovered in a Roman vineyard on January 14, 1506, it was appropriated by Pope Julius II for his collection, which already included the Apollo Belvedere, and placed in a niche at the end of the Cortile del Belvedere constructed especially to house it.

The rarity of such free-standing large-scale figures made them so desirable

that a virtual cottage industry of replication—and forgery—developed to meet the demand. Early in his career Michelangelo deliberately forged an Eros figure for sale in Rome as an antique. He may have done the same with the Bacchus (Fig. 6.55), seen in a drawing from the period standing amid antique fragments in the sculpture garden of Jacopo Galli, a Florentine banker and friend of Michelangelo's. Today it is valued as an early work of outstanding delicacy and sensuality by Michelangelo, but when it was made in 1496, by a young and virtually unknown sculptor, and grouped with ancient sculpture, it could well have seemed an exceptionally well-preserved antique statue. By the time Heemskerck drew this view of Jacopo Galli's garden, the family was apparently dispersing the collection. Nonetheless the drawing does give some indication of the picturesque nature of such gardens, themselves giving every appearance of a site of classical ruins. Some of the sculptural fragments lie propped against walls as if they were put down in the first available space when they were carried in, while others, like the figural relief, were set into the wall and still others, like the reclining figure in the background, were placed on columns, themselves probably antique fragments.

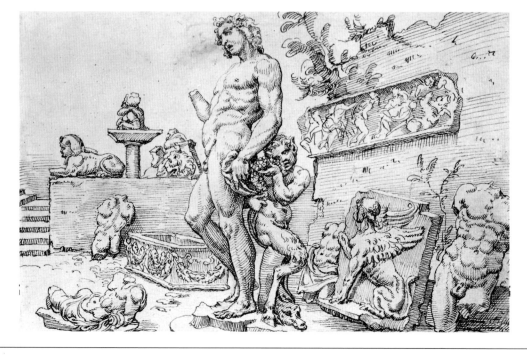

6.55 *Jacopo Galli's Garden in Rome*, c. 1532–35, MARTIN VAN HEEMSKERCK. Pen and ink on paper (Staatliche Museen, first volume of Heemskerck's sketchbook, fol. 72r, Berlin)

The central standing figure is Michelangelo's *Bacchus* (1496).

be an elaborate allegory on marriage for Lorenzo di Pierfrancesco's wedding to Semiramide d'Appiano in 1482. Whether the painting need be connected to a particular event is debatable. What is certain is that Botticelli invented a new type of monumental painting which defies all the conventions of naturalism and narrative focus traditionally considered to typify the Renaissance. Along with Filippino Lippi, Botticelli generated a new courtly art—a visual poetry comparable to the Petrarchan love poetry written by Lorenzo the Magnificent and his close associates—for a city that still believed in its republican traditions.

Antiquarianism

From the beginnings of humanist study in the fourteenth century, objects of antiquity were prized because—like ancient manuscripts—they helped people to form a truer picture of classical civilization. By the later part of the fifteenth century princely connoisseurs throughout central and northern Italy were amassing significant collections of ancient sculpture, coins, and gems. Lorenzo de' Medici added to the collections of these objects begun by earlier generations of his family and added ancient goblets and plates made of semiprecious stone which were displayed on special occasions as a sign of his magnificence. In fact the first mention of Donatello's *David* (see Fig. 5.17) focuses on a display of gold plate that was arranged beneath its column support. In an inventory of Lorenzo's collections made at his death in 1492 the costliest object was a sardonyx cameo cup 8 inches (20 centimeters) in diameter, now known as the Farnese Cup, which was valued at 10,000 florins, roughly one-third the cost of the Strozzi Palace (see Fig. 6.52). As a further comparison, twelve years later Michelangelo received approximately 400 florins for over three years' work carving the *David* (see Fig. 7.2).

When the antique is refabricated in a self-conscious manner, however, its feigned presence requires careful scrutiny. In one of his most noteworthy acts of patronage, Lorenzo the Magnificent commissioned Giuliano da Sangallo to build a country villa at Poggio a Caiano. Different from traditional irregularly shaped, crenellated villas (see example in background of Fig. 5.21), the residence Sangallo designed was worthy of a humanist prince (Figs. 6.56 and 6.57). He arranged the rooms symmetrically, raised the building on a platform (recalling Vitruvius's comments about the nobility of raised buildings), and marked the entrance itself with a Roman temple portico. Like Botticelli's *Primavera* or Filippino Lippi's now ruined fresco of the Laocoön myth in the entrance portico of the villa itself, the villa creates another world,

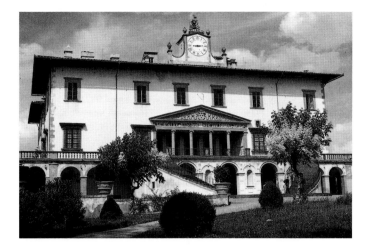

6.56 Villa Medici, Poggio a Caiano (outside Florence), 1480s, commissioned by Lorenzo de' Medici from GIULIANO DA SANGALLO

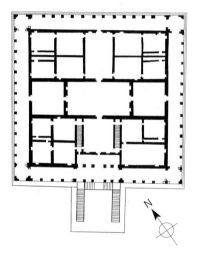

6.57 Villa Medici, Poggio a Caiano, plan of upper floor

This plan shows the presumed original position of the outside stair ramps.

evocative in its claims to the ideal, but fundamentally romantic in its artificiality.

The appropriation of the antique seen at Poggio a Caiano is taken to much greater lengths in an early work by an artist destined to be antiquity's greatest rival, Michelangelo Buonarroti (1475 Caprese–1564 Rome). Most likely carved in a studio maintained by Lorenzo the Magnificent in a garden area bordering the piazza in front of the monastery church of San Marco, the *Battle of the Lapiths and the Centaurs* (Fig. 6.58) is a small relief masquerading as a work of antique sculpture. As on Roman battle sarcophagi, the figures twist not just to suggest the animated frenzy of the battle but also to maintain the relief plane of the sculpture. Space for the densely compacted figures extends vertically rather than into a recessional background. The relief seems to adhere both to antique conventions in sarcophagi and to late medieval

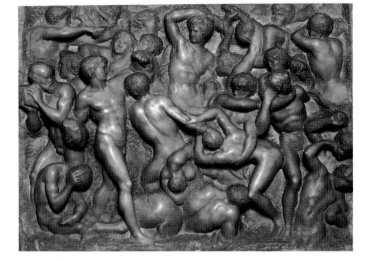

6.58 *Battle of the Lapiths and the Centaurs*, c. 1492, MICHELANGELO. Marble, 33¼ × 35⅛" (84 × 89 cm) (Casa Buonarroti, Florence)

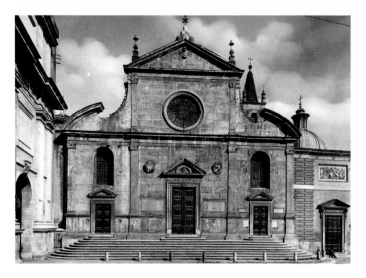

6.59 Santa Maria del Popolo, Rome, 1472–c. 1480, commissioned by Sixtus IV from BACCIO PONTELLI (?)

The Porta del Popolo is at the left.

uses of those same conventions (see Fig. 1.15). Here Michelangelo consciously rejected the pictorial illusionism of Donatello that he had emulated in other youthful work, selectively experimenting with a wide range of sculptural styles. The *Battle of the Lapiths and the Centaurs*, like Pollaiuolo's *Hercules and Anteus* (see Fig. 5.22) and the Villa Medici at Poggio a Caiano, blurs the boundaries between the real and the counterfeit so that the possessor can claim the attributes—and the power—of the culture he recreates. This is not a new idea in the history of art. But to counterfeit objects as collectors' items suggests that the value of the image—and its message—resides in its being perceived as an object of art. The connection between collector and ruler would have been obvious, since great rulers in antiquity were known to have amassed extensive and notable collections of art.

The Florence of Lorenzo the Magnificent was one in which republican and civic imagery and values were increasingly displaced by princely and aristocratic ones. While bank managers like Francesco Sassetti continued to commission works rooted in a formal everyday reality, the elite in the social hierarchy—notably the Medici and the Strozzi—supported artists who created lyrical visions of classical antiquity.

Roma Caput Mundi

The history of the papacy—and of the city of Rome—during Francesco della Rovere's reign as Sixtus IV (r. 1471–84) is one of expanding power, expressed in increasingly monumental artistic commissions. Although Sixtus had begun his clerical life as a Franciscan, he had a clear sense that the character of the papal office was most appropriately conveyed through lavish display. His intention, following upon the groundwork laid by Nicholas V, was to re-establish Rome as the *caput mundi*, the "head of the world."

In one of his first public acts after his election, Sixtus placed a collection of antique sculpture on the Capitoline Hill (see Fig. 5.34), the civic center of the city, which Sixtus—like Nicholas V before him—wished to control. The statues came from the papal collections at the Lateran and included two colossal heads: one in marble, known to represent Constantine, and one in bronze, believed also to represent this emperor who, according to tradition, had given the popes control over Rome when he re-established the capital of the empire in Constantinople in 330. The gift of these statues was a manifestation of Sixtus's power in Rome at the very site where it might be the most contested—especially since, like most popes, he was not a Roman.

Santa Maria del Popolo

Sixtus was also conscious of his role as spiritual head of the Church and of the need to enhance the religious life of the city. One of his first projects as pope was the complete rebuilding of the church of Santa Maria del Popolo (Fig. 6.59). The church held the miraculous image of the Virgin and Child thought to have been painted by St. Luke and a relic of Pope St. Sixtus I (r. 115–125?), a patron saint of Sixtus IV. Significantly, Santa Maria del Popolo stood immediately adjacent to the gate to the city used by virtually all visitors traveling along the Via Flaminia from the north. In rebuilding Santa Maria del Popolo, Sixtus visually dominated access to the city along this important route. Subsequent popes acknowledged this symbol of papal control by making it the first stop on their ceremonial entrance into the city to assume their office.

Sixtus's architect for Santa Maria del Popolo was probably the Florentine-trained woodworker and architect Baccio Pontelli (Bartolomeo di Fino; c. 1450 Florence–

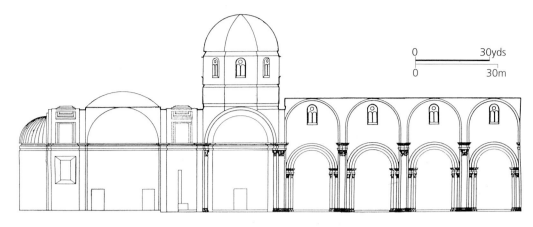

6.60 Santa Maria del Popolo, Rome, 1472–c. 1480, reconstruction of the original interior on the longitudinal axis

1492 Urbino). For the façade Pontelli echoed the recently completed façade of Santa Maria Novella in Florence (see Fig. 5.29), although in this case using travertine rather than the typically Florentine geometric marble revetment. The temple form of the upper story is echoed in the pediments of the doors. The lower part of the façade extends the width of the building, although the pilasters are set in high enough relief to suggest the constituent units of the interior spaces that lie behind. The partial segmental pediment form arching up from the left and right wings of the façade (taking the place of Alberti's scrolls) intersect—somewhat awkwardly—with garland forms descending from the top of the upper story, but provide brackets for the extremities of the building that turn attention back toward the center. Where these segments continued into the central unit of the façade they would just graze the frame of the round window, indicating that Pontelli, like Alberti, used a precise geometry to determine the composition of the façade.

Pontelli designed a grand interior space (Fig. 6.60) now transformed by later remodeling. The pentagonal chapels along the side aisles were the first of their kind in Rome and established discrete spaces for individual patronage within the church. Three of these chapels were patronized by members of Sixtus's family, the Della Rovere. The groin vaulting, the massing of the travertine piers, with their attached columns, and the steady rhythm of the arches of the nave recalled the monumentality of classical Roman architecture.

The Vatican Library Portrait

Nowhere is Sixtus's concept of an imperial papacy more clearly evident than in the fresco by Melozzo da Forlì recording the pope's generosity to the Vatican library and his support of humanist scholarship. The fresco (Fig. 6.61) shows the pope seated in a pose familiar from Roman imperial sculptural reliefs, in which only the emperor is shown seated. Bartolomeo Platina, the humanist scholar whom Sixtus had made papal librarian in 1475, kneels before the pope. The cardinal standing to

the right of Platina is Giuliano della Rovere, Sixtus's nephew and later pope as Julius II. The cardinal behind Sixtus is Raffaello Riario, another nephew. Each of the

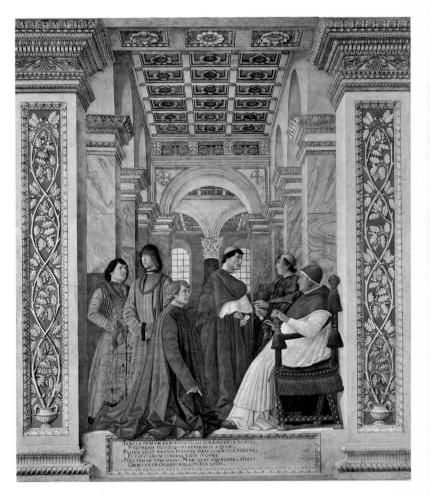

6.61 *Sixtus IV Confirming Platina as Papal Librarian*, variously dated 1477/78 or 1480–81, commissioned by Sixtus IV from MELOZZO DA FORLÌ for the Vatican Library, Rome. Fresco now detached and transferred to canvas, 12' 1½" × 10' 4" (3.7 × 3.15 m) (Musei Vaticani, Rome)

The inscription beneath the figures, over which Platina's cape extends, reads: "Sixtus, because you restored the churches, palace, streets, forums, walls, bridges, and the Acqua Vergine (Trevi) which had been abandoned, [and] though you are determined to restore the ancient benefits of a harbor to sailors, and to encircle the Vatican Hill, yet the city owes more to you for the library which was in obscure decay and is now in a famous location."

figures presents a careful study in portraiture, Melozzo having both captured the physical features and suggested the personality behind them.

The life-sized figures are placed in an imposing room, constructed with meticulous attention to perspective and adorned with a wealth of classical details. The capitals and the coffered ceiling are embellished with gold to suggest the grandeur of Sixtus's reign. Sixtus's support of letters and his fondness for his family (leading to an extraordinary degree of nepotism) are clear messages carried by the fresco. At the same time the classically inspired inscription that forms the base of the painting, and which is formally integrated into it by the way that Platina's drapery illusionistically overlaps its border, refers more broadly to Sixtus's role as patron of the arts throughout the city. It specifically mentions Sixtus's work to bring the city back from squalor, to build churches (*templa* is the first word of the inscription), a hospital, piazzas, walls, and roads, and to repair fountains, especially the Acqua Vergine, later reworked and known today as the Trevi Fountain. The statement is hardly inflated, given the scale of Sixtus's artistic projects.

Commemorative Monuments

During the reign of Sixtus IV the grandly scaled classicizing funerary monument became a common designation of status for the church hierarchy. Papal tombs had previously been large and made of costly materials; now cardinals, too, and other important clerics emulated the popes with elaborate wall tombs in their titular churches. The leading workshop in developing this type of monument was that of Andrea Bregno (1418 Osteno, near Como–1503 Rome), who had arrived in Rome from northern Italy in the 1460s. The tomb of Cardinal Pietro Riario (Fig. 6.62), Sixtus's favorite nephew, who died unexpectedly at age 28, is a fully developed example of this type of tomb. The effigy of the dead cardinal lies on a bier above a sarcophagus decorated with festoons, putti, and other motifs. The decoration of the pilasters and entablature and the mourning erotes at either side of the base all employ a classical vocabulary. Riario appears a second time, in the relief above his effigy, being presented by his name saint, Peter, to the Virgin and Child. His brother Girolamo kneels at the right with St. Paul. His connection to Sixtus IV is marked by the papal crest at the top of the monument and again by an inscription in good Roman lettering at the base, which describes his virtues and success in the Church and indicates Sixtus as the donor. Sixtus used this monument, as he was later to do with Melozzo's library fresco (see Fig. 6.61), to assert the presence of the papal family in a city where they were for-

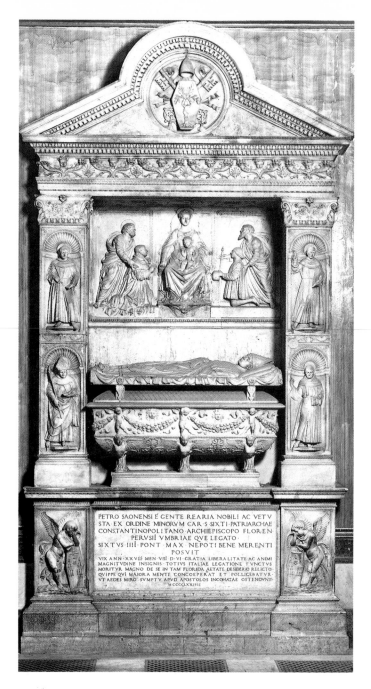

6.62 Tomb of Cardinal Pietro Riario, 1474–77, commissioned by Sixtus IV from Andrea Bregno (?), with assistance from Mino da Fiesole and Giovanni Dalmata, for Santi Apostoli, Rome. Marble, 21′ 4″ × 11′ 2″ (6.5 × 3.41 m)

eigners and where their success was in large measure dependent on the papal office holder.

The Hospital of Santo Spirito

The old hospital of Santo Spirito (Fig. 6.63) which Sixtus rebuilt is located near the entrance to the Vatican, in the Borgo, a neighborhood then inhabited by Rome's English colony. Situated on the banks of the Tiber (see Fig. 1.31), the hospital faces the Ponte Sant'Angelo, the bridge connecting the Vatican to the rest of Rome. As appropriate for

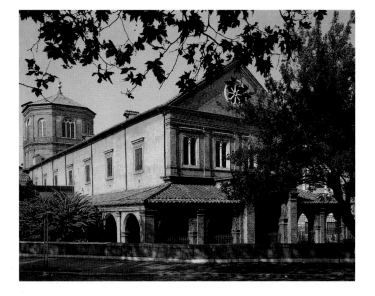

6.63 Hospital of Santo Spirito, Rome, 1473, commissioned by Sixtus IV

The high octagon at the left is the chapel that separated the men's and women's wards of the hospital.

its function, the hospital's architecture is simple and direct. A two story gabled hall allowed unobstructed floor space for the patients' beds. Regularly placed windows at the upper level allowed light and air into the hospital, which was divided into men's and women's wards, with a chapel between them. A cycle of frescoes (Fig. 6.64) by an unknown painter or studio, executed in a manner as direct and unassuming as the building itself, provides a carefully constructed history of Sixtus IV, including his mother's purported vision that he would be a Franciscan and then rise to power within the Church. Unlike Melozzo's grand image of Sixtus in his library (see Fig.

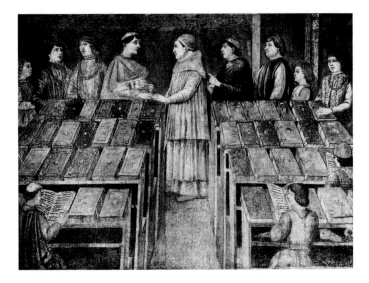

6.64 *Sixtus IV with His Nephews in the Papal Library*, detail of biographical cycle, Hospital of Santo Spirito, Rome, Fresco

6.61), these frescoes, with their doll-like figures representing the same members of the papal court who appear in Melozzo's fresco, use a didactic and popular style, appropriate for the audience of patients in this charity hospital for the poor. For the benefit of literate visitors, each image of the cycle was accompanied by a long inscription, thus making Sixtus's beneficence clear both visually and verbally.

The Sistine Chapel

The monument for which Sixtus IV is best remembered is a chapel built within the Vatican Palace to accommodate the increasing size of the papal court and to house the conclaves of cardinals that met to choose a new pope. Designed most likely by Baccio Pontelli, who had already worked for Sixtus at Santa Maria del Popolo (see Fig. 6.59), the Sistine Chapel (Fig. 6.65) was built from 1479 to 1481 between the existing papal palace and Old St. Peter's; it replaced an existing fourteenth-century structure known as the Great Chapel. The chapel retains a crenellated fortress-like appearance on the exterior, conforming to the refortification of the Vatican initiated by Nicholas V. The simple rectangular, box-like interior (Fig. 6.66) was designed without protruding architectural elements other than the molding running beneath the windows, suggesting that the extensive fresco cycles that cover its walls were intended from the outset. The chapel has the same proportions as the Temple of Solomon described in the Old Testament, an architectural conceit that would have implied a connection between King Solomon's position as ruler of Jerusalem (and Israel) and the pope's claim to rule Rome.

Sistine Chapel Frescoes Sixtus's claims to temporal sovereignty are implied with more complexity in the frescoes he commissioned for the Sistine Chapel. Beginning under a vaulted ceiling, which may have been painted with gold stars on a blue ground, all four walls of the chapel were completely frescoed (see Fig. 6.66); even the architectural frames of the paintings are painted illusions.

Sixtus brought a number of painters to Rome to work on the frescoes to guarantee their completion in a short period of time and to insure their high quality. The participation of Florentine painters such as Botticelli, Ghirlandaio, and Cosimo Rosselli (1439 Florence–1507 Florence) suggests that Lorenzo de' Medici may have arranged for a group of Florentine artists to work for the pope as a gesture toward re-establishing amicable Florentine-papal relations after Sixtus's ill-advised participation in the Pazzi Conspiracy of 1478. Two other painters, Pietro Vanucci, called Perugino (c. 1450 Città

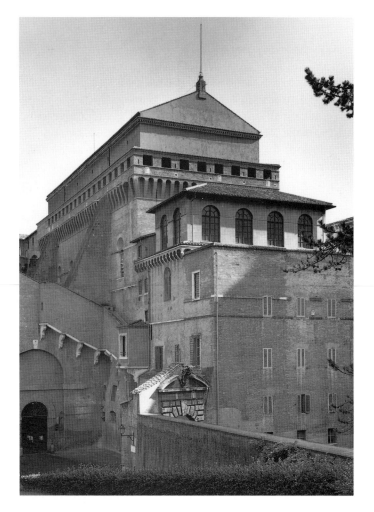

6.65 Sistine Chapel, Rome, 1477–81, commissioned by Sixtus IV from BACCIO PONTELLI (?)

del Pieve–1523 Fontignano), and Bernardino di Betto, called Pinturicchio (c. 1452 Perugia–1513 Siena), were Umbrian artists. It was Perugino who painted the fresco altarpiece (later covered by Michelangelo's *Last Judgment* but known from a drawing by a member of Perugino's shop), representing the Assumption of the Virgin, to which the chapel was dedicated. Sixtus assumed a prominent role in the altarpiece as a kneeling donor, his papal tiara placed conspicuously on the ground in front of him. St. Peter stood behind Sixtus, touching him on the shoulder with his key, simultaneously presenting the pope to the Virgin and symbolically conferring the papal office on his successor, a reference to the unbroken succession of papal authority.

Between the windows of the upper walls of the chapel, Botticelli and his assistants painted standing figures of the popes who were saints of the Church, beginning with Peter, on the wall over the altar (also later destroyed for Michelangelo's *Last Judgment*). These popes establish a continuous lineage for the papacy and repeat an iconography used in St. John Lateran, where roundels containing painted portrait busts of the popes ran the length of the nave on both walls. At the lowest level of the chapel the walls are painted to look as if they were hung with draperies woven in alternating panels with gold and silver thread. Sixtus's coat of arms and the papal keys form part of the woven pattern, again clearly identifying the patron.

A double cycle of biblical narratives occupies the middle level of the chapel and constitutes the main theme of Sixtus's decorative program. Stories from the life of Moses run the length of the left wall, and parallel stories from the life of Christ decorate the right wall (Figs. 6.67 and 6.68). The rare appearance of Moses as a subject in painting of this period suggests that Sixtus intended to remind viewers of the biblical patriarch's role as priest, lawgiver, and ruler, three critical aspects of his own office.

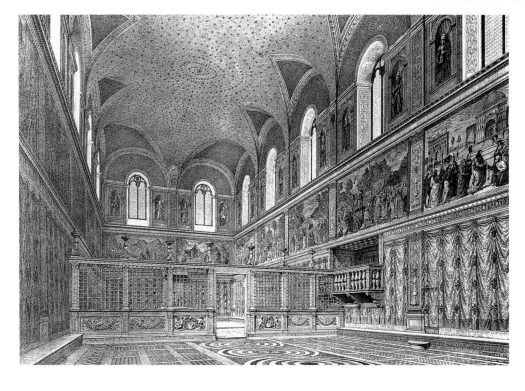

6.66 Sistine Chapel, Rome, reconstruction of the interior at the time of Sixtus IV. Frescoes completed 1481–82

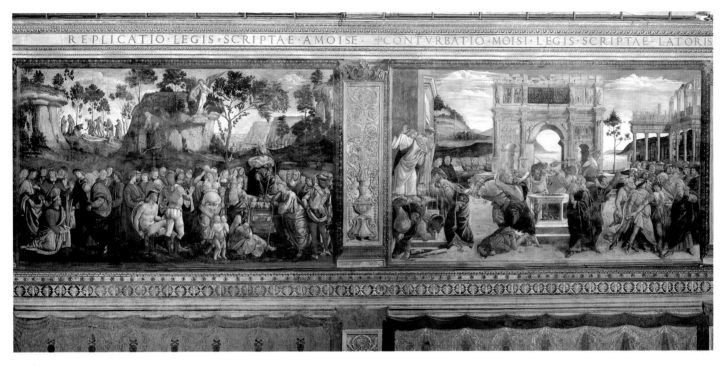

6.67 *Testament of Moses* and *Punishment of Corah*, 1481–82, commissioned by Sixtus IV from LUCA SIGNORELLI and BOTTICELLI for the left wall of the Sistine Chapel, Rome. Fresco, each scene c. 11′ 6″ × 18′ 9″ (3.5 × 5.72 m)

The inscription over the *Punishment of Corah* reads: "Challenge to Moses, bearer of the written law."

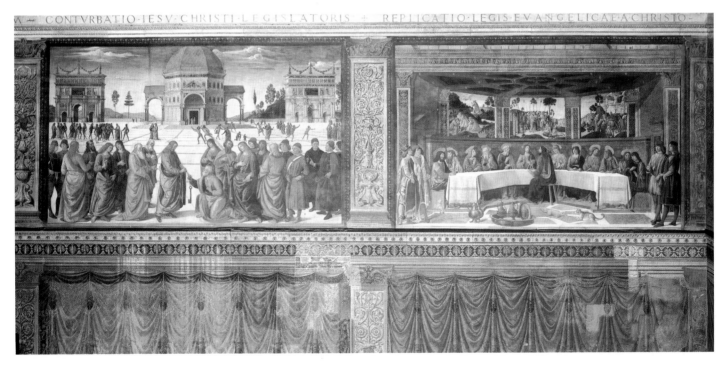

6.68 *Christ Giving the Keys to Peter* and the *Last Supper*, 1481–82, commissioned by Sixtus IV from PIETRO PERUGINO and COSIMO ROSSELLI for the right wall of the Sistine Chapel, Rome. Fresco, each scene 11′ 5½″ × 18′ 8½″ (3.49 × 5.7 m)

The inscription over *Christ Giving the Keys to Peter* reads: "Challenge to Jesus Christ, bearer of the law".
The two arches in the background contain a single inscription between them: "You, Sixtus IV, unequal in riches, but superior in wisdom to Solomon, have consecrated this vast temple."

Botticelli's *Punishment of Corah* (Numbers 16:1–35) shows Corah and three others rebelling against the authority of Moses and Aaron (see Fig. 6.67, right section). When they and 250 of their followers attempted to make an unlawful offering to Yahweh (the Hebrew name for God), Moses raised his rod, and the earth opened and swallowed up the four leaders, and their families, as depicted at the left of Botticelli's fresco. At the center of the painting Moses appears again before the sacrificial altar condemning those who unlawfully assumed a priestly role; the censers of the rebels become unnaturally agitated as they are consumed by fire. At the right of the scene the Israelites flee Yahweh's punishment. As in other paintings of this period, the figures extend across a band of space at the front of the composition while a vast expanse of landscape opens into the background, adding to the monumentality of the whole image. This fresco glitters with gold leaf throughout—the metal censers, the light emanating from Moses's head, and decorative details of clothing and architecture. Despite the horrific tale it tells, the *Punishment of Corah* conveys a sense of lavishness and wealth. The triumphal arch that anchors the center of the composition is a close rendering of the Arch of Constantine in Rome. The gilded Latin inscription on it translates as "No one can assume the honor [of the priesthood] unless he is called by God, just as Aaron was." Thus the fresco is a warning to anyone who might challenge the divinely ordained power of the pope.

The *Testament of Moses* (see Fig. 6.67, left section) is by Luca Signorelli (c. 1441 Cortona–1523 Cortona?), a pupil of Piero della Francesca. Signorelli may have gained access to this important commission from Piero, who is documented in Rome as early as 1459, where he had painted at Santa Maria Maggiore and at the Vatican Palace—or, more likely, through the intervention of Lorenzo the Magnificent, since Signorelli, sitting on the town councils of Arezzo, a client state of the Medici, seems to have supported Medicean positions and claims. Signorelli's scene from the life of Moses is, like others in the cycle, heavily decorated with gold, and, like Botticelli's scene, presents several moments of the narrative. To the right Moses reads, presumably from the Laws, to the Israelites, while at the left he hands the rod of leadership to Joshua. His death is depicted in the distant left landscape. The nude in the center of the composition has been interpreted as a reference to the Gentiles, "the stranger in the camp" referred to in Deuteronomy 29:11.

On the other side of the chapel Perugino's *Christ Giving the Keys to Peter* (see Fig. 6.68, left section) emphasizes the continuity between the New Law and the Old. Perugino set his scene in an unnaturally open piazza whose perspective system leads quickly to the ideal centrally planned temple in the distance. Triumphal arches like

that in Botticelli's fresco again recall ancient Rome. An inscription continuing over both of the arches compares Sixtus's patronage of his chapel to Solomon's building of the Temple and suggests that Sixtus is greater than Solomon because the new religion has supplanted the Old Law. Sixtus's control of the New Law is asserted in the foreground as Christ hands the keys of temporal and spiritual power to a kneeling Peter. In virtually all of the narrative scenes in the Sistine Chapel frescoes members of the papal court stand as mute witnesses to the events depicted and as manifest records of their allegiance to what was arguably the most impressive and learned court in Europe.

Innocent VIII (r. 1484–92) and Alexander VI (r. 1492–1503)

Sixtus's successors continued his references to Roman imperial rulership and elaborate contemporary court life. The tomb of Innocent VIII (Fig. 6.69), by the Florentine sculptors Antonio and Piero (1443 Florence–1496 Rome) del Pollaiuolo, transforms the traditional wall tomb type by showing the deceased not only as a recumbent effigy but also seated and gesturing as in life, reclaiming imagery first used in the burial chapel of Pope Boniface VIII (see Fig. 1.40). In the original form of the tomb the seated figure with its flanking virtues was below the effigy, which lay immediately beneath the crowning lunette. Innocent holds in his left hand a replica of Longinus's lance, reputed to have pierced the body of Christ, a relic he had received in 1492 from the Sultan Bajazet II (r. 1481–1512) for having detained the Sultan's threatening brother in Rome. To enshrine this lance Innocent commissioned a reliquary tabernacle comparable to that holding the head of St. Andrew ordered by Pius II (see Fig. 5.38). Innocent's tomb is novel, however, insofar as he appears in the seated pose typical of an emperor (used by earlier popes in civic monuments) and insofar as his double representation adheres to the type of the prince's tomb (see Fig. 2.55), further stressing his temporal powers. The figures of the pope appropriately use a naturalistic representation to recall the dead pontiff, whereas the female personifications of virtues in the niches and in the mandorla at the top are idealized, classicizing figures.

The Borgia Apartments   Roderigo Borgia, a Spaniard and the nephew of Pope Calixtus III (r. 1455–58), became pope as Alexander VI in 1492. He maintained a lavish court for himself and his family which has become a byword for licentiousness and corruption. Having bribed his way to the papacy, he lived openly at the Vatican with his mistress and made gifts of papal properties to his family—particularly to his son Cesare Borgia, one of the most feared courtiers and *condottieri* of his time.

As a patron, Alexander concentrated on works that would enhance his image as a Renaissance prince. The most famous of these are the decorations for the papal apartments in the Vatican palace, which had been built by Nicholas V. Pinturicchio, who had worked as Perugino's assistant in the Sistine Chapel, frescoed each of the rooms with a degree of lavishness unsurpassed in the papal residences. Although his *Disputation of St. Catherine* (Fig. 6.70) imitates the decorous poses and disposition of figures seen in the Sistine Chapel frescoes, the entire surface of the painting is elaborately patterned with different luxurious materials and further adorned with gold. Even the landscape takes on a decorative cast, with trees silhouetted against the sky. Not unlike Flemish paintings of landscape, their leaves provide abstract patterns comparable to those on the costumes of the figures. A replication of the Arch of Constantine in the distance—appropriately crowned with the Borgia heraldic bull—is prominently inscribed with gold letters "To the Cultivator of Peace," a reference to Alexander but also to Constantine, whose triumphal arch bears comparable inscriptions. Since Turkish advances into Europe were one of the threats to peace, the appearance at the right of the mounted Prince Djem, the Sultan's brother who was a threat to his power, seems particularly ironic. Djem was detained in the Vatican and was a pawn in papal politics with the Sultan, an attempt to give him free rein in exchange for staving off Turkish advances in the Christian west.

Cardinals' Commissions

Members of Sixtus's court aided the pope in transforming the city into a vision of a grand and prosperous state. Cardinals' commissions—in architecture, funerary monuments, and private chapels—were, like the pope's, also remarkable acts of self-aggrandizement. The economic power of the cardinals is evident particularly in their architectural projects. Between 1479 and 1483 the long-lived Guillaume d'Estouteville (see pages 261–62) rebuilt his titular church of Sant'Agostino (Fig. 6.71) and marked his extraordinary patronage—rivaling that of the pope at Santa Maria del Popolo—by having his name prominently inscribed across its façade, much as Giovanni Rucellai had done at Santa Maria Novella in Florence (see Fig. 5.29). Despite the awkwardness of the heavy-handed scrolls added to conceal the buttressing and to distract attention from the disproportion between the central and side doors, this church is important in helping to establish a model for church façades. The upper story accommodates the height of the nave, the lower story extends laterally to include the aisles, its cornice doubling to suggest a broken pediment and to unite—however tentatively—the lower and upper storys. Scrolls, as at Santa Maria Novella, effect the transition between the two stories. Confined in a small space near the Piazza Navona, Sant'Agostino rises grandly from a high podium, its pilasters springing from a tall base. The

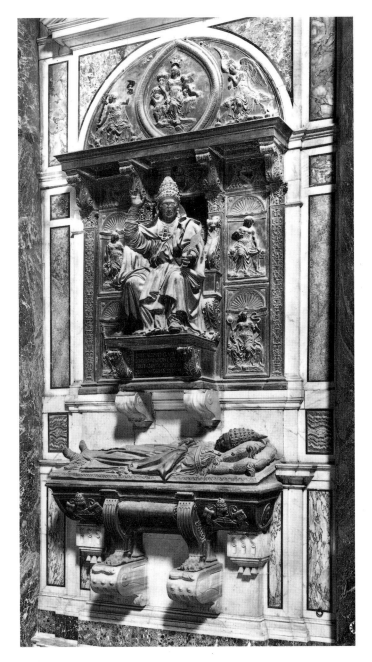

6.69 Tomb of Innocent VIII, c. 1492–98, commissioned by Lorenzo Cibo from ANTONIO AND PIERO POLLAIUOLO for St. Peter's, Rome. Bronze with gilding

The tomb was first moved in 1507 with the beginning of the new St. Peter's; it was disassembled in 1606 and reconstructed in its current position in 1621.

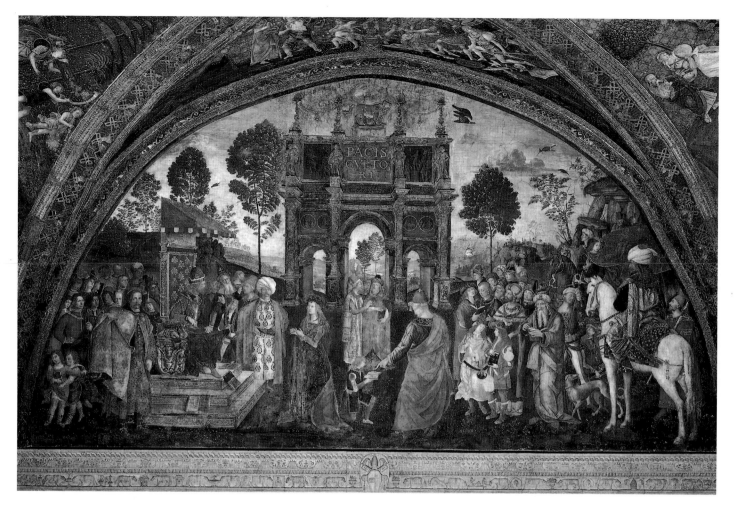

6.70 *Disputation of St. Catherine*, 1492–95, commissioned by Alexander VI from Pinturicchio for the Room of the Saints, Vatican Palace, Rome. Fresco with gold leaf

whole is topped by a pediment, suggesting a temple. The interior also employed a classical Roman vocabulary, with a Composite order and lofty arches.

The Cancelleria   The most important—and certainly the most imposing—palace built in Rome during the late fifteenth century was that of the Cancelleria (Fig. 6.72). It was built as a cardinal's palace by Sixtus's nephew Raffaello Riario, who appears in Melozzo's Vatican Library fresco (see Fig. 6.61). The architect is unknown. To make space for his huge palace, Cardinal Riario tore down pre-existing structures at the site, including his titular church which he rebuilt as part of his new building. Its finely dressed stone courses and rhythmic alternation of windows and pilasters recall Alberti's Rucellai Palace (see Fig. 34) and the papal palace in Pienza (see Fig. 5.40). The slightly projecting bays at the ends help to give a sense of completion to the 300-foot (92-meter) façade (and are a feature previously used only on government buildings). The great size, regular composition, and

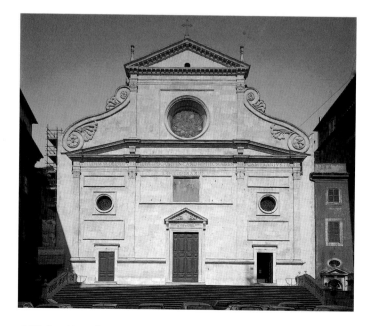

6.71 Sant'Agostino, Rome, 1479–83, commissioned by Guillaume d'Estouteville perhaps from Giacomo da Pietrasanta

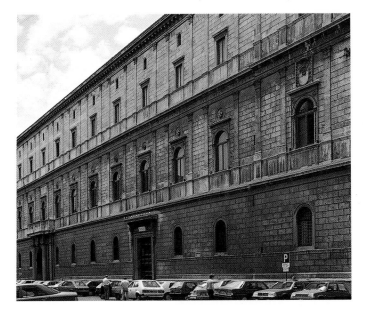

6.72 Palazzo della Cancelleria, Rome, planned shortly after 1483, underway by 1485, mostly complete in 1489, façade finished in 1495, additions between 1503 and 1511, commissioned by Raffaello Riario

When Cardinal Riario was discovered to have participated in a plot against Pope Leo X in 1516 he was forced to deed the palace to the papacy as part of his fine. The building was then used as offices for the papal chancellery, thus giving it its current name.

classicizing decoration of this building, as well as its domination over the urban landscape, its creation of a piazza on its entrance façade and its presence on the papal processional route, all made it a model for later Roman palaces.

The Carafa Chapel The private chapel was another means of denoting status within the Church hierarchy. The Carafa Chapel at Santa Maria sopra Minerva (Fig. 6.74), commissioned by Cardinal Oliviero Carafa from Filippino Lippi, is among the most ornate of the period. It intervened in Filippino's painting of the Strozzi Chapel in Florence (see Figs. 6.50 and 6.51) and provided an important incentive to the painter's stylistic development. Every decorative detail displays an archaeological accuracy, suggesting the new discoveries of ancient Roman buildings on the Palatine Hill. The frescoed altarpiece shows the Dominican Carafa as a witness to the Annunciation, his patron St. Dominic standing behind him as his advocate. In the fresco surrounding the altarpiece, Lippi painted an Assumption, thus presenting the first and last miraculous moments of the Virgin's life. Lippi opened the wall of the chapel illusionistically to landscape beyond, giving an even grander sense of space and scale than the already very large chapel would allow. The sumptuousness of the decorative details and the elegance of the individual figures give this prince of the Church an image comparable to that of temporal princes

in Italy and testifies to the secure re-establishment of the papacy and its extensive court in Rome by the end of the fifteenth century.

Michelangelo's *Pietà* The lure of patronage at the papal court brought large numbers of artists from across Italy to Rome, as it had since the time of Giotto. Not the least among these was Michelangelo. Having completed his *Bacchus* (see Fig. 6.55) for the Florentine banker Jacopo Galli in 1496, Michelangelo received a commission from the French cardinal Jean Bilhères de Lagraulas (Jean de Villiers de la Groslaye) for a *Pietà* for his funerary chapel (Fig. 6.73). The contract for the work bravely asserts that the completed statue would be the most beautiful statue in Rome, leaving open just what was meant by such a claim. Nonetheless, the finished statue is a technical *tour de force*: palpable flesh, distended veins, extended limbs, lustrously polished surfaces, and complexities of drapery folds and gatherings whose only excuse could have been to show off the skill of the sculptor. The group is

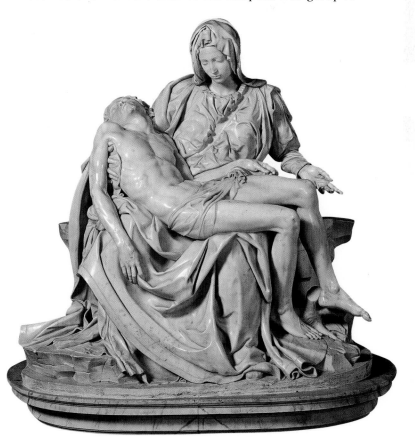

6.73 *Pietà*, 1498–9, commissioned by Cardinal Jean Bilhères de Lagraulas (Jean de Villiers de la Groslaye) from MICHELANGELO for his funerary chapel at St. Peter's, Rome. Marble, 5′ 8″ (1.74 cm) high, width at base 6′ 5″ (1.95 cm) (Rome, St. Peter's)

The cardinal's burial site was in the round domed church of St. Petronilla attached to the left nave of Old St. Peter's. This chapel was also known as the Chapel of the Kings of France.

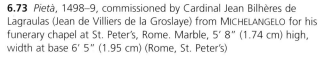

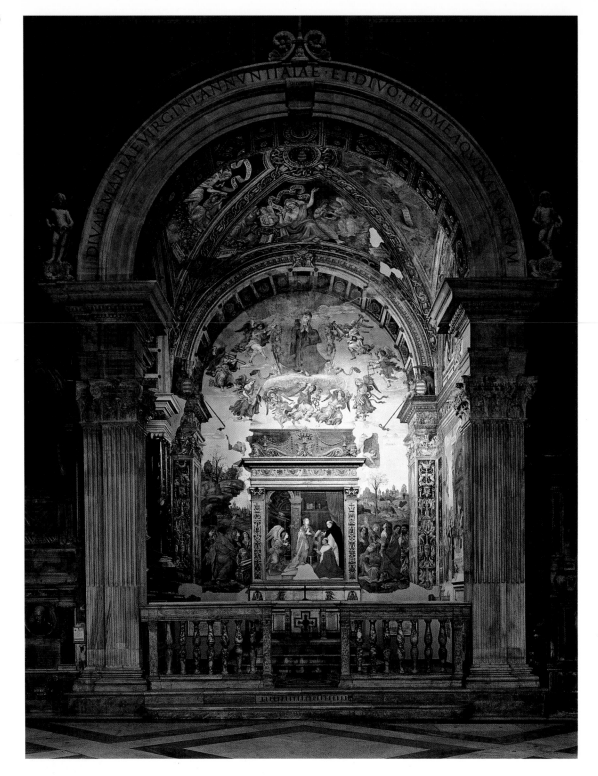

6.74 Carafa Chapel, 1489–93, commissioned by Oliviero Carafa from FILIPPINO LIPPI for Santa Maria sopra Minerva, Rome. Fresco

On the right wall of the chapel is a representation of the *Triumph of St. Thomas Aquinas* over heresy and, in the lunette above, scenes from the life of the saint. The four reclining female figures in the vaults are figures of sibyls.

unprecedented in Italian sculpture in its iconographic form, but relates instead to northern wooden sculpture groups of this devotional type, perhaps a gesture to Michelangelo's French patron. As he was to do repeatedly in his long career, the young Michelangelo here quite deliberately set himself apart from the norm as one way of establishing his presence in the competitive environment of Rome. The story told by his biographer that Michelangelo hid in St. Peter's in order to add his signature (on the belt of the Virgin) to the sculpture after he had heard it attributed to a Lombard artist, illustrates his

keen sense of this as a demonstration piece for his talent. His signature also proudly declares that he is Florentine. Moreover, in using the imperfect verb form of the Latin *faciebat*, he not only references his work to that of Praxiteles, whom ancient writers credit with this verbal oddity; he also suggests, like Praxiteles, that the statue is still in process. This boast, that as extraordinary as the sculpture may now be, it will only get better, also refers to the trajectory of his career as a sculptor. Such a claim—for himself, and for the history of Roman art—was truer than even Michelangelo could have imagined.

Milan: The Sforza and a Grand Classical Style

Sforza Milan

Francesco Sforza became ruler of Milan in 1450. A brilliant *condottiere*, he earned the honor of marrying Duke Filippo Visconti's illegitimate daughter and sole heir, Bianca Maria, because of his military successes for the Visconti. However, when Filippo died in 1447, the Milanese citizenry rebelled and set up their own government, the so-called Ambrosian Republic (1447–50), named for St. Ambrose, the founder of Christianity in the city. Francesco spent the next three years gaining control of Milan's subject cities and then, after a three-month siege, recaptured Milan. Having been assisted financially by the Medici Bank and politically by the Medici family in Florence—then interested both in dominating international finance and in eliminating Milanese threats to Florence's liberty—Francesco welcomed central Italian merchants, bankers, and artists to Milan. At the same time, his shaky claims to legitimate rulership impelled him to forge visible links with the Visconti past to which he was tenuously linked through his marriage. He encouraged his artists to restore and enhance frescoes at the Castello Visconteo in Pavia (see Fig. 3.37), and he resumed construction of the nearby Certosa. As if to drive the point home, he even played the role of Giangaleazzo Visconti, one of his predecessors, in a court costume ball.

Francesco's sons, especially Ludovico Sforza (1451–1508), followed the same policy of claiming the right of rulership through appropriation of Visconti imagery. Called "il Moro" because of his dark complexion, Ludovico dominated Milanese culture and politics for the entire last quarter of the fifteenth century, in spite of the fact that he was the illegitimate and younger son of Francesco Sforza. After the death in 1476 of his elder brother, the wanton Galeazzo Maria Sforza, Ludovico managed to oust his sister-in-law as regent for his young nephew, Gian Galeazzo Maria, and secured effective control of the state. In 1494 he succeeded in having himself proclaimed Duke of Milan—a title he would enjoy for only five years. Obviously, both he and his father needed to deploy the visual arts to legitimate their rule.

Completing Visconti Ecclesiastical Foundations

The Certosa No monument was more intimately linked with the Visconti—and therefore crucial to the Sforzas—than the Certosa di Pavia (Fig. 6.75). As we have seen (see Fig. 4.2), it was built in conscious emulation of similar foundations by the dukes of Burgundy and was intended to house the remains of Giangaleazzo Visconti, the first Duke of Milan. Construction at the monastery had proceeded haltingly throughout the first half of the century. Under Francesco's patronage, work sped up on the nave and on the cloister nearest the church (Fig. 6.76), which is embellished with a profusion of terracotta reliefs. Gaily cavorting putti and lush garlands and vegetation decorate the arches and friezes, making reference to Milan's proud Roman imperial heritage. Busts emerging from roundels in the spandrels recall the classical prototype of the *imago clipeata*, often found along with putti and garlands on ancient sarcophagi. Everything is full of movement, every figure and molding fresh and exuberant, testifying to Lombard delight in decorative complexity and to native facility with clay and brick.

The present façade of the Certosa (see Fig. 6.75) reflects the overall design by Giovanni Antonio Amadeo (1447 Pavia–1522 Milan), approved by Ludovico in 1492. Amadeo was the leading local sculptor, architect, and engineer in Lombardy, active in Bergamo as well as Pavia and Milan. His façade incorporates marble reliefs that

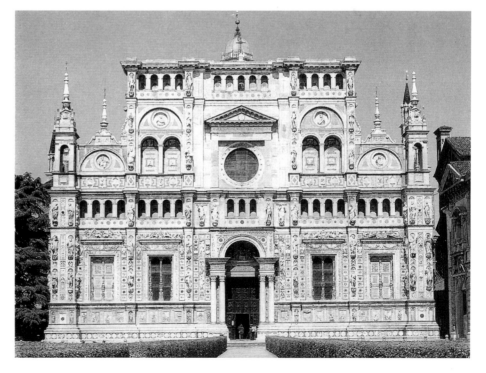

6.75 The Certosa, Pavia, façade commissioned by Galeazzo Maria Sforza from ANTONIO AND CRISTOFORO MANTEGAZZA and GIOVANNI AMADEO in 1473, present arrangement of lower stories commissioned by Ludovico Sforza in 1492

had been commissioned in 1473 by Galeazzo Maria Sforza for a somewhat less elaborate design. Neither façade was to have been less than sumptuous, however; the Sforza brothers were renowned throughout Italy for their extravagant pomp and display. For example, Galeazzo's state visit to Florence in 1471 had overwhelmed spectators with a parade of 2,000 horses, 500 pairs of dogs, and 1,000 courtiers and attendants dressed in velvet and silk. The marble façade of the Certosa is as intricate and unabashedly costly, for its size, as the ivory altarpiece that its founder, Giangaleazzo Visconti, had commissioned for the high altar (see Fig. 4.3). The source of patronage of the project is suggested by a series of medallions at the base of the façade depicting Roman emperors. Like the images on the ceiling of the Camera Picta in Mantua (see Fig. 6.23), they point to the historical roots of Ludovico's autocratic power. Biblical reliefs on the next level Christianize the program, completed by dozens of standing saints and prophets.

All of the reliefs have suffered damage and weathering, but *The Mocking of Christ* (Fig. 6.77) is sufficiently well preserved to sustain closer examination. It was produced by the Mantegazza brothers—Antonio (active 1473–95 Milan and Pavia) and Cristoforo (active 1464–81 Milan and Pavia)—Lombard sculptors who specialized in intricate carving of flattened figures evoking the character of ancient gems and cameos. The relief centers around the seated Christ, covered in drapery executed in the wet, clinging manner seen in some ancient sculpture. A triumphal arch leads back to another antique image: a fanciful equestrian statue on a very tall pedestal which may recall the Mantegazzas' model for a never-executed equestrian monument of Francesco Sforza. A crowd of onlookers, the two most forward of whom taunt Christ with their coarse faces and clenched fists, recall north Italian traditions of narrative **verism** (see Fig. 3.46). The Roman street scene is a sculptural variation on Andrea Mantegna's archaeological reconstructions in Padua (see Fig. 5.61) and the spatial illusionism of Vincenzo Foppa in Milan (see Fig. 6.82). Typically Lombard in its complexity and extravagant decoration, the relief also calls to mind the terracotta decorations in one of the Certosa's own cloisters (see Fig. 6.76), here in the more prestigious material of marble.

The Cathedral As work on the Certosa neared completion, Ludovico pushed forward with plans to enhance Milan's chief shrine, the cathedral. In 1487 the original tower over the crossing was dismantled because it was structurally unsound; but instead of merely replacing the tower, the Fabbrica called a competition for a new, more elaborate structure. All the leading builders and sculptors in Milan submitted plans, including Giovanni

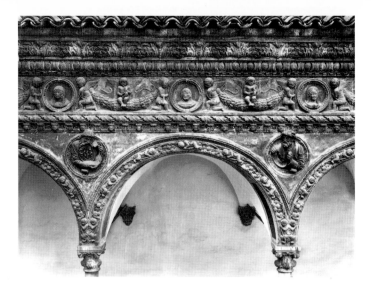

6.76 Cloister, Certosa, Pavia, 1460s, commissioned by the Carthusians with the support of Francesco Sforza from GUINIFORTE SOLARI. Terracotta

Amadeo, Leonardo da Vinci, and Donato Bramante. Tellingly, the judges decided in favor of Amadeo's Gothic spire, with its spiraling exterior staircases (Fig. 6.78). They justified their decision on the grounds that it was more important for the tower to match the style of the rest of the building than to follow the fashion for

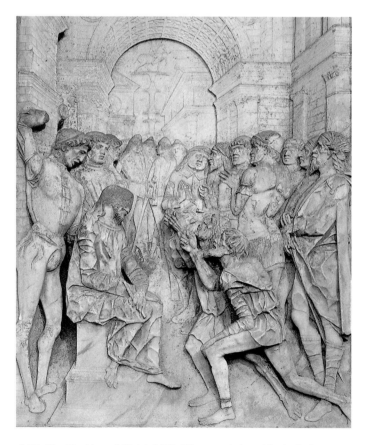

6.77 *The Mocking of Christ*, 1482–92, commissioned by Ludovico Sforza from ANTONIO AND CRISTOFORO MANTEGAZZA for the façade of the Certosa, Pavia. Marble

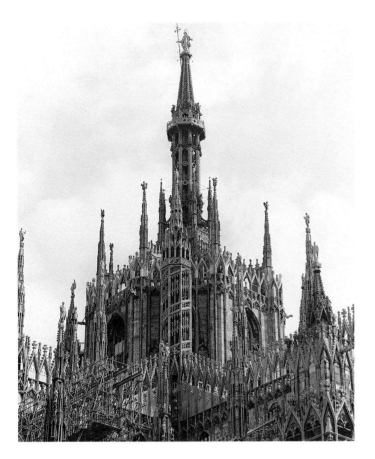

6.78 Crossing tower, Milan Cathedral, designed 1487/90, commissioned by the Fabbrica of Milan Cathedral with the support of Ludovico Sforza from GIOVANNI AMADEO

Commissions continued to be granted for Gothic architectural designs throughout the sixteenth and seventeenth centuries, especially for the completion of unfinished churches.

classical forms. The structure also gave Milan a cathedral unlike any of the other major Italian city-states and underscored its relations with transalpine cities. In addition, the tower was much less heavy than a classical dome might have been, requiring no reinforcement of the pre-existing church.

Private Commissions

Local tastes and traditions also affected the form of commissions undertaken by foreigners in Sforza Milan. When officials of Cosimo de Medici established the Medici Bank headquarters in the city, in a building given him by Francesco Sforza in 1456, his branch manager, Pigello Portinari, rebuilt the structure to resemble those currently being erected in Florence, but enhanced it with more opulent decoration. The façade of the Medici Bank (Fig. 6.79), known through a drawing in the *Treatise on Architecture* by the Florentine sculptor and architect Filarete, imitates the heavy roof cornice, double-lancet windows, and fortress-like ground story of the Medici Palace in Florence (see Fig. 5.14), but the scheme was enriched with lush terracotta decoration, as in the new cloister at the Certosa. Paying homage to Milan's rich Gothic heritage, the windows of the upper story were set within pointed arches; the main portal was overlaid with numerous heraldic motifs and devices. Sober Tuscan models took on a courtly, celebratory air.

Pigello Portinari also supervised the construction of a burial chapel for his family at the church of Sant'Eustorgio (Figs. 6.80 and 6.81). Its Florentine and specifically Medici-associated patronage is evident in its plan and elevation, which consciously recall the Old Sacristy at San Lorenzo in Florence (see Fig. 5.9). Here again, however, there are significant alterations to both the proportions and the decoration. In deference to Milanese traditions, Pigello's architect inserted a drum under the dome, increasing the height and providing a field in which polychromed terracotta angels dance and swing heavily laden festoons. The delight in color, so different from Brunelleschi's spare, bichromatic scheme, continues in the vault, where frescoes simulate multiple

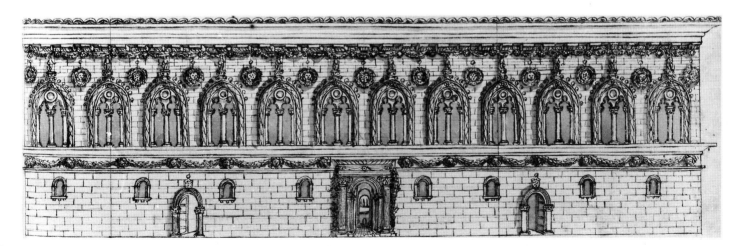

6.79 Medici Bank, Milan, façade, c. 1465, from FILARETE, *Treatise on Architecture* (Biblioteca Nazionale, Magl. 11.1. 140 fol. 20, Florence)

In this treatise, Filarete also imagined and described the buildings of a great new city he called Sforzinda in honor of Francesco Sforza.

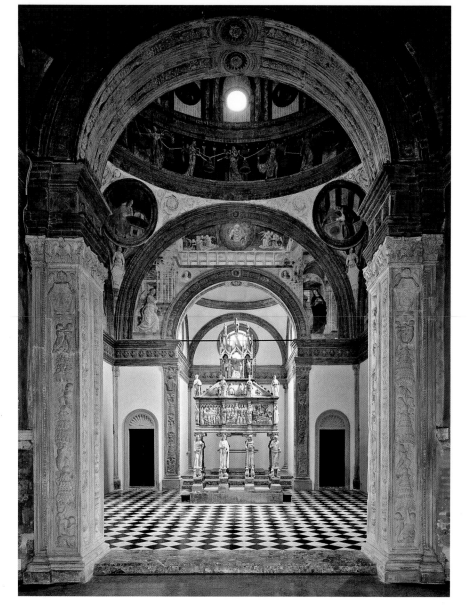

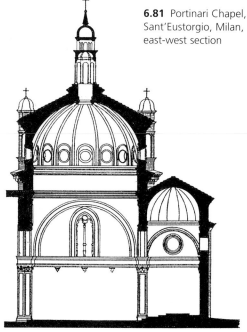

6.80 Portinari Chapel, Sant'Eustorgio, Milan, c. 1468, commissioned by Pigello Portinari, frescoes by VINCENZO FOPPA

The tomb of St. Peter Martyr at the center of the chapel originally stood in its own chapel in the nave of the church. During the Renaissance, the head of the saint was displayed in the chapel.

6.81 Portinari Chapel, Sant'Eustorgio, Milan, east-west section

rings of red, yellow, green, and blue overlapping tiles. The sequence of colors is that codified by Dominicans in the early fourteenth century as constituting the rainbow: a heavenly vision for Pigello, who was buried in the floor directly under the dome and whose coat of arms appeared in the lantern above.

Highly illusionistic frescoes by the Milanese painter Vincenzo Foppa (c. 1428–1515) bring the walls to life. Their primary subjects, the *Annunciation* and *Scenes from the Life of St. Peter Martyr* (Fig. 6.82) ingratiated Pigello to the Sforza

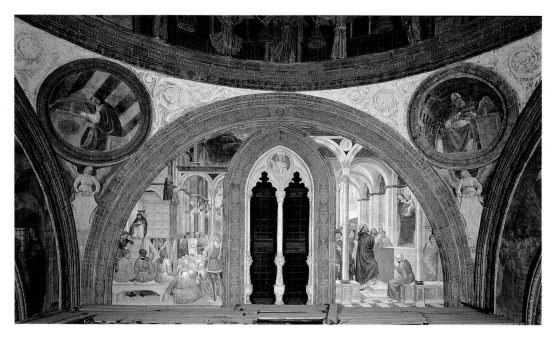

6.82 *Miracle of the Cloud and Miracle of the False Madonna*, c. 1468, commissioned by Pigello Portinari from VINCENZO FOPPA for the right wall of the Portinari Chapel, Sant'Eustorgio, Milan. Fresco

regime: Francesco Sforza had formally entered Milan on Annunciation Day 1450, and Peter Martyr, buried at Sant'Eustorgio (though not as now in the Portinari Chapel), continued to be honored as the city's most important Dominican saint.

On the right wall Foppa cunningly exploits scientific perspective and clear, rich color to place figures and architecture into deep illusionistic space. The scene on the left, showing the saint preaching, repeats the basic configuration of Andrea da Firenze's earlier fresco of St. Peter Martyr in Florence (see Fig. 3.20). Now, however, figures diminish in size according to their distance from the viewer, and their reactions to his preaching are more subtle and varied. In the middle background Foppa steeply foreshortens one of the men's faces so that he can be seen to observe a black thunder-cloud in the upper sky. According to legend, the cloud was a blessing to the crowd, which had been suffering in the blazing August sun.

On the right Peter Martyr steps up to an altar with the Eucharistic host in his hand to reveal that what seems to be a statue of the Madonna and Child is actually an idol. Both mother and child suddenly sprout horns. Onlookers, several of them clearly portrait likenesses,

react in shock and amazement. A Cathar priest garbed in a red turban holds a sulphurous yellow cloak up to his nose, visualizing the stench of abomination. He skulks away discredited, much as Giotto had shown the sultan's priests doing in St. Francis's trial by fire (see Fig. 2.8). Admirably straightforward, the frescoes recall, too, nearly contemporary scenes from saints' lives by Benozzo Gozzoli, one of the artists favored by Pigello Portinari's employers, the Medici. The frescoes as well as the architecture, then, make reference to the patron's Florentine origins, translated into a rich Lombard mode.

Santa Maria delle Grazie

In the early 1490s, Ludovico Sforza put the finishing touches on his brilliantly successful scheme to marry his niece Bianca Maria Sforza to Emperor Maximilian and so secure imperial investiture as Duke of Milan (in 1494, the year after the marriage). It seemed an appropriate time to build a dynastic mausoleum in a grand, classically inspired style for himself and his family. The site he chose was the still quite new church of Santa Maria delle Grazie not far from his residence, the Castello Sforzesco.

The resulting building (Figs. 6.83 and 6.84) may have been a collaboration among Bramante (Donato di Angelo di Antonio; 1443/44 Monte Asdrualdo/ Fermignano–1514 Rome), Amadeo (whose workshop

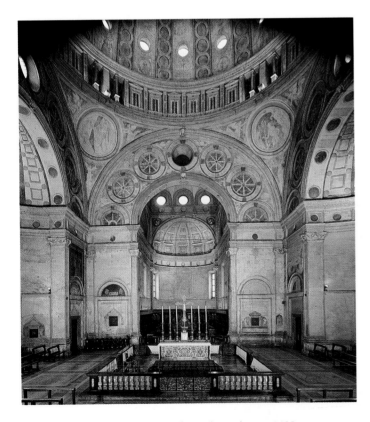

6.83 Santa Maria delle Grazie, Milan, tribune, begun 1493, commissioned by Ludovico Sforza possibly from DONATO BRAMANTE collaborating with AMADEO and LEONARDO DA VINCI

The roundels in the tympanum arches are fictive, painted architectural decorative details.

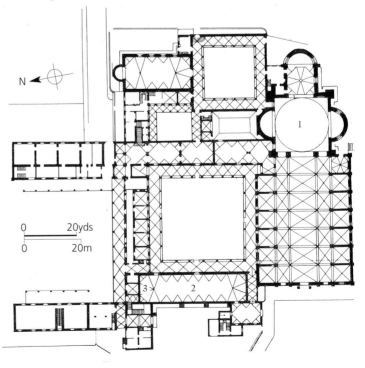

6.84 Santa Maria delle Grazie, Milan, plan of the church and monastery

1 Tribune; **2** Refectory; **3** Leonardo da Vinci, *Last Supper*

probably provided much of the exterior detail), and Leonardo da Vinci, whose notebooks from the early 1490s include several drawings of centrally planned, domed churches. While retaining the long nave of the existing church, the architect(s) added a large tribune consisting of a domed crossing, a choir, and three semicircular apses, which evoke associations with the triple apses in the transepts and choir of the Visconti burial site at the Certosa (see Fig. 4.2). The shallow dome rests on a typically Lombard drum, encircled on the exterior by an arcade.

The general scheme of the tribune ultimately derives from Brunelleschi's Old Sacristy (see Fig. 5.9)—a suitable model insofar as the Florentine structure served as a burial place for the Medici family—but the design departs remarkably from this precedent and other fifteenth-century variations of it (for example, Pigello Portinari's chapel at Sant'Eustorgio in Milan, see Fig. 6.80, and the chancel of Santa Maria dei Miracoli in Venice, see Fig. 6.39). All the prior buildings were modestly dimensioned, recalling antiquity in their constituent parts, but lacking Roman scale and monumentality. Likely inspired by the impressive size of late antique buildings in Milan itself (see Fig. 9.7) and by Ludovico's ambitions, the tribune of Santa Maria delle Grazie is an essay in volumetric expanse, the space, not the walls, being of primary architectural interest. Its scale and grandeur ensured that, when Bramante moved to Rome upon Ludovico's fall from power in 1499, he was both ready to learn from the imposing ruins of the ancient city and fashion his architectural masterpiece: the original centralized plan for the new St. Peter's basilica (see Figs. 7.19 and 7.20).

In keeping with the imposing scale of Santa Maria delle Grazie's tribune, nearly 65 feet (20 meters) square, the architectural details within it are relatively simple. The numerous oculi in the pre-existing church and in the new apses are echoed by the large painted roundels that adorn the arches and by the laced circles between the ribs of the dome. The monochrome *sgraffito* decoration on the walls respects the Dominican commitment to austerity. The effect is one of luminous expansiveness.

When Beatrice d'Este, Ludovico's young wife, died unexpectedly in 1497, he commissioned a tomb (Fig. 6.85) for the new tribune at Santa Maria delle Grazie from Cristoforo Solari (Il Gobbo; 1468/70 Milan–1524 Milan). Solari came from Milan's foremost family of builders and architects, some of its members having supervised construction both at the Certosa and on the earlier nave of Santa Maria delle Grazie. He was very popular in courtly circles, working as well for Beatrice's sister, Isabella d'Este, in Mantua and their brother, the duke of Ferrara. Cristoforo's recumbent effigies of Beatrice and Ludovico show his own accomplishments as a sculptor. He has worked the marble slab so that it appears as malleable and silken as the cloth and flesh it portrays. The couple seems merely resting, ready to rise to meet their ducal obligations, Ludovico in his flowing cloak, Beatrice in her satin gown overlaid with the braided and knotted cords she had popularized in courtly fashions. The two recumbent figures are also remarkable insofar as double tombs of this sort are quite rare in Italy. Most Italian men were buried with their male relatives, women with other women. Pairing Ludovico and Beatrice speaks of more than their affection: it also reinforced Sforza claims to high aristocratic status. French royal tombs brought king and queen together, if only in effigy (see Fig. 2.40), emphasizing dynasty and lineage, much as we must assume Ludovico intended.

Leonardo da Vinci

The Last Supper   The Sforzas also commissioned artists to enhance the living quarters of the Dominicans at Santa Maria delle Grazie. For the refectory they

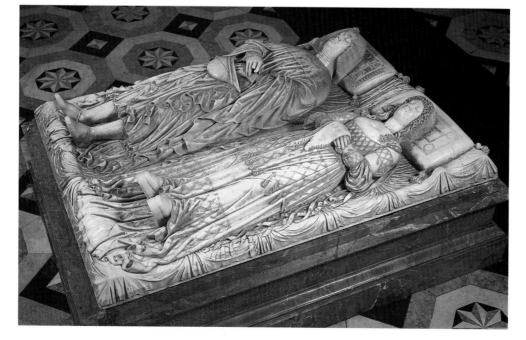

6.85 Tomb of Beatrice d'Este and Ludovico Sforza, after 1497, commissioned by Ludovico Sforza from CRISTOFORO SOLARI for Santa Maria delle Grazie, Milan. Marble (Certosa, Pavia)

commissioned a fresco of *The Last Supper* (Fig. 6.86) from Leonardo da Vinci. Ludovico's and Beatrice's names and coats of arms appear proudly in the central lunette over the composition; to either side are the emblems of their sons and successors, Massimiliano (r. 1512–15) and Francesco II (r. 1521–4, 1525, 1529–35), yet another dynastic image.

Leonardo had been in Milan since 1481 or 1482 when he wrote a letter to Ludovico offering his services as a military and city planner, sculptor, and sometime painter, an indication that whereas we now esteem Leonardo mainly for his surviving paintings and drawings, he gauged that his skills in engineering were more likely to be appreciated by a potential patron.

The subject of the Last Supper was traditional for refectories (see Figs. 2.14 and 5.28), but Leonardo invested it with a new sense of drama, which has made it one of the most memorable images in Western art. Selecting the moment just after Christ announces that one of his disciples will betray him, Leonardo imagined the apostles'

confusion and self-doubt, and portrayed their agitated reactions. He arranged them in four groups, linked by their gestures and turning bodies. Christ becomes the calm fulcrum in the midst of this turbulence, with all the human energy, as well as the strong diagonals of the deeply tunneling space, resonating around his stable, pyramidal form. Casting his eyes down toward his open left hand, Christ makes a gesture of sacrifice, offering his mystical body through the symbol of a piece of bread. At the same time, he embraces his destiny, reaching out with his right hand to share a portion with Judas, whose shadowed face and body—and the fact that he alone is not protesting—indicate his treachery. By placing Christ against a luminous landscape, Leonardo was able to dispense with a conventional halo; nature here embodies and symbolizes the divine.

Leonardo's perspective system is also highly expressive. Constructed from Christ's eye level, just to the left of his head, it creates a deep and measurable space, much more capacious than earlier versions of the scene (see Fig.

CONTEMPORARY VOICE

A Man of Many Talents

When, in 1481/82, Leonardo da Vinci wrote to Ludovico il Moro offering his services, it was his prowess as a military engineer that he stressed. A few brief references to his artistic abilities were added near the end of the letter, almost as an afterthought.

MOST ILLUSTRIOUS LORD,—Having now sufficiently considered the specimens of all those who proclaim themselves skilled contrivers of instruments of war, and that the invention and operation of the said instruments are nothing different to those in common use: I shall endeavour, without prejudice to anyone else, to explain myself to your Excellency, showing your Lordship my secrets, and then offering them to your best pleasure and approbation to work with effect at opportune moments on all those things which, in part, shall be briefly noted below.

(1) I have a sort of extremely light and strong bridges, adapted to be most easily carried, and with them you may pursue, and at any time flee from the enemy; and others, secure and indestructible by fire and battle, easy and convenient to lift and place. . . .

(2) I know how, when a place is besieged, to take water out of the trenches, and make endless variety of bridges, and covered ways and ladders, and other machines pertaining to such expeditions. . . .

(4) Again, I have kinds of mortars; most convenient and easy to carry; and with these I can fling small stones almost resembling a storm; and with the smoke of these cause great terror to the enemy, to his great detriment and confusion.

(9) [8] And if the fight should be at sea I have kinds of many machines most efficient for offence and defence. . . .

(5) *Item.* I have means by secret and tortuous mines and ways, made without noise to reach a designated [spot], even if it were needed to pass under a trench or a river.

(6) *Item.* I will make covered chariots, safe and unattackable. . . . And behind these, infantry could follow quite unhurt and without any hindrance.

(7) *Item.* In case of need I will make big guns, mortars, and light ordnance of fine and useful forms, out of the common type.

(8) Where the operation of bombardment might fall, I would contrive catapults . . . and

other machines of marvellous efficacy and not in common use.

(10) In time of peace I believe I can give perfect satisfaction and to the equal of any other in architecture and the composition of buildings, public and private; and in guiding water from one place to another.

Item. I can carry out sculpture in marble, bronze, or clay, and also I can do in painting whatever may be done, as well as any other, be he whom he may.

[32] Again, the bronze horse may be taken in hand, which is to be the immortal glory and eternal honour of the prince your father of happy memory, and of the illustrious house of Sforza.

And if any one of the above-named things seem to anyone to be impossible or not feasible, I am most ready to make the experiment in your park, or in whatever place may please your Excellency, to whom I commend myself with the utmost humility.

(from J.P. and I.A. Richter. *The Literary Works of Leonardo da Vinci.* 2 vols. London: Oxford University Press, 1939, pp. 273–5)

5.28). Doorways between the tapestries on the left wall—revealed in recent restorations—and niches between the ones on the right create cross axes, extending the space beyond the perimeters of the room. And yet Leonardo has pushed the apostle's table curiously close to the picture frame, locking his figures in the embrace of the receding walls. He also extended the orthogonals along the edges of his ceiling to the upper corners of the refectory in which the fresco is located, that is, from above and to the sides of the lunettes containing the Sforza family's coats of arms, causing the illusionistic space to tunnel much more quickly than the actual space occupied by the viewer. These devices serve to focus special attention on Christ and the apostles, creating an exalted vision of an event central to the Christian theology of redemption.

Leonardo's wall painting was like none that ever had been seen before. Novel in its composition and emotional tenor, it was also produced in an experimental technique, largely applied *a secco* using a mixture of tempera and oil, allowing Leonardo time to achieve effects similar to oil painting. But for the most part Leonardo's pigments did not adhere to the wall, causing the surface to deteriorate soon after it was completed. A doorway later punched into the center of the base literally added insult to injury. Modern conservation has been able to do little more than consolidate spotty patches of pigment. Had it not been for the strength of the overall composition and for copies the work immediately inspired, it would be impossible to imagine the impact it once made, however briefly.

Madonna of the Rocks   In commissioning Leonardo to paint the *Last Supper*, Ludovico was doubtless confident that it would display at least some of the pictorial subtlety Leonardo had already demonstrated in court portraits and in an altarpiece that the artist began soon after arriv-

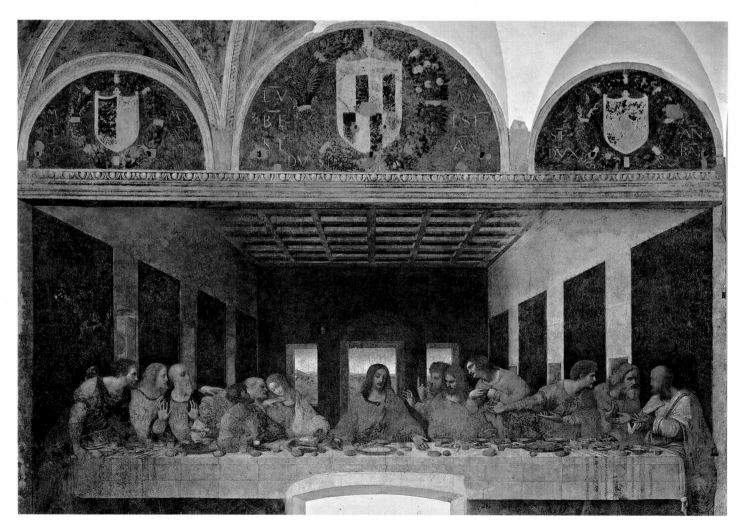

6.86 *Last Supper*, 1494?–97/98, probably commissioned by Ludovico Sforza and Beatrice d'Este from LEONARDO DA VINCI for the Refectory, Santa Maria delle Grazie, Milan. Painting (tempera and oil) on plaster, 13' 9" × 29' 10" (4.60 × 8.80 m)

The work is ruinous, having been painted in an experimental medium that began deteriorating soon after it was applied.

ing in Milan, the *Madonna of the Rocks* (Fig. 6.87). Commissioned by the Confraternity of the Immaculate Conception for their new chapel in the Franciscan basilica of San Francesco Grande, the painting was the centerpiece of a larger wooden structure which included side panels by the Milanese de Predis brothers—Ambrogio (c. 1455 Milan–after 1508) and Cristoforo (d. 1486)—who probably assisted Leonardo in breaking into the Milanese market prior to Ludovico's offer of employment at court. Thick, yellowed varnish has dulled Leonardo's coloristic effects, but otherwise the painting is well preserved. Dramatic but soft spotlighting picks out the figures, recalling a remark Leonardo made in his note-

books about the beauty of faces seen in the subdued light of a courtyard. Exquisitely detailed rocks, mists, water, and plant life, all studied carefully from nature, surround the figures.

Curiously, for a commission that requested only a Madonna and Child accompanied by angels, Leonardo's *Madonna of the Rocks* includes a prominent figure of an infant John the Baptist kneeling to adore the Christ Child from under the protective right arm of the Virgin. Christ reciprocates with a blessing, accompanied by a figure traditionally identified as an angel, who points at the Baptist. Coming from Florence, Leonardo would have seen numerous images of that city's patron saint as a child, often in the company of a Madonna and Child in a rocky setting, such as Filippo Lippi's *Adoration of the Christ Child* (see Fig. 5.19). Even so, once Leonardo had the idea of using this imagery, he must have had to be sure that it also made sense for its Milanese context. Efforts to connect the unusual subject with the cult of the Immaculate Conception, to which the commissioning confraternity was dedicated, have proven fruitless: but since the confraternity's chapel was located in a Franciscan church, the identification of St. Francis as a second John the Baptist by Francis's official biographer, Bonaventure, may have made the confraternity amenable to John's inclusion. They were impressed enough with Leonardo's preliminary work that even though the work remained unfinished for several decades, they neither commissioned another altarpiece nor assigned its completion to another artist—though they did instigate legal action that finally forced Leonardo to complete the work in 1508.

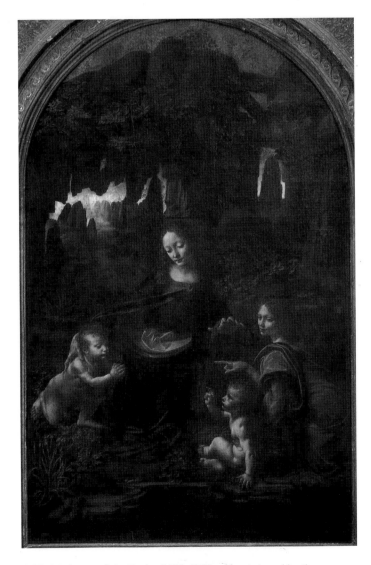

6.87 *Madonna of the Rocks*, 1483–1508, commissioned by the Confraternity of the Immaculate Conception from LEONARDO DA VINCI for their chapel in San Francesco Grande, Milan. Oil on panel, 6' 6½" × 4' (2 × 1.22 m) (Musée du Louvre, Paris)

Another version of this painting survives in the National Gallery, London. The precise relationship between the two—one probably replaced the other—remains much debated.

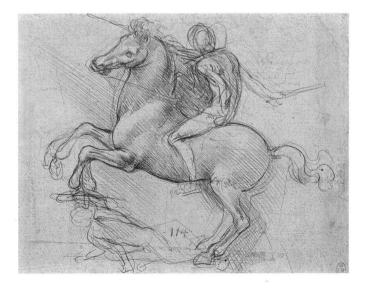

6.88 Study for the Sforza Monument, c. 1488, commissioned by Ludovico Sforza from LEONARDO DA VINCI. Silverpoint on white paper covered with a blue preparation, 5¾ × 7¼" (14.8 × 18.5 cm) (Royal Library, RL12358r, The Royal Collection, Windsor, England © Her Majesty Queen Elizabeth II)

Leonardo at Ludovico's Court   Although it was not uncommon for Leonardo to leave his paintings incomplete—his inquisitive nature impelled him on to new studies and experiments—the confraternity may have been willing to exercise extreme patience since Leonardo's services were also claimed by Ludovico Sforza; it is not wise to antagonize an autocrat. Leonardo's notebooks were full of designs for fortifications and machinery that were potentially of use to the Milanese state. Many of his "inventions" are actually ingenious improvements upon military equipment already described by ancient authors and in fifteenth-century military treatises, including designs for crossbows, catapults, lightweight bridges, cannons, and armoured vehicles; but Leonardo's extraordinary powers of visual analysis and description make his renditions more convincing than prior illustrations. Leonardo also turned his intelligence to new matters, including the possibility of human flight (Fig. 6.89),

which distinguished him from his contemporaries. His design for an enormous bowl-shaped helicopter—Leonardo's notes indicate he was imagining a structure 40 feet (12 meters) across with a wingspan twice that size—depends on a man standing in the middle of the machine moving treadles with his head as well as his feet. Unaware of the principles of airflow and lift, in spite of his careful study of the flight of birds, Leonardo was unable to design a workable vehicle. Nonetheless, his sheer inventiveness and knowledge of pulleys and gears, essential to his work as a military consultant, gave him a technological base upon which to build.

Leonardo challenged (and nearly overcame) the limits of his generation's mechanical expertise in plans for a twice life-sized, bronze equestrian monument honoring Ludovico's father, Francesco Sforza. Preparatory drawings (Fig. 6.88) show that Leonardo once again rethought a standard artistic type (see Fig. 5.60), imagining a rearing horse whose hoofs rise over a fallen enemy while the rider leans back and to his side to fight off any other challengers. After turning the rider to a more usual, frontal pose, he was able to complete a full-scale model for the imperial wedding in 1493. Set in the courtyard of the Castello Sforzesco, the group declared the authority and legitimacy of the Sforza dynasty on a colossal scale that ancient authors said was more appropriate to the gods than mere mortals. Never cast because Ludovico requisitioned the necessary bronze to produce cannons in an ill-fated attempt to keep French troops from invading Italy, the model was destroyed when it was used for target practice by soldiers after Ludovico's fall from power in 1499.

Ludovico and Leonardo were well suited to one another. Both were masters of grand gestures and dreams, more than practical accomplishments. Their mutual delight in addressing complex problems, as much for intellectual stimulation as for practical purposes, is evident in Leonardo's paintings for Ludovico's audience chamber in the Sforza Castle, the Sala delle Asse (Fig. 6.90). Leonardo's design has been heavily overpainted, but its witty complexity is still evident. In place of classical motifs, as used by Mantegna on the ceiling of the Camera Picta in Mantua (see Fig. 6.23), Leonardo turned to natural "architecture," imagining the room as a vast tent of interlacing mulberry trees, one of Ludovico's heraldic devices. At their apex appears Ludovico's coat of arms, quartered with those of his recently deceased wife, Beatrice d'Este. Since Beatrice popularized knotted ornament at court, the intertwining branches may refer on a personal level to the bonds that united Ludovico and Beatrice. However, plaques knitted into the branches on each of the four sides of the room announce Ludovico's primary aim: a celebration of his dealings with and ties to the court of Emperor Maximilian.

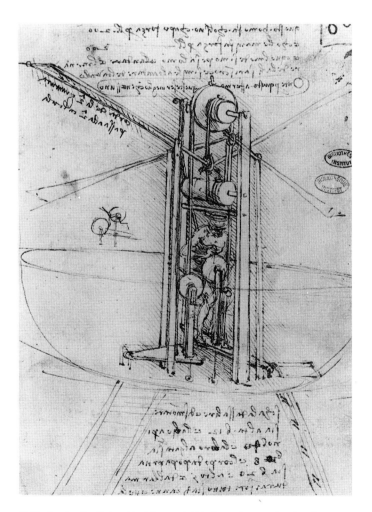

6.89 Study of a Flying Machine, c. 1490, from the notebooks of LEONARDO DA VINCI (Institut de France, ms. B, fol. 80r, Paris)

Leonardo's notes are written in a mirror script as they are throughout his notebooks.

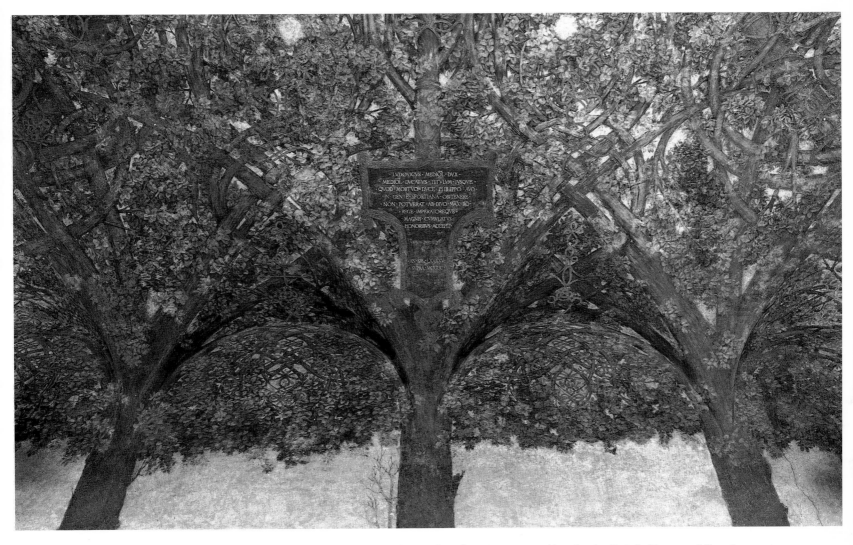

6.90 Decorations of the Sala delle Asse, c. 1497, commissioned by Ludovico Sforza from LEONARDO DA VINCI for the Castello Sforzesco, Milan. Fresco

The work has been heavily repainted, but the intricate interlace design is original. The inscription on the illusionistic tablet in this section of the ceiling records that Ludovico had been named duke by the Emperor Maximilian.

Still, imperial connections could not save Ludovico from his own ineptitude. In 1499 the French royal army deposed him, claiming authority for their king through earlier intermarriage with the Visconti. Leonardo, Bramante, and others fled Milan to Florence and Rome, where patrons readily embraced the grand manner which had been promoted by Ludovico Sforza.

Epilogue: Milan under Foreign Rule

Milan now entered a thirty-six-year period of political turbulence, ruled alternately by the French, the Spanish, and Ludovico's two eldest sons. In these circumstances there was little new building in Milan, but the need for military and engineering expertise, as well as talents in the arts of pageantry and display, continued unabated. In May 1506, the French governor, Charles d'Amboise, Lord of Chaumont, petitioned the Signoria of Florence to allow Leonardo to return to Milan. Charles, like so many Milanese leaders before him, did not seek a radical break with the past. Instead, he employed Leonardo, the most famous artist of the Sforza court, to create works that would, he hoped, seamlessly insert his regime into Milanese history. Leonardo, unusually apolitical for a person of his era, seems to have found no difficulty in working for Charles in spite of his eighteen years of service for Ludovico Sforza. That the Florentine Signoria agreed to release Leonardo to the governor, even though he had not completed painting a fresco commissioned for the Palazzo della Signoria (see Fig. 7.7), indicates prudent respect for the power of Milan's French conquerors.

For a while Leonardo traveled back and forth between Milan and Florence, but in the summer of 1508 he settled

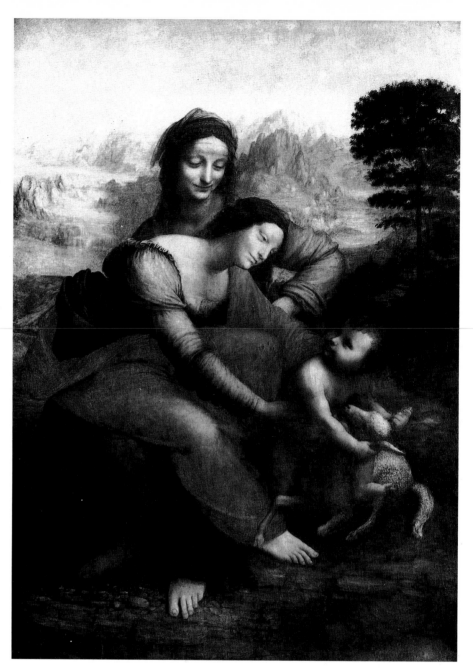

6.91 *Madonna and Child with St. Anne*, c. 1505 (?)–13, commissioned from LEONARDO DA VINCI. Oil on canvas, 5′ 7″ × 4′ 2¾″ (1.7 × 1.29 m) (Musée du Louvre, Paris)

This work, like the *Mona Lisa* (see Fig. 7.9), remained in the artist's personal possession until his death.

in Milan, where he remained until 1513. Once again he became the chief court artist, designing pageants, advising on the choir stalls of the Duomo, proposing architectural and urban projects, and attending to military matters. Leonardo traveled widely for Charles. During this period he also began his first series of systematic notes on geology and atmospheric effects, including an examination of marine fossils on mountain heights which led him to the radical conclusion that these objects had not been deposited there by the biblical Flood, as generally believed, but that this land had once formed part of the ocean floor. His studies of the Alps bore artistic results in the background of his altarpiece of the *Madonna and Child with St. Anne* (Fig. 6.91). Leonardo never completed the drapery on the main figures, gracefully and dynamically interlaced with one another, focusing his attention rather on the mist-covered mountains in the background. His astute observations on the perception of color and light under differing atmospheric conditions, carefully recorded in his notebooks, led him to a radically different depiction of nature than appears in his earlier *Madonna of the Rocks* (see Fig. 6.87). Abandoning the uniformly precise rendition of details characteristic of much fifteenth-century art, Leonardo expands his vision to planetary dimensions. At the foot of the painting he describes every rocky striation and pebble, but as he moves to the back, his brushstrokes soften and then dissolve into light-saturated mists enveloping Alpine crags. He also enlarges the scale of his figures so that they themselves form a mountainous mass, making the entire work seem larger and more imposing than the *Madonna of the Rocks* in spite of the fact that the earlier painting is actually somewhat taller.

When Charles d'Amboise died in 1511, Leonardo continued in the service of the new co-governors, the French nobleman Gaston de Foix and the Milanese aristocrat Giangiacomo Trivulzio. Both were renowned military men. Trivulzio, for whom Leonardo designed a com-

memorative tomb monument (Fig. 6.92) had served as *condottiere* for Ludovico il Moro before joining and then leading the French forces that toppled the Sforza government. As soon as he assumed power he began building a centralized burial chapel, reminiscent of a Roman emperor's mausoleum, at the church of San Nazaro Maggiore, a potent civic site which had been founded by St. Ambrose and was, until the late sixteenth century, lined with splendid Roman revetments and reliefs, which must have given the church a distinctly imperial air. Leonardo's drawings indicate that Trivulzio intended to appropriate the triumphant imagery that the artist had devised for the ill-fated Sforza equestrian monument (see Fig. 6.88): a galloping horse and rider rearing over a cowering foe. Reduced to life size, the group was to have stood over a chamber containing Trivulzio's effigy and sarcophagus. The smallest of Leonardo's sketches

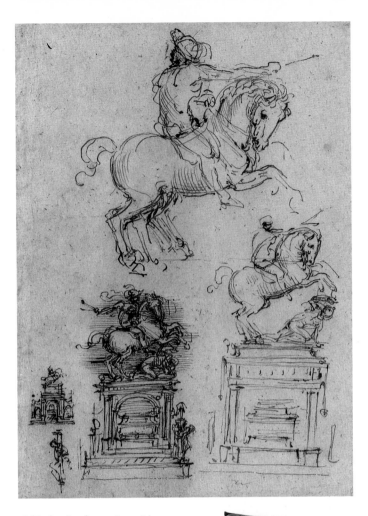

suggest that he was considering a tripartite structure in the form of a triumphal arch; another shows the same theme of conquest expressed in the form of human captives tied to columns.

Trivulzio was not a popular ruler. His heavy hand is already evident in commissions that pre-date his assumption of full power, including a series of twelve huge tapestries depicting the months of the year (Fig. 6.93). Commissioned from Bramantino (Bartolomeo Suardi; c. 1465 Milan–1530 Milan), a local artist who earned his nickname from the fact that he was the protégé of Bramante, the tapestries were woven throughout 1508 and 1509 by masters who worked into the night so that the hangings could be displayed during the traditionally lavish court festivities at Christmas. Unlike the frescoes depicting the same subject at the Castello del Buonconsiglio in Trent (see Fig. 4.12), which feature people dressed in contemporary garb in real settings, Bramantino's cycle consists of allegories populated by figures in Roman guise. To specify their patronage, a huge roundel with Trivulzio's coat of arms hangs from a heraldic border composed of the arms of the noble houses with which he was allied. Inside this self-celebratory frame, figures stand before reconstructions of Roman porticoes and cityscapes wearing brilliantly

6.92 Studies for an Equestrian Tomb Monument, c. 1511, tomb commissioned by Giangiacomo Trivulzio, co-governor of Milan, from LEONARDO DA VINCI for San Nazaro Maggiore, Milan. Pen and bistre (?) on coarse grayish paper, 11 × 7¾" (28 × 19.8 cm) (Royal Library, RL12355r, The Royal Collection, Windsor, England © Her Majesty Queen Elizabeth II)

6.93 *April*, 1508–9, commissioned by Giangiacomo Trivulzio from MASTER BENEDETTO, following designs by BRAMANTINO. Tapestry (Museum of Castello Sforzesco, Milan)

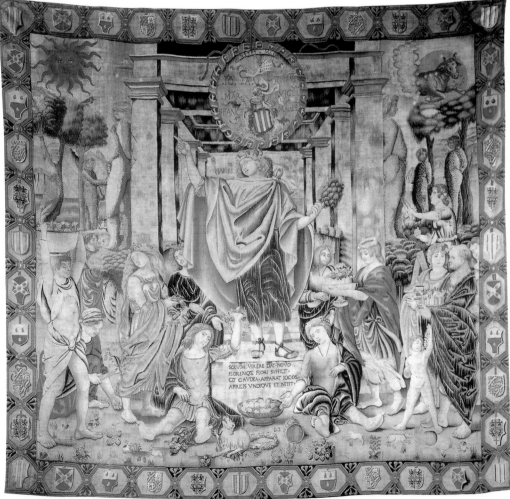

colored Roman togas and armor. Oversized male orators represent each month, Latin inscriptions at their feet giving words to their gestures of praise and exhortation. Since the verse for the month April states that the earth becomes green once again and breaks into flower, preparing for joys and games, Bramantino's figures approach the orator with bowls filled with flowers. In the background human-headed topiaries glisten with new leaves. Despite such ingenious devices, the tapestries are impressive more for their size than for their quality, compromised by the speed of their execution. What was remarkable was the precocious attempt at classicism in a medium that had for so long been dominated by chivalric themes.

Trivulzio's co-governor Gaston de Foix died at the Battle of Ravenna on April 11, 1512, less than a year after taking office. He thus had little opportunity to develop his own visual iconography, but the French royal house immediately seized upon the occasion of his death to commission an extravagant tomb monument exalting his accomplishments and celebrating French rule in Milan. The project, commissioned from Agostino Busti, known as Il Bambaia (1483 Busto Arsizio?–1548 Milan), who had trained in the somewhat precious manner of the Pavia workshops (see Fig. 6.77), called for an idealized effigy resembling Cristoforo Solari's reclining figures of Ludovico il Moro and Beatrice d'Este (see Fig. 6.85), as well as a great number of highly detailed historical reliefs in marble (Fig. 6.94) to be set within a free-standing architectural framework which would have borne similarities to the lower level of the Trivulzio monument, as well as the structure of French royal tombs. The effect was to have been exquisite. Each relief pulsates with innumerable figures that are so fully carved that the entire foreground seems composed of freely modeled statuettes. Landscape settings and intricately entwined figures rival the complexity of even the most remarkable of earlier Lombard reliefs (see Fig. 6.77). The work was so labor-intensive that in 1517 it was estimated that Bambaia and his assistants from the cathedral workshops would require at least four to six years to complete the work—wishful thinking, it turns out, for a monument that was eventually abandoned unfinished.

Continuity of Fifteenth-Century Ideals

The extravagant complexity, preciosity, and sheer costliness of works of art commissioned by the rulers of Milan in the early sixteenth century contrast sharply with another popular but more prosaic strand of artistic production. Led by the native Lombard painter Bernardino Luini (1480–85 Luini–1532 Lugano), artists working

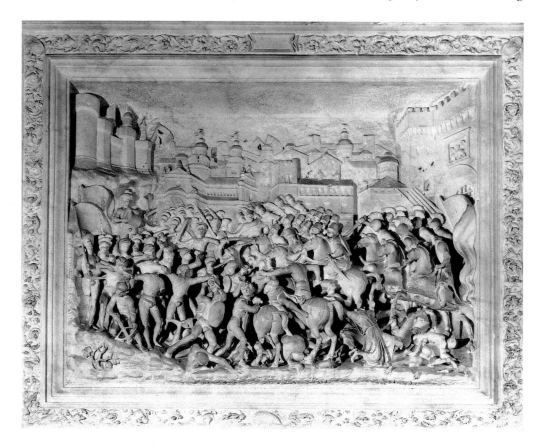

6.94 *The Capture of Brescia*, after 1517, probably commissioned by Odet de Foix, governor of Milan, and financed by the French royal family, including Francis I, from IL BAMBAIA for Santa Marta, Milan. Marble, 37¾ × 46½ × 7½" (96 × 118.5 × 19 cm) (Museum of Castello Sforzesco, Milan)

in this mode appealed to patrons who still appreciated the realism that had characterized much Lombard art since at least the days of Giovannino de' Grassi in the late fourteenth century (see Fig. 4.9). Luini's *Madonna, Child, and Infant St. John the Baptist* (Fig. 6.95) indicates that he knew Leonardo's compositions (see Fig. 6.91) but that he took little interest in that master's highly evolved and sophisticated compositions and subjects.

However, Leonardo's influence may account for the accessible qualities in Luini's work, such as the child's expressively extended arms and playful interaction with the lamb. Luini essentially translated Leonardo's composition back into the artistic language of the fifteenth century. Rather than suggesting cosmic grandeur, Luini's figures bridge the gap between the sacred and the secular, insisting on a religious experience that is humble and rooted in everyday reality—themes that Church reformers, too, were soon to stress. As in the Florence of Lorenzo the Magnificent, the grand manner was not for everyone. Elite and popular sometimes mingled, but remained distinct.

Synopsis

The later fifteenth century offers students of art history a challenge in categorization. Inconveniently for some, Leonardo da Vinci invented a visual language—one that was to form the basis of much sixteenth-century art—in a court that collapsed by the beginning of the new century. In addition, earlier forms persisted unabated in the face of his style. To further complicate matters, Leonardo spent the bulk of his most productive years in Milan, not Florence, Rome, or sixteenth-century Venice—cities where Vasari and most subsequent historians of Renaissance art have focused their attention. Supposedly anachronistic in time and place, Leonardo demands re-situating.

Or does he? Rather than reposition Leonardo, we need to reconfigure the development of the arts of the fifteenth century to recognize the extraordinary energy and ambition of artists and patrons in this period. From the physical renewal of the *scuole* in Venice, to Federico da Montefeltro's massive expansion of his palace when he was named duke, to Pope Sixtus IV's splendid new chapel, to his successors' glittering apartments, and Lorenzo de' Medici's skillful orchestration of the arts in Florence, remarkably ambitious patrons worked hand in hand with artists to create a visual environment that was the envy of Europe. Leonardo would have been at home in almost any of these centers. However, the particular shape of his creations—like those of all his contemporaries—would not have been the same, for patronage and place once again shaped and conditioned what artists were able to accomplish.

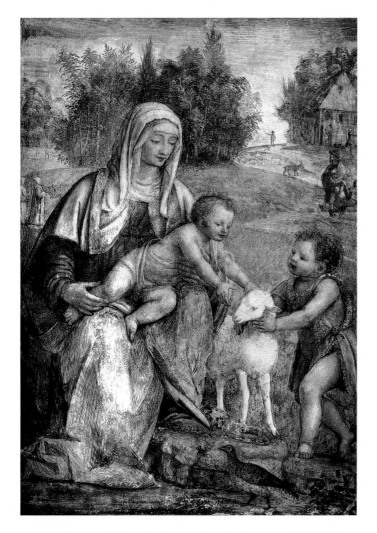

6.95 *Madonna, Child, and Infant St. John the Baptist*, c. 1510–20 (?), commissioned from BERNARDINO LUINI for the Carthusian Hospice of San Michele alla Chiusa, Milan. Fresco transferred to canvas, 5' 5⅛" × 3' 8¾" (1.66 × 1.14 m) (Brera Gallery, Milan)

Two monks of the Carthusian Order for whom this fresco was commissioned can be seen walking across the landscape in their white hooded habits.

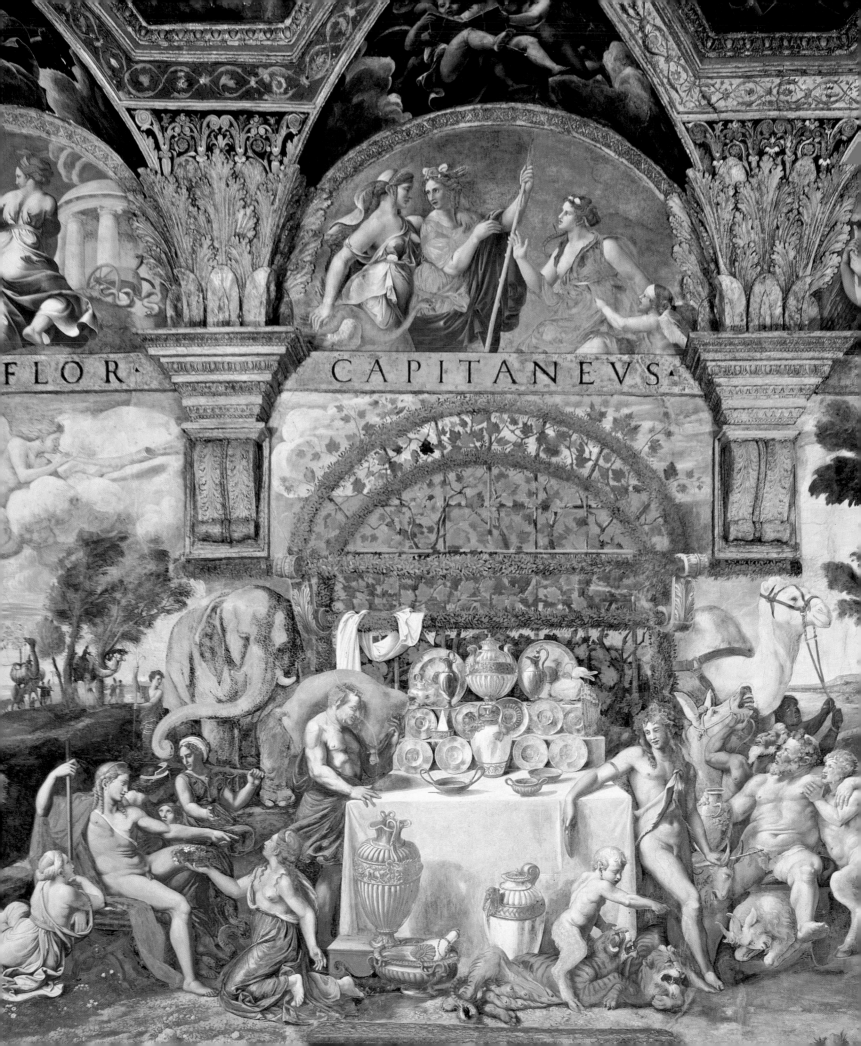

FLOR· CAPITANEVS·

7

Rivaling Ancient Rome:
The Early Sixteenth Century

The first third of the sixteenth century was an era of stylistic and political realignment. Invasions by foreign troops, challenges to Church authority by Protestant reformers, and a return to inter-city warfare shattered the tranquility of prior decades. Many patrons and artists worked together to create a wide variety of works that purposefully masked these hard realities. In Rome Pope Julius II encouraged Raphael and Michelangelo to paint the walls of the papal apartments and chapel with optimistic visions of stability and harmony, and he commissioned Bramante to envision a new St. Peter's and papal palace that implied a universal order under the Roman papacy. In a Venice threatened by the pan-European military force of the League of Cambrai, noble patrons responded enthusiastically to Giorgione's and Titian's poetic evocations of an idyllic golden age, when humans supposedly lived harmoniously with nature and one another. In both centers altarpieces and narrative frescoes became increasingly dynamic and imposing. Everyday reality became subject to ever grander notions of a perfect world modeled on classical idealizations. These inclinations were confirmed by the discovery of such awe-inspiring works of ancient art as the Hellenistic *Laocoön* group, whose exaggerated musculature and compositional tour de force artists soon sought to surpass, not just to emulate.

Artists and patrons were also increasingly willing to bend and sometimes even reject the rules and principles of composition and design that had been formulated over the course of the fifteenth century. Looking more at the underlying concerns of narrative presentation than at formal compositional rules, many artists experimented with new, sometimes non-canonical ways of organizing their compositions and articulating their buildings, counting on sophisticated patrons to appreciate novelty and invention in their own right.

At the north Italian courts art continued to reflect the aristocratic environments in which it was produced, as it had for the previous 200 years. Often charged with eroticism and sensuality, it had a conscious artifice and refinement that appealed to aristocrats who sought to distance themselves from the general populace. It was often playful as well, unfettered by the high moral purpose that tended to characterize art both at the Vatican and in the newly restored Florentine and Genoese republics.

Florence: The Renewed Republic

In November 1494, after sixty years of *de facto* rule, Medici control of Florence came, temporarily, to an end. Having ruled for a mere two years, Piero de' Medici (known to history as "the Unfortunate," in marked contrast to his father, Lorenzo "the Magnificent") was forced by a mob of his fellow Florentines to leave the city. Politically inept, he had responded to threats from rival factions within the city and from the French by allying himself with Naples and then, when the French invader was on the doorstep, by allying himself with the French king, Charles VIII.

One of the strongest political voices in the city at this time was that of the Dominican friar Girolamo Savonarola (1452–98), abbot of the monastery of San Marco. As a member of the clergy and also a native of Ferrara, Savonarola could not hold office; yet his powerful preaching of Christian reform gave such a theological cast to republican reform that the meeting room of the Great Council was referred to as the Hall of Christ. In 1498, Savonarola's interventions in the workings of the state proved his undoing; in particular, his castigation of the notorious Pope Alexander VI had led to diplomatic difficulties between Florence and Rome. Savonarola was

7.1 (opposite) *Wedding Feast of Cupid and Psyche* (detail), 1527–30, commissioned by Federigo Gonzaga from GIULIO ROMANO for the Sala di Psiche, Palazzo del Tè, Mantua. Fresco. See also Fig. 7.67.

eventually forcibly hauled out of San Marco, tortured, tried as a heretic, hanged with two of his companions until they were nearly dead, and then burned at the stake. His ashes were later thrown into the Arno. Thus twice in a decade, in 1494 and in 1498, Florence had freed itself from what it perceived as tyranny.

The Republic as Patron

With Piero in exile and Savonarola dead, the citizens of Florence turned to the task of reconstructing their cherished republic and reinventing a visual mythology and stylistic language to express its ideals. The Signoria thus embarked on a number of commissions which were to transform the iconography of the Florentine state. These commissions for the renewed republic did two things. They provided the physical site of government with a powerful new series of images designed to establish an iconography of restored republican power, and they evoked the history of the earlier republican city, both in their iconography and in their placement.

Even before the new works were commissioned, the intentions of the new government were clear. In 1495, not quite a year after Piero's forced exile, the Signoria ordered the removal of several works of art from the Medici Palace. Donatello's bronze *David* (see Fig. 5.17) was placed inside the Palazzo della Signoria, joining both his marble *David* (see Fig. 4.34), which had been moved there in 1416, and Verrocchio's bronze *David*, which Lorenzo and Giuliano de' Medici had sold to the Signoria in 1476. Donatello's bronze *Judith* (see Fig. 5.18) was moved from the garden of the Medici Palace to the platform immediately to the left of the main entrance of the Palazzo della Signoria. An inscription was added to the statue at that time which said that the citizens placed the statue there as an "exemplum" of public well-being. In both cases references to the protection of the state from tyrannical forces could not have been clearer. Paintings by Pollaiuolo of the Labors of Hercules, a civic hero central to the mythology of Florence, and by Uccello of the Battle of San Romano, an important event in the political history of the state, were also taken to the Palazzo della Signoria from the Medici Palace.

Besides reclaiming civic imagery which had been appropriated by a private family, the placement of these sculptures and paintings at the Palazzo della Signoria initiated a program of state symbolism whose most memorable component is Michelangelo's *David* (Fig. 7.2). The statue was originally commissioned for the north tribune of the cathedral to continue the decorative program begun by Nanni di Banco and Donatello in 1408–09 (see Figs. 4.33 and 4.34) during a golden age of the Republic.

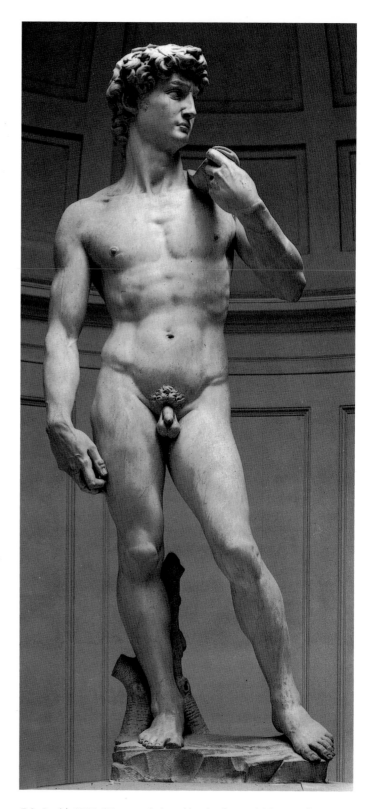

7.2 *David*, 1501–04, commissioned by the Opera del Duomo from MICHELANGELO for the north tribune of Florence Cathedral, but on completion installed in front of the Palazzo della Signoria, Florence. Marble, height 17′ ⅛″ (5.22 m) (Accademia, Florence)

In October 1504 the tree stump supporting the *David* was gilded, a gilt garland was placed on the figure's head, and a belt of twenty-eight gilt-bronze leaves was fixed around its waist.

When completed in 1504 the *David* was, instead, placed just to the left of the entrance of the Palazzo della Signoria, displacing Donatello's *Judith*.

The *David* is striking both for its realistic representation of the male human body and for the idealism that Michelangelo has projected onto the body. The figure is simultaneously understandable as an ordinary man, essentially free of attributes that would readily identify him (the sling being virtually hidden from sight), and as a hero. The colossal size of the figure—nearly three times life size—implies a link with colossal sculptures of antiquity; the greatness of Greece and Rome now is equalled by that of Florence. But concentration on the statue's formal classical antecedents misses the deliberate tension in the figure between real and ideal, the suggestion that the ordinary can be transformed into the extraordinary by a decisive moment of action.

Just as the figure is both real and ideal, it is also both David and other heroes as well. The nudity of the figure was unusual for the representation of David, Donatello's bronze *David* (see Fig. 5.17) notwithstanding. Although the biblical text (I Samuel 17:38–39) leaves room for interpreting David as a nude, the pose of the figure, along with the nudity, suggests a classical statue of Hercules. Moreover, the rocky terrain on which the figure stands, as well as the blasted tree trunk behind David's right leg, suggests a tale with moral dimensions from the mythology of Hercules (who had appeared on the state seal of Florence since the end of the thirteenth century). Faced with a choice between virtue and vice, allegorically represented as, respectively, a sere and rocky landscape and a lush and flowering landscape, Hercules chooses the first. No one entering the Palazzo della Signoria could have missed the moral and political meaning of the statue.

Other sculptural commissions at the cathedral indicate the seriousness of the Republic's intentions to associate itself with the artistic commissions of the city before the Medici assumption of power. In 1503, even before the *David* had been completed, Michelangelo was commissioned by the Opera of the cathedral to carve twelve apostle figures, like the *David* recalling the projects of the earlier period. Michelangelo began only one of these statues, the unfinished *St. Matthew* (Fig. 7.3), a figure expressionistically torqued around its central axis, before his contract was dissolved in 1505 when, at the behest of Pope Julius II, he went to Rome to work for the papacy. After a brief delay, however, the apostle commission was begun anew in 1511, with a contract to Jacopo Sansovino (Jacopo Tatti; 1486 Florence–1570 Florence; Fig. 7.4), a sculptor and architect who trained under Andrea Sansovino and, like other artists, took his master's name. This led to the completion of four apostle statues by four different sculptors by 1518. While indebted to

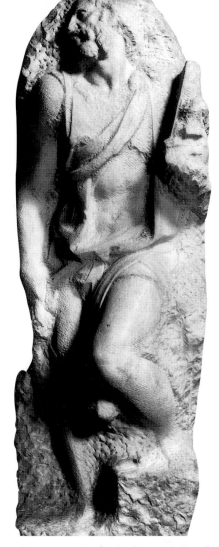

7.3 *St. Matthew*, 1503–8 (unfinished), commissioned by the Opera del Duomo from MICHELANGELO. Marble, height 8′ 11″ (2.71 m) (Florence, Accademia)

Michelangelo's *St. Matthew* in its *contrapposto* movement, the *St. James* does not have the coiled torsion of that figure. Like the *St. Matthew* it also refers to earlier figures such as Donatello's *St. Mark* (see Fig. 4.40) in the pose and relationship to the niche. The apostle commission seems not only to be linked to earlier moments in Florentine republican history, but also to be an active attempt to regain the civic space of the cathedral interior that Lorenzo de' Medici had begun to appropriate for himself, especially with plans from the early 1490s to decorate its main chapel (dedicated to St. Zenobius, one of Florence's chief patron saints) with mosaics.

The Imagery of State

A major renovation project was underway within the Palazzo della Signoria, during the time that Michelangelo was carving the *David*. Expansion of the Florentine Great Council to 500 members in 1495 in imitation of the Maggior Consiglio of Venice necessitated the enlargement

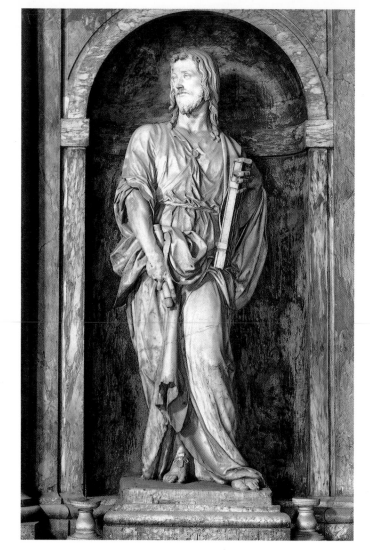

7.4 *St. James*, 1511–18, commissioned by the Opera of the Duomo from JACOPO SANSOVINO for the interior of Florence Cathedral. Marble (nave of Florence Cathedral)

7.5 Sala del Gran Consiglio (Hall of the Great Council), Palazzo della Signoria, Florence, reconstruction of the walls and ceiling showing proposed decorative projects initiated by the renewed Republic (after Johannes Wilde)

This plan depicts the ceiling of the room with the walls extending from it, as if hanging from their upper edges. Folding the walls along the lines of juncture with the ceiling would provide a three-dimensional model of the room.
1 Michelangelo, *Battle of Cascina*; **2** Leonardo da Vinci, *Battle of Anghiari*; **3** Fra Bartolomeo, *St. Anne Altarpiece*; **4** Jacopo Sansovino, *San Salvatore*, marble statue projected for architrave over the bench of the Gonfaloniere

of spaces in the building to accommodate that number, meant to ensure that no single family or faction would once more gain the power over the state that the Medici had enjoyed. Although little remains of this project for the Hall of the Great Council (Sala dei Cinquecento [Room of the 500] or the Sala del Gran Consiglio) the program for its decoration is known (Fig. 7.5).

An impressive altarpiece, two large frescoes, carved wooden benches, and a marble sculpture were the main components of the program. In 1498 Filippino Lippi received a commission to paint an altarpiece for the center of one of the long walls of the room, directly opposite the Gonfaloniere's bench. His death in 1504 caused delays in the project, but it was eventually assigned to Fra Bartolomeo (Baccio della Porta; 1472 Florence–1517 Florence), then a monk at San Marco, the very monastery from which the forces of the Republic had taken Savonarola in 1498. Fra Bartolomeo had trained with Cosimo Rosselli and then set up a workshop with his fellow student Mariotto Albertinelli (1474 Florence–1515 Florence) until 1500, when he began a term as a Dominican novice, ultimately joining the order in 1501 at San Marco. Fra Bartolomeo's *St. Anne Altarpiece* (Fig. 7.6) was probably similar in iconography to Lippi's earlier, unexecuted work. In this painting (left unfinished in 1512 when the Medici returned to power and aborted the program of the Hall of the Great Council) the Virgin and Child sit raised on a platform in the center of the

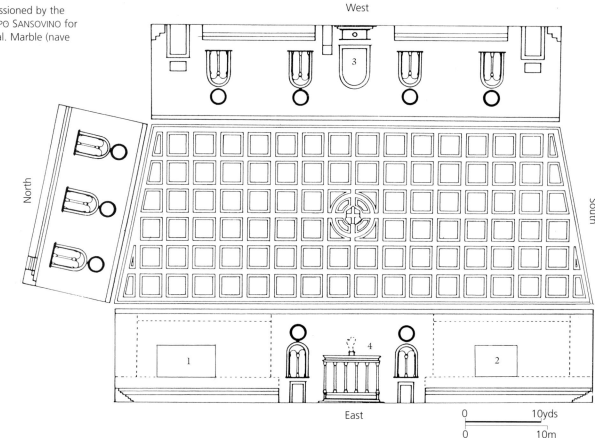

West

North

South

East

0   10yds

0   10m

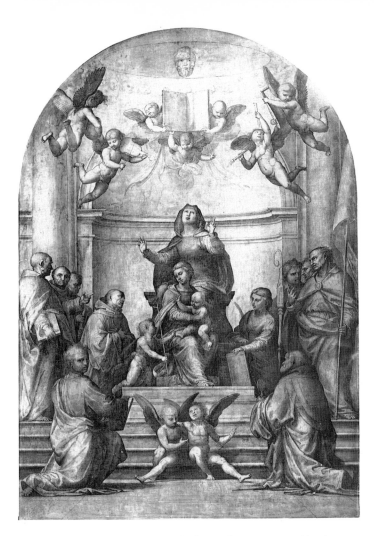

7.6 *St. Anne Altarpiece*, 1510–12 (unfinished), commissioned by the Signoria from FRA BARTOLOMEO for the Sala del Gran Consiglio, Palazzo della Signoria, Florence. Oil on canvas (Museo di San Marco, Florence)

symmetrically constructed scheme, with St. Anne, the Virgin's mother, sitting behind them. These three figures link with the kneeling male saints in the foreground in a triangular composition which, along with the stately background architecture, provides a stable armature for the animation of the figures. Each of the principal figures is conceived in an active pose, his or her body turning in a *contrapposto* so that the surrounding space is enlivened and attention directed to other forms in the composition. The Virgin looks toward her right, but her lower body turns in the opposite direction toward the kneeling figure in the right foreground. The interlocking forms of the Virgin and Child, their simplified ovoid faces, and their placement at the center of the composition—where they receive the energy directed toward them by the other figures and are, at the same time, the source of it—recall the work of Leonardo (see Fig. 6.91), who had been an active presence in Florence from 1500, when he returned from Milan, to 1506 when he again left the city for Milan.

At the same time, the altarpiece is thoroughly integrated into its political context. Each saint depicted in it was intended as a reference to a specific Florentine historical event that had occurred on the day of the saint's feast. The painting, then, is both a devotional image and a record of civic achievement. The image of St. Anne symbolizes the expulsion in 1343 of Walter of Brienne from Florence. Walter had actually been invited by the Florentines to serve as ruler of the city, but he overstepped his power and was expelled on the feast day of St. Anne, a day that henceforward was freighted with overtones of freedom from tyranny. The original contract for Lippi's painting explicitly called for representations of St. John the Baptist, the main patron saint of Florence; St. Zenobius, the city's first bishop; and St. Victor, on whose feast day in 1364 the Florentines defeated the Pisans at the Battle of Cascina. The connection between past and present was also manifest in plans to have Andrea Sansovino (Andrea Contucci; 1467/70 Monte San Savino–1529 Monte San Savino) carve a figure of the Redeemer to be placed over the Gonfaloniere's seat opposite the *St. Anne Altarpiece*, for it was on the feast of the Savior (November 9) that Piero de' Medici had been expelled from the city in 1494 and that the new government had legislated as a civic holiday.

In fact, in 1501 Leonardo had apparently exhibited a cartoon (now lost) for a painting of St. Anne with the Virgin and Child and a lamb (associated with the early history of Fig. 6.91) in a room attached to the church of SS. Annunziata in Florence, one of the city's major cult churches. Since preparatory drawings seem to have had little intrinsic value at this time outside the artist's studio, the tale told by Vasari that large numbers of Florentines lined up over the course of two days to see the drawing because it was by a famous native son does not ring completely true. Given that Leonardo subsequently modified this iconography in another large cartoon (London, National Gallery) by substituting for the lamb a figure of the infant John the Baptist, the patron saint of Florence, this story suggests that the image participated in the history of St. Anne as a civic symbol at just the time that Michelangelo was asked to complete work on the unfinished block of the *David*.

Civic history was also to be represented on the walls of the room on either side of the Gonfaloniere's seat. In 1503 the Signoria commissioned Leonardo to paint the Battle of Anghiari against the Milanese (1440) on one side, and in 1504 they commissioned the younger Michelangelo to paint the Battle of Cascina on the other side. Michelangelo's subject had particular resonance since the Florentines were again warring with Pisa in a protracted conflict which lasted until 1509. Such battle paintings enlivened the walls of many Italian town halls, commemorating great moments in communal history (see Fig. 2.37). The Signoria pitted Leonardo and Michelangelo against one another in a clear attempt to urge each to his creative limits and at the same time to push for a speedy completion of the project—a familiar mode of

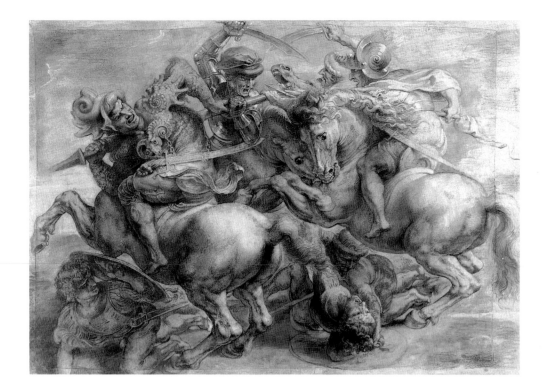

7.7 *Battle of Anghiari*, commissioned by the Signoria from Leonardo in 1503 for the Sala del Gran Consiglio, Palazzo della Signoria, Florence; central section of the projected fresco representing the battle for the standard, copy by PETER PAUL RUBENS, 1600–08. Black chalk, pen and ink, heightened with gray and white, 17¾ × 25″ (45.2 × 63.5 cm) (Musée du Louvre, Paris)

Leonardo began the fresco in 1505, and left it in 1506. His unfinished section was framed in 1513 and ultimately replaced by Vasari's paintings after 1563. The Rubens drawing was, therefore, not done from Leonardo's actual fresco, but from some copy made of it before its destruction.

assigning projects. They were successful in the first respect but not in the second, for Leonardo completed only a small part of the actual fresco, and Michelangelo apparently never moved beyond the stage of the cartoon. Yet the preparatory drawings for their frescoes were to influence Florentine artistic developments for years to come, and they still offer a textbook description of the range of pictorial possibilities for the early years of the sixteenth century.

The section of Leonardo's *Battle of Anghiari* shown here (Fig. 7.7) in a copy by Peter Paul Rubens (1577–1640) was to form the center of the whole fresco, embedded in a vast expanse of landscape containing various moments of the battle. Horses and bodies twist violently, their movement accentuated by details of realistically rendered costume and musculature. Despite the frenzied action, the figures form a tightly structured unit, in which arms and swords link with one another, providing both a stable composition and movement through it; each figure demands individual attention. The movement implicit in Leonardo's early *Adoration of the Magi* (see Fig. 6.44) is here unleashed so that it becomes part of the subject of the painting.

Michelangelo's *Battle of Cascina* is known only from his preliminary drawings and from copies (Fig. 7.8). Fresh from carving the *David*, he chose a moment when the Florentine troops, bathing in a river, were called to readiness by their leader. This choice allowed Michelangelo to concentrate on the nude body in motion, providing a virtual studio portfolio of poses. Unlike Leonardo,

Michelangelo pushed his figures forward in the composition, in a frieze-like manner reminiscent of the placement of figures on Roman sarcophagi. Opportunities to depict spatial volume seem deliberately rejected as figures move laterally across the space, both physically and psychologically independent of one another. Leonardo's insistent naturalism is here subordinated to the hard sculptural form of the male nude and to the invention of complex, yet graceful, poses for the figures—almost as if Michelangelo wished deliberately to provide an alternative to the *Battle of Anghiari*. Where Leonardo's figures fuse in the shadows of his *sfumato* technique, Michelangelo's are each clearly delineated, with crisp outlines separating light from dark. Where the torsions of Leonardo's figures are determined by the immediate moment of the battle in which they participate, the poses of Michelangelo's soldiers are isolated depictions of self-conscious grace and willed complexity that seem only tangentially connected to the moment of alarm.

Private Patrons

Like the public commissions for the Palazzo della Signoria, private commissions during the early years of the sixteenth century indicate a development of earlier painting styles. The presence of the revered Leonardo in Florence coincided with the emerging power of the mature Michelangelo and the assimilative mind of the young Raphael (Raffaello Santi; 1483 Urbino–1520

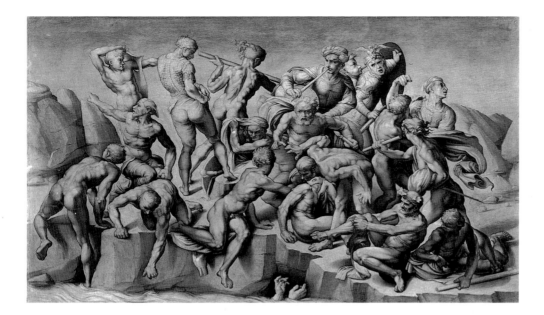

7.8 *Battle of Cascina*, commissioned by the Signoria from MICHELANGELO in 1504, copy of 1542 by Sebastiano da Sangallo (?). Grisaille panel (Lord Leicester Collection, Holkham Hall, England)

Rome), newly arrived in the city from his native Urbino, where he had trained with his father, Giovanni Santi, also a painter, and from Perugia, where he had been impressed by the light and jewel-like coloring of Perugino's painting. Although we have virtually no documentation concerning interactions among Raphael, Leonardo, and Michelangelo, the intellectual and artistic exchanges among them are manifest in their work.

One of Leonardo's greatest accomplishments as a painter was his transformation of the portrait from an icon of status to a representation of a person fully engaged with the viewer, something he had begun with his portrait of Ginevra de' Benci before his move to Milan. His *Mona Lisa*, showing an unidentified woman, seated, against the background of a rocky and watery landscape (Fig. 7.9), epitomizes this achievement although it is based on contemporary developments in Venetian painting which Leonardo would have seen when he visited that city in 1500 on his way to Florence after having fled Milan. Her crossed arms form the base of a triangle with her head as its apex. Her face is an idealized oval, emphasized by the sharp, semicircular delineation between the crown of her head and the sky behind. The contours of her face, hands, and body are rendered with the utmost sensitivity, so that convex merges into concave in a continuous movement. Leonardo's use of the *sfumato* technique blends light and dark and one form with another to enhance the unity of the composition. The lady turns gently to recognize the presence of the viewer, her slight smile—the subject of endless speculation—inviting conversation. Unlike many portraits of women during this period, Mona Lisa is represented without any of the normal attributes of wealth; she wears no rings or other jewelry, although her dress seems made of fine materials. Her hair hangs loose, and a scarf seems casually thrown over her left shoulder, adding an unusual air of informality to the picture. These anomalies, tied to contemporary accounts indicating that Leonardo worked on the painting while he was in Rome after 1513, suggest that, like many of the artist's paintings, the *Mona Lisa* had a long history. Whatever painting Leonardo may have begun in Florence, he may well have modified it at a later date so that it became much more than a portrait. It seems to be a meditation on ideal feminine beauty and an exploration of the sitter's (and perhaps the artist's) psyche.

When Raphael painted the wedding portraits of Agnolo Doni and Maddalena Strozzi (Fig. 7.10) the *Mona Lisa* (at some early stage in its conception) was clearly his inspiration. Nonetheless he reverted to earlier formal conventions, in which a woman's social position was marked by her fine dress and jewelry (provided by her husband) and in which the formality of the image is enhanced by the staring gaze and stiff pose of the figure, as was the case with Ghirlandaio's *Giovanna de' Tornabuoni* (see Fig. 6.48). The few strands of hair that escape on Maddalena's right side are a rather cautious attempt at a natural effect, far removed from the flowing tresses of the *Mona Lisa*. Despite Raphael's technical facility and the rapidity with which he assimilated the new work being produced in Florence after his arrival in 1504/05, *Maddalena Strozzi Doni* relies strongly on older portrait models, as if the new elite in the city wished to ensure their position by lip-service to established conventions.

Raphael's *Madonna of the Baldachin* (Fig. 7.11), painted for the Dei family but left unfinished, uses the conventional symmetrical composition of the enthroned Virgin and Child flanked by saints. The figures are placed in an austerely classical architectural setting. Despite the

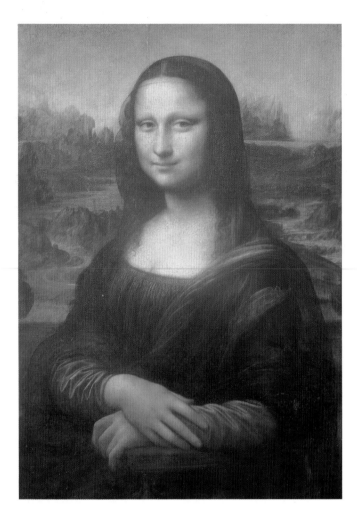

7.9 *Mona Lisa*, c. 1503–1513(?), LEONARDO DA VINCI. Oil on panel, 38½ × 21″ (97.8 × 53.3 cm) (Musée du Louvre, Paris)

At one time the figure was flanked by columns whose bases are just visible on the ledge behind her. The identity of the figure is uncertain. Vasari was the first to use the name Mona [Madonna] Lisa, leading to an identification of the figure as Lisa Gherardini, who married Francesco Bartolomeo del Giocondo in 1495. Another writer who had seen the painting in France in 1517 when he visited Leonardo indicated that the painting had been made for Giuliano de' Medici when Leonardo was in Rome, making the identification of Mona Lisa unlikely.

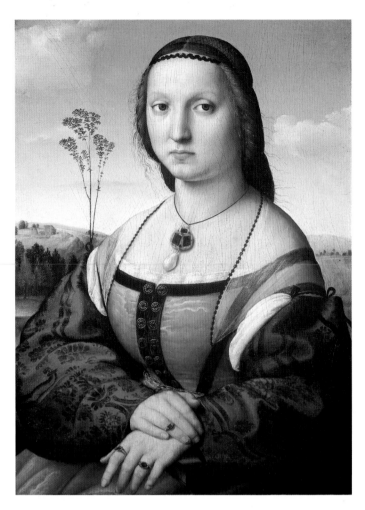

7.10 *Maddalena Strozzi Doni*, c. 1506, commissioned by Agnolo Doni from RAPHAEL as a pendant to Doni's own portrait. Oil on panel, 24¾ × 17¾″ (63 × 45 cm) (Galleria Pitti, Florence)

availability of Leonardo's and Michelangelo's studies for their battle paintings, Raphael here shows little sign of sharing the older artists' fascination with movement and physical energy. Although Mary's legs are directed left while her torso turns to the right, only the angels holding the drapery of the *baldacchino* at the top of the painting are animated, suggesting that Raphael may have been incorporating the new vocabulary slowly, in ancillary figures. He may also have been constrained by the commission itself to produce a familiar image, in which movement was by convention restrained.

Raphael's interest in the new work of Leonardo and Michelangelo is evident, however, in his *Entombment* (Fig. 7.12), painted for Atalanta Baglione of Perugia to

commemorate her dead son killed at his mother's door by relations of relatives he had murdered. The group of men around the dead Christ creates a centrifugal movement away from the body at the same time that the Magdalene moves toward it, her golden hair blowing sensuously across her bodice. The stances of the two men holding the body seem determined by the dead weight they support. The pristine clarity of the landscape, with trees and crosses silhouetted against open sky, betray Raphael's training with Perugino and the contemporary popularity of Flemish painting. Raphael's interest in classical models is evident in the simplified facial features of the standing man at the right center of the composition—the only figure separated from a group—and in the figural group as a whole, which is a quotation from a Roman sarcophagus representing the dead Meleager, an appropriate reference for Atalanta's dead son in this painting. The seated figure at the right is also a quotation, this time from a painting of the Holy Family by Michelangelo made just before Raphael painted this work.

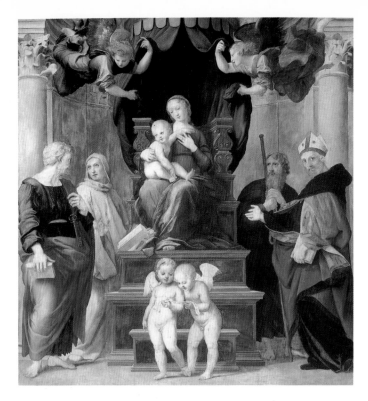

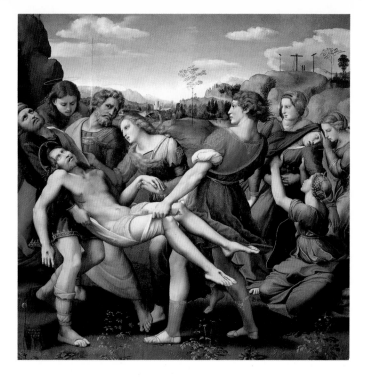

7.11 *Madonna of the Baldachin*, 1508, commissioned by Rinieri di Bernardo Dei from RAPHAEL for the Dei Chapel, Santo Spirito, Florence, left unfinished when Raphael moved to Rome in 1508. Oil on canvas, 9' × 7' 4" (2.74 × 2.24 m)

The illustration shows the painting in its original state, without the additions of a later date to the upper part of the altarpiece.

7.12 *Entombment*, 1507, commissioned by Atalanta Baglioni of Perugia from RAPHAEL to commemorate the death of her son, Grifonetto Baglione. Oil on panel, 5' 11½" × 5' 9¼" (1.82 × 1.76 m) (Borghese Gallery, Rome)

But clearly what distinguishes this painting from the *Madonna of the Baldacchin* is the dynamic movement of the figures, each of whom adds a dramatic energy to the action. Although Raphael's composition derives from an engraving of the same subject by Mantegna, a drawing for the painting (Fig. 7.13)—one of a series—suggests how concerned Raphael was to follow the lead of Leonardo and Michelangelo in activating the movement of his figures to give them a greater sense of participating in an ongoing narrative action rather than a static *tableau vivant*. Whereas the drawing—an intermediate stage in the development of the final composition—shows the figure of Christ parallel to the picture plane, with the other figures in a frieze-like arrangement, perhaps inspired by an antique Roman sarcophagus relief of Meleager, the painting shows Christ turned at an angle into space. The shoulders of the painted Christ have a slight torsion and his head both falls heavily back and turns off axis with the body towards the viewer, giving the figure a decided physical tension despite the fact that Christ is dead. The muscular young man lifting Christ's legs in the painting thrusts back, countering the movement of Christ into space, different from his frontally disposed predecessor in the drawing. And what had begun in the drawing as a rather conventional lamentation scene has in the finished painting been transformed into an astonishing conflation of deposition, lamentation, and entombment iconographies, their narrative carried by the dynamics of the figures.

By the time Raphael completed the *Entombment* he had obviously integrated into his work the recent innovations

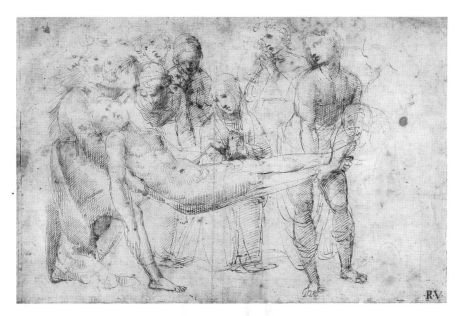

7.13 *The Entombment*, c. 1507, RAPHAEL, preparatory drawing for Fig. 7.12. Ink on paper, 8¼ × 12⅞" (20.9 × 32 cm) (British Museum, London)

of Florentine painting, but he also equally clearly understood their implicit contradictions. Like the *Battle of Cascina*, the *Entombment* deviates from the commonly accepted idea that painting of the early sixteenth century is characterized by a single focus within the narrative, a stable symmetrical composition, and a clear relationship between the individual forms—in short, that it adheres to classical principles. Clearly, neither Michelangelo's projected Cascina fresco nor Raphael's painting conforms to these ideals. Rather, the artists pushed beyond classical models in an attempt to make the dramatic content of their subjects more palpable. It is no accident that both paintings are narratives with a strongly implied story line, rather than conventional religious images. Moreover, Raphael obviously struggled in his search for a solution to the opposing possibilities for narrative and compositional structures presented by the Battle paintings of Leonardo and Michelangelo (see Figs. 7.7 and 7.8). The rupture in the composition of the *Entombment* at the right, where Mary and her attendants are separated from the main group, and the residual planar structure of the males at the left, despite the illusion of a deep space beyond, attest to the difficulties facing any painter of this period —even one with Raphael's extraordinary skills—in coming to terms with the divergent visions for the future of painting embedded in the two Battle paintings.

Rome: The Imperial Style under Julius II and the Dissolution of Papal Power under the Medici Popes

When Giuliano della Rovere became pope as Julius II (r. 1503–13) he already had a long history as a generous patron of the arts. As the nephew of Sixtus IV he had taken responsibility for completion of his uncle's tomb by Pollaiuolo and had renovated his own titular church of San Pietro in Vincoli, adding to it a palace where he kept his collection of antique sculpture, the most famous example of which was the *Apollo Belvedere*. This early patron-

age, while extensive, fell comfortably within the boundaries of late fifteenth-century Roman conventions.

When Julius became pope, however, his patronage needs changed dramatically. Having been elected on a platform of reform, specifically opposing himself to the hedonistic life that characterized the papacy of his predecessor, Alexander VI, Julius had to find a new visual language to express this change. Such a language also needed to reflect an enlarged Church, which now reached to the Americas and to southern and eastern Asia. The very name he took upon becoming pope (not to mention his self-stylization as "Julius Caesar" on one of his commemorative medals) leaves little doubt that Julius wished his office to be viewed in terms of Roman imperial models.

For his first commissions as pope, Julius concentrated on the Vatican, choosing Donato Bramante to express architecturally his vision of power. Before moving to Rome in 1499, Bramante had worked for the Sforza in Milan (see Fig. 6.83), and he was thus already familiar with the requirements of absolute rulers.

The earliest collaboration between Julius and Bramante resulted in the transformation of the existing papal palace by the addition of a huge enclosed courtyard uniting the medieval living quarters with a summer house, called the Belvedere because of its view, which Innocent VIII had built at the top of the Vatican Hill (Figs. 7.14 and 7.15). Although considerably altered later in the century, the Belvedere Courtyard clearly illustrates the imperial scale of Julius's thinking from the outset of his papacy. Long arms of architecture some 300 yards (275 meters) in length engulfed a vast open space, ordering the sloping hill into three discrete levels connected by

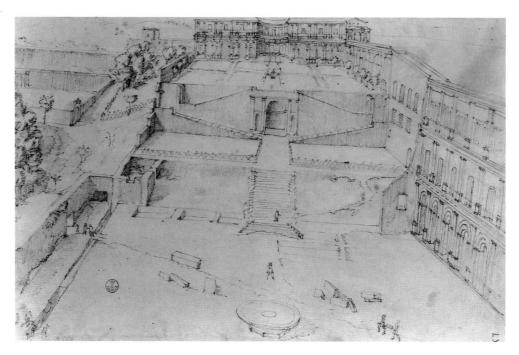

7.14 Belvedere Courtyard, Vatican Palace, Rome, begun 1504, commissioned by Julius II from DONATO BRAMANTE, drawing by Antonio Dosio, c. 1558–61, showing the courtyard under construction

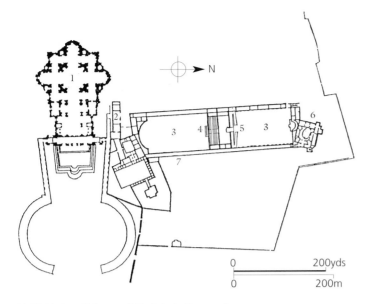

7.15 Vatican Palace and St. Peter's, Rome, plan

1 St. Peter's (Michelangelo's plan, with seventeenth-century extension by Carlo Maderna); **2** Sistine Chapel; **3** Belvedere Courtyard; **4** Stairs; **5** Ramps; **6** Statue Court; **7** Porta Giulia

stairs and ramps. The courtyard provided both a formal garden space at the upper level and a space for theatrical display with viewing loggias at the lower level adjacent to the formal rooms of the palace. The sources for such a grandiose scheme lay in the multi-storied Roman imperial palace, in ancient Roman country villas stretching horizontally over the landscape, and—in the lower level—in the three-storied, arcaded Colosseum. The iconography of the architecture was therefore appropriate to Julius's self-representation as a caesar.

A New St. Peter's

The boldest of Julius's early projects was his plan to demolish the Old St. Peter's, which dated to around 330, and to replace it with an entirely new church. In doing so Julius wiped away 1,200 years of accumulated history at the site, placing himself at the beginning of its new history. Since Old St. Peter's had been built by Constantine as an imperial donation, Julius's commission also equated him with the power of that Roman emperor, the last to have controlled all of Europe and the Mediterranean basin and the first to legitimize Christianity as a state religion.

Bramante's plan for the new St. Peter's supplanted the Early Christian basilica composed of nave and side aisles with a domed centralized plan (see Fig. 7.19). This type of structure, also tied to architecture of the Early Christian period, was known as a **martyrium** and typically marked the place where a saint was buried, its domical form carrying the cosmological symbolism of heaven. Insofar as the building was built over the site of the tomb of St. Peter, the first pope, the centralized plan was, therefore, iconographically appropriate for the new St. Peter's.

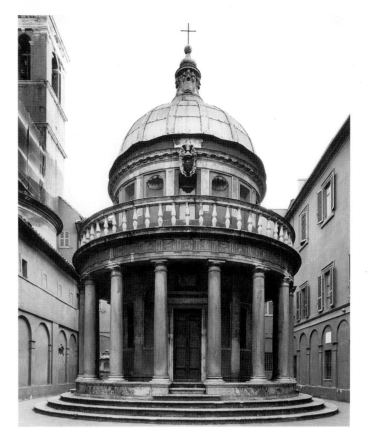

7.16 Tempietto, San Pietro in Montorio, Rome, inscription of 1502, commissioned by Ferdinand and Isabella of Spain from DONATO BRAMANTE

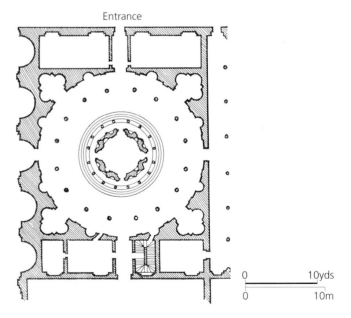

7.17 Tempietto, San Pietro in Montorio, Rome, proposed plan by DONATO BRAMANTE (after Sebastiano Serlio)

The colonnaded courtyard planned by Bramante to surround the Tempietto was never built.

Bramante had already used the martyrium form for the small free-standing chapel he had designed for King Ferdinand and Queen Isabella of Spain to mark the site revered as the place of St. Peter's crucifixion (Figs. 7.16 and 7.17). Known as the Tempietto because of its small

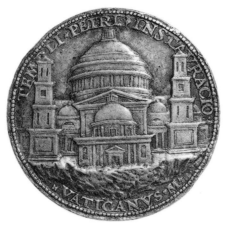

7.18 Foundation medal of St. Peter's, Rome, showing DONATO BRAMANTE'S first plan for St. Peter's, 1506, Caradosso. Bronze (© British Museum, London)

size and classical allusions, this pilgrimage chapel exists in what was to have been the central unit of a redesigned courtyard at San Pietro in Montorio, one of the Spanish churches in Rome. Bramante's plan for the Tempietto, with its columns aligned to columns of the surrounding loggia, its niches aligned to niches and openings in the redesigned courtyard, was completely ordered and symmetrical, providing a space for the pilgrim which mirrored the forms of the symbolic cosmos of the building at the center.

Participation in the divine was also at the heart of Bramante's plans for the new St. Peter's. A commemorative medal coined at the time of the groundbreaking for the building in 1506 and Bramante's still extant plans indicate his original scheme for the new St. Peter's (Figs. 7.18–7.20). His references to the Pantheon in the dome of the building and to colossal Roman basilicas remained consistent points of departure for all subsequent plans for the building. In its simplest form the plan for the new St.

Peter's is an elaboration of circles and squares, the perfect geometrical units mentioned by Vitruvius (active 46–30 B.C.E.), the architect of the Roman emperor Augustus. Leonardo's drawing of Vitruvius's text from *De architectura* (Fig. 7.21) places the human figure at the center of a perfectly ordered universe, the same geometrical metaphor used by Bramante for his plan for St. Peter's and for the Tempietto. Bramante added the additional symbolic form of the cross in the open spaces extending out from the domed area at the center of the building, fusing Christian and pagan in architectural form as Julius sought to combine Roman imperial splendor with his role as the spiritual leader of Christendom.

Although the actual building of the new St. Peter's did not begin until 1506, plans for such a structure must have been under way long before then. Thus it is possible to see both the Belvedere Courtyard and the new St. Peter's as part of an overall scheme for the Vatican, uniting palace and church in an architectural iconography of sovereignty known since classical antiquity and most brilliantly exemplified in Italy in the uniting of the Doge's Palace and St. Mark's Basilica in Venice (see Fig. 1.7).

The Tomb of Julius II   At the very time that his building projects were getting under way in 1505, Julius commissioned Michelangelo to design his tomb. Michelangelo's first scheme for the tomb was for a colossal free-standing, three-storied monument containing an internal oval burial chamber (Fig. 7.22). The free-standing tomb type recalls Pollaiuolo's tomb of Julius's uncle, Sixtus IV, whose construction Julius had overseen. The tiered shape of the tomb with a door to an interior burial chamber, niches and sculpture at the lowest level, and a figure of

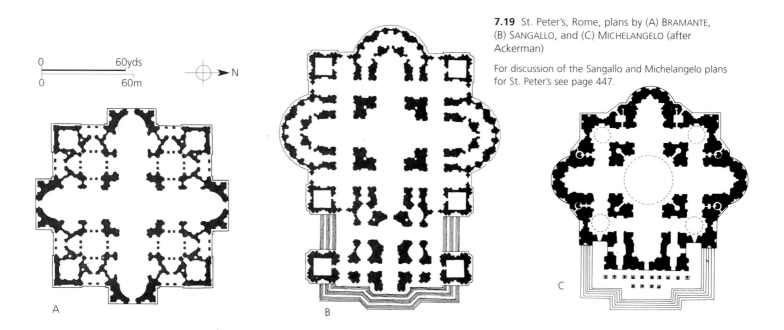

7.19 St. Peter's, Rome, plans by (A) BRAMANTE, (B) SANGALLO, and (C) MICHELANGELO (after Ackerman)

For discussion of the Sangallo and Michelangelo plans for St. Peter's see page 447.

0 ——— 60yds
0 ——— 60m   ⊕ ► N

A   B   C

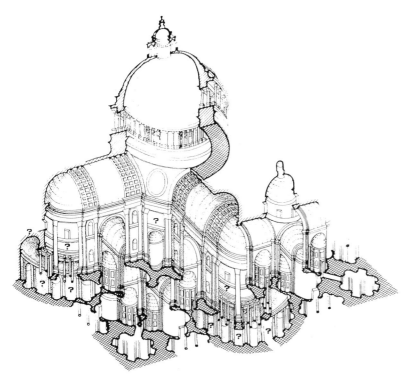

7.20 St. Peter's, Rome, axonometric view after DONATO BRAMANTE'S second plan of 1506 (after Bruschi)

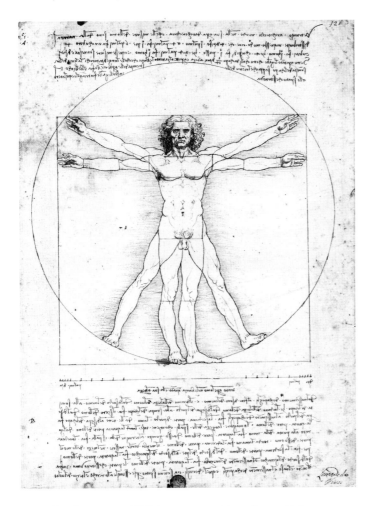

7.21 *Vitruvian Man*, c. 1487, LEONARDO DA VINCI. Pen and ink, 13½ × 9½″ (34.3 × 24.5 cm) (Galleria dell'Accademia, Venice)

the deceased at the top recalls Roman imperial funeral pyres shown on the backs of imperial coins; thus the abstract shape of the tomb, like the formal properties of Julius's architecture, gives it an imperial significance and once again marks Julius's pretensions as a new caesar.

The tomb was to measure approximately 23 feet 6 inches by 35 feet 6 inches (7.2 by 10.8 meters), which would have made it Michelangelo's first real essay in architecture and a patent challenge to the restrained forms of Bramante. Around the lower level Michelangelo planned niches containing sculptures of allegorical representations of Victories standing over conquered territories—a reference to Julius's military attempts to reconquer papal lands given away by his predecessor. Each of the niches was to be flanked by an over-life-sized male nude; only six of the projected total of at least sixteen such figures were ever begun. At each corner of the middle level there would have been a seated figure: Moses, St. Paul, and personifications of the active and the contemplative life. Moses, the only one of the figures to have been carved, refers to the same aspects of leadership—priest, lawgiver, ruler—that Sixtus IV had signified in his commission for the fresco cycle of the Sistine Chapel (see Fig. 6.66). At the apex of the tomb Michelangelo probably intended to place a figure of Julius himself.

The meaning of the standing male nudes (Fig. 7.23) still remains incompletely understood. Michelangelo's biographer, Ascanio Condivi, maintained in 1553 that they represented the arts, expiring at the death of Julius II, their greatest patron. They are also commonly—and misleadingly—referred to as "slaves" or "captives," a terminology deriving from the bands of material that seem to constrict the movement of the most completely carved of these figures. Such an identification also relates to the Victory figures which they were to flank, although each Victory seems to have stood astride its own captive. The torsion of the pose heightens the sense of movement only implied in the earlier *David* (see Fig. 7.2).

In the uncarved rock supporting two of the nudes there is a monkey, barely sketched in the stone but unmistakably looking out toward the right, just beneath the left thigh of the illustrated figure. Although often used as a symbol for lust, the monkey also stood for the concept of art aping nature (*ars simia natura*), a realism emphasized in this sculpture by the sliding pose and by the soft sensuousness of the figure. Thus Michelangelo seems to have entered into the dispute known as the *Paragone* which debated whether painting or sculpture was the more noble of the arts. One of the lines of argument in this debate concerned whether painting or sculpture more convincingly depicts a narrative, the former by placing figures in an illusionistic setting, the latter by creating

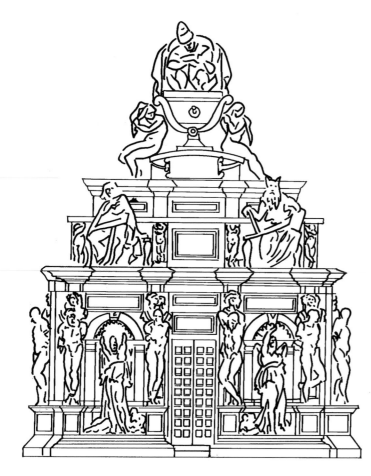

7.22 Tomb of Julius II, reconstruction of plan of 1505 (after Tolnay), commissioned by Julius II from MICHELANGELO

The figure of the pope on the top tier of the tomb is conjectural. Michelangelo's biographer, Ascanio Condivi, states simply that the tomb was to have been capped by two angels carrying a sarcophagus. Conventionally, papal sarcophagi (and others) showed a recumbent figure of the deceased on the lid.

figures in actual space. The palpably sensual realism of this nude figure for Julius's tomb, his right hand beginning a slow slide along the surface of his undulant torso, provides Michelangelo's response to the debate in favor of sculpture.

The Sistine Ceiling

There are indications that as early as 1506 Julius II intended to have the ceiling of the Sistine Chapel painted, but Michelangelo did not sign a contract until May 1508. The first plan for the ceiling called for figures of twelve Apostles in the spandrels between the windows and various ornamental motifs in the main section. However, Michelangelo apparently persuaded the pope that this initial project was unworthy of the chapel and embarked on the program which exists today (Figs. 7.24 and 7.25).

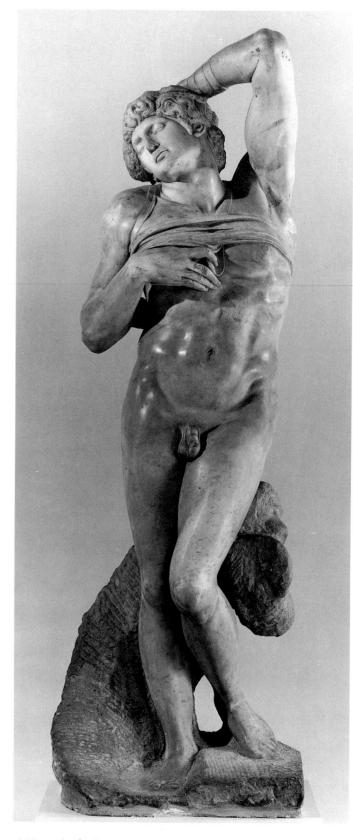

7.23 Tomb of Julius II, commissioned by Julius II in 1505 from MICHELANGELO, detail of male nude, begun after 1512, offered in 1546 as a gift by Michelangelo to Ruberto Strozzi in Lyon, who gave it to Francis I who in turn gave it to the Connétable Anne de Montmorency for his château at Ecouen. Marble, height 7' 6" (2.29 m) (Musée du Louvre, Paris)

C O N T E M P O R A R Y   V O I C E

Michelangelo the Poet

In addition to his formidable gifts in the visual arts, Michelangelo possessed considerable talent as a poet, and his poems were greatly admired by his contemporaries. In this sonnet, one of his best known, he compares the struggle of finding love to the failure of art to ward off death.

Sonnet 151 (c. 1538–44)
  Not even the best of artists has any conception
that a single marble block does not contain
within its excess, and *that* is only attained
by the hand that obeys the intellect.

The pain I flee from and the joy I hope for
are similarly hidden in you, lovely lady,
lofty and divine; but, to my mortal harm,
my art gives results the reverse of what I wish.
  Love, therefore, cannot be blamed for my pain,
nor can your beauty, your hardness, or your scorn,
nor fortune, nor my destiny, nor chance,
  if you hold both death and mercy in your heart
at the same time, and my lowly wits, though burning,
cannot draw from it anything but death.

(from James Saslow. *The Poetry of Michelangelo*. New Haven: Yale University Press, 1991, p. 302)

Michelangelo worked until 1512 on the ceiling, standing on a bridge-like scaffold which he had had constructed across the width of the building at the upper cornice level and which was moved from the entrance to the altar wall of the chapel as work progressed. During the course of his painting, Michelangelo's style changed. This is most immediately evident in the figures of the prophets and sibyls, whose bodies become larger and whose poses become more active as one approaches the altar end. For example, in painting the *Libyan Sibyl* (see Fig. 7.26) Michelangelo contrived an impossibly contorted figure, whose pose, like that of the nudes, recalls the experiments of the unexecuted *Battle of Cascina* and whose complexity is a tour de force of artistic virtuosity.

Michelangelo ordered the smooth vaulted space of the chapel with fictive architecture similar to the forms he had proposed for Julius's tomb. At the extremities of the ceiling narrow bands of blue sky appear as if through an opening in the architecture, illusionistically suggesting a limitless space beyond the vault of the ceiling. Particularly at the altar end of the ceiling the large unframed narrative panels seem to participate in this vision of space beyond the confines of the room. Three groups of three alternating large and small narrative panels extend the length of the ceiling. These tell the Genesis story of Creation (from the altar wall), the creation and fall of Adam and Eve (in the center), and the story of Noah (at the entrance end of the chapel), a human fall from grace and a promise of redemption. The paintings, however, are oriented for a viewer facing the altar. Looking up and moving from the entrance of the chapel toward the altar, one sees the figures right side up and traces the history of the fall of humankind backwards in time towards Creation, as if to emphasize a new beginning and a return to

pre-lapsarian grace. Insofar as the chapel is dedicated to the Virgin it is appropriate that the center panel shows the creation of Eve, the archetype of Mary, who, according to tradition, began the redemption necessitated by the sin of Eve and Adam.

Eve also appears as an incipient companion for Adam in the *Creation of Adam* panel, where she looks out anxiously toward Adam from under the left arm of God (see Fig. 18). Adam rests on a schematic brown mound since his name translates as "Earth," although nowhere in the ceiling (or anywhere else in his paintings) does Michelangelo show any interest in depicting anything more than the most minimal landscape features. Adam's body, modeled after the ancient *Belvedere Torso* in the papal collections, has its left hip raised to display his genitals, a reference to his future procreation of humankind. Adam's lifeless lassitude is paired with the whirling energy of God the Father (depicted in the same pose as in the *Creation of the Sun and the Moon* in the second panel of the ceiling). At the moment before their figures touch in life-giving energy, however, there is a powerfully charged void as if two like-charged magnetic fields were inhibiting contact. Prophets and sibyls (Fig. 7.26)—men and women who Christians claimed foretold the birth of the redeemer in both the Jewish and the ancient Roman traditions—alternate in the large spandrels between the windows. Jonah, in the spandrel over the altar (originally also between windows), is a symbol of redemption as well since, like Christ in the tomb, he was in the belly of the whale for three days before being released.

The pendentive areas in the corners of the room show male and female heroes of the Old Testament. David and Judith carry overtones of Julius's wars against usurpers of papal territories. Moses and Esther in the pendentives at

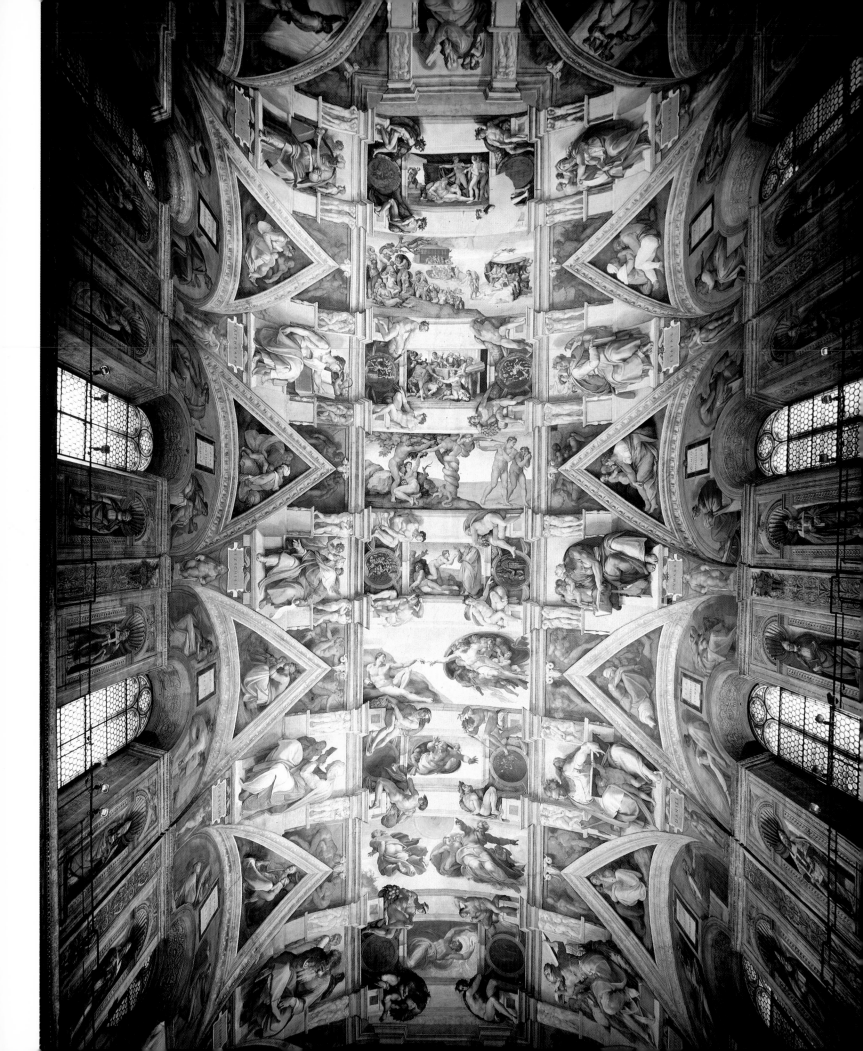

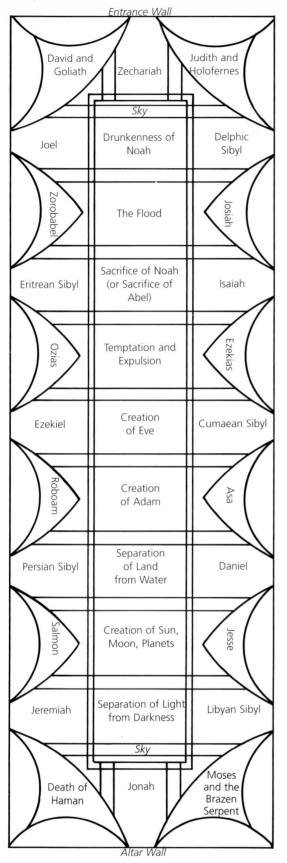

7.25 Sistine Chapel, Rome, plan of ceiling scenes (after Hibbard)

A recent suggestion that the panel traditionally identified as the *Sacrifice of Noah* represents instead the *Sacrifice of Abel* would both remove the single chronological inconsistency in the arrangement of the narratives on the ceiling and also conform to the identification of the panel given by Michelangelo's early biographers.

7.24 (opposite) Sistine Chapel, Rome, ceiling as seen from entrance end, 1508–12, commissioned by Julius II from MICHELANGELO. Fresco, 45 × 128′ (13.7 × 39 m)

Within the plan (figure 7.25), the following labels appear:

Entrance Wall

David and Goliath — Zechariah — Judith and Holofernes

Sky

Joel — Drunkenness of Noah — Delphic Sibyl

Zorobabel — The Flood — Josiah

Eritrean Sibyl — Sacrifice of Noah (or Sacrifice of Abel) — Isaiah

Ozias — Temptation and Expulsion — Ezekias

Ezekiel — Creation of Eve — Cumaean Sibyl

Roboam — Creation of Adam — Asa

Persian Sibyl — Separation of Land from Water — Daniel

Salmon — Creation of Sun, Moon, Planets — Jesse

Jeremiah — Separation of Light from Darkness — Libyan Sibyl

Sky

Death of Haman — Jonah — Moses and the Brazen Serpent

Altar Wall

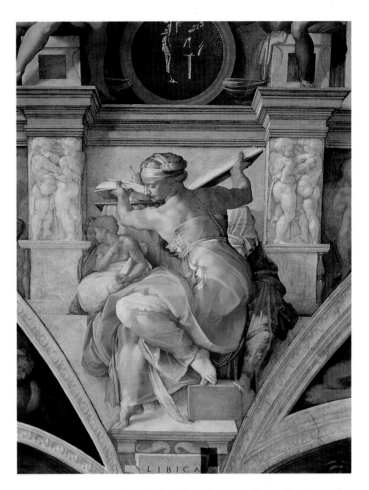

7.26 *Libyan Sibyl*, the first sibyl on the right as one faces the altar wall of the Sistine Chapel, Rome. Fresco

the altar end of the building again suggest Julius's power as a divinely ordained leader of his people. The nudes framing the smaller narrative panels present the most insistent projections into the space of the chapel as they are posed in front of the illusionistic architecture. They recall both the tensely movemented figures of the *Battle of Cascina* (see Fig. 7.8) and the sensuousness of the nudes for Julius's tomb (see Fig. 7.23). The gilt bronze military shields they carry again suggest Julius's persistent warfare and their illusionistic reality—paired with the architecture—the notion of art imitating nature. The della Rovere heraldic symbols of the oak (*rovere* in Italian) and acorn appear throughout the ceiling to identify Julius as the patron of the work. With Michelangelo's frescoes Julius completed the program begun by his uncle, Sixtus IV, on the walls of the room below (see Figs. 6.66, 6.67 and 6.68), so that all of Christian history—from the Creation on the ceiling to the Resurrection on the short entrance wall—is represented in the chapel.

The colors of the ceiling, newly revealed in the recent cleaning of the frescoes, are intense and often applied in broad areas. Michelangelo also used the technique of

Art and Dissent

It is a commonplace to refer to art "speaking" to the viewer, but during the Renaissance this idea was given a more literal sense. The painted wooden crucifix in the church of San Damiano in Assisi that allegedly spoke to St. Francis in 1205, admonishing him to "rebuild my church" and thus setting the stage for the foundation of the Franciscan order, is the most familiar of a number of such painted and sculpted crucifixes believed to act as conduits of divine will.

The tradition of speaking sculpture also extended to works of antique art—found mostly in Rome—that carried written messages for the public weal. Perhaps the most famous of these was the Pasquino (Fig. 7.27), a fragment (6 feet 3 inches [1.92 m] high) of a sculptural group representing *Menelaus Carrying the Body of Patroclus* (although during the Renaissance it was also thought to represent Hercules vanquishing Geryon). According to one local tradition, the statue received its name because it had lain in the yard of a schoolmaster named Pasquino. A story from the mid-sixteenth century claimed that the sculpture had really been found near the shop of a free-speaking tailor—also called Pasquino—famous for his criticisms of the pope and the papal court. The Pasquino was installed near its present location, at what was then the

corner of the Palazzo Orsini, by Cardinal Oliviero Carafa in 1501. It quickly became the source of witty, scandalous, and politically and religiously charged comments which were written in humanist Latin (scholarly rather than ecclesiastical Latin) on scraps of paper and attached both to it and to the wall behind it. These pithy jibes passed for the words of the Pasquino itself, allowing

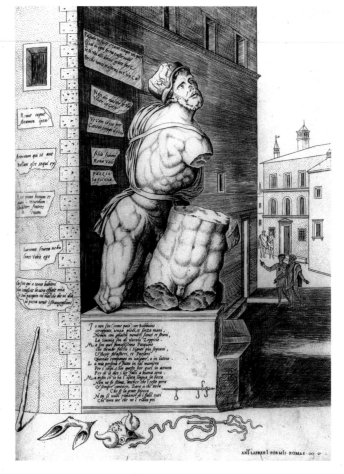

7.27 Pasquino, c. 1550, Nicholas Beatrizet, collected and published by Antoine Lafréry (Antonio Lafreri) in *Speculum Romanae Magnificentiae*, Rome, 1550. Engraving

the venting of popular opinions in the safety of anonymity and with a commonly accepted understanding that since the Pasquino was responsible for their coining, no one would be prosecuted for the sentiments expressed. Cardinal Carafa arranged that the statue be dressed each April (near the feast of Easter—Pasqua in Italian) in the costume of a different classical Roman mythological figure, lending a festive atmosphere of street theater to the city in the spring. In 1513 the statue appeared as Apollo, in honor of the election of Giovanni de' Medici as Pope Leo X (a reference to the new pope's passion for music). Beginning in 1509 the comments of the Pasquino were collected, provided with a printed frontispiece, and published on an annual basis as political and social satire of a sharply critical and sometimes obscene nature. Humanist writers, who delighted in the rhetorical skills of the Pasquino, accused the morally conservative Pope Hadrian VI of wanting to throw the statue into the Tiber in order to rid the city of its corrupting influence. Threats against the sculpture were also made during the religious reformation of the mid-sixteenth century, but the Pasquino continued to issue a running commentary on the foibles of the famous and on the social order of the city well into the nineteenth century.

changeable color, in which contrasting colors are placed side by side to produce highlighting effects, rather than modeling the dominating color with shadows and highlights. This technique may have been chosen in order to accommodate the great distance between the viewer on the floor of the chapel and the figures on the ceiling, but it also served as an alternative to Leonardo's *sfumato* technique, just as Michelangelo's composition for the *Battle of Cascina* had been opposed to Leonardo's companion painting. The ceiling was not only a complex Old Testament exegesis but a demonstration of the possibilities for painting at the beginning of the sixteenth century, making it a constant source of study for painters of the next generation.

The Stanza della Segnatura

Julius commissioned Raphael to decorate his private apartments in the Vatican Palace, now called simply the Stanze ("rooms"). His choice of artist was an implicit rejection of the style and history of his predecessor, Alexander VI, whose own apartments on the floor immediately below had recently been painted by Pinturicchio (see Fig. 6.70). In its grand stateliness Raphael's style directly opposed the lush elegance of Pinturicchio's frescoes.

The work began in the Stanza della Segnatura (Fig. 7.28). There Raphael's images portray four main bodies of human knowledge: Philosophy in the *School of Athens*, where the best known philosophers and intellectuals of the ancient world group around Plato and Aristotle at the center (Fig. 7.29); Religion in the *Disputà*, where theologians present their writings about the true presence of Christ in the Eucharist, which is displayed at the very center of the painting (Fig. 7.31); Poetry in the *Parnassus*, where writers from both the ancient and the modern worlds group around a seated Apollo and figures of the Muses (Fig. 7.30); and Law, where the cardinal virtues of Prudence, Temperance, and Fortitude sit beneath Justice depicted immediately overhead in a roundel in the ceiling.

The *School of Athens* and the *Disputà*, facing one another across the room, have become the paradigms for the classical style in painting under Julius. In each case, Raphael painted an architectural frame much like a proscenium (the wall itself is actually flat and unadorned architecturally), which effects a transition between the real space of the room and the illusionistic space of the fresco. He also used the arching shape of the wall as the underlying geometrical structure for the composition, so that in the *Disputà*, for example, banks of clouds create a semicircular, apse-like space in the picture, as do the figures at the ground level. A similar arched shape appears on the vertical axis for the mandorla around the central figure of Christ, echoed by a complete circle for the radiance around the dove of the Holy Spirit and for the monstrance on the altar. Every element of the painting is locked into this geometrical order.

In the *School of Athens* the arch is repeated in the barrel vaults of the architecture behind the figures, a building that reflects the contemporary plans of Bramante for the new St. Peter's. In this image the single-point perspective system is structured so that it moves to a point between the heads of Plato and Aristotle, emphasizing their seminal importance for the discipline of philosophy.

Raphael repeatedly broke the limitations of the frame in these frescoes. In the *School of Athens*, figures rush into the scene at the left and out of it at the right. In the *Disputà* the figure at the right foreground leans over painted

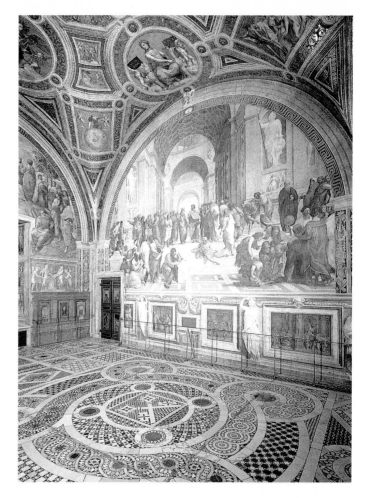

7.28 Stanza della Segnatura, Vatican Palace, Rome, 1508–11, commissioned by Julius II from RAPHAEL, view showing *Parnassus* wall on the left and the *School of Athens* on the right. Fresco

In Julius's time the room was a library. It became a room where papal documents were signed only later, when it received its modern designation of the "Room of the Signature."

architecture as if into the space of the room. In the *Parnassus* (see Fig. 7.30), Raphael achieved an illusionistic tour de force where figures like the seated Sappho on the left are depicted as if in front of the painted frame of the window, even casting illusionistic shadows on the fictive architecture. The *contrapposto* pose of Sappho indicates that Raphael had looked carefully at Michelangelo's figures in the nearby Sistine Chapel and was quickly incorporating their formal innovations in his own work.

Pope Julius's presence is constantly evident in this room, whether in the symbolic oaks of the *Parnassus* which transform the ancient Mount Parnassus into the Vatican Hill or in the far more obvious double inscription of Julius's name in the interlace pattern on the altar frontal in the *Disputà*. Equations between Julius and ancient imperial patrons appear in the *grisaille* paintings under the *Parnassus*, where Alexander is shown placing the poems of Homer in the tomb of Achilles and Augustus is depicted saving the *Aeneid* of Virgil from the flames, just as Julius preserved the work of other writers in his library. In the wall of the Law fresco Julius appears

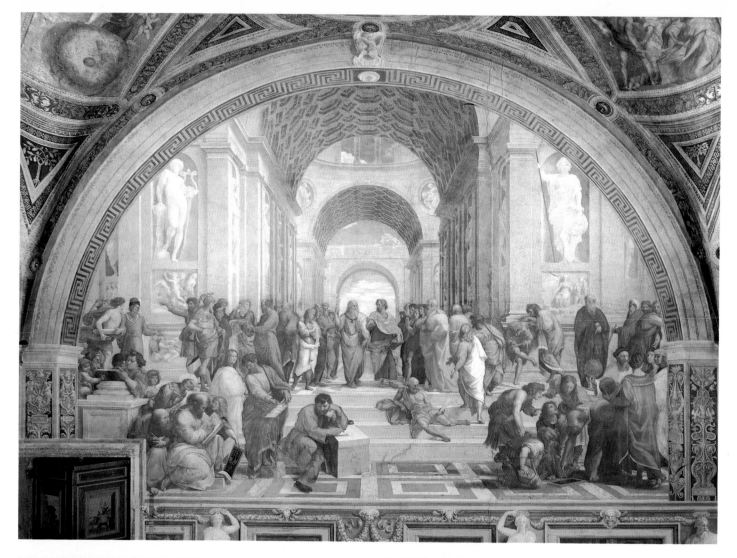

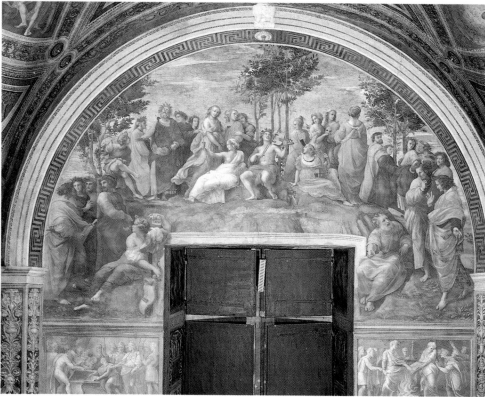

7.29 *School of Athens*, 1510–11, commissioned by Julius II from RAPHAEL for the Stanza della Segnatura, Vatican Palace, Rome. Fresco, height 19′ (5.79 m)

The statues in the two facing niches represent Apollo and Minerva. Plato is thought to represent Leonardo da Vinci, the seated figure of Heraclitus leaning on the block in the center foreground Michelangelo, and the bending bald-headed Euclid at the right Bramante. Raphael included his own youthful self-portrait in the foreground at the far right, next to a figure sometimes identified as the painter Sodoma.

7.30 *Parnassus*, c. 1511, commissioned by Julius II from RAPHAEL for the Stanza della Segnatura, Vatican Palace, Rome. Fresco, height 19′ (5.79 m)

Apollo is seated top center, flanked by the muses. To the left of the image Dante appears in profile, in red, and to his right the blind Homer. To the right of Homer, looking toward Dante, is the Roman poet Virgil who guided Dante through Hell and Purgatory in the Divine Comedy. The hooded man just behind the tree at the left is Petrarch; the seated female leaning out from the window embrasure is the Greek poet Sappho.

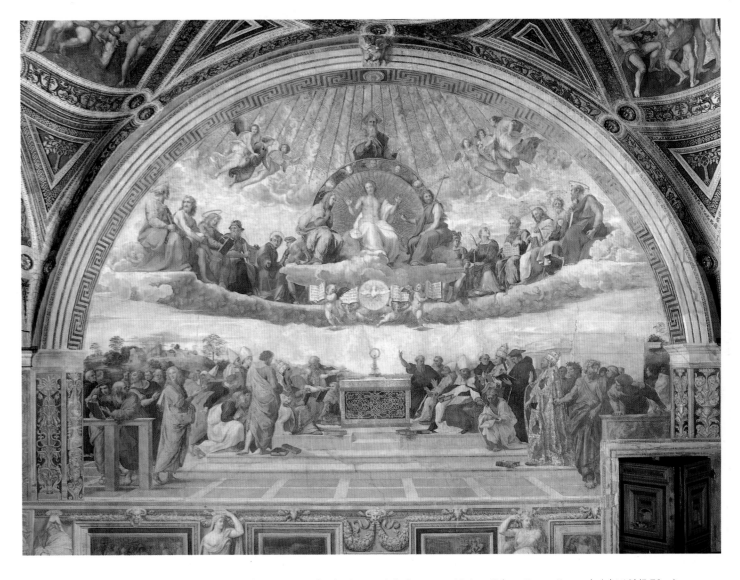

7.31 *Disputà*, 1510–11, commissioned by Julius II from RAPHAEL for the Stanza della Segnatura, Vatican Palace, Rome. Fresco, height 19′ (5.79 m)

The standing figure in full papal regalia on the right side of the fresco is a portrait of Sixtus IV, Julius's uncle. Seated at the left and right of the altar are the four doctors of the church, Gregory the Great and Jerome at the left, Ambrose and Augustine at the right. The figures seated on the cloud bank are from the left St. Peter, Adam, St. John the Evangelist, David, St. Stephen, Jeremiah, and, to the right of Christ, Judas Maccabeus, St. Stephen, Moses, St. Matthew (?), Abraham, and St. Paul.

beneath the Cardinal Virtues in a life-size portrait as Gregory IX receiving the code of canon law. No one could have entered this room without being struck by Julius's presence as a patron and as a ruler.

The Portrait of Julius II

Despite the triumphal images of order and control which Raphael produced for Julius II in the Stanza della Segnatura, Julius's hold on the Christian empire was not secure. Toward the end of his reign, papal territories were in revolt, and his absolutist control over the institution of the Church was threatened from within by some cardinals and bishops who wished for shared rule through open councils, leading finally to a movement to depose him. When Raphael painted Julius's portrait (Fig. 7.32), showing the pope with a beard he had grown when the papal city of Bologna declared independence from his rule in 1510, he depicted the pope as a slightly stooped old man, pensively staring into space. The painting functioned as an ex voto for the high altar area of Santa Maria del Popolo, a church built for Julius's uncle, Sixtus IV (see Figs. 6.59 and 6.60) and to which Julius had added a new

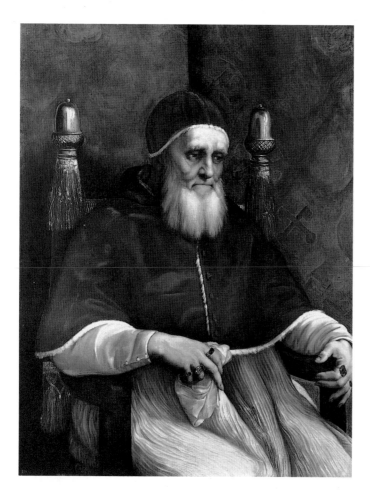

7.32 *Julius II*, c. 1512, commissioned by Julius II for the altar area of Santa Maria del Popolo from RAPHAEL. Oil on panel, 42½ × 31½″ (108 × 80 cm) (National Gallery, London)

finials on the chair back, his costume defines his office and the handkerchief held in his hand refers to the *mappa*, a symbol of office carried by Roman consuls who held power throughout the empire. The representation is both intimate and official.

Roman Civic Imagery

Not all art in the city of Rome was controlled by the papacy. Constant tensions between the Roman civic government and the papacy over control of the city led both bureaucracies to assert their presence on the Capitoline Hill, the traditional seat of Roman civil government. While the popes marked the place with their collections of antique sculpture (see page 320), city authorities evolved a visual vocabulary decidedly distinct from that employed by the papacy. Jacopo Ripanda's (b. Bologna?; active 1490–1516 Rome) frescoes depicting scenes of the Punic Wars in the Palazzo dei Conservatori on the Capitoline Hill are a case in point (Fig. 7.33). Each of the walls of the room in which they are painted retells a story from Livy's history of Rome's war with Carthage. Importantly, the narratives chosen are histories, not mythologies, suggesting a continuous link between the Rome of antiquity and its later governors meeting in this room. Insofar as the frescoes are in a formal seat of civic governance, they use a stately and formal language deriving from Roman sculpture then visible in the city. Even though Ripanda had worked with Pinturicchio (see Fig. 6.70), he avoided the overtly decorative vocabulary of his teacher's painting, instead employing a didactic classicism in some ways appropriate to the illustration of a Roman historian's narrative. The quadriga, for example, is a slightly modified quotation from one of the reliefs of the Arch of Titus, while

choir designed by Bramante. There is even one instance in which the image was placed on the main altar, although it seems more likely to have hung on a nearby pier. The psychological insight of the painting marks a new departure in the history of portraiture, a strangely personal, introspective, and melancholic image for such a public and formal space. Yet Raphael still surrounded Julius with symbols of his power: the papal keys are woven into the brilliant green fabric behind the pope, the della Rovere acorn appears as the

7.33 *Triumph of Rome over Sicily*, 1507–08, commissioned by the Conservators of Rome from JACOPO RIPANDA, Palazzo dei Conservatori, Room of the Punic Wars

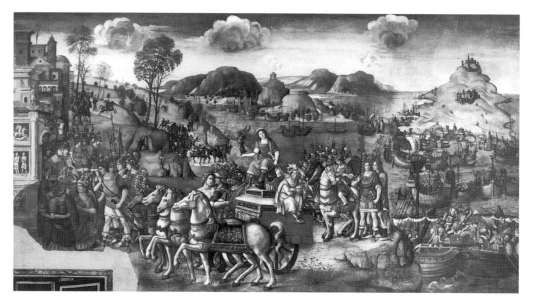

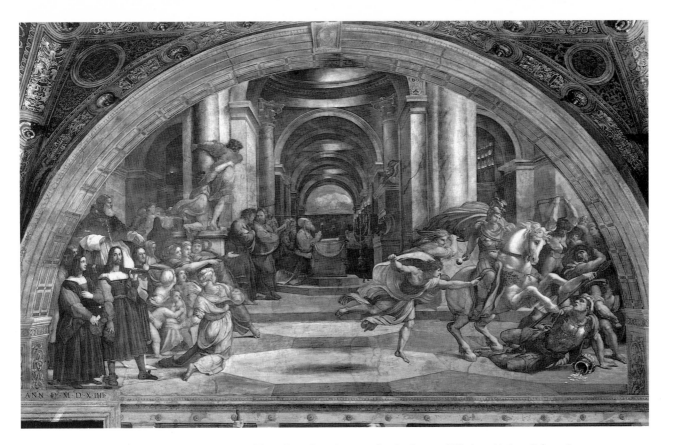

7.34 *Expulsion of Heliodorus*, 1512, commissioned by Julius II from RAPHAEL for the Stanza d'Eliodoro, Vatican Palace, Rome. Fresco, base 21' 8" (6.6 m)

other figures in the painting are direct copies of figures from those antique reliefs and others. It is just this straightforward antiquarianism—unassimilated as it had been in earlier paintings, such as the frescoes for the Sistine Chapel (see Figs. 6.67 and 6.68) and not transformed into new idealized models as contemporaries like Raphael were doing (see Fig. 7.29)—that give these frescoes their curious timelessness. As in other painting of the time, the figures in this fresco spread across a stage apron at the foreground of the composition, while a grand landscape stretches like stage scenery behind them. Yet, in choice of subject matter and in mode of depiction, the *Triumph of Rome over Sicily* provides a telling, albeit brief, moment in the history of Roman art when the civic government asserted its connections to its Roman past and therefore its legitimacy, and did so, moreover, with a style that itself can be said to distinguish the paintings from those commissioned by the papacy.

The Stanza d'Eliodoro

Raphael's invention of a powerful language of personal and institutional leadership in the *Stanza della Segnatura* led to a commission to paint an adjoining room. Containing frescoes on the theme of divine intervention, it is named for the fresco depicting the *Expulsion of Heliodorus* (Fig. 7.34). In this story, from the Second Book

of Maccabees (3:1–33) in the Old Testament, the chancellor of King Seleucus, Heliodorus, was ordered by the king to confiscate the treasure of the Temple in Jerusalem. As he was fleeing with the booty, a mounted horseman and two other figures appeared miraculously and beat him to the ground, thus preserving the Temple treasury intact. Later, the high priest, Onias, seen kneeling in the center background of the fresco, prayed for Heliodorus' recovery. The apparitions reappeared, healing Heliodorus and leading to his belief in the sacredness and inviolate nature of the Temple, here an antetype for the Church. Julius, carried on a papal throne, appears at the left of the painting—a thinly veiled reference to the fate awaiting contemporaries who would despoil the papal territories. The frescoes in the room—all miracle scenes—suggest that Julius, a passive witness to the event, had lost confidence in his power and now had to rely on miraculous divine power to ensure the success of his policies, an idea comparable to the placement of his portrait at Santa Maria del Popolo.

Despite the success of the balanced composition and perfected geometrical order of the Stanza della Segnatura frescoes, the style which they exemplify seems to have been short lived. Although Raphael structured the *Expulsion*, like the paintings in the Stanza della Segnatura, around a single-point perspective system, the composition fragments into three distinct sections, with the critical action of the priest virtually lost in the background because of the welter of figures to the left and right. A number of pictorial curiosities also distinguish the composition from the stately order of the Segnatura frescoes. Heliodorus, fallen at the right of the fresco, and the twisting female figure kneeling in front of Julius's entourage are of a different scale from nearby figures, thus calling attention to themselves and their poses. Heliodorus derives from an antique river god statue, then on the Quirinal Hill, but moved to the Capitoline in 1517 during the time that Raphael served as Prefect of the Antiquities of Rome (1515–1520). The female figure seems to have no role to play in the narrative except to enhance the drama of the moment by her expressive pose. The figure climbing up the wall and clutching the column at the left certainly breaks the decorum of behavior appropriate for a temple. In each case the figure rewards the viewer's own cleverness in recognizing its source in antique art or appreciation of the artist's skill in rendering complex and dramatic forms, issues far removed from the narrative content of the fresco.

Leo X (r. 1513–21)

When Julius died in 1513 he was succeeded by Leo X (Giovanni de' Medici, the son of Lorenzo the Magnificent). Leo completed the Stanza d'Eliodoro and began his own project in another room of the papal apartments. By 1514 Raphael was at work for him in the Stanza dell'Incendio, which takes its name from the painting of *The Fire in the Borgo* (Fig. 7.35) on one of its walls. Each of the walls in this room depicts an event in the life of a previous pope named Leo. In the *Fire* it is Leo IV (r. 847–55), who put out a fire in the area known as the Borgo in front of Old St. Peter's, merely by raising his hand in a gesture of blessing. Once again the clearly defined perspective system disguises the fact that very little in the painting makes logical sense. There are shifts in scale among the figures, the water carrier at the far right could hardly balance the vase on her head if she were in a hurry to get to the fire, the nudity of the male figures on the left seems gratuitous, the man hanging from the wall

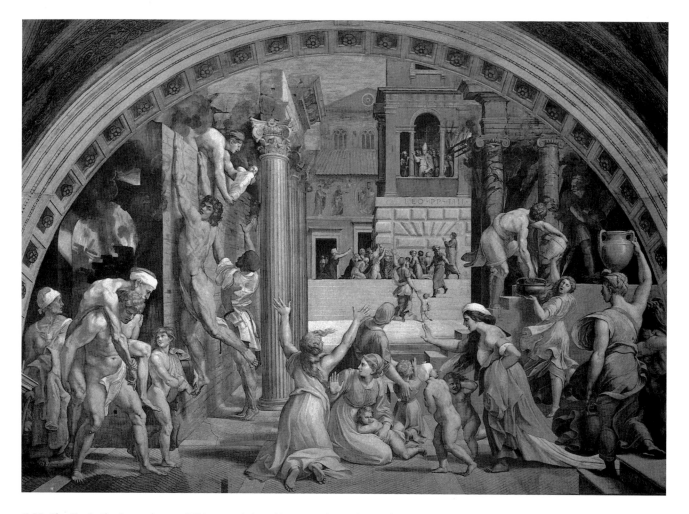

7.35 *The Fire in the Borgo*, begun 1514, commissioned by Leo X from RAPHAEL for the Stanza dell'Incendio, Vatican Palace, Rome. Fresco, base 22′ 1″ (6.73 m)

at the left with all his muscles tensed does so for no reason, since the ground is only a short distance beneath his feet. Leo IV, in the loggia in the distance, is barely visible although he is supposedly the main character in the painting. While tied to the history of the papacy and to its traditional iconography (see Fig. 1.39), this fresco relaxes the narrative focus so that each element in the painting becomes interesting in its own right rather than as a component of the story. Leo X is reputed to have said, "God has given us the papacy, let us enjoy it"; in *The Fire in the Borgo* Raphael provided an essay in visual enjoyment.

The Sistine Tapestries

The compositional oddities of the *Fire* disappear in another commission for Leo X that Raphael worked on at approximately the same time. In a series of cartoons for tapestries for the lower walls of the Sistine Chapel (see Fig. 6.66, which shows the fictive tapestries that then covered the lower walls of the chapel) Raphael used a pictorial decorum that both took into account the official nature of the papal chapel (where Leo himself had been elected pope) and the grand classicism of the frescoes already in the room. The tapestries depict scenes from the lives of Peter and Paul, appropriate for a papal chapel.

They also carry the narrative of the 1481–82 cycle immediately above them (see Fig. 6.68) into the future, giving a completion of the history of mankind begun on the ceiling (see Fig. 7.24) into the early Church and its leadership by Peter. In *The Miraculous Draught of Fishes* (Fig. 7.36), the heroically muscled fishermen at the right make reference to Michelangelo's nudes on the ceiling above and yet are appropriately strong for the labor that they pursue. In fact the tensed musculature is directly responsive to the heavy net loaded with fish that the two men are attempting to lift into the boat. The boatman does suggest a rather self-conscious quotation of an antique river god statue, yet the overall composition of the cartoon is compellingly naturalistic, with an apparently unbroken movement into a deep recessional space that adds a heroic frame to the entire narrative. The two Apostles gesturing toward Christ reveal—as conventional theory since Alberti had postulated—the workings of their minds through the motions of their bodies. Yet the uncertain pose of the standing Apostle suggests the very real precariousness of a person standing in a small boat. Here, where the site demanded grand drama, Raphael brought a dramatic realism to the history of Christ and the Apostles who were, theologically, the predecessors of the pope and the cardinal bishops who met in this building.

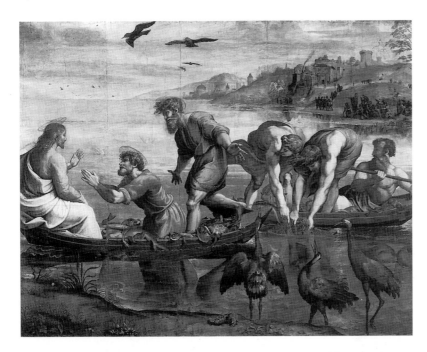

7.36 *The Miraculous Draught of Fishes*, c. 1515–16, commissioned by Leo X from RAPHAEL for the lower walls of the Sistine Chapel. Gouache on paper, later laid on canvas lining, 10′ 5½″ × 13′ 1″ (26.6 × 33.3 cm) (London, Victoria and Albert Museum)

As the tapestries for which these cartoons were designed were woven from behind, the cartoons were themselves created in reverse to accommodate this technical process.

A Suburban Villa

Outside the papal court, fascination with the elegant and mannered style of the later Stanze is evident among the wealthy elite. When Agostino Chigi, a rich Sienese banker, built a palace in an undeveloped area along the Tiber, he intended it as a suburban villa where he and his guests would be free of the formal cares of the city. For a ground-floor loggia facing out into the garden, Chigi commissioned Raphael and his studio to paint an illusionistic arbor through whose fruit- and flower-decorated trellis shines a painted sky, imitating an actual garden bower (Fig. 7.37). Along the length of the ceiling Raphael designed two large painted fields depicting the marriage of Cupid and Psyche and Psyche being received on Mount Olympus as if they were tapestries strung overhead (Fig. 7.38). This lush and seductive arbor is populated with nude figures of gods and goddesses, painted in a cool, classical vocabulary as if they were part of a painted sculptural relief. Many are depicted in suggestive poses that are glossed by the phallic vegetables and opened fruits of the garlands.

The erotic pleasures so vividly suggested in this private palace found another form in a set of erotic drawings by Giulio Romano (1499? Rome–1546

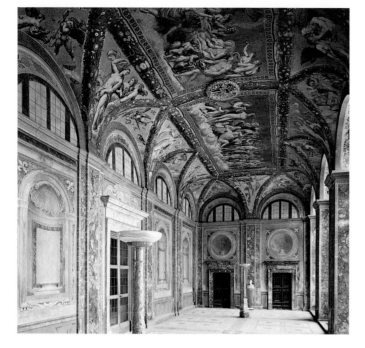

7.37 Loggia of Psyche, view, 1518–19, commissioned by Agostino Chigi from RAPHAEL and his studio for the Villa Farnesina (formerly Villa Chigi), Rome. Fresco

Mantua), then working in Raphael's studio and soon to take over his master's shop when Raphael died. Known as *I Modi* ("The Positions"), they were engraved by Marc'Antonio Raimondi (1470/82 Argini–1527 Rome) (Fig. 7.39). Raimondi established an active engraving school in Rome and popularized the art of his contemporaries in the print medium. His engravings of *I Modi*

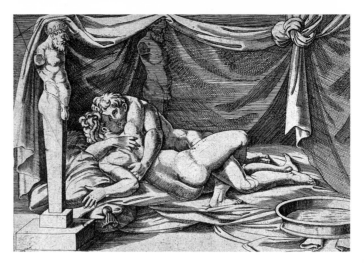

7.39 *I Modi*, c. 1517, drawn by GIULIO ROMANO and engraved by MARC'ANTONIO RAIMONDI (© British Museum, London)

were not the only prints of this type in Rome at the time, but these acrobatic variations of positions for sexual intercourse landed the engraver in jail, even in the sybaritic environment of Leo's Rome. The scopophilic pleasures of the print were apparently condemned not simply because of the subject's pornographic nature, but because they presumably extended such imagery to an audience outside the narrow circle of court intimates. These courtiers would know that the imagery derived from antique texts and images, particularly from ancient coins (*spintria*) that depict sexual activity, some of which Giulio Romano may have owned. So sexual pleasure could be overlaid with a veneer of classical, humanistic scholarship.

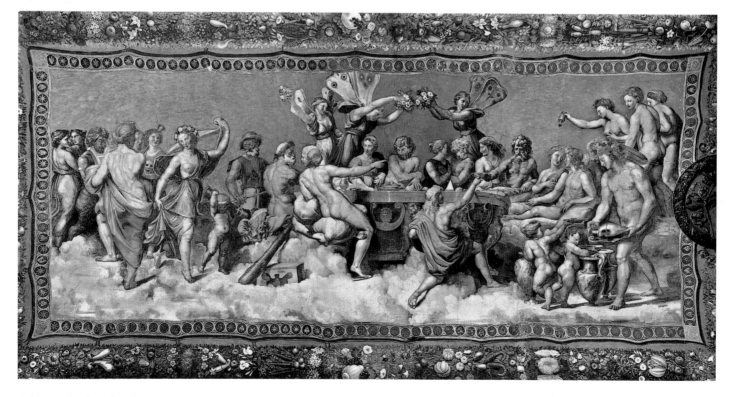

7.38 Loggia of Psyche, detail showing arbor and the *Marriage of Cupid and Psyche* from the western half of the ceiling, 1518–19, commissioned by Agostino Chigi from RAPHAEL and his studio for the Villa Farnesina, Rome. Fresco

Nonetheless Raphael's transformation of Chigi's garden loggia into Olympus created an environment of luxury and license for the Sienese banker, his mistress, and his guests unmatched in the city. For a patron whose gestures of grandeur included having served a banquet on gold plate only to toss the gold dishes out of the window into the Tiber as a demonstration of his enormous wealth (although servants were stationed below to retrieve the plate), Raphael was obviously challenged to provide a loggia of fanciful illusionism, classical learning, and erotic pleasure.

Raphael and Michelangelo

In 1518 Cardinal Giulio de' Medici ordered two paintings for the cathedral of Narbonne, France, where he was bishop. This commission for Raphael's *Transfiguration*

(Fig. 7.40) and *The Raising of Lazarus* (Fig. 7.41) by Sebastiano del Piombo (Sebastiano Luciani; c. 1485 Venice–1547 Rome) renewed the competition between Raphael and Michelangelo initiated by Julius II a decade earlier in the Stanze and the Sistine Chapel since Michelangelo apparently provided drawings as well as advice for Sebastiano's painting, as he did on numerous other occasions to help his friend. Although he was in Florence working for the Medici, Michelangelo's canny intervention in Sebastiano's commission allowed him to maintain an active presence in Rome where Raphael was the dominating artist in papal circles. Thus although Cardinal Giulio established the project as a competition between Raphael and Sebastiano, he undoubtedly knew that he would be engaging the talents of Michelangelo as well. Collaboration was every bit as much a part of artistic practice as competition.

Sebastiano's painting shows Lazarus removing the winding sheets from his body after Christ, still gesturing at the center of the painting, has miraculously brought him

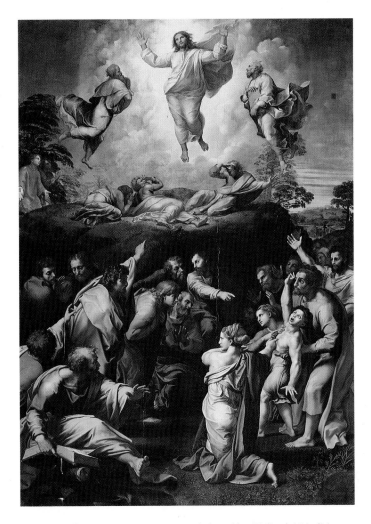

7.40 *Transfiguration*, 1518–20, commissioned by Giulio de' Medici (later Clement VII) from RAPHAEL for Narbonne Cathedral, where he was bishop. Oil on panel, 13' 5½" × 9' 2" (4.1 × 2.79 m) (Musei Vaticani, Rome)

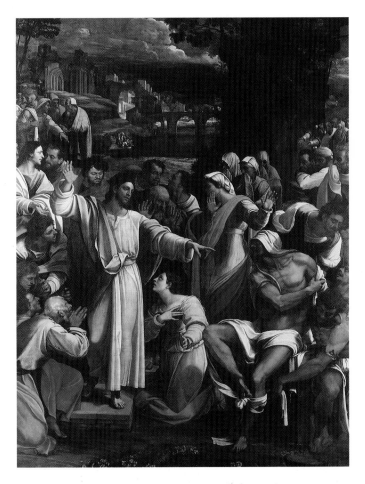

7.41 *The Raising of Lazarus*, 1517–19, commissioned by Giulio de' Medici (later Clement VII) from SEBASTIANO DEL PIOMBO for Narbonne Cathedral. Oil on canvas, 12' 6" × 9' 6" (3.81 × 2.9 m) (National Gallery, London)

back to life. Raphael's painting depicts two distinct but consecutive biblical narratives: one in which Moses and Elijah miraculously appear with the transfigured Christ, witnessed by Peter, James, and John, and a subsequent episode in which the other Apostles, failing to cure a boy possessed by demons, await the return of Christ from the mountain above (Matthew 17:1–20). Giulio Romano, Raphael's heir, may have painted some of the figures in the lower background area of the *Transfiguration* since the painting was apparently not finished when Raphael died in 1520. The importance of the painting in Raphael's career was apparently recognized immediately since it was placed on Raphael's tomb in the Pantheon at the time of his burial.

These two paintings exemplify many of the artistic currents in Rome at the time of their commissioning and suggest that an integration of new ideas from a variety of sources had been achieved. Since being cleaned, the paintings indicate that the brilliant coloring of the Sistine ceiling had finally had an impact on panel painting. The kneeling woman at the foreground of the *Transfiguration* (virtually a mirror image of the comparable figure in Raphael's *Expulsion of Heliodorus*; see Fig. 7.34) wears an icy pink tunic whose sash uses a changeable color technique. Each of the major figures is clothed in a bright color, perhaps to respond to the large size of the painting. Both Sebastiano, who was Venetian, having been trained in the shop of Giovanni Bellini, and Raphael use typically Venetian **chiaroscuro** techniques which add luminous effects to the surface and enhance the sense of changing atmospheric conditions in the background. Both the possessed boy and Lazarus have the heavy musculature characteristic of **Hellenistic** sculpture such as the *Laocoön* and of Michelangelo's figures. The animated gesturing of the figures in each painting is thrown into sharp relief by being highlighted against a dark ground. Active poses are given added tension because of the compacted space in which they are placed. Pose, highlighting, and gesture enhance figural motion throughout the paintings.

Clement VII (r. 1523–34)

The stylistic developments so notable in the *Transfiguration* and the *Raising of Lazarus* were cut short in Rome by a number of historical events. Raphael died in 1520, leaving Giulio Romano in charge of his studio; four years later Giulio left Rome for Mantua. Leonardo, who had been a ghostly and idiosyncratic presence in the court of Leo X from 1513 to 1516, where he apparently involved himself predominantly with theater and scientific investigations, had moved to France, where he died in 1519. Michelangelo had left Rome for Florence, where he was working on Medici commissions at San Lorenzo. And Bramante, who had provided Julius II with plans with an architectural vocabulary for a Roman renewal, had died in 1514. Artists and artistic personalities alone, however, are not the sole engines driving artistic development.

When Leo X died in 1521 he was succeeded by a Dutch cardinal who took the name Adrian VI (r. 1522–23). Adrian began a series of long-overdue reforms in the government of the Church and in the morals of the papal court. These reforms led to a drastic reduction of artistic patronage—seen as the manifestation of an extravagant court—at just the time that a younger group of artists such as Rosso Fiorentino and Parmigianino (Girolamo Francesco Maria Mazzola; 1503 Parma–1540 Casalmaggiore) had come to Rome from Florence and Parma respectively, and were promising to develop a new International Style there. By the time of Adrian's short reign, Protestant reformers, led by the German monk Martin Luther, had issued a serious challenge to the Church that was to lead to a split in Western Christendom. Thus, at the very time that the boundaries of the Church had expanded to encompass newly explored territories in the Americas and in Asia, its center began to collapse.

Although there was loud rejoicing when Giulio de' Medici became pope as Clement VII in 1523, he was never able, in his eleven-year reign, to reinstitute the impressive scale of patronage of Julius II and Leo X. The decline of the myth of Rome's sacrosanctity in the European imagination was given concrete expression in 1527 when the troops of the Hapsburg emperor Charles V (1500–58), ostensibly in Italy to fight the French, sacked the city and despoiled many of its most hallowed sites. Given the short period of time between Clement's accession to the office of the papacy and the Sack as well as the destruction of artists' workshops by the German soldiers, it is not surprising that little concrete evidence remains for artistic activity in Rome during the early years of Clement's reign. The *Dead Christ* (Fig. 7.42) by Rosso Fiorentino is one of the few paintings that can be assigned with any security to this period. Painted for Lorenzo Tornabuoni, a relative of the pope who in 1523 or 1524 had been made bishop of Sansepolcro (meaning "Holy Sepulchre," thus perhaps explaining its subject matter), the painting shows a nude dead Christ flanked by angels. Symbols of the passion lie on the foreground step and illusionistically extend into space. The creamy expanse of Christ's sagging body—modeled in part on one of the sons in the antique statue group of the *Laocoön* in the papal collections since 1506—glows in the sharp light coming in from the left; its details—the red hair, the disembodied hand touching the wound in his side, the pubic hair—only enhance the sensuality of the figure. The sharp contrasting colors of the

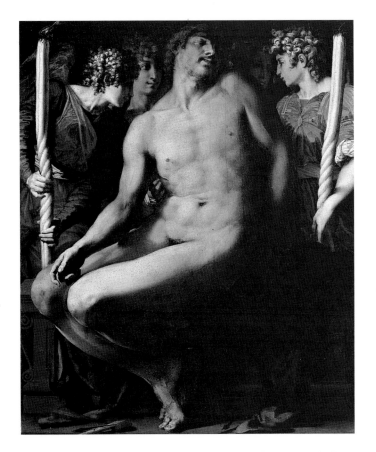

7.42 *Dead Christ*, c. 1524–27, commissioned by Bishop Leonardo di Lorenzo Tornabuoni probably for his cathedral church at Sansepolcro, from ROSSO FIORENTINO. Oil on panel, 52½ × 41″ (133.5 × 104.1 cm) (Museum of Fine Arts, Boston)

At the time of the Sack of Rome in 1527 Rosso apparently left this painting with the Franciscan nuns of the church of San Lorenzo in Panisperna for safe-keeping. Immediately after the Sack, Rosso was imprisoned in the palace of Cardinal della Valle. When he subsequently tried to retrieve the painting the nuns at first refused to give it up. Sometime shortly afterward it entered into a private collection and never served as an altarpiece, although that was its original purpose.

angels' clothing—deep red, green, and white on the left angel and orange, blue, and violet on the right—play against the white candles they hold and their golden corkscrew curls are reminiscent of the hair of the Sistine Ceiling nudes (see Fig. 7.24). The soft eroticism of the painting suggests that imagery in the Clementine court would have returned to the refined and charged sensibilities of Leonine Rome, a deliberate rejection of the austerities under Adrian VI. The Sack all too quickly put an end to this style of painting in Rome, leaving artists like Rosso a hostage to German troops and causing them eventually to abandon the city that had only recently promised extraordinary new patronage possibilities.

Despite the sacrilege of the Sack, Clement crowned Charles Holy Roman Emperor in Bologna in 1530 and established improved relations between the papacy and some European rulers. Perhaps inevitably, he paid relatively little attention to artistic patronage in Rome, though he endowed his own city, Florence, with two splendid commissions at San Lorenzo (see Figs. 7.46–7.48). Clement seemed unable to define a new vision of the papacy, and the revival of Roman art thus had to wait for his successor.

Florence II: Return of the Medici

The Medici had returned to power in Florence in 1512. Even with French support, the new Florentine Republic was unable to withstand the combined opposition of the papacy and its allies who supported the Medici. A Spanish army forced the Republic to submit to Medici rule, first to Piero the Unfortunate's brother Giuliano and then, a year later, to his son Lorenzo. The Medici's position in the city was guaranteed when, as we have seen, Giovanni de' Medici, the second son of Lorenzo the Magnificent, became pope in 1513. As Leo X, he brought the full weight (and wealth) of the papacy to bear on their control of Florence.

Mannerism

Not surprisingly, the change in the power structure in Florence to a *de facto* principate led in time to a new style in the visual arts. The shift was caused partly by the fact that the three greatest exponents of the classicizing style in early sixteenth-century painting had left Florence—Leonardo in 1506, Michelangelo and Raphael in 1508. The new style, commonly called Mannerism (after *maniera*, "manner" or "style"), manifested itself in painting and sculpture, and less so in architecture. It lasted until the end of the century, spreading from Florence and Rome to other parts of Italy and beyond the Alps.

The character and meaning of the style and the reasons for its evolution have aroused much scholarly debate. Some of its more obvious stylistic aspects, however, can be discerned rather quickly by comparing two paintings: the *Madonna of the Harpies* (Fig. 7.43) by Andrea del Sarto (Andrea d'Agnolo; 1486 Florence–1530 Florence) and the *Visdomini Altarpiece* (Fig. 7.44) by Jacopo Pontormo (Jacopo Carucci; 1494 Pontormo–1557 Florence). Andrea probably trained with the quirky painter Piero di Cosimo, though his works reveal the varied influences of Leonardo, Raphael, Michelangelo, and Fra Bartolomeo. Pontormo was Sarto's student (and may also have studied with Leonardo), but his painting deviates noticeably from the classicizing ideals that Sarto had helped to establish as a norm in Florence and which he practiced virtually all of his life. In the *Madonna of the Harpies*, the simple *sacra conversazione* is set within a severe architecture broken only by the harpies at the corners of the Virgin's pedestal. The niche behind the Virgin is shadowed to suggest depth. St. Francis looks out at the left and St. John the Evangelist at the right. Each figure stands in a pose that suggests imminent movement, while at the same time the figures are given stability by the architecture behind them. The bright, fully saturated primary colors of the drapery give each of the figures an independent presence within the overall compositional structure.

In the *Visdomini Altarpiece* Pontormo flattened the space. Its shallowness is emphasized by his deployment of the figures across the picture plane. There is no overlap to suggest spatial recession, but, rather, a vertical space with figures appearing to be above rather than behind one another in the composition. If the kneeling St. Francis at the right were to stand, he would be considerably taller than the figure next to him—a drastic inconsistency of scale. None of the figures seems to focus within the composition. While a viewer looks in toward the figures they look outward in different directions, scattering any possible focus in several directions at once. Yet Pontormo simultaneously indicated that he knew the "rules" of good painting. The Virgin is on a central axis and the figures create a carefully structured and stable dia-

mond shape in the center of the composition (although there is nothing at the center of that shape). Almost as a jest, the small putti and the child Jesus and John the Baptist playfully betray a knowledge of *contrapposto* figural structure; by contrast all the adult male figures are flattened, with areas of possible spatial recession and volume—such as overlapping legs or twisting shoulders—deliberately repressed by drapery or impenetrable shadow.

Although there is little disagreement about the formal organization of these paintings, interpretation of the style of a work like the *Visdomini Altarpiece* remains one of the most contested areas within art history. The stylistic properties evident in Pontormo's *Visdomini Altarpiece* could be read simply as attempts on the part of a new generation of painters to distinguish, and to distance, themselves from the rules of classicism which had so carefully and painstakingly been developed in painting practice by Leonardo and other artists, including Pontormo's own teacher, Andrea del Sarto. Thus "anti-classicism" or a deliberate breaking of rules and self-conscious opposition to the stylistic properties of classicism would be a characteristic of this new style. Such an anti-classicism, if that is what it really is, must be understood in terms of artistic practice of the early sixteenth century in Florence and not as a denial of the art of classical antiquity,

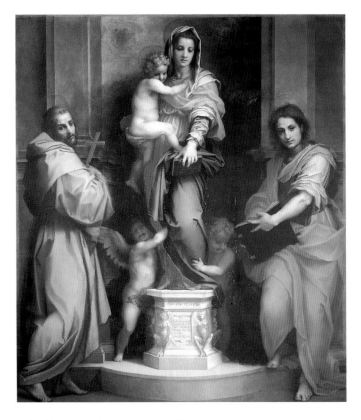

7.43 *Madonna of the Harpies*, 1517, commissioned from ANDREA DEL SARTO for the high altar of San Francesco, Florence. Oil on panel, 6′ 9½″ × 5′ 10″ (2.07 × 1.78 m) (Galleria degli Uffizi, Florence)

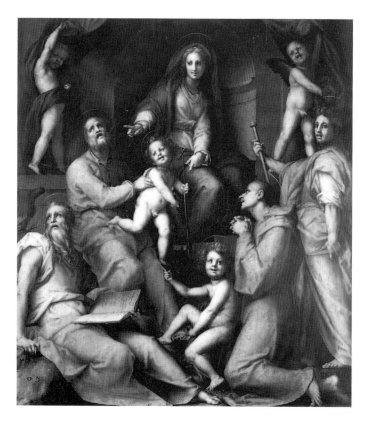

7.44 *Visdomini Altarpiece*, 1518, commissioned by Francesco di Giovanni Pucci from JACOPO PONTORMO for San Michele in Visdomini, Florence. Oil on paper, 7′ × 6′ 1″ (2.13 × 1.85 m)

for Pontormo seems to be quoting the head of the antique statue *Laocoön* in the figure second from the left, thus maintaining definitive references to ancient art. Pontormo's self-consciousness in the manipulation of forms and in inverting accepted rules in the *Visdomini Altarpiece* emphasizes artifice at the expense of a clear reading of the subject matter of the painting, again a change from the classical style. This mannered style calling attention to the hand of the artist provides a source for the term *maniera* whose root word in Italian is the same as hand (*mano*).

Pontormo's commission from Ludovico di Gino Capponi marks one of the few extant decorative ensembles of early Mannerism (Fig. 7.45). The chapel itself was

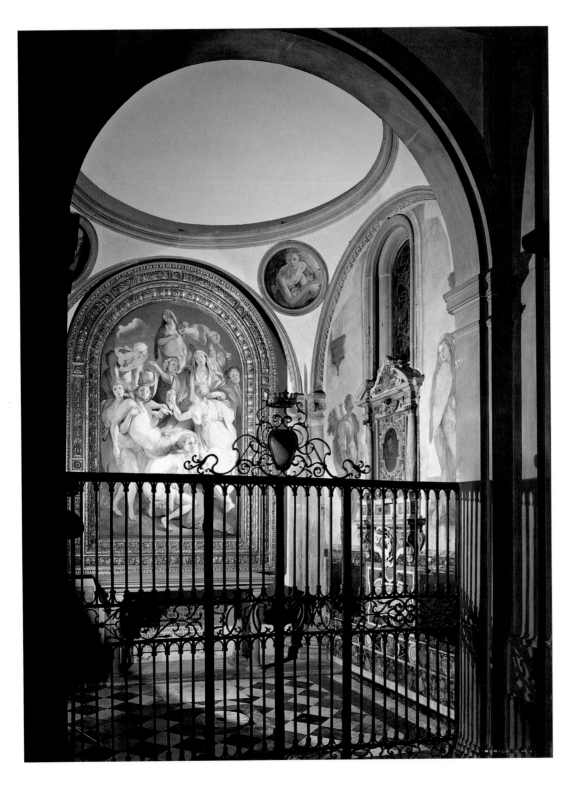

7.45 *Capponi Chapel*, 1525–8, commissioned by Ludovico di Gino Capponi from JACOPO PONTORMO, Santa Felicità, Florence

The commission included a now lost fresco in the ceiling of God the Father, pendentive roundels of the four Evangelists (with assistance from Agnolo Bronzino), a stained-glass window by Guillaume de Marcillat, the *Entombment* altarpiece (oil and tempera on panel, 10′ 3″ × 6′ 4″ [3.1 × 1.9 m]), and a fresco of the *Annunciation*.

built against the entrance wall of the convent church of Santa Felicità by Brunelleschi for the Barbadori family at the beginning of the fifteenth century. When Capponi acquired the space in 1525 as a funerary chapel for himself and his male heirs he retained a reference to the earlier dedication to the Annunciation with frescoes of that subject on the window wall. An inscription also indicates a dedication to "pietà," suggesting not only piety but the subject of Pontormo's altarpiece: the dead Christ in the company of his mother and other mourners (see Fig. 6.73). If this is an *Entombment*—the precise title of the work is contested by art historians—it is curiously dissociated from identifying elements of the historical narrative, unlike Raphael's painting of this subject (see Fig. 7.12), in which Golgotha is shown in the distance and the rock tomb is indicated at the left. In the Capponi Chapel those narrative elements appear in a separate stained-glass window on the wall over the *Annunciation*. In the altarpiece itself both the Virgin, larger in size than any other figure in the painting and captivating in her cascading blue drapery, and the coolly liquid figure of the dead Christ command attention as the dedications of the chapel would demand.

Yet these very figures are embedded in a welter of billowing drapery and empty hand gestures, which make any single focus impossible. The color, deriving in part from the Sistine Ceiling (especially in the shot hues of the foreground figure), also disperses attention in its brilliant areas of pink against blue, even though the light that spotlights the figures suggests that it comes from the window of the chapel itself—and perhaps from the now lost figure of God the Father in the dome of the chapel. The space of the painting, like the earlier *Visdomini Altarpiece*, is sharply vertical, with no indication of where the background figures are standing, although the overall composition and figural poses take into account the semicircular form of the upper part of the painting.

While the individual details of the painting are compelling in their realistic depiction of form and volume, the figures are both idealized in their simplified volumes and gracefully attenuated both at their extremities and in their overall proportions. This is perhaps most evident in the Virgin, whose legs (at the center of the composition), hands, and head are thinned in comparison with the mass of her body. Curious impossibilities occur throughout the painting: it is difficult, for example, to understand how the Virgin's legs, shown on a diagonal, connect to her torso, shown parallel to the picture plane, or how the kneeling male figure in the foreground could possibly support a dead body, balletically positioned as he is on his toes, or how the male figure on the left can support that same dead body apparently with one hand, again an exploration of weight and support quite contrary to

Raphael's *Entombment*. The perplexing aspects of the painting are nowhere more evident than in the left hand of Christ, which seems to be held out by two disembodied hands. These hands apparently belong to a figure whose head is immediately above the head of Christ, but who is all but indistinguishable from the overall blue coloration of the surrounding figures and the consciously showy patterns of drapery that flow through the painting; there seems, furthermore, to be little actual space for any body beneath that head.

In this work Pontormo transformed the devotional altarpiece into a spasm of emotional reactions to the event of Christ's death. Depicted through the dramatic gestures of the bodies and through the icy brilliance of the intensely contrasted colors, this piety is clearly directed outward by the kneeling foreground male, who looks pointedly out of the painting in a gaze of communion with the viewer. Without undermining the purpose of the altarpiece as an incentive to piety, Pontormo has both upped its emotional charge and clothed it with an elegance that responds to the idealizations of the previous generation of painters and the changing social needs of the patron.

An interpretation based on the concept of a reaction "against" the prevailing classicizing style is but one possible way to read Mannerism. It isolates the shift in style obvious in Pontormo's painting within the formal aspects of the work and ignores the context in which the work was created. Since the classical style had been employed as the language of the republic after 1494 it would have been inappropriate for the newly restituted Medici rule after 1512 and their deliberate dismantling of the republic. Mannerism provided the language for the emerging social aristocracy under the Medici in Florence.

Yet even within the self-conscious artifice of Mannerism there are characteristics suggesting a development of the classicizing tradition rather than a mere rejection of it. From Leonardo onward, painters seemed to have realized that regardless of how realistically they were able to reconstruct the physical forms of nature, they could never capture the critical element of motion. The curiously slipping poses of Pontormo's figures and their unstable positions are formal means of suggesting incipient movement, analogous to the contorted figures in Leonardo's and Michelangelo's fresco drawings for the Palazzo della Signoria Battle paintings.

Michelangelo and the Medici

When Pope Leo X (Giovanni de' Medici; 1475–1521) entered Florence in triumph in 1515, he and his cousin Giulio (later Pope Clement VII) initiated a series of commissions at San Lorenzo which built upon the projects of their Medici ancestors at that church. The New Sacristy, now generally known as the Medici Chapel (Figs. 7.46 and 7.47), was designed as a burial pantheon for the Medici family (see genealogical chart, page 486), especially for the brothers Lorenzo the Magnificent (Leo X's father) and Giuliano (Cardinal Giulio's father), and also for Giuliano, Duke of Nemours (1478–1516; Leo's brother), and Lorenzo, Duke of Urbino (1492–1519; Piero di Lorenzo's son). Michelangelo's New Sacristy was designed to mirror Brunelleschi's Old Sacristy (see Fig. 5.9). Yet within these constraints, Michelangelo provided new expressive possibilities for architecture. Where Brunelleschi's decorative elements respected the plane of the wall, Michelangelo transformed surface into sculpture. The structural integrity of the space is enhanced visually by the framework of gray *pietra serena* stone outlining the main architectural features. Within this ordering system Michelangelo pushed the central units of the side walls back into tripartite marble triumphal arches and forward with tombs and sculpture, which, if executed as planned, would have included reclining river gods on the floor in front of the sarcophagi. Drawings for a Resurrection indicate that Michelangelo also intended

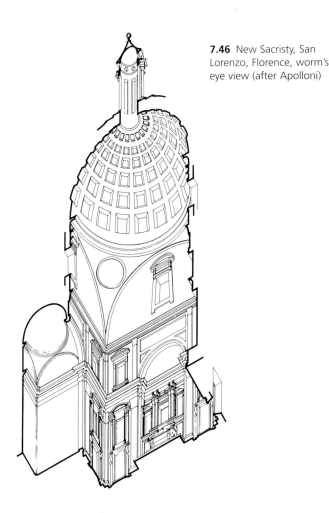

7.46 New Sacristy, San Lorenzo, Florence, worm's eye view (after Apolloni)

to fill the lunettes over the tombs with frescoes. The coffered ceiling was painted by Giovanni da Udine (1487 Udine–1564 Rome), Raphael's chief decorative assistant at the Vatican Palace. Thus the room was envisaged as an integrated work of painting, sculpture, and architecture, thus giving the coloristic effects of earlier non-Florentine renditions of the Old Sacristy (the Portinari Chapel in Milan, for example; see Fig. 6.80) an only slightly more Florentine cast.

The tombs of the two dukes show an active Giuliano and a contemplative Lorenzo, both turning away from the altar to face the wall where their forebears Lorenzo the Magnificent and his brother were to be buried in a double tomb (unfortunately never built). Thus the dukes would have directed attention to their ancestors, and also to the Virgin and Child, now provisionally installed on that wall—the traditional fusion of devotional and familial images. But Michelangelo endowed the chapel with allegorical complexities well beyond any funerary monument then existing in Florence. The four river gods projected for the base of the tombs were to represent the four rivers of eternal Paradise, while the allegorical figures of Dusk and Dawn on the sarcophagus of Duke Lorenzo and Night and Day on the sarcophagus of Duke Giuliano represent diurnal time. Thus the chapel's iconography was to embrace issues of time and immortality. The centralized plan of a martyrial structure and the dome with which it is crowned imply both Christian resurrection and the cosmological order under the Medici princes.

If there are competing interpretations of Mannerism in painting there is little coherent discussion of what would constitute a definition of Mannerism in architecture. Although Michelangelo's architecture at San Lorenzo is often called Mannerist, this designation is made solely on the basis of its individual formal components rather than on the overall structure, thus seriously compromising the applicability of the term.

Michelangelo was undoubtedly boldly inventive in his manipulation of canonic forms in the New Sacristy. The tabernacle niches over the doors of the room are good examples as they are the largest architectural forms in the chapel and overwhelm the doors beneath them in scale. The segmental pediment extends so far out from the wall that its support by the thin pilasters is compromised; at the same time its base rests on a line with the bases of the Corinthian *pietra serena* capitals, giving it visual stability within the overall structure of the room. These pediments have interrupted bases and their arcs are broken, undermining their visual power as a capping architectural form. However a rectangular niche intrudes into the pediment and spills into its sides, supporting the pediment at just the point where it breaks forward and creating a richly textured movement both into and out from the wall. Here

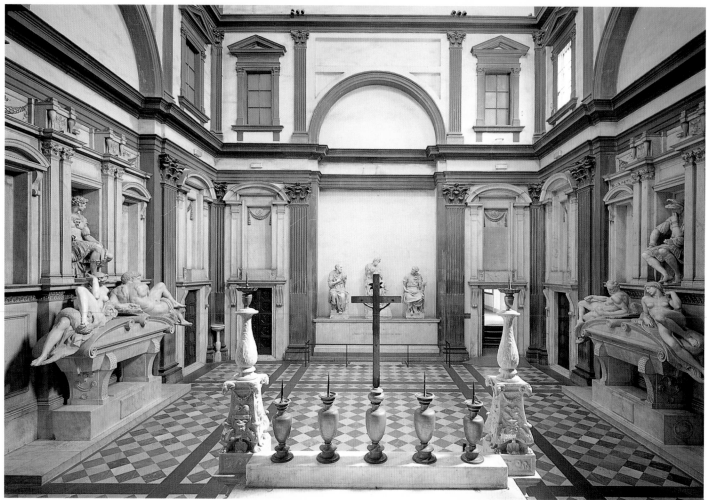

7.47 New Sacristy (also known as the Medici Chapel), San Lorenzo, Florence, 1519–34, commissioned by Leo X and Giulio de' Medici from MICHELANGELO as a funerary chapel for their fathers and for recently deceased members of their family who had played leadership roles in restoring Medici power in Florence; left unfinished when Michelangelo moved to Rome in 1534

The photograph is taken from the position of the priest celebrating mass at the altar of the Chapel.

as in other places in the chapel no single architectural unit functions as a discrete form but interacts in a lively manner with adjacent forms, tying the entire surface of the wall together. Although each form—niche, tabernacle, pediment—echoes canonic structures, none falls comfortably within convention.

If willful manipulation of classical form were enough for a definition of Mannerism, then these tabernacles would qualify for placement within that stylistic category. But just as such willfulness is not sufficient to provide a convincing definition for Mannerism in painting, it is also not adequate for designating the New Sacristy as Mannerist architecture. Regardless of how playful Michelangelo may have been with individual architectural forms, he was also conscious of the overall space of the room and of the commemorative and devotional practices which took place there. Thus had the chapel been completed, the priest at the altar would have stood on axis with the Virgin and Child on the opposite wall and would have been able to see the tombs of all four of the Medici family members for whom he was praying. The two Medici dukes on the side

walls would have emphasized the focal point of the devotions by their gaze toward the image of the Virgin and Child. The clarity of this visual order precludes a description of the space simply as Mannerist.

The Laurentian Library Michelangelo experimented even more boldly with architectural form in the vestibule (*ricetto*) of the Laurentian Library (Fig. 7.48). Giulio de' Medici commissioned the library complex when he rose to the papacy as Clement VII in 1523, most likely as a way to leave his own imprint on the fabric of San Lorenzo. The library with its long reading room and vestibule was built over the pre-existing cloister of San Lorenzo to house the enormous book and manuscript collection of the Medici family and to provide a place for study.

Michelangelo used the same skeletal membering of gray *pietra serena* stone against a painted off-white stucco in the vestibule that had characterized building at San Lorenzo since the beginning of the Brunelleschian plan at the start of the fifteenth century. He originally planned a glass ceiling for the room, but the pope complained it would be impossible to keep clean. Michelangelo clearly intended that the room be a light-filled and pleasant environment, complemented by the cleverness of the architecture. Paired columns are atypically recessed in the walls where they actually function as weight-bearing elements and allow Michelangelo to thin the wall and lessen its weight so that the earlier walls beneath would support the room. In the corners of the room Michelangelo bundled the energies of the columns by placing a pier between them which reads as a reverse corner. The pilasters of the wall tabernacles taper downward, again providing an atypical architectural language, although from the space below their tapering is optically corrected.

The staircase leading from the vestibule to the library reading room a story above nearly fills the entire space of the room and pressures the remaining space outward against the walls. A number of drawings (see Fig. 33) indicate that Michelangelo developed the plan for this staircase through a series of designs, beginning with a simple double staircase extending left and right along the side walls from the library door to the complex one which today spills into the space of the room. Since this room was also left unfinished when Michelangelo left for Rome in 1534 the stairs were built from a model which he later sent back to Florence. The staircase of the vestibule provides a dramatic entrance to the library and is the first of its kind in the early modern period. Had it been built out of rich walnut, as early designs seem to indicate, it would have provided a warm coloristic link to the wooden desks, intricately coffered ceiling, and inlaid terracotta floor of the reading room just beyond.

The stairwell is trapezoidal in overall form so that it creates a visual perspective towards the entrance of the library. Each of the steps in the central flight of stairs bulges forward at the center, setting up a contrary slow flowing movement toward the bottom of the stairs. Small

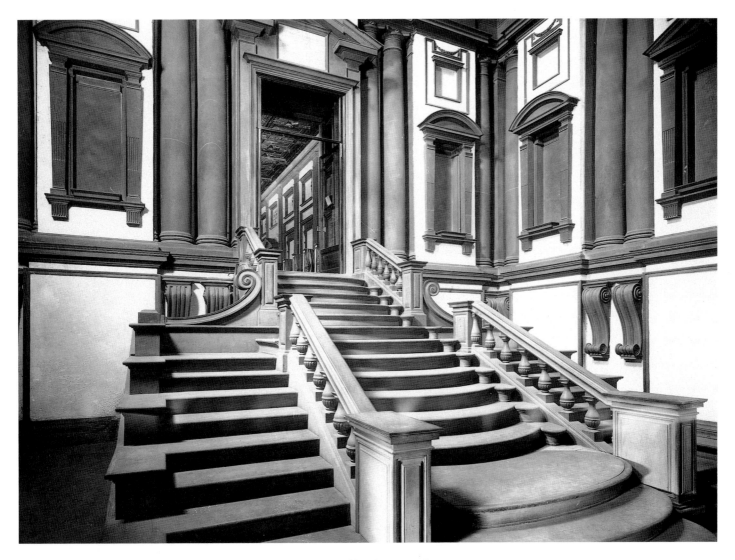

7.48 Laurentian Library, San Lorenzo, Florence, 1523–59, commissioned by Clement VII from MICHELANGELO

sworls are carved into the ends of the central stairs, adding to their organic, sculptural quality, but also making it difficult to walk at the edges of the staircase where the balustrade would offer some support. The connection of the side stairs to the central flight of steps is screened by the balustrade, making them independent units whose bordering podia double as seats and disguising the fact that there are ten risers on the central flight and eleven on the side stairs to reach the same platform two-thirds of the way up the stairwell.

Although every unit in the vestibule of the Laurentian Library has been imaginatively reinvented, providing diversion for the readers coming from the serene and serious space of the reading room, the staircase focuses the viewer's attention on the door to the reading room and access to the library. From the top of the stairs looking back into the vestibule the viewer is at a level with the niches whose forms, despite their innovations, are simple and unbroken, unlike the tabernacles of the Medici Chapel, and whose sobriety befits the seriousness of the study taking place in the reading room behind. Clearly Michelangelo responded to the complex needs of the library spaces—for serious study and for respite, for grand entrance and for serene and light-filled study space—and united them in an environment in which the viewer is conscious of purpose and direction, despite the witty play of form along the way. For Michelangelo wit was a form of intelligence and his architecture a visual response to the high seriousness of the library.

Public Sculpture

When the Medici returned to Florence in 1512 they quickly realized that they had to overcome the very powerful and successful visual propaganda that the Republic had initiated. Thus, with clear understanding of the new political order, the Signoria revoked all laws passed since 1494 and aborted the outstanding artistic commissions that had been undertaken by the Republic, most notably the projects undertaken for the Hall of the Great Council (see Figs. 7.5, 7.7, 7.8). In fact, in that case, the Medici ordered that the elaborately carved and very expensive wooden benches already made for the new Council Hall be burned, in an attempt to erase the memory of the recent Republic. Medici awareness of the power of earlier commissions in the public imagination was evident in their response to Baccio Bandinelli's (Bartolomeo Bandinelli; 1493 Gaiole in Chianti–1560 Florence) suggestion that they replace Donatello's bronze *David* (see Fig. 5.17) with a new sculpture of the same subject for the courtyard of the Medici Palace. Donatello's figure had been taken by the Signoria to the courtyard of the Palazzo della Signoria

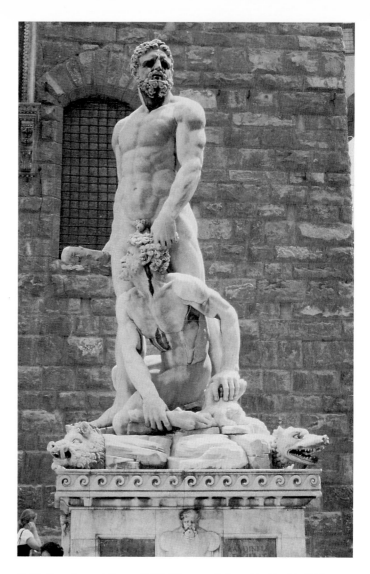

7.49 *Hercules and Cacus*, 1525–34, commissioned by the Medici from BACCIO BANDINELLI for the Piazza della Signoria, Florence. Marble, height 16' 3" (4.96 m)

in 1495, where it became a symbol for the Republic's victory over Medici tyranny and thus a loaded political image. Cardinal Giulio de' Medici, the illegitimate son of Giuliano de' Medici (who had been assassinated in the Pazzi Conspiracy of 1478), refused the suggestion of a David. Instead he commissioned Bandinelli (whose father had been a goldsmith in the Medici employ, thus giving him an opening wedge into Medici employment) to carve an Orpheus for the courtyard (see Fig. 5.15). Given the interest in music of Pope Leo X, the family's most eminent member, Orpheus was a reasonable choice of subject since his return from the Underworld also served as a fitting metaphor for Medici return to power. But importantly, Orpheus could not be associated with earlier public sculpture so the Medici could not be accused of placing a civic image within their private dwelling.

The same is not true of the commission for Bandinelli's *Hercules and Cacus* (Fig. 7.49). Originally the commission for this colossal statue had been given by the

Gonfaloniere of the Republic to Michelangelo in 1508 as a companion piece to his *David*, thus making overt the Hercules iconography that Michelangelo had so carefully built into his earlier figure. The block from which the statue was to be carved was not delivered until 1525, however. At that time the Medici assumed the commission and gave it to Bandinelli rather than Michelangelo, even though Michelangelo was then in their employ. When the Medici again fell from power briefly between 1527 and 1530, Michelangelo was once more asked by the renewed republican government to take over the carving of the stone. During this time Bandinelli traveled to Genoa to work for Andrea Doria (see Fig. 7.78), giving clear indication that he was so closely associated with the Medici family that it would be unwise—not to say unprofitable—to remain in Florence. But when the Medici returned to power in 1530 they returned the project to Bandinelli, who had by then been commissioned to make the tombs (now in Santa Maria sopra Minerva in Rome) for the two Medici popes, Leo X and Clement VII.

Hercules and Cacus was put in place in 1534 to the right side of the door of the Palazzo della Signoria. This event marked the beginning of Medici transformation of the Piazza della Signoria and the Palazzo itself into a family site by appropriating civic symbols such as the *Hercules* as their own. Indebted to extant colossal Roman sculpture such as the *Horse Tamers* in Rome, Bandinelli's *Hercules* seems both to claim an ancient precedent of greatness and imperial patronage and at the same time to distance itself from Michelangelo's *David* with which it is paired, as if to distinguish the style under the victorious Medici rulers of the city from that of the Republic. The shifting back and forth of this commission between Michelangelo and Bandinelli marks the political fortunes of the city, the role that art played in reinforcing the dominant political order, and the association of individual artists with particular power structures in the city. Tellingly, Michelangelo, who worked both for the Republic and for the Medici in what must have been a very complicated psychological situation for him, seems to have eliminated all identifying Medici imagery from the New Sacristy, where he even erased the individual physical features from the portraits of the two dukes. Artists, like the art that they made, were participants in the political culture in which they worked.

Venice: Vision and Monumentality

By the beginning of the 1500s a century of successful expansion onto the Italian mainland had earned Venice the jealous enmity of the pope, the Holy Roman Emperor, the king of France, and the lords of Milan. In 1509 these powers formed the League of Cambrai, a military alliance dedicated to stripping Venice of its mainland possessions. Psychologically and militarily unprepared, Venice watched incredulously as its empire dissolved and foreign troops advanced on Mestre, just across the lagoon from the city. Over eight centuries of independence seemed on the verge of ending.

Through immense sacrifice, self-determination, and a good deal of luck, Venice did prevail. It regained its prize possession, Verona, in January 1517. Twelve years later, in 1529, the city obtained a final peace, which affirmed its right to holdings nearly as extensive as before the war. Nigh miraculous in its recovery, Venice became the subject of a carefully formulated civic myth which stressed that the city had been saved because of its unique site and history, its maritime origins having produced an especially stouthearted and selfless citizenry, willing to sacrifice personal profit for communal gain. Although modern historical research has shown that the Venetians were as likely as other Italians to avoid civic duty, especially when it conflicted with their business interests, it is true that traditional communal values helped to bolster local pride and encouraged the Venetians to persevere.

In the midst of often bleak and dangerous times, harshly contrasting with the prized values of stability and serenity which had earned La Serenissima its epithet, some Venetian patrons naturally preferred the familiar artistic styles of the past, continuing to commission works from such "eyewitness" painters as Carpaccio (see Fig. 6.37). But many others embraced a new style, which was evocative and often ambiguous rather than descriptive. They also sought solace and delight in nostalgia for the remote classical past, many of whose myths and idyllic images had become newly accessible through Venice's printing industry. Faced with challenges for which local history and civic rhetoric did not provide ready answers, artists created ideal and elevated images of reassuring beauty.

Visual Poetry

An important innovation in Venetian art of this period was the *poesia*, or painting that was meant to operate in the indirect manner of poetry. Foremost among painters of the new manner was Giorgione (Zorzi da Castelfranco; c. 1477/78 Castelfranco–1510 Venice), a painter from Castelfranco, a small town northwest of Venice. A painting known since 1530 as the *Tempesta* (Fig. 7.50) because of the storm that thunders in the background clearly demonstrates his originality. Despite the drama of the storm and the commanding presence of the landscape— itself a novelty in Italian painting at this time—it is the figures that command our attention. A virtually nude

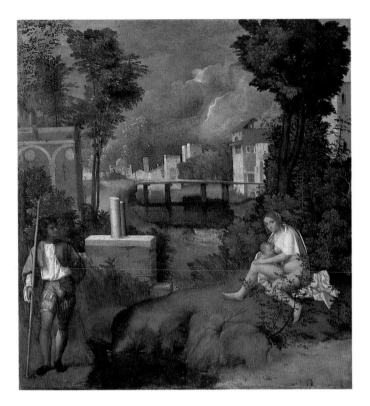

7.50 *La Tempesta*, c. 1509 (?), perhaps commissioned by Gabriele Vendramin from GIORGIONE. Oil on canvas, 32½ × 28¾" (82 × 73 cm) (Galleria dell'Accademia, Venice)

woman sits on a hillock at the right nursing a baby. A man carrying a halberd but dressed in an unkempt manner hardly appropriate for a soldier stands looking toward them from the left. Contrary to accepted traditions, Giorgione has pushed these figures to the sides of the painting, so that attention is drawn back to the watery middle ground and to a bolt of lightning that flashes eerie light across the walls of a city.

X-ray photographs of the painting reveal that Giorgione originally painted a female nude bathing where the man now stands. The change in figures, their ambiguous relationship to the landscape and to each other, and the unpopulated cityscape and ruins have led some writers to believe that the painting simply lacks a subject, in the traditional sense of that word. The soft, feathery leaves, moist landscape, and sparkling highlights give the painting the air of a romantic tale that the viewer's imagination must complete.

Other scholars have sought explanations in ancient mythology and the Bible, seeing the woman as representing such diverse and contradictory characters as Eve, Venus, Ceres (the goddess of grain), or Mater Tellus (Mother Earth). Others see the work not as a narrative concerning one of these figures but as allegorical, more easily accounting for but not fully explaining its compositional peculiarities and abstruse subject.

Yet another reading sees the painting as a martial allegory. This interpretation depends on the assumption that the Venetian nobleman Gabriele Vendramin, in whose collection the work is first documented in 1530, was the patron of the work. His uncle and brothers were heavily involved in the Cambrai Wars, especially the early and successful campaign to regain Padua. The arms of the Carrara family, who ruled Padua until its annexation by Venice in 1406, appear on some of the towers in the background of Giorgione's painting along with a separate representation of Venice's Lion of St. Mark. The specific imagery may be related to a statement ascribed by later historians to Doge Leonardo Loredan (r. 1501–21), who asked young Venetian noblemen to take up arms to regain Padua, which had been lost due "to a certain fatal tempest." Vendramin's uncle led the successful recapture of the city, and two of his brothers joined 174 other young patricians in guarding the gates of Padua. In combination with the image of the broken columns at the left of the painting, which may refer to fortitude, and the nursing mother at the right, who evokes traditional images of charity, the painting could then be an allegory of patriotism—the storm in the background referring to war and unpredictable fortune.

Whatever the painting's intended subject, it is clearly a revolutionary work, one in which evocative color, form, and light seem both to demand and to frustrate attempts at a literal reading. With this small painting visual poetry had been born.

Eroticism and Antiquity

One way in which Giorgione and his patrons exploited the new style was through sensual subject matter. The *Sleeping Venus* (Fig. 7.51) is a case in point. The reclining figure was originally accompanied by a small figure of Cupid holding a bird at the right side of the painting, but this figure was painted over in 1843, most likely to focus attention solely on the female nude.

Giorgione placed the Venus across the whole width of the painting. She stretches one arm behind her head, making a long, continuous slope of body whose gentle curves echo the hills of the landscape and suggest some form of connection between the female depicted and nature behind. Painted at just the moment when Venice was defending its claims on the *terra firma*, it may, therefore, be possible to read Venus (*Venere*) as Venice (*Venezia*).

Venus's sensuality is heightened by her red lips and by the deep red velvet and white satin drapery upon which her creamy body lies. Significantly, she is asleep, so the issue of decorum is bypassed, although for modern critics she thus becomes an object for the voyeuristic gaze

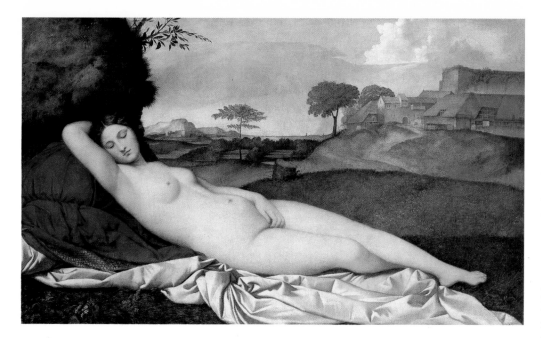

7.51 *Sleeping Venus*, c. 1507–1510, perhaps commissioned by Girolamo Marcello from GIORGIONE, completed by Titian. Oil on canvas, 3′ 6½″ × 5′ 8⅞″ (1.08 × 1.75 m) (Gemäldegalerie, Dresden)

The thatched, steeply-sloping roofs of the buildings in the background are not typically Italian and suggest that Giorgione copied them from Northern European prints.

of the viewer. But her sleep also implies dreaming and transport of the figure to another world like Poliphilus, whose dream took him, accompanied by a nymph, through an imagined ancient bucolic world in the bestseller printed by Aldus Manutius in Venice in 1499, the *Hypnerotomachia Poliphili* ("The Dream of Poliphilus"; see Fig. 37, from the same book). Thus the painting may be interpreted as a poetic evocation of a classical idyll.

But no amount of poetic mythology or political allegory can override the sensual nature of the image. Apart from her pose, this Venus bears no resemblance to female nudes from ancient Roman sculpture. Instead, she looks like a contemporary Venetian woman who has removed her clothes. Her left hand seems not to be modestly hiding her genitals but apparently pleasuring them (and at the exact vertical center of the painting). According to gynaecological treatises of the time, female masturbation made a woman more fertile. Such a representation of Venus would have been appropriate if—as the horizontal format of the painting suggests—it was integrated into a piece of bedroom furniture, perhaps commissioned around October 1507 when Girolamo Marcello (who owned the *Sleeping Venus*) married Morosina Pisani. Reclining nude men or women appeared regularly on the inside covers of dowry chests, alluding to the fertility hoped for in marriage. In fact, the first reference to a sleeping Venus in classical literature seems to have been in a poem by the Roman poet Claudianus, written in 399 to celebrate the wedding of two friends. Since the primary goal of marriage was to produce a male child, Venus may well have been a talisman to guarantee Morosina and Girolamo an heir.

Perhaps even more obvious an example of the poetic, pastoral tradition initiated by Giorgione's *Tempest* is his *Pastoral Concert* (Fig. 7.52), a painting sometimes also attributed to the young Titian (Tiziano Vecelli; c. 1488 Pieve di Cadore–1576 Venice), a painter from the Dolomites who early in his career collaborated with Giorgione and then went on to become Venice's most eminent Renaissance painter. Here pastoral references, with a shepherd and his flock in the middle distance to the right, are obvious, as is Giorgione's poetic juxtaposition of opposites. Two men are seated in the lush country landscape, one dressed in the elegant

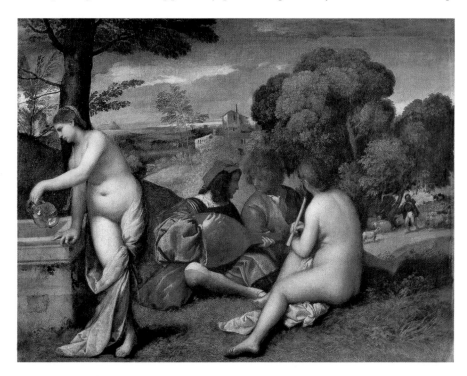

7.52 *Pastoral Concert*, c. 1509–10, probably by GIORGIONE, although the painting is sometimes attributed to TITIAN. Oil on canvas, 43¼ × 54⅜″ (110 × 138 cm) (Musée du Louvre, Paris)

The landscape in this painting extends remarkably far into the distance to a misty plain and mountains reminiscent of Leonardo da Vinci (see Fig. 6.91).

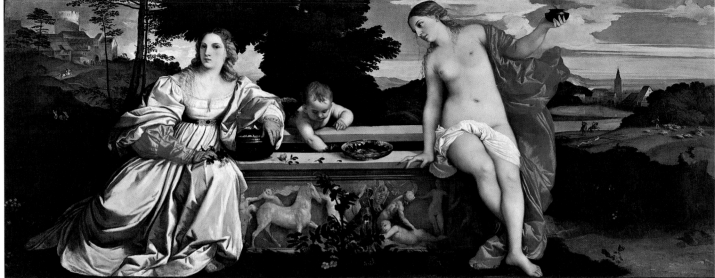

7.53 *Sacred and Profane Love*, c. 1514, commissioned by Niccolò Aurelio on his marriage to Laura Bagarotto in 1514 from TITIAN. Oil on canvas, 46½ × 109⅞" (118 × 279 cm) (Galleria Borghese, Rome)

costume of a Venetian nobleman, the other barefoot and wearing rustic clothing. They are accompanied by two nude women. Despite their sixteenth-century costumes, the men in this *poesia* are enveloped in a romantic evocation of pastoral antiquity. The men's faces are shadowed as they turn toward one another, creating a private interaction between themselves from which the viewer—not to mention their companions—is excluded. In fact, they seem completely oblivious of the women, one of whom is seated immediately in front of them and facing them. The other stands outside the central group to the left, her body in a complicated *contrapposto* position as she empties a glass ewer, reversing the normal practice of taking water from a well. The painting is held together compositionally by the soft light that suffuses the entire landscape, uniting the psychologically distant figures. The compositional elements all point to peace between city and country, but once again a precise meaning and subject seem purposefully avoided. This was the sort of painting over which learned friends might muse. Since it allowed a variety of interpretations, viewers could have made allusions to classical literature and have demonstrated their learning in their comments.

The integration of landscape painting and mythology into the traditions of Venetian art is evident in *Sacred and Profane Love* (Fig. 7.53) by Titian, Even more elongated than the *Sleeping Venus*, the painting almost certainly served to adorn a piece of furniture. The facial resemblance between the two women suggests that they may be the same person in two guises. The presence of the Cupid behind the sarcophagus indicates that the nude figure is the celestial Venus, representing divine love. She holds a burning lamp aloft, its tiny flame silhouetted against the clear blue sky, while her fluttering red satin cloak billows dramatically along the left side of her body, a marked contrast to her creamy smooth flesh. The woman at the left, dressed in heavy, luxurious clothing and wearing gloves, would then be the earthly Venus, for the materials of her clothing appeal to the human senses, as do her low-cut dress and open bodice. The slash of red sleeve against the cool blue of her dress adds to the sensuousness of the satin.

The painting reflects the new classical learning of the period and the new Venetian fascination with landscape while it simultaneously celebrates married sexual love. The floral wreath in the hair and flowers in the lap of the dressed Venus signal fertility, surrounded by emblems of fecundity: the stallion on the sarcophagus and the rabbits in the landscape at the left. The shield on the sarcophagus identifies the patron as Niccolò Aurelio, the vice-chancellor of the Venetian republic. Nearly hidden in the silver bowl on the edge of the sarcophagus is a second crest belonging to Laura Bagarotto, whom Aurelio married in 1514. The *Sacred and Profane Love* is certainly a marriage painting for this couple, its purpose to remind the wife of her virtuousness and her procreative powers by the double guise of Venus and, unsubtly, by the small rabbits in the fields at the left. It was also to provide the husband with a charged erotic image whose moral message nonetheless maintains the boundaries of decorum.

Poetic Altarpieces

A more poetic approach also characterized religious painting in Venice at this time. Perhaps around 1505, Giorgione painted an altarpiece for the cathedral of his home town, Castelfranco (Fig. 7.54). The painting shares the shimmering light and *trompe l'oeil* effects of Giovanni Bellini's *San Giobbe Altarpiece* of two decades earlier (see Fig. 6.32), making specific reference to Bellini's figure of St. Francis, here shown in a mirror image, again inviting

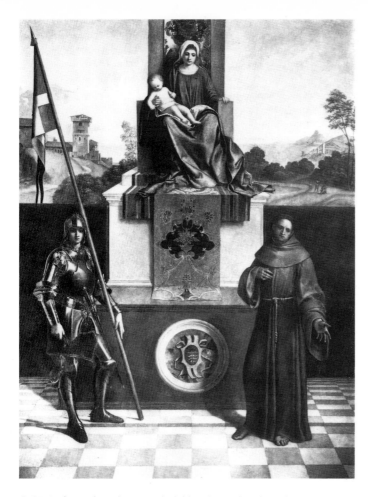

7.54 *Enthroned Madonna and Child with St. Liberale and St. Francis*, c. 1504 (?), commissioned by Tuzio Costanzo, perhaps to commemorate the death of his son, Matteo, in 1504, from GIORGIONE for Castelfranco Cathedral. Panel, 6′ 6¾″ × 5′ (2 × 1.52m)

the worshiper to enter a sacred realm. But Giorgione's figures are set at a distance, no longer existing in a world directly adjacent to the viewer's space. Instead, a pavement intervenes, and the Madonna and Child appear as in a vision on top of an altar-shaped throne. Giorgione's considerable illusionistic and descriptive powers do more than counterfeit reality: they enhance and exalt it. Balancing the armor-clad St. Liberale and the fortified landscape on the left with a barefoot St. Francis and a glowing scene of peaceful nature on the right, Giorgione groups his figures into a highly calculated, pyramidal organization very different from the almost casual gathering of Bellini's earlier altarpiece. What is lost in accessibility is compensated for by an increase in monumentality and grandeur.

This new manner finds parallels in the late work of Giovanni Bellini himself, exemplified by an altarpiece for one of the side chapels of San Zaccaria (Fig. 7.55). As at San Giobbe (see Fig. 6.32), Bellini surrounds his figures with classicizing architecture, but the space inhabited by the holy figures is no longer a literal extension of the actual church. Instead, the scene opens to trees and sky at left and right, suggesting an airy setting for contemplation. As in Giorgione's exactly contemporaneous work, Bellini sets

his figures farther back in space, reduces their number (seven, rather than the eleven in the San Giobbe painting), and casts their eyes down or slightly obscures them with shadows. Bellini may have been inspired by Giorgione's work, though it is just as likely that the younger artist drew inspiration from Bellini's example. Whatever the precise relationship between the two artists, they both promoted a new, more evocative style which quickly came to dominate Venetian painting.

One of the most gifted young artists to follow and promote the new style was Sebastiano del Piombo. Between March 1510 and spring 1511, when he left Venice for the papal court in Rome, Sebastiano painted an altarpiece for the parish church of San Giovanni Crisostomo (Fig. 7.56). The church had recently been reconstructed on a Byzantine-inspired Greek cross plan devised by Mauro

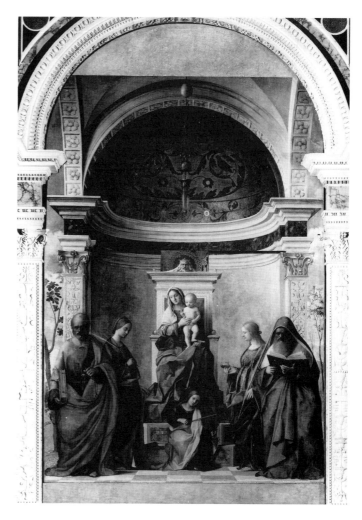

7.55 *Enthroned Madonna, Child, and Saints*, completed 1505, commissioned for the Benedictine nuns of San Zaccaria from GIOVANNI BELLINI for San Zaccaria, Venice. Oil on canvas transferred from wood, 16′ 5½″ × 7′ 9″ (5 × 2.35 m)

The painting was cut down by 29″ (76 cm) when it was in Paris between 1797 and 1816 before being reunited with its original frame.

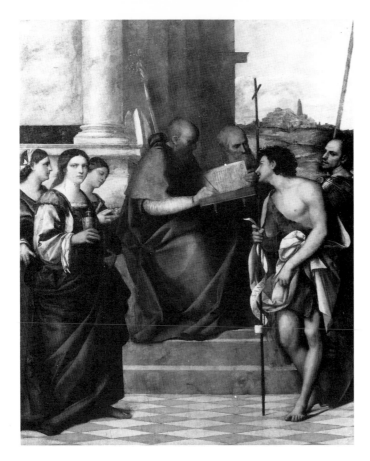

7.56 *San Giovanni Crisostomo Altarpiece*, 1510–11, SEBASTIANO DEL PIOMBO, San Giovanni Crisostomo, Venice. Oil on canvas (perhaps transferred from panel), 6' 6¾" × 5' 5" (2 × 1.65 m)

The painting is now in poor condition, but its novel composition merits special attention.

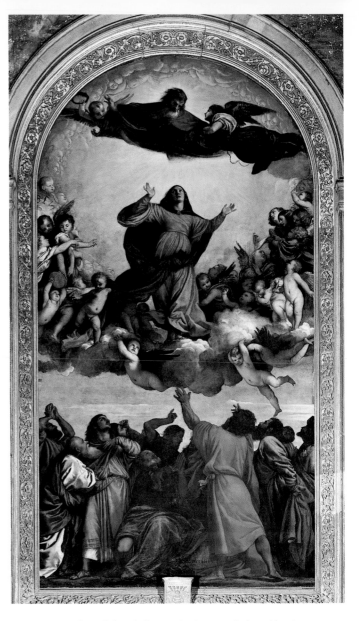

7.57 *Assumption of the Virgin*, 1516–18, commissioned by Germano da Caiole from TITIAN for the main apse of Santa Maria Gloriosa dei Frari, Venice. Oil on panel, 22' 7½" × 11' 9¾" (6.9 × 3.6 m)

The painting stands in its original frame, which is inscribed with the name of the patron. Statues of the Risen Christ, St. Francis, and St. Anthony stand on its summit.

Codussi, and Sebastiano responded to its open and essentially centralized plan by turning his composition at an angle into space. This necessitated a break with the traditional frontal placement of his saints, allowing for more complex groups, who are set before a monumental colonnade which reaches above and beyond the frame. Moving from the left, the figures are disposed in a diagonal back into space. This axis is then countered by the tilt and gaze of John the Baptist from the opposite side of the canvas, crossing at the central figure of the seated St. John Chrysostom.

The work, like Giorgione's and Titian's secular *poesie*, is psychologically complex and offers the attuned viewer numerous visual surprises. First there is the reaction of the woman on the left, who looks rather askance at the presumed viewer. Next, while St. John Chrysostom, the major dedicatee of the altarpiece, serves as the central fulcrum of the composition, he is lost in both shadow and thought as he writes in a large tome. John the Baptist at the far right poses gallantly and peers inquisitively at the saint, the inscription on his unfurling banderole changed from the usual "Ecce Agnus Dei" ("Behold the Lamb of God," referring to Christ) to "Ecce Sanctus" ("Behold the Saint"), returning the worshipper's attention to John

Chrysostom. It is an evocative rather than descriptive painting, creating a mood of mystic reverie.

In 1516 Germano da Caiole, prior of the Franciscan basilica of Santa Maria Gloriosa dei Frari, commissioned Titian to produce a large *Assumption of the Virgin* for the church's high altar (Fig. 7.57). The painting was unveiled on May 19, 1518, a day significant for Venice as well as for the Franciscans because it was the eve of the feast of San Bernardino of Siena, a Franciscan reformer and one of the city's official saintly protectors. It immediately set a new standard for monumentality and drama, confirming Titian's position as the undisputed leader of Venetian painting. In the altarpiece, whose subject derived from the principal dedication of the church to the "glorious" Virgin, Titian created a highly charged representation of the Virgin's bodily ascent into heaven. He also succeeded in establishing a focal point for this spacious church. Flanked by two of the largest ducal tombs in the city (see Fig. 6.40), the altarpiece stands directly in front of a multi-storied screen of stained-glass windows that fill the apse with rich, glowing light. Titian responded to this imposing setting by breaking his composition into two stories, coordinated with clear divisions in the tracery in front of which it stands. He also made his figures larger than life, dressing them in sonorous shades of red, blue, and green, and directing their gestures heavenward, where God the Father hovers in a circle of golden clouds. A golden aureole of angel heads echoes the curving top of the altarpiece, completed as a full circle in the clouds and cherubs below who surround the Virgin. Even seen from as far away as the church's entrance, Titian's bold composition dominates the church's elaborate interior.

Given the resounding success of the painting, as a celebration of the Virgin's Assumption, a central element in Franciscan theology, and the visual culmination of nearly two centuries of construction at the Frari, it may seem surprising that Titian's patrons expressed concern about the composition while he was painting it. In particular, they complained that the Apostles at the bottom of the composition were too large. But Titian repudiated their complaints, knowing that his strategic shadowing of the Apostles' gesticulating forms would diminish their apparent importance in the church, while still retaining their function as an essential foil to the light-drenched, heavenly realm above. His self-assurance was a milestone in relations between artist and patron, furthering the then novel idea of the artist as main begetter of the work.

In an altarpiece commissioned for a side chapel in the Frari by the Pesaro family (Fig. 7.58), Titian built on the example of Sebastiano's *San Giovanni Crisostomo Altarpiece* (see Fig. 7.56), placing his figures against enormous columns, steps, and the corner of a classically detailed palace. The setting seems as grand as, if not grander than the vast space of the Frari. He also set his figures on a diagonal, so that the worshiper walking down the nave is drawn up and into the composition from the kneeling donor to the Virgin and Child.

The clarity of the composition masks the complexity of its program, which addresses doctrinal, personal, and familial concerns. The altar above which it stands had been dedicated to the Virgin of the Immaculate Conception before Jacopo Pesaro, donor of the altarpiece, acquired patronage rights to it. Since the doctrine of the Immaculate Conception was so dear to the Franciscans, and because a confraternity dedicated to the doctrine celebrated its feast at this altar, Jacopo seems to have been unwilling or unable to alter the dedication. Titian may have underscored the theme with his two columns and ring of clouds, which evoke a phrase in Ecclesiasticus 24:7 used

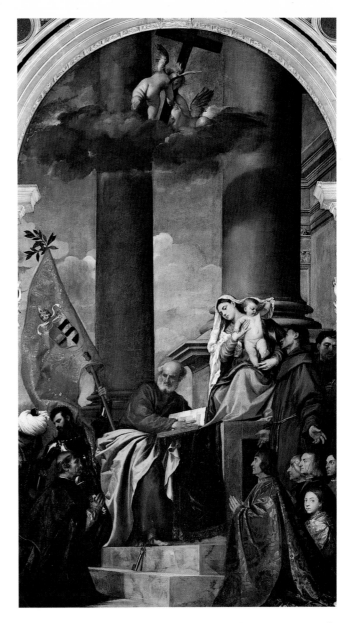

7.58 *Pesaro Altarpiece*, 1519–26, commissioned by Jacopo Pesaro from TITIAN for the Pesaro Chapel, Santa Maria Gloriosa dei Frari, Venice. Oil on canvas, 15' 11" × 8' 10" (4.85 × 2.69 m).

The kneeling figures at the bottom are all Pesaro family members.

by the Franciscans to defend the doctrine: "my throne was in a pillar of cloud." The unusual inclusion of St. Peter at the physical center of a Marian altarpiece—though deftly handled by placing him at a less exalted height than the Virgin—is accounted for by an incident in Jacopo Pesaro's life. In 1502 Jacopo was the leader of papal forces who defeated the Turks at the Ionian island of Santa Maura for Pope Alexander VI, whose arms appear on the shimmering victory banner held by a soldier behind him. The turbaned figure at the left, behind the kneeling figure of Jacopo, represents the conquered Turk brought to Christianity, whose leadership is symbolized by St. Peter. Some of Jacopo's male relatives, kneeling at the right, are recommended to the Virgin and Child by St. Francis, who points with his right hand to his namesake Francesco Pesaro, the head of the clan.

San Salvatore

The grandeur of Titian's altarpieces was matched architecturally by new churches such as San Salvatore (Figs. 7.59 and 7.60), laid out by the head of civic works in Venice, Giorgio Spavento (active 1486–1509 Venice), but continued by Tullio Lombardo (c. 1455 Venice–1532 Venice), son of Pietro Lombardo. Abandoning his father's rather precious and sometimes fussy detail, Tullio successfully emulated the dignity and monumentality of ancient Roman architecture, filtering it, as was usual in Venice, through Byzantine sources.

During the Cambrai Wars, only the most urgent projects (which included the rebuilding of the Rialto business district after a fire in 1514) went forward; this included work on nearby San Salvatore. Construction was favored by the fact that Antonio Contarini, the prior who commissioned the work in 1507, continued to support the project after he became patriarch of Venice the following year. The church's link with St. Mark's Basilica can be seen in the nave, which consists of three interlocking centrally planned units, each surmounted by a dome and flanked at the corners by smaller domes. Tullio Lombardo, who had already evolved a spare, impressive classicism in his reliefs for the façade of the Scuola Grande di San Marco (see Fig. 6.38) gave visual coherence to the interior with a series of proportionally interrelated pilasters distributed between the nave and the corner units. Crisp but substantial moldings, elegant Corinthian capitals, and broad barrel vaults add to the building's serene elegance.

The revived classicism evident at San Salvatore also informs Tullio's work for the Santo in Padua. His relief of the *Miracle of the Miser's Heart* (Fig. 7.61) forms part of an unprecedentedly rich scheme of nine large compositions lining the walls of the saint's chapel in the left transept of the Santo. The entire program was designed to bolster the cult of the city's miracle-working saint at the very moment that Protestants in northern Europe and even some of the professors at Padua's university were attacking traditional notions of saints and relics. Tullio and his collaborators went on the offensive, presenting the saint's miracles as nobly and dramatically as possible. Tullio's work centers around the corpse of a miser who St. Anthony, shown preaching at the left, predicted would be found to have lost his heart in his money box—here poised at the back corner of his classically designed bier. The whole composition reads like a Roman imperial relief, its large figures deeply carved and arranged in a uniform row across the composition. Inspired no doubt by the dramatic intensity of Donatello's bronze reliefs in the same church (see Fig. 5.58), Tullio also exploits the vigor and emotional gestures of Hellenistic sculpture, such as the recently discov-

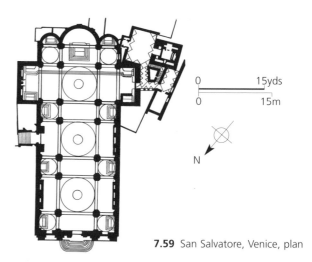

7.59 San Salvatore, Venice, plan

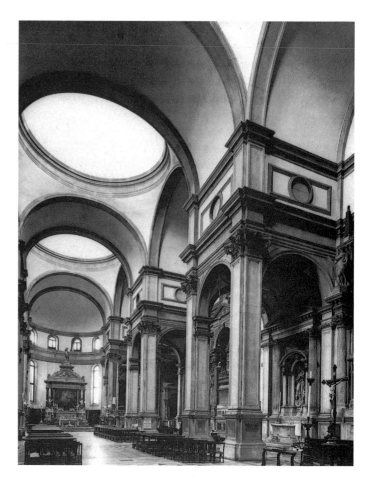

7.60 San Salvatore, Venice, 1507–32, commissioned by Antonio Contarini from GIORGIO SPAVENTO and TULLIO LOMBARDO

A silver gilt altarpiece on the high altar resembles the *Pala d'Oro* (see Fig. 3.2). It is exposed only from August 3–5; otherwise it is covered by a badly damaged *Transfiguration* (c. 1560–65) by Titian.

ered *Laocoön*. Classicism, which in the hands of painters had opened new possibilities for sensuous, secular subject matter, could also be marshalled to promote more traditional values, thus ensuring its widespread adoption and popularity.

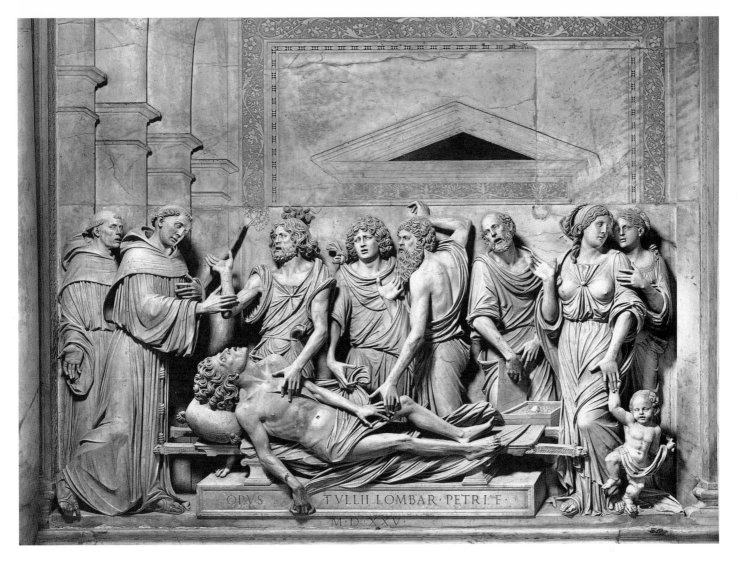

7.61 *Miracle of the Miser's Heart*, 1520–25, commissioned as a result of a bequest given by Francesco Sansone (1414–99), minister general of the Franciscan order, by the governors of the Santo from TULLIO LOMBARDO for the Chapel of St. Anthony, The Santo, Padua. Marble, 51¼ × 96" (130 × 245 cm)

Tullio boldly asserted his authorship of this relief by inscribing it on the base of the dead man's bier: "This is the work of Tullio the Lombard, son of Pietro, 1525." All the figures are daringly undercut, leaving them nearly freestanding.

Ferrara, Mantua, Parma, and Genoa: Exquisite Delights

The small cities of Ferrara, Mantua, and Parma and the major maritime center of Genoa were centers of particularly sophisticated artistic production in the early sixteenth century. Following the lead of the self-absorbed papal courts of Leo X and Clement VII, provincial aristocratic patrons commissioned works intended to appeal to elite audiences, promoting artifice and formal invention as primary values. Unabashedly luxurious and often precious, the arts were shaped to appeal to connoisseurs and *literati* who had developed a seemingly insatiable appetite for classical antiquity, scholarly allusions, visual puns, and illusionistic effects. Instead of art mimicking life, life now mimicked art—every aspect of speech, dress, and comportment shaped to create a purposefully artifi-

cial and refined effect. This is the world of Baldassare Castiglione's *Book of the Courtier*, published in 1528 but nostalgically recalling the learned conversations and witty repartee at the court of Urbino earlier in the century when it was actually written (1508–18). Emphasizing artistic grace, decorum, and nonchalance, the speakers in Castiglione's book address such topics as speech, dress, effortless work by the amateur, desirable qualities in women, duties of good government, and the true nature of love. Their seemingly casual but highly calculated remarks are palpably visible in Raphael's portrait of the author (Fig. 7.62). Castiglione quietly but intensely looks out at the viewer, his utter composure and self-confidence manifest in his firmly clasped hands. As was the fashion at court in the sixteenth century, he wears subdued but luxurious black velvet, silvered fur, and white silk. Nothing—not a chair nor a window nor an inscription—distracts from his spot-lit visage. Only the silhouette of

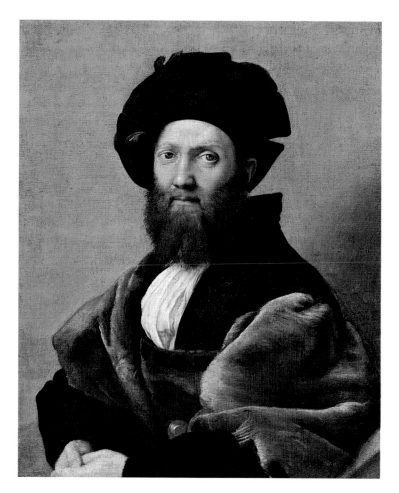

7.62 *Baldassare Castiglione*, c. 1514, commissioned by Baldassare Castiglione from RAPHAEL, Musée du Louvre, Paris. Oil on canvas, c. 32¼ × 26½" (81.9 × 67.3 cm)

his sleeves, cloak, hat, and collar relieve the potential monotony of such a radically spare picture. While Castiglione and his contemporaries regularly commissioned and enjoyed elaborately complex works of art, Raphael has captured their self-ideal: understated, sophisticated, and intelligent.

Ferrara: The Private *Studiolo*

Since at least the time of Leonello d'Este in the first half of the fifteenth century (see Fig. 4.25), Ferrara's ruling family had embraced and cultivated humanist learning and the arts, also promoting themselves as noble defenders of peace and concord. The Este enhanced their reputation as enlightened rulers through works of urban renewal and splendid self-celebration, epitomized in the late 1400s by Duke Ercole's creation of an entire district of classically inspired buildings emanating directly from the Este palace compound at the center of the city. At the crossroads of the district's main axes Ercole's brother, Sigismondo (1433–1507), erected the extraordinary Palazzo dei Diamanti, so-called for the 8,500 diamond-faceted blocks that erupt from its façades (Fig. 7.63). Designed by the court architect Biagio Rossetti, who was responsible for the layout of the neighborhood as well as for numerous churches and residences within it, the building subtly evokes the fortified character of the Este Castle in its raked plinth and insistent rustication. Rossetti domesticated these forms by applying them decoratively to a classically organized rectangular structure recalling the Palazzo Medici in Florence (see Fig. 5.14). Reversing the usual Tuscan practice of a dominant ground story, Rossetti enlarged the main, upper story, punctuating it with large pedimented windows. Smaller windows, those on the entrance side capped by entablatures, illuminate the lower story.

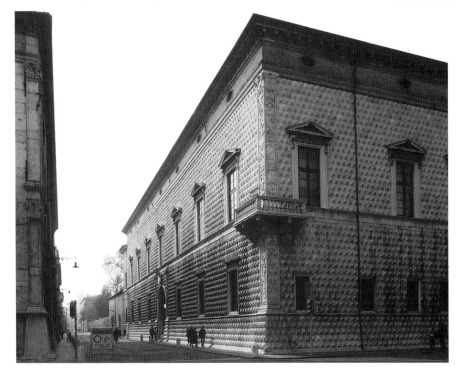

7.63 Palazzo dei Diamanti, Ferrara, 1493, commissioned by Sigismondo d'Este from BIAGIO ROSSETTI

The palace stands midway between the Este Castle in the old city and what was to have been the site of a 55-foot (17-meter) tall equestrian statue of Duke Ercole.

The corner, from which the Este were both to admire their new straight streets and appear splendidly to their subjects, is accented with two lavishly carved, superimposed pilasters and a balcony. Every element is exquisitely detailed, down to the diamond-shaped blocks, whose facets shift from level to level so that they point upward from the bottom, appear perfectly centered in the middle zone, and slightly tilt downward from the *piano nobile*.

Alfonso d'Este

The Este family's sophisticated taste found yet another exponent in Ercole's son and Sigismondo's nephew, Duke Alfonso (r. 1505–34). At the castle in the center of the city Alfonso assembled some of the most sophisticated decorative ensembles of the early sixteenth century. An avid antiquarian, like most members of his family (especially his sister Isabella), Alfonso employed agents to purchase Roman antiquities and commissioned artists to revive ancient subject matter in classical style. Ferrara was to be yet another new Athens.

The Studio di Marmi   Alfonso selected for special elaboration an elevated passageway bridging a moat between the family's medieval castle and their more modern palace—perhaps because in childhood he, his mother, and his sisters had fled through this corridor for safety during an infamous attempted coup. Linking the private and public parts of the palace compound, it was also both easily accessible from his private chambers and conveniently available for display to visiting dignitaries. Here he asked Antonio Lombardo (c. 1438 Venice?–1516 Ferrara), brother of Tullio, to create a "Studio of Marbles" (*Studio di Marmi*), a private study lined entirely in marble, making it even more precious and expensive than Federico da Montefeltro's renowned *studiolo* in Urbino (see Fig. 6.19), which itself had been inspired by Este precedents. Antonio was well suited to the task, having worked alongside Tullio Lombardo on the recent Santo reliefs (see Fig. 7.61). In Ferrara he was responsible for narrative reliefs, friezes, inscriptions from classical authors, and even the marble floor. For the most part Antonio adopted the calm and idealized manner of ancient Greek and **Augustan** art, underlining the room's

CONTEMPORARY VOICE

The Courtier as Artist

Baldassare Castiglione (1478–1529) was himself a courtier at the highly civilized court of Guidobaldo da Montefeltro, in Urbino. *The Book of the Courtier*, his best-known work, sets out in detail the characteristics of a cultivated person, including good manners and various accomplishments, such as drawing and painting.

"Before we launch into this subject," the Count replied, "I should like us to discuss something else again which, since I consider it highly important, I think our courtier should certainly not neglect: and this is the question of drawing and of the art of painting itself. And do not be surprised that I demand this ability, even if nowadays it may appear mechanical and hardly suited to a gentleman. For I recall having read that in the ancient world, and in Greece especially, children of gentle birth were required to learn painting at school, as a worthy and necessary accomplishment, and it was ranked among

the foremost of the liberal arts; subsequently, a public law was passed forbidding it to be taught to slaves. It was also held in great honour among the Romans, and from it the very noble family of the Fabii took its name, for the first Fabius was called *Pictor*. He was, indeed, an outstanding painter, and so devoted to the art that when he painted the walls of the Temple of Salus he signed his name: this was because (despite his having been born into an illustrious family, honoured by so many consular titles, triumphs and other dignities, and despite the fact that he himself was a man of letters, learned in law and numbered among the orators) Fabius believed that he could enhance his name and reputation by leaving a memorial pointing out that he had also been a painter. And there was no lack of other celebrated painters belonging to other illustrious families. In fact, from painting, which is in itself a most worthy and noble art, many useful skills can be derived, and not least for military purposes: thus a knowledge of the art gives one the facility to sketch towns, rivers, bridges,

citadels, fortresses and similar things, which otherwise cannot be shown to others even if, with a great deal of effort, the details are memorized. To be sure, anyone who does not esteem the art of painting seems to me to be quite wrong-headed. For when all is said and done, the very fabric of the universe, which we can contemplate in the vast spaces of heaven, so resplendent with their shining stars, in the earth at its centre, girdled by the seas, varied with mountains, rivers and valleys, and adorned with so many different varieties of trees, lovely flowers and grasses, can be said to be a great and noble painting, composed by Nature and the hand of God. And, in my opinion, whoever can imitate it deserves the highest praise. Nor is such imitation achieved without the knowledge of many things, as anyone who attempts the task well knows."

(from Baldassare Castiglione. *The Book of the Courtier*. Trans. George Bull. Harmondsworth: Penguin, 1967, pp. 96–7)

function as a meditative retreat intended for the duke's leisure and tranquility; but for the dramatic subject of *The Birth of Athena at the Forge of Vulcan* (Fig. 7.64) Antonio turned to the pathos of Hellenistic sculpture. At the left a writhing, bearded figure representing Zeus is one of the earliest surviving direct quotations from the recently excavated (1506) *Laocoön* group. The quotation served to enhance Alfonso's reputation as a patron and collector who had up-to-date knowledge of ancient art. It also gave expression to the pain Zeus must have experienced after Vulcan's axe (being forged by the nude figures at the brazier in the center of the relief) released Athena, fully formed, from his head. The leg of the priest who performed the act can be seen behind Zeus, while Athena, calm patroness of wisdom and peace, stands sedately in the niche above.

The Camerino d'Alabastro   In October 1511, just as work was coming to a conclusion on the Studio di Marmi, Duke Alfonso asked his sister Isabella's court humanist, Mario Equicola, to devise a program of bacchanalian subjects for his Camerino d'Alabastro (Alabaster Room), a small chamber containing alabaster decoration, also by Antonio Lombardo, adjacent to the study. This room too was to present classical subject matter, but in the form of frankly sensual and celebratory paintings, counterbalancing the lofty themes of wisdom, peace, and strength

dominating the Studio. Alfonso sent Equicola's written instructions to Giovanni Bellini, Titian, Fra Bartolomeo, and Raphael, who were each assigned a composition. For the painters it was an opportunity to pit their talents against one another; for Alfonso, an opportunity to create a gallery of works by the most renowned painters of his day—a conscious ploy to compete with Isabella (see Fig. 6.25) and other eminent patrons. In the end Fra Bartolomeo and Raphael died before they could fulfill the commission, and Bellini completed only one, so Titian painted three canvases, and yet another was allotted to the resident court artist, Dosso Dossi (Giovanni Luteri; 1480–1542), who also provided friezes with ten scenes from Virgil's *Aeneid*.

Bellini's contribution, known as the *Feast of the Gods* (Fig. 7.65), initiated the cycle with a depiction of ancient gods and goddesses associated with the winter solstice. Like the rest of the paintings it revolves around themes of love, in this case represented by three couples: a nature goddess and Neptune (actually a portrait of Alfonso) sitting behind the large bowl of fruit to the right of center, Ceres (Mother Earth) and Apollo (the sun god) to the right, and the lusty Priapus leering over the sleeping nymph Lotis at the far right. They originally rested in front of a continuous background, the grove of trees at the right extending across the entire canvas until Titian added the hill, trees, and sky at the left and repainted the

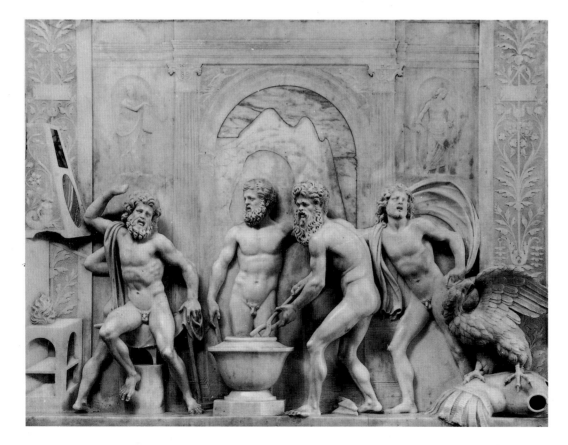

7.64 *The Birth of Athena at the Forge of Vulcan*, c. 1508–11, commissioned by Alfonso d'Este from ANTONIO LOMBARDO for the Studio di Marmi, Palazzo Ducale, Ferrara. Marble, width 41¾" (1.06 m) (Hermitage Museum, St. Petersburg)

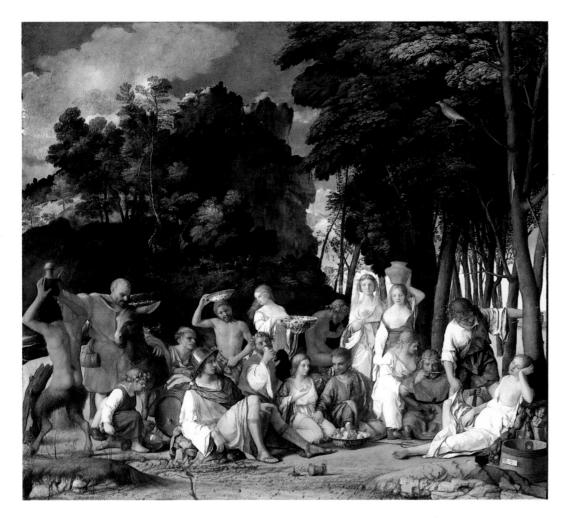

foliage (already altered by Dosso Dossi) to coordinate with his later paintings in the same room. The celebration, first described in the first book of Ovid's *Fasti*, takes place during the peaceful, so-called halcyon days, marked explicitly by the tiny kingfisher ([*h*]*alcyon* in Latin), who was said to mate at this time and so is shown perched on a little twig at the left foreground. Though it is the end of a long day of revelry, the infant Bacchus, god of wine, stoops to fill yet another crystal pitcher from a wine cask just above the bird. Behind him is Silenus, another god of revelry, whose donkey will soon start braying, warning Lotis of the lascivious intentions of her would-be suitor, clearly indicated by the protruding drapery between his loins

Probably in his eighties when he painted this canvas, Bellini was in full control of his art, turning a complex literary subject into a visually satisfying painting—a task that his almost exact contemporary Andrea Mantegna had approached with less sympathy in his heavily labeled allegory for Isabella d'Este (see Fig. 6.25). Here Bellini exploits the unifying effects of light, shadow, and figural grouping and the sensuous pleasure of brilliantly clear colors, proving himself one of the most sensitive painters

of his age. At the same time there is something delightfully naive about this work, marking it as the product of an older generation, whose approach to antiquity is very different from that of Antonio Lombardo, for example, whose gods and goddesses capture both the spiritual and fleshly aspects of antiquity. In this regard, Mantegna had surpassed Bellini, but even his passion for archaeology had not allowed him to revivify the sensuous spirit of antiquity fully.

It was left to Titian to bring classical mythology to full, pulsating life. In the second of his paintings for Alfonso's Camerino, the *Meeting of Bacchus and Ariadne* (Fig. 7.66), an exuberant Bacchus leaps from his triumphal chariot (drawn by cheetahs Titian had observed in Alfonso's menagerie) to rescue Ariadne, shown in a reciprocating but wary half-turning pose at the left. Having been abandoned by her former lover, Theseus, on the island of Naxos, she can hardly be reassured by Bacchus's noisy parade of carousing nymphs and satyrs, their frenzy intensified by the inclusion of another direct quotation from the snake-entwined *Laocoön* group. The head of a stag has been dropped on the ground in front of the figure, while behind him another Bacchic reveler wields an animal's leg. It has been freshly torn from its socket, presumably in the wild frenzy that ancient sources said Bacchus induced in his followers. Maidens clang cymbals and tambourines, signaling the way for the debauched, paunchy Silenus in the background—small in scale but highly visible thanks to Titian's brightening the green of the tree over his head. Titian contains these unruly figures in an isosceles triangle defined by an imaginary line that runs from the lower left to the upper right corner of the canvas. It grazes the edge of a bronze vase and yellow drape—seemingly casually thrown on the ground but essential to the pictorial structure—and proceeds under Bacchus's foot, through the trees, and into a small patch of blue sky. This diagonal is echoed in Bacchus's leap from his chariot in the relatively tranquil left portion of the composition. Still, a calm resolution is in sight, the limpid sky displaying the constellation that will commemorate Ariadne's peaceful marriage to Bacchus. A safe harbor also awaits her at the city in the background, its subdued color and execution a deliberate contrast with the splashily painted revelers at the right. Titian reserved his most splendid effects for his protagonists, whose alluring, pearlescent flesh and brilliant blue and red draperies assure their primacy even amid so much potentially distracting, carnal delight.

Mantua: The Pleasure Palace

Alfonso was hardly alone in his appreciation of ancient erotic subjects. At Mantua, where Isabella d'Este attempted to impose moralistic propriety on the court, her son Federigo Gonzaga engaged Giulio Romano to satisfy his considerable libido with bawdy decorations for a pleasure palace on the outskirts of the city where he stabled his horses and housed his mistress. Giulio arrived in Mantua from Rome in 1524, personally recommended and escorted by the Gonzaga's cultural agent in Rome, Baldassare Castiglione (see Fig. 7.62), and set to work in the Palazzo del Tè, a name deriving from the island on which it was situated. The general decorative scheme of the room that contains his *Wedding Feast of Cupid and Psyche* (Fig. 7.67) is indebted to Raphael's designs for the Villa Farnesina in Rome (see Fig. 7.38), but Giulio and his patron flaunted the bawdy delights of the gods with a fine disregard for decorum. Everything that is cool and idealized in Raphael is here flush with color and heat. Cupid has matured into a fleshy adult, reclining on his marriage couch at the right, nude along with his voluptuous bride, Psyche, and their lascivious and inebriated guests. The lovers turn their heads to receive marriage wreaths from an *amorino* who balances at the top of their couch, while the rumpled and cascading sheets beneath them suggest a heated and energetic coupling. (Snidely Giulio echoes the poses and cupidity of the two through a pet dog stretched out in the lower folds of the sheets.) To the left of the couple Bacchus barely holds himself upright on the corner of a table displaying fine gold and silver plate. Behind him Silenus's donkey brays uncontrollably. Even Apollo—depicted at the left of the table in a serene profile pose derived directly from ancient cameos—receives the

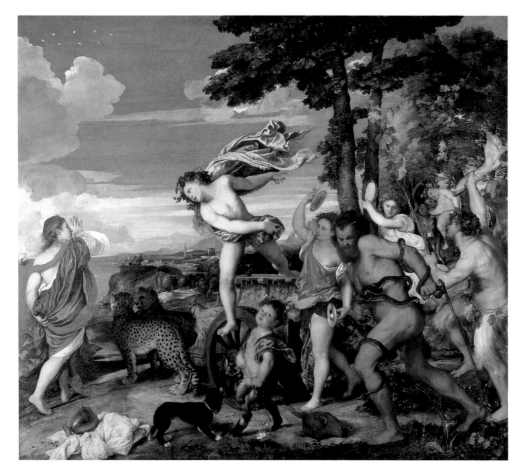

7.66 *Meeting of Bacchus and Ariadne*, 1522–23, commissioned by Alfonso d'Este from TITIAN for the Camerino d'Alabastro, Palazzo Ducale, Ferrara. Oil on canvas, 5′ 9″ × 6′ 3″ (1.75 × 1.9 m) (National Gallery, London)

This painting has been over cleaned, with most of the varnishes removed, resulting in some flattening of form, too brilliant and sharp coloration, and an absence of the atmospheric subtleties present in better preserved works by Titian.

attention of the muses. Above in the lunettes and ceiling Giulio tells the story of Cupid and Psyche and the conquests of Jupiter with similar sexual energy. Nothing is immune from playful, erotic commentary, all knit together with long, sinuous line and graceful exaggerations.

In the frescoes of the Sala dei Giganti, which were created for the second visit of Emperor Charles V to Mantua, Giulio reproduced in paint the spectacular effects of court entertainments. For these productions, designed by artists such as himself, vast machinery was employed to hoist figures up and down from the heavens. In the *Fall of the Giants from Mount Olympus* (Fig. 7.70), the densely crowded dome of heaven culminates in a vertiginous and off-center gallery, clearly meant to recall and surpass the oculus in Mantegna's palace decorations for Federigo's great grandfather (see Fig. 6.23). In so doing, Giulio underlined Federigo's distinguished pedigree as a patron of the arts while also asserting the superiority of his generation to those who came before him. Beneath the gods, in a

melodramatic representation which neither Ludovico Gonzaga nor Mantegna would have countenanced, the giants tumble to earth, seeming to destroy the walls around them and threatening the merely human-sized spectator. Giulio's paintings entertain with all the subtlety and grace of an amusement park fun house, offering coarse humor as an antidote to the potentially tedious idealism of much antique-revival art.

The playful and extravagant, at times even wanton, flavor of Giulio's paintings was intended to complement the tongue-in-cheek architectural forms he designed for additions to the palace itself (Fig. 7.68). In this suburban retreat, Giulio expanded a modest, pre-existing rectangular building (now incorporated into the northern wing of the courtyard) into an impressive, multi-zoned complex (Fig. 7.69). Entering through a rustic portico, the visitor is surrounded by the four wings of an ample courtyard, which leads on to a larger portico, fish tanks, and eventually a large open expanse for exercising and displaying

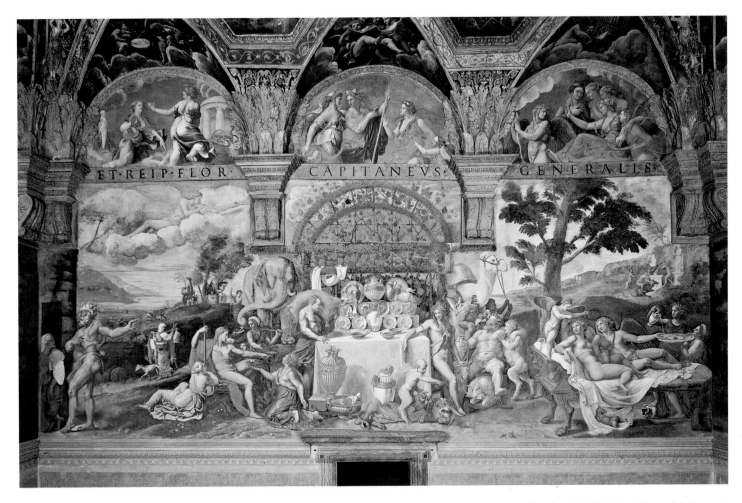

7.67 *Wedding Feast of Cupid and Psyche*, 1527–30, commissioned by Federigo Gonzaga from GIULIO ROMANO for the Sala di Psiche, Palazzo del Tè, Mantua. Fresco.

Emperor Charles V enjoyed dining alone in this room with Federigo as his steward. As a complement to the frescoes on the walls, a marble statue of Venus stood at the center of the room.

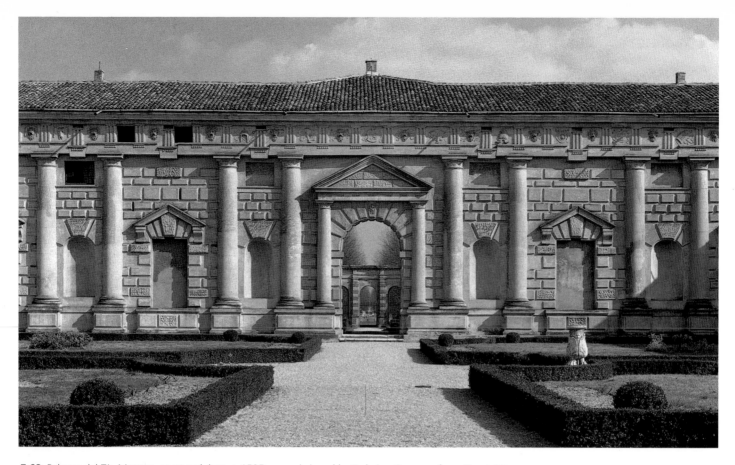

7.68 Palazzo del Tè, Mantua, courtyard, begun 1525, commissioned by Federigo Gonzaga from GIULIO ROMANO

Federigo's prize horses. While Giulio articulated the eastern façade of the palace facing the horse field with a pedimented façade, in the courtyard he employed unorthodox combinations of seemingly finished and unfinished forms, different architectural orders, and varying wall systems. Many of them collide, delighting connoisseurs who knew the rules of ancient architecture so well that they enjoyed seeing them willfully disobeyed. Equal bays appear on the northern and southern wings but alternating narrow and wider bays on the east and west. The ends are further distinguished from the sides by Giulio's witty violation of the **architrave**, a **triglyph** hanging down as though dislodged over every bay. Throughout, baseless pediments are invaded by keystones —more appropriate to arches—which split them at their apex. For all this building's apparent massiveness, Giulio seems to say, it is really a stage set, which the architect and his sophisticated patron can shape at will, exploiting stucco and brick to mimic carved masonry and columns and playing on normal expectations of courtly decorum.

Some critics have seen Giulio's fantastic paintings and architecture as symptoms of a troubled and shattered world embodying the so-called "psychosis" of Mannerism. But in the context of a pleasure palace, none of Giulio's aberrations were actually disturbing. Instead, they served to give Federigo and his guests a sense of superiority over normal mortals, reinforcing increasingly autocratic and authoritarian political and social realities.

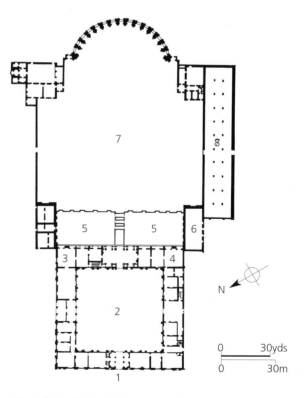

7.69 Palazzo del Tè, Mantua, plan of lower floor

1 Entrance; **2** Courtyard; **3** Sala di Psiche; **4** Sala dei Giganti; **5** Fishponds; **6** Tennis court; **7** Garden; **8** Stables
The hemicycle at the far end of the garden was built much later and may not correspond to Giulio's intentions.

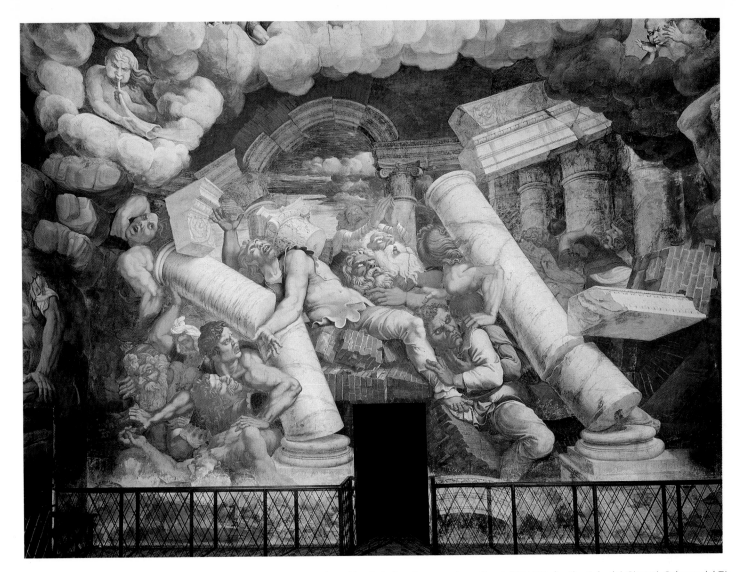

7.70 *Fall of the Giants from Mount Olympus*, 1530–32, commissioned by Federigo Gonzaga from GIULIO ROMANO for the Sala dei Giganti, Palazzo del Tè, Mantua. Fresco.

This room has very peculiar reverberating acoustics that turn any conversation into cacophony. The floor was originally set with pebbles making it difficult to walk as well as hear.

The Loves of Jupiter In his main palace in Mantua Federigo Gonzaga intended to create his own version of Alfonso d'Este's set of paintings for the Camerino d'Alabastro. Combining his interest in erotic subject matter and identification with the Olympian gods, Federigo asked Antonio Allegri, known as Correggio (1489 Correggio–1534 Correggio), to paint a series of works depicting the loves of Jupiter. Correggio complied with some of the most sensuous paintings of the sixteenth century. In his *Jupiter and Io* (Fig. 7.71) the king of the gods appears to the mortal Io in the guise of a cloud. Enfolding her in his nebulous form, Jupiter plants a kiss upon her receptive cheek. Io abandons herself to intense, physical pleasure, her outstretched limbs, fingers, and toes charged with delight. Although Correggio seems to have developed his painter's skills without any direct contact with progressive centers such as Venice and Rome, relying on prints after Raphael for Io's complex pose, his native ability in rendering the different textures and

temperatures of cloud, flesh, fabric, and other materials made him well suited to provide visual delights for Federigo's intimate retreat.

Parma: Elegance and Illusionism

Correggio spent most of his career working in Parma, a short distance from Mantua. Though the city had established a proud artistic tradition in the Middle Ages with the construction of its Romanesque cathedral and pink and white baptistry, it had fallen into provincial obscurity as a dependency of the Visconti and Sforza of Milan. On becoming part of the Papal States in the early sixteenth century, the city experienced a cultural revival. Among the first patrons to exploit Correggio's talents was Giovanna da Piacenza, the sophisticated abbess of the Benedictine nunnery of San Paolo. Correggio's decorations for a room in her private apartments (Fig. 7.72) demonstrate the extent to which antique subject matter

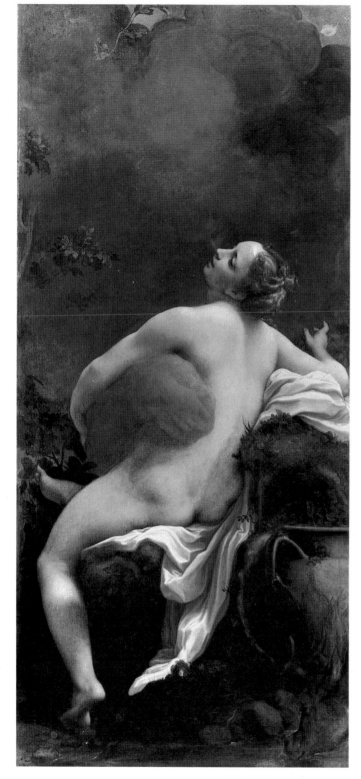

7.71 *Jupiter and Io*, early 1530s, commissioned by Federigo Gonzaga from CORREGGIO for his pleasure chamber in the Palazzo Ducale, Mantua. Oil on canvas, 29¼″ × 64″ (74 × 163 cm) (Kunsthistorisches Museum, Vienna)

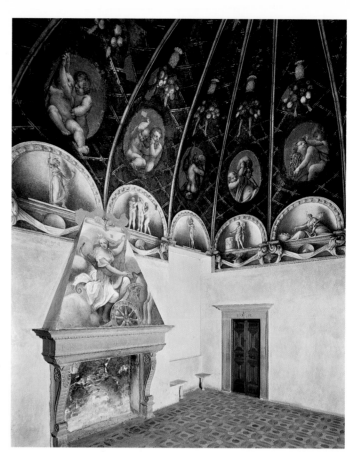

7.72 *Camera di San Paolo*, 1519, commissioned by Abbess Giovanna da Piacenza from CORREGGIO, Parma. Fresco

had become accepted and perhaps even expected in any major commission from an educated patron. Unlike Federigo Gonzaga, however, the abbess predictably stipulated chaste and uplifting subject matter. The precise meaning of the program has yet to be unraveled—an indication that it was specially prepared by a scholar

familiar with a wide range of antique texts—but the dominating presence over the fireplace of Diana, the chaste huntress, indicates its high moral character. Correggio used grisaille to depict figures from antiquity in the lunettes around the room, reserving rich color for a verdant trellis on the vaulted ceiling. Innocent putti displaying emblems of Diana cavort in the oval openings of the trellis, adding symbolic purpose to their usual playfulness.

Correggio was a consummate illusionist. Being particularly adept at theatrical visual effects, he was the logical choice to decorate the domes of two of the city's largest churches, San Giovanni Evangelista and the cathedral. His frescoes for Parma Cathedral (Fig. 7.73) catch the Virgin of the Assumption, to whom the cathedral is dedicated, in a luminous vortex of swirling clouds, saints, and angels. The Virgin's ascent seems especially dramatic by contrast with calm representations of the four patron saints of Parma in the squinches: Bernard, Thomas, Hilary of Poitiers, and John the Baptist. Above them, a fictive balustrade barely constrains excited onlookers, who crane their necks to catch a glimpse of the rapidly disappearing Virgin, visible only when one has begun to climb the broad stairs leading from the nave to the much higher transept and apse. The viewer's identification with the Virgin's ascent is intensified by the progressively smaller

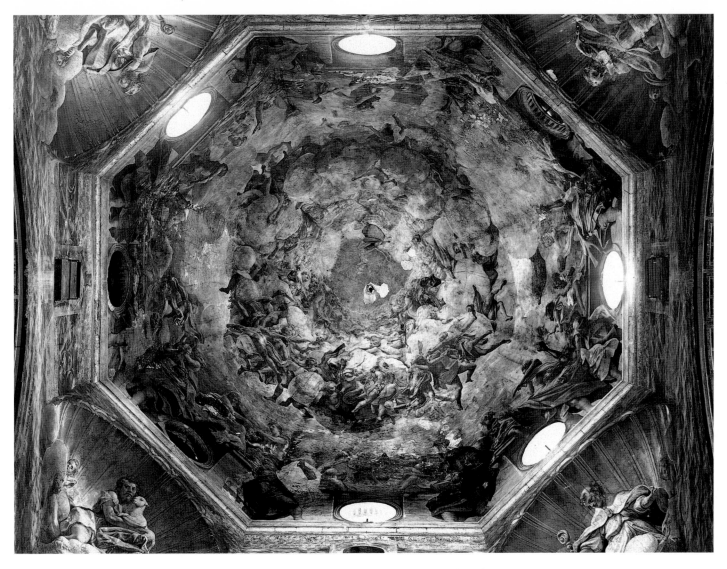

7.73 *Assumption of the Virgin*, 1522–30, Correggio, Parma Cathedral. Fresco, diameter c. 36′ (11 m)

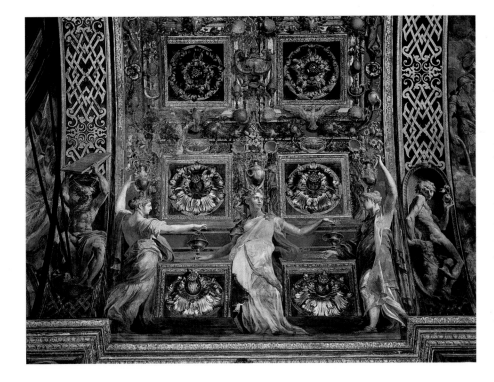

scale of the figures in each ring of the composition, far exceeding what would be necessary to achieve normal foreshortening. At the very center, the composition finally comes to rest in a peaceful and cloudless sky.

Correggio left Parma immediately after completing the dome frescoes. Because the details of his composition must always have been difficult to read—Correggio was more interested in the bold, overall effect than the precise rendition of any single figure—it was rumored that his patrons were dissatisfied with the work. However, admiring remarks from

7.74 *Three Foolish Virgins Flanked by Moses and Adam*, 1531–39, commissioned by the Confraternity of the Madonna della Steccata from Parmigianino for the vault in front of the main apse, Madonna della Steccata, Parma. Fresco

contemporary visitors—including Queen Christina of Sweden, who would not believe that the balustrade around the base of the dome was a fiction until she climbed to its base to see for herself—indicate that he may merely have sought a rest after having completed an extraordinarily demanding commission.

In Correggio's absence, a young native painter trained by his printmaker father and uncles returned to Parma from Rome, having established himself as the darling of the cultural elite. While in his teens, Parmigianino (Girolamo Francesco Maria Mazzola; 1503 Parma–1540 Casalmaggiore) had worked alongside Correggio. At the papal court he acquired an international reputation and cosmopolitan sophistication. Hailed upon his arrival in Rome in 1524 as a new Raphael, he was young, intelligent, and suave, both in personal manner and in his work, epitomizing the courtly ideal of an artist.

Parmigianino's initial commission in Parma involved decorating the vaults and main apse of a new centrally planned church dedicated to the Virgin (Fig. 7.74), that of the Madonna della Steccata. This project gave him the opportunity to refine Correggio's illusionistic effects and promote an even more elegant and graceful style which allied his patrons with the most sophisticated developments in contemporary Roman art. Parmigianino transformed the broad barrel-vault in front of the main apse into a sumptuous gilt, blue, and red field which seems to be bounded by protruding arches overlaid with interlacing gilt strapwork. Only the bosses at the center of the coffers are actually three-dimensional, every other figure, niche, and decorative detail a fiction. The three female figures who perform a balletic balancing act on a fictive ledge carry empty lamps which characterize them as the unprepared Foolish Virgins of one of Christ's parables; their wise, mirror-image counterparts appear on the opposite side of the vault.

Parmigianino's art offered the Parmesan aristocracy extraordinary opportunities for self-promotion. In his portrait of Gian Galeazzo Sanvitale, Count of Fontanellato (Fig. 7.75), whose villa Parmigianino brightened with inspired variations on Correggio's frescoes in the Camera di San Paolo, the sitter's self-confidence is extraordinary. The count stares out at the viewer, calmly daring anyone to challenge his innate physical and intellectual superiority. In his right hand he displays a bronze medal marked with the mysterious ciphers "7" and "2," which must have had significance for him and his close circle of friends, but whose inscrutability serves to distance him from the rest of humanity. Even so, the portrait is engaging; Parmigianino's artful arrangement of the count's helmet, mace, and costume, along with his masterly coordination of the simple background with the figure in front of it, fully embody Castiglione's courtly value of *sprezzatura* (confident but relaxed grace and ease).

Exquisitely contrived beauty also gave power to Parmigianino's religious paintings, their refinement employed as a metaphor for the perfection of God and the saints. One of his most famous religious paintings and an outstanding example of Mannerism is the altarpiece known as the *Madonna of the Long Neck* (Fig. 7.76). Commissioned by the noblewoman Elena Baiardi for her family chapel in the church of Santa Maria dei Servi in Parma, the painting takes its subject from a simile in medieval hymns to the Virgin which likened her neck to a great ivory tower or column. Highly appropriate to the traditional understanding of the Virgin as an allegorical representation of the Church, this imagery was also exploited in poems penned by Andrea Baiardi, the patron's father. Consciousness of such recondite medieval literary conceits pervaded courtly circles, not only in literature but in art as well. Thus the exaggerated length of the limbs of the Virgin and her son, as well as the presence of a column in the background of the painting, are not contrived merely for their decorative value, but clearly signal the painting's religious meaning. Similarly, the Virgin's engorged nipples need to be understood as emblems of her ability to nourish the faithful. When Vasari saw the painting in the mid-sixteenth century he noted another religious emblem in it: a cross, now barely visible, on the vase that one of the angels offers to the Madonna and Child, indicative of Christ's fate as sacrifice and spiritual food for humanity.

Admittedly, Parmigianino's expression of these religious concepts is so refined and contrived that both the uneducated worshiper of his own day and the modern, secular viewer could easily mistake his intentions. Because there is hardly an element in the painting that faithfully reproduces nature, the viewer is constantly required to question the artist's decisions, to comment on his skill, and to recognize that the subject of the painting is as much the craft of painting and the artist's intellectual agility as it is a Madonna and Child. Typical of the Mannerist style, the shift in scale is so great that there is no way to move from foreground to background in the painting. The five angels at the left are compacted into a space so constricted that one cannot imagine how their bodies fit into it. The Madonna is much larger than any other figure in the painting; her proportions are distended unnaturally and her hands and head have been elongated to emphasize their elegance. The perfect oval of the Virgin's head is crowned with a complicated braided hair style reminiscent of some figures in Leonardo drawings—a reminder that, regardless of its distortions of form, Mannerism often drew its inspiration from older masters.

Elements of overt sensuality belie the commission of this work as an altarpiece. The Virgin's right hand moves

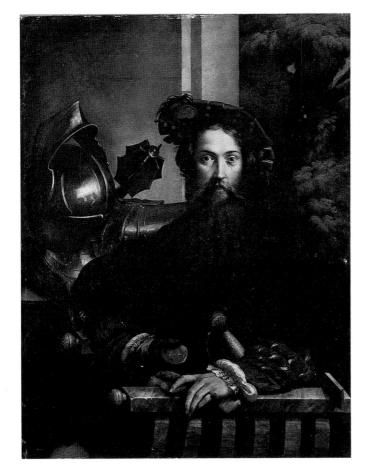

7.75 *Gian Galeazzo Sanvitale, Count of Fontanellato*, 1524, commissioned by Gian Galeazzo Sanvitale from PARMIGIANINO. Oil on panel, 43 × 31¾" (109 × 81 cm) (Museo Nazionale, Pinacoteca, Naples)

caressingly over her breast, which is revealed by a wet drapery technique borrowed from antique sculpture. Sliding along the left side of the painting is a smooth, long leg whose sensuous nudity is emphasized by the big toe of the Christ Child which presses suggestively against it. It is easy to understand how the metaphor linking artificial and elegant physical grace to a spiritual state of grace could be lost in the sheer artfulness and beauty of the painting.

Genoa: A Princely Republic

Genoa suddenly emerged as a major center of courtly patronage in the late 1520s. Nominally a republic, this great maritime center on the northern coast of the Ligurian Sea had always been dominated by powerful clans of nobles. Now Andrea Doria (1466–1560), an extraordinarily talented naval commander from an impoverished branch of an ancient local family, catapulted himself and the city into the international arena. By commanding impressive fleets and driving hard

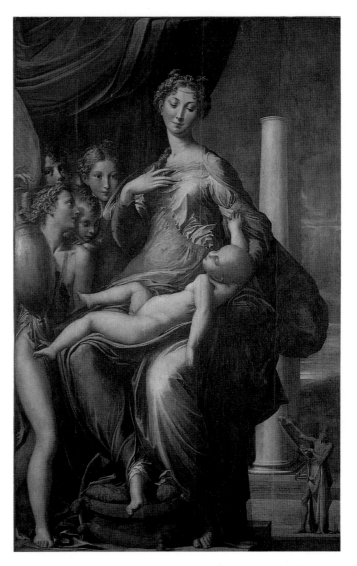

7.76 *Madonna of the Long Neck*, begun 1534, commissioned by Elena Baiardi from PARMIGIANINO for the Baiardi Chapel, Santa Maria dei Servi, Parma. Oil on panel, 85 × 52" (216 × 132 cm) (Galleria degli Uffizi, Florence)

The painting was left unfinished in 1540, accounting for some of its visual peculiarities, including numerous column bases and shadows but only a single distinct column in the background, and a disembodied foot next to the prophet at the lower right of the frame.

bargains for compensation with King Francis I of France, Pope Clement VII, and Emperor Charles V, he succeeded in enriching himself and reestablishing Genoese independence after protracted domination by the French. Charles V admitted him to the prestigious imperial Order of the Golden Fleece, and his fellow citizens named him Prince ("Principe") and Father of the Homeland ("Pater Patriae"). He and Genoa's oldest noble families set to refashioning their city—still markedly medieval in its dense urban fabric and precipitously narrow streets—to reflect the city's reemergence as a major player in Italian and international politics.

7.77 *Andrea Doria*, 1526, commissioned by Pope Clement VII from SEBASTIANO DEL PIOMBO. Oil on panel, 5' × 3' 6" (1.53 × 1.07 m) (Palazzo del Principe, Genoa)

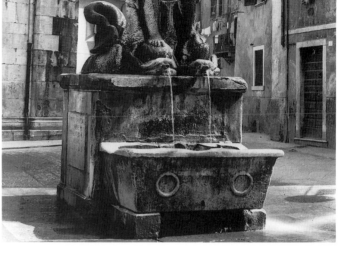

7.78 *Andrea Doria as Neptune*, 1528–29 and 1537–38, commissioned by the Signoria of Genoa from BACCIO BANDINELLI for a city square. Marble (Piazza del Duomo, Carrara)

This work was left incomplete and never was shipped to Genoa.

Doria Portraits Doria's commanding presence and indefatigable will—he lived to the remarkable age of 94—is ably captured in a portrait by Sebastiano del Piombo, produced in Rome for his employer Pope Clement VII (Fig. 7.77). This is a man of conspicuous determination whose grasp on the control of Genoa was singularly fierce. When, for example, the rival Fieschi family conspired to overthrow him in 1547, he had the clan obliterated. Dressed in black, Doria stares coldly at the viewer, staccato light catching prickly white stubble on the right side of his face. Shadows mask his features—and full intentions—on the left, leading the viewer's eye down to the half round shadow of his head on the back wall and his imperious, gesticulating right hand below. All that is calm and reserved in Raphael's similarly monochromatic portrait of Baldassare Castiglione (see Fig. 7.62) is charged with ominous drama. While scholars have succeeded in identifying the actual Roman relief on which Sebastiano based the naval motifs to which Doria is pointing, their precise meaning remains obscure, adding to the powerful allure of this portrayal.

Doria's self-assured virility—not to mention his position as commander of the imperial navy—allowed him to identify easily with Neptune, the ancient god of the sea. Soon after liberating the city from the French in 1528, city fathers (presumably with Doria's blessing) commissioned an over-life-sized marble statue of him as Neptune from the Florentine sculptor Baccio Bandinelli (Fig. 7.78). This, the first Renaissance portrayal of a contemporary ruler as a Roman god, presented Doria as the pacific (peaceful) Neptune astride two dolphins. The image is alert and vigilant, a bearded counterpart to Michelangelo's Florentine *David* (see Fig. 7.2), whose stance and bearing Bandinelli clearly emulated. Like David, Doria was to be seen as the city's liberator and a man of the people—a useful conceit for a "prince" in a republic.

Villa Doria Befitting his unique status in Genoa, Doria built himself a splendid seaside villa just outside the city's western gate (Fig. 7.79). An inscription running across its façade claimed it was his "retirement" home, but here he hosted dignitaries for months at a time and played the effective lord of Genoa. As was typical of many autocratic rulers' palaces (see Fig. 2.38), the villa stood adjacent to but outside the city proper. The site afforded superb views of the city and its harbor, while also practically and symbolically isolating the structure from its urban context, so as to exalt its owner.

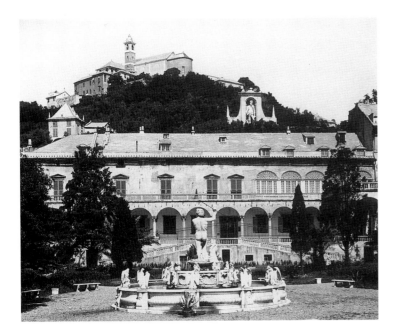

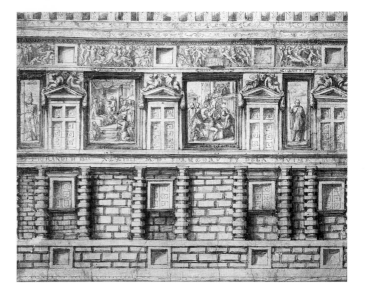

7.79 Villa Doria (now called Palazzo del Principe), Genoa, 1521–33, commissioned by Andrea Doria from PERINO DEL VAGA and others

7.80 Design for the north façade of the Villa Doria (Palazzo del Principe), Genoa, c. 1532, commissioned by Andrea Doria from PERINO DEL VAGA. Ink drawing on paper, 11½ × 14¼" (29.4 × 36.2 cm) (Rijksmuseum, Amsterdam)

The Villa Doria also resembled Roman suburban retreats like Agostino Chigi's villa in Rome (see Fig. 7.37) in its general form, incorporation of loggias, and the surrounding gardens. The importance of gardens is suggested by the formidable effort needed to carve terraces from the promontory against which the villa is situated. On the southern, seaward side, a three-armed portico reaches out to a terrace on which stood a fountain featuring an over-life-sized stucco version of Doria as Neptune (the statue visible in Fig. 7.80 is a permanent replacement carved in 1599). Divine imagery was as at home in his villa as in the public square.

Doria entrusted the design and decoration of much of this complex to Perino del Vaga (Pietro di Giovanni Buonaccorsi; 1501 Florence–1547 Rome), one of Raphael's students, who, like Bandinelli, escaped papal Rome during its fateful sack by imperial troops in 1527. Perino's common artistic roots with Giulio Romano, another of Raphael's talented pupils, is evident in the designs he made for the street-side façade of the Villa Doria (Fig. 7.80). As Giulio had done at the Palazzo del Tè for Federigo Gonzaga in Mantua (see Fig. 7.68), Perino conceived of the

7.81 *Fall of the Giants*, c. 1530, commissioned by Andrea Doria from PERINO DEL VAGA for the Salone dei Giganti, Villa Doria (Palazzo del Principe), Genoa. Fresco

Perino was responsible for the entire decoration of the room, which included very large and elaborate fireplaces built according to his designs.

façade as a field for architectural and decorative fantasies. Befitting the "rustic" setting of a villa, both designers employed what look like large rusticated blocks of stone, even imbedding the shafts of some of their columns in stacked blocks of stone—though Perino's façade is likely to have been executed almost entirely in illusionistic fresco, not three dimensions. Perino's basic attitude toward ancient-inspired motifs is also very different than Giulio's. Raphael's artistic example at the Vatican allowed for many possible responses. Giulio tended toward the grandiloquent and sometimes even melodramatic, especially at Federigo's pleasure palace, where he intended to entertain and delight. For Doria's more stately civic villa, on the other hand, Perino developed the elegant side of both Raphael and Michelangelo. The clearly composed scenes of Furius Camillus expelling the Gauls from Rome (a clear reference to Doria's having driven the French from

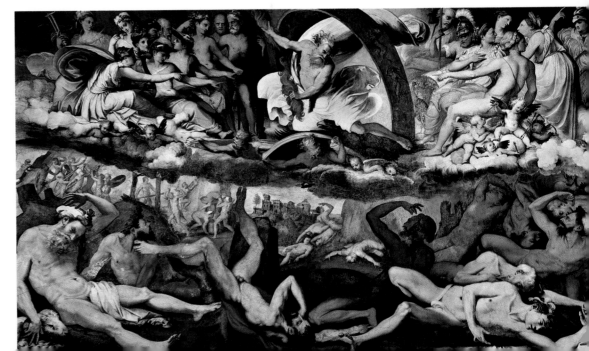

Genoa) recall Raphael's narrative genius, while the paired nudes reclining above the pedimented windows derive from the *ignudi* on the Sistine Ceiling (see Fig. 7.24).

Inside the villa, further allegories and scenes from antiquity thinly veiled Doria's autobiographical intents. His ancestors appear in Roman military garb on the upper loggia, reestablishing his distinguished lineage, while in the main reception hall Perino crowned the splendidly appointed room—hung with gold and silver tapestries illustrating the loves of Jupiter—with a representation of the *Fall of the Giants* (Fig. 7.81). Once again the contrast with Giulio Romano's rendition of the same theme, obviously a popular one (see Fig. 7.70), is dramatic. Perino, like Parmigianino, seized upon the artificial beauty of Raphael's art, arranging the Olympian gods at the top of the panel in a semicircle recalling the form of the Vatican *Disputà* and the relaxed grace of the *Parnassus* (see Figs. 7.31 and 7.30). At the center Jupiter swings through the blue ring of the zodiac like God the Father in Michelangelo's *Creation of Sun, Moon and Planets* (see Fig. 7.24). He is supported by an eagle that is fortuitously both the imperial symbol, and thus a complement to Emperor Charles V, and a reference to Charles' commander Doria, whose family emblem was the eagle. The indecorously posed yet elegantly distributed bodies of the giants in the lower half of the composition display Perino's skillful knowledge of anatomy and lighting effects. At the far left appears a lamb's head and fleece, yet another Dorian reference, in this case to the Order of the Golden Fleece, whose legend had it that the fleece was stolen by one of the giants.

Coda: Genoa in the Second Half of the Sixteenth Century

Doria's wholesale adoption of Roman artists and artistic models initiated a period of remarkable creativity in Genoa that was to endure well into the seventeenth century. In his *Palazzi Moderni di Genova* (Modern Palaces of Genoa, 1622) Peter Paul Rubens extolled the city as one of the most spectacular urban ensembles in Europe. He was particularly impressed with the Strada Nuova ("new" street, Figs. 7.82 and 7.83) and published engravings of its grand residential structures as well as many of the city's churches. Laid out for a select group of "old" noble families whose status was being challenged by newer clans around 1550, the street was promoted by them as a civic rather than private project. Profits from the sale of lots were shared with the cathedral. Still, only a few noble families benefited from the construction, and others—notably the Franciscans, who found the city brothel relocated near their doorstep—definitely suffered. Urban renewal has always had its problems.

Built up against a hill on what was then the edge of the city, the Strada Nuova is not technically a *strada* (street). It was never meant to be a thoroughfare but a modernized version of a traditional Genoese *albergo* (extended family compound). Entered at one end from a small existing piazza and ending at a garden wall, it was a closed space primarily intended for friends and relatives of the very exclusive group of families who lived there. One scholar has usefully described the Strada Nuova as a "street piazza," reflecting its function as gathering space as well as communication route.

In its initial stages, the street was also notable for its bilateral symmetry. The first six buildings on the street function as pairs: their main portals are located directly opposite one another, and they are grouped by size. The first two are the shortest and narrowest on the street, the next were the same height but wider than the first (renovations and additions have subsequently altered their proportions), and the third were as wide as the second but taller yet. Given the effects of perspective diminution, reinforced by the substantial length and straightness of the street, the distinctions would have blurred somewhat, contributing to the sense of an organized and coherent

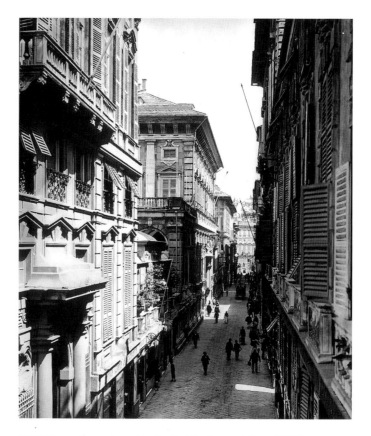

7.82 Strada Nuova (now Via Garibaldi), Genoa, initiated 1550, construction begun 1558, commissioned by the city government and noble families of Genoa perhaps from GALEAZZO ALESSI

Some of the buildings on the far end of the street date from as late as the eighteenth century.

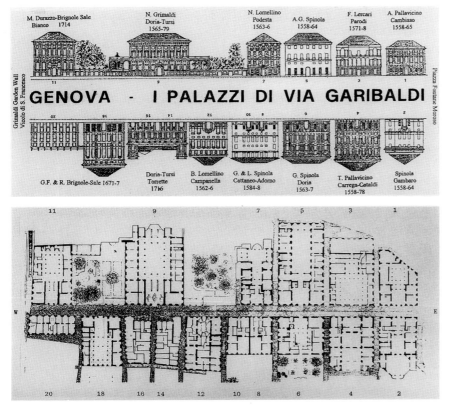

GENOVA - I PALAZZI DI VIA GARIBALDI

7.83 Strada Nuova, Genoa, plan

popularity, there was general agreement on appropriate models for imitation and emulation. This did not, however, result in a single, classical style. Instead, artists and patrons embraced ancient models and subjects in part because they offered an extraordinarily varied repertoire, not a restrictive standard. Ancient art itself had been heterogeneous, tolerating many local variations. Because each Renaissance city state had its own version of its ancient past, differences were inevitable. Thus in Venice a classicizing building like San Salvatore is anchored not in a generic style but draws on models from the imperial, Byzantine tradition that had provided civic inspiration for generations. Bramante's imperial forms were inspired by his contact with Italy's two ancient capitals: Milan and Rome.

Painters, having fewer specific remains to emulate than sculptors and architects—the impressive ruins of Pompeii on which modern accounts of ancient painting so heavily rely were not uncovered until the eighteenth century—exercised particular freedom in their stylistic inventions. After painting the balanced and centralized compositions of the Stanza della Segnatura, for example, Raphael went on to invent more dynamic and unsettled compositions in the other papal apartments. In Mantua and Genoa his students developed these ideas in their own distinctive ways. In the spandrels of the Sistine ceiling, Michelangelo called forth a new appreciation for brilliant and high-pitched color very different than the subdued mono- and bichromism of his sculpture and architecture. In Venice, Giorgione's and Titian's *poesie* contain few overt quotations from antiquity; rather, their classicism resides in the successful evocation of ancient elegies. Similarly, artists such as Parmigianino offered aristocratic patrons freely invented visual essays on the ancient values of grace and eloquence.

Increasingly pitted against one another in artistic competitions—whether in papal Rome, republican Florence, or Alfonso d'Este's Ferrara—artists were encouraged to develop distinctive styles and outdo one another in their inventiveness. Thus art was always in flux: at times balanced, at others dynamic, alternately serious and playful, licentious and high-minded, depending on the needs and status of the patron and the private or public nature of the commission. Only in subsequent centuries did critics define certain supposedly "classic" works—the Stanza della Segnatura and the Sistine ceiling, for example—as representing *the* singular standard of artistic achievement.

program. Variety reigned, however, in the decoration of the façades. Each clan adopted its own general scheme—a rustic and highly sculptural Doric mode for the Pallavicino palaces, flat frescoed blocks for the Spinola, for example—even though each clan's palaces were scattered along the street, not always opposite one another. Familial ties and loyalties overruled strict symmetry. The interiors of the palaces on the Strada Nuova are particularly distinctive insofar as they had to accommodate the steeply sloping site along which they were built. Those on the city side of the street required the construction of vast underpinnings to elevate terraces and viewing loggias; those on the hillside required just the opposite: complex engineering to move up the hill in elegant, broad stages. The expense and difficulty of their construction, the sheer amplitude and splendor of their spaces and interior furnishings, and the glorious vistas and gardens made these residences the epitome of aristocratic urban life for generations to come.

Synopsis

The early sixteenth century saw the wholesale acceptance of ancient Greece and Rome as the dominant sources of artistic and cultural inspiration throughout Italy. For the first time since the early fifteenth century, when the International Gothic style had experienced wide

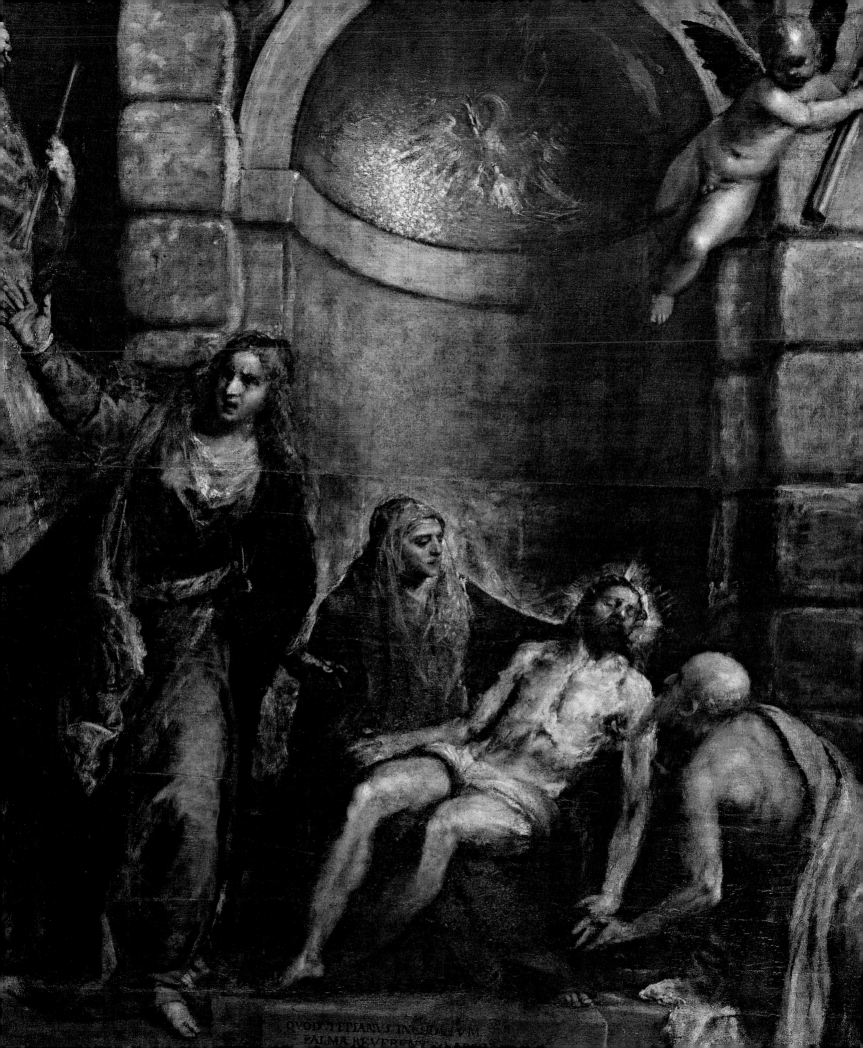

8
Renewing the City: The Mid-Sixteenth Century

The mid-sixteenth century was an era of artistic and political consolidation. Patrons and artists, chastened by the Sack of Rome in 1527, the Cambrai Wars (1509–29), and Protestant revolts, cultivated a renewed sense of order and discipline. Although painting in Florence and Rome, for example, continued to be dominated by stylishly elongated and elegant figures, patrons there set a new premium on clear exposition and subdued sensuousness. Gone were the freewheeling inventions and caprices that were so popular earlier in the century. Even Michelangelo caught criticism for his nudes in the Sistine Chapel, especially those in his *Last Judgment*, which were considered lewd and unseemly in a religious setting. Sensual themes and subjects continued to find ready patrons, but only for private delectation, not as subcurrents in religious imagery.

In Florence the reappearance of the Medici and the consolidation of their control over the city imposed new parameters on patronage and artistic expression. Duke Cosimo and his wife Eleonora of Toledo favored restrained and often haughty imagery to confirm their autocratic rule.

In Venice, state imagery was somewhat less forbidding but no less forceful. City officials took advantage of Jacopo Sansovino's and Andrea Palladio's intimate knowledge of Roman architecture—both contemporary and ancient—to determine the form of major public buildings and churches throughout the city, as well as for mainland palaces and villas. Classicizing structures increasingly punctuated and dominated the Byzantine and Gothic fabric of the city. Likewise in Rome, Pope Paul III reshaped major civic sites, including the Capitoline Hill and St. Peter's, which Michelangelo redirected back to the bold spatial concepts of Bramante.

In all major urban centers painters continued to receive commissions for grand allegories and extensive narratives, while producing impressively dramatic altarpieces and portraits as well. The creators of these works enjoyed increased social status in this period, earning individual recognition and organizing themselves into artistic academies that were to define artistic standards for generations to come.

Venice and the Veneto: The City Triumphant

In the years following the Cambrai Wars, which ended with the peace of Bologna in 1529, Venetians had cause to celebrate. They had triumphed over their adversaries, affirming their right to dominion over cities as far west as Bergamo and, to the east, beyond Dubrovnik on the Istrian coast. The city was once again the capital of an undisputed empire, and funds formerly earmarked for the war effort could now be lavished on construction at home. The moving force behind this extraordinary urban renewal was Doge Andrea Gritti (r. 1523–38), assisted by the Venetian Senate, the Procurators of San Marco, religious and lay groups, and private patrons, all of whom were intent on making Venice truly worthy of her claim to be the New Rome. With both Constantinople and Rome humiliated by foreign armies—the Byzantine capital in 1453 and Rome in the fateful Sack of 1527— Venice alone among the major Italian cities could boast of being inviolate. The Venetians were also beneficiaries of their rivals' woes, opening their arms to fleeing artists and scholars.

8.1 (opposite) *Pietà* (detail), begun c. 1570, left unfinished in 1576, painted by TITIAN for his own burial site at the Altar of the Holy Cross, Santa Maria Gloriosa dei Frari, Venice, completed by PALMA GIOVANE. Oil on canvas, 11' 6⅜" × 12' 9¼" (3.51 × 3.89 m) (Galleria dell'Accademia, Venice). See also Fig. 8.27.

Sansovino: Refashioning the City

Among the illustrious refugees fleeing to Venice was the forty-one-year-old Jacopo Sansovino (Jacopo Tassi; 1486 Florence–1570 Venice), who intended to stay only a few months but instead spent the second half of his extremely long life reshaping the face of the city. Sansovino had spent his youth in Florence (see Fig. 7.4) and his early adulthood in Rome, where he was deeply impressed by the works of Bramante, Michelangelo, and Raphael. He thus brought with him a thorough appreciation of the grand manner of ancient Roman architecture which had been revived by Julius II; but instead of merely importing and imposing Roman prototypes, he produced a distinctively Venetian interpretation of classical forms. Always extremely sensitive to the purpose and function of the buildings commissioned from him, Sansovino worked in a number of different modes, adjusting his architectural vocabulary, massing, and ornamentation to the problem at hand.

The Zecca   Soon after arriving in Venice, Sansovino employed his considerable technological knowledge of ancient and modern vaulting to strengthen and restore the domes of St. Mark's, a job that earned him the position of *proto* (architect and chief building superintendent) of St. Mark's from 1529 until his death in 1570. This position, along with commissions from the Venetian government, gave him extraordinary opportunities within the city's center, beginning in 1535, when Sansovino entered the competition to rebuild the Zecca, the state mint, on the quay facing the city's ceremonial waterfront entrance. As can be seen just below and to the left of the Campanile in Jacopo Barbari's print of Venice (see Figs. 1.2, 1.3), this area was occupied by a motley series of buildings, many of which were leased as shops and hostelries.

Venice's Council of Ten selected Sansovino's design for the Zecca in 1536. The massive new building (Fig. 8.2), originally only two stories high, confidently announced the city's recovery from the economic difficulties of the preceding decades of war. Its great cost was financed by government orders that freed slaves in Venice's dependency of Cyprus for 50 ducats a head. Fireproof, thanks to Sansovino's use of stone vaulting throughout the structure, the Zecca proclaims its impregnability through a bold use of rustication. Above the rugged ground story arcade (leased to cheese sellers, who had traditionally sold their products at the site), the second story employs the Doric order in a highly original way, with banded attached columns that appear to be squeezed at the top between the double lintels over the large windows. Making use of forms he would have known from his experience in Rome and from contemporary work such as Guilio Romano's more playful buildings in Mantua (see Fig. 7.68), Sansovino thus suggests the compressive processes used to create coins as well as the strength and dignity of a city gate or fortress—themes well suited to the building's site and function.

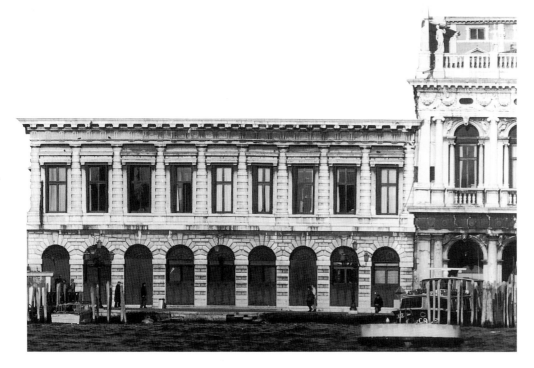

The Library   When Sansovino began work on the Zecca, he was also engaged by the government to rebuild the residence of the Procurators on the south side of the Piazza San Marco (their old residences are visible on the right in Gentile Bellini's *Procession in St. Mark's Square* (see Fig. 1.7), pushing back the façade so as to enlarge the piazza and also make the Campanile a free-standing

8.2 The Zecca (Mint), Venice, 1535–47, commissioned by the Council of Ten from JACOPO SANSOVINO

An upper story later added to the building has been removed from this photograph to give a better sense of the Zecca's original relationship to the Library at the right.

monument. Before he could make much progress, however, the Procurators switched their attention to the site alongside the Zecca facing the Doge's Palace on the Piazzetta. Seeking to add greater decorum to the city, the Procurators evicted hostelries and food shops from the site in order to establish a public library, one of the first of its kind (Fig. 8.3). It was intended to redress the embarrassing lack of a permanent home for the renowned collection of Greek and Latin manuscripts that Cardinal John Bessarion, a Greek emigré, had given to the state in 1468 and to display publicly the city's rich intellectual patrimony. The anteroom adjoining the main reading room was to be home to a school, ensuring the ongoing promotion of humanist values among young Venetian nobles. In its conscious emulation of the public libraries of classical antiquity, it also underscored Venice's image as successor to the legacy of imperial Rome and Constantinople.

The forceful architectural vocabulary of the adjacent Zecca was inappropriate to such a commission, so Sansovino's patrons must have requested more elegant forms. He complied by creating an airy palace, which purposefully contrasts in height, scale, and detail with the Zecca (see Fig. 8.2). Taking his cue from the Doge's Palace, directly opposite, Sansovino set two open arcades one upon another but interpreted the scheme in classical language—a Doric order on the ground floor, Ionic above, and, on the top, a balustrade punctuated with statues—to create effective counterparts to the earlier building's tracery, inlaid marbles, and exotic crenellations. Lush garlands bedeck the friezes, and sensuous figures recline in all the spandrels. The effect is lavish and ornate, in emulation of the most splendid examples from antiquity.

A showpiece of classical values, the library won international renown for its elegance and Sansovino's clever solution to a previously unresolved dictum of Vitruvius. The Roman architect had stipulated that a Doric frieze should end with a half **metope**, the blank surface between triglyphs; but since triglyphs were placed over columns it would have been impossible to have even a half metope at the corner of a building supported by a colonnaded loggia without altering the proportions of the triglyphs and metopes or extending the architrave awkwardly beyond the corner column. Sansovino provided an elegant solution by ending his colonnade with a pier rather than a column, at the same time reinforcing the solidity of the building's corners. He was so proud of his solution—and convinced that no one else would think of it—that in 1539 he sent out disingenuous requests for assistance from architects across Italy, to establish that the idea was his alone. The subsequent publication of his solution marked a new level of concern for, and success in, self-promotion.

Still, Sansovino's bravura did not free him from subservience to his patrons. When the stone vault of the main reading room of the library collapsed during unusually cold weather in December 1545, Sansovino was unceremoniously thrown in jail. Though soon released—following intervention from Titian and the ambassador of Emperor Charles V, among others—Sansovino was further penalized by having his salary suspended for two years and was commanded to make repairs at his own expense. At issue seems to have been the fact that he had ignored his patrons' preference for a traditional wooden ceiling, whose elasticity had proved more amenable to Venice's unstable subsoil. Roman prototypes and precedents could be adopted only when they were also well suited to local conditions.

The Loggetta In 1537 the Procurators had added to Sansovino's responsibilities by commissioning him to design a new loggia at the base of the Campanile (Fig. 8.3). Known as the Loggetta, it was to replace a pre-existing structure which had been the traditional meeting place of Venetian noblemen but was now considered inadequate for its location among such imposing buildings. The new Loggetta was intended to serve as a permanent civic stage set, providing a handsome gathering place for the city's nobles and celebrating Venice as a wise, imperial power. Adopting the appropriately symbolic form of a Roman triumphal arch, Sansovino placed allegorical reliefs alluding to Venice's maritime possessions

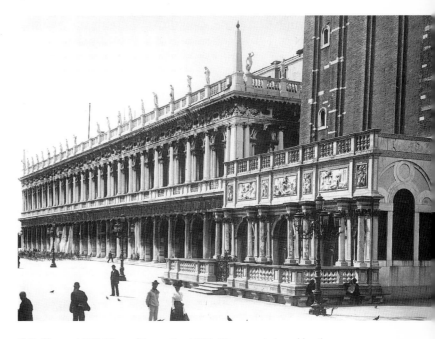

8.3 Library, 1537–91, and Loggetta, 1537–45, commissioned by the Procurators of St. Mark's from JACOPO SANSOVINO, Piazzetta San Marco, Venice

The Loggetta was rebuilt after the Campanile collapsed in 1902.

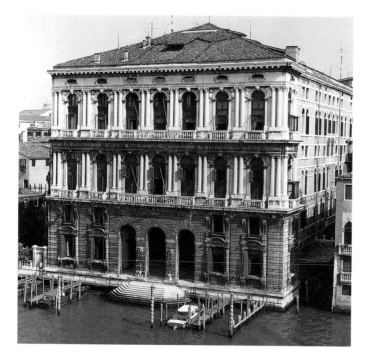

8.4 Palazzo Corner, Venice, c. 1545, commissioned by Zorzi Corner from JACOPO SANSOVINO

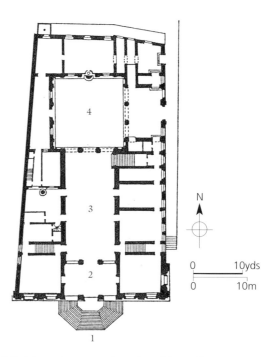

8.5 Palazzo Corner, Venice, plan of lower floor

1 Grand Canal; **2** Entrance portico (*riva*); **3** Central hall (*androne*); **4** Courtyard

Cyprus and Crete on the attic story and filled the ground-story niches with bronze statues of ancient gods and goddesses. Pallas, at the far left, stood for the wisdom of Venice's patriciate; Apollo, the sun god, represented the city's uniqueness and its remarkable harmony; Mercury, messenger of the gods, symbolized eloquence; and Peace emphasized the republic's commitment to non-belligerence. Sansovino's deft use of red Verona and other white and grey marbles enriched the site beyond its relatively modest dimensions while linking it visually to the brick tonalities of the Campanile, the then brick piazza, and the pink and white detailing of the Doge's Palace.

The Palazzo Corner   Sansovino's elegant and monumental classicism proved a powerfully expressive vehicle for one of Venice's wealthiest families, the Corner. The Palazzo Corner della Ca Grande, although only half as large as the family once contemplated, set a new standard for its huge size and rigorous Vitruvian detail (Figs. 8.4 and 8.5). The Corner (rhymes with "forbear") were an old patrician family whose wealth was greatly enhanced in the late fifteenth century by their success in persuading their kinswoman, Caterina Corner, to abdicate the throne of Cyprus that she had inherited from her husband so as to return control of the island to the Venetian government. Already wealthy merchants, they received special concessions and huge land holdings from the government, and also claimed rights to Caterina's dowry, which was deposited with the state. After a fire completely

destroyed the family's palace in 1532, they successfully petitioned to release half the dowry for the new construction. However, divisions of the family inheritance prevented major work from beginning until around 1545.

Sansovino organized the palace in typical Venetian fashion, providing three large openings on the canal for the receipt of merchandise. The rest of the structure—including an unprecedentedly large courtyard—resembled contemporary Roman palaces. Above the rusticated Doric ground story, he set an Ionic and then a Corinthian story, each of their seven bays divided from its neighbors by attached double columns set on pedestals. These features give the façade unprecedented weight and substance.

The Rialto Bridge

It is hard to imagine Venice without the Rialto Bridge, a sleek arc of white Istrian stone gliding over the Grand Canal in the heart of the city's commercial district (Fig. 8.6). The bridge dates from the late sixteenth century, when it replaced an earlier wooden bridge (visible in Carpaccio's *Miracle at Rialto*; see Fig. 6.37). By the mid-1500s this wooden bridge had become very dilapidated, but despite numerous complaints, followed by official discussions and plans submitted by Sansovino, as well as Michelangelo and others, the Venetian government did not commit to its reconstruction until 1588, making it the last of the century's major urban renewal projects.

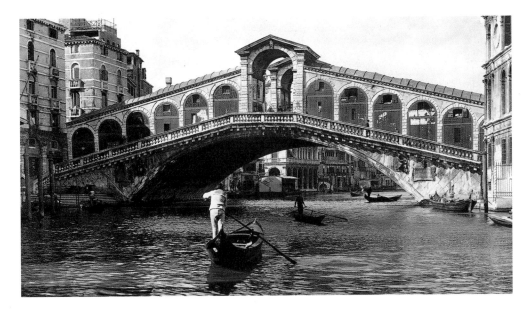

8.6 Rialto Bridge, Venice, 1588–91, commissioned by the Venetian government from ANTONIO DA PONTE

Throughout the fifteenth and sixteenth centuries the Venetians replaced hundreds of small wooden bridges with stone structures. A local chronicler indicated that bridges took on new, higher profiles to accommodate the cabins that had become popular on the gondolas of the nobles. At Rialto, the steep curve allowed large ships and barges to pass easily.

The chosen design is by Antonio da Ponte (1512 Venice?–1597 Venice), a master builder who worked on some of the most important civic projects in Venice, including military fortifications. His design is consummately Venetian, leaping the canal in a single 157-foot (48-meter) span and avoiding much of the complication of earlier proposals. It is also pragmatic, respecting the necessity of providing shops, lit from front and back, on both sides of the bridge and tall enough at the center to allow boats to pass under it easily. The bridge is also sensitive to human needs, featuring a gentle gradient and the reward of an open viewing platform at its summit.

Churches for Monastic and State Patrons

One of the architects whose design for the Rialto Bridge was rejected (probably because government officials were not keen to disturb private businesses by expropriating land on either end of the bridge necessary to fulfill his plans) was Andrea di Pietro of Padua, known as Palladio (1508 Padua–1580 Vicenza). Palladio was given his classical nickname (after Pallas Athene, goddess of wisdom) by Gian Giorgio Trissino, a humanist patrician of Vicenza who discovered the young stonemason and provided him with the education that both unleashed and harnessed his formidable creative talents. Palladio had learned the building trades from the ground up; with tutoring from Trissino and several trips accompanying his patron to Rome, he became his generation's most eloquent promoter of antique building types and by the 1550s had established a thriving practice in Vicenza. In 1554 he published his own little guidebook to the antiquities of Rome, followed in 1556 by illustrations for Daniele Barbaro's commentaries on Vitruvius. Palladio's writings culminated in 1570 with *The Four Books on Architecture*, a treatise organized by building types in which he laid out the rules of ancient architecture, illustrating them with numerous examples from his own buildings. The clean lines and clear geometry of his designs made them suited to graphic representation, assuring the dispersion of his ideas throughout Europe and to colonial America.

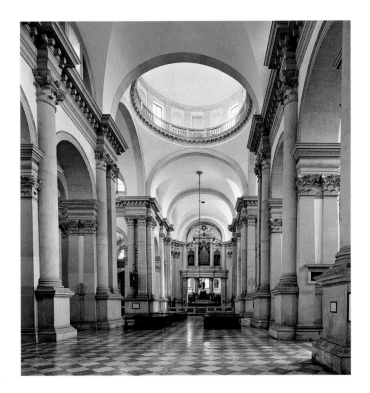

8.7 San Giorgio Maggiore, Venice, begun 1565, commissioned by Abbot Andrea Pampuro da Asolo from ANDREA PALLADIO

The doge and the Venetian senators made an annual visit to San Giorgio on the feast of St. Stephen (December 26).

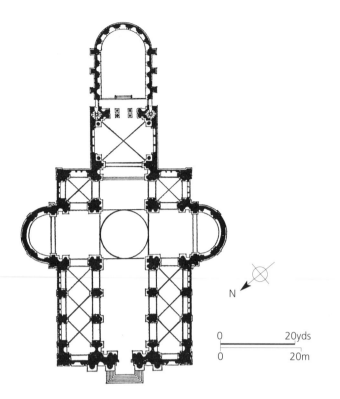

8.8 San Giorgio Maggiore, Venice, plan

San Giorgio Maggiore   In 1565 Palladio began work on one of his most prestigious commissions: rebuilding the Benedictine church and monastery of San Giorgio Maggiore, on an island directly across the lagoon from the Doge's Palace (Figs. 8.7 and 8.8). In his *Four Books*, Palladio advocated a central plan as the most suitable for a church because it was "most apt to demonstrate the Unity, the infinite Essence, the Uniformity and Justice of God." Here as elsewhere, however, he respected the preference of ecclesiastical authorities for a long nave, devising a Latin cross plan crowned with a dome at its crossing. He also made concessions to the needs of his monastic patrons by placing their choir in the apse, behind the high altar, rather than in the traditional rows in front of it; this was in response to new Church directives that the laity have an unobstructed view of the altar. Palladio's nave, with its rhythmic interplay of attached columns and pilasters, is impressive and yet welcoming (see Fig. 8.7). Unlike the imposing but dark churches of the Byzantine revival, whose domes were originally unilluminated, the church is filled with light from large thermal windows directly under the vaults. The rigorous geometry underlying the plan and determining the relationship between all the structural members is relieved by the slight swelling of the applied columns and pilasters, here the classical principles of **entasis** used inaccurately with the Corinthian order rather than the usual Doric. A softly bulging cushion molding intervenes between the columnar supports and the strongly projecting **entablature**. The effect is lucid and

harmonious, space modeled by, and yet flowing around, the building's structural supports.

The Redentore   The end of a particularly virulent outbreak of the plague in the summer of 1576 resulted in Palladio's receiving a commission for another church, this one built on the adjacent island of the Giudecca. During the plague the doge had vowed that when it ended the city would erect a church to Christ the Redeemer in gratitude. Work began on the church almost immediately; and the following year, on the feast of the Redeemer (the third Sunday in July), the Venetian government established the custom—still observed—of a civic procession over a bridge of boats to a service of thanksgiving in the church.

Palladio's design for the Redentore (Fig. 8.9) gives great prominence to the façade. Raised on a podium and approached by a broad stairway, well suited to the frontal approach dictated by the annual ceremony, the façade employs a subtle arrangement of interlocking triangles, pilasters, and attached columns. Palladio's design provided an ingenious solution to the problem of adapting a Roman temple front to the high nave and lower side aisles of the church. He combined two temple fronts: a tall, narrow one for the center unit fronting the nave with pilasters at either side and attached columns emphasizing the entrance, and a broad, lower one recessed behind the first. For all its complexity, the design manages to convey

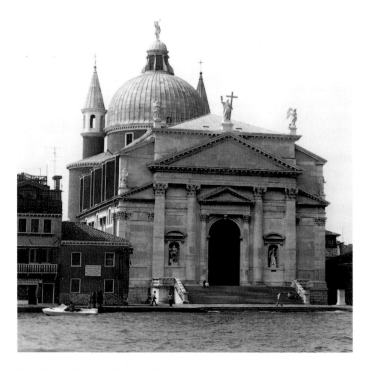

8.9 The Redentore (Church of the Redeemer), Venice, begun 1577, commissioned by the Venetian government from ANDREA PALLADIO

Plague in Venice

This account of the plague that devastated Venice in 1576–7 was written by a Venetian notary, Rocco Benedetti, some years after the event, in 1630. Nevertheless, it conveys vividly the terror and despair experienced by the citizens at the time.

The plague continued, killing more people with every hour that passed, and every day inspiring greater terror and deeper compassion for its poor infected victims. Onlookers wept as these people were carried down to their doors by their sons, fathers and mothers, and there in the public eye their bodies were stripped naked and shown to the doctors to be assessed. The same had to be done for the dead, and I myself had to carry down three whom I had lost: my mother, my brother, and a nephew. Neither in life nor in death had they shown any symptom of plague, but they were assessed by the parish doctor as "of concern" and, since there was an order that [two] cases "of concern" were equivalent to one "of suspicion,"

I was compelled to spend forty days confined at home.

The fate of those who lived alone was wretched, for, if they happened to fall ill, there was no one to lend them any assistance, and they died in misery. And, when two or three days had passed without their appearing and giving an account of themselves, their deaths were suspected. And then the corpse-bearers, entering the houses by breaking down the doors or climbing through the windows, found them dead in their beds or on the floors or in other places to which the frenzy of the disease had carried them . . . .

When the bodies could no longer be burned because of the great stench, a cemetery was established a little way off on the Lido, at a place called Cavanella, and there very deep pits were dug. Following the practice at the Lazzaretto, a layer of corpses was placed in them, and then a layer of lime, and then a layer of earth, and so on from layer to layer until they were full, in such a way that from one day to the next all bodies were buried. The dead from the city who had been

assessed as "of concern" were taken for burial in their coffins at Sant'Avario di Torcello. And, because neither the Certosa nor any of the other places assigned for airing goods was big enough, and because goods had to be aired for as long as forty days, so that most were ruined by exposure to air, wind and rain by day and by night, permission was given to those with spacious houses to air [their goods] themselves at home or in other suitable places.

To sum it all up, in maintaining so many people and bearing such expense the Doge spent a huge sum of money. Administration became chaotic, so that all the Savi [officials] were bewildered, not seeing how to provide for so great a need, nor which course to take to protect us from such a hail of arrows, showered down in all directions by the plague.

(from D.S. Chambers and B. Pullan with J. Fletcher. *Venice: A Documentary History*. Oxford: Blackwell, 1992, pp. 117–19)

an impression of serene simplicity. The attic story over the main pediment evokes associations with the Pantheon in Rome, while, rising triumphantly above these classical forms, the bulbous Venetian dome flanked by turrets proudly proclaims the city's Byzantine heritage.

Villas on the Venetian Mainland

By the mid-sixteenth century, Venice's maritime activities were in permanent decline, weakened both by the Turks and by fellow Europeans, who had rounded the Cape of Good Hope and had begun exploring the Americas. Venetian nobles acquired land in the countryside between their city and Vicenza and built impressive villas, not only because they wanted and needed a country retreat, but also as a gesture of defiance in the face of challenges to their mainland empire. Unlike the suburban villas of papal Rome (see Figs. 8.55 and 8.56) or such pleasure palaces as that built by Federigo Gonzaga in Mantua (see Fig. 7.68), these buildings were the functional centers of large working farms, many built on recently drained swamps. To ennoble these sites and bring them into con-

formity with Venetian nostalgia for the supposedly idyllic rural life of antiquity, a number of Venetian noblemen hired Palladio as the architect for their villas very soon after his return from Rome in 1541. Palladio centered his villa designs around a main residence fronted by a classical portico.

The Villa Barbaro At the Villa Barbaro in Maser (Figs. 8.10 and 8.11), his patrons, the brothers Daniele and Marc'Antonio Barbaro, explicitly sought to re-create a Triclinium described by Pliny the Younger at his commodious seaside villa outside ancient Rome, opening all four sides of the building to a cross-shaped, barrel-vaulted, central hall. Given the paucity of physical evidence on Roman villas available to Palladio and his patrons, the complex fails as an archaeological reconstruction, but it is an inspired evocation of antiquity; some of its unusually ornate sculptural decoration may be the work of Marc'Antonio Barbaro himself, who was an amateur painter and sculptor. Making a virtue of necessity, Palladio increased the apparent size of the house by extending it with an arcaded gallery which joins

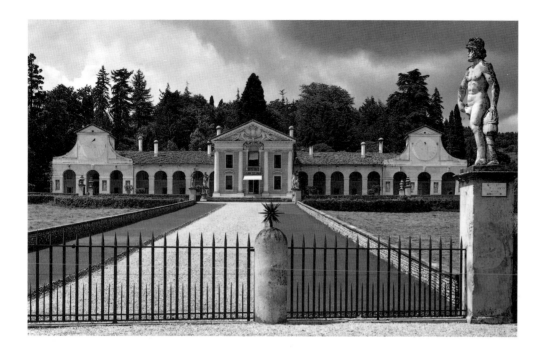

8.10 Villa Barbaro, Maser, 1555–59, commissioned by Daniele and Marc'Antonio Barbaro from ANDREA PALLADIO

Palladio's villas were built of economical materials faced in tinted stucco, unlike his city palaces, which were usually faced in stone.

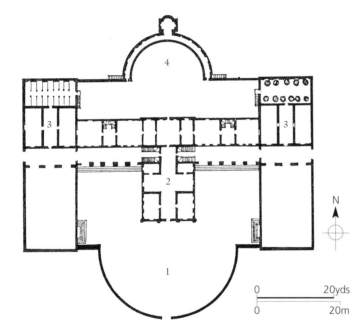

8.11 Villa Barbaro, Maser, plan, from ANDREA PALLADIO, *Quattro Libri dell'Architettura*, 1570

1 Courtyard; **2** Main residence; **3** Service wings; **4** Nymphaeum

it to twin service buildings accommodating stables, storerooms, and wine cellars. The plan Palladio published in his *Four Books* (see Fig. 8.11) indicates that the side buildings and the agrarian activities that took place in them were to have been partially obscured by enclosed forecourts, while the residence itself was to have been preceded by a classically inspired hemispherical entrance wall,

repeated in the shape of a **nymphaeum** at the far side of the house. Rigorously symmetrical, as were all his designs, the plan established two clear axes, giving order to the villa's multiple functions.

The decoration inside the villa seems to have been entirely assigned to Paolo Cagliari, known as il Veronese (1528 Verona–1588 Venice), whose frescoes and stucco works enhance and elaborate Palladio's rather severe architectural forms. Veronese's rich decorative style and sumptuous but delicate colors made him the favorite painter of the Venetian nobility. The specific program is difficult to elucidate and is often described as lacking a specific subject, but in his translation and commentary on Vitruvius, Daniele Barbaro said that painting, like literature and music, "must have intentions and represent some effect that controls or directs the entire composition." The predominance of allegorical figures and landscapes suggests that Barbaro intended to celebrate the natural world and the virtues of his family.

On the ceiling of the central room at the back of the residence (Fig. 8.12), overlooking the nymphaeum, Veronese took inspiration from Mantegna's famous illusionistic composition in the Camera Picta in Mantua (see Fig. 6.23). At the sides, arching above idealized landscapes, are illusionistic balconies. On one side stands the splendidly garbed lady of the house, Giustiniana Giustinian, next to a swarthy old servant woman whose one exposed breast may indicate that she is Giustiniana's loyal nursemaid (a small dog, symbol of fidelity, sits pertly in front of her). The jarring contrast between the two serves to emphasize Giustiniana's superior social status and fecund youth, while at the same time suggesting

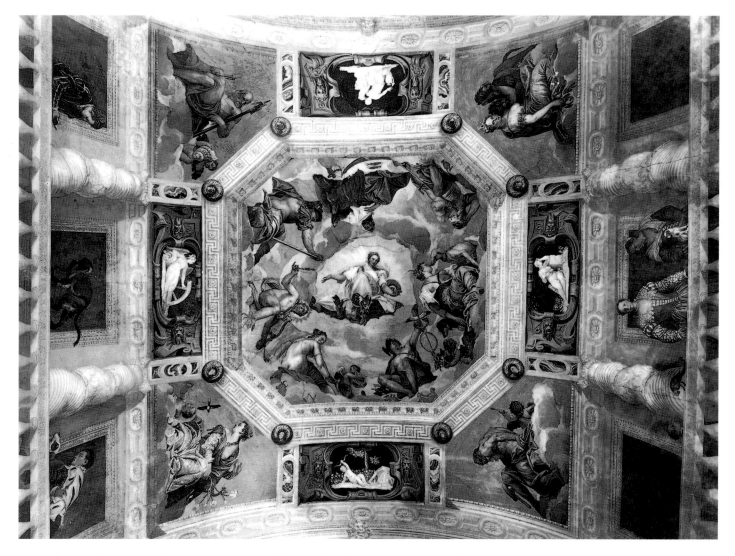

8.12 *Allegory of Divine Love*, after 1559, commissioned by Daniele and Marc'Antonio Barbaro from PAOLO VERONESE for Villa Barbaro, Maser. Fresco

the close bonds among all female members of the household. Next to them, the youngest Barbaro boy, still presumably directly in his mother's care, peers at a parrot from the left side of one of the spiraling columns. On the opposite side of the room, two older and presumably more independent boys read and attend to a hunting dog, while a pet monkey gambols across the parapet. Together these figures declare this a domestic space, one which was ordered and administered by Giustiniana in the Barbaro brothers' frequent absences. Tellingly, at the center, in an octagonal oculus, a female figure dressed in white and sitting on a beast probably represents Divine Love, who has conquered strife (the beast) and now imposes order on the universe. Personifications of the signs of the zodiac surround her. Vulcan, Cybele, Neptune, and Juno fill the corner spandrels, alluding to the four elements of fire, earth, water, and air; gods associated with each of the four seasons recline in the spandrels between them.

The Villa La Rotonda The church dignitary and humanist Monsignor Paolo Almerico chose a site overlooking the gentle hills outside Vicenza, his main place of residence, for his villa. Known as La Rotonda (Fig. 8.13), it differs from other countryside residences in that it was built primarily as a suburban retreat rather than as a working farm. As was the case with all of Palladio's villas, the exterior is rather plain. The setting made it grand and inspired Palladio to give each side of the house, built on a centralized plan (Fig. 8.14), a pedimented loggia, so as to enjoy, in the architect's words, "beautiful views on every side, some of which are limited, others more distant, and still others that reach the horizon." Each portico is approached by a broad staircase. The sensitive deployment of simple forms—square, rectangle and triangle—combined with Palladio's unerring sense of proportion culminates in a shallow dome which forms a surrogate crest to the hill, uniting the building and the

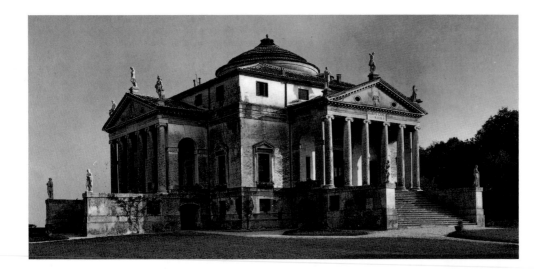

8.13 Villa La Rotonda, Vicenza, begun late 1560s, commissioned by Paolo Almerico from ANDREA PALLADIO

A later owner, Mario Capra, inserted his name on tablets in the middle of each entablature. The interior of the villa was thoroughly redecorated in the eighteenth century.

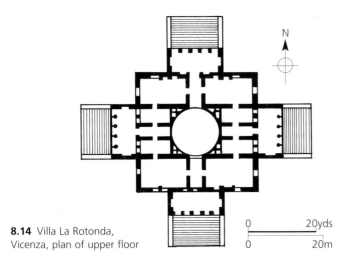

8.14 Villa La Rotonda, Vicenza, plan of upper floor

0   20yds
0   20m

land upon which it rests. Passageways originally interrupted the center of each of the building's four exterior staircases to allow carts easy access to ground-floor work areas, which contained internal staircases leading to an attic granary. The building's main floor was designed for gracious entertaining, with symmetrically disposed rectangular reception rooms encircling a domed central hall.

The Teatro Olimpico

Vicenza's leading citizens were especially appreciative of Palladio's classicism. The architect himself enjoyed the unusual honor of being a member of the Olympic Academy, formed in 1555 to encourage the revival and production of ancient theatrical works. For this group of scholars, Palladio designed his most thoroughly archaeological creation, the Teatro Olimpico (Figs. 8.15 and 8.16), which was completed after his death—as were many of Palladio's projects—by the Veronese architect

Vincenzo Scamozzi (1548 Vicenza–1616 Venice). The seating was arranged as a series of concentric steps facing a richly articulated proscenium resembling the façade of a grand palace, with several openings. Scamozzi added street vistas set in perspective behind the openings so as to increase the apparent depth of the stage. Following classical practice, however, nearly all the dramatic action took place in front of the proscenium. Members who contributed funds for the construction received commemoration with a statue, inscription, and their coat of arms on one of the pedestals of the columns on the proscenium and in niches surrounding the seating. Many donors were negligent in their payments, however; the inaugural performance, in 1585, of Sophocles' *Oedipus Rex*, was made possible only because the Academy's president (known as the "prince") took out a personal loan to underwrite the costs.

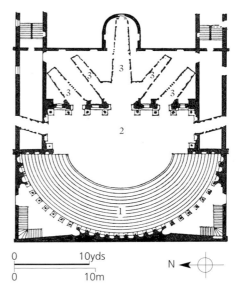

0   10yds
0   10m   N ◄

8.15 Teatro Olimpico, Vicenza, plan

1 Seating; **2** Proscenium; **3** Street scenes extending stage area

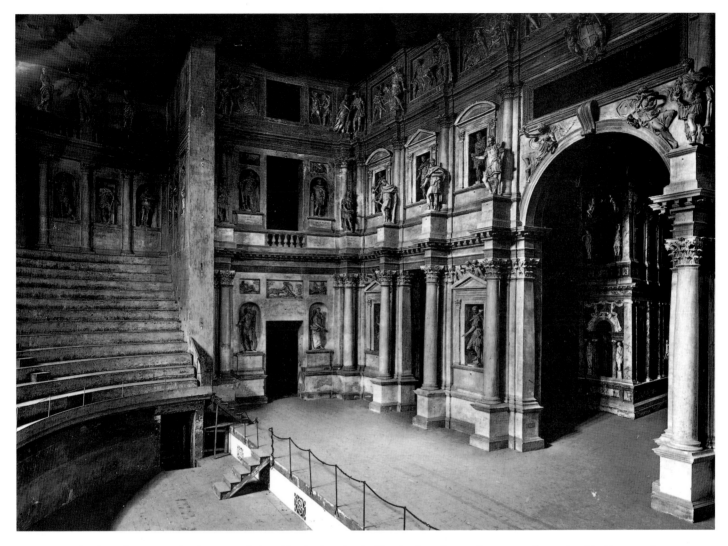

8.16 Teatro Olimpico, Vicenza, 1555–1616, commissioned by the Accademia Olimpica from ANDREA PALLADIO and completed by VINCENZO SCAMOZZI

Titian: Fashioning Images of the International Elite

In attempting to lure benefactors with the promise of inscriptions inside the Teatro Olimpico, the members of Vicenza's Academy were attempting to capitalize (if somewhat unsuccessfully) on a current pan-European enthusiasm for grand portraiture. Titian, for one, cultivated a remarkably international clientele, who called upon him because, as a painter of altarpieces and narrative works, he was already more famous than a "mere" portraitist. He was comfortable creating works that were larger than life and was committed, like Leonardo da Vinci and Raphael, to capturing a sitter's psychological as well as physical being.

The character Titian imparted to his sitters, however, depended as much on their social status, gender, and traditional conventions of representation as it did on the individual sitter's personality or the artist's innate talent. Titian was hardly free to paint a portrait as he chose. In creating a pair of paintings of the duke and duchess of Urbino, Francesco Maria della Rovere and Eleonora Gonzaga (Figs. 8.18 and 8.19), he predictably reprised many of the themes seen in Piero della Francesca's double portrait of their predecessors, Federico da Montefeltro and Battista Sforza (see Fig. 6.13). Once again, the male portrait is more rugged and individualized, emphasizing military exploits and adventures. Francesco Maria poses alert in his stunningly rendered, glinting armor, his right arm and baton dramatically thrust out into the viewer's space. Behind him a splendid, plumed parade helmet, reflecting the vibrant, pulsating red of a velvet drape, faces a jauntily angled set of lances. In marked contrast, Eleonora Gonzaga sits primly in her chair, immobile within her highly detailed but much less lovingly depicted court dress. Described by Castiglione as embodying

Art and Country Life

Virulent outbreaks of malaria and plague in Renaissance cities during the oppressive heat of July and August induced people of means to retreat for safety, as well as relaxation, to the cooler and healthier climes of the countryside. Such was the setting of Boccaccio's *Decameron*, in which young nobles retreat to the hills outside Florence to tell amusing stories as they wait out the plague. Many landowners spent a full third of the year at their villas, staying at their rural estates from late spring well into September and early October to oversee the grape harvest and wine production.

As one might expect, life at country estates was more casual than in cities. Chickens and other small farm animals wandered freely in the large walled courtyards around the living and dining quarters—scenes that easily spring to mind when one visits the villas designed by Andrea Palladio, most of which, despite their elegance, were the center of working farms. Gentlemen donned work clothes and experimented with grafting trees and rooting unusual specimens. Nevertheless, the upper class always tamed part of their surroundings as a setting for elegant entertainments. In Figure 8.17, a painting attributed to Benedetto

Cagliari (1538–98), brother of Paolo Veronese, noblewomen dressed in stylish silks are about to take a boat ride, while a more plainly garbed woman, perhaps a servant, dangles a fishing pole over the back of a stone bench, which has been softened with a velvet cover. A vine-covered pergola just above the landing will

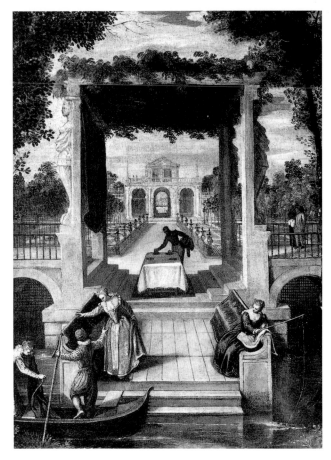

8.17 View of a garden, late sixteenth century, perhaps commissioned from BENEDETTO CAGLIARI, possibly for a Bergamese villa (Accademia Carrara, Bergamo)

provide a breezy and shady setting for the main meal of the day, taken at midday. A servant sets the table, while at the far right, on a bridge over a canal, a young boy strolls with an old man, much as the owners and their guests will do in the garden before and after the meal.

Pastimes at such country estates included reading, story telling, and card and board games. The most distinctive entertainments, though, were provided by *giochi d'aqua* (water games), the play of cascading waters in fountains, some of which were controlled by servants. Hidden from view, confederates of the host would suddenly surround an unsuspecting guest with a wall of water or surprise the ear by precipitously increasing or diminishing the water flow. Respite from the heat was provided by the gently dripping waters inside an artificial grotto like that of the Villa Giulia (see Fig. 8.55) or within a fountain house like the structure in the background of Cagliari's painting. Seeking harmony with and pleasure from nature, visitors felt refreshed and restored, "better able," as Francesco Doni put it in *Le Ville* of the 1550s, "to tolerate the irritating annoyances, and unbearable toils" of responsibilities in the city.

"wisdom, grace, beauty, intelligence, discreet manners, humanity and every other gentle quality," she was confined to a much more circumspect existence. Even her pet dog lies bored on a table in front of a window. Titian's landscape is expansive but untraversable, marked by a church tower in its idealized blue distance. Only when Titian was painting ideal women—always young—do they seem to come alive. A nearly contemporary portrait of the fiery and determined Isabella d'Este is as lacking in verve and emotion as Eleonora's. This is partly due

to the fact that Isabella asked him to copy an earlier, youthful portrait, a clear sign that she, like Eleonora, was complicit with the roles and ideals men held about women. In offering a lackluster portrait of Eleonora, Titian was most likely exercising decorum and restraint, flattering her even as he confirmed societal stereotypes.

In male portraits, artists had a greater range of behaviors and emotions to explore, but again sitters' depicted behavior depended on their age and social status. When Titian returned from a trip to Rome in 1546 he exploited

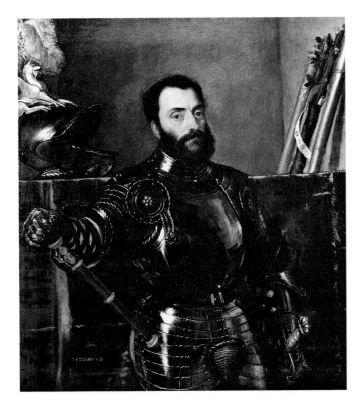

8.18 *Francesco Maria della Rovere*, 1536–38, commissioned by the sitter from TITIAN. Oil on canvas, 45 × 39⅜" (114.3 × 100.3 cm) (Galleria degli Uffizi, Florence)

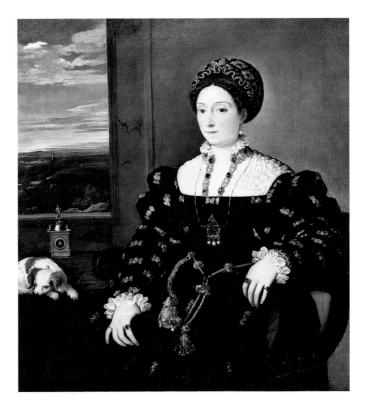

8.19 *Eleonora Gonzaga*, c. 1538, commissioned by the sitter or Francesco Maria della Rovere from TITIAN. Oil on canvas, 44⅞ × 40¼" (114 × 102.2 cm) (Galleria degli Uffizi, Florence)

his experience there in a group portrait of the male members of the Vendramin family (Fig. 8.20). Here Titian adapted elements such as the steps, massive altar, flickering candles, and groups of onlookers from Raphael's *Mass of Bolsena* in the papal apartments as a suitably impressive setting for the Vendramin family's adoration of a reliquary of a fragment of the True Cross. Although the relic was owned by the Scuola Grande di San Giovanni Evangelista, the Vendramin family was closely associated with it: one of their ancestors had donated the relic to the Scuola, and Andrea Vendramin, namesake of Titian's patron, was famous for having rescued it when it earlier fell into a canal. Titian suggests the intimacy of the family's relation to the relic by placing the

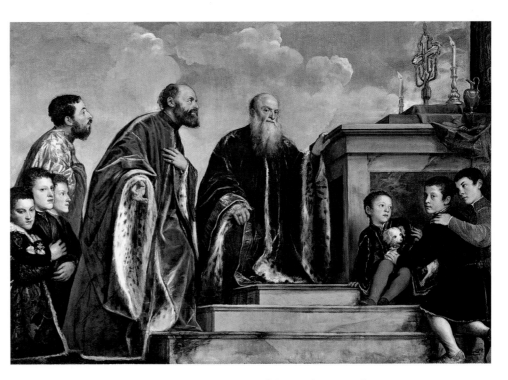

8.20 *Male Members of the Vendramin Family*, c. 1547, commissioned by Andrea Vendramin from TITIAN, probably for the Palazzo Vendramin, Venice. Oil on canvas, 6' 7" × 9' 10½" (2.06 × 3 m) (National Gallery, London)

current head of the family (also named Andrea) in the center of the composition, with one hand on the altar as he looks out of the picture, inviting the viewer's participation. At the left, two other family members, dressed in senatorial red, pay their eloquent devotion to the relic, the middle-aged man reaching out as if to share his adoration with others. Titian records and contrasts the emotions of his subjects; the sober obedience of the adolescents at left and the innocent play of the children at right serve to underscore the maturity and depth of the adults' piety.

Titian excelled not only at depicting character and emotion but also in suggesting the qualities of leadership possessed (or claimed) by the highest-ranking members of society—qualities that set them above their subjects. In 1548 Emperor Charles V called Titian to Augsburg, where he painted a life-sized equestrian portrait, the first of its kind, which set the standard for regal portraiture for well over a century (Fig. 8.21). Titian captured the Emperor at the height of his powers, calm and erect upon a charging horse. The contrast between the Emperor's resolute confidence and the horse's bowed, obedient head eloquently conveys Charles's authority over it. His power and invincibility are underscored by the aura of gleaming light reflecting off his armor and the glowing, radiant sky toward which he advances from

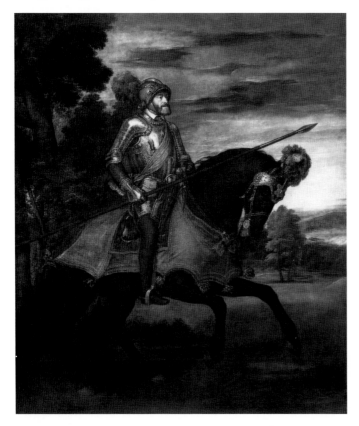

8.21 *Equestrian Portrait of Emperor Charles V*, 1548, commissioned by Charles V from TITIAN. Oil on canvas, 10' 10⅜" × 9' 1⅞" (3.31 × 2.79 m) (Museo del Prado, Madrid)

Charles wears the armor he actually wore in the decisive battle of Muhlberg where he trounced his Protestant opponents. The armor is preserved in the Royal Armory in Madrid.

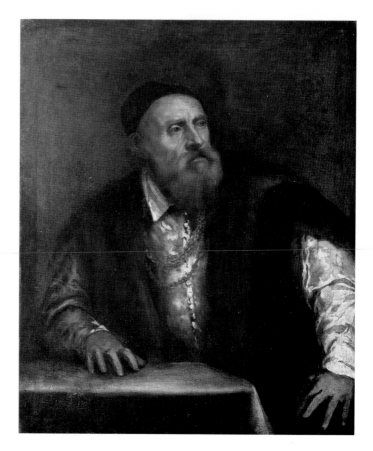

8.22 *Self-Portrait*, 1560s, TITIAN. Oil on canvas, 29½ × 37¾" (75 × 96 cm) (Gemäldegalerie, Berlin)

the dark trees and ominous clouds at the left. In keeping with traditions of royal portraiture, Charles appears as virtuous as a saint and as stoic as a Roman hero. Yet he is also vigorously alive, chin set high and eyes focused forward, the epitome of a human ruler with superhuman powers and responsibilities.

Titian knew his sitters well. The intimate of popes, kings, and princes, he was himself knighted by Charles in 1533. In a self-portrait from the 1560s (Fig. 8.22), Titian proudly wears the gold chains and fur jacket that marked his membership of the international elite. He does not look straight out at the viewer—the simplest pose for an artist who must study his own features in a mirror—but instead lifts his head to the side as if in recognition of some person or force beyond him. Since Titian had earlier used a similar pose for a portrait of his good friend the poet Pietro Aretino, he may have intended this self-portrait as a meditation on his own intellectual and creative powers. The painting is unfinished, especially in the hands and arms, but here Titian is in full control of his medium, with bold dashes of paint on the artist's collar, buttons, and sleeves suggesting the vigor of his intensely engaged mind and spirit. Titian declares himself worthy of his international fame and recognition.

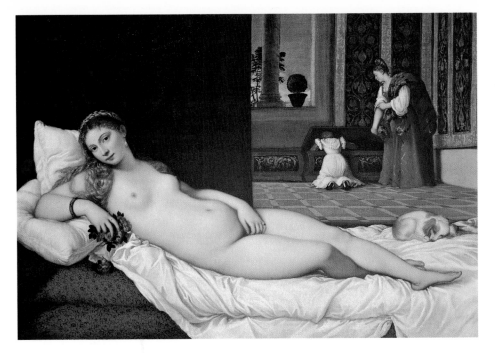

8.23 *Reclining Nude* ("*Venus*" *of Urbino*), c. 1538, commissioned by Guidobaldo della Rovere from TITIAN. Oil on canvas, 3' 11" × 5' 5" (1.19 × 1.65 m) (Galleria degli Uffizi, Florence)

Mythology and Sensuality for Court Sophisticates

As is evident from early sixteenth-century painting in Venice and at the court of Alfonso d'Este in Ferrara, artists such as Titian found a ready market for sensuous, purportedly mythological subject matter. Especially popular were paintings of reclining women, dubbed "Venus" by later generations, but which sixteenth-century documents unabashedly call "nude woman." Titian made their erotic intent unmistakable in a painting that he completed for Duke Guidobaldo della Rovere of Urbino around 1538 (Fig. 8.23). Instead of placing her in a poetic landscape (see Fig. 7.51), Titian presents his object of

desire inside a handsome palace, displaying herself on white satin sheets and pillows upon a luxurious red couch. Her golden tresses cascade alluringly over her shoulder to her braceleted right arm and hand, which toys with a small bouquet of flowers, while her left is placed provocatively over her genitals. Cool and dispassionate as the morning light which appears in the window at the rear of the room, this woman is nonetheless alert and available—her small pet dog, a traditional twin symbol of fidelity or lust, having fallen asleep at her feet. Servants in the background search diligently for garments to adorn her alluring and self-confident beauty. Calling to mind the sophisticated and renowned world of Venetian courtesans and court mistresses, whose physical beauty was expected to be accompanied by pleasant and learned conversation—unlike the conventional verbal reticence usually expected of Renaissance women—Titian's "nude woman" is a woman "worthy" of male companionship.

For the most part, however, male patrons of such paintings imagined themselves as far superior to females, a point made explicit in a series of paintings Titian produced for King Philip II of Spain (r. 1555–98) illustrating the loves of Jupiter. The king was to imagine himself as a god; all his conquests are mere mortals. One of the most openly sensual of these images, the *Danaë* of 1554 (Fig. 8.24), represents a further development of ideas informing earlier images of female nudes. The myth relates how Jupiter transformed himself into a shower of gold in order to possess a lovely young woman guarded by an old crone. Given the old woman's avaricious collection of some of the gold in the form of actual coins, and Danaë's receptivity to Jupiter's advances expressed by her parted legs and dreamy expression, the story's associations with prostitution are

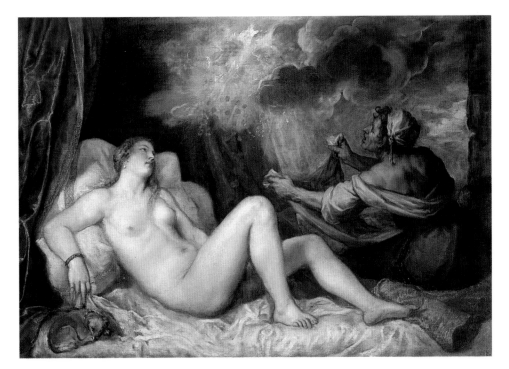

8.24 *Danaë*, 1554, commissioned by Philip II of Spain from TITIAN. Oil on canvas, 4' 2⅜" × 5' 10" (1.28 × 1.78 m) (Museo del Prado, Madrid)

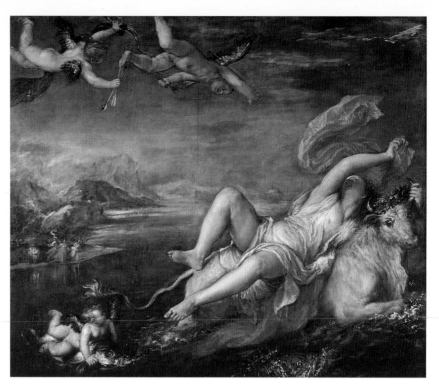

8.25 *Rape of Europa*, 1559–62, commissioned by Philip II of Spain from TITIAN. Oil on canvas, 5' 9¼" × 7' 8¼" (1.76 × 2.04 m) (Isabella Stewart Gardner Museum, Boston)

clear. Titian had earlier offered to paint Donna Olimpia, a famous Roman courtesan and reputed lover of Cardinal Alessandro Farnese, in the appropriate guise of Danaë. According to the cardinal's agent, who saw Titian working on that painting in Venice, the image made the Duke of Urbino's reclining nude (see Fig. 8.23) look like a nun. In this version for Philip II, Titian's extraordinarily free brushwork, especially on the curtain and sheets, and in the orgasmic outburst in the sky, further enhance Danaë's palpably physical reactions to Jupiter's approach. Only the ostensibly mythological subject and Danaë's classically inspired pose, adapted from statues of ancient Roman river gods, made the painting socially acceptable, although King Philip apparently kept curtains over some of these images so that women in the court would not have their modesty offended.

Titian's imagination and painterly technique continued to expand as he worked on further paintings for Philip II's erotic cycle. In the *Rape of Europa* (Fig. 8.25), the story of a nymph's abduction by Jupiter in the guise of a bull, whose horns she had been plaiting with flowers—itself a sexually charged image—Titian abandoned the usual representation of a sedate, side-saddle trot. He chose instead to represent an impassioned romp, moving in an ascending diagonal across the picture surface, as in his earlier *Meeting of Bacchus and Ariadne* (see Fig. 7.66). Pushed to the foreground of the composition, the scantily clad Europa rolls on the bull's back in what a male viewer was surely intended to read as ecstatic sexual abandon, her right leg bent up, her left leg and right arm swept in a single, slightly curving line up the painting. Her raised arm casts a shadow across her face, her own serious expression suggesting that Europa may yet need to be incited to passion by the three *amorini* (companions of Cupid) who rush after her. In the background at an enormous distance from Europa, her maidservants run to the shore vainly flailing their arms, their gestures and forms reflected in the passive waters in front of them, so different than the seething, foamy brine around Europa and the bull. Titian's extremely free brushwork is superbly adapted to the composition and contrasts markedly with the more polished surfaces of his earlier work. Here he exploits the actual physical texture and presence of his paint, not just its color. Light glints off thick deposits of color suspended in oil, especially in the foreground, and softens when it encounters more thinly painted surfaces in the distance. Shifting color as well as texture, Titian

masterfully turns his brown rocky coast blue and then dissolves it into the sunset tones of the evening sky. Europa's textural, billowing blood-red drape seems all the more dramatic for being set in front of such a remarkable, freely painted sky.

Colorito versus *Disegno*

The loose, painterly quality of Titian's mature and late works contrasts markedly with the more precise, essentially graphic approach of central Italian painting. Venetian painters had always been more interested than others in effects of glimmering color and light, whether in the gilded richness of Jacobello del Fiore's *Justice* (see Fig. 3.11) or the impressionistic refraction of light in the mosaic-encrusted apse of Giovanni Bellini's *San Giobbe Altarpiece* (see Fig. 6.32). In the mid-sixteenth century, literary praise and defense of this propensity became more systematic and took on distinctly patriotic tones. While central Italians such as Vasari were promoting the values they saw most evident in the art of Michelangelo—sculptural solidity, tightly controlled compositions and space, clear delineation, anatomical accuracy—in Venice critics including Pietro Aretino championed an alternative set of values epitomized by Titian—spontaneity, mobility, evanescent colors, and evocative rather than analytic description. To express the central Italian conception of art as something predominately cogitated and rational, Vasari adopted the noun **disegno**, meaning a combination of drawing and good design. The Venetians, on the other hand, chose **colorito**, a past participle which by its linguistic nature acts as both a verb and adjective. Literally signifying the quality of being "colored" and the state of "having been colored," the term emphasized the rich textural and visual effects of oil paint and glazes laid thickly on rough canvas. The values encapsulated in *colorito* and *disegno* effectively divided sixteenth-century art into opposing camps.

Communicating Religious Values: Titian's Late Altarpieces

For all their sensuosity, Titian's flashing color and bravura technique could also be harnessed to intensify a religious experience. In a towering altarpiece dedicated to St. Lawrence (Fig. 8.26), Titian dramatically depicted the saint's horrific martyrdom on a grill, whose fire blazes out in the nocturnal darkness—an ironic counterpart of St. Lawrence's words in the *Golden Legend* (a book of lives of the saints): "My night hath no darkness; all things shine with light!" The bright color and thick impasto form a bold diagonal from lower right up toward the left. Thus the composition exploits the painting's original location on the right side of the church by drawing the worshiper into the martyr's world, a device Titian previously used, in reverse, in the *Pesaro Altarpiece* (see Fig. 7.58). Embers burn white-hot under the grill, torches flare red and yellow in the night air, and rays of light break through the dense clouds to offer the saint divine recognition and reassurance. All other forms are left in shadow, suggesting the transience of worldly glory which Titian imagines in terms of imperial Rome. This classical imagery, which includes a representation of the goddess Vesta on the pedestal at the left, probably derives from Titian's reading of a poem by the fourth-century Roman Christian writer, Prudentius, whose work was published in Italian in Venice by the Aldine Press: "The death the holy martyr died was in truth the death of the temples. That day Vesta saw her Palladian house-spirits deserted and no vengeance follow. All the Romans who used to reverence Numa's libation cup now crowd the churches of Christ and sound the martyr's name in hymns." The saint's searing torture is thus to be understood as an image of ultimate Christian victory.

Titian's own belief in the redemptive power of Christian suffering is made explicit in his *Pietà*, which he painted for the altar above his own tomb in the right aisle of Santa Maria Gloriosa dei Frari (Fig. 8.27 and Fig. 8.1). The huge canvas remained partly unfinished at Titian's death on August 27, 1576. The flying angel and certain parts of the architectural moldings were judiciously completed by Palma Giovane (Jacopo Negretti; c. 1548–1628), who understood that the painting was Titian's personal testament and so chose neither to emulate nor to disturb the master's freely painted forms. Only decades of painterly exploration had made it possible for Titian to

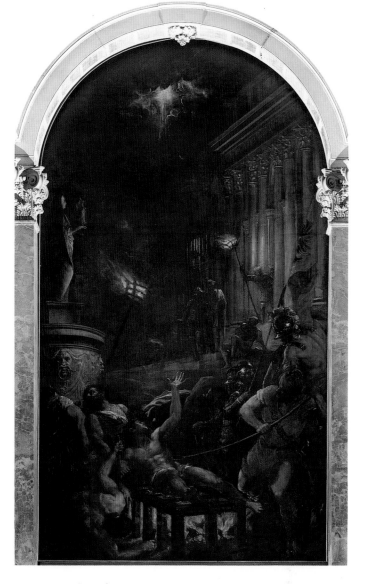

8.26 *Martyrdom of St. Lawrence*, 1548–57, commissioned by Lorenzo Massolo in 1548 (and confirmed by his widow, Elisabetta Querini, in 1557) from TITIAN for his chapel in the right aisle of Santa Maria dei Crociferi. Oil on canvas, 16′ 4⅞″ × 9′ 2¼″ (5 × 2.8 m) (Chiesa dei Gesuiti, Venice)

This is Titian's first major depiction of a nocturnal event.

create a work of such evocative intensity. Here again he built his figural composition on a diagonal. At lower right, a balding penitent kneels and reaches out to touch the dead but radiant body of Christ. A small votive panel leans against Titian's family coat of arms and the base of the sibyl, suggesting that the penitent should be understood as Titian himself. At the left, a grieving Magdalene runs forward, giving voice to the silent agony at the center. In the background, a massive rusticated niche reverberates with light, suggesting the burnished glow of Byzantine altarpieces and more recent evocations of the style in paintings such as Giovanni Bellini's *San Giobbe Altarpiece* (see Fig. 6.32). Although never placed over the altar for which it was intended, the painting continues to elicit deep emotions about life and death, a fitting testimony to Titian, his art, and his beliefs.

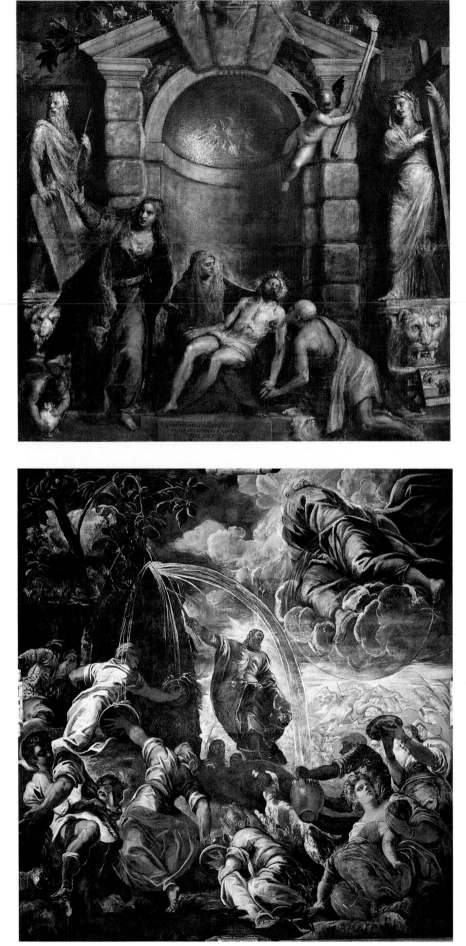

8.27 *Pietà*, begun c. 1570, left unfinished in 1576, painted by TITIAN for his own burial site at the Altar of the Holy Cross, Santa Maria Gloriosa dei Frari, Venice, completed by PALMA GIOVANE. Oil on canvas, 11' 6⅜" × 12' 9¼" (3.51 × 3.89 m) (Galleria dell'Accademia, Venice)

Titian's tomb in the Frari is now marked by an extravagant marble monument created 1838–52 by Pietro and Luigi Zandomeneghi.

Tintoretto's Narrative Imagery in the *Scuole*

Only one other artist in late sixteenth-century Venice was capable of approaching Titian's spiritual intensity: his sometime student Jacopo Tintoretto (Jacopo Robusti; 1519 Venice–1594 Venice). Though not always as rigorous and methodical as Titian—he often took on more commissions than he could handle and completed many works at breakneck speed—Tintoretto shared Titian's enthusiasm for complex human drama and used painting to evoke strong emotions. He made his reputation in Venice with the *Miracle of St. Mark*, which he completed in 1548 for the altar in the main hall of the Scuola Grande di San Marco (Fig. 8.29). No earlier surviving depiction of a story from a saint's life for a Venetian *scuola* had been so charged with energy—perhaps the reason why its members were uncertain whether to accept the finished work. They may also have disapproved because much of the work dedicated to Venice's patron saint depends on Tintoretto's adaptation of non-Venetian, specifically Roman sources. At the center of the composition is a tumbling apparition of St. Mark based on Tintoretto's study of Michelangelo's Sistine ceiling. At the left, the pivoting mother and child evoke similar figures in Raphael's *Fire in the Borgo* (see Fig. 7.35). They and other agitated figures provide the frame for the foreshortened, nude body of a devotee of St. Mark whom legend

8.28 *Moses Drawing Water from the Rock*, c. 1577, commissioned by the Scuola Grande di San Rocco, from JACOPO TINTORETTO for the ceiling of their main meeting hall. Oil on canvas, 18' × 17' 1" (5.50 × 5.20 m) (Scuola Grande di San Rocco, Venice)

The ceilings and walls of the entire Scuola are covered with paintings by Tintoretto. A commission of three Scuola members was charged with examining, judging, and approving the paintings.

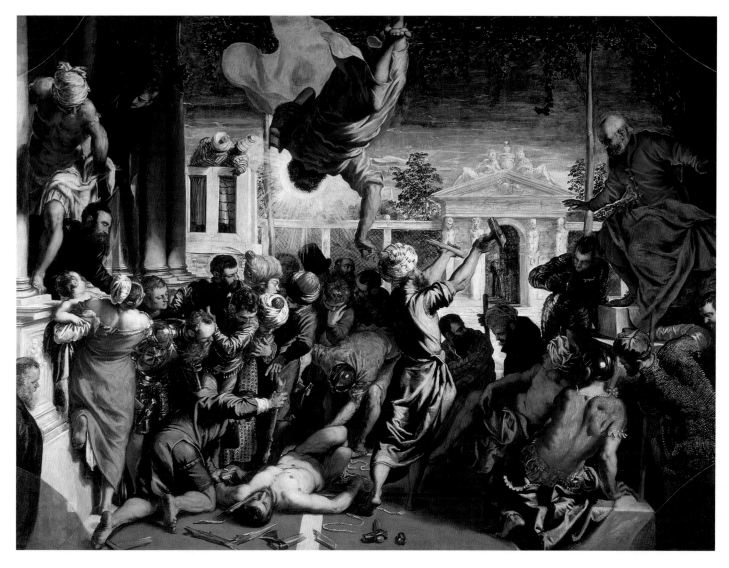

8.29 *Miracle of St. Mark*, 1548, commissioned by the Scuola Grande di San Marco from JACOPO TINTORETTO for the main hall of the Scuola Grande di San Marco, Venice. Oil on canvas, 12' 10¾" × 10' 4¾" (3.93 × 3.17 m) (Galleria dell'Accademia, Venice)

said infidels repeatedly attempted to mutilate and martyr. Every time they attempted to crush the man's body, St. Mark's intercession rendered their tools ineffective, as shown by the broken implements in the foreground of the painting and the splintered axe held aloft by the turbaned executioner. Pulsating with color, the work gave the Scuola, which finally accepted it in 1562, a vivid means of promoting the cult of their patron saint.

Soon Tintoretto earned commissions from other *scuole* as well. None was more successful in securing his services than the Scuola Grande di San Rocco, founded as recently as the late fifteenth century but very popular because its patron saint was renowned for offering protection from the plague, an increasingly common threat. The Scuola's headquarters were not complete until the mid-sixteenth century, so when Tintoretto began working there in 1564 he found an essentially blank slate. After

winning the competition by sneaking into the officers' chamber (*albergo*) of the Scuola and installing his full-scale painting of a triumphant San Rocco on the ceiling, he covered the walls with tumultuous scenes of Christ's passion. In 1577 he promised to provide three paintings a year free to the Scuola (of which he was a member). His paintings, then, became signs of his personal devotion.

For the main upper meeting hall Tintoretto covered the ceiling and walls with parallel scenes from the Old Testament and the life of Christ that emphasize the charitable aims of the Scuola. In *Moses Drawing Water from the Rock* (Fig. 8.28) the subject alludes to the brothers' commitment to provide food and drink for the poor. At the center of the canvas, Moses strikes a rock and powerful streams of water erupt from it, filling plates, bowls and jars held out eagerly by the parched Israelites. Tintoretto uses many of the same dramatic devices he had employed nearly thirty years earlier for the Scuola di San Marco: sharp contrasts between light and dark, rich color, forceful gestures, exaggerated foreshortenings, and even a figure flying through the sky (in this case God the Father). Appropriate to its placement on the ceiling rather than on a wall, however, the subject is composed from well below. The Israelites seem in danger of slipping down a steep hill into the viewer's space; streams of water appear to pour out over the room. Thanks to the artist's lightning-quick brushstrokes and highlights, the action seems caught for just a moment, not frozen in a tableau as in the earlier painting.

Celebrating the City Triumphant

Artists working for the Venetian government felt greater restraints as they worked to promote and celebrate their city. Major fires in the Doge's Palace in 1574 and 1577 necessitated the wholesale renovation of its pictorial decoration, and artists received explicit instructions about subject and even composition, the idea being to emulate the visual authority of the destroyed works as closely as possible. Tintoretto painted several large ceiling panels for the elaborate program, which emphasized Venice's military achievements (especially in the eastern Mediterranean), celebrated the city's unique form of government, touted civic freedom, and claimed Venice's parity with the papacy and the Holy Roman Empire. Tintoretto's most important contribution to the enterprise was the replacement of Guariento's 1365 *Coronation of the Virgin* (see Fig. 3.9), located behind the dais on which the doge and leading patricians sat during meetings of the Great Council (Fig. 8.30). Perhaps because of his artistic willfulness and discussions about the relative lack of finish in many of his works, Tintoretto was not the first choice for this commission, which was initially assigned to Paolo Veronese and Francesco Bassano

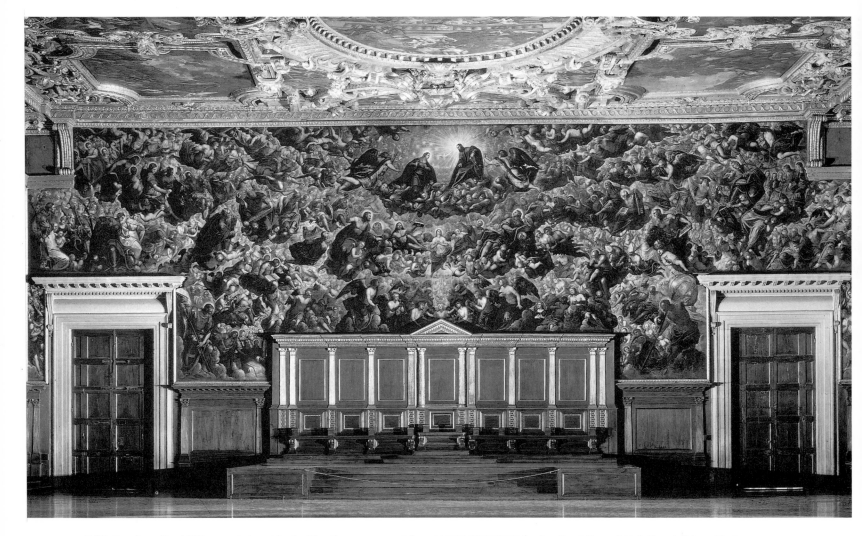

8.30 *Paradise*, after 1588, commissioned by the Venetian government from JACOPO TINTORETTO for the Great Council Hall, Doge's Palace, Venice. Oil on canvas

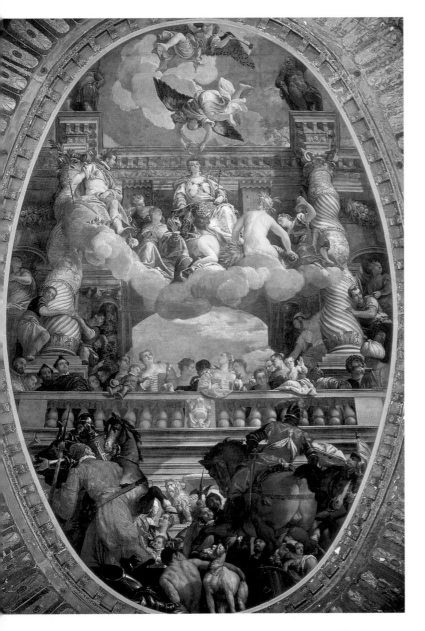

8.31 *Apotheosis of Venice*, probably 1585, commissioned by the Venetian government from PAOLO VERONESE for the ceiling of the Great Council Hall, Doge's Palace, Venice. Oil on canvas, 29′ 8″ × 19′ (9.04 × 5.79 m)

(Francesco dal Ponte the Younger; 1549 Bassano–1592 Venice). When Veronese died in 1588 the work had not been begun, but it had been decided that it would continue to center around Christ and Mary, preserving the general paradisical theme of Guariento's composition. However, the focus of Tintoretto's composition was to be Christ rather than Mary, eliminating the flanking scenes of the Annunciation and setting Christ as the supreme authority, to whom Mary is subsidiary. The seething crowds of saints and angels purposefully suggest a Last Judgment, reminding Great Council members of the

gravity and enduring significance of their deliberations and actions.

Tintoretto's painting had its secular counterpart in Veronese's *Apotheosis of Venice*, one of thirty-five panels on the ceiling of the same room (Fig. 8.31). Rising above a bank of clouds, the royally garbed Venice sits enthroned between the twin towers of the city's Arsenal, about to be crowned with laurel by flying victories. Arrayed at her feet and offering her wise counsel are personifications of peace, abundance, fame, happiness, honor, security, and freedom. An especially splendid triumphal arch, fronted by twisting columns, marks the top of an enormous balcony which accommodates the multitudes of celebrating people stipulated in the commission. At the base, Venice's smiling subjects seem undisturbed by the enormous size and energy of careening horsemen in their midst, reminders of Venice's considerable military might. The same illusionistic devices that Veronese had used on the ceiling at the Villa Barbaro (see Fig. 8.12) here take on monumental dimensions, serving to give political allegory a previously unimagined dynamism and visual excitement. Masking the realities of a slow and inevitable decline in Venice's fortunes throughout the sixteenth century, the *Apotheosis of Venice* and other works like it helped to sustain the city's independence and triumphalist self-imaging well into the eighteenth century.

Florence under Cosimo I (1537–74) and his Successors

The last expulsion of the Medici family from Florence lasted from 1527 to 1530 and was directly tied to the fortunes of the papacy under the Medici pope Clement VII. When armies of the German emperor sacked Rome in 1527, forcing the pope to flee to the protection of the Castel Sant'Angelo and, ultimately, to leave the city, the Florentines took the opportunity to oust the Medici regime and declare the restitution of the Republic yet again. Three years later, after restoring relations with Charles V, Clement was able to restore the Medici to power by using the same imperial forces that had sacked Rome against his native city. But it was not until an eighteen-year-old boy, a Medici on both his father's and his mother's side of the family, assumed power after the Battle of Montemurlo in 1537 and slaughtered his political enemies that the Medici regime was truly secure in the city. Providently named Cosimo at the time of his birth through the intervention of Leo X, who envisioned him as the reviver of his family's fortunes, just as his namesake had been at the beginning of the fifteenth century, he was ultimately crowned Grand Duke of Tuscany by Pius V.

Portraiture

From the time of the Medici return to power in 1512 members of the family had used portraiture to build historical connections to the past as support for their control of the present. Cosimo I seems to have sensed the importance both of repeating his own image (and that of other individuals in his family) as a form of propaganda and of developing new types of portraiture which would add credibility to his position as ruler.

Immediately upon his return from working for King Francis I at the French court of Fontainebleau, the Florentine goldsmith and sculptor Benvenuto Cellini (1500 Florence–1571 Florence) made an over-life-sized bronze bust of Cosimo (Fig. 8.32). Active as a superb goldsmith at the papal court in Rome from 1519 to 1540 and in France for the next five years, Cellini probably created the exquisitely detailed portrait as a way of ingratiating himself with a potential patron. Shown wearing a military breastplate, Cosimo appears both in the guise of a Roman emperor and as a contemporary military leader whose ruthlessness is indicated by the roaring lion's head on the armor at his right shoulder, an iconographical refer-

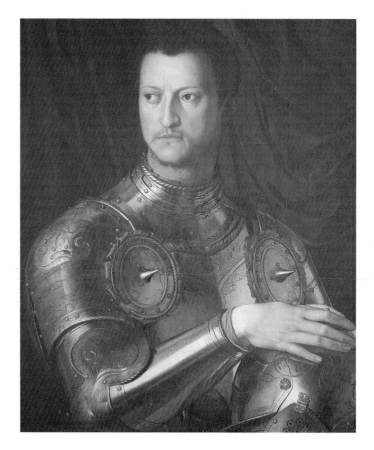

8.33 *Cosimo I*, c. 1545–46, commissioned by Cosimo I from AGNOLO BRONZINO. Tempera on panel, 29 × 22¾" (74 × 58 cm) (Galleria degli Uffizi, Florence)

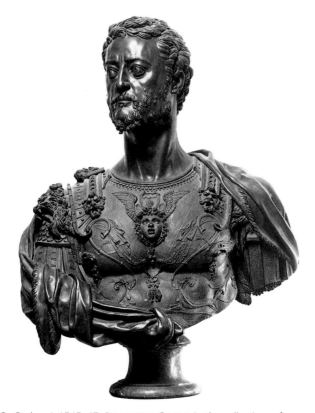

8.32 *Cosimo I*, 1545–47, BENVENUTO CELLINI, in the collections of Cosimo I by 1553, probably having been purchased shortly after its completion. Bronze, originally partially gilt with enamel eyes, height 3′ 7¼″ (1.1 m) (Museo Nazionale, Florence)

Cellini claims to have made the bust for his own "pleasure" but it was most likely a way to curry favor with Cosimo I.

ence that also connects Cosimo with the old Florentine political symbol of the Marzocco, or lion, here subordinated to the city's new leader. The active turn of his head and the precise details of his features give vitality to the portrait. Another contemporary portrait of Cosimo, by Agnolo Bronzino (Agnolo di Cosimo di Mariano; 1503 Monticelli–1572 Florence), also shows him in military armor (Fig. 8.33), providing Cosimo with an image reflecting his control over the state and a reminder that his father, Giovanni delle Bande Nere, was a respected Florentine military leader who had fought against the imperial troops on their way through Italy to Rome. Cellini's portrait was sent to the fortress of Stella (the Star) in Portoferraio on the island of Elba in 1557 to mark Cosimo's conquest of the island and control of shipping in this part of the Mediterranean. Its banishment to Elba gives a telling insight into Cosimo's reaction to it, especially in comparison to the Bronzino portrait. Apparently Cellini's bronze bust, with its vivid sense of motion and its soft depiction of flesh of Cosimo's face, was simply too naturalistic, representing what Cellini himself called the "fiery movements of life." Official court portraiture, it seems, demanded the impassive icon of rulership that Bronzino so aptly provided.

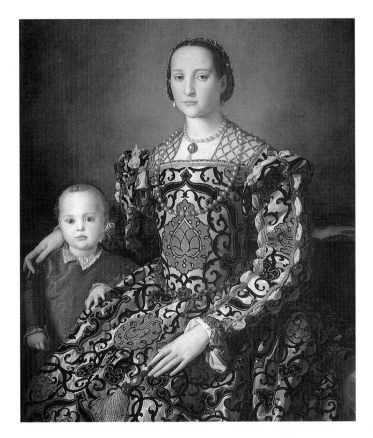

8.34 *Eleonora of Toledo and Her Son, Giovanni*, c. 1546, commissioned by Cosimo I from AGNOLO BRONZINO. Oil on panel, 45¼ × 37¾" (115 × 96 cm) (Galleria degli Uffizi, Florence)

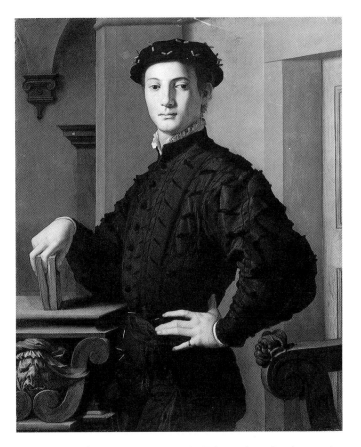

8.35 *Portrait of a Young Man*, c. 1540–45 (sometimes dated as much as a decade earlier), AGNOLO BRONZINO. Oil on panel, 37½ × 29½" (95.5 × 74.9 cm) (H. O. Havemeyer Collection, Bequest of Mrs H. O. Havemeyer, 1929 [29.100.16], Metropolitan Museum of Art, New York)

Cosimo's concerns for dynastic continuity are evident in the images of himself, his family, and his ancestors that began to crowd his living quarters. Bronzino's portrait of Cosimo's wife, Eleonora of Toledo, and their son Giovanni (Fig. 8.34) is typical of the portraiture of Cosimo's court. Eleonora is virtually imprisoned in the elaborately embroidered dress she wears. Her social position is proclaimed in a traditional manner by the extraordinary size of her jewels. Unlike the images of Cosimo, Eleonora looks directly out of the painting, yet the alabastrine perfection of her features—flattened by the strong lighting—distances her from the viewer. Bronzino refers to paintings like the *Mona Lisa* (see Fig. 7.9) in the pose, the shape of the face, and even in the slight smile of the figure, but Eleonora still becomes an iconic representation of the state whose continuity is assured by her progeny.

Other portraiture of the period betrays this same aloofness and detachment. For example, Bronzino's *Portrait of a Young Man* (Fig. 8.35) shows an elegantly dressed man in an architectural space that is as difficult to comprehend as he is. His every gesture is self-conscious, from his slow gaze downward toward the viewer to his claw-like finger, marking his place in the book, perhaps identifying him as

a friend from within the literary circles familiar to Bronzino and his wife Laura Battiferri, themselves both accomplished writers and poets. His left hand, resting on his hip, shows an unnatural arrangement of thumb and fingers. The costume is elaborately cut in the latest fashion, with multiple slashes through which another material appears. Laces with gold points decorate both the hat and the codpiece, itself a curious development in the history of costume at this time, calling attention to the sexuality of the figure. For all the detailing of the costume, the face of the man is exceedingly bland and refined—in striking contrast to the grotesque head carved on the arm of the chair to the right. The man's eyes, moreover, are not aligned, making any attempt at communication tentative at best. Bronzino includes a witty internal comment on the impenetrable mask-like aspect of the figure with the swag of material carved into the table at the lower left corner; it, too, reads as a flaccid grotesque head, quite unlike the crisp perfected features of the young man. Complexity, refined elegance, self-consciousness (on the part of both sitter and artist), and wit make this portrait a touchstone of Mannerism within the courtly environment of Cosimo's Florence.

The Myth of the State

Though Cellini lacked the reticence preferred at court—he had a flamboyant and openly counter-cultural lifestyle that included dressing one of his male assistants as a young woman to accompany him to a party and gilding another's skin—he possessed both the technical knowledge and artistic vision to continue the Medicean decorative program for the exterior of the Palazzo della Signoria initiated by Bandinelli's *Hercules and Cacus* (see Fig. 7.49). His over-life-size bronze *Perseus* (Fig. 8.36) depicts the slaying of the Gorgon Medusa, so hideous that to look upon her meant instant death. Designed for the place where it still stands, under the left arch of the Loggia della Signoria, the *Perseus* would have been a companion piece not only for the *Hercules and Cacus* but, more notably, for Donatello's *Judith and Holofernes* (see Fig. 5.18), which then stood under the right arch of the loggia. The act of decapitation, the arm extended in space, and the sensuality of the male body are comparable in each statue, so it is not unreasonable to see Cellini's bronze in competition with Donatello's great sculpture of the previous century. The *Perseus* is also a critique of the extravagantly muscled body and tormented face of Bandinelli's male nude immediately to its left. Inscriptions on the base of Cellini's group indicate that the *Perseus* was conceived as a reference to the Medici as saviors of the public good who had freed the citizenry from tyrants. Its spatial pairing with the *Judith and Holofernes* would, then, have undermined the inscription placed on that statue in 1495 when it was moved to the Palazzo della Signoria (see page 348) and would once again have claimed it for the Medici.

Cosimo's plans for the Piazza della Signoria, the civic heart of Florence, did not stop at such oblique propaganda as the *Perseus*. Bandinelli received a commission for a large fountain in this space and, with the intervention of Eleonora of Toledo, who apparently despised Cellini, was eventually awarded the central marble statue of Neptune. Bandinelli's death in 1560 unleashed a frenetic competition among a number of sculptors vying for Bandinelli's privileged position as artist within the court. The major part of the work was ultimately awarded to Bandinelli's student and a friend of Michelangelo, Bartolomeo Ammanati (1511 Settignano–1592 Florence). He gave the gigantic marble Neptune surmounting the *Fountain of Neptune* (Fig. 8.37) the features of Cosimo, leaving little doubt that the generous gift of water to the center of the city was the duke's. In this fountain Cosimo, like a Roman emperor, was deified, repeating an image of power that Bandinelli had used for Andrea Doria in Genoa (see Fig. 7.78).

Representing Cosimo as Neptune, the god of the sea was also historically appropriate since he had recently conquered Pisa, thus opening the Mediterranean to Florentine interests. By the time of the fountain's completion in 1575 (after Cosimo's death) the Neptune/Cosimo was aligned spatially with both Michelangelo's *David* and Bandinelli's *Hercules and Cacus*, toward which it looked, thus assimilating their meanings as biblical and mythological heroes into Cosimo's propagandistic aims.

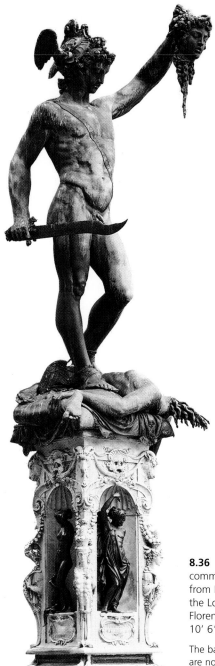

8.36 *Perseus*, 1545–54, commissioned by Cosimo I from BENVENUTO CELLINI for the Loggia della Signoria, Florence. Bronze, height 10' 6" (3.2 m)

The base and bronze statuettes are now in the Museo Nazionale del Bargello.

Casting the *Perseus*

This passage from Cellini's unfinished autobiography is one of the most famous of the artist's descriptions of his own technical brilliance. In it he pairs his own return to life with that of the bronze cast and plays on his role as Creator through his revivification of the near-failed casting. In this case his divine spark is one of superb technical know-how rather than of intellectual design, itself a witty inversion of the academic arguments then current.

I clothed my Perseus with the clays I had prepared some months previously in order to ensure that they would be properly seasoned. When I had made its clay tunic, as it is called, I carefully armed it, enclosed it with iron supports, and began to draw off the wax by means of a slow fire. It came out through the air vents I had made—the more of which there are, the better a mould fills. After I had finished drawing off the wax, I built round my Perseus a funnel-shaped furnace. It was built, that is, round the mould itself, and was made of bricks piled on on top of the other, with a great many gaps for the fire to escape more easily. Then I began to lay on wood, in fairly small amounts, keeping the fire going for two days and nights.

When all the wax was gone and the mould well baked, I at once began to dig the pit in which to bury it, observing all the rules that my art demands. That done, I took the mould and carefully raised it up by pulleys and strong ropes, finally suspending it an arm's length above the furnace, so that it hung down just as I wanted it above the middle of the pit. Very, very slowly I lowered it to the bottom of the furnace and set it in exact position with the utmost care: and then, having finished that delicate operation, I began to bank it up with the earth I had dug out. As I built this up, layer by layer, I left a number of air holes by means of little tubes of terracotta of the kind used for drawing off water and similar purposes.

I had had the furnace filled with a great many blocks of copper and other bronze scraps, which were placed according to the rules of our art, that is, so piled up that the flames would be able to play through them, heat the metal more quickly, and melt it down. Then, very excitedly, I ordered the furnace to be set alight. . . . the workshop caught fire and we were terrified that the roof might fall in on us, and at the same time the furnace began to cool off because of the rain and wind that swept in at me from the garden.

I struggled against these infuriating accidents for several hours, but the strain was more than even my strong constitution could bear, and I was suddenly attacked by a bout of fever. . . .

I told my housemaids to bring into the workshop enough food and drink for everyone, and I added that I myself would certainly be dead by the next day. They tried to cheer me up, insisting that my grave illness would soon pass and was only the result of excessive tiredness. Then I spent two hours fighting off the fever, which all the time increased in violence, and I kept shouting out: "I'm dying!" . . .

In the middle of this dreadful suffering I caught sight of someone making his way into my room. His body was all twisted, just like a capital S, and he began to moan in a voice full of gloom, like a priest consoling a prisoner about to be executed.

"Poor Benvenuto! Your work is all ruined—there's no hope left!"

On hearing the wretch talk like that I let out a howl that could have been heard echoing from the farthest planet, sprang out of bed, seized my clothes, and began to dress. My servants, my boy, and everyone else who rushed up to help me found themselves treated to kicks and blows, and I grumbled furiously at them . . .

I went at once to inspect the furnace, and I found that the metal had all curdled, had caked as they say. I ordered two of the hands to go over to Capretta, who kept a butcher's shop, for a load of young oak that had been dried out a year or more before and had been offered me by his wife, Ginevra. When they carried in the first armfuls I began to stuff them under the grate. The oak that I used, by the way, burns much more fiercely than any other kind of wood, and so alder or pinewood, which are slower burning, is generally preferred for work such as casting artillery. . . .

When they saw the metal beginning to melt my whole band of assistants were so keen to help that each one of them was as good as three men put together.

Then I had someone bring me a lump of pewter, weighing about sixty pounds, which I threw inside the furnace on to the caked metal. By this means, and by piling on the fuel and stirring with pokers and iron bars, the metal soon became molten. And when I saw that despite the despair of all my ignorant assistants I had brought a corpse back to life, I was so reinvigorated that I quite forgot the fever that had put the fear of death into me.

At this point there was a sudden explosion and a tremendous flash of fire, as if a thunderbolt had been hurled in our midst. Everyone, not least myself, was struck with unexpected terror. When the glare and noise had died away, we stared at each other, and then realized that the cover of the furnace had cracked open and that the bronze was pouring out. I hastily opened the mouths of the mould and at the same time drove in the two plugs.

Then, seeing that the metal was not running as easily as it should, I realized that the alloy must have been consumed in that terrific heat. So I sent for all my pewter plates, bowls, and salvers, which numbered about two hundred, and put them one by one in front of the channels, throwing some straight into the furnace. When they saw how beautiful the bronze was melting and the mould filling up, everyone grew excited. . . .

[I] cried out loud: "O God, who by infinite power raised Yourself from the dead and ascended into heaven!" And then in an instant my mould was filled. So I knelt down and thanked God with all my heart. . . .

I left the cast to cool off for two days and then, very, very slowly, I began to uncover it. The first thing that I found was the head of Medusa, which had come out beautifully because of the air vents, just as I had said to the Duke that the nature of fire was to ascend. Then I began uncovering the rest, and came to the other head—that is the head of the Perseus—which had also succeeded beautifully. This came as much more of a surprise because, as can be seen, it's a good deal lower than the Medusa. . . .

It was astonishing to find that there was not the slightest trace of metal left in the channels, nor on the other hand was the statue incomplete. This was so amazing that it seemed a certain miracle, with everything controlled and arranged by God.

(Benvenuto Cellini. *Autobiography*. Trans. George Bull. Harmondsworth, UK: Penguin, 1956)

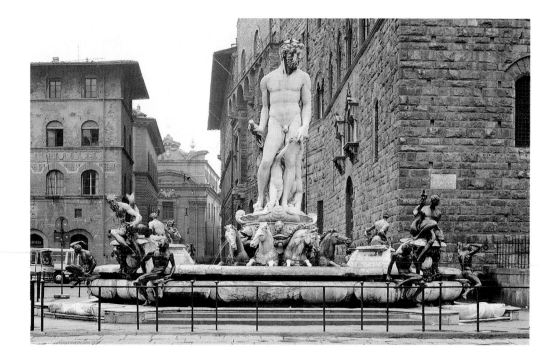

8.37 *Fountain of Neptune*, 1550–75, Neptune figure completed in 1565, commissioned by Cosimo I from BACCIO BANDINELLI, ultimately made by BARTOLOMEO AMMANATI and others for the Piazza della Signoria, Florence. Marble and bronze, height 18′ 4½″ (5.6 m)

Restructuring Civic Space: The Uffizi

In conjunction with Cosimo's sculptural commissions he also ordered the building of the Uffizi (Fig. 8.38). Built to house all the civil offices (the meaning of *uffizi*), the guilds, and Medici court artists, the Uffizi is an architectural symbol of a unified bureaucracy under Medici rule. Giorgio Vasari (1511 Arezzo–1574 Florence), the architect of the complex, built a long, U-shaped building whose colonnades at ground level imitate those in the Roman Forum. The reference to imperial rule was made explicit by the inclusion of Vincenzo Danti's (1530 Perugia–1576 Perugia) statue of *Cosimo as Augustus* (Fig. 8.39) in a niche in the cross-arm of the building. The statue, showing the emperor in military costume, was appropriate for Cosimo I, whose reputation as a military leader was well known (see Fig. 8.33). Although the appropriateness of such an image within this civic (not military) context might be questioned, it is true that the Arno, flowing west to Pisa, which

Cosimo had taken for Florence, could be seen through the open archway at the end of the axis of the building. Danti had studied with Michelangelo and Daniele da Volterra in Rome before going to Florence in 1557, and thus he know both the traditions of ancient military statues of emperors and the conventions of twisting body poses and fantastical armor (see Fig. 7.47) that were part of contemporary artistic vocabulary.

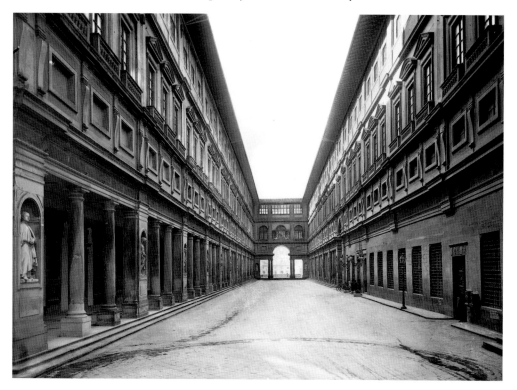

8.38 Uffizi, Florence, 1560–80, commissioned by Cosimo I from GIORGIO VASARI, completed by BERNARDO BUONTALENTI and ALFONSO PARIGI

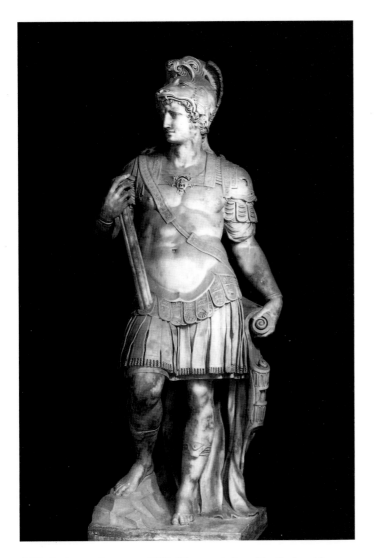

8.39 *Cosimo as Augustus*, 1568–72, commissioned by Cosimo I from VINCENZO DANTI for the cross-arm of the Uffizi, Florence. Marble, height 9' 2¼" (2.8 m) (Museo Nazionale del Bargello, Florence)

The statue repeats the pose of Michelangelo's *Bacchus* (see Fig. 6.55), which Francesco de' Medici bought for the ducal collection in 1572. Francesco seems to have been involved with this commission, at least in its early stages. He replaced the statue in 1595 with Giambologna's figure of a standing Cosimo I now still in place.

Vasari ordered the difficult site by dividing the façades into tripartite bays in which triangular and segmented pediments alternate over the windows in an *a–b–a* pattern and by breaking and extending the cornice lines forward at the separation of each bay. Nonetheless, the unremitting repetition of forms sets up a sense of oppressive order in the urban landscape which could be related to Cosimo's order over the state. As an extension of the Piazza della Signoria and with its virtual attachment to the Palazzo della Signoria and the Loggia della Signoria (see Fig. 1.18), the Uffizi marks the imposition of Cosimo's government over all aspects—political, mercantile, and artistic—of civic life.

Dynasty Supported by History and Myth

Cosimo marked his takeover of the government in a definitive manner when, in 1540, he left the ancestral Medici Palace and moved with his new wife to the Palazzo della Signoria, taking over the rooms that had earlier been reserved for the priors of the city. Cosimo remodeled the building to accommodate his expanding family and commissioned elaborate decorative programs of the histories of his ancestors, of his own military conquests, and of dynastic portraiture to fill its vast spaces. In 1569, during the work at the Palazzo, Cosimo was given the title of Grand Duke of Tuscany by Pope Pius V, a title that Emperor Charles V had refused to confer on him in 1537 at the time of his assumption of control of the Medici family and of the state. In addition to rooms explicitly dedicated to his ancestors—Cosimo Pater Patriae, Lorenzo the Magnificent, and Leo X (Giovanni de' Medici)—Cosimo had commissioned Giorgio Vasari in 1562 to design a program for the Sala del Gran Consiglio. Vasari's scheme covered ceiling, **soffits**, and walls, necessitating the destruction of the remains of Leonardo's *Battle of Anghiari* and erasing all memory of the projects for this room initiated by the Republic of 1494–1512 (see pages 348–352). The program merged the history of the city of Florence with Cosimo's military victories. Each narrative carries a didactic inscription. At the center of the enormous room, in a circular panel in the ceiling, is an image of the *Apotheosis of Cosimo* (Fig. 8.40), surrounded by the heraldic shields of the commune, the people and the city of Florence and of the twenty-one guilds of the city. This image replaced one of the Glorification of Florence in an earlier plan. Now Flora (Florence) obediently crowns a mask-like Cosimo, dressed in formal military attire, and a small putto holds the ducal crown in the background.

In addition to their commissions for government buildings, the Medici returned to other well-known places in the city where both their ancestors and the Republic had earlier been active. The most obvious focus of their patronage was the church of San Lorenzo (see Fig. 5.8). In 1546 Cosimo commissioned Jacopo Pontormo to fresco the unfinished choir which Cosimo Pater Patriae had reserved for his own in 1442 and before which he was buried. Thus Cosimo I not only inserted himself in the long and illustrious tradition of Medici patronage in San Lorenzo but he also associated himself with his namesake, the founder of Medici hegemony in Florence.

Pontormo's fresco cycle included scenes from Genesis, a Last Judgment, and the martyrdom of St. Lawrence, the titular saint of the church. The scenes from the story of Noah which would have been on the left wall of the chapel were part of a revival of an old myth which

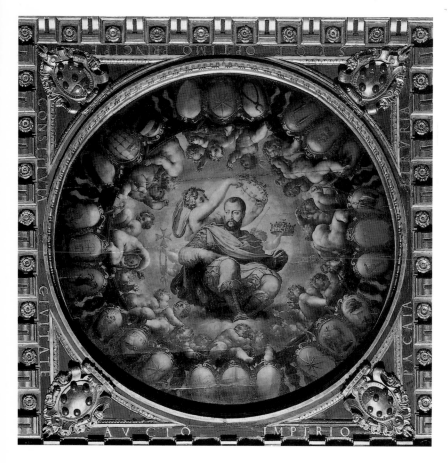

8.40 *Apotheosis of Cosimo*, 1562, commissioned by Cosimo I from GIORGIO VASARI for the centerpiece of an elaborately coffered and painted ceiling in the Sala del Gran Consiglio, Palazzo della Signoria, Florence

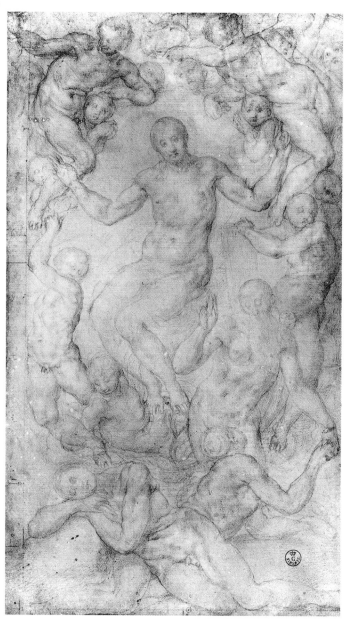

8.41 *Christ in Glory and the Creation of Eve*, preparatory drawing for the frescoes of the choir of San Lorenzo, Florence, frescoes painted 1546–56, destroyed in 1742, commissioned by Cosimo I from JACOPO PONTORMO. Black chalk on paper, 12¾ × 7" (32.6 × 18 cm) (Galleria degli Uffizi, Florence)

proposed that Noah had founded Florence after the Flood. Thus, as ruler of the city, Cosimo I was also connected with the leaders of the Old Testament. Known mostly from drawings, the figural style of these frescoes recalls the work of Michelangelo, despite the soft fluidity of Pontormo's own draftsmanship. In the *Christ in Glory and the Creation of Eve* (Fig. 8.41), drawn for a fresco on the center of the upper wall of the choir aligned axially with the nave, the ambiguous sitting/standing pose of the Christ figure imitates the comparable figure in Michelangelo's *Last Judgment* (see Fig. 8.45) and the roiling nudes around Christ repeat in a slightly more languid fashion the complex poses of their counterparts. Pontormo's friendship with Michelangelo allowed reverberations of Michelangelo's style in the main chapel at San Lorenzo, although the master himself steadfastly refused to work for the city's new ruler, who had so thoroughly subverted the old republican principles which Michelangelo had supported by carving figures such as the *David* (see Fig. 7.2) and by designing fortifications for the short-lived Republic during the siege of 1527–30.

Art as a Symbol of the Advanced State

At least since the time of Lorenzo the Magnificent, the Medici—like other statesmen—had used objects of art and artists themselves as ways to build alliances between themselves and other powerful rulers. Bronzino's *Allegory with Venus and Cupid* (Fig. 8.42) was commissioned as one of a long series of important gifts of art to Francis I of France, who in his later years increasingly preferred subject matter of an overtly erotic nature. The lasciviously entwined figures of an adolescent Cupid and his mother, Venus, were obviously aimed at this sensibility, but there is more than salaciousness to the painting. The golden orb which Venus holds in her left hand represents the golden apple given her by Paris when he judged her more beautiful than Juno and Minerva, but it also refers to the orb of royal rule. In her right hand she suggestively displays an arrow plucked from Cupid's quiver. A third brightly lit figure, this of a young boy identified as Giuoco or playfulness, appears ready to shower them with the roses he holds in his hand, oblivious of the thorn at his foot. Above Giuoco is another well-lit figure, albeit more swarthy in appearance, representing Chronos or Time. He extends a blue drapery across the background of the composition, essentially throwing the figures before it into relief. This drapery extends to the front of the painting, where it functions as a rumpled sheet on which Venus is seated, its icy blue color playing against the steely red of the cushion on which Cupid kneels.

Chronos and Giuoco are paired in a set of visual oppositions: young/old, light/dark, curly-headed/bald, smiling/frowning. These suggest an interior dialogue on the

actions of Venus and Cupid, although neither Giuoco nor Chronos actually looks at the main protagonists. Chronos looks towards the upper left corner of the painting at a figure variously identified as Fraud or Oblivion, whose head is really an empty shell, cut off behind the ear in mask-like fashion, not unlike the two masks of Deceit lying at the bottom right. She is one of a trio of troubling shadowy figures in the cramped middle ground that includes a haggard, howling male tearing his hair at the far left and, just behind Giuoco, a beautiful young woman extending a sweet honeycomb. The male figure, once identified as a female Jealousy, is now thought to be a representation of pain ("dolor" is gendered male) or the "*morbo gallico*," known now as syphilis. At the time syphilis was called the "French disease" in part because its first recorded epidemic appearance occurred with the French troops who had invaded Italy in 1494. The female figure represents either a problematic Pleasure or Fraud, since her body, seen to the right of Giuoco, is that of a dragon, its tail curving past the two masks of Deceit to end in a stinger held in the figure's own right hand.

The esoteric imagery, still disputed by scholars, accords with elaborate Mannerist conceits and parallels the complexity of the poses. Cosimo sent this painting not only as a demonstration of painterly excellence, but as a demonstration of Florentine intellectual cleverness, necessary both for the invention of the imagery and for its unraveling. A princely ruler addressing a king chose an elevated and artificial language as the appropriate one to convey their mutual god-like status while at the same time playing to the king's taste for the erotic.

The Florentine Academy

Just as the government of Florence was re-ordered in the 1530s, so were the arts in Florence by the founding of the Accademia del Disegno (Academy of Design) by Vasari and others in 1562. The patron and sponsor of the Academy was Cosimo I, to whom Vasari had dedicated the first edition of his *Lives* in 1550. Art and the state were clearly linked, even as artists were encouraged to invent new conceptual structures for their work. The Academy placed a strong emphasis on history and theory, thus removing the arts from the craft traditions which had previously governed their existence.

It also encouraged artists to develop their talents and ideas free of traditional conventions relating to content. The work of Giambologna (1529 Douai–1608 Florence) is a case in point. Trained in his native Flanders by an Italianate sculptor, he himself went to Rome in 1554 and then to Florence in 1556, where he soon came to the attention of the Medici. His *Rape of the Sabines* (Fig. 8.43)

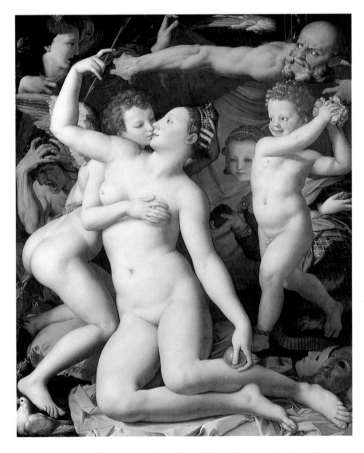

8.42 *Allegory with Venus and Cupid*, mid-1540s, commissioned by Cosimo I from AGNOLO BRONZINO as a gift to Francis I of France. Oil on panel, 61 × 56¼" (155 × 143 cm) (National Gallery, London)

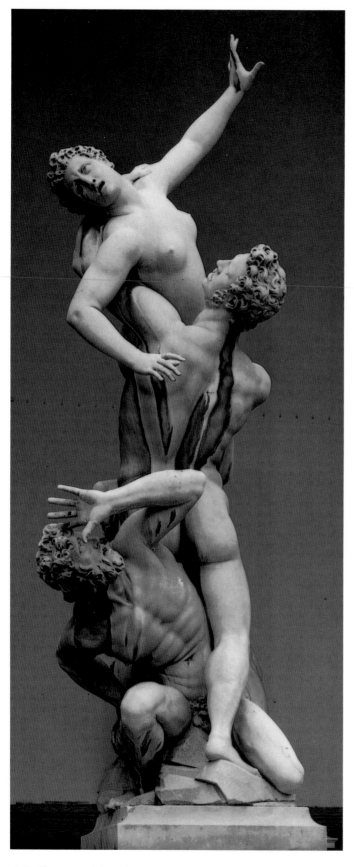

8.43 *The Rape of the Sabines*, 1579–83, GIAMBOLOGNA, Loggia della Signoria, Florence, replaced Donatello's *Judith and Holofernes* in 1582 and was completed the following year. Marble, height c. 13′ 5½″ (c. 4.1 m)

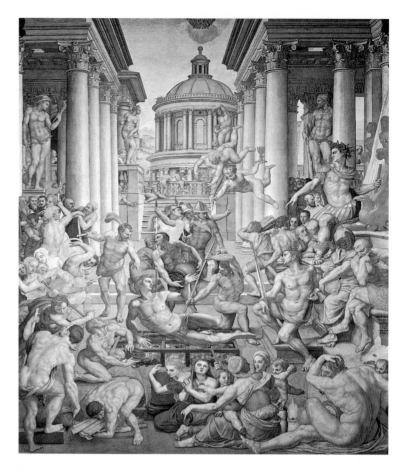

8.44 *Martyrdom of St. Lawrence*, 1565–69, commissioned by Cosimo I from AGNOLO BRONZINO. Fresco (Florence, San Lorenzo)

was apparently begun as a free invention during his stay at the Academy, intended as a demonstration of his ability to solve difficult compositional problems, in this case with no particular narrative in mind. When Cosimo's son, Grand Duke Ferdinand I (r. 1587–1609), saw the work, he decided it should be placed in the Loggia della Signoria as a pendant to his father's *Perseus*. Asked to name the work, Giambologna suggested that the woman could be Andromeda, the wife of Perseus, clearly an attempt to unify the program of the Loggia and to connect father and son as patrons/rulers of the city. But Raffaello Borghini, a leading member of the Academy, proposed the Sabines as the subject, a designation which has remained ever since. Although the self-conscious complexities of the physical movements and interactions—interesting in themselves, divorced from content—place this sculptural group well within the conventions of Mannerism, it is the changed role of the artist, supported by the Academy, which made the exploration of formal issues a content in its own right.

These purely artistic concerns—at least as they appear in the fully developed *maniera*—reached its climax in such paintings as Bronzino's *Martyrdom of St. Lawrence* (Fig. 8.44). There is hardly a stylistic reference that does not appear in this feverish painting: an academic recreation of a Roman city, decorated with quotations from classical sculpture; quotations from the paintings of Michelangelo, the father figure of the Academy; figures, like that in the lower right, who are part of the narrative space, but whose inclusion is more for their references to classical sculpture; a gratuitous use of nudity as a reference to classical antiquity; animated figures whose poses are notable more for their inventiveness and complexity than as reasonable depictions of the actions they pursue; a *tour de force* of complex compositional arrangements, as if the painter had a limitless supply of imagination from which he could effortlessly draw; a peopling of the painting by people who seem emotionally unaffected by the grisly martyrdom of the central figure, who himself reacts rather too gracefully to the flames that begin to burn his body; portraits inserted at a reduced scale in the midground, as if the men represented wished to assert their presence within an artistic event rather than participate in a narrative at which none of them bothers to look.

This focus on art and artfulness could serve both the artists in their attempts to claim an elevated social role in the culture and Cosimo I, as the titular head of the Academy, in his efforts to bring all aspects of Florentine life under his control.

Roma Restaurata: Paul III (r. 1534–49) and Michelangelo

When Alessandro Farnese was elected to the papacy as Paul III in 1534, he was the first Roman to hold that office since Martin V in the early fifteenth century. As a Roman he must have felt keenly the city's humiliation in the Sack of 1527. He now faced the task of bringing new order to the social and political life of the city. He also had to renew the tenets and practices of the Church that had been severely challenged by the Protestant reformers. Since Paul enjoyed the longest reign of any of the popes of the sixteenth century, he had ample time to reconstruct the image of the papacy and of the Church.

Having spent some years of his youth in the Florentine court of Lorenzo the Magnificent, Paul was well versed in the power of art to enhance the position of the patron. Made a cardinal in 1493 (although not ordained as a priest until 1519), he had also witnessed the development of the arts in Rome under Julius II and Leo X. Paul's projects were carefully chosen, historically charged in their siting and context, and ultimately of a magnitude comparable to those of Julius II and appropriate for someone who, like Julius, claimed a universal rulership. Moreover, they were at a scale indicating that, despite the Reformation and the Sack, the Church had triumphed.

Paul's two greatest legacies to the Church were his support of new religious orders, especially the Jesuits, to whom he gave official recognition in 1540, and his opening, albeit reluctantly, of the Council of Trent in 1545. The Jesuits, a powerful new teaching order, soon had an international network of communities. The Council of Trent, which continued intermittently until 1563, gave new guidelines for a post-Reformation Roman Church which were to affect its teachings and its liturgy, and therefore its art for the next four hundred years.

Michelangelo's *Last Judgment*

Paul's first major commission in 1534 was for the Sistine Chapel, giving little doubt of his intentions to affiliate his papacy with those of Sixtus IV and Julius II. For the fresco of the *Last Judgment* (Fig. 8.45) Paul brought Michelangelo back to Rome from Florence, where he had been working on Medici commissions at San Lorenzo. Michelangelo had previously discussed with Clement VII the possibility of a large fresco of the Fall of the Rebel Angels for the entrance wall of the Chapel; but Paul changed both the subject and the placement of Michelangelo's work, insisting on a *Last Judgment* for the altar wall. The commission entailed the destruction of pre-existing frescoes on that wall, including Perugino's frescoed altarpiece and Michelangelo's own work from earlier in the century.

For many years the *Last Judgment* was so obscured by grime that its outlines, not to mention its original colors, were all but indiscernible. The recent cleaning of the fresco, finished in 1994, shows that Michelangelo used some of the same intense colors that he had employed on the ceiling of the chapel and that even in the darker areas of the painting at the lower edge, where the dead arise from their graves at the left and the damned are faced with hell on the right, he was concerned with details of the human (and demonic) bodies. The heroically scaled and dramatically posed bodies may be considered a development of Michelangelo's figural style seen in the ceiling above (see Fig. 7.24). Yet their fleshy, overdeveloped muscles also refer to Hellenistic sculpture like the bronze Hercules given by Sixtus IV in 1471 to the Capitoline Hill (where Michelangelo was also working in these years) and to the Roman copy in marble of Lysippus's statue *Hercules Resting* in the collection of Francesco Piccolomini (Pius III), another of Michelangelo's patrons.

The fresco is unusual in that Michelangelo did not include an architectural frame, as he had done for the ceiling. Its absence implies absence of wall, as if the chapel had been blasted out by the Judgment Day itself. In this terrifying vision, Christ appears in the band

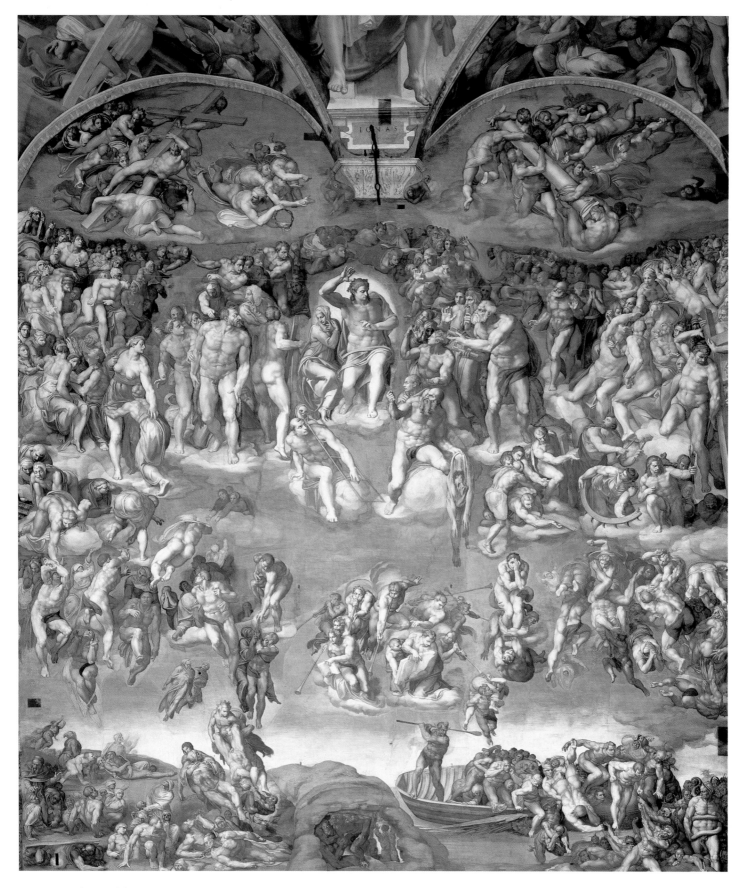

8.45 *Last Judgment* (after cleaning), 1534–41, commissioned by Paul III from MICHELANGELO for the Sistine Chapel, Rome. Fresco, 48 × 44′ (14.6 × 13.41 m)

A Word of Advice

In this letter from the poet Pietro Aretino (1492–1557) to Michelangelo, the writer takes the artist to task for what he claims are indecencies in the *Last Judgment*. The irony is that Aretino was himself the author of many lascivious works, including the famous *Sonnetti lussuosi* ("Luxurious Sonnets"), which were illustrated with pornographic images comparable to *I Modi* (see Fig. 7.39). After his hypocritical closing, Aretino adds a postscript promising to tear up his own copy of the letter; but when Michelangelo did not reply, he published a slightly altered version of the letter.

To the Great Michelangelo Buonarroti in Rome
SIR,
When I inspected the complete sketch of the whole of your Last Judgment, I arrived at recognizing the eminent graciousness of Raffaello in its agreeable beauty of invention.

Meanwhile, as a baptized Christian, I blush before the license, so forbidden to man's intellect, which you have used in expressing ideas connected with the highest aims and final ends to which our faith aspires. So, then, that Michelangelo stupendous in his fame, that Michelangelo renowned for prudence,

that Michelangelo whom all admire, has chosen to display to the whole world an impiety of irreligion only equalled by the perfection of his painting! Is it possible that you, who, since you are divine, do not condescend to consort with human beings, have done this in the greatest temple built to God, upon the highest altar raised to Christ, in the most sacred chapel upon the earth, where the mighty hinges of the Church, the venerable priests of our religion, the Vicar of Christ, with solemn ceremonies and holy prayers, confess, contemplate and adore his body, his blood, and his flesh?

If it were not infamous to introduce the comparison, I would plume myself upon my discretion when I wrote *La Nanna*. I would demonstrate the superiority of my prudent reserve to your immodesty, seeing that I, while handling themes lascivious and immodest, use language comely and decorous, speak in terms beyond reproach and inoffensive to chaste ears. You, on the contrary, presenting so awful a subject, exhibit saints and angels, these without earthly decency, and those without celestial honors.

The pagans when they made statues I do not say of Diana who is clothed, but of naked Venus, made them cover with their hand the parts which should not be seen. And here there comes a Christian who, because he

rates art higher than faith, deems a royal spectacle martyrs and virgins in improper attitudes, men dragged down by their genitals, things in front of which brothels would shut their eyes in order not to see them. Your art would be at home in some voluptuous bagnio [bathhouse], certainly not in the highest chapel of the world. Less criminal were it if you were an infidel, than, being a believer, thus to sap the faith of others. Up to the present time the splendor of such audacious marvels has not gone unpunished; for their very superexcellence is the death of your good name. Restore it to good repute by turning the indecent parts of the damned to flames, and those of the blessed to sunbeams; or imitate the modesty of Florence, who hides your David's shame beneath some gilded leaves [see Fig. 7.2]. And yet that statue is exposed upon a public square, not in a consecrated chapel.

As I wish that God may pardon you, I do not write this out of any resentment . . . .

(November 1545, in Venice. Your servant, The Aretine)

(from J.A. Symonds, trans. *The Life of Michelangelo*. London: J.C. Nimmo, 1899, pp. 333–6)

---

of figures aligned with the window area of the side walls. He is neither seated, in the traditional manner, nor standing, but half-crouched, his body turning in a corkscrew movement suspended in space. The Virgin, readily visible in her ice-blue drapery, turns in on herself, the only figure in the composition psychologically disengaged from the sur-rounding tumult, perhaps because her intercessory powers no longer pertain at the moment of the Last Judgment. St. Peter stands in the group of figures to the right; he is the largest figure in the fresco and clearly a potent image of the papal office, wielding the keys to the Kingdom of Heaven symbolically given to him by Christ. Michelangelo gave the flayed skin held by St. Bartholomew, at the center right, his own features—perhaps a mordant comment on his fears about his own salvation, since he is the only one of the resurrected

throng not to have regained his bodily form. By and large, however, the saints who fill the wide upper band of the fresco are unidentified. Still, St. Lawrence appears paired with St. Bartholomew and St. Simon of Cyrene, who helped Christ carry his cross, has a prominent position at the far right edge of the fresco. St. Blaise and St. Catherine of Alexandria (both later partly chiseled out and reconfigured by Michelangelo's student Daniele da Volterra so that Blaise would not appear to be approaching a nude Catherine from the rear) can be identified by their symbols of the carding comb and broken spiked wheel at the right. Diminution of scale within these large groups of figures suggests a vastness of space, although there are abrupt changes of scale throughout the group, conventionally giving prominence through size.

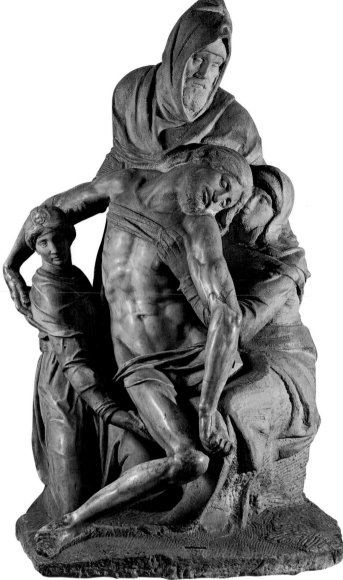

8.46 *Deposition*, c. 1546–55, MICHELANGELO; smashed by the sculptor in 1555 and pieced together and continued by his student, TIBERIO CALCAGNI. Marble, height 7′ 8″ (2.34 m) (Museo dell'Opera del Duomo, Florence)

Calcagni seems largely to have completed the small female figure at the left thought to represent Mary Magdalene.

The inclusion of the Virgin in the mandorla of the Divinity suggests references to earlier Last Judgment iconography (see Fig. 3.15), where Mary, as the personification of Ecclesia, enjoys a position of equality with Christ. Mary's shrinking pose in Michelangelo's *Last Judgment* is a notable change in this iconography and may have opened questions about the Church's power to grant salvation, despite Peter's dominating presence. Thus contemporary criticism of the *Last Judgment*, which focused on the propriety of so much nudity in a papal chapel, may have had, as a subtext, a response to the painting's disguised message about the role of the Church in salvation.

The *Deposition*

Michelangelo's own intense personal questioning of the routes to salvation increased after his meeting with the poet Vittoria Colonna shortly after beginning work on the *Last Judgment*. Through his friendship with Colonna, he was introduced to some of those within the Church—such as Cardinal Reginald Pole of England and the Spaniard Juan de Valdés—who wished to introduce reforms into Church beliefs and structures which many within the hierarchy found heretical.

Michelangelo's *Deposition* (Fig. 8.46), planned by the sculptor for his own tomb when he was about seventy, suggests the intensity of his concern for his own salvation. The vertical axis of the group is defined by the sinking but severely torqued and muscular body of Christ and the standing hooded figure of Nicodemus who had provided myrrh and aloes for Christ's burial (John 19:39). Michelangelo gave Nicodemus his own features (a much more positive self-representation than the skin held by Bartholomew in the *Last Judgment*), thus clearly aligning himself with the promise of redemption offered by Christ. Although the Virgin receives the body of Christ, as in conventional "Pietà" iconography (see Fig. 6.73), Michelangelo displaced her to the right, assuming for himself the primary role, on the central axis of the composition. If the Virgin is interpreted as Ecclesia, Michelangelo would then have been suggesting that he could take salvation (Christ) into his own hands, thus supplanting the intervention of the Church—a view close to heresy. It is perhaps not surprising that he smashed the unfinished statue in 1555.

Triumphalist History

Although these works by Michelangelo may give some insight into the deeply felt religious questions shared by the artist and others of this time about Reformation theology and new efforts of reform within the Roman Church, Paul III consistently attempted to declare that his papacy was strong and to blur over the difficulties of the previous decades in ways that would suggest unbroken institutional strength. One sign of this was his decision to restore the Castel Sant'Angelo, the fortress at the entrance to the Vatican to which Clement VII had fled in 1527 at the time of the Sack of Rome. By turning what had been a place of shame for his predecessor into a splendid retreat, Paul, in effect, suppressed its previous ignominious history. In the major room of the building, he hired Perino del Vaga, newly returned to Rome after having worked in Genoa (see Fig. 7.81) after the Sack, to paint a series of frescoes depicting ancient emperors—

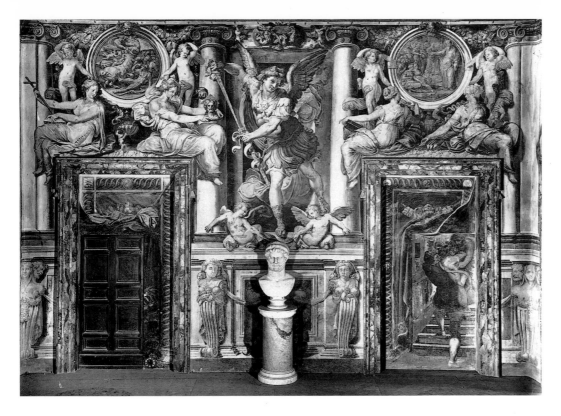

8.47 Sala Paolina, 1545–47, commissioned by Paul III from PERINO DEL VAGA for Castel Sant'Angelo, Rome. Fresco

The room is named for the pope, a clear indication that it met his propaganda needs.

including Alexander the Great, since Paul's name was Alessandro Farnese—and a figure of the Archangel Michael overcoming evil (Fig. 8.47). One entire wall of the building imitates an earlier image of St. Michael by Raphael and the nudes and shields of the Sistine ceiling by Michelangelo (see Fig. 7.24). Since Perino had worked in Raphael's workshop, these quotations may not seem unusual, especially given the frequency with which works by Raphael and Michelangelo were quoted during the sixteenth century. But the overtones of the Sistine commission are so strong as to suggest that Paul actively encouraged these stylistic references as a way to equate his own papacy with the accomplishments of Julius and Rome before the Sack.

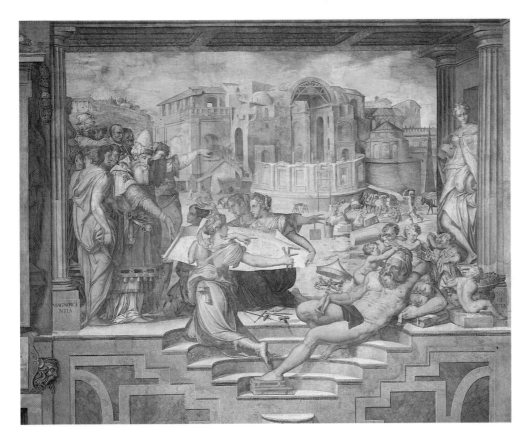

8.48 *Paul III Directing the Construction of St. Peter's,* detail of *Life of Paul III,* 1544, commissioned by Alessandro Farnese from GIORGIO VASARI for the Sala dei Cento Giorni, Cancelleria, Rome. Fresco

This room is called the Room of the Hundred Days because it was supposedly completed in the amazingly rapid time of 100 days. When Michelangelo was told of this feat he purportedly replied in a typically sharp and succinct manner, "Si vede" or "It looks it."

Paul's grandson, also named Alessandro Farnese, used a comparably grand rhetorical vocabulary in paintings that he commissioned from Vasari for his palace of the Cancelleria (Fig. 8.48). As in ancient Roman art, the paintings recording the deeds of Paul III combine history and allegory. In *Paul III Directing the Construction of St. Peter's*, the standing pope points to St. Peter's in the background, whose building he had immediately taken up upon becoming pope. The colossal size of the project asserts the renewed strength of the Church as well as the centrality of the papacy, since the building celebrates the first pope. Allegorical figures of Architecture hold out the plans of the building for Paul to see, much as personifications of abstract concepts accompany classical images of Roman emperors. Despite the elegant and complex poses of the foreground figures, the didacticism and clarity of this imagery—far removed from the fashionable esoteric conceits of Mannerism—suggest that the patron had called for a grand yet relatively straightforward narration of the deeds of his uncle.

The complex workings of the papal family within the larger papal court are evident in a psychologically charged

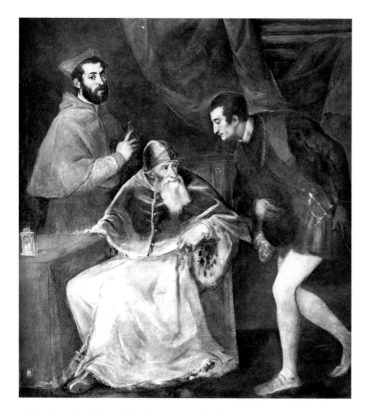

8.49 *Pope Paul III and His Grandsons, Cardinal Alessandro Farnese and Ottavio Farnese*, 1546, commissioned by Paul III from TITIAN. Oil on canvas, 6' 6¾" × 5' 8½" (2 × 1.74 m) (Gallerie Nazionali di Capodimonte, Naples)

This painting is usually euphemistically called "Pope Paul and his Nephews," obscuring the fact that many church leaders had illegitimate children in this period.

portrait of Paul III with two of his grandsons (Fig. 8.49). As the guest of the pope in the Vatican, Titian painted the group portrait either for Paul III, as a gift with political overtones for the Holy Roman Emperor, Charles V, or for the pope's cardinal-"nephew" (in reality his grandson), Alessandro Farnese, who appears at the pope's right hand as the apex of a weighty red and white pyramid anchored by Paul III and the table. Titian captured the undiminished mental powers of the seventy-eight-year-old pope, physically stooped but obviously alert (perhaps even suspicious) of Ottavio Farnese's fawning approach. The painting, never finished, is far from the tradition of formal papal family images typified by the fresco of *Sixtus IV Confirming Platina as Papal Librarian* (see Fig. 6.61), and even from earlier somewhat introspective papal portraits such as Raphael's votive portrait of Julius II (see Fig. 7.32), which Titian had used as a model for an earlier portrait of Paul III. Here Titian transformed the personal relations into an emotionally and intellectually compelling narrative, his brushstrokes leaving lightning reflections on the pope's velvet cape and a charged emphasis on the pope's left hand far in excess of its sketchy description.

The pope's grandsons serve as a study in contrasts. Alessandro, one of the most important Roman patrons in his own right (see Fig. 9.17) and a man of fabulous wealth, stands as an embodiment of the official Church, one assured of his power in a volatile court environment. Ottavio, however, subservient and meek in his bent approach to his grandfather, appears to understand that his role in the world was dependent on the aged Paul III. In 1547, aware that Paul had been unsuccessful in arranging with the Emperor for his assumption of the control of the Duchy of Parma and Piacenza, Ottavio associated with his father's murderer to gain possession of the cities, an act that undermined Paul's papal and family authority. Paul's shift of political allegiance from Charles V to the French king, and Titian's perceptive—one might say unflinching and unflattering—reading of the personalities involved may explain why the painting was never completed. Yet the astuteness of Paul III remains a dominant feature of the painting, a witness to his awareness of his office, its history, and the demands that lay at the heart of his patronage.

Urbi et Orbi: The City

The papal blessing is traditionally given *urbi et orbi* ("to the city and to the world"). This double focus of the papacy governed its commissions throughout the early modern period. The popes had to speak to Rome, which they ruled, despite the existence of a Roman senate

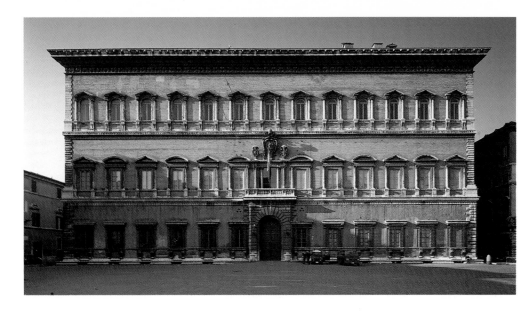

8.50 Palazzo Farnese, Rome, begun 1517, commissioned by Alessandro Farnese (later Paul III) from ANTONIO DA SANGALLO the Younger, continued by Michelangelo in 1546

markets and a site of civic justice (see Fig. 5.33), again extending the presence of the building—and of the Farnese—through the urban fabric.

The Capitoline Hill

After becoming pope, Paul used his experience of space and scale at the Palazzo Farnese in a more sophisticated manner on the Capitoline Hill (Campidoglio; Figs. 8.51 and 8.52). For the visit to Rome in 1536 of the Holy Roman Emperor, Charles V, Paul planned a triumphal procession through the city which was to include the Capitoline Hill. Since classical times this site had been the political center of the city—and in ancient times its religious center also, crowned by the Temple of Jupiter. Embarrassingly the area was too rough and overgrown to accommodate the procession (see Fig. 5.34).

and civil government, and to the world, for which they claimed to be spiritual rulers and which, in the sixteenth century, had ever-increasing parameters. In 1517, while still a cardinal, Paul III had begun building a palace in Rome that was clearly intended to broadcast his pre-eminence to his fellow citizens. The design for the Palazzo Farnese (Fig. 8.50), by Antonio da Sangallo the Younger (1483 Florence–1546 Terni), then one of Raphael's assistants as architect at St. Peter's, made the building one of the greatest private residences in the city, comparable to Cardinal Riario's Cancelleria (see Fig. 6.72). When Paul became pope in 1534, he enlarged the original design for the façade from eleven to thirteen bays. At Sangallo's death in 1546, Paul assigned the completion of the building to Michelangelo, who planned the third story with its colossal cornice and added the large central window in the façade as a papal benediction loggia. Since Paul III never lived in the building after assuming office, the building functioned as a propagandistic symbol of papal power rather than as an actual papal residence. The building is larger than any other in the area. The huge public square in front of it was apparently meant to be paved in a grid design tied to the width of each bay, thus locking the building with the urban space. The stolid regularity of the façade, with its alternating triangular and curved pediments on the second story, creates an overwhelming impression of strength and grandeur. The central axis of the palace was aligned with a short street leading to the Campo dei Fiori, one of the oldest of the city's

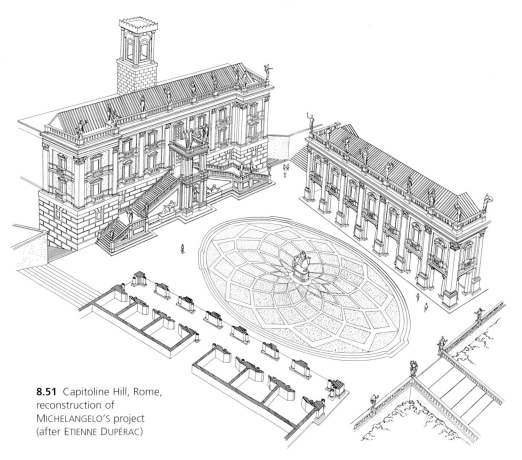

8.51 Capitoline Hill, Rome, reconstruction of MICHELANGELO'S project (after ETIENNE DUPÉRAC)

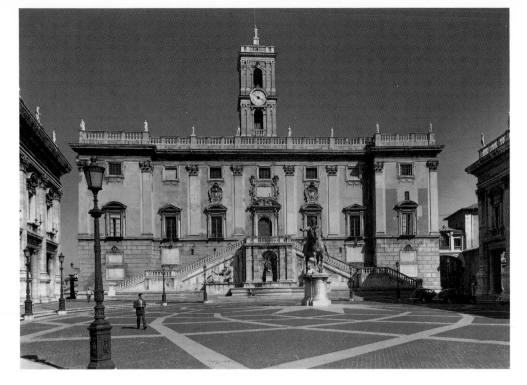

8.52 Capitoline Hill, Rome, decision to rebuild made in 1536, commissioned by Paul III from MICHELANGELO; double stair begun in 1544, *cordonata* (ramp) begun under Pius IV in 1561, Conservators' Palace begun in 1563

The pavement, although apparently planned by Michelangelo, was not laid until 1940 when Mussolini recognized the historical importance of the Capitoline as a symbol of governance. The gilded bronze equestrian statue of Marcus Aurelius, which stood at the center of this architectural complex, has recently been cleaned and removed to the protection of the museum in the Palazzo Nuovo at the left of the site.

This incident inspired Paul to renovate the area—probably in cooperation with the Conservators (urban magistrates responsible for finances and administration), whose palace stood there. For the project he engaged Michelangelo. Paul's first move—opposed by Michelangelo—was to transfer the bronze equestrian statue of Emperor Marcus Aurelius from the papal palace at St. John Lateran to the center of the piazza. Paul thus echoed the gesture made by Sixtus IV who, in 1471, had donated other ancient statues to the site including fragments of a colossal statue of Constantine. Paul's own gift was considered particularly significant, for at the time it was thought that the equestrian statue also represented Constantine, the emperor who had legitimated Christianity as a state religion and who, according to papal political fiction (exposed as such by Nicolas of Cusa in 1433 and again by Lorenzo Valla in 1440) had ceded temporal power over Rome to the papacy when he moved the seat of Roman government to Constantinople in 330.

Whatever misgivings Michelangelo may have had about repositioning the statue, he designed a magnificent architectural space to frame it. The statue stood at the center of the complex on a slightly mounded pavement which was to have been decorated by an interlocking stellate pattern, whose twelve points refer to the signs of the zodiac, thus adding cosmological significance to the site. A long ramp, or *cordonata*, led from the medieval city below to the top of the hill, directly on axis with the Marcus Aurelius and the center portal of the Senators' Palace, approached by a long double-ramped staircase, one of the first of the renovations to be built (see Fig. 5.34). The niche at the center of the staircase was intended to house a large statue of Jupiter, the king of the gods (it now houses a too-small figure of Roma). A baldachin, another symbol of rulership, was to crown the staircase before the main door of the building. The Conservators' Palace, to the right, was also to be given a new façade, one bay in depth, and an identical building façade was to be constructed across from it.

The scheme was not completed until the late seventeenth century, a hundred years after Michelangelo's death, and it was modified in some respects by the Lombard-trained Giacomo della Porta (c. 1532 Porlezza–1602 Rome). However, the result is essentially as Michelangelo intended: a spacious exterior room which could function as a stage set for ceremonial events. Michelangelo's renovations and additions had to take into account already existing buildings and also be responsive to the meanings attached to the site.

The trapezoidal shape of the plan was forced upon Michelangelo by the fact that the old Senators' and Conservators' palaces stood at an 80-degree angle to each other; however, visual distortions at the top of the *cordonata* make the trapezoid look like a square and the oval pavement like a circle—geometrical figures considered ideal by Renaissance theorists.

Michelangelo structured the façade of the Conservators' Palace, and that of the Palazzo Nuovo across the piazza, with a colossal order, uniting the entire façade. Corinthian pilasters rise up through both stories—rather than through only one in the traditional manner—and support a proportionately heavy cornice topped with a balustrade. This colossal order unites the entire façade. Within this majestic framework Michelangelo introduced a wryly playful Ionic order, flanking the piers at ground level. The **volutes** of the capitals twist elastically around each column, and grotesque masks peek out at the very top of the capitals. Michelangelo's inventiveness is everywhere evident in the complex. Two vocabularies are employed at the Conservators' Palace—one decorous and

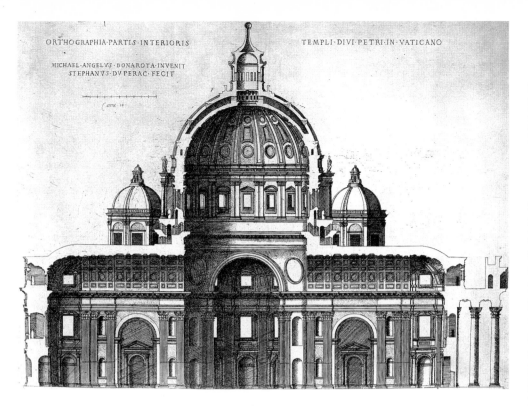

ORTHOGRAPHIA·PARTIS·INTERIORIS TEMPLI·DIVI·PETRI·IN·VATICANO

MICHAEL·ANGELVS·BONAROTA·INVENIT
STEPHANVS·DVPERAC·FECIT

8.53 St. Peter's, Rome, reconstruction of interior presumably based on MICHELANGELO'S plans (after ETIENNE DUPÉRAC) (Metropolitan Museum of Art, New York)

formal, the other willfully manipulating the rules of the order. The first is appropriate as an official language of the state, the second perhaps for the diurnal activities of the site as a commercial center.

St. Peter's

In 1546 Paul appointed Michelangelo chief architect of St. Peter's in a push to complete the project begun by Julius II in 1506. Paul had earlier entrusted the continuation of the construction to Antonio da Sangallo the Younger, his preferred architect. Sangallo's plan for St. Peter's (see Fig. 7.19) had maintained some of the characteristics of Bramante's second plan for the building, although he extended one arm of the cross to create a nave, thus destroying the centrally planned scheme so important to Bramante. Sangallo constructed a huge wooden model of his plan between 1539 and 1546; by 1543 he had actually vaulted part of the nave, as can be seen in the Cancelleria fresco (see Fig. 8.48).

Michelangelo reverted to Bramante's initial central plan, thickened the exterior walls, removed secondary spaces, and in so doing unified the spatial volumes of the structure and made the interior especially luminous (Fig. 8.53). This plan necessitated the destruction of an ambulatory on Sangallo's south **hemicycle** (1548–49), a bold move considering the building costs already incurred.

For the exterior of the building (Fig. 8.54) Michelangelo again used a colossal order and maintained an appropriately formal vocabulary throughout. His employment of the huge flat pilasters around the building's curves and corners creates a rippling, muscular surface,

accentuated by the step-like movement of the cornice. Where the hemicycles meet the central square of the plan, Michelangelo added a diagonal wall unit which softens the contours of the building, eliminating the sharp corners indicated on the Sangallo plan. Michelangelo's original design called for a hemispherical dome, which, like Bramante's, would have symbolized cosmological power for St. Peter buried beneath and, by extension, for the papacy. Even in the form of the ogival dome which was ultimately built, this symbolism remains. The dome is raised on a high drum (partially constructed 1555–57) to give it visibility over the mass of the building. Like the walls of the building, the drum is treated as a sculptural volume, with applied double columns disguising the mass of the buttresses that support the dome and with large pediments breaking the wall mass over the windows.

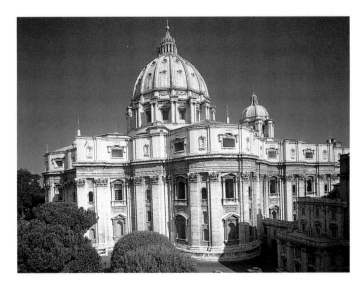

8.54 St. Peter's, Rome, new project of 1546 using plans by MICHELANGELO.

The building continued after Michelangelo's death in 1564 under Giacomo Vignola. On the death of Vignola in 1573 Giacomo della Porta became the architect of St. Peter's; his project for the dome, significantly altering the hemispherical shape originally planned by Michelangelo, was approved in 1586 and was brought to completion from 1588 to 1590. The lantern was completed between 1590 and 1593.

The Villa Giulia

After Paul III's grand schemes for the restoration of the city of Rome, the villa planned by his successor, Julius III (r. 1550–55), seems quite playful, even given its nature as a suburban retreat (Figs. 8.55 and 8.56). It is the work of several different architects: Vasari, Ammanati, and Giacomo Barozzi da Vignola (1507 Vignola–1573 Rome), with contributions from Julius himself. Although there is a formal entrance—including a papal benediction loggia facing the roadway from the city—the remainder of the villa plays games with the viewer's expectations. There is a clear axis set up through the center of the villa, but no way to follow it from the entrance to the small garden at the opposite end of the complex. A loggia screens the first courtyard from the succeeding spatial areas. Beyond that loggia, the space drops two stories into a nymphaeum, access to which is hidden by doorways and stairwells in the walls. At the lowest level of the nymphaeum all of the preceding areas disappear from sight, leaving the viewer isolated in a small space with cool, quiet pools and water-spouting statues imitating classical **herms**, a magical evocation of an actual Roman nymphaeum.

From the entrance of the building the viewer is also invited to follow a semicircular vaulted loggia which leads on either side of the complex to walled gardens, completely unadorned architecturally and thus totally different from the building itself. Within the villa, wit and play disorient the viewer; views are clear but access is denied, and passage from one area to another is enlivened by a continual shift of scale and decoration. The architects have manipulated not only canonic forms but also the visitor's experience of space. In this building both formal elements and the handling of space provide one of the clearest explorations of Mannerism in architecture of the period.

The Farnese Hours

Private patronage for personal enjoyment, rather than for public effect, also flourished in Rome. Cardinal Alessandro Farnese commissioned Giulio Clovio (Juraj Klovic; 1498 Grisone [Grizane], Croatia–1578 Rome) to paint a private book of hours now known as the *Farnese Hours* (Fig. 8.57). Biblical narratives are paired with apocryphal stories; all are framed with elaborate architectural

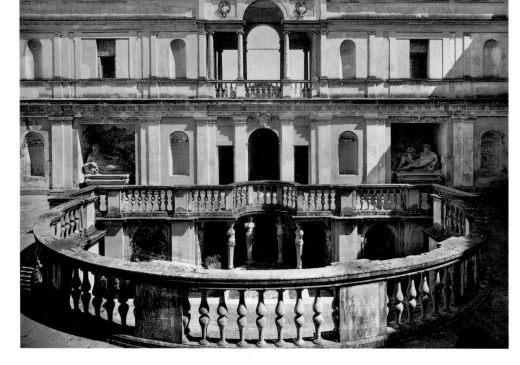

8.55 Villa Giulia, Rome, view into the nymphaeum from the southeast, 1551–55, commissioned by Julius III from GIACOMO VIGNOLA, with assistance from BARTOLOMEO AMMANATI and GIORGIO VASARI

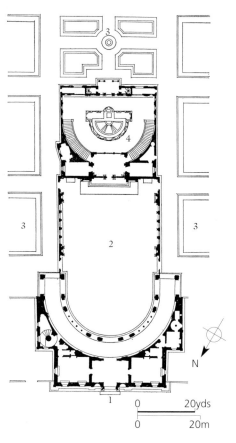

8.56 Villa Giulia, Rome, plan of lower floor

1 Entrance to the villa (Vignola);
2 Courtyard (Ammanati, 1552); **3** Gardens;
4 Nymphaeum (Ammanati)

8.57 *Farnese Hours*, pages showing *Annunciation to the Shepherds* and *Augustus and the Sibyl*, 1538–46, commissioned by Alessandro Farnese from GIULIO CLOVIO. Vellum, each page 6¾ × 4¼" (17.2 × 11 cm) (The Pierpont Morgan Library, New York).

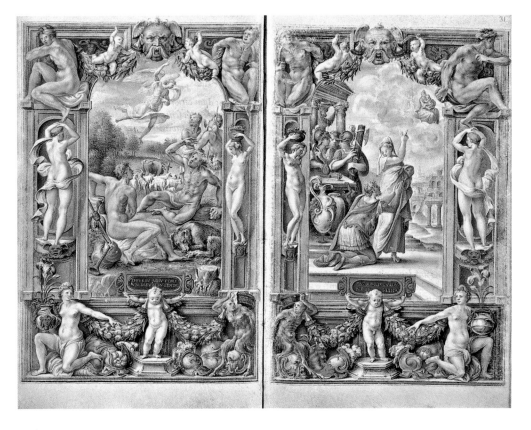

borders decorated with sensuous nudes, masks, and floral swags, hardly a manifestation of the biblical accuracy and decorum demanded by the Protestant or Catholic Reformation, but certainly something Clovio would have remembered from his training with Giulio Romano before the latter left for Mantua in 1524.

In addition to the wonderfully fanciful *Farnese Hours*, Alessandro Farnese also commissioned a variant of one of Titian's more lascivious paintings, the *Danaë* (see Fig. 8.24), where Jupiter has transformed himself into a shower of gold in order to possess the female figure reclining nude on her bed. Even in the works of a single artist such as El Greco (Domenico Theotocopouli; 1541 Candia, Crete–1614 Toledo), who lived for a short time in the Palazzo Farnese while he was in Rome between 1570 and 1575, Alessandro's catholicity of taste is evident. The two El Greco paintings he owned, the traditional biblical scene of *Christ Healing the Blind* (c. 1570) and an enigmatic and very unusual genre-like image of a *Boy Lighting a Candle* (c. 1570—75), illustrate the breadth of subject matter in his collection. Such commissions are reminders of the cosmopolitan nature of Rome, a city with an international court and an itinerant international artistic community. No single style or type of subject matter could maintain exclusive control in such an environment.

Synopsis

Vasari did not publish the first comprehensive history of art in Renaissance Italy until 1550, contemporary with the works of art discussed in this chapter. His history was adamantly anti-Gothic and decisively biased toward Florentine art. An eminently successful courtier and impresario in the papal and Florentine courts, he emphasized grace, visual elegance, and classicism as defining characteristics of the best art at this time. He also did much to elevate the status of artists, seen elsewhere in this period in the establishment of academies of design and such self-promotional activities as Palladio's publication of designs for his own buildings and Titian's and Michelangelo's obsession with their own funerary monuments. Charles V's interest in owning a "Titian," whatever its subject, and Giambologna's carving of a figural group without a pre-determined subject or patron both indicate how much artist/patron relationships were changing.

At the same time, certain patrons were more powerful than ever. The Venetian state imprisoned Sansovino for structural failures in one of his buildings, and Michelangelo's work at St. Peter's, the Palazzo Farnese, and the Capitoline Hill depended on the will of Pope Paul III. In Vasari's case, his very livelihood depended on pleasing Duke Cosimo, to whom he dedicated the *Lives*.

This period codified the language employed ever since to describe Renaissance art, providing useful ways to articulate distinctions among various artistic traditions in Italy—though once again caution is required to avoid the temptation to apply such terminology anachronistically. For Vasari, the mid-sixteenth century marked the height of the Renaissance; for students of Renaissance art today, it is but one fascinating chapter among many.

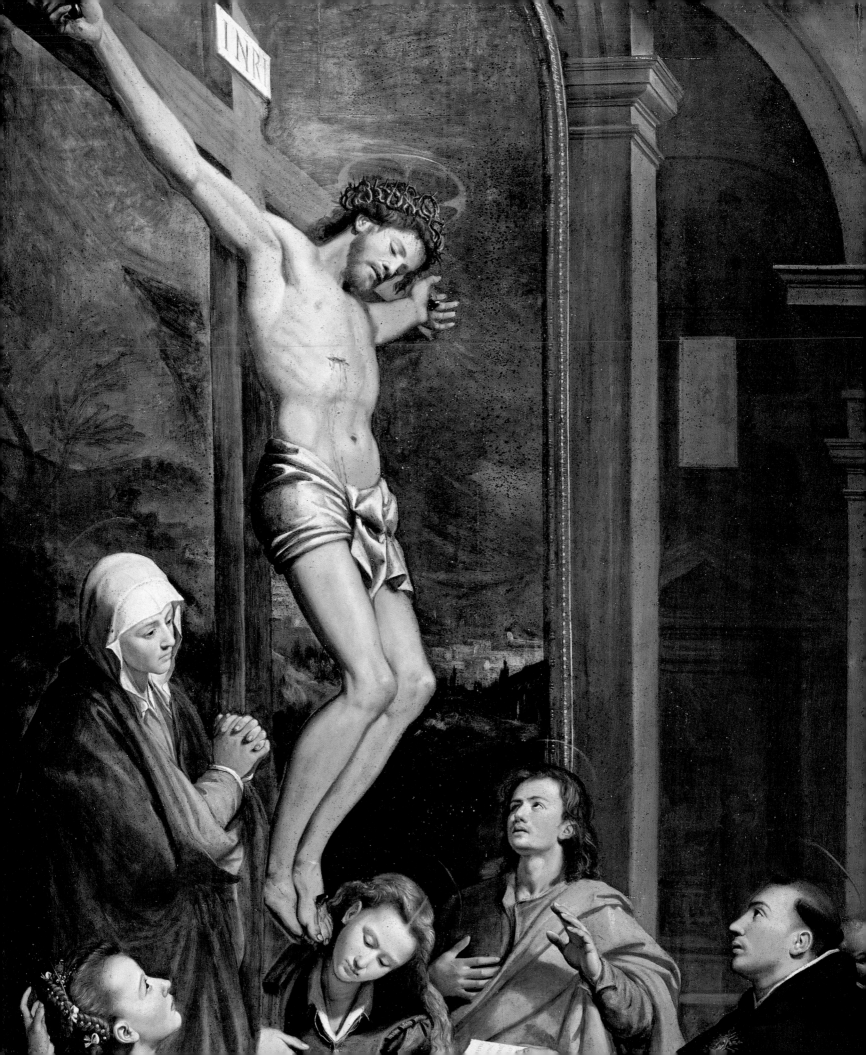

9

Innovation and Reform: The Later Sixteenth Century

A serious discussion of works produced in the last third of the sixteenth century often fails to appear in books on art in Renaissance Italy. Beyond the chronological limits of Vasari's canonical *Lives of the Artists* these decades are, nonetheless, critical, underscoring the decisive relationship that existed between artists and patrons throughout the Renaissance. In the midst of reform, ecclesiastical authorities profoundly altered stylistic expectations throughout Italy by reining in artistic license and reclaiming traditional patronage roles.

Major religious reforms, the coalescence of national states, a renewed and truly universal Church in a radically reordered geographical world, the waning of small independent city-states in Italy, and the emergence of new economic forces within the cultures of Europe as a whole changed the nature of artistic production irrevocably during the later part of the sixteenth century. The wholesale clearing out and transformations of church interiors left many earlier buildings as we see them today: not elegantly subdivided, densely filled, colorful, and accumulative as they were intended to be, but sober and spare. Churches like Santa Croce and Santa Maria Novella in Florence, for example, were scrubbed and their choir screens removed—acts that responded to changes in liturgical practice promulgated by the Council of Trent, but equally importantly asserted the hegemony of a classical artistic vocabulary over the styles of earlier periods.

The Demands of the Council of Trent

The Council of Trent was convened by Paul III in response to the call for reform within the Catholic Church and to the criticisms made of Rome by Protestant leaders. The four plenary sessions of the Council were held in the north Italian city of Trent beginning in 1545. The Council argued for liturgical and ecclesiastical reform and a return to the principles of the early Church—issues on which Rome concurred with the Protestants. It also stated unambiguously, however, that the cult of the Virgin and the saints and their relics which had grown to such enormous proportions through the Middle Ages was to be retained, maintaining that the saints were not only aids to devotion but also efficacious intercessors for the redemption of the faithful. Additionally, the Council accorded special devotion to the Eucharist as embodying the true presence of Christ. These two points—the intercessions of the saints and the nature of the Eucharist—were obvious reinforcements of traditional positions and in clear opposition to Protestant theology. Thus the changes in the Roman Church legislated by the Council at its closing in 1563 can be seen both as a reformation and as a counter-reformation, one directed to ongoing processes from within, the other directed to challenges from without. To see the changes in Church teachings—and consequently in its art—merely as a "Counter-Reformation" is to see only one part of the picture.

The needs of the reformed Roman Church after the last session of the Council of Trent stimulated both renewed and revised artistic activity, not only in Rome but throughout Catholic Europe. As a Church newly secure after the threats of the Protestant Reformation, Rome attempted once again to assert its universality, now in a world that included the Americas and parts of Africa, India, and eastern Asia. The arts were an effective form of propaganda with which to articulate the new confidence of the Church and its claims to dominance over the Christian faith. Regulations for the arts resulting from the decrees of the Council were, like earlier Protestant treatises, promulgated through the print medium and

9.1 (*opposite*) *Vision of St Thomas Aquinas*, 1593 (detail), commissioned by Sebastiano Pandolfini del Turco from SANTI DI TITO for the del Turco Chapel, San Marco, Florence. Oil on panel, 11′ 9″ × 7 7″ (3.62 × 2.33m). See also Fig. 9.13.

helped to bring about a uniformity of style and common concerns for propagating orthodoxy not only to the arts of Italy but to all of Catholic Europe and its colonies as well.

Long after the closing of the Council of Trent its importance was underscored in a didactic and journalistic fresco (Fig. 9.2) painted as part of an otherwise elegant and classicizing decorative program for a chapel built by Vignola's protegé Martino Longhi the Elder (c. 1534 Viggiù–c. 1591 Rome) for one of Rome's leading churchmen, Cardinal Marco Sittico Altemps. Participants in the Council session are spread row upon row across the top of the composition, their faces directed forward or turned in profile as if to record as completely and accurately as possible the individual members. At the lower right of this pictorial chronicle of the event, however, allegorical personifications of the virtues crown a figure representing the Roman Church with a papal tiara. A globe at the lower left shows Europe, Africa, and parts of Asia. Thus the Church appears not only victorious, but extending far beyond Europe, where Protestantism had recently made such dramatic inroads. In this fresco the didactic stylistic language of the historical chronicle is spliced—albeit somewhat awkwardly—with a classical stylistic revival appropriate for allegories of dominating political power.

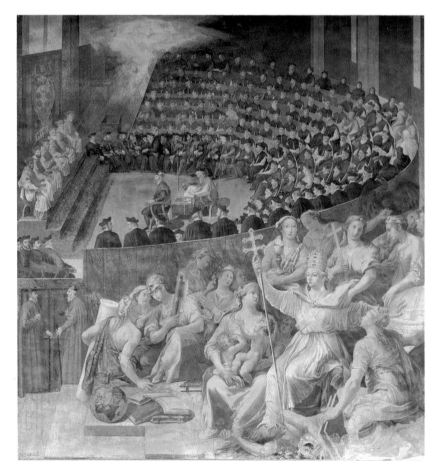

Decrees on the Arts

The decrees of the Council of Trent stipulated that art was to be direct and compelling in its narrative presentation, that it was to provide an accurate presentation of the biblical narrative or saint's life, rather than adding incidental and imaginary moments, and that it was to encourage piety. The Council also maintained the efficacy of religious images to convey the messages of the new Church, contrary to the belief of some—although not all—of the Protestant churches:

> . . . the images of Christ, of the Virgin Mother of God, and of other saints are to be placed and retained especially in the churches. . .
>
> . . . let the bishops diligently teach that by means of the stories of the mysteries of our redemption portrayed in paintings and other representations the people are instructed and confirmed in the articles of faith.
>
> . . . through the saints the miracles of God and salutary examples are set before the eyes of the faithful, so that they may give God thanks for those things, may fashion their own life and conduct in imitation of the saints and be moved to adore and love God and cultivate piety.

Perhaps because the Council's formal decrees on art were both limited and vague in their directives, treatises on art and architecture provoked by the Council proliferated in the last third of the sixteenth century. Those written by churchmen, such as Charles Borromeo's *Instructiones fabricae et supellectilis ecclesiasticae* (Instructions on Ecclesiastical Buildings and Furnishings, 1577), Robert Bellarmine's *Disputationes* (1586 edition dedicated to Pope Sixtus V), Gabriele Paleotti's *De imaginibus sacris* (On Sacred Images, published in Germany in 1594), and G. A. Gilio da Fabriano's *Degli Errori de' Pittori* (On the Errors of Painters, 1564) were prescriptive; but in general all called for a style different from the courtly conceits of Mannerism. And, importantly, because they were printed they reached an even wider audience than the International Style of the early fifteenth century, opening the way for the first truly pan-national style in the arts since classical antiquity.

9.2 *The Council of Trent*, 1588, Pasquale Cati da Iesi (?), Chapel of Cardinal Marco Sittico Altemps, Santa Maria in Trastevere, Rome, built by MARTINO LONGHI the Elder. Fresco

The Council is sometimes called the Tridentine Council, after the Latin name for the city, Tridentum. The coat of arms on the left wall behind the cardinals in red is that of Pius IV, the pope at the time of the closing of the Council.

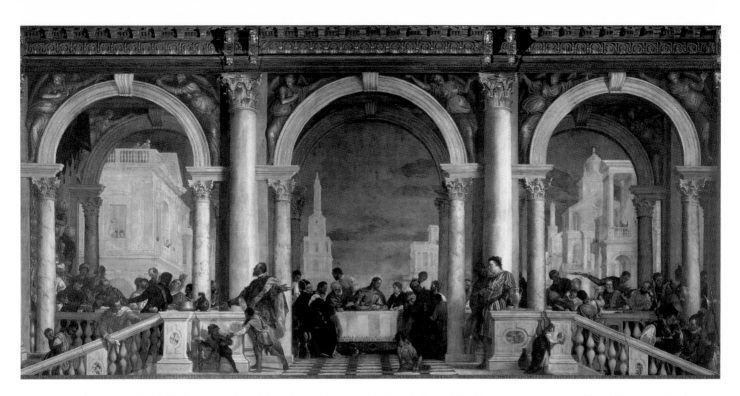

9.3 *Feast in the House of Levi*, 1573, commissioned from PAOLO VERONESE for the refectory of the Dominican monastery of Santi Giovanni e Paolo, Venice. Oil on canvas, 18′ 3″ × 42′ (5.56 × 12.8 m) (Galleria dell'Accademia, Venice)

Reform and Censorship

During the nearly twenty years when the Council of Trent was in session, reforms begun under Paul III took unforeseen and stringently moralistic forms. The Roman Inquisition (or official inquiry into heresy) instituted under Paul III in 1542 took a particularly virulent turn under Paul IV Carafa (r. 1555–59) as an active effort to assert orthodoxy. One of the concerns of the "reformers"—one quite familiar to modern ears—was to expunge perceived lasciviousness from religious images. It should be noted, however, that overt eroticism continued unabated and uncontested in images made for private contexts. Johannes Molanus's *De picturis et imaginibus sacris* (On Sacred Pictures and Images), published in Louvain in 1570, quotes an earlier writer in saying that "[t]he most disgusting aspect of this age is the fact you come across pictures of gross indecency in the greatest churches and chapels, so that there one can look at all the bodily shames that nature has concealed, with the effect of arousing not devotion but every lust of the corrupt flesh." Paintings such as Parmigianino's *Madonna of the Long Neck* (see Fig. 7.76) come to mind when reading such passages. The sensuality of Parmigianino's Virgin cannot help but intrude on any devotional thoughts of the viewer, especially since the Christ Child seems to be slipping away from his mother in order to reveal more of her torso beneath the clinging drapery. It is perhaps not surprising that the painting remained unfinished. But incompleteness is relatively benign in comparison to defacement. Michelangelo's *Last Judgment* (see Fig. 8.45) stands as a primary example of contemporary attacks on religious images that were considered offensive (see page 441). Immediately after Michelangelo's death in 1564 Daniele da Volterra (Daniele Ricciarelli; 1509 Volterra–1566 Rome) and others painted pants over the genital areas of a number of the nude figures in the fresco, which earned them the nickname *"braghettoni,"* or "breeches-painters." (These "breeches" were left in place during the recent cleaning of the fresco.) Within the heart of the Vatican, support for such a modification of Michelangelo's work by pope and cardinals—as well as by secular writers like the scurrilous Venetian poet Pietro Aretino—could only have supported the efforts of "reformers" like Molanus.

Although regulations proliferated, they were not, of course, always followed. Veronese's grand painting with life-sized figures of the *Feast in the House of Levi* (Fig. 9.3), originally painted as a Last Supper for the Dominican monastery of Santi Giovanni e Paolo in Venice, is a case in point. On July 18, 1573, Veronese was called before the court of the Inquisition because it found his treatment of the subject inappropriate. Since the figures about which he was questioned were certainly not part of the biblical narrative, Veronese's reply that he thought such figures would enliven the story did not satisfy the Inquisition. Although Veronese did not substantially alter the painting, the Inquisition took no formal action against him, perhaps because of his judicious tactic of changing the title of the painting from the *Last Supper* to the *Feast in the House of Levi*, thereby providing a context for which the festive courtly figures he had already depicted would be appropriate. Although Veronese's response

Veronese before the Inquisition

Called before the Inquisition to answer charges against his painting of the *Last Supper* (now known as the *Feast in the House of Levi*), Veronese acquitted himself well, giving some indication of his working practice and of his awareness of art outside Venice.

VENICE, JULY 18, 1573. The minutes of the session of the Inquisition Tribunal of Saturday, the 18th of July, 1573. . . .

Questioned about his profession:
Answer: I paint and compose figures.
Question: Do you know the reason why you have been summoned?
A: No, sir.
Q: Can you imagine it?
A: I can well imagine.
Q: Say what you think the reason is.
A: According to what the Reverend Father, the Prior of the Convent of SS. Giovanni e Paolo, . . . told me, . . . Your Lordships had ordered him to have painted [in the picture] a Magdalen in place of a dog. I answered him by saying I would gladly do everything necessary for my honor and for that of my painting, but that I did not understand how a figure of Magdalen would be suitable there for many reasons which I will give at any time, provided I am given an opportunity.
Q: What picture is this of which you have spoken?
A: This is a picture of the Last Supper that Jesus Christ took with His Apostles in the house of Simon . . .
Q: At this Supper of Our Lord have you painted other figures?
A: Yes, milords.
Q: Tell us how many people and describe the gestures of each.
A: There is the owner of the inn, Simon; besides this figure I have made a steward, who, I imagined, had come there for his own pleasure to see how the things were going at the table. There are many figures there which I cannot recall, as I painted the picture some time ago . . .

Q: In this Supper which you made for SS. Giovanni e Paolo what is the significance of the man whose nose is bleeding?
A: I intended to represent a servant whose nose was bleeding because of some accident.
Q: What is the significance of those armed men dressed as Germans, each with a halberd in his hand? . . .
A: We painters take the same license the poets and the jesters take and I have represented these two halberdiers, one drinking and the other eating nearby on the stairs. They are placed there so that they might be of service because it seemed to me fitting, according to what I have been told, that the master of the house, who was great and rich, should have such servants.
Q: And that man dressed as a buffoon with a parrot on his wrist, for what purpose did you paint him on that canvas?
A: For ornament, as is customary. . .
Q: Who do you really believe was present at that Supper?
A: I believe one would find Christ with His Apostles. But if in a picture there is some space to spare I enrich it with figures according to the stories.
Q: Did any one commission you to paint Germans, buffoons, and similar things in that picture?
A: No, milords, but I received the commission to decorate the picture as I saw fit. It is large and, it seemed to me, it could hold many figures.
Q: Are not the decorations which you painters are accustomed to add to paintings or pictures supposed to be suitable and proper to the subject and the principal figures or are they for pleasure—simply what comes to your imagination without any discretion or judiciousness?
A: I paint pictures as I see fit and as well as my talent permits.
Q: Does it seem fitting at the Last Supper of the Lord to paint buffoons, drunkards, Germans, dwarfs and similar vulgarities?
A: No, milords.
Q: Do you not know that in Germany and in

other places infected with heresy it is customary with various pictures full of scurrilousness and similar inventions to mock, vituperate, and scorn the things of the Holy Catholic Church in order to teach bad doctrines to foolish and ignorant people?
A: Yes that is wrong; but I return to what I have said, that I am obliged to follow what my superiors have done.
Q: What have your superiors done? Have they perhaps done similar things?
A: Michelangelo in Rome in the Pontifical Chapel painted Our Lord, Jesus Christ, His Mother, St. John, St. Peter, and the Heavenly Host [see Fig. 8.45]. These are all represented in the nude—even the Virgin Mary—and in different poses with little reverence.
Q: Do you not know that in painting the Last Judgment in which no garments or similar things are presumed, it was not necessary to paint garments, and that in those figures there is nothing that is not spiritual? There are neither buffoons, dogs, weapons, or similar buffoonery. And does it seem because of this or some other example that you did right to have painted this picture in the way you did and do you want to maintain that it is good and decent?
A: Illustrious Lords, I do not want to defend it, but I thought I was doing right. I did not consider so many things and I did not intend to confuse anyone, the more so as those figures of buffoons are outside of the place in a picture where Our Lord is represented.

After these things had been said, the judges announced that the above named Paolo would be obliged to improve and change his painting within a period of three months . . . and that if he did not correct the picture he would be liable to the penalties imposed by the Holy Tribunal. Thus they decreed in the best manner possible.

(from E.G. Holt. *Literary Sources of Art History*. Princeton: Princeton University Press, 1947, pp. 245–8)

was opportunistic and clever, benefiting from relaxed Venetian attitudes toward the Inquisition, the whole episode does indicate a new concern on the part of the Church authorities for regulating the accuracy of religious painting and asserting a renewed orthodoxy.

Milan

Milan was an early center for reform in the visual arts. Bereft of native rulers (the last Sforza had died in 1536) and dominated by Spain, Milan in the mid-sixteenth century looked to its local bishop for leadership as it had done earlier in its history. Charles Borromeo (1538–84; canonized in 1610) was appointed cardinal and archbishop of Milan in 1560 by his very conservative uncle Pope Pius IV (r. 1559–65). While holding this position, he actively directed the last session of the Council of Trent and was instrumental in drafting the decrees it published in 1563. As a personal witness to the demands for reform made by the Council, Charles gave away all his considerable personal wealth, thus providing the Milanese with a compelling model of religious simplicity and severity. With the assistance of new religious orders such as the Jesuits and the Theatines, both of whom Charles brought to Milan, the city led all of northern Italy in implementing Church reforms.

Ecclesiastical Commissions   Lombard religious leaders had from the outset of the Reformation been quick to counter Protestant challenges to the Roman Church, perhaps because of their proximity to Germany and also perhaps because of constant threats of northern political domination. Encouraging art that was simple, powerful, direct, and free of preciosity and artificiality, they had laid the groundwork for the prescriptions of the Council of Trent long before the formal publication of the Council's decrees in 1563. It was this Lombard tradition, typified by works such as the *Ecce Homo* ("Behold the Man"; Fig. 9.4) by Moretto da Brescia (Alessandro Bonvicino; 1498 Brescia–1554 Brescia) which Borromeo may well have had in mind as he directed the discussions of the Council and as he wrote his own treatise on church art and architecture. Moretto worked largely in Brescia, although he assimilated Venetian painting technique early in his career. Given its proximity to Milan, Brescia was culturally and religiously dependent upon the Lombard capital as part of its archdiocese in spite of belonging to Venice's mainland empire. In the altarpiece Moretto placed the Cross and the pathetic figure of Christ accusingly before the worshiper, the weeping angel in the background demonstrating an appropriately repentant and grieving response. Very limited in its palette and chilled by a gray,

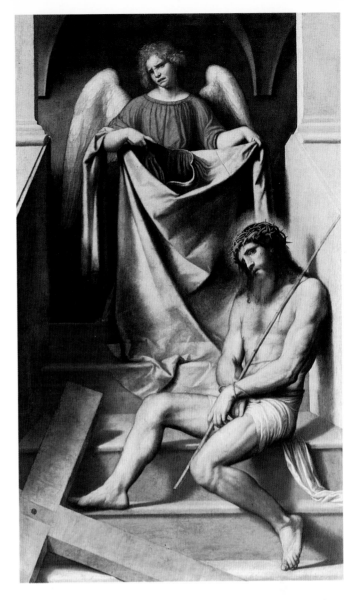

9.4 *Ecce Homo*, c. 1550–54, commissioned by the Confraternity of the Holy Cross from MORETTO DA BRESCIA for their chapel in Brescia Cathedral. Oil on canvas, 84½ × 49¼″ (214.6 × 125 cm) (Pinacoteca Tosio Martinengo, Brescia)

sepulchral light, the altarpiece was probably inspired by contemporary devotional books such as Giovanni da Fano's *L'arte dell'unione* (The Art of Union), which set its mystical reunion with Christ in a palace where the spat-upon, beaten, and crowned Christ was attended by an anguished and sorrowful angel. The dull orange-red steps serve as a none-too-subtle reminder of Christ's blood, shed for humanity. Nothing in the painting detracts the viewer's attention from the object of devotion or from the appropriate response one should have to this tragic (and a-historical) icon. The painting could hardly be more different from Rosso's Mannerist version of essentially the same subject (see Fig. 7.42).

Even subjects that were not concerned directly with Christ's Passion and Crucifixion took on a new severity in this period. The altarpiece of the *Virgin in Glory with St. Barbara and St. Lawrence* (Fig. 9.5), painted by Moretto's pupil Giovanni Battista Moroni (c. 1520/24 Albino?–1578 Albino) for a church in Bergamo, is also spare and somewhat forbidding. In keeping with the Church's reaffirmation of the crucial intercessory role of saints, Barbara stands as a gatekeeper to heaven, while the Madonna and Child are set distantly in the clouds. There is little to distract or beguile the eye, the relative emptiness of the landscape and prosaic description of the sky encouraging the worshiper to meditate upon the arduous task of seeking salvation through the Church.

While altarpieces emphasized sacrificial aspects of Christianity, appropriate to their placement above altars where priests celebrated Christ's sacrifice in the mass, dome frescoes invited worshipers to contemplate the awe-inspiring splendors of heaven. In Milan Gian Paolo Lomazzo (1538 Milan–1600 Milan) painted the half-dome over the Foppa Chapel in the church of San Marco with an ambitious scene of the *Glory of Angels* (Fig. 9.6), building on the dual example of Correggio (see Fig. 7.73) and Giulio Romano. Rank upon rank of sober-faced but rapturously intertwined angels stand with their heads tipped back to contemplate the vertiginous heights of heaven. Extravagant and self-consciously clever foreshortenings and dense figural groupings could be tolerated because they so effectively evoked a vision of heaven.

Lomazzo ended his career early because of blindness, but he dictated and published two treatises that promulgated his artistic ideas: the *Trattato dell'arte de la pittura,*

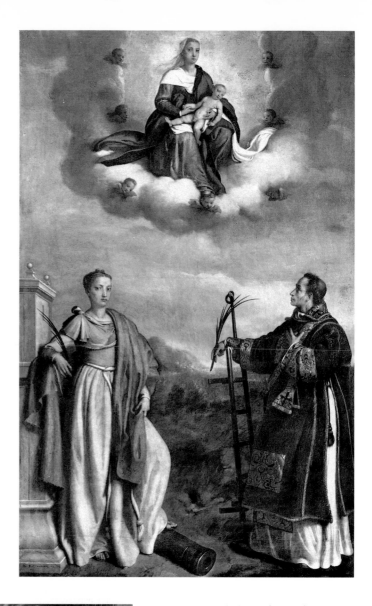

9.5 (above) *Virgin in Glory with St. Barbara and St. Lawrence*, 1550s, GIOVANNI BATTISTA MORONI. Oil on canvas (Brera Gallery, Milan)

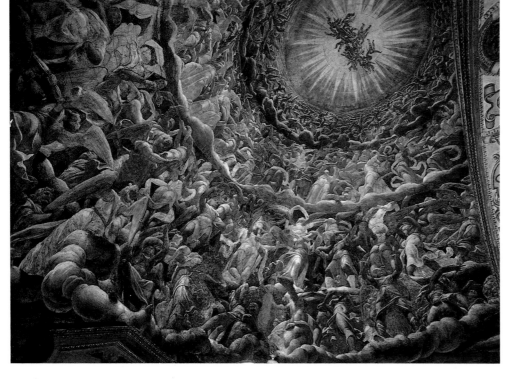

9.6 *Glory of Angels*, c. 1570, commissioned from GIAN PAOLO LOMAZZO for the Foppa Chapel, San Marco, Milan. Fresco

scoltura et architettura (Treatise on the Art of Painting, Sculpture, and Architecture, 1584) and *Idea del tempio della pittura* (Idea of the Temple of Painting, 1590). These books were to be as influential for northern Italy as Vasari's *Lives* were for central Italian art and art theory. Typical of artists participating in painting academies, Lomazzo constructed a system of ideals—in his case based on neo-Platonism—to which he believed artistic practice should aspire. He uses a round temple form recalling Bramante's *Tempietto* (see Fig. 7.16) as a device to structure his discussion. The imaginary building's very form recalls the cosmological significance of centralized structures and the concept of the divine that they embody. At the same time, his temple is an idealized fantastical concoction with statues of seven exemplary artists serving as the columnar support system for the entire structure. While somewhat arcane in its elaboration of painterly attributes of these seven sixteenth-century artists, each of whom Lomazzo associates with a planet and the conventional astrological notion of personality traits identified with that planet, the *Idea del tempio* is nevertheless an important discussion of beauty as reflective of divine order. Other parts of Lomazzo's temple give him a chance to talk about such central issues as proportion, perspective, and light.

Milanese Churches When the mid-fourth-century octagonal church of San Lorenzo Maggiore (Fig. 9.7) suddenly collapsed on June 5, 1573, Borromeo immediately recognized the propaganda value of reconstructing the building on its ancient foundations. It had, after all, been built when Milan was serving as the capital of the western Roman Empire. The project was sure to feed civic pride and offered a unique opportunity for demonstrating that the institutional church of his own day was capable of replicating the accomplishments of Christian antiquity. The technical challenges of building this large structure were brilliantly overcome by the architect and engineer Martino Bassi (1544 Seregno–1591 Milan), who supervised a team that carefully sifted through and measured the ruins. While replicating the quatrefoil plan and general elevation of the original church, including its classical vocabulary, the reconstructed building is, however, cold and austere. In Charles Borromeo's Milan, austerity had become a primary value which even the example of Roman antiquity could not dislodge.

Some exceptions were made for church façades, but only if, as at Santa Maria presso San Celso (Fig. 9.8), elaboration served a didactic purpose. In this case the Genoese architect Galeazzo Alessi laid out a scheme of unfluted pilasters to serve as a foil for sculptures of prophets and reliefs of scenes from the life of the Virgin. As at the earlier Certosa in Pavia (see Fig. 6.75), the

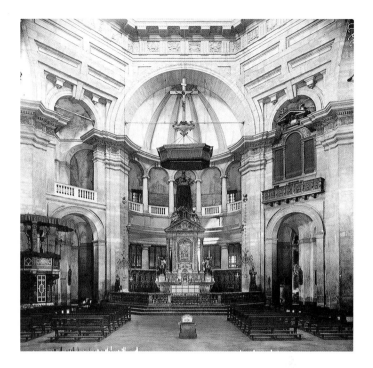

9.7 San Lorenzo Maggiore, Milan, fourth century (rebuilt after 1573 respecting the original plan)

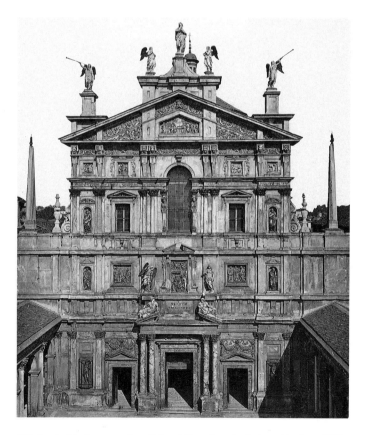

9.8 Santa Maria presso San Celso, Milan, façade designed before 1570 by GALEAZZO ALESSI and completed by MARTINO BASSI.

Alessi was responsible only for the façade of the building. The building project was begun in 1485; by 1493 Gian Giacomo Dolcebuono appears as its architect. A number of other architects and sculptors contributed their expertise to the building before Alessi added the façade.

design is largely additive, a distinctively Lombard accumulation of stories and levels unconcerned with accurately reproducing classical precedents which both vexed and inspired architects in other parts of Italy (see Fig. 8.9). Even though the sculptural reliefs and free-standing figures recall Michelangelo's unexecuted plan for the façade of San Lorenzo in Florence, and the reclining figures over the doors his Times of Day for the Medici Chapel (see Fig. 7.47), the façade still subordinates the sculpture to the tightly structured architectural composition, itself rather severe despite the doubled columns and stepped surfaces.

Secular Commissions Charles Borromeo and the reforms he promoted cast a long shadow over Lombardy and Milan, dampening, though never completely suppressing, the region's propensity for conspicuous display. The archbishop must have looked askance at projects such as the gargantuan family palace built by Tommaso Marino, not far from Milan Cathedral (Fig. 9.9). Marino was a nouveau-riche banker intent on claiming a place for himself among the patriciate. The building's architect, Galeazzo Alessi, emblazoned his patron's newly purchased title, "Duke of Terranova," across the palace's densely detailed façade, where every window is framed by both aedicules and a columnar main order. The emphasis is on novelty and luxury: bold rusticated blocks alternate with smooth shafts around the ground-floor windows; tapering surrounds, many capped by human and animal heads, enrich the upper stories. The extraordinarily costly

construction was abandoned for lack of funds in 1565. Marino died insolvent in 1572, and the unfinished building was confiscated to pay debts—an architectural warning against self-promotion and reliance on worldly wealth. Yet the extravagant vocabulary of Italian suburban villas (see Figs. 7.79, 7.80), which Alessi would have known from his time in Genoa, had entered the city.

In a climate where individuals found it increasingly in their best interest to avoid ostentation for fear of accusations of vanity, or even heresy, the art of portraiture was necessarily suspect. Fortunately, painters such as Moroni had already devised a type of individual representation that was appropriately sober and restrained. In his *Portrait of Gian Gerolamo Grumelli* (Fig. 9.10) the figure is dressed in splendid red attire; bits of classical antiquity along with an obscure motto in Spanish ("more the last than the first") attest to his worldly sophistication. Yet Moroni presents Grumelli's features with a disarming honesty, distinctly different from the elegant, idealized portraits of Parmigianino (see Fig. 7.75) or the heroic state imagery of Titian (see Fig. 8.21). Moroni's cavalier seems not so much sitting for a portrait as caught off guard as he goes about his daily business. Crumbling architecture, piles of dust, and fragmented sculpture attest to the fleeting and transitory nature of human fame and endeavor. The image is distinctly self-deprecating—appropriate for the man who hosted Charles Borromeo on the latter's visit to Grumelli's home city of Bergamo. The realism of the depiction sharpens the sense of Grumelli as the main subject of a framing allegory.

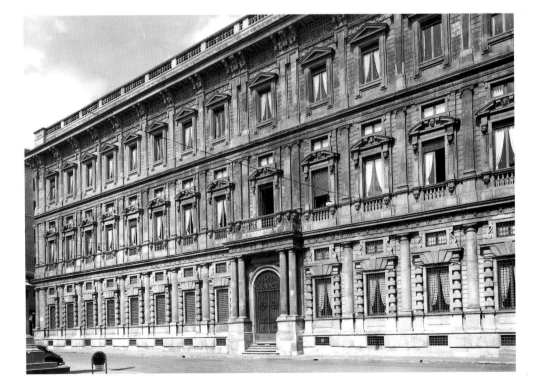

9.9 Palazzo Marino, Milan, begun 1558, commissioned by Tommaso Marino from GALEAZZO ALESSI

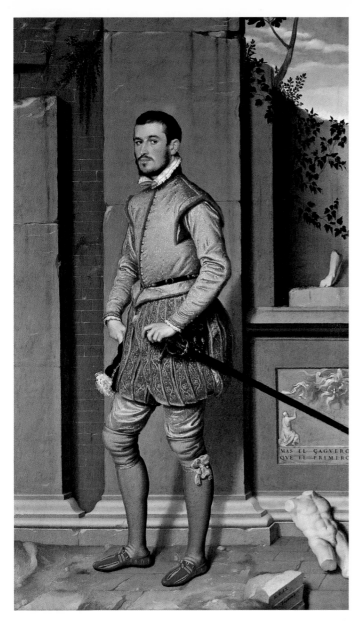

9.10 *Portrait of Gian Gerolamo Grumelli*, 1560, commissioned by the sitter from GIOVANNI BATTISTA MORONI. Oil on canvas (Collection of Count Antonio Moroni, Bergamo)

Florence: Renovation and Reform

Artistic change and renewal—even when ostensibly responding to the Council of Trent—could also refer to issues of state power; political orthodoxy thus mirrored the new religious orthodoxy. This was the case in the renovation projects begun in 1565 at the Florentine churches of Santa Croce and Santa Maria Novella (see Figs. 1.21 and 1.23). Cosimo I initiated the redecoration of these major Franciscan and Dominican churches, choosing Giorgio Vasari as his architect in both instances. Vasari removed existing choir screens to permit the laity to see the altar, in accordance with the Council's dictate; he also whitewashed fourteenth-century frescoes and supplanted their outdated style with classicizing architectural tabernacles framing new devotional paintings. The resulting

interiors of the buildings have a stripped-down, uniform, and modern appearance. For Santa Croce, Vasari also designed a huge Eucharistic tabernacle which dominated the newly opened central space of the church, giving a focus to the Sacrament, as explicitly demanded by Trent.

Cosimo's reasons for funding these extensive renovations stemmed from his desire to ingratiate himself with the papacy. His generosity was rewarded in 1569 when Pius V named him Grand Duke of Tuscany, a title that Cosimo had sought virtually from the moment he took power in Florence. The extensive obliteration of the past in these churches left their interiors appropriate for the new golden age under his rule. The awareness of Cosimo's other-than-religious motives is evident in the suit that the Alberti family brought against him, claiming that, in removing the choir-screen of Santa Croce, Cosimo was ostensibly claiming the space before the main altar of the church where their ancestors had been buried for over

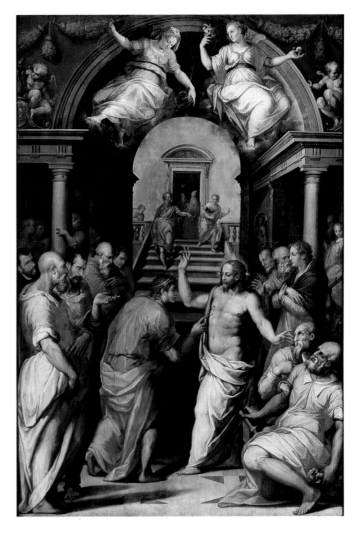

9.11 *Incredulity of St. Thomas*, 1572, commissioned by Tommaso and Francesco Guidacci from GIORGIO VASARI for the Guidacci Chapel, Santa Croce, Florence. Oil on panel

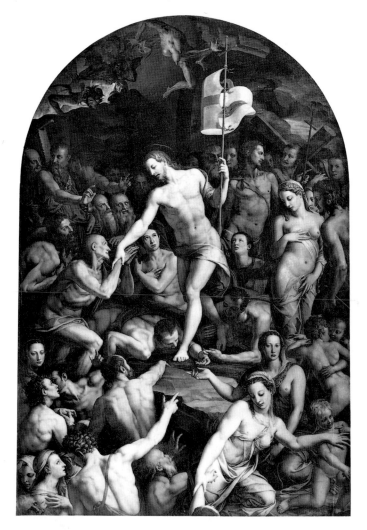

9.12 *Christ in Limbo*, 1552, commissioned by Giovanni Zanchini from AGNOLO BRONZINO for the Zanchini Chapel, Santa Croce, Florence. Oil on panel, 14′ 6¼″ × 9′ 6½″ (4.43 × 2.91m) (Soprintendenza alle Gallerie; formerly Museo di Santa Croce, damaged in the flood of November 1966 and in restoration ever since)

two hundred years. The Alberti claimed the presbytery and choir as their own—a space still today marked by their coats of arms high on the piers to the left and right of the main altar. Not surprisingly, the Alberti lost their suit. It is also no surprise that the building committees for these projects were composed of men loyal to Cosimo I and that in most cases these men were allotted the new altar chapels for their own use. Local politics and Church reform enjoyed reciprocal benefits in Florence.

Unlike previous practice, the owners of the new private chapels at Santa Croce and Santa Maria Novella were not allowed to determine the architectural forms of their chapels or to select the subject of the altarpieces that adorned them. The altarpieces were prescribed in Vasari's program. All are of narrative events, as if to bring the viewer into a closer relation with the historical fact of the biblical text and to ensure a more active involvement with its message, as the Council of Trent had stipulated; conventional Madonna and Child representations are com-

pletely absent. For Santa Croce Vasari devised a program of Christ's Passion and post-Passion histories which provided a continuous narrative from one altar to the next (see Fig. 1.22). A comparison of Bronzino's *Christ in Limbo* (Fig. 9.12), already in Santa Croce when Vasari began his renovations, and Vasari's own *Incredulity of St. Thomas* (Fig. 9.11) also demonstrates a change in style from Mannerism to what has come to be known as the **counter-maniera**, indicating its opposition to the complexities of Mannerism. Bronzino's altarpiece, painted before Cosimo's and Vasari's renovations, is distinctly Mannerist. Although the figure of Christ is centrally placed in Bronzino's painting, the welter of figures around him and the torsions of their poses compete for the viewer's attention. The complex positions of the limbs, the soft sensuality of the bodies and the vagueness of the figures were all criticized by Vasari's friend and advisor Raffaello Borghini in his *Il Riposo* of 1584. Vasari's painting, by contrast, shows Christ and St. Thomas at the center, framed by arches, with the subordinate figures focusing attention toward the narrative center of the painting. Space is rationally constructed and ordered around a single-point perspective system. Although the twisted pose of the crouching St. Peter to the far right employs Mannerist conventions, the allegories of Hope and Sorrow floating above are decorously clothed, unlike the fetching angelic figure in Parmigianino's *Madonna of the Long Neck* (see Fig. 7.76). Vasari, adept in the Mannerist style, could bring it to conform to the demands of the Council of Trent in programs that demanded new naturalism and accuracy to the narrative text.

Perhaps the most developed example of this new style and the devotional reforms that lie behind its appearance is Santi di Tito's (1536 Sansepolcro–1602 Florence) *Vision of St. Thomas Aquinas* (Fig. 9.13; see also Fig. 9.1) depicting a miraculous event in the life of the Dominican saint when Christ spoke to him from a painted crucifix. This painting shows Thomas kneeling in religious rapture before a crucified Christ, flanked by St. Catherine of Alexandria, the Virgin Mary, Mary Magdalene, and St. John, who seem to have moved out of the painting depicted on the walls of the niche behind them into physical space. Here Thomas's devotion is so intense that the icon has disappeared to be replaced by the real event. Contrary to the hagiographic story, Thomas does not levitate in the painting, but exists as a surrogate for the devout viewer kneeling before it, in this case perhaps members of a confraternity dedicated to the saint. Protestant criticisms of icon worship are here answered by the Catholic claim that images are merely a means to approach the figures depicted—in this case a successful means—in order to transform devotional practice into an immediate experience of the divine. A diagonal axis into

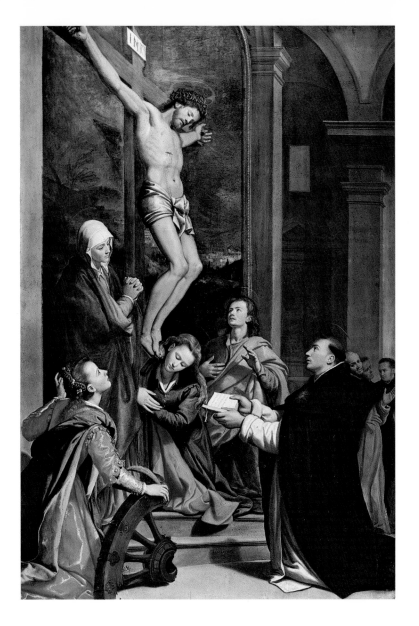

the painting invites the viewer to imitate the experience, assisted by the gesturing St. Catherine at the left, who, like a figure in a flanking panel in a traditional altarpiece, stands atemporally in relation to the Crucifixion. In this devotional moment she acts as another human to collapse the lived moment of the prayerful viewer into the ever-present, sacral redemptive moment of Christ's sacrifice.

The realism of the figures and the intensity of their engagement in the drama of the narrative are a radical shift away from the work of Bronzino (see Fig. 8.44), who had been one of Santi's teachers, and from the bombast and quotational classicism of Bandinelli (see Figs. 7.49 and 7.78), who had also taught him. Santi's stay in Rome between 1558 and 1564 where he worked in the papal court put him in touch with the new spiritual movements there and with the return to the classical traditions of Raphael that he had already known in Florence. Santi also apparently visited Venice in 1571–72 and assimilated at that time both Venetian colorism and dramatic composition. He was able to integrate these various experiences when he returned to Florence, joined the Accademia del Disegno (1564), and worked with its leader, Vasari, ultimately developing a style quite different from Vasari's and attaining a position as the outstanding painter in the city at the end of the century.

9.13 *Vision of St. Thomas Aquinas*, 1593, commissioned by Sebastiano Pandolfini del Turco from SANTI DI TITO for the del Turco Chapel, San Marco, Florence. Oil on panel, 11′ 9″ × 7′ 7″ (3.62 × 2.33 m). See also Fig. 9.1.

Extending the Faith

Gregory Martin, an English Jesuit living in Rome, wrote a guidebook to the city in 1581. In it he details the major sites of Rome and indicates the importance of contemporary pilgrimage to the city's holy places. He also conveys the excitement of a Church successfully responding to the threats of the Protestant Reformation through the institution of new religious orders, like his own order of the Society of Jesus. One of its goals was the conversion of peoples in newly penetrated areas of the world through the teaching of men like Francis Xavier.

After him [Francis Xavier] folowed others, with such successe, by the mightie hand of God in external miracles and internal touching of the peoples hartes, that within few yeres Kings and Queens and countries and peoples were Christened, and are at this day every yere, sometime so many hundred, then so many thousand, as in the yerely Relations of the Fathers there to their General . . .; namely in Terra S. Bartolomaei [on the island of Chora off the coast of Goa] . . . first 20,000, then 15,000; in the Ile Japona within a short time above 40,000, as in the Italian Epistles from thence of the yeres 1576 and 1577 appeareth.

Whereby it groweth, that now in the east India there are six Colleges [of Jesuits] and above sixtene places of smaller Residence: in Brasil, three Colleges, and five Residences; in the West India (most under the Spaniardes) namely in two Provinces, to wit, in Peru three Colleges, foure Residences: in Mexicum, foure Colleges, one house of Probation for Novices, one Residence.

(from Gregory Martin. *Roma Sancta* (1581). George Bruner Parks, ed. Rome: Edizioni di Storia e Letteratura, 1969)

Reform and New Religious Orders

In Rome and throughout the rest of the Catholic world, the reforms of the Council of Trent were helped enormously by the new religious orders founded during the sixteenth century. Like the Franciscans and Dominicans in the thirteenth century, these orders—most notably the Jesuits (formally, the Society of Jesus), the Oratorians, and the Theatines—were soon enlisted by the papacy to instill orthodoxy and devotion on the part of the faithful and to convert new members to their ranks. The Jesuits were founded by a Spaniard, Ignatius of Loyola (1491?–1556); their order was confirmed by Paul III in 1540 and grew to worldwide prominence as an agent of teaching, conversion, and reform. Although it is overstating the case to read a "Jesuit style" in the visual arts, their home church of the Gesù in Rome (Figs. 9.14–9.17) clearly illustrates architectural and pictorial responses to the Council's directives.

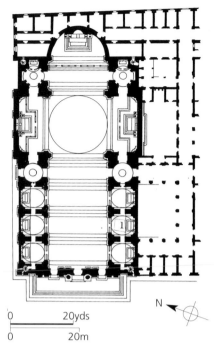

0   20yds

0   20m

N

9.14 The Gesù, Rome, plan

1 Chapel of the Passion

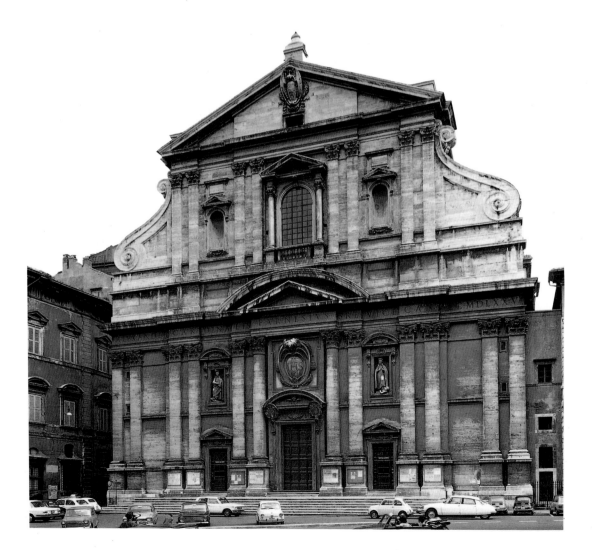

9.15 The Gesù, Rome, present building begun in 1568, commissioned by the Jesuits with the patronage of Cardinal Alessandro Farnese from GIACOMO VIGNOLA; façade and dome by GIACOMO DELLA PORTA

The Gesù   The importance of the Gesù in its own time can perhaps be understood by the simple fact that it was the largest church to have been built in Rome since the sack of the city in 1527. Although Ignatius had hoped for a new church for his order virtually from the time of its confirmation, the slow process of acquiring property in the center of Rome and raising adequate funds delayed its construction until December 1550; and then it was based on a rather pedestrian plan for both church and cloister by Nanni di Baccio Bigio (Giovanni Lippi; 1512/13 Florence–1568 Rome), the Florentine assistant of Antonio da Sangallo the Younger). Difficulties with the site ultimately led the Jesuits to involve Michelangelo with the project; he agreed in 1554 to produce drawings and a model, but apparently nothing came of this—in part perhaps because of Ignatius's death in 1556 and tensions between the Jesuits and Paul IV, who had been elected in 1555. Cardinal Alessandro Farnese intervened in

1561 when the project was floundering, providing funding for much of the building, with the stipulation that no other patron be allowed at the site and that he be buried in the church. A commemorative double portrait of Alessandro and his grandnephew Odoardo with a view of the interior of the Gesù behind them (see Fig. 9.17) shows the church before the ceiling areas had been painted and decorated in the seventeenth century. It underscores the generosity of the Farnese family to the order, naming both Alessandro and Odoardo as "munificent founders" of the church and the adjacent residence—yet another example of familial rather than purely personal patronage. Alessandro's name is emblazoned across the façade of the church as a public statement of his patronage.

Giacomo Vignola, whose work at the Palazzo Farnese (see Fig. 8.50) from 1549 brought him in close contact with the family, was associated with the Gesù from 1563, when he provided an unusual oval plan (ultimately not

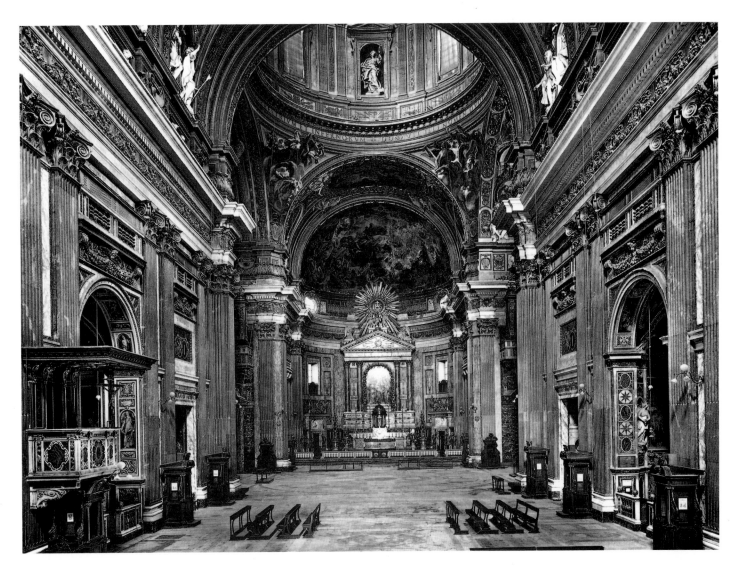

9.16 The Gesù, Rome

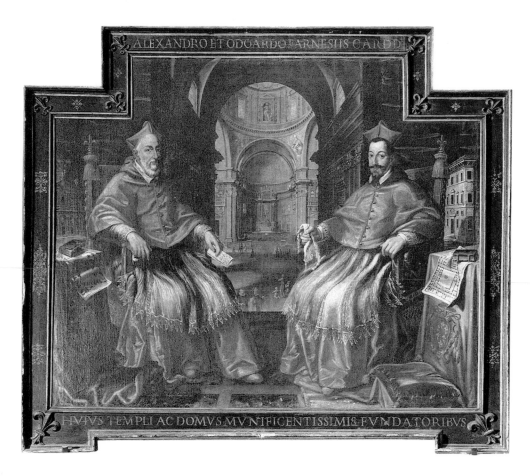

9.17 *Cardinals Alessandro and Odoardo Farnese seated before models of their donations to the Jesuits, the Church of the Gesù and the Casa del Gesù*, seventeenth century, corridor to Sacristy, the Gesù, Rome. Oil on canvas

This is the same Alessandro Farnese whom Titian had earlier depicted with his grandfather, Paul III (see Fig. 8.49), and who had commissioned a particularly lascivious version of Titian's *Danaë* (see fig. 8.24).

accepted) for the building. The publication in 1562 of his treatise on the five architectural orders, *Regole delli cinque ordini di architettura*, had made him one of the best-known architects in Europe. After Vignola's death the dome of the church was completed by Giacomo della Porta.

The exterior of the Gesù reflects the sculptural treatment of architectural surfaces employed by Michelangelo in his commissions for the papacy. Typically for this period, the façade of the building was considered a separate commission. Alessandro Farnese chose the design of the Giacomo della Porta over those submitted by Vignola and Galeazzo Alessi. Although della Porta retained the integrity of the architectural surface by using pilasters throughout the façade, he did frame, and thus accentuate, the door with columns. Della Porta doubled the pilaster and the pilaster/column supports as well as the pediments over the main portal, giving the surface a muscular strength which he emphasized by breaking the entablatures and stepping the central unit of the building forward toward the piazza. Despite the energy of the façade, however, its decoration is quite restrained and decorous (the statues were not added until the seventeenth century), and is thus appropriate to the concept of reform in the Church, supported by the Jesuits.

The interior of the Gesù is an open, single-vessel barrel-vaulted space with truncated transepts and a single wide apse (see Figs. 9.14 and 9.16). Side chapels line the nave, and although there are connecting passages between them, they function as distinct spaces. The paired pilasters provide a dynamic surface comparable to the exterior of the building. The colossal order, like that used by Michelangelo for St. Peter's (see Figs. 8.53 and 8.54) gives a sense of grandeur to the interior, whose thick cornice extends the length of the nave, and at the same time connects the Gesù to the central church of Christianity and to the papacy. The unified space of the church affords an uninterrupted focus on the altar, as demanded by the Council of Trent, and facilitates preaching by concentrating the congregation in one area.

The importance of the Gesù to church design is evident in the contemporary Jesuit church of San Fedele in Milan (Fig. 9.18), commissioned by Charles Borromeo. In this instance Borromeo forced the Jesuits to accept the plans of his favorite architect, Pellegrino Tibaldi (1527 Puria di Vasolda–1596 Milan) rather than those of an architect member of their own order, furthering a consistence of his reforming designs throughout his diocese. Tibaldi had been in Rome with Borromeo in 1564 when the Gesù was in its final design stages and when Michelangelo had begun his work at Santa Maria degli Angeli, a project (begun 1563) that involved converting part of the huge complex of the Roman Baths of Diocletian into a

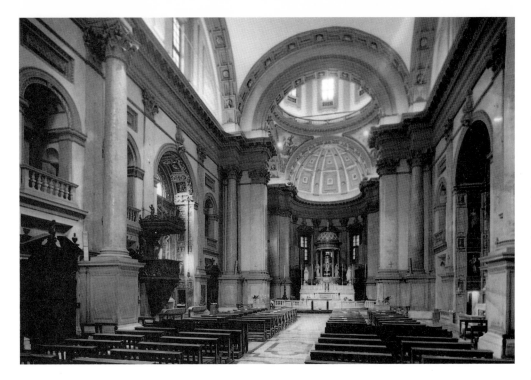

9.18 San Fedele, Milan, designed 1567, commissioned by Charles Borromeo for the Jesuits from PELLEGRINO TIBALDI

Painting for the Gesù The painted decoration of the chapels of the Gesù is among the earliest in Rome to respond to the concerns for clarity, historical accuracy, and compelling emotional impact voiced by the Council of Trent and its interpreters. More importantly, the decorative program for the high altar and the side chapels is directly related to Ignatius's *Spiritual Exercises* (1548), a very popular form of directed prayer and meditation that in its most extensive form involved a retreat of thirty days. The entire project was apparently overseen by Giuseppe Valeriani (1542 L'Aquila–1596 Naples), himself a Jesuit priest who had joined the order in 1572, thus guaranteeing a faithfulness to the wishes of the order's founder for sequenced and cumulative devotional practices. In the chapel dedicated to the Passion of Christ, Valeriani and Gasparre Celio (1571 Rome–1640 Rome) planned and painted the *Crucifixion* (Fig. 9.19) under the direction of another Jesuit, Giovanni Battista Fiammeri. In this painting they dramatically lit the body of Christ nailed to the cross, pushing it forward and isolating it at the center of the composition, so that it

Christian church. In the extremely wide church of San Fedele, Tibaldi surpassed Vignola at the Gesù in subordinating the side chapels to the nave, treating them as niches in the nave's supporting walls rather than as discrete and therefore competing elements. Bold but simple moldings and large clerestory windows ensure that the Milanese space is bright and clearly ordered, while giant, freestanding columns and tympanum windows, deriving from Michelangelo's Santa Maria degli Angeli, bring a classical austerity to the church, despite the pink coloration of the surfaces. This triumphalist language of forms seems to have developed in several places at once, a suitable style for the reformed Church in Europe.

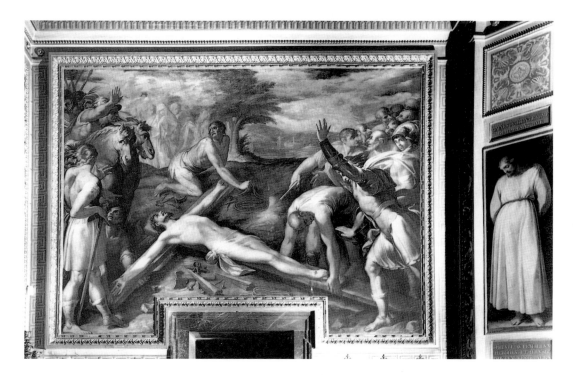

9.19 *Crucifixion*, c. 1589–90, commissioned by Bianca Mellini from GIUSEPPE VALERIANI and GASPARRE CELIO for the Chapel of the Passion in the Gesù, Rome. Oil on canvas

becomes a devotional icon within the historical narrative. The Christ is immediately over the passageway leading from one side chapel to another, suggesting that the figures to the left and right may spill forward into the viewer's space. Jerusalem can be seen over the hillside in the background. The Roman soldier on the right, modeled on an antique statue and thus well within the academic conventions of the period, rushes into the scene, his arms extended in a spasm of emotion, which adds to

the immediacy of the scene and is clearly intended to induce a similar internal response in the worshiper. The *Lamentation* (Fig. 9.20) painted by Scipione Pulzone (Scipio Gaetano; 1500 Gaeta–1598 Rome) for the altar of this chapel, like the Valeriani painting, also demonstrates the new style of religious art following the Council of Trent. Pulzone was a pupil of the Mannerist painter Jacopino del Conte and had studied Flemish and Venetian painting as well as the work of Raphael. Christ's body takes central place in the composition close to the picture plane. The close focus and the naturalistic rendering of the figures—red-eyed with weeping and yet decorously restrained—give immediacy to the drama as each figure shows a concentrated personal reaction to the event, inviting viewers to share their emotions.

Women as Patrons

Bianca Mellini, a Roman patrician, was the patron of the Chapel of the Passion at the Gesù which contained Pulzone's *Lamentation*. Although women had always played roles in commissioning works of art, most notably as executors of their husbands' estates, the continued growth of the size of dowries over the course of the fifteenth century gave widows increased economic power within the arts during the sixteenth century. Particularly in Rome—where the restitution of the papacy, the success of the Council of Trent, the founding of new religious orders, and the growth of the city as a pilgrimage center called for an astonishing amount of building activity, renovation, and decoration, and where estates were divided between all children rather than just between the male heirs—women played important roles as patrons of the arts. They were especially active with new religious orders which needed their help and which were perhaps more receptive to non-traditional avenues of patronage.

Although most of these women came from wealthy families and had powerful connections in the Roman civil and ecclesiastical hierarchies, they built mainly to provide housing and security for other women wishing sequestered, conventual living and to free themselves from the social strictures of their widowhood. They modeled themselves mainly on earlier female donors, some of whom were known from the first developments of church architecture in the early Christian period. Fulvia Conti Sforza, for example, chose to rebuild for her convent the church of Sant'Urbano in Rome, originally built by Giacoba Bianchi in 1264; she retained the inscription of the first patron over the door of the new building as if to assert a continuing female presence at the site.

Since the goal of such women was to leave the world for the convent or for a female lay religious community

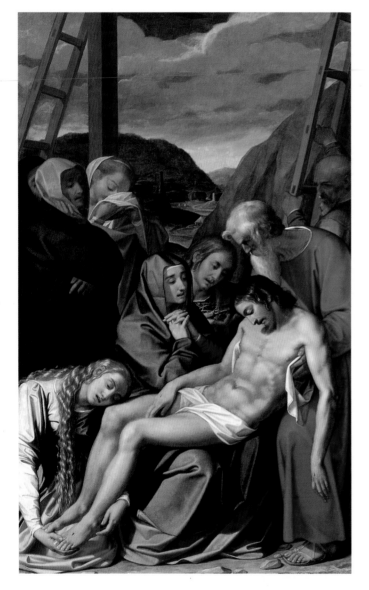

9.20 *Lamentation*, 1591, commissioned 1589/90 by Bianca Mellini from SCIPIONE PULZONE for the altar of the Chapel of the Passion in the Gesù, probably through the intervention of the Jesuits and Giuseppe Valeriani. Oil on canvas, 9′ 6″ × 5′ 8″ (2.9 × 1.27m) (Purchase, Anonymous Gift, in memory of Terence Cardinal Cooke, 1984 [1984.74] © 1984 Metropolitan Museum of Art, New York)

The painting was most likely removed from the Gesù in 1798 during the French occupation of Italy when virtually everything of value in the church was appropriated by the occupying forces.

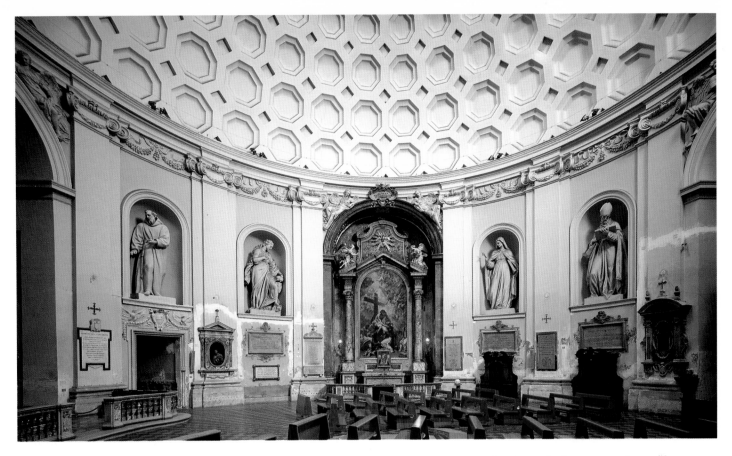

9.21 (above) San Bernardo alle Terme, Rome, consecrated in 1600, commissioned by Caterina de' Nobili Sforza, stucco statues by CAMILLO MARIANI and others

9.22 (below) San Stefano Rotondo, Rome, martyrdom scenes commissioned in 1582 by the German and Hungarian College from NICCOLÒ CIRCIGNANI and MATTEO DA SIENA

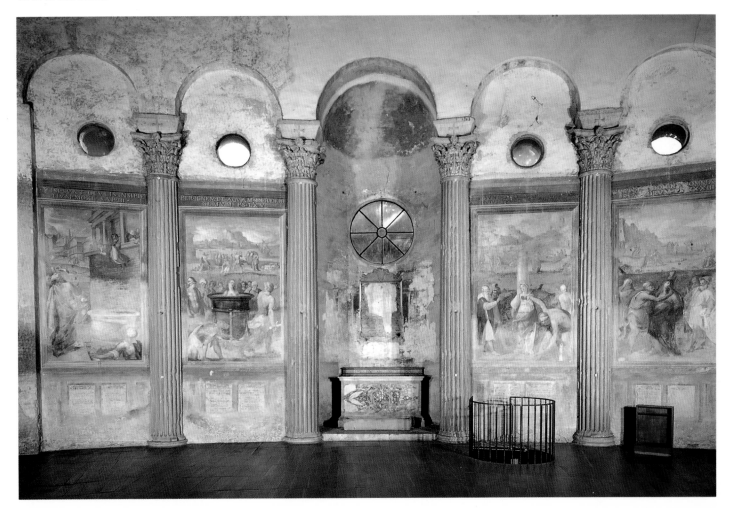

and not to use their patronage to advance their position in society at large, their building projects were generally modest and unostentatious. Yet women patrons could also match their male counterparts in asserting their family's prominence through the visual arts. Caterina de' Nobili Sforza built the circular church of San Bernardo alle Terme (Fig. 9.21) out of the ruins of one of the circular pavilions at the corners of the ancient Baths of Diocletian. Each of the bays around the Pantheon-like structure is decorated with an inscription commemorating members of her family. She commissioned Camillo Mariani (1567? Vicenza–1611 Rome), newly arrived from the Veneto, where he had specialized in decorative plasterwork for Palladian villas, to fill the niches with heroic-sized statues referring to her family and to herself (St. Catherine of Alexandria and St. Catherine of Siena). For the first time outside of royal commissions, the independent (and sometimes contested) patronage of women took on a public scale equal to that of male donors.

Gregory XIII (r. 1572–85)

Gregory XIII (Ugo Boncompagni) is perhaps best remembered as the pope who initiated the reform of the calendar that produced the one in use today. With the regularization of the liturgy demanded by the Council of Trent, the calendar became an important issue because of the need to regulate saints' feasts and Easter. From a scientific point of view, the old Julian calendar was obsolete because it was too long, in relation to the movement of the Earth around the sun, with the result that by the sixteenth century the spring equinox (March 21) occurred on March 11. After an extraordinary international effort on the part of the scientific community, including support from the German astronomer Johannes Kepler, Gregory issued a papal bull, or decree, on February 24, 1582, that changed the means of measuring the solar year and corrected accumulated errors. The extra ten days were simply dropped. (England and some other Protestant nations adhered to the Julian calendar for many more years—in the case of England until 1752.) The Gregorian calendar was just one way in which the pope attempted to bring the Church up to date. Gregory also opened colleges and seminaries throughout the Catholic world which would teach the new theology defined by the Council of Trent; he singled out Japan for special missionary activity; and he refounded the Roman painting Academy of St. Luke in 1577, changing it from its former craft guild status to a teaching academy comparable to its counterpart in Florence founded by Cosimo I.

On being elected pope in 1572, Gregory announced that Rome would celebrate a Holy Year in 1575. This announcement prompted new artistic activity throughout the city in an attempt to demonstrate to the pilgrims who would come to Rome that the Church had weathered the crises of the Reformation, had re-established itself on a sound footing through the Council of Trent, and was once again a powerful force in the world. Gregory Martin, an English priest living in Rome from 1576 to mid-1578, wrote a guide to the city in 1581 in which he mentioned the building in the city and its effect:

> It were to[o] long to number and name the Churches, Chappels, Oratories, and aultars, built, garnished, enriched, namely agaynst this last year of Jubilee 1575. And so we see concerning this poynte also that Rome daily florisheth and excelleth, advancing Christian and Catholike Religion not without cause of the Auncient fathers called Romanum, that is the Romane religion.

The completion of the façade for the Gesù in 1575 (see Fig. 9.15) is but one manifestation of this activity. There were many others. Old altars were removed from the central spaces of the major pilgrimage basilicas such as Santa Maria Maggiore to provide large unencumbered spaces for pilgrims, as well as to respond (as Vasari had done at Santa Croce and Santa Maria Novella in Florence) to the Council's wishes that congregations have a clear view of the altar and the Eucharistic celebration there.

One goal of the leaders of the newly reformed Church was to bring it back to the purity of its Early Christian beginnings—the very point made by reformers both within the Church, like Erasmus, and outside it, like Luther. Renovations of the main Early Christian basilicas for the Holy Year served to reaffirm this goal. Like his predecessors, Gregory also initiated a program of widening streets and building new fountains as a way of making the city a welcome place for pilgrims. His papal bull of 1574 supported the confiscation of private property by stating explicitly that the "common good and the beautifying of the city must always be considered before the cupidity or even the desires of individuals."

San Stefano Rotondo The centrally planned sixth-century church of San Stefano Rotondo was restored under Gregory XIII, partly in accordance with his papal bull of 1580 uniting the colleges for German and Hungarian Jesuits at the site. This church was a center for clergy being trained to return to their home countries to propagate the faith, and in many instances to meet the hostility of the Protestant reformers. Around the periphery of its interior, Niccolò Circignani (Il Pomarancio; c. 1517/24 Pomerance– 1596 Città di Pieve), who had worked for the pope at the Vatican Palace, led a team of artists that painted a fresco cycle (Fig. 9.22) of thirty-one scenes of explicitly graphic martyrdoms. Beginning with Christ's Crucifixion, it continues through the executions of the Apostles and the early Christian saints—appropriate subjects for this Early Christian martyrial structure. The cycle derives from a book commissioned by Ignatius of Loyola to instruct the faithful and to provide a focus for meditation on the Gospel stories through both notes and images. The frescoes are notable for their blatant didacticism, uniting words to images—rather like captions in a newspaper article—so there can be no doubt about the desire to instruct. Each martyrdom carries a hortatory biblical inscription across the top and each has a double caption below—one text in Latin, another translating the Latin into Italian—which identifies the figures in the paintings.

In one of the last scenes in the cycle, representing the *Martyrdom of St. John, St. Paul, St. Bibiana, and St. Artemius* (Fig. 9.23), the bodies of the four dead saints are sequenced in a neat row from the foreground into the space of the painting, each extending the entire width of the image; other scenes of martyrdom are depicted in the background. Far removed from the conventions of Mannerism, these frescoes depict in a naturalistic, almost journalistic, manner the grisly details of martyrdom. The heads of the closest two men are severed from their bodies, and blood trickles from the neck of St. Bibiana, the third figure from the front. The body of St. Artemius, crushed under the weight of a huge stone, pours blood over the lower stone on which it is laid; his eyes are gouged out and his entrails ooze from his torso. Large black letters label each group of figures and are coordinated with the legends in Latin and Italian under each scene. The paintings were intended as a meditation on saintly martyrdoms which had strengthened the early

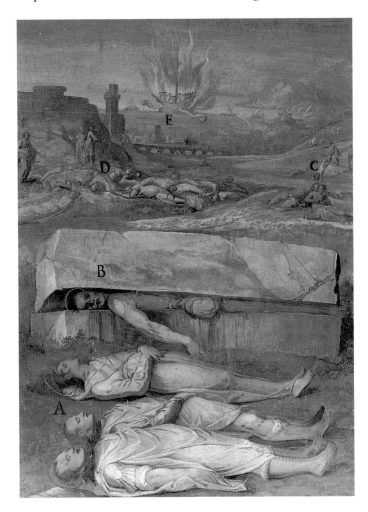

9.23 *Martyrdom of St. John, St. Paul, St. Bibiana, and St. Artemius*, 1582, commissioned by the German and Hungarian College from NICCOLÒ CIRCIGNANI and MATTEO DA SIENA for San Stefano Rotondo, Rome. Fresco, 10′ × 6′ 10¼″ (3.05 × 2.1m)

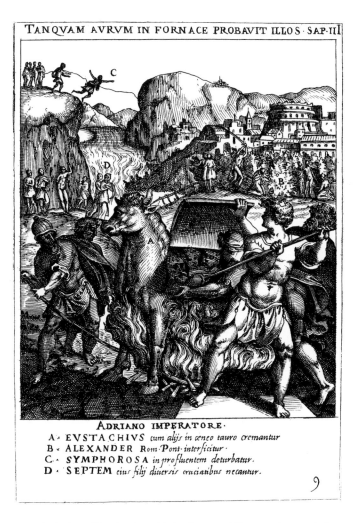

9.24 *Ecclesiae militantis triumphi sive Deo amabilium martyrum gloriosa pro Christi fide certamina*, Rome, 1583, GIOVANNI BATTISTA DE CAVALLIERI, scene from the ninth fresco of San Stefano Rotondo, Rome, showing St. Eustache and his companions being cremated in a bronze bull, one of the torture instruments of the period. Engraving

The inscription at the top from the Book of Wisdom recalls Old Testament prototypes: Like gold were they tested in the furnace.

Church, and as exemplars of the courage that the students in the German and Hungarian College would need in their dangerous missions. In images such as these—an art of instruction—issues of aesthetics played a minimal role.

The power of the martyrdom scenes at San Stefano Rotondo led to their immediate reproduction in printed form, which made them accessible to an even wider audience. Just as the Lutherans had used the new print medium as an effective mode of proselytizing, so did the later reformers in the Roman Church. In Giovanni Battista de Cavallieri's *Ecclesiae militantis triumphi . . .* published in Rome in 1583 and again (a measure of its popularity) in 1585, the frescoes of San Stefano Rotondo are reproduced along with their inscriptions (Fig. 9.24) as if they were a catechism for the newly reformed Church returning to its Early Christian roots, an incentive both to piety and to action.

Sixtus V and the Replanning of Rome

Like so many of his predecessors, Pope Sixtus V (Felice Peretti; r. 1585–90) sought to assert the legitimacy of his office with references to papal history and established Rome as the dominant European power by adding his own contributions to its physical splendor. Despite the brevity of his reign, he significantly furthered its development as the model European capital city, already begun by Paul III and Michelangelo. Although he was a Franciscan, Sixtus V, like Sixtus IV and Nicholas IV before him, commissioned projects whose scope and grandeur belie the rule of poverty central to the Franciscan order. For all these Franciscan popes, the demands of their office and their responsibilities as temporal rulers overrode whatever Franciscan qualms they may have had.

To ensure that his extensive rebuilding of Rome would be remembered, Sixtus commemorated his architectural commissions in a series of prints and publications. One of these (Fig. 9.25) shows him surrounded by his building projects in much the same way that early saints' altar-

pieces showed saints surrounded by narratives of their miracles (see Figs. 1.25 and 1.26). Each of the small illustrations is diagramatically represented and carefully labeled so that there can be no doubt about Sixtus's accomplishments.

Each of the projects depicted on Sixtus's didactic print fits within an overall scheme of urban planning designed to make Rome more accommodating and more impressive to the visitor. Drawing on earlier traditions of widening and straightening streets to provide safety and clear access within the warren of medieval Rome, Sixtus and his architects, most notably Domenico Fontana (1543 Melide, Lake Lugano–1607 Naples) planned major axes through the urban fabric to unite its main pilgrimage basilicas (Fig. 9.26).

Unlike Pope Nicholas V's plans to unite the bureaucratic offices of the papacy in his urban renewal of the

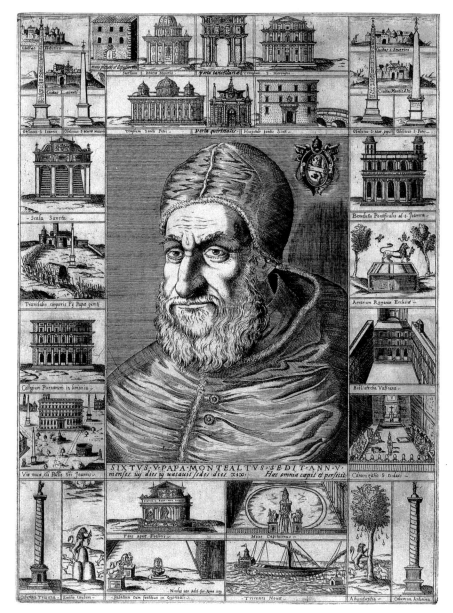

9.25 *Invicti quinarii numeri series quae summatim a superioribus pontificibus et maxime a Sixto Quinto res praeclare quadriennio gestas adnumerat*, fol. 3, showing a portrait of Sixtus V surrounded by images of his building projects, Rome, 1589, GIOVANNI PINADELLO (apud FRANCISCUM ZANNETTUM) (Metropolitan Museum of Art, New York)

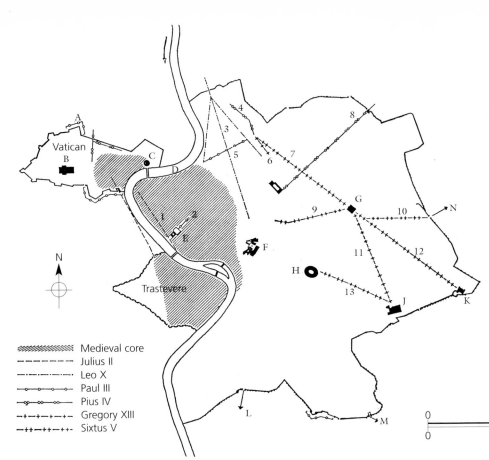

9.26 Rome, showing Sixtus V's urban planning and that of his sixteenth-century predecessors (after Gerhard Krämer)

1 Via Giulia; **2** Piazza Farnese and Via dei Baullari; **3** Via del Corso (Via Flaminia); **4** Via Babuino (Via Paolina); **5** Via Condotti; **6** Via Gregoriana; **7** Via Sistina; **8** Strada Pia; **9** Via Panisperna; **10** Street linking Santa Maria Maggiore and Porta San Lorenzo; **11** Via Merulana; **12** Via Santa Croce di Gerusalemme; **13** Street linking St. John Lateran and the Colosseum

A Fortifications around Belvedere; **B** St. Peter's; **C** Castel Sant'Angelo; **D** River Tiber; **E** Palazzo Farnese; **F** Campidoglio and Santa Maria in Aracoeli; **G** Santa Maria Maggiore; **H** Colosseum; **J** St. John Lateran and Lateran Palace; **K** Santa Croce in Gerusalemme; **L** Porta San Paolo and road to San Paolo fuori le Mura; **M** Porta San Sebastiano and road to San Sebastiano fuori le Mura; **N** Porta San Lorenzo and road to San Lorenzo fuori le Mura; **O** Porta Pia (Michelangelo); **P** Porta del Popolo

Borgo Leonino stretching from St. Peter's to the Tiber, or Pope Julius II's plans to link historically important areas of the city with the Via Giulia, Sixtus's concentration on the major basilicas simultaneously suggests the vitality of the reformed Church and recalls its unbroken history back to the Early Christian period. The major axis of Sixtus's grand urban plan extended across the entire city from the Piazza del Popolo at the north, one of the main gateways into Rome and a prominent ceremonial site (see Fig. 6.59) to Santa Maria Maggiore, which was the major basilica within the Roman city and also a Franciscan church. The street then further extended to Santa Croce in Gerusalemme at the southeast, another pilgrimage basilica built near the wall at the opposite side of the ancient city. Named the Strada Felice in honor of Sixtus, whose given name was Felice, and to suggest a new happiness in the city under his rule, the street was built for most of its projected length, from Santa Croce as far as Santa Trinità dei Monti, above the Spanish Steps; it still exists as a prominent axis on the plan of modern Rome.

The Obelisks   At considerable expense and through the impressive engineering skills of his architects, particularly Domenico Fontana, Sixtus also moved a number of Egyptian obelisks from their ancient Roman sites to new ones, which pinned down the axes of his urban plan and established new focal points in the city. The prominence of the obelisks in the upper corners of the 1589 print (see Fig. 9.25) indicates Sixtus's pride in these accomplishments. The obelisk now in the piazza in front of St. Peter's (Fig. 9.28) was the most notable example of these reposi-

tioned obelisks; others include the one in the Piazza del Popolo, one flanking a chapel built by Sixtus at Santa Maria Maggiore, and one at the Lateran Palace. Others were earmarked for relocation, but these projects were delayed because of time and cost constraints. Sixtus claimed the relocated obelisks as his own and as a manifestation of the triumph of the Church over antiquity, both by adding inscriptions to that effect and by capping each of them with his emblem of three stylized mountains (seen in the lower left of the 1589 print) and, in the case of the St. Peter's obelisk, a Christian cross.

The obelisks were associated with the Roman emperors who had originally brought them to Rome from Egypt. Those that Sixtus chose for St. Peter's and for Santa Maria Maggiore were taken from monuments of Augustus and were carefully inscribed as such, providing a clear reference not only to the international power of the first Roman emperor, but to the concept of the *pax augustana* (age of peace under Augustus) and the ensuing golden age for which he was known. The engineering feats involved in moving these obelisks were also of a magnitude reminiscent of ancient Roman technology and were perceived to be so remarkable that Fontana published a folio volume detailing the various stages of the moving process (Fig. 9.27).

Of course the obelisks are also freighted with Christian references. The Augustan obelisk for Santa Maria Maggiore served as a visual reminder that Christ was born during the reign of Augustus, and that the main relics of this event, the cave of the Nativity and the crib, were housed at that basilica. But all the resituated imperial obelisks are associated with churches and thus under-

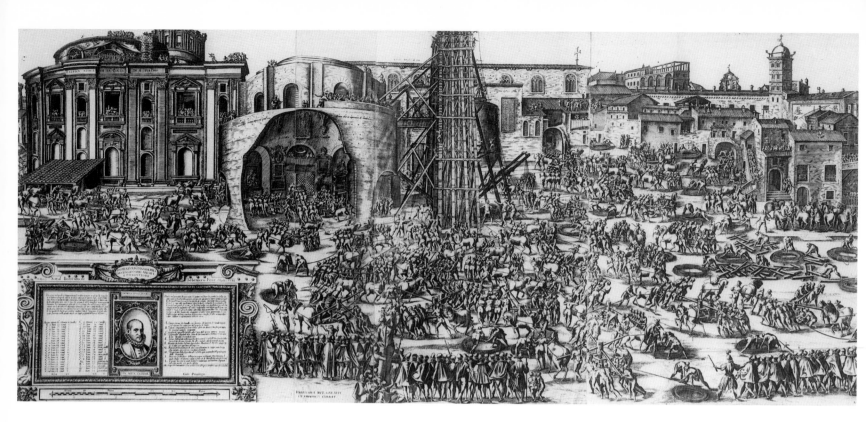

9.27 *Moving the Augustan Obelisk to the Piazza in front of St. Peter's*, detail, 1586, NATALE BONIFACIO after GIOVANNI GUERRA. Engraving, 19⅜ × 43¾″ (49.2 × 111.1 cm) (Elisha Whittelsey Collection, Elisha Whittelsey Fund, 1959 [59.508.102], Metropolitan Museum of Art, New York)

The print shows the south flank of Old St. Peter's, the atrium of the old basilica with Giotto's mosaic of the *Navicella* on the inside entrance wall, a view into the sacristy of St. Peter's through the wall breached to make room for the pulleys and winches used for moving the obelisk, and the new St. Peter's under construction. See Fig. 9.28 for the completed process which lasted from April to September 1586.

score one of the traditional tenets of the papacy—that it was both a spiritual and a secular power.

The Roman Columns In the lower corners of the 1589 print are images of the historiated columns of Trajan and Marcus Aurelius, too large to consider moving, but appropriated by Sixtus nonetheless. On December 4, 1587, he capped Trajan's Column with a large bronze statue of St. Peter (Fig. 9.29), and on October 27 of the following year he placed a bronze figure of St. Paul atop that of Marcus Aurelius. The artists for these two statues, Leonardo Sormani (? Savona–1589 Rome) and Bastiano Torrigiani (? Bologna–1596 Rome), were part of a stable of artists and architects whom Sixtus used for his numerous proj-

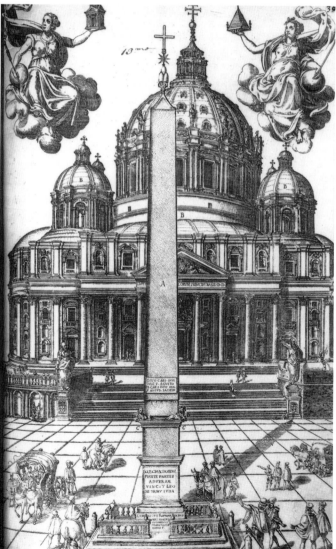

9.28 *Della trasportatione dell'obelisco vaticano et delle fabriche di nostro signore papa Sisto V*, Rome, 1590, DOMENICO FONTANA, DOMENICO BASA, fol. 35r. Engraving

This page from Fontana's book shows the obelisk of Augustus newly moved to the piazza in front of St. Peter's. 800 men, 140 horses, and 40 winches were involved in moving and erecting it, accompanied by the ringing of bells and music by Palestrina. Moving the obelisk was such an extraordinary accomplishment that Sixtus made Fontana a Knight at the Golden Spur and gave him the status of a Roman patrician.

ects. Essentially as house artists, they worked together and understood their patron's wishes. Although working on different projects, they were essentially part of a large workshop directed by Sixtus's master architect, Domenico Fontana, and controlled by the pope. Sormani's muscular *St. Peter* has an active striding pose, the figure turning on axis as he extends his keys into space. The exaggerated facial features, perhaps necessitated by the great height of the figure from the ground, recall those of earlier papal images as well as the leonine portrait type seen also in the fearsome lion-like features of Michelangelo's *David* (see Fig. 7.2).

In the case of Trajan's Column, Sixtus was returning to a monument that Paul III had had excavated and around which Michelangelo had planned a new piazza, a scheme

accepted by the Communal Council in 1558. Sixtus allowed his artists to despoil both Roman and Early Christian monuments to cast these statues. The St. Peter, for example, was made from bronze melted down from half a cannon from the Castel Sant'Angelo; from medieval bronze doors from Sant'Agnese, Old St. Peter's, and the Scala Santa at the Lateran; and from part of a bronze pilaster stripped from the Pantheon. The presence of these two saints on top of monuments to Roman emperors gave graphic expression to the triumph of the papacy and the Church over the ancient world. As if to underscore this triumph, the statues were positioned so that they faced St. Peter's.

The Acqua Felice Sixtus provided special gifts to the Roman people in the form of fountains, the most notable of which is the rather heavy-handed Acqua Felice (Fig. 9.30), whose name refers to his own name, to the water's

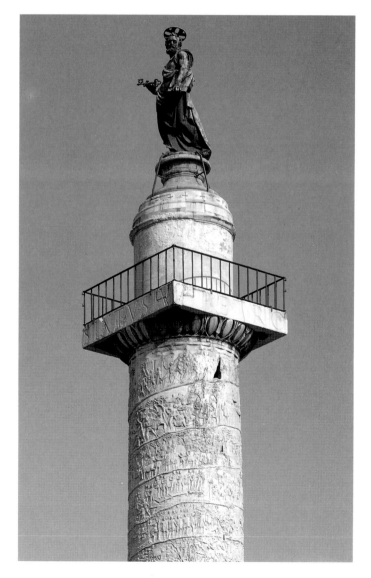

9.29 Column of Trajan crowned with the statue of St. Peter, statue finished and put in place in 1587, statue commissioned by Sixtus V from LEONARDO SORMANI, TOMMASO DELLA PORTA, and BASTIANO TORRIGIANI. Bronze, height of statue 13′ 1½″ (4 m)

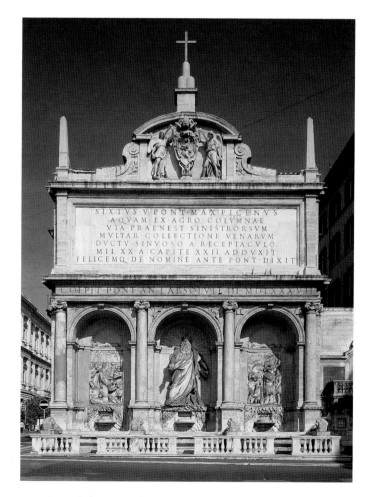

9.30 Acqua Felice, Rome, begun 1589, commissioned by Sixtus V from LEONARDO SORMANI (statue of Moses), GIOVANNI BATTISTA DELLA PORTA (the relief on the left depicting *Aaron Leading the Jews to a Well*), and FLAMINIO VACA and PIETRO PAOLO OLIVIERI (the relief on the right depicting *Gideon Leading His Soldiers and the Jewish People over the Jordan*). Marble

ability to make the populace happy (*felice*), and to the pleasant sound of the flowing water in the urban setting. It is difficult now to imagine how important this project was for a city whose aqueducts had been in a ruinous condition for centuries and whose limited water sources occasionally forced its inhabitants to carry water from the Tiber. But the Acqua Felice—which appears just below Sixtus's name in the 1589 print—was of such significance that it is mentioned on Sixtus's tomb, along with one other project, the completion of St. Peter's. The fountain takes the form of a triumphal arch, in keeping with the triumphal theme of Sixtus's plan as a whole. In the center arch is a marble statue of Moses striking the rock in the desert to produce a miraculous flow of water for the Israelites. Sormani, again Sixtus's choice of sculptor for the major figure, produced a dramatically posed Moses whose scale not only fills the central arch but carries the power of the figure across the piazza in front of the fountain. Like the *St. Peter* atop Trajan's column, the Moses had to function within a large urbanistic context, in this case addressing both the piazza and the street at the left, the Via Pia that had been built by Pope Pius IV (r. 1559–65) and that terminated at the city walls with a fantastical gate designed by Michelangelo.

The connection between Moses and Sixtus as leaders of their people is obvious and carries much of the same meaning that Sixtus IV had wished to convey with the frescoes on the lower walls of the Sistine Chapel from a century earlier (see Fig. 6.67), and that Julius II had intended with the Moses for his tomb (see Fig. 7.22).

Santa Maria Maggiore   Sixtus's projects for Santa Maria Maggiore demonstrate that his determined association with earlier important popes began even before his election to office. Sixtus first became a patron of the building in 1573 when the tomb of Nicholas IV, the first Franciscan pope (see page 66), was rediscovered in the left transept. At that time old altars were being cleared from the crossing of the building in preparation for the Holy Year of 1575 and in response to the legislation of the Council of Trent which had stipulated that the main altar should be clearly visible to the congregation. In Nicholas's honor, Sixtus, then a cardinal and like Nicholas a Franciscan, ordered Domenico Fontana to design a new tomb for the remains of the thirteenth-century pope (Fig. 9.31) and commissioned Leonardo Sormani to provide the sculpture of the seated pope and allegorical figures of Religion and Justice. The effect of the tomb is of a decorously correct, if chilly, classicism—a foretaste of Sormani's imperial stylistic associations in Sixtus's later projects. The tomb is as interesting for the inscriptions that the future pope had placed on it as it is for its sculpture and architecture. Explicit mention is

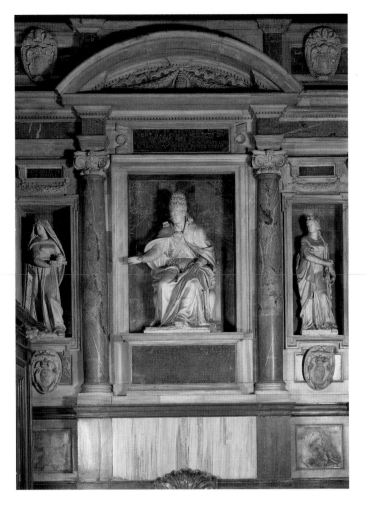

9.31 Tomb of Nicholas IV, commissioned in 1573 by Felice Peretti (later Sixtus V) from DOMENICO FONTANA and LEONARDO SORMANI for Santa Maria Maggiore, Rome. Marble

made of Nicholas IV as a professor, philosopher, and theologian; as a converter of heretics; as a foreign legate; as a peacemaker between kings; as a restorer of the papacy; as a patron of St. John Lateran and Santa Maria Maggiore; and as a man of justice and religious duty. Although the inscription praises the thirteenth-century pope, the words could not but echo as a description of the patron. They provide an autobiographical self-fashioning for Sixtus as cardinal that gives a clear picture of his own intentions as patron and later as pope.

Immediately upon his election to the papacy in 1585 Sixtus began work on a large chapel off the right aisle of Santa Maria Maggiore (Fig. 9.33) which was ultimately to house his own tomb as well as that of the saintly Pius V (r. 1566–72), who had been his own great patron. The centrally planned Cappella Sistina, designed by Sixtus's favorite architect Domenico Fontana, is the size of a small church. It is decorated with marble revetment, two large opposing wall tombs (probably also designed by Fontana, but carved by at least four different sculptors,

Art, Pilgrimage, and Processions

Pilgrimage and procession were familiar aspects of urban life in the Middle Ages and the Renaissance. Sites of major relics such as Rome, Assisi, Padua, Chartres, Cologne, Santiago de Compostela, and Canterbury drew pilgrims in a constant stream, their attention focused on the redemptive powers of the saint or saints whose relics they had come to venerate and upon whose intercessions they believed their salvation depended. As the hub of Christianity, Rome had the greatest concentration of shrines and relics in Europe, and its seven (an appropriately symbolic number) major basilicas formed a well-defined pilgrimage route within and immediately outside the walls of the city itself, imitating the extended pilgrimage routes that crisscrossed Europe and extended to the shrines of the Holy Land. An engraved depiction of the Holy Year of 1575 (Fig. 9.32) shows the pilgrims greeted by apparitions of the name saints of the major basilicas. St. Peter with his keys is at the bottom of the print, standing outside his own church in the Vatican, as it appeared at that time, before the lengthening of the nave and the addition of the façade we know today; the dome is only partially completed. Pilgrims kneel before him.

Apart from the basilicas, most of the city has disappeared into barren terrain, a metaphor for the penitential role that pilgrimage was meant to play. The depiction of pilgrims marching two by two

from basilica to basilica is misleading, however, in its suggestion of order and decorum. Pilgrimages had their unruly moments: in the Holy Year of 1450 pilgrims pushed and jostled so on the bridge crossing the Tiber from the main part of the city to the Castel Sant'Angelo and the Vatican that a number fell off the bridge and drowned in the river below.

Such processions served to mark the destined site as a place of importance within the culture and also to suggest the idea of a spiritual journey of preparation for their destination. Processions for religious holidays intensified the piety of the participants through spoken prayer and song, a public reaffirmation of communal devotion to the saints that protected both individuals and state. For example, the procession of Duccio's *Maestà* through the city of Siena in 1311 was used as an opportunity to reaffirm

the city's dedication to the Virgin. Icons, banners (see Fig. 5.46), wooden statues (see Donatello's naturalistically painted crucifix, Fig. 24), or precious relics (see the reliquaries of San Gennaro in Naples, Fig. 2.41, and the jaw of St. Anthony in Padua, Fig. 3.47) often provided a visual focus for such processions. But processions through cities were not limited to religious events or even to civic celebrations. Criminals were paraded through cities (see Fig. 5.33) to the place of their execution, the route punctuated with stops to exhort the prisoner to prayerful penitence or to torture him as an example to bystanders of the dangers of criminal behavior. Processions such as these were intended to strengthen the social order by bringing its structures into the visual field of the population at large, just as processions of confraternity members (see Fig. 1.7) enhanced individual social position within the community.

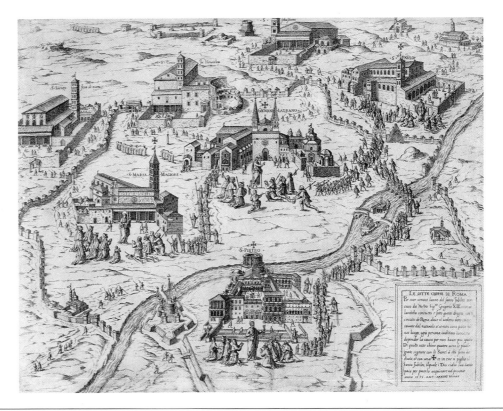

9.32 *Pilgrims Visiting the Seven Churches of Rome during the Holy Year of 1575,* c. 1575, ANTOINE LAFRÉRY (ANTONIO LAFRERI). Engraving (Metropolitan Museum of Art, New York)

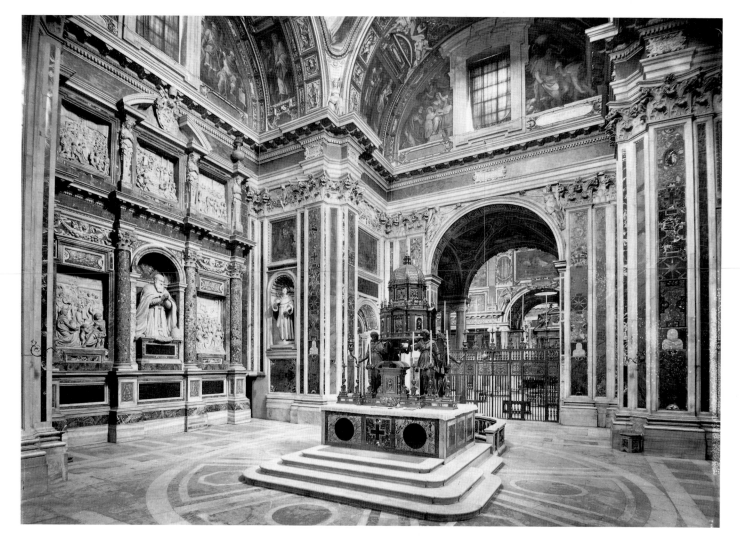

9.33 Cappella Sistina, Santa Maria Maggiore, Rome, begun 1585, commissioned by Sixtus V from DOMENICO FONTANA

including two Flemish ones) and an extensive painting project. Fontana also masterminded another major engineering feat to enhance the prestige of the chapel. The reliquary shrine of the crib of Christ from Bethlehem was extracted from the rock of the crypt of Santa Maria Maggiore, where it had been the site of pilgrimage throughout the Middle Ages. Encased in a wooden frame, it was moved to Sixtus's new chapel, where it was lowered into a new subterranean site (Fig. 9.34). Thus Sixtus essentially commandeered one of the major relics of the city for his own use and was later to have the honor of being buried adjacent to its miraculous powers.

A decree of the Council of Trent stipulating that the Eucharistic host be conserved on the main altar of a church in full view of the congregation, rather than in some nearby tabernacle or chapel, as had traditionally been the case, required building renovation in virtually every Catholic church. This decree was obviously a response to Protestant denial of Christ's true presence in

the Eucharist. Nevertheless, contrary to this liturgical reform (which as a theological adviser to the Council he knew only too well) Sixtus transformed his chapel into a Sacrament Chapel and commissioned Bastiano Torrigiani to make a large and dramatic container for the Eucharist in a form imitating the building itself, which is now the focal point of the chapel, aligned with the entrance to the crypt housing the crib. Given the size of the Cappella Sistina, it is possible to argue that Sixtus thus provided a worthy position for the Eucharist which allowed the faithful to focus their worship in a manner intended by the Council. Notably, the two most prominent "worshipers" in the space are the sculpted kneeling figures of the two popes, Pius and Sixtus, who, from the central niches of their tombs, provide a model for the laity.

The messages of the Cappella Sistina are complex and are conveyed through a variety of means. The imperial scale and lavishness of appointment alone convey the enormous power and assurance of the patron as a univer-

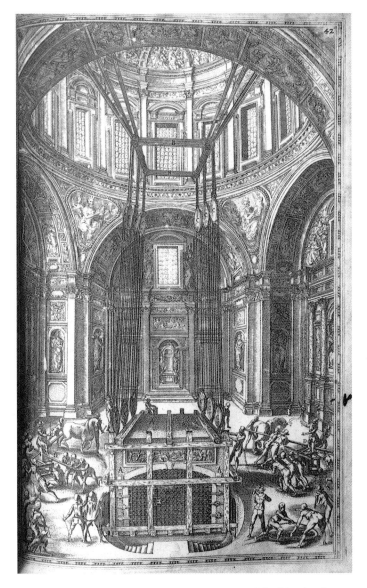

9.34 *Della trasportatione dell'obelisco vaticano et delle fabriche di nostro signore papa Sisto V*, Rome, 1590, DOMENICO FONTANA, DOMENICO BASA, fol. 53, showing the installing of the manger of Christ in the Cappella Sistina, Santa Maria Maggiore, Rome. Engraving

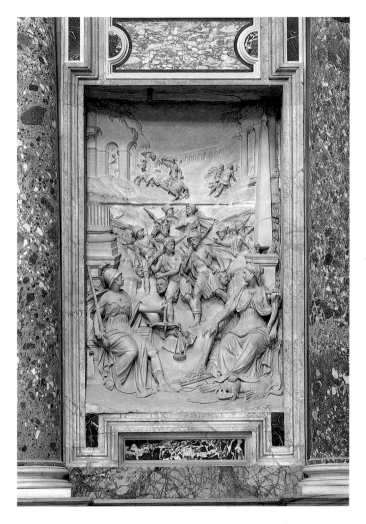

9.35 *Sixtus V's Temporal Government with Justice and Peace*, detail of Tomb of Sixtus V, commissioned by Sixtus V, design by DOMENICO FONTANA, sculpture by EGIDIO DELLA RIVIERA (GILLIS VAN DER VLIETE), NICCOLÒ PIPPI OF ARRAS (MOSTAERT), and VASOLDO (GIOVANNI ANTONIO PARACCA DA VASOLDO), Cappella Sistina, Santa Maria Maggiore, Rome. Marble

The soldiers carry the severed heads of bandits, against whom Sixtus was especially severe.

sal ruler. The siting of the funerary chapel at Santa Maria Maggiore rather than at St. Peter's, then nearing completion, manifests Sixtus's Franciscan background, as well as his devotion to the cult of the Virgin, revered in this church in a miracle-working icon, the *Salus Publica* (the public well-being) and thus carrying civic overtones. His initiative in providing a suitable funerary monument for Pius V demonstrates filial devotion to the man responsible for supporting Sixtus in his career and for making him cardinal. The two popes facing one another across the expanse of the chapel—Sixtus a Franciscan and Pius a Dominican, their monastic background precisely noted both by inscription and by the saints that flank the tombs (Francis and Anthony for Sixtus, Dominic and Peter

Martyr for Pius)—also provide an image of dynastic continuity for the papacy, as well as an image of concord and conversion within the newly reformed Church. The marble reliefs decorating the tombs are typical of sixteenth-century papal tombs in containing both illustrations of important events in the individual papacies and personifications of virtues. They are therefore much like Roman imperial historical reliefs: conventional in their iconography and didactic in their intentions. Interestingly, in the case of Sixtus, the reliefs depict his attempts to make Rome a safe city. Thus, emulating Augustus's establishment of peace throughout the Empire, Sixtus freed the countryside from bandits (Fig. 9.35) and attempted—with only partial success—to make it secure.

The Cappella Sistina in Santa Maria Maggiore also shows signs of its patron's wish to emulate its more famous namesake built by an earlier Sixtus across the Tiber (see Fig. 6.66). Its papal status is clearly indicated by the bishop's chair, centrally placed before the wall opposite the entrance. And the painted figures of Old Testament ancestors of Christ in the ceiling echo those of Michelangelo in their style. Such artistic emulation reflects not only reverence for the stylistic models but also the need of a pope to forge links with his predecessors and thus assert his legitimacy.

Sixtus also employed an international group of artists for the sculpture of the Chapel. Although their early histories are undocumented, it seems that both Egidio della Riviera (Gillis van den Vliete; ?Mechelen/Malines–1602 Rome) and Niccolò Pippi (Nicolas Piper;? Arras–1601/04 Rome) came from northern Europe and brought with them traces of a Flemish style, visible in the decorative aspects of the drapery patterns and the vertical placement of the figures against an increasingly shallow plane to suggest space. Egidio also worked at restoring ancient sculpture early in his career, as did Vasoldo (Giovanni Antonio Paracca; ?Vasoldo–1597 Rome), so the relief maintains a classicizing style appropriate for the new ruler of Rome, whose heraldic lions appear as supports for the obelisk behind Peace.

The Dome of St. Peter's   Perhaps Sixtus's greatest symbolic architectural triumph was the completion of the dome of St. Peter's (see Figs. 8.53 and 8.54). Covering the tomb of St. Peter, the dome emphasized Sixtus's lineage from the first pope and also connected him to Julius II, who had begun the building, and to Paul III, who had reinitiated the construction after Rome was sacked. It also provided him with a cosmological form traditionally connoting power. The dome completed the transformation of St. Peter's into a building that differed stylistically from all the other early Christian pilgrimage sites in the city, thus providing a symbol for a renewed, invigorated, and modern Church.

Although Michelangelo seems to have planned an ogival dome, della Porta most likely intervened with his own version after Michelangelo's death to give it its present form, resolving the complex engineering problems of the dome's lateral thrusts. The double shell construction (planned by Michelangelo at the early stages of its development when he envisioned a hemispherical interior dome) allows the dome to rise high above the skyline of the city, providing a focus for attention among all the competing structures and activities of urban life and marking the power of the papacy that was able to build such an extraordinary structure. Over a century earlier Alberti had written that Brunelleschi's dome for the

cathedral of Florence "covered the entire Tuscan people with its shadow." Such a metaphorical claim to territorial control certainly would have applied to the dome of St. Peter's as well, suggesting renewed order, stability, and power in the Church in an ever more complicated and expanding world. The potency of that symbolic message was so great that over the next two centuries the dome of St. Peter's echoed repeatedly in both the ecclesiastical and secular architecture of Europe and the Americas, claiming a universal presence for a state religion and an ideal social order as well. The domes of St. Paul's in London, the Pantheon in Paris, and the Capitol in Washington are the most obvious of a long line of such symbolic forms.

The search initiated by Nicholas III at the end of the thirteenth century for a visual language which would convey the dual nature of the papacy—temporal and spiritual—ends with Sixtus, whose plans for the urban transformation of Rome definitely changed European cityscapes, ultimately providing a language of temporal, not spiritual authority. The world—mirrored in the microcosm of the city—had changed, and with it so had the visual vocabulary necessary to express its meaning.

Synopsis and Conclusion

The evolving of both the Protestant and Catholic reformations, the coalescing of new nation states, the explosion of mass communication through the printed word, and the astonishing expansion of the known boundaries of the physical world had drastically altered social structures throughout Italy and the rest of Europe. Once again the visual arts responded and gave meaning to experience. Tied to economic sources, they flourished most expansively in the ever enlarging urban centers of Europe, as they had in the major cities of Milan, Venice, Florence, Rome, and Naples discussed in this book. Balancing tradition and innovation, artists and patrons shaped their cities and the art within them with renewed strength and power, more often than not employing a classicizing vocabulary which was to remain a norm until the nineteenth century.

Grand urban centers like the piazza before St. Peter's or the Capitoline Hill, wider streets, and points of triumphal focus—like Sixtus's obelisks or the Loggetta in front of the Doge's Palace in Venice or Cosimo I's Neptune Fountain in Florence—all provided messages about the importance of the site and the people who governed it. Although the monumentality of these forms and the classical style used to carry their messages were more marked in the arts of the sixteenth century, they were also part of a long series of developments which this book has charted. Paul III's decision to place the equestrian statue of Marcus Aurelius on the Capitoline Hill, for example, was much more than a simple act of Roman revival. It recognized a lively tradition of equestrian imagery from the previous several centuries, encompassing fourteenth-century works such as the monuments of Bernabò Visconti in Milan and Cansignorio della Scala in Verona and the more classicizing fifteenth-century imagery of Donatello's *Gattamelata* in Padua and Leonardo's Sforza monument in Milan. History and the meanings attached to types of artistic form continued to matter, tying the future to the past by providing a vocabulary that was familiar, accessible, and therefore meaningful to the population at large.

Within such continuities it is important to underscore changes in artistic production. Although artists were by and large still economically tied to a patronage system at the end of the sixteenth century, the Renaissance had begun a transformation of that hierarchical relationship which led ultimately in the modern world to the creation of works of art free of the demands of the purchaser. Ironically, this development also allowed art to be treated as an economic commodity divorced from the functional roles it had previously played within society; independence seems to have entailed marginalization of the very work that the artists produced.

Not only did the relationship between patron and artist alter, but so did the social order of the patron. Shifts in the economic structures of Europe and the emergence of a middle class meant that a new type of patron with radically different needs made new demands on artists. Furthermore, the removal of traditional religious imagery

from some Protestant churches initiated a rethinking of appropriate subjects for painting and sculpture. This led to an explosive expansion of new genres such as portraiture, still-life, and landscape within a burgher culture not only in northern European countries but in Italy as well.

One particularly notable example is the evolution of still life (Fig. 9.36) as a distinct genre of painting. At the moment poorly charted, the history of still life seems to have begun in Lombardy with the work of Vincenzo Campi (1530/35 Cremona–1591 Cremona). Similar explorations of the genre appeared in Bologna with the work of Bartolomeo Passerrotti (1529 Bologna–1592 Bologna) and Annibale Carracci (1560 Bologna–1609 Rome). A number of reasons might be given for the appearance of still life in northern Italy at this time, especially in Campi's native city of Cremona, which had been controlled by Milan from 1334 (except for a brief period of Venetian domination from 1499 to 1510, a result of the French invasion of Milan in 1499). The Holy Roman Emperor Charles V took the city in 1522, eventually passing it on to his son, Philip II of Spain. Situated on a major trading route from Italy to Germany, Cremona seems to have had equal access to both the Italian and northern traditions of painting, with commerce in art moving in both directions. With no local ruling family, the citizenry was essentially made up of merchants and tradespeople with a strong middling class. This social situation is not reason enough to explain the appearance of still life in Cremona, but it is a beginning. Not only did there seem to be a local market for Campi's still life paintings

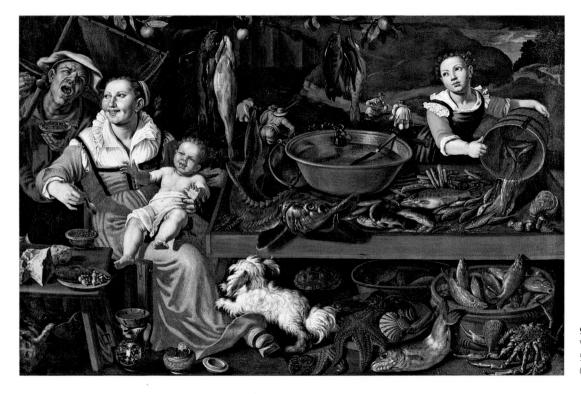

9.36 *Fishmongers*, c. 1580, by VINCENZO CAMPI. Oil on canvas, 57 × 84⅝″ (145 × 215 cm) (Milan, Pinacoteca di Brera)

(perhaps sold out of the studio outside the normal patronage systems, if the mystery of their early histories is any indication), a foreign market is documented as well. In 1580 Hans Fugger, a member of the leading German banking family, ordered a set of five still life paintings from Campi for his home in Kirchheim, where they still are. Clearly by then Campi had a reputation for such pictures, which themselves derive from similar images by Dutch artists like Pieter Aertsen (1507/08–74) and Joachim Beuckelaer (c. 1533–73), themselves part of a commercial and burgher culture.

Nevertheless, it is important to realize that contemporaries saw paintings such as the *Fishmongers* as an expression of compositional and technical skill, a piling up of countless different textures, colors, and surface lights that was a test of the artist's skill as well as a visual delight to the viewer. They may also have been amused by disguised visual puns of a social or a sexual nature: the coarse man at the far left holding a bowl of beans is a cue both for stupidity and incipient sexual intercourse since beans were thought to increase the production of sperm in males; the small dog seeming to want to jump on to the lap of the woman is a cue for lust; the raw meat ("carne" as both meat and flesh) is a cue for cupidity and unbridled sexuality. Such paintings can also be read as moralizing allegories; in this case one can be warned about the sinfulness of voluptuousness and greed and at the same time enjoy the lavishness and cleverness of the image. Recent study also suggests that, at least in later paintings, such imagery disguises enormously erudite references to classical and contemporary humanistic literature, even if such references are themselves also scatological. One ancient writer even postulated that the term "satire" stems from the Roman word "satura," a plate heaped with food offering to the gods. Thus images like Campi's *Fishmongers* suggest the richness of doubled meanings in satire. Even Pliny wrote favorably in his *Natural History* of a painter, Piraeicus, who had painted "barbers' shops and cobblers' stalls, asses, viands and the like," who had been called a "painter of sordid subjects." Interesting for the commercial culture of the Italian middling class of the sixteenth century, Pliny also indicated with a verbal pun that these paintings gave "exquisite pleasure [*consummata voluptas*]" and that "they fetched bigger prices than the largest works of many masters." New subject matter, new patronage classes, and expanded modes of artistic commerce, all suggest an increasing independence for artists of the period and an expanding role for their imaginations.

Local developments like the still life were paralleled by the evolution of official histories of art which, initiated by Vasari in 1550, grew by the seventeenth century into a significant cottage industry in European intellectual history. In tandem with these histories were increasing numbers of treatises on the arts, beginning with Alberti in the mid-fifteenth century. Some were written by practicing painters, sculptors, and architects, but many of the authors came from outside the arts. Charles Borromeo, for example, published his treatise in 1577 giving explicit instructions for church building and decoration. Thus artists had to respond not only to the traditions inherent in the objects they produced but also to the literary constructions of their history and to the increasingly academic canons of artistic treatises, all disseminated by the still novel printed book—a medium that made for a wider and better informed public.

Changes such as these occurred within the period itself. To these must be added subsequent re-evaluation of the Renaissance in our own time. Emerging feminist studies, for example, have rediscovered the names of women artists of the Renaissance and have begun to reinstate their work into accounts of the history of the period. More importantly, they have focused attention on the critical roles women played as patrons within the economic structures of the culture and have analyzed how the very structures of presentation of women—and men—in Renaissance art can throw new light on social order. Interdisciplinary work by economic and political historians and by cultural anthropologists has also expanded understanding of the period by suggesting the richness of the relationships between artists and the various publics they addressed. Rather than discussing simply the artists and their work or the particular iconography of the art, studies of the period now consider the relationship between artist and patron, between patron and public, between artist and public, between art and the history of the site in which it was placed. They also look at a range of objects that had earlier been outside the frame narrowly construed as art—the domestic and liturgical arts, for example, where artists are for the most part anonymous, thus existing outside the biographical methods defined by Vasari for constructing artistic history. Recently the increased overlap between material culture and art has provided new ways to construct the visual field of the period and to suggest the vitality of artistic ideas as they traveled from place to place and as they entered the lived realities of their viewers.

The facts of the Renaissance are continually reconstructed by new interpretation. This book is part of that process. It has attempted to suggest some of the diversity of current historical thought while still focusing on art as a compelling, provocative, and instructive carrier of meaning. At the same time it has attempted to point out that each work of art is not an independent aesthetic object, but a site embodying a complex nexus of social relationships where both the coordinated and the conflicted ideas of a culture can be viewed and analyzed.

Map of Italy

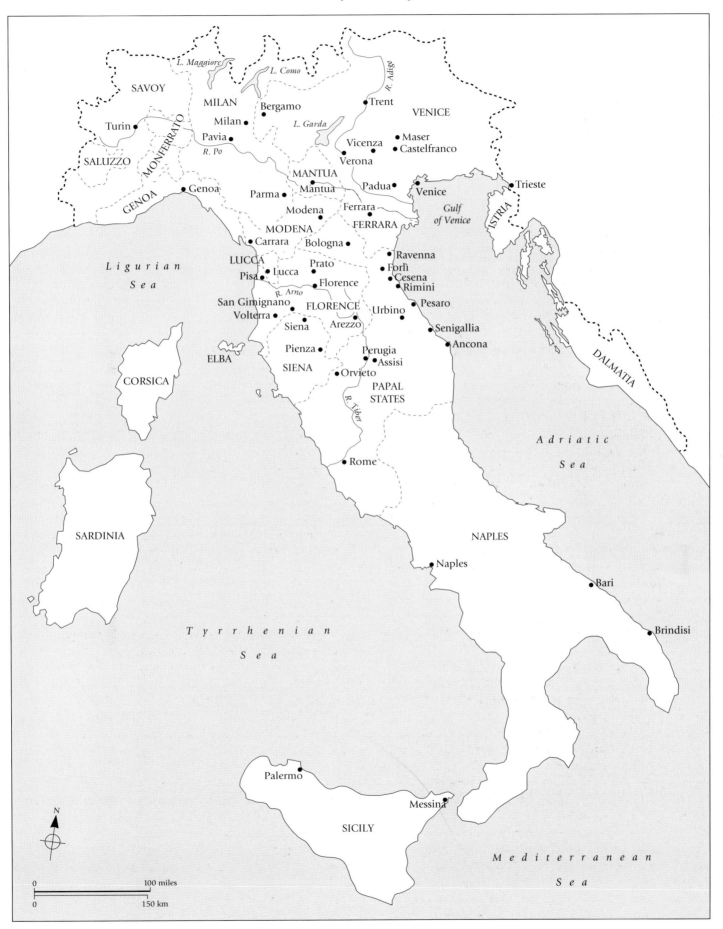

SAVOY

L. Maggiore

L. Como

R. Adige

MILAN

Bergamo

Trent

VENICE

Turin

MONFERRATO

Milan

L. Garda

Pavia

Maser

Vicenza

Castelfranco

SALUZZO

R. Po

Verona

MANTUA

Padua

GENOA

Genoa

Parma

Mantua

Venice

Trieste

ISTRIA

Gulf
of Venice

Modena

Ferrara

MODENA

FERRARA

Carrara

Bologna

Ravenna

Ligurian

Sea

LUCCA

Prato

Forlì

Cesena

Pisa

Lucca

Rimini

R. Arno

Florence

Pesaro

San Gimignano

FLORENCE

Urbino

Senigallia

Volterra

Arezzo

Ancona

Siena

DALMATIA

Pienza

Perugia

ELBA

SIENA

Assisi

Orvieto

PAPAL
STATES

CORSICA

R. Tiber

Adriatic

Sea

Rome

SARDINIA

NAPLES

Naples

Bari

Tyrrhenian

Sea

Brindisi

Palermo

Messina

SICILY

Mediterranean

Sea

N

0   100 miles

0   150 km

Genealogies

The following genealogies have been simplified where necessary in the interests of clarity.

·················· Illegitimate line

1. Angevin rulers of Naples

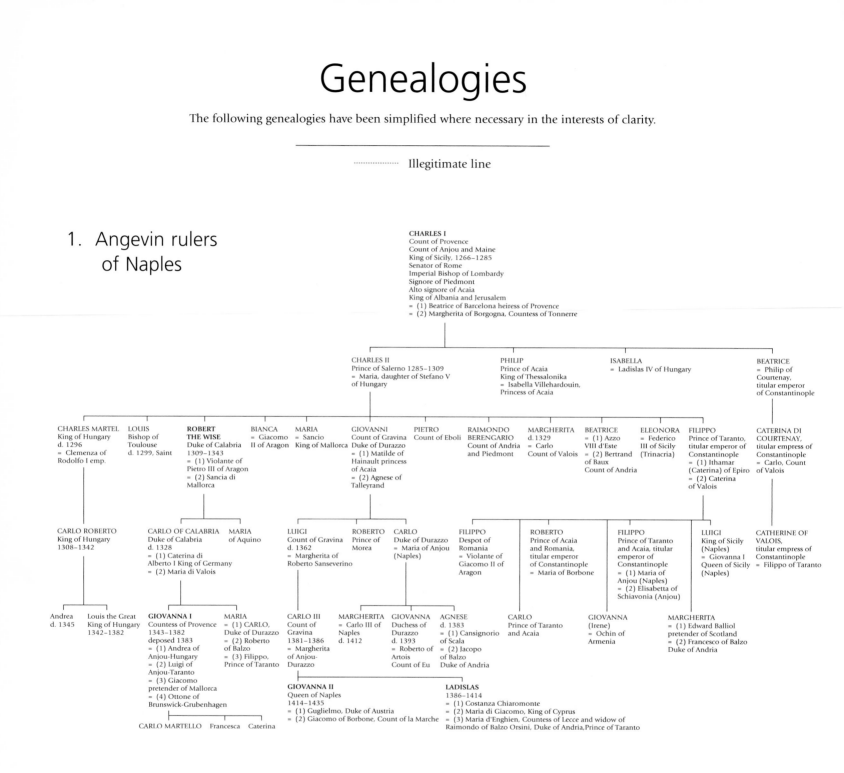

CHARLES I
Count of Provence
Count of Anjou and Maine
King of Sicily, 1266–1285
Senator of Rome
Imperial Bishop of Lombardy
Signore of Piedmont
Alto signore of Acaia
King of Albania and Jerusalem
= (1) Beatrice of Barcelona heiress of Provence
= (2) Margherita of Borgogna, Countess of Tonnerre

CHARLES II
Prince of Salerno 1285–1309
= Maria, daughter of Stefano V of Hungary

PHILIP
Prince of Acaia
King of Thessalonika
= Isabella Villehardouin, Princess of Acaia

ISABELLA
= Ladislas IV of Hungary

BEATRICE
= Philip of Courtenay, titular emperor of Constantinople

CHARLES MARTEL
King of Hungary
d. 1296
= Clemenza of Rodolfo I emp.

LOUIS
Bishop of Toulouse
d. 1299, Saint

ROBERT THE WISE
Duke of Calabria 1309–1343
= (1) Violante of Pietro III of Aragon
= (2) Sancia di Mallorca

BIANCA
= Giacomo II of Aragon

MARIA
= Sancio King of Mallorca

GIOVANNI
Count of Gravina Duke of Durazzo
= (1) Matilde of Hainault princess of Acaia
= (2) Agnese of Talleyrand

PIETRO
Count of Eboli

RAIMONDO BERENGARIO
Count of Andria and Piedmont

MARGHERITA
d. 1329
= Carlo Count of Valois

BEATRICE
= (1) Azzo VIII d'Este
= (2) Bertrand of Baux Count of Andria

ELEONORA
= Federico III of Sicily (Trinacria)

FILIPPO
Prince of Taranto, titular emperor of Constantinople
= (1) Ithamar (Caterina) of Epiro
= (2) Caterina of Valois

CATERINA DI COURTENAY,
titular empress of Constantinople
= Carlo, Count of Valois

CARLO ROBERTO
King of Hungary
1308–1342

CARLO OF CALABRIA
Duke of Calabria
d. 1328
= (1) Caterina di Alberto I King of Germany
= (2) Maria di Valois

MARIA
of Aquino

LUIGI
Count of Gravina
d. 1362
= Margherita of Roberto Sanseverino

ROBERTO
Prince of Morea

CARLO
Duke of Durazzo
= Maria of Anjou (Naples)

FILIPPO
Despot of Romania
= Violante of Giacomo II of Aragon

ROBERTO
Prince of Acaia and Romania, titular emperor of Constantinople
= Maria of Borbone

FILIPPO
Prince of Taranto and Acaia, titular emperor of Constantinople
= (1) Maria of Anjou (Naples)
= (2) Elisabetta of Schiavonia (Anjou)

LUIGI
King of Sicily (Naples)
= Giovanna I Queen of Sicily (Naples)

CATHERINE OF VALOIS,
titular empress of Constantinople
= Filippo of Taranto

Andrea
d. 1345

Louis the Great
King of Hungary
1342–1382

GIOVANNA I
Countess of Provence
1343–1382
deposed 1383
= (1) Andrea of Anjou-Hungary
= (2) Luigi of Anjou-Taranto
= (3) Giacomo pretender of Mallorca
= (4) Ottone of Brunswick-Grubenhagen

MARIA
= (1) CARLO, Duke of Durazzo
= (2) Roberto of Balzo
= (3) Filippo, Prince of Taranto

CARLO III
Count of Gravina
1381–1386
= Margherita of Anjou-Durazzo

MARGHERITA
= Carlo III of Naples

GIOVANNA
Duchess of Durazzo
d. 1393
= Roberto of Artois Count of Eu

AGNESE
d. 1383
= (1) Cansignorio of Scala
= (2) Jacopo of Balzo Duke of Andria

CARLO
Prince of Taranto and Acaia

GIOVANNA
(Irene)
= Ochin of Armenia

MARGHERITA
= (1) Edward Balliol pretender of Scotland
= (2) Francesco of Balzo Duke of Andria

CARLO MARTELLO   Francesca   Caterina

GIOVANNA II
Queen of Naples
1414–1435
= (1) Guglielmo, Duke of Austria
= (2) Giacomo of Borbone, Count of la Marche

LADISLAS
1386–1414
= (1) Costanza Chiaromonte
= (2) Maria di Giacomo, King of Cyprus
= (3) Maria d'Enghien, Countess of Lecce and widow of Raimondo of Balzo Orsini, Duke of Andria, Prince of Taranto

2. Aragon rulers of the Kingdom of Naples

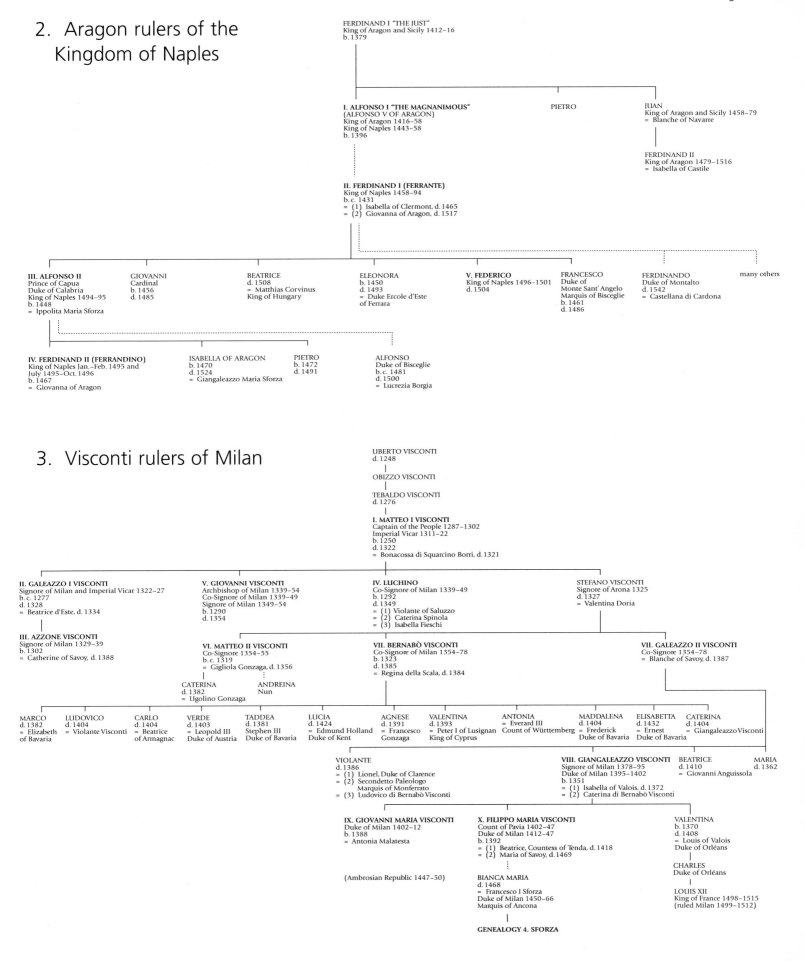

FERDINAND I "THE JUST"
King of Aragon and Sicily 1412–16
b. 1379

I. ALFONSO I "THE MAGNANIMOUS"
(ALFONSO V OF ARAGON)
King of Aragon 1416–58
King of Naples 1443–58
b. 1396

PIETRO

JUAN
King of Aragon and Sicily 1458–79
= Blanche of Navarre

FERDINAND II
King of Aragon 1479–1516
= Isabella of Castile

II. FERDINAND I (FERRANTE)
King of Naples 1458–94
b. c. 1431
= (1) Isabella of Clermont, d. 1465
= (2) Giovanna of Aragon, d. 1517

III. ALFONSO II
Prince of Capua
Duke of Calabria
King of Naples 1494–95
b. 1448
= Ippolita Maria Sforza

GIOVANNI
Cardinal
b. 1456
d. 1485

BEATRICE
d. 1508
= Matthias Corvinus
King of Hungary

ELEONORA
b. 1450
d. 1493
= Duke Ercole d'Este
of Ferrara

V. FEDERICO
King of Naples 1496–1501
d. 1504

FRANCESCO
Duke of
Monte Sant'Angelo
Marquis of Bisceglie
b. 1461
d. 1486

FERDINANDO
Duke of Montalto
d. 1542
= Castellana di Cardona

many others

IV. FERDINAND II (FERRANDINO)
King of Naples Jan.–Feb. 1495 and
July 1495–Oct. 1496
b. 1467
= Giovanna of Aragon

ISABELLA OF ARAGON
b. 1470
d. 1524
= Giangaleazzo Maria Sforza

PIETRO
b. 1472
d. 1491

ALFONSO
Duke of Bisceglie
b. c. 1481
d. 1500
= Lucrezia Borgia

3. Visconti rulers of Milan

UBERTO VISCONTI
d. 1248

OBIZZO VISCONTI

TEBALDO VISCONTI
d. 1276

I. MATTEO I VISCONTI
Captain of the People 1287–1302
Imperial Vicar 1311–22
b. 1250
d. 1322
= Bonacossa di Squarcino Borri, d. 1321

II. GALEAZZO I VISCONTI
Signore of Milan and Imperial Vicar 1322–27
b. c. 1277
d. 1328
= Beatrice d'Este, d. 1334

V. GIOVANNI VISCONTI
Archbishop of Milan 1339–54
Co-Signore of Milan 1339–49
Signore of Milan 1349–54
b. 1290
d. 1354

IV. LUCHINO
Co-Signore of Milan 1339–49
b. 1292
d. 1349
= (1) Violante of Saluzzo
= (2) Caterina Spinola
= (3) Isabella Fieschi

STEFANO VISCONTI
Signore of Arona 1325
d. 1327
= Valentina Doria

III. AZZONE VISCONTI
Signore of Milan 1329–39
b. 1302
= Catherine of Savoy, d. 1388

VI. MATTEO II VISCONTI
Co-Signore 1354–55
b. c. 1319
= Gigliola Gonzaga, d. 1356

VII. BERNABÒ VISCONTI
Co-Signore of Milan 1354–78
b. 1323
d. 1385
= Regina della Scala, d. 1384

VII. GALEAZZO II VISCONTI
Co-Signore 1354–78
= Blanche of Savoy, d. 1387

CATERINA
d. 1382
= Ugolino Gonzaga

ANDREINA
Nun

MARCO
d. 1382
= Elizabeth
of Bavaria

LUDOVICO
d. 1404
= Violante Visconti

CARLO
d. 1404
= Beatrice
of Armagnac

VERDE
d. 1403
= Leopold III
Duke of Austria

TADDEA
d. 1381
Stephen III
Duke of Bavaria

LUCIA
d. 1424
= Edmund Holland
Duke of Kent

AGNESE
d. 1391
= Francesco
Gonzaga

VALENTINA
d. 1393
= Peter I of Lusignan
King of Cyprus

ANTONIA
= Everard III
Count of Württemberg

MADDALENA
d. 1404
= Frederick
Duke of Bavaria

ELISABETTA
d. 1432
= Ernest
Duke of Bavaria

CATERINA
d. 1404
= Giangaleazzo Visconti

VIOLANTE
d. 1386
= (1) Lionel, Duke of Clarence
= (2) Secondetto Paleologo
Marquis of Monferrato
= (3) Ludovico di Bernabò Visconti

VIII. GIANGALEAZZO VISCONTI
Signore of Milan 1378–95
Duke of Milan 1395–1402
b. 1351
= (1) Isabella of Valois, d. 1372
= (2) Caterina di Bernabò Visconti

BEATRICE
d. 1410
= Giovanni Anguissola

MARIA
d. 1362

IX. GIOVANNI MARIA VISCONTI
Duke of Milan 1402–12
b. 1388
= Antonia Malatesta

X. FILIPPO MARIA VISCONTI
Count of Pavia 1402–47
Duke of Milan 1412–47
b. 1392
= (1) Beatrice, Countess of Tenda, d. 1418
= (2) Maria of Savoy, d. 1469

VALENTINA
b. 1370
d. 1408
= Louis of Valois
Duke of Orléans

(Ambrosian Republic 1447–50)

BIANCA MARIA
d. 1468
= Francesco I Sforza
Duke of Milan 1450–66
Marquis of Ancona

CHARLES
Duke of Orléans

LOUIS XII
King of France 1498–1515
(ruled Milan 1499–1512)

GENEALOGY 4. SFORZA

4. Sforza rulers of Milan

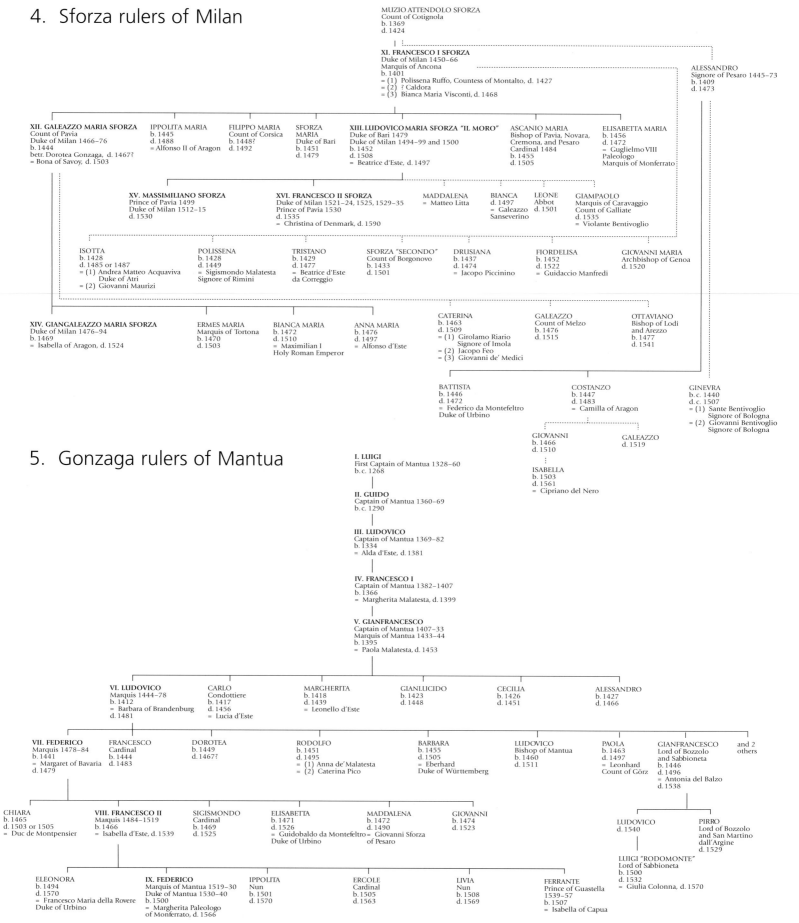

MUZIO ATTENDOLO SFORZA
Count of Cotignola
b. 1369
d. 1424

XI. FRANCESCO I SFORZA
Duke of Milan 1450–66
Marquis of Ancona
b. 1401
= (1) Polissena Ruffo, Countess of Montalto, d. 1427
= (2) ? Caldora
= (3) Bianca Maria Visconti, d. 1468

ALESSANDRO
Signore of Pesaro 1445–73
b. 1409
d. 1473

XII. GALEAZZO MARIA SFORZA
Count of Pavia
Duke of Milan 1466–76
b. 1444
betr. Dorotea Gonzaga, d. 1467?
= Bona of Savoy, d. 1503

IPPOLITA MARIA
b. 1445
d. 1488
= Alfonso II of Aragon

FILIPPO MARIA
Count of Corsica
b. 1448?
d. 1492

SFORZA MARIA
Duke of Bari
b. 1451
d. 1479

XIII. LUDOVICO MARIA SFORZA "IL MORO"
Duke of Bari 1479
Duke of Milan 1494–99 and 1500
b. 1452
d. 1508
= Beatrice d'Este, d. 1497

ASCANIO MARIA
Bishop of Pavia, Novara,
Cremona, and Pesaro
Cardinal 1484
b. 1455
d. 1505

ELISABETTA MARIA
b. 1456
d. 1472
= Guglielmo VIII
Paleologo
Marquis of Monferrato

XV. MASSIMILIANO SFORZA
Prince of Pavia 1499
Duke of Milan 1512–15
d. 1530

XVI. FRANCESCO II SFORZA
Duke of Milan 1521–24, 1525, 1529–35
Prince of Pavia 1530
d. 1535
= Christina of Denmark, d. 1590

MADDALENA
= Matteo Litta

BIANCA
d. 1497
= Galeazzo
Sanseverino

LEONE
Abbot
d. 1501

GIAMPAOLO
Marquis of Caravaggio
Count of Galliate
d. 1535
= Violante Bentivoglio

ISOTTA
b. 1428
d. 1485 or 1487
= (1) Andrea Matteo Acquaviva
Duke of Atri
= (2) Giovanni Maurizi

POLISSENA
b. 1428
d. 1449
= Sigismondo Malatesta
Signore of Rimini

TRISTANO
b. 1429
d. 1477
= Beatrice d'Este
da Correggio

SFORZA "SECONDO"
Count of Borgonovo
b. 1433
d. 1501

DRUSIANA
b. 1437
d. 1474
= Jacopo Piccinino

FIORDELISA
b. 1452
d. 1522
= Guidaccio Manfredi

GIOVANNI MARIA
Archbishop of Genoa
d. 1520

XIV. GIANGALEAZZO MARIA SFORZA
Duke of Milan 1476–94
b. 1469
= Isabella of Aragon, d. 1524

ERMES MARIA
Marquis of Tortona
b. 1470
d. 1503

BIANCA MARIA
b. 1472
d. 1510
= Maximilian I
Holy Roman Emperor

ANNA MARIA
b. 1476
d. 1497
= Alfonso d'Este

CATERINA
b. 1463
d. 1509
= (1) Girolamo Riario
Signore of Imola
= (2) Jacopo Feo
= (3) Giovanni de' Medici

GALEAZZO
Count of Melzo
b. 1476
d. 1515

OTTAVIANO
Bishop of Lodi
and Arezzo
b. 1477
d. 1541

BATTISTA
b. 1446
d. 1472
= Federico da Montefeltro
Duke of Urbino

COSTANZO
b. 1447
d. 1483
= Camilla of Aragon

GINEVRA
b. c. 1440
d. c. 1507
= (1) Sante Bentivoglio
Signore of Bologna
= (2) Giovanni Bentivoglio
Signore of Bologna

GIOVANNI
b. 1466
d. 1510

GALEAZZO
d. 1519

ISABELLA
b. 1503
d. 1561
= Cipriano del Nero

5. Gonzaga rulers of Mantua

I. LUIGI
First Captain of Mantua 1328–60
b. c. 1268

II. GUIDO
Captain of Mantua 1360–69
b. c. 1290

III. LUDOVICO
Captain of Mantua 1369–82
b. 1334
= Alda d'Este, d. 1381

IV. FRANCESCO I
Captain of Mantua 1382–1407
b. 1366
= Margherita Malatesta, d. 1399

V. GIANFRANCESCO
Captain of Mantua 1407–33
Marquis of Mantua 1433–44
b. 1395
= Paola Malatesta, d. 1453

VI. LUDOVICO
Marquis 1444–78
b. 1412
= Barbara of Brandenburg
d. 1481

CARLO
Condottiere
b. 1417
d. 1456
= Lucia d'Este

MARGHERITA
b. 1418
d. 1439
= Leonello d'Este

GIANLUCIDO
b. 1423
d. 1448

CECILIA
b. 1426
d. 1451

ALESSANDRO
b. 1427
d. 1466

VII. FEDERICO
Marquis 1478–84
b. 1441
= Margaret of Bavaria
d. 1479

FRANCESCO
Cardinal
b. 1444
d. 1483

DOROTEA
b. 1449
d. 1467?

RODOLFO
b. 1451
d. 1495
= (1) Anna de' Malatesta
= (2) Caterina Pico

BARBARA
b. 1455
d. 1505
= Eberhard
Duke of Württemberg

LUDOVICO
Bishop of Mantua
b. 1460
d. 1511

PAOLA
b. 1463
d. 1497
= Leonhard
Count of Görz

GIANFRANCESCO
Lord of Bozzolo
and Sabbioneta
b. 1446
d. 1496
= Antonia del Balzo
d. 1538

and 2
others

CHIARA
b. 1465
d. 1503 or 1505
= Duc de Montpensier

VIII. FRANCESCO II
Marquis 1484–1519
b. 1466
= Isabella d'Este, d. 1539

SIGISMONDO
Cardinal
b. 1469
d. 1525

ELISABETTA
b. 1471
d. 1526
= Guidobaldo da Montefeltro
Duke of Urbino

MADDALENA
b. 1472
d. 1490
= Giovanni Sforza
of Pesaro

GIOVANNI
b. 1474
d. 1523

LUDOVICO
d. 1540

PIRRO
Lord of Bozzolo
and San Martino
dall'Argine
d. 1529

LUIGI "RODOMONTE"
Lord of Sabbioneta
b. 1500
d. 1532
= Giulia Colonna, d. 1570

ELEONORA
b. 1494
d. 1570
= Francesco Maria della Rovere
Duke of Urbino

IX. FEDERICO
Marquis of Mantua 1519–30
Duke of Mantua 1530–40
b. 1500
= Margherita Paleologo
of Monferrato, d. 1566

IPPOLITA
Nun
b. 1501
d. 1570

ERCOLE
Cardinal
b. 1505
d. 1563

LIVIA
Nun
b. 1508
d. 1569

FERRANTE
Prince of Guastella
1539–57
b. 1507
= Isabella of Capua

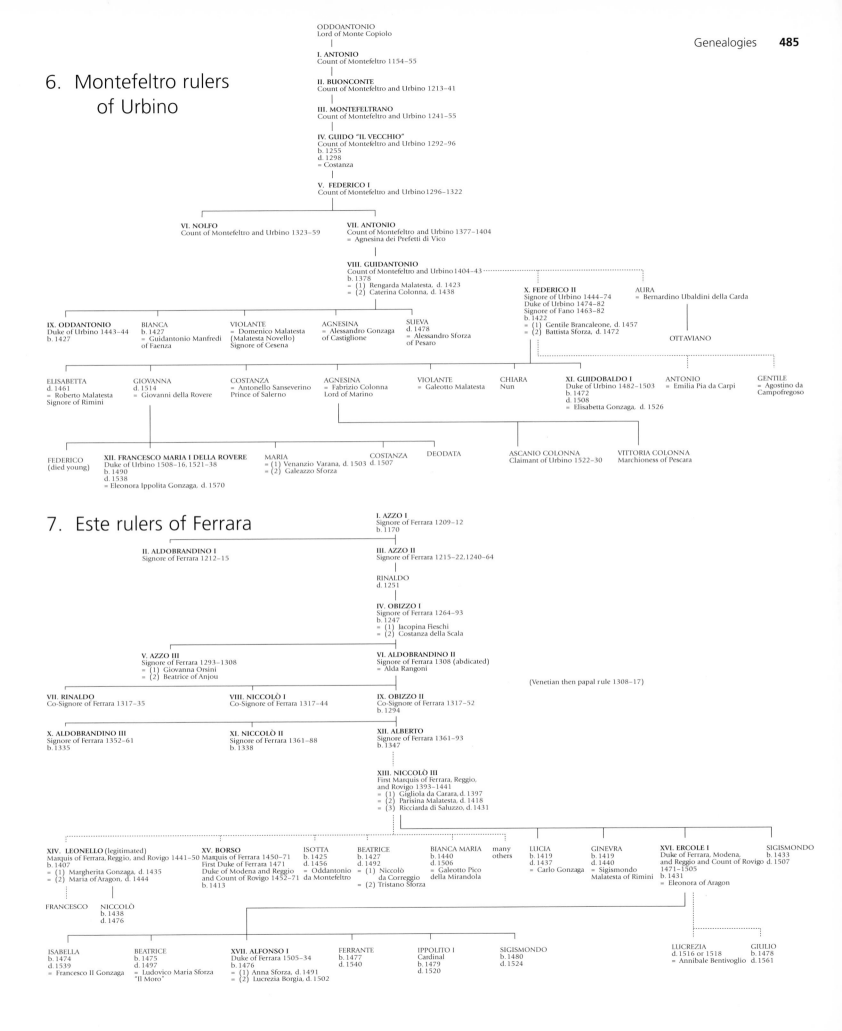

6. Montefeltro rulers of Urbino

ODDOANTONIO
Lord of Monte Copiolo

I. ANTONIO
Count of Montefeltro 1154–55

II. BUONCONTE
Count of Montefeltro and Urbino 1213–41

III. MONTEFELTRANO
Count of Montefeltro and Urbino 1241–55

IV. GUIDO "IL VECCHIO"
Count of Montefeltro and Urbino 1292–96
b. 1255
d. 1298
= Costanza

V. FEDERICO I
Count of Montefeltro and Urbino 1296–1322

VI. NOLFO
Count of Montefeltro and Urbino 1323–59

VII. ANTONIO
Count of Montefeltro and Urbino 1377–1404
= Agnesina dei Prefetti di Vico

VIII. GUIDANTONIO
Count of Montefeltro and Urbino 1404–43
b. 1378
= (1) Rengarda Malatesta, d. 1423
= (2) Caterina Colonna, d. 1438

X. FEDERICO II
Signore of Urbino 1444–74
Duke of Urbino 1474–82
Signore of Fano 1463–82
b. 1422
= (1) Gentile Brancaleone, d. 1457
= (2) Battista Sforza, d. 1472

AURA
= Bernardino Ubaldini della Carda

IX. ODDANTONIO
Duke of Urbino 1443–44
b. 1427

BIANCA
b. 1427
= Guidantonio Manfredi
of Faenza

VIOLANTE
= Domenico Malatesta
(Malatesta Novello)
Signore of Cesena

AGNESINA
= Alessandro Gonzaga
of Castiglione

SUEVA
d. 1478
= Alessandro Sforza
of Pesaro

OTTAVIANO

ELISABETTA
d. 1461
= Roberto Malatesta
Signore of Rimini

GIOVANNA
d. 1514
= Giovanni della Rovere

COSTANZA
= Antonello Sanseverino
Prince of Salerno

AGNESINA
= Fabrizio Colonna
Lord of Marino

VIOLANTE
= Galeotto Malatesta

CHIARA
Nun

XI. GUIDOBALDO I
Duke of Urbino 1482–1503
b. 1472
d. 1508
= Elisabetta Gonzaga, d. 1526

ANTONIO
= Emilia Pia da Carpi

GENTILE
= Agostino da
Campofregoso

FEDERICO
(died young)

XII. FRANCESCO MARIA I DELLA ROVERE
Duke of Urbino 1508–16, 1521–38
b. 1490
d. 1538
= Eleonora Ippolita Gonzaga, d. 1570

MARIA
= (1) Venanzio Varana, d. 1503
= (2) Galeazzo Sforza

COSTANZA
d. 1507

DEODATA

ASCANIO COLONNA
Claimant of Urbino 1522–30

VITTORIA COLONNA
Marchioness of Pescara

7. Este rulers of Ferrara

I. AZZO I
Signore of Ferrara 1209–12
b. 1170

II. ALDOBRANDINO I
Signore of Ferrara 1212–15

III. AZZO II
Signore of Ferrara 1215–22, 1240–64

RINALDO
d. 1251

IV. OBIZZO I
Signore of Ferrara 1264–93
b. 1247
= (1) Jacopina Fieschi
= (2) Costanza della Scala

V. AZZO III
Signore of Ferrara 1293–1308
= (1) Giovanna Orsini
= (2) Beatrice of Anjou

VI. ALDOBRANDINO II
Signore of Ferrara 1308 (abdicated)
= Alda Rangoni

(Venetian then papal rule 1308–17)

VII. RINALDO
Co-Signore of Ferrara 1317–35

VIII. NICCOLÒ I
Co-Signore of Ferrara 1317–44

IX. OBIZZO II
Co-Signore of Ferrara 1317–52
b. 1294

X. ALDOBRANDINO III
Signore of Ferrara 1352–61
b. 1335

XI. NICCOLÒ II
Signore of Ferrara 1361–88
b. 1338

XII. ALBERTO
Signore of Ferrara 1361–93
b. 1347

XIII. NICCOLÒ III
First Marquis of Ferrara, Reggio,
and Rovigo 1393–1441
= (1) Gigliola da Carara, d. 1397
= (2) Parisina Malatesta, d. 1418
= (3) Ricciarda di Saluzzo, d. 1431

XIV. LEONELLO (legitimated)
Marquis of Ferrara, Reggio, and Rovigo 1441–50
b. 1407
= (1) Margherita Gonzaga, d. 1435
= (2) Maria of Aragon, d. 1444

XV. BORSO
Marquis of Ferrara 1450–71
First Duke of Ferrara 1471
Duke of Modena and Reggio
and Count of Rovigo 1452–71
b. 1413

ISOTTA
b. 1425
d. 1456
= Oddantonio
da Montefeltro

BEATRICE
b. 1427
d. 1492
= (1) Niccolò
da Correggio
= (2) Tristano Sforza

BIANCA MARIA
b. 1440
d. 1506
= Galeotto Pico
della Mirandola

many
others

LUCIA
b. 1419
d. 1437
= Carlo Gonzaga

GINEVRA
b. 1419
d. 1440
= Sigismondo
Malatesta of Rimini

XVI. ERCOLE I
Duke of Ferrara, Modena,
and Reggio and Count of Rovigo
1471–1505
b. 1431
= Eleonora of Aragon

SIGISMONDO
b. 1433
d. 1507

FRANCESCO

NICCOLÒ
b. 1438
d. 1476

ISABELLA
b. 1474
d. 1539
= Francesco II Gonzaga

BEATRICE
b. 1475
d. 1497
= Ludovico Maria Sforza
"Il Moro"

XVII. ALFONSO I
Duke of Ferrara 1505–34
b. 1476
= (1) Anna Sforza, d. 1491
= (2) Lucrezia Borgia, d. 1502

FERRANTE
b. 1477
d. 1540

IPPOLITO I
Cardinal
b. 1479
d. 1520

SIGISMONDO
b. 1480
d. 1524

LUCREZIA
d. 1516 or 1518
= Annibale Bentivoglio

GIULIO
b. 1478
d. 1561

8. Medici rulers of Florence*

*Although the Medici functioned as de facto rulers of Florence after 1434 they did not act officially in that capacity until after their return from exile in 1512.

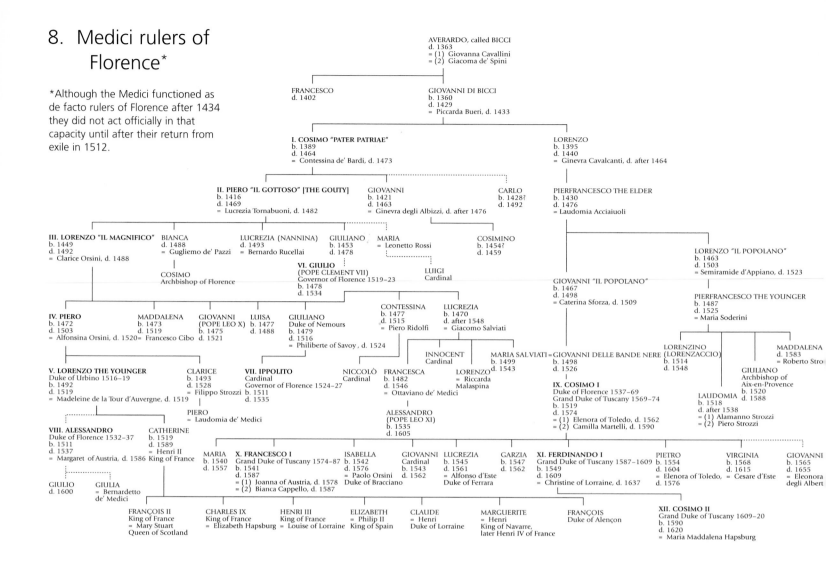

List of Popes

Nicholas III (Giovanni Gaetano Orsini, of Rome), 1277–80

Martin IV (Simon de Brion, of Montpincé in Brie), 1281–85

Honorius IV (Iacopo Savelli, of Rome), 1285–87

Nicholas IV (Girolamo Masci, of Lisciano di Ascoli), 1288–92

St. Celestine V (Pietro Angeleri da Morrone, of Isernia), July 5–December 13, 1294 (abdicated; d. 1296)

Boniface VIII (Benedetto Gaetani, of Anagni), 1294–1303

Blessed Benedict XI (Niccolò Boccasini, of Treviso), 1303–04

Clement V (Bertrand de Got, of Villandraut, near Bordeaux), 1305–14

John XXII (Jacques d'Euse, of Cahors), 1316–34

Benedict XII (Jacques Fournier, of Saverdun, near Toulouse), 1334–42

Clement VI (Pierre Roger de Beaufort, of Château Maumont, near Limoges), 1342–52

Innocent VI (Etienne d'Aubert, of Mont, near Limoges), 1352–62

Blessed Urban V (Guillaume de Grimoard, of Grisac, Languedoc), 1362–70

Gregory XI (Pierre Roger de Beaufort, of Château Maumont, near Limoges), 1370–78

Urban VI (Bartolomeo Prigano, of Naples), 1378–89

Boniface IX (Pietro Tomacelli, of Naples), 1389–1404

Innocent VII (Cosimo de' Migliorati, of Sulmona), 1404–06

Gregory XII (Angelo Correr, of Venice), 1406–15 (deposed by Council of Pisa 1409; abdicated 1415; d. 1417)

POPES AT AVIGNON

Clement VII (Robert of Savoy, of Geneva), 1378–94

Benedict XIII (Pedro de Luna, of Aragon), 1394–1423

ANTIPOPES AT AVIGNON

Clement VIII (Gil Sanchez Muñoz, of Barcelona), 1423–29

Benedict XIV (Bernard Garnier), 1425–30 [?]

POPES AT PISA

Alexander V (Pietro Filargis, of Candia), 1409–10

John XXIII (Baldassare Cossa, of Naples), 1410–15 (deposed; d. 1419)

Martin V (Oddo Colonna, of Genazzano, near Rome; b. 1368), 1417–31

Eugenius IV (Gabriele Condulmer, of Venice; b. 1383), 1431–47

[Felix V (Amadeus, duke, of Savoy), 1439–49, d. 1451]

Nicholas V (Tommaso Parentucelli, of Sarzana; b. 1397), 1447–55

Callixtus III (Alfonso Borgia, of Xativa, Spain; b. 1378), 1455–58

Pius II (Aeneas Silvius Piccolomini, of Corsignano, now Pienza; b. 1405), 1458–64

Paul II (Pietro Barbo, of Venice; b. 1417), 1464–71

Sixtus IV (Francesco della Rovere, of Savona; b. 1414), 1471–84

Innocent VIII (Giovanni Battista Cibo, of Genoa; b. 1432), 1484–92

Alexander VI (Rodrigo Borgia, of Valencia, Spain; b. c. 1431), 1492–1503

Pius III (Francesco Todeschini-Piccolomini, of Siena; b. 1439), September 22–October 18, 1503

Julius II (Giuliano della Rovere, of Savona; b. 1443), 1503–13

Leo X (Giovanni de' Medici, of Florence; b. 1475), 1513–21

Adrian VI (Adrian Florisz Dedel, of Utrecht, Netherlands; b. 1459), 1522–23

Clement VII (Giulio de' Medici, of Florence; b. 1478), 1523–34

Paul III (Alessandro Farnese, of Camino, Rome, or of Viterbo [?]; b. 1468), 1534–49

Julius III (Giovanni Maria Ciocchi del Monte, of Monte San Savino, near Arezzo; b. 1487), 1550–55

Marcellus II (Marcello Cervini, of Montefano, Macerata; b. 1501), April 9–30, 1555

Paul IV (Giovanni Pietro Carafa, of Capriglio, Avellino; b. 1476), 1555–59

Pius IV (Giovanni Angelo de' Medici, of Milan; b. 1499), 1559–65

Pius V (Antonio Ghislieri, of Bosco Marengo, near Tortona; b. 1504), 1566–72

Gregory XIII (Ugo Boncompagni, of Bologna; b. 1502), 1572–85

Sixtus V (Felice Peretti, of Grottammare; b. 1520), 1585–90

List of Venetian Doges

Marino Morosini, 1249–53

Raniero Zen, 1253–68

Lorenzo Tiepolo, 1268–75

Iacopo Contarini, 1275–80

Giovanni Dandolo, 1280–89

Pietro Gradenigo, 1289–1311

Marino Zorzi, 1311–12

Giovanni Soranzo, 1312–28

Francesco Dandolo, 1329–39

Bartolomeo Gradenigo, 1339–42

Andrea Dandolo, 1343–54

Marin Falier, 1354–55 (deposed and decapitated)

Giovanni Gradenigo, 1355–56

Giovanni Dolfin, 1356–61

Lorenzo Celsi, 1361–65

Marco Corner, 1365–68

Andrea Contarini, 1368–82

Michele Morosini, 1382

Antonio Venier, 1382–1400

Michele Steno, 1400–13

Tomaso Mocenigo, 1414–23

Francesco Foscari, 1423–57 (deposed)

Pasquale Malipiero, 1457–62

Cristoforo Moro, 1462–71

Nicolò Tron, 1471–73

Nicolò Marcello, 1473–74

Pietro Mocenigo, 1474–76

Andrea Vendramin, 1476–78

Giovanni Mocenigo, 1478–85

Marco Barbarigo, 1485–86

Agostino Barbarigo, 1486–1501

Leonardo Loredan, 1501–21

Antonio Grimani, 1521–23

Andrea Gritti, 1523–38

Pietro Lando, 1539–45

Francesco Donato, 1545–53

Marcantonio Trevisan, 1553–54

Francesco Venier, 1554–56

Lorenzo Priuli, 1556–59

Girolamo Priuli, 1559–67

Pietro Loredan, 1567–70

Alvise I Mocenigo, 1570–77

Sebastiano Venier, 1577–78

Nicolò da Ponte, 1578–85

Pasquale Cicogna, 1585–95

Marino Grimani, 1595–1605

Time Chart

	1200–1300	1300–40	1340–90	1390–1430
Politics	**1204** Venetians sack Constantinople **1215** King John of England signs the Magna Carta **1265** Charles of Anjou claims Kingdom of Naples **1295** Visconti assume power in Milan **1297** The *serrata* in Venice closes and defines membership in the governing noble class	**1339** Beginning of the Hundred Years' War	**1346** Bardi and Peruzzi banks fail in Florence **1347** Cola di Rienzo takes control of Rome **1347** First reported outbreak of Black Death; it strikes Italy with devastating losses in summer 1348 **1355** The Nine fall from power in Siena **1385** Giangaleazzo Visconti unites rule of Milan and Pavia	**1395** Giangaleazzo Visconti named Duke of Milan **1397** Medici Bank founded in Florence **1406** Venetians gain control of Padua **1409** King Ladislas of Naples gains control of Rome and Papal States **1425** Florence, Venice, and the papacy ally against Milan **1427** *Catasto* (property tax) established in Florence
Religion	**1215** Fourth Lateran Council codifies major aspects of Church doctrine **1223** St. Francis establishes first Nativity scene at Greccio **1228** Canonization of St. Francis **1234** Canonization of St. Dominic **1262** Bonaventure commissioned to write the *Legenda Maior*; completed 1266 **1300** Pope Boniface VIII declares first Jubilee in Rome	**1309** Papacy establishes permanent residence in Avignon	**1368** St. Catherine of Siena experiences a mystical marriage with Christ **1378** Beginning of the Great Schism	**1417** Council of Constance deposes competing popes and elects Martin V **1420** Pope Martin V enters Rome **1431** Joan of Arc burnt at the stake
Literature and Learning	**1225** St. Francis composes *Canticle of the Sun*	**1308** Dante begins the *Divine Comedy* in Ravenna **c. 1330** Galvano Fiamma revives classical notion of magnificence	**1341** Petrarch crowned poet laureate on Capitoline Hill **1351** Boccaccio completes the *Decameron* **1379** Publication of Petrarch's *Famous Men* **1387** Chaucer begins the *Canterbury Tales*	**1396** Florentines invite the Byzantine scholar Manuel Chrysoloras to revive the study of Greek in Italy **1410** Rediscovery of Ptolemy's *Geography*
Visual Arts	**1265** Operai of Siena Cathedral commission pulpit from Nicola Pisano **1266** Venetians enlarge and pave Piazza San Marco **c. 1290** *Last Judgment* for Santa Cecilia in Trastevere commissioned from Cavallini **1299** Palazzo della Signoria begun in Florence	**1302** Enrico Scrovegni commissions Giotto to fresco Arena Chapel, Padua **1308** Operai of Siena Cathedral commission *Maestà* from Duccio **1310** Queen Sancia of Mallorca founds Santa Chiara, Naples **1330** Arte del Calimala commissions bronze doors for Florence Baptistry from Andrea Pisano **c. 1330** Azzone Visconti builds palace complex at San Gottardo, Milan	**c. 1343** King Robert of Anjou gives directions for his tomb monument in Santa Chiara, Naples **1345** Doge Andrea Dandolo renovates Pala d'Oro in Venice **c. 1363** Bernabò Visconti commissions equestrian monument from Bonino da Campione **1370s** Lupi family commissions frescoes for St. James Chapel in the Santo, Padua, from Altichiero **1373** Florentines begin construction of Loggia della Signoria	**1390** Francesco the Younger Carrara commissions antique coins of his father in Padua **1390s** Giangaleazzo Visconti commissions Ivory Triptych from Baldassare Embriachi for the Certosa, Pavia **1401** Competition for Baptistry doors, Florence **1414** Queen Giovanna of Naples commissions tomb for her brother King Ladislas from Andrea and Matteo Nofri **1421** Marco Contarini oversees construction and decoration of his family home, the Ca' d'Oro, Venice **c. 1424** Felice Brancacci commissions Masaccio and Masolino to fresco the family chapel, Santa Maria del Carmine, Florence

1430–65	1465–1500	1500–30	1530–60	1560–1600
1433 Medici exiled from Florence; return following year **1443** Triumphal entry of Alfonso of Aragon into Naples **1447** Establishment of Ambrosian Republic in Milan **1450** Francesco Sforza assumes power in Milan **1452** Borso d'Este acquires title of Duke of Ferrara and Reggio **1453** Fall of Constantinople to the Turks **1454** Peace of Lodi establishes boundaries of major powers in Italy for most of the rest of the century	**1478** Pazzi Conspiracy fails in its attempt to overthrow the Medici in Florence **1479** Venetians establish peace with Turks and Sultan Muhammad II **1486** Portuguese explorers round the Cape of Good Hope **1492** Columbus lands in the Indies **1494** Ludovico Sforza named Duke of Milan **1494** King Charles VIII of France invades Italy **1494** Medici expelled from Florence	**1501** Amerigo Vespucci sails to South America **1509** League of Cambrai unites major powers against Venice **1512** Medici return to control in Florence **1519** Magellan begins circumnavigation of the globe **1527** Mercenaries of Charles V sack Rome **1530** Charles V crowned Emperor in Bologna by Pope Clement VII	**1537** Cosimo I de' Medici assumes power in Florence	**1565** Foundation of St. Augustine, Florida **1569** Cosimo I de' Medici named Grand Duke of Tuscany **1571** Turkish fleet defeated by Spaniards and Venetians at Battle of Lepanto
1438 Council of Ferrara **1439** Council of Florence unites Eastern and Western Churches **1444** St. Bernardino of Siena dies **1450** Pope Nicholas V declares Jubilee in Rome	**1497** Savonarola institutes "Bonfires of the Vanities" in Florence	**1507** Pope Julius II issues indulgences to rebuild St. Peter's **1517** Luther issues his 95 Theses calling for Church reform **1521** Diet of Worms condemns Luther	**1536** John Calvin publishes *Institutes of the Christian Religion* **1540** Ignatius Loyola founds Society of Jesus (Jesuits) **1545** Pope Paul III opens Council of Trent **1557** Cardinal Carafa issues first Index of Prohibited Books	**1563** Council of Trent issues final decrees **1566** Publication of the *Roman Catechism* **1573** Veronese appears before the Inquisition **1582** Pope Gregory XIII reforms the calendar
1435 Alberti's treatise *On Painting* **1443** *Della famiglia* by Alberti **1456** Gutenberg produces first printed Bible	**1465** First printing press in Italy set up in Subiaco, near Rome **1466** Marsilio Ficino begins translations of Plato's *Dialogues* **1468** Cardinal Bessarion leaves his library to the Venetian state **1475** Sixtus IV establishes the Vatican Library **1490** Aldus Manutius establishes Aldine Press in Venice	**1509** Publication of *Praise of Folly* by Erasmus **1513** Machiavelli writes *The Prince* **1516** Publication of *Orlando Furioso* by Ariosto **1516** Publication of Thomas More's *Utopia* **1528** Publication of Castiglione's *Book of the Courtier*	**1537** Aretino declares Titian's manner as his aesthetic model **1543** Publication of Copernicus' *On the Revolution of Heavenly Orbs* **1543** Andrea Vesalius publishes first scientific text on human anatomy **1550** Vasari publishes first edition of *Lives of the Artists* **1555** Olympic Academy founded in Vicenza	**1561** Francesco Guicciardini begins publishing *History of Italy* **1562** Vasari founds Accademia del Disegno, Florence **1570** Palladio publishes *The Four Books of Architecture* **1575** Tasso at work on *Jerusalem Liberated* **1577** Charles Borromeo publishes treatise on church decoration **1596** Shakespeare's *Romeo and Juliet*
1431 Doge Francesco Foscari commissions the decoration of the Cappella Nova, St. Mark's, Venice **1442** Cosimo de' Medici commits to paying for construction of nave of San Lorenzo, Florence **1447** Ludovico Gonzaga commissions Lancelot frescoes in Mantua from Pisanello **1452** Alfonso of Aragon commissions Sala dei Baroni, Naples, from Guillermo Sagrera **1462** Pope Pius II transforms birthplace into Pienza	**1469** Abbot Donà commissions San Michele in Isola from Mauro Codussi **1476** Federigo da Montefeltro commissions intarsia decorations for his *studiolo* in Urbino **1477–81** Pope Sixtus IV builds the Sistine Chapel **1481** Monks of San Donato, Scopeto, commission *Adoration of the Magi* from Leonardo da Vinci **1485** Scuola di San Marco, Venice, commissions new headquarters from Mauro Codussi after fire **c. 1493** Ludovico Sforza commissions new tribune for Santa Maria delle Grazie, Milan, probably from Bramante	**1506** Pope Julius II breaks ground for new St. Peter's **1508** Michelangelo signs contract with Julius II for Sistine Ceiling **1516** Abbot Germano Gaiole commissions *Assumption Altarpiece* from Titian for high altar, Santa Maria Gloriosa dei Frari, Venice **1525** The Medici commission *Hercules and Cacus* from Baccio Bandinelli	**1534** Pope Paul III commissions *Last Judgment* for Sistine Chapel from Michelangelo **1537** Venetian government commissions Library from Jacopo Sansovino **1548** Titian in Augsburg working for Emperor Charles V **c. 1560** Duke Cosimo commissions Uffizi from Giorgio Vasari	**1565** Cosimo de' Medici and Giorgio Vasari strip and refurbish Santa Croce and Santa Maria Novella, Florence **1566** Benedictines of San Giorgio Magggiore, Venice, commission new church from Palladio **1568** Cardinal Farnese provides funds for the Gesù **1573** Charles Borromeo orders rebuilding of San Lorenzo Maggiore, Milan

City Plans

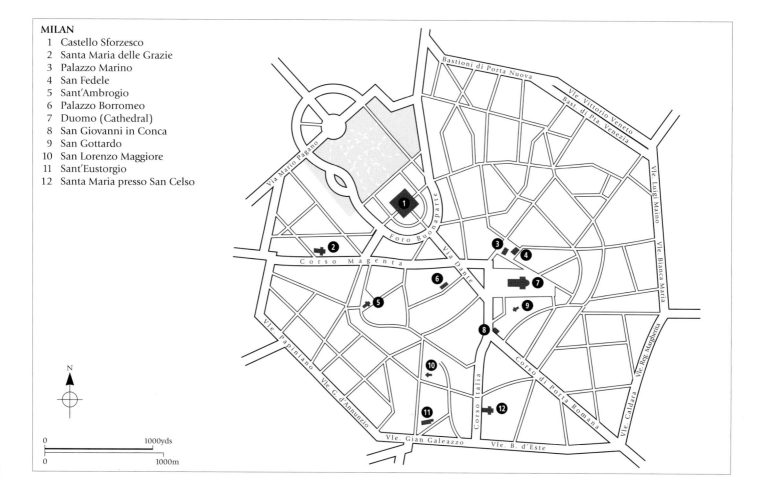

NAPLES

1 San Giovanni a Carbonara
2 Santa Maria Donna Regina
3 Duomo (Cathedral)
4 Castel Capuano
5 San Lorenzo Maggiore
6 San Domenico
7 Sant'Angelo a Nilo
8 Santa Chiara (Franciscan)
9 Palazzo Penna
10 Sant'Eligio
11 Piazza del Mercato
12 Santa Maria dell'Incoronata
13 Castel Nuovo (Castello Aragonese)
14 Castel dell'Ovo

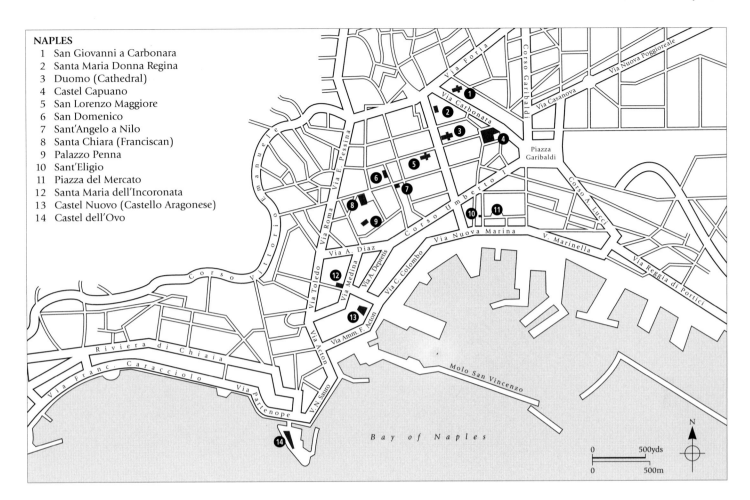

ROME

1 Villa Giulia
2 Porta del Popolo
3 Santa Maria del Popolo
4 Sistine Chapel
5 St. Peter's Basilica
6 Vatican Palace and Belvedere Courtyard
7 Castel Sant'Angelo
8 Acqua Felice (fountain)
9 San Bernardo alle Terme
10 Hospital of Santo Spirito
11 Sant'Agostino
12 Column of Marcus Aurelius
13 Santa Maria della Pace
14 Santa Maria sopra Minerva
    (Dominican)
15 Pantheon
16 Santi Apostoli
17 Santa Maria Maggiore
18 Cancelleria
19 Palazzo Venezia and San Marco
20 Il Gesù (Jesuit)
21 Column of Trajan
22 Palazzo Farnese
23 Imperial Fora
24 Capitoline Hill
25 Tor dei Specchi
26 Colosseum
27 Porta Maggiore
28 San Pietro in Montorio
29 Santa Maria in Trastevere
30 Santa Cecilia in Trastevere
31 San Stefano Rotondo
32 Lateran Palace
33 San Giovanni in Laterano
34 Sancta Sanctorum (Scala Santa)

34 Sancta Sanctorum
    (Scala Santa)
35 Santa Croce in
    Gerusalemme

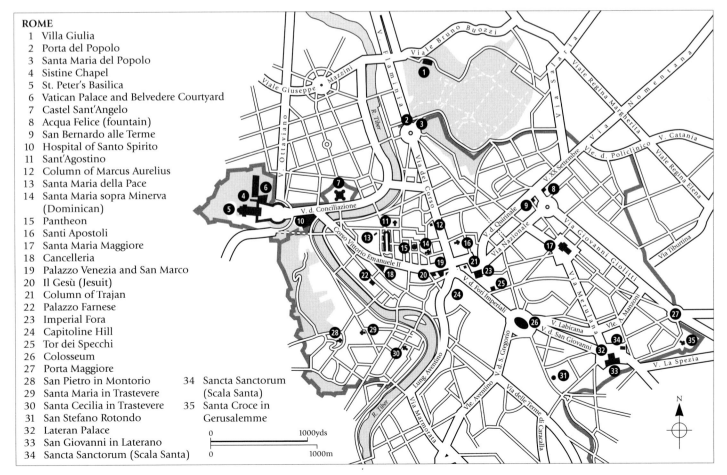

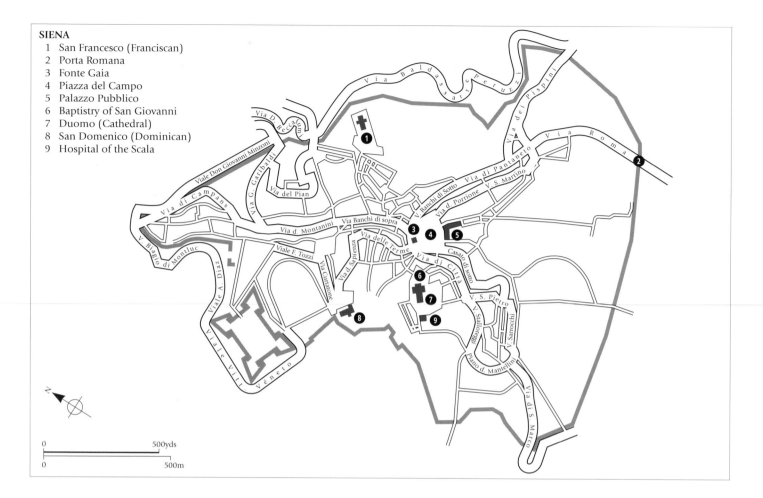

SIENA

1 San Francesco (Franciscan)
2 Porta Romana
3 Fonte Gaia
4 Piazza del Campo
5 Palazzo Pubblico
6 Baptistry of San Giovanni
7 Duomo (Cathedral)
8 San Domenico (Dominican)
9 Hospital of the Scala

0   500yds
0   500m

VENICE

1 San Michele in Isola
2 San Giobbe
3 Ca' d'Oro
4 Scuola Grande di San Marco
5 Santi Giovanni e Paolo (Dominican)
6 Scuola Grande di San Giovanni Evangelista
7 Scuola Grande di San Rocco
8 Santa Maria Gloriosa dei Frari (Franciscan)
9 Ponte Rialto
10 Palazzo Foscari
11 San Zaccaria
12 Arsenal
13 San Pietro di Castello
14 St. Mark's
15 Piazza San Marco
16 Campanile and Loggetta
17 Library (Biblioteca Marciana)
18 Mint (Zecca)
19 Piazzetta San Marco
20 Doge's Palace (Palazzo Ducale)
21 Palazzo Corner della Ca' Grande
22 Accademia (formerly Scuola Grande della Carità)
23 San Giorgio Maggiore
24 Il Redentore

0   1000yds
0   1000m

Glossary

a secco See fresco.

aedicule A decorative architectural frame around a door, window, or niche consisting of an entablature and pediment supported by two columns or pilasters.

all'antica In Greek or Roman classical style.

ambulatory A vaulted passageway or aisle that leads around the apse of a Christian church.

antipope Any pope elected in opposition to another held to have been canonically chosen.

apse A semicircular or polygonal recess at the end of the major axis of a Roman basilica or Christian church.

architectonic Relating to architecture or resembling the spatial and structural aspects peculiar to architecture.

architrave The lowest part of an entablature, beneath the frieze and cornice, resting directly on the capital of a column; also the frame over a door or window.

articulated Defined, normally by distinct architectural features.

attached column A column that is attached to a background wall and is therefore not completely cylindrical; also referred to as an engaged column.

attic story In classical architecture the story above the main entablature.

Augustan Relating to the reign of the Roman Emperor Augustus from 27 B.C.E. to 14 C.E.

baldacchino A canopy placed over an honorific or sacred space such as a throne or church altar.

banderole A narrow handheld scroll, usually flowing free as if blown by the wind, and normally carrying an inscription.

barrel vault A ceiling in the form of a semicircular vault.

basilica In ancient Roman architecture, a large rectangular public building with an open interior space, usually with side aisles separated from the main space by rows of evenly spaced columns. The structure was later adopted as a building type for Early Christian churches.

basket capital A column capital decorated with a latticework pattern resembling basketweave.

bole A red claylike pigment used as the ground for gold leaf.

burin A tool with a sharp, triangular-shaped metal point used for cutting lines to be printed from metal and wood blocks.

cantoria The Italian word for a balcony for singers and musicians.

cartoon A full-scale preparatory drawing on paper which is used to transfer the outline of a design onto the surface to be painted; from the Italian "cartone," meaning heavy paper.

cassone Italian for "large case" or "large chest," referring to carved and painted chests used to hold clothing, often given as gifts to a prospective bride for her dowry by her future husband.

centering Temporary wooden scaffolding and supports erected in the construction of vaults, arches, or domes.

chancel The eastern portion of a Christian church, reserved for the clergy and choir and often separated from the main body of the church by a screen, rail, or steps. The term is also used to describe the entire east end of a church beyond the crossing.

chiaroscuro An Italian word literally meaning "light-dark," used to describe the dramatic contrast of light and dark in painting to create effects of three-dimensionality.

ciborium A type of *baldacchino*: a canopy supported on columns over the altar or other place of sacred significance in a Christian church; also used to refer to small architectural wall enclosures used for the reservation of the elements of the Eucharist between religious services.

cloisonné A multicolored surface made by pouring enamels into compartments outlined by bent wire fillets or strips.

coffering Recessed panels, square or polygonal, that decorate a vault, ceiling, or the underside of an arch (soffit).

colorito A term characterizing Venetian painting of the sixteenth century where form is created by the pre-application of pigment on the painted surface and by the building of forms through a successive layering and interaction of pigment; opposite of *disegno*.

Composite order Architectural system using a column capital consisting of two rows of acanthus leaves at the bottom and Ionic volutes above.

compound pier A pier or large column with several engaged shafts or pilasters attached to it on one or all sides. These structural supports are found in both Romanesque and Gothic architecture.

console A bracket, usually formed of volute scrolls, projecting from a wall to support a lintel or other member.

contrapposto Italian for "set against" or "counter-posed." Derived from ancient art, it gives freedom to the representation of the human figure by counterpoising parts of the body around a central vertical axis. Most of the weight is placed on one leg with an S-curve in the torso. Normally movement of engaged and relaxed parts alternates left-right through the figure.

Corinthian column An order in Greek architecture characterized in part by its elongated and refined forms, including column capitals composed of deeply cut and symmetrically arranged acanthus leaves.

cornice The uppermost, projecting portion of an entablature; also the crowning ornamental molding along the top of a wall or arch.

counter-maniera Term used to indicate a style opposed to Mannerism, using direct and naturalistic presentation of the subject.

crenellation A pattern of open notches built into the top parapets and battlements of many fortified buildings for the purpose of defense.

crocket In Gothic architecture, a decorative feature, usually shaped like a curling leaf, projecting at regular intervals from the angles of spires, pinnacles, and gables.

cruciform Shaped like a cross, such as the plan of a church.

cupola A rounded, convex roof or vaulted ceiling (dome).

cusping In architecture, a pair of curves tangent to the line defining the area, decorated and meeting at a point within the area.

diaper A pattern of small, identical, nonfigurative, usually geometrical, units adopted as a means of covering a surface or as a background for figurative work.

diaphragm arch A transverse arch across the nave of a church partitioning the roof and the space of the building into sections.

diptych A work consisting of two images (usually paintings on panel) side by side, traditionally hinged to be opened and closed.

disegno Literally "design" or "drawing," a term used in central Italian art to describe the creation of figures and volume through a sharply defined drawn line; opposite of *colorito*.

elevation The vertical organization of the face of a building; also an architectural drawing made as if projecting on a vertical plane to show any one side, exterior or interior, of a building.

entablature The upper part of a classical architectural order above the columns and capitals and comprising architrave, frieze, and cornice.

entasis The slight swelling in the shaft of a column as it tapers toward the top to give added vertical thrust to the column and a visual vitality to the form.

ex voto An offering made by a worshiper to the deity or saint being prayed to, either in thanksgiving or supplication.

fictive Surrogate, or painted to look as if the image represents an actual object; normally used as part of wall decorations, for example feigning tapestry or niches.

figural (or figurative) Representing the likeness of a recognizable human (or animal) figure; also a work whose principal subject consists of representations of human beings.

fresco A wall painting technique in which pigments are applied to a surface of wet plaster (called *buon fresco*). Painting on dry plaster (called *fresco a secco*) is a less durable technique as the paint tends to flake off with time.

frieze The flat middle division of an entablature usually decorated with moldings, sculpture, or painting. Also used loosely to describe any sculpted or decorated horizontal band.

gonfaloniere Literally the standard-bearer or the person who carried the flag (*gonfalone*), a term referring to an elected head of a republican state or, sometimes, a confraternal order.

gesso A fluid white coating of finely ground plaster and glue used to prepare a painting surface (such as a wooden panel for tempera painting) so that it will accept paint readily and allow controlled brushstrokes.

giant (colossal) order A form of architectural decoration in which applied columns or pilasters extend over more than one story of a building from the ground to the cornice, uniting the entire structure in a single compositional scheme.

glair A glaze or size made of egg white.

grisaille A painting in various shades of gray, sometimes suggesting low relief.

Hellenistic Relating to the time from the death of Alexander the Great in 323 B.C.E. to the first century B.C.E.

hemicycle A semicircle or semicircular structure.

herm Used in architectural decoration, this is a rectangular plain pillar which terminates in the head and torso of a human.

iconography Visual conventions and symbols used to portray ideas and identify individuals and attributes in a work of art.

illusionistic A type of art in which space and objects are intended to appear real by the use of artistic devices such as perspective and foreshortening.

impasto Oil paint thickly applied.

impost block A decorative block with splayed sides placed between the abacus and capital on a column or pier.

intarsia The decoration of wood surfaces (panelled walls, chests, and choirstalls) with inlaid designs created from colorful and contrasting woods and other materials such as ivory, metal, and shell.

lancet window A tall, slender window with a sharply pointed arch (like a lance), common in Gothic architecture.

lantern In architecture, a small circular turret with windows all around, crowning a roof or dome.

loggia The Italian term for a room or small building open on one or more sides with columns to support the roof.

lost-wax method Also known as *cire-perdue*. A method of casting metal such as bronze by a process in which wax is used to coat an original rough model, which is then worked in finer detail. The finished model is coated with plaster, then heated so that the wax melts away, leaving an empty space into which molten metal is poured.

mandorla An upright almond (*mandorla*) shape representing a radiance of light in which a sacred figure, such as Christ, is represented.

Mannerism A style most commonly associated with the arts of central Italy during the sixteenth century, characterized by its extreme artificiality and elegance.

martyrium A church or other building erected on a site sacred to Christianity, symbolizing a place of martyrdom or marking the grave of a martyr.

membering The subordinate architectural structural features of a building.

metope In architecture, the square area between the triglyphs of a Doric frieze, often decorated with relief sculpture.

narthex An enclosed rectangular porch or vestibule at the main entrance of a church which extends across the entire façade of the structure.

niche A concave recess in a wall, often used to house statuary.

nymphaeum A form of secluded antique garden architecture often involving pools or fountains, meant to call up the playful woodland environments of nymphs.

oculus In architecture, a circular opening in a wall or dome.

Opera The board of works of a cathedral, normally presided over by an official—sometimes elected, sometimes appointed—called an *operaio*.

order One of the architectural systems (Doric, Ionic, Corinthian) used by the Greeks and Romans to decorate and define the post and lintel system of construction; also a monastic society or fraternity.

orthogonals Diagonal lines moving to the centric point in a painting or relief, in accordance with the laws of linear perspective.

pastiglia Raised plaster detailing.

pendentive An inverted, concave, triangular area of wall serving as the transition from a square support system to the circular base of a dome.

pietra serena A clear gray Tuscan limestone used in Florence.

pilaster A decorative structural feature looking like a flattened column, projecting slightly from the face of a wall.

plate tracery Decorative framing within an opening, usually a window, in which details are inscribed on the surface rather than cut free.

podestà A chief magistrate in Italian medieval towns and republics.

poesia Literally "poetry," an evocative form of narrative presentation meant to suggest rather than describe possible interpretations.

polychromy The use of many colors in a painting, sculpture, or building; also the coloring applied to the surface of sculpture and architectural details.

polyptych A painting or relief, usually an altarpiece, constructed from multiple panels and sometimes hinged to allow for movable side panels or wings.

predella The platform on which an altarpiece is set, often decorated with narrative sculpture or painting relating to the main subject.

punch work Decorative designs that are stamped onto a surface such as leather, metal, or the gilded plaster background of panel paintings using a handheld metal tool (punch).

putto(i) The Italian term for a full-length cherub figure—normally male.

quatrefoil panel A decorative four-leaf clover shape superimposed on a diamond, used in Gothic architecture and art.

reliquary A receptacle, often made of precious materials, used to house a sacred relic.

rinceau(x) A garland of leafwork.

Romanesque An artistic style of the Middle Ages (c. 1000–1200) drawing its name from the use of rounded arches, tunnel vaults, and other features of Roman architecture. In painting and sculpture works are often broad and monumental, with an emphasis on two- rather than three-dimensional design.

rondels Small round windows, or motifs resembling such apertures.

rustication The appearance of rough-cut masonry blocks on a wall achieved by beveling edges so that the apparent joints are indented.

sacra conversazione Italian term for "sacred conversation"; in art, the depiction of the Virgin and Child flanked by saints in such a way that they occupy a single pictorial space.

sacristy In a Christian church, the room where the priest's vestments and the sacred vessels are housed.

schiacciato Italian for "squashed," referring to very thin reliefs often barely incised on a surface.

scuola A Venetian term for a religious confraternity of laypeople.

sgraffito A decorative technique in which a surface layer of paint, plaster, or slip is incised to reveal a ground of contrasting color.

soffit The underside of an arch.

squinch An arch or system of concentrically wider and gradually projecting arches placed diagonally to support a polygonal or circular dome on a square base.

stele An upright slab with an inscription or relief carving, usually commemorative.

stringcourse A continuous horizontal band decorating the face of a wall.

tabernacle A canopied recess containing an image; or an ornamental receptacle for the consecrated host, usually in the form of a miniature building placed on an altar.

tempera Paint consisting of pigment dissolved in water and mixed with a binding medium, usually the yolk (but sometimes also the white) of an egg. Egg tempera was the principal technique for panel painting from the thirteenth to the fifteenth centuries, when it was gradually superseded by oil painting.

tempietto A small temple-like structure, usually round or polygonal.

terra verde Italian for "green earth," the color used for the underpaint of flesh tones in tempera painting; sometimes used for monochrome painting.

tondo A painting or relief of circular shape.

trabeated An architectural system using a horizontal beam over supports (synonymous with post and lintel).

tribune The apse of a basilica; also an alternative term for a gallery—the upper story over an aisle—in a Romanesque or Gothic church.

triglyph In a Doric frieze, the rectangular area between the metopes, decorated with three vertical grooves.

trilobed Having three lobes.

triptych A painting, usually an altarpiece, made up of three panels, the center one of which is usually larger than the other two.

trompe-l'oeil An illusionistic painting intended to "deceive the eye" into believing that the subject depicted actually exists in three-dimensional reality.

truss In architecture, a framework of wood or metal beams, usually based on triangles, used to support a roof or bridge.

two-point perspective In linear perspective drawings, the representation of a three-dimensional form viewed from an angle, so that the lines formed by its horizontal edges will appear to diminish to two different vanishing points on the horizon.

tympanum A semicircular area formed by the intersection of a wall and an arch or vault; often decorated with sculpture.

vault An arched ceiling or roof made of stone, brick, or concrete which spans an interior space.

verism A style capturing the exterior likeness of an object or person, usually by rendering its visible details in a finely executed, meticulous manner.

volute The spiral scroll on capitals of Ionic columns.

Bibliography

General

Ames-Lewis, Francis. *The Intellectual Life of the Early Renaissance Artist*. New Haven: Yale University Press, 2000.

Barkan, Leonard. *Unearthing the Past: Archaeology and Aesthetics in the Making of Renaissance Culture*. New Haven: Yale University Press, 1999.

Barker, Emma, Nick Webb, and Kim Woods. *The Changing Status of the Artist*. New Haven/London: Yale University Press, 1999.

Barolsky, Paul. *Michelangelo's Nose: A Myth and its Maker*. University Park: Pennsylvania State University Press, 1990.

——. *Why Mona Lisa Smiles and Other Tales by Vasari*. University Park: Pennsylvania State University Press, 1991.

——. *Giotto's Father and the Family of Vasari's Lives*. University Park: Pennsylvania State University Press, 1992.

Baxandall, Michael. *Giotto and the Orators, Humanist Observers of Painting in Italy and the Discovery of Pictorial Composition 1350–1450*. Oxford: Clarendon Press, 1971.

Blunt, Anthony. *Artistic Theory in Italy 1450–1600*. Oxford: Clarendon Press, 1959.

Bober, Phyllis Pray, and Ruth Olitski Rubinstein. *Renaissance Artists and Antique Sculpture: A Handbook of Sources*. New York: Oxford University Press, 1986.

Burckhardt, Jacob. *The Civilization of the Renaissance in Italy*. Oxford: Phaidon, 1965.

Cole, Alison. *Virtue and Magnificence: Art of the Italian Renaissance Courts*. New York: Abrams/Prentice Hall, 1995.

Cole, Bruce. *The Renaissance Artist at Work: from Pisano to Titian*. New York: Harper & Row, 1983.

Cropper, Elizabeth. "On Beautiful Women, Parmigianino, *Petrarchismo*, and the Vernacular Style," *Art Bulletin*, 58, 1976, 374–94.

Freedberg, David. *The Power of Images*. Chicago: University of Chicago Press, 1989.

Gilbert, Creighton E. *Italian Art 1400–1500*. Englewood Cliffs, NJ: Prentice Hall, 1980.

——. "What Did the Renaissance Patron Buy?," *Renaissance Quarterly*, 51, 1998, 392–450.

Goldthwaite, Richard A. *Wealth and the Demand for Art in Italy 1300–1600*. Baltimore: Johns Hopkins University Press, 1993.

Hartt, Frederick. *History of Italian Renaissance Art* (fourth edition revised by David G. Wilkins). New York: Harry N. Abrams Inc. and Prentice Hall, 1994.

Jacobs, Fredrika H. *Defining the Renaissance Virtuosa: Women Artists and the Language of Art History and Criticism*. New York: Cambridge University Press, 1997.

Kempers, Bram. *Painting, Power, and Patronage: The Rise of the Professional Artist in the Italian Renaissance*. London: Penguin, 1992.

Kent, F.W. and Patricia Simmons, with J.C. Eade. *Patronage, Art and Society in Renaissance Italy*. Oxford: Oxford University Press, 1987.

King, Catherine. *Renaissance Women Patrons: Wives and Widows in Italy, c. 1300–1550*. Manchester: Manchester University Press, 1998.

Klein, Robert, and Henri Zerner. *Italian Art 1500–1600*. Englewood Cliffs, NJ: Prentice Hall, 1966.

Larner, John. *Culture and Society in Italy, 1290–1420*. London: Batsford, 1971.

Lazzaro, Claudia. *The Italian Renaissance Garden*. New Haven: Yale University Press, 1990.

Martindale, Andrew. *The Rise of the Artist in the Middle Ages and the Early Renaissance*. New York: McGraw-Hill, 1972.

Norman, Diana (ed.). *Siena, Florence and Padua: Art, Society and Religion 1280–1400* (2 vols.). London/New Haven: Yale University Press, 1995.

Panofsky, Erwin. *Renaissance and Renascences*. New York: Harper & Row, 1960.

Parshall, Peter. "Imago contrafacta: Images and Facts in the Northern Renaissance," *Art History*, 16, 1993, 554–79.

Shearman, John. *Mannerism*. Harmondsworth/Baltimore: Penguin, 1967.

Smyth, Craig Hugh. *Mannerism and Maniera*. Locust Valley, NY: J.J. Augustin, 1961.

Steinberg, Leo. *The Sexuality of Christ in Renaissance Art and Modern Oblivion*. New York: Pantheon, 1983.

Tinagli, Paola. *Women in Italian Renaissance Art*. Manchester: Manchester University Press, 1997.

Vasari, Giorgio. *Lives of the Most Eminent Painters, Sculptors, and Architects* (3 vols., trans. Gaston Du C. de Vere, ed. Kenneth Clark). New York: Abrams, 1979.

Verdon, Timothy, and John Henderson. *Christianity and the Renaissance*. Syracuse: Syracuse University Press, 1990.

Waley, Daniel. *The Italian City-Republics*. New York/Toronto: McGraw-Hill, 1969.

Warnke, Martin. *The Court Artist, On the Ancestry of the Modern Artist* (trans. David McLintock). Cambridge: Cambridge University Press, 1993.

Welch, Evelyn S. *Art and Society in Italy, 1350–1500*. Oxford: Oxford University Press, 1997.

White, John. *Art and Architecture in Italy, 1250–1400* (3rd ed.). New Haven: Yale University Press Pelican History of Art, 1993.

——. *Studies in Late Medieval Italian Art*. London: Pindar Press, 1984.

Wohl, Hellmut. *The Aesthetics of Italian Renaissance Art: A Reconsideration of Style*. New York: Cambridge University Press, 1999.

Architecture

Goldthwaite, Richard A. *The Building of Renaissance Florence: An Economic and Social History*. Baltimore: Johns Hopkins University Press, 1980.

Heydenreich, Ludwig H., and Wolfgang Lotz. *Architecture in Italy 1400–1600*. Harmondsworth: Penguin, 1974.

Toker, Franklin L. "Building on Paper: the Role of Architectural Drawings in Late-Medieval Italy," in *L'Art et les Révolutions. Section 8. Table ronde: Technique, structure et style de l'architecture gothique* (ed. A.M. Romanini), *XXVIIe congrès international d'histoire de l'art*. Strasbourg: Société Alsacienne pour le Développement de l'Histoire de l'Art, 1992, 31–50.

Wagner-Rieger, Renate. *Die italienische Baukunst zu Beginn der Gotik* (Part II *Süd- und Mittelitalien*). Graz-Cologne: H. Bohlaus, 1957.

Painting, Drawing, and Printmaking

Ames-Lewis, Francis. *Drawing in Early Renaissance Italy*. New Haven/London: Yale University Press, 1981.

Bambach, Carmen C. *Drawing and Painting in the Italian Renaissance Workshop: Theory and Practice, 1300–1600*. New York: Cambridge University Press, 1999.

Baxandall, Michael. *Painting and Experience in Fifteenth-Century Italy: A Primer in the Social History of Pictorial Style*. New York: Oxford University Press, 1988.

Belting, Hans. "The New Role of Narrative in Public Painting of the Trecento: *Historia* and Allegory," *Studies in the History of Art*, 16, 1985, 151–68.

Bomford, David, Jill Dunkerton, Dillian Gordon, and Ashok Roy. *Art in the Making: Italian Painting Before 1400*. London: National Gallery Publications, 1989.

Borsook, Eve. *The Mural Painters of Tuscany from Cimabue to Andrea del Sarto* (2nd ed.). Oxford: Oxford University Press, 1979.

Burckhardt, Jacob. *The Altarpiece in Renaissance Italy*. Cambridge, England/New York: Cambridge University Press, 1988.

Castelnuovo, Enrico (ed.). *La Pittura in Italia: Il Duecento e il Trecento* (2 vols.). Milan: Electa, 1986.

Cennini, Cennino d'Andrea. *The Craftsman's Handbook: Il Libro dell'Arte* (trans. Daniel V. Thompson, Jr.). New York: Dover, 1954.

Dunkerton, Jill, Susan Foister, Dillian Gordon, and Nicholas Penny. *Giotto to Dürer: Early Renaissance Painting in The National Gallery*. New Haven/London: Yale University Press, 1991.

Freedberg, Sidney J. *Painting in Italy, 1500–1600*. Harmondsworth: Penguin, 1990.

Hall, Marcia. *After Raphael: Painting in Central Italy in the Sixteenth Century*. Cambridge: Cambridge University Press, 1998.

Landau, David, and Peter Parshall. *The Renaissance Print, 1470–1550*. New Haven/London: Yale University Press, 1994.

Roettgen, Steffi. *Italian Frescoes*, vol. 1, *The Early Renaissance 1400–1470*; vol. 2, *The Flowering of the Renaissance 1470–1510*. New York: Abbeville, 1996/97.

Smart, Alastair. *The Dawn of Italian Painting, c. 1250–1400*. Ithaca: Cornell University Press, 1978.

Thomas, Anabel. *The Painter's Practice in Renaissance Tuscany*. Cambridge and New York: Cambridge University Press, 1995.

Sculpture

Ames-Lewis, Francis. *Tuscan Marble Carving 1250–1350*. Aldershot: Ashgate, 1997.

Jacobs, Frederika H. "The Construction of a Life: Madonna Properzia de' Rossi *'Scultrice' Bolognese*," *World & Image*, 9, 1993, 122–32.

Pope-Hennessy, John. *Italian Gothic Sculpture* (3rd ed.). Oxford: Phaidon, 1986.

——. *Italian Renaissance Sculpture* (3rd ed.). Oxford: Phaidon, 1986.

——. *Italian High Renaissance and Baroque Sculpture* (3rd ed.). Oxford: Phaidon, 1986.

Seymour, Charles, Jr. *Sculpture in Italy 1400–1500*. Baltimore: Penguin, 1966.

Assisi

Belting, Hans. *Die Oberkirche von San Francesco in Assisi, Ihre Dekoration als Aufgabe und die Genese einer neuen Wandmalerei*. Berlin: Mann, 1977.

Mather, Frank Jewett. *The Isaac Master; A Reconstruction of the Work of Gaddo Gaddi*. Princeton: Princeton University Press, 1932.

Meiss, Millard. *Giotto and Assisi*. New York: Norton, 1960.

Offner, Richard. "Giotto, Non-Giotto," *The Burlington Magazine*, 74, 1939, 259–68 and 75, 1939, 96–113.

Smart, Alastair. *The Assisi Problem and the Art of Giotto*. Oxford: Clarendon Press, 1971.

Stubblebine, James H. *Assisi and the Rise of Vernacular Art*. New York: Harper & Row, 1985.

White, John. *The Birth and Rebirth of Pictorial Space*. New York: Harper & Row, 1972.

——. "The Date of the 'St. Francis Legend' at Assisi," *The Burlington Magazine*, 98, 1956, 344–51.

Wood, Jeryldene. "Perceptions of Holiness in Thirteenth-Century Italian Painting: Clare of Assisi," *Art History*, 14, 1991, 301–28.

Ferrara and Bologna

Bull, David. "Conservation Treatment and Interpretation," *Studies in the History of Art*, 40, 1990, 21–52.

Colantuono, Anthony. "*Dies Alcyoniae*: The Invention of Bellini's Feast of the Gods," *Art Bulletin*, 73, 1991, 237–56.

Goodgal, Dana. "The Camerino of Alfonso I d'Este," *Art History*, 1, 1978, 162–90.

Gould, Cecil. *The Paintings of Correggio*. Ithaca: Cornell University Press, 1976.

Hope, Charles. "The 'Camerini d'Alabastro' of Alfonso d'Este," *The Burlington Magazine*, 113, 1971, 641–50 and 712–21.

Lippincott, Kristen. "The Iconography of the *Salone dei Mesi* and the Study of Latin Grammar in Fifteenth-Century Ferrara," *La corte di Ferrara e il suo mecenatismo 1441–1598, The Court of Ferrara & its Patronage, Atti del convegno internazionale Copenhagen maggio 1987* (ed. Marianne Pade, Lene Waage Petersen, Daniela Quarta). Copenhagen, 1990, 93–109.

Longhi, Roberto. *Officina ferrarese*. Florence: Sansoni, 1968.

Macioce, Stefania. "Le 'Borsiade' di Tito Vespasiano Strozzi e la 'Sala dei Mesi' di Palazzo Schifanoia," *Annuario dell'Istituto di Storia dell'Arte, Università degli Studi di Roma "La Sapienza,"* N.S. 2, 1982–3, 3–13.

Molfino, Alessandra Mottola, and Mauro Natale (ed.). *Le muse e il principe, Arte di corte nel Rinascimento padano* (Exhibition Museo Poldi-Pezzoli, Milan, September 20 to December 1, 1991, 2 vols.). Milan, 1991.

Rosenberg, Charles M. "The Sala degli Stucchi in the Palazzo Schifanoia in Ferrara," *Art Bulletin*, 61, 1979, 377–84.

——. "Courtly Decorations and the Decorum of Interior Space," in *La corte e lo spazio: Ferrara estense* (ed. Giuseppe Papagno and Amedeo Quondam). Rome: Bulzoni, 1982, 529–44.

——. "Per un atlante di Schifanoia, Borsian and Ferrarese imagery in the heavenly zone in the Salone dei mesi," *Schifanoia, Notizie dell'Istituto di studi rinascimentali di Ferrara*, 5, 1988, 43–9.

——. *The Este Monuments and Urban Development in Renaissance Ferrara*. Cambridge and New York: Cambridge University Press, 1997.

Ruhmer, Eberhard. *Tura, Paintings and Drawings*. London: Phaidon, 1958.

Sheard, Wendy Stedman. "Antonio Lombardo's Reliefs for Alfonso d'Este's *Studio di Marmi*: Their Significance and Impact on Titian," in *Titian 500* (Studies in the History of Art, 45, Center for Advanced Study in the Visual Arts, Symposium Papers XXV), Hanover/London: University Presses of New England, 315–57.

Shearman, John. "Alfonso d'Este's Camerino," *Il se rendit en Italie: Etudes offerts à André Chastel*, Rome/Paris: CNRS, 1987, 209–29.

Travagli, Anna Maria Visser. *Ferrara, Palazzo Schifanoia a Ferrara e Palazzina Marfisa a Ferrara*. Milan, 1991.

Tuohy, Thomas. *Herculean Ferrara: Ercole d'Este (1471–1505) and the Invention of a Ducal Capital*. Cambridge and New York: Cambridge University Press, 1996.

Florence

General

Brucker, Gene. *Renaissance Florence*. New York: John Wiley, 1969.

Fremantle, Richard. *Florentine Gothic Painters from Giotto to Masaccio*. London: Secker & Warburg, 1975.

Paatz, Walter. *Die Kirchen von Florenz* (5 vols.). Frankfurt am Main: V. Klostermann, 1952–5.

Turner, Richard. *Florence, The Invention of a New Art*. New York: Harry N. Abrams, 1997.

Wackernagel, Martin. *The World of the Florentine Renaissance Artist: Projects and Patrons, Workshop and Art Market* (trans. Alison Luchs). Princeton: Princeton University Press, 1981.

Thirteenth and Fourteenth Centuries

Baldini, Umberto, and Bruno Nardini. *Santa Croce: La Basilica, Le Cappelle, I Chiostri, Il Museo*. Florence: Centro Internazionale del Libro, 1983.

—— (ed.). *Santa Maria Novella: Kirche, Kloster und Kreuzgänge*. Stuttgart: Urachaus, 1982.

Chiellini, Monica. *Cimabue*. Florence: Scala, 1988.

Gardner, Julian. "Andrea di Bonaiuto and the Chapterhouse Frescoes in Santa Maria Novella," *Art History*, 2, 1979, 107–38.

Hueck, Irene. *Das Programm der Kuppelmosaiken im Florentiner Baptisterium.* Dissertation Ludwig-Maximilans-Universität, Munich, 1962.

Kent, F.W. "The Black Death of 1348 in Florence: A New Contemporary Account," in *Renaissance Studies in Honor of Craig Hugh Smyth* (ed. Andrew Morrough, Fiorella Superbi Giofredi, Piero Morselli, and Eve Borsook). Florence: Giunti Barbèra, 1985, 117–28.

Ladis, Andrew. *Taddeo Gaddi: Critical Reappraisal and Catalogue Raisonné.* Columbia: University of Missouri Press, 1982.

Meiss, Millard. *Painting in Florence and Siena after the Black Death.* Princeton: Princeton University Press, 1951.

Moskowitz, Anita. *The Sculpture of Andrea and Nino Pisano.* Cambridge: Cambridge University Press, 1986.

Romano, Serena. "Due affreschi del Cappellone degli Spagnoli: Problemi iconologici," *Storia dell'arte*, 28, 1976, 181–213.

Tintori, Leonetto, and Eve Borsook. *Giotto. The Peruzzi Chapel.* New York: Abrams, 1961.

Trachtenberg, Marvin. "What Brunelleschi Saw: Monument and Site at the Palazzo Vecchio in Florence," *Journal of the Society of Architectural Historians*, 47, 1988, 14–44.

Fifteenth Century

Alberti, Leon Battista. *On Painting* (trans. Cecil Grayson, ed. Martin Kemp). London: Penguin, 1991.

Ames-Lewis, Francis (ed.). *Cosimo 'il Vecchio' de' Medici 1389–1464.* Oxford: Clarendon Press, 1992.

Baskins, Cristelle. "Donatello's Bronze David: Grillanda, Goliath, Groom?" *Studies in Iconography*, 15, 1993, 113–34.

Beck, James. *Masaccio: The Documents.* Locust Valley, NY: J.J. Augustin, 1978.

Bennett, Bonnie, and David G. Wilkins. *Donatello.* Oxford: Phaidon, 1984.

Bent, George R. "A Patron for Lorenzo Monaco's Uffizi *Coronation of the Virgin*," *Art Bulletin*, 82, 2000, 348–54.

Beyer, Andreas, and Bruce Boucher (ed.). *Piero de' Medici "il Gottoso" (1416–1469).* Berlin: Akademie Verlag, 1993.

Borsook, Eve. "L'Hakwood [sic] d'Uccello et la *Vie de Fabius Maximus* de Plutarque," *Revue de l'art*, 55, 1982, 44–51.

—— and Johannes Offerhaus. *Francesco Sassetti and Ghirlandaio at Santa Trinita.* Doornspijk: Davaco Publishers, 1981.

Boskovits, Miklòs. *Pittura Fiorentina alla vigilia del Rinascimento.* Florence: Edam, 1975.

Brown, David Alan. *Leonardo da Vinci: Origins of a Genius.* New Haven: Yale University Press, 1998.

Butterfield, Andrew. "Verrocchio's Christ and St. Thomas: Chronology, Iconography and Political Context," *The Burlington Magazine*, CXXXIV, 1992, 225–33.

Cherubini, Giovanni, and Giovanni Fanelli (ed.). *Il Palazzo Medici Riccardi di Firenze.* Florence: Giunti, 1990.

Dempsey, Charles. *The Portrayal of Love: Botticelli's Primavera and Humanist Culture at the Time of Lorenzo the Magnificent.* Princeton: Princeton University Press, 1992.

Edgerton, Samuel Y., Jr. *The Renaissance Rediscovery of Linear Perspective.* New York: Basic Books, 1975.

Eisenberg, Marvin. *Lorenzo Monaco.* Princeton: Princeton University Press, 1989.

Friedman, David. "The Burial Chapel of Filippo Strozzi in Santa Maria Novella in Florence," *Arte*, 9, 1970, 109–31.

Goldthwaite, Richard. "The Building of the Strozzi Palace: The Construction Industry in Renaissance Florence," *Studies in Medieval and Renaissance History*, X, 1973, 97–194.

——. *Wealth and the Demand for Art in Italy 1300–1600.* Baltimore: Johns Hopkins University Press, 1993.

Haines, Margaret. "Brunelleschi and Bureaucracy: The Tradition of Public Patronage at the Florentine Cathedral," *I Tatti Studies*, 3, 1989, 89–125.

Herlihy, David, and Christiane Klapisch-Zuber. *Tuscans and Their Families; a Study of the Florentine Catasto of 1427.* New Haven/London: Yale University Press, 1985 (abridged trans. of *Les Toscans et leurs families*).

Hood, William. *Fra Angelico at San Marco.* London/New York: BCA, 1993.

Hyman, Isabelle. "The Venice Connection: Questions about Brunelleschi and the East," in *Florence and Venice: Comparisons and Relations* (ed. Nicolai Rubinstein and Craig Hugh Smyth), Florence: La Nuova Italia, 1979, I, 193–208.

Janson, H.W. *The Sculpture of Donatello.* Princeton: Princeton University Press, 1957.

Joannides, Paul. *Masaccio and Masolino: A Complete Catalogue.* London: Phaidon, 1993.

Kent, Dale. *Cosimo de' Medici and the Florentine Renaissance: The Patron's Oeuvre.* London: Yale University Press, 2000.

Kent, W.F. "Più superba di quella di Lorenzo: Courtly and Family Interest in the Building of Filippo Strozzi's Palace," *The Renaissance Quarterly*, 1977, 311–23.

Krautheimer, Richard. *Lorenzo Ghiberti.* Princeton: Princeton University Press, 1956.

Lavin, Irving. "Donatello's Bronze Pulpits in San Lorenzo and the Early Christian Revival," in Lavin, *Past-Present; Essays on Historicism in Art From Donatello to Picasso.* Berkeley/Los Angeles: University of California Press, 1993, 1–27.

Lightbown, Ronald. *Botticelli* (2 vols.). Berkeley: University of California Press, 1978.

——. *Sandro Botticelli: Life and Work.* New York: Abbeville, n.d.

Manca, Joseph. "The Gothic Leonardo: Towards a Reassessment of the Renaissance," *Artibus et Historiae*, 34, 1996, 121–58.

Manetti, Antonio di Tuccio. *The Life of Brunelleschi* (ed. Howard Saalman). University Park: Pennsylvania State University Press, 1970.

Molho, Anthony. "The Brancacci Chapel: Studies in its Iconography and History," *Journal of the Warburg and Courtauld Institutes*, 40, 1977, 50–98, 322.

Pope-Hennessy, John. *Fra Angelico.* Ithaca: Cornell University Press, 1974.

——. *Donatello.* New York: Abbeville, 1993.

Rubin, Patricia Lee and Alison Wright (eds). *Renaissance Florence: the Art of the 1470s.* London: National Gallery Publications Ltd., 1999.

Ruda, Jeffrey. *Fra Filippo Lippi.* London: Phaidon, 1993.

Saalman, Howard. *Filippo Brunelleschi: The Cupola of Santa Maria del Fiore.* London: Zwemmer, 1980.

——. *Filippo Brunelleschi: The Buildings.* University Park: Pennsylvania State University Press, 1993.

Sale, J. Russell. *Filippino Lippi's Strozzi Chapel in Santa Maria Novella.* New York: Garland, 1979.

Seymour, Charles, Jr. *The Sculpture of Verrocchio.* London: Studio Vista, 1971.

Spencer, John R. *Andrea del Castagno.* Durham: Duke University Press, 1991.

Sperling, Christine M. "Donatello's Bronze 'David' and the Demands of Medici Politics," *Burlington Magazine*, 134, 1992, 218–24.

White, John. *The Birth and Rebirth of Pictorial Space.* London: Faber & Faber, 1957.

Wohl, Hellmut. *The Paintings of Domenico Veneziano.* New York: New York University Press, 1980.

Zervas, Diane Finiello. *The Parte Guelfa, Brunelleschi and Donatello.* Locust Valley, NY: J.J. Augustin, 1987.

Sixteenth Century

Ackerman, James. *The Architecture of Michelangelo* (2 vols.). London: Zwemmer, 1961.

Barzman, Karen-edis. *The Florentine Academy and the Early Modern State.* New York: Cambridge University Press, 2000.

Cochrane, Eric. *Florence in the Forgotten Centuries 1527–1800: A history of Florence and the Florentines in the Age of the Grand Dukes.* Chicago: University of Chicago Press, 1973.

J.F. Conway. "Syphilis and Bronzino's London Allegory," *Journal of the Warburg and Courtland Institutes*, 49, 1986, 250–55.

Cox-Rearick, Janet. *Dynasty and Destiny in Medici Art.* Princeton: Princeton University Press, 1984.

——. *Bronzino's Chapel of Eleonora of Toledo in the Palazzo Vecchio.* Berkeley/Los Angeles: University of California Press, 1992.

Crum, Roger. "Cosmos, the World of Cosimo: The Iconography of the Uffizi Façade," *Art Bulletin*, 71, 1989, 237–53.

Forster, Kurt W. "Metaphors of Rule. Political Ideology and History in the Portraits of Cosimo I de' Medici," *Mitteilungen des Kunsthistorischen Institutes in Florenz*, XV, 1971, 65–104.

Franklin, David. *Rosso in Italy*. New Haven/London: Yale University Press, 1994.

Freedberg, Sidney. *Painting of the High Renaissance in Rome and Florence*. New York: Harper & Row, 1972.

Gaston, Robert W. "Love's Sweet Poison: A New Reading of Bronzino's London *Allegory*," *I Tatti Studies*, 4, 1991, 249–88.

——. "Sacred Erotica: The Classical *figura* in Religious Painting of the Early Cinquecento," *International Journal of the Classical Tradition*, 2, Fall 1995, 238–64.

Hall, Marcia. *Renovation and Counter-Reformation: Vasari and Duke Cosimo in Sta Maria Novella and Sta Croce 1565–1577*. Oxford: Clarendon Press, 1979.

Hibbard, Howard. *Michelangelo*. New York: Harper & Row, 1974.

Mendelsohn, Leatrice. "Saturnian Allusions in Bronzino's London *Allegory*," *Saturn from Antiquity to the Renaissance*. M. Ciaralella and A.A. Iannucci (eds). Ottawa: Dove House, 1992, 101–50.

Muccini, Ugo. *The Salone dei Cinquecento of Palazzo Vecchio*. Florence: Le Lettere, 1990.

Parker, Deborah. *Bronzino: Renaissance Painter as Poet*. Cambridge: Cambridge University Press, 2000.

Poma Swank, Annamaria. "Iconografia controriformistica negli altari delle chiese fiorentine di Santa Maria Novella e Santa Croce," *Altari controriformati in Toscana: architettura e arredi*. Carlo Cresti (ed.). Florence: Angelo Pontecorboli Editore, 1997, 95–131.

Rubin, Patricia Lee. *Giorgio Vasari: Art and History*. New Haven: Yale University Press, 1995.

Seymour, Charles, Jr. *Michelangelo's David: A Search for Identity*. Pittsburgh: University of Pittsburgh Press, 1967.

Wilde, Johannes. "The Hall of the Great Council of Florence," *Journal of the Warburg and Courtauld Institutes*, VII, 1944, 65ff. (reprinted, Creighton E. Gilbert, *Renaissance Art*, New York, 1970, 92–132).

Genoa

Caraceni, Fiorella. *A Renaissance Street: Via Garibaldi in Genoa*. Genoa: Sagep, 1993.

Gorse, George, "A Classical Stage for the Old Nobility: The *Strada Nuova* and Sixteenth-Century Genoa," *Art Bulletin*, 79, 1997, 301–27.

—— "The Villa of Andrea Doria in Genoa: Architecture, Gardens, and Suburban Setting," *Journal of the Society of Architectural Historians*, 44, 1985, 18–36.

Mantua

Boorsch, Suzanne, Keith Christiansen, David Ekserdjian, Charles Hope, David Landau, *et al*. *Andrea Mantegna* (Exhibition, Metropolitan Museum of Art, New York, and Royal Academy of Arts, London). Milan: Electa, 1992.

Jones, Mark. "The First Cast Medals and the Limbourgs," *Art History*, 2, 1979, 35–44 and illustration.

Lightbown, Ronald. *Mantegna, with a Complete Catalogue of the Paintings, Drawings and Prints*. Oxford: Phaidon/Christie's, 1986.

Paccagnini, Giovanni. *Pisanello*. London: Phaidon, 1974.

San Juan, Rose Marie. "The Court Lady's Dilemma: Isabella d'Este and Art Collecting in the Renaissance," *The Oxford Art Journal*, 14, 1991, 67–78.

Weiss, Roberto. *Pisanello's Medallion of the Emperor John VIII Palaeologus*. London, 1966.

Woods-Marsden, Joanna. "'Ritratto al Naturale': Questions of Realism and Idealism in Early Renaissance Portraits," *Art Journal*, 46, Fall 1987, 209–16.

——. *The Gonzaga of Mantua and Pisanello's Arthurian Frescoes*. Princeton: Princeton University Press, 1988.

Milan and Lombardy

General

La Storia di Milano. Milan: Treccani, 1953–62.

Fourteenth Century

Baroni, Costantino. *Scultura gotica lombarda*. Milan: E. Bestetti, 1944.

Gilbert, Creighton E. "The Fresco by Giotto in Milan," *Arte lombarda*, 47/48, 1977, 31–72.

Green, Louis. "Galvano Fiamma, Azzone Visconti and the Revival of the Classical Theory of Magnificence," *Journal of the Warburg and Courtauld Institutes*, 53, 1990, 98–113.

Merlini, Elena. "Il trittico eburneo della Certosa di Pavia: Iconografia e committenza," *Arte cristiana*, 73, 1985, 369–84; 74, 1986, 139–54.

Moskowitz, Anita. "Giovanni di Balduccio's Arca di San Pietro Martire: Form and Function," *Arte lombarda*, 96/97, 1991, 7–18.

Pächt, Otto. "Early Italian Nature Studies and the Early Calendar Landscape," *Journal of the Warburg and Courtauld Institutes*, 13, 1950, 13–47.

Sutton, Kay. "Milanese Luxury Books, The Patronage of Bernabò Visconti," *Apollo*, 134, 1991, 322–6.

Toesca, Pietro. *La pittura e la miniatura nella Lombardia*. Turin: Einaudi, 1966.

Fifteenth and Sixteenth Centuries

Sacro e profano nella pittura di Bernardino Luini (Catalogue of exhibition in Luino, August 9 to October 8, 1975). Milan: Silvana Editoriale d'Arte, 1975.

Algeri, Giuliana. "La pittura in Lombardia nel primo Quattrocento," in *La Pittura in Italia, Il Quattrocento*. Milan: Electa, 53–71.

Bernstein, Joanne Gitlin. "A Florentine Patron in Milan: Pigello and the Portinari Chapel," in *Florence and Milan: Comparisons and Relations* (ed. Sergio Bertelli, Nicolai Rubinstein, and Craig Hugh Smyth). Florence: La Nuova Editrice, 1989, 171–200.

—— "Science and Eschatology in the Portinari Chapel," *Arte Lombarda*, n.s. 60, 1981, 33–40.

Brambilla Barcilon, Pinin, and Pietro C. Marani. *Leonardo, L' Ultima Cena*. Milan: Electa, 1999.

Bush, Virginia. "Leonardo's Sforza Monument and Cinquecento Sculpture," *Arte lombarda*, 50, 1978, 47–68.

Castelnuovo, Enrico. *Il ciclo dei Mesi di Torre Aquila a Trento*. Trent, 1987.

Chamberlin, E.R. *The Count of Virtue, Giangaleazzo Visconti, Duke of Milan*. New York: Scribner, 1965.

Clark, Kenneth. *Leonardo da Vinci* (rev. and introduced by Martin Kemp). London: Penguin, 1988.

Cohen, Charles E. "Pordenone's Cremona Passion Scenes and German Art," *Arte lombarda*, 42/43, 1975, 74–96.

Curlee, Kendall. *The Sforza Court, Milan in the Renaissance 1450–1535* (Exhibition, curator Andrea Norris, Archer M. Huntington Art Gallery, University of Texas at Austin, October 27 to December 18, 1988).

de Klerck, Bram. *The Brothers Campi: Images and Devotion: Religious Painting in Sixteenth-Century Lombardy*. Amsterdam: Amsterdam University Press, 1999.

Fiorio, Maria Teresa. *Bambaia, Catalogo completo delle opere*. Florence: Cantini, 1990.

Garrard, Mary D. "Here's Looking at Me: Sofonisba Anguissola and the Problem of the Woman Artist," *Renaissance Quarterly*, 47, 1994, 556–622.

Kemp, Martin. *Leonardo da Vinci: The Marvelous Works of Nature and Man*. Cambridge, MA: Harvard University Press, 1981.

Kiang, Dawson. "Gasparo Visconti's Pasitea and the Sala delle Asse," *Achademia Leonardi Vinci*, 2, 1989, 101–9.

Kirsch, Edith. *Five Illuminated Manuscripts of Giangaleazzo Visconti*. University Park/London: Pennsylvania State University Press, 1991.

McGrath, Thomas. "Color and the Exchange of Ideas between Patron and Artist in Renaissance Italy," *Art Bulletin*, 82, 2000, 298–308.

Martindale, Andrew. "Painting for Pleasure—some lost 15th century secular decorations of Northern Italy," in *The Vanishing Past, Studies of Medieval Art, Liturgy and Metrology presented to Christopher Hohler* (ed. Alan Borh and Andrew Martindale). Oxford: BAR, 1981, 109–31.

Moffitt, John F. "Leonardo's Sala delle Asse and the Primordial Origins of Architecture," *Arte lombarda*, 92/93, 1990/1–2, 76–90.

Morassi, Antonio. "Come il Fogolino restaurò gli affreschi di Torre Aquila a Trento," *Bollettino d'arte*, 8, 1928, 337–67.

Morscheck, Charles R. *Relief Sculpture for the Façade of the Certosa di Pavia, 1473–1499*. New York: Garland, 1978.

Neher, Gabriele. *Moretto and Romanino: Religious Painting in Brescia 1510–1550: Identity in the Shadow of la Serenissima*. Unpublished dissertation, University of Warwick, 2000.

Norris, Andrea S. "The Sforza of Milan," *Schifanoia, Notizie dell'Istituto di studi rinascimentali di Ferrara*, 10, 1990, 19–22.

Ottino Della Chiesa, Angela. *Pittura Lombarda del Quattrocento*. Bergamo: Istituto Italiano d'Arti Grafiche, 1961.

Rossi, Laura Mattioli. *Vincenzo Foppa: La cappella Portinari*. Milan: Federico Motta, 1999.

Shell, Janice. "Il problema della ricostruzione del monumento a Gaston de Foix," *Il Bambaia, Il monumento a Gaston de Foix, Castello Sforzesco di Milano: un capolavoro acquisito*. Milan: Finarte e Longanesi, 1990, 32–61.

Smyth, Carolyn. *Correggio's Frescoes in Parma Cathedral*. Princeton: Princeton University Press, 1997.

Sullivan, Margaret A. "Aertsen's Kitchen and Market Scenes: Audience and Innovation in Northern Art," *Art Bulletin 81*, 1999, 236–66.

Tasso, Francesca. "I Giganti e le vicende della prima scultura del Duomo di Milano," *Arte lombarda*, 92/93, 1990/1–2, 55–62.

Welch, Evelyn S. *Art and Authority in Renaissance Milan*. New Haven: Yale University Press, 1995.

Wind, Barry. "Annibale Carracci's 'Scherzo': The Christ Church *Butcher Shop*," *Art Bulletin*, 58, 1976, 93–6.

Naples

General

Storia di Napoli. Naples: Edizioni del Giglio, 1981–7.

Bacco, Enrico. *Naples, An Early Guide*. New York: Italica Press, 1991.

Causa, Raffaello. *Pittura napoletana dal XV al XIX secolo*. Bergamo: Istituto italiano d'arti grafiche, 1957.

De Seta, Cesare. *Napoli (La città nella storia d'Italia)* (5th ed.). Roma-Bari: Laterza, 1991.

——. *Napoli fra Rinascimento e Illuminismo*. Naples: Electa, 1991.

Thirteenth and Fourteenth Centuries

Bologna, Ferdinando. *I pittori alla corte angioina di Napoli, 1266–1414*. Rome: Ugo Bozzi Editore, 1969.

Bottari, Stefano. "Il monumento alla Regina Isabella nella Cattedrale di Cosenza," *Arte antica e moderna*, 1, 1958, 339–44.

Bruzelius, Caroline A. "'Ad modum franciae' Charles of Anjou and Gothic Architecture in the Kingdom of Sicily," *Journal of the Society of Architectural Historians*, 50, 1991, 402–20.

——. "Hearing is Believing: Clarissan Architecture, c. 1213–1340," *Gesta*, 31, 1992, 83–91.

Buchtal, Hugo. "Historia Troiana," *Studies in the History of Medieval Secular Illustration*. London: Warburg Institute, 1971.

Gardner, Julian. "Saint Louis of Toulouse, Robert of Anjou and Simone Martini," *Zeitschrift für Kunstgeschichte*, 39, 1976, 12–33.

Joost-Gaugier, Christiane L. "Giotto's Hero Cycle in Naples: A Prototype of *Donne Illustre* and a Possible Literary Connection," *Zeitschrift für Kunstgeschichte*, 43, 1980, 311–18.

Leone de Castris, Pierluigi. *Arte di corte nella Napoli angioina*. Florence: Cantini, 1986.

Lipinsky, Angelo. "L'arte orafa napoletana sotto gli Angiò," in *Dante e l'Italia meridionale*, Atti del congresso nazionale di Studi Danteschi, 10–16 October 1965. Florence: Olschki, 1966, 169–215.

Musca, Giosuè, Francesco Tateo, Enrico Annoscia, and Pierluigi Leone de Castris. *La Cultura Angioina* (Civiltà del Mezzogiorno), Cinisello Balsamo (Milan): Silvana Editoriale d'Arte, 1985.

Strazzullo, Franco. *Saggi sul Duomo di Napoli*. Naples, 1959.

Venditti, Arnaldo. "Urbanistica e architettura angioina," in *Storia di Napoli* (vol. 3). Naples: Edizioni del Giglio, 1987, 667ff.

Fifteenth Century

Bentley, Jerry H. *Politics and Culture in Renaissance Naples*. Princeton: Princeton University Press, 1987.

Bologna, Ferdinando. *Napoli e le rotte mediterranee della pittura, Da Alfonso il Magnanimo a Ferdinando il Cattolico*. Naples, 1977.

Castelfranchi Vegas, Liana. "Aspetti e problemi della pittura fiamminga nell'Italia del Quatttrocento," *ACME, Annali della Facoltà di lettere e filosofia dell'Università degli Studi di Milano*, 32, 1, 1979, 81–111.

Causa, Raffaello. *Pittura napoletana dal XV al XIX secolo*. Bergamo: Istituto italiano d'arti grafiche, 1957.

Cirillo Mastrocinque, Adelaide. "Cultura e mode nordiche nell'opera di Baboccio da Piperno," *Napoli nobilissima*, 8, 1969, 16–25.

de Rinaldis, Alda. "Forme tipiche dell'architettura napoletana nella prima metà del Quattrocento," *Bollettino d'arte*, 4, 1924–5, 162–83.

Ferrari, Oreste. "Per la conoscenza della scultura del primo Quattrocento a Napoli," *Bollettino d'arte*, ser. 4, 39, 1954, 11–24.

Filangieri, Riccardo. *Castel Nuovo, Reggia Angioina ed Aragonese di Napoli* (preface Bruno Molajoli). Naples: L'Arte Tipografia, 1964.

Hersey, George L. *Alfonso II and the Artistic Renewal of Naples, 1485–1495*. New Haven/London: Yale, 1969.

——. *The Aragonese Arch at Naples, 1443–1475*. New Haven/London: Yale University Press, 1973.

Lightbown, R.W. *Donatello & Michelozzo, An Artistic Partnership and Its Patrons in the Early Renaissance* (2 vols.). London: Harvey Miller, 1980.

Pane, Roberto. *Il rinascimento nell'Italia meridionale* (2 vols.). Milan, 1975 and 1977.

Ryder, A.F.C. *Alfonso the Magnanimous: King of Aragon, Naples and Sicily, 1396–1458*. Oxford: Clarendon Press, 1990.

Serra, Luigi. "Gli affreschi della Rotonda di S. Giovanni a Carbonara a Napoli," *Bollettino d'arte*, 3, 1909, 121–36.

Wethey, Harold E. "Guillermo Sagrera," *Art Bulletin*, 21, 1939, 42–60.

Woods-Marsden, Joanna. "Art and Political Identity in Fifteenth-Century Naples: Pisanello, Cristoforo di Geremia, and King Alfonso's Imperial Fantasies," in *Art and Politics in Late Medieval and Early Renaissance Italy: 1250–1500* (ed. Charles M. Rosenberg). Notre Dame/London: Notre Dame University Press, 1990, 11–37.

Padua

Edwards, Mary D. "The Tomb of Raimondino de' Lupi and Its Setting," *The Rutgers Art Review*, 3, 1982, 36–49.

Mommsen, Theodor E. "Petrarch and the Decoration of the Sala Virorum Illustrium in Padua," *Art Bulletin*, 34, 1952, 95–116.

Plant, Margaret. "Patronage in the Circle of the Carrara Family: Padua, 1337–1405," in *Patronage, Art, and Society in Renaissance Italy* (ed. F.W. Kent and Patricia Simons with J.C. Eade). Oxford: Clarendon Press, 1987, 177–99.

——. "Portraits and Politics in Late Trecento Padua: Altichiero's Frescoes in the S. Felice Chapel, S. Antonio," *Art Bulletin*, 63, 1981, 406–25.

Saalman, Howard. "Carrara Burials in the Baptistery of Padua," *Art Bulletin*, 69, 1987, 376–94.

Stubblebine, James H. (ed.). *Giotto: The Arena Chapel Frescoes*. New York: Norton, 1969.

Thomas, Hans Michael. "Sonneneffekte in der Giotto-Kapelle in Padua," *Sterne und Weltraum*, 4, 1995, 278–85.

Pisa

Camposanto Monumentale di Pisa: Affreschi e Sinopie. Pisa: Opera della Primaziale Pisana, 1960.

Jolly, Penny Howell. "Symbolic Landscape in *The Triumph of Death*: The Garden of Love and the Desert of Virtue," *Politeia*, 1985, 27–42.

Luzzati, Michele. "Simone Saltarelli arcivescovo di Pisa (1323–1342) e gli affreschi del Maestro del Trionfo della Morte," *Annali della Scuole Normale Superiore di Pisa, Classe di Lettere e Filosofia*, ser. III, XVIII, 4, 1988, 1645–64.

Morpurgo, S. "Le epigrafi volgari in rima del 'Trionfo della Morte', del 'Giudizio Universale e Inferno,' e degli 'Anacoreti' nel Camposanto di Pisa," *L'Arte*, 2, 1899, 51–87.

Polzer, Joseph. "The Role of the Written Word in the Early Frescoes in the Campo Santo of Pisa," in *World Art: Themes of Unity in Diversity* (ed. Irving Lavin), University Park: Pennsylvania State University Press, 1989, I, 361–66.

Testi Cristiani, Maria Laura. "Voci dialoganti e coro nella 'Umana Commedia' del Trionfo della Morte," *Critica d'arte*, 54, no. 19, 1989, 57–68.

Watson, Paul F. *The Garden of Love in Tuscan Art of the Early Renaissance*. Philadelphia: Art Alliance Press, 1979.

Rimini

Ettlinger, Helen S. "The Sepulchre on the Façade: A Re-evaluation of Sigismondo Malatesta's Rebuilding of San Francesco in Rimini," *Journal of the Warburg and Courtauld Institutes*, 53, 1990, 133–43.

Lavin, Marilyn Aronberg. "Piero della Francesca's Fresco of Sigismondo Malatesta before St. Sigismond," *Art Bulletin*, 56, 1974, 345–74.

Mitchell, Charles. "Il tempio Malatestiano," *Studi Malatestiani*, 1978, 71–103.

Ricci, Corrado. *Il tempio Malatestiano*. Milan/Rome: Bestitti and Tumminelli, 1924 (reprinted Rimini, 1974).

Woods-Marsden, Joanna. "How Quattrocento Princes Used Art: Sigismondo Pandolfo Malatesta of Rimini and *cose militari*," *Renaissance Studies*, 3, 1989, 387–414.

Rome

General

Partridge, Loren. *The Art of Renaissance Rome, 1400–1600*. London: Calmann & King and New York: Abrams, 1996.

Thirteenth and Fourteenth Centuries

Gardner, Julian. "Nicholas III's Oratory of the Sancta Sanctorum," *The Burlington Magazine*, 115, 1973, 283–94.

——. "Pope Nicholas IV and the Decoration of Santa Maria Maggiore," *Zeitschrift für Kunstgeschichte*, 36, 1973, 1–50.

——. *The Tomb and the Tiara, Curial Tomb Sculpture in Rome and Avignon in the Later Middle Ages*. Oxford: Clarendon Press, 1992.

Hetherington, Paul. *Pietro Cavallini, A Study in the Art of Late Medieval Rome*. London: Sagittarius Press, 1979.

Kempers, Bram, and Sible de Blaauw. "Jacopo Stefaneschi, Patron and Liturgist," *Mededelingen van het Nederlands Instituut*, 47, 1987, 83–113.

Kessler, Herbert L. and Johanna Zacharias. *Rome 1300: On the Path of the Pilgrim*. New Haven: Yale University Press, 2000.

Krautheimer, Richard. *Rome, Profile of a City, 312–1308*. Princeton: Princeton University Press, 1980.

Mitchell, Charles. "The Lateran Fresco of Boniface VIII," *Journal of the Warburg and Courtauld Institutes*, 14, 1951, 1–6.

Nichols, Francis Morgan (ed.). *The Marvels of Rome: Mirabilia Urbis Romae*. New York: Italica Press, 1986.

Rash, Nancy. "Boniface VIII and Honorific Portraiture: Observations on the Half-Length Image in the Vatican," *Gesta*, 26, 1987, 47–58.

Redig de Campos, Deoclecio. *I Palazzi Vaticani*. Bologna: Cappelli, 1967.

Righetti Tosti-Croce, Marina (ed.). *Bonifacio VIII e il suo tempo: anno 1300 il primo Giubileo*. Milan: Electa, 2000.

Romanini, Angiola Maria (ed.). *Roma anno 1300, Atti della IV settimana di studi di storia dell'arte medievale dell'Università di Roma "La Sapienza", 19–24 maggio*, Rome: L'Erma di Bretschneider, 1983.

—— (ed.). *Roma nel Duecento, L'arte nella città dei papi da Innocenzo III a Bonifacio VIII*. Rome: SEAT, 1991.

Tomei, Alesandro. *Jacobus Torriti Pictor, Una vicenda figurativa del tardo Duecento romano*. Rome, 1990.

Fifteenth Century

Burroughs, Charles. *From Signs to Design: Environmental Process and Reform in Early Renaissance Rome*. Cambridge, MA: MIT Press, 1990.

Ettlinger, Leopold D. *The Sistine Chapel before Michelangelo*. Oxford: Clarendon Press, 1965.

Lee, Egmont. *Sixtus IV and Men of Letters*. Rome: Edizioni di Storia e Letteratura, 1978.

Magnuson, Torgil. *Studies in Roman Quattrocento Architecture [Figura, 9]*. Stockholm: Almquist & Wiksell, 1958.

Miglio, Massimo et al. (ed.). *Un Pontificato ed una Città: Sisto IV (1471–1484)*. Vatican City: Scuola Vaticana di Paleographia, Diplomatica e Archivista, 1986.

Piccolomini, Aeneas Silvius (Pius II). *The Commentaries of Pius II*. Northampton: Smith College Studies in History, volumes XXII/1–2 (1937), XXV/1–4 (1939–40), XXX (1947), XLIII (1957), XXXV (1951).

Rubinstein, Ruth Olitsky. "Pius II's Piazza S. Pietro and St. Andrew's Head," *Enea Silvio Piccolomini, Papa Pio II. Atti del Convegno per il Quinto Centenario della Morte e altri scritti raccolti da Domenico Maffei*. Siena: Accademia Senese degli Intronati, 1968, 221–43.

Smith, Christine. *Architecture in the Culture of Early Humanism: Ethics, Aesthetics, and Eloquence 1400–1470*. New York/Oxford: Oxford University Press, 1992.

Westfall, Carroll William. *In This Most Perfect Paradise*. University Park: Pennsylvania State University Press, 1974.

Zuraw, Shelley E. "Mino da Fiesole's First Roman Sojourn: The Works in Santa Maria Maggiore," in *Verrocchio and Late Quattrocento Italian Sculpture* (ed. Steven Bule, Alan Phipps Darr, and Fiorella Superbi Gioffredi). Florence: Casa Editrice Le Lettere, 1992, 303–19.

Sixteenth Century

Ackerman, James. *The Architecture of Michelangelo* (2 vols.). London: Zwemmer, 1961.

Bailey, Gauvin Alexander. "The Jesuits and Painting in Italy, 1550–1690: The Art of Catholic Reform," *Saints and Sinners: Caravaggio and the Baroque Image*. Franco Mormando (ed.). Newton (Mass): McMullen Museum of Art, Boston College, 1999 (distributed by University of Chicago Press).

Bruschi, Arnaldo. *Bramante*. London: Thames & Hudson, 1977.

Burroughs, Charles. "Michelangelo at the Campidoglio: Artistic Identity, Patronage, and Manufacture," *Artibus et Historiae*, 28, 1993, 85–111.

Buser, Thomas. "Jerome Nadal and Early Jesuit Art in Rome," *Art Bulletin*, 58, 1976, 424–33.

Chastel, André. *The Sack of Rome, 1527*. Princeton: Princeton University Press, 1983.

Ebert-Schifferer, Sybille. "Ripandas Kapitolinischer Freskenzyklus und die Selbstdarstellung der Konservatoren um 1500," *Römisches Jahrbuch für Kunstgeschichte*, 23/24, 1988, 75–218.

Fontana, Domenico. *Della trasportatione dell'obelisco vaticano et delle fabriche di nostro signore Papa Sisto V*. Rome: Domenico Basa, 1590 (reprinted Milan: Edizioni il Polifilo, 1978, ed. Adriano Carugo).

Freedberg, David. "Johannes Molanus on Provocative Paintings," *Journal of the Warburg and Courtauld Institutes*, 34, 1971, 229–45.

Freiberg, Jack. *The Lateran in 1600: Christian Concord in Counter-Reformation Rome*. Cambridge: Cambridge University Press, 1995.

Hersey, George. *High Renaissance Art in St. Peter's and the Vatican*. Chicago: University of Chicago Press, 1993.

Herz, Alexandra. "Imitators of Christ: The Martyr-Cycles of Late Sixteenth Century Rome Seen in Context," *Storia dell'Arte*, 62, 1988, 54–70.

Hibbard, Howard. "*Ut picturae sermones*: The First Painted Decorations of the Gesù," *Baroque Art: The Jesuit Contribution*. Rudolf Wittkower and Irma B. Jaffe (eds.). New York: Fordham University Press, 1972, 29–50.

Hirst, Michael. *Sebastiano del Piombo*. Oxford: Clarendon Press, 1981.

Jones, Roger, and Nicholas Penny. *Raphael*. New Haven: Yale University Press, 1983.

Joost-Gaugier, Christiane L. "Michelangelo's Ignudi, and the Sistine Chapel as a Symbol of Law and Justice," *Artibus et Historiae*, 34, 1996, 19–43.

Madonna, Maria L. (ed.). *Roma di Sisto V: Le arti e la cultura*. Rome: De Luca, 1993.

Magnuson, Torgil. *Rome in the Age of Bernini*. Atlantic Highlands, NJ: Humanities Press, 1982, vol. 1, 1–38.

Mâle, Emile. *L'Art religieux après le Concile de Trente*. Paris, 1932.

Mancinelli, Fabrizio (ed.). *The Sistine Chapel*. New York: Knopf, 1991.

Martin, Gregory. *Roma Sancta (1581)* (ed. George Bruner Parks). Rome: Edizioni di Storia e Letteratura, 1969.

Monssen, Lief Holm. "The martyrdom cycle in Santo Stefano Rotondo," *Acta ad Archaeologiam et Artium Historiam Pertinentia*, series altera, II, 1982, 175–319 and III, 1983, 11–106.

Ostrow, Steven F. *The Sistine Chapel at S. Maria Maggiore: Sixtus V and the Art of the Counter Reformation*. Ann Arbor: University Microfilms, 1987.

—— *Art and Spirituality in Counter-Reformation Rome: The Sistine and Pauline Chapels in S. Maria Maggiore*. Cambridge/New York: Cambridge University Press, 1996.

Partridge, Loren, and Randolph Starn. *A Renaissance Likeness: Art and Culture in Raphael's* Julius II. Berkeley: University of California Press, 1980.

Pecchiai, Pio. *Il Gesù di Roma*. Rome: Società Grafica Romana, 1952.

Pietrangeli, Carlo (ed.). *The Sistine Chapel: the art, the history, and the restoration*. New York: Harmony Books, 1986.

Robertson, Clare. *"Il gran cardinale": Alessandro Farnese, Patron of the Arts*. New Haven: Yale University Press, 1992.

Rowland, Ingrid D. *The Culture of the High Renaissance: Ancients and Moderns in Sixteenth-Century Rome*. New York: Cambridge University Press, 1998.

Sette, Maria Piera (ed.). *Sisto V: Architetture per la Città*. Rome: Multigrafica Editrice, 1992.

Shearman, John. "The 'Dead Christ' by Rosso Fiorentino," *Bulletin: Museum of Fine Arts, Boston*, 64. 338, 1966. 148–72.

Talvacchia, Bette. *Taking Positions: On the Erotic in Renaissance Culture*. Princeton: Princeton University Press, 1999.

Valone, Carolyn. "Roman Matrons as Patrons: Various Views of the Cloister Wall," in *The Crannied Wall: Women, Religion, and the Arts in Early Modern Europe* (ed. Craig A. Monson). Ann Arbor: University of Michigan Press, 1992, 49–72.

Zeri, Federico. *Pittura e controriforma*. Turin: Giulio Einaudi, 1957.

Siena

General

Bortolotti, Lando. *Siena*. Rome, 1983.

Cole, Bruce. *Sienese Painting from Its Origins to the Fifteenth Century*. New York: Harper & Row, 1980.

Riedl, Anselm and Max Seidel (eds.). *Die Kirchen von Siena*. Munich: Bruckmann, 1985–.

van Os, Henk. *Sienese Altarpieces, 1215–1460* (2 vols.). Groningen: Bouma's Boekhuis, 1984/Groningen: Egbert Forsten Publishing, 1990.

Thirteenth and Fourteenth Centuries

Deuchler, Florens. *Duccio*. Milan: Electa, 1984.

Kempers, Bram. "Icons, Altarpieces, and Civic Ritual in Siena Cathedral, 1100–1530," in *City and Spectacle in Medieval Europe* (ed. Barbara A. Hannawalt and Kathryn L. Reyerson). Minneapolis: University of Minnesota Press, 1994, 89–136.

Kosegarten, Antje Middeldorf. *Sienesische Bildhauer am Duomo Vecchio, Studien zur Skulptur in Siena 1250–1330*. Munich: Bruckmann, 1984.

Maginnis, Hayden B.J. "The Lost Façade Frescoes from Siena's Ospedale di S. Maria della Scala," *Zeitschrift für Kunstgeschichte*, 51, 1988, 180–94.

Martindale, Andrew. *Simone Martini*. Oxford: Phaidon, 1988.

Norman, Diana. *Siena and the Virgin: Art and Politics in a Late Medieval City State*. New Haven: Yale University Press, 1999.

Pietramellara, Carla. *Il Duomo di Siena, Evoluzione della forma dalle origini alla fine del Trecento*. Florence, 1980.

Rowley, George. *Ambrogio Lorenzetti* (2 vols.). Princeton: Princeton University Press, 1958.

Rubinstein, Nicolai. "Ambrogio Lorenzetti and Taddeo di Bartolo in the Palazzo Pubblico," *The Journal of the Warburg and Courtauld Institutes*, 21, 1958, 179–207.

Starn, Randolph. *Ambrogio Lorenzetti. The Palazzo Pubblico, Siena*. New York: Braziller, 1994.

Stubblebine, James H. *Duccio di Buoninsegna and his School* (2 vols.). Princeton: Princeton University Press, 1979.

White, John. *Duccio: Tuscan Art and the Medieval Workshop*. London: Thames & Hudson, 1979.

Fifteenth Century

Christiansen, Keith, Laurence B. Kanter, and Carl Brandon Strehlke. *Painting in Renaissance Siena 1420–1500*. New York: Metropolitan Museum and Abrams, 1988.

Mallory, Michael, and Gaudenz Freuler. "Sano di Pietro's Bernardino altarpiece for the Compagnia della Vergine in Siena," *The Burlington Magazine*, 133, 1991, 186–92.

Seymour, Charles, Jr. *Jacopo della Quercia*. New Haven: Yale University Press, 1973.

Southard, Edna Carter. *The Frescoes in Siena's Palazzo Pubblico, 1289–1539: Studies in Imagery and Relations to other Communal Palaces in Tuscany*. New York: Garland, 1979.

Symeonides, Sibilla. *Taddeo di Bartolo*. Siena: Accademia Senese degli Intronati, 1965.

Urbino

Piero e Urbino, Piero e le corti rinascimentali (ed. Paolo dal Poggetto). Venice: Marsilio, 1992.

Cheles, Luciano. *The Studiolo of Urbino, An Iconographic Investigation*. Wiesbaden: Dr. Ludwig Reichert Verlag, 1986.

Clough, Cecil. "Federigo da Montefeltro's Artistic Patronage," *Journal of the Royal Society of Arts*, 126, 1978, 718–34.

——. "Federigo da Montefeltro's Patronage of the Arts," *Journal of the Warburg and Courtauld Institutes*, 36, 1973, 129–44.

Heydenreich, Ludwig Heinrich. "Federico da Montefeltro as a Building Patron, Some Remarks on the Ducal Palace of Urbino," in *Studien zur Architektur der Renaissance, Ausgewählte Aufsätze*. Munich: Wilhelm Fink, 1981.

Lavin, Marilyn Aronberg. "Piero della Francesca's Montefeltro Altarpiece: A Pledge of Fidelity," *Art Bulletin*, 51, 1969, 367–71.

Lightbown, Ronald. *Piero della Francesca*. New York, Abbeville, 1992.

Meiss, Millard. "*Ovum Struthionis*: Symbol and Allusion in Piero della Francesca's Montefeltro Altarpiece," in *The Painter's Choice: Problems in the Interpretation of Renaissance Art*. New York: Harper & Row, 1976.

—— with Theodore G. Jones. "Once Again Piero della Francesca's Montefeltro Altarpiece," in *The Painter's Choice: Problems in the Interpretation of Renaissance Art*. New York: Harper & Row, 1976.

Rotondi, Pasquale. *Il palazzo ducale di Urbino* (2 vols.). Urbino: Istituto statale d'arte per il libro, 1950–51.

Venice

General

Brown, Patricia Fortini. "Painting and History in Renaissance Venice," *Art History*, 7, 1984, 263–94.

——. "The Self-Definition of the Venetian Republic," in *City and State in Classical Antiquity and Medieval Italy* (ed. Anthony Molho, et al.). Ann Arbor: University of Michigan Press, 1991, 511–48.

—— *Art and Life in Renaissance Venice*. New York: Harry N. Abrams and Prentice Hall, 1997.

Concina, Ennio. *A History of Venetian Architecture* (trans. Judith Landry). Cambridge and New York: Cambridge University Press, 1998.

Davis, Robert C. *The War of the Fists, Popular Culture and Public Violence in Late Renaissance Venice*. New York/Oxford: Oxford University Press, 1994.

Howard, Deborah. *The Architectural History of Venice*. New York: Holmes & Meier, 1981.

—— .*Venice and the East*. London: Yale University Press, 2000.

Humfrey, Peter. *Painting in Renaissance Venice*. New Haven: Yale University Press, 1995.

Huse, Norbert, and Wolfgang Wolters. *The Art of Renaissance Venice: Architecture, Sculpture, and Painting*. Chicago: University of Chicago Press, 1990.

Perry, Marilyn. "Saint Mark's Trophies: Legend, Superstition, and Archaeology in Renaissance Venice," *Journal of the Warburg and Courtauld Institutes*, 40, 1977, 27–49.

Pincus, Debra. "Venice and the Two Romes: Byzantium and Rome as a Double Heritage in Venetian Cultural Politics," *Artibus et historiae*, 26, 1992, 101–14.

——. *The Tombs of the Doge of Venice*. New York: Cambridge University Press, 2000.

Rosand, David. "Venetia Figurata: The Iconography of a Myth," in *Interpretazioni Veneziane, Studi di Storia dell'Arte in onore di Michelangelo Muraro* (ed. David Rosand). Venice: Arsenale Editrice, 1984, 177–96.

Schulz, Juergen. "Urbanism in Medieval Venice," in *City and State in Classical Antiquity and Medieval Italy* (ed. Anthony Molho, et al.). Ann Arbor: University of Michigan Press, 1991, 419–45.

Thirteenth and Fourteenth Centuries

Arslan, Edoardo. *Gothic Architecture in Venice* (trans. Anne Engel). London: Phaidon, 1972.

Demus, Otto. *The Mosaics of San Marco in Venice*. Chicago: University of Chicago Press, 1984.

Pincus, Debra. "Andrea Dandolo (1343–1354) and Visible History: The San Marco Projects," in *Art and Politics in Late Medieval and Early Renaissance Italy: 1250–1500* (ed. Charles M. Rosenberg). Notre Dame/London: University of Notre Dame Press, 1990, 191–206.

Wolters, Wolfgang. *La scultura veneziana gotica.* Venice: Alfieri, 1976.

Fifteenth Century

Brown, Patricia Fortini. *Venetian Narrative Painting in the Age of Carpaccio.* New Haven: Yale University Press, 1988.

——. "The Antiquarianism of Jacopo Bellini," *Artibus et historiae*, 26, 1992, 65–84.

Degenhart, Bernhard, and Annegrit Schmitt. *Jacopo Bellini, L'Album dei disegni del Louvre.* Milan: Jaca, 1984 (original edition in English New York: Braziller, 1984).

Dyggve, E. "Il frontone ad arco e trilobato veneziano, Alcune osservazioni sulla sua origine," in *Venezia e l'Europa, Atti del XVIII congresso internazionale di storia dell'arte.* Venice, 226–30.

Eisler, Colin. *The Genius of Jacopo Bellini, The Complete Paintings and Drawings.* New York: Abrams, 1989.

Fiocco, G. "Michele Giambono," *Venezia, Studi di arte e storia a cura della Direzione del Museo Civico Correr*, 1, 1920, 206–36.

Fleming, John. *From Bonaventure to Bellini: An Essay in Franciscan Exegesis.* Princeton: Princeton University Press, 1982.

Goffen, Rona. "Bellini, S. Giobbe, and Altar Egos," *Artibus et historiae*, 14, 1986, 57–70.

——. *Giovanni Bellini.* New Haven: Yale University Press, 1989.

Goy, Richard J. *The House of Gold, Building a Palace in Medieval Venice.* Cambridge: Cambridge University Press, 1992.

Gnudi, Cesare. "Jacobello e Pietro Paolo da Venezia," *La Critica d'Arte*, 2, 1937, 26–38.

Humfrey, Peter. *The Altarpiece in Renaissance Venice.* New Haven/London: Yale University Press, 1993.

Lieberman, Ralph. *Renaissance Architecture in Venice 1450–1540.* New York: Abbeville, 1982.

—— "Real Architecture, Imaginary History: The Arsenal Gate as Venetian Mythology," *Journal of the Warburg and Courtauld Institutes*, 54, 1991, 117–26.

Maek-Gérard, Michael. "Die *Milanexi* in Venedig— Ein Beitrag zur Entwicklungsgeschichte der Lombardi-Werkstatt," *Wallraf-Richartz-Jahrbuch*, 41, 1980, 105–131; 142.

Merkel, Ettore. "Un problema di metodo: La *Dormitio Virginis* dei Mascoli," *Arte veneta*, 27, 1973, 65–80.

Munman, Robert. "Antonio Rizzo's Sarcophagus for Niccolò Tron: A Closer Look," *Art Bulletin*, 55, 1973, 77–85.

Muraro, Michelangelo. "The Statues of the Venetian *Arti* and the Mosaics of the Mascoli Chapel," *Art Bulletin*, 43, 1961, 263–74.

——. "La Scala senza giganti," *De artibus opuscula XL. Essays in Honor of Erwin Panofsky* (ed.

Millard Meiss). New York: New York University Press, 1961, 350–70.

Niero, Antonio. *Chiesa di Santo Stefano in Venezia.* Padua: Edizioni Messaggero, 1978.

Pallucchini, Rodolfo. *La pittura veneta del Quattrocento, Il gotico internazionale e gli inizi del rinascimento.* Bologna, 1956.

——. *La pittura veneta del Quattrocento, Il Rinascimento, Parte I* (typescript). Istituto di Storia dell'Arte, Università di Padova, Anno accademico 1956–7.

——. *La pittura veneta del Quattrocento, Parte II, La diffusione del Mantegnismo nel Veneto dal Crivelli a Giovanni Bellini* (typescript). Istituto di Storia dell'Arte, Università di Padova, Anno accademico 1957–8.

——. *I Vivarini (Antonio, Bartolomeo, Alvise).* Venice: Neri Pozza, [1961].

Pesaro, Cristina. "Per un catalogo di Michele Giambono," *Atti dell'Istituto Veneto di Scienze, Lettere ed Arti*, 136, 1977–8, 19–33.

Pincus, Debra. "The Tomb of Niccolò Tron and Venetian Renaissance Ruler Imagery," in *Art the Ape of Nature: Studies in Honor of H.W. Janson* (ed. Moshe Barasch and Lucy Freeman Sandler). New York: Abrams, 1981, 127–52.

Planiscig, Leo. *Venezianische Bildhauer der Renaissance.* Vienna: Anton Schroll, 1921.

Puppi, Loredana Olivato, and Lionello Puppi. *Mauro Codussi e l'architettura veneziana del Primo Rinascimento.* Milan: Electa, 1977.

Robertson, Giles. *Giovanni Bellini.* Oxford, 1968.

Schulz, Anne Markham. *Antonio Rizzo, Sculptor and Architect.* Princeton: Princeton University Press, 1983.

Sheard, Wendy Stedman. "The Birth of Monumental Classicizing Relief in Venice on the Façade of the Scuola di San Marco," in *Interpretazioni Veneziane, Studi di Storia dell'Arte in onore di Michelangelo Muraro* (ed. David Rosand). Venice: Arsenale Editrice, 1984, 149–74.

Sixteenth Century

Ackerman, James S. *Palladio's Villas.* New York: J.J. Augustin for the Institute of Fine Arts, 1967.

——. "The Geopolitics of Venetian Architecture in the Time of Titian," in *Titian: His World and His Legacy* (ed. David Rosand). New York: Columbia University Press, 1982, 41–71.

Anderson, Jayne. "Giorgione, Titian and the Sleeping Venus," in *Tiziano e Venezia.* Vicenza: Neri Pozza, 1980, 337–42.

Calabi, Donatella, and Paolo Morachiello. *Rialto: Le fabbriche e il ponte, 1514–1591.* Turin, 1987.

Cocke, Richard. "Veronese and Daniele Barbaro: The Decoration of Villa Maser," *Journal of the Warburg and Courtauld Institutes*, 35, 1972, 226–46.

Ettlinger, Helen S. "The Iconography of the Columns in Titian's Pesaro Altarpiece," *Art Bulletin*, 61, 1979, 59–67.

Fehl, Phillip. "Saints, Donors and Columns in Titian's Pesaro Madonna," in *Renaissance

Papers 1974* (ed. Dennis G. Donovan and A. Leigh Deneef). Durham, NC: The Southeastern Renaissance Conference, 1975, 75–85.

Gaston, Robert W. "Vesta and the *Martyrdom of St. Lawrence* in the Sixteenth Century," *Journal of the Warburg and Courtauld Institutes*, 37, 1974, 358–62.

Goedicke, Christian, Klaus Slusallek, and Martin Kubelik. "Thermoluminescent Dating in Architectural History: The Chronology of Palladio's Villa Rotonda," *Journal of the Society of Architectural Historians*, 45, 1986, 396–407.

Goffen, Rona. *Titian's Women.* New Haven/London: Yale University Press, 1997.

Gordon, D.J. "Academicians Build a Theatre and Give a Play: The Accademia Olimpica, 1579–1585," in *The Renaissance Imagination, Essays and Lectures by D.J. Gordon.* Berkeley: University of California Press, 1975, 247–68.

Howard, Deborah. "Giorgione's *Tempesta* and Titian's *Assunta* in the Context of the Cambrai Wars," *Art History*, 8, 1985, 271–89.

——. *Jacopo Sansovino, Architecture and Patronage in Renaissance Venice.* New Haven/London: Yale University Press, 1975 (second printing with corrections, 1987).

Huse, Norbert. "Palladio und die Villa Barbaro in Maser: Bemerkungen zum Problem der Autorschaft," *Arte veneta*, 28, 1974, 106–22.

Kaplan, Paul H.D. "The Storm of War: The Paduan Key to Giorgione's Tempest," *Art History*, 9, 1986, 405–25.

Libbey, L. "Venetian History and Political Thought after 1509," *Studies in the Renaissance*, 20, 1973, 7–45.

Palladio, Andrea. *I quattro libri dell'architettura.* Venice, 1570 (facsimile reprint Milan: Hoepli, 1951).

Reist, Inge Jackson. "*Divine Love* and Veronese's Frescoes at the Villa Barbaro," *Art Bulletin*, 67, 1985, 614–35.

Rogers, Mary. "An Ideal Wife at the Villa Maser: Veronese, the Barbaros and Renaissance Theorists on Marriage," *Renaissance Studies*, 7, 1993, 379–97.

Schulz, Juergen. "Tintoretto and the First Competition for the Ducal Palace 'Paradise'," *Arte veneta*, 34, 1980, 112–26.

Settis, Salvatore. *Giorgione's Tempest: Interpreting the Hidden Subject.* Chicago: University of Chicago Press, 1990.

Sinding-Larsen, Staale. *Christ in the Council Hall: Studies in the religious Iconography of the Venetian Republic (Acta ad Archaeologiam et Artium Historiam Pertinentia) (Institutum Romanum Norvegiae, V).* Rome: L'Erma di Bretschneider, 1974.

Tafuri, Manfredo. *Venice and the Renaissance* (trans. Jessica Levine) (Chapter 2: Republican pietas, Neo-Byzantinism, and Humanism. San Salvador: A Temple *in visceribus urbis*). Cambridge, MA: MIT Press, 1989.

Literary Credits and Picture Credits

Literary Credits

The authors and publishers wish to thank the following for permission to use copyright material. Every effort has been made to trace or contact all copyright holders. The publishers would be pleased to rectify any omissions notified at the earliest opportunity.

Harry N. Abrams Inc.: from *Lives of the Most Eminent Painters, Sculptors, and Architects: Volume II* by Giorgio Vasari, translated by Gaston de Vere, edited by Kenneth Clark (New York: Harry N. Abrams, 1979). All rights reserved; **Blackwell Publishers**: from *Venice: A Documentary History* by D. S. Chambers and B. Pullan with J. Fletcher (Oxford: Blackwell, 1992); **Cambridge University Press**: from *The House of Gold: Building a Palace in Medieval Venice* by Richard J. Goy (Cambridge: Cambridge University Press, 1992); **Dover Publications Inc.**: from *The Craftsman's Handbook*, translated by Daniel V. Thompson, Jr. (New York: Dover Publications, 1960); **Franciscan Press**: from *St Francis of Assisi: Writings and Early Biographies*, edited by Marion Habig, OFM (Chicago: Franciscan Herald Press, 1972); **Paulist Press**: from *Catherine of Siena: The Dialogue*, translated by Susan Noffke (New York: Paulist Press, 1980); **Penguin Books Ltd.**: from *The Book of the Courtier* by Baldassare Castiglione, translated by George Bull (Penguin Classics, 1967), © George Bull, 1967; from *The Autobiography of Benvenuto Cellini*, translated by George Bull (Penguin Classics, 1956), © George Bull, 1956; **Pennsylvania State University**: from *The Life of Brunelleschi* by Antonio Manetti, edited by Howard Saalman (University Park: Pennsylvania State University Press, 1970); **Princeton University Press**: from "Ghiberti: Commentaries," in *A Documentary History of Art* by Elizabeth G. Holt (New York: Doubleday, 1957), © 1947, renewed 1957, 1981 by Princeton University Press; from *Literary Sources of Art History* by E. G. Holt (Princeton University Press, 1947), © 1947, renewed 1975 by Princeton University Press; **Yale University Press**: from *On Painting* by Leon Battista Alberti, translated/edited by John Spencer (New Haven: Yale University Press, 1956); "Sonnet 151" from *The Poetry of Michelangelo* by James Saslow (New Haven: Yale University Press, 1991).

Picture Credits

Collections are given in the captions alongside the illustrations. Sources for illustrations not supplied by museums or collections, additional information, and copyright credits are given below. Boldface numbers refer to figure numbers unless otherwise indicated. The following abbreviations have been used: Alinari—© Fratelli Alinari, Florence; Böhm—© Osvaldo Böhm, Venice; Cameraphoto—© CAMERAPHOTO Arte, Venice; Lensini—© Foto 3 di Lensini Fabio, Siena; Morris—© James Morris, London; Quattrone—© Studio Fotografico Quattrone, Florence; RMN—© Réunion des Musées Nationaux, Paris; Scala— © Scala, Florence.

Frontispiece Cameraphoto; **1** © British Museum, London; **2** Museo Bardini, Florence; **3** Quattrone; **4** Böhm; **6** Lensini; **7** Duke of Northumberland, photo Courtauld Institute of Art, London; **8** RMN/Michèle Bellot; **9** Quattrone; **10,11** Lensini; **12** © foto Berardi/Index, Florence; **14** Quattrone; **15, 16** Scala; **17** Quattrone; **18** Vatican Museums, Rome; **19** Yale University Art Gallery, University Purchase from James Jackson Jarves; **20** Alinari; **22** Foglia; **24** Quattrone; **25** Foglia; **26** Scala; **27** courtesy Francesca G. Bewer, Harvard University; **28** Frick Collection, N.Y.; **29** RMN; **30** The Governing Body, Christ Church, Oxford; **31** Lensini; **32** Alinari; **33** Scala; **34** Alinari; **36** Devonshire Collection, Chatsworth. Reproduced by permission of the Chatsworth Settlement Trustees; **1.1** Courtesy of the Vicar Capitular and Administrator, Basilica Santa Maria Maggiore; **1.2, 1.3** Böhm; **1.4** Quattrone; **1.5, 1.6** Alinari; **1.7** Cameraphoto; **1.8** Böhm; **1.9** Calmann & King Archives, London/Ralph Lieberman; **1.10** Scala; **1.11** Alinari; **1.13** Lensini; **1.14** Quattrone; **1.15, 1.16, 1.17** Alinari; **1.19** from Marvin Trachtenberg, *Dominion of the Eye: Urbanism, Art, and Power in Early Modern Florence*, Cambridge University Press, 1997; **1.20, 1.21**, Alinari; **1.23** Scala; **1.25** Quattrone; **1.26** Scala; **1.27** Quattrone; **1.28** Scala; **1.29, 1.30** Quattrone; **1.31** Fotomas Index, Kent; **1.32** Photo Vatican Museums; **1.33** Photo Vatican Museums/A.Bracchetti, 1994; **1.34** Photo Vatican Museums/D.Pivato, 1994; **1.35** Courtesy of the Vicar Capitular and Administrator, Basilica Santa Maria Maggiore; **1.36** Scala; **1.37** Canali Photobank, Capriolo; **1.38, 1.39** Scala; **1.40, 1.41** Alinari; **1.42** Photo Biblioteca Vaticana (Vat.Barb. Lat 2733, ff 146v/147r); **1.43** Scala; **1.44, 1.46** Quattrone; **1.47** Alinari; **1.48** Quattrone; **2.1** Foglia; **2.2** Scala; **2.4** Studio Deganello, Padua; **2.5** Scala; **2.6, 2.7** Quattrone; **2.8** Alinari; **2.9, 2.10** Quattrone; **2.11** Raffaello Bencini, Florence; **2.13** Quattrone; **2.14** Raffaello Bencini, Florence; **2.16** Scala; **2.17** Quattrone; **2.18** Alinari; **2.19, 2.20, 2.21, 2.22, 2.23** Quattrone; **2.24** Scala; **2.25** Quattrone; **2.26** Böhm; **2.27, 2.28, 2.29** Quattrone; **2.30, 2.31, 2.32** Scala; **2.33, 2.34** Alinari; **2.35, 2.36** Lensini; **2.37** Scala; **2.38** Foglia; **2.39** Pierpont Morgan Library/Art Resource, N.Y.; **2.41** Canali Photobank, Capriolo; **2.42, 2.43** Foglia; **2.45** Alinari; **2.47** Index, Florence; **2.48** Foglia; **2.49** Alinari; **2.50** Foglia; **2.51, 2.52, 2.54** Alinari; **2.55** Foglia; **2.56** Alinari; **2.59** Studio Fotografico Perotti, Milan; **2.60** Alinari; **3.1** Scala; **3.2** Cameraphoto; **3.3** Böhm; **3.4** Cameraphoto; **3.5** Böhm; **3.6** Alinari; **3.7, 3.8** Böhm; **3.9, 3.11** Cameraphoto; **3.12, 3.13** Böhm; **3.14, 3.15** Alinari; **3.16** Quattrone; **3.17** Scala; **3.18** Quattrone; **3.19** Alinari; **3.20** Quattrone; **3.21** Alinari; **3.22** Scala; **3.23** Quattrone; **3.24** Scala; **3.25** Quattrone; **3.26, 3.27, 3.28** Alinari; **3.29** Scala; **3.30, 3.31, 3.32** Alinari; **3.33** Scala; **3.34, 3.35, 3.36** Alinari; **3.37** Gary Radke; **3.45** Scala; **3.46** Canali Photobank, Capriolo; **3.47** Veneranda Arca di S. Antonio, Padua; **3.48** Alinari; **4.3** Alinari; **4.5** A. F. Kersting, London; **4.7** Alinari; **4.8** photo Pineider, courtesy Index Florence; **4.9, 4.12, 4.13** Scala; **4.14** The Pierpont Morgan Library/Art Resource, N.Y.; **4.16, 4.17** Alinari; **4.18** Foglia; **4.19, 4.20** Alinari; **4.21** Scala; **4.22** Index, Florence/ © Soprintendenza B.A.S. del Veneto, Verona; **4.24, 4.25** Alinari; **4.26** Scala; **4.27** Conway Library, Courtauld Institute of Art, London; **4.28** Alinari; **4.29, 4.30** Quattrone; **4.31, 4.32** Scala; **4.33** Alinari; **4.34** Quattrone; **4.35, 4.36, 4.37, 4.38, 4.39, 4.40** Alinari; **4.41** Quattrone; **4.42** Alinari; **4.43, 4.44** Scala; **4.46** Quattrone; **4.48** Scala; **4.49, 4.50, 4.51** Alinari; **4.52** Scala; **4.53** Alinari; **4.54** Scala; **4.55** Quattrone; **4.56** Alinari (side panels only); **4.58, 4.59, 4.60** Quattrone; **4.62, 4.63, 4.64** Scala; **4.63, 4.64** Scala; **4.65, 4.66, 4.67** Alinari; **4.68** Lensini; **4.69, 4.70, 4.71, 4.72** Alinari; **5.1** Photo Vatican Museums, Rome; **5.2, 5.4, 5.5** Scala; **5.6** Quattrone; **5.8** Alinari; **5.9, 5.10** Raffaello Bencini, Florence; **5.11** Scala; **5.12** Index, Florence © Soprintendenza B.A.A. Florence; **5.13** Quattrone; **5.14** Scala; **5.15** Austin; **5.16, 5.17, 5.18** Alinari; **5.19, 5.21** Quattrone; **5.22, 5.23, 5.24** Alinari; **5.25, 5.26** Scala; **5.27, 5.28** Quattrone; **5.29** Index, Florence © Soprintendenza B.A.A. Florence; **5.30** Scala (centre panel); **5.31, 5.32** Morris; **5.33** Araldo De Luca, Rome; **5.34** RMN, Paris; **5.36, 5.37** Photo Vatican Museums, Rome; **5.38** Photo Biblioteca Apostilica Vaticana (Vat.Barb. Lat 2733, ff 104v/105r); **5.39** Morris; **5.40** Scala; **5.41, 5.43, 5.44** Alinari; **5.45** Canali Photobank, Capriolo; **5.46** Alinari; **5.47** Böhm; **5.48, 5.49** Cameraphoto; **5.51** Böhm; **5.53, 5.54** Cameraphoto; **5.55** Böhm; **5.56** RMN, Paris; **5.57** Cameraphoto; **5.58** Scala; **5.59, 5.60, 5.61** Alinari; **5.62** Scala; **6.1, 6.2, 6.4, 6.5** Foglia; **6.7, 6.8** Alinari; **6.9** Biblioteca Estense, Modena (Ms Lat. 422 V.G. 12, I, c.280 V.); **6.10** Scala; **6.12** Alinari; **6.13, 6.14** Raffaello Bencini, Florence; **6.15** Alinari; **6.17, 6.18** © James Austin, Cambridge; **6.19** Scala; **6.20, 6.21** Calmann & King Archives, London/Ralph Lieberman; **6.22, 6.23** Quattrone; **6.24** The Royal Collection © Her Majesty Queen Elizabeth II; **6.25** RMN; **6.26** Cameraphoto; **6.27, 6.29** Böhm; **6.30** Calmann & King Archives, London/Ralph Lieberman; **6.31** Cameraphoto; **6.32** Böhm; **6.35** © Frick Collection, N.Y.; **6.36** Alinari; **6.37** Cameraphoto; **6.38** Böhm; **6.39** Cameraphoto; **6.40, 6.41** Böhm; **6.42** Alinari; **6.43** Scala; **6.44** Quattrone; **6.45** Andrew W. Mellon Collection, © 1996 Board of Trustees, National Gallery of Art, Washington, D.C.; **6.46** Scala; **6.47** © 2001 Board of Trustees, National Gallery of Art, Washington (Ailsa Mellon Bruce Fund); **6.48** © Museo Thyssen-Bornemisza, Madrid; **6.49** Quattrone; **6.50** Nicolò Orsi Battaglini, Florence; **6.51** © Studio Fotografico Quattrone, Florence; **6.52** Alinari; **6.54** Quattrone; **6.55** Bildarchiv Preussischer Kulturbesitz, Berlin; **6.56** Calmann and King archives; **6.58** Quattrone; **6.59** Alinari; **6.61** Scala; **6.62** Alinari; **6.63** Morris; **6.64** Alinari; **6.65** Morris; **6.67, 6.68** Photo Vatican Museums; **6.69** Alinari; **6.70** Scala; **6.71** Morris; **6.72** Tim Benton, Cambridge; **6.73** © Araldo De Luca, Rome; **6.74** Morris; **6.75** Gugliemo Chiolini, Pavia; **6.76** Alinari; **6.77** Istituto Geografico De Agostini, Milan; **6.78** © James Austin, Cambridge; **6.79** photo Pineider, courtesy Index Florence; **6.80, 6.82** Mauro Ranzani/Index, Florence; **6.83** Scala; **6.85** Gugliemo Chiolini, Pavia; **6.86, 6.87** Quattrone; **6.88** Bulloz, Paris; **6.89** The Royal Collection © 2001 Her Majesty Queen Elizabeth II; **6.90** Civiche Raccolte d'Arte, Castello Sforzesco, Milan; **6.91** RMN; **6.93, 6.94** Civiche Raccolte d'Arte, Castello Sforzesco, Milan; **6.95** Alinari; **7.1** Scala; **7.2** Quattrone; **7.3** © Tosi/Index, Florence; **7.4, 7.6** Alinari; **7.7** RMN; **7.8** By kind permission of the Earl of Leicester and the Trustees of the Holkham Estate, photograph Courtauld Institute of Art, London; **7.9, 7.10, 7.11** Quattrone; **7.12** Scala; **7.13** © British Museum, London; **7.14** Gabinetto Disegni e Stampe degli Uffizi, Florence, courtesy Quattrone; **7.16** Calmann & King Archives/Ralph Lieberman; **7.21** Böhm; **7.23** RMN; **7.24** Photo Vatican Museums; **7.26** Photo Vatican Museums (A.Bracchetti); **7.27** Conway Library, Courtauld Institute of Art, London; **7.28** Photo Vatican Museums; **7.29** Scala; **7.30, 7.31** Photo Vatican Museums; **7.33** © Archivio Musei Capitolini/Index, Florence; **7.34, 7.35** Photo Vatican Museums; **7.36** Victoria & Albert Museum Picture Library, London; **7.37** Scala; **7.38** Alinari; **7.40** Photo Vatican Museums (M.Sarri); **7.42** Charles Potter Kling Fund. 58.527. Courtesy, Museum of Fine Arts, Boston. Reproduced with permission. © 2001 Museum of Fine Arts, Boston. All Rights Reserved; **7.43** Quattrone; **7.44** Alinari; **7.45** Index, Florence/Tosi; **7.47** Raffaello Bencini, Florence; **7.48** Alinari; **7.49** John Paoletti; **7.50** Quattrone; **7.52** RMN; **7.53** © Araldo de Luca, Rome; **7.54** Alinari; **7.55, 7.56** Böhm; **7.57, 7.58** Cameraphoto; **7.60** Calmann & King Archives, photo Ralph Lieberman; **7.61** Alinari; **7.62** RMN; **7.63** Index, Florence; **7.65** Widener Collection, © 1996 Board of Trustees, National Gallery of Art, Washington, D.C.; **7.67** Scala; **7.68** © James Austin, Cambridge; **7.70, 7.72** Scala **7.73** Alinari; **7.74, 7.75** Scala; **7.76** Quattrone; **7.77** Scala; **7.78** © Index, Florence/ Kunsthistorisches Institut; **7.79** Index, Florence; **7.80** © Rijksmuseum-Stichting, Amsterdam; **7.81** Scala; **7.82** Alinari; **8.1** Cameraphoto; **8.2, 8.3, 8.6** Böhm; **8.7** Cameraphoto; **8.9** Böhm; **8.10** A. F. Kersting, London; **8.12** Alinari; **8.13** Phyllis D. Massar, N.Y.; **8.16, 8.17** Alinari; **8.18, 8.19** Scala; **8.21** © Museo del Prado, Madrid; **8.22** Staatliche Museen zu Berlin-Preußischer Kulturbesitz Gëmaldegalerie, photo Jörg P. Anders; **8.23** Quattrone; **8.24** © Museo del Prado, Madrid; **8.26, 8.27, 8.28** Cameraphoto; **8.29, 8.30, 8.31** Böhm; **8.32, 8.33, 8.34** Quattrone; **8.35** Metropolitan Museum of Art, H.O. Havemeyer Collection, Bequest of Mrs H.O. Havemeyer, 1929 (29.100.16); **8.36, 8.37** Scala; **8.38, 8.39** Alinari; **8.40** Scala; **8.41** Alinari; **8.43** Quattrone; **8.44** Scala; **8.45** © Nippon Television Network Corporation Tokyo, 1991 **8.46** Quattrone; **8.47** Alinari; **8.48** Scala; **8.49** Alinari; **8.50** Morris; **8.52** A. F. Kersting, London; **8.53** Metropolitan Museum of Art, Harris Brisbane Dick Fund, 1941. [41.72 (3) pl. 26]; **8.54** Morris; **8.55** Alinari; **8.57** Pierpont Morgan Library/Art Resource, N.Y.; **9.1** Scala; **9.2** Morris; **9.3** Böhm; **9.4** Scala; **9.5** Alinari; **9.6** Studio Fotografico Perotti, Milan; **9.7, 9.8, 9.9** Alinari; **9.10** © Archivio Electa/Index, Florence; **9.11** Scala; **9.12** Alinari; **9.13** Scala; **9.15** Conway Library, Courtauld Institute of Art, London; **9.16** Alinari; **9.17** Morris; **9.18** Publifoto, Milan; **9.19** Morris; **9.20** The Metropolitan Museum of Art, purchase, anonymous gift, in memory of Terence Cardinal Cooke, 1984. (1984.74) © 1984 Metropolitan Museum of Art; **9.21** Morris; **9.22** Canali Photobank, Capriolo; **9.23** Morris; **9.25** Metropolitan Museum of Art, N.Y., Elisha Wittelsey Collection, Elisha Whittelsey Fund, 1949 (49.95.146 pl. 4); **9.27** Biblioteca Hertziana, Rome; **9.28** Conway Library, Courtauld Institute of Art, London; **9.29, 9.30, 9.31** Morris; **9.32** Metropolitan Museum of Art, N.Y., Harris Brisbane Dick Fund, 1941 (41.72 1[12]); **9.33** Alinari; **9.34** Conway Library, Courtauld Institute of Art, London; **9.35** Morris; **9.36** Scala.

Index